Steck-Vaughn

COMPLETE CANADIAN

GED

PREPARATION

Editorial Consultant:
Jim Barlow, B.A., M.Ed.
Adult Educator
Legacy 5 Consultants, Inc.

NELSON EDUCATION

ISBN-13: 978-0-7747-1631-4
ISBN-10: 0-7747-1631-2

Nelson Education Ltd.
1120 Birchmount Road
Toronto, Ontario M1K 5G4
1-800-668-0671
www.nelson.com

National Library of Canada Cataloguing in Publication

Complete Canadian GED preparation.

Includes index.
ISBN 0-7747-1631-2

1. **General educational development tests—Study guides.** 2. **High school equivalency examinations—Study guides.**

LB3060.33.G45C65 2003   **373.126'2**   **C2003-902148-3**

Contributors:

Roy C. Baillieul
Instructor
New Brunswick Community College
Moncton, NB

Vivian Bodnar
Teacher
Nanaimo Correctional Centre

Joe Dardano
Education Coordinator
Hope Learning Centre
Union Gospel Mission
Vancouver, BC

Clayton Graves
Teacher
e-learning Division, tv Ontario
Toronto, ON

Rochelle McCarthy
Waterloo Regional District School Board
Waterloo, ON

Arthur Prudham
(formerly) Waterloo Regional District School
Board
Waterloo, ON

Reviewers:

Jack Maga
Principal of Continuing Education
Hamilton Wentworth Catholic District School
Board
Hamilton, ON

M. Dwight Stuart
(formerly) Instructor
New Brunswick Community College
Saint John, NB

Project Manager: Tony Luengo
Supervising Editor: Julie Kretchman
Editors and Text Researchers: Su Mei Ku and Kelly V. Cochrane, SMK Editorial Services
Production Editor: Shefali Mehta
Production Coordinator: Kimberly Sullivan
Permissions Editor: Paula Joiner
Map Illustrator: Crowle Art Group
Page Composition: Darlene Eiler and Beth Crane, Heidy Lawrance Associates
Printing and Binding: RR Donnelley

Printed and Bound in the United States
15 16 17   16 15 14

Contents

To the Learner

After leaving high school at 16, Tommy Gallant worked as a manual labourer before successfully taking the GED Tests in 1989. A native of Prince Edward Island, Gallant won a scholarship from Atomic Energy of Canada, and has earned university degrees in biology.

You have taken a big step in your life by deciding to take the GED Tests. When you opened this book, you made a second important decision: to put in the time and effort to prepare for the tests. You may feel nervous about what is ahead. This is natural. Just relax and read the following pages to find out more about the GED Tests.

What Are the GED Tests?

The GED Tests cover the same subjects that people study in high school. The five subject areas are Language Arts, Writing; Language Arts, Reading; Social Studies; Science; and Mathematics. You will not be required to know all the information that is usually taught in high school. However, you will be tested on your ability to read and process information, solve problems, and communicate effectively.

Who administers the GED Tests?

The GED Tests are the five tests of General Educational Development. The GED Testing Service makes them available to adults who did not graduate from high school. When you pass the GED Tests, you will receive a diploma or certificate that is equivalent to a high-school diploma. Employers in private industry and government, as well as admissions officers in colleges and universities, accept the GED certificate as they would a high-school diploma.

Who takes the GED Tests?

Since 1969, when the GED Tests were first put into place in Canada, over 350 000 people have taken them. Of those completing the test battery, about 70 percent earn their GED certificates. *Steck-Vaughn Complete Canadian GED Preparation* will help you pass the GED Tests by providing (1) instruction and practice in the required skill areas; (2) practise with test items like those found on the GED Test; (3) test-taking tips; (4) timed-test practice; and (5) evaluation charts to help track your progress.

How are the GED Tests scored?

The chart on page 2 gives you information on the content, number of items, and time limit for each GED test. Because each province has its own requirement for how many tests you take in a day or testing period, you must check with your local adult education centre for the requirements in your province or territory.

The GED (General Educational Development) Tests

Test	Content Areas		Items	Time Limit
Language Arts, Writing, Part I	Sentence Structure Organization Usage Mechanics	30% 15% 30% 25%	50 questions	75 minutes
Language Arts, Writing, Part II	Essay			45 minutes
Social Studies	Canadian History World History Civics and Government Economics Geography	25% 15% 25% 20% 15%	50 questions	70 minutes
Science	Life Science Earth and Space Science Physical Science	45% 20% 35%	50 questions	80 minutes
Language Arts, Reading	Nonfiction Texts Literary Texts • Prose Fiction • Poetry • Drama	25% 75%	40 questions	65 minutes
Mathematics	Numbers and Operations Geometry Measurement and Data Analysis Algebra	20–30% 20–30% 20–30% 20–30%	Part I: 25 questions with optional use of a calculator Part II: 25 questions without a calculator	90 minutes

Some items in each test are based on business- and consumer-related documents. These do not require any specialized knowledge but will ask you to draw on your own observations and life experiences.

The Language Arts, Writing Test will ask you to detect and correct common errors in Canadian English; you will also be asked to decide on the most effective organization of text. The Essay portion of the Writing Test will ask you to write an essay offering your opinion or an explanation on a single topic of general knowledge.

The tests for Social Studies; Science; and Language Arts, Reading will ask you to answer questions. You will complete these tasks by interpreting reading passages, diagrams, charts and graphs, maps, cartoons, and practical and historical documents.

The Mathematics Test will ask you to solve a variety of word problems (many with graphics) using basic computation, analytical, and reasoning skills.

GED Scores

After you take each GED Test, you will receive a score. Once you have completed all five GED Tests, you will receive a total score, which is an average of all the scores. The highest score possible on a single test is 800. The minimum score required for you to pass the GED depends on where you live. Contact your local adult education centre for the minimum passing scores required for your province or territory.

Where can you go to take the GED Tests?

The GED Tests are offered year-round throughout Canada. For more information contact one of these institutions in your area:

- an adult education centre
- a continuing education centre
- a local community college
- a public library
- a private business school or technical school
- the board of education

These institutions can give you information regarding required identification, testing schedules, testing fees, and test supplies. They can also provide information about the scientific calculator to be used on the GED Mathematics Test.

Other GED Resources

- www.acenet.edu/calec/ged This is the official site for the GED Testing Service. Just follow the GED links throughout the site for information on the test.

- www.steckvaughn.com Follow the Adult Learners link to learn more about available GED preparation materials and www.gedpractice.com. This site also provides other resources for adult learners.

- www.nald.ca/nls.htm The National Literacy Secretariat provides information on instruction, federal policies, and national initiatives that affect adult education.

Why Should You Take the GED Tests?

A GED certificate is widely recognized as the equivalent of a high-school diploma and can help you in the following ways:

Employment

Many employers will not hire someone who does not have a high-school diploma or GED certificate. Future promotions and job changes will also be easier for GED graduates.

Education

Technical schools, vocational schools, and apprenticeship and training programs usually require a high-school diploma or the equivalent for enrollment. Other postsecondary institutions and programs always require a high-school diploma or the equivalent.

Personal Development

Attaining a GED certificate can be an ultimate aspiration, or the first step toward other educational aims. It is a positive move toward reaching your full potential.

Using This Book

- Start by taking the Entry Test for each unit and record your answers on a copy of the Answer Sheets at the back of this book. These tests will give you an idea of what the GED Test is like. Then use the Performance Analysis Chart at the end of each test to identify your areas of strength and the areas you need to review. The chart will refer you to specific pages or lessons in this book for further study.

- As you study, read the instruction and Tips carefully. Then answer the questions and check your work in the Answers and Explanations. Use the GED Review and GED Unit Review for each content area to find out if you need to review any lessons before continuing.

- After you complete the GED Unit Review, take the corresponding Simulated GED Test and record your answers on a copy of the Answer Sheets at the back of this book. It is identical to the real test in format and length. It will give you an idea of what the real test is like and if you are ready to take it. The Simulated GED Test Performance Analysis Chart for each test will help you determine if you need additional review.

- Additional resources including a GED Study Planner, Essay Self-Assessment form, Writing Checklists, and a GED Calculator Handbook can be found in Appendix B on pages 895–916. Extra practice in reading and interpreting tables, graphs, maps, and diagrams is included on pages 878–894.

What You Need to Know to Pass the GED Tests

Test One: Language Arts, Writing, Part I

Time: 75 minutes with 50 questions

The GED Language Arts, Writing Test has two parts. Part I is a proofreading and editing test in multiple-choice format, and Part II is an essay.

Part I consists of several passages, 12–22 sentences long. These include instructional or "how-to" texts, business communications, and informational articles. Always read the entire passage before you start answering questions. When you see an error, expect that there will be a question about it, but wait until you have finished reading the passage to address that question. Some questions require you to have a sense of the passage as a whole.

Content Areas

Questions on Part I of the Writing Test cover four general content areas: sentence structure, organization, usage, and mechanics.

Sentence structure (30%) You will be asked to correct sentence fragments, run-on sentences, and comma splices. You will also correct improperly subordinated ideas, misplaced modifiers, and lack of parallel structure.

Organization (15%) You will be expected to restructure ideas within a paragraph, choose an effective topic sentence, remove irrelevant ideas, and unify a document.

Usage (30%) Usage includes correct use of pronouns, nouns, and verbs.

Mechanics (25%) You will be asked to use standard conventions in the use of punctuation, capitalization, and spelling. Spelling items focus on possessives, contractions, homonyms, and other commonly confused words.

Item Types

Various questions will ask you to

- Correct sentences from the passage which may or may not contain a mistake. Choose the best way to correct the mistake or choose the alternative "(5) no correction is necessary."

- Revise an underlined part of a sentence. The sentence part may or may not include an error. You will choose the best correction or option (1) which has no change.

- Choose alternate ways to present ideas. These items test your ability to restructure or combine sentences.

Test One: Language Arts, Writing, Part II, the Essay

Time: 45 minutes for one assigned essay topic

For the GED Language Arts, Writing Test, Part II, you will write an expository essay. An essay gives a writer's views on a particular topic. You will be given an essay topic describing a situation and asking you to present your opinion or explanation. Topics cover general knowledge, so that you may draw on personal observations and experiences to write the essay.

Within the allotted time, you should plan, write, and proofread your essay. The test booklet contains scratch paper for planning and two lined pages for the final draft. On pages 22 and 23, you can read over the directions and an assignment that are representative of Part II of the Writing Test.

Scoring

A sample of the GED Essay Scoring Guide is on page 185. Two trained readers score the essay, judging how well you

- focus and develop your main points
- organize your essay
- develop your ideas, using examples and details
- demonstrate effective word choice
- use correct sentence structure, grammar, spelling, and punctuation

Two readers will each assign your essay a score between 1 and 4. These two scores are averaged to find your total score. An average score of 1 or 1.5 means that both parts of the GED Language Arts, Writing Test must be repeated. If the average score is 2 or higher, a formula is used to find a combined score for Parts I and II of the Writing Test.

Test Two: Social Studies

Time: 70 minutes with 50 questions

The GED Social Studies Test examines your ability to understand and use information about social studies. You will be asked to think about what you read. You will not be tested on any outside knowledge about social studies.

Content Areas

Questions on the GED Social Studies Test cover five general content areas: Canadian history, world history, civics and government, economics, and geography.

Canadian History (25%) Items include excerpts from the *Charter of Rights and Freedoms*.

World History (15%) You will read and answer questions about global events and how people have responded to them.

Civics and Government (25%) The questions cover the organization and operation of Canada. At least one practical document (for example, a voters' guide or tax form) will be included.

Economics (20%) You will read about the production of goods and services and how they are marketed and used. You will find practical documents, such as budgets and other workplace materials, in this part of the test.

Geography (15%) This area covers relationships between people and the environment.

Test Three: Science

Time: 80 minutes with 50 questions

The GED Science Test examines your ability to understand and interpret science information presented as text or graphics such as maps, charts, graphs, or diagrams. You will be asked to think about what you read. You will not be tested on any outside knowledge about science.

Content Areas

Questions on the GED Science Test cover general content areas, including life science, earth and space science, and physical science.

Life Science (45%) You will find topics such as cells, heredity, and health, and functions such as respiration, photosynthesis, and the behaviour and interdependence of organisms.

Earth and Space Science (20%) These topics include Earth's structure; earthquakes and volcanoes; weather and climate; and the origin and development of our solar system and universe.

Physical Science (35%) These topics include atoms, elements, compounds, radioactivity, matter, energy, and magnetism.

Test items in the above content areas also reflect the following content standards, as described in the National Science Education Standards: **Science as Inquiry** (the principles behind scientific methods, reasoning, and processes); **Science and Technology** (use of technology in scientific processes and findings); **Unifying Concepts and Processes** (major concepts such as "constancy and change"); **Science in Personal and Social Perspectives** (contemporary issues such as personal and community health); and **History and Nature of Science** (pursuit of scientific knowledge and historical perspectives on it).

Test Four: Language Arts, Reading

Time: 65 minutes with 40 questions

The GED Language Arts, Reading Test focuses on how well you understand and analyze what you read. You will not be tested on your knowledge of literature. Each selection will be preceded by a "purpose question" that helps to direct your reading of the text.

Types of Selections

- Two **nonfiction** selections of 200–400 words: These may include informational or persuasive texts, critical reviews of the fine arts and the performing arts, and business documents.

- Three **prose fiction** selections of 200–400 words: These are excerpts from novels or short stories. There will be one selection written before 1920, one from 1920 to 1960, and one written after 1960.

- One **poetry** selection of 8 to 25 lines

- One **drama** selection of 200–400 words

Thinking Skills

The GED Social Studies Test, the GED Science Test, and the GED Reading Test require you to think about information in several ways. To answer the questions, you will use five types of thinking skills: comprehension, application, analysis, evaluation, and synthesis.

Comprehension questions require a basic understanding of materials presented. They measure your ability to recognize a restatement, paraphrasing, or summary or to know what is implied in the text.

Application questions require you to apply information in a new situation or context. You'll need to know how to support a generalization, principle, or strategy and then apply the generalization, principle, or strategy to a new problem.

Analysis questions require you to break down information and find relationships between ideas in order to draw a conclusion, make an inference, distinguish fact from opinion and conclusions from supporting detail, identify cause-and-effect relationships, compare and contrast ideas, or recognize unstated assumptions.

Evaluation questions require you to make judgments, draw conclusions, and identify values and beliefs. You will also need to recognize the role that values and beliefs play in decision-making.

Synthesis questions require you to put elements together to form a whole. They require analysis of the overall text (for example: comparing and contrasting), interpreting tone, point of view, or purpose, or integrating new information with information in the text.

Test Five: Mathematics

Time: 90 minutes with 25 questions on each of two parts

The GED Mathematics Test has both formal mathematical problems and real world situations. About 50 percent of the test involves drawings, diagrams, charts, and graphs. For Part I, you will be able to use a calculator issued to you at the test site.

Approximately 20 percent of the test will entail entering your answer on either a standard grid or a coordinate plane grid. The test includes directions on the use of these "alternative" formats.

Some questions ask you to show *how* you would solve problems. Others test your ability to do basic math operations or test your understanding of concepts such as ratio and proportion, estimation, and formulas. A formulas page, which includes all the formulas you will need to take the test, will be provided.

Content Areas

The GED Mathematics Test covers the following four content areas.

Numbers and Operations (20%–30%) This area tests your ability to work problems involving whole numbers, fractions, decimals, percents, and ratios and proportion. You will use numbers in equivalent forms, compare numbers, and draw conclusions. You will also relate basic arithmetic operations to each other, use them in the proper order, and compute with and without a calculator.

Measurement and Data Analysis (20%–30%) Measurement questions involve length, perimeter, circumference, area, volume, and time. You will need to understand both the U.S. measurement system and the metric system.

Data Analysis questions test your skills with tables, charts, and graphs. You may be asked to find the mean (average), median, mode, or the probability that a given event will occur.

Algebra (20%–30%) These questions test your understanding of variables, algebraic expressions, and equations. Some questions test concepts such as square roots, exponents, and scientific notation. Percent, ratio, and proportion are also applied to algebra questions. A few questions may include powers and roots, factoring, solving inequalities, graphing equations, or finding the slope of lines. Algebra questions also test your understanding of the coordinate grid and ordered pairs. The new coordinate grid alternative answer format requires you to mark your answer by bubbling in the location of the ordered pair.

Geometry (20%–30%) Geometry questions cover lines and angles, circles, triangles, and quadrilaterals, and indirect measurement. You will use basic arithmetic operations to find values of angles and line segments. Some items require understanding of congruence, similarity, and the Pythagorean Relationship.

How to Prepare for the GED Tests

Classes are available to anyone who wants to prepare to take the GED Tests. Most GED preparation programs offer individualized instruction and tutors who can help you identify areas in which you may need help. The classes are usually informal and allow you to work at your own pace and with other adults who also are studying for the GED Tests. For information about classes available near you, contact one of the resources listed on page 3.

If you prefer to study by yourself, *Steck-Vaughn Complete GED Preparation* has been developed to guide your study through skill instruction and practice exercises. In addition to working on specific skills, you will be able to take practice GED Tests (like those in this book) in order to check your progress.

Test-Taking Skills

Steck-Vaughn Complete Canadian GED Preparation will help you prepare for the GED Tests. In addition, there are some specific ways that you can improve your performance on the test.

Answering the Test Questions

- Never skim the directions. Read them carefully so that you know exactly what to do. If you are unsure, ask the test-giver whether the directions can be explained.

- Read each question carefully to make sure that you know what it is asking.

- Read all the answer options carefully, even if you think you know the right answer. Some of the answers may not seem wrong at first glance, but only one answer will be correct.

- Before you answer a question, be sure that there is evidence in the passage to support your choice. Don't rely on what you know outside the context of the passage.

- Answer all the questions. If you cannot find the correct answer, reduce the number of possible answers by eliminating all the answers you know are wrong. Then go back to figure out the correct answer. If you still cannot decide, make your best guess.

- Fill in your answer sheet carefully. To record your answers, fill in one numbered circle on the answer sheet beside the number that corresponds to the question. Fill in only one answer space for each question; multiple answers will be scored as incorrect.

- Remember that the GED is a timed test. When the test begins, write down the time that you must be finished. Then keep an eye on the time. Do not take a long time on any one question. Answer each question as best you can and go on. If you are spending a lot of time on one question, skip it, making a very light mark next to the question number on the sheet. If you finish before time is up, go back to the questions you skipped or were unsure of and give them more thought. Be sure to erase any extraneous marks you have made.

- Don't change an answer unless you are certain your answer was wrong. Usually, the first answer you choose is the correct one.

- If you begin to feel nervous, stop working for a moment. Take a few deep breaths and relax. Then begin working again.

Study Skills

Study Regularly

- Distractions can ruin your concentration. Explain to others why it is important that you are left alone during your scheduled study time.

- Find a comfortable place to study. If you cannot study at home, consider going to the library. Most public libraries have quiet areas for reading and studying. Is there a college or university near you? Find out if you can use the library there.

Organize Your Study Materials

- Select a place to keep your books, pencils, and paper, so that you don't waste valuable study time looking for your materials.

- Create a folder for each subject you are studying. Folders with pockets are useful for storing notes and loose papers.

Read Regularly

- Get a library card. Become a regular at the library where there is reading material on every topic imaginable. Do you have hobbies? Check the magazine section for publications of interest to you. If you are not familiar with the library, ask for help.

Take Notes

- Find a system for note-taking that works well for you. Perhaps you need only a few key words to help you remember a concept. You may prefer a question-and-answer format: *What is the main idea? The main idea is.* ... Some people like to outline ideas or put them into charts or diagrams. The goal is to restate important information in a way that will help you remember it.

Improve Your Vocabulary

- When you encounter an unfamiliar word in your reading, do your best to figure out what it means. Try reading the sentence by replacing the word you don't know with another. Does it make sense with the rest of the paragraph?

- If you can't figure out what the word means on your own, use a dictionary. Look up the word while the passage is in front of you, because many words have more than one meaning. You may need to try several meanings in the sentence, to see which one applies.

- Start a list of new words. Use your own words to write definitions.

Taking the Tests

Before the Test

- If you have never been to the test centre, go there the day before you take the test. If you drive, find out where to park.

- Prepare the things you need for the test: your admission ticket (if necessary), acceptable identification, some sharpened No. 2 pencils with erasers, a watch, glasses, a jacket or sweater (in case the room is cold), and a snack to eat during breaks.

- Eat a nutritious meal and get a good night's sleep. If the test is early in the morning, set the alarm.

The Day of the Test

- Eat a good meal before the test. If you are going to be at the test centre all day, consider packing a lunch. Finding a restaurant or waiting to be served may make you late for the rest of the test.

- Wear comfortable clothing, and make sure that you have all the materials you need.

- Try to arrive at the test centre about 20 minutes early. This allows sufficient time in case there is a last-minute change of room.

LANGUAGE ARTS, WRITING, PART I

Directions

The Language Arts, Writing Entry Test is intended to measure your ability to use English clearly and effectively. It is a test of English as it should be written, not as it might be spoken.

This test consists of paragraphs with numbered sentences. Some sentences have errors in sentence structure, organization, usage, or mechanics (spelling, punctuation, and capitalization). Read the sentences and answer the multiple-choice questions that follow. Some questions refer to sentences that are written correctly. The best answer for these questions is the one that leaves the sentence as originally written. The best answer for some questions is the one that creates a sentence that is consistent with the verb tense and point of view used throughout the paragraph.

You should spend no more than 37.5 minutes answering the 25 questions on this test. Work carefully, but do not spend too much time on any one question. Do not skip any items. Make a reasonable guess when you are not sure of an answer. You will not be penalized for incorrect answers.

When time is up, note the last item you finished. This will tell you whether you can finish the real GED Test in the time allowed. Then complete the Entry Test.

Record your answers to the questions on a copy of the answer sheet on page 917. Be sure that all required information is properly recorded on the answer sheet.

To record your answers, mark the numbered space on the answer sheet that corresponds to the answer you choose for each question on the test.

Example

Sentence 1: **We were all honoured to meet lieutenant governor Phillips.**

Which correction should be made to sentence 1?

(1) change honoured to honouring
(2) insert a comma after honoured
(3) change meet to met
(4) change lieutenant governor to Lieutenant Governor
(5) no correction is necessary

In this example, the words lieutenant governor should be capitalized; therefore, answer space 4 would be marked on the answer sheet.

Do not rest the point of your pencil on the answer sheet while thinking about your answer. Do not make any stray or unnecessary marks. If you change an answer, erase your first mark completely. Mark only one answer space for each question; multiple answers will be scored as incorrect. Do not fold or crease your answer sheet.

When you finish the test, use the Performance Analysis Chart on page 21 to determine whether you are ready to take the real GED Test and, if not, which skill areas need additional review.

Directions: Choose the one best answer to each question.

Questions 1 through 9 refer to the following memo.

MEMORANDUM

To: Cariboo Company Staff
From: Aisha Smith, Director of Community Relations
Re: Holiday Gift Drive

(A)

(1) This year our employees collected a record 120 presents for the annual gift drive for smithville children's hospital. (2) Last year we didn't collect as many presents. (3) Every department participated, so congratulations are due all around! (4) Now we're looking for at least ten volunteers. (5) The volunteers will wrap the presents. (6) It's faster and more fun with more people. (7) The present wrapping will start at 3 P.M. on Monday.

(B)

(8) Will you drive or distribute the presents on Tuesday? (9) We are especially eager for drivers with station wagons vans or trucks. (10) Even if you can't drive, you can help distribute gifts at the hospital. (11) If you've never been to the children's hospital and seen the kids' faces when they receive his presents, you should make time to come. (12) Seeing the children's eyes light up is an experience you wouldn't forget. (13) Please sign up by this Friday, we can assign everyone to a car pool. (14) Cariboo Company—and the children at the hospital—will thank you for your effort!

---

1. Sentence 1: **This year our employees collected a record 120 presents for the annual gift drive for smithville children's hospital.**

   Which is the best way to write the underlined portion of the sentence? If the original is the best way, choose option (1).

   (1) smithville children's hospital
   (2) the smithville children's Hospital
   (3) Smithville Children's Hospital
   (4) the Smithville Children's hospital
   (5) Smithville Childrens' Hospital

2. Sentence 2: **Last year we didn't collect as many presents.**

   Which revision should be made to the placement of sentence 2?

   (1) move sentence 2 to follow sentence 3
   (2) move sentence 2 to follow sentence 5
   (3) move sentence 2 to the end of paragraph A
   (4) move sentence 2 to the beginning of paragraph B
   (5) remove sentence 2

3. Which revision would improve the effectiveness of the memo?

   (1) begin a new paragraph with sentence 4
   (2) begin a new paragraph with sentence 5
   (3) begin a new paragraph with sentence 6
   (4) combine paragraphs A and B
   (5) no revision is necessary

4. Sentences 4 and 5: **Now we're looking for at least ten volunteers. The volunteers will wrap the presents.**

   The most effective combination of sentences 4 and 5 would include which group of words?

   (1) to wrap the presents
   (2) who can wrap the presents
   (3) In order to wrap the presents
   (4) Now we need to wrap the presents
   (5) for the wrapping of the presents

5. Sentence 8: **Will you drive or distribute the presents on Tuesday?**

   Which is the most effective rewrite of sentence 8?

   (1) replace sentence 8 with We need some help Tuesday.
   (2) replace sentence 8 with Let's not forget about Tuesday.
   (3) replace sentence 8 with Can you distribute presents on Tuesday?
   (4) replace sentence 8 with On Tuesday, we will need help delivering the presents.
   (5) replace sentence 8 with The presents will need to be delivered, of course.

6. Sentence 9: **We are especially eager for drivers with station wagons vans or trucks.**

   Which is the best way to write the underlined portion of this sentence? If the original is the best way, choose option (1).

   (1) station wagons vans or trucks
   (2) station wagons, vans, or trucks
   (3) station wagons vans, or trucks
   (4) station wagons or vans or trucks
   (5) station wagons, vans or, trucks

7. Sentence 11: **If you've never been to the children's hospital and seen the kids' faces when they receive his presents, you should make time to come.**

   Which correction should be made to sentence 11?

   (1) replace his with her
   (2) replace they with he
   (3) replace his with their
   (4) remove the comma between presents and you
   (5) no correction is necessary

8. Sentence 12: **Seeing the children's eyes light up is an experience you wouldn't forget.**

   Which correction should be made to sentence 12?

   (1) change wouldn't to won't
   (2) change is to was
   (3) add a comma after light up
   (4) change seeing to having seen
   (5) no correction is necessary

9. Sentence 13: **Please sign up by this Friday, we can assign everyone to a car pool.**

   Which is the best way to write the underlined portion of this sentence? If the original is the best way, choose option (1).

   (1) Friday, we can
   (2) Friday so we can
   (3) Friday we can
   (4) Friday and we can
   (5) Friday. We can

A Woman of Distinction

(A)

(1) Emily Howard Stowe was born in 1831 in Norfolk, Ontario. (2) She lived there until moving to Toronto to study teaching at the Toronto Normal School. (3) Stowe taught for ten years, becoming the first female principal of a public school in Canada. (4) This, however, was just the beginning of her professional journey.

(B)

(5) Stowe decided to become a doctor. (6) This was despite the fact that her husband bedridden by tuberculosis. (7) Stowe was also raising three children. (8) She trained at the New York Medical College for Women since no medical college in Canada were accepting female applicants. (9) Suddenly Stowe was a caregiver, a parent, and studying. (10) She received her degree in 1867, and though Canadian law denied Stowe a medical licence, it will not prohibit her from practising without one.

(C)

(11) Stowe was determined to be the first woman to have a medical practice in Canada. (12) She was also determined to break down the social and professional barriers facing women. (13) She helped organize the Ontario Medical College for Women in 1883. (14) She also founded the Toronto Women's Literary Club and Canada's first suffrage group, and she was the principal founder and first president of the Dominion Women's Enfranchisement Association in 1889. (15) Stowe was finally granted a medical licence 13 years after starting her practice. (16) Though it could then be argued that Stowe was not Canada's first female doctor, it can't be denied that she opened the door for women. (17) Dr. Stowe died in 1903, but her legacy has lived on. (18) Their was a ceremony in 1935 to award her the Jubilee Medal posthumously. (19) In 1981, the 150th anniversary of her birth, Stowe's image was put on a Canadian postage stamp.

10. Sentence 3: **Stowe taught for ten years, becoming the first female principal of a public school in Canada.**

    If you rewrote sentence 3 beginning with

    After she taught for ten years, Stowe

    the next word(s) should be

    (1) is becoming
    (2) was becoming
    (3) will become
    (4) became
    (5) becomes

11. Sentence 6: **This was despite the fact that her husband bedridden by tuberculosis.**

    Which correction should be made to sentence 6?

    (1) replace husband bedridden with husband was bedridden
    (2) insert a comma after bedridden
    (3) change tuberculosis to Tuberculosis
    (4) remove the fact that
    (5) no correction is necessary

12. Sentence 8: **She trained at the New York Medical College for Women since no medical college in Canada were accepting a female applicant.**

Which correction should be made to sentence 8?

(1) replace she with Stowe
(2) change trained to trains
(3) change were accepting to was accepting
(4) change no medical college to no Medical College
(5) no correction is necessary

13. Sentence 9: **Suddenly Stowe was a caregiver, a parent, and studying.**

Which is the best way to rewrite the underlined portion of this sentence?

(1) was studying
(2) a student
(3) will be studying
(4) has been studying
(5) studied

14. Sentence 10: **She received her degree in 1867, and though Canadian law denied Stowe a medical licence, it will not prohibit her from practising without one.**

Which is the best way to write the underlined portion of this sentence? If the original is the best way, choose option (1).

(1) will not prohibit
(2) did not prohibit
(3) were not prohibiting
(4) have not prohibited
(5) do not prohibit

15. Sentence 12: **She was also determined to break down the social and professional barriers facing women.**

Which correction should be made to the sentence?

(1) change was also determined to is also determined
(2) change facing women to that face women
(3) change facing women to women were to face
(4) change women to women's
(5) no correction necessary

16. Sentence 18: **Their was a ceremony in 1935 to award her the Jubilee Medal posthumously.**

Which correction should be made to the sentence?

(1) replace Their with There
(2) replace Their with They're
(3) replace Medal with Meddle
(4) replace posthumously with posthumosly
(5) no correction is necessary

17. Which revision would improve the effectiveness of the article?

Begin a new paragraph with

(1) sentence 15
(2) sentence 16
(3) sentence 17
(4) sentence 18
(5) sentence 19

Buying a Used Car

(A)

(1) Today, there are more options than ever for buying a used car.
(2) Manufacturer-certified used car's are available from many brand name dealers.
(3) Certified cars have been reconditioned and usually come with a warranty. (4) If you want to see a variety of makes and models you can visit a used car dealer.
(5) Of course, you can also shop the old fashioned way by reading the classified ads and contacting individuals. (6) No matter how you shop, it can't be too careful when buying a used car. (7) Examine the car carefully and, if your province has "lemon laws," know how to use them in case of fraud.

(B)

(8) Before you take a used car for a test drive, inspect it thoroughly. (9) Look for rust on the underside of the body and check the tires. (10) Tires that are badly worn or shows uneven wear may indicate that the car has not been well maintained. (11) Look for a lot of wear on the foot pedals, that tells you the car was heavily driven. (12) Oily spots under a car may indicate further problems. (13) Excessive oil is also a bad sign on the engine. (14) Check the odometer to see how many kilometres the car has been driven. (15) If a car that appears to be old and worn shows a low kilometrage the odometer may have been set back.

(C)

(16) After you test drive the car, look at the engine make sure it is running smoothly, and check for smells, such as burnt oil and coolant, that might signal a problem. (17) Finally, have the car inspected by a mechanic whom you trust.
(18) If you are careful, you should be able to find an affordable, reliable used car.

18. Sentence 2: **Manufacturer-certified <u>used car's</u> are available from many brand name dealers.**

Which is the best way to write the underlined portion of the sentence? If the original is the best way, choose option (1).

(1) used car's
(2) used-car's
(3) used cars
(4) used cars'
(5) used-cars'

19. Sentence 4: **If you want to see a variety of makes and models you can visit a used car dealer.**

Which correction should be made to sentence 4?

(1) change <u>want</u> to <u>wants</u>
(2) insert a <u>comma</u> after <u>models</u>
(3) change <u>dealer</u> to <u>Dealer</u>
(4) replace <u>and</u> with <u>or</u>
(5) no correction is necessary

20. Sentence 6: **No matter how you shop, it can't be too careful when buying a used car.**

Which is the best way to write the underlined portion of this sentence? If the original is the best way, choose option (1).

(1) No matter how you shop, it
(2) No matter how you shop,
(3) No matter how you shop, you
(4) Shopping for a used car? It
(5) Shopping for a used car, it

21. Sentence 10: **Tires that are badly worn <u>or shows</u> uneven wear may indicate that the car has not been well maintained.**

Which is the best way to write the underlined portion of this sentence? If the original is the best way, choose option (1).

(1) or shows
(2) or show
(3) yet shows
(4) yet show's
(5) nor show

22. Sentence 11: **Look for a lot of wear on the foot pedals, that tells you the car was heavily driven.**

Which correction should be made to sentence 11?

(1) change <u>pedals, that</u> to <u>pedals. That</u>
(2) remove the comma after <u>pedals</u>
(3) insert <u>can</u> before <u>that</u>
(4) insert <u>and</u> before <u>that</u>
(5) no correction is necessary

23. Sentence 13: **Excessive oil is also a bad sign on the engine.**

Which correction should be made to sentence 13?

(1) replace <u>Excessive</u> with <u>Expressive</u>
(2) change <u>is</u> to <u>are</u>
(3) remove <u>also</u>
(4) move <u>on the engine</u> after <u>oil</u>
(5) no correction is necessary

The article has been repeated for your use in answering the remaining questions.

Buying a Used Car

(A)

(1) Today, there are more options than ever for buying a used car. (2) Manufacturer-certified used car's are available from many brand name dealers. (3) Certified cars have been reconditioned and usually come with a warranty. (4) If you want to see a variety of makes and models you can visit a used car dealer. (5) Of course, you can also shop the old fashioned way by reading the classified ads and contacting individuals. (6) No matter how you shop, it can't be too careful when buying a used car. (7) Examine the car carefully and, if your province has "lemon laws," know how to use them in case of fraud.

(B)

(8) Before you take a used car for a test drive, inspect it thoroughly. (9) Look for rust on the underside of the body and check the tires. (10) Tires that are badly worn or shows uneven wear may indicate that the car has not been well maintained. (11) Look for a lot of wear on the foot pedals, that tells you the car was heavily driven. (12) Oily spots under a car may indicate further problems. (13) Excessive oil is also a bad sign on the engine. (14) Check the odometer to see how many kilometres the car has been driven. (15) If a car that appears to be old and worn shows a low kilometrage the odometer may have been set back.

(C)

(16) After you test drive the car, look at the engine make sure it is running smoothly, and check for smells, such as burnt oil and coolant, that might signal a problem. (17) Finally, have the car inspected by a mechanic whom you trust. (18) If you are careful, you should be able to find an affordable, reliable used car.

24. Sentence 15: **If a car that appears to be old and worn shows a low kilometrage the odometer may have been set back.**

Which correction should be made to sentence 15?

(1) change appears to appear
(2) change shows to showing
(3) insert a comma after kilometrage
(4) remove the odometer
(5) no correction is necessary

25. Sentence 16: **After you test drive the car, look at the engine make sure it is running smoothly, and check for smells, such as burnt oil and coolant, that might signal a problem.**

Which is the best way to write the underlined portion of this sentence? If the original is the best way, choose option (1).

(1) the engine make sure
(2) the engine and make sure
(3) the engine, however, make sure
(4) the engine. Make sure
(5) the engine, so make sure

Language Arts, Writing

This chart can help you determine your strengths and weaknesses on the content and skill areas of the Language Arts, Writing Test. Use the Answers and Explanations starting on page 718 to check your answers to the test. Then circle on the chart the numbers of the test items you answered correctly. Put the total number correct for each content area and skill area in each row and column. If you answered fewer than 25 questions correctly, look at the total items correct in each column and row and decide which areas need more study. Use the page references to study those areas.

Item Type / Content Area	Correction	Revision	Construction Shift	Number Correct	Page References
Sentence Structure					**68–95**
Sentences/Sentence Fragments	11			____/1	68–71
Compound Sentences/ Combining Ideas				____/0	72–75
Subordinating Ideas			4	____/1	76–79
Run-ons/Comma Splices	22	9, 25		____/3	80–83
Modifiers	23			____/1	84–86
Parallel Structure		13		____/1	87–89
Organization					**96–113**
Paragraph Structure/ Unity and Coherence	2			____/1	96–99
Topic Sentences			5	____/1	100–102
Paragraph Divisions			3, 17	____/2	103–105
Transitions				____/0	106–108
Usage					**114–131**
Subject-Verb Agreement	12	14		____/2	114–117
Verb Forms	8, 15		10	____/3	118–120
Verb Tenses		21		____/1	121–123
Pronouns	7	20		____/2	124–127
Mechanics					**132–144**
Capitalization	1			____/0	132–134
Commas	19, 24	6		____/3	135–137
Spelling	16	18		____/2	138–141

1–20 → You need more review.
21–25 → Congratulations! You're ready to write the Official Language Arts Writing Part I

LANGUAGE ARTS, WRITING, PART II

Essay Directions and Topic

Look at the box on the next page for your assigned topic and the letter of that topic.

You must write on the assigned topic **only**.

You will have 45 minutes to write on your assigned essay topic. Return to the multiple-choice section after you complete your essay, if you have time remaining in this test period. Do not return the Language Arts, Writing booklet until you finish both Parts I and II of the Language Arts, Writing Test.

Two evaluators will score your essay according to its overall effectiveness. Their evaluation will be based on the following features:

- Well-focused main points
- Clear organization
- Specific development of your ideas
- Control of sentence structure, punctuation, grammar, word choice, and spelling

Remember, you must complete both the multiple-choice questions (Part I) and the essay (Part II) to receive a score on the Language Arts, Writing Test. To avoid having to repeat both parts of the test, be sure to do the following:

- Do not leave the pages blank.
- Write legibly *in ink* so that the evaluators will be able to read your writing.
- Write on the assigned topic. If you write on a topic other than the one assigned, you will not receive a score for the Language Arts, Writing Test.
- Write your essay on the lined pages of the separate answer sheet booklet. Only the writing on these pages will be scored.

Part II is a test to determine how well you can use written language to explain your ideas.

In preparing your essay, take the following steps:

- Read the **directions** and the **topic** carefully.
- Plan your essay before you write. Use the scrap paper provided to make notes and a brief outline. These notes will be collected but not scored.
- Before you hand in your essay, reread what you have written and make any changes that will improve your essay.

Your essay should be long enough to develop the topic adequately.

TOPIC F

Why do people continue doing things that are bad for them, even when there is clear evidence that these activities are harmful?

In your essay, give reasons for this behaviour.

When you finish your essay, see page 720 of the Answers and Explanations to evaluate and score your essay.

SOCIAL STUDIES

Directions

This Social Studies Entry Test is intended to measure your knowledge of general social studies concepts.

The questions are based on short readings or on graphs, maps, charts, cartoons, or illustrations. Study the information given and then answer the questions that follow. Refer to the information as often as necessary in answering the questions.

Spend no more than 35 minutes answering the 25 questions on this test. Work carefully, but do not spend too much time on any one item. Do not skip any items. Make a reasonable guess when you are unsure of an answer. You will not be penalized for incorrect answers. When time is up, note the last item you finished. This will tell you whether you can finish the real GED Test in the time allowed. Then complete the Entry Test.

Record your answers to the questions on a copy of the answer sheet on page 918. Be sure that all required information is recorded on the answer sheet.

To record your answers, fill in the numbered circle on the answer sheet that corresponds to the answer you choose for each item on the test.

Example

Early pioneers of the western frontier looked to settle on land that had adequate access to water. To ensure access to water, many early pioneers settled on land near which type of geographic feature?

(1) forests
(2) grasslands
(3) rivers
(4) glaciers
(5) oceans

The correct answer is <u>rivers</u>; therefore, answer circle 3 should be filled in on the answer sheet.

Do not rest the point of your pencil on the answer sheet while considering your answer. Do not make any stray or unnecessary marks. If you change an answer, erase your first mark completely. Mark only one answer for each question; multiple answers will be scored as incorrect. Do not fold or crease your answer sheet.

When you finish the test, use the Performance Analysis Chart on page 32 to determine whether you are ready to take the real GED Test and, if not, which skill areas need additional review.

Questions 1 through 4 refer to the following passage and cartoon.

As World War II drew to a close, the United Nations was created in the hope of preventing future wars. UN agencies help reduce world tensions by providing loans, food, and other aid to nations in need. Most of the UN's services are generally considered worthwhile. Its role as a peacekeeper, however, is more controversial. The UN has no army. It depends on member nations to provide it with troops. Sometimes international politics make it difficult for UN peacekeepers to accomplish their goal. Such was the case when the first Canadian and French forces were sent to Bosnia in the early 1990s. Their mission was to protect the Bosnian Muslims from the atrocities committed against them by the Christian Bosnian Serbs. This Canadian cartoon assessed the effectiveness of the UN peacekeeping mission.

Malcolm Mayes/artizans.com.

1. According to the passage, why was the United Nations formed?

   (1) to end World War II
   (2) to provide loans to member nations
   (3) to donate food to starving people
   (4) to promote world peace
   (5) to protect Bosnians from ethnic violence

2. What was the reason UN troops were sent to Bosnia in the early 1990s?

   (1) The French and Canadians were fighting.
   (2) The Christians were attacking the Muslims.
   (3) The Muslims were attacking the Christians.
   (4) The UN was assembling its army.
   (5) The UN was avoiding a controversy.

3. Which situation from daily life is most like the one pictured in the cartoon?

   (1) purchasing a rifle at a gun shop
   (2) getting your hair done at a new salon in town
   (3) hearing a teacher threaten to suspend a bully but not following through
   (4) getting mugged by a gang of hoodlums on a street corner near your home
   (5) being unjustly arrested by the police for a crime you did not commit

4. The passage and the cartoon support which of the following conclusions?

   (1) The UN should be disbanded.
   (2) The UN should have its own army.
   (3) The UN should get out of Bosnia.
   (4) The UN should be able to enforce its missions.
   (5) The UN should relocate Bosnian refugees to France and Canada.

Questions 5 and 6 refer to the following passage and document.

Section 10 (C) of the *Constitution Act of 1982* states, "everyone has the right on arrest or detention to have the validity of the detention determined by way of *habeas corpus* and to be released if the detention is not lawful." This fundamental right in Canada originated in British law when the *Habeas Corpus Act* was created in 1679. The term *habeas corpus* literally means "you shall have the body." When someone is arrested in Canada, a lawyer can obtain a writ or court order of *habeas corpus* to justify the arrest or force the case to trial.

FORM 83A
IN THE SUPREME COURT — TRIAL DIVISION

IN THE MATTER OF _____ of _____, Province of Prince Edward Island, confined or restrained of his liberty at_____.

ELIZABETH THE SECOND, by the Grace of God, of the United Kingdom, Canada and Her other Realms and Territories, Queen, Head of the Commonwealth, Defender of the Faith.

TO: The Superintendent of _____ at _____

GREETING:

WE COMMAND YOU, that you bring _____ in person before the presiding Judge of the Supreme Court — Trial Division at _____, _____ County, on _____ day, the _____ day of _____, 19_____, at the hour of _____ o'clock in the ___ noon, together with this Writ, so that such judge of our court may then and there cause to be done with _____ what is right and just according to law.

WE DO FURTHER COMMAND you to send forthwith to the Registrar's Office at the said place true copies of all orders, warrants, committals or other documents pursuant to which the said _____ is confined or restrained of his liberty and which are in your possession or control, together with your certificate that the documents listed in such certificate are all of the documents pursuant to which the said _____ is confined or restrained as aforesaid.

_____
Registrar

Habeas Corpus writ from PEI, Law Courts Education Society, Vancouver.

5. What important value of Canada's judicial system is suggested by the right of *habeas corpus*?

   (1) Government can keep anyone in jail for an indefinite period.
   (2) Lawyers have the right to issue writs.
   (3) British law has influenced Canadian law.
   (4) Individual freedom is protected by law.
   (5) Democratic principles are enshrined in the *Constitution Act of 1982*.

6. A writ of *habeas corpus* is most similar to which of the following documents?

   (1) a credit card
   (2) a restraining order
   (3) a marriage certificate
   (4) a constitutional amendment
   (5) a certificate of insurance

Questions 7 and 8 refer to the following photograph and paragraph.

Maurice Duplessis and Archbishop Joseph Charbonneau (centre) at Ste-Thérèse in 1946.

From 1935 to 1959, Maurice Duplessis, leader of the conservative Union Nationale party, dominated Quebec provincial politics. Duplessis' goal was to prevent secularism and modernism from overtaking Quebec society. In 1949, a strike by unionized mine workers at Asbestos challenged three pillars of power in the province: the Duplessis regime, the hierarchy of the Catholic church, and the American owners of the asbestos mine. The strike was settled only after much violence took place.

7. What conclusion is supported by details in the paragraph?

   (1) Quebec society in the decade after World War II was open and progressive.
   (2) The province was ripe for political and social change.
   (3) Quebeckers saw the church as their best hope for modernization.
   (4) Maurice Duplessis wanted American companies to raise the wages of Quebec workers.
   (5) The Union Nationale party was the only party in Quebec provincial politics.

8. What does the photograph reveal about the power structure of Quebec under Premier Duplessis?

   (1) Duplessis championed the common people.
   (2) The premier was a devout Catholic.
   (3) Maurice Duplessis allied himself with the church, big business, and the police.
   (4) Lawyers dominated Quebec society.
   (5) The Catholic church was not involved in Quebec politics.

Questions 9 through 11 refer to the following passage.

A lone worker has only one small voice, but not workers who speak as a group through a labour union. When these workers threaten to stop production by striking, their employer must pay attention.

In 1940, to avoid workers' strikes in critical wartime industries, the federal government passed emergency regulations that forced employers to bargain with workers organized in unions. The regulations forbade companies from discriminating against workers who joined a union and said the employers had to bargain "in good faith." This set the stage across Canada for the process of collective bargaining.

Collective bargaining is the discussion between company managers and union leaders who speak for the company's employees. The two groups negotiate and attempt to come to agreement on a contract that sets the workers' wages and conditions of employment. Often both sides will give up something that is important to them to get something else that they want even more.

Since the 1930s, collective bargaining has improved wages and salaries, health and vacation benefits, working and safety conditions, and company liability for accident and health hazards. If, after collective bargaining, the labour union and management cannot agree on a contract, the union may choose to strike. Often, the mere threat of a strike will cause management to agree to workers' demands. Sometimes, however, even a long strike does not help workers get their way.

9. What would probably happen first if a school board did not want to increase teachers' salaries?

   (1) The teachers would strike.
   (2) The teachers would take a cut in pay.
   (3) The teachers would quit.
   (4) The school board would close the schools.
   (5) The teachers' union would bargain with the school board.

10. Which of the following is an opinion about labour unions?

   (1) They are too powerful.
   (2) They improve the lives of workers.
   (3) They engage in collective bargaining.
   (4) They give workers a voice in their jobs.
   (5) They negotiate about work safety and other issues.

11. Which value is most strongly related to the use of collective bargaining in resolving labour disputes?

   (1) power
   (2) wealth
   (3) control
   (4) compromise
   (5) freedom

Question 12 refers to the following graph.

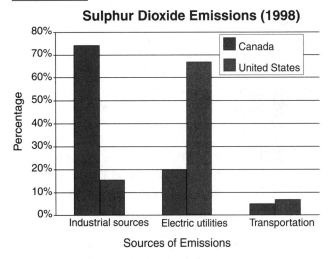

Sulphur Dioxide Emissions (1998)

12. Which of the following statements is implied by the graph?

   (1) Both Canadians and Americans need better transportation systems.
   (2) Canadian industries are more successful than American industries.
   (3) Sulphur dioxide emission is caused mostly by industrial sources in Canada and by electrical utilities in the United States.
   (4) Sulphur dioxide emissions are a more serious problem in Canada than in the United States.
   (5) Both Canada and the United States had the same level of sulphur dioxide emissions during 1998.

Questions 13 and 14 refer to the following table.

Unemployment as a Percentage of the Labour Force, 1930–1941 and 1992–2001			
Year	Unemployment (%)	Year	Unemployment (%)
1930	13.1	1992	11.2
1933	32.4	1995	9.5
1934	26.5	1998	8.3
1938	15.8	2000	6.8
1941	3.2	2001	7.2

Source: Statistics Canada.

13. According to the table, in which year was the rate of unemployment the highest?

   (1) 2001
   (2) 1933
   (3) 1941
   (4) 1993
   (5) 1999

14. How did the rate of unemployment in the 1990s compare with the rate of unemployment during the 1930s?

   (1) The rates in the 1990s are lower than any earlier year shown in the table.
   (2) The rates in the 1990s are higher than any earlier year shown in the table.
   (3) The rates in the 1990s are about the same as the rates in the 1930s.
   (4) The rates in the 1990s are lower than the rates during the 1930s.
   (5) The rates in the 1990s are higher than the rates during the 1930s.

Questions 15 and 16 refer to the following passage.

Until recently, our knowledge of early Canada was strongly influenced by the writings of European travellers and missionaries. This approach to history is referred to as Eurocentric, since historical events were explained and understood from a European point of view. From a Eurocentric perspective, the Aboriginal inhabitants of North America played only a minor, supporting role in the story of Canada.

Recently, Canadian historians have widened their focus, thanks in part to the work of archaeologists. Archaeological findings place Aboriginals at the centre of our early history. The Aboriginal peoples of North America had been coping with the severities of climate and the shifting relations among different cultures for several millennia before the Spanish, French, and English arrived.

15. What is the main idea of the passage?

   (1) Early Canadian history is more interesting than early American history.
   (2) The history of early Canada was primarily written from a European point of view.
   (3) Early Europeans in North America were fearless in the face of hostile Aboriginal inhabitants.
   (4) Aboriginal peoples lived on this continent long before the Europeans arrived.
   (5) The work of archaeologists has given us a new appreciation of Aboriginal history and its importance.

16. According to the passage, what is the main problem with a Eurocentric approach to our early history?

   (1) It paints an exciting picture of early Canada.
   (2) Its focus is mainly on the social and economic lives of Aboriginal peoples.
   (3) It undervalues the role of the European explorers.
   (4) It tries to justify European expansion in the Americas.
   (5) It gives us an incomplete picture of what really happened and why.

Questions 17 and 18 refer to the following map.

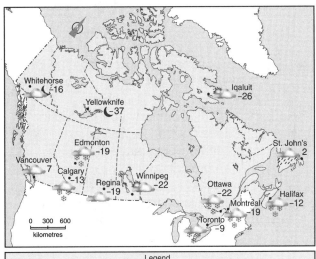

17. Which statement is best supported by the information in the map?

(1) Icy roads in Regina will cause accidents.
(2) Vancouver is expecting snow.
(3) St. John's is expecting near-freezing temperatures and rain.
(4) Ottawa is the warmest city in Ontario.
(5) Whitehorse will have more daylight than usual.

18. What is the most likely effect of the weather?

(1) Heavy snowfall in Toronto will delay traffic.
(2) Weather will disrupt electrical power in Vancouver.
(3) Fishermen will be warned of high winds in Halifax.
(4) Edmonton's above average temperatures will increase tourism.
(5) Sunshine in Montreal will melt winter snow.

Question 19 refers to the following cartoon.

Copyright © 2003 Ingrid Rice

19. Which of the following is an opinion expressed in the cartoon?

(1) Provincial premiers have little influence on federal healthcare policies.
(2) The federal and provincial governments work together on healthcare policies.
(3) In Canada, there is often intergovernmental conflict over social programs.
(4) The premier was admitted to the hospital with an ulcer.
(5) Hospital patients need more clothing.

Question 20 refers to the following paragraph.

The executive branch of the federal government creates royal commissions to investigate important matters of public interest. Through this process the government receives input from Canadians regarding existing problems and ways to solve them.

20. Which of the following recommendations would a Royal commission most likely suggest?

(1) Create more royal commissions.
(2) Pay higher salaries to politicians.
(3) Grant Aboriginal self-government.
(4) Raise the standard of living in developing countries.
(5) Do ballot recounts in close election results.

Questions 21 and 22 refer to the following passage and cartoon.

The railway promised to British Columbia for entering Confederation was to serve only 11 000 white people and 30 000 Aboriginals. This fact became an issue in the 1872 federal election.

Sir John A. Macdonald knew that Ontario voters thought the railway would cost too much. To win the election, he would need money, but where would it come from?

The answer was from Sir Hugh Allan, president of the Canadian Pacific Railway Company, who was competing for the charter to build the railroad. Allan was prepared to pay—secretly, of course.

As the 1872 election campaign began, Allan was sent a letter: "Dear Sir Hugh, The friends of the government will expect to be assisted with funds in the pending elections, and any amount which you or your Company shall advance for that purpose will be recouped by you." The total would come to more than $350 000—an astronomical sum in those days.

The money came, and it did help re-elect Macdonald and the Conservatives. Allan got his charter, too. What Macdonald didn't know, however, was that much of the money came from American investors in the CPR Company.

When word about the money leaked in 1873, the whole affair blew up into a tremendous scandal, and Macdonald was forced to resign in disgrace.

21. According to the passage, what deal was implied in the letter to Sir Hugh Allan?

(1) Contributions from Allan would be paid back to him after the 1872 election.
(2) If the Conservatives won the election, they would cancel the deal to build the railway to British Columbia.
(3) If the CPR Company contributed to Macdonald's Conservative Party, Macdonald would leave politics.
(4) If Allan provided money to the Conservatives, he would be guaranteed the lucrative charter to build the railway.
(5) If Macdonald didn't win the election, Allan would hire him to work for the CPR.

22. What impression of John A. Macdonald did the cartoonist want to convey?

(1) that he was an innocent and morally upright politician
(2) that he was cynical and corrupt
(3) that he was truthful
(4) that he wanted to deceive Canadians
(5) that he would never take a bribe again

Question 23 refers to the following graph.

The federal government's expenditure ratio measures the net budgetary expenditures as a percentage of net budgetary revenues.

NET BUDGETARY EXPENDITURES

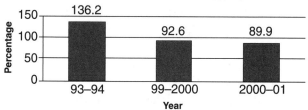

23. Which statement accurately reflects the trend in the above graph?

(1) Revenues are less than expenditures.
(2) Expenditures exceed revenues.
(3) The government is earning less and spending more.
(4) The government needs to collect more taxes.
(5) In recent years, the federal government has not been overspending.

Question 24 refers to the following passage.

The media's pervasive influence on Canadian culture has led to scrutiny about its power to affect elections. The publication of public opinion polls to broadcast probable election results before an election has been an issue of debate for many years. In Canada, election polls have been taken since 1945 with a high degree of accuracy. Supporters of opinion polls argue for the right of free speech, but opponents believe that publishing an election poll just before the election can dramatically affect voter attitudes and behaviour.

Advocates for election-poll regulation were pleased with changes to the *Canada Elections Act* in 1993. The amendment stated: "No person shall broadcast, publish or disseminate the results of an opinion survey respecting how electors will vote at an election or respecting an election issue that would permit the identification of a political party or candidate from midnight the Friday before polling day until the close of all polling stations." This initiative was similar to restrictions put into law in France almost 20 years earlier.

Members of the Canadian press challenged this amendment in an Ontario court in 1996 but were defeated. Eventually, they took their case to the Supreme Court of Canada, arguing that this legislation hindered the freedom of the press and infringed on Canadians' freedom of thought and expression. In 1998 the Supreme Court reversed the provincial court ruling, allowing media to publish election polls before elections without conditions.

24. Identify an opinion based on the above passage.

(1) The *Canada Elections Act* was amended in 1993.
(2) For a time, the media could not publish election poll results before an election.
(3) Some believed that amendment to the *Canada Elections Act* in 1993 infringed on the freedom of the press.
(4) The media wields too much power in Canadian politics.
(5) The *Canada Elections Act* was challenged in 1996.

Question 25 refers to the following map.

25. What conclusion about Japan does the map support?

(1) Japan's highest mountains are found on Hokkaido.
(2) Kyushu is Japan's smallest main island.
(3) There are fewer farms on the western coasts of Japan's main islands than on the eastern coasts.
(4) Industry is more important than agriculture to Japan's economy.
(5) More Japanese live on Honshu than on any of the other islands.

Entry Test Performance Analysis Chart
Social Studies

This chart can help you determine your strengths and weaknesses in the content and skill areas of the GED Social Studies Test. Use the Answers and Explanations starting on page 720 to check your answers to the test. Then circle on the chart the number of test items you answered correctly. Put the total number correct for each content area and skill area in each row and column. Look at the total items correct in each column and row and decide which areas are difficult for you. Use the lesson references to study those areas.

Thinking Skill / Content Area	Comprehension (Lessons 1, 2, 7, 16, 18)	Analysis (Lessons 3, 4, 6, 9, 10, 11, 12, 19)	Application (Lessons 14, 15)	Evaluation (Lessons 5, 8, 13, 17, 20)	Total Correct
Canadian History (Lessons 1–6)	15	**7**, 16, **21**	8	**22**	___/6
World History (Lessons 7–10)	**1**	**2**	**3**	**4**	___/4
Civics and Government (Lessons 11–14)	**23**	**19**, 20, 24	**6**	**5**	___/6
Economics (Lessons 15–17)	**13**	10, **14**	9	11	___/5
Geography (Lessons 18–20)	**12**	**17**	**18**	**25**	___/4
Total Correct	___/5	___/10	___/5	___/5	___/25

> 1–20 → You need more review.
> 21–25 → Congratulations! You're ready for the GED!

Boldfaced numbers indicate questions based on charts, graphs, diagrams, photographs, and drawings.

SCIENCE

Directions

The Science Entry Test consists of multiple-choice questions intended to measure your understanding of general science concepts. The questions are based on short readings, graphs, charts, or diagrams. Study the information given, and then answer the questions that follow. Refer to the information as often as necessary in answering the questions.

Spend no more than 40 minutes answering the 25 questions on the Science Entry Test. Work carefully, but do not spend too much time on any one question. Do not skip any items. Make a reasonable guess when you are unsure of an answer. You will not be penalized for incorrect answers.

When time is up, note the last item you finished. This will tell you whether you can finish the real GED Test in the time allowed. Then complete the Entry Test.

Record your answers to the questions on a copy of the answer sheet on page 919. Be sure that all required information is properly recorded on the answer sheet.

To record your answers, mark the numbered circle on the answer sheet that corresponds to the answer you choose for each question on the test.

Example

Which of the following is the smallest unit in a living thing?

(1) tissue
(2) organ
(3) cell
(4) muscle
(5) capillary

The correct answer is "cell"; therefore, answer circle 3 should be marked on the answer sheet.

Do not rest the point of your pencil on the answer sheet while considering your answer. Do not make any stray or unnecessary marks. If you change an answer, erase your first mark completely. Mark only one answer circle for each question; multiple answers will be scored as incorrect. Do not fold or crease your answer sheet.

When you finish the test, use the Performance Analysis Chart on page 41 to determine whether you are ready to take the real GED Test and, if not, which skill areas need additional review.

Directions: Choose the one best answer to each question.

Questions 1 through 3 refer to the following diagram and paragraph.

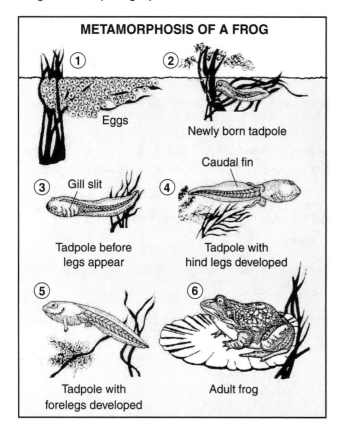

METAMORPHOSIS OF A FROG

① Eggs

② Newly born tadpole

③ Gill slit — Tadpole before legs appear

④ Caudal fin — Tadpole with hind legs developed

⑤ Tadpole with forelegs developed

⑥ Adult frog

The life cycle of the frog is an example of metamorphosis. Metamorphosis refers to an animal's changing form as it grows. A frog's immature form, called a tadpole, gradually changes into an adult form. The tadpole lives in water and breathes through gills. As it matures, the tadpole loses the gills and develops lungs. The adult frog can live on land because it can breathe through its lungs.

1. What is metamorphosis?

   (1) the process of reproduction in frogs and similar organisms
   (2) the process by which an immature form changes into a different adult form
   (3) the growth of any young organism into an adult
   (4) changes in an adult organism caused by aging
   (5) the process by which tadpoles absorb oxygen from water

2. Which of the following is most similar to the development of a tadpole into a frog?

   (1) growth of a puppy into a dog
   (2) development of a child into an adult
   (3) growth of a lamb into a sheep
   (4) development of a caterpillar into a butterfly
   (5) development of a chick into a chicken

3. Which of the following statements does the author assume you know?

   (1) All animals go through metamorphosis.
   (2) All plants go through metamorphosis.
   (3) Different body structures are suitable for different environments.
   (4) Almost all frog eggs eventually develop into adults.
   (5) Metamorphosis occurs in humans.

Question 4 refers to the following line graph.

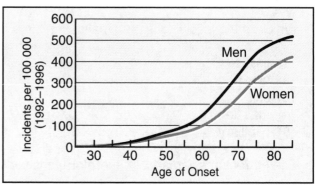

Incidents per 100 000 (1992–1996)

Men

Women

Age of Onset

Source: National Cancer Institute

4. "Colon cancer is a man's disease." Based on the graph, why is this statement illogical?

   (1) Very few people under age 50 get colon cancer.
   (2) There are almost as many women as men with colon cancer.
   (3) More women than men get colon cancer.
   (4) More young men than old women get cancer.
   (5) More men die of lung cancer than of colon cancer.

Question 5 refers to the following diagram.

LUNAR ECLIPSE

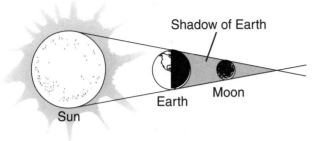

5. A lunar eclipse occurs when Earth moves into a certain position relative to the sun. Why is this statement an oversimplification?

(1) The position of the moon is also a factor in the occurrence of a lunar eclipse.
(2) A lunar eclipse occurs only during the spring and the autumn months.
(3) A lunar eclipse is not visible while Earth is revolving around the sun.
(4) A lunar eclipse is visible only at night.
(5) The position of Earth is not a factor in the occurrence of a lunar eclipse.

Question 6 refers to the following diagram.

WATER MOLECULE (H_2O)

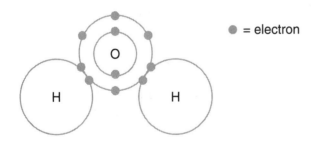

6. Covalent bonding involves each atom contributing one electron to form the bond. Therefore, how many total electrons did the oxygen atom have <u>before</u> it bonded covalently with the hydrogen atoms to form a water molecule?

(1) one
(2) two
(3) six
(4) eight
(5) ten

7. The Search for Extraterrestrial Intelligence (SETI) uses radio telescopes to scan the sky for evidence of intelligent life in the form of patterned radio waves. It is difficult for SETI scientists to obtain time on the world's largest radio telescopes, because many people in the scientific community consider their project to be science fiction rather than valid scientific research.

Which of the following is an opinion about SETI rather than a fact?

(1) Some scientists are searching for signs of extraterrestrial intelligence.
(2) Radio telescopes pick up radio waves from space.
(3) Radio waves sent by intelligent beings would show regular patterns.
(4) It is difficult for SETI scientists to get observation time on the large telescopes.
(5) SETI projects are based on dreams rather than realistic possibilities about space.

8. Deep V-shaped depressions of the sea floor are called trenches. At the trenches, one plate is descending below another. The deepest trenches, which are in the Pacific, Atlantic, and Indian Oceans, are listed below.

TRENCH DEPTHS		
Ocean	**Trench**	**Depth in Metres**
Pacific	Mariana	10 924
	Tonga	10 800
Atlantic	Puerto Rico	8 605
	S. Sandwich	8 325
Indian	Java	7 235
	Ob'	6 874

Which of the following is supported by the information in the table?

(1) The Ob' trench is 8335 m.
(2) The sea floor spreads apart at a trench.
(3) The deepest trench is the Puerto Rico trench.
(4) The Java trench is deeper than the Tonga trench.
(5) The world's deepest trenches are in the Pacific Ocean.

Carbon dioxide is a waste product of cellular respiration. It leaves the body in the air you exhale and can be measured. First, breathe for one minute exhaling through a straw into a flask containing 100 mL of water. The CO_2 in your breath dissolves in the water to form a weak acid. Add five drops of phenolphthalein, an acid-base indicator. Then, add sodium hydroxide, a basic solution, drop by drop. The more drops needed to neutralize the acid and turn the water pink, the more carbon dioxide in the water and in your exhaled breath.

To test whether exercise affects the amount of carbon dioxide in exhaled air, Jason ran in place for five minutes and then tested his breath using the method described above. It took five drops of sodium hydroxide solution to turn the water pink.

9. Jason hypothesized that exercise would result in an increased level of carbon dioxide in his exhaled breath. What was the assumption underlying Jason's hypothesis?

(1) Plants use the carbon dioxide produced during cellular respiration in the process of photosynthesis.
(2) Plants release oxygen into the air as a result of photosynthesis.
(3) Less cellular respiration is needed to produce the energy required by five minutes of exercise.
(4) The rate of cellular respiration goes up during exercise to give additional energy to the body.
(5) The capacity of the lungs to hold air decreases during exercise.

10. In addition to the flask, water, straws, phenolphthalein, and sodium hydroxide solution, which of the following items would be useful for this procedure?

(1) a Bunsen burner
(2) a dropper
(3) a measuring spoon
(4) a test tube
(5) a centrifuge

In diffusion, molecules move from an area where they are highly concentrated to an area where they are less concentrated, until a balance has been reached. Osmosis is the diffusion of water molecules across a membrane, such as a cell membrane.

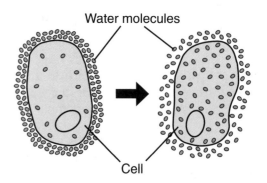

Water molecules

Cell

11. Which of the following is an example of osmosis?

(1) The genetic material of a cell duplicates itself and the cell divides.
(2) The cells of plant roots absorb water from the surrounding soil.
(3) Blood cells pick up oxygen in the lungs and get rid of carbon dioxide.
(4) Water vapour leaves a plant through pores in the leaves.
(5) Transport proteins let amino acids pass through the cell membrane.

12. During an ice age, weather becomes colder, and the ice caps and glaciers spread south and north from the poles. If there were a new ice age, what would people in the northern regions of North America be most likely to do?

(1) move to the Southern Hemisphere
(2) move toward the equator
(3) stay in northern North America
(4) quickly die out because of the ice
(5) enjoy shorter, milder winters

Question 13 refers to the following passage and graph.

The ability to learn and remember certain types of things varies with age. This was demonstrated in an experiment in which 1205 people were asked to learn some names. They watched videotapes on which 14 people introduced themselves by name and said where they were from. As shown in the line graph, everyone tested recalled more names after the second and third playing of the video, but younger adults consistently outperformed older adults.

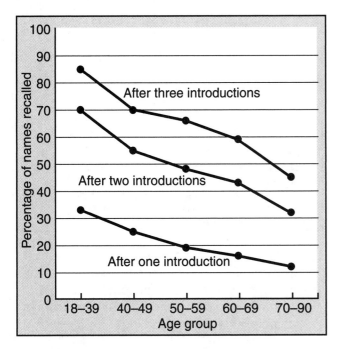

13. Which group remembered the fewest names?

(1) age 18–39 after one introduction
(2) age 50–59 after one introduction
(3) age 50–59 after two introductions
(4) age 70–90 after one introduction
(5) age 70–90 after three introductions

Question 14 refers to the following paragraph and diagram.

Many species have vestigial structures—organs or limbs that are small and lack any recognizable function. Scientists believe that vestigial structures are the remains of structures that were well-developed and functional in the ancestors of present-day organisms.

Remains of leg bones in porpoise

14. Which of the following is a conclusion rather than a supporting detail?

(1) The modern porpoise has small, vestigial leg bones.
(2) Vestigial structures serve no recognizable purpose.
(3) Vestigial structures are the remains of well-developed and functional structures.
(4) Many species, including the porpoise, have structures with no function.
(5) Vestigial structures like the porpoise's legs are often small.

15. Energy on Earth comes from nuclear reactions in the sun. The sun's energy reaches Earth in the form of heat and light. On Earth, green plants convert light energy to chemical energy through photosynthesis. Animals get their energy by eating plants or other animals.

If this energy conversion through photosynthesis decreased, what would be the effect on Earth?

Earth would have

(1) greater light energy from the sun
(2) less light energy from the sun
(3) greater heat energy from the sun
(4) less energy available for living things
(5) more energy available for living things

Question 16 refers to the following passage.

Frequency is the number of waves that pass a given point in a specific unit of time. For example, if you watched an object in the ocean bob up and down ten times in one minute, the frequency of the wave would be ten cycles per minute. In order to count one complete cycle, both a crest and a trough of the wave must pass.

If you know the wavelength (distance between two consecutive crests) and frequency of a wave, you can find its speed. If the frequency of the wave is measured in Hertz (waves per second), and the wavelength is measured in metres, then the speed in metres per second is given by this equation:

$$\text{speed} = \text{wavelength} \times \text{frequency}$$

16. What relationship does a wave's frequency involve?

    (1) height and distance between crests
    (2) height and distance between troughs
    (3) distance between crests and amplitude
    (4) number of cycles that pass a given point and unit of time
    (5) number of cycles that pass a given point and distance

17. An object moving in a circle is always changing direction. The force that keeps an object moving in a circle is called centripetal force. For example, when you whirl a ball at the end of a string, the force of the string pulls the ball to the centre. The ball's inertia keeps it from falling into the centre.

    Which of the following is most similar to centripetal force as described above?

    (1) a bullet eventually falling to Earth
    (2) the force of friction on a slide
    (3) the pull of Earth's gravity on a space station
    (4) the attraction between opposite electric charges
    (5) a sky diver reaching terminal velocity

Question 18 refers to the following information.

Ecology is the study of organisms and their relationships with one another and their environment. Ecologists can analyze these relationships at different levels of complexity.

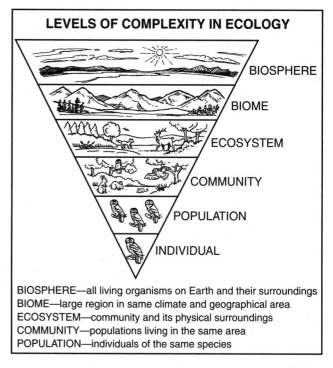

LEVELS OF COMPLEXITY IN ECOLOGY

BIOSPHERE
BIOME
ECOSYSTEM
COMMUNITY
POPULATION
INDIVIDUAL

BIOSPHERE—all living organisms on Earth and their surroundings
BIOME—large region in same climate and geographical area
ECOSYSTEM—community and its physical surroundings
COMMUNITY—populations living in the same area
POPULATION—individuals of the same species

18. Scientists have attempted to create a large sealed, self-sustaining environment, similar to Earth, with a variety of soils, air, plants, animals, and microclimates. At what level of complexity are they working?

    (1) population
    (2) community
    (3) ecosystem
    (4) biome
    (5) biosphere

Question 19 refers to the following paragraph and diagram.

An embryo is an early stage in the development of an organism from a fertilized egg. Similarities in the embryos of fish, birds, and humans suggest that they evolved from a common ancestor. For example, at first, these embryos all have gill slits, but later only fish develop true gills.

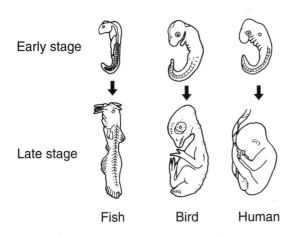

19. Which of the following is supported by information in the paragraph and the diagram?

    (1) Humans are more closely related to fish than to birds.
    (2) Birds and fish are more closely related to one another than to humans.
    (3) The similarity among embryos is greatest at the late stage of development.
    (4) As fish, birds, and humans evolved, their embryos looked more similar.
    (5) The common ancestor of fish, birds, and humans was probably a water animal.

Question 20 refers to the following table.

Heat Energy Released by Combustion with Oxygen	
Fuel	Heat Energy Released per Gram of Fuel (in kilojoules)
Methane	55.9
Natural gas	48.7
Heating oil	47.5
Coal (anthracite)	30.7
Wood	18.9

20. Which of the following comparisons is supported by the information in the table?

    (1) Natural gas releases less heat than oil.
    (2) Methane provides the most heat.
    (3) Wood gives off half as much heat as oil.
    (4) Wood gives off more heat than coal.
    (5) Coal gives off more heat than oil.

Question 21 refers to the following passage.

A glacier is a thick mass of ice. Most glaciers form in mountains where snow builds up faster than it can melt. As snow falls on snow year after year, it is compacted into ice. When the ice becomes heavy enough, the pull of gravity causes it to move slowly down the mountain. As the glacier moves, it picks up blocks of rock. As the rocks become frozen into the bottom of the glacier, they carve away more rock. Some of this rock is left behind at the edges of the glacier.

Sometimes a glacier enters a V-shaped river valley that is narrower than the glacier. As the glacier squeezes through the valley, it erodes both the floor and sides of the valley. As a result, the valley changes to a U-shaped valley.

21. Which is the best title for this passage?

    (1) Glaciers Past and Present
    (2) Agents of Erosion
    (3) How Glaciers Form
    (4) How Glaciers Carve Valleys
    (5) Causes and Effects of Glaciers

Question 22 refers to the following passage and diagram.

An ear thermometer contains a sensor whose electrical conductivity is affected by infrared radiation. The infrared radiation given off by the eardrum is converted to an electrical signal that is interpreted by a microprocessor in the handle. The body's temperature is then displayed.

EAR THERMOMETER

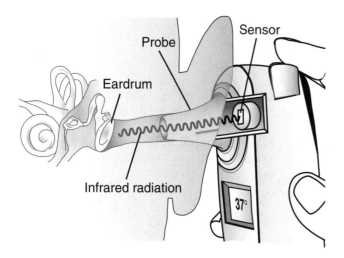

22. What property of infrared radiation allows it to change the electrical conductivity of the sensor?

(1) its mass
(2) its density
(3) its electromagnetic fields
(4) its wavelength
(5) its frequency

23. The average speed of an object is found by dividing the total distance travelled by the time. Instantaneous speed is the object's speed at any given moment. Which of the following is an example of instantaneous speed?

(1) a bird flitting from branch to branch
(2) a baseball traveling 30 m in 3 s
(3) a 1000 km drive that takes two days
(4) a car accelerating from 0 to 50 km/h
(5) a car whose speedometer reads 100 km/h

Question 24 refers to the following paragraph.

Speed is the distance an object travels in a given amount of time. Velocity is different from speed because it includes both speed and direction of motion.

24. Which of the following provides information about velocity as well as about speed?

(1) 100 km at 60 km per hour
(2) 17 m at 3 m/s
(3) 100 dm at 10 dm/m
(4) 900 km at 110 km/h
(5) 20 m north at 5 m/s

Question 25 refers to the following passage.

In 1998, the government of Iceland granted a biotechnology company the right to develop a computerized database. The database will contain the DNA profile, genealogical background, and medical history of every person in Iceland. Supporters of the plan argue that the database will produce a wealth of new and useful knowledge. Opponents claim it violates the rights of individuals to their privacy.

25. For which of the following would the database be most useful?

(1) preventing the spread of HIV/AIDS
(2) identifying bacterial infections
(3) improving the diets of Icelanders
(4) screening for genetic diseases
(5) vaccinating infants

Entry Test Performance Analysis Chart
Science

This chart can help you determine your strengths and weaknesses on the content and skill areas of the GED Science Entry Test. Use the Answers and Explanations on page 723 to check your answers to the test. Then, on the chart, circle the numbers of the test items you answered correctly. Put the total number correct for each content area and skill area in each row and column. Look at the total items correct in each column and row and decide which areas are difficult for you. Use the lesson references to study those areas.

Thinking Skill / Content Area	Comprehension (Lessons 1, 2, 6, 9, 13)	Application (Lessons 8, 15)	Analysis (Lessons 3, 4, 7, 10, 14, 17, 19)	Evaluation (Lessons 5, 11, 12, 16, 18, 20)	Total Correct
Life Science (Lessons 1–8)	**1, 13**	**2, 11, 18,** 25	**3,** 9, 10, **14**	**4, 19**	_____/12
Earth and Space Science (Lessons 9–13)	21	12	7	**5, 8**	_____/5
Physical Science (Lessons 14–20)	16	**6,** 17, 23, 24	15, **22**	**20**	_____/8
Total Correct	_____/4	_____/9	_____/7	_____/5	_____/25

1–20 → You need more review.
21–25 → Congratulations! You're ready for the GED!

Boldfaced numbers indicate questions based on charts, graphs, diagrams, or drawings.

LANGUAGE ARTS, READING
Directions

The Language Arts, Reading Entry Test consists of excerpts from fiction, nonfiction, poetry, and drama. Each excerpt is followed by multiple-choice questions about the reading material.

Read each excerpt first and then answer the questions that follow. Refer to the reading material as often as necessary in answering the questions.

A "purpose question" in bold face precedes each excerpt. The purpose question gives a reason for reading the material. Use these purpose questions to help focus your reading. You do not have to answer the purpose questions. They are given only to help you concentrate on the ideas presented in the reading material.

Spend no more than $32\frac{1}{2}$ minutes answering the 20 questions on this test. Work carefully, but do not spend too much time on any one question. Do not skip any items. Make a reasonable guess when you are not sure of an answer. You will not be penalized for incorrect answers.

When time is up, make a note of the last item you finished. This will tell you whether you can finish the real GED Test in the time allowed. Then complete the Entry Test.

Record your answers to the questions on a copy of the answer sheet on page 920. Record all required information properly on the answer sheet.

To record your answers, fill in the numbered circle on the answer sheet that corresponds to the answer you choose for each question on the test.

Example

It was Susan's dream machine. The metallic blue paint gleamed, and the sporty wheels were highly polished. Under the hood, the engine was no less carefully cleaned. Inside, flashy lights illuminated the instruments on the dashboard, and the seats were covered by rich leather upholstery.

What does "It" <u>most likely</u> refer to in this excerpt?

(1) an airplane
(2) a stereo system
(3) an automobile
(4) a boat
(5) a motorcycle 　　　①　②　●　④　⑤

The correct answer is "an automobile"; therefore, answer circle 3 would be filled in on the answer sheet.

Do not rest the point of your pencil on the answer sheet while you are considering your answer. Do not make any stray or unnecessary marks. If you change an answer, erase your first mark completely. Mark only one answer circle for each question; multiple answers will be scored as incorrect. Do not fold or crease your answer sheet.

When you finish the test, use the Performance Analysis Chart on page 51 to determine whether you are ready to take the real GED Test and, if not, which skill areas need additional review.

Directions: Choose the one best answer to each question.

Questions 1 through 3 refer to the following excerpt from a short story.

WHAT ARE THIS FATHER'S VIEWS?

I am not unsympathetic, Jack, to your views on the war. I am not unsympathetic to your views on the state of the world in general. From the way you wear your hair
(5) and from the way you dress I do find it difficult to decide whether you or that young girl you say you are about to marry is going to play the male role in your marriage—or the female role. But even that I don't find
(10) offensive. And I am not trying to make crude jokes at your expense. You must pardon me, though, if my remarks seem too personal. I confess I don't know you as well as a father *ought* to know his son, and
(15) I may seem to take liberties. …
I don't honestly know when I decided to go into college teaching, Jack. I considered doing other things—a career in the army or navy. Yes, I might have gone to Annapolis
(20) or West Point. Those appointments were much to be desired in the Depression years, and my family did still have a few political connections. One thing was certain, though. Business was just as much
(25) out of the question for me as politics had been for my father. An honest man, I was to understand, had too much to suffer there. Yes, considering our family history, an ivory tower didn't sound like a bad thing at all for
(30) an honest man and a serious man. …

Peter Taylor, "Dean of Men," *The Collected Stories.*

1. Which of the following is most likely true of the narrator's past?

    (1) He became a college teacher reluctantly.
    (2) He was extremely conventional.
    (3) He had a brief career in the army.
    (4) He did not follow in his father's footsteps.
    (5) His father was dishonest.

2. What is the main effect of the phrase "ivory tower" (lines 28–29)?

    (1) It emphasizes that the narrator wanted to escape into a safer world.
    (2) It shows how much the narrator reveres the college where he works.
    (3) It shows that the narrator realizes he has not been a good father.
    (4) It reflects the narrator's opinion that Jack is not facing real life.
    (5) It shows how much the narrator and his son have in common.

3. If Jack told his father that he was becoming a vegetarian, how would his father most likely react, based on the information in the excerpt?

    (1) He would tell Jack he was being illogical.
    (2) He would conclude that Jack was acting out of rebellion.
    (3) He would assume that Jack's wife was pushing him into it.
    (4) He would predict that Jack would soon change his mind.
    (5) He would do his best to accept Jack's views.

WHAT WAS IT LIKE TO BE A SLAVE DURING THE WAR?

I had no schooling whatever while I was a slave, though I remember on several occasions I went as far as the schoolhouse door with one of my young mistresses to
(5) carry her books. The picture of several dozen boys and girls in a schoolroom engaged in study made a deep impression upon me, and I had the feeling that to get into a schoolhouse and study in this way
(10) would be about the same as getting into paradise.

So far as I can now recall, the first knowledge that I got of the fact that we were slaves, and that freedom of the
(15) slaves was being discussed, was early one morning before day, when I was awakened by my mother kneeling over her children and fervently praying that Lincoln and his armies might be successful, and that one
(20) day she and her children might be free. In this connection I have never been able to understand how the slaves throughout the South, completely ignorant as were the masses so far as books or newspapers
(25) were concerned, were able to keep themselves so accurately and completely informed about the great National questions that were agitating the country. From the time that Garrison, Lovejoy, and
(30) others began to agitate for freedom, the slaves throughout the South kept in close touch with the progress of the movement. Though I was a mere child during the preparation for the Civil War and during the
(35) war itself, I now recall the many late-at-night whispered discussions that I heard my mother and the other slaves on the plantation indulge in. These discussions showed that they understood the situation,
(40) and that they kept themselves informed of events by what was termed the "grape-vine" telegraph.

Booker T. Washington, *Up from Slavery.*

4. Who were Garrison and Lovejoy, based on the information in the excerpt?

   (1) friends of the author
   (2) members of Lincoln's cabinet
   (3) well-known slavery opponents
   (4) wealthy slaveholders
   (5) troublemakers

5. Based on the context in which it is used, what is "the 'grape-vine' telegraph" (lines 41–42)?

   (1) telegraph messages sent from the North to the South
   (2) telegraph wires that looked like grapevines
   (3) a person-to-person means of transmitting information
   (4) a direct pipeline from the Union forces' command posts
   (5) a means of communication using secret codes

6. The author of this excerpt, Booker T. Washington, built Tuskegee Institute into a respected and important college. What quality exhibited in this excerpt does this accomplishment reflect?

   (1) the author's fervent desire for freedom
   (2) the author's desire for fame
   (3) the author's lack of schooling
   (4) the author's deep interest in education
   (5) the author's exposure to knowledgeable slaves

HOW DO YOU DESCRIBE A KITE?

A Kite Is a Victim

A kite is a victim you are sure of.
You love it because it pulls
gentle enough to call you master,
strong enough to call you fool;
(5)   because it lives
like a desperate trained falcon
in the high sweet air,
and you can always haul it down
to tame it in your drawer.

(10)   A kite is a fish you have already caught
in a pool where no fish come,
so you play him carefully and long,
and hope he won't give up,
or the wind die down.

(15)   A kite is the last poem you've written
so you give it to the wind,
but you don't let it go
until someone finds you
something else to do.

(20)   A kite is a contract of glory
that must be made with the sun,
so you make friends with the field
the river and the wind,
then you pray the whole cold night before,
under the travelling cordless moon,
to make you worthy and lyric and pure.

Leonard Cohen, "A Kite is a Victim," *Stranger Music*.

7. The poet uses a number of images to describe. To which of the following images does he *not* compare the kite?

   (1) a fish you've already caught
   (2) a victim you are sure of
   (3) the wind
   (4) the last poem you've written
   (5) a contract (of glory)

8. To what is the kite further compared in lines 5 to 9?

   (1) to the high sweet air of the skies
   (2) to a desperate trained falcon
   (3) to a drawer
   (4) to a tamed, caged pet
   (5) to a stuffed bird you can pull down from a shelf

9. The kite is finally contrasted to the moon in lines 25 to 26 by the use of one word. Which word is it?

   (1) cordless
   (2) travelling
   (3) worthy
   (4) lyric
   (5) pure

WHAT DOES RENTERS INSURANCE COVER?

Renters insurance is an important commodity that too many renters overlook. Two key terms that are used in discussing renters insurance are *peril* and *risk.* Perils

(5) are the potential causes of a loss, such as a fire, windstorm, hail, theft, and vandalism. Risk is the chance of experiencing a loss.

Two other key terms that pertain to

(10) renters insurance are *actual cash value* and *replacement cost coverage.* Both have to do with ways in which a claim to a property loss can be settled.

Actual cash value means, in many

(15) provinces, that if a loss occurs, you will be paid the current replacement cost minus depreciation (wear and tear due to age and use). The total amount to be paid is subject to the terms of your policy.

(20) *Replacement cost coverage* means that in case of loss, you will be repaid for the cost you incur to replace the damaged property with comparable new property, subject to the terms of your policy.

(25) Other key terms in a renters insurance policy are *deductible,* the portion of the loss the insured is willing to pay out of pocket, and coverage *limits,* the maximum amounts the insurer will pay a policyholder

(30) for a covered loss. Keeping the coverage limits low correspondingly keeps the cost of the insurance low.

Renters insurance offers the following coverage options: personal property

(35) protection, family liability protection, and guest medical protection. Personal property protection is protection against loss to *movable* property. Family liability protection is protection against certain

(40) liability claims brought against you because of property damage or bodily injury you may have accidentally caused. Guest medical protection is reimbursement for expenses incurred if visitors to your

(45) home are injured, regardless of who was at fault.

10. According to the information in this excerpt, which of the following types of insurance should a person with a large collection of valuable dolls buy?

(1) replacement cost coverage renters insurance
(2) actual cash value renters insurance
(3) a policy with a high deductible
(4) a family liability policy
(5) fire insurance

11. Which of the following best describes the style in which this excerpt is written?

(1) legal and technical
(2) informative and direct
(3) scholarly and dull
(4) casual and conversational
(5) light and breezy

Questions 12 and 13 refer to the following excerpt from a novel.

WHY IS JOHN DISTRACTED BY HIS NEW TEACHER?

When he was young, John had paid no attention in Sunday school, and always forgot the golden text, which earned him the wrath of his father. Around the time of
(5) his fourteenth birthday, with all the pressures of church and home uniting to drive him to the altar, he strove to appear more serious and therefore less conspicuous.[1] But he was distracted by his
(10) new teacher, Elisha, who was the pastor's nephew and who had but lately arrived from Georgia. He was not much older than John, only seventeen, and he was already saved and was a preacher. John stared at
(15) Elisha all during the lesson, admiring the timbre of Elisha's voice, much deeper and manlier than his own, admiring the leanness, and grace, and strength, and darkness of Elisha in his Sunday suit,
(20) wondering if he would ever be holy as Elisha was holy. But he did not follow the lesson, and when, sometimes, Elisha paused to ask John a question, John was ashamed and confused, feeling the palms
(25) of his hands become wet and his heart pound like a hammer. Elisha would smile and reprimand him gently, and the lesson would go on.

Roy never knew his Sunday school
(30) lesson either, but it was different with Roy—no one really expected of Roy what was expected of John. Everyone was always praying that the Lord would change Roy's heart, but it was John who was
(35) expected to be good, to be a good example.

_____
[1] noticeable

James Baldwin, *Go Tell It on the Mountain.*

12. What does the author mean by the phrase "with all the pressures of the church and home uniting to drive him to the altar" (lines 5–7)?

(1) The pressure from his parents is driving John from his home.
(2) The church has been pressuring John to become a member.
(3) John's parents have been pressuring him to join the church.
(4) John is being pressured to become a preacher.
(5) John is being pressured to get married.

13. The style of this excerpt is characterized by which of the following?

(1) use of many descriptive words
(2) frequent use of figurative language
(3) reliance on dialect
(4) sprinkles of humour throughout
(5) use of first-person narration throughout

Questions 14 through 16 refer to the following excerpt from a play.

WHAT DECISION HAS MRS. BROOKS MADE AND WHY?

RUBY: (RUBY and MRS. BROOKS *enter through the front door.*) Girl, I sure wish I could get my hands on whoever that is keeps pushing every one of them
(5) buttons on the elevator before they get off. The old elevator door banging shut on every floor just about drove me out of my mind. I don't see how you can be so good-natured about it, Gladys.
(10) MRS. BROOKS: Sometimes I think that's my trouble, I'm too good-natured about everything.
RUBY: Ah, girl.
MRS. BROOKS: It's true, and you know it.
(15) I just let everybody push me around.
RUBY: Don't be so hard on yourself, Gladys.
MRS. BROOKS: But, girl, this morning I made up my mind, I'm leaving
(20) Mr. Brooks.
RUBY: Gladys, it's not that bad, is it? Remember it ain't the easiest thing in the world to leave a man after all these years.
(25) MRS. BROOKS: Humph. Telling me I couldn't buy a new dress for Gail's wedding; that was the last straw.
RUBY: You know, Gladys, there is such a thing as going from the refrigerator into
(30) the frying pan.
MRS. BROOKS: Oh, Ruby, be serious.
RUBY: I am just as serious as cancer. I mean, it's not as though the man won't work. Everybody knows that he ain't
(35) known to mess up a piece of money.
MRS. BROOKS: A lot of good it does me. Everything in the house is in his name. My name don't appear on nothing except the income tax deductions. …
(40) MRS. BROOKS: Last week I overspent buying groceries, and talking about a man carrying on! You'd have thought that seventeen cents was going to cause a panic down on Wall Street.
(45) RUBY: Now, Gladys, you know sometimes he does have good intentions.

MRS. BROOKS: My granny always said that the road to hell is paved with good intentions.
(50) RUBY: My granny always said that there's some good in everybody.
MRS. BROOKS: If there's some good in Mr. Brooks he's done done a Houdini with it, and made it disappear. 'Cause
(55) you sure can't see it.

Charlie Russell, *Five on the Black Hand Side.*

14. Which of the following sentences best describes what Mrs. Brooks' grandmother meant by "the road to hell is paved with good intentions" (lines 48–49)?

(1) Never trust people who say that they mean well.
(2) Bad things can result even when someone means well.
(3) It is obvious that Mr. Brooks was always an evil person.
(4) Spending too much money will get you into trouble.
(5) All good things will eventually disappear.

15. Based on this excerpt, which of the following statements can you infer about Mrs. Brooks?

(1) She has thought for a long time about leaving Mr. Brooks.
(2) She needs Ruby's approval before she will leave Mr. Brooks.
(3) She will not leave Mr. Brooks until she has found a job.
(4) She probably will not leave Mr. Brooks at all.
(5) She will probably move in with Ruby.

16. Which of the following best describes the theme of this excerpt?

(1) Spouses sometimes complain unnecessarily.
(2) People who work hard often do not like to spend money.
(3) Disagreements over money can affect relationships.
(4) Friends are not always supportive.
(5) Wealthy people have problems too.

Questions 17 through 20 refer to the following excerpt from a short story.

WHY IS THIS WOMAN WEARING BLACK?

I should have known the minute I saw her, holding court in her widow's costume, that something had cracked inside Doña Ernestina. She was in full *lato*—black from
(5) head to toe, including a mantilla. …
Doña Ernestina simply waited for me to join the other two leaning against the machines before she continued explaining what had happened when the news of
(10) Tony had arrived at her door the day before. She spoke calmly, a haughty expression on her face, looking like an offended duchess in her beautiful black dress. She was pale, pale, but she had a
(15) wild look in her eyes. The officer had told her that—when the time came—they would bury Tony with "full military honors"; for now they were sending her the medal and a flag. But she had said, *"No, gracias,"*
(20) to the funeral, and she sent the flag and medals back marked *Ya no vive aqui:* Does not live here anymore. "Tell the Mr. President of the United States what I say: *No, gracias."* Then she waited for
(25) our response.
Lydia shook her head, indicating that she was speechless. And Elenita looked pointedly at me, forcing me to be the one to speak the words of sympathy for all of
(30) us, to reassure Doña Ernestina that she had done exactly what any of us would have done in her place: yes, we would have all said *No, gracias,* to any president who had actually tried to pay for a son's life
(35) with a few trinkets and a folded flag.

Judith Ortiz Cofer, "Nada," *The Latin Deli: Prose and Poetry.*

17. Why does the narrator begin to believe Doña Ernestina has "cracked"?

(1) She spoke of her son's death too calmly.
(2) She was dressed too beautifully for such a sad occasion.
(3) She was dressed as a widow in mourning.
(4) Her only son was killed in Vietnam.
(5) She sent the flag and the medals back to the military.

18. Based on the information in this excerpt, if the president invited Doña Ernestina to a ceremony to honour war heroes, how would she most likely react?

She would

(1) wear her widow's costume to the ceremony
(2) refuse to attend the ceremony
(3) implore him to end the war
(4) ask to give a speech about her son
(5) thank the president for honouring her son

19. Which of the following descriptions best indicates Doña Ernestina's state of mind?

    (1) She was dressed in black from head to toe.
    (2) She had a haughty expression on her face.
    (3) She looked like a duchess.
    (4) She had a wild look in her eyes.
    (5) She wore a beautiful dress.

20. In this excerpt, what technique does the author use to add authenticity?

    (1) third-person narration
    (2) a president's name
    (3) formal language
    (4) Spanish phrases
    (5) figurative language

Entry Test Performance Analysis Chart
Language Arts, Reading

This chart can help you determine your strengths and weaknesses on the content and skill areas of the GED Language Arts, Reading Entry Test. Use the Answers and Explanations starting on page 725 to check your answers to the test. Then circle on the chart the numbers of the test items you answered correctly. Put the total number correct for each content area and skill area in each row and column. Look at the total items correct in each column and row and decide which areas need more work and study. Use the page references to study those areas.

Thinking Skill / Content Area	Comprehension	Application	Analysis	Synthesis	Total Correct
Nonfiction (Lessons 1–9)	4	10	5	6, 11	____/5
Fiction (Lessons 10–19)	1, 12	3, 18	2, 17, 19	13, 20	____/9
Poetry (Lessons 20–24)	7, 8			9	____/3
Drama (Lessons 25–28)	15		14	16	____/3
Total Correct	____/6	____/3	____/5	____/6	____/20

1–16 → You need more review.
17–20 → Congratulations! You're ready for the GED!

Entry Test

MATHEMATICS
Part I

Directions

The Mathematics Entry Test consists of multiple-choice and alternate format questions intended to measure your general mathematical skills and problem-solving ability. The questions are based on short readings that often include a graph, chart, or diagram.

You will have 22 minutes to complete the 12 questions in Part I. Work carefully, but do not spend too much time on any one question. Be sure to answer every question; you will not be penalized for incorrect answers. When time is up, mark the last item you finished. This will tell you whether you can finish the real GED Test in the time allowed. Then complete the Entry Test.

Formulas you may need are given on page 55. Only some questions will require a formula. Not all the formulas given will be needed.

Some questions contain more information than you will need to solve the problem; other questions do not give enough information. If the question does not give enough information to solve the problem, the correct answer choice is "Not enough information is given."

You may use a calculator in Part I. Calculator directions for the CASIO *fx-260SOLAR* scientific calculator can be found on page 54.

Record your answers on a copy of the separate answer sheet provided on page 921. Be sure all required information is properly recorded on the answer sheet.

To record your answers, mark the numbered circle on the answer sheet that corresponds to the answer you select for each question on the test.

Example: If a grocery bill totalling $15.75 is paid with a $20.00 bill, how much change should be returned?

(1) $5.25
(2) $4.75
(3) $4.25
(4) $3.75
(5) $3.25

The correct answer is $4.25; therefore, answer space 3 would be marked on the answer sheet.

Do not rest the point of your pencil on the answer sheet while you are considering your answer. Make no stray or unnecessary marks. If you change an answer, erase your first mark completely. Mark only one answer for each question; multiple answers will be scored as incorrect. Do not fold or crease your answer sheet.

When you finish the test, use the Performance Analysis Chart on page 65 to determine whether you are ready to take the real GED Test and, if not, which skill areas need additional review.

MATHEMATICS

Mixed numbers, such as $3\frac{1}{2}$, cannot be entered in the alternate format grid. Instead, represent them as decimal numbers (in this case, 3.5) or fractions (in this case, 7/2). No answer can be a negative number, such as -8.

To record your answer for an alternate format question

- begin in any column that will allow your answer to be entered.
- write your answer in the boxes on the top row.
- fill in the circle representing that character in the column beneath a fraction bar or decimal point (if any) and each number in your answer.
- leave blank any unused column.

Example

The scale on a map indicates that $\frac{1}{2}$ cm represents an actual distance of 120 km. In centimetres, how far apart on the map will two towns be if the actual distance between them is 180 km?

The answer to the above example is 3/4, or 0.75, cm. The answer could be gridded using any of the methods below.

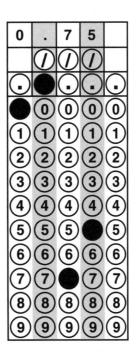

Points to remember

- The answer sheet will be machine scored. **The circles must be filled in correctly.**
- Mark no more than one circle in any column.
- Grid only one answer even if there is more than one correct answer.
- Mixed numbers, such as $3\frac{1}{2}$, must be gridded as a decimal (3.5) or fraction (7/2).
- No answer can be a negative number.

Adapted with permission of the American Council on Education.

CALCULATOR DIRECTIONS

To prepare the calculator for use the **first** time, press the (ON) (upper-rightmost) key. "DEG" will appear at the top-centre of the screen and "0." at the right. This indicates the calculator is in the proper format for all your calculations.

To prepare the calculator for **another** question, press the (ON) or the red (AC) key. This clears any entries made previously.

To do any arithmetic, enter the expression as it is written. Press (=) (equal sign) when finished.

EXAMPLE A: 8 − 3 + 9

> First press (ON) or (AC).
> Enter the following:
>
> $\quad$ 8 (−) 3 (+) 9 (=)
>
> The correct answer is 14.

If an expression in parentheses is to be multiplied by a number, press (×) (multiplication sign) between the number and the parenthesis sign.

EXAMPLE B: 6(8 + 5)

> First press (ON) or (AC).
> Enter the following:
>
> $\quad$ 6 (×) ((---) 8 (+) 5 (---)) (=)
>
> The correct answer is 78.

To find the square root of a number

- enter the number.
- press (SHIFT) (upper-leftmost) key ("SHIFT" appears at the top-left of the screen).
- press (x^2) (third from the left on top row) to access its second function: square root.
  DO NOT press (SHIFT) and (x^2) at the same time.

EXAMPLE C: $\sqrt{64}$

> First press (ON) or (AC).
> Enter the following:
>
> $\quad$ 64 (SHIFT) (x^2)
>
> The correct answer is 8.

To enter a negative number such as −8

- enter the number without the negative sign (enter 8).
- press the "change sign" ((+/−)) key, which is directly above the 7 key.

All arithmetic can be done with positive or negative numbers.

EXAMPLE D: −8 − −5

> First press (ON) or (AC).
> Enter the following:
>
> $\quad$ 8 (+/−) (−) 5 (+/−) (=)
>
> The correct answer is −3.

Adapted with permission of the American Council on Education.

FORMULAS

AREA of a

square	Area = side^2
rectangle	Area = length × width
parallelogram	Area = base × height
triangle	Area = $\frac{1}{2}$ × base × height
trapezoid	Area = $\frac{1}{2}$ × (base$_1$ + base$_2$) × height
circle	Area = π × radius^2; π is approximately equal to 3.14

PERIMETER of a

square	Perimeter = 4 × side
rectangle	Perimeter = 2 × length + 2 × width
triangle	Perimeter = side$_1$ + side$_2$ + side$_3$

CIRCUMFERENCE of a circle Circumference = π × diameter; π is approximately equal to 3.14

VOLUME of a

cube	Volume = edge^3
rectangular container	Volume = length × width × height
square pyramid	Volume = $\frac{1}{3}$ × (base edge)^2 × height
cylinder	Volume = π × radius^2 × height; π is approximately equal to 3.14
cone	Volume = $\frac{1}{3}$ × π × radius^2 × height; π is approximately equal to 3.14

COORDINATE GEOMETRY

distance between points = $\sqrt{(x_2 - x_1)^2 + (y_2 - y_1)^2}$; (x_1, y_1) and (x_2, y_2) are two points in a plane

slope of a line = $\frac{y_2 - y_1}{x_2 - x_1}$; (x_1, y_1) and (x_2, y_2) are two points on a line

PYTHAGOREAN RELATIONSHIP

$a^2 + b^2 = c^2$; a and b are legs and c the hypotenuse of a right triangle.

MEASURES OF CENTRAL TENDENCY

mean = $\frac{x_1 + x_2 + \ldots + x_n}{n}$, where the x's are the values for which a mean is desired and n is the total number of values for x

median = the middle value of an odd number of <u>ordered</u> scores, and halfway between the two middle values of an even number of <u>ordered</u> scores

SIMPLE INTEREST interest = principal × rate × time

DISTANCE distance = rate × time

TOTAL COST total cost = (number of units) × (price per unit)

Adapted with permission of the American Council on Education.

Part I

Directions: You will have 22 minutes to complete questions 1–12. Choose the <u>one best answer</u> to each question. You <u>may</u> use your calculator.

1. Sondra buys an insurance policy that costs $7.43 for every $2500 of insurance. If she buys $30 000 of insurance, how much does it cost her?

   (1) $86.08
   (2) $87.16
   (3) $88.08
   (4) $89.16
   (5) $90.08

Question 2 refers to the following figure.

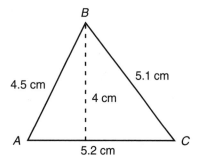

2. What is the area to the nearest <u>square centimetre</u> of △*ABC*?

   (1) 10
   (2) 14
   (3) 17
   (4) 19
   (5) 21

3. Teresa sold 2 cameras for $175 each and 3 cameras for $150 each. If she earns a $35 commission for each sale, which expression shows how much she earned in commissions?

   (1) ($175 + $150)$35
   (2) (2 × $175) + (3 × $150)
   (3) $35 × 2 × 3
   (4) (2 + 3)$35
   (5) $\frac{(\$175 + \$150)}{\$35}$

4. On a number line, −2 is located halfway between which of the following points?

   (1) −3 and 0
   (2) −4 and 1
   (3) −4 and −1
   (4) −4 and 0
   (5) −5 and 0

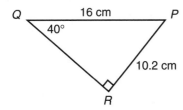

5. What is the measure of ∠RPQ?

    (1) 40°
    (2) 50°
    (3) 60°
    (4) 90°
    (5) 140°

6. What is the length of $\overline{QR}$ to the nearest tenth centimetre?

    Mark your answer in the circles in the grid on your answer sheet.

SNACK SALES IN MAY
Total: $12 Million

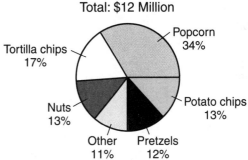

7. How much money, in millions of dollars, was spent on popcorn in May?

    (1) $1.32
    (2) $1.44
    (3) $1.56
    (4) $2.04
    (5) $4.08

8. What was the ratio of the amount spent on popcorn to the amount spent on tortilla chips in May?

    (1) 34:13
    (2) 2:1
    (3) 17:13
    (4) 13:34
    (5) 1:2

9. The expression $4(x + 2y) - (x + y)$ is equal to which of the following expressions?

   (1) $3x + y$
   (2) $3x + 3y$
   (3) $3x + 5y$
   (4) $3x + 7y$
   (5) $3x + 9y$

Question 10 refers to the following figure.

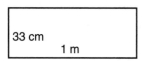

33 cm

1 m

10. What is the area of the rectangle in <u>square centimetres</u>?

   (1) 330
   (2) 33
   (3) 3300
   (4) 3030
   (5) 300

11. What is the approximate area in square metres of the bottom of a circular pool with a diameter of 8 m?

   (1) 50
   (2) 48
   (3) 40
   (4) 20
   (5) 16

12. Show the location of the point whose coordinates are $(-3, 2)$.

   Mark your answer on the coordinate plane grid on your answer sheet.

MATHEMATICS
Part II

Directions

The Mathematics Entry Test consists of multiple-choice and alternate format questions intended to measure your general mathematical skills and problem-solving ability. The questions are based on short readings that often include a graph, chart, or diagram.

You will have 23 minutes to complete the 13 questions in Part II. Work carefully, but do not spend too much time on any one question. Be sure to answer every question. You will not be penalized for incorrect answers. When time is up, mark the last item you finished. This will tell you whether you can finish the real GED Test in the time allowed. Then complete the Entry Test.

Formulas you may need are given on page 61. Only some questions will require a formula. Not all the formulas given will be needed.

Some questions contain more information than you will need to solve the problem; other questions do not give enough information. If the question does not give enough information to solve the problem, the correct answer choice is "Not enough information is given."

The use of calculators is not allowed in Part II.

Continue to record your answers on a copy of the separate answer sheet provided on page 921. Be sure all required information is properly recorded on the answer sheet.

To record your answers, mark the numbered circle on the answer sheet that corresponds to the answer you select for each question on the test.

Example: If a grocery bill totalling $15.75 is paid with a $20.00 bill, how much change should be returned?

(1) $5.25
(2) $4.75
(3) $4.25
(4) $3.75
(5) $3.25

The correct answer is $4.25; therefore, answer space 3 would be marked on the answer sheet.

Do not rest the point of your pencil on the answer sheet while you are considering your answer. Make no stray or unnecessary marks. If you change an answer, erase your first mark completely. Mark only one answer for each question; multiple answers will be scored as incorrect. Do not fold or crease your answer sheet.

When you finish the test, use the Performance Analysis Chart on page 65 to determine whether you are ready to take the real GED Test and, if not, which skill areas need additional review.

Adapted with permission of the American Council on Education.

MATHEMATICS

Mixed numbers, such as $3\frac{1}{2}$, cannot be entered in the alternate format grid. Instead, represent them as decimal numbers (in this case, 3.5) or fractions (in this case, 7/2). No answer can be a negative number, such as -8.

To record your answer for an alternate format question

- begin in any column that will allow your answer to be entered.
- write your answer in the boxes on the top row.
- fill in the circle representing that character in the column beneath a fraction bar or decimal point (if any) and each number in your answer.
- leave blank any unused column.

Example

The scale on a map indicates that $\frac{1}{2}$ cm represents an actual distance of 120 km. In centimetres, how far apart on the map will two towns be if the actual distance between them is 180 km?

The answer to the above example is 3/4, or 0.75, cm. The answer could be gridded using any of the methods below.

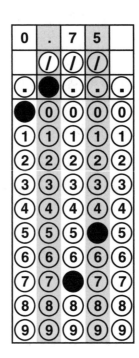
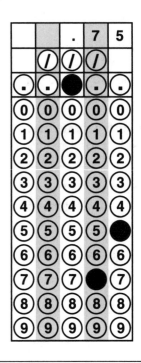

Points to remember

- The answer sheet will be machine scored. **The circles must be filled in correctly.**
- Mark no more than one circle in any column.
- Grid only one answer even if there is more than one correct answer.
- Mixed numbers, such as $3\frac{1}{2}$, must be gridded as a decimal (3.5) or fraction (7/2).
- No answer can be a negative number.

Adapted with permission of the American Council on Education.

FORMULAS

AREA of a

square	Area = side^2
rectangle	Area = length $\times$ width
parallelogram	Area = base $\times$ height
triangle	Area = $\frac{1}{2} \times$ base $\times$ height
trapezoid	Area = $\frac{1}{2} \times$ (base$_1$ + base$_2$) $\times$ height
circle	Area = $\pi \times$ radius^2; π is approximately equal to 3.14

PERIMETER of a

square	Perimeter = 4 $\times$ side
rectangle	Perimeter = 2 $\times$ length + 2 $\times$ width
triangle	Perimeter = side$_1$ + side$_2$ + side$_3$
CIRCUMFERENCE of a circle	Circumference = $\pi \times$ diameter; π is approximately equal to 3.14

VOLUME of a

cube	Volume = edge^3
rectangular container	Volume = length $\times$ width $\times$ height
square pyramid	Volume = $\frac{1}{3} \times$ (base edge)$^2 \times$ height
cylinder	Volume = $\pi \times$ radius$^2 \times$ height; π is approximately equal to 3.14
cone	Volume = $\frac{1}{3} \times \pi \times$ radius$^2 \times$ height; π is approximately equal to 3.14

COORDINATE GEOMETRY

distance between points = $\sqrt{(x_2 - x_1)^2 + (y_2 - y_1)^2}$; (x_1, y_1) and (x_2, y_2) are two points in a plane

slope of a line = $\frac{y_2 - y_1}{x_2 - x_1}$; (x_1, y_1) and (x_2, y_2) are two points on a line

PYTHAGOREAN RELATIONSHIP

$a^2 + b^2 = c^2$; a and b are legs and c the hypotenuse of a right triangle.

MEASURES OF CENTRAL TENDENCY

mean = $\frac{x_1 + x_2 + \ldots + x_n}{n}$, where the x's are the values for which a mean is desired and n is the total number of values for x

median = the middle value of an odd number of ordered scores, and halfway between the two middle values of an even number of ordered scores

SIMPLE INTEREST

interest = principal $\times$ rate $\times$ time

DISTANCE

distance = rate $\times$ time

TOTAL COST

total cost = (number of units) $\times$ (price per unit)

Part II

Directions: You will have 23 minutes to complete questions 13–25. Choose the <u>one best answer</u> to each question. You may <u>not</u> use your calculator.

13. The sum of three consecutive even numbers is 138. What is the greatest number?

    (1) 52

    (2) 50

    (3) 48

    (4) 46

    (5) 44

Questions 14 and 15 refer to the following diagram.

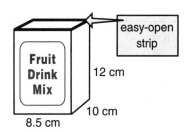

14. A new drink mix is packaged in rectangular containers. An easy-open strip goes around the top of the package as shown. What is the length in centimetres of the strip?

    (1)　 30.5

    (2)　 37

    (3)　 61

    (4)　 85

    (5) 1020

15. A label completely covers the front of the container. Which of the following expressions could be used to find the area of the label?

    (1) 8.5 + 12 + 8.5 + 12

    (2) (8.5 × 2) + (12 × 2)

    (3) 8.5 × 4

    (4) 8.5 × 12

    (5) 8.5 × 10 × 12

16. Which of the following expressions is equal to 2 − (x + 7)?

    (1) x − 9

    (2) −x − 5

    (3) −x − 9

    (4) −x + 9

    (5) −x + 14

17. The Jordans borrow $5000 for 3 years at 14% interest. What is the total amount they will pay back to the bank?

    (1) $2100

    (2) $5042

    (3) $6400

    (4) $7100

    (5) $8000

18. Kathy cuts a piece of board 19.6 cm long into 4 equal parts. How many centimetres long is each piece?

    Mark your answer in the circles in the grid on your answer sheet.

Question 19 refers to the following figure.

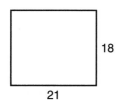

19. The figure shows a rectangle attached to a half-circle. Which of the following expressions represents the perimeter of the figure?

(1) $16 + 2\pi$

(2) $10 + 2\pi$

(3) $10 + 4\pi$

(4) $16 + 4\pi$

(5) $24 + 4\pi$

20. Which expression can be used to find the perimeter of the figure below?

18
21

(1) $21 + 21 + 12 + 12$

(2) $21 + 21 + 18 + 18$

(3) $2(12 + 18)$

(4) $12 + 18$

(5) 21×18

Question 21 refers to the table below.

Game	Score
1	94
2	73
3	86
4	102
5	96
6	71

21. What was the median score for the games shown?

(1) 94.0

(2) 90.0

(3) 87.0

(4) 86.5

(5) 86.0

Question 22 refers to the following figure.

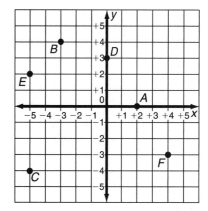

22. The graph of the equation $y = -\frac{3}{2}x + 3$ would pass through which of the following points on the coordinate grid?

(1) A and B

(2) A and C

(3) A, D, and F

(4) A and E

(5) C and D

23. Janet has worked out a payment schedule to pay off an $1800 debt. The schedule calls for her to pay $300 the first month and $150 per month after that. Which expression shows how many $150 payments it will take for Janet to pay off the debt?

(1) $\frac{(\$1800 - \$300)}{\$150}$

(2) $\$1800 - \$300 - \$150$

(3) $\frac{(\$1800 - \$150)}{\$300}$

(4) $\$1800 - (\$300 + \$150)$

(5) $\$1800 - \$300 \times \$150$

24. A box contains 15 cards, each one numbered with a different whole number from 1 to 15. If a card is chosen at random, what is the probability that it is an even number?

(1) $\frac{1}{15}$

(2) $\frac{7}{15}$

(3) $\frac{1}{2}$

(4) $\frac{7}{8}$

(5) $\frac{14}{15}$

25. Beatta has five weeks to study for two final exams. Each day she can spend exactly four hours on studying. How many minutes can she spend studying for each exam?

(1)   10

(2) 1200

(3) 4200

(4) 2100

(5) 8400

Entry Test Performance Analysis Charts
Mathematics

The following charts can help you determine your strengths and weaknesses in the content and skill areas of the GED Mathematics Test. Use the Answers and Explanations starting on page 727 to check your answers to the test. Then circle on the charts for Part I and Part II the numbers of the test items you answered correctly. Put the total number correct for each content area and skill area in each row and column. Look at the total items correct in each column to determine which areas are difficult for you. Use the lesson references to study those skills.

Part I

Content Area	Concept	Procedure	Application	Total Correct
Numbers and Operations (Lessons 1–13)		3	1	____/2
Measurement (Lessons 14–15)			**10**	____/1
Data Analysis (Lessons 16–17)			**7, 8**	____/2
Algebra (Lessons 18–22)	4, 12	9		____/3
Geometry (Lessons 23–27)	**5**		**2, 6**, 11	____/4
Total Correct	____/3	____/2	____/7	____/12

Part II

Content Area	Concept	Procedure	Application	Total Correct
Numbers and Operations (Lessons 1–13)		23	17, 18	____/3
Measurement (Lessons 14–15)	25	**20**	**14**	____/3
Data Analysis (Lessons 16–17)	**21**, 24			____/2
Algebra (Lessons 18–22)		16	13, **22**	____/3
Geometry (Lessons 23–27)		**15, 19**		____/2
Total Correct	____/3	____/5	____/5	____/13

The item numbers in **bold** are based on graphics.

> 1–20 → You need more review.
> 21–25 → Congratulations! You're ready for the GED!

Unit 1

LANGUAGE ARTS, WRITING

The GED Language Arts, Writing, Part I Test will cover the following content and skills.

The Test

- 50 multiple-choice questions
- 75 minutes to complete

The Content

- Sentence structure
- Organization
- Usage
- Mechanics

The Questions

- Correction
- Revision
- Construction shift

Sharp writing skills are vital to all of us—at home, on the job, and in many other aspects of our lives. Writing, after all, is communication, whether it's a business letter, a note to a teacher, a short story, or an e-mail sent to a friend. Is there anyone who doesn't want to communicate better?

When you find mistakes in your writing, you should not be discouraged. Use them as an opportunity to learn and to improve your writing skills. Through the process of review and revision, a sentence or paragraph that is awkward and unclear can become powerful. This unit provides sentences that contain mistakes or that could be written more effectively. Your job is to correct or revise them. As you do so, you will be sharpening your writing skills and making sure that what you want to say is stated clearly. That also means that whoever reads your piece of written communication will understand immediately what you are thinking or what you want.

Study Tip

Writing helps keep your mind on the task.

Taking notes as you study helps you understand and remember difficult concepts, and it keeps distractions at bay.

- Jot down key ideas as you read.
- Write out new words to help you remember spellings.
- Stay focused on the material by writing a summary, either in sentences or in point form.
- Paraphrase material—restate information and ideas in your own words to make sure you understand them.
- Review your notes to make sure they're clear, rewriting them if necessary.
- Jot down questions for follow-up.

Sentence Structure

Part I of the GED Language Arts, Writing Test will test your ability to recognize and revise problems in sentences and paragraphs. Thirty percent of the questions on the test are about sentence structure, or the way sentences are put together. These lessons focus on key topics in sentence structure. They will show you ways to express your ideas in clear, correct, and logical sentences.

Sentences and Sentence Fragments

Complete Sentences

To write clearly, you should use complete sentences. A sentence is complete when it meets the following requirements.

subject
tells who or what a sentence is about

predicate
tells what the subject is or does; it must include a verb to be complete

Identify a complete sentence by asking yourself some questions: *Does the sentence have a subject? Does it have a complete predicate? Does it express a complete thought?* If the answer to each question is yes, the sentence is complete.

RULE 1 A complete sentence has a subject and a verb. The **subject** names who or what the sentence is about. The **predicate** tells what the subject is or does.

No Subject: Teaches her son to drive a car with a stick shift.
Complete: Gloria teaches her son to drive a car with a stick shift.

No Predicate: A car with an automatic transmission.
Complete: A car with an automatic transmission is easy to drive.

Sometimes the subject of a sentence is not stated, but it is understood to be the word *you*.

Complete: Learn to drive safely.

RULE 2 A complete sentence expresses a complete thought.

Incomplete: Because it gets better kilometrage.
Complete: Ramon plans to buy a car with a standard transmission because it gets better kilometrage.

RULE 3 A complete sentence ends with punctuation. Most statements end with a period. A question ends with a question mark. A strong statement or command ends with an exclamation point.

Statement: Gloria prefers to drive a car with a stick shift.
Question: Is Ramon a good driver?
Exclamation: Get out of his way!

Sentence Fragments

sentence fragment
an incomplete
sentence

You have been working with complete sentences. If you mistakenly write an incomplete sentence, you have written a **sentence fragment.** When you edit a piece of writing and you see a sentence fragment, you can use one of these methods to correct it. The method that you choose will depend on the situation and on what you think will most improve the piece of writing.

METHOD 1 If a fragment is missing a subject, add a subject.

Fragment: Went to the interview with her résumé.
Correct: <u>Lia</u> went to the interview with her résumé.

You can fix a fragment in various ways. However, on the GED Test, there will always be **only one** correct answer.

METHOD 2 If a fragment is missing a complete predicate, complete the predicate by adding a verb.

Fragment: Dr. Parks <u>asking</u> about her last job.
Correct: Dr. Parks <u>is asking</u> about her last job.

METHOD 3 Add or change words to make an incomplete thought complete.

Fragment: Not a bad job, only boring.
Correct: Her last job was not bad, only boring.

METHOD 4 Attach the fragment to a complete sentence. This is a good method to use when a fragment has a subject and predicate but still does not express a complete thought.

Fragment: Lia took the job. <u>Because she wanted a challenge.</u>
Correct: Lia took the job because she wanted a challenge.
Correct: Because she wanted a challenge, Lia took the job.

The second correction shows that when you attach a fragment to a sentence, you may also need to add or rearrange words.

The underlined statement that follows is a fragment. Put a check mark next to the best way to correct it.

Jay lost weight. <u>Once he started exercising.</u>

_____ a. add a subject

_____ b. add a verb

_____ c. add words to complete the thought

_____ d. attach it to the sentence before it

You are correct if you chose *option d.* The fragment already has the subject *he* (*option a*) and the verb *started* (*option b*), but it is not a complete thought. You could add words to the fragment to make it a complete thought (*option c*). However, the best way to correct it is to attach it to the preceding sentence because that sentence is short and choppy, and the meaning of the fragment is related closely to it.

GED Practice

Directions: Choose the one best answer to each question.

Questions 1 through 4 refer to the following paragraph.

Microwave Ovens

(1) Microwave ovens have transformed cooking because of their convenience in today's fast-paced society. (2) In the past, most people cooked with gas or electricity. (3) Today, many people prefer microwave ovens for their speed of cooking. (4) Which is one of their best qualities. (5) Less expensive than gas or electric ranges, too. (6) Where space is a consideration, microwave ovens are also conveniently small. (7) In fact, most people use the microwave as an addition to, not a replacement for, a full-size gas or electric oven. (8) Stove manufacturers not being worried.

1. Sentence 1: **Microwave ovens have transformed cooking because of their convenience in today's fast-paced society.**

   Which correction should be made to sentence 1?

   (1) insert they after ovens
   (2) change have to having
   (3) change cooking because to cooking. Because
   (4) change convenience in to convenience. In
   (5) no correction is necessary

2. Sentences 3 and 4: **Today, many people prefer microwave ovens for their speed of cooking. Which is one of their best qualities.**

   Which is the best way to write the underlined portion of these sentences? If the original is the best way, choose option (1).

   (1) cooking. Which is one
   (2) cooking, which is one
   (3) cooking. One
   (4) cooking and one
   (5) cooking. Being one

3. Sentence 5: **Less expensive than gas or electric ranges, too.**

   Which correction should be made to sentence 5?

   (1) replace Less with Microwaves are less
   (2) insert to use after expensive
   (3) insert either after than
   (4) change gas or to gas. Or
   (5) insert are after ranges

4. Sentences 7 and 8: **In fact, most people use the microwave as an addition to, not a replacement for, a full-size gas or electric oven. Stove manufacturers not being worried.**

   If you rewrote sentences 7 and 8 beginning with

   Stove manufacturers, however,

   the next words should be

   (1) not being worried because most
   (2) not worrying because, in fact
   (3) they aren't worried because most
   (4) are not worried because most
   (5) not worried because in fact,

Some GED questions give the option "no correction is necessary." If you think that is the correct answer, reread the sentence carefully to make sure there really aren't any errors.

Questions 5 through 8 refer to the following paragraphs.

Finesse Computer Systems

To Our Valued Customers:

(A)

(1) Finesse Computer wants to make it easier for you to visit our Web sites. (2) We've set up our systems to help you store the information you want to share with us. (3) Your name, street and e-mail addresses, and telephone number. (4) Then you select your unique Finesse password, which you will be asked to enter at the beginning of your Web search. (5) You won't have to reenter all your personal information. (6) To download an article from our archives or to purchase a new product. (7) Simply type in your password, and the system will access the information automatically.

(B)

(8) The information we store for you will not be shared with anyone else, and your personal information cannot be accessed by others. (9) Your information updated at any time by typing in your password and editing the information on file.

5. Sentences 2 and 3: **We've set up our systems to help you store the information you want to share with us. Your name, street and e-mail addresses, and telephone number.**

Which is the best way to write the underlined portion of these sentences? If the original is the best way, choose option (1).

(1) us. Your
(2) us your
(3) us, such as your
(4) us being your
(5) us because your

6. Sentence 4: **Then you select your unique Finesse password, which you will be asked to enter at the beginning of your Web search.**

Which correction should be made to sentence 4?

(1) insert as after Then
(2) change you select to selecting
(3) change password, which to password. Which
(4) replace your with you're
(5) no correction is necessary

7. Sentences 5 and 6: **You won't have to reenter all your personal information. To download an article from our archives or to purchase a new product.**

The most effective combination of sentences 5 and 6 would include which group of words?

(1) for the reason of downloading
(2) when you want to download
(3) reenter and download
(4) information and for
(5) information because

8. Sentence 9: **Your information updated at any time by typing in your password and editing the information on file.**

Which correction should be made to sentence 9?

(1) insert can be before updated
(2) change updated to updating
(3) change time by to time. By
(4) change editing to having edited
(5) insert you have after the information

Answers start on page 729.

Lesson 2

Compound Sentences
Coordinating Conjunctions

You have been writing complete sentences, which are also called independent clauses. An independent clause can stand by itself as a simple sentence. Two or more independent clauses can be combined into one compound sentence. Writing a compound sentence is an effective way for you to show how the ideas in the clauses are related.

METHOD To write a compound sentence, combine independent clauses with a **coordinating conjunction.** The coordinating conjunction shows the relationship between the clauses.

coordinating conjunction
a word that connects the independent clauses in a compound sentence

Coordinating conjunction	Relationship
and	connects two related ideas
but, yet	contrasts two ideas
for	shows a cause
so	shows an effect
or	gives choices
nor	gives negative choices

RULE When you write a compound sentence with a coordinating conjunction, use a comma before the conjunction.

To combine two sentences effectively, read both sentences and look for the relationship between their ideas. Then use a comma and a coordinating conjunction that correctly expresses that relationship.

Separate: Jack joined a group of actors. They are quite talented.
Combined: Jack joined a group of actors, and they are quite talented. (The word *and* connects the two related ideas.)

Separate: Their first play is a hilarious comedy. It's sure to be a hit.
Combined: Their first play is a hilarious comedy, so it's sure to be a hit. (The word *so* shows an effect.)

Put a check mark next to the compound sentence that correctly combines independent clauses.

_____ a. My mother works at High Mills, she's worked there ten years.

_____ b. She started as a sewer, but she wanted to be a designer.

_____ c. After six years she finished college so she was promoted to the design department.

You are correct if you decided that *option b* is a correct compound sentence. Its two independent clauses are joined by both a comma and the coordinating conjunction *but. Option a* contains only a comma with no conjunction. *Option c* does not include a comma.

Other Connectors

There are two other ways to combine independent clauses in compound sentences.

METHOD 1 Combine sentences using a semicolon when the ideas are closely related.

Separate: Nuclear weapons threaten all our lives. Failure to solve this problem could have serious consequences.

Combined: Nuclear weapons threaten all our lives; failure to solve this problem could have serious consequences.

METHOD 2 Combine sentences using a semicolon and a conjunctive adverb. The conjunctive adverb you choose should show the relationship between the two ideas being combined.

Conjunctive adverbs	Relationship
also, furthermore, moreover, besides	connect two ideas
however, still, nevertheless, instead, nonetheless	contrast two ideas
similarly, likewise	compare two ideas
therefore, thus, consequently	show a result
next, then, meanwhile, finally, subsequently	show time order
for example, for instance	give examples

RULE When you use a conjunctive adverb to connect two clauses, put a semicolon before it and a comma after it.

Separate: People are interested in avoiding nuclear war. They do not always agree on the best way to do so.

Combined: People are interested in avoiding nuclear war; however, they do not always agree on the best way to do so. (*However* contrasts the two ideas.)

Put a check mark next to the sentences that correctly combine ideas in compound sentences.

_____ a. Social Insurance provides many forms of financial help; it currently pays retirement, disability, and other benefits.

_____ b. Most people retire at age 65; meanwhile, some people want to retire much later.

_____ c. Some people retire at age 62; consequently, they receive lower benefits.

_____ d. Retirees also continue to receive health benefits; which cover medical services.

You are correct if you chose *options a* and *c. Option b* incorrectly uses *meanwhile*, a time-order connecting word, when the relationship is a contrast. *Option d* is incorrect because *which cover for medical services* is not an independent clause.

GED Practice

Directions: Choose the <u>one best answer</u> to each question.

<u>Questions 1 through 4</u> refer to the following paragraphs.

Tour Jackets

(A)

(1) During the Vietnam War, many of the sailors and soldiers wore personally decorated jackets known as "Pleiku" or tour jackets. (2) The jackets were hand-sewn with colourful designs. (3) Maps, dragons, flags, and the like. (4) Later, the owners added elaborate patches, or they embroidered messages that indicated where they were stationed. (5) The jackets became completely personalized; each individual's was different.

(B)

(6) The first to wear the tour jackets were sailors. (7) The U.S. Navy issued each sailor a complete working uniform yet the jacket was the only U.S. Navy clothing that could be embellished. (8) Decorating jackets, then, began with sailors. (9) Became more common among soldiers later in the war.

1. Sentences 2 and 3: **The jackets were hand-sewn with colourful designs. Maps, dragons, flags, and the like.**

   The most effective combination of sentences 2 and 3 would include which groups of words?

   (1) designs, and maps
   (2) designs such as maps
   (3) hand-sewn maps with
   (4) The maps were hand-sewn
   (5) Their jackets with maps

2. Sentence 4: **Later, the owners added elaborate patches, or they embroidered messages that indicated where they were stationed.**

   Which is the best way to write the underlined portion of this sentence? If the original is the best way, choose option (1).

   (1) patches, or they
   (2) patches or they
   (3) patches. Or they
   (4) patches or, they
   (5) patches, or, they

3. Sentence 7: **The U.S. Navy issued each sailor a complete working uniform yet the jacket was the only U.S. Navy clothing that could be embellished.**

   Which is the best way to write the underlined portion of this sentence? If the original is the best way, choose option (1).

   (1) uniform yet
   (2) uniform, thus
   (3) uniform. And
   (4) uniform yet,
   (5) uniform, yet

4. Sentence 9: **Became more common among soldiers later in the war.**

   Which correction should be made to sentence 9?

   (1) change <u>Became</u> to <u>Becoming</u>
   (2) change <u>Became</u> to <u>It became</u>
   (3) insert a comma after <u>war</u>
   (4) change <u>war</u> to <u>War</u>
   (5) no correction is necessary

Questions 5 through 8 refer to the following paragraph.

Internet Tax Filing

(1) Canada Customs and Revenue Agency (CCRA) has simplified tax time with NETFILE, an electronic filing system. (2) You can prepare and file your tax forms very quickly over the Internet, so your tax refund may arrive in three weeks instead of six. (3) To file electronically, you'll need a personal computer with a modem and commercial tax preparation software. (4) The software records all your personal and financial information and the modem transmits it to the CCRA. (5) The CCRA then checks your forms for errors. (6) Some forms may be rejected. (7) The CCRA has a customer service department to help in such cases. (8) A service representative can tell you what's missing or incomplete, so that you can correct it and file again. (9) Once your return is accepted, you may be asked to send in additional documents, such as recipts and information slips. (10) You can also pay electronically, you can have the CCRA deposit your refund directly into your bank account.

5. Sentence 2: **You can prepare and file your tax forms very quickly over the Internet, so your tax refund may arrive in three weeks instead of six.**

Which is the best way to write the underlined portion of this sentence? If the original is the best way, choose option (1).

(1) Internet, so your
(2) Internet, your
(3) Internet so, your
(4) Internet so your
(5) Internet. So your

6. Sentence 4: **The software records all your personal and financial information and the modem transmits it to the CCRA.**

Which correction should be made to sentence 4?

(1) remove and after information
(2) insert a comma after and
(3) insert a comma after information
(4) remove the modem
(5) no correction is necessary

7. Sentences 6 and 7: **Some forms may be rejected. The CCRA has a customer service department to help in such cases.**

The most effective combination of sentences 6 and 7 would include which group of words?

(1) rejected, the
(2) rejected the,
(3) rejected therefore the
(4) rejected but the
(5) rejected, but the

8. Sentence 10: **You can also pay electronically, you can have the CCRA deposit your refund directly into your bank account.**

Which correction should be made to sentence 10?

(1) remove the comma
(2) insert or after the comma
(3) insert however after the comma
(4) insert a comma after deposit
(5) no correction is necessary

Some questions on the GED Test ask, "Which way is the best way to write the underlined portion of the text?" In those question types, option (1) is always the same as the original.

Answers start on page 729.

complex sentence contains an independent clause and a subordinate clause, connected by a subordinating conjunction

Subordinating Ideas

Complex Sentences

You know that an independent clause has a subject and predicate and expresses a complete thought. A dependent clause, or subordinate clause, has a subject and predicate but does not express a complete thought.

Subordinate clause: Until the sun set.

You also know that a compound sentence consists of two independent clauses joined by a coordinating conjunction. You can create a **complex sentence** when you join an independent clause and a subordinate clause. The subordinate clause adds information or details to the main independent clause.

Complex sentence: The fireworks did not start until the sun set.

A subordinate clause is introduced by a subordinating conjunction. Here are some subordinating conjuctions and relationships they show.

> **Time:** after, before, once, since, until, when, whenever, while
> **Result/effect:** in order that, so, so that
> **Location:** where, wherever
> **Condition:** if, even if, unless
> **Choice:** whether
> **Concession:** although, even though, though
> **Reason/cause:** as, because, since

METHOD A subordinate clause is a sentence fragment if it is not connected to an independent clause. You can correct the fragment by attaching it to an independent clause to create a complex sentence.

Independent clause
and fragment: The game was cancelled. Because it rained.
Complex sentence: The game was cancelled because it rained.

RULE Use a comma after a subordinate clause at the beginning of a sentence. You usually do not need a comma before a subordinate clause at the end of a sentence.

Complex sentence: Because it rained, the game was cancelled.
Complex sentence: The game was cancelled because it rained.

Put a check mark next to the correct complex sentence.

_____ a. Once the tow truck removed the broken-down truck.

_____ b. Once the truck was removed, the traffic jam was cleared.

You are correct if you chose *option b*. It is a correctly punctuated complex sentence. *Option a* is a subordinate clause (fragment).

Combining Details

Tip

Very simple ideas or single details often don't need their own sentences. Try combining them with sentences nearby to smooth choppy writing.

A simple sentence has a subject, a verb, and one idea. Simple sentences are often short. Too many short, simple sentences—or too many short, simple clauses in a compound sentence—will make your writing seem choppy and repetitious.

There are several methods for combining details to make your writing flow more smoothly. Notice that although all three methods solve the problem in a slightly different way, each contains the same details, eliminates repetition, and shows the relationship of ideas.

METHOD 1 Combine details into one longer simple sentence.

Choppy: Many different needles are required for hand sewing. The needles vary according to eye shape. They vary according to length. They vary according to point.

Choppy: The needles vary according to eye shape, and they vary according to length, and they vary according to point.

Smooth: Needles for hand sewing vary according to eye shape, length, and point.

METHOD 2 Combine details into one compound sentence.

Smooth: Hand sewing requires different needles, so they vary according to eye shape, length, and point.

METHOD 3 Combine details into one complex sentence.

Smooth: Because hand sewing requires different needles, they vary according to eye shape, length, and point.

Put a check mark next to the smoothest, most effective writing.

_____ a. On average, women in Canada live longer than men. They live about five years longer than men who are generally stronger than women.

_____ b. On average, women in Canada live five years longer than men, even though men are physically stronger.

_____ c. On average, women in Canada live five years longer than men. That means men, on average, have shorter lives than women. Men are typically stronger than women.

You are correct if you chose *option b*. It combines all the ideas smoothly and shows how they are related in one clear complex sentence. *Option a* combines some ideas, but repeats information unnecessarily. *Option c* does not combine any of the ideas and repeats the same information in different ways.

GED Practice

Directions: Choose the <u>one best answer</u> to each question.

<u>Questions 1 through 4</u> refer to the following paragraphs.

Moving Tips

(A)

(1) Whether you're going across town or across the country. (2) Moving is one of life's stressful experiences. (3) So that you have an easier time experienced movers suggest making a "home change-over" list.

(B)

(4) For example, let the utility companies know the date that you're moving. (5) Fill out a Change of Address form at the post office. (6) Be sure you know your new address. (7) Know the date you want your mail switched, too. (8) Some movers recommend packing a survival kit. (9) This kit contains items such as basic tools, snacks and drinks, and tissue. (10) You will probably need these things at some point on moving day, so make sure you keep your kit with you.

1. Sentences 1 and 2: **Whether you're going across town or across the <u>country. Moving is one of life's stressful experiences.</u>**

   Which is the best way to write the underlined portion of these sentences? If the original is the best way, choose option (1).

   (1) country. Moving
   (2) country moving
   (3) country, moving
   (4) country, and moving
   (5) country because moving

2. Sentence 3: **So that you have an easier time experienced movers suggest making a "home change-over" list.**

   Which correction should be made to sentence 3?

   (1) replace <u>So that</u> with <u>Because</u>
   (2) insert a <u>comma</u> after <u>time</u>
   (3) change <u>suggest</u> to <u>suggested</u>
   (4) insert a <u>comma</u> after <u>suggest</u>
   (5) no correction is necessary

3. Sentences 6 and 7: **Be sure you know your new address. <u>Know</u> the date you want your mail switched, too.**

   Which is the best way to write the underlined portion of these sentences? If the original is the best way, choose option (1).

   (1) address. Know
   (2) address, know
   (3) address, while knowing
   (4) address. And know
   (5) address and

4. Sentences 8 and 9: **Some movers recommend packing a survival kit. This kit contains items such as basic tools, snacks and drinks, and tissue.**

   The most effective combination of sentences 8 and 9 would include which group of words?

   (1) survival kit, and this
   (2) survival kit such as
   (3) survival kit containing
   (4) packing basic tools
   (5) movers recommending a kit with

Questions 5 through 8 refer to the following paragraph.

Fit and Healthy

(1) Being fit is practically a national obsession. (2) Fitness books are numerous. (3) So are commercial exercise programs. (4) Unfortunately, there is no magic formula for getting into shape. (5) How do you become fit and stay fit? (6) If you really want to get into shape you need to make serious, permanent lifestyle changes. (7) Exercise must be one of those changes. (8) You don't need to pay for membership in an expensive health club. (9) You can simply buy a good pair of shoes and take a brisk walk in them several times a week, and the shoes should be made especially for walking. (10) Finally, keep a positive attitude. (11) Frequently remind yourself how much better you look and feel. (12) Since you've changed your behaviour.

5. Sentences 2 and 3: **Fitness books are numerous. So are commercial exercise programs.**

   The most effective combination of sentences 2 and 3 would include which group of words?

   (1) numerous, so are
   (2) books and commercial exercise programs are
   (3) in addition, commercial exercise programs
   (4) but so are commercial exercise programs
   (5) Numerous fitness books and commercial

One way to combine details is to combine subjects. For example, *Stan worked at the warehouse. Ivan did too.* becomes *Stan and Ivan worked at the warehouse.* You can also combine predicates: *Stan unloaded shipments. He also checked inventory.* becomes *Stan unloaded shipments and checked inventory.*

6. Sentence 6: **If you really want to get into shape you need to make serious, permanent lifestyle changes.**

   Which correction should be made to sentence 6?

   (1) replace If you with You
   (2) insert a comma after want
   (3) insert a comma after shape
   (4) change shape you to shape. You
   (5) no correction is necessary

7. Sentence 9: **You can simply buy a good pair of shoes and take a brisk walk in them several times a week, and the shoes should be made especially for walking.**

   The most effective revision of sentence 9 would include which group of words?

   (1) make sure that the shoes
   (2) Buying a good pair of shoes and walking
   (3) You can simply buy and walk
   (4) the shoes should be good for walking
   (5) a good pair of walking shoes

8. Sentences 11 and 12: **Frequently remind yourself how much better you look and feel. Since you've changed your behaviour.**

   Which is the best way to write the underlined portion of these sentences? If the original is the best way, choose option (1).

   (1) feel. Since you've
   (2) feel, and since you've
   (3) feel since you've
   (4) feel although you've
   (5) feel. You've

Answers start on page 730.

Lesson 4

Run-ons and Comma Splices

Run-on Sentences

A **run-on sentence** consists of two or more independent clauses joined incorrectly. There are several ways to correct run-ons.

METHOD 1 Separate the clauses in a run-on sentence by making two sentences.

Run-on: It's easy to get caught up in the excitement of an auction it's so fast and noisy.

Correct: It's easy to get caught up in the excitement of an auction. It's so fast and noisy.

METHOD 2 Separate the clauses with a semicolon alone or with a semicolon, conjunctive adverb, and comma.

Run-on: A man at an auction sneezed he wound up owning a moth-eaten moose head.

Correct: A man at an auction sneezed; he wound up owning a moth-eaten moose head.

Correct: A man at an auction sneezed; consequently, he wound up owning a moth-eaten moose head.

METHOD 3 Separate the clauses with both a comma and a coordinating conjunction. Remember that the seven coordinating conjunctions are *and, but, or, nor, for, so,* and *yet.*

Run-on: Decide ahead of time how much to spend you won't be tempted to overbid.

Correct: Decide ahead of time how much to spend, and you won't be tempted to overbid.

METHOD 4 Make one independent clause a dependent clause with a subordinate conjunction. Use a comma if necessary.

Correct: If you decide ahead of time how much to spend, you won't be tempted to overbid.

Put a check mark next to the correct sentence.

_____ a. Agnes is not efficient, but she's learning quickly.

_____ b. Agnes is not efficient she's learning quickly.

You are correct if you chose *option a*. It correctly creates a compound sentence with a comma and the coordinating conjunction *but*. *Option b* is a run-on sentence.

run-on sentence
two or more independent clauses that are run together without proper punctuation or connecting words

To decide whether a long sentence is a run-on, check to see whether there are too many ideas that are not connected with the correct punctuation and connecting words.

Comma Splices and Run-ons Connected with *And*

comma splice
a run-on sentence in which independent clauses are connected only by a comma

A **comma splice** occurs when independent clauses are joined only with a comma; the coordinating conjunction is missing.

METHOD 1 The easiest way to correct a comma splice is to add a coordinating conjunction after the comma.

Comma splice: A learning disorder is a disability, you can't see any obvious signs like other disabilities.

Correct: A learning disorder is a disability, yet you can't see any obvious signs like other disabilities.

You can also fix a comma splice by using any of the methods for fixing a run-on explained on page 80.

Another kind of run-on is created when too many independent clauses are strung together, connected only by the word *and*. Often, these lengthy sentences connect ideas that are not closely enough related to be combined in one sentence.

METHOD 2 Correct a run-on with too many independent clauses by dividing it into more than one sentence. One or more sentences may become compound sentences.

Run-on: There are many types of learning disorders and they can interfere with a person's speaking or writing and these disorders sometimes produce problems with reading or math and they may affect attention or self-control.

Correct: There are many types of learning disorders. They can interfere with a person's speaking or writing. These disorders sometimes produce problems with reading and math, and they may affect attention or self-control.

Put a check mark next to the correct sentences.

_____ a. Babies like toys that make noise, but be sure no small pieces can break off for babies to swallow.

_____ b. Big, lightweight toys are fun, and they are easy to grab and hold.

_____ c. They shouldn't have sharp edges, avoid points as well.

_____ d. You can buy a tube and you place toys or toy parts in it and if the parts can fit in it then they are too small for a baby and you should get rid of the toy.

You are correct if you chose *options a* and *b*. They are correctly combined compound sentences. *Option c* is a comma splice because it combines two independent clauses with only a comma. *Option d* has too many clauses connected with just the word *and*.

GED Practice

Directions: Choose the <u>one best answer</u> to each question.

Questions <u>1 through 4</u> refer to the following application.

Conditions of Credit

(1) I have read this application everything I have stated in it is true. (2) I authorize Ocean Pacific Bank to check my credit, employment history, and any other relevant information. (3) I agree to be responsible for all bills charged to the account, I am at least 18 years of age. (4) I also understand that information about me or my account may be shared by the Bank with its related companies. (5) However, refuse to allow such sharing of personal or credit information with outside companies. (6) If I refuse, I agree to inform Ocean Pacific in a letter and I need to include my name, address, and home telephone number, as well as any applicable Ocean Pacific Bank account numbers. (7) The information in this application is accurate as of the date signed below.

1. Sentence 1: **I have read this application everything I have stated in it is true.**

   Which is the best way to write the underlined portion of this sentence? If the original is the best way, choose option (1).

   (1) application everything
   (2) application, everything
   (3) application, therefore everything
   (4) application and everything
   (5) application, and everything

2. Sentence 3: **I agree to be responsible for all bills charged to the account, I am at least 18 years of age.**

   Which correction should be made to sentence 3?

   (1) change <u>bills charged</u> to <u>bills. Charged</u>
   (2) remove the comma
   (3) change the comma to a period
   (4) insert <u>yet</u> after the comma
   (5) replace <u>I am</u> with <u>being</u>

3. Sentence 5: **However, refuse to allow such sharing of personal or credit information with outside companies.**

   Which correction should be made to sentence 5?

   (1) insert <u>I can</u> after the comma
   (2) change <u>refuse</u> to <u>refusing</u>
   (3) replace <u>refuse</u> with <u>my refusal</u>
   (4) insert a comma after <u>personal</u>
   (5) no correction is necessary

4. Sentence 6: **If I refuse, I agree to inform Ocean Pacific in a letter and I need to include my name, address, and home telephone number, as well as any applicable Ocean Pacific Bank account numbers.**

   The most effective revision of sentence 6 would include which group of words?

   (1) If I refuse yet agree
   (2) including a letter to Ocean Pacific
   (3) letter, needing to include
   (4) letter and include my name,
   (5) I agree to include, if I refuse,

Questions 5 through 9 refer to the following paragraph.

On-the-Job Injuries

(1) Not all on-the-job injuries involve heavy equipment, some office occupations can also involve injuries. (2) Workers who type constantly, such as data entry operators, may suffer from carpal tunnel syndrome their fingers may literally seize up from the repetitive finger movements. (3) Both changing position frequently and keeping the keyboard lower than the elbows help avoid injury. (4) Studies have uncovered other injuries at seemingly "safe" jobs, staring for long periods at computer screens can cause severe eyestrain. (5) To reduce eyestrain, stay at least 50 cm from the screen, and use diffuse overhead lighting. (6) In some offices back injuries are common workers can lower their risk by squatting when they lift objects off the floor.

5. Sentence 1: **Not all on-the-job injuries involve heavy equipment, some office occupations can also involve injuries.**

   Which is the best way to write the underlined portion of this sentence? If the original is the best way, choose option (1).

   (1) equipment, some
   (2) equipment some
   (3) equipment, however some
   (4) equipment so that some
   (5) equipment. Some

6. Sentence 2: **Workers who type constantly, such as data entry operators, may suffer from carpal tunnel syndrome their fingers may literally seize up from the repetitive finger movements.**

   Which is the best way to write the underlined portion of this sentence? If the original is the best way, choose option (1).

   (1) syndrome their
   (2) syndrome, their
   (3) syndrome. Their
   (4) syndrome for their
   (5) syndrome and their

7. Sentence 3: **Both changing position frequently and keeping the keyboard lower than the elbows help avoid injury.**

   Which correction should be made to sentence 3?

   (1) replace Both with By both
   (2) insert a comma after frequently
   (3) remove and
   (4) insert to after elbows
   (5) no correction is necessary

8. Sentence 4: **Studies have uncovered other injuries at seemingly "safe" jobs, staring for long periods at computer screens can cause severe eyestrain.**

   The most effective revision of sentence 4 would include which group of words?

   (1) jobs and staring
   (2) Whereas studies have uncovered
   (3) because staring for long periods
   (4) jobs; for example,
   (5) have uncovered that staring

9. Sentence 6: **In some offices back injuries are common workers can lower their risk by squatting when they lift objects off the floor.**

   Which correction should be made to sentence 6?

   (1) replace In with Because in
   (2) insert a comma after common
   (3) insert and after common
   (4) change common workers to common. Workers
   (5) no correction is necessary

Be careful to distinguish between two compound clauses separated by *and* (which require a comma) and two subjects separated by *and.* Do not use a comma between two subjects.

Answers start on page 730.

Misplaced and Dangling Modifiers

When you write, you can use a modifier to describe another word or phrase. A modifier can be a single word, such as the adjective *soft* in *soft pillow* or the adverb *soundly* in *sleep soundly*. A modifier can also be a phrase, such as *on the bed* in *My husband is sleeping on the bed.*

When a modifier is put in the wrong place in a sentence, it can confuse the reader or change the meaning of the sentence. Then it is called a **misplaced modifier.** A misplaced modifier appears to describe the wrong word or phrase, or it is unclear which word or phrase the modifier is describing.

RULE 1 Place a modifier near the word or phrase it describes.

Misplaced: Our hands blistered when we paddled painfully. (Does *painfully* modify *paddled*?)
Correct: Our hands blistered painfully when we paddled.
Unclear: Our canoe was wooden, which was the only choice. (Does the phrase *which was the only choice* modify *canoe* or *wooden*?)
Correct: Our canoe, which was the only choice, was wooden.

A **dangling modifier** is another problem modifier. A modifier is dangling when the sentence lacks the subject that the modifier is describing.

RULE 2 Avoid dangling modifiers.

METHOD 1 Fix a dangling modifier by making it into a subordinate clause.

METHOD 2 Fix a dangling modifier by changing the subject of the sentence to the word that the modifier is describing.

Dangling: Paddling down the river, the canoe overturned. (Who is the subject of *Paddling down the river*? As written, it seems that the canoe is!)
Correct: As we paddled down the river, the canoe overturned.
Correct: Paddling down the river, we overturned the canoe.

Put a check mark next to the sentence that has a misplaced or dangling modifier.

_____ a. I made dinner for a friend at his house.

_____ b. Looking in the refrigerator, the vegetables were rotten.

You are correct if you chose *option b*. There is no subject for the opening phrase (*who* is looking in the refrigerator—the vegetables?), so it has a dangling modifier.

---

misplaced modifier
a word or phrase placed too far from the word or phrase it describes

dangling modifier
a phrase placed at the beginning of a sentence that lacks the subject the modifier is describing

Misplaced modifiers can be hard to spot because a reader automatically tries to interpret a sentence even if it's confusing. Be sure to read exactly what a sentence is saying, rather than what you think it means to say.

GED Practice

Directions: Choose the one best answer to each question.

Questions 1 through 4 refer to the following paragraph.

Lower Your Insurance

(1) Is your car insurance too high? (2) By installing anti-theft devices, your insurance cost will decrease. (3) The best way to save money is by etching your vehicle identification number into the windows, costing about $20. (4) Etched windows make it hard to break down a car into sellable pieces for car thieves. (5) Etched windows can save you up to $50 on your comprehensive rate, depending on where you live. (6) Other popular devices cost between $300 and $800 but can save you as much as 35% on insurance rates. (7) Whichever you choose, installing anti-theft devices gives you both lower rates and peace of mind.

1. Sentence 2: **By installing anti-theft devices, your insurance cost will decrease.**

   Which correction should be made to sentence 2?

   (1) replace By installing with If you install
   (2) remove the comma
   (3) insert and after the comma
   (4) change will decrease to decreasing
   (5) no correction is necessary

When a GED Test question asks you how best to revise or rewrite a sentence, change the words around in your head first. Then match how you would change the sentence with one of the options given.

2. Sentence 3: **The best way to save money is by etching your vehicle identification number into the windows, costing about $20.**

   The most effective revision of sentence 3 would begin with which group of words?

   (1) Costing about $20,
   (2) Being the cheapest way to save,
   (3) To save money,
   (4) Etching your vehicle identification number,
   (5) Your vehicle identification number

3. Sentence 4: **Etched windows make it hard to break down a car into sellable pieces for car thieves.**

   The most effective revision of sentence 4 would include which group of words?

   (1) By etching windows, it
   (2) If you etch windows, you make
   (3) making it hard to break
   (4) hard for car thieves to break
   (5) break into sellable pieces

4. Sentence 7: **Whichever you choose, installing anti-theft devices gives you both lower rates and peace of mind.**

   Which correction should be made to sentence 7?

   (1) replace Whichever you choose with Selecting either one,
   (2) remove the comma
   (3) replace installing with you can install
   (4) insert a comma after rates
   (5) no correction is necessary

Questions 5 through 9 refer to the following letter of recommendation.

Dear Ms Lang:

(1) As senior crew supervisor, Erica Ortiz supervises 24 gardeners in six landscaping crews for Strong Landscapers, Inc. (2) She makes sure when leaving each morning that the crews have their job assignments and tools. (3) Erica started as the only female supervisor at Strong Landscapers, quickly gaining the respect of crew members in 1998. (4) Hardworking, well-organized, and dedicated, she has done a commendable job of supervising the gardening crews. (5) Erica also has a great reputation among our customers, representing Strong Landscapers proudly in the community. (6) With pleasure, Erica Ortiz is recommended for a managerial position in the landscaping field.

5. Sentence 1: **As senior crew supervisor, Erica Ortiz** supervises 24 gardeners in six landscaping crews for Strong Landscapers, Inc.

Which is the best way to write the underlined portion of this sentence? If the original is the best way, choose option (1).

(1) As senior crew supervisor, Erica Ortiz
(2) As Erica Ortiz, senior crew supervisor,
(3) Erica Ortiz is senior crew supervisor
(4) Erica Ortiz being senior crew supervisor
(5) Erica Ortiz, she is senior crew supervisor

6. Sentence 2: **She makes sure when leaving each morning that the crews have their job assignments and tools.**

The most effective revision of sentence 2 would include which group of words?

(1) Making sure that the crews have
(2) When leaving each morning, she
(3) makes sure that the morning job assignments
(4) sure that the crews have their job assignments and tools when
(5) when the crews have their job assignments

7. Sentence 3: **Erica started as the only female supervisor at Strong Landscapers, quickly gaining the respect of crew members in 1998.**

Which is the best way to write the underlined portion of this sentence? If the original is the best way, choose option (1).

(1) Landscapers, quickly gaining the respect of crew members in 1998
(2) Landscapers quickly gaining the respect in 1998 of crew members
(3) Landscapers in 1998 and quickly gained the respect of crew members
(4) Landscapers, and she quickly gained the respect of crew members in 1998
(5) Landscapers, in 1998 she quickly gained the respect of crew members

8. Sentence 5: **Erica also has a great reputation among our customers, representing Strong Landscapers proudly in the community.**

If you rewrote sentence 5 beginning with

Proudly representing Strong Landscapers,

the next words should be

(1) Erica also has
(2) a great reputation
(3) the community has
(4) customers have
(5) and having a great reputation

9. Sentence 6: **With pleasure, Erica Ortiz is recommended for a managerial position in the landscaping field.**

Which correction should be made to sentence 6?

(1) change the comma to a period
(2) change Erica Ortiz is recommended to I recommend Erica Ortiz
(3) remove is
(4) insert a comma after recommended
(5) no correction is necessary

Answers start on page 731.

Parallel Structure

When a sentence contains a series of equal and related items, all the items should be in the same form. That is, each item should match grammatically with the others. This is called **parallel structure.** You will express your ideas more clearly if you use parallel structure.

RULE 1 Match items in a series in form and part of speech.

Not Parallel: I hunted, searched, and was begging for an apartment.
Parallel: I <u>hunted</u>, <u>searched</u>, and <u>begged</u> for an apartment.

Not Parallel: My routine was to wake at six, to run for the paper, and checking every rental ad before breakfast.
Parallel: My routine was <u>to wake</u> at six, <u>to run</u> for the paper, and <u>to check</u> every rental ad before breakfast.
Parallel: My routine was <u>waking</u> at six, <u>running</u> for the paper, and <u>checking</u> every rental ad before breakfast.

Not Parallel: A renter must look sensibly, carefully, and with caution at new apartments.
Parallel: A renter must look <u>sensibly, carefully</u>, and <u>cautiously</u> at new apartments.

RULE 2 Match phrases with phrases.

Not parallel: Look in the rooms, at the building, and the lease.
Parallel: Look in the rooms, at the building, and <u>at</u> the lease.

RULE 3 Do not mix words or phrases with clauses.

Not Parallel: Make sure that the building is clean, safe, and you can afford it.
Parallel: Make sure that the building is clean, safe, and <u>affordable</u>.

Write _P_ if a sentence has parallel structure. Write _N_ if it does not.

_____ a. We love our pets because they live with us, know us well, but loving us anyway.

_____ b. We need them to charm, entertain, and comfort us.

_____ c. To eat enough, daily exercise, and a safe home are all they ask of us.

You are correct if you labelled only _option b_ parallel. _Option a_ should be _We love our pets because they live with us, know us well, but love us anyway. Option c_ should be _Enough food, daily exercise, and a safe home are all they ask of us._

parallel structure
writing in which all the elements in a series are written in the same grammatical form

Tip

When items in a series are connected by _and, but, or, nor, yet,_ or _as well as,_ check that the items are parallel.

GED Practice

Directions: Choose the <u>one best answer</u> to each question.

<u>Questions 1 through 4</u> refer to the following paragraph.

An Effective Interview

(1) Displaying interest, with a lot of experience, and carrying a good résumé are not enough for a successful job interview. (2) To get a good job, you should arrive at your interview on time and appropriately dressed. (3) You don't create a good impression when you arrive late, breathing hard, and loudly apologetic. (4) If you walk in wearing jeans, a sweatshirt, and sneakers, you won't impress anyone, either. (5) Wear clothes that are businesslike, conservative, and look serious. (6) If you are confident, professional, and be friendly, you stand a good chance of getting the job. (7) Even if you aren't hired at the very first interview, the experience of preparing for it should improve your chances at the next one.

1. Sentence 1: **Displaying interest, with a lot of experience, and carrying a good résumé are not enough for a successful job interview.**

   Which correction should be made to sentence 1?

   (1) change <u>Displaying</u> to <u>To display</u>
   (2) remove the comma after <u>interest</u>
   (3) replace <u>with a lot of</u> with <u>having</u>
   (4) remove <u>carrying</u>
   (5) insert a comma after <u>résumé</u>

2. Sentence 3: **You don't create a good impression when you arrive late, breathing hard, and loudly apologetic.**

   If you rewrote sentence 3 beginning with

   <u>By arriving late, breathing hard,</u>

   the next words should be

   (1) and loudly apologetic
   (2) as if you were apologizing loudly
   (3) and to apologize loudly
   (4) and apologizing loudly
   (5) and with loud apologies

3. Sentence 4: **If you walk in wearing jeans, a sweatshirt, <u>and sneakers,</u> you won't impress anyone, either.**

   Which is the best way to write the underlined portion of this sentence? If the original is the best way, choose option (1).

   (1) and sneakers
   (2) and in sneakers
   (3) and with sneakers on
   (4) and wearing sneakers
   (5) and sneakers on your feet

4. Sentence 5: **Wear clothes that are businesslike, conservative, and look serious.**

   Which correction should be made to sentence 5?

   (1) change <u>Wear</u> to <u>Wearing</u>
   (2) change <u>Wear</u> to <u>To wear</u>
   (3) remove the comma after <u>businesslike</u>
   (4) insert <u>and</u> before <u>conservative</u>
   (5) remove <u>look</u>

Directions: Choose the one best answer to each question.

Questions 5 through 9 refer to the following paragraph.

Elevator Music

(1) You either love it, hate it, or ignore the music playing while you're shopping, riding in an elevator, or waiting for appointments. (2) The music that plays in the background of our lives is soft, vague, and we can recognize it. (3) It's well known that music can calm us, lower our heart rate, as well as reducing our blood pressure. (4) Businesses play so-called "elevator music" to affect our behaviour in stores, at work, and while waiting in stressful situations. (5) Offices that use this music report less absenteeism better job performance, and less turnover of employees. (6) Stores think elevator music makes customers shop longer and buy more. (7) If you detest this background hum, you can try singing to yourself, wearing earplugs, or leaving.

5. Sentence 2: **The music that plays in the background of our lives is soft, vague, and we can recognize it.**

Which correction should be made to sentence 2?

(1) change plays to can play
(2) change soft to softly
(3) change vague to vagueness
(4) replace and with so
(5) replace and we can recognize it with and recognizable

6. Sentence 3: **It's well known that music can calm us, lower our heart rate, as well as reducing our blood pressure.**

Which correction should be made to sentence 3?

(1) change can calm to calming
(2) insert to before lower
(3) remove as well as
(4) change reducing to reduce
(5) no correction is necessary

7. Sentence 4: **Businesses play so-called "elevator music" to affect our behaviour in stores, at work, and while waiting in stressful situations.**

Which is the best way to write the underlined portion of this sentence? If the original is the best way, choose option (1).

(1) in stores, at work, and while waiting in stressful situations
(2) in stores, while at work, and waiting in stressful situations
(3) in stores, at work, and waiting in stressful situations
(4) in stores, at work, and in stressful situations
(5) in stores, working, and stressful situations

8. Sentence 5: **Offices that use this music report less absenteeism better job performance, and less turnover of employees.**

Which correction should be made to sentence 5?

(1) insert a comma after music
(2) change report to reporting
(3) insert a comma after absenteeism
(4) change performance to performing
(5) no correction is necessary

9. Sentence 7: **If you detest this background hum, you can try singing to yourself, wearing earplugs, or leaving.**

Which correction should be made to sentence 7?

(1) remove the comma after hum
(2) change singing to to sing
(3) remove wearing
(4) replace leaving with you can leave
(5) no correction is necessary

Answers start on page 732.

Directions: Choose the <u>one best answer</u> to each question.

<u>Questions 1 through 5</u> refer to the following business letter.

Dear Sir:

    (1) On June 15, I ordered a pair of blue pants in boys' size 8 from your outlet catalogue. (2) I was sent a pair of green pants instead. (3) Which I promptly returned. (4) Then I received the right colour, but in size 4, not 8. (5) I was transferred to voice mail when I called the customer service line to complain. (6) 15 days since I left that message. (7) This unacceptable treatment of a customer. (8) I will cancel my store charge account. (9) An apology and full reimbursement within one week.

1. Sentences 2 and 3: **I was sent a pair of green pants instead. Which I promptly returned.**

   Which is the best way to write the underlined portion of these sentences? If the original is the best way, choose option (1).

   (1) instead. Which
   (2) instead! Which
   (3) instead, which
   (4) instead and
   (5) instead. And which

2. Sentence 5: **I was transferred to voice mail when I called the customer service line to complain.**

   Which correction should be made to sentence 5?

   (1) insert <u>Even though</u> before <u>I was</u>
   (2) change <u>mail when</u> to <u>mail! When</u>
   (3) change <u>mail when</u> to <u>mail. When</u>
   (4) remove <u>when</u>
   (5) no correction is necessary

3. Sentence 6: **15 days since I left that message.**

   Which correction should be made to sentence 6?

   (1) insert <u>It has been</u> before <u>15</u>
   (2) change <u>15</u> to <u>Fifteen</u>
   (3) insert <u>ago</u> after <u>days</u>
   (4) insert <u>with your voice mail</u> after <u>message</u>
   (5) no correction is necessary

4. Sentence 7: **This unacceptable treatment of a customer.**

   Which correction should be made to sentence 7?

   (1) replace <u>This</u> with <u>Making this</u>
   (2) insert <u>is</u> after <u>This</u>
   (3) change <u>treatment of</u> to <u>treatment. Of</u>
   (4) replace <u>of</u> with <u>given to</u>
   (5) insert <u>by your store</u> after <u>customer</u>

5. Sentences 8 and 9: **I will cancel my store charge account. An apology and full reimbursement within one week.**

   The most effective combination of sentences 8 and 9 would include which group of words?

   (1) account give me an
   (2) account demanding an
   (3) account unless I receive an
   (4) account and an
   (5) account with an

Read a GED selection carefully. Think about how you could correct or improve it. Then when you read the questions, you may already have an idea about the correct answers.

Questions 6 through 10 refer to the following business letter.

Dear New Cellular Phone Customer:

(1) Your monthly access charges will be billed on the twenty-fifth of every month. (2) Your first bill includes prorated charges from April 8, the date you began service, and the regular access charge for May. (3) Two months are combined on the first bill, it may be larger than subsequent bills. (4) In addition, you get one free hour of cellular airtime each month. (5) That airtime must be used within the month. (6) Additional taxes, tolls, and special charges will be recorded separately. (7) Charges for calls begin at the time of pickup and, they end at the time of disconnection. (8) You are billed for all answered calls but there is no charge for busy signals or unanswered rings. (9) Calls are billed in full minutes; for example, a call of 5 minutes and 15 seconds will be billed as a 6-minute call.

6. Sentence 3: **Two months are combined on the first bill, it may be larger than subsequent bills.**

   Which correction should be made to sentence 3?

   (1) insert , and after combined
   (2) insert similarly after the comma
   (3) insert so after the comma
   (4) remove the comma
   (5) no correction is necessary

7. Sentences 4 and 5: **In addition, you get one free hour of cellular airtime each month. That airtime must be used within the month.**

   The most effective combination of sentences 4 and 5 would include which group of words?

   (1) month for example that
   (2) month and airtime
   (3) month however airtime
   (4) month so, the airtime
   (5) month, but it

8. Sentence 7: **Charges for calls begin at the time of pickup and, they end at the time of disconnection.**

   Which correction should be made to sentence 7?

   (1) change pickup and, to pickup, and
   (2) replace and with nonetheless
   (3) remove and
   (4) remove the comma
   (5) no correction is necessary

9. Sentence 8: **You are billed for all answered calls but there is no charge for busy signals or unanswered rings.**

   Which is the best way to write the underlined portion of this sentence? If the original is the best way, choose option (1).

   (1) calls but
   (2) calls, but
   (3) calls, however,
   (4) calls and
   (5) calls. But

10. Sentence 9: **Calls are billed in full minutes; for example, a call of 5 minutes and 15 seconds will be billed as a 6-minute call.**

    Which correction should be made to sentence 9?

    (1) replace for example with nevertheless
    (2) replace for example with but
    (3) remove the comma
    (4) insert a comma after 5 minutes
    (5) no correction is necessary

On the GED Test, you may see an option that uses a conjunctive adverb without a semicolon to connect two clauses. Remember, that type of sentence construction is never correct.

Questions 11 through 14 refer to the following letter.

Dear Dr. Winger:

(A)

(1) Thank you for responding to our evaluation of your program at City Hospital you are correct in observing the difference in the evaluation this year. (2) The reason is that our agency is shifting its emphasis from hospital-based programs to community-based settings. (3) We also had more time for our evaluations this year, so the report is more detailed.

(B)

(4) Your program is in noncompliance in several areas, there is no reason to be too concerned. (5) We evaluate many hospital programs and almost all fail to comply in one or more areas and total compliance is not an absolute requirement for funding. (6) We will provide an objective view of your operation and an explanation of our new evaluation process in our annual report.

11. Sentence 1: **Thank you for responding to our evaluation of your program at City Hospital you are correct in observing the difference in the evaluation this year.**

    Which is the best way to write the underlined portion of this sentence? If the original is the best way, choose option (1).

    (1) City Hospital you are correct
    (2) City Hospital, You are correct
    (3) City Hospital, you are correct
    (4) City Hospital. You are correct
    (5) City Hospital and you are correct

12. Sentence 3: **We also had more time for our evaluations this year, so the report is more detailed.**

    Which correction should be made to sentence 3?

    (1) insert a comma after <u>time</u>
    (2) remove the comma
    (3) insert <u>and</u> after the comma
    (4) remove <u>so</u>
    (5) no correction is necessary

13. Sentence 4: **Your program is in noncompliance in several areas, there is no reason to be too concerned.**

    Which correction should be made to sentence 4?

    (1) replace <u>Your</u> with <u>Because your</u>
    (2) remove the comma
    (3) replace the comma with <u>and</u>
    (4) insert <u>however</u> after the comma
    (5) insert <u>but</u> after the comma

14. Sentence 5: **We evaluate many hospital programs and almost all fail to comply in one or more areas and total compliance is not an absolute requirement for funding.**

    The most effective revision of sentence 5 would include which group of words?

    (1) programs, and almost all fail to comply in one or more areas. Total
    (2) While evaluating many hospital programs,
    (3) Many hospital programs fail evaluation
    (4) total compliance not being an absolute requirement
    (5) hospital programs that fail to comply

Questions 15 through 18 refer to the following memo.

Memorandum

To: All Project Members
From: Ken Lopez

(A)

(1) I evaluated Pinto Software in three areas: record of reliability, ease of installation, and how easy it is to use. (2) Pinto seems completely reliable. (3) Pinto users report their computers run for months without crashing and the program does not interfere with other applications. (4) Unfortunately, its installation process is not for the faint of heart. (5) I had to change my hard drive and I had to reconnect my mouse three times and I had to reinstall my Internet connection twice. (6) Finally, I'm afraid it's not easy to use either. (7) The graphics are complicated the commands are confusing.

(B)

(8) In conclusion, I recommend we keep searching for more appropriate software.

15. Sentence 1: **I evaluated Pinto Software in three areas: record of reliability, ease of installation, and how easy it is to use.**

    Which correction should be made to sentence 1?

    (1) remove the comma after reliability
    (2) change installation to being installed
    (3) replace how easy it is to use with ease of use
    (4) change is to will be
    (5) no correction is necessary

16. Sentence 3: **Pinto users report their computers run for months without crashing and the program does not interfere with other applications.**

    Which correction should be made to sentence 3?

    (1) change report to reporting
    (2) change run to running
    (3) insert a comma after crashing
    (4) replace and with without
    (5) change does not to don't

17. Sentence 5: **I had to change my hard drive and I had to reconnect my mouse three times and I had to reinstall my Internet connection twice.**

    The most effective revision of sentence 5 would include which group of words?

    (1) Changing my hard drive and reconnecting my mouse three times and reinstalling
    (2) to change, to reconnect, and to reinstall
    (3) drive, reconnecting my mouse three times and reinstalling
    (4) drive, reconnect my mouse three times, and reinstall
    (5) drive, and I also had to reconnect my mouse three times, and I also had to reinstall

18. Sentence 7: **The graphics are complicated the commands are confusing.**

    Which is the best way to write the underlined portion of this sentence? If the original is the best way, choose option (1).

    (1) complicated the
    (2) complicated and the
    (3) complicated however the
    (4) complicated, the
    (5) complicated, and the

Questions 19 through 22 refer to the following paragraph.

Impulse Shopping

(1) Supermarkets are designed to encourage us to buy on impulse. (2) When we enter we generally move in the direction the store has chosen, down the "power" aisle. (3) It is a rare shopper who can reach the dairy products in the rear of the store without picking up unplanned items. (4) Then we stand in the checkout line and see more impulse buys. (5) We see magazines. (6) We see candy and other small items. (7) Even though we may have wanted only a litre of milk. (8) We'll probably walk out with several items. (9) We can avoid impulse buying. (10) We have to understand why we do it.

19. Sentence 2: **When we enter we generally move in the direction the store has chosen, down the "power" aisle.**

   Which correction should be made to sentence 2?

   (1) replace When with Because
   (2) insert a comma after enter
   (3) change enter we to enter. We
   (4) insert a comma after generally
   (5) insert a comma after direction

A subordinating conjunction, a subject, and a predicate at the beginning of the sentence will help you determine whether you need to use a comma.

20. Sentences 4, 5, and 6: **Then we stand in the checkout line and see more impulse buys. We see magazines. We see candy and other small items.**

   The most effective combination of sentences 4, 5, and 6 would include which group of words?

   (1) Standing in the checkout line and seeing
   (2) Then we stand and see
   (3) buys such as magazines, candy, and
   (4) buys, we see magazines
   (5) buys, seeing magazines

21. Sentences 7 and 8: **Even though we may have wanted only a litre of milk. We'll probably walk out with several items.**

   Which is the best way to write the underlined portion of these sentences? If the original is the best way, choose option (1).

   (1) milk. We'll
   (2) milk, and we'll
   (3) milk, so we'll
   (4) milk we'll
   (5) milk, we'll

22. Sentences 9 and 10: **We can avoid impulse buying. We have to understand why we do it.**

   The most effective combination of sentences 9 and 10 would include which group of words?

   (1) buying, and we
   (2) buying, so we
   (3) Because we can
   (4) if we understand
   (5) although we do not

Questions 23 through 26 refer to the following paragraphs.

Recycling

(A)

(1) Recycling has become a priority in this country because landfills are at capacity. (2) That's why residents are required to separate their trash in certain provinces. (3) Each household must separate bottles, cans, and paper in containers. (4) When left at the curb, they help the recycling effort.

(B)

(5) Many companies in the recycling industry have found creative new uses for used products. (6) Industries with a promising future forming to help replace biodegradable items. (7) Factories create new glass and aluminum products from melted down cans and bottles. (8) One innovative shoe manufacturer makes soles and it uses worn-out tires to make them and the soles are for athletic shoes. (9) Publishing companies are trying to increase the amount of recycled paper in their products.

(C)

(10) With such continued efforts by both individuals and companies, the waste problem in this country can be greatly reduced.

23. Sentence 2: **That's why residents are required to separate their trash in certain provinces.**

    The most effective revision of sentence 2 would include which group of words?

    (1) separating trash in certain provinces
    (2) requirements in certain provinces
    (3) residents in certain provinces
    (4) separate in certain provinces
    (5) trash required in certain provinces

For more information about Sentence Structure, see the Writer's Checklist on page 898.

24. Sentence 4: **When left at the curb, they help the recycling effort.**

    Which correction should be made to sentence 4?

    (1) replace When with Being
    (2) replace When left with Left
    (3) replace left with residents leave these items
    (4) remove the comma
    (5) change help to helping

25. Sentence 6: **Industries with a promising future forming to help replace biodegradable items.**

    Which correction should be made to sentence 6?

    (1) replace Industries with a promising future with With a promising future, industries
    (2) replace with with have
    (3) insert are after future
    (4) insert a comma after forming
    (5) no correction is necessary

26. Sentence 8: **One innovative shoe manufacturer makes soles and it uses worn-out tires to make them and the soles are for athletic shoes.**

    The most effective revision of sentence 8 would include which group of words?

    (1) uses worn-out tires and is making soles for athletic shoes
    (2) out of worn-out tires makes soles for athletic shoes
    (3) is making using worn-out tires soles for athletic shoes
    (4) shoe and sole manufacturer uses worn-out tires for athletic shoes
    (5) makes soles for athletic shoes using worn-out tires

Answers start on page 733.

Lesson 7

Organization

Organization is an important content area on the GED Language Arts, Writing Test. Fifteen percent of the multiple-choice questions will be based on organization issues. Paying attention to the organization of the entire piece of writing will help you answer all the questions on the test.

Organizing your ideas into paragraphs will help your reader understand your meaning. Paragraphs are groups of sentences that are organized around one main idea. The main idea of a paragraph is expressed in a topic sentence and supported by other sentences with examples, facts, and specific details. You can use transition words and phrases to show the relationship between sentences and between paragraphs.

Effective Paragraphs

Paragraph Structure

An effective paragraph clearly develops an idea by presenting specific information in a logical order. A **paragraph** is a group of sentences about one main idea. It has a **topic sentence,** which states the main idea, as well as several sentences that supply supporting details. These **supporting details** help the reader understand the main idea of the paragraph by giving examples, facts, reasons, and specific details.

Read this paragraph from a letter in response to a help wanted ad. Notice how each of the other sentences helps explain and support the main idea stated in the topic sentence.

> I would be a knowledgeable and effective sales clerk at Handy Works Hardware. I have studied carpentry and advanced home repairs at Brookline Adult School, where I learned about electric and hand tools, paint mixing, and plumbing. I am also familiar with computerized registers, which I used at my summer job at Standard Stores. As my previous employer will confirm, I am friendly, polite, and helpful when dealing with the public. Finally, I am a quick learner and will be a great asset to your staff.

paragraph
a group of related sentences that develops a single main idea

topic sentence
states the main idea of a paragraph

supporting details
statements that explain the main idea of a paragraph by giving specific details, examples, and reasons

Remember to show the beginning of a paragraph by indenting. This tells your reader that you are moving on to a new idea.

Unity and Coherence

Unity and coherence are the results of good writing. A paragraph has unity when all the sentences support one main idea as stated in the topic sentence. When all the sentences are presented in a sensible, logical order, a paragraph has coherence. Irrelevant details or disorganized ideas make a paragraph seem sloppy and confusing.

For example, read this paragraph and notice the lack of unity and coherence:

> A lot of people want to own their homes, but owning can be expensive and stressful. Repairs can be costly, and you need to come up with a down payment. Repair companies can be unreliable. Our teenaged babysitter is pretty unreliable, too. Overall, home ownership can be worrisome and costly. Property taxes are another hidden expense.

In contrast, read this edited paragraph. Pay attention to the changes in colour. Notice how they make the ideas unified and coherent:

> A lot of people want to own their homes, but owning can be expensive and stressful. First, you need to come up with a down payment. Repairs can be costly, and repair companies can be unreliable. ~~Our teenaged babysitter is pretty unreliable, too.~~ Property taxes are another hidden expense. Overall, home ownership can be worrisome and costly.

Tip

Be sure that every sentence in your paragraph is related to the main idea. Delete any unrelated sentences.

Put a check mark next to the sentence that could be used in this paragraph. Then indicate where you would place the sentence in the paragraph on the line below.

We have been having problems with sales reports. Some sales team members have been turning them in late or incomplete. Sales reports must be in your Team Folder each Thursday by 4:00. Inform your team leader if you have an unavoidable delay in turning in your reports.

_____ a. The promotion list is in the sales team office.

_____ b. Others have not been turning sales reports in at all.

_____ c. The sales team incentive program starts on Friday.

You are correct if you chose *option b*. It is the only sentence that relates to problems with turning in sales reports, the main idea. The other options mention sales teams, but they don't relate to the same main idea. The best place to add this detail in the paragraph is at the third sentence. The most logical relation of ideas is that some team members have been turning in reports late or incomplete and then that others have not been turning them in at all.

GED Practice

Directions: Choose the <u>one best answer</u> to each question.

Questions 1 through 3 refer to the following paragraphs.

A Rising Star

(A)

(1) Are Canadian sports fans giving golfer Mike Weir the kind of recognition he deserves? (2) Ask a Canadian about a Canadian sports hero and, almost without fail, you will hear names such as Richard, Gretzky, Orr, and Howe. (3) These responses may be understandable since these players dominated their sport. (4) Fans went to games just to watch these players, and teams made a lot of money from the players' popularity. (5) But how many Canadians would have to be asked the question before Weir's name came up the players?

(B)

(6) Before winning The Masters, consider the obstacles Weir overcame in his golfing career. (7) Weir plays a sport that is dependent on summer weather, yet he's from Ontario. (8) Also, Weir is left-handed. (9) Most of the players who are winning on the tour grew up playing golf 11 and 12 months of the year. (10) Growing up, Weir would be lucky to get an eight-month golf season if the weather was unseasonably warm! (11) Golf courses are just not set up for "lefties." (12) This is clear from the historical performance of left-handers on the tour. (13) More and more, Mike Weir is a rising star.

(C)

(14) Weir shines in his play, he shines in his approach to the game, and he shines in his manner on the course. (15) He is increasingly becoming a Canadian sports figure who deserves our respect and recognition.

1. Which revision would improve the effectiveness of paragraph A?

   (1) remove sentence 4
   (2) move sentence 4 to the beginning of the paragraph
   (3) move sentence 4 to the end of the paragraph
   (4) move sentence 2 to the beginning of the paragraph
   (5) no revision is necessary

2. Which revision would improve the effectiveness of sentence 9?

   (1) remove sentence 8
   (2) move sentence 8 to follow 9
   (3) move sentence 8 to follow sentence 10
   (4) move sentence 8 to the beginning of paragraph C
   (5) no revision is necessary

3. What revision would improve the effectiveness of sentence 14?

   (1) move sentence 13 to the beginning of paragraph A.
   (2) move sentence 13 to the end of paragraph A
   (3) remove sentence 13
   (4) move sentence 13 to the beginning of paragraph C
   (5) no revision necessary

Be sure that you read the entire passage before you answer the questions. As you read, consider whether all the sentences support the main idea. Also, think about whether the sentences are in logical order.

Questions 4 and 5 refer to the following paragraphs.

Winter Safety Tips

(A)

(1) Winter snow can be just as dangerous to children on sleds as it can be to adults in cars. (2) Here are some ideas for building safety into your children's sledding fun.

(B)

(3) Most important, choose a sled that can be steered so that your children won't crash into trees or rocks, or go smashing into other sledders. (4) If using last year's sled, make sure the steering mechanism hasn't rusted or broken. (5) The sledding area should not be too steep or icy and there must be a flat area at the bottom for slowing down. (6) Your children shouldn't sled near or onto water. (7) Teach your children to wait their turn and to walk back to the top of the hill around, not up, the slopes.

(C)

(8) Your children should wear helmets to avoid head injuries. (9) Gloves and boots are essential to protect them from cold and scrapes. (10) These you can buy at any store. (11) Finally, don't forget to bundle up too. (12) The top of a sledding hill can be very cold, windy, and bone-chilling for waiting parents.

4. Sentence 12: **The top of a sledding hill can be very cold, windy, and bone-chilling for waiting parents.**

   Which correction should be made to sentence 12?

   (1) insert it after hill
   (2) change can be to being
   (3) remove the comma after cold
   (4) insert it can be after and
   (5) no correction is necessary

5. Which revision would improve the effectiveness of paragraph C?

   (1) remove sentence 9
   (2) remove sentence 10
   (3) move sentence 11 to the beginning of the paragraph
   (4) remove sentence 12
   (5) no revision is necessary

Question 6 refers to the following passage.

The Whooping Crane

(1) The whooping crane, with its noisy songs and distinctive dances, has always fascinated observers. (2) Whooping cough, the common name for pertussis, was named after the sound the whooping crane makes. (3) This elegant, white, 1.5-m-tall bird is the largest native North American fowl. (4) In flight, whooping cranes have wingspans of more than two metres. (5) People travel great distances to view these lovely creatures.

6. Which revision would improve the effectiveness of the passage?

   (1) remove sentence 1
   (2) move sentence 1 to the end of the paragraph
   (3) remove sentence 2
   (4) remove sentence 5
   (5) no revision is necessary

Answers start on page 735.

Lesson 8

Try writing your topic sentence after deciding which supporting details to include in the paragraph.

Topic Sentences

A topic sentence states the main idea of a paragraph. It is a reader's guide to understanding the ideas in the paragraph. For that reason, many writers begin their paragraphs with the topic sentence, even though it may be placed anywhere in a paragraph.

Avoid writing topic sentences that are either too specific or too general. If you are too specific, your reader will not see the big picture or main idea. A topic sentence that is too general will not help your reader focus on what you are saying about the topic. Every topic sentence should clearly answer the question, "What is the main point of this paragraph?"

RULE A topic sentence states the main idea of the entire paragraph without being too general or too specific.

For example, read this group of sentences. Then consider the possible topic sentences.

> Most air pollution is caused by forms of transportation. We flush polluting exhaust into the air every time we drive our cars. The diesel engine exhaust of commercial trucks is also very harsh. In addition, fuel combustion for heating our homes, offices, and factories contributes to pollution. Industrial processes such as oil refining do, too. Natural sources, such as volcanoes, contribute some pollutants but not nearly as many as people think.

Too general: The air is polluted.
Too specific: Most air pollution comes from cars and trucks.
Effective: Air pollution is most often caused by human activity.

The effective topic sentence sums up the details, which point to things done by humans that cause air pollution.

Put a check mark next to the best topic sentence for a paragraph on this topic.

Topic: How to obedience-train your puppy

_____ a. There are four major steps in obedience training.

_____ b. Reward good behaviour with lots of praise.

_____ c. You can train your dog.

You are correct if you chose *option a* as the best topic sentence. It states the main idea and gives the reader clear information about what to expect. *Option b* is too specific. *Option c* is too general.

GED Practice

Directions: Choose the <u>one best answer</u> to each question.

<u>Questions 1 through 3</u> refer to the following article.

Change of Address Notification Forms

(A)

(1) Every post office and postal outlet has Change of Address Notification forms for your mail. (2) You can fill out this form at the post office or outlet, or take it home, fill it out, and return it. (3) Postal workers recommend you turn in the form at least one month before you move so that your mail isn't delayed. There is a fee for this service.

(B)

(4) Forwarded personal mail includes standard mail and Xpresspost. (5) The post office will also forward newspapers and magazines that are addressed to you. (6) It is your responsibility to notify those publications that you've moved.

(C)

(7) Most businesses can process your change of address within three months, so tell them early. (8) The post office won't deliver circulars, catalogues, or advertisements unless you specifically request it to do so.

1. Which sentence would be most effective if inserted at the beginning of paragraph A?

   (1) Moving is a very stressful experience.
   (2) To keep receiving mail when you move, notify the post office of your new address.
   (3) Change of Address Notification forms take very little time to complete.
   (4) The post office forwards your mail to your new address.
   (5) There is a form called Change of Address Notification.

2. Which revision would improve the effectiveness of paragraph B?

   (1) insert at the beginning of the paragraph <u>The post office will forward your personal mail and most packages.</u>
   (2) remove sentence 4
   (3) move sentence 4 to the end of the paragraph
   (4) replace sentence 4 with <u>Not all mail will be forwarded.</u>
   (5) no revision is necessary

3. Which sentence would be most effective if inserted at the beginning of paragraph C?

   (1) Then there's business mail.
   (2) Many businesses send you mail, too.
   (3) Some businesses send what people consider "junk mail."
   (4) Many people forget to tell businesses that they are moving.
   (5) Don't forget to notify businesses you deal with that you have moved.

Once you choose a topic sentence for a paragraph on the GED Test, read the whole paragraph with the topic sentence at the beginning. That will help you "hear" whether the topic sentence that you chose is effective.

Questions 4 and 5 refer to the following paragraph.

Nail Colour

(1) White nails may indicate liver disease. (2) Half white and half pink nails may indicate kidney disease. (3) A heart condition may show up along with a red nail bed. (4) Nails that are thick, yellow, and have bumps may be telling you that your lungs are in trouble. (5) Pale nail beds show anemia. (6) Nails that are yellow with a slight pinkness at the base may indicate diabetes. (7) As for nail polish, it can dry nails out, especially the frequent use of nail polish remover. (8) You don't need to worry about white spots. (9) They seem to be caused by external damage rather than internal disease.

4. Which sentence would be most effective if inserted at the beginning of the paragraph?

(1) Sometimes nails change colours.
(2) Some nails are white or pink; others are reddish or yellow.
(3) Changes in the natural colour of your nails can warn you of disease.
(4) Examine your nails every day for disease.
(5) Some nail colour changes are serious, while others are not.

5. Which revision would improve the effectiveness of the text?

(1) remove sentence 3
(2) move sentence 5 to the end of the paragraph
(3) move sentence 6 to the end of the paragraph
(4) remove sentence 7
(5) move sentence 7 to the end of the paragraph

Questions 6 and 7 refer to the following letter.

Dear Grade Seven Parent,

(A)
(1) We will be attending the Winter Lights Show and "Mysteries of Ancient Mesopotamia." (2) The bus will leave the school at 8:30 A.M. and will return at 2:30 P.M.

(B)
(3) The fee includes museum admission, a morning snack, and transportation. (4) Please make cheques payable to the *Easton School Fund.* (5) Please do not send extra money because there will be no free time to go to the Museum Shop.

(C)
(6) There's a permission form attached. (7) If your child will need to be administered medication during the day, be sure to sign the attached medication form as well. (8) Your child's science teacher will collect the money and signed forms.

6. Which sentence would be most effective if inserted at the beginning of paragraph A?

(1) The grade seven students will visit the Science Museum on Monday, October 5.
(2) Grade seven field trips are usually educational in nature.
(3) This year the Cell Exhibit is temporarily closed, so the grade seven students will view other Science Museum offerings.
(4) The grade seven students always takes one field trip a year.
(5) Students in grade seven learn a great deal from field trips to the Science Museum.

7. Which sentence would be most effective if inserted at the beginning of paragraph B?

(1) Parents will be notified of the cost of the trip.
(2) The cost of the trip includes three items.
(3) The cost of the trip is $8.00 payable by cash or cheque.
(4) Most of the trip will be paid by the School Department, but parents will be asked to contribute a portion of the cost.
(5) The cost to each student will be less than $10.

Answers start on page 735.

Lesson 9

Paragraphing

Paragraphs are a way to organize your ideas. Each paragraph develops only one main idea. Also, writing is much easier to read when it is broken into paragraphs rather than presented in one long block of text.

RULE 1 Start a new paragraph when the main idea of a group of sentences shifts.

RULE 2 Both the introduction and conclusion are organized into paragraphs. The introduction is the first paragraph; the conclusion is the final paragraph.

Note where each paragraph starts in this article. The introduction is in a separate paragraph, but the conclusion is not.

Introduction ⟶

> E-mail is fast becoming the most popular means of communication. E-mail users even predict that it will soon replace letters and stamps. Certainly, many individuals and companies use it daily.
>
> E-mail does have many advantages over regular mail. The speed of e-mail has made communication almost instantaneous. You can send messages to faraway places in almost no time at all. E-mail doesn't cost much, either. In fact, many people get free e-mail. A lot of people also like the informality of e-mail.
>
> Still, a lot of people function without e-mail. Some people do not have access to or experience with computers. Others feel e-mail is too impersonal. They think less care and thought are put into an e-mail than a letter. Sooner or later, however, everyone will be getting e-mail. It's easy to imagine that within a few years, regular letters will go the way of manual typewriters. They will be seen as funny, old-fashioned antiques that your grandparents barely remember.

Conclusion ⟶

Put a check mark next to the sentence from the third paragraph that should begin the concluding paragraph.

_____ a. Sooner or later, however, everyone will be getting e-mail.

_____ b. It's easy to imagine that within a few years, regular letters will go the way of manual typewriters.

You are correct if you chose *option a*. The third paragraph is about people who function without e-mail. *Option a* introduces a new idea, the future of e-mail, which is the conclusion of the essay.

Most paragraphs have a topic sentence and three or four supporting sentences. Introductory and concluding paragraphs may be shorter.

GED Practice

Directions: Choose the one best answer to each question.

Question 1 refers to the following notice.

From: The Desk of the Town Manager
To: The Residents of Mapleville

(A)

(1) Town residents may now purchase recycling permits at the Town Hall. (2) They may also purchase permits at the Recycling Station during normal operating hours. (3) Permits cost $10 and are valid for one year. (4) If you want to obtain a permit, you must appear in person with a valid vehicle registration certificate. (5) Permits will not be issued by mail, nor will they be issued without proof of registration. (6) Upon purchasing your permit, you must attach it to the rear driver's side window. (7) Permits are not valid unless they are permanently attached and visible. (8) Please remove permits from prior years.

(B)

(9) Yard waste can now be disposed of at the Recycling Station, or you can continue bringing it to the brush dump on Riel Street. (10) This area will be open on Monday, Wednesday, and Saturday to coincide with the recycling division.

1. Which revision would improve the effectiveness of the notice?

   (1) begin a new paragraph with sentence 5
   (2) begin a new paragraph with sentence 6
   (3) remove sentence 6
   (4) remove sentence 8
   (5) move sentence 8 to the beginning of paragraph B

Question 2 refers to the following letter.

Dr. Eli Brownwood
Central Clinic
4201 Bethune Avenue
Vancouver, BC V3A 2N8

Dear Dr. Brownwood:

(1) I am typing this letter with one hand because I broke my wrist last week when I fell on the ice in the parking lot at work. (2) I want to thank the staff members at Central Clinic for their extraordinary care, gentleness, and professionalism in treating my injury. (3) When I entered the clinic, I was almost fainting from pain and unable to remove the glove from my injured hand. (4) The first person I met was Marge Freeman at Reception, whose warmth and concern immediately calmed me down. (5) Next, Dr. Rayford managed to remove the glove from my swollen hand with care. (6) Then I moved on to Emergency Care. (7) Everyone I met was incredibly helpful. (8) Corey Clay administered the novocaine painlessly and efficiently. (9) The technician, Bill Stone, was extremely gentle and concerned. (10) Dr. Chan's surgery was professional, and she contacted me three times before my follow-up visit. (11) I am so grateful for my treatment by your staff. (12) I hope you will share this letter with all the people I mentioned and extend to them my deepest appreciation.

Sincerely,
Maria Santini

2. Which revision would improve the effectiveness of the letter?

   Begin a new paragraph

   (1) with sentence 2
   (2) with sentence 3
   (3) with sentence 4
   (4) with sentence 5
   (5) with sentence 6

Questions 3 through 5 refer to the following school memo.

Evaluating a Student's Writing

(A)

(1) We use three levels of mastery to evaluate a student's writing. (2) The lowest level is novice, the middle level is proficient, and the highest level is superior. (3) The work of a novice may show flashes of quality, but it needs improvement in several important ways. (4) For example, a novice's description may be superficial or demonstrate incomplete understanding of the subject matter. (5) The writing may also contain serious errors in spelling, grammar, punctuation, or capitalization, or it may be poorly organized. (6) Overall, the final product may be untidy. (7) At the next level of mastery, the proficient student's writing is acceptable, but it could be improved in a few important ways. (8) For example, the writer's comprehension of the subject matter may seem at times incomplete or inaccurate. (9) The writing may contain several errors in grammar, punctuation, spelling, or capitalization. (10) The final product, however, is generally neat.

(B)

(11) Superior writers show an excellent understanding of their subject matter. (12) Specific, accurate details are plentiful. (13) The writing is well organized, words are well chosen, and mistakes in grammar, punctuation, spelling, and capitalization are generally avoided. (14) The final product is neat and professional. (15) Each student may submit two original pieces for competency evaluations per semester. (16) We suggest students who were previously evaluated as novices revise and resubmit those writings for reevaluation.

3. Which revision would improve the effectiveness of the text?

   Begin a new paragraph

   (1) with sentence 2
   (2) with sentence 3
   (3) with sentence 4
   (4) with sentence 5
   (5) with sentence 6

4. Which revision would improve the effectiveness of sentences 7 through 10?

   Begin a new paragraph

   (1) with sentence 7
   (2) with sentence 8
   (3) with sentence 9
   (4) with sentence 10
   (5) no revision is necessary

5. Which revision would improve the effectiveness of the text?

   Begin a new paragraph

   (1) with sentence 12
   (2) with sentence 13
   (3) with sentence 14
   (4) with sentence 15
   (5) with sentence 16

Answers start on page 736.

Clear Transitions

You have learned how certain words and phrases—coordinating conjunctions, subordinating conjunctions, and conjunctive adverbs—indicate that ideas are related in particular ways. These words and phrases are called **transitions.**

If you use transitions effectively, your writing will flow smoothly from idea to idea, from sentence to sentence, and from paragraph to paragraph. (To review transitional words and phrases with correct punctuation, see Lessons 2 and 3.)

RULE 1 Use transitions and punctuation to show the relationship between ideas in two sentences. A transition at the beginning of a sentence requires a comma after it. Within a sentence, it requires a comma before and after it.

No transition:	Discount fees vary from bank to bank. Average ATM fees are $1.25 at some banks, but can be as low as 50¢ at others.
With transition:	Discount fees vary from bank to bank. <u>For example,</u> average ATM fees are $1.25 at some banks, but can be as low as 50¢ at others.
With transition:	Discount fees vary from bank to bank. Average ATM fees, <u>for example,</u> are $1.25 at some banks, but can be as low as 50¢ at others.

RULE 2 Use transitions and punctuation when moving from one paragraph to another to show how ideas are related.

A study of charges at different banks shows some interesting data. In almost every category, from chequing account minimums to bounced cheque fees, small banks give consumers a better deal.

<u>Nevertheless,</u> consumers continue to put their money into big banks for several reasons. For instance, the big banks offer services that small banks cannot. . . .

Put a caret (^) where you would place the transitional word *However* in this short paragraph.

Manitoba's Riel House is a National Historic Site of Canada. Ontario's Casa Loma is much more famous. One reason it is more famous may be that it is situated in Toronto, an urban centre.

You are correct if you chose to place *However* between the first and second sentences: *Manitoba's Riel House is a National Historic Site of Canada. Ontario's Casa Loma is much more famous.* The addition of the transition makes the relationship between the ideas clear.

transition
a word or phrase that signals the relationship from one idea to the next

Other common transitions are *in other words* (definition), *in the first place* (order), *as a matter of fact* (supporting detail), *on the other hand* (contrast), and *as a result* or *for this reason* (cause and effect).

GED Practice

Directions: Choose the one best answer to each question.

Questions 1 through 4 refer to the following information.

Varnished Wood Furniture

(A)

(1) Wood that is varnished stands up well to normal wear and tear. (2) That's because varnish is a tough finish. (3) It protects for decades. (4) The major problem with varnished wood is that scratches show up very easily.

(B)

(5) Dust it regularly. (6) Wash it occasionally with paint thinner, which dissolves dirt. (7) Paint thinner may dull the finish, however, so be prepared to restore the shine with a good buffing. (8) A mild solution of a good detergent and water will also clean varnished furniture, but water should be used sparingly. (9) Polish isn't needed on varnished furniture. (10) Polish can build up and dull the finish. (11) It can even collect dirt.

(C)

(12) Follow this advice, and your varnished wood furniture will look good and last for a long, long time.

1. Sentence 4: **The major problem with varnished wood is that scratches show up very easily.**

   Which revision would improve the effectiveness of sentence 4?

   (1) replace The with Unfortunately, the
   (2) insert unfortunately, after wood
   (3) insert , unfortunately after scratches
   (4) insert unfortunately after up
   (5) no revision is necessary

2. Which sentence would be most effective if inserted at the beginning of paragraph B?

   (1) Moreover, the following is advice for wood maintenance.
   (2) Most important, you can always clean the wood.
   (3) Fortunately, you can keep varnished wood looking good if you follow this advice.
   (4) Nevertheless, dusting wood is important, but polishing it isn't.
   (5) In contrast, rugs look good on clean, varnished floors.

3. Sentences 5 and 6: **Dust it regularly. Wash it occasionally with paint thinner, which dissolves dirt.**

   The most effective combination of sentences 5 and 6 would include which group of words?

   (1) and, of course,
   (2) and, in addition,
   (3) and, as a result,
   (4) and, for example,
   (5) and, in contrast,

4. Sentences 9 and 10: **Polish isn't needed on varnished furniture. Polish can build up and dull the finish.**

   Which is the best way to write the underlined portion of these sentences? If the original is the best way, choose option (1).

   (1) furniture. Polish
   (2) furniture, polish
   (3) furniture, so polish
   (4) furniture. In fact, polish
   (5) furniture, likewise polish

Questions 5 and 6 refer to the following paragraph.

Credit Checks

(1) Have you been turned down for a credit card or mortgage? (2) Here's how to check your credit rating to find out why. (3) You have the right to read your credit report and correct any errors. (4) To do so, request the name and address of the credit bureau employed by the bank or credit card company that denied you a loan or credit. (5) The credit bureau must furnish you a copy of its report. (6)

5. Sentence 3: **You have the right to read your credit report and correct any errors.**

    The most effective revision of sentence 3 would begin with which words?

    (1) It's your right,
    (2) Having the right to read
    (3) To read your credit report and correct
    (4) Start by exercising your right,
    (5) You have, you should be aware, the right

6. Sentence 4: **To do <u>so, request</u> the name and address of the credit bureau employed by the bank or credit card company that denied you a loan or credit.**

    Which is the best way to write the underlined portion of this sentence? If the original is the best way, choose option (1).

    (1) so, request
    (2) so. Request
    (3) so, requesting
    (4) so, in fact, request
    (5) so, therefore request

Questions 7 and 8 refer to the following paragraph.

Childcare in the Workplace

(1) In some European countries, the government runs daycare centres for children. (2) In Canada, most parents who work are on their own. (3) Many find themselves late for work or even absent because of childcare problems, so some employers are providing childcare for their employees. (4) One factory in Ontario runs a three-shift, on-site day-care centre. (5) Grateful fathers and mothers can bring their children to work with them. (6) Lateness and absenteeism have been greatly reduced. (7) This program satisfies both employer and employee. (8) Employees don't have to worry about childcare. (9) They tend to be far more productive than those who do worry.

7. Sentence 2: **In Canada, most parents who work are on their own.**

    Which revision would improve the effectiveness of sentence 2?

    (1) insert <u>however,</u> after the comma
    (2) insert <u>however,</u> after <u>parents</u>
    (3) insert <u>however</u> after <u>who</u>
    (4) insert <u>, however</u> after <u>work</u>
    (5) insert <u>however</u> after <u>own</u>

8. Sentence 6: **Lateness and absenteeism have been greatly reduced.**

    Which revision would improve the effectiveness of sentence 6?

    (1) replace <u>Lateness</u> with <u>Consequently, lateness</u>
    (2) insert <u>, consequently,</u> after <u>Lateness</u>
    (3) insert <u>, consequently,</u> after <u>and</u>
    (4) insert <u>consequently</u> after <u>absenteeism</u>
    (5) no revision is necessary

Answers start on page 736.

Language Arts, Writing • Organization

Directions: Choose the one best answer to each question.

Questions 1 through 3 refer to the following passage.

Saving the Whooping Crane

(A)

(1) In 1941 the whooping crane was nearly extinct. (2) Then, with government assistance, a program was begun to rescue the species. (3) Today, there are almost 400 surviving "whoopers." (4) Thanks to scientist-inventors, eggs were hatched in incubators made to look like female whooping cranes. (5) In order to teach "whooping behaviour" to young chicks, biologists dressed up like whooping cranes, waddled into marshes with the chicks, and pecked and scratched for food.

(B)

(6) If efforts to save the crane continue to succeed, these fascinating birds may be removed from the endangered species list soon. (7) Most wild animals don't get such personal attention. (8) The cranes' survival will be a natural success story.

Tip

When you are not sure whether a sentence belongs in a paragraph, read the paragraph without it. Then decide whether the paragraph seems complete or whether the missing sentence helps to develop the main idea.

1. Which revision would improve the effectiveness of paragraph A?

   (1) move sentence 1 to the end of paragraph A
   (2) remove sentence 2
   (3) remove sentence 3
   (4) move sentence 3 to the end of the paragraph
   (5) move sentence 5 to the beginning of paragraph B

2. Which revision should be made to the placement of sentence 7?

   (1) move sentence 7 to the beginning of paragraph B
   (2) remove sentence 7
   (3) move sentence 7 to the end of paragraph B
   (4) replace sentence 7 with However, other wild animals will still be on the list.
   (5) no revision is necessary

3. Which revision should be made to the placement of sentence 8?

   (1) move sentence 8 to the end of paragraph A
   (2) move sentence 8 to the beginning of paragraph A
   (3) move sentence 8 to the beginning of paragraph B
   (4) remove sentence 8
   (5) no revision is necessary

Question 4 refers to the following paragraphs.

Handy Around the House

(A)

(1) Anyone can learn to be a handy person around the house. (2) Start with simple things such as changing a light bulb, oiling a lock, and tightening screws in the door. (3) Many reference guides are full of helpful hints even for such simple jobs. (4) Nowadays, you can probably even order these books over the Internet.

(B)

(5) As you try more difficult jobs, you first need to analyze the steps. (6) It often helps to consider what preparations are necessary and to make a list before you start. (7) For example, if you decide to paint the walls in your bedroom, figure out the tasks to be done and their order.

(C)

(8) If you want to try more technical jobs, you should first consult someone who has experience. (9) No one is born with handy skills: the best way to learn is by doing.

4. Which revision would improve the effectiveness of paragraph A?

   (1) remove sentence 1
   (2) move sentence 2 to the end of the paragraph
   (3) remove sentence 2
   (4) remove sentence 4
   (5) no revision is necessary

Question 5 refers to the following paragraphs.

How to Shop Online Safely

(A)

(1) Shopping online has become popular now that more and more people are connected to the Internet. (2) Everything is available online with a credit card. (3) This includes everything from discount clothing to bus or train tickets. (4) Many people find Internet shopping fast and convenient.

(B)

(5) There are, however, some risks involved. (6) Delivery of orders is not always reliable, and shipping and handling fees can add a whopping 15 percent to the cost.

(C)

(7) Laws about returning unwanted purchases don't always apply to online businesses. (8) Giving out credit card numbers on an unsecured site might allow someone to steal your personal information.

(D)

(9) Consumer advocates say there are several things you can do to protect yourself. (10) For example, one should stick to well-known businesses when shopping online. (11) Online retailers who don't list a telephone number are sometimes fakes. (12) Make sure you check the return policy and shipping fees before making a purchase. (13) As long as you are careful, online buying can be a helpful new way to shop.

5. Which revision would improve the effectiveness of the text?

   (1) move sentence 6 to the beginning of paragraph B
   (2) combine paragraphs B and C
   (3) move sentence 7 to the end of paragraph C
   (4) move sentence 8 to the beginning of paragraph D
   (5) remove sentence 8

How to Change a Tire Safely

(A)

(1) These safety rules are important to follow if you ever have a flat tire while driving. (2) The first thing you should do is to stop in a safe place. (3) Put on your hazard signal, and if you are on a multi-lane highway, move carefully into the far right lane. (4) Then, slowly pull over to the curb or onto the shoulder and continue until you have driven to an area as free from traffic as possible.

(B)

(5) Try to park the car on firm, level ground. Turn the ignition off, and set the parking brake. (6) If you have any passengers, let them out on the passenger side.

(C)

(7) As you change the tire, remember these suggestions. (8) Never get under a car that is raised on a jack. (9) It is easy for a car to roll off the jack; anyone underneath may be seriously injured. (10) After you have removed the flat, place it carefully on the ground with the outside surface up so that the wheel's finish won't get scratched. (11) Next, mount your spare tire and tighten the wheel nuts. (12) When the spare fits tightly against the hub, lower the car to the ground and remove the jack. (13) Tighten the wheel nuts as securely as you can, stow your tools safely, and store the flat.

(D)

(14) With your spare tire in place, your next stop should be at an auto repair shop. (15) Let mechanics there check the spare. (16) They may also be able to repair or replace the flat, so you can, finally, be safely on your way.

6. Which revision would improve the effectiveness of the text?

(1) move sentence 5 to the end of paragraph A
(2) combine paragraphs A and B
(3) remove sentence 6
(4) move sentence 7 to the end of paragraph B
(5) remove sentence 8

How to Find a Job

(A)

(1) Successful job hunting requires careful preparation. (2) Here are some useful steps those just entering the job market can take.

(B)

(3) First, list the kinds of jobs you'd like to do. (4) You can determine the skills, training, and experience required by talking to people who have those types of jobs. (5) Next, list your qualifications and see whether they match any of the jobs you've selected. (6) If not, you need to think again about the kinds of work you want. (7) For example, you can't start as a restaurant manager, but you may be able to start as a waiter or cashier and work your way up. (8) Once you select work that matches your qualifications and find a job opening in a company, you need to set up an interview. (9) Try to learn about the workplace before you go for the interview. (10) In order to make a good impression, you need to look, speak, and act your best. (11) Stress your qualifications, your positive work habits, and your interest in the job.

7. Which revision would improve the effectiveness of the text?

Begin a new paragraph

(1) with sentence 5
(2) with sentence 6
(3) with sentence 7
(4) with sentence 8
(5) with sentence 9

Questions 8 and 9 refer to the following paragraph.

A Family Health Tree

(1) Here are some facts about members of your family you need to make a family health tree. (2) The family members you need to know about are your parents, grandparents, siblings, children, grandchildren, aunts, and uncles. (3) More distant relatives, such as great-grandparents, cousins, nieces, and nephews, are added bonuses. (4) The basic facts you need to know for each relative are date of birth and major diseases. (5) Also ask them for information about allergies, disabilities, weight or blood pressure problems, and general health habits such as diet or smoking. (6) Relatives who are overweight should diet, and smokers should definitely stop smoking. (7) For relatives who are deceased, record their ages and causes of death. (8) Give copies of your family health history to your doctor, your pediatrician, and other family members.

8. Which sentence would be most effective if inserted at the beginning of the paragraph?

   (1) A family health tree shows medical histories.
   (2) Charting your family's health history may help save a life because heredity plays a role in many illnesses.
   (3) Illnesses such as allergies and diabetes should be listed on a family health tree.
   (4) Get your relatives to help you make a family health tree.
   (5) It's good to have information about your family's diseases.

9. Which revision would improve the effectiveness of the text?

   (1) move sentence 5 to follow sentence 2
   (2) remove sentence 6
   (3) move sentence 6 to the end of the paragraph
   (4) remove sentence 7
   (5) remove sentence 8

Question 10 refers to the following paragraphs.

Daydreaming

(A)

(1) Daydreaming is a common pastime for most people. (2) Songs, legends, and movies often contain stories about daydreaming. (3) Daydreaming is fine as long as you are the one in control and don't let it control you.

(B)

(4) Daydreaming has several positive psychological aspects. (5) For example, it can help you relax, unwind, and improve your mood when you're having a bad day. (6) Sometimes you may daydream while doing a boring, repetitive job, such as pushing a lawn mower around the yard. (7) Daydreaming is a good way to occupy your mind while your body is otherwise engaged.

(C)

(8) For one thing, it can be dangerous to daydream while supervising children, using machinery, or operating electrical controls. (9) You might find yourself daydreaming while driving a car alone along a straight road for a long time. (10) Most of all, you need to be careful that you don't get to the point where you will begin to confuse dreams with reality. (11) Daydreaming, like many other things, is usually all right if not done to excess.

10. Which sentence would be most effective if inserted at the beginning of paragraph C?

    (1) Like most things, however, daydreaming can have a negative side as well.
    (2) Sometimes people daydream at other times too.
    (3) It's common to daydream during boring classes or sermons.
    (4) You might daydream on a long car trip.
    (5) Intense daydreaming can make you miss important conversations or phone calls.

Question 11 refers to the following paragraphs.

How to Deal with a Feverish Child

(A)

(1) Unless describing a child, it is accurate to say that a person's normal temperature is 37° C. (2) According to pediatricians, a child's normal temperature falls within the range of 36° C to 37.75° C. (3) What should parents do when their child is feverish? (4) Here are some helpful guidelines.

(B)

(5) For infants under three months, all temperatures above 37.75° C need medical attention. (6) Be aware that an illness is not always symptomatized by fever. (7) Your baby's temperature may fall within normal range, but he or she may still be vomiting or gasping for air. (8) In such cases, call your doctor immediately.

(C)

(9) For an older child with a fever, a sponge bath with cool water is a good idea. (10) Non-aspirin pain relievers may also help. (11) Make sure you don't give a child more than the recommended dose. (12) If you're not sure of how much medicine to give your child, call your doctor for advice. (13) A child's dosage is usually determined by weight.

11. Which revision would improve the effectiveness of paragraph C?

    (1) move sentence 9 to the end of paragraph B
    (2) remove sentence 11
    (3) move sentence 12 to follow sentence 10
    (4) move sentence 12 to the end of paragraph C
    (5) remove sentence 12

Question 12 refers to the following memo.

TO: All Employees
FROM: A. Desai, Human Resources Specialist
RE: Job Opening

(A)

(1) The Human Resources Department is pleased to announce a new job opening. (2) The department is looking for a full-time assistant to the supervisor of personnel records.

(B)

(3) Candidates for the position must have proven skills and be able to perform certain duties. (4) The assistant needs to have strong typing skills, be well organized, and pay attention to details. (5) The assistant will be responsible for distributing, collecting, and recording time sheets, sick-time authorization forms, and vacation vouchers for all branches. (6) He or she will verify the accuracy of employee time records each week. (7) The assistant will also be involved in distributing information to the branches. (8) Finally, the selected candidate will report to the supervisor.

12. Sentence 3: **Candidates for the position must have proven skills and be able to perform certain duties.**

    Which revision should be made to the placement of sentence 3?

    (1) move sentence 3 to the end of paragraph A
    (2) remove sentence 3
    (3) move sentence 3 to follow sentence 4
    (4) move sentence 3 to the end of paragraph B
    (5) no revision is necessary

For more information about organization, see the Writer's Checklist on page 898.

Answers start on page 737.

Usage

Usage is an important content area on the GED Language Arts, Writing Test. About 30 percent of the multiple-choice questions will be based on usage concepts. These concepts include subject-verb agreement, verb forms and tenses, and pronoun use and agreement. Mastery of grammar rules and usage concepts will help you to avoid some common errors and to produce effective pieces of writing.

Subject-Verb Agreement

Agreement in Number

The subject and the verb in a sentence must both be singular (referring to one) or plural (referring to more than one). That is called subject-verb agreement. To check that these two parts of a sentence agree, first decide whether the subject is singular or plural. Then make the verb match the subject.

RULE 1 With a singular subject, use a singular verb.

Don't agree: Ms Lopez plan the company party every year.
Agree: Ms Lopez plans the company party every year.

The singular subject *Ms Lopez* needs a singular verb, *plans*.

RULE 2 With a plural subject, use a plural verb.

Don't agree: Volunteers helps with the planning.
Agree: Volunteers help with the planning.

The plural subject *Volunteers* needs a plural verb, *help*.

RULE 3 With compound subjects joined by *and,* use a plural verb.

Don't agree: Pauline and Ray knows some great activities.
Agree: Pauline and Ray know some great activities.

The subject *Pauline and Ray* refers to two people. The plural verb *know* agrees with the compound subject.

Tip

Most verbs ending in *s* are singular: *she walks, he sings.* Most verbs not ending in *s* are plural: *we walk, they sing.* Verbs used with the pronouns *I* and singular *you* are exceptions: *I am, I walk, you are, you sing.*

Interrupting Phrases and Inverted Order

When a subject is separated from the verb by a word or phrase, it may be hard to decide which word is the subject. It also may be difficult to find the subject when it comes after the verb.

Decide on the subject of the sentence by asking yourself *who* or *what* the sentence is about. Then check for agreement between the subject and the verb.

RULE 1 Make the verb agree with the subject, not with the words or phrases that come between them.

Don't agree: <u>Directions</u> to the company party is easy.

Agree: <u>Directions</u> to the company party <u><u>are</u></u> easy.

If you didn't ask yourself what the sentence was about, you might think the subject is the singular *party,* not the plural *directions.*

RULE 2 Make the subject and verb agree even when the subject comes after the verb, as in a question or in a sentence that starts with *there* or *here.*

Don't agree: <u><u>Is</u></u> her <u>assistant</u> and Ms Gross car pooling to the party?

Agree: <u><u>Are</u></u> her <u>assistant</u> and Ms Gross car pooling to the party?

Don't agree: There <u><u>are</u></u> a <u>map</u> showing three different routes.

Agree: There <u><u>is</u></u> a <u>map</u> showing three different routes.

Agree: There <u><u>are</u></u> <u>maps</u> showing three different routes.

Put a check mark by the sentence in which the subject and the verb do not agree.

_____ a. There are three computer science courses still open for this semester.

_____ b. Students in one computer course learn how to search the Internet.

_____ c. Professor Hardy, along with his teaching assistants, have them surfing the Internet the first day of class.

You are correct if you chose *option c.* The subject of that sentence is *Professor Hardy,* so the verb should be the singular *has: Professor Hardy, along with his teaching assistants, has them surfing the Internet the first day of class.*

> ## Tip
>
> Interrupting phrases often begin with words showing relationships, such as *along with, as well as, among, at, between, of, in,* or *with.* Some interrupting phrases are set off by commas: *Sam, of all the brothers, is single.*

Special Cases in Subject-Verb Agreement

collective noun
a word that refers to a group of people or things

RULE 1 A **collective noun** refers to a group of people or things. When the subject of a sentence is a collective noun in which the group is acting as one, use a singular verb.

Don't agree: The budget <u>committee</u> <u>are meeting</u> today.
Agree: The budget <u>committee</u> <u>is meeting</u> today.

A committee is made up of more than one person, but the people in the committee are acting together as one, so the subject is singular.

RULE 2 Some words do not refer to a specific person or thing. It is not always clear whether a word like this is singular or plural. Use this chart to help you determine subject-verb agreement.

Always Singular			Always Plural	Singular or Plural	
one	anybody	someone	several	all	any
each	anyone	something	few	some	part
much	anything	nobody	both	none	half
other	everybody	no one	many	most	
another	everyone	nothing			
either	everything	somebody			
neither					

Don't agree: <u>Everyone</u> <u>are</u> welcome!
Agree: <u>Everyone</u> <u>is</u> welcome!

Tip

If you can substitute the pronoun *it* for a collective noun used as a subject, use a singular verb.

RULE 3 When compound subjects are joined by *or, nor, either-or,* or *neither-nor,* make the verb agree with the nearest subject.

Don't agree: Neither the managers nor <u>Jay Holt</u> <u>are</u> planning to attend.
Agree: Neither the managers nor <u>Jay Holt</u> <u>is</u> planning to attend.

The compound subject is joined by *neither-nor,* so the verb should agree with the singular *Jay Holt,* which is the nearest subject.

Write *A* if the subject and verb agree and *D* if they do not.

_____ a. My family has two vehicles: a van and a pickup truck.

_____ b. Both has fairly low insurance rates.

_____ c. Neither my husband nor I has ever had an accident.

You are correct if you wrote *A* for *sentence a.* The collective noun *family* is singular. You were also correct if you wrote *D* for *sentences b* and *c.* The pronoun *Both* means two, so it is plural: *Both have fairly low insurance rates.* With the pair *neither-nor,* the verb should agree with the nearest subject: *Neither my husband nor I have ever had an accident.*

GED Practice

Directions: Choose the one best answer to each question.

Questions 1 through 4 refer to the following warranty.

Fair Point Company

(A)

(1) Fair Point Company guarantee that the Excel Disk Player will be free from defects in materials and quality of work for a period of one year. (2) Occasionally, however, a defect occurs. (3) Then the company, at no charge to the owner for parts, have the option of replacing or repairing the machine. (4) The customer, because of misuse, might cause a defect, malfunction, or failure in which case this warranty becomes invalid.

(B)

(5) This warranty is valid only when the *Model JDS-23* is returned to a Fair Point Products dealer. (6) This warranty cover a period of one year from the date of purchase. (7) To establish that your warranty is valid, you must also submit a copy of the original sales slip.

1. Sentence 1: **Fair Point Company guarantee that the Excel Disk Player will be free from defects in materials and quality of work for a period of one year.**

   Which correction should be made to sentence 1?

   (1) change guarantee to have guaranteed
   (2) change guarantee to guarantees
   (3) insert a comma after materials
   (4) insert a comma after quality of work
   (5) no correction is necessary

2. Sentence 3: **Then the company, at no charge to the owner for parts, have the option of replacing or repairing the machine.**

   Which is the best way to write the underlined portion of this sentence? If the original is the best way, choose option (1).

   (1) have
   (2) having
   (3) has
   (4) it has
   (5) is having

3. Sentence 4: **The customer, because of misuse, might cause a defect, malfunction, or failure in which case this warranty becomes invalid.**

   If you rewrote sentence 4 beginning with

   If a defect, malfunction, or failure

   the next words should be

   (1) are caused
   (2) might cause
   (3) will be caused
   (4) is caused
   (5) being caused

4. Sentence 6: **This warranty cover a period of one year from the date of purchase.**

   Which correction should be made to sentence 6?

   (1) replace This with However, this
   (2) change cover to covers
   (3) change cover to covering
   (4) insert a comma after year
   (5) no correction is necessary

Answers start on page 738.

Verb Forms

Regular Verbs

Every verb has four principal parts: present, present participle, past, and past participle. **Regular verbs** form these parts by adding *-d, -ed,* or *-ing* to their present forms. Most verbs are regular verbs.

RULE 1 Form the present participle by adding *-ing* to the present form of the verb. The present participle always uses a **helping verb** in a form of the verb *be.*

Present: Scientists <u>remind</u> us to reduce the amount of trash right now.
Present participle: They <u>are reminding</u> us that we must act immediately.

RULE 2 Form the past by adding *-d* or *-ed* to the present form of a verb. The past tense does not use a helping verb.

Present: Today, many towns <u>require</u> people to recycle paper, wood, and plastic.
Past: Years ago, towns <u>required</u> people to recycle paper only.

RULE 3 Form the past participle by adding *-d* or *-ed* to the present form of the verb and use a helping verb. The helping verbs used with the past participle are forms of the verb *be* or *have.*

Present: Today, towns <u>recycle</u> everything they can.
Past: In 2002 alone, my town <u>recycled</u> 178 tonnes of plastic.
Past participle: In fact, my town <u>has recycled</u> more plastic than any other town in the province.

Put a check mark next to the sentence in which a verb form is used incorrectly.

_____ a. Researchers have <u>learned</u> that optimistic people live longer.

_____ b. One study <u>looked</u> at more than 800 Newfoundlanders for 30 years.

_____ c. About 20 percent more optimists than pessimists <u>living</u> today.

_____ d. Apparently, optimists <u>watch</u> out for themselves more carefully and are less prone to depression.

You are correct if you chose *option c.* The sentence needs a helping verb to go along with the present participle *living*:
About 20 percent more optimists than pessimists are living today.

---

regular verb
a verb that forms its principal parts by adding *-d, -ed,* or *-ing* to the present form

helping verb
(also called **auxiliary verb**) a form of the verb *be* or *have* used with the main verb to make participle forms

A sentence with a present participle without a helping verb is often a sentence fragment: *About 20 percent more optimists than pessimists living today.*

Irregular Verbs

irregular verb
a verb whose past forms are not made by adding *-d* or *-ed* to the simple present

Unlike regular verbs, **irregular verbs** usually change their spelling pattern in a variety of ways to form the past and past participle. Study the irregular verbs in these charts.

RULE 1: Form the past participle for some irregular verbs by adding *-en* or *-n* to the present.

Present	Past	Past Participle
blow	blew	blown
drive	drove	driven
eat	ate	eaten
fall	fell	fallen
give	gave	given

Present	Past	Past Participle
know	knew	known
rise	rose	risen
see	saw	seen
take	took	taken
write	wrote	written

RULE 2: Form the past participle for some irregular verbs by adding *-en* or *-n* to the past.

Present	Past	Past Participle
break	broke	broken
choose	chose	chosen

Present	Past	Past Participle
freeze	froze	frozen
speak	spoke	spoken

RULE 3: Form the past and past participle for some irregular verbs by changing the vowel from *i* in the present to *a* in the past and *u* in the past participle.

Present	Past	Past Participle
begin	began	begun
drink	drank	drunk
ring	rang	rung

Present	Past	Past Participle
sing	sang	sung
sink	sank	sunk
swim	swam	swum

RULE 4: Some irregular verbs do not follow a pattern.

Present	Past	Past Participle
buy	bought	bought
come	came	come
do	did	done

Present	Past	Past Participle
fly	flew	flown
go	gone	went
lose	lost	lost

Put a check mark next to the sentence that uses the irregular verb form incorrectly.

_____ a. It has begun snowing hard.

_____ b. I have drove my car into a snow bank.

You are correct if you chose *option b*. The correct past participle of *drive* is *driven: I have driven my car into a snow bank.*

GED Practice

Directions: Choose the <u>one best answer</u> to each question.

Questions <u>1 through 4</u> refer to the following article.

New Teenage Concern

(A)

(1) The priorities of teenagers been changed over the years. (2) Of course, many teens are still concerned about grades, friends, dates, and jobs. (3) In recent years, however, they have taken on a new and very adult issue, the fear of violence.

(B)

(4) A major newspaper and television poll has indicated that teens thinking between 15 percent and 50 percent of their peers carry knives in school. (5) About 40 percent feeling personally afraid. (6) Yet more than 80 percent also said that no one in their families was a victim of violence in the past two years. (7) Sadly, speaking about their fears is not something many teens have done with their parents.

1. Sentence 1: **The priorities of teenagers been changed over the years**.

   Which is the best way to write the underlined portion of this sentence? If the original is the best way, choose option (1).

   (1) been changed
   (2) have changed
   (3) has changed
   (4) changing
   (5) are changed

2. Sentence 4: **A major newspaper and television poll has indicated that teens thinking between 15 percent and 50 percent of their peers carry knives in school.**

   Which correction should be made to sentence 4?

   (1) insert a comma after <u>newspaper</u>
   (2) change <u>has indicated</u> to <u>indicating</u>
   (3) insert <u>be</u> before <u>thinking</u>
   (4) change <u>thinking</u> to <u>think</u>
   (5) change <u>carry</u> to <u>carries</u>

3. Sentence 5: **About 40 percent <u>feeling</u> personally afraid.**

   Which is the best way to write the underlined portion of this sentence? If the original is the best way, choose option (1).

   (1) feeling
   (2) is feeling
   (3) been feeling
   (4) feeled
   (5) feel

4. Sentence 7: **Sadly, speaking about their fears is not something many teens have done with their parents.**

   If you rewrote sentence 7 beginning with

   <u>Sadly, many teens</u>

   the next words should be

   (1) not been speaking
   (2) have not spoke
   (3) have done speaking
   (4) have not spoken
   (5) not speaking

Answers start on page 738.

Lesson 13

Verb Tenses

Simple and Perfect Tenses

Verbs change to show when an action takes place or when a condition is true. These are called **verb tenses.**

RULE 1 Use the simple tenses for actions or for conditions that are usually true.

- The **present tense** expresses that an action takes place now or that a condition is true now.
- The **past tense** expresses that an action took place or that a condition was true in the past.
- The **future tense** expresses that an action will take place or that a condition will be true in the future. Use the helping verbs *will* or *shall* with the present form.

Present: Mr. Sarkar <u>advises</u> Paula to apply for another job.
Past: He <u>worked</u> with Paula on a special project last year.
Future: Paula <u>will bring</u> her résumé to the office next Thursday.

RULE 2 Use perfect tenses for more complex time relationships.

The perfect tenses always use a helping verb that is a form of the verb *have* plus the past participle.

- The **present perfect tense** expresses an action that began in the past and is already completed or continues into the present. Use *have* or *has* with the past participle.
- The **past perfect tense** expresses an action that was completed in the past before another past action began. Use *had* with the past participle.
- The **future perfect tense** expresses a future action that will begin and end before another future action begins. Use *will have* with the past participle.

Present perfect: I <u>have sent</u> her application to Ms Hall.
Past perfect: Previously, Ms Hall <u>had considered</u> only graduates.
Future perfect: Paula <u>will have graduated</u> by June.

Put a check mark next to the correct sentence.

_____ a. The conference has ended before we arrived.

_____ b. The conference had ended before we arrived.

You are correct if you checked *option b.* In that sentence, the past perfect tense is correctly used because it describes a past action that was completed (*conference ended*) before the second action began (*we arrived*).

---

verb tense
tells when an action takes place or when a condition is true

In perfect tenses, only the helping verb, *have,* changes form. The past participle stays the same:
We have worked.
We had worked.
We will have worked.

Consistency and Sequence

The verb tenses within a sentence or paragraph should be consistent—all present, all past, or all future—unless the meaning requires a change in verb tense.

Clues in the sentence or paragraph often show which tense should be used. Sometimes other verbs in a sentence can tell you what tense you need. Other times you may have to read a whole paragraph to figure out the correct tense.

RULE 1 Avoid unnecessary shifts in verb tense within a sentence or paragraph.

Inconsistent: Last Wednesday, a woman from my office <u>sat</u> down next to me. She <u>acts</u> as if she had never seen me before.

Consistent: Last Wednesday, a woman from my office <u>sat</u> down next to me. She <u>acted</u> as if she had never seen me before.

In the first sentence, *Last Wednesday* indicates the past tense, so the verb *sat* is correct. Because the action in the second sentence takes place at the same time, it, too, should be the past tense, *acted*.

RULE 2 In a complex sentence, use the same verb tense in each clause unless the action in the second clause occurs at a different time.

Incorrect: When I <u>said</u> hello, she <u>does</u> not react.

Correct: When I <u>said</u> hello, she <u>did</u> not react.

Both actions occurred in the past, so both should be past tense. But look at this example:

Incorrect: If she <u>behaves</u> this rudely again, I <u>become</u> very upset.

Correct: If she <u>behaves</u> this rudely again, I <u>will become</u> very upset.

In the first sentence, the verbs *behave* and *become* are both in the present tense. However, the action in the second clause will occur *after* the action in the first clause, so the verb *become* should be changed to the future tense *will become*.

Put a check mark next to the sentence with an incorrect tense shift.

_____ a. Huan needs a job, so he goes to an employment agency.

_____ b. Huan took an application form and sat down to fill it out.

_____ c. He was interviewed after he completes the form.

_____ d. He was told that Mr. Fry will let him know next week.

You are correct if you chose *option c*. Both actions were completed in the past, so the verbs should be consistent: *He was interviewed after he completed the form.*

Tip

Look for time words that give clues about verb tense, such as *now, last, next, after, during, while,* and *since.* Phrases can give clues, too. For example, *at this time* shows present tense; *in the 1900s* shows past tense; *next year* shows future tense.

GED Practice

Directions: Choose the <u>one best answer</u> to each question.

Questions 1 through 5 refer to the following letter.

Dear Customer:

(A)

(1) Thank you for shopping with Way More Sales. (2) We have been pleased to be your resource for quality home goods. (3) We regret that your order has been delayed. (4) We are waiting for the product from our vendors and will ship it within the next thirty days. (5) Upon arrival of this product at our warehouse, we will ship it to you.

(B)

(6) If you prefer to cancel your order, please be calling our service department at any time. (7) Credit card orders will not be charged until shipment is made. (8) We will appreciate your patience and look forward to serving you again.

1. Sentence 2: **We have been pleased to be your resource for quality home goods.**

   Which correction should be made to sentence 2?

   (1) change <u>have</u> to <u>had</u>
   (2) change <u>have been</u> to <u>are</u>
   (3) change <u>be</u> to <u>have been</u>
   (4) insert a comma after <u>resource</u>
   (5) no correction is necessary

2. Sentence 4: **We are waiting for the product from our vendors and <u>will ship</u> it within the next thirty days.**

   Which is the best way to write the underlined portion of this sentence? If the original is the best way, choose option (1).

   (1) will ship
   (2) had shipped
   (3) are shipping
   (4) shipped
   (5) be shipping

3. Sentence 5: **Upon arrival of this product at our warehouse, we will ship it to you.**

   If you rewrote sentence 5 beginning with

   <u>We will ship the product as soon as it</u>

   the next word or words should be

   (1) will have arrived
   (2) were arriving
   (3) arrives
   (4) is arriving
   (5) arriving

4. Sentence 6: **If you prefer to cancel your order, please be calling our service department at any time.**

   Which correction should be made to sentence 6?

   (1) change <u>prefer</u> to <u>are preferring</u>
   (2) remove the comma after <u>order</u>
   (3) change <u>order, please</u> to <u>order. Please</u>
   (4) change <u>be calling</u> to <u>call</u>
   (5) no correction is necessary

5. Sentence 8: **We <u>will appreciate</u> your patience and look forward to serving you again.**

   Which is the best way to write the underlined portion of this sentence? If the original is the best way, choose option (1).

   (1) will appreciate
   (2) have appreciated
   (3) are appreciating
   (4) will have appreciate
   (5) appreciate

Answers start on page 739.

Pronouns
Subject and Object Pronouns

A **personal pronoun** is a word that can be used in place of the name of a person, animal, place, or thing. Depending on the way you use it in a sentence, a personal pronoun can be a subject or an object.

Subject Pronouns		Object Pronouns	
Singular	**Plural**	**Singular**	**Plural**
I	we	me	us
you	you	you	you
he, she, it	they	him, her, it	them

personal pronoun
a word used in place of a noun, which names a person, animal, place, or thing

RULE 1 Use a subject pronoun as the subject of a sentence.

Correct: I am writing about the nomination of Andy Walker for union representative.
Incorrect: Andy and me work in the same department.
Correct: Andy and I work in the same department.

RULE 2 Use a subject pronoun when the pronoun that refers to the subject follows a form of the verb *be*.

Incorrect: The winner of the election will be him.
Correct: The winner of the election will be he.

Pronouns in compound subjects with nouns can be tricky. To "hear" whether a pronoun is correct, mentally cross out the noun and the word *and*. Which sounds better: ~~Andy and~~ me work or ~~Andy and~~ I work? *I work* sounds better.

RULE 3 Use an object pronoun as the object of a verb.

Correct: Joe Burnitz also knows him.
Incorrect: Andy invited Joe and I to run his campaign.
Correct: Andy invited Joe and me to run his campaign.

RULE 4 Use an object pronoun as the object of a preposition—a word such as *in, on, of, for, with,* and *between.*

Correct: Please vote for him.

Put a check mark next to the sentence that uses the correct personal pronoun.

_____ a. Mary asked my husband and I to visit her home.

_____ b. Mary asked my husband and me to visit her home.

You are correct if you checked *option b* because *my husband and me* is the object of the verb *asked.*

Possessive Pronouns

Personal pronouns can also be used to show possession.

Possessive Pronouns	
Singular	**Plural**
my, mine	our, ours
your, yours	your, yours
his, her, hers, its	their, theirs

Possession: Greta has <u>her</u> problems. I have <u>mine</u>.

Agreement with Antecedents

antecedent
the noun that a pronoun takes the place of

The noun that a pronoun stands for is its **antecedent.** A subject, object, or possessive pronoun must agree with its antecedent.

RULE 1 A pronoun must agree with its antecedent in **number—** singular or plural.

Agree: The <u>Greens</u> are in Room 1215. <u>They</u> love the view.

RULE 2 A pronoun must agree with its antecedent in **gender—** masculine, feminine, or neutral.

Agree: There's a <u>fax</u> for Ms. Vasquez. Bring <u>it</u> to Room 1580.

RULE 3 A pronoun must agree with its antecedent in **person.**

First person:	I, we, me, us, my, mine, our, ours
Second person:	you, your, yours
Third person:	he, she, it, they, him, her, them, his, hers, its, their, theirs

Agree: <u>Martin and I</u> are leaving. <u>We</u> can be reached at home.

RULE 4 When compound antecedents are joined by *or, either-or,* or *neither-nor,* the pronoun should agree with the nearest antecedent.

Correct: Neither the <u>Livingstons</u> nor <u>Kevin</u> is happy with <u>his</u> room.

RULE 5 Use singular pronouns for collective nouns unless the meaning clearly expresses the individuals in the group.

As a unit:	The <u>board</u> meets monthly. <u>It</u> is meeting now.
As individuals:	The <u>board</u> put <u>their</u> signatures on the budget.

Tip

To determine which pronoun to use in a sentence, find its antecedent. Decide whether the antecedent is singular or plural and feminine, masculine, or neutral. Then choose a pronoun that agrees with its antecedent on both points.

Put a check mark next to the correct sentence.

_____ a. The members of the audience leapt to their feet.

_____ b. The members of the audience leapt to its feet.

You are correct if you chose *option a.* The pronoun refers to *members,* so it should be plural.

Pronoun Shifts and Clear References

A pronoun shift occurs when the person or number of a pronoun changes incorrectly within a sentence or paragraph.

RULE 1 Avoid shifts in pronoun person or number.

Incorrect: When you hear the shriek of a fire truck's siren, one should pull over and let it pass.

Correct: When you hear the shriek of a fire truck's siren, you should pull over and let it pass.

In the first sentence, there is a shift from the second-person pronoun *you* to the third-person pronoun *one.*

Incorrect: It makes an unbelievable amount of noise; in fact, they sometimes cause temporary deafness.

Correct: It makes an unbelievable amount of noise; in fact, it sometimes causes temporary deafness.

In the first sentence, the pronoun shifts from the singular *it* to the plural *they.*

An unclear antecedent means that a reader cannot be sure of the antecedent of a pronoun.

RULE 2 Avoid ambiguous pronouns with more than one possible antecedent.

Ambiguous: There are special devices firefighters use to open locked doors. They are helpful when a building is on fire.

A reader cannot be sure if *They* refers to *devices* or *firefighters.*

Clear: There are special devices firefighters use to open locked doors. The devices are helpful when a building is on fire.

RULE 3 Avoid vague pronouns without any antecedents.

Vague: Georgia wants to join the fire department because they are community heroes.

There is no antecedent for the pronoun *they.*

Clear: Georgia wants to join the fire department because firefighters are community heroes.

Underline two pronoun problems in these sentences.

I use a monthly bus pass. They say passes are good for public transportation. Some companies can buy passes for their workers at a discount. The passes make them happy.

You are correct if you underlined *They* in the second sentence (it has no antecedent) and *them* in the last sentence (it could refer to either *companies* or *workers*).

GED Practice

Directions: Choose the <u>one best answer</u> to each question.

Questions 1 through 4 refer to the following passage.

Avoiding Lyme Disease

(A)

(1) Summer is the time to watch for the symptoms of Lyme disease, a skin rash or flu-like symptoms. (2) The disease, which has become a major health problem, is caused by the bite of a deer tick.

(B)

(3) There are sensible things you can do to avoid it. (4) When you walk in tall grass, woodlands, or sand dunes, always wear long pants. (5) They say to tuck the bottom of your pants into your socks, too. (6) If you wear light colours, you will be able to see them and pull them off before they have a chance to bite you.

(C)

(7) There are tick collars that your pets— both cats and dogs—can wear to protect themselves. (8) They are very important during tick season, which usually lasts from May until September.

1. Sentence 3: **There are sensible things you can do to avoid it.**

   Which correction should be made to sentence 3?

   (1) change <u>There are</u> to <u>There is</u>
   (2) replace <u>you</u> with <u>one</u>
   (3) replace <u>you</u> with <u>I</u>
   (4) replace <u>it</u> with <u>the disease</u>
   (5) no correction is necessary

2. Sentence 5: **They say to tuck the bottom of your pants into your socks, too.**

   Which is the best way to write the underlined portion of this sentence? If the original is the best way, choose option (1).

   (1) They say to tuck
   (2) You should tuck
   (3) One advises tucking
   (4) We always tuck
   (5) Everyone should tuck

3. Sentence 6: **If you wear light colours, you will be able to see them and pull them off before they have a chance to bite you.**

   Which correction should be made to sentence 6?

   (1) change <u>you wear</u> to <u>one wears</u>
   (2) remove the comma after <u>colours</u>
   (3) insert a comma after <u>see them</u>
   (4) replace <u>see them</u> with <u>see the ticks</u>
   (5) change <u>they have</u> to <u>it has</u>

4. Sentence 8: **They are very important during tick season, which usually lasts from May until September.**

   Which correction should be made to sentence 8?

   (1) replace <u>They</u> with <u>Tick collars</u>
   (2) replace <u>tick season</u> with <u>it</u>
   (3) change <u>season, which</u> to <u>season. Which</u>
   (4) change <u>lasts</u> to <u>is lasting</u>
   (5) no correction is necessary

Read the entire passage when deciding which pronoun is the correct answer for a GED question.

Answers start on page 739.

GED Review Usage

Directions: Choose the one best answer to each question.

Questions 1 through 4 refer to the following letter.

Highland Park Delivery Service
304 Park Blvd. N.
Winnipeg, MB R3P 0G7

Dear Mr. Brand:

(A)

(1) Please accept my application for the job of van driver that you listed in the *Hamlet News*. (2) I have driven a car for four years, and I have holded a licence for five years. (3) In your ad, you mentioned that you need a driver in Winnipeg. (4) I know the city well because I growed up in that area.

(B)

(5) I also have very suitable work experience. (6) I drived a delivery van for Economy Stores for two years. (7) In addition, I have been a substitute driver for Metro Service since May.

(C)

(8) Please consider me for the job. (9) I look forward to hearing from you.

Regards,
Jason May

1. Sentence 2: **I have driven a car for four years, and I have holded a licence for five years.**

   Which correction should be made to sentence 2?

   (1) remove have before driven
   (2) change driven to drove
   (3) remove the comma after years
   (4) change holded to held
   (5) insert a comma after licence

2. Sentence 4: **I know the city well because I growed up in that area.**

   Which correction should be made to sentence 4?

   (1) change I know to Knowing
   (2) change know to knowed
   (3) remove because
   (4) change growed to grew
   (5) no correction is necessary

3. Sentence 6: **I drived a delivery van for Economy Stores for two years.**

   Which is the best way to write the underlined portion of this sentence? If the original is the best way, choose option (1).

   (1) drived
   (2) drove
   (3) done drove
   (4) driven
   (5) been driving

4. Sentence 7: **In addition, I have been a substitute driver for Metro Service since May.**

   Which is the best way to write the underlined portion of this sentence? If the original is the best way, choose option (1).

   (1) have been
   (2) has been
   (3) am been
   (4) am being
   (5) been

Questions 5 through 9 refer to the following memo.

Memo

To: All Employees
From: Gene McKinney
RE: Car pooling

(1) Recently, Rick Fredericks informed my staff and I that 76 percent of the company's employees drive to work alone. (2) I am concerned that this statistic is so high. (3) We need to encourage more voluntary car pooling among ourselves. (4) For example, Rick and me realized we drive in separately from Kirkland Street every day. (5) We started car pooling on Monday. (6) Sharon Michaels has already offered to organize them for her department. (7) If you are interested in organizing your department or signing up for a car pool, give your name and phone number to Rick. (8) He will give it to me, and I will compile the information and get back to everyone shortly.

5. Sentence 1: **Recently, Rick Fredericks informed my staff and I that 76 percent of the company's employees drive to work alone.**

   Which correction should be made to sentence 1?

   (1) insert he after Rick Fredericks
   (2) change I to me
   (3) change drive to drove
   (4) change drive to drives
   (5) no correction is necessary

6. Sentence 4: **For example, Rick and me realized we drive in separately from Kirkland Street every day.**

   Which is the best way to write the underlined portion of this sentence? If the original is the best way, choose option (1).

   (1) Rick and me
   (2) me and Rick
   (3) him and I
   (4) he and me
   (5) Rick and I

7. Sentence 6: **Sharon Michaels has already offered to organize them for her department.**

   Which correction should be made to sentence 6?

   (1) replace Sharon Michaels with She
   (2) insert she after Michaels
   (3) change offered to been offering
   (4) replace them with car pool groups
   (5) replace her with their

8. Sentence 7: **If you are interested in organizing your department or signing up for a car pool, give your name and phone number to Rick.**

   Which correction should be made to sentence 7?

   (1) change you are to one is
   (2) change are to be
   (3) insert a comma after department
   (4) remove the comma after car pool
   (5) no correction is necessary

9. Sentence 8: **He will give it to me, and I will compile the information and get back to everyone shortly.**

   The most effective revision of sentence 8 would include which group of words?

   (1) to me, compiling it and getting back
   (2) He will and I will compile all the information
   (3) give the information to me, and I will compile it
   (4) so that I can compile the information and get back
   (5) compile the information, and then I will get back

Questions 10 through 14 refer to the following paragraph.

Houseplant Care

(1) Here are some advice for taking care of your houseplants if you need to be away for a period of time. (2) First, don't worry about fertilizing them. (3) Houseplants from the African violet to a zonal geranium lasts for months without needing fertilizer. (4) However, nothing survive without water. (5) To simplify watering, put the plants in a bathtub that gets light from a window. (6) Layers of paper protects the tub from getting scratched, so place them down first. (7) Then place bricks on the paper and the plants on the bricks. (8) Finally, fill the tub so that you cover all the bricks with water, but you don't cover the pots. (9) Then the roots can absorb the water through the holes in the bottoms of their pots.

10. Sentence 1: **Here are some advice for taking care of your houseplants if you need to be away for a period of time**.

    Which correction should be made to sentence 1?

    (1) replace Here are some with Some
    (2) change are to is
    (3) insert a comma after houseplants
    (4) change need to needs
    (5) insert a comma after away

11. Sentence 3: **Houseplants from the African violet to a zonal geranium lasts for months without needing fertilizer.**

    Which correction should be made to sentence 3?

    (1) insert a comma after violet
    (2) insert a comma after geranium
    (3) change lasts to lasting
    (4) change lasts to last
    (5) no correction is necessary

12. Sentence 4: **However, nothing survive without water.**

    Which correction should be made to sentence 4?

    (1) replace However, nothing with Not
    (2) replace nothing with not one
    (3) change survive to survives
    (4) change survive to surviving
    (5) no correction is necessary

13. Sentence 6: **Layers of paper protects the tub from getting scratched, so place them down first.**

    Which is the best way to write the underlined portion of this sentence? If the original is the best way, choose option (1).

    (1) protects
    (2) protect
    (3) protecting
    (4) is protecting
    (5) are protecting

14. Sentence 8: **Finally, fill the tub so that you cover all the bricks with water, but you don't cover the pots.**

    If you rewrote sentence 8 beginning with

    Finally, fill the tub so that the bricks, but not the pots,

    the next words should be

    (1) is covered
    (2) are covered
    (3) covered
    (4) covering
    (5) be covered

Tip

Use the passage as a whole to decide which tense is correct in a GED item. In some cases, a verb may be grammatically correct in the sentence but may not work with the meaning of the passage as a whole.

Questions 15 through 18 refer to the following article.

Safe Produce

(A)

(1) Consumers know for many years that growers treat produce with pesticides and other chemicals. (2) For example, a number of years ago consumers become angry when they learned about Alar, a chemical used to make apples and grapes larger and more colourful. (3) The problem, both then and today, is that consumers often choose produce that looked appealing. (4) Such consumer behaviour only encourages growers to use chemicals that make fruits and vegetables more attractive.

(B)

(5) The Alar issue, however, did drive some consumers to organic groceries and farmers' markets instead. (6) As there is an increase in consumer demand for pesticide-free produce, there will be more produce growers focusing on organic growing methods. (7) Others may turn to genetic engineering of fruits and vegetables, which raises its own safety issues.

15. Sentence 1: **Consumers know for many years that growers treat produce with pesticides and other chemicals.**

    Which is the best way to write the underlined portion of this sentence? If the original is the best way, choose option (1).

    (1) know
    (2) known
    (3) knowed
    (4) will know
    (5) have known

For more information about Usage, see the Writer's Checklist on page 898.

16. Sentence 2: **For example, a number of years ago consumers become angry when they learned about Alar, a chemical used to make apples and grapes larger and more colourful.**

    Which correction should be made to sentence 2?

    (1) remove the comma after example
    (2) change become to became
    (3) insert a comma after angry
    (4) insert have after they
    (5) change become to have become

17. Sentence 3: **The problem, both then and today, is that consumers often choose produce that looked appealing.**

    Which is the best way to write the underlined portion of this sentence? If the original is the best way, choose option (1).

    (1) looked
    (2) had looked
    (3) has looked
    (4) looks
    (5) is looking

18. Sentence 6: **As there is an increase in consumer demand for pesticide-free produce, there will be more produce growers focusing on organic growing methods.**

    If you rewrote sentence 6 beginning with

    As consumer demand for pesticide-free produce increases, more produce growers

    the next words should be

    (1) will be focusing
    (2) will have focused
    (3) will focus
    (4) are focusing
    (5) focusing

Answers start on page 739.

Mechanics

Mechanics is an important content area on the GED Language Arts, Writing Test. About 25 percent of the multiple-choice questions will be based on these topics. Mechanics concepts include capitalization, punctuation, and spelling. Writing that is mechanically correct—that is, writing that has correct capitalization, punctuation, and spelling—always makes a better impression than writing that contains errors.

Capitalization

When to Capitalize

You probably already know that the first word in a sentence and the pronoun *I* are always capitalized. These additional rules will help you decide when to capitalize other words.

proper noun
a word that names a specific person, animal, place, or thing

RULE 1 Capitalize a **proper noun,** a word that names a specific person, animal, place, group, or thing.

William Boyle invented the credit card in 1951.
He lived on Spark Street in West Stead on Long Island.
Mr. Boyle worked for the Franklin National Bank.

proper adjective
a descriptive word formed from a proper noun

RULE 2 Capitalize a **proper adjective,** a descriptive word that comes from the name of a specific person or place.

Franklin's main competitor was First American Bank.

RULE 3 Capitalize a title that comes directly before a person's name.

On the bank's board of directors was Mayor Graham.
A depositor, Ms. Ailey, asked for credit to pay a big heating bill.

Titles and family names (for example, *mother, father, grandmother*) are capitalized when they are used to address a person directly.

Ms. Ailey said, "How do you do, Mayor."
"Mr. Boyle, Sir, I would appreciate a line of credit, just like you give to wealthy depositors and businesses."

RULE 4 Capitalize the names of holidays, days of the week, and months of the year.

Statements were sent out on the first Monday of the month.
By New Year's Day in January 1952, Franklin National Bank had set up more than 700 credit card accounts for its customers.

When Not to Capitalize

Some writers overcapitalize; that is, they capitalize words that should not be capitalized. You need to avoid using unnecessary capital letters.

RULE 1 A title or a family name that is preceded by *a, the,* or a possessive pronoun such as *my* is not capitalized.

Incorrect: Alice went to see the Dean.
Correct: Alice went to see the dean.
Correct: Alice went to see Dean Asher.

Incorrect: She went with her Uncle.
Correct: She went with her uncle.
Correct: She went with her Uncle William.

RULE 2 The names of the seasons are not capitalized.

Incorrect: Both are going back to school in the Fall.
Correct: Both are going back to school in the fall.

RULE 3 A school subject is not capitalized unless it is the name of a specific course or a language.

Incorrect: Alice wants to take a History course.
Correct: Alice wants to take a history course.
Correct: Alice wants to take Canadian History 101 and French.

RULE 4 A direction word is not capitalized unless it refers to a specific place, such as a region of the country.

Incorrect: They walked West to the administration building.
Correct: They walked west to the administration building.
Correct: Alice was born here, but William grew up out West.

RULE 5 A geographic place is not capitalized unless it is part of a specific name you can find on a map.

Incorrect: The school is next to a huge Lake.
Correct: The school is next to a huge lake.
Correct: The school is next to Lake Ontario.

Tip

Proper nouns are sometimes abbreviated. When a word should be capitalized, its abbreviation should be capitalized too: *Mount Shasta, Mt. Shasta.*

Put a check mark next to the sentence that has a capitalization error.

_____ a. Joe and his cousin, Dino, are taking Geometry and English in school this summer.

_____ b. Hank is staying with his Aunt Carol on this side of the River, so he doesn't have a long commute from north of town.

You are correct if you checked *option b.* There is no reason to capitalize *river* because it is not part of a specific place name.

GED Practice

Directions: Choose the <u>one best answer</u> to each question.

Questions 1 through 4 refer to the following paragraphs.

From Gifts to Gardens

(A)

(1) Many people throw out potted Easter lilies or mother's day plants soon after they bloom. (2) The National Lily foundation, however, claims that, with some care and rest in your garden, potted lilies can recover and bloom the next year.

(B)

(3) Wait until the last frost in your region. (4) In far northern areas, this usually means waiting until mid-june. (5) Knock the bulb out of its pot, keeping the leaves and stem because they provide food for the bulb. (6) Plant the bulb about eight inches deep in a sunny spot and feed it about once a month. (7) At the end of Summer when the leaves are dead, cut the plant back, and cover it with pine needles or mulch. (8) Your lily should blossom for many years.

1. Sentence 1: **Many people throw out potted Easter lilies or mother's day plants soon after they bloom.**

   Which correction should be made to sentence 1?

   (1) change throw to threw
   (2) change Easter to easter
   (3) insert a comma after lilies
   (4) change mother's day to Mother's Day
   (5) insert a comma after plants

The names of many holidays and other proper nouns consist of more than one word. Be sure to capitalize all the relevant words in a proper noun.

2. Sentence 2: **The National Lily foundation, however, claims that, with some care and rest in your garden, potted lilies can recover and bloom the next year.**

   Which correction should be made to sentence 2?

   (1) change National Lily to national lily
   (2) change foundation to Foundation
   (3) change claims to claim
   (4) replace potted lilies with they
   (5) change bloom to be blooming

3. Sentence 4: **In far northern areas, this usually means waiting until mid-june.**

   Which correction should be made to sentence 4?

   (1) change northern to Northern
   (2) change means to meant
   (3) insert a comma after waiting
   (4) change mid-june to Mid-june
   (5) change mid-june to mid-June

4. Sentence 7: **At the end of Summer when the leaves are dead, cut the plant back, and cover it with pine needles or mulch.**

   Which correction should be made to sentence 7?

   (1) change Summer to summer
   (2) remove the comma after dead
   (3) change dead, cut to dead. Cut
   (4) change pine to Pine
   (5) no correction is necessary

Answers start on page 741.

Language Arts, Writing • Mechanics

Commas

Items in Series and Compound Sentences

The comma is a guide for readers. It tells when to pause in a sentence or which elements in a sentence need to be separated in a meaningful way. Learning the rules for using commas will help you become a better writer and a better reader.

RULE 1 Use a comma to separate items in a series—a list of three or more. The items in the series may be words or phrases.

Correct: Cakes, pies, and cookies will be sold at the charity bake sale. Committees have helped with getting publicity, soliciting donations, and decorating booths.

When there are only two items, do not use a comma.

Correct: The advertising committee wants more posters and flyers.

When three or more items are all separated by the conjunction *and* or *or,* do not use commas.

Correct: The advertising committee wants more posters and flyers and mailings.

RULE 2 Use a comma between the clauses in a compound sentence. Remember that a compound sentence contains two or more complete thoughts, called independent clauses, joined by a coordinating conjunction: *and, but, or, for, nor, so,* or *yet.*

Everyone is helping, so the bake sale should be a hit.

Put a check mark next to the sentence with a comma error.

_____ a. Old-fashioned vending machines were usually filled with stale candy or sandwiches.

_____ b. Some newer vending machines contain rolls pizza coffee and fresh fruit.

_____ c. The newer ones also make change for five-dollar, ten-dollar, or twenty-dollar bills.

You are correct if you checked *option b.* The series needs commas: *Some newer vending machines contain rolls, pizza, coffee, and fresh fruit.*

A comma before the final *and* in a series is optional. However, using commas throughout the rest of a series is required.

Do not use a comma to separate two subjects in a compound subject or two verbs in a compound predicate: *Mary and Jim* fished. Liz *fished and swam.*

Introductory Elements and Appositives

Words and phrases that introduce or interrupt the main idea of a sentence are usually set off from the rest of the sentence with commas.

RULE 1 Use a comma to separate introductory elements—words or phrases at the beginning of a sentence—from the rest of the sentence.

<u>No,</u> the bank is closed on Victoria Day.
<u>As a result of overspending,</u> Ron's funds are low.

RULE 2 Use a comma after a dependent clause that comes at the beginning of a sentence. Remember that a dependent clause contains a subject and a verb but is not a complete thought and cannot stand alone. It begins with a subordinating conjunction such as *before* or *if*.

<u>When all his bills came in,</u> he was stunned.
But: He was stunned when all his bills came in.

An **appositive** is a noun phrase that further explains or describes another noun or pronoun. If the appositive is necessary to identify the noun or pronoun, it is essential. If the appositive simply adds some information but is not necessary in order to identify the noun or pronoun, it is nonessential.

RULE 3 Use commas to separate a nonessential appositive from the rest of the sentence. Do not use commas for essential appositives.

Nonessential: Ron, <u>my friend,</u> has 13 credit cards.
Essential: He is reading the library book *Ten Ways to Get Out of Debt.*

A **parenthetical expression** is a word or phrase that adds nothing essential to the meaning of a sentence. Many parenthetical expressions are transitions. Some common parenthetical expressions are *for example, incidentally, of course, however,* and *on the one hand.*

RULE 4 Use commas to set off parenthetical expressions.

Ron has cards, <u>for example,</u> for most stores in the mall.

Put a check mark next to the sentence that uses commas correctly.

_____ a. In addition to skills, appearance is important at an interview.

_____ b. My job counsellor, Della Rollins helped me pick an interview outfit.

You are correct if you checked *option a* because *In addition to skills* is an introductory phrase that should be followed by a comma. In *option b,* a second comma is needed after the nonessential appositive *Della Rollins.*

GED Practice

Directions: Choose the <u>one best answer</u> to each question.

<u>Questions 1 through 4</u> refer to the following memo.

Memo

TO: Staff
DATE: September 12, 2003
RE: Deli Opening

(A)

(1) Next Friday Saturday, and Sunday, the Four Corners Supermarket will hold an in-store sale to introduce our new deli department. (2) We will have tasty cooking demonstrations for customers. (3) All deli-made sandwiches, soups, and salads will be half-price. (4) In addition samples of our delicious smoked ham, roast beef, and tuna salad will be served throughout the store.

(B)

(5) Before the event, you will have the opportunity to meet all the new staff in the deli department. (6) The new deli manager, Jin Tan expects that the new department will increase store sales by 50 to 75 percent during the special event. (7) You can help by encouraging your friends, and relatives to visit our new department.

1. Sentence 1: **Next Friday Saturday, and Sunday, the Four Corners Supermarket will hold an in-store sale to introduce our new deli department.**

   Which is the best way to write the underlined portion of this sentence? If the original is the best way, choose option (1).

   (1) Friday Saturday, and Sunday,
   (2) Friday Saturday and Sunday,
   (3) Friday, and Saturday and Sunday
   (4) Friday Saturday, and Sunday
   (5) Friday, Saturday, and Sunday,

2. Sentence 4: **In addition samples of our delicious smoked ham, roast beef, and tuna salad will be served throughout the store.**

   Which correction should be made to sentence 4?

   (1) insert a comma after <u>In addition</u>
   (2) remove the comma after <u>ham</u>
   (3) insert a comma after <u>salad</u>
   (4) change <u>will be</u> to <u>was</u>
   (5) <u>no correction</u> is necessary

3. Sentence 6: **The new deli manager, Jin Tan expects that the new department will increase store sales by 50 to 75 percent during the special event.**

   Which correction should be made to sentence 6?

   (1) change <u>manager</u> to <u>Manager</u>
   (2) insert a comma after <u>Tan</u>
   (3) insert a comma after <u>sales</u>
   (4) change <u>expects</u> to <u>expected</u>
   (5) replace <u>the special event</u> with <u>it</u>

4. Sentence 7: **You can help by encouraging your friends, and relatives to visit our new department.**

   Which correction should be made to sentence 7?

   (1) replace <u>You</u> with <u>One</u>
   (2) change <u>help</u> to <u>be helping</u>
   (3) remove the comma after <u>friends</u>
   (4) insert a comma after <u>relatives</u>
   (5) <u>no correction</u> is necessary

Answers start on page 741.

Spelling

Possessives

Possessives are words that show ownership. You make a noun show possession by using an apostrophe (') and usually the letter -*s*. Plural nouns that do not show possession do not use an apostrophe.

RULE 1 Add '*s* to show the possessive for a singular noun and for a plural noun that does not end in -*s*.

Singular Possessive: John's sons are going fly-fishing next week.
Singular Possessive: Jess's old reel is oiled and ready.
Plural Possessive: The children's rods are stacked in the garage.

RULE 2 Add only an apostrophe to show the possessive for a plural noun ending in -*s*.

Plural Possessive: Both sons' fishing flies are already tied.
Plural Possessive: The flies' hooks have been carefully inserted.

RULE 3 Don't use an apostrophe with the possessive pronouns *his, hers, its, ours, yours, theirs*, and *whose*.

Incorrect: That big catch of trout is their's.
Correct: That big catch of trout is theirs.

Put a check mark by the sentence in which all possessives are spelled correctly.

_____ a. Here is Jills' picture in the photo album.

_____ b. Who's pictures are these?

_____ c. They are of my Grandmother Tess and her two younger sister's, Bess and Jess.

_____ d. Her brothers' names are Fess and Les Rimes.

You are correct if you checked *option d*. The possessive plural *brothers'* is spelled correctly. In *option a,* the singular possessive *Jills'* should be spelled *Jill's*. In *option b,* the possessive pronoun *Who's* should be spelled *Whose*. In *option c,* the plural noun *sister's* should be spelled *sisters*.

possessive
a word that shows
ownership

Tip

To check for possession, try to turn the words into a phrase with *of*.
Possessive: *Bob's sister = the sister of Bob*

Contractions

contraction
a word formed from
two words that
are combined and
shortened by
leaving out letters.
An apostrophe takes
the place of the
missing letter(s).

A **contraction** is a shortened way to write two words by combining them and omitting one or more letters. Like possessives, contractions use apostrophes.

RULE 1 Use an apostrophe to take the place of the missing letters in a contraction: *I + am = I'm.*

Incorrect: Do'nt put the apostrophe in the wrong place.
Correct: Don't put the apostrophe in the wrong place.

Most contractions combine a personal pronoun and a verb:

you've = you have	we're = we are
she'd = she had	he'd = he would
it's = it is	they'll = they will

Negative contractions combine a verb and the word *not:*

isn't = is not	wasn't = was not
aren't = are not	weren't = were not
don't = do not	didn't = did not
doesn't = does not	won't = will not
haven't = have not	hasn't = has not
can't = cannot	shouldn't = should not
couldn't = could not	wouldn't = would not

To check the spelling of a contraction, look at the placement of the apostrophe. An apostrophe replaces a letter or letters in one word of a contraction. For example: *We're = We are.* The apostrophe replaces the *a* in *are.*

RULE 2 Do not confuse contractions with possessives that sound the same.

Incorrect: Its a common spelling problem.
Correct Contraction: It's a common spelling problem.

Incorrect: Make sure each word has it's apostrophe in the correct place.
Correct Possessive: Make sure each word has its apostrophe in the correct place.

To decide whether a word is a contraction or a possessive, mentally substitute the two words that form the contraction. If the sentence makes sense, the word is a contraction.

You can substitute *it is* in the first sentence, so that is a contraction and needs the apostrophe. You cannot substitute *it is* in the second sentence, so *its* is a possessive.

Put a check mark by the sentence that uses a contraction correctly.

_____ a. It's a library book.

_____ b. It's due date was last month.

You are correct if you checked *option a.* You can substitute *It is* in the sentence: *It is a library book.*

Homonyms

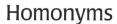

homonyms
words that sound alike but have different spellings and meanings

To avoid errors with homonyms, read the entire sentence before you decide how to spell the word. That way, you will know the intended meaning of the word.

Homonyms are words that sound alike but have different spellings and different meanings. There are no rules to help you write homonyms. You simply have to learn how to spell the particular homonym you want to use.

As you have learned, some contractions and possessives are homonyms: *it's/its, you're/your, who's/whose.*

Here are some other commonly confused homonyms:

board (piece of wood)
bored (not interested)

brake (to stop)
break (to damage or destroy; rest period)

coarse (rough, textured)
course (path, track)

feat (achievement)
feet (plural of *foot*)

grate (to shred)
great (extremely good)

hear (to listen)
here (in this place)

hole (opening)
whole (entire)

knew (past tense of *know*)
new (latest, additional)

passed (went by)
past (a time before)

principal (main; head of a school)
principle (rule, belief)

right (correct; opposite of left)
write (to form words)

their (belonging to them)
there (in that place)
they're (contraction of *they are*)

to (in the direction of)
too (also)
two (the number 2)

way (path, direction)
weigh (to measure heaviness)

weak (not strong)
week (seven days)

wear (to have on clothing)
where (what place)

weather (climate)
whether (if)

wood (what trees are made of)
would (verb expressing a want)

Some words are not actual homonyms, but they are often confused because they sound so similar:

accept (to receive or get)   affect (to influence)   than (comparison)
except (excluding)   effect (a result)   then (after that)

Put a check mark by the sentence with no misspelling.

_____ a. The instructor's lesson will positively affect the class.

_____ b. The instructor's lesson will positively effect the class.

You are correct if you chose *option a*. The instructor's actions will influence the class positively.

For more information on homonyms see the Writer's Checklist on page 898.

Language Arts, Writing • Mechanics

GED Practice

Directions: Choose the <u>one best answer</u> to each question.

Questions 1 through 4 refer to the following letter.

Dear Thomas Peters:

(A)

(1) Don't miss this special renewal opportunity. (2) If you act now, you'll receive 48 weakly issues of *Online Emblem,* plus 12 monthly special reports for the great rate of only $18.95.

(B)

(3) Don't miss the only newsmagazine covering the people, local news, and community actions shaping the Internet economy. (4) Our magazines' coverage provides you with breaking news on e-mail, shopping discounts, jobs, and sports. (5) With your paid renewal, well send you an additional 12 monthly special reports covering exciting Internet issues.

(C)

(6) Don't wait another minute to continue the service that Professor Jane Notch of Dwyer University's School of Computer Science calls "the best, most accurate publication" covering the Internet today!

1. Sentence 2: **If you act now, you'll receive 48 weakly issues of *Online Emblem,* plus 12 monthly special reports for the great rate of only $18.95.**

   Which correction should be made to sentence 2?

   (1) change <u>you act</u> to <u>one acts</u>
   (2) remove the comma after <u>now</u>
   (3) change <u>receive</u> to <u>have received</u>
   (4) replace <u>weakly</u> with <u>weekly</u>
   (5) replace <u>great</u> with <u>grate</u>

> **Tip**
>
> As you work through these exercises, note the homonyms that give you trouble. Study them and practise writing sentences with them.

2. Sentence 4: **Our magazines' coverage provides you with breaking news on e-mail, shopping discounts, jobs, and sports.**

   Which correction should be made to sentence 4?

   (1) change <u>magazines'</u> to <u>magazine's</u>
   (2) change <u>provides</u> to <u>provide</u>
   (3) replace <u>you</u> with <u>one</u>
   (4) replace <u>breaking</u> with <u>braking</u>
   (5) no correction is necessary

3. Sentence 5: **With your paid renewal, well send you an additional 12 monthly special reports covering exciting Internet issues.**

   Which correction should be made to sentence 5?

   (1) replace <u>your</u> with <u>you're</u>
   (2) remove the comma
   (3) replace <u>well</u> with <u>we'll</u>
   (4) change <u>special reports</u> to <u>Special Reports</u>
   (5) no correction is necessary

4. Sentence 6: **Don't wait another minute to continue the service that Professor Jane Notch of Dwyer University's School of Computer Science calls "the best, most accurate publication" covering the Internet today!**

   Which correction should be made to sentence 6?

   (1) replace <u>wait</u> with <u>weight</u>
   (2) insert a comma after <u>service</u>
   (3) change <u>Professor</u> to <u>professor</u>
   (4) change <u>University's</u> to <u>Universities</u>
   (5) no correction is necessary

Answers start on page 741.

GED Review Mechanics

Directions: Choose the one best answer to each question.

Questions 1 through 4 refer to the following paragraphs.

How to Take Phone Messages

(A)

(1) In these days of voice mail and automated phone menus, the art of answering the telephone may be part of our past. (2) Yet some companies still recognize the value of personal contact. (3) Here are some great tips for receiving incoming calls and taking customer's messages.

(B)

(4) After greeting a customer, say the name of the company and "How may I help you?" as politely as possible. (5) Its important to listen carefully to callers and ask them to repeat any names or numbers you don't understand. (6) To take a message for an employee who isn't available, note the employee's name and the time of the call. (7) Than write down the caller's name, company, phone number, and any message he or she wants to leave. (8) Verify both the name by spelling it back and the telephone number by repeating the numbers. (9) Finally, thank the caller and make sure the message gets to the right person promptly.

1. Sentence 1: **In these days of voice mail and automated phone menus, the art of answering the telephone may be part of our past.**

   Which correction should be made to sentence 1?

   (1) insert a comma after voice mail
   (2) remove the comma after menus
   (3) replace our with hour
   (4) replace past with passed
   (5) no correction is necessary

2. Sentence 3: **Here are some great tips for receiving incoming calls and taking customer's messages.**

   Which correction should be made to sentence 3?

   (1) replace Here with Hear
   (2) change are to is
   (3) replace great with grate
   (4) insert a comma after calls
   (5) change customer's to customers'

3. Sentence 5: **Its important to listen carefully to callers and ask them to repeat any names or numbers you don't understand.**

   Which correction should be made to sentence 5?

   (1) replace Its with It's
   (2) change callers to callers'
   (3) replace and with a comma
   (4) insert a comma after names
   (5) change don't to do'nt

4. Sentence 7: **Than write down the caller's name, company, phone number, and any message he or she wants to leave.**

   Which correction should be made to sentence 7?

   (1) replace Than with Then
   (2) replace write with right
   (3) change caller's to callers
   (4) remove the comma after name
   (5) insert a comma after message

Questions 5 through 9 refer to the following paragraphs.

Getting Your Calcium

(A)

(1) Calcium is a mineral needed for strong, healthy, and lasting, teeth and bones. (2) Doctors generally agree that 2000 mg of calcium a day is safe for most people.

(B)

(3) Although many people take calcium in pills nutritionists recommend eating foods naturally rich in calcium. (4) Dairy products are the foods richest in calcium and now many of them are also low-fat or non-fat. (5) For people with difficulty digesting milk there are now low-lactose alternatives. (6) In addition, foods such as orange juice can be fortified with calcium. (7) Non-dairy products that are rich in calcium, include broccoli, leafy green vegetables, and fortified bread and cereals.

5. Sentence 1: **Calcium is a mineral needed for strong, healthy, and lasting, teeth and bones.**

   Which correction should be made to sentence 1?

   (1) change is to has been
   (2) insert a comma after mineral
   (3) remove the comma after lasting
   (4) insert a comma after teeth
   (5) no correction is necessary

6. Sentence 3: **Although many people take calcium in pills nutritionists recommend eating foods naturally rich in calcium.**

   Which correction should be made to sentence 3?

   (1) change take to were taking
   (2) insert a comma after calcium
   (3) insert a comma after pills
   (4) change nutritionists to Nutritionists
   (5) no correction is necessary

7. Sentence 4: **Dairy products are the foods richest in calcium and now many of them are also low-fat or non-fat.**

   Which is the best way to write the underlined portion of this sentence? If the original is the best way, choose option (1).

   (1) calcium and
   (2) calcium
   (3) calcium. And
   (4) calcium, and
   (5) calcium and,

8. Sentence 5: **For people with difficulty digesting milk there are now low-lactose alternatives.**

   Which correction should be made to sentence 5?

   (1) insert a comma after difficulty
   (2) insert a comma after milk
   (3) replace there are with they have
   (4) change are to is
   (5) no correction is necessary

9. Sentence 7: **Non-dairy products that are rich in calcium, include broccoli, leafy green vegetables, and fortified bread and cereals.**

   Which correction should be made to sentence 7?

   (1) replace that with they
   (2) change are to have been
   (3) remove the comma after calcium
   (4) remove the comma after broccoli
   (5) insert a comma after bread

Avoid unnecessary commas in a series by counting the items. For only two, do not use a comma. For three or more, subtract one from the number of items. That is the number of commas you need.

Questions 10 through 13 refer to the following paragraphs.

Elections

(A)

(1) Every four years in the Fall, Americans go to the polls on Election Day to elect a president. (2) The largest number of presidents have come from the South. (3) Interestingly, the nation's most populous State, California, has produced only two presidents, Richard Nixon and Ronald Reagan.

(B)

(4) Although the job of a vice president seems comparatively unimportant, it is a vital transitional position for the nation. (5) For example, after Nixon resigned from the White House, vice president Ford succeeded him. (6) Ford had been a representative in congress from the Midwest before Nixon named him to succeed Spiro Agnew. (7) Even though Ford was not returned to office by the voters, the country had been spared a serious gap in leadership.

10. Sentence 1: **Every four years in the Fall, Americans go to the polls on Election Day to elect a president.**

    Which correction should be made to sentence 1?

    (1) change Fall to fall
    (2) change go to goes
    (3) change go to went
    (4) change president to President
    (5) no correction is necessary

For more information on Mechanics, see the Writer's Checklist on page 898.

11. Sentence 3: **Interestingly, the nation's most populous State, California, has produced only two presidents, Richard Nixon and Ronald Reagan.**

    Which correction should be made to sentence 3?

    (1) change nation's to Nation's
    (2) change State to state
    (3) change has to have
    (4) insert they were after presidents,
    (5) change presidents to Presidents

12. Sentence 5: **For example, after Nixon resigned from the White House, vice president Ford succeeded him.**

    Which correction should be made to sentence 5?

    (1) remove the comma after example
    (2) change White House to white house
    (3) remove the comma after House
    (4) change president to President
    (5) change vice president to Vice President

13. Sentence 6: **Ford had been a representative in congress from the Midwest before Nixon named him to succeed Spiro Agnew.**

    Which correction should be made to sentence 6?

    (1) change had to has
    (2) change had been to was being
    (3) change representative to Representative
    (4) change congress to Congress
    (5) change Midwest to midwest

Answers start on page 742.

Directions: Choose the <u>one best answer</u> to each question.

Questions <u>1 through 3</u> refer to the following letter.

West Star Insurance Company
570 Nanaimo Avenue
Victoria BC V9A 7J4

Dear Ms. Santos:

(A)

(1) Thank you for doing business with West Star Insurance. (2) We certainly hope you never have damage or loss to you're car. (3) If you do, however, we at West Star are committed to settling your claim with the least inconvenience to you.

(B)

(4) In addition to providing speedy claim service, West Star offers top-quality repairs at any of our recommended body shops. (5) When replacing a cracked or broken windshield, our preferred list has the best glass shops in your area. (6) West Star also can negotiate special rates for car rentals.

(C)

(7) Please find enclosed a special kit that West Star provides for every new client. (8) It contains instructions on what to do if you are in an accident. (9) The kit also contains an accident information card on which to record important facts about an accident. (10) It is a good idea to keep the kit in the glove compartment of your car, so you have it on hand when you need it. (11) There's a list of toll-free numbers to call when reporting an accident, too.

(D)

(12) Everyone at West Star Insurance looks forward to serving you for many years to come. (13) We also wish you safe, accident-free driving.

Yours truly,
West Star Claims Department

1. Sentence 2: **We certainly hope you never have damage or loss to you're car.**

   Which correction should be made to sentence 2?

   (1) insert <u>will</u> after <u>certainly</u>
   (2) change <u>have</u> to <u>had</u>
   (3) insert a <u>comma</u> after <u>damage</u>
   (4) replace <u>you're</u> with <u>your</u>
   (5) no <u>correction</u> is necessary

2. Sentence 5: **When replacing a cracked or broken windshield, our preferred list has the best glass shops in your area.**

   The most effective revision of sentence 5 would begin with which group of words?

   (1) A cracked or broken windshield needs replacing
   (2) When you need a cracked or broken windshield replaced,
   (3) With a cracked or broken windshield
   (4) Needing to repair a cracked or broken windshield
   (5) Upon cracking or breaking a windshield

3. Sentence 12: **Everyone at West Star Insurance looks forward to serving you for many years to come.**

   Which correction should be made to sentence 12?

   (1) change <u>looks</u> to <u>will look</u>
   (2) change <u>looks</u> to <u>look</u>
   (3) change <u>serving</u> to <u>serve</u>
   (4) insert a <u>comma</u> after <u>you</u>
   (5) no correction is necessary

Questions 4 through 8 refer to the following notice.

Notice to Diggers

(A)

(1) Every Spring, landlords and homeowners throughout the province begin construction, renovation, and landscaping projects. (2) Please be warned, however, that anyone who uses large machinery to dig holes must follow these digging guidelines. (3) A person digging with hand tools are the only exception.

(B)

(4) Provincial law requires that a digger must provide plans to the local building department at least five days before work begins. (5) They will issue a permit and notify the utility companies. (6) The utility companies, in turn, will locate and mark all their underground systems. (7) Once marked, a digger can safely proceed with plans.

(C)

(8) This process helps avoid damaging homes or other structures. (9) Provincial law also mandates that a contractor or other digger "pre-mark" the boundary of any proposed hole. (10) White paint, taped stakes, or other clearly visible signs, are acceptable. (11) Such markings will further ensure that no underground cables or pipes will be damaged by digging.

4. Sentence 1: **Every Spring, landlords and homeowners throughout the province begin construction, renovation, and landscaping projects.**

   Which correction should be made to sentence 1?

   (1) change Spring to spring
   (2) remove the comma after Spring
   (3) change province to Province
   (4) change begin to will begin
   (5) remove the comma after construction

5. Sentence 3: **A person digging with hand tools are the only exception.**

   Which correction should be made to sentence 3?

   (1) insert is after person
   (2) insert a comma after digging
   (3) change tools to tool's
   (4) insert a comma after tools
   (5) change are to is

6. Sentence 5: **They will issue a permit and notify the utility companies.**

   Which is the best way to write the underlined portion of this sentence? If the original is the best way, choose option (1).

   (1) They
   (2) It
   (3) One
   (4) The building department
   (5) The diggers

7. Which revision would improve the effectiveness of paragraph C?

   (1) move sentence 8 to the end of paragraph B
   (2) remove sentence 8
   (3) move sentence 8 to follow sentence 9
   (4) remove sentence 9
   (5) no revision is necessary

8. Sentence 10: **White paint, taped stakes, or other clearly visible signs, are acceptable.**

   Which correction should be made to sentence 10?

   (1) remove the comma after paint
   (2) remove the comma after signs
   (3) change are to being
   (4) change are to is
   (5) no correction is necessary

Questions 9 through 11 refer to the following paragraphs.

Protect Yourself from Home-Repair Fraud

(A)

(1) Billions of dollars are wasted each year on home repairs that are shoddy, unfinished, or never started at all. (2) Here are some ways to avoid becoming a victim of such consumer fraud.

(B)

(3) First of all, recognize the warning signs. (4) Extravagant promises or free merchandise are usually cause for suspicion. (5) Another questionable tactic is an offer of a lower price if you refer potential customers, called a kickback. (6) Contracts should be free of tricky phrases or vague language, and they should match the promises of the sales pitch. (7) Take your time before signing, and resist pressure to sign right away.

(C)

(8) Once you have chosen a home-repair contractor, there are additional ways to protect your investment. (9) You should never pay in cash, and do not pay the whole amount before the work begins. (10) Reputable contractors rarely expect this kind of payment. (11) Instead, they usually agree to payments in thirds or quarters. (12) For example, the contractor will receive one third at the start, one third halfway through the job, and the final third upon completion of the job. (13) Ask to see the licences of the workers who are hired. (14) Make sure written contracts clearly spell out the cost of materials and labour, as well as the start and finish dates.

(D)

(15) In summary, be alert to the warning signs when someone offers to repair your home. (16) Do'nt hesitate to refuse an offer that seems too good to be true. (17) Finally, contact the authorities if you believe that you have been a victim of fraud.

9. Sentence 4: **Extravagant promises or free merchandise are usually cause for suspicion.**

Which correction should be made to sentence 4?

(1) change promises to promise's
(2) insert a comma after promises
(3) change are to is
(4) replace for with four
(5) no correction is necessary

10. Sentence 5: **Another questionable tactic is an offer of a lower price if you refer potential customers, called a kickback.**

The most effective revision of sentence 5 would begin with which group of words?

(1) Another questionable tactic for referring potential customers,
(2) Another questionable tactic, called a kickback,
(3) For referring potential customers, a questionable tactic
(4) A kickback for referring potential customers, known as a questionable tactic,
(5) Offering a lower price for a kickback is another

11. Sentence 16: **Do'nt hesitate to refuse an offer that seems too good to be true.**

Which correction should be made to sentence 16?

(1) change Do'nt to Don't
(2) change hesitate to have hesitated
(3) replace seems with seams
(4) replace too with to
(5) no correction is necessary

Questions 12 through 14 refer to the following memo.

TO: All Fitness Staff
FROM: Rikke Benson
RE: Committee Report on Temporary Staff

(A)

(1) This is a summary of last month's report on Bellmore fitness centres' use of temporary staff. (2) Bellmore hires about 60 temporary office workers each season. (3) These temps help in various departments among our 36 fitness centres. (4) Temps cover reception desks, complete filing, order sportswear and equipment, and fill in for regular staff. (5) Bellmore hires temps so that various departments can complete projects as well as screen prospective permanent workers.

(B)

(6) In their report, the committee identified and explored the following issues. (7) Without direct fitness-centre experience, problems for our clients are created by more than one half of the temporary hires. (8) Because temps are hired for a maximum of three months, they receive very little training. (9) These workers are not motivated to solve problems. (10) Unresolved problems create a poor atmosphere for clients and staff alike. (11) In response to this report, Human Resources Director Jane Chu and I are looking for volunteers to work on a brief and practical employee manual for temporary workers.

(C)

(12) Such a handbook would define roles, clarify procedures, and orient new workers quickly and efficiently. (13) If you want to participate in this worthwhile project, please contact Jane or I. (14) I'm sure that this project will make everyone's job a little easier.

12. Sentence 1: **This is a summary of last month's report on Bellmore fitness centres' use of temporary staff.**

Which correction should be made to sentence 1?

(1) change month's to months
(2) change Bellmore to bellmore
(3) change fitness centres' to Fitness Centres'
(4) change centres' to centre's
(5) no correction is necessary

13. Sentence 7: **Without direct fitness-centre experience, problems for our clients are created by more than one half of the temporary hires.**

If you rewrote sentence 7 beginning with

Because they have no direct fitness-centre experience,

the next words should be

(1) more than one half of the temporary hires create
(2) problems are created for our clients by more than one half
(3) creating problems for our clients by more than one half
(4) and because they create problems for more than one half
(5) our clients have problems created by more than one half

14. Sentence 13: **If you want to participate in this worthwhile project, please contact Jane or I.**

Which correction should be made to sentence 13?

(1) change want to wants
(2) replace to with too
(3) remove the comma
(4) insert so after the comma
(5) replace I with me

Questions 15 through 18 refer to the following business report summary.

Annual Report of
United Grain Operations, Inc.

(A)

(1) United Grain Operations (UGO) has much to celebrate in this, its centennial year. (2) It was one century ago that two grain magnates, May Foods and Brans United, merged their rival firms. (3) In a stroke, they created the great UGO. (4) UGO's cereal products soon became household names and spawned an empire. (5) Today, not only does UGO continue to dominate the ready-to-eat cereal industry, but its other divisions compete strongly as well. (6) We were quite pleased with United Corn Oil's performance last year, and this was despite a tough business environment. (7) UCO listed record profits and began negotiations with several Western ethanol processors. (8) In addition, United Seed Company continues to dominate their market. (9) Sales have reached record levels for the third straight year. (10) Finally, United Mills was named one of the top 100 performers of the year by *Investors* magazine.

(B)

(11) The full annual report will detail UGO's on-going, as well as proposed, business ventures for its second century. (12) The report will be on your desks next week.

15. Sentences 3 and 4: **In a stroke, they created the great UGO. UGO's cereal products soon became household names and spawned an empire.**

    The most effective combination of sentences 3 and 4 would include which group of words?

    (1) UGO, whose cereal
    (2) UGO, and their cereal
    (3) creating the great UGO cereal products
    (4) UGO, becoming household names
    (5) created cereal products and became

16. Sentence 6: **We were quite pleased with United Corn Oil's performance last <u>year, and this was despite</u> a tough business environment.**

    Which is the best way to write the underlined portion of this sentence? If the original is the best way, choose option (1).

    (1) year, and this was despite
    (2) year and this despite
    (3) year. And this despite
    (4) year, despite
    (5) year. This being despite

17. Sentence 8: **In addition, United Seed Company continues to dominate their market.**

    Which correction should be made to sentence 8?

    (1) remove the comma after <u>addition</u>
    (2) change <u>Company</u> to <u>company</u>
    (3) change <u>continues</u> to <u>continue</u>
    (4) replace <u>to</u> with <u>too</u>
    (5) replace <u>their</u> with <u>its</u>

18. Which revision would improve the effectiveness of this business report?

    Begin a new paragraph

    (1) with sentence 5
    (2) with sentence 6
    (3) with sentence 7
    (4) with sentence 8
    (5) with sentence 10

Questions 19 through 21 refer to the following paragraphs.

The Oscars

(A)

(1) "May I have the envelope, please?" (2) Just hearing those words is enough to send a shiver of anticipation through the whole audience. (3) Soon a film nominee will receive an Oscar, the oldest and best known award of the academy of Motion Picture Arts and Sciences. (4) The statue is one of the most coveted awards. (5) Stands only 25.5 cm high and weighs about three kilograms.

(B)

(6) Some of the awards are for artistic work, such as best picture, best director, best actor, or best song. (7) Other awards are also given in a number of technical categories, such as film editing or sound effects. (8) Occasionally, the academy also presents a special prize called the Lifetime Achievement Award. (9) This prize is given to a member of the motion picture industry, based on his or her entire body of work rather than on a particular film.

(C)

(10) The Academy Awards ceremony has also become a popular television show each spring. (11) It is a showcase of talent, films, and personalities in the entertainment industry. (12) Oscars are the most sought-after awards by actors and actresses because Oscars are universally admired. (13) In addition, any film that wins one or more Oscars is almost guaranteed to see its profits soar.

19. Sentence 3: **Soon a film nominee will receive an Oscar, the oldest and best known award of the academy of Motion Picture Arts and Sciences.**

    Which correction should be made to sentence 3?

    (1) change nominee to Nominee
    (2) remove the comma
    (3) insert a comma after oldest
    (4) change Arts and Sciences to arts and sciences
    (5) change academy to Academy

20. Sentences 4 and 5: **The statue is one of the most coveted awards. Stands only 25.5 cm high and weighs about three kilograms.**

    Which is the best way to write the underlined portion of these sentences? If the original is the best way, choose option (1).

    (1) awards. Stands
    (2) awards, yet it
    (3) awards, it
    (4) awards, stands
    (5) awards stands

21. Which sentence would be most effective if inserted at the beginning of paragraph B?

    (1) Oscars are awarded in many film categories.
    (2) Most people are thrilled to be presented with the awards.
    (3) Stars wear glamorous clothing to the ceremony.
    (4) Some nominees do not attend the ceremony.
    (5) Sometimes an entire group wins an Oscar.

Questions 22 through 25 refer to the following paragraphs.

Postal Delivery: Then and Now

(A)

(1) The U.S. Postal Service has come a long way since its founding by Ben Franklin in the late 1700s. (2) A multi-talented man, Franklin represented the new nation in Europe and gave us countless clever inventions. (3) Back then, it took weeks for mail to travel across the 13 states. (4) About 100 years later, the Pony Express took up to ten days to carry mail from Missouri West to California. (5) In this century, however, came the swift trains, the efficient trucks, and finally, fastest of all, came the speedy airplanes. (6) Today, according to the post office, most first-class mail within the 50 states is delivered within three days, while mail out of the country takes five to six days.

(B)

(7) In addition to speed, the cost of mailing a letter has also changed. (8) The cost of first class mail has rose dramatically since colonial days. (9) One ounce of first class mail cost less than 5 cents to mail in 1800. (10) By 2000, the cost was up to 33 cents. (11) Many people are upset by the cost of postage. (12) Costs relatively less now than in 1800. (13) The U.S. Postal Service, despite its faults, do the finest job in the world delivering mail fast and accurately.

22. Sentence 4: **About 100 years later, the Pony Express took up to ten days to carry mail from Missouri West to California.**

    Which correction should be made to sentence 4?

    (1) remove the comma after <u>later</u>
    (2) change <u>Pony Express</u> to <u>pony express</u>
    (3) change <u>took</u> to <u>been taken</u>
    (4) insert a <u>comma</u> after <u>days</u>
    (5) change <u>West</u> to <u>west</u>

23. Sentence 8: **The cost of first class mail has rose dramatically since colonial days.**

    Which correction should be made to sentence 8?

    (1) change <u>has</u> to <u>have</u>
    (2) change <u>rose</u> to <u>risen</u>
    (3) insert a comma after <u>dramatically</u>
    (4) change <u>colonial</u> to <u>Colonial</u>
    (5) no correction is necessary

24. Sentences 11 and 12: **Many people are upset by the cost of <u>postage. Costs</u> relatively less now than in 1800.**

    Which is the best way to write the underlined portion of these sentences? If the original is the best way, choose option (1).

    (1) postage. Costs
    (2) postage, costs
    (3) postage, costing
    (4) postage costs
    (5) postage, yet it costs

25. Sentence 13: **The U.S. Postal Service, despite its faults, <u>do</u> the finest job in the world delivering mail fast and accurately.**

    Which is the best way to write the underlined portion of this sentence? If the original is the best way, choose option (1).

    (1) do
    (2) are doing
    (3) have done
    (4) will do
    (5) does

Questions 26 through 29 refer to the following paragraphs.

Safe Bunk Beds

(A)

(1) Bunk beds have long been a favourite space-saving solution for cramped quarters and children usually love the drama of climbing up the ladder to bed. (2) Unfortunately, for years these beds have also been a safety hazard. (3) Recently, the government issued strict standards to protect children from injury. (4) Here is some useful tips that can help every "bunker" have a safe night's sleep.

(B)

(5) First of all, find out whether your bunk bed was manufactured after the standards were issued. (6) Look for a permanent label with information about the bed's date of manufacture, company of distribution, and model. (7) Missing this label, you can assume the bed does not meet the standards. (8) You will probably want to buy a new one.

26. Sentence 1: **Bunk beds have long been a favourite space-saving solution for cramped quarters and children usually love the drama of climbing up the ladder to bed.**

    Which is the best way to write the underlined portion of this sentence? If the original is the best way, choose option (1).

    (1) quarters and
    (2) quarters, and
    (3) quarters and,
    (4) quarters. And
    (5) quarters, and,

27. Sentence 4: **Here is some useful tips that can help every "bunker" have a safe night's sleep.**

    Which correction should be made to sentence 4?

    (1) change is to are
    (2) insert a comma after tips
    (3) change have to has
    (4) change night's to nights'
    (5) change night's to nights

28. Sentence 7: **Missing this label, you can assume the bed does not meet the standards.**

    The most effective revision of sentence 7 would begin with which group of words?

    (1) You don't have the label
    (2) Not having information labeling,
    (3) If this label is missing,
    (4) It doesn't have a label
    (5) A label that is missing

29. Sentence 8: **You will probably want to buy a new one.**

    Which revision would improve the effectiveness of sentence 8?

    (1) move sentence 8 to follow sentence 5
    (2) replace You with If that's the case, you
    (3) replace You with Finally, you
    (4) move sentence 8 to the beginning of paragraph B
    (5) remove sentence 8

Questions 30 through 32 refer to the following letter.

Ms Elaine Stockwell, Hiring Manager
Fare Safe Hotels
Halifax, NS B3J 2S9

Dear Ms Stockwell:

(A)

(1) The customer service trainee position that you advertised in Sunday's *Daily News* greatly interests me. (2) Fare Safe Hotels have always stood for comfortable accommodations with courteous service, and they are reasonably priced. (3) I would like to be part of Fare Safe's continued growth. (4) My aunt always stays at the Fare Safe Hotel when she visits, and she thinks it's great.

(B)

(5) As you seen from the résumé I have attached, I possess the qualifications and determination needed for the trainee position. (6) In June, I received my high-school equivalency certificate. (7) While I was attending school and studying to pass the GED Test, I developed strong organizational skills. (8) Furthermore, my part-time job at the information desk of the Halifax infirmary requires extensive interpersonal and public relations skills. (9) My supervisor gave me high scores on all my work reviews. (10) I received a commendation for exceptional service to patients. (11) I believe that these experiences are fine preparation for your training program in customer service.

(C)

(12) I would appreciate the opportunity to discuss my qualifications with you. (13) To set up an interview, please call me at 902-500-0000. (14) Thank you for your kind consideration.

Sincerely,
William Beaupré

30. Sentence 5: **As you seen from the résumé I have attached, I possess the qualifications and determination needed for the trainee position.**

    Which is the best way to write the underlined portion of this sentence? If the original is the best way, choose option (1).

    (1) seen
    (2) will have seen
    (3) have been seeing
    (4) will be seen
    (5) will see

31. Which revision would improve the effectiveness of the letter?

    (1) move sentence 1 to the end of paragraph A
    (2) remove sentence 3
    (3) remove sentence 4
    (4) move sentence 5 to the end of paragraph A
    (5) no revision is necessary

32. Sentence 8: **Furthermore, my part-time job at the information desk of the Halifax infirmary requires extensive interpersonal and public relations skills.**

    Which correction should be made to sentence 8?

    (1) remove the comma after Furthermore
    (2) insert a comma after job
    (3) change infirmary to Infirmary
    (4) change requires to require
    (5) change relations to relation's

Customer Service Department
Fuller Stores
67 Sunset Avenue
Edmonton, AB T5K 0L2

To Whom It May Concern:

(A)

(1) Yesterday morning, I had gone to the Fuller Store in St. Albert to purchase the Media Radio that was advertised in the Sunday paper. (2) According to the advertisement, the model X12 radio would be available at all stores for $47.95.

(B)

(3) Unfortunately, I had several problems in the home entertainment department in St. Albert. (4) First, I had to wait ten minutes before even seeing any sales clerk. (5) When I finally spoke to a clerk, he said that the store didn't carry the model at all. (6) Then a second clerk said the model was out of stock. (7) At that point, I found Joe Forest, who was the supervisor. (8) Joe Forest said that the store did carry the radio, but it wasn't on sale. (9) Since I hadn't brought the ad with me I could not show it to him. (10) Before I could ask him to check, he disappeared. (11) I was about to leave when I spotted the radio, on sale at the right price. (12) I purchased it immediately and left. (13) My experience at the store was so frustrating, however, that I won't shop there again. (14) If you want to keep customers, I suggest you improve your staff training right away.

Sincerely,

Arvis Black

33. Sentence 1: **Yesterday morning, I had gone to the Fuller Store in St. Albert to purchase the Media Radio that was advertised in the Sunday paper.**

Which is the best way to write the underlined portion of this sentence? If the original is the best way, choose option (1).

(1) had gone
(2) have went
(3) has gone
(4) was going
(5) went

34. Sentences 7 and 8: **At that point, I found Joe Forest, who was the supervisor. Joe Forest said that the store did carry the radio, but it wasn't on sale.**

The most effective combination of sentences 7 and 8 would include which group of words?

(1) Joe Forest, the supervisor, who said
(2) Joe Forest, who was the supervisor and who said
(3) Joe Forest, being the supervisor, who said
(4) supervisor, and Joe Forest said
(5) supervisor, so he said

35. Sentence 9: **Since I hadn't brought the ad with me I could not show it to him.**

Which correction should be made to sentence 9?

(1) remove Since
(2) change hadn't to had'nt
(3) insert a comma after me
(4) change show to shown
(5) replace it with the ad

Questions 36 through 39 refer to the following paragraphs.

Transforming Inventions

(A)

(1) We have come a long way since the fifteenth century, when johannes gutenberg invented the printing press. (2) Today's Internet sends bookloads of text around the world in seconds. (3) Yet the printing press had its own dramatic effect on human culture and the flow of ideas.

(B)

(4) All written material was done by hand. (5) There were few books and very little written information. (6) It took an hour or more to hand print a page. (7) An entire book such as the Bible would take months or even years to finish. (8) With the printing press, many copies could quickly and easily be made of a page once type for that page had been set. (9) It meant information could spread more widely and rapidly, allowing people to become more educated and knowledge to advance. (10) The printing press may be the single most important invention ever made and yet exception may be taken to that if you consider the personal computer.

(C)

(11) Today, computers give us the Internet and instant access to millions of books and massive amounts of information. (12) In fact, some people say we have too much information. (13) Perhaps people would have felt overwhelmed by the printing press. (14) Everyone just needs time to get used to inventions that change their lives.

36. Sentence 1: **We have come a long way since the fifteenth century, when johannes gutenberg invented the printing press.**

    Which correction should be made to sentence 1?

    (1) insert a comma after way
    (2) change century to Century
    (3) change johannes gutenberg to Johannes Gutenberg
    (4) change invented to was inventing
    (5) no correction is necessary

37. Sentence 4: **All written material was done by hand.**

    Which revision would improve the effectiveness of sentence 4?

    (1) move sentence 4 to the end of paragraph A
    (2) replace All with For instance, all
    (3) replace All with Before the invention of the printing press, all
    (4) remove sentence 4
    (5) no revision is necessary

38. Sentence 10: **The printing press may be the single most important invention ever made and yet exception may be taken to that if you consider the personal computer.**

    The most effective revision of sentence 10 would include which group of words?

    (1) made, yet taking exception to that
    (2) Either the printing press or the personal computer is the single most important
    (3) Taking exception to the printing press being
    (4) made except, perhaps, for the personal computer
    (5) made, yet considering the personal computer

39. Sentence 13: **Perhaps people would have felt overwhelmed by the printing press.**

    Which is the best way to write the underlined portion of this sentence? If the original is the best way, choose option (1).

    (1) would have felt
    (2) have felt
    (3) felt
    (4) had felt
    (5) feel

Answers start on page 743.

Unit 2

ESSAY

The GED Language Arts, Writing, Part II Test will cover the following content and skills.

The Test

- One assigned essay topic
- 45 minutes to complete

The Content

Two evaluators will score your essay based on the following features:
- Well-focused main points
- Clear organization
- Specific development of your ideas
- Control of sentence structure, punctuation, grammar, word choice, and spelling

The Essay

On the essay you must
- Write legibly in ink
- Write on the assigned topic
- Write your essay on the lined pages of the separate answer sheet booklet

"SNL [Saturday Night Live] was a valuable experience. I learned how to write on a deadline."

~Chris Rock
GED graduate

Comedian Chris Rock has made a name for himself as a writer. Week after week, Rock wrote skits under unforgiving deadlines for *Saturday Night Live.* After three seasons with the late-night comedy series, he moved on to star in movies, comedy specials, and his own TV series, making two Grammy-winning recordings, and authoring the book *Rock This!* In 1997, he won two Emmy awards for his comedy special *Bring On the Pain!* and was nominated for best writing for his work on *Politically Incorrect with Bill Maher.* The year 1999 brought Rock another Emmy for outstanding writing, and in 2000 he was nominated four times.

By writing high-quality skits each week for *Saturday Night Live,* Chris Rock polished his writing skills. Unit 2 presents a step-by-step approach to the skills you need to write an effective essay, then offers many opportunities to polish these skills. You will have plenty of practice developing and organizing your ideas and then stating your thoughts clearly. The Unit Review includes essay topics, so you can practise writing a well-developed essay within the time allowed for the GED Test.

Don't be intimidated by the 45-minute deadline on the GED Essay Test. Just as GED graduate Chris Rock learned to write on a deadline, you can learn to organize your ideas and get them on paper within the time limit. It just takes practice.

Study Tip

Knowing the test formats helps you to prepare.

Avoid nervousness and mistakes by familiarizing yourself with the format for each section of the GED Test.

- Know what skills you need to do well in each section.
- Know what types of questions to expect.
- Know how much time you have to complete each section.

Planning

On Part II of the GED Language Arts, Writing Test, you will have 45 minutes to write an essay on an assigned topic. Because you are expected to write only one draft, you should spend about five minutes planning your essay. Thinking about the topic and then gathering ideas, examples, and supporting details are critical to creating a successful GED essay. That is why the first step in the writing process is planning.

Understanding the Writing Assignment

The second part of the GED Language Arts, Writing Test is a **writing assignment** for an essay. This test requires you to state your view on a topic and to support that view with examples. For instance, here is a typical GED writing assignment.

writing assignment directions to write about a given topic

The **topic** is the subject of your essay. All the ideas in your essay should relate to this topic.

> Has modern technology, such as the computer, made people's lives better or worse?
>
> Write an essay to explain your view on that topic. Use your personal observations, experience, and knowledge to support your view.

The **instructions** tell what kind of information to give in your essay.

The key words *explain your view* tell what you should do in your essay. This chart contains key words commonly used in essay instructions that are clues to the kind of information you should give.

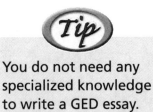

Tip

You do not need any specialized knowledge to write a GED essay.

If the instructions say	You should
explain why state the reasons	write about causes or reasons
explain the effects discuss the advantages and disadvantages	write about effects
describe	discuss the qualities of something
state your position present your view give your opinion	tell what you think about an issue and why

discuss the similarities and
    differences
compare and contrast
	explain how things are alike
	    and different

GED Practice

Read each GED writing assignment. Then underline key words and write the kind of information you should give. Use the chart on page 158 to help you.

TOPIC 1

What is a true friend?

Write an essay that describes what a true friend is. Use your personal observations, experience, and knowledge to support your view.

Kind of information: _____

TOPIC 2

Some people believe it is harmful for both parents of a preschool child to work outside the home, others do not feel this way.

State your point of view in an essay. Give specific examples to support your view. Use your personal observations, experience, and knowledge.

Kind of information: _____

TOPIC 3

How does the climate in your region affect you and the other people who live there?

Write an essay explaining both the advantages and disadvantages of living in your climate. Use your personal observations, experience, and knowledge to support your view.

Kind of information: _____

TOPIC 4

Despite laws that require people to wear seat belts, many people still do not wear them.

Write an essay that explains why people do not buckle up. Use your personal observations, experience, and knowledge to support your view.

Kind of information: _____

TOPIC 5

How important is having a GED or a high-school diploma when you apply for a job?

In an essay, tell your point of view. Give specific examples to support your view. Use your personal observations, experience, and knowledge.

Kind of information: _____

Answers start on page 747.

Gathering Your Ideas

gathering ideas
when a writer lists related ideas about a topic to support a main idea

list
when a writer jots down ideas in the order he or she thinks of them

idea map
a way of recording ideas that shows their relationship to the topic and to each other

Once you understand the writing assignment, you are ready to begin **gathering ideas.** For your essay to receive a good grade, you need a variety of specific ideas and examples. Use your own observations, experience, and knowledge to gather ideas that you can write about easily.

To gather ideas, spend about five minutes thinking about the topic and writing down all the ideas that come to mind. Then stop and review what you have written. This review may help you think of more ideas.

One way to record your ideas is to make a **list.** When you make a list, you write your ideas in the order you think of them.

Another way to record your ideas for an essay is to make an **idea map.** When you make an idea map, you write down ideas in a way that shows their relationship to the topic and to each other.

Look at how two students wrote their ideas about seat belt laws. One student wrote a list and the other made an idea map.

Student 1's List

Topic: *Should seat belt laws be enforced?*

– *save lives*

– *people are more careful*

– *cities make money on fines*

– *people would not use them*

Student 2's Idea Map

can't get out of car after accident

Topic: Should seat belt laws be enforced?

people should make their own decisions

government controls too much

GED Practice

Read each essay topic. Then write a list of five or six ideas or create an idea map about it. Create your own idea map or use a copy of the blank idea map on page 897.

TOPIC 1: How watching television affects people

TOPIC 2: How being a sports fan affects your life

TOPIC 3: The importance of having a GED or high-school diploma

TOPIC 4: The influence of popular music on young people

Answers start on page 747.

Determining Your Main Idea

After you gather ideas on a topic, you need to determine the **main idea** of your essay. The main idea is the most important point you are trying to make about the topic. To determine your main idea, look at all your ideas and try to figure out what they have in common.

For example, if the topic is about the positive and negative effects of technology, see whether your ideas are mostly positive effects, negative effects, or both. If you wrote mostly positive effects, your main idea might be *Overall, technology has had many positive effects on society.*

Look at the list of ideas gathered for this topic.

TOPIC: Are there more advantages or disadvantages to owning a car?

> have to pay for insurance
> pollutes the air more than public transportation
> buying and upkeep cost more than taking the bus
> can go where you want, when you want
> not always easy to find parking
> have privacy in a car

Put a check mark by the sentence that best states the main idea of this list.

_____ (a) Owning a car has many advantages.

_____ (b) Car ownership has many disadvantages.

Most of the ideas relate to the problems that car owners have. Therefore, a good main idea for this list would be *option (b).*

Read the topic and ideas below. Write a main idea statement.

TOPIC: Is it better to own or rent your home?

> renters have to depend on the landlord for repairs
> buying a home is a good investment
> if you own, you're responsible for repairs and maintenance
> renters can be forced to move when lease is up
> rents can increase suddenly
> have to pay property taxes if you own

Main idea statement: _____

_____

Most of the ideas listed are advantages of owning a home. Therefore, your main idea statement should be something such as *Owning your home is better than renting.*

GED Practice

A. Read the topics and ideas below. Write a main idea statement for each.

TOPIC 1: Causes of homelessness

> living paycheque to paycheque, costly crisis happens
> drug use
> abused kids go live on the street
> not enough low-income housing available

Main idea statement: _____

TOPIC 2: How can you take an affordable trip?

> stay with friends or family
> get list of cheap restaurants
> drive or take bus instead of flying
> book tickets early
> travel with friends and split the cost

Main idea statement: _____

B. Look at the ideas that you wrote on page 161. Write a main idea statement for each list or idea map.

TOPIC 1: How watching television affects people

> **Main idea statement:** _____

TOPIC 2: How being a sports fan affects your life

> **Main idea statement:** _____

TOPIC 3: The importance of having a GED or high-school diploma

> **Main idea statement:** _____

TOPIC 4: The influence of popular music on young people

> **Main idea statement:** _____

C. Here are some additional topics. Make an idea map or list and then write a main idea statement for each.

TOPIC 1: The benefits of regular exercise

> **Main idea statement:** _____

TOPIC 2: The similarities and differences between men's and women's personalities

> **Main idea statement:** _____

TOPIC 3: Causes of stress in modern life

> **Main idea statement:** _____

Answers start on page 747.

Review your understanding of planning skills by answering the questions about the sample GED essay topic below. For more tips on developing your personal writing strategy, see pages 909 and 911.

TOPIC

Is life better in a city or in a small town?

Explain your point of view in an essay. Use your personal observations, experience, and knowledge to support your view.

---

1. Underline the key words in the instructions.

2. What kind of information do these key words tell you to include in your essay?

   _____

   _____

3. Think about the topic. What are two methods that you could use to gather your ideas about this topic?

   _____

   _____

   _____

4. Once you have gathered ideas on the topic, see what the ideas have in common. What do you do once you recognize what your ideas have in common?

   _____

   _____

   _____

   _____

Answers start on page 747.

Organizing

The second step in the writing process is organizing. In this lesson, you will learn how to divide your ideas into groups and how to label the groups. Because an effective GED essay depends on having many good ideas and examples, you will also practise expanding your groups of ideas and putting them in logical order. These idea groups will become the basis for your paragraphs.

Grouping and Labelling

Once you have some ideas about a topic, your next step is grouping the ideas and labelling the groups. Each group of ideas will become a paragraph that supports the main idea of your essay.

To group ideas, see what the ideas on your list have in common. Put these ideas in a group and label, or name, the group to show how it relates to the main idea. Then group other related ideas and label them. If an idea does not fit in any group, cross it out.

Here is the way one student grouped her ideas about how watching TV affects people. First, she listed all the ideas that came to mind.

Tip

Get rid of unrelated ideas before you start writing. This can keep you on the topic.

Main idea: Watching TV has both good and bad effects.

The Effects of Watching TV
violence seems to be everywhere
keeps people from reading
keeps people from doing active things
TVs cost a lot
informs
provides an escape from everyday life
entertainment
ads make people want things

Next, she looked for ways to group her ideas. To do this, she looked for ideas that were related. She circled all the ideas that were good effects and labelled them. Then she did the same for the bad effects.

After sorting out her ideas, she realized that one idea—*TVs cost a lot*—was not an effect at all, so she crossed that idea off her list.

The student's groups of ideas looked like this:

The Effects of Watching TV

> violence seems to be everywhere
> keeps people from reading
> keeps people from doing active things

~~TVs cost a lot~~

Bad effects

> informs
> provides an escape
>   from everyday life
> entertainment

— Good effects

> ads make people want things

It is usually not difficult to divide your list of ideas into two groups. However, to write a well-developed essay, it is helpful to have three groups of related ideas. These three groups will contain the ideas for the three middle, supporting paragraphs of your essay. If you divide your larger group into two groups, each of your three groups can become a supporting paragraph of your essay.

To make her three groups, the student noticed that she could make two groups from the larger group—*the bad effects of TV*. One group could include things that were unrealistic about TV. The other could include things that watching TV kept people from doing.

Bad Effects

False Sense of Life

want too many
    things (ads)

violence seems to
    be everywhere

_Keeps People from
Better Things_

reading

doing active
    things

If the writer had used an idea map, many of her ideas would already be grouped and connected. She would need only to label the different groups, like this:

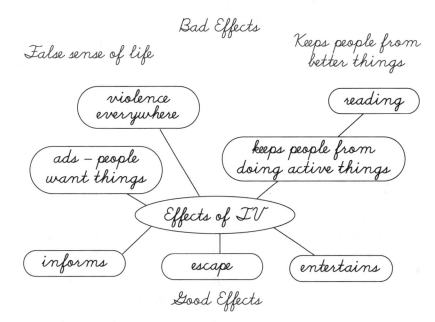

Read the three groups of ideas for the topic "What are the pros and cons of having a hobby?" Put a check mark next to the idea that does not fit with any of the groups. In which group does the other idea belong?

____ (a) bowling is my hobby

____ (b) may become too involved, lose interest in other things

The Pros and Cons of Having a Hobby

Pros		Cons
Practical Reasons	**Emotional or Social Reasons**	
can learn things	have fun	may neglect things that need to be done
can develop new skills	relieve stress	
	may meet people with similar interests	may spend too much money

You are correct if you chose *option (a)* because it does not fit in any of the groups. *Option (b)* belongs in the group *Cons* because it is another possible negative effect of having a hobby.

Ordering Your Groups

You need to take one more step before you write your essay. You must choose a logical order in which to present your groups. Because each of your three groups of ideas will become a paragraph in your essay, the order is important. You want the paragraphs ordered in a way that makes your essay strong and convincing.

There are several ways to order ideas. For a GED essay, two useful methods are order of importance and compare and contrast.

Order of Importance

order of importance a method of essay writing that starts with the least important ideas and ends with the most important

You can rank your groups of ideas from least important to most important and write about them in **order of importance.** Because this kind of organization builds from the weakest ideas to the strongest ideas, the last thing a reader sees and the thing that stays in a reader's mind is the most important point.

The paragraphs below are from an essay about seat belt laws. The ideas are in order of importance. Notice how the words in colour help you, the reader, understand the order of ideas.

> Seat belt laws are a source of money for cities. People ticketed for not wearing seat belts must pay fines, and this money can be used for roadway maintenance.
> Even more important, seat belt laws improve traffic safety. Just by buckling up, people are reminded to drive more safely.
> But the most important reason that seat belt laws are wise is that they save lives. Countless numbers of people are alive today because they were wearing their seat belts when they had accidents. Countless more have been saved from serious injury.

The writer placed his reasons for supporting seat belt laws in order from least important to most important. The most important reason, saving lives, is the last one to be read. It leaves you, the reader, with the strongest impression.

Try reading the paragraphs in the opposite order of the way they are written. How does it change the effectiveness of the essay?

_____

_____

If you read the most important reason first, the other reasons seem less significant. But when you read the least important reason first, it seems valid, and each additional reason adds to the argument.

These words signal that ideas are organized in order of importance: _more important, most important, better, best._

Compare and Contrast

When you compare things, you show how they are alike. When you contrast things, you show how they are different. A GED writing assignment may ask you to **compare and contrast** two things, such as the problems of the past and those we encounter today. Or it may ask you to **contrast** different sides of a topic, such as the advantages and disadvantages (or pros and cons) of a night-shift job.

The student organized her essay about the effects of watching TV by contrasting the positive and negative effects. Pay attention to the phrases in colour. They show how the ideas are ordered.

> There is no doubt that watching television can have positive effects. On the one hand, adults can keep informed about current events by watching the evening news. They may even gain some practical knowledge about their health and other personal concerns. Children can learn from educational shows such as *Sesame Street*. In addition, everyone can be entertained and even escape a little with cartoons, comedies, and action shows.
>
> On the other hand, watching television has some definite negative effects. Instead of just using it as a temporary escape, some people may watch television rather than deal with their problems. TV also keeps people from spending time with their family or from reading. In fact, it turns some people into couch potatoes, keeping them from any physical activity.
>
> In addition, television gives people a false sense of what life is like. They see commercials on TV and feel they must have what's being advertised. They see violence on shows and think modern life is more violent than it really is, or they may even think it is all right to act violently.

By contrasting the negative and positive effects of watching television, the student got her main idea across effectively. She used her first paragraph to discuss the good effects. She used her second paragraph to discuss some of the bad effects, and she signalled this contrast with the words *on the other hand*. She used her third paragraph to discuss more negative effects.

Try reading the paragraphs in the opposite order of the way they are written. How does it change the effectiveness of the essay?

_____

_____

A writer's strongest arguments should come near the end of the essay. Because there are more negative effects than positive effects—enough for two paragraphs—placing them last focuses attention on them. When the paragraph on positive effects is placed at the end, the essay is less effective. It weakens the writer's negative view of TV. Is that how you felt as you read the paragraphs in the opposite order?

These words signal a comparison: *both, also, similarly, like.* These words signal a contrast: *on the other hand, in contrast, however, but, whereas, while.*

GED Practice

For each essay topic, determine the method of organization and the order of ideas you think would best support the main idea. Number the groups in that order. For Topics 2 and 3, write a main idea statement.

TOPIC 1: What are the qualities of swimming that make it worthwhile?

Main idea statement: Swimming is a worthwhile sport.

Organization: _____

Benefits ___	**Little Equipment** ___	**Ease and Convenience** ___
healthy exercise	swimsuit	can do year-round
little stress on body	towel	park district pools
fun	maybe swimming goggles	beach in summer
mental relaxation		easy to learn

TOPIC 2: What effect would passing the GED Tests have on a person?

Main idea statement: _____

Organization: _____

Personal Reasons ___	**Job-Related Reasons** ___	**Educational Reasons** ___
feel good about yourself	get a more satisfying job	stronger reading and
learn how not to quit	earn more money	math skills
more confidence	better chance for promotion	chance to go on to further
		education or training

TOPIC 3: What are the positive and negative effects of society's emphasis on being thin?

Main idea statement: _____

Organization: _____

Bad Effects on Society ___	**Good Effects on Health** ___	**Bad Effects on Individuals** ___
children learn to make fun of overweight people	many people eat well and exercise	feel bad about yourself if not thin
people judge by appearance	fewer health problems	some become obsessed with thinness
overweight people are discriminated against	fewer medical costs related to obesity	some try unsafe diets
		could lead to anorexia

Answers start on page 747.

Review your understanding of organizing skills by answering the questions about the sample GED essay topic below. For more tips on developing your personal writing strategy, see pages 909 and 911.

> **TOPIC**
>
> Is life better in a city or in a small town?
>
> Explain your point of view in an essay. Use your personal observations, experience, and knowledge to support your view.

1. You have already made a list of ideas or an idea map for this topic. What should be your first step in organizing those ideas?

   _____

   _____

2. What methods can you use to think of more ideas?

   _____

   _____

   _____

   _____

   _____

3. What is the best kind of organization for an essay like this one? Why?

   _____

   _____

4. In what order would you put your three groups? Why?

   _____

   _____

   _____

Answers start on page 747.

Writing

After you plan and organize your thoughts and ideas, you will be ready to write. That is why the third step in this process is writing your essay. You should spend about 25 minutes writing the first draft of your essay.

The Three Parts of an Essay

An essay has three basic parts: an introduction, a body, and a conclusion, in that order. Each part has a specific purpose.

To write a well-developed essay for the GED Test, one student read the following topic and then completed the first two steps.

> Is regular exercise important in maintaining good health?
>
> Write an essay explaining your point of view. Use your personal observations, experience, and knowledge.

Main idea: *Regular exercise is important.*

Better Health	*Look Better*	*Feel Better*
stronger heart	*lose weight*	*feel good about*
breathe better	*firm muscles*	*how you look*
more endurance	*healthier skin*	*more self-esteem*
burns calories	*and hair*	*reduces tension*
		feel more relaxed

Then the student wrote the following essay. Read it and notice how the three parts of an essay are contained in the five paragraphs.

Introduction
- one paragraph
- includes the essay topic
- tells the main idea

Many people exercise regularly, yet many others do not. If those who don't exercise knew how important it is, they would all start exercise programs. Regular exercise makes and keeps you fit. In fact, it helps you look and feel fit in addition to being fit.

Body
- three paragraphs
- develops the topic
- supports the main idea

First of all, regular exercise is good for your health. When you run, bicycle, or do some other aerobic activity regularly, your heart becomes stronger, and your breathing improves. These physical changes increase your endurance. You actually have more energy. Also, muscles that are working burn more calories.

Exercise can help improve not only your health but also your looks. Because your body burns more calories, you lose weight and look slimmer and trimmer. Your muscles become firm. You seem more youthful and energetic. In addition, better circulation gives your skin a healthy glow and your hair lots of shine.

All these physical benefits lead to perhaps the most important result of regular exercise—it makes you feel better. Exercise reduces tension in your muscles and makes you more relaxed. You feel rested and ready to go during the day, and you sleep better at night. Because you look better, you also feel better about your body and about yourself. Your self-esteem increases.

Conclusion
- one paragraph
- sums up and reviews information in the body

With all these benefits of regular exercise, it's hard to understand why someone would <u>not</u> work out. If you exercise regularly, your body and your mind will appreciate it.

Paragraphs and Topic Sentences

Before you write your essay, you need to know how to develop a good paragraph. To do so, focus on the groups of ideas you wrote in step 2. Each group will become a paragraph in your essay.

Each paragraph will have a **topic sentence** that tells the main idea of the paragraph. The other ideas become the **supporting details** of the paragraph. You can write the topic sentence at the beginning, middle, or end of a paragraph. A paragraph may be written in these three ways:

Topic Sentence – Supporting Details

Supporting Details – **Topic Sentence** – Supporting Details

Supporting Details – **Topic Sentence**

Read the following paragraphs. Where are the topic sentences?

1. The cost of living has risen steadily over the past several decades. Although a loaf of bread cost 30 cents 40 years ago, today it can cost six or seven times that. Just 30 years ago, you could purchase a new car for about $4000. Today the average cost of a new car is closer to $20 000. The price of housing is another example of rising costs. In the 1960s, an apartment rented for as little as $125 a month. With today's rents, that same apartment would cost at least $600 per month.

2. Many city pools are open for free or for just a few dollars admission during the summer. Picnics are a great way to enjoy the outdoors, especially on cool summer evenings. Some local parks have theater productions or live music for free—you only need to bring your lawn chair. Recreational centres provide a variety of activities for all ages, from movies to bowling. Amusement parks and long vacations may be the summer tradition, but even a family on a budget can have a great summer.

The first sentence of paragraph 1 is the topic sentence. It tells the main idea of the paragraph. The rest of the sentences support the paragraph's main idea with details that contrast the prices of bread, cars, and housing with their prices a few decades ago. In paragraph 2, the topic sentence is the last sentence. It states the main idea of the paragraph.

topic sentence
the sentence that tells the main idea of the paragraph

supporting details
additional ideas that give more information about the main idea

GED Practice

Read the paragraph. Then answer the questions.

1.   A good worker is someone who understands how important it is not to be absent too often and who gets the job done. People seldom get fired because the quality of their work is poor. Instead, more people lose their jobs for such things as not showing up for work or not doing their job. Managers need to know that they can count on their workers to be on the job. Employers have little tolerance for workers who talk so much with their co-workers that they can't finish a job.

a. What is the paragraph about? _____

_____

b. Underline the topic sentence.

c. List some supporting details. _____

_____

_____

_____

_____

Write a topic sentence for each paragraph.

2.   Smoking cigarettes is bad for your health. In fact, tobacco use in any form has been proven harmful. Thousands of people die each year from lung cancer, and thousands more die from heart disease that is linked to smoking. In addition, smoking is an expensive habit. Heavy smokers may spend more than $7 per day on cigarettes. That adds up to about $210 a month! Think of all the things a person could buy with that money.

_____

_____

_____

3.   There are consumer groups you can go to for financial help. They will review your finances and advise you on how to reduce your debt. They will help you make a budget to pay your creditors. They will even tell you if your financial situation is so complicated that you need to see a lawyer. People to whom you owe money will often work with you as well. They may be willing to reduce your monthly payments so that you can afford to pay them. Most important, you can learn to live within your means.

_____

_____

_____

Answers start on page 748.

Writing Your Introductory Paragraph

A good introductory paragraph does several things:
- It tells what your topic and main idea are.
- It gives a preview of your essay.
- It may provide background information.

thesis statement
a sentence that tells the topic of an essay

The topic of an essay is stated in a sentence called the **thesis statement.** This sentence is the main idea of the whole essay. You can write the thesis statement by rewriting your main idea from step 1. Expand the main idea by adding words that help explain or strengthen the statement. This example shows how a student expanded her main idea into a thesis statement.

Main idea: I like TV comedies.
Thesis statement: Of all the many different kinds of TV shows, comedies are my favourite.

preview sentences
sentences in the introduction that tell your reader what to expect in the essay

A good introductory paragraph has one or more **preview sentences.** Preview sentences tell your reader what to expect in the essay. To write preview sentences, use your labelled groups, from step 2, and tell about them in a brief, general, and interesting way.

Finally, you can add one or two background sentences that give general information about the topic. Background sentences are not necessary, but they can help introduce your topic.

Here is the introductory paragraph from the essay on pages 172–173. In the planning stage, the main idea was "Regular exercise is important."

Underline the thesis statement. Circle the preview sentence.

Many people exercise regularly, yet many others do not. If those who don't exercise knew how important it is, they would all start exercise programs. Regular exercise makes and keeps you fit. In fact, it helps you look and feel fit in addition to being fit.

Sometimes your main idea becomes clearer after you've planned your essay. Your thesis statement can pinpoint exactly what you want to say.

The thesis statement is *Regular exercise makes and keeps you fit.* The preview sentence is *In fact, it helps you look and feel fit in addition to being fit.* It tells in general what the three middle paragraphs of the essay are about. The first two sentences of the introduction are background information.

GED Practice

Write introductory paragraphs for the topic assignments below. Follow these steps.

a. Read each topic assignment. Use steps 1 and 2 to create groups of ideas, label them, and write a main idea for each topic. Topic 1 has been done for you. Use it as a model.

b. Write an introductory paragraph for each essay. Use a separate sheet of paper for each topic.

TOPIC 1

Is it fair for professional athletes to receive such high salaries?

Explain your viewpoint in an essay. Use your personal observations, experience, and knowledge.

Main idea: Athletes earn their money.

Physical Work	**Professionals**	**Serve the Community**
requires intense training	train for a long time	act as positive role models
can be hurt or hospitalized	work hard to become pro	do commercials against drugs
chance of long-term injury	have to stay on a strict diet	work for charities
lots of effort during game	have no privacy	

TOPIC 2

How does rock music influence young people?

Write an essay that explains positive influences, negative influences, or both. Use your personal observations, experience, and knowledge.

TOPIC 3

What is the role of being a parent?

Write an essay that discusses the responsibilities, the pleasures, or both. Explain your view with details and examples. Use your personal observations, experience, and knowledge.

Answers start on page 748.

Writing Body Paragraphs

Tip

You can place a topic sentence at the beginning, middle, or end of a paragraph, but it's a good idea to put it first so that your reader knows what the paragraph is about.

Now you're ready to write the body paragraphs of your essay. The three body paragraphs develop your topic. They back up the thesis statement in your introductory paragraph with supporting ideas.

To write three body paragraphs, use your expanded groups of ideas from step 2. Follow the order you chose for the groups. Use the label you gave to the first group to help you write a topic sentence for that paragraph. Then use the ideas from the group to write supporting sentences for the paragraph. To be sure your supporting sentences stay on the topic, keep your list handy as you write.

Follow those same steps to write your next two body paragraphs.

Here are the body paragraphs from the essay about exercise on pages 172–173. Compare the paragraphs with the three groups of ideas. Notice how each underlined topic sentence tells the main idea of the paragraph. Notice also that the writer has added details that aren't in the groups. While he was writing the body paragraphs, new ideas occurred to him.

Better Health

stronger heart
breathe better
more endurance
burns calories

First of all, regular exercise is good for your health. When you run, bicycle, or do some other aerobic activity regularly, your heart becomes stronger, and your breathing improves. These physical changes increase your endurance. You actually have more energy. Also, muscles that are working burn more calories.

Look Better

lose weight
firm muscles
healthier skin
  and hair

Exercise can help improve not only your health but also your looks. Because your body burns more calories, you lose weight and look slimmer and trimmer. Your muscles become firm. You seem more youthful and energetic. In addition, better circulation gives your skin a healthy glow and your hair lots of shine.

Feel Better

feel good about
   how you look
more self-esteem
reduces tension
feel more relaxed

Tip

You can use new ideas that occur to you during any of the steps. Just be sure they support the thesis statement of the essay as well as the topic sentence of the paragraph.

All these physical benefits lead to perhaps the most important result of regular exercise — it makes you feel better. Exercise reduces tension in your muscles and makes you more relaxed. You feel rested and ready to go during the day, and you sleep better at night. Because you look better, you also feel better about your body and about yourself. Your self-esteem increases.

Look at the first group of ideas on page 177 for the essay on athletes' salaries. On a separate sheet of paper, write a topic sentence. Then write supporting sentences.

Compare your work with this sample body paragraph. The topic sentence is underlined: *A professional athlete's job requires demanding physical work. Athletes must train intensely to keep in shape. They put forth a great deal of effort during every game. In addition, athletes may be hurt during a game, and their injuries may require hospitalization. The possibility of long-term injury is a constant threat.*

GED Practice

Use your work from the GED Practice on page 177. Use the following steps for each topic assignment. Use the same paper that you used to write the introductory paragraphs.

a. Review the lists of ideas and the introductory paragraph you wrote.

b. Follow the order you chose for the lists.

c. Use the labels to write topic sentences.

d. Use the ideas in the group to write supporting sentences.

e. Add details as they come to you.

1. Write three body paragraphs justifying the high salaries of professional athletes.

2. Write three body paragraphs about whether rock music is a bad influence on young people, a positive influence, or both.

3. Write three body paragraphs about the responsibilities of being a parent, the pleasures, or both.

Answers start on page 748.

Developing Body Paragraphs

To write an effective essay, you need to develop your ideas. To develop ideas means to explain with details and examples.

When you develop the ideas in a body paragraph, you provide support for the paragraph's topic sentence. In turn, the three topic sentences of the body paragraphs support the thesis statement of your entire essay. In this way, you write a strong essay.

See how the writer of the essay on exercise gave support to some of his original ideas by adding details to explain them.

Supporting Ideas	Details in Body Paragraph
• burns calories	muscles that are working burn more calories
• lose weight	you lose weight and look slimmer and trimmer

An example names a person or explains a situation that helps illustrate what you mean. Read these examples that the writer added to the essay on exercise to illustrate his supporting ideas.

Supporting Ideas	Examples in Body Paragraph
• regular exercise	running, bicycling, or some other aerobic activity regularly
• feel more relaxed	you feel rested and ready to go during the day, and you sleep better at night

In the essay on athletes' salaries, one of the supporting ideas in the third paragraph is: "Athletes act as positive role models."

To develop this idea, think of an athlete who acted as a positive role model. What did he or she do?

_____

_____

A possible answer is *By admitting that he was HIV positive, basketball player Magic Johnson helped reduce the stigma of the disease.*

Writing Your Concluding Paragraph

The last paragraph of your essay is the concluding paragraph. It gives the same information that the introductory paragraph gives, but it is written from a different perspective. Instead of previewing the ideas in your essay, a concluding paragraph reviews them. It restates your thesis statement and sums up your supporting ideas. For example, reread the concluding paragraph from the essay about exercise.

With all these benefits of regular exercise, it's hard to understand why someone would not work out. If you exercise regularly, your body and your mind will appreciate it.

Tip

As you write your essay, you may want to add or change phrases or sentences. Leave wide margins so that you can make changes easily.

The thesis statement in the introductory paragraph was *Regular exercise makes and keeps you fit.* The last sentence in the concluding paragraph restates this idea as *If you exercise regularly, your body and your mind will appreciate it.*

The supporting details in the essay discussed three benefits of exercise—being healthy, looking better, and feeling better. These details are summed up in the phrase *With all these benefits of regular exercise.*

Finally, the conclusion also includes this strong statement about the topic that leaves an impression in the reader's mind: *it's hard to understand why someone would not work out.*

Reread the introductory and body paragraphs you wrote for the essay on athletes' salaries on pages 177 and 179. Write a concluding paragraph for the essay on the same paper.

Here is a possible concluding paragraph:
Professional athletes provide us with hours of entertainment as well as valuable service to the community, and they work extremely hard to make that possible. Considering what athletes contribute, their high salaries are more than justified. In fact, they should be paid even more.

Your concluding paragraph may be different, but it should restate your thesis statement and sum up the three main ideas from your body paragraphs. You might also have included a strong, last-impression statement.

GED Practice

Look back at the introductory and body paragraphs you wrote for the essays on rock music and parenting on pages 177 and 179. Then complete the exercises below.

1. Write a concluding paragraph for the essay about the ways that rock music influences young people.

_____

_____

_____

_____

_____

_____

_____

_____

2. Write a concluding paragraph for the essay about the responsibilities, the pleasures, or both of being a parent.

_____

_____

_____

_____

_____

_____

_____

_____

_____

Answers start on page 748.

Essay • Writing

Review your understanding of writing a first draft by answering the questions about the sample GED essay topic below. For more tips on developing your personal writing strategy, see pages 909 and 911.

TOPIC

Is life better in a city or in a small town?

Explain your point of view in an essay. Use your personal observations, experience, and knowledge to support your view.

---

1. What are the three parts you would include in an essay on this topic?

_____

_____

2. What kind of information should be in the introductory paragraph?

_____

_____

_____

3. How would you decide how many body paragraphs you should write?

_____

_____

_____

4. How would you write the topic sentence and supporting details for the body paragraphs?

_____

_____

_____

5. What kind of information should be in the concluding paragraph? How is it different from the introductory paragraph?

_____

_____

_____

Answers start on page 748.

Writing • Review
183

Evaluating

Once you have submitted your GED essay, trained essay scorers read it and assign it a score. That's why the fourth step in the writing process is evaluating your essay.

Holistic Scoring

Your essay will be scored holistically. This means that it will be judged on its overall effectiveness. To the essay scorers, the most important aspects of your essay are how clearly you present your thesis statement and how well you support it. A few errors in spelling or grammar will not cause your essay to receive a low score, although too many errors might. The essay scorers will evaluate your essay by judging how well you

- focus and develop your main points
- organize your essay
- provide specific examples and details to support your main points
- use clear and precise word choice
- use correct sentence structure, grammar, spelling, and punctuation

A sample of the complete GED Essay Scoring Guide with explanations of the characteristics that the evaluators look for when they read an essay is on page 185.

An essay that is scored 1 or 1.5 is considered failing, and that person must repeat both the multiple-choice and essay parts of the GED Language Arts, Writing Test. If your essay scores a 2 or higher, a formula is used to find a combined score for Parts I and II of the Writing Test.

Leave wide margins on your paper so that you can add ideas when you revise. Leave space between the lines to correct errors.

Remember that to score an essay holistically, you should read it once carefully, but not too slowly.

Scoring an Essay

	1 Inadequate	2 Marginal	3 Adequate	4 Effective
			Reader understands the writer's ideas and easily follows the writer's expression of ideas.	
Response to the Prompt	Reader has difficulty identifying or following the writer's ideas.	Reader occasionally has difficulty understanding or following the writer's ideas.	Reader understands the writer's ideas.	
	Attempts to address prompt but with little or no success in establishing a focus.	Addresses the prompt, though the focus may shift.	Uses the writing prompt to establish a main idea.	Presents a clearly focused main idea that addresses the prompt.
Organization	Fails to organize ideas.	Shows some evidence of an organizational plan.	Uses an identifiable organizational plan.	Establishes a clear and logical organization.
Development and Details	Demonstrates little or no development; usually lacks details or examples or presents irrelevant information.	Has some development but lacks specific details; may be limited to a listing, repetitions, or generalizations.	Has focused but occasionally uneven development; incorporates some specific detail.	Achieves coherent development with specific and relevant details and examples.
English Language Conventions (ELC)	May exhibit minimal or no control of sentence structure and the ELC.	May demonstrate inconsistent control of sentence structure and the ELC.	Generally controls sentence structure and the ELC.	Consistently controls sentence structure and ELC.
Word Choice	Exhibits weak and/or inappropriate words.	Exhibits a narrow range of word choice, often including inappropriate selections.	Exhibits appropriate word choice.	Exhibits varied and precise word choice.

Read this sample essay and the score it would likely receive.

TOPIC

Is life better in a city or in a small town?

Explain your point of view in an essay. Use your personal observations, experience, and knowledge to support your view.

Life in the big city, and life in a small town vary sharply. There are advantages as well as disadvantages to life in the city, just as there are good and bad things about small towns.

Some of the bad points to city life are high crime, over crowded housing, and heavy traffic. Life can also be very rewarding in the city, as there are more places of employment as well as intertainment.

Life in a small town moves at a slower rate. The people are friendlier, because of a lower crime rate. The housing is spaced more openly, and the highways are not as crowded, because there are less intertainment and employment oppurtunities.

In my oppinion life in the small town far out weighs life in the city because life at a slower pace is more rewarding.

This essay would likely receive a score of 2. It is organized, but the introduction does not address the topic directly by stating whether the writer believes life is better in a small town or a city. There are also some errors in the conventions of English—mainly in spelling.

Look at the scoring guide and read about the development and details in an essay that scores 2. What is another reason this essay received a 2?

The essay does not develop the details. It merely lists details in the first body paragraph and repeats them in the second body paragraph.

Essay • Evaluating

Evaluating an Essay

Five areas are considered when evaluating a GED essay—response to the prompt, organization, development and details, conventions of standard Canadian English (sentence structure, usage, spelling, capitalization, and punctuation), and word choice. You can use this checklist to help you evaluate your essay.

Tip

Trained GED evaluators read an essay once and then assign a score to it. However, when you evaluate your essay, read it more than once to see how to improve it and get a higher score.

Yes	No	**Response to the Prompt**
☐	☐	(1) Is there a clear main idea?
☐	☐	(2) Does the essay stick to the topic?

Organization

☐	☐	(3) Does the introductory paragraph include a thesis statement and a preview?
☐	☐	(4) Does each body paragraph have a topic sentence and details related to the topic sentence?
☐	☐	(5) Does the concluding paragraph restate the thesis statement and review the ideas?
☐	☐	(6) Are there smooth transitions between paragraphs and between sentences?

Development and Details

☐	☐	(7) Do the paragraphs include specific details and examples that support the topic sentences?
☐	☐	(8) Does the essay support the thesis statement?
☐	☐	(9) Is the essay free from irrelevant details?

Conventions of Edited Canadian English

☐	☐	(10) Are the ideas written in complete sentences?
☐	☐	(11) Is there a variety of sentence structures?
☐	☐	(12) Do all the subjects and verbs agree?
☐	☐	(13) Are verbs in the correct tense?
☐	☐	(14) Are punctuation marks used correctly?
☐	☐	(15) Are words spelled correctly?
☐	☐	(16) Are capital letters used correctly?

Word Choice

☐	☐	(17) Is the use of words varied and appropriate?
☐	☐	(18) Are words used precisely?

Tip

When you evaluate your GED essay, read it carefully to be sure that your ideas are presented clearly. Ask yourself, "Would another reader understand what I am writing?"

To evaluate your essay, read it at least twice. During the first reading, concentrate on the first three areas of the checklist—response to the prompt, organization, and development and details. These questions help you evaluate your presentation of ideas. During the second reading, concentrate on the last two areas of the checklist—the conventions of edited Canadian English and word choice.

GED Practice

The two essays on this and the following page were written for the writing assignment on page 186 on living in a city versus living in a small town. Work independently or with a partner to evaluate the essays. Use these steps to evaluate them.

1. Read each essay once to evaluate it as a GED evaluator would. Use the GED scoring guidelines on page 185 to assign a score of 1 to 4.

2. Evaluate each essay again to improve the presentation of ideas. Answer the questions in the first three areas of the checklist that follows these essays.

3. Check over the essay a third time to evaluate the control of the conventions of Canadian English and word choice. Answer the questions in the last two areas of the checklist that follows these essays.

Essay 1

I think that rural life is better than urban. Because you save time and money. You don't have to go to the grocery store as much. You don't have to commute back & forth on a bus. You can do your washing on hand. It is less complicated. The crime rate is very low. Less traffic. Don't worry that much about being mugged or robbed because the town is so small. The people within the community. They seem very nice. The atmosphere smells very clean.

Essay 2

I prefer to live in a small town. Rural life is more relaxed and less expensive than life in a large city.

The pace of life in a small town is far more relaxed than ~~life~~ living in a large city. People are not in such a hurry in a small town. They have time for one another and for the little pleasures in life. Because there are fewer people, there are shorter lines at the bank, the grocery, and the post office. People don't get so tense because these everyday activities take less time than in a big city. Drivers don't get stuck in traffic and worry about being late for appointments. This little things add up to fewer hassles and a more relaxed atmosphere.

The cost of living in a big city is a disadvantage, too. ~~Rural~~ Housing in rural towns is cheaper and food cost less. Kids don't go to private schools much so education is not as much. There are fewer reasons to have to dress up and buying clothes is not so important. Keeping up with the Jones is not nearly so important. People can just be theirselves.

Living in a small town is a more relaxed and less expensive way to live. I would rather live in a small town anyday.

	Essay 1				**Essay 2**		
○	○	○	○	○	○	○	○
1	2	3	4	1	2	3	4

Essay 1   Essay 2

Yes	No	Yes	No	
				Response to the Prompt
☐	☐	☐	☐	(1) Is there a clear main idea?
☐	☐	☐	☐	(2) Does the essay stick to the topic?
				Organization
☐	☐	☐	☐	(3) Does the introductory paragraph include a thesis statement and a preview?
☐	☐	☐	☐	(4) Does each body paragraph have a topic sentence and details related to the topic sentence?
☐	☐	☐	☐	(5) Does the concluding paragraph restate the thesis statement and review the ideas?
☐	☐	☐	☐	(6) Are there smooth transitions between paragraphs and between sentences?
				Development and Details
☐	☐	☐	☐	(7) Do the paragraphs include specific details and examples that support the topic sentences?
☐	☐	☐	☐	(8) Does the essay support the thesis statement?
☐	☐	☐	☐	(9) Is the essay free of irrelevant details?
				Conventions of Edited Canadian English
☐	☐	☐	☐	(10) Are the ideas written in complete sentences?
☐	☐	☐	☐	(11) Is there a variety of sentence structures?
☐	☐	☐	☐	(12) Do all the subjects and verbs agree?
☐	☐	☐	☐	(13) Are verbs in the correct tense?
☐	☐	☐	☐	(14) Are punctuation marks used correctly?
☐	☐	☐	☐	(15) Are words spelled correctly?
☐	☐	☐	☐	(16) Are capital letters used correctly?
				Word Choice
☐	☐	☐	☐	(17) Is the use of words varied and appropriate?
☐	☐	☐	☐	(18) Are words used precisely?

Answers start on page 748.

Because you cannot take an evaluation checklist with you to the GED essay test, it's a good idea to remember as many of the criteria as you can. Write the criteria you remember for each element below. For more tips on developing your personal writing strategy, see pages 909 and 911.

1. Response to the Prompt

_____

_____

_____

2. Organization

_____

_____

_____

_____

3. Development and Details

_____

_____

_____

4. Conventions of Edited Canadian English

_____

_____

_____

_____

_____

5. Word Choice

_____

_____

_____

Answers start on page 748.

Lesson 5

Revising

On the GED essay, you will have 45 minutes to plan, write, and revise an essay. You will not have time to write a second draft, but you need to leave some time to review your work and make revisions. That is why the next step in the writing process is revising.

Revising Ideas and Organization

When you evaluate your essay, you identify areas that need strengthening or correcting. When you revise your essay, you decide how to change those areas and then make the changes.

First, evaluate and revise your ideas and organization. Then evaluate and revise your use of the conventions of English. This second step of revision is sometimes called proofreading.

When you evaluated your presentation of ideas, you asked yourself three groups of questions:

Yes	No	**Response to the Prompt**
☐	☐	(1) Is there a clear main idea?
☐	☐	(2) Does the essay stick to the topic?

Organization

Yes	No	
☐	☐	(3) Does the introductory paragraph include a thesis statement and a preview?
☐	☐	(4) Does each body paragraph have a topic sentence and details related to the topic sentence?
☐	☐	(5) Does the concluding paragraph restate the thesis statement and review the ideas?
☐	☐	(6) Are there smooth transitions between paragraphs and between sentences?

Development and Details

Yes	No	
☐	☐	(7) Do the paragraphs include specific details and examples that support the topic sentences?
☐	☐	(8) Does the essay support the thesis statement?
☐	☐	(9) Is the essay free from irrelevant details?

Tip

You can revise your essay at any time. For example, correct a misspelled word or punctuation error when you first notice it. But do not spend too much time correcting until you have written your first draft.

Your answers to the questions tell you which parts of your essay need revising. For example, if your answer to question 3 is *no,* decide how to add a thesis statement for the essay topic. Use revision marks to add sentences. If your answer to question 9 is *no,* decide which sentences or phrases discuss things not directly related to the topic. Then cross them out.

Look at how one writer revised her essay on the topic assignment "State whether you think it is better to stay in one place or to move often and live in different places."

Note that the writer used some of these revision methods:
- Make corrections or add ideas between the lines or in the margin.
- Use a caret (^) to show where additions belong.
- Cross out any unwanted words or phrases.
- Rewrite any part that is illegible or too messy to read.

Main idea: *It's better to live in different places than to stay in just one place.*

Many people live in one place their entire lives and enjoy it, but I prefer experiencing different places. Living in one place provides security, but there are many disadvantages to this lifestyle. Living in new places is exciting and educational.

Living in one place for a long time does have some advantages. You know where everything is and have the security of a routine. If you need help, you can ask a friend or neighbour.^ It is easy to cash cheques and conduct other business because everyone knows you.

For me these advantages are overshadowed by the disadvantages of staying in one place. A comfortable routine can easily turn into a rut. You see the same people and do the same things over and over, and for me that means boredom!^ Finally, You never get exposed to fresh ideas and new ways of thinking.
you begin to have a narrow concept of what the world is like.

Moving to a different city or town is an adventure. Everything will be unfamiliar to you. You will have new experiences you will have different things to see and do. Maybe you will be near mountains or by the ocean. You could learn to ski or surf. ~~But remember, long distance phone calls are expensive.~~ Moving can give you opportunities you didn't have before. Best of all, you will be able to meet many people and make many new friends.

So brave! Find a place you think you'd like, then pack up and move. Decide whether you will move yourself or whether you will hire a moving company. You'll have many more exciting experiences than people who stay in one place all their lives.

When the writer began evaluating her essay, she looked for ideas that did not relate to the main idea. She found a sentence in the fourth paragraph that did not seem to fit, so she crossed it out.

Then she looked at the ideas she had gathered and organized in steps 1 and 2. She added a sentence to the second paragraph about the advantage of cashing cheques. Next, she thought of another supporting detail and added a sentence about getting exposed to new ideas to her third paragraph.

Evaluate the last paragraph of the essay again, using the checklist on page 192. Find another revision that could be made.

You should have crossed out *Decide whether you will move yourself or whether you will hire a moving company*. It does not relate to the topic of the paragraph.

When you revise your essay, compare it with your planning list of ideas. That will help you determine whether you included all your ideas.

Essay • Revising

Editing for the Conventions of English

After you make revisions to the ideas and organization of your essay, you should evaluate your use of the conventions of English and your choice of words and revise, if necessary. To evaluate (step 4), you asked yourself these two groups of questions:

Yes	No	**Conventions of standard Canadian English**
☐	☐	(10) Are the ideas written in complete sentences?
☐	☐	(11) Is there a variety of sentence structures?
☐	☐	(12) Do all the subjects and verbs agree?
☐	☐	(13) Are verbs in the correct tense?
☐	☐	(14) Are punctuation marks used correctly?
☐	☐	(15) Are words spelled correctly?
☐	☐	(16) Are capital letters used correctly?

Yes	No	**Word Choice**
☐	☐	(17) Is the use of words varied and appropriate?
☐	☐	(18) Are words used precisely?

Your answers to the questions tell you which corrections to make. For example, correct a sentence fragment by adding the necessary words and using a caret to show where they should be inserted. For a misspelled word, cross it out and write the correct spelling above it.

Look again at the essay about living in one place versus living in different places. The writer finished the second revision step and corrected her errors in the conventions of English. Her revision marks are in colour.

Many people live in one place their entire lives and enjoy it, but I prefer experiencing different places. Living in one place provides security, but there are many disadvantages to this lifestyle. Living in new places is exciting and ~~educationel~~ educational.

Living in one place for a long time does have some advantages. You know where everything is and have the security of a routine. If you need help, you can ask a friend or neighbour. ^It is easy to cash cheques and conduct other business because everyone knows you.

For me these advantages are overshadowed by the disadvantages of staying in one place. A comfortable routine can easily turn into a rut. You see the same people and do the same things over and over, and for me that means boredom! ^Finally, *You never get exposed to fresh ideas and new ways of thinking.* *you begin to have a narrow concept of what the world is like.*

Moving to a different city or town is an adventure. Everything will be unfamiliar to you. You will have new experiences. ~~Y~~you will have different things to see and do. Maybe you will be near mountains or by the ocean. You could learn to ski or surf. ~~But remember, long distance phone calls are expensive.~~ Moving can give you opportunities you didn't have before. Best of all, a variety of *you will be able to meet ~~many~~ people and make many new friends.*

So brave! Find a place you think you'd like, and then pack up and move. ~~Decide whether you will move yourself or whether you will hire a moving company.~~ You'll have many more exciting experiences than people who stay in one place all their lives.

The writer corrected a misspelled word in the first paragraph and a run-on sentence in the fourth paragraph. Then she realized she could improve her word choice in the last sentence of that paragraph by changing *many* to *a variety of.*

Use the checklist on page 195 to help you proofread for errors in the final paragraph. Revise if necessary.

You should have inserted the word *be* to correct the fragment at the beginning of the paragraph.

Be sure to use all the steps when you write your GED essay. You may allow more or less time for a step than the time suggested, but following the steps will help you write a better essay.

Essay • Revising

GED Practice

Read the following essay on the popularity of fast-food restaurants. Edit the essay for its use of the conventions of English. Use a copy of the checklist on page 195 if you need to. Make your revisions directly on the essay.

Over the past few years, there has been an increase in the number of fast-food restaurants across the country. Its easy to see why. The increase is due to their convenience, their prices, and the rising number of families in which both husband and wife work outside the home.

Fast-food restaurants are conveniently located. They're built near companies, and along highways. In addition, they usually offer short menus you can make a quick, easy decision about what you want to order.

These restaurants also offer low prices. Hamburgers for a couple of dollars. Salad bars are usually inexpensive, too. Also, if you eat at a fast-food restaurant, you don't spend money on food at home or on the gas or electricity to cook it.

Finaly, more and more families is made up of working couples. The husband and wife are tired when they come home and don't want to cook they want to spend time with their kids. Therfore, they get everybody into the car and head out to the nearest fast-food restaurant.

The poplarity of fast food and the increase in restaurants serving it are easy to understand. These restaurants offer tired, hungry people just what they want.

Answers start on page 748.

Review your understanding of revising by answering the questions about the sample GED essay topic below. For more tips on developing your personal strategy, see pages 909 and 911.

see pages 909 and 911.

> **TOPIC**
>
> Is life better in a city or in a small town?
>
> Explain your point of view in an essay. Use your personal observations, experience, and knowledge to support your view.

1. Once you have written a first draft for this essay, what should you do next—evaluate and revise the ideas in your essay or evaluate and edit for the use of conventions of English? Why?

_____

_____

_____

2. How can you make changes on your essay without rewriting it? List at least three methods.

_____

_____

_____

_____

_____

3. How should you decide what to change?

_____

_____

_____

4. How can you determine whether you included all the ideas you intended to include?

_____

_____

_____

Answers start on page 749.

Use these topics to gain additional experience writing GED essays. Use your personal test-taking strategy to follow all the writing steps you have learned. Take no more than 45 minutes to write each essay. Your essay should be long enough to develop the topic adequately. For more tips on writing an effective essay, see the Writing Checklist on page 912.

TOPIC 1

Describe the ways in which computers have affected our lives.

In your essay, you may want to deal with the good effects, the bad effects, or both.

TOPIC 2

Why do many people love to watch sports?

Write an essay explaining the reasons.

TOPIC 3

What are the advantages and disadvantages of a "child-free" lifestyle?

In your essay, explore the advantages and disadvantages of choosing not to have children.

TOPIC 4

Compare and contrast the person you are now with the person you were five or ten years ago.

In your essay, explain how you have changed.

TOPIC 5

How are people affected by constantly seeing ads in magazines and newspapers and on TV and hearing them on radio?

Write an essay stating the effects of ads on the buying public.

Answers start on page 749.

SOCIAL STUDIES

The GED Social Studies Test will cover the following content and skills.

The Test

- 50 multiple-choice questions
- 70 minutes to complete

The Content

- History—Canada and the world
- Civics and government
- Economics
- Geography

The Questions

- Comprehension
- Application
- Analysis
- Evaluation

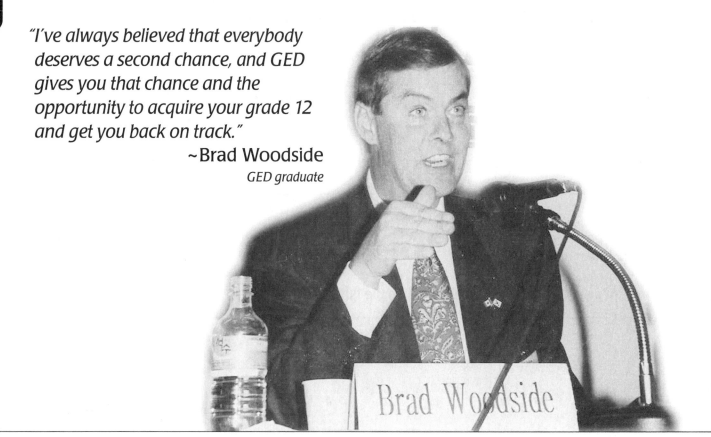

"I've always believed that everybody deserves a second chance, and GED gives you that chance and the opportunity to acquire your grade 12 and get you back on track."
~Brad Woodside
GED graduate

Social Studies

The longest serving mayor in the history of Fredericton is a GED graduate. Brad Woodside, now the owner of his own tour company, was mayor of the capital of New Brunswick for 13 years – serving five consecutive terms, from 1986 to 1999. Before that, he was a city counsellor for five years. Woodside has also been a top-rated radio-show host, served on the University of New Brunswick Board of Governors, acted as president of the Fredericton Tourism Association, and delivered keynote speeches to volunteer organizations around the world. In addition to his many other activities, Woodside writes a weekly column for *The Daily Gleaner*, a Fredericton newspaper.

In his many activities, Woodside must stay informed. That means he must do a lot of reading about issues and events. Next, he must be able to take what he has read and digest it. He must consider the implications and then use what he has learned to make decisions. You, too, use these skills as you read and digest information you find at work, in the newspaper, and in books. The Social Studies unit exercises your ability to read and consider information and then use it to make decisions.

Brad Woodside believes that everyone deserves a second chance to do their part. There's no way to know what opportunities you will have to support your beliefs. Perhaps earning your GED, as Brad Woodside did, will be among them.

Study Tip

To enhance reading comprehension, read.

A large part of the GED tests your ability to understand and apply what you have read. Practise as often as you can.

- Read and discuss newspaper articles with friends.
- Read the editorials to see what others think.
- Join a club where members read and discuss books.

Lesson 1

Canadian History

Studying Canadian history helps us understand who we are and how we came to be that way. Canadian history is an important part of the GED Social Studies Test, making up 25 percent of the test questions.

European Colonization of North America

Identifying the Main Idea

main idea
what the paragraph or article is about; the broadest, most important idea

topic sentence
a sentence that tells the reader what the paragraph is about

The most important idea, or point, of a story or paragraph is the **main idea.** You need to look for the main idea when you read and study and when you take the GED Test.

How can you find the main ideas of a passage? First note how many paragraphs it has. You should find a main idea in each paragraph. Looking at these main ideas all together will point you to the main idea for the whole passage.

Each paragraph focuses on a single topic—the main idea. The main idea is presented in the **topic sentence**, which often appears as the first or last sentence of the paragraph. Every other sentence in the paragraph supports this main idea. Sometimes the main idea is not stated clearly in one sentence. In that case, ask yourself, "What one thing is the writer discussing throughout the paragraph?"

To find the main idea of a paragraph, look at the first or last sentence. One of these is often the topic sentence. If you can't find a topic sentence, look at the details. What main idea do they point to or support?

Read the passage and answer the question below.

The term *Iroquois* has several meanings. It applies to a group of Aboriginal people, their language, and their way of life. The Iroquois-speaking people lived in a region of North America called the Eastern Woodlands. More than 500 years ago, the Iroquois practised agriculture and lived in rectangular longhouses that lodged a dozen or more families.

In the fifteenth century, the Iroquois formed a league or council of five peoples so that they could stand together against invasion. The council had complex systems for choosing leaders and making important decisions.

Write *M* next to the sentence that best expresses the main idea of the passage.

_____ a. The term *Iroquois* refers to a group of North American Aboriginal tribes who practised agriculture and lived in longhouses.

_____ b. The people referred to as Iroquois spoke the same language and had a distinct way of life and an advanced system of self-government.

You are correct if you chose *option b.* The idea it expresses is broad enough to include the information from both paragraphs.

GED Practice

Directions: Choose the <u>one best answer</u> to each question.

<u>Questions 1 through 3</u> refer to the following passage.

Aboriginal societies were kept intact by adherence to a set of principles that included acting with generosity, sacrificing one's own needs for those of the family, and accepting hardships stoically.

The societies were based on communal sharing rather than private accumulation of wealth. Hospitality and helping less fortunate people were considered great virtues. Those who did acquire wealth were expected to be generous to others. Prestige was acquired by giving, not by getting.

Spiritual beliefs shaped all daily activities, since Aboriginal peoples believed that all aspects of nature—sun, moon, rain, and disease, for example—as well as some objects such as fishing nets were animate. The belief system included a supernatural world. Hunters, would contact the spirits of prey animals to ensure success, and they disposed of inedible animal parts according to a strict code, to avoid offending the animal's family. The bones of a bear, for example, were carefully buried rather than thrown away or fed to the dogs.

1. What is the main idea of this passage?

   (1) Aboriginal peoples based their lives on the profit motive.
   (2) Trade among Aboriginal peoples began after the arrival of the first Europeans.
   (3) Aboriginal peoples believed that the natural world was inhabited by supernatural creatures
   (4) Aboriginal peoples had well-ordered societies that included a set of spiritual beliefs.
   (5) Aboriginal cultures had a set of myths that explained the mysteries of the universe.

2. Based on the passage, which values did Aboriginal cultures stress?

   (1) Each person should be independent.
   (2) Children should respect their elders.
   (3) There should be respect for all forms of life—both in society and in nature.
   (4) Look after your own needs before the needs of others.
   (5) Eat, drink, and be merry, for tomorrow you will die.

3. Which of the following was the most likely reason for the priority of group needs?

   (1) Individuals did not matter in the society.
   (2) The group's survival depended on conformity and cooperative behaviour.
   (3) Groups could acquire more wealth than individuals.
   (4) Everyone had to share in the decision-making.
   (5) Food was very scarce.

<u>Question 4</u> refers to the following paragraph.

When early Europeans first saw totem poles in the villages of the Pacific Northwest, they assumed that the carved figures represented pagan gods or even demons either worshipped or feared by the Tsimshian and Kwakiutl peoples. In fact, the totem poles had another purpose; they were used as physical and artistic symbols of specific clans of people, rather like a family coat-of-arms. Totem poles were also a means of displaying wealth and status in the society.

4. What idea might have led Europeans to conclude that totem poles had a religious function in Aboriginal societies?

   (1) The totem poles were in front of Christian churches.
   (2) Totem poles seemed to be everywhere.
   (3) The poles were made of cedar.
   (4) Artistic products are always used to symbolize religious beliefs.
   (5) Public statues and carved figures often represented religious figures in Christian European societies.

HURON SUBSISTENCE CALENDAR

Activity	Months of the Year J/F/M/A/M/J/J/A/S/O/N/D	Division of Labour Major	Division of Labour Minor
Fishing		M	F
Hunting		M	F
Trading		M	
Warfare		M	
Gathering firewood		F	
Preparing fields		F	M
Planting		F	
Weeding		F	C
Harvesting		F	
Gathering		F	C
Manufacturing		MF	
Socializing		MF	

━━ Primary period for activity
········· Activity also carried on
M, F, C Males, Females, Children

5. What is the main idea of the Huron Subsistence Calendar?

   (1) to show that tasks were not equally divided among men, women, and children
   (2) to compare the relative importance of fishing to agriculture in Huron society
   (3) to emphasize that the harvesting of crops took very little effort
   (4) to identify the variety of activities that the Huron people engaged in during the year
   (5) to demonstrate that a lot of time was spent socializing in the winter months

6. Which of the following cannot be determined from the table?

   (1) Women were heavily involved in the agricultural activities.
   (2) Among the Huron people, participation in warfare was primarily a male activity.
   (3) The Huron people produced tools and other implements for their daily use.
   (4) It was too cold to hunt and fish in the winter months.
   (5) The Hurons participated in economic activity with neighbouring Aboriginal peoples.

Of all the European goods traded with the Aboriginal peoples, the kettle probably had the greatest impact on the daily life of Aboriginal families. Kettles and pots made of metal were durable and transportable and could be used over an open fire. This method of cooking was much more efficient than putting heated stones in a birchbark container. As a result, soups and stews became a staple in the Aboriginal diet. European blankets and cotton or woollen fabrics also became important trade items. Woven cloth wasn't as warm as fur, but it dried more quickly, and wool provided warmth even when it was wet. When it came to making clothes out of animal skins, European-produced tools such as knives, metal awls, needles, and scissors made women's tasks much easier.

For Aboriginal men, firearms brought about the greatest change. Traditionally they had hunted by stalking and killing their prey at close range, using bows and arrows and lances. The problem was that prey animals often travelled great distances before they bled to death. With guns, however, death was instant; thus, hunting efficiency increased dramatically.

Although Aboriginal peoples spent a relatively small part of their income on glass beads, their low cost and easy availability led to the wide-scale appearance of decorative beadwork on clothing. It wasn't long before beads replaced the traditional decorations of porcupine quills and shells.

7. Which of the following titles best expresses the main idea of this passage?

   (1) The Division of Labour in Aboriginal Villages
   (2) The Advantages of Wool over Fur
   (3) The Impact of European Goods on Aboriginal Life
   (4) The Effect of Guns on Hunting
   (5) Systems of Survival in Early Canada

8. According to the information in the passage, which of the following European products probably brought about the greatest change in daily life?

   (1) scissors
   (2) glass beads
   (3) cotton shirts
   (4) kettles
   (5) felt hats

Questions 9 through 12 refer to the following passage and graph.

The French fur trade depended on the labour, trading networks, and know-how of Aboriginal peoples in the St. Lawrence Valley. Each nomadic Aboriginal family annually used about 30 beavers for food and clothing. After being worn for a year, the beaver pelts shed their long guard hairs, exposing the short hairs required for felt-making. Based on population estimates of Aboriginals in the St. Lawrence-Great Lakes region, several hundred thousand beaver pelts were available to trade annually at the end of the sixteenth century.

The fur trade was a precarious economy, however; it depended on Aboriginal populations who did not respond to increased demand for furs the same way as Europeans did. The periodic warfare among Aboriginal nations in the region also disrupted the supply of beaver pelts.

Disease added another variable. With no immunity to European diseases such as smallpox and influenza, entire villages were decimated in the late 1630s. The Aboriginal peoples allied with the French were particularly vulnerable, since they were in constant contact with European missionaries and interpreters.

**THE POPULATION OF THE
ST. LAWRENCE VALLEY, 1530–1650**

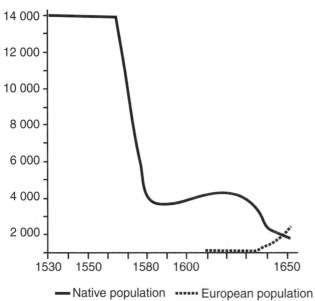

9. In what way did the Native people's domestic use of fur help the fur trade?

   (1) The furs that dropped off the pelts could be collected by Aboriginal children and sold for a profit.
   (2) Fur pelts worn for a year dropped their thick outer hairs and left more usable, soft fur.
   (3) Aboriginal women made the fur pelts into finished commercial products.
   (4) The Aboriginal groups were proud of the quality of the fur.
   (5) Wearing fur robes helped keep Aboriginal people warm in winter.

10. What was the estimated Aboriginal population in the St. Lawrence Valley in 1560?

   (1) approximately 14 000
   (2) nearly 1.4 million
   (3) about 56 000
   (4) more than 140 000
   (5) slightly less than 1400

11. Which of the following statements is implied by the graph and the passage?

   (1) Europeans discovered the St. Lawrence Valley about 1610.
   (2) The arrival of Europeans resulted in a population explosion.
   (3) Floods wiped out thousands of Aboriginal people in 1570.
   (4) Aboriginal people migrated south in winter.
   (5) The Aboriginal population fell dramatically after contact with the Europeans.

12. According to the passage, what cultural factor contributed to the uncertainty of the fur trade in New France?

   (1) Speaking differrent languages prevented good communication.
   (2) Aboriginal peoples did not trade.
   (3) Materialism was a weaker motivator in European society than in Aboriginal societies.
   (4) Aboriginal peoples did not see the need to respond to European economic demand with an increased supply of furs.
   (5) Aboriginal peoples scorned the whims of European fashion.

Answers start on page 750.

New France and the British Conquest
Summarizing Ideas

Lesson 2

summary
a brief account of the main points of a piece of writing or a graphic

Tip

To summarize a passage, look for the main idea in each paragraph. Ask *who, what, when, where, why,* and *how.*

Has anyone ever asked you, "What was that movie about?" Usually, instead of explaining the entire plot of the movie, you give a brief account or a summary of the main characters and events.

Summarizing is also an important skill for reading and understanding social studies material. A **summary** is a short, accurate account of the main points of a piece of writing or a graphic. It always includes the main idea of the material, which is often in the title. When you summarize a piece of writing, you restate the main points in a shortened fashion. These are usually the topic sentences or main points of all the paragraphs that support the overall main idea.

To summarize visual material such as maps and graphs, look at the title and the key, headings, and labels. Then restate the information in a sentence or two. To write a summary, you should answer as many of these questions as you can: *Who? What? When? Where? Why? How?*

Read the passage and answer the question below.

After the British defeated the French at Quebec in 1759, peace talks began in the spring of 1761. Discussions went very slowly at first, partly because the two country's negotiators hated each other. Many British businessmen and politicians wanted England to keep the Caribbean island of Guadeloupe and give Canada back to the French. They argued that Guadeloupe's sugar exports produced twice the revenue of Canada's fur exports, without the problem of governing 65 000 Catholics.

The French negotiator at last grew so impatient with the slow pace of negotiations that in a fit of anger he wrote down a list of terms: France would give back the island of Minorca to England and England would return Guadeloupe. The English would keep Canada, but the French would get fishing rights in the Gulf of St. Lawrence and the two tiny islands of St. Pierre and Miquelon off the coast of Newfoundland and Labrador. The French negotiator thought this agreement was the best they could hope for. So they signed the Treaty of Paris in 1763.

Put a check mark next to the sentence that is the best summary of the entire passage.

_____ a. Many Englishmen thought that Britain should give back Canada to the French and keep the sugar-rich Caribbean island of Guadeloupe instead.

_____ b. The 1763 Treaty of Paris solved the frustrating impasse between English and French negotiators by giving Canada to Britain while France retained two fishing islands off Newfoundland and Labrador and the island of Guadeloupe in the Caribbean.

You are correct if you chose *option b*. This sentence tells who, what, where, when, and why. *Option a* gives information from the first paragraph only.

GED Practice

Directions: Choose the <u>one best answer</u> to each question.

<u>Questions 1 through 3</u> refer to the following passage and map.

Samuel de Champlain was one of the great explorers of early North America. From Quebec in 1608, he directed the colony of New France. He cemented the French position by establishing alliances with the Aboriginal peoples along the St. Lawrence and Ottawa Rivers, and with the Huron and Algonquian people around the southern Great Lakes. Venturing inland, he explored and mapped the upper St. Lawrence River, the Ottawa River, the area around Lake Huron called Huronia, and the lake south of Montreal, which is named after him.

But French settlers did not flock to the colony of New France as he had hoped. Moreover, in 1627, the colonial government decided to expel the Huguenots from the colony. These French Protestants had already been exiled from France itself and had brought their great entrepreneurial skills and energy to New France. Their exclusion undoubtedly robbed New France of the very things it needed to thrive—leadership, brainpower, and initiative. Sadly, when Champlain died in 1635, there were only about 100 Europeans in Quebec. It is just possible that if the Huguenots had been allowed to stay in New France, the British might never have been able to conquer the French in the next century.

CHAMPLAIN'S MAP 1612

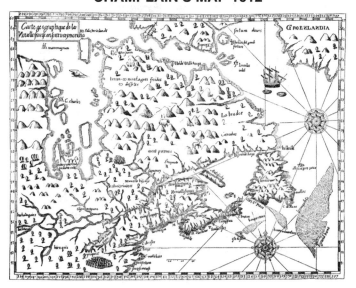

1. What important body of water in eastern North America is not on Champlain's map, likely meaning that he had not yet discovered it?

   (1) Hudson Bay
   (2) the Gulf of St. Lawrence
   (3) the Bay of Fundy
   (4) the Fraser River
   (5) the Great Lakes

2. In what way did the geography of eastern North America help the French to build a communications system that opened up virtually the whole continent in the seventeenth century?

   (1) The rivers all ran to the Atlantic Ocean.
   (2) The land was exceedingly flat and easy to cross.
   (3) The system of lakes and rivers allowed easy access to the interior of the continent.
   (4) There were passages through the Rocky Mountains.
   (5) The lakes and rivers were completely frozen for eight months of every year.

3. What conclusion could you draw from the information in the passage?

   (1) The expulsion of the Huguenots from New France was probably a serious mistake.
   (2) The Huguenots possessed great business talents.
   (3) Champlain does not deserve much credit for his work in New France.
   (4) The Protestant religion was strong in the French colony.
   (5) French missionaries had little success in converting the Hurons to the Catholic religion.

Question 4 refers to the following passage.

To pay for the recent wars against France and to finance the governing of the new territories in the West, the British decided to raise some of the money in the Thirteen Colonies of North America. They levied new taxes on the already resentful American colonists, fuelling idea of rebelling against England.

Coincidentally, with the French gone from North America, fewer British troops were needed in the colonies. This fact enticed those colonists who had been calling for independence from England to assert their strength and encourage others to join them. So, in some ways, one might conclude that the British success in conquering New France paved the way for the American Revolution.

4. According to the passage, how did the victory over the French at Quebec lead to the American Revolution?

   (1) The American colonists saw that the British could easily be defeated.
   (2) The colonists realized that Britain needed a rest.
   (3) The Americans knew the Spanish would help them if they revolted against the British.
   (4) The Americans resented having to pay for Britain's wars through taxes in which they had no say.
   (5) The settlers in the Thirteen Colonies knew that they could now freely expand westward in the Ohio River Valley.

Questions 5 and 6 refer to the following passage.

By 1750, the stage was set for a war to determine who would control North America—the British or the French. The main point of contention was the string of French forts along the Ohio-Mississippi Valley.

In 1754, a young English colonel, George Washington, led a small army into the Ohio Valley to drive out the French and clear the way for English traders and settlers. The war, often called the French and Indian War, soon became part of a wider, worldwide struggle for trade and territory between France and England.

In 1758, the English captured Louisbourg, and the next year they took Quebec, winning the famous battle on the Plains of Abraham. In the peace treaty of 1763, New France became a British colony. The victors assumed that the *Canadiens* would quickly accept the blessings of British rule and be assimilated into the North American English Empire. It seemed that the struggle to control the continent of North America was over.

5. According to this passage, what was the main reason the English wanted to drive the French out of North America?

   (1) to get rid of the Catholic church
   (2) to keep George Washington occupied
   (3) to impose the English language on the *Canadiens*
   (4) to allow English settlers to move west unhindered
   (5) to break up the French alliances with the Aboriginal peoples

6. As the dominant force in North America, what did the English assume about the future?

   (1) The *Canadiens* would be easily assimilated.
   (2) They should attack the Spanish in Florida next.
   (3) George Washington was a poor military leader.
   (4) The English should leave North America.
   (5) The French would stir up a lot of trouble in Quebec.

Answers start on page 751.

Building a Country
Recognizing Unstated Assumptions

"I'll see you at Jenna's party tonight," a friend might say. This friend just made at least two unstated assumptions: (1) that you've been invited to the party and (2) that you plan to go. Writers make unstated **assumptions** too. You must read carefully to recognize unstated assumptions and to understand the material fully.

Writers often make assumptions about what you already know. For example, you read a report in the newspaper that mentions that the prime minister is having a reception at 24 Sussex Drive. Without being told, you know this story is about the prime minister of Canada because 24 Sussex Drive is the prime minister's official residence in Ottawa. Sometimes writers assume that particular principles are true. For example, a writer may make the assumption that the Europeans who colonized North America had a right to move Aboriginal peoples out of their way. Others may disagree strongly with this assumption.

To recognize unstated assumptions in a piece of writing, read slowly and carefully. Ask yourself, "What is this writer assuming to be true?"

Read the passage and answer the question below.

After Confederation, waves of settlers from eastern Canada began to move westward. Life in the west at that time was both difficult and dangerous. Settlers required courage and endurance to establish farms and homes on uncleared land, deal with the Aboriginal inhabitants, and form new communities under harsh climatic conditions.

For the easterner who migrated to the area, Winnipeg represented the very end of civilization. Henri Julien was a French-Canadian artist who visited the area. He wrote in his journal: "This narrow strip of planking [the railway station's platform] was the dividing line between civilization and the wilderness. Behind us lay the works of man, with their noises: before us stretched out the handiwork of God, with its eternal solitudes."

Put a check mark next to the sentence that is an unstated assumption made by Henri Julien.

_____ a. There was no civilization in the western territories before the settlers from the east arrived.

_____ b. The territory that lay to the west of Winnipeg was immense, uninhabited wilderness.

You are correct if you chose *option a*. Henri Julien was assuming that the Aboriginal peoples and the Métis who lived in the West before the arrival of easterners were not civilized. Many people would disagree with that assumption. *Option b* is incorrect because it is not an unstated assumption. It is a direct restatement of Henri Julien's sentences in the second paragraph.

assumption
an idea, theory, or principle that a person believes to be true

An assumption is something the writer takes for granted and does not explain. Read carefully to recognize unstated assumptions.

GED Practice

Directions: Choose the <u>one best answer</u> to each question.

<u>Questions 1 and 2</u> refer to the following.

John Graves Simcoe, the first lieutenant governor of Upper Canada, was determined to transform the rough, backward colony into a civilized "little England," attractive enough to Americans that they would clamour to be let in. To sweeten the deal, he offered free land to all who would renew their allegiance to the British king and come north to settle.

Simcoe sent land surveyors into the forests to lay out the grid plan of concessions and side roads that still organize rural Ontario. He used both settlers and soldiers to build the highways of the future through the swamps and the bush. He also moved the capital from Niagara to the village of York, later renamed Toronto.

By 1811, almost 90 000 people had settled in Upper Canada, an increase of 75 000 in 20 years. Towns and villages sprang up with growing businesses and a colonial aristocracy not unlike that in Britain. All the while, a new and definitely unaristocratic republic was taking shape to the south, with a population of six million.

1. Which of the following best expresses the main idea of this passage?

    (1) Under Simcoe, an elite class was established in Upper Canada.
    (2) The road and highway systems of Ontario were laid out under Simcoe.
    (3) Simcoe was the first lieutenant governor of Upper Canada.
    (4) Simcoe's administration was a period of dynamic growth and development in Upper Canada.
    (5) Simcoe was pessimistic about the future of the British colonies in North America.

2. What assumption can be made from the details in this passage?

    (1) Allegiance to the British king was required for settlement in Upper Canada.
    (2) Upper Canada would become a republic.
    (3) York was more protected than Niagara.
    (4) The short distance to the United States was the main reason for Americans coming to settle in Upper Canada.
    (5) There would be trouble between the United States and Upper Canada.

<u>Question 3</u> refers to the following passage.

In 1812, while Britain fought Napoleon in Europe, the Americans saw their chance to capture Canada and redress the wrongs they had suffered when British ships had seized American vessels as they attempted to trade with France. Thomas Jefferson, a former president, said the conquest of Canada would be "a mere matter of marching," for the American population was 7.5 million and Upper Canada's just 80 000. The confident Americans declared war on June 18, 1812.

Unfortunately, they hadn't counted on the strength that an Aboriginal alliance under Tecumseh gave to the British side. This alliance brought goals, too. It wanted to stop American expansion into their western lands and secure a native homeland from the Great Lakes to Florida, territory that the United States insisted they now "owned."

Under Isaac Brock and De Salaberry, the badly outnumbered British defeated the invading forces in several critical battles, culminating in the capture and burning of the American capital city. A treaty ended the war in 1814 and restored the territorial status quo. Unfortunately, Britain kept its Aboriginal allies out of the negotiations and they lost their hope of an autonomous homeland forever. One of the legacies of the War of 1812, however, was a uniting of the people of British North America against a common enemy.

3. What assumption can be made from the information in this passage?

    (1) A result of the War of 1812 was an autonomous homeland for the Aboriginal people.
    (2) Canada's population was a fraction of that of the United States.
    (3) Isaac Brock was the main British hero of the War of 1812.
    (4) British North America would one day become its own country—Canada.
    (5) Thomas Jefferson hated the British.

Questions 4 through 6 refer to the following passage and cartoon.

The push for Confederation came from Upper and Lower Canada. Their union into one province in 1841 was failing and government had come to a standstill. In fact, both colonies wanted some form of self-government and the freedom to run their own affairs, but they still wanted to maintain their historical connection.

One possible solution to the stalemate was to separate, but each was too economically and politically weak to survive as a country on its own. Another option was to create a new country with one central (or federal) government to look after common interests—the economy, transportation, defence— and two separate governments to handle local issues.

That is exactly what the Canadians proposed to the Atlantic colonies in 1864 in Charlottetown. Later that year, in Quebec, they hammered out the details. In the new country, each colony would become a province, and each province would have its own provincial government. The four provinces would elect members to a House of Commons patterned on Britain's. The number depended on their populations. There would also be an appointed Senate, with members equally representing the three regions, the Maritimes, Quebec, and Ontario. The constitution would divide up the powers between the two levels of government, federal and provincial.

The British government was very supportive of the idea and played an important role in encouraging New Brunswick and Nova Scotia to join Confederation. So in 1867 the British Parliament passed the *British North America Act* that brought Canada into existence.

MOTHER BRITANNIA — *"See! Why, the dear child can stand alone!"*
UNCLE SAM. — *"Of course he can! Let go of him Granny; if he falls I'll catch him!"*

Source: National Archives of Canada, C-050336.

4. In what way was Canada's achievement of independence different from that of the United States?

   (1) Canada bought her independence from England.
   (2) Canadians voted for their independence.
   (3) The British forced Canada to become independent.
   (4) Canada relied on American support in the British House of Commons.
   (5) Canada's independence was achieved with the stroke of a pen; America's was achieved by a revolution.

5. Which of the following government powers was most likely assigned to the federal government in the *British North America Act*?

   (1) control over municipal governments
   (2) tourism and recreation
   (3) defence
   (4) highways and roads
   (5) education

6. What assumption can be made from the information and images in the cartoon?

   (1) If the new country faltered, the United States might "help out" by annexing Canada and making it part of the United States.
   (2) Britain might try to revoke Canada's independence and turn it into a colony again.
   (3) Canada might foolishly declare war on either Britain or the United States if it had its own army.
   (4) British and American fighting over Canada might tear the new country apart.
   (5) The new country was so unstable and young that it might destroy itself.

Answers start on page 752.

Lesson 4

cause
what makes something happen

effect
what happens as a result of a cause

Tip

The words and phrases *because, since, therefore,* and *as a result* are clues that indicate a cause-and-effect relationship.

Settling the West
Analyzing Cause and Effect

"I can barely keep my eyes open today," a friend says. "My baby was up all night coughing." The friend has identified the reason, or cause, for her tiredness: her baby kept her up all night. A **cause** is what makes something happen. An **effect** is what happens as a result of a cause. In this case, the effect is that your friend is tired.

Writing is often organized in a cause-and-effect pattern. For example, a writer may explore the causes behind a particular event—say, Confederation. Or a passage may explore the effects of a particular event—say, the Yukon gold rush. History is concerned with causes and effects of events.

To recognize causes and effects when you read, focus on how the events are connected. Ask yourself, "Does the passage explain how or why an event occurred (the causes)? Does it focus on the results (effects) of an event?"

Read the passage and answer the question below.

When the first Europeans arrived on the North American Great Plains, there were probably as many as 50 million buffalo. The great herds of grassland bison—the largest North American terrestrial animal at 900 kg—had provided food, shelter, and clothing for the Plains Aboriginal people for millennia.

In 1860, there were still herds of plains buffalo so large that it took several days to ride by them on horseback. However, two technological advances led to a dramatic and quick decimation of the great herds. First, a new method was invented for tanning buffalo hide so that it was sturdy enough to make belts rather than just soft chamois. Second, hunters now had access to the fast-shooting repeating rifle. But a third reason for the great slaughter was the U.S. government's deliberate policy of mass buffalo kills as a way of destroying the Aboriginal peoples' food supply. Within five years, tens of millions of the great mammals had been slaughtered for sport, profit, or military reasons. The result was that the buffalo was hunted to the edge of extinction. In fact, when Canadian settlers started to farm the Prairies, often their first cash crop was buffalo bones, sold by the tonne as fertilizer.

1. Put a check mark next to the statement that is an effect of settlers coming to the North American Great Plains.

_____ a. the use of the fast-shooting repeating rifle

_____ b. the slaughter of the Great Plains buffalo almost to the point of extinction

You are correct if you chose *option b.* This is stated in the second last sentence of the passage. *Option a* is a cause, not an effect.

GED Practice

Directions: Choose the one best answer to each question.

Question 1 refers to the following passage.

By 1867, as Americans moved in large numbers into the Great Plains, they came face to face with the Cree, Ojibwa, and Assiniboine inhabitants. As far as the American settlers were concerned, however, the area had no borders.

In that same year, the United States bought Alaska from Russia for $7 million. Canada now had Americans both to the north and to the south. John A. Macdonald viewed this American expansion as a threat to his goal of creating a Canada from sea to sea.

To avoid losing the West altogether, Canada bought all the land from the Great Lakes to the Rockies from the Hudson's Bay Company in 1869 for $1.5 million and named it the "North-West Territories." It was the biggest real estate deal in Canadian history.

Unfortunately, neither the Canadians nor the British had considered the 6000 Métis people living in the Red River area. The Métis feared that an influx of English settlers from the East would overrun and dominate their way of life, religion, and language. Under Louis Riel, they set up their own government. Riel then demanded that Macdonald agree to create a new province with its own government, protection for the French language and Catholic religion, and Métis ownership of the land they already occupied. Macdonald, reluctantly, had to agree, and in 1870 Manitoba became Canada's fifth province.

1. What effect did American expansion into the Great Plains and purchase of Alaska have on Macdonald's plans for Canada?

   (1) Macdonald realized he would have to attack the United States.
   (2) He decided that if Canada didn't act quickly, the Americans might annex all of western North America.
   (3) He thought that he could probably annex for Canada all the lands being occupied by Americans .
   (4) Macdonald concluded that Canada would never extend "from sea to sea."
   (5) He assumed that the Americans would abandon the western half of the continent.

Questions 2 and 3 refer to the following passage.

John A. Macdonald had always intended the federal government to be the overriding authority in Canada. He thought the provincial governments would decline in importance until they were as weak as municipalities. In fact, a series of provincial premiers, beginning with Oliver Mowat in Ontario, proved him wrong. Mowat, one of the original Fathers of Confederation, argued that in the Confederation deal the provinces were equal powers and not subordinate to the federal government. He was joined in this opinion by Quebec Premier Honoré Mercier. When the two provinces took constitutional cases to the British courts, they often won. The power of the federal government to disallow provincial laws, for example, was severely curbed, and ever since there has been a federal-provincial power struggle in Canada.

2. According to the passage, what was the effect of Mowat and Mercier's battles with the federal government?

   (1) The provinces lost.
   (2) The British courts often sided with the provinces.
   (3) The federal government won.
   (4) Each side won about half of its cases.
   (5) The courts refused to hear the cases.

3. What conclusion can be drawn from the passage?

   (1) John A. Macdonald was a weak leader.
   (2) Ontario and Quebec wanted to dominate Confederation.
   (3) Macdonald's idea of Confederation was proved correct.
   (4) There were different opinions about how Confederation should operate.
   (5) Confederation wasn't working.

Question 4 refers to the following poster and paragraph

Source: Department of Immigration, Canada; National Archives of Canada, C-85854

To unite Canada from sea to sea and attract settlers to western Canada, Sir John A. Macdonald planned to build a railroad to the Pacific. The land that the railroad would pass through was advertised in pamphlets and posters distributed in central Canada, England, Scotland, and Europe. For English industrial workers, the posters focused not just on land, but also on a new, classless society. For city-dwellers, the promotional material stressed clean air, clean morals, and the chance to escape miserable factory jobs. In short, the advertising depicted a dream, and, for men at least, the opportunity to reinvent themselves by building muscles of iron and nerves of steel.

4. What effect would the poster most likely have on a potential immigrant?

(1) increased desire for an easy life
(2) increased desire to live in an urban setting
(3) renewed hope for economic security and happiness
(4) heightened expectation that western Canada would resemble rural England
(5) interest in Aboriginal cultures

Question 5 refers to the following passage.

In 1885, the Canadian Pacific Railway Company (CPR), which was building the railway to the west coast, teetered on the verge of bankruptcy. The project was over budget, and the federal government, underwriting the cost, refused to provide any more funds. As a result, work came to a halt.

Just at this point, the Northwest Rebellion broke out in Saskatchewan. Louis Riel had set up his own independent government to preserve the autonomy of the Métis and secure equitable land rights for his people. But thousands of new Anglo-Canadians were arriving and settling on the land. At the same time, the Cree people saw their land being taken; in response, they attacked several English-Canadian settlements.

What was Macdonald to do? To achieve his grand goal, he quickly arranged more financing for the CPR. In so doing, he could complete the railway, fulfill the Confederation deal with British Columbia, and crush Riel by sending 5000 troops to Saskatchewan quickly via train. Riel's insurrection was put down at the Battle of Batoche, and the Métis leader was executed after a controversial trial. At the same time, the CPR was spurred to completion.

Unfortunately, the aftermath of these events divided Canada for decades. The French claimed Riel as a martyr and hero, while the English condemned him as a dangerous fanatic and a traitor to Canada.

5. What two outcomes could Macdonald arrange by providing more financing for the CPR in 1885?

(1) Troops could be sent to crush the rebellion and the transcontinental railroad would be completed.
(2) The animosity between English and French would end and Macdonald would be reelected.
(3) Louis Riel would be pacified and the Cree would get their own province.
(4) The plains bison could be saved from extinction and western settlers could begin to plant crops.
(5) The people in Quebec would renounce Riel and vote for Macdonald's Conservative Party.

Answers start on page 752.

Turmoil and Triumph

Recognizing Values

Values are the goals and ideals that make life meaningful. They include what people think is important, good, beautiful, worthwhile, or sacred. Recognizing values helps us understand that human beings often make decisions about what to do based on their values.

Most writing expresses some values. For example, a writer may say that the building of the Pacific railroad was a magnificent accomplishment by and for the people of Canada. Another writer might say that the railroad was built with the blood and sweat of poor workers. Both statements are based on historical fact, but they express different values. The first focuses on the values of progress and accomplishments; the second focuses on values about and concern for the suffering of individuals.

values
goals and ideals; what people think is important, good, beautiful, worthwhile, or sacred

To recognize the values expressed in a piece of writing, read carefully and look behind the words. What is the writer's attitude about the subject? How are the people discussed in the passage behaving? Ask yourself, "What matters most to the writer or to the people discussed in the passage?"

Read the passage and complete the exercise below.

Norman Bethune of Gravenhurst, Ontario, was renowned for his medical innovations and dedication to the care of the ill. Between 1929 and 1936, he invented 12 medical and surgical instruments, and he was convinced that the medical system should be changed so that it provided adequate care for everyone, rich or poor. In 1936—now one of the most highly paid doctors in Canada and one of the world's top thoracic surgeons—Bethune went to Spain to head a medical unit during the Spanish Civil War, fighting against the fascists. In Spain, he developed the world's first mobile medical unit, which could travel to the soldiers, allowing practitioners to provide blood transfusions and perform operations. On many occasions Bethune risked his own life delivering blood to the front lines. In 1938, Bethune went to China to help Mao Zedong fight the Japanese. He became the Army's medical chief and trained thousands of Chinese as doctors and medics. He redesigned his mobile medical unit and saved the lives of many soldiers. Bethune died from blood poisoning in 1939 and is revered as a hero in China.

To understand the values in a piece of writing, ask yourself "What do the writer or the people depicted in the passage think is important?"

Put a check mark next to each statement that expresses a value in Bethune's life.

_____ a. Those with skill and knowledge must share it with others.

_____ b. When you see a problem, invent a solution.

_____ c. We must first take care of the home front.

You are correct if you chose *options a* and *b*. Both were ideals, or values, in Bethune's life. *Option c* would be incorrect because Bethune sacrificed the stability of wealth and a successful career in Canada to help others in great need in other countries.

GED Practice

Directions: Choose the <u>one best answer</u> to each question.

Questions 1 through 4 refer to the following passage and photograph.

When soldiers returned to Canada at the end of World War I, they found few jobs. A wave of labour unrest soon swept the country, and some even spoke of revolution to overthrow the capitalist system.

Tensions exploded in Winnipeg in May and June of 1919. More than 35 000 workers joined a general strike that paralyzed the city. The government sided with the employers, claiming the strike was a threat to the whole country. They sent in troops to break up demonstrations, arrested strike leaders, and charged them with conspiracy to overthrow the government. At a demonstration on June 21, police killed one man and many were injured in the melee. More arrests followed and some strikers, identified as "foreign agitators," were deported.

The royal commission appointed to investigate the strike concluded that the strikers were not revolutionaries, but simply workers seeking the right to bargain collectively about their wages and working conditions.

The Winnipeg General Strike was a short-term defeat for the workers, but in the long run it encouraged people to organize new political parties that represented the interests of workers and ordinary people. In the next decade, voters elected labour leaders to all levels of government in Canada.

1. As described in the passage, what do the government's actions suggest was most important to it during the strike?

   (1) helping workers to achieve a fair wage
   (2) supporting the work of churches
   (3) raising the moral standards of the poor
   (4) maintaining peace and civil order
   (5) correcting those who questioned political or economic leaders

2. What term is used for the process in which a group of workers collaborates in negotiating for better wages and working conditions?

   (1) worker confrontation
   (2) collective bargaining
   (3) labour demonstrations
   (4) collaborative investigation
   (5) group action

3. Based on the passage, how did the strike change Canadian society?

   (1) It drew attention to poor social and economic conditions and caused workers and others to become more politically active.
   (2) It brought about a violent revolution that almost destroyed Canada.
   (3) It proved that governments always sided with employers.
   (4) Unions were shown to be powerless.
   (5) It immediately led to the arrest of eight strike leaders who were charged with conspiracy to overthrow the government.

4. Which of the following can be determined from the photograph?

   (1) The city government sent negotiators to talk with workers and their leaders.
   (2) The prime minister encouraged workers to visit Ottawa and petition Parliament.
   (3) Churches held prayer meetings to try and end the violence.
   (4) The police set up barricades around stores to stop looting and bombing.
   (5) The civil authorities used mounted police to break up labour demonstrations.

Questions 5 and 6 refer to the following passage.

The October 1929 stock market crash is easily identified in hindsight as the beginning of the Great Depression that gripped the world for almost a decade. But at the time, many business leaders, government officials, and economists thought that it was just a normal downturn in the business cycle and that prosperity would soon return.

The evidence that this wouldn't happen came quickly, however, as the price for farm products such as wheat dropped by one half between 1929 and 1933. Farmers' incomes fell as a result, and they stopped buying tractors, cars, appliances, and other manufactured goods. This drop in demand caused factories to cut back on production, putting employees out of work, which meant that they bought fewer things. Since all sectors of the economy were interrelated, everyone began to suffer. By 1933 about 30 percent of Canadians were unemployed; in fact, thousands had no job for the rest of the decade. Many others were underemployed as they took whatever job they could find and most took big pay cuts.

5. Based on the passage, what values did leaders, officials, and economists exhibit at the first signs of economic troubles in 1929?

    (1) a belief in socialism
    (2) a desire for a new challenge
    (3) a commitment to compassion
    (4) a mistrust of bankers
    (5) trust in the integrity of the capitalist economic system

6. According to the passage, why did the Depression spread to the whole economy?

    (1) All parts of the economy were interrelated.
    (2) People panicked and started to spend unwisely.
    (3) Canada's economy was based on the production of staples.
    (4) The stock market prices went up and down.
    (5) Railway companies stopped transporting goods.

Questions 7 and 8 refer to the following passage.

Canada did not enter the World War II with Britain on September 1, 1939. Canada officially declared war against Nazi Germany after a full debate and a vote in the Canadian House of Commons. One member of Parliament voted against going to war, the pacifist J. S. Woodsworth.

Some regard this independent declaration of war as an important symbolic act for Canada. It signified that Canada now had full control over both its internal and external affairs. The road to this full independence had been paved by the passing of a British law in 1931, the Statute of Westminster. This statute recognized the dominions of the old British Empire as fully independent countries. Britain could no longer pass laws binding on them. Three centuries of colonial control had ended.

Canadian historian Arthur Lower wrote that there was a good reason for marking December 11, 1931, as Canada's independence day, "for on that day she became a sovereign state."

7. Based on the passage, which of following best reflects a set of values?

    (1) Canada struggled to convince Britain to pass the Statute of Westminster.
    (2) Britain passed the Statute of Westminster only to control Canada.
    (3) Britain was not only willing but eager to pass the Statute of Westminster.
    (4) J. S. Woodsworth voted against the war.
    (5) The best way to achieve independence is through violent means.

8. What did historian Arthur J. Lower imply by his statement that December 11, 1931 was Canada's real independence day?

    (1) Canada should change its national holiday from July 1 to December 11.
    (2) Before the Statute of Westminster was passed, Canada was still a colony.
    (3) Canada should still allow Britain to dictate when a state of war was officially proclaimed.
    (4) Canada should have the same Indepen-dence Day as Australia and New Zealand.
    (5) Independence for Canada was still a long way off.

Answers start on page 753.

Canada and the Modern World

Distinguishing Conclusions from Supporting Details

A **conclusion** is a judgment or decision based on facts and details. **Supporting details** are the evidence that leads to the conclusion. Sometimes a writer points the reader to the conclusion by using words such as *thus* or *therefore*. Other times, the reader must distinguish the conclusion from the details without such clues.

One way to identify a writer's conclusion is to draw a conclusion yourself. Add the details in the passage together and see what larger idea you get. For example, consider these details about early immigrants to Canada: They left homes and families behind. Their sea journey was difficult. Customs authorities could send them back to Europe for many reasons. What conclusion can you come to? Immigrants must have had courage and determination.

Read carefully to distinguish details from the conclusion in a piece of writing. Ask yourself two questions: "What facts and details are given in the passage? What larger idea do they point to?"

conclusion
a judgment or decision based on facts and details

supporting details
the evidence or facts that lead to a conclusion

Read the passage and answer the question below.

Emily Murphy was one of the most remarkable Canadians of the twentieth century. Through her writing she mobilized public opinion that forced the Alberta government to pass a law protecting a wife's right to a one-third share in her husband's property. She was also prominent in helping women to get the vote in Canada. A self-taught legal expert, she was the first woman in the British Empire to be appointed a judge in 1916 in Edmonton. On her first day in court, however, a lawyer told Murphy that her judgments would not count because, in the eyes of the *British North America Act*, "persons" did not include women. Murphy was outraged and she began a struggle to overturn this injustice. When the federal government used the "persons" argument to refuse to appoint a woman as a senator, she found a little-known law that allowed her to challenge the government's position in the Supreme Court of Canada. But in 1928 even that high court ruled that under the law women were not persons. Undaunted, Murphy appealed to the British Privy Council in London, and a year later the Privy Council declared that women were persons.

Tip

Sometimes a conclusion follows such words as *therefore, thus,* and *so,* or *what we can learn from this.* Use these words as guides to identify the conclusion.

Put a check mark next to the sentence that states the conclusion of the passage.

_____ a. Emily Murphy discovered a little-known law that allowed her to challenge the discriminatory practice against appointing women Senators.

_____ b. Emily Murphy was a courageous activist for women's equality in Canada.

Option b is a conclusion drawn in the passage. *Option a* is just one example of Emily Murphy's activism for women.

GED Practice

Directions: Choose the <u>one best answer</u> to each question.

<u>Question 1</u> refers to the following passage.

Most adult Canadians in the 1950s and 1960s remembered the hardships of the Great Depression clearly. In fact, they wanted governments to provide social security for all citizens and they were willing to pay for that security through taxes. In the 1950s, as Canada's economy improved, the tentative measures of the first social security programs were broadened to include healthcare for everybody.

Saskatchewan became the model for all of Canada when it introduced a hospital insurance plan in 1947. Ten years later, the federal government offered to share the costs of hospital insurance with all provinces. By 1961, every province was part of the plan. In 1962, Saskatchewan again led the way with medical services insurance, so that when people went to the doctor, their medical insurance paid for the treatment. The federal government followed suit with the *Medical Care Insurance Act* of 1966. This act provided the funds to support all provincial medical insurance plans.

By the end of the 1960s, Canadians had both government-provided hospital care and access to doctors no matter where they lived. This provision of universal healthcare still differentiates Canada from the United States.

1. What conclusion is supported by the details in the passage?

   (1) There was no agreement that governments should provide social security for people.
   (2) A national consensus in favour of social programs for all Canadians emerged in Canada.
   (3) Doctors opposed socialized medicine.
   (4) The federal government was the first to provide medical insurance.
   (5) Canada followed the American lead in providing free universal access to medical care.

<u>Question 2</u> refers to the following passage.

On October 5, 1970, a cell of the FLQ movement (Front de libération du Québec) kidnapped British Trade Commissioner James Cross in Montreal. The captors demanded that Quebec free imprisoned FLQ members and publish their separatist Manifesto. The FLQ Manifesto was read on the radio, but no prisoners were released.

Five days later, Quebec Labour Minister Pierre Laporte was kidnapped. To some Canadians, the events looked like the start of a full-scale political revolution.

When newly elected Quebec Premier Robert Bourassa asked for federal help, Prime Minister Pierre Trudeau invoked the *War Measures Act* to control the "apprehended insurrection." This Act gave the police exceptional powers to search for the kidnappers and led to 400 arrests of suspected terrorists.

On October 17, Pierre Laporte was found strangled. In December, the FLQ agreed to release James Cross, and later that month, Laporte's murderers were arrested.

In English Canada, Trudeau's actions were well received at first. But as time passed, very few charges were actually laid against the detainees. The FLQ was shown to be a mere handful of people, and in fact, it appeared that there really had been no insurrection at all. But faced with the irrational violence of the FLQ radicals, even the Parti Québécois began to tone down its rhetoric on independence for Quebec.

2. What conclusion about why the October Crisis of 1970 ended as it did is supported by the details in the passage?

   (1) The people of Quebec preferred to deal with their political issues peacefully.
   (2) The prime minister was indecisive.
   (3) Montreal was a dangerous city.
   (4) The Quebec government could not keep law and order in its own province.
   (5) Canada attracted political terrorists.

Questions 3 through 5 refer to the following information and document.

In 1900, the concept of rights for individuals in Canada was very limited. Individuals did have rights, of course, in both law courts and in voting, but only if they were men over the age of 21 and owned property. Much of life was governed by traditional beliefs such as the idea that women were not equal to men, the belief that certain racial and ethnic groups were superior, and the feeling that Christian beliefs should be the nation's moral guide.

One hundred years later, many of those beliefs and traditions have changed. In fact, many rights unimagined a century ago are now entrenched in our laws. The document that spells them out is the *Canadian Charter of Rights and Freedoms*. It is part of our Constitution and cannot be changed except by a constitutional amendment, a process not easily achieved. The Charter sets out guarantees and rights in general language, but it is up to the courts to interpret their precise meaning. Since the adoption of the Charter in 1982, there have been thousands of court cases in which judges have interpreted the Charter's meaning.

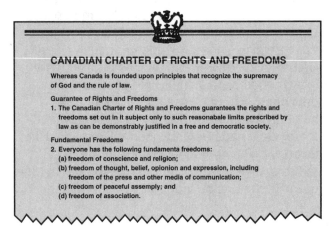

CANADIAN CHARTER OF RIGHTS AND FREEDOMS

Whereas Canada is founded upon principles that recognize the supremacy of God and the rule of law.

Guarantee of Rights and Freedoms

1. The Canadian Charter of Rights and Freedoms guarantees the rights and freedoms set out in it subject only to such reasonabale limits prescribed by law as can be demonstrably justified in a free and democratic society.

Fundamental Freedoms

2. Everyone has the following fundamenta freedoms:
   (a) freedom of conscience and religion;
   (b) freedom of thought, belief, opionion and expression, including freedom of the press and other media of communication;
   (c) freedom of peaceful assemply; and
   (d) freedom of association.

Source: *Canadian Charter of Rights and Freedoms*, Department of Justice, Canada.

3. What conclusion about the *Canadian Charter of Rights and Freedoms* is supported by details in the passage?

   (1) The Charter causes a glut of cases in the courts.
   (2) Traditional Canadian beliefs are entrenched in the Charter.
   (3) The courts bear the burden of interpreting the Charter.
   (4) Women are major supporters of the Charter.
   (5) The United States Constitution was a source of inspiration for the Charter.

4. Only laws or acts of government or governmental agencies such as the police can be used as the basis for an appeal to the courts based on the Charter. Protection of a person's rights against private discrimination, for example, can't be used as an appeal to the courts. Which of the following could be the basis of a Charter appeal in a court case?

   (1) Your neighbour's loud rock music constantly wakes you up at night so you can't work effectively at your job.
   (2) The police don't inform you that you have the right to speak to a lawyer when they arrest you.
   (3) A person next to you starts to smoke a cigarette even though there is a sign requesting "no smoking" in view.
   (4) Someone makes fun of your clothing in front of others.
   (5) A sign in a protest demonstration declares that a business discriminates against gays in their hiring practices.

5. According to the Charter, what are the two fundamental principles that underlie all of the Charter's sections?

   (1) fair play and honesty
   (2) the right to own property and pursue happiness
   (3) personal security and integrity
   (4) the supremacy of God and the rule of law
   (5) compassion and understanding

Answers start on page 754.

Social Studies • Canadian History

GED Review Canadian History

Directions: Choose the one best answer to each question.

Question 1 refers to the following passage.

Lord Durham was sent to Canada in 1838 to investigate the reasons for the two violent rebellions in Upper and Lower Canada the previous year. His report made three central recommendations: (1) unite the two provinces under one government (he hoped the English would overwhelm and assimilate the French); (2) force the colonial governor to use elected Assembly members as his ruling advisors (instead of the appointed cronies on the executive councils); and (3) give the colonies power over their own internal affairs. Durham blamed the haughty elite of Upper Canada and the outdated system for the rebellion there, but in describing the situation in Lower Canada (Quebec) he found "two nations warring in the bosom of a single state … a struggle not of principles but of race." He also dismissed the French Canadians as "a people with no history and no literature."

1. What might one expect the reaction of the French in Quebec to be to Durham's report?

   (1) They would agree with his conclusions.
   (2) They would call for a new report.
   (3) They might invite him back for a second look.
   (4) They would be indifferent to his conclusions.
   (5) They would find the report both insulting and threatening.

Questions 2 and 3 refer to the following paragraph.

Lieutenant Governor John Graves Simcoe had deep-seated feelings against slavery. His revulsion increased when he found that many of the Loyalists who were coming to Upper Canada from the United States were bringing slaves with them. Simcoe's anti-slavery attitudes were not shared by everyone in Upper Canada, however, and he had a very difficult time forcing through a law banning slavery in Upper Canada. He succeeded, thanks to the help of Peter Martin, a representative of the black community in the province. The *Slave Act of 1793* did not free existing slaves, but it did outlaw the slave trade. The Assembly was outraged by Simcoe's action and introduced a bill of its own to reinstate slavery. The lieutenant governor stalled the passage of this bill in the Assembly for so long, however, that it eventually died. So, Upper Canada became not only the first place in North America, but also in all the British colonies, to formally abolish slavery.

2. What evidence in the passage reveals that Simcoe exercised not only strong moral leadership, but also political skill?

   (1) He publicly attacked those who owned slaves.
   (2) He encouraged slave owners to sell their slaves.
   (3) He imposed law and order on the province.
   (4) He enacted a law without any discussion.
   (5) He used effective tactics to delay and ultimately kill a morally repugnant bill.

3. What general principle of history does the passage reveal?

   (1) The power of groups is always stronger than the power of the individual.
   (2) There was nothing morally wrong with the institution of slavery.
   (3) Upper Canada was the first colony to pass a law banning slavery.
   (4) A strong individual can set the moral standard for a whole continent, if not the world.
   (5) Might makes right.

Questions 4 through 7 refer to the following passage and map.

In 1900, when Canada was 33 years old, it had seven provinces and two territories. The population was 5.4 million people in 1901, when the first national census of the twentieth century was taken. At that time, most Canadians claimed they were of British, French, or Aboriginal background. The remaining people identified themselves as being German or northern European. More than 60 percent of Canadians lived in rural areas.

Today, Canada has a population of more than 33 million, and most live in urban areas. One out of three Canadians lives in the four largest cities: Toronto, Montreal, Vancouver, and Ottawa-Hull. Although many Canadians are still from the four ethnic backgrounds identified in the 1901 census, the ethnic composition of Canada has changed dramatically. Canada has become a multicultural country. So much so, in fact, that on their census forms many Canadians don't just tick off a box to identify their ethnic background; they write it in. In the most recent census, for example, more than 30 percent chose the multiple category (more than one ethnic background). And almost 20 percent chose the relatively new category of just plain "Canadian."

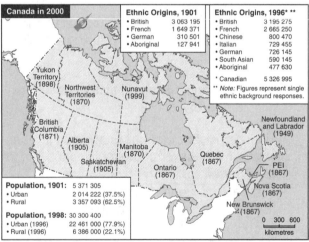

Note: Date under each province/territory name indicates when it joined Canada.

Source: Ian M. Hundey and Michael L. Magarrey, *Canadian History 1900–2000*. Toronto: Irwin, 2000, p. 424.

4. According to the passage and the map, the ethnic composition of Canada's population changed dramatically in the twentieth century. What other remarkable change occurred?

   (1) Canada's population shifted from the Maritime provinces to British Columbia.
   (2) There was a large rural-to-urban shift.
   (3) Most Canadians left for the U.S.
   (4) The population declined.
   (5) Most immigrants declared that they were Canadian.

5. In what way does the recent census form emphasize the fact that Canada has become a multicultural country?

   (1) Canadians can write in their ethnic background(s) rather than just select from a limited number.
   (2) The form is available in English and French.
   (3) The form allows people to identify their favourite foods.
   (4) Everyone fills out census forms.
   (5) The form only allows you to choose one ethnic identity.

6. What is one likely explanation of the fact that almost 20 percent chose the relatively new census category of "Canadian" to indicate their national or ethnic origin?

   (1) They wanted to indicate that they consume a certain brand name of beer.
   (2) They found it difficult to choose any other category.
   (3) They wanted to express a new identity.
   (4) They couldn't understand the question.
   (5) They didn't want to be identified as American.

7. According to the map, what is the most recently established administrative area in Canada with its own government?

   (1) Newfoundland and Labrador
   (2) the city of Edmonton
   (3) the Yukon territory
   (4) the territory of Nunavut
   (5) the Greater Toronto Area (GTA)

Questions 8 and 9 to refer to the following passage and cartoon.

In 1990, the United Nations Development Programme (UNDP) published its first annual Human Development Report. This report ranks 175 countries to produce a global index of human development. The definition of human development includes factors considered important for living a long, healthy life, being educated, and having access to the resources needed for a decent standard of living.

Japan was ranked first overall in 1990, 1991, and 1993. Canada was ranked first in 1992, and consistently from 1994 to 1999. Canada was ranked above the United States, Japan, France, the Netherlands, Iceland, Norway, Finland, and Sweden.

Interestingly, the report concludes that there is no automatic link between economic growth and human progress. Even if a nation has a relatively low national income, human development can be very positive. In countries where people participate widely in nongovernmental organizations, the human development index goes up. But the report also notes that there is still a gap in many countries between the development opportunities for men and women. Closing this gap is thought to be essential for raising human development worldwide.

In recent years, the report has added a Human Poverty Index, a Gender-Related Development Index, and a Gender Empowerment Measure. Despite its overall first ranking in 1999, Canada ranked fourth on the gender-related index and ninth out of the seventeen richest industrialized countries in the poverty index.

Source: Cartoonist Dusan Petricic.

8. If Canada wanted to work at raising its rank on the index of human development, which of the following might it address?

   (1) make strong efforts to ensure pay equity for men and women
   (2) increase its per capita military spending budget
   (3) improve the salaries of professional baseball players
   (4) impose strict controls on immigration to Canada
   (5) build more coal-burning energy plants

9. What opinion about Canada's high rank on the Human Development Index does the cartoon imply?

   (1) Canada should get a medal for its good performance.
   (2) Poverty also exists in the so-called "best" country in the world.
   (3) Grinding poverty only exists on the other side of the globe, in developing countries.
   (4) Begging on the streets is a serious concern in Canadian cities.
   (5) Poor countries should model themselves after Canada.

Answers start on page 754.

Lesson 7

World History

The record of world history is an ongoing struggle of some groups to control others—and of the unquenchable desire of people for freedom. Studying world history helps us understand and value the progress and remaining challenges that exist in today's world. World history is an important part of the GED Social Studies Test, making up 15 percent of the test questions.

Ancient Empires of the World

Identifying Implications

implication
something that is not openly stated but is hinted at or suggested

Most spoken and written information is presented to you directly. However, sometimes information is only hinted at, or implied. When an author implies something, he or she is making an **implication.** To get the most out of the information you receive, you must understand not only the stated information, but also its implications.

Identifying implications is an important skill for reading and understanding the social studies material you will encounter on the GED Test. This skill may seem difficult, but you already identify implications every day. For example, suppose your boss tells you to be extra helpful in your dealings with a particular customer. Even though your boss does not tell you why you should be helpful, you will probably understand the implication that this is an important customer.

To identify implications in what you read, you must first identify the facts and any conclusions that the author has stated directly. Then see whether any other conclusions that are not directly stated can be drawn from the material. Also, look for phrases that suggest emotions or attitudes. For example, if the author writes that someone gritted her teeth before making a decision, the author's implication is that the decision was unpleasant or difficult.

 Read between the lines to identify implications. Remember that what is suggested but is not stated can be as important as what is stated.

GED Practice

Directions: Choose the one best answer to each question.

Questions 1 through 3 refer to the following passage and chart.

In about 800 B.C.E., organized society developed on the Greek peninsula when clans (group of people with a common ancestor) and tribes established hundreds of city-states. At first, each city-state was ruled by a tribal chief or king. By about 700 B.C.E., most of these rulers had been overthrown by wealthy landowners. The Greeks referred to these new governments as *aristokratika,* or aristocracies, meaning "rule by the best." Eventually, some aristocracies were replaced by governments in which the common people, or *demos,* had a voice in the city-state's rule. These governments were called democracies. The greatest democracy was Athens, which became the centrepiece of what is called Greece's Golden Age around 400 B.C.E.

Although it lasted fewer than a hundred years, Greece's Golden Age was a time of great achievement in science, the arts, and ways of thinking about the world. Wars and the various rivalries among the city-states gradually wore down Athens' cultural leadership, but the accomplishments of that short period affected Greek civilization and the entire world for centuries to come.

Science and Thought	Art and Drama
Socrates (470 B.C.E.–399 B.C.E.): developed methods of seeking truth and knowledge that became the basis of modern education	**Aeschylus** (525 B.C.E.–456 B.C.E.): wrote the world's first dramas, or plays that contain action and dialogue
Hippocrates (460 B.C.E.–377 B.C.E.): founded medicine by teaching that diseases had natural causes and were not punishment of the gods	**Euripedes** (484 B.C.E.–406 B.C.E.): wrote the first dramas to focus on ordinary people and social issues rather than on actions of the gods
Democritus (460 B.C.E.–370 B.C.E.): developed the idea that the universe is made up of tiny particles of matter that he called atoms	**Myron** (480 B.C.E.–440 B.C.E.): sculpted *The Discus Thrower,* one of the most famous examples of ancient Greek art

1. Which of the following is implied by the passage?

   (1) Greek culture drew heavily on Egyptian civilization.
   (2) The English word *democracy* comes from the Greek term meaning "the people."
   (3) The Greek city-states were very large.
   (4) An aristocracy is a better form of government than a democracy.
   (5) Warfare encourages cultural growth.

To identify and understand a writer's implications, look for clues in word and sentence order that imply important ideas and connections.

2. What can you conclude from the chart?

   (1) The greatest playwrights came from Athens.
   (2) Myron was executed because of his art.
   (3) Socrates inspired Hippocrates's teachings.
   (4) Socrates influenced the writing of Euripedes.
   (5) The early Greeks influenced modern science.

3. What reason is implied for Athens' cultural leadership in the Golden Age?

   (1) its military victory over Sparta
   (2) its desire to influence the rest of the world
   (3) its democratic form of government
   (4) the rivalries among city-states
   (5) the contributions of Aeschylus and Myron

Questions 4 through 6 refer to the following passage and map.

In South America, advanced civilizations first appeared along the coast of what is now Peru. The Nazca people farmed the region as early as 3000 B.C.E., and by 1800 B.C.E. they were working with metals and building large temples. A later people, the Moche, created an elaborate system of canals to irrigate their fields and raised llamas and guinea pigs for meat. By 400 C.E., the Moche kingdom extended 645 km along the coast, linked by roads that the Inca would use about a thousand years later to rule their own empire in the same region.

Between 1800 B.C.E. and 900 C.E., the Maya developed a civilization across much of Central America that rivaled the ancient Mediterranean cultures. Like the early Greeks, the Maya lived in independent city-states. They cleared the forest outside each city and raised crops to feed the city's population. Some of these cities were very large. Tikal in present-day Guatemala covered 80 km^2 and had a population of 75 000–100 000 in 400 C.E.

Trade was also important to the Maya. Even without pack animals or knowledge of the wheel, they carried trade goods great distances on their backs. One of Tikal's trading partners was Teotihuacán, 1600 km away in central Mexico. With a population as high as 200 000 Teotihuacán was the largest city in ancient America.

For reasons that are still unclear, Teotihuacán, like the Mayan civilization, was gone by 900 C.E. However, around 1200 C.E., a new people, the Aztec, built a new civilization near the ruins of the great abandoned city.

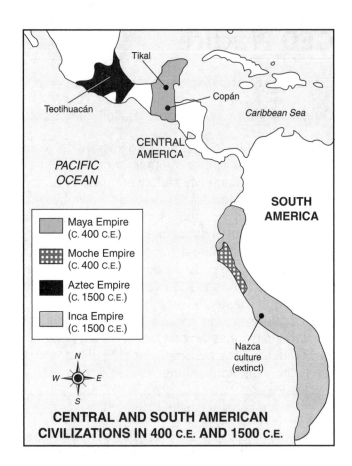

CENTRAL AND SOUTH AMERICAN CIVILIZATIONS IN 400 C.E. AND 1500 C.E.

4. Based on the passage, which of the following is a similarity among the Nazca, Moche, and Mayan civilizations?

   (1) They each formed city-states and lived in cities.
   (2) Extensive road systems existed in each empire.
   (3) Farming was important in each culture.
   (4) They all arose in South America.
   (5) They each declined and disappeared for reasons that are not clear.

5. Which of the following is supported by evidence presented on the map?

   (1) The cities of Teotihuacán, Tikal, and Copán traded with each other.
   (2) The Aztec and Inca empires existed at the same time.
   (3) The Inca made use of Moche roads to conquer Copán.
   (4) The Aztec built their empire on Tikal's ruins.
   (5) The Aztec were active in Central America before the Maya.

6. Which of the following does Moche road building suggest was important in the Moche culture?

   (1) self-government
   (2) cities
   (3) learning
   (4) religion
   (5) trade

As Greece was entering its Golden Age, a new power was rising on the Italian peninsula to the west. In 509 B.C.E., the Latin people of Rome overthrew the Etruscan kings who ruled them. They set up a republic in which the city's citizens elected representatives to govern them. However, an aristocracy of certain clans quickly gained control of the elected offices.

Roman laws were not written down, so it was easy for elected officials to interpret them in ways that kept their clans in power. Citizens of Rome soon demanded change. Around 450 B.C.E., Roman law was put in writing and became more democratic. For example, all citizens gained the right to hold public office. Citizens who owned property were also required to serve in the Roman army.

Democracy spread as Rome extended its power. By 272 B.C.E., Rome controlled all of Italy. The peninsula's conquered peoples all became citizens of the Roman Republic.

Moving beyond Italy, Rome invaded and defeated the powerful city of Carthage in 202 B.C.E. and gained control of North Africa. Next, Roman armies moved west into Spain. They also marched east, conquering Greece and its colonies in present-day Turkey. By 133 B.C.E., Rome's supremacy in the Mediterranean was complete.

The Romans did not grant citizenship or democratic government to peoples outside Italy. Instead, the conquered peoples were ruled by an official appointed by Rome and backed by a Roman army of occupation. These subject peoples were forced to pay high taxes to their Roman masters. Some, like the citizens of Carthage, were even enslaved by the Romans.

7. What implication does the passage make about Carthage?

   (1) It was located in North Africa.
   (2) It was defeated by Rome's armies.
   (3) It was more democratic than Rome.
   (4) Its conquest gave Rome supremacy in the Mediterranean region.
   (5) Its citizens became citizens of Rome.

Government of the Roman Republic

Senate
Citizens elected upper-class Romans to a 300-member Senate, which passed laws, set foreign policy, and controlled government funds.

Popular Assemblies
Assemblies of citizens voted on laws and elected officials called tribunes. Tribunes could block acts of the Senate that were not in the public interest.

Consuls
Two elected consuls ran the government. Each consul had the power to veto (the Latin word meaning "I forbid") the actions of the other.

Praetors
These elected officials oversaw the legal system and interpreted questions about the law.

Censors
These officials registered citizens according to their wealth, selected candidates for the Senate, and oversaw the moral conduct of all Romans.

8. Which officials of the Canadian government are most like the Roman praetors?

   (1) the prime minister, who can veto acts of Parliament
   (2) the members of the senate who pass the nation's laws
   (3) the members of the provincial legislatures, who pass the laws for each province
   (4) the justices of the Supreme Court, who determine whether laws agree with the Constitution
   (5) the premiers, who head the provinces and territories

9. What does the information suggest that the ancient Romans valued most?

   (1) wealth and trade
   (2) political and military power
   (3) freedom and equality for all peoples
   (4) equal rights for women
   (5) Greek art and culture

Answers start on page 755.

How Nations Arose

Assessing the Appropriateness of Information

People often make unsupported **generalizations** and reach unsupported **conclusions.** You probably hear them all the time: "The shipping clerks don't work as hard as the sales clerks." "There is a lot more crime in this neighbourhood than there used to be." Without evidence to back them up, these statements have little or no value.

Appropriate information consists of facts and other details that make a generalization or conclusion true, understandable, and believable. For a generalization or conclusion to be useful, there must be appropriate information to support it. The information must have some basis in fact. It should illustrate or provide an example, describe a cause, or explain the reasoning behind the generalization or conclusion. Any information that fails to do one of these things is probably not appropriate information, even if it is interesting and true.

generalization
a broad statement applied to an entire class of things or people

conclusion
a judgment or decision about someone or something

appropriate information
information that supports an idea, a generalization, or a conclusion

Read the passage and complete the exercise below.

Today we think of a nation as the land where people live under the rule of a single government. For much of history, however, a nation was defined by culture rather than by boundaries or politics. All people who shared a language and ethnic background were a nation, even if they were governed by different rulers. The Tang emperors of China in the eighth century supported Buddhism and encouraged Chinese arts. The Franks were a nation in the sixth century, a thousand years before the Bourbon kings united them to form the political nation of France. Indeed, the goal of turning a cultural nation into a political nation has been a major force in world history.

To determine whether information is appropriate to other material, first determine the central idea, generalization, or conclusion presented in the material.

Put a check mark next to the information that supports the conclusion that a nation is a people, not a geographic area with set boundaries.

_____ a. The Franks were a nation in the sixth century, a thousand years before the Bourbon kings united them to form the political nation of France.

_____ b. The Tang emperors of China in the eighth century supported Buddhism and encouraged Chinese arts.

You are correct if you chose *option a.* The passage is about the difference between the historic and modern definitions of the word *nation. Option a* illustrates this difference. The information in *option b* does not help you understand what a nation is.

GED Practice

Directions: Choose the <u>one best answer</u> to each question.

Questions 1 and 2 refer to the following passage.

In the mid-seventh century, Muslim traders spread their religion, Islam, beyond their homelands in the Middle East. By 750 C.E., Muslim influence had stretched across North Africa into Spain and east into India. Where Muslims gained control, science, learning, and the arts became important.

Arabs held the greatest power in the Muslim world for about 500 years. Between 1000 and 1100, however, the Turks swept out of Central Asia, conquered much of the Middle East, and converted to Islam. Eventually, leadership of the Muslim world passed to the Turks.

Around 1400, a group of Turks called Ottomans invaded Europe. By 1450, the Ottoman Empire included most of Greece and present-day Bulgaria. By 1550, the Ottomans had gained control over most of eastern Europe, the Middle East, and North Africa.

1. What is the best title for this passage?

   (1) The Influence of Religion in the Middle Ages
   (2) The Growth and Spread of Islam, 650–1550
   (3) Arab Domination in the Middle Ages
   (4) Ottoman Domination in the Middle Ages
   (5) Muslim Domination of North Africa

2. Which conclusion about the Ottoman Empire is supported by the information in the passage?

   (1) The Turks persecuted the Arabs.
   (2) The Muslims in Spain were Ottomans.
   (3) The Turks ended the Renaissance in Europe.
   (4) The arts flourished in the Ottoman Empire.
   (5) The Muslims persecuted the Christians.

Question 3 refers to the following passage.

Between the time the Roman Empire collapsed and the first English settlers arrived in North America, three great civilizations rose and fell in West Africa. The earliest of these was Ghana, which developed in the fourth century along a caravan route between North Africa and West Africa. By 1000, Ghanaians had become rich in the salt, gold, and slave trades. But religious conflict erupted when the kingdom was invaded by Muslim Berbers from North Africa. By the mid-thirteenth century, Ghana had ceased to exist.

Ghana's decline allowed the rise of a neighbouring kingdom—Mali. Eventually, Ghana became a part of Mali's empire that stretched from the West African interior to the Atlantic Coast. At the height of Mali's culture and power in the early fourteenth century, Timbuktu, its capital city, was an important centre of learning. Its Islamic university attracted scholars from Egypt and Arabia. Then a series of weak rulers caused Mali to decline. However, Mali managed to keep control of the trade routes to North Africa until the mid-fifteenth century when it was conquered by Songhay, a kingdom that it had once ruled.

Under Songhay control, West African culture thrived. Trade in gold, ivory, and slaves flourished. Timbuktu grew to include 180 Islamic schools and three Islamic universities that taught astronomy, poetry, medicine, and religion. Their libraries held large collections of ancient Greek and Roman writings. By the mid-sixteenth century, education rivaled trade as Timbuktu's major activity.

3. According to the passage, which value seems to have been <u>least</u> important in Songhay culture?

   (1) human rights
   (2) education
   (3) wealth
   (4) literature
   (5) religion

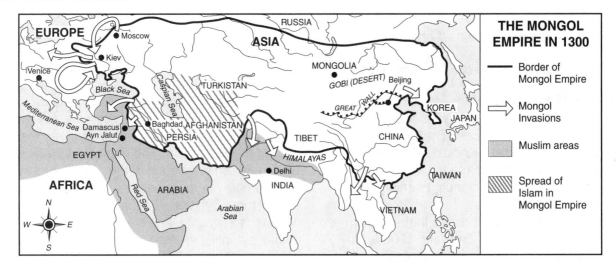

In the early 1200s, a people called the Mongols expanded west and south from a region in Central Asia now called Mongolia. In the next hundred years, led by Genghis Khan and then by his three grandsons, the Mongols established the greatest empire the world had ever seen.

Genghis Khan had conquered northern China by 1215. He then turned his attention to the west. Before he died in 1227, his empire reached to the Black Sea.

Mongols led by Genghis Khan's grandson Batu swept across Russia and invaded Europe in the 1240s. Only politics saved Europe from conquest. Mongol forces had defeated Polish and Hungarian armies and were threatening Vienna in 1242 when Batu called off the attack and returned to Asia to help choose the next Mongol leader. Meanwhile, another grandson, Halagu, had conquered Persia by the 1250s. His invasion of the Middle East failed when he was defeated by Muslim forces in Syria in 1260.

By 1279, the third grandson, Kublai Khan, had completed his grandfather's conquest of China and extended the Mongol empire into Korea and Tibet. He also attacked Burma and Vietnam. In 1281, he attempted to add Japan to the empire.

Mongol armies struck terror wherever they went. Archers on horseback could cover 160 km a day and, while at a full gallop, send an arrow to its target. Mongol warriors looted and destroyed places that resisted them and often put the people who lived there to death.

4. What is the topic of this passage and map?

   (1) clashes between Mongols and Muslims
   (2) Genghis Khan and his grandsons
   (3) the growth of the Mongol Empire
   (4) invasion routes of Mongol armies
   (5) the Mongol threat to Europe

5. Which assumption can be made based on the passage and the map?

   (1) The Mongol Empire extended into Africa.
   (2) The Mongols attacked Vietnam by sea.
   (3) The Mongols eventually conquered Arabia.
   (4) A Mongol invasion of Japan did not succeed.
   (5) All Mongols were Muslims.

6. What conclusion is best supported by the information in the passage and the map?

   (1) The Mongols were not good at governing their empire.
   (2) The Mongols were the fiercest warriors that the world has ever seen.
   (3) The Mongols used superior technology to overwhelm their enemies.
   (4) The Mongol Empire declined after the death of Genghis Khan.
   (5) The Mongols had a major impact on world history.

Answers start on page 756.

Global Expansion

Analyzing Cause and Effect

As you learned in Lesson 4, a **cause** is what makes something happen; the **effect** is the result. Often an event has more than one cause, and a single cause can have many effects. Suppose that the place where you work is destroyed by fire. This one event would have many effects. Traffic would be disrupted around the site. Customers would have to go elsewhere. Employees might lose their jobs. Each of these effects in turn would be the cause of other effects. For example, losing your job because of the fire might mean that you must sell the new car you just bought because you cannot afford the car payments.

Written history, the record of real life, contains multiple causes and effects. In addition, some causes may be **implied causes**—that is, causes that are not directly stated. For example, a writer may describe a series of events and depend on the reader to understand that each event resulted from the prior event.

Another way to imply a cause is to state two or three related effects. Suppose you read in a novel that the main character's TV suddenly went blank. That could have happened for several reasons. But if you then read that the character was unable to turn on a light, the author is implying that a power failure was the cause.

cause
something that produces a result or consequence

effect
something brought about by a cause; a result or consequence

implied cause
a cause that is not directly stated but is only suggested or hinted at

To identify an implied cause, start with the known effect. Then look for a reason to explain why the effect happened.

Read the passage and complete the exercise below.

In the 1490s and early 1500s, Christopher Columbus made several voyages for Spain in which he explored the Caribbean islands and the coast of Central America. Meanwhile, in 1499, Spain's rival Portugal sent an expedition to explore the region farther south. On board for this voyage was an Italian-born navigator named Amerigo Vespucci. As his expedition explored the region, Vespucci decided that Columbus was wrong. This was not Asia, he concluded. Instead, he wrote, the lands were a "New World, because our ancestors had no knowledge of them." Soon mapmakers began using the name "America" on their maps to identify Amerigo Vespucci's New World.

Put a check mark next to the statement the passage indicates is the reason the Western Hemisphere is known as America.

_____ a. Spain and Portugal were competing to explore it.

_____ b. Vespucci was first to recognize it as a New World.

You are correct if you chose *option b*. The passage clearly suggests a connection between the name *America* and the first name of the man who realized the land was not Asia. The facts do not support *option a* as the cause.

GED Practice

Directions: Choose the <u>one best answer</u> to each question.

<u>Questions 1 through 5</u> refer to the following passage.

The Panama Canal makes Central America an important region in world trade. Central America is also important to the North American economy because North American companies have large investments in bananas, coffee, and other resources there. For both of these reasons, North America has long supported Central American governments that were not democratic but that brought stability to the region. Concern about stability increased after 1977, when the United States agreed to turn the canal over to Panama in 2000.

In the late 1970s, it became clear that Fidel Castro, the communist dictator of Cuba, was aiding rebels in Central America, including those in El Salvador. Supported by the United States, El Salvador's government fought back. The Salvadoran army and government death squads killed thousands of citizens suspected of siding with the rebels before peace was restored in the 1990s. American aid to Guatemala led to a similar chain of events during the same period.

In 1979, communists overthrew the U.S.-backed dictator of Nicaragua, whose family had ruled since the 1930s. The United States responded by financing, training, and arming a force known as the contras to overthrow the new government. In 1990, after a decade of war, the communists agreed to hold new elections. The U.S.-backed candidate, the daughter of a wealthy Nicaraguan family, became president.

1. What is the main purpose of this passage?

   (1) to tell about the Panama Canal
   (2) to show how imperialism affected Central America
   (3) to compare unrest in El Salvador, Guatemala, and Nicaragua
   (4) to show how North American investment caused imperialism in Central America
   (5) to describe the wars in Central America

2. According to the passage, what was the effect of U.S. involvement in Nicaragua?

   (1) the deaths of thousands of innocent citizens
   (2) wealthy Nicaraguans' loss of land to the poor
   (3) unhappiness in the United States over the government's policies in Nicaragua
   (4) Nicaraguans' dislike of U.S. policies
   (5) the ultimate failure of the communists in Nicaragua

3. Which cause for U.S. actions in Central America is implied in the passage?

   (1) concern for Panama Canal security
   (2) the location of Central American nations south of the United States
   (3) the importance of bananas and coffee to North American consumers
   (4) the perception of Central American nations as weak
   (5) the desire of U.S. leaders to seize control of Central America

4. Which countries mentioned in the passage practised imperialism?

   (1) the United States and Nicaragua
   (2) Nicaragua and Cuba
   (3) Cuba and the United States
   (4) the United States and El Salvador
   (5) El Salvador and Nicaragua

5. Which value was <u>least</u> important to the United States in its Central American policies?

   (1) the security of the Panama Canal
   (2) stable Central American governments
   (3) protecting North American investments
   (4) strengthening democracy in Central America
   (5) preventing the spread of communism

Social Studies • World History

Questions 6 through 9 refer to the following passage and map.

For centuries, China dealt with outsiders on its own terms. The government severely limited the movement of foreign traders in China. Chinese merchants accepted only gold and silver for their tea, silks, and other trade goods. In about 1800, however, British traders began offering opium from their colonies in India to pay for goods they bought in China. When China's government demanded that the drug imports be stopped, the result was a war that lasted from 1839 to 1842.

Great Britain's easy victory over China in the Opium War proved how powerful the Industrial Revolution had made European nations. To restore peace, China was forced to turn Hong Kong over to Great Britain and to give British traders special privileges in five Chinese ports.

Britain's special trade advantage with China did not last long. France and other nations soon demanded similar trade concessions. By the late nineteenth century, large areas of China had come under foreign control. These spheres of influence technically remained part of China. However, foreigners in each nation's sphere obeyed only the laws of their own nation. They were exempt from Chinese authority. Each sphere became a market for that country's products and a source of raw materials for its factories at home.

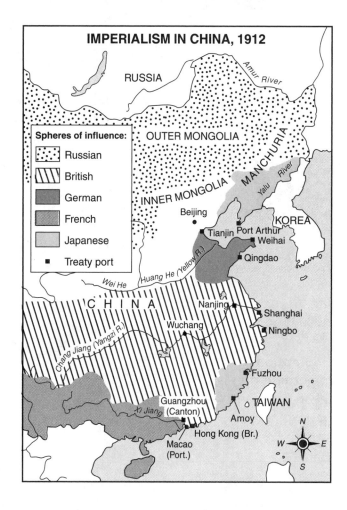

IMPERIALISM IN CHINA, 1912

Spheres of influence:
- Russian
- British
- German
- French
- Japanese
- ■ Treaty port

6. Which effect of the Industrial Revolution is implied in the passage?

  (1) The British began to produce opium.
  (2) Europe no longer desired Chinese silk.
  (3) The Industrial Revolution caused the Opium War.
  (4) Industrialized countries became more powerful than nonindustrial countries.
  (5) The Industrial Revolution caused spheres of influence to develop in China.

7. Which nation had the smallest sphere of influence in China in 1912?

  (1) France
  (2) Germany
  (3) Great Britain
  (4) Japan
  (5) Russia

8. Based on the passage, what value was <u>most</u> important to China when it fought the British in the Opium War?

  (1) holding on to the profits of the drug trade
  (2) convincing Japan that China was still strong
  (3) controlling trade coming into China
  (4) ending all trade with India
  (5) ending the spheres of influence in China

9. What is the <u>only</u> appropriate conclusion about Japan that can be supported by the information on the map and in the passage?

  (1) Japan was an ally of Britain and France.
  (2) Japan and Russia were at war in 1912.
  (3) Japan intended to conquer China and Korea.
  (4) Japan wanted to expand its spheres of influence in China.
  (5) Japan was an industrial nation in 1912.

Answers start on page 757.

The Post–Cold War World

Recognizing Unstated Assumptions (in Political Cartoons)

As you learned in Lesson 3, when people talk or write about a topic, they usually don't tell everything they know about it. They assume that you already know some things. Since a cartoon uses very few words to make its point, it makes many **assumptions** about what you know. To understand a political cartoon, you must recognize the cartoonist's assumptions. Examine this cartoon that was published in the early 1990s.

assumption
something that is taken for granted and not explained

To identify the assumptions in a political cartoon, you must look for visual clues to the cartoonist's message, such as the appearance of the figures drawn in the cartoon.

In this cartoon, you see a bear, labelled *Russia* on the cap, looking at a recipe labelled *Democracy* and holding a burning pot.

Put a check mark next to the sentence that gives an unstated assumption important for understanding the cartoon.

_____ a. Russia has no tradition of democracy so it is trying to use a "recipe."

_____ b. The burning pot represents the problems Russia is having making democracy work.

You are correct if you chose *option a.* You need to know that information (the *why*) in order to understand the cartoon's message, that Russia is having difficulty changing from communism to democracy. Recognizing the meaning of the pot in *option b* (the *what* of the cartoon) does not help you understand the cartoon's significance.

Social Studies • World History

GED Practice

Directions: Choose the one best answer to each question.

Questions 1 through 3 refer to the following passage and cartoon.

Since ancient times, there has been recurring yet intermittent conflict between Arabs and Jews in Palestine. During the centuries the region was part of the Ottoman Empire, few Jews lived in Palestine, and few conflicts arose. With the fall of the Ottoman Turks after World War I and with an influx of Jewish settlers to the region, tensions increased. They were aggravated by the British, who had made conflicting promises to both Arabs and Jews to gain their support against the Turks during the war.

Britain governed Palestine between the world wars. After World War II, the United Nations voted to divide Palestine into Arab and Jewish states. Arabs, who were the majority, felt betrayed. When Jews formed the state of Israel in 1948, surrounding Arab countries attacked. More than half of Palestine's Arabs fled. Ever since, Palestinians have sought to regain land they regard as their home. Jews, who consider their claims to the land equally valid, have resisted. Violence has often been the result. In 1956, for example, Egypt nationalized the Suez Canal, drawing Israel, Britain, and France into the conflict and causing a world crisis. Lester Pearson, Canada's top diplomat at the time, used his considerable skills at the United Nations to defuse the situation with a proposal for a neutral peace-keeping force in the area. For his efforts, Pearson was awarded the Nobel Prize for peace in 1957.

Since 1973, the United States has been trying to help settle the continuing disputes between Israel and the Palestinians. Israel and the Palestinian Liberation Organization (PLO), which represents Palestinian Arabs, reached several agreements during the 1990s. However, for various reasons, each agreement collapsed before it was fully implemented. In October 1998, encouraged by U.S. President Bill Clinton, the two sides concluded yet another agreement, which inspired the above cartoon.

1. Why does the cartoonist depict the three figures on a platform of playing cards?

   (1) to express the view that agreements between the two sides have been shaky
   (2) to recognize the Palestinian leader's love of card-playing
   (3) to show that making treaties is like gambling
   (4) to state that the United States should stay out of Middle Eastern issues
   (5) to honour President Clinton for his role in bringing peace to the Middle East

2. According to the passage, what is the basis of the Arab-Jewish conflict in the Middle East?

   (1) They practise different religions.
   (2) They fought each other in World War II.
   (3) They both lay claim to the same land.
   (4) The Ottomans set them against each other.
   (5) The British set them against each other.

3. What essential knowledge must you have in order to understand this 1998 cartoon?

   (1) The Arab is Yasser Arafat, the PLO head.
   (2) The figure on the right is Israel's prime minister, Benjamin Netanyahu.
   (3) Israel's parliament approved the peace agreement that Netanyahu is holding.
   (4) Most agreements between Israel and the PLO have not been fully carried out.
   (5) The Knesset is Israel's parliament.

Questions 4 through 7 refer to the following cartoon and passage.

Jeff Koterba/*Omaha World-Herald*. Reprinted by permission.

In the early 1980s, it seemed as if the Cold War between the Soviet Union and the West would never end. But by 1989, Soviet political control began to break down. The next year, the Soviet Union split into independent nations. Most of the Soviet Union's satellite nations in Europe had also overthrown their communist rulers and established democratic governments. Nowhere were these events more dramatic than in Berlin, a city surrounded by communist East Germany. Since 1961, the people of East Berlin had been separated from democratic West Berlin by a wall erected by the East German government.

On November 9, 1989, thousands of Germans on both sides of the Berlin Wall began to tear it down. The collapse of the Berlin Wall signalled the end of the Cold War and doom for European communism.

4. Which assumption can be made from the information in the passage?

   (1) The Soviet government opposed the Berlin Wall.
   (2) East Germany's rulers kept their people under tight control as communism was collapsing elsewhere.
   (3) Communism collapsed in the Soviet Union's satellite nations.
   (4) A communist government controlled East Berlin.
   (5) The countries formed from the breakup of the Soviet Union remained communist nations.

5. Which of the following has a relationship most similar to the one between East Germany and West Germany?

   (1) Canada and the United States
   (2) Great Britain and the United States
   (3) North Korea and South Korea
   (4) North Carolina and South Carolina
   (5) West Virginia and Virginia

6. Which assumption is important for you to make to understand this 1990 cartoon?

   (1) The dinosaur represents European communism under Soviet leadership.
   (2) The dinosaur represents West Berlin.
   (3) The Soviet Union built the Berlin Wall.
   (4) The Berlin Wall was located in Germany.
   (5) The Soviet Union was responsible for carrying out the destruction of the Berlin Wall.

7. If the cartoonist had given this cartoon a title that expresses its message, which title would he most likely have used?

   (1) Moving the Berlin Wall
   (2) The Fall of the Berlin Wall
   (3) European Communism Becomes Extinct
   (4) The Collapse of the Soviet Union
   (5) Communism Remains Big and Dangerous

Answers start on page 758.

Social Studies • World History

Directions: Choose the <u>one best answer</u> to each question.

<u>Questions 1 through 4</u> refer to the following passage.

The policy of one nation extending its power over weaker nations or peoples is known as imperialism. Imperialism has been practised in every period of history and in all regions of the world. Ancient Greeks invaded what is now western Turkey. The Macedonians conquered the Greeks and, under the leadership of Alexander the Great, extended their control eastward to India. The Romans commanded a huge empire stretching from England to Egypt. Much later, in the seventeenth century and eighteenth century, the English colonized and controlled India and much of North America.

In the 1800s, many European nations established empires. There were several reasons for this increase in imperialism. First, Europeans felt superior to other cultures. They wanted to spread their way of life and their Christian religion to other parts of the world. Second, as a result of the Industrial Revolution that started in the mid-eighteenth century, factories could produce huge amounts of goods. With more products to sell, the industrial nations of Europe needed more places to market their goods. Third, industrial nations needed secure sources of raw materials that would allow their factories and workers to keep producing the goods.

By the early twentieth century, nearly all of Africa had been colonized and divided by various European nations. France controlled most of West Africa; Britain controlled much of North and South Africa; and Belgium claimed Central Africa. Germany, Italy, Portugal, and Spain also held territory in Africa. Most of Southeast Asia, large parts of China, and many islands in the South Pacific also came under European control.

1. What is the subject of this passage?

   (1) the ancient Greek and Roman empires
   (2) European colonization in Asia
   (3) the spread of the Industrial Revolution
   (4) Great Britain's world empire
   (5) imperialism in world history

2. What is the reason that Europeans spread their culture and religion?

   (1) The Greeks and Romans had done this.
   (2) Europeans felt superior to other peoples.
   (3) Imperialism required them to do it.
   (4) They needed raw materials for their factories.
   (5) The people the Europeans met had no culture.

3. Which is an example of imperialism?

   (1) Spanish soldiers conquer the Inca Empire in the sixteenth century.
   (2) The United States declares its independence from Great Britain in the 1770s.
   (3) The world powers form the United Nations after World War II and invite other nations to join.
   (4) Japan protects its industries in the 1970s by banning competing foreign goods.
   (5) The United States and its allies free Kuwait in the Persian Gulf War in the 1990s.

4. Which of the following developments was a cause of European imperialism in the nineteenth century?

   (1) the lack of armies in other nations
   (2) the Industrial Revolution and the need for more markets to sell goods
   (3) the need for more markets to sell goods and the desire to subjugate the people of Africa
   (4) the need for more markets to sell goods and an excess of raw materials
   (5) the lack of religion in other nations

To decide whether a cause-and-effect relationship exists, ask yourself whether the second event would have happened if the first event had not taken place.

In 1949, Chinese communists led by Mao Zedong overthrew that nation's government. They converted China's economy to communism, silenced Chinese who opposed them, and ended what little democracy existed in China. After Mao died in 1976, China's leaders relaxed government control of the economy and began to let people operate their own small businesses.

This economic freedom encouraged some Chinese to push for political freedom, so in 1989, protesters gathered in the capital to demand democracy. China's leaders cracked down, sending troops to attack the protesters, killing hundreds. China's government continued its attempts to crush the pro-democracy movement in the 1990s. The movement's leaders and many other Chinese were arrested, tortured, and imprisoned. The world community condemned China for violating the human rights of its people, but China resisted demands for political reform.

5. Which title best relates the content of this passage to the cartoon?

   (1) The Communist Revolution in China
   (2) Mao Zedong's Contributions to China
   (3) China Makes Political Reforms
   (4) China Moves Toward a Capitalist Economy
   (5) The Pro-Democracy Movement in China

6. What was the effect of the event referred to in the cartoon?

   (1) The standard of living in China increased.
   (2) Mao Zedong was replaced as China's leader.
   (3) The world community criticized China.
   (4) Political freedom in China increased.
   (5) China's government made economic changes.

One way to decide if information supports a conclusion is to look for cause-and-effect relationships. Information that shows a cause of the conclusion is appropriate support for the conclusion.

Linda Boileau, *Frankfort State Journal*, Rothco Cartoon Syndicate. Reprinted by permission.

7. What does the figure on the ground in the cartoon represent?

   (1) the communist leaders of China
   (2) the United States
   (3) Mao Zedong
   (4) the protesters who demanded democracy
   (5) the overthrown 1949 government

8. Based on the cartoon and passage, what do China's leaders seem to value most?

   (1) control
   (2) truth
   (3) life
   (4) equality
   (5) human rights

9. What is the implication of this cartoon?

   (1) The desire for democracy is dead in China.
   (2) The desire for democracy is alive in China.
   (3) China's army was not in charge of the killing.
   (4) The killing of Chinese protesters is a myth.
   (5) Americans should stay out of China's affairs.

Questions 10 through 13 refer to the following chart.

THE LANGUAGE OF IMPERIALISM

Annexation	one country adds all or part of the territory of another country to its own territory; can be accomplished by agreement or by military action
Colonialism	formal control by one nation over another with the loss of identity and independence by the nation being controlled; contrast with protectorate
Cultural imperialism	pushing a form of government, lifestyle, values, or other parts of a culture on another people; does not require conquest or political control
Dependent colony	colony in which a few officials of the controlling nation rule the population of the controlled people; contrast with settlement colony
Military intervention	one nation uses force in the territory of another, not to conquer it, but to control events there; troops are usually uninvited, but the weaker country may be pressured to "invite" intervention
Neo-imperialism	one country exploits the natural resources of another, uses its people for labour, takes unfair advantage of investment opportunities, or uses it as a market to dump surplus products, sometimes called economic imperialism
Protectorate	arrangement in which a stronger country protects a weaker one: the weaker country retains its identity as a nation, but the stronger country takes full or partial control of its affairs; contrast with colonialism
Settlement colony	colony in which large numbers of people from the controlling nation occupy the land of the controlled people; contrast with dependent colony

10. In the 1820s, Protestant missionaries from New England introduced Christianity to Hawaii. When King Kamehameha III opposed laws they wanted passed, they tried to overthrow him.

    Which type of imperialism occurred in Hawaii?

    (1) neoimperialism
    (2) cultural imperialism
    (3) annexation
    (4) creation of a dependent colony
    (5) creation of a settlement colony

11. Angola had a civil war before Portugal granted the colony independence in 1975. The United States backed a group called the FNLA, the Soviet Union favoured the MPLA, and neighbouring South Africa aided UNITA. When South African forces entered Angola, Soviet-backed Cuban troops arrived to support the MPLA.

    What action were the Cubans taking?

    (1) colonialism
    (2) annexation
    (3) establishing a protectorate
    (4) cultural imperialism
    (5) military intervention

12. Vietnam gained independence from China in 939 C.E. after more than 1000 years of rule. Chinese Buddhism had become the guiding force in its culture. Even today, Vietnam uses the government systems introduced by the Chinese.

    Which types of imperialism are illustrated here?

    (1) settlement and dependent colonies
    (2) military intervention and colonialism
    (3) colonialism and cultural imperialism
    (4) cultural imperialism and neoimperialism
    (5) neoimperialism and settlement colonies

13. In 1876, Japan forced an unwanted trade agreement on Korea; by 1910, Korea had been annexed. Thousands of people left Japan and relocated in Korea. Korea did not regain its independence until Japan's defeat in World War II.

    Which types of imperialism did Korea experience?

    (1) neoimperialism and dependent colony
    (2) protectorate formation and cultural imperialism
    (3) cultural imperialism and colonialism
    (4) neoimperialism and settlement colony
    (5) colonialism and creation of a protectorate

Answers start on page 759.

Civics and Government

Understanding how our government and political system work is key to preserving our position as a free people. That is why civics and government is an important part of the GED Social Studies Test, making up 25 percent of the test questions.

Modern Government

Distinguishing Fact from Opinion

A **fact** is information about something that actually happened or actually exists. For example, when a news reporter covers a political demonstration and writes about what demonstrators are doing and saying, the reporter is reporting on things that exist and events that are taking place. These things and events are facts.

An **opinion** is an interpretation of the facts. Opinions are influenced by people's interests, by what they know about a subject, and by their experience with related facts. Opinions can lead people to act on the facts they know. Demonstrators express their opinions in the slogans on their signs and in their speeches. They support one view of a political issue and reject contrary views that other people may hold.

Political arguments are full of opinions. Although opinions are always *about* facts, they are not always *based on* facts or on sound reasoning. However, political opinions usually are presented as if they are facts. It is up to you to decide whether the statements are logical and based on valid information.

fact
a real occurrence or event

opinion
someone's beliefs or feelings about something

Remember that a fact can be proven to be true; an opinion is a judgment that may or may not be true. Certain words provide a clue that a statement is an opinion. These words include *should, ought to, better,* and *worse.*

Read the following passage and complete the exercise below.

When a political party captures the majority of seats in the House of Commons after an election, it forms a *majority government*. If the governing party does not claim the majority of seats, it then forms a *minority government*. Although having more than one dominating party in Parliament appears, in theory, to promote more dialogue and compromise, some political analysts believe this type of government is ineffective. The longest-serving minority government in Canada was between 1922 and 1925, and it remained in power for just over three and a half years.

Put a check mark next to the statement that is a fact.

_____ a. The longest serving minority government in Canada lasted over three and a half years.

_____ b. Some believe minority governments are ineffective.

You are correct if you chose *option a.* The length of time a minority government is in power is a fact that can be verified. The belief that minority governments are ineffective is an opinion.

GED Practice

Directions: Choose the <u>one best answer</u> to each question.

<u>Questions 1 through 4</u> refer to the following passage.

Canadians are used to hearing that they have certain rights and privileges. But what are rights and how do they differ from privileges? In legal terms, rights are powers and freedoms that government must protect. For example, the *Canadian Charter of Rights and Freedoms* provides all Canadians with the right to a public trial before a jury if they are accused of a crime. In addition to such legal rights, the Charter also protects fundamental freedoms. In the seventeenth century, the great political thinker John Locke expressed these fundamental freedoms as the right to life, liberty, and property. The Canadian Charter says that everyone has "freedom of conscience and religion; freedom of thought, belief, opinion and expression, including freedom of the press and other means of communication; freedom of peaceful assembly; and freedom of association."

In contrast to rights are entitlements. These can best be thought of as privileges or benefits that government provides by law to people who meet certain requirements. Examples include the Canada Pension Plan and Employment Insurance. Unlike rights, entitlements are more easily limited or changed in time and can even be taken away.

1. Which is an example of a fundamental freedom?

   (1) freedom of speech
   (2) a public trial
   (3) a licence to practise medicine
   (4) paying taxes
   (5) government payments to the unemployed

2. What is an example of an entitlement?

   (1) freedom of the press
   (2) trial by a jury
   (3) a government-guaranteed student loan
   (4) the ability to quit your job
   (5) the ability to put your house up for sale

3. Which of the following is an opinion expressed in or implied by the passage?

   (1) Privileges are more important to Canadians than fundamental freedoms.
   (2) Fundamental freedoms are more important to Canadians than entitlements.
   (3) Canadians have the right to freedom of conscience and religion.
   (4) People who have no job should receive payments from the government.
   (5) John Locke was a great political thinker.

4. Why are rights and freedoms more important to Canadians than entitlements?

   (1) People do not need entitlements.
   (2) Rights and freedoms are protected in the Canadian Charter.
   (3) Entitlements are protected by the Charter, but rights and freedoms are not.
   (4) Rights and freedoms apply only to Canadian citizens, but entitlements apply to all Canadian residents.
   (5) These rights and freedoms originated in the seventeenth century with the work of John Locke.

5. Democracies and totalitarian governments have different goals as well as different structures. An important goal in a democracy is to ensure freedom and dignity for all individuals. The major goal of a totalitarian government is to maintain control over all aspects of people's lives.

   Based on the information above, if you lived under a totalitarian government, which of the following could you expect?

   (1) to be able to choose your nation's leader
   (2) to send your children to a private school
   (3) to be able to choose where you live
   (4) to be limited in where you could travel
   (5) to always have a job

The presidential system in the United States is one of the forms that democratic government may take. Another democratic form of government is the parliamentary system, which exists in Canada. In this system, an elected legislature, or Parliament, directs both the legislative and the executive functions of government.

In a presidential system, the chief executive, or president, is chosen by the voters. In a parliamentary system, the chief executive is the prime minister. He or she must be a member of the Parliament. With the Parliament's approval, the prime minister selects other members from its ranks to form a ruling cabinet. These ruling officials are not only part of the legislature, but they are also subject to its direct control. They stay in office only as long as their policies have the support of the legislature.

The parliamentary system is the most common form of democratic government in the world today. In addition to Canada, Great Britain, Japan, and India are among the nations using this system.

TWO BASIC FORMS OF DEMOCRATIC GOVERNMENT

*Parliamentary system is based on the British model.

6. Who chooses the prime minister in a parliamentary system of government?

    (1) the president
    (2) the voters
    (3) the cabinet
    (4) the legislature
    (5) the judiciary

7. Which of the following statements is an opinion?

    (1) In a parliamentary system, the legislature has more power than in a presidential system.
    (2) The parliamentary system is a more common form of government than the presidential system.
    (3) The parliamentary system is a better form of government than the presidential system.
    (4) The prime minister in a parliamentary system is similar to the president in a presidential system.
    (5) Both the presidential and the parliamentary systems include a cabinet.

8. Who chooses the judges for the court system in a parliamentary form of government?

    (1) the cabinet
    (2) the Parliament
    (3) the prime minister
    (4) the voters
    (5) the prime minister and the legislature

9. What evidence best supports the conclusion that the prime minister of Great Britain is a less independent leader than the U.S. president?

    (1) The prime minister must be a member of the legislature.
    (2) The prime minister must resign if he or she loses an important vote in the legislature.
    (3) The prime minister must appoint a cabinet.
    (4) The prime minister is directly responsible to the voters.
    (5) The parliamentary system is the most common form of democratic government.

Democracy will not continue in Canada merely because most Canadians believe it is essential to government policies and decisions. It is made possible only by a strong belief in and strict practice of the following five principles.

The Five Pillars of Democracy
The Importance of the Individual Each person's worth and dignity must be recognized and respected by all others at all times. At the same time, however, each person's individual interests must be secondary to the interests of all the individuals who make up the society.
The Equality of All Persons Each person is entitled to equal opportunity and equal treatment by the law. The principle does not mean that all people are born with the same abilities or that they have a right to an equal share of the nation's wealth.
Majority Rule and Minority Rights Majority rule is the basis of democracy. However, majority rule without minority rights destroys democracy. The majority must be willing to listen to the minority and recognize its right by lawful means to become the majority.
The Need for Compromise In a society that emphasizes individualism and equality, few public questions will have only two points of view. The blending of competing interests through compromise is needed to find the position most acceptable to the largest number.
Individual Freedom Democracy cannot exist in an atmosphere of absolute freedom. That would eventually lead to rule by the strongest members of society. However, in democracy, each person has as much freedom as possible without interfering with the rights of others.

For Canadians, these principles do more than guide a system of government. They have become part of our way of life. We expect to be able to choose our own way of doing things in our day-to-day living. However, because personal freedom is taken for granted, there is a danger of imposing our own ways and values on someone else. We must recognize that one person's choice may not be good for another person. We must also keep in mind that our rights and freedoms are not without limits. In 1987, Supreme Court Justice Gérard La Forest asked, "What is liberty? What should the limits be to it? We all know what we think ourselves. But when it comes to defining liberty, each and every state restriction exists in a proper context." In a democratic society, personal freedoms exist in relation to others' rights and freedoms, which naturally creates restrictions.

10. What opinion about freedom is expressed in the passage?

    (1) that it has accompanying restrictions
    (2) that it is an important entitlement
    (3) that exercising it is not really possible
    (4) that it is leading the nation into danger
    (5) that it should have no limits

11. Which of the following is true of a democracy?

    (1) The majority must always have its way.
    (2) People should share equally in the nation's resources.
    (3) Equality is its most important principle.
    (4) It is built on respect for individual differences.
    (5) It will always exist in Canada.

12. What democratic value was Supreme Court Justice Gérard La Forest expressing when he said that "when it comes to defining liberty, each and every state restriction exists in a proper context"?

    (1) Personal freedom is not important in a democratic society.
    (2) In a democracy no person's rights can be allowed to interfere with the rights of others.
    (3) All people in a democracy should be allowed to have an equal opportunity to succeed.
    (4) Fighting and violence are not rights in democratic society.
    (5) Democratic government cannot succeed in an atmosphere where differences of opinion exist.

Answers start on page 760.

comparing
looking for similarities and differences in things

contrasting
looking only for differences in things

Tip

When comparing and contrasting things, look for similarities among them first. When you know how things are the same, it will be easier to see how they are different.

Structure of the Canadian Government
Comparing and Contrasting

Suppose you want to buy a used car. You find some cars with features you want, but the cars have been driven many kilometres. Others have low kilometrage and the right features, but they are not the model you want or a colour you like. The prices also differ, so choosing a car is even more confusing. The only way to make a good decision is to compare and contrast the characteristics of each car.

Comparing and **contrasting** involve examining two or more things to understand how they are the same and how they are different. Looking for similarities and differences in things often helps you evaluate them.

The most important step in using this skill is to establish the categories of things to be compared and contrasted. The categories you use must be parallel. For example, it would not be helpful to compare the sound system in one car to the colour of another. Creating broad categories also increases the chances of finding similarities and differences. Sound systems would be a better category than CD players, since some cars may have only radios and others may have radios with CD players.

Read the following passage and complete the exercise below.

In 1920 the House of Commons passed the *Dominion Elections Act*, which created the position of the Chief Electoral Officer, or CEO. To ensure fairness, this individual works independently from any political party or government body and is accountable to Parliament. The CEO serves until retirement or removal from office for a valid reason by a majority vote in both the House of Commons and the Senate.

The Chief Electoral Officer is charged with carrying out the requirements of the *Elections Act* and *Referendum Act* by managing an office that comprises the CEO and several assistants who oversee different aspects of the electoral process. One of the CEO's assistants is the Commissioner of Canada Elections. The commissioner is the one who implements the terms and conditions outlined in each Act.

Put a check mark next to the statement that explains how the roles of the chief electoral officer and the commissioner of Canada Elections are different.

_____ a. Both work within the guidelines of the *Elections Act* and *Referendum Act*.

_____ b. The Chief Electoral Officer administers elections and referendums and the Commissioner of Canada Elections enforces the rules.

You are correct if you chose *option b*. In *option a*, the statement describes a similarity between the two positions. In *option b*, the statement outlines the subtle differences between the two positions.

GED Practice

Directions: Choose the <u>one best answer</u> to each question.

<u>Questions 1 through 3</u> refer to the following passage.

    Canada's government is a federal system, which means that power is divided or shared between the central authority in Ottawa and regional powers, which include provinces and territories. The nature of Canada's federation has changed over the years. In 1867, the national government exercised dominance over the provinces. This same centralizing tendency was evident in the 1930s during the Great Depression. However, recent events such as the 1980 and 1995 Quebec referendums, the *Constitution Act of 1982*, and the subsequent Meech Lake and Charlottetown Accords suggest that provinces are gaining more political autonomy.

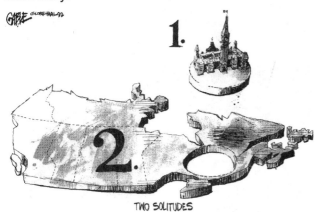

TWO SOLITUDES

Source: From *Another Day, Another Doom: Brian Gable's Cartoon Commentary*. Vancouver: Greystone Books, 1995. Reprinted with permission from *The Globe & Mail*.

1. According to the passage and cartoon, what is the nature of a federal system of government?

    (1) a central governing authority
    (2) a system for national dominance
    (3) a source of provincial autonomy
    (4) a way of dividing powers between federal and provincial governments
    (5) a system of direct democracy

2. What statement <u>best</u> describes the cartoonist's view?

    (1) The provinces are too strong.
    (2) Canada comprises two nations.
    (3) The federal government is exercising too much power.
    (4) Parliament has dissolved.
    (5) Quebec wants to separate from Canada.

3. To what kind of organization or institution can we compare a federal system of government?

    (1) a political dictatorship
    (2) an absolute monarchy
    (3) the military
    (4) federal prisons
    (5) a family

4. Section 4(1) of the *Constitution Act of 1982* states: "No House of Commons and no legislative assembly shall continue for longer than five years from the date fixed for the return of the writs at a general election of its members."

What rights does this section ensure?

    (1) democratic rights
    (2) mobility rights
    (3) legal rights
    (4) minority language rights
    (5) equality rights

5. Many cities have neighbourhood groups that meet regularly so that the residents can deal with issues that affect the neighbourhood. Which kind of political activity do these neighbourhood group meetings <u>most closely</u> resemble?

    (1) writing political party platforms
    (2) speaking at a meeting of a city council
    (3) electing government representatives
    (4) ratifying an amendment
    (5) making decisions in a direct democracy

Canada's constitutional history is characterized by progressive autonomy from Britain. The *British North America Act of 1867* (*BNA Act*) established a federal union, with the national government having authority over concerns like trade and defence, and the provinces having jurisdiction over matters such as education. However, at that time Britain's Parliament retained exclusive power to amend the *BNA Act*.

This balance of power endured until the *Statute of Westminster* was passed in 1931. By then, Britain could not unilaterally legislate for Canada without formal request by Canada's government. Momentum for increased Canadian autonomy continued in 1949, when the *BNA Act* was amended to give Canada further power to make constitutional amendments except in certain cases.

The 1980 Quebec referendum gave rise to political activity for Canada gaining full authority over constitutional issues. The movement toward patriation of Canada's constitution ended in 1982 with the *Constitution Act.* This historic amendment to Canada's constitution did not alter the structure of government, but it did establish the *Charter of Rights and Freedoms* and a legal process for making constitutional amendments. Depending on what sections need change, there are five formulas to make constitutional amendments. The chart below illustrates the five formulas, with examples.

Formula 1
Issues that need to be passed by House of Commons, Senate, and every provincial legislature (e.g., the use of English and French languages)

OR

Formula 2
Issues that need to be passed by House of Commons, Senate, and two-thirds of the provinces representing one-half of Canada's population (e.g., the powers of the Senate)

OR

Formula 3
Issues that need to be passed by House of Commons, Senate, and legislatures of affected provinces (e.g., changes to provincial boundaries)

OR

Formula 4
Issues that can be changed by an act of the Canadian Parliament (e.g., changes to Canada's executive government)

OR

Formula 5
Issues that concern any provincial legislature only (e.g., changes to a province's constitution)

6. What effect did the *Statute of Westminster* have on the Canadian government?

   (1) It abolished British legislative power in Canada.
   (2) It established the *Charter of Rights and Freedoms*.
   (3) It was one step toward Canadian autonomy from Britain.
   (4) It weakened the Canadian Parliament.
   (5) It gave Britain more legislative powers.

7. When reading the five formulas inserted into the *Constitution Act* of 1982, what value do you think was evident in the framers' minds?

   (1) weakening the office of the prime minister
   (2) increasing government power
   (3) increasing judicial power
   (4) disassociation from Britain
   (5) increasing provincial power

8. What is implied by amendments that need to follow Formula 1?

   (1) The Senate needs to approve any proposed constitutional amendment.
   (2) The House of Commons now has more power.
   (3) Any province can veto a proposed constitutional amendment.
   (4) All provinces need to agree on proposed constitutional amendments.
   (5) The prime minister is not involved in the process.

Answers start on page 762.

Canadian Politics in Action

Identifying Faulty Logic

Identifying faulty logic means recognizing errors in reasoning. A person who is presenting an argument might begin with a logical progression of ideas but then draw conclusions from these ideas that are not fully logical. It is important to be aware of faulty logic because a speaker or writer might use such erroneous thinking convincingly. It is up to the reader or listener to note whether reasoning has gone wrong and to reject conclusions based on faulty logic.

One example of faulty logic is hasty generalization. This happens when someone makes a broad statement based on inadequate evidence. A common type of hasty generalization is the **stereotype.** You can suspect a stereotype in almost any statement about someone or something that is based on its connection to a larger group. Be especially wary if the group has religion, race, nationality, or gender in common. For example, one stereotype is that men are better than women at math and science. In fact, many women are better than men in these areas.

A related type of faulty logic is **oversimplification.** This often results when someone links two things that are not directly connected in a cause-and-effect relationship. For example, one common oversimplification is that poverty causes crime. If that were true, then all poor people would be criminals—which, of course, they are not. The causes of crime are much more complicated than whether or not a person is poor.

stereotype
a fixed idea or image of a particular type of person or thing that is often not true

oversimplification
a description of something in terms that make it seem less complicated than it really is

Read the following passage and complete the exercise below.

Cheri Lynn for MP! It's time for a change! Ian Murphy is responsible for the legislation that raised your taxes and created unemployment. Cheri Lynn will work to amend this law and find more jobs for the average Canadian. Politicians are controlled by interest groups who donate money to their campaigns. But Cheri Lynn will be a member of Parliament who will be a voice for the people! Elect Cheri Lynn for Parliament!

Mark the oversimplification in this campaign ad with an *O* and the stereotype with an *S*.

In looking for faulty logic, ask yourself: Does the information presented support the conclusion? Is more information needed to support this conclusion?

_____ a. Politicians are controlled by interest groups that donate money to their campaigns.

_____ b. Ian Murphy is responsible for the legislation that raised your taxes and created unemployment.

You are correct if you chose *option a* as the stereotype and *option b* as the oversimplification. Not all politicians are controlled by special interests. Saying that a member of Parliament is responsible for a tax increase and unemployment is an oversimplification. Tax increases and unemployment result from many factors.

GED Practice

Directions: Choose the <u>one best answer</u> to each question.

<u>Questions 1 through 4</u> refer to the following passage.

The Liberal and Conservative parties have been the most dominant parties in Canadian history, but other parties have arisen over the years. In the 1921 general election, the Progressive party captured 69 seats in the House of Commons, the first time a third party had made a significant impact in a federal election. Eventually, the Progressive party joined forces with the Conservative party in the 1940s and the Progressive Conservative party emerged.

Often, third parties begin because established parties fail to address some important social issues. During the 1930s, when Canada was beset by the economic and social trauma of the Great Depression, the Co-operative Commonwealth Federation (CCF) arose in the West to represent the interests of working class Canadians. In 1961, the CCF party became the New Democratic party (NDP).

In recent Canadian electoral history, the third party has evolved into a multi-party phenomenon, with parties appearing in response to regional discord. Founded in 1990, the Bloc Québécois has been a voice in federal politics for disgruntled Quebec separatists. In the 1993 general election, the Bloc won 54 seats and became the Official Opposition in the House of Commons. However, its purpose as a political party is solely to win support for Quebec separation from Canada. In the Canadian West the Reform Party, established in 1987, was similarly created because of regional discontent and a feeling of alienation from the rest of Canada. The Reform Party achieved Official Opposition status after the 1997 and 2000 general elections.

1. What does the passage imply about third parties in Canada?

   (1) They are dangerous to Canadians.
   (2) Their members do not support them.
   (3) They have been influential in politics.
   (4) Their issues are not truly important.
   (5) They contribute nothing to the nation.

2. Which of the following <u>best</u> summarizes the third paragraph of the passage?

   (1) The Reform Party has twice attained Official Opposition status.
   (2) The main purpose of third parties is to separate provinces or regions from Canada.
   (3) Both the Bloc Québécois Party and the Reform Party have short histories.
   (4) Canadians prefer third parties as the Official Opposition in Parliament.
   (5) Regional differences have led to the creation of more parties.

3. What is the <u>most likely</u> reason that many Canadian voters support third parties and their candidates?

   (1) Canadians are increasingly afraid of taking a stand on political issues.
   (2) Third-party candidates are more exciting than the candidates of the major parties.
   (3) Many Canadians want to change the nation into a socialist state.
   (4) Voters feel that the major parties are not addressing important problems.
   (5) Growing numbers of Canadians have become indifferent about politics.

4. Which type of party system would Canada have if the Progressive Conservative party regains its former popularity and the Bloc Québécois party and the Reform party decline in power?

   (1) a democracy
   (2) a republic
   (3) a multiparty system
   (4) a third-party system
   (5) a two-party system

Arguments and conclusions that are based on judgments or opinions are more likely to contain faulty logic than those that are based on facts.

Social Studies • Civics and Government

Questions 5 and 6 refer to the following paragraph and cartoon.

Political cartoonists often depict their subjects through common cultural symbols. Canada is usually visualized as a beaver. Below, the cartoonist imagines the consequences of a by-election victory in Quebec. A by-election is held between general elections to fill a vacant seat in legislature.

Source: From *Another Day, Another Doom: Brian Gable's Cartoon Commentary*. Vancouver: Greystone Books, 1995. Reprinted with permission from *The Globe and Mail*.

5. What is the main idea of the cartoon?

  (1) The PQ is too overpowering.
  (2) Canada is being crushed in Olympic events.
  (3) A PQ election victory will destroy the Canadian union.
  (4) Canada is ignorant.
  (5) The Québécois control the country.

6. What is the cartoonist assuming the reader knows about by-election victories?

  (1) Canada is losing interest in Quebec politics.
  (2) The PQ wins the luge event at the Olympics.
  (3) By-elections are more important than general elections.
  (4) By-election victories control a nation.
  (5) By-election results in a constituency measure the probable outcome of a provincial or national election.

Questions 7 through 9 refer to the following passage.

Interest groups play an important role in Canadian politics. During election campaigns, these groups are free to make financial contributions to one or more political parties. In the 1988 federal election, pressure groups from both sides of the issue spent millions of dollars trying to win over candidates on the subject of free trade. Interest groups continue to persuade politicians, even after elections, by forming relationships with powerful members of government such as members of Cabinet, individual MPs, or civil servants. One recent and noteworthy example is the persistent work of the tobacco companies to change restrictions on cigarette advertising during sports and cultural events.

7. What evidence in the passage supports the conclusion that interest groups help shape government policies?

  (1) They promote smoking.
  (2) They form relationships with powerful members of government.
  (3) Interest groups give money to many political parties.
  (4) Interest groups are concerned with free trade.
  (5) Interests groups are influential during elections.

8. The work of interest groups indicates that they are concerned with

  (1) promoting sports and cultural events
  (2) health care costs
  (3) free trade with the United States
  (4) influencing legislation
  (5) influencing elections

9. The role of interest groups in Canada is an example of

  (1) bureaucracy
  (2) individualism
  (3) competition
  (4) representative government
  (5) democratic politics

Answers start on page 763.

The Canadian Government and Its Citizens

Applying Information to New Contexts

Frequently, things you have already learned in one **context** can be applied to other situations that you encounter. To apply information to a new context means to take information that you learned in one situation and use it to help you understand a related situation. It is a useful life skill as well as an aid in understanding social studies material.

For example, you might read that the Supreme Court of Canada has declared that a law must not be enforced because it violates the *Canadian Charter of Rights and Freedoms*. Later, you find out that the local police can no longer enforce another law that was in effect in your community. You can apply what you learned about the first law to conclude that the second law was probably also unconstitutional.

Sometimes information is presented in a general way. If you understand the general idea, you can then apply it to a specific situation. Other times you may learn something through a specific example. You may then find out about another situation. If the two situations are similar, the information you learned about the first situation can be applied to help you better understand the second.

Read the following passage and complete the exercise below.

Many industries benefit from government assistance or from the creation of Crown corporations. In 1935, the Canadian Wheat Board was created by the federal government to help farmers earn a fair living by marketing their grains and setting prices for their commodities. In times of economic hardship when grain prices reach very low levels, this Crown corporation has aided many Canadian farmers.

Mark the federal government program that provides similar help to an industry.

____ a. Tax increases for foreign-based corporations

____ b. TAGS, a federal strategy to financially assist people in the fishing industry in Atlantic Canada

You are correct if you checked *option b*. Tax increases for foreign-based corporations do not help those companies, but federal assistance to Atlantic fisheries is similar to the function of the Canadian Wheat Board, because it helps people who work in a major Canadian industry.

context
the circumstances or setting in which an event occurs

The more two contexts are similar, the more information about one situation will apply in helping to understand the other. Knowing the effect of one government program helps you understand the effect of a different program.

GED Practice

Directions: Choose the <u>one best answer</u> to each question.

<u>Questions 1 through 3</u> refer to the following graph and passage.

The federal government gets the money to pay for its programs and operating expenses in two ways: taxing and borrowing. The main source of revenue is federal income tax. Canadians who receive more than a minimum amount of income must pay part of their earnings to the federal government in the form of income taxes. Other government revenue comes from duties on imported goods and excise taxes on such products as gasoline, tobacco, and alcohol.

The Treasury Board borrows from Canadian citizens and from citizens of foreign countries by offering treasury notes and bonds for sale. Although the person is "buying" the note or bond, the transaction is really a loan and thus a debt owed by the government. After a set number of years, the government must repay the cost of the bond or note and pay the buyer interest on the loan. The total amount the government owes to purchasers of its notes and bonds is known as the national debt.

COMPOSITION OF NET EXPENDITURES, 2001–2002

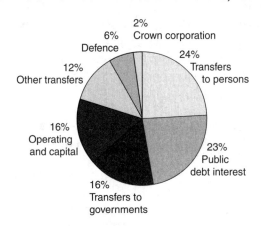

Note: Numbers do not add to 100 percent because of rounding.

1. Which statement is true of government programs and spending?

   (1) All government services are provided to citizens for free.
   (2) The smallest portion of the budget was spent on Crown corporations.
   (3) Government programs are supported solely by the taxes Canadians pay.
   (4) The interest on the national debt helps pay for government programs.
   (5) The government spends more on defence than it does on "other transfers."

2. Which is <u>most likely</u> to happen if the government spends more money than it collects?

   (1) Income taxes will go down.
   (2) Excise taxes will go down.
   (3) Taxes will increase.
   (4) The government will offer fewer bonds.
   (5) Canadians will have to earn more money.

3. Which part of the graph would include Employment Insurance benefits?

   (1) transfers to governments
   (2) transfers to persons
   (3) defence
   (4) Crown corporations
   (5) public debt interest

When applying information in a new context, ask: What is similar? Are the events similar? Are the results similar?

PER CAPITA PROVINCIAL DEBT BY PROVINCE

Year	New Brunswick	Quebec	Ontario	Alberta
1989–90	$4 196	$5 163	$3 692	$6 400
1993–94	$7 407	$7 235	$7 431	$8 500
1997–98	$7 620	$12 119	$10 021	$5 276
2001–02	$8 610	$12 084	$9 306	$1 957

Source: Courtesy of the Canadian Taxpayer's Federation, www.Taxpayer.com.

4. Which provinces show an inconsistent pattern of debt?

   (1) New Brunswick and Ontario
   (2) Quebec and New Brunswick
   (3) Ontario and Alberta
   (4) Alberta and New Brunswick
   (5) Quebec and Ontario

5. Which of the following statements is supported by the information in the table?

   (1) From 1989 to 2002, the per capita provincial debt has increased for each province.
   (2) In 1989–90, Quebec had the lowest per capita provincial debt.
   (3) New Brunswick has had a marked decline in its per capita provincial debt.
   (4) Alberta is the only province with an overall decline in its per capita provincial debt.
   (5) Ontario has the largest provincial debt in the country.

6. In 1993–94, how much more did Ontario owe per person than New Brunswick?

   (1) $24
   (2) $124
   (3) $1024
   (4) $69
   (5) $1069

7. If trends continued in a similar manner, what would be the effect on the per capita debt in 2004–05?

   (1) Quebec's per capita provincial debt would be reduced by half.
   (2) Ontario's per capita provincial debt would continue to increase.
   (3) Alberta's per capita provincial debt would increase.
   (4) New Brunswick's per capita provincial debt would show a marked decrease.
   (5) Alberta would have a negative provincial debt per capita.

8. The Canadian general election in 2000 was distinguished by a lack of voter participation. Only 61 percent of eligible voters cast a ballot, provoking some people to wonder if Canada was experiencing a crisis in democracy.

   What generalizations about electoral attitudes does this information best support?

   (1) Many Canadians have become cynical about politics.
   (2) More and more young people are becoming interested in political issues.
   (3) Political parties are more popular than ever.
   (4) Political scandals are more pervasive.
   (5) Federal politicians are more visible in the media.

Answers start on page 764.

Directions: Choose the one best answer to each question.

Questions 1 through 4 refer to the following passage.

Power is the ability to control people's behaviour. There are three basic ways to get power over people: through force, through authority, and through influence.

Force is based on making people do things against their will. Because physical force makes people afraid, they will do things they do not want to do.

Authority is the power of leaders to get the people to obey the laws. It is based on the belief that those leaders have a right to rule.

Influence is a form of persuasion. An individual who has a strong personality, who is important or wealthy, or who has the support of many other people can persuade people to do things. However, the power to govern usually requires more than influence.

A stable government is based on what is called legitimate power. Such power is considered proper and acceptable by the people who obey it. It comes from having a leader who has the authority to make decisions that people will follow, even if they do not always agree with the decisions. Force is considered illegitimate power because it does not have the support or consent of the people governed. Legitimate power generally results in better and more effective government than does illegitimate power.

1. Which of the following statements is an opinion of the writer of this passage?

   (1) Legitimate power is power that is considered to be proper and acceptable.
   (2) Force is illegitimate power.
   (3) Legitimate power results in better government than does illegitimate power.
   (4) Force makes people do things that they do not want to.
   (5) Some people can be persuaded to do things by a person who is important or wealthy.

2. After the death of King Baudouin in 1993, his son Albert became king of Belgium. Which type of power is illustrated by the rule of King Albert?

   (1) influence
   (2) force
   (3) persuasion
   (4) authority
   (5) elective office

3. According to the passage, how are people's opinions important to the exercise of power?

   (1) People's opinions are not at all important to the exercise of power.
   (2) People's support is necessary for power to be legitimate.
   (3) People's opinions can be easily changed.
   (4) People's opinions can be influenced by force.
   (5) Public opinion is the basis for all types of power.

4. What effect does force have in the exercise of power?

   (1) It has little, if any, effect.
   (2) It turns illegitimate power into legitimate power.
   (3) It allows wealthy people to have power.
   (4) It causes people to believe what the government tells them.
   (5) It makes people behave in ways that government leaders desire.

The words *believe, think, feel, best,* and *worst* often signal that an opinion is being stated.

Questions 5 though 8 refer to the following passage.

The Canadian government's power is organized into three separate institutions: the executive, the legislature, and the judiciary. The executive is further divided into two branches comprising the governor general (the British monarch's representative in Canada) and the prime minister, his cabinet, and various governmental ministries. Unlike the president of the United States, each Canadian prime minister is not limited to governing for two terms. Historically, Canadian prime minister's terms have ranged from as little as 69 days to 22 years.

The House of Commons, the Senate, and the Crown regulate Canada's legislative process. As the Crown's agent, the governor general's approval of legislation is necessary before a government bill becomes law. Before the governor general's assent, a bill passes through Canada's bicameral legislature—the elected lower house known as the House of Commons, and the appointed upper house, called the Senate. Since Canadian voters do not elect members of the Senate, its function has been criticized since the late nineteenth century, and proposals have been made to reform its present power.

The *Canadian Charter of Rights and Freedoms* recognizes the "supremacy of God and the rule of law." Canadian laws are mediated and interpreted by the judiciary system, headed by the Supreme Court of Canada. Members of the Supreme Court are appointed by the prime minister and his cabinet with approval by the governor general. The Supreme Court is networked to provincial and federal trial and appeal courts throughout the country.

5. What is the main purpose of this passage?

   (1) to compare the functions of the Canadian prime minister with those of the American president
   (2) to explain the role of the court system
   (3) to describe Canada's governing institutions
   (4) to demonstrate the Senate's undemocratic power
   (5) to illustrate the governor general's power

6. Which of the following states an opinion about the passage?

   (1) Canadian prime ministers' terms in office are not limited.
   (2) Members of the Supreme Court are appointed, not elected.
   (3) The governor general gives assent to bills passing through Parliament.
   (4) The Senate exercises too much power in the Canadian government.
   (5) The Canadian legislature is bicameral.

7. What is a logical conclusion supported by the above passage?

   (1) The governor general reflects public opinions.
   (2) No Canadian citizen or institution is above the law.
   (3) American presidents have more power than Canadian prime ministers.
   (4) The Senate will someday be eliminated from the Canadian legislature.
   (5) The Supreme Court drafts all laws in Canada.

8. Which system best describes Canada's government?

   (1) a dictatorship
   (2) a republic
   (3) a direct democracy
   (4) a parliamentary government
   (5) a bicameral legislature

Tip

In comparing and contrasting, consider only information that fits the category being compared or contrasted.

A referendum is a way for voters to express their views on important political issues within a province or nation. Politicians have employed referendums to determine public opinion before making policy decisions. Canadians have experienced an increased number of referendums recently, prompting some to argue that citizens want more involvement in the political process to strengthen Canada's democracy. Similarly, others maintain that Canadians are drawn together by referendums during periods of regional discord, building national unity and identity.

However, referendums do not appeal to everyone. Skeptics contend that referendums subvert the power of elected officials in Parliament and that voters are not fully prepared to decide these important questions. Other adversaries claim that the will of minority groups is unfairly sacrificed. In other instances, the question(s) asked in the referendum could oversimplify complex matters that need subtle compromise and negotiation.

Significant Canadian Referendums		
Year	Region	Issue
1898	National	Sale of alcohol
1942	National	Conscription to fight in World War II
1980	Quebec	Sovereignty-association with federal government
1991	Saskatchewan	Use of referendums to approve constitutional amendments
1992	National	Constitutional amendment: Charlottetown Accord
1995	Quebec	Quebec sovereignty

9. Which person would likely vote to approve the sale of alcohol in the 1898 referendum?

(1) a preacher
(2) a merchant
(3) a prohibitionist
(4) a doctor
(5) a farmer

10. What possibility did voters face during the 1980 referendum?

(1) increased federal power in Quebec
(2) debate over language rights
(3) dissolution of Quebec's legislature
(4) Quebec separating from Canada
(5) abuse of democratic privileges

11. According to the passage, what would be the most likely reaction if Canada were to hold another national referendum in the near future?

(1) Minority groups would be against it.
(2) Politicians would be indifferent to future referendums.
(3) Some would welcome the use of a referendum; others would criticize.
(4) New immigrants would participate.
(5) Canadian nationalists would praise its advantages.

12. To which person would the result of the 1942 referendum have most value?

(1) a retired butcher
(2) a gold miner in British Columbia
(3) a real estate agent
(4) an 18-year-old male
(5) the leader of the Official Opposition in Parliament

Answers start on page 765.

Economics

Economics is the study of the decisions involved in the way goods and services are produced, distributed, consumed, or used. Understanding economics equips us to be better consumers and to make wiser choices that will bring us greater satisfaction when we spend our time and money.

Economics is also part of our everyday lives. We deal with economics when we collect a paycheque, shop, or pay taxes. Many of the choices we make involve economics in some way, whether we realize it or not. Economics is also an important part of the GED Social Studies Test, making up 20 percent of the test questions.

General Economic Principles

Using Ideas in New Contexts

concept
an idea or principle that applies to many individual circumstances or situations

You already have learned that a piece of information from one specific context or situation can help you understand similar situations. However, you can also apply a general idea called a **concept** to situations that may not even be related. For instance, the concept of "distance" helps determine how long it takes to get somewhere. It also helps you understand that you can increase your time to eat lunch at work if you eat in the lunchroom rather than going out to a restaurant. You are using the concept of distance in analyzing how to spend your lunch break.

Applying concepts from economics to your daily shopping helps you to be a smarter consumer. One such concept in consumer economics is getting value for your money. Perhaps you have considered buying shirts with the logo of a popular sportswear maker. The shirts are attractive, but they cost much more than other shirts. Your clothing budget is limited. But you should consider quality. The brand name shirts may be of higher quality and may last longer than less-costly shirts. Thus, they may provide more value for the money. You are applying the economic concept of quality versus cost to your shopping.

To apply an idea to a situation, look for how the idea helps explain, define, or reveal a cause or effect of the situation.

To use ideas in new contexts, you apply other skills that involve analysis and evaluation. These include identifying cause-and-effect relationships, making comparisons, and drawing conclusions.

GED Practice

Directions: Choose the one best answer to each question.

Questions 1 through 4 refer to the following passage and graph.

The principles of supply and demand help determine workers' wages. If more people want to work at a certain occupation than there are jobs available, the pay for that work will be lower than if there are a lot of jobs and few people to fill them. If the supply of or demand for workers changes, so may the wages in that occupation. For example, at one time there was a shortage of lawyers, and high pay prompted many people to go to law school. Eventually, the supply of lawyers exceeded demand, resulting in a surplus. Many beginning lawyers had to settle for lower wages than they expected, and some law-school graduates had to take low-paying jobs not directly related to the practice of law.

Another factor that influences pay is the value of the work performed. A doctor earns more than a doctor's receptionist because the doctor does specialized work that is important to society.

Of course, it takes a lot of training to become a doctor. But training also relates to supply and demand. Fewer people are qualified to fill jobs that involve difficult training. So those jobs generally pay more than jobs that require less training. Unpleasant or hazardous work is the exception. Jobs in plants that process nuclear materials require little training. However, these jobs expose workers to potentially harmful radiation. Thus, these jobs pay well since few people want them.

WHAT PEOPLE EARNED, 1997

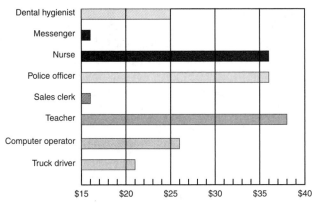

Average Annual Starting Pay (in thousands of $)

1. Which two occupations are closest in pay?

   (1) teacher and dental hygienist
   (2) nurse and sales clerk
   (3) messenger and computer operator
   (4) sales clerk and doctor's office receptionist
   (5) police officer and nurse

2. Which is the most likely explanation of why nurses earn more than messengers?

   (1) Nursing is a dangerous job.
   (2) There is less demand for nurses.
   (3) Messenger is a more desirable job.
   (4) There are many more messengers than nurses.
   (5) Nurses require more training than messengers.

3. The chart shows that police officers have a high starting pay. What gives the best explanation for the high salary police make?

   (1) The job of police officer is dangerous.
   (2) The demand for police officers is smaller than the supply of people who want the job.
   (3) Training is required for the job.
   (4) Most police officers are men.
   (5) Police officers provide a more valuable service to society than doctors do.

4. What conclusion about the starting pay of lawyers is supported by the information?

   (1) It is better than the pay for teachers.
   (2) It is rising rapidly.
   (3) It is better than the pay of any of the occupations shown on the graph.
   (4) It was better in the past than it is today.
   (5) It is below that of police officers.

Questions 5 through 7 refer to the following passage.

Businesses are organized in three basic ways. A proprietorship is a business that is owned by one person. The single owner gets all the profits and has to pay all the debts. The owner also has total control of how the company is managed.

A partnership is owned by at least two people. The owners share the management decisions. The profits and debts are also shared, usually according to the percentage of the company that each partner owns. However, each partner is usually legally responsible for all the company's debts if any other partner fails to pay his or her share.

A corporation is owned by one or more people but is itself a legal unit. Each owner holds shares of ownership of the corporation called stock. How much stock each owner holds depends on how much money he or she has invested in the company. The profits of a corporation are divided among the owners according to how much stock each owner holds. Each share receives the same amount. The company itself is responsible for its debts. If a corporation cannot pay its bills, the individual owners (shareholders) cannot be forced to pay.

5. In what way are proprietorships and partnerships alike?

   (1) Both are large businesses.
   (2) Both are small businesses.
   (3) One person makes the business decisions.
   (4) Both raise money by selling stock.
   (5) The owners of each get the profits.

6. Based on the passage, what is the biggest difference between a partnership and a corporation?

   (1) the size of the business
   (2) the way business profits are divided
   (3) responsibility for business debt
   (4) the party who manages the daily operations of the business
   (5) the number of people who own the business

7. Dan and Ann are opening a print shop. Ann owns two-thirds of the business, and Dan owns one-third. Dan runs the presses, and Ann takes customers' orders. What do both Dan and Ann most likely assume?

   (1) They will share equally in the profits.
   (2) Dan's job is more important than Ann's.
   (3) Ann will be responsible for all the bills.
   (4) They will agree about business decisions.
   (5) Ann will manage the business.

Questions 8 and 9 refer to the passage below.

One of the most important factors in the economy is the consumer. Sales of items from candy to cars are a major part of what keeps the economy growing. When people have the money to buy more than just what they need to live, businesses profit.

When interest rates go down, the amount of money people borrow and spend goes up. But when consumers begin to feel a pinch in the pocketbook, they spend less. A decrease in spending hurts business. It often results in unemployment so that people have even less money to spend. Then the economy slows.

8. According to the passage, which is an effect of declining interest rates?

   (1) Business activity slows down.
   (2) People borrow more money.
   (3) People have less money to spend.
   (4) Fewer people buy houses.
   (5) Consumers lose confidence in the economy.

9. The owner of Joe's Diner learns that unemployment is rising sharply. Based on this information and on the passage, what should he assume will happen to affect his business?

   (1) The economy will grow.
   (2) The interest rate on his loan will rise.
   (3) He will have fewer customers.
   (4) Other restaurants will raise prices.
   (5) Many of his employees will quit.

Answers start on page 766.

The Government and the Economy
Identifying Implications from Graphs

You have already learned that maps provide information in a visual format. Graphs are another device for presenting information visually. Writers sometimes use graphs to show relationships between things so that they do not need to explain those relationships in writing. It is the reader's responsibility to identify the implications of this graphic material.

Graphs are often used to show changes over time. This allows readers to easily make comparisons and see trends. The bar graph below shows how the minimum wage that employers must pay workers has changed in one Canadian province since 1975. Setting a minimum wage rate is one way that the government affects the nation's economy.

Various dollar amounts are listed on the left side of the graph. Along the bottom of the graph, each year between 1975 and 2000 is indicated. Above each year is a vertical bar. The top of each bar corresponds to a dollar amount on the left side of the graph. For example, the graph shows that the minimum legal wage in 1975 was $2.40 per hour. In 1979 and 1980, it rose to $3.00 an hour.

Study the graph and answer the question below.

MINIMUM WAGE

Wages per Hour

$8.00 — $6.50 — $5.00 — $3.50 — $2.00

1975 1976 1977 1978 1979 1980 1981 1982 1983 1984 1985 1986 1987 1988 1989 1990 1991 1992 1993 1994 1995 1996 1997 1998 1999 2000

To interpret a graph, examine its vertical and horizontal axes to see what kinds of data are shown.

Which information is implied by the graph?

_____ a. The minimum wage has risen steadily since 1995.

_____ b. The minimum wage increased the most in the 1980s.

You are correct if you chose *option b*. The graph shows that the rise in the minimum wage was the sharpest during that period. *Option a* is incorrect because, as the graph shows, the minimum wage did not rise steadily—it did not rise at all from 1995 to 2000.

Additional practice material available on page 878

GED Practice

Directions: Choose the <u>one best answer</u> to each question.

<u>Questions 1 through 4</u> refer to the following passage.

Three major economic systems exist in the world today: capitalism, communism, and socialism. The main differences in the systems are the ways ownership and decision-making are treated.

Capitalism, the economic system favoured by the industrialized western world, allows for private ownership of goods and the means of production. Decisions and planning are in private hands.

Under communism, the economic system of countries such as North Korea and Cuba, the state owns the means of production and plans the economy. The basis of communism is that, in theory, all individuals contribute their best effort to the good of the community and in return receive everything they need.

Socialism is similar to communism in that the state owns all major means of production and plans the economy for the good of all. But socialism encourages competition among small businesses. The state provides certain social services for its citizens, such as free or inexpensive health care.

In the modern world, these economic systems have become confused with political systems. Because communism and socialism depend so much on central planning, they have become associated in people's minds with dictatorship. Capitalism, because it is built around private ownership and free enterprise, is associated with democratic or representative government.

1. According to the passage, how are capitalism and socialism similar?

   (1) The state owns production.
   (2) The state plans the economy.
   (3) Small businesses can compete.
   (4) All people have everything they need.
   (5) People have economic and political freedom.

2. What do capitalism and communism have in common?

   (1) Economic planning is in private hands.
   (2) Individuals work for the common good.
   (3) They require democratic government.
   (4) They are economic systems.
   (5) The state owns all businesses.

3. Which conclusion is supported by the passage?

   (1) Individual freedom is associated with capitalism.
   (2) In the past, socialist economies have failed.
   (3) Under communism, people can get rich.
   (4) Capitalism can do well under a dictatorship.
   (5) Politics and economics have nothing to do with each other.

4. What additional information do you need to draw the conclusion that the theory of communism differs from the reality?

   (1) only what is stated in the passage
   (2) what the theory of communism is
   (3) what the reality of communism is
   (4) more details about communist theory
   (5) how socialism differs from communism

5. Many manufactured products carry a warranty. A warranty promises that, if the product is defective, the manufacturer will repair it. What concept of economics do warranties illustrate?

   (1) capitalism
   (2) consumer protection
   (3) the gross domestic product
   (4) supply and demand
   (5) communism

Questions 6 through 8 refer to the following passage and chart.

One way government is involved in the economy is in its attempts to protect the consumer. In the past, people had little protection. Every store should have posted large signs saying "Buyer, beware!" If bakers bought flour that was full of bugs, they could take the time to sift them out, include them in the products they baked, or toss out the flour and lose money. Today, the Canadian Food Inspection Agency, Health Canada, Transport Canada, and other agencies protect consumers from careless or unethical people who might otherwise put profits ahead of public health and safety.

Public awareness of consumer rights, public relations on the part of manufacturers and store owners, and self-policing by various businesses have also increased consumer protection. For example, food stores today replace food that has gone stale or sour or that is contaminated in some way. In fact, they figure in the losses from not being able to sell such food when they decide what prices to charge for the groceries.

FEDERAL CONSUMER PROTECTION AGENCIES	
Agency	**Consumer Protection Functions and Activities**
Canadian Food Inspection Agency	Sets up and enforces food standards, such as the grading of meat and fresh produce, and accurate labelling of the contents of food labels; issues warnings about unsafe or potentially unsafe food products, possible allergens
Transport Canada	Cooperates with the provincial and territorial governments to improve road safety and reduce death, injuries, damage to property and the environment, and reduce energy consumption; issues warnings about unsafe tires, mechanical problems
Health Canada	Sets product safety regulations to prevent product-related death, illness and injury; protects consumers from hazardous and potentially hazardous products, such as chemicals, toys, cosmetics, and drugs

6. Which of the following is implied by the passage and the chart?

   (1) Self-policing protects consumers more effectively than government action.
   (2) Health Canada is a more effective consumer protection agency than Transport Canada.
   (3) The most serious product safety issues involve toys.
   (4) Self-policing by industry groups makes government regulation unnecessary.
   (5) If consumers didn't have government protections, companies might knowingly sell products that harm people.

7. Who <u>most likely</u> pays the cost of a manufacturer's recall of a defective product?

   (1) the government
   (2) the manufacturer
   (3) consumers
   (4) Transport Canada
   (5) the Canadian Food Inspection Agency

8. What is the common goal of the agencies and departments described in the chart?

   (1) to help prevent Canadians from buying potentially harmful cosmetics
   (2) to control prices so that all goods and services are affordable
   (3) to ensure that food is of a high quality
   (4) to make sure that car tires are safe
   (5) to ensure that Canadian consumers can purchase safe goods and services and be able to deal effectively with problems

Answers start on page 767.

Labour and the Economy
Assessing the Adequacy of Supporting Data

When you evaluate a conclusion, you must decide if you have been given *enough* facts to support it. This applies to conclusions that you draw, as well as to those that you read or hear. It also applies to **data** as well as to other supporting information.

To decide whether the data presented are adequate, or enough, to support a conclusion, you need to understand the main idea and all the supporting details. When you are sure that you understand these ideas and data, ask yourself, "Are these facts enough to support the conclusion?" Also be sure to ask whether there is anything else you would need to know to draw that conclusion logically. If you find enough solid, relevant supporting information, then the conclusion is probably accurate. Sometimes, however, you might not find enough information or the conclusion may not be adequately supported. In either case, the conclusion is probably not valid or accurate.

data
facts, statistics, or measurements used as a basis for reasoning, discussion, or calculation

Read the passage and answer the question below.

The first labour unions in Canada were organized among longshoremen in Halifax and Saint John during the War of 1812. The power of workers to achieve better wages and working conditions was limited, however. Surprisingly, in 1872 the federal government passed a law legalizing unions, but it also enacted a tougher law against most union activities. Nevertheless, between 1900 and 1911, union membership in Canada grew from 20 000 to 120 000—8 percent of the labour force, even though internal fighting often left unions ineffective. Employers countered union growth with anti-union tactics such as: hiring strikebreakers and pressuring governments to use the militia against striking workers. One of the most important events in Canada's labour history came out of a bitter coal miner's strike in Alberta in 1906. To calm the situation, the following year the federal government passed the *Industrial Disputes Investigation Act*, which forced employers and unions to negotiate contracts rather than settle their disputes the old way—with crowbars and fists.

After identifying supporting data and other facts, look for unstated assumptions, implications, and stated or unstated cause-and-effect relationships in the information related to the conclusion.

Which of the following conclusions is supported by adequate data?

_____ a. The *Industrial Labour Disputes Investigation Act* brought about an end to strikes in Canada.

_____ b. The growth of labour unions in the nineteenth century was difficult, marked as it was by strong employer opposition, violence, and internal union struggles.

You are correct if you chose *option b*. The passage provides examples of the difficulties labour unions experienced in the nineteenth century—opposition from politicians and employers, strikebreakers, and violence. In spite of these problems, membership in labour unions grew to 8 percent of the total labour force by 1911. To conclude option a would require supporting examples of the effect of the *Industrial Disputes Investigation Act* on labour disputes.

GED Practice

Directions: Choose the <u>one best answer</u> to each question.

<u>Questions 1 through 4</u> refer to the following passage and table.

Mergers between companies and takeovers by one company of part or all of another have become facts of Canadian economic life. These actions occur when companies large and small run into trouble and put themselves up for sale. Even some businesses that are not for sale can be the targets of hostile takeovers by competitors or other buyers who find the business attractive.

Workers who are employed by companies that are taken over often worry about job security, fearing that the new owners might hire new staff or eliminate their jobs. The new owners may decide to stop producing or selling some of the products of the company they purchased.

Many of the people who lost their jobs in 1998 became unemployed because their company moved or closed a plant. Almost a third were let go because their positions were eliminated.

Even so, some workers benefit from the shifting business scene. Stable companies sometimes take advantage of shakeups elsewhere by offering good jobs to the skilled employees of companies in transition.

Mergers and Company Acquisitions in the 1990s					
Activity	**1990**	**1992**	**1994**	**1996**	**1998**
Company Mergers and Acquisition	838	551	1066	1185	1163

Source: *Directory of Mergers and Acquisitions in Canada* and *The Toronto Stock Exchange Review 1999*.

Tip

To support a conclusion, imagine having to explain the conclusion to someone else. Ask "Will these facts convince another person that the conclusion is correct?"

1. According to the passage, when does a hostile takeover <u>always</u> occur?

   (1) when the company being bought does not want to be purchased
   (2) when the buyer is a competitor of the company it is buying
   (3) when the buyer is a foreign company
   (4) when the buyer has no real interest in the company it is purchasing
   (5) when the buyer eliminates jobs in the company it acquires

2. What would be the <u>most likely</u> effect of one company buying a competitor?

   (1) Workers' wages will go down.
   (2) More jobs will become available.
   (3) Consumers will have fewer product choices.
   (4) The new company will put itself up for sale.
   (5) Both companies' prices will drop.

3. What information would you need to determine the accuracy of the conclusion drawn in the first sentence of the passage?

   (1) names of big companies that have merged
   (2) the number of hostile takeovers
   (3) the percentage of workers who have lost their jobs through mergers
   (4) the number of jobs lost in any given year
   (5) only the information in the table

4. Which information presents the <u>best</u> evidence for answering the question "Should employees of companies that are taken over worry about their jobs?"

   (1) the information in paragraph two
   (2) the information in paragraph three
   (3) the information in paragraph four
   (4) the data on mergers in the table
   (5) the information in paragraph one

Questions 5 through 7 refer to the following passage and graph.

Teenage unemployment is a serious problem in Canada. Many teenagers drop out of high school. Many high-school graduates do not go on for further training or degrees. Although the statistics vary somewhat from region to region, they are cause for concern. About 16 percent of teenagers who are not in school are unemployed, and a number of them have children. Many young women are not part of the workforce because they need to work in their own homes cooking, cleaning, and caring for their young children. Lack of paying jobs can cause financial hardship for these families.

For other teenagers who drop out of school, fast-food restaurants or part-time retail clerk positions provide short-term employment solutions. But few teenagers look forward to a lifetime of waiting on other people. The looming question is how these teenagers will support themselves and others who depend on them financially.

EDUCATIONAL LEVEL AND AVERAGE ANNUAL EARNINGS, 1995

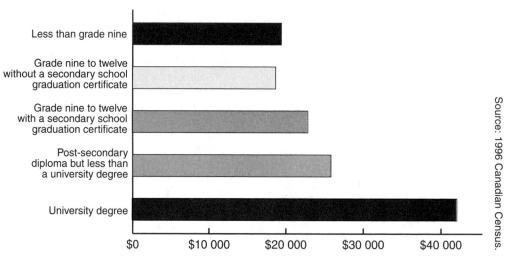

Source: 1996 Canadian Census.

5. Which information would best support the conclusion that the teenage dropout rate is cause for alarm?

   (1) that provided in the graph
   (2) that in the first paragraph of the passage
   (3) that about teenage mothers
   (4) that in the passage and graph together
   (5) more about what becomes of teenagers who drop out of school

6. Based on the information, what factor is most important in determining whether a person will get a well-paying job?

   (1) gender
   (2) previous work experience
   (3) level of education
   (4) marital status
   (5) a high school diploma

7. Which of the following is a likely effect of teenagers dropping out of high school?

   (1) more teenage mothers
   (2) more children in poverty
   (3) higher wages for high-school graduates
   (4) fewer workers for fast-food industries
   (5) fewer part-time retail clerks

8. About 15 percent of all adults 55 or older enroll in adult education courses. Data for enrollment for adults 17–34 and 35–54 are 39 percent and 32 percent, respectively.

   Which conclusion do these statistics support?

   (1) Adults take courses to learn new skills.
   (2) Most adult students are under age 35.
   (3) Young adults earn the most money.
   (4) Adult education is popular in Canada.
   (5) Older adults are busier than younger adults.

Answers start on page 768.

GED Review Economics

Directions: Choose the one best answer to each question.

Questions 1 through 4 refer to the following passage and graph.

The economy of every country is based on exchange—either through the barter of goods and services or through the payment of money for them. Goods are physical objects like food, cars, or housing. Services refer to work that people do that does not produce new goods. Services include car repair, house painting, and healthcare.

A common way to measure how well a country's economy is performing is by its gross domestic product, or GDP. The GDP is the total monetary value of all goods and services produced in that country during a year.

The Canadian GDP doubled between 1970 and 1992. This does not mean that Canada's economy doubled in size or that Canadians were twice as well off economically. We must take into account inflation and population growth. Prices rose almost 40 percent between 1980 and 1992, so a large part of the GDP increase resulted from higher prices, not increased production. The so-called real GDP—the value of annual production adjusted for increases due to inflation—was smaller. Added to this was the increase in Canada's population due to natural increase and a large influx of immigrants. So, although, more goods and services were produced in 1991 than in 1980, they had to be divided among more people.

GROWTH IN THE GDP, 1992–1998

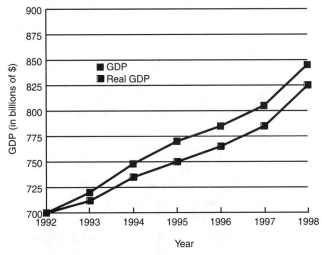

Source: Statistics Canada.

1. What is the real GDP?

   (1) all the goods and services produced and sold in a country in one year
   (2) the total value of a country's production divided by its population
   (3) a country's overseas trade in goods and services
   (4) the GDP adjusted for price increases that are due to inflation
   (5) the personal income that a country's people earn

2. Which of the following is a good that would be included in this year's GDP?

   (1) a used car purchased in New Brunswick
   (2) legal advice from a lawyer in British Columbia
   (3) an ear of corn grown in Manitoba
   (4) an operation on a family pet in Alberta
   (5) a CD player imported from Japan

3. What does the information in the graph imply about the 1990s?

   (1) Most Canadians became wealthier.
   (2) The nation's economy grew steadily.
   (3) The value of manufactured goods declined.
   (4) Canadian companies sold more overseas.
   (5) Canadians bought more foreign goods.

4. What conclusion about the Canadian economy is supported by the graph?

   (1) If growth continued at the same rate, Canada's GDP would have reached one trillion dollars by 2002.
   (2) Canada's economy was less healthy in the 1990s than it was in the 1980s.
   (3) The nation's economy was healthier in the 1990s than it was in the 1980s.
   (4) Canada is changing from a manufacturing-based economy to a service-based economy.
   (5) The unemployment rate falls as GDP rises.

Questions 5 through 8 refer to the following passage and table.

Income in Canada is distributed unequally. The richest 20 percent of our population earn almost 50 percent of the income. In contrast, the poorest 20 percent of Canadians earn less than 10 per cent of the income. In 1995, about 14 percent of Canadian families and 25 percent of children lived below the poverty line. Many people lack the education and training necessary to hold jobs in our increasingly technological society.

The gap between rich and poor continues to grow. As prices for necessities such as food and shelter have risen, the poor have become less able to pay for them. The use of food banks and sheltered accommodation continues to grow, yet Canada consistently ranks in the United Nations' Index of Human Development as the world's most livable country.

PERCENTAGE OF FAMILIES LIVING IN POVERTY				
Region	1980	1985	1990	1995
Atlantic provinces	16.5	16.4	12.7	15.6
Quebec	16.5	16.9	12.7	15.6
Ontario	11.5	11.4	9.6	12.6
Prairie provinces	11.7	14.4	14.0	14.2
British Columbia	10.5	16.7	11.7	13.0

Source: Canadian Council on Social Development.

5. Which of the following regions had a generally lower level of family poverty than the others?

   (1) Quebec
   (2) the Prairie provinces
   (3) Ontario
   (4) the Atlantic provinces
   (5) British Columbia

6. Wealth in Canada is distributed unevenly. What would you expect to find in a country where wealth is distributed more evenly?

   (1) All people would spend similar proportions of their income on food and housing.
   (2) Most people would buy the same make and model of car.
   (3) All families would have the same number of children.
   (4) Everyone would have the same amount of education.
   (5) People would spend their money on the same kind of leisure-time activity.

7. In Canada, there are more children living in poverty than families living in poverty. What is the most likely reason?

   (1) Children are poorer than their parents.
   (2) Most families in poverty have more children than wealthy families do.
   (3) Raising a child costs money.
   (4) Children in poverty are more likely to drop out of school.
   (5) It is not legal for children to work at most jobs.

8. Would a claim that poverty rates are rising be believable?

   (1) Yes, because the table shows that poverty rates generally rose between 1980 and 1995.
   (2) No, because the passage fails to relate rising prices to rising poverty rates.
   (3) Yes, because the passage shows that the distribution of income has become more unequal.
   (4) No, because the table shows that poverty rates have generally declined in recent years.
   (5) Yes, because the passage establishes that 25 percent of children were poor in 1995.

Social Studies • Economics

Questions 9 through 12 refer to the following passage and chart.

The North American economy is said to go through an eight- to-ten-year business cycle. This cycle has four phases: expansion, peak, contraction, and trough. During expansion, business activity increases until it reaches a high point, or peak. During contraction, business activity decreases until it reaches a low point, or trough. Although minor upswings and downswings happen all the time, the overall pattern of the business cycle is to rise, then fall, and then rise again.

Movement in the economy is classified by many different terms that explain the effects that wages, production, and money supply have on one another—and on the business cycle—at any given time. The chart identifies some of these terms and briefly defines the economic trends they describe.

ECONOMICS TERMS AND DEFINITIONS

Term	Description
inflation	a general increase in prices resulting from a decline in the value of money; occurs when there is more money in the economy than there are goods to buy
demand-pull inflation	an increase in prices that occurs when there is a greater demand for goods than there is a supply; results from too much money and relatively too few goods
cost-push inflation	an increase in prices caused by an increase in the cost of production; often results from a general rise in wages; cost-push inflation related to wages is sometimes called the wage-price spiral
recession	a period of general economic decline; characterized by production declines, rising unemployment, and people having less money to spend
depression	a severe reduction or slowing of business activity and in the flow of money in the economy; many people are unemployed and have little money to spend

9. Which word best describes the North American economy?

   (1) positive
   (2) negative
   (3) changing
   (4) unchanging
   (5) large

10. Which economics term relates to both a recession and a depression?

   (1) inflation
   (2) peak
   (3) trough
   (4) expansion
   (5) upswing

To apply an idea to a new situation, analyze the situation to make sure the idea clearly relates to it. Look for similarities between the original context and the new situation.

11. In 2000, it cost $2 to purchase an item that cost $1 in 1990. Which economic condition does this illustrate?

   (1) inflation
   (2) recession
   (3) depression
   (4) expansion
   (5) contraction

12. Which is an unstated assumption the passage makes about the North American economy?

   (1) It is currently on the rise.
   (2) Inflation has no effect on it.
   (3) Contraction is preferable to expansion.
   (4) Minor variations in the pattern can lead to recession or depression.
   (5) It is not seriously affected by minor variations in the pattern.

Answers start on page 769.

Geography

Over the course of human history, people have spread over all of Earth's usable land. Understanding the planet and its resources has always been essential to human survival. People need to know where there is sufficient water, where the land will provide enough food, and where materials needed for shelter can be found.

Geography is the study of the physical environment and the human environment, and how each of these environments affects the other. Knowing about geography helps us understand the land we occupy and how we can make better use of it. Geography is also an important part of the GED Social Studies Test, making up 15 percent of the test questions.

Places and Regions

Restating Information from Maps

Suppose you are hosting a party and not all the guests know where you live. Some of them want a map to your home, and others prefer written directions. People learn in different ways. Verbal **restatements** help some people better understand the content of visual material. When you write out directions, you are restating the map's visual information in a verbal format.

Maps give information about land. This information may include the way the land is shaped; the location, direction, and distance of objects; and even the land's climate, resources, and population. To accurately restate information from maps, you must be able to read them.

To find out what is in a map, first look at the map's title. On many maps, a list of symbols—called a **legend**—explains information that is shown on the map. A map tool called a **compass rose** indicates north and the other directions. Distance measurements are given in a map scale.

restatement
information that is provided in another way

legend
the map tool that explains the meaning of the map's symbols

compass rose
the map tool that indicates the four cardinal directions— north, south, east, and west—on the map

 Before using a map, read its title and study the legend. This helps you determine what you can learn from the map.

GED Practice

Directions: Choose the <u>one best answer</u> to each question.

Questions 1 through 4 refer to the following passage and map.

Of all the continents, only Antarctica has not attracted permanent settlers. Antarctica is one of the most difficult places in the world to live. The average temperature is 56 degrees below zero.

Even though it is a cold land covered by snow and ice, Antarctica is considered a desert. Only a small amount of precipitation falls every year. It falls in the form of snow. The snow almost never melts, and over the centuries, the light snowfalls have built up to form a sheet or "cap" of ice that is hundreds of metres thick.

Only a few types of plants survive in the rare, rocky places that are not covered by ice. Except for a few insects, animals are able to live only on the edges of this vast frozen continent. Penguins and seals gather food in Antarctica's offshore waters, which, although studded with icebergs, are warmer than the land.

ANTARCTICA

1. Which of the following correctly restates information about Antarctica from the map?

   (1) Because of its location at the South Pole, it does not have seasons.
   (2) Many nations have research stations, but the United States has the most.
   (3) The Transantarctic Mountains divide it into eastern and western regions.
   (4) It consists mostly of shelf ice, but with mountain ranges and an ice cap, too.
   (5) The highest point is found at the South Pole in the continent's interior.

2. What does the passage imply about deserts?

   (1) Deserts exist only in Africa and Asia.
   (2) A place that is cold cannot be a desert.
   (3) Snow almost never occurs in a desert.
   (4) Deserts have sand, even if covered by ice.
   (5) Places with little precipitation are deserts.

3. Why do Antarctica's largest animals live along the coasts, not in the interior, of the continent?

   (1) The interior is too cold.
   (2) The interior is too mountainous.
   (3) Most of the interior is covered with ice.
   (4) The interior has no good food source.
   (5) Researchers in the interior have hunted large animals to extinction.

4. Which value has most likely caused nations to establish research stations in Antarctica?

   (1) curiosity—to learn more about the continent
   (2) courage—lack of fear of the climate
   (3) compassion—to help the people there
   (4) love of nature—to save its animals
   (5) efficiency—to build industry on unused land

Additional practice material available on page 878.

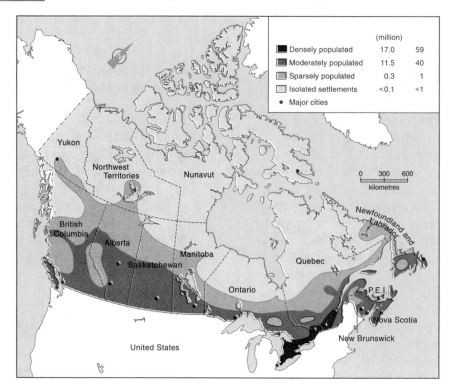

5. On average, which Canadian provinces or territories have the highest population density?

    (1) British Columbia and Yukon
    (2) Nova Scotia and PEI
    (3) Ontario and Quebec
    (4) the Northwest Territories and Nunavut
    (5) Alberta and Saskatchewan

6. Which statement accurately reports information shown by this map?

    (1) Most Canadians live near the American border.
    (2) There are more people living in Alberta than in Saskatchewan.
    (3) More Canadians now live in the northern territories.
    (4) Quebec and New Brunswick have the highest population in Canada.
    (5) The United States is attracting more Canadian immigrants.

7. Which reason best explains why some areas on the map show very high population density?

    (1) Many tourists visit these areas.
    (2) They are near major lakes.
    (3) The soil is most fertile in these areas.
    (4) The climate in these areas is warm.
    (5) Major cities are located in these areas.

8. Suppose that you wanted to open a chain of restaurants across a province. Based on the information given, which of the following provinces or territories would be the best in which to do this?

    (1) Yukon
    (2) Newfoundland and Labrador
    (3) Ontario
    (4) Manitoba
    (5) Nunavut

Additional practice material available on page 878.

In relation to other major land masses, Canada lies in the middle and high latitudes of the world, which greatly affects its climate. Oceans on both the west and east coasts also affect Canadian climate. Because Canada's land surface ranges from 42° N to 83° N latitude and borders both the Pacific and Atlantic Oceans, this geographical diversity creates seven different climate zones. For instance, the climate in the Canadian north is extremely cold and dry, resulting in long, harsh winters and brief summers. In more southern regions, such as the Great Lakes and St. Lawrence River, however, the climate is more moderate throughout each year. Also, the Labrador Current on the east coast brings cool water to Atlantic Canada, making that region colder than the Pacific climate zone in British Columbia, which receives a corresponding warmer Japanese Current.

9. Which sentence summarizes the passage?

(1) Like weather, climate is unpredictable.
(2) Geographic latitude and oceans affect climate.
(3) Climate varies because of land features.
(4) Climate depends on ocean patterns.
(5) Canada has seven climate zones.

10. Which sentence accurately restates information from the map?

(1) The climates along the west coast and along the east coast are similar.
(2) Most Canadians live near the American border.
(3) Canadian lakes affect climate.
(4) The Atlantic Ocean has a greater influence on climate than the Pacific Ocean does.
(5) Much of Canada's climate is either Subarctic or Arctic.

11. If Canada were bordered by land on three sides instead of water, what would be the likely effect on the climate of the east and west regions?

(1) Seasonal temperatures would be more consistent.
(2) Winters would be warmer and summers colder.
(3) Winters would be colder and summers warmer.
(4) There would be more rain and wind.
(5) There would be no change.

12. What features would be least likely to appear on a map of physical regions?

(1) mountains
(2) lakes
(3) plains
(4) roads
(5) deserts

Answers start on page 770.

Resources Affect Where People Live

Distinguishing Conclusions from Supporting Details

As you have already learned, it is important to be able to tell a conclusion from its supporting details in order to judge whether the conclusion is accurate. Not every paragraph of written material will contain a conclusion. However, when writers reach a conclusion about a topic of a paragraph, they generally structure the paragraph so that their conclusion is stated either at the beginning of the paragraph or at the end.

When a conclusion appears at the beginning of a paragraph, the remainder of the paragraph usually contains evidence and other details that the writer includes to make the conclusion believable. This paragraph structure has some advantages for the reader. Knowing the conclusion first makes it easier to judge whether the details that follow actually support that conclusion.

Paragraphs in which the conclusion occurs at the end can be more difficult to comprehend. This is because the supporting details are stated before the reader learns the conclusion that the details are intended to support. In analyzing such materials, the reader must either remember the details or look back in the paragraph to see whether they truly support the conclusion stated at its end.

Read the paragraph and answer the question below.

Resources play an important role in determining where people live. Though Canada's indigenous people occupied most areas of the country before European contact, the development of towns and cities in the Canadian West (then known as Rupert's Land) was greatly influenced by the activities of European explorers. Europeans travelled across Western Canada in search of furs. They explored this vast area by canoe through the many lakes and rivers, and established a series of fur trading forts along these travel routes. Eventually many of these forts became modern cities. Fort William, located on the edge of Lake Superior, is known today as Thunder Bay; Fort Garry, located along the Red River, is now known as Winnipeg; and Fort George, situated along the Fraser River, is now named Prince George.

Which sentence from the paragraph states its conclusion?

_____ a. Resources play an important role in determining where people live.

_____ b. Fur trading forts developed into modern Canadian cities.

You are correct if you chose *option a*. The rest of the paragraph shows how this statement is true. *Option b* is a fact that supports the opinion that resources are important in determining where people live.

When a paragraph contains information about a cause-and-effect relationship, the conclusion will likely be stated at the end of the paragraph.

Social Studies • Geography

GED Practice

Directions: Choose the <u>one best answer</u> to each question.

<u>Questions 1 through 3</u> refer to the following passage.

On a map, a river looks like it follows a set path. But a river can change its course. A riverboat captain who lived one hundred years ago would be able to detect many changes in how the Mississippi River looks today. The water pushing against the mud and trees has changed all the bends and small islands in the river.

Humans also can change the course of a river by digging channels and building dams, and the changes can affect the way people live. Before the Aswan High Dam was completed in 1970, the Nile River in Egypt flooded every autumn. As the floodwaters receded, a layer of silt—small particles of soil that were suspended in the water—was left behind on the ground. These silt deposits enriched the land, increasing the harvests and profits of farmers.

Since the dam ended flooding, farmers along the Nile have had to replenish their land with expensive chemical fertilizers. Some of these chemicals get into the river, killing fish on which other Egyptians depend for their living. However, damming the Nile has also brought electricity into the homes and businesses of millions of Egyptians.

1. How did the flooding of the Nile River affect Egyptian farmers?

   (1) The floods made farming more difficult.
   (2) Frequent flooding required them to use expensive fertilizer on their farmland.
   (3) The floods made it impossible for farmers to harvest their crops during the summer months.
   (4) The flooding allowed farmers to produce more crops.
   (5) The floods washed away the land's rich top layer of soil.

2. Which detail supports the conclusion that changes in a river can affect how people live?

   (1) A river can change its course.
   (2) Humans can change the course of a river by digging channels and building dams.
   (3) Before the Aswan High Dam was completed in 1970, the Nile River flooded every year.
   (4) Silt deposits enriched the land, increasing the harvests and profits of farmers.
   (5) Farmers along the Nile have had to enrich their soil with expensive chemical fertilizers.

3. Which conclusion is supported by the passage?

   (1) Rivers can be dangerous and deadly.
   (2) Rivers are economically important.
   (3) The Nile flooding made travel and trade more difficult.
   (4) Egyptian farmers use more fertilizer than Canadian farmers do.
   (5) The fishing industry in Egypt is growing.

4. Large parts of Earth are very different now from the way they used to be. Many of the changes, like climate changes, have natural causes. Others are caused by people. For example, much of southern Ontario was farmland in the 1800s. Today, much of it is urban.

   What is the main idea of this paragraph?

   (1) Southern Ontario was mainly farmland in the 1800s.
   (2) Cities now stand where farms used to be.
   (3) Changes in Earth are caused by nature and by people.
   (4) Although Earth has changed in the past, it no longer does so.
   (5) Much of the eastern Canada is urban today.

In the mid-nineteenth century, industrial manufacturing developed in southern Ontario. Its geography became appealing because of its proximity to water—an urgently needed resource for both power and transportation. In those days of Canada's industrial infancy, manufacturing operations relied on power generated by water. Therefore, small industries (such as sawmills) blossomed in towns and cities in close proximity to a lake or river.

Settlements in urban areas grew as people moved from rural areas to find work. A pattern of urban growth in what is known today as the "Golden Horseshoe" evolved as many towns formed around Lake Ontario. Toronto, Canada's largest city, is located along this Golden Horseshoe. Oshawa, a leading centre for automobile manufacturing in Canada, is the northeastern boundary of the horseshoe. Hamilton, known for its steel production, extends south on the western shores of Lake Ontario. Along with these major cities are several others similarly located near a water source, whose manufacturing contributes to the Canadian economy.

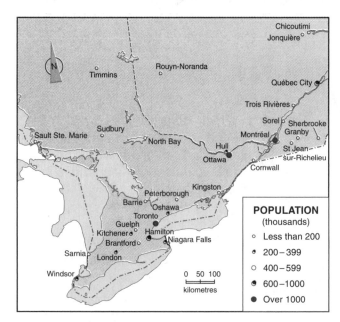

5. Which sentence from the passage best restates the map's information about the geography in southern Ontario?

   (1) Toronto, Canada's largest city, is located along this Golden Horseshoe.
   (2) Therefore, small industries (such as sawmills) blossomed in towns and cities in close proximity to a lake or river.
   (3) Settlements in urban areas grew as people moved from rural areas to find work.
   (4) Hamilton, known for its steel production, extends south on the western shores of Lake Ontario.
   (5) A pattern of urban growth in what is known today as the "Golden Horseshoe" evolved as many towns formed around Lake Ontario.

6. What information about southern Ontario is implied by the passage?

   (1) Early settlers liked the area because it had good soil.
   (2) Urbanization helped to staff this industry-rich area.
   (3) Access to water was a critical aspect of the development of industry and urbanization in southern Ontario.
   (4) People wanted to leave because of the pollution of the Great Lakes.
   (5) Manufacturing forms the core of Ontario's economy.

7. Which statement is an accurate conclusion about the above passage?

   (1) Automobile manufacturing drives Ontario's economy.
   (2) Toronto is Ontario's largest city.
   (3) Water power helped develop Ontario's manufacturing industry.
   (4) People tend to migrate to cities for employment.
   (5) Water resources created most of the major cities in southern Ontario.

Often a conclusion contains words like *consequently, thus, therefore,* or *as a result.* Look for such words to identify conclusions.

Answers start on page 772.

How People Change the Environment
Recognizing Values

You have already learned that values are principles, qualities, and goals people think are desirable and worthwhile. People often make decisions about what to do based on their values.

You have also previously learned that the values people share are among the things that hold a society together. These shared values—as well as the values of the individual members of a society—affect the decisions that people make about the use and conservation of the society's resources. For example, many people make an effort to conserve water during a shortage. But some people continue to soak their lawns with little apparent concern about whether others will have enough water. These two approaches toward using this resource result from very different sets of values.

Two types of values can be present in written material—the values of the people being written about and the writer's values. Being able to recognize the values of the people being written about helps us understand why they act as they do. It is also important to recognize the writer's values in order to be aware of any **biases** in his or her writing. Look for words in the material that provide clues about the writer's attitude toward the subject.

bias
a strong opinion that a person holds about a topic, sometimes unfairly or without good reason

To recognize values in written materials, pay close attention to accounts of people's actions as well as to accounts of their words. How people behave often reveals more of their values than what they say.

Read the passage and answer the question below.

In the early part of the 1970s, the Quebec government introduced the James Bay Project, a strategy to produce more hydroelectric energy. One incentive for this venture lay in the generation and sale of vast amounts of electrical energy to Canadian and American markets. After spending billions of dollars, the first part of the project was completed in 1985. However, this undertaking greatly affected the surrounding environment because it affected many rivers that flow into James Bay. The Cree nation, who depend on fishing, hunting, and trapping, had voiced strong concerns to the Quebec government from the very beginning because the extensive pollution and waste threatened their way of life. Although both parties have cooperated to decide on compensation, the Cree still resist future development in the area.

Which belief did people hold that encouraged them to develop hydroelectric energy?

_____ a. Each person's comfort and happiness is important.

_____ b. Economic prosperity for some is more important than threats to Aboriginal ways of life.

You are correct if you chose *option b*. Hydroelectric power benefits many Québécois, but the resulting impact on Aboriginal ways of life shows that, for some people, economic development is more important than Aboriginal concerns.

GED Practice

Directions: Choose the <u>one best answer</u> to each question.

Questions 1 through 4 refer to the following cartoon.

Cartoon by Peter Porges. © 1975. Reprinted by permission.

1. Which statement <u>best</u> describes what is happening in the cartoon?

   (1) A fisherman has caught the largest fish on record.
   (2) A fish is being prepared for processing and eating.
   (3) A fish is hanging over a dock or the deck of a boat.
   (4) A fisherman has caught a fish that has eaten people's trash.
   (5) A large fish was used to help clean up the ocean.

2. What opinion is the cartoon expressing about how people are changing the environment?

   (1) Fishing is exhausting the supply of fish.
   (2) The world's oceans are polluted.
   (3) Fishing is cleaning up the environment.
   (4) Pollution is causing birth defects in fish.
   (5) Fishing is polluting the environment.

3. What does the cartoon suggest are some polluters' values and attitudes about pollution?

   (1) Sport fishing kills more fish than pollution.
   (2) Fishermen are among the worst polluters.
   (3) It is all right to litter if people cannot see it.
   (4) Clean air is more important than clean water.
   (5) Ocean pollution is not a big problem.

4. What conclusion is supported by the information in the cartoon?

   (1) It is not safe to eat fish.
   (2) Pollution of the oceans kills fish.
   (3) Fishing with a pole is less harmful to the environment than fishing with a net.
   (4) The government should regulate fishing.
   (5) Pollution affects the ocean's animals.

5. Natural barriers like oceans and deserts have long slowed the movement of ideas. Today, satellites allow telephones and the Internet to reach almost anywhere in the world, to spread ideas and reduce differences among societies.

   Which of the following is <u>most</u> like a communications satellite?

   (1) a wall
   (2) a floor
   (3) a window
   (4) a room
   (5) a ceiling

Tremendous growth has occurred along the nation's coasts in recent decades. Shores that were once deserted are now covered with homes and businesses. From a geographical standpoint, these shores often are not good places for such development.

Over time, waves and currents reshape shorelines and beaches. Waves that strike a beach "head on" wash the sand directly out to sea. This produces islands called sand bars just offshore. Where the waves hit the shore at an angle, they create a current, called a longshore current, that flows parallel to the coastline. Sand washed from the beach is carried by this current and deposited elsewhere along the coast.

To resist these natural forces, property owners and communities have constructed breakwaters, jetties, and seawalls. Breakwaters are barriers placed offshore; jetties jut out from the shore. The diagrams show how these structures work. Seawalls can be thought of as on-shore breakwaters. They are often a last-ditch effort to save buildings. Although seawalls protect land behind them, they accelerate erosion on their seaward side, causing beaches to rapidly disappear.

Breakwaters and jetties slow the erosion of nearby beaches. Breakwaters can even create new beach by keeping sand deposited by the longshore current from being washed away. But neither prevents the shoreline from changing, and some experts believe that they increase long-term erosion by interfering with the natural cycles.

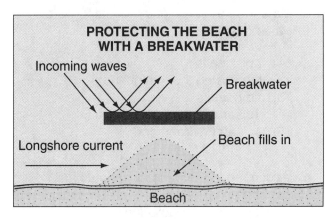

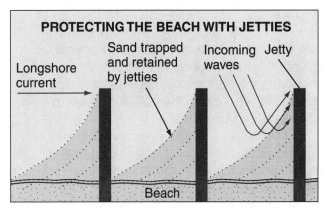

6. Based on the diagram, what do jetties do?

   (1) break the energy of incoming waves
   (2) stop incoming waves
   (3) trap the sand
   (4) create the longshore current
   (5) create sand bars

7. Which sentence expresses a value that best relates to the construction of breakwaters, jetties, and seawalls?

   (1) Protecting property is important.
   (2) Natural environment must be preserved.
   (3) People should accept forces of nature.
   (4) Natural beauty is worth preserving.
   (5) People have a responsibility to help others.

8. Which of the following is most similar in function to the breakwater in the diagram?

   (1) a ski lift on a mountainside
   (2) a bridge over a river
   (3) a TV station's transmission tower
   (4) a guardrail along a highway
   (5) an underground bomb shelter

9. Which of the following is an opinion?

   (1) The shoreline is constantly changing shape.
   (2) Waves can wash beach sand away.
   (3) Jetties and breakwaters function differently.
   (4) The building of seawalls destroys beaches.
   (5) Breakwaters and jetties accelerate erosion.

Answers start on page 772.

Directions: Choose the one best answer to each question.

Questions 1 through 4 refer to the following passage.

One of the greatest challenges to our environment is water pollution. For years, industries across Canada buried harmful chemicals or dumped them into streams. Most water pollution cannot be seen. Only its effects on plants and animals provide evidence of poor water quality.

Water pollution is not confined to places where the contamination actually happens. In the cycle of nature, the water supply is used and reused. Surface water evaporates and later returns to Earth in the form of rain or snow. Some of this water soaks through the soil and slowly seeps down between cracks in rocks to become part of large pools, lakes, and rivers of water that exist beneath Earth's surface. Eventually, this groundwater returns to the surface in the springs that create streams. Because of this cycle, the pollution of any water becomes the pollution of all water.

Groundwater is also tapped by wells and provides drinking water for many Canadians. Many people use water filters or drink bottled water because they question whether their household water is safe. Older homes often have lead pipes. Lead from these pipes can sometimes get into the water that passes through them. Lead is absorbed very slowly by the body. But if high levels build up, damage to the brain and central nervous system can result.

1. Which of the following expresses the main idea of the passage?

   (1) Lakes and rivers are being polluted.
   (2) Water pollution is hazardous to human health.
   (3) Water pollution is a widespread problem.
   (4) There is no solution for water pollution.
   (5) People should start drinking bottled water.

2. Which of the following is a conclusion supported by the passage?

   (1) Polluted water can be detected by its appearance.
   (2) Groundwater is more polluted than water from rivers and lakes.
   (3) Water from rivers and lakes is more polluted than groundwater.
   (4) People who get their drinking water from wells should have it periodically tested.
   (5) People will become seriously ill if they drink water from the pipes of older homes.

3. What do people who drink bottled water value most?

   (1) their health
   (2) impressing their neighbours
   (3) old houses
   (4) conserving resources
   (5) a clean environment

4. According to the passage, should the burying of harmful chemicals be considered a source of water pollution?

   (1) Yes, because water pollution is one of the greatest challenges to our environment.
   (2) No, because these chemicals are buried on land, not dumped into bodies of water.
   (3) Yes, because the chemicals are harmful to humans.
   (4) No, because when the chemicals were buried, it was not against the law to do so.
   (5) Yes, because seepage from rainwater could carry these chemicals into the groundwater.

Remember that the things considered to be important indicate people's values.

Questions 5 through 8 refer to the following passage and map.

Each autumn, monarch butterflies across eastern and central North America fly south for the winter. They reappear every spring. In 1975, a Canadian scientist located the winter home of the monarchs in the Sierra Madre Mountains of central Mexico. In just 100 km² there are 14 colonies of monarchs, or about 150 million of these regal creatures. They turn the sky orange and black and cover the trunks of trees, and branches bend under their weight.

When word of this wondrous place spread, it began to attract sightseers. By the early 1980s, thousands of tourists were visiting the area every weekend from December through March. They filled the monarchs' home with litter and stuffed butterflies into plastic bags as souvenirs. Local residents, seeing an economic opportunity, began to supply small wood and glass cases with monarchs mounted inside.

As tourism brought development, the threat to the monarchs became even more severe. The region's growth created a need for wood, and local residents increased logging in the forest where the monarch colonies lived. In 1986, Mexico's government created a preserve to protect 5 of the 14 colonies. But the owners of the land received little compensation for the loss of their timber resources; illegal logging continues today in the area that is supposed to shelter the monarchs.

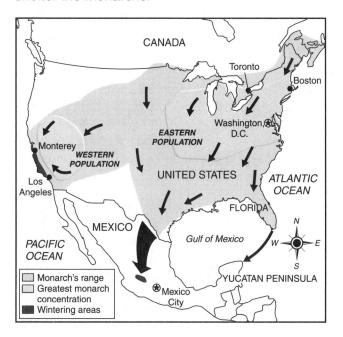

Map legend:
- Monarch's range
- Greatest monarch concentration
- Wintering areas

5. According to the map, in what other region besides central Mexico do monarch butterflies spend the winter?

(1) Canada
(2) Central America
(3) Mexico City
(4) the west coast of the United States
(5) Mexico's Yucatan Peninsula

6. Which of the following is an unstated fact important for understanding the first paragraph of the passage?

(1) Butterflies are smaller than birds.
(2) The monarchs' winter home is in Mexico.
(3) Air quality in the monarch preserve is poor.
(4) Birds also fly south for the winter.
(5) A monarch has orange-and-black wings.

7. If the U.S. government wanted to protect monarch butterflies along the west coast, what might it establish that would be similar in intention to Mexico's monarch preserve?

(1) a zoo
(2) a wildlife refuge
(3) a farm
(4) a tourist resort
(5) a national recreation area

8. What cause-and-effect relationship is implied by the information in the passage?

(1) Logging the forest threatens the well-being of the monarchs.
(2) The government created the preserve at the request of the tourists.
(3) Economic growth has brought an end to logging in the area.
(4) Establishing the preserve has increased the number of monarchs.
(5) Most of the damage to the forest is caused by the monarchs themselves.

The environment we live in is not just air, land, and water. It also includes cities and towns. Much of the world's population lives in cities. In Canada, about 78 percent of people live in urban areas.

Unfortunately, the nation has not prepared well for urban growth. Even though the majority of Canadians live in cities, the space they occupy is only about 1 percent of the land. Cities face problems related to overcrowding, air pollution, trash disposal, water supply and treatment, inadequate housing, and more. The problems that cities face result from many people being concentrated in a small area. If the urban environment does not get more attention, these problems are likely to get worse.

Recently, Canadians have increasingly come to understand and appreciate cities' problems. Politicians have begun to pay attention to cities, too. Some are beginning to pass laws that help make cities better places to live.

9. What is the main idea of the first paragraph of the passage?

(1) The environment includes all land as well as air and water.
(2) More people live in suburbs than in cities.
(3) Cities take up more land than farms do.
(4) Cities and suburbs are part of the environment, but farms are not.
(5) Most Canadians live in urban areas, which are part of the environment.

10. Which of the following statements from the passage is a conclusion?

(1) Much of the world's population now lives in cities.
(2) The majority of Canadians live in cities.
(3) The problems that cities face result from many people being concentrated in a small area.
(4) Urban problems include overcrowding, air and water pollution, and inadequate housing.
(5) The majority of Canadians live on only 1 percent of the land.

11. Which is the most likely cause of the water supply problems that cities face?

(1) not enough rain
(2) too many people
(3) polluted wells
(4) too much rain
(5) urban flooding

12. Which information is the writer's opinion?

(1) About 78 percent of Canadians live in urban areas.
(2) Trash disposal is an issue affecting cities.
(3) Urban growth has not been well planned.
(4) Some politicians work to help cities.
(5) New laws address some issues cities face.

13. Which cause-and-effect relationship is suggested by the passage?

(1) As more Canadians move to cities, the amount of land cities occupy decreases.
(2) Canadians have become aware of urban problems because the news media are paying more attention to cities.
(3) As Canadians have become more aware of urban problems, government has come under more pressure to improve cities.
(4) Because cities have so many problems, most people living there are unhappy.
(5) Politicians know about urban problems because the problems are worldwide.

14. North America's worst oil spill in history occurred in 1989. An oil tanker struck a reef off Alaska's coast, and 50 million litres of oil leaked into the sea. Almost 2000 km of coastline was polluted and 100 000 birds died.

What conclusion is supported here?

(1) The oil spill was an environmental disaster.
(2) Transporting oil by ship should be outlawed.
(3) Many birds died from drinking the oil.
(4) The ship was not operating safely.
(5) People can clean up their environment.

Answers start on page 773.

GED Unit Review Social Studies

Directions: Choose the one best answer to each question.

<u>Questions 1 through 3</u> refer to the following map and information.

Earth's climate changes gradually over thousands of years. When Earth's average temperature rises, parts of the polar ice caps melt, and the sea level rises everywhere. This map shows areas that might be harmed by a rise in sea level.

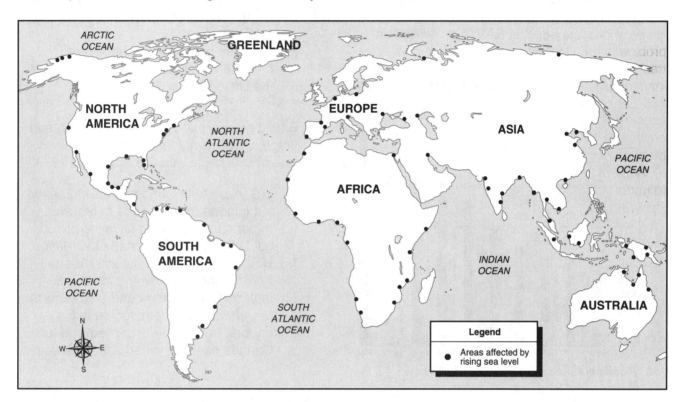

1. What is <u>most likely</u> to be the result of a slowly warming climate?

   (1) a gradual rise in the sea level
   (2) a sudden rise in the sea level
   (3) colder winters all over the world
   (4) tidal waves along the coasts
   (5) more ice trapped in the polar caps

2. On which two continents is the threat of flooding due to rising sea levels <u>most similar</u>?

   (1) North America and South America
   (2) Africa and South America
   (3) North America and Africa
   (4) Africa and Australia
   (5) Australia and North America

3. People living in which of the following places would be <u>most interested</u> in the information on this map?

   (1) Europe
   (2) coastal cities
   (3) Australia
   (4) the west coast of South America
   (5) close to the North Pole

Questions 4 through 6 refer to the following paragraph and graph.

On January 1, 1994, the North American Free Trade Agreement (NAFTA) went into effect. The agreement provided for the gradual removal of trade barriers among Canada, the United States, and Mexico. This means that goods produced in any of these nations may be sold in the other two without payment of the taxes normally placed on foreign-made goods. The graph shows the effect of NAFTA on Canadian trade with the United States.

CANADIAN TRADE WITH THE UNITED STATES

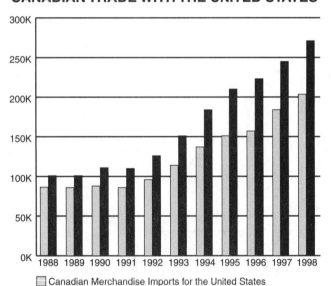

☐ Canadian Merchandise Imports for the United States
■ Canadian Merchandise Exports to the United States
(in millions of $CAN)

Source: Statistics Canada.

4. Which of the following most likely explains the increased trade between Canada and the United States in 1992 and 1993?

   (1) More Canadians visited the United States as tourists.
   (2) More Americans visited Canada as tourists.
   (3) There had been no change in the value of Canadian-American trade in the previous four years.
   (4) Trade increased in anticipation of the introduction of NAFTA.
   (5) The Canadian dollar increased sharply in value.

5. Which of the following statements about NAFTA is supported by the information?

   (1) NAFTA made the United States the chief trading partner of Mexico.
   (2) NAFTA reversed the trade relationship between the United States and Mexico.
   (3) NAFTA made Mexico more important than Canada as a U.S. trading partner.
   (4) Canadian exports to the United States sharply increased in the first year under NAFTA.
   (5) Because of NAFTA, Canada has become the chief supplier of clothing to the United States.

6. Based on information in the paragraph and graph, which of the following is most likely true of U.S. trade with Canada since 1994?

   (1) U.S. exports to Canada have increased, but imports from Canada decreased.
   (2) Imports from Canada have increased, but U.S. exports to Canada decreased.
   (3) U.S. exports to Canada and imports from Canada have both increased.
   (4) Imports from Canada and U.S. exports to Canada have both decreased.
   (5) Imports from Canada and exports to Canada have remained about the same.

Question 7 refers to the following paragraph.

After World War II, the United States and its allies adopted a policy toward communism called "containment." This policy was based on the idea that communism should be prevented from spreading beyond the countries where it already existed.

7. Which of the following world events is an example of containment?

   (1) creation of the United Nations to help the nations of the world work together
   (2) creation of the European Union to help improve the economy of Europe
   (3) independence of India and Pakistan
   (4) a limited war in Korea to drive communist invaders of South Korea back into North Korea
   (5) a revolution in Cuba that brought a communist government to power

Canada's 100th birthday was in 1967. Perhaps the greatest celebration of that anniversary was Expo '67, an international exposition, held in Montreal. Millions of visitors came to Canada to visit the country and share in the birthday party. One of the most famous guests was French President General Charles de Gaulle.

During his visit, the French leader gave a speech from the balcony of the City Hall in Montreal, praising Quebec and its French heritage. Near the end of his speech, he stretched out his arms and called out, "Vive Montréal! Vive le Québec! Vive le Quebéc libre!" ("Long live Montreal! Long live Quebec! Long live free Quebec!") This was the very slogan of Quebec independence.

The Canadian government, under Prime Minister Lester B. Pearson, was furious when these remarks were reported in the media, and as protests poured in, Pearson sent a telegram (excerpted below) to the French leader, calling the old general's remarks "unacceptable."

When de Gaulle heard Prime Minister Pearson's angry response to his speech, he quickly cancelled the rest of his trip in Canada and returned to France.

> The people of Canada are free. Every province of Canada is free. Canadians do not need to be liberated. Indeed, many thousands of Canadians gave their lives in two world wars in the liberation of France and other European countries. Canada will remain united and will reject any effort to destroy her unity.

8. In what way did the French leader contribute to political and social tensions in Canada?

   (1) De Gaulle seemed to criticize Expo '67.
   (2) The French president appeared to support Quebec separatism.
   (3) His remarks caused a revolution in Montreal.
   (4) The speech aroused patriotism back in France.
   (5) The French leader reminded Quebeckers that their culture came from France.

9. What historical reminder did the Canadian prime minister deliver to the French president?

   (1) Canada was a bilingual country.
   (2) France was not a democratic country.
   (3) The Canadian government had just recently granted freedom to Quebec.
   (4) Many Canadians had died to help liberate France.
   (5) Canada's survival depended on France.

Question 10 refers to the following passage and excerpt.

In 1865, the Legislative Assembly of the united province of Canada was debating the proposed scheme of a British North American confederation. One politician from Canada East (Quebec), Henri Gustave Joly, made the following suggestion:

> I propose the adoption of the rainbow as our emblem. By the endless variety of its tints the rainbow will give an excellent idea of the diversity of races, religions, sentiments, and interests of the different parts of the Confederation. By its slender and elongated form the rainbow would afford a perfect representation of the geographical configuration of the Confederation. … An emblem we must have, for every great empire has one; let us adopt the rainbow.

10. What feature of Canada might make the rainbow an even more appropriate symbol for the country today?

    (1) Canada's diverse technologically driven economy
    (2) the modernity of Canada's large cities
    (3) Canada's multicultural society
    (4) Canada's political institutions
    (5) Canada's British heritage

Questions 11 through 13 refer to the following passage and graph.

In the 1997 and 2000 general elections a record 62 female candidates were elected to office each time. In 1921, Agnes Campbell Macphail paved the way for women running for office when she became the first woman to be elected to the House of Commons as a member of the Progressive party.

In 1957 Ellen Louks Fairclough was the first woman to hold a Cabinet post when she was appointed secretary of state of Canada. In 1980, Jeanne Sauvé was the first female Speaker of the House of Commons. Four years later she also became Canada's first female governor general. Later, Kim Campbell was the first woman to become prime minister of Canada after Brian Mulroney resigned from office in June 1993.

NUMBER OF WOMEN ELECTED TO PARLIAMENT

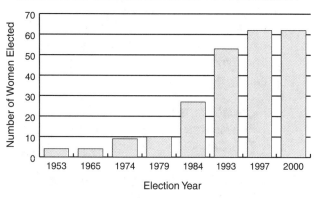

11. Which statement best illustrates the significance of the 1993 election for women?

(1) Not enough women ran as candidates for office from 1953 to 1979.
(2) Women were discriminated against from 1953 to 1979.
(3) More women were elected to Parliament than ever before.
(4) Kim Campbell's election as prime minister influenced Canadians to vote for women candidates.
(5) Voters elected almost twice the number of women to Parliament than in the previous election.

12. What concluding statement is consistent with the information in the passage and the graph?

(1) In recent years, fewer women have been elected to public office.
(2) Political parties have run more women candidates in recent years.
(3) Women have made few or no gains in provincial politics.
(4) More female candidates are needed in federal politics.
(5) Over time, women have gained more power in federal politics.

13. Which attitudes most likely influenced the role of women in federal politics before 1921?

(1) Canadian media generally ignored female candidates.
(2) Political parties tended to promote younger women in their ranks.
(3) Women were encouraged to run in federal elections.
(4) Women should not run in federal elections.
(5) Too many women were involved in federal politics.

Question 14 refers to the following passage.

One of the first and most important acts of the United Nations was to pass a Universal Declaration of Human Rights in 1948. The Declaration asserts individual rights as the basis of international law. It seeks to protect people on the basis of their gender, race, religion, language, and political beliefs. It also declares that everyone has the right to education, healthcare, and employment.

The Declaration is an assertion about the inherent value of every human life. Most people don't know that it was drafted by a Canadian, John Humphrey of New Brunswick. The Declaration has been recognized by almost every country as a landmark document. It has also served as the basis of the constitution in many countries.

14. To what other common document is the Universal Declaration of Human Rights similar?

   (1) the Ten Commandments of the Bible
   (2) the *Highway Traffic Act*
   (3) the National Gun Registry
   (4) the *Canadian Charter of Rights and Freedoms*
   (5) the *British North America Act*

Questions 15 and 16 refer to the following advertisement.

BOOKKEEPER / PAYROLL

Long-established firm seeks person to handle payroll and bookkeeping. Ideal candidate is high-school grad with 2 years bookkeeping and computer experience. Payroll experience a plus, but will train. We offer flexible hours and a competitive salary and benefits, including dental. Small, nonsmoking office. Send résumé with salary history to:
Barr & Co. 34 East Blvd., Ottawa, ON K1K 0V2

---

15. Prakash is applying for the job described in the ad. What fact should he emphasize in an interview?

   (1) He speaks two languages.
   (2) He is married and has a child.
   (3) He has worked as a bookkeeper.
   (4) He is in excellent health.
   (5) He had a B average in high school.

16. Which statement about the job expresses an opinion rather than a fact?

   (1) The firm is located in Ottawa.
   (2) The job offers a dental plan.
   (3) Flexible hours can be arranged.
   (4) A person without payroll experience probably won't be hired.
   (5) Smoking is not permitted in the office.

Question 17 refers to the following cartoon map.

Source: Reprinted with permission from *The Globe and Mail*.

17. Which statement best restates the information in the cartoon map?

   (1) There are more elderly ladies living in Ontario.
   (2) There are regionalized tensions in Canada.
   (3) The east coast wants to separate from Canada.
   (4) The Canadian north is colder than southern Canada.
   (5) Canada is an angry country.

Question 18 refers to the following paragraph.

   A small city has no public transportation system. Aside from walking or riding a bicycle, residents of this city who don't have cars can get around only by hiring the ABC Taxi Company. The city has no laws regulating taxi fares.

18. Which of the following is most likely to be true of the ABC Taxi Company?

   (1) The price of a taxi ride is high.
   (2) The price of a taxi ride is low.
   (3) The company's service is good.
   (4) The city will purchase the taxi company.
   (5) The company will go out of business.

Question 19 refers to the following graph.

Percentage Distribution of Seats in the House of Commons by Province or Territory

Distribution of Seats in the House of Commons

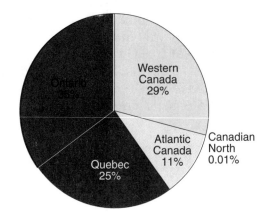

19. According to the pie chart, what part of Canada has the *least* number of seats in the House of Commons?

   (1) Ontario
   (2) Atlantic Canada
   (3) Western Canada
   (4) the Canadian North
   (5) Quebec

Question 20 refers to the following illustrations.

Source: John Henry Walker, Ink. Notman Photographic Archives, McCord Museum of Canadian History, Montreal/M930.50.5.142 and M930.50.262.

20. How do the illustrations demonstrate that the Industrial Revolution arrived in Canada about the same time as in the rest of the world?

   (1) They show that workers were joining craft unions.
   (2) They contrast early handwork with later mechanized production.
   (3) They compare the quality of shoes in two eras.
   (4) They reveal that industrial work was less interesting than farming.
   (5) They romanticize the shoemaker.

Question 21 refers to the following graph.

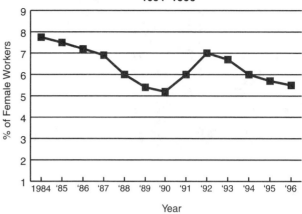

21. Which of the following is a conclusion based on the graph?

   (1) In 1989, women experienced the lowest level of unemployment.
   (2) Unemployment among women declined steadily between 1984 and 1996.
   (3) In 1987 and 1992, the rate of unemployment was the same, at 6 percent.
   (4) The rate of unemployment among women declined overall between 1984 and 1996.
   (5) Unemployment increased between 1992 and 1996.

Question 22 refers to the following paragraph and photograph.

   This photograph shows the famous "last spike," completing the CPR in November 1885. Noticeably absent are any Chinese labourers, hired at half the wage rate of white workers and given the dangerous job of setting the dynamite. At the completion of work, all Chinese workers were laid off. Neither the government nor the CPR honoured their pledge of free passage back to China, leaving most of the 15 000 workers destitute.

22. What do the photograph and the passage suggest many Canadians then believed?

   (1) All Chinese workers should be made citizens.
   (2) Europeans should be excluded from Canada.
   (3) Discrimination against non-Europeans was acceptable.
   (4) Chinese workers were good at their jobs.
   (5) Wages for Chinese workers should be raised.

Answers start on page 775.

unit 4

SCIENCE

The GED Science Test will cover the following content and skills.

The Test

- 50 multiple-choice questions
- 80 minutes to complete

The Content

- Life science
- Earth and space science
- Physical science

The Questions

- Comprehension
- Application
- Analysis
- Evaluation

". . . without my GED I would not have been successful as a businesswoman."
~Linda Torres-Winters
GED graduate

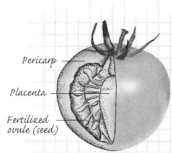

Pericarp

Placenta

Fertilized
ovule (seed)

Linda Torres-Winters has discovered many ways to use her GED. In 1994, she started a company called Lindita's, making instant salsa mixes from traditional recipes. After years of doing research, learning about spices, developing a marketing plan, and putting in lots of hard work, Torres-Winters introduced her product. Sales continue to soar as Lindita's Instant Salsa Mix conquers new markets. For Torres-Winters, involvement in her community is part of her position as a successful businesswoman. She hosts a local television show and works with charitable groups. Success, for "Lindita," has been a process of discovering all that she can do.

Discovery is part of what makes science exciting: the understanding that dawns as you reason through new concepts. You will use this process of discovery on the GED Science Test. First, you will read and analyze all the information carefully. In some cases, you will take general science information and apply it to specific situations. In others, you will evaluate information and judge its accuracy.

When she studied for the GED Test, Linda Torres-Winters may not have known exactly how she would use her certificate. She certainly could not have predicted the many ways in which she would find success. You, too, may discover unexpected ways to use your GED.

Study Tip

Break your study time into scheduled blocks.

You will remember more if you study in several shorter blocks of time, rather than long, exhaustive sessions.

- Make a study schedule and stick to it.
- Choose a time of day to study that works for you.
- Schedule study blocks no longer than two or three hours.

Life Science

Although we may not always realize it, life science information helps us make decisions every day. On a personal level, life science can help us learn how to improve our health and quality of life. On a larger scale, life science helps us to understand how humans and other organisms function and interact with their surroundings and how we can enhance the quality of this interaction. Life scientists are concerned with everything about life systems from the cellular makeup of organisms through the variations among like organisms to the ecosystems found on Earth.

Understanding life science is also very important for success on the GED Science Test. Life science topics are the basis for about 50 percent of the questions on the test.

Cell Structures and Functions

Identifying the Main Idea

main idea
the central topic of a paragraph or passage

When you take the GED Test, you will read science passages and study graphics for understanding. This means that as you read, you must look for **main ideas** and details that support the main ideas. How can you find the main ideas of a passage? Look over the passage quickly, counting the paragraphs. If there are three paragraphs, you should find three main ideas. Together, the main ideas of the paragraphs form the main idea of the passage.

Each paragraph is a group of sentences about a single topic—the main idea. The main idea of a paragraph is usually stated in the topic sentence. Often the topic sentence is the first or last sentence of the paragraph, but sometimes it is in the middle of the paragraph. Wherever it is, the sentence with the main idea has a meaning general enough to cover all the points in the paragraph.

Sometimes the main idea of a paragraph is not stated clearly in one sentence. In that case, you must read and think about the whole paragraph to understand the main idea. Look for supporting details that will help you. These may be facts, examples, explanations, or proofs that illustrate or tell more about the main idea.

GED Practice

Directions: Choose the <u>one best answer</u> to each question.

<u>Questions 1 through 3</u> refer to the following passage and diagram.

As living things, all cells have a life cycle. The cell life cycle has five stages: interphase, prophase, metaphase, anaphase, and telophase. During its life cycle, the cell grows, carries out its special jobs, and divides.

The most important part of cell division is mitosis—the division of the nucleus. During mitosis, the chromosomes in the parent cell duplicate and divide into two identical sets. One set will go to each of two new daughter cells.

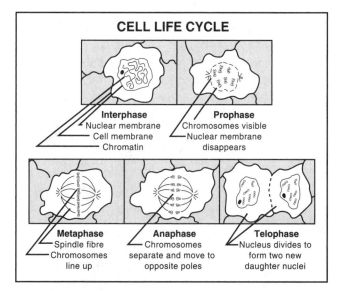

CELL LIFE CYCLE

Interphase
Nuclear membrane
Cell membrane
Chromatin

Prophase
Chromosomes visible
Nuclear membrane
disappears

Metaphase
Spindle fibre
Chromosomes
line up

Anaphase
Chromosomes
separate and move to
opposite poles

Telophase
Nucleus divides to
form two new
daughter nuclei

For most cells, interphase is the longest part of the life cycle. During interphase, the cell carries out many different life processes important for its growth and survival. Near the end of interphase, the cell prepares to divide. The chromatin in the nucleus duplicates.

Mitosis begins with prophase. During prophase, the chromatin shortens and thickens to form chromosomes. Each chromosome is made of two identical chromatids, which attach at their centres. A network of fibres called the spindle spans the cell. The nuclear membrane dissolves.

The next phase of mitosis is called metaphase. During metaphase, the chromosomes line up across the middle of the cell. They attach to the spindle fibres.

During anaphase, the chromatids in each chromosome separate. They migrate toward the poles along the spindle fibres. Once separated, the chromatids are called daughter chromosomes. The spindle pulls the two sets of daughter chromosomes to opposite ends of the cell.

The last phase of mitosis is telophase. During this phase, a new nuclear membrane forms around each set of daughter chromosomes. The chromosomes become longer and thinner. With mitosis complete, the cytoplasm divides, producing two daughter cells. They enter interphase and the cell life cycle begins again.

1. Which title tells the main idea of the passage?

   (1) Interphase—the Longest Phase
   (2) The Disappearing Nuclear Membrane
   (3) The Process of Mitosis
   (4) What the Spindle Does
   (5) Why Cell Division Is Important

2. Which of the following is a detail about mitosis that is supported by the diagram?

   (1) The nuclear membrane dissolves during prophase.
   (2) Spindle fibre formation begins in prophase.
   (3) If any of the spindle fibres get cut, mitosis cannot proceed normally.
   (4) Near the end of interphase, the protein content of the cell increases.
   (5) Anaphase is the shortest phase in the process of mitosis.

3. If a parent cell has 6 chromosomes at the start of interphase, how many chromosomes will each daughter cell eventually have?

   (1) 1
   (2) 3
   (3) 6
   (4) 12
   (5) 15

Questions 4 through 6 refer to the following information and diagram.

People once made fun of the notion that someday cell scientists would grow cells in the lab and fashion them into living body parts. Believe it or not, that day has come. The diagram below describes how new blood vessels can be created cell by cell, outside a human body.

BUILDING BLOOD VESSELS, CELL BY CELL

1. The scientist coats the inside of a tube of plastic scaffolding with muscle cells.

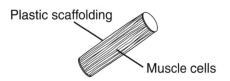

Plastic scaffolding

Muscle cells

2. The scientist places the tube in nutrient-rich liquid that washes over and through the tube in gentle waves.

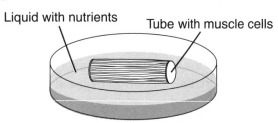

Liquid with nutrients

Tube with muscle cells

3. After eight weeks, the muscle cells have broken down the plastic scaffolding and they begin replacing it with connective tissue.

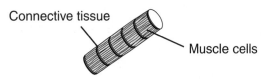

Connective tissue

Muscle cells

4. The scientist paints the inside of the tube with skin cells. A blood vessel has been built, cell by cell.

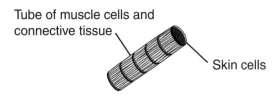

Tube of muscle cells and connective tissue

Skin cells

---

4. Which sentence best summarizes the main idea of the paragraph and the diagram?

  (1) Cell biologists have worked hard to meet human needs.
  (2) Cell biologists do not think that they can grow living body parts from cells.
  (3) Blood vessels are not the first body parts cell biologists have been able to grow.
  (4) Cell biologists have succeeded in growing blood vessels from living cells.
  (5) The first step in growing blood vessels is to coat plastic scaffolding with muscle cells.

5. What is the unstated assumption behind this information?

  (1) Artificial body parts are superior to body parts formed from living cells.
  (2) Scientists may someday be able to form replacement body parts from living cells.
  (3) It is extremely easy to form body parts from living cells.
  (4) The process of forming body parts from living cells takes too long to be practical.
  (5) Plastic scaffolding must support new body parts formed from living cells.

6. It may soon be possible that when nerves are cut, doctors can place a type of plastic between the cut nerves to help the nerve cells grow back. What is the most likely function of the plastic?

  (1) to reconnect the two cut nerves
  (2) to supply living nerve cells for reconnecting the damaged nerves
  (3) to provide a physical support for the growing nerve cells
  (4) to carry away the waste products of the damaged nerves
  (5) to allow both muscle cells and nerve cells to grow

Questions 7 through 9 refer to the following passage and diagram.

Plant cells have certain structures that animal cells do not have. For example, plant cells have a cell wall surrounding the cell membrane. Cell walls are made of bundles of cellulose and serve to support the plant.

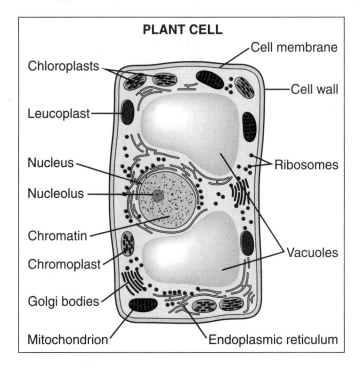

PLANT CELL

Cell membrane
Chloroplasts
Cell wall
Leucoplast
Nucleus
Ribosomes
Nucleolus
Chromatin
Vacuoles
Chromoplast
Golgi bodies
Mitochondrion
Endoplasmic reticulum

Plant cells also gain support from large, water-filled sacs called vacuoles. In a mature plant cell, one or two vacuoles may take up most of the space inside the cell. Animal cells rarely contain vacuoles and when they are present, they are tiny.

Also unique to plant cells are organelles called plastids. Chloroplasts are one kind of plastid. Chloroplasts contain the green pigment chlorophyll. Plants need chlorophyll to carry out the sugar-making process of photosynthesis. Chromoplasts are another type of plastid containing pigment. Yellow, orange, and red pigments are stored in a plant's chromoplasts. Leucoplasts are a third type of plastid. They make starches and oils for the plant.

7. Which is the best title for the passage and diagram together?

(1) Plant Cell Structures and Their Functions
(2) How a Plant Cell Reproduces
(3) How Plant and Animal Cells Are Alike
(4) How Plastids Function in Plant Cells
(5) Parts of a Green Plant

8. Based on the information in the passage, which type of structure gives daffodil and rose petals their colour?

(1) cell membrane
(2) cell wall
(3) mitochondria
(4) chromoplasts
(5) leucoplasts

9. Kenisha did not water her plants for three weeks, and they wilted. Why did the plants wilt?

(1) The cellulose in the cell walls disintegrated.
(2) The vacuoles shrank as their water was used up.
(3) The leucoplasts made too many starches.
(4) The chloroplasts lost all their chlorophyll and stopped functioning.
(5) The chromoplasts produced too much pigment.

To identify the main idea, look for the general idea of the passage. To identify supporting details, watch for names, numbers, dates, and examples. Look for key words including *like, such as,* and *for example.*

Answers start on page 778.

Lesson

2

restate information
to say something in
another way

When restating
information, be sure
all the facts and ideas
stay the same. Only
the words or the
arrangement of
information should
change.

Cells and Energy

Restating Information

When you **restate information,** you say it in another way. Sometimes you simply use different words. Other times you may restate information by putting it in the form of a diagram, graph, chart, or formula. Restating information is a good strategy to use to make sure you understand important science concepts.

The most common way to restate information is to paraphrase, or rewrite an idea, sentence, or paragraph in your own words. When you take notes in class or while reading, you usually paraphrase.

When information is restated, all the facts remain the same. However, the way the facts are presented changes. For example, the order of the information may be rearranged, or information presented in sentences may be restated in pictorial form.

Read the passage and answer the questions below.

Runners pace themselves during a long race. Their muscle cells need a steady supply of energy. Cells usually get energy through a chemical process called cellular respiration. In this process, cells use oxygen to break down sugar, which releases energy. When a runner can't breathe fast enough to keep her muscle cells supplied with oxygen, the cells switch to another energy-releasing process, called fermentation (anaerobic respiration). Fermentation also breaks down sugar to release energy, but it does not require oxygen. Lactic acid is a byproduct of fermentation. As lactic acid collects in the cells, the runner's muscles start to ache. This may cause the runner to slow down or even stop running.

1. Put a check mark by the restatement of the fermentation process.

_____ a. a chemical process in which energy and lactic acid are released from the breakdown of sugar in the absence of oxygen

_____ b. a chemical process in which muscle cells use lactic acid to release energy

You are correct if you chose *option a.* Fermentation is explained in the fifth and sixth sentences of the paragraph. *Option a* paraphrases those sentences. *Option b* is not true; lactic acid is a byproduct of fermentation.

2. Put a check mark by the restatement of the passage's last idea.

_____ a. A runner's legs ache because of a build-up of oxygen.

_____ b. A runner's legs ache because of a build-up of lactic acid.

You are correct if you chose *option b.* It restates the idea in slightly different words. *Option a* is not true; muscle fatigue results from too little oxygen.

GED Practice

Directions: Choose the one best answer to each question.

Questions 1 through 3 refer to the following passage and diagram.

People and other animals get their energy from food. When you eat, your digestive system breaks down the carbohydrates in food into simple sugar, called glucose. Glucose enters the cells of the body, where it is broken down to release energy. This complex chemical process is called cellular respiration.

CELLULAR RESPIRATION

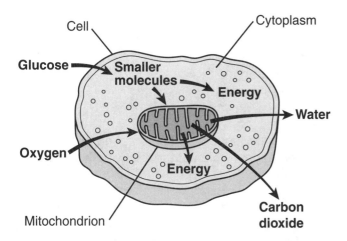

During cellular respiration, oxygen combines with glucose to release chemical energy and the byproducts carbon dioxide and water. Cellular respiration occurs in stages. The stage in which most of the energy is released takes place in the mitochondria.

$$C_6H_{12}O_6 + 6O_2 \longrightarrow 6CO_2 + 6H_2O + energy$$
glucose + oxygen $\longrightarrow$ carbon + water + energy
dioxide

1. In which cell structure is most of the energy resulting from cellular respiration released?

   (1) cell membrane
   (2) cytoplasm
   (3) chloroplast
   (4) mitochondrion
   (5) nucleus

2. Which of the following sentences restates the equation for cellular respiration?

   (1) Carbon dioxide and water combine in the presence of light energy and chlorophyll to yield glucose, oxygen, and water.
   (2) Glucose and water combine to yield carbon dioxide, oxygen, and energy.
   (3) Glucose and carbon dioxide combine to yield oxygen, water, and energy.
   (4) Glucose, oxygen, and energy combine to yield carbon dioxide and water.
   (5) Glucose and oxygen combine to yield carbon dioxide, water, and energy.

3. Which of the following is likely to result if the supply of oxygen to the cell is reduced?

   (1) Less energy is released.
   (2) More energy is released.
   (3) Cellular respiration speeds up.
   (4) More carbon dioxide is released.
   (5) Cellular respiration is not affected.

4. Cellular respiration and photosynthesis are opposite processes. In cellular respiration, oxygen is used, and energy and carbon dioxide are released. In photosynthesis, energy and carbon dioxide are used, and oxygen is released. Together, the processes help keep the levels of oxygen and carbon dioxide in the air in balance.

   Which of the following statements does this information support?

   (1) More green plants means less oxygen in the air.
   (2) More green plants means more oxygen in the air.
   (3) Fewer green plants means less carbon dioxide in the air.
   (4) Fewer green plants means more energy is stored in glucose.
   (5) There is more oxygen than carbon dioxide in the air.

Questions 5 through 8 refer to the following passage and diagram.

Metabolism is the total of all the chemical reactions that take place in a cell. There are two basic metabolic processes: anabolism and catabolism.

In anabolic reactions, raw materials that enter the cell are used to make more complex molecules, such as proteins and fats. These complex molecules are used for cell growth and maintenance. In catabolic reactions, such as cellular respiration, energy is released from the breakdown of organic materials.

ANABOLISM AND CATABOLISM

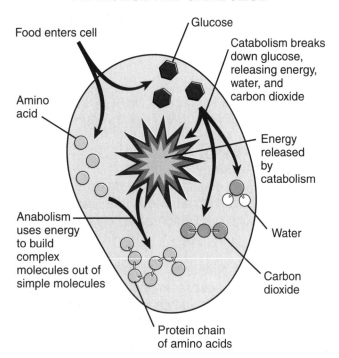

When an organism's anabolism is greater than its catabolism, then the organism grows or gains weight. When catabolism is greater than anabolism, an organism loses weight. When the two processes are balanced, the organism is in a state of equilibrium.

5. What is metabolism?

(1) the process by which organisms capture energy from sunlight
(2) the sum of all the chemical processes carried out by a cell
(3) the process by which energy is released from glucose
(4) the total amount of energy released by cellular respiration
(5) the total amount of raw material used by the cell to get energy

6. Which symbol or symbols in the diagram represent the energy released by catabolic reactions?

(1) arrows
(2) circles
(3) chained circles
(4) hexagons
(5) sunburst

7. If the amount of glucose entering the cell decreases, which of the following is likely to happen?

(1) Light energy decreases.
(2) Fewer amino acids enter the cell.
(3) More proteins are produced.
(4) There are fewer catabolic reactions.
(5) The cell produces more energy.

8. Kayla wants to lose weight by exercising more each day. If she succeeds, what change will she have made in her cell metabolism?

(1) increased photosynthesis
(2) increased catabolic reactions
(3) increased anabolic reactions
(4) decreased photosynthesis
(5) decreased catabolic reactions

Answers start on page 778.

Science • Life Science

Genetics

Distinguishing Fact from Opinion

A **fact** is something that has objective reality. A fact can be proved to be true. An **opinion** is what someone thinks is true. An opinion may or may not be true, and it cannot be proved true or false.

You deal with facts and opinions all the time. For example, your friend's hairline forms a widow's peak just like her mother's. It is a fact that her hairline comes to a point in the middle of her forehead. It is a fact that she inherited this trait, or the way a characteristic is displayed, from her mother. You may think your friend's hair is pretty. This is your opinion. You cannot prove that your friend's hair is pretty. Others may not agree.

Much of what you read in science is fact. However, you will also read scientists' opinions. Scientists observe things and then form an opinion. They may use their opinion to formulate a hypothesis to explain their observations. Then they experiment to learn whether the hypothesis is supported by the data collected.

Read the passage. Then complete the fact and opinion table below.

Scientists have produced a type of squash that is resistant to a deadly virus. They did this by changing some of the squash's genetic material. The new squash was approved for human consumption by the government despite controversy over the risks it may pose to the environment. Some scientists think that the genetically engineered squash will breed with wild squash. The offspring may inherit the resistance to the virus. Then wild squash may spread like a "superweed" throughout farmers' fields or in the wild. Other scientists think that the government was right to approve the new squash. They say the environmental risks are exaggerated, and the benefits of the new squash outweigh the risks.

fact
something that can be
proved true

opinion
a belief that may
or may not be true

When distinguishing fact from opinion, watch for words and phrases that signal opinions. These include *according to, it is possible, believe, think, feel, suggest, may, might, should, agree,* and *disagree.*

Tip

Also look for words that express an evaluation or degree of quality such as *best, worst, prettiest, easier, harder,* and *preferable.*

Fact	Opinion
Scientists genetically engineered squash to make it resistant to a deadly virus.	Some scientists believe approval of the genetically engineered squash is a mistake; others think the government was right to approve it.

Facts from the passage include the following sentences: *The government approved the squash. There is controversy over it.* From the fourth sentence to the end, the author presents opinions about the squash. You should have written two of these in the Opinion column.

GED Practice

Directions: Choose the <u>one best answer</u> to each question.

<u>Questions 1 through 3</u> refer to the following passage and diagram.

In 1903 American geneticist Walter Sutton, who was studying the egg and sperm cells of grasshoppers, discovered that Mendel's units of heredity—genes—were located on the chromosomes. Chromosomes are composed of a chemical called DNA. The structure of the DNA molecule was not known until 1953, when an American biologist, James D. Watson, and a British biophysicist, Francis Crick, worked it out. They described DNA as a double helix, or spiral, made up of two strands wound around each other and connected by crosspieces. The DNA molecule looks like a twisted ladder.

DNA MOLECULE

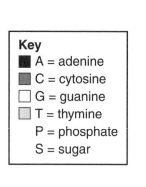

Key
A = adenine
C = cytosine
G = guanine
T = thymine
P = phosphate
S = sugar

The sidepieces of DNA are made of sugar and phosphate. The rungs of the DNA ladder are composed of pairs of four nitrogen bases: adenine, cytosine, guanine, and thymine. On the rungs, adenine always pairs with thymine, and guanine always pairs with cytosine. The sequence of bases along the ladder varies in different organisms (but each cell in a given organism has the same sequence in its copy of DNA). These variations form a genetic code that controls the production of proteins in the organism's cells. The proteins help determine the characteristics and functions of an organism.

1. Which of the following is a function of DNA?

   (1) controlling the production of proteins in the cell
   (2) breaking down proteins in the cell
   (3) producing energy from food molecules inside the cell
   (4) controlling substances that enter and leave the cell
   (5) joining adenine with guanine and cytosine with thymine

2. Suppose the sequence of bases along one side of a particular section of DNA is ATGTCAGC. Which of the following is the correct sequence of bases with which this sequence would be paired?

   (1) CTAGATAT
   (2) CTAGTGCT
   (3) TACACTCG
   (4) TACAGTCG
   (5) ATGTCAGC

3. Which of the following statements is supported by the information shown in the diagram?

   (1) Sugars and phosphates form the crosspieces of DNA molecules.
   (2) Of the two sidepieces of DNA, one is formed of only sugar and the other of only phosphate.
   (3) The base thymine is always attached to a guanine base.
   (4) Only the base adenine can attach to the sidepieces of the DNA.
   (5) The sidepieces of DNA are formed of alternating units of sugar and phosphate.

Science • Life Science

Questions 4 and 5 refer to the following passage and diagram.

A gene is a portion of the genetic molecule that determines a particular trait. Plants and animals that result from sexual reproduction inherit one gene for each trait from each parent. The set of genes that a plant or animal inherits is called its genotype.

To depict the traits that will be inherited, scientists use a Punnett square. The Punnett square below shows the possible combination of genes in the offspring of two parents with cleft chins. A cleft chin is one with a vertical groove. It is a dominant trait.

The genotype of the male parent is CC. Letters representing the genes from the father are across the top of the square. The genotype of the female parent is Cc. Letters representing the mother's genes are down the left side of the square. Each child inherits one gene from each parent.

	C	C
C	CC	CC
c	Cc	Cc

C = cleft chin
c = smooth chin

The Punnett square shows the possible genotypes of the offspring, but what appearance does each genotype represent? That is, what would a child with each genotype actually look like? To figure out the phenotype, or appearance, you must look at the dominant trait of each individual, shown by a capital letter. For example, individuals with the genotypes CC or Cc have cleft chins. When an individual has the dominant gene for a trait, that trait always shows, even when it is paired with the recessive gene for the trait. Only when an individual has two recessive genes in his or her genotype does the recessive trait actually show.

4. How many phenotypes are shown in the Punnett square?

(1) 0
(2) 1
(3) 2
(4) 3
(5) 4

5. If you saw a girl with a cleft chin, what could you tell with the greatest accuracy?

(1) the phenotype of her chin
(2) the genotype of her chin
(3) whether she has a recessive gene for chin type
(4) whether her mother has a cleft chin
(5) whether her father has a cleft chin

6. Traits are not always dominant or recessive. Sometimes the inheritance of traits occurs in a pattern called incomplete dominance. For example, the four o'clock plant has three genotypes for flower colour. The genotype RR results in a red flower; rr results in a white flower; and Rr results in a pink flower.

If you crossed a white-flowered four o'clock plant with a red-flowered four o'clock plant, what is the chance of producing a plant with pink flowers?

(1) no chance
(2) 1 out of 4
(3) 2 out of 4
(4) 3 out of 4
(5) 4 out of 4

Some questions are easier to answer if you draw a sketch, diagram, or chart. Making a Punnett square can help you answer genetics questions correctly.

Answers start on page 779.

Lesson

4

Human Body Systems

Recognizing Unstated Assumptions

When people communicate, they often assume that the listener or reader knows certain facts. These facts or ideas are called **unstated assumptions.** You need to be able to identify such facts.

You make unstated assumptions all the time. For example, when you tell a friend that there may be a thunderstorm this afternoon, you assume she knows what a thunderstorm is. Therefore, you do not describe the thunder, lightning, wind, and rain.

When you read about science, you will find that there are many unstated assumptions. Writers take for granted that you know certain common facts. In order to understand what you read, you must be able to identify the assumptions the writer makes.

unstated assumption
a fact or idea that is taken for granted and not actually stated

Read the passage and graph and answer the question below.

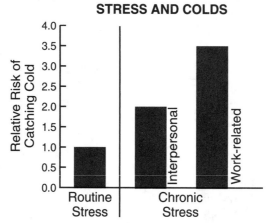

STRESS AND COLDS

According to researcher Dr. Sheldon Cohen, you are more likely to catch a cold when under chronic stress than when under mild, routine stress. Dr. Cohen is now trying to pinpoint how stress affects the body's immune system, lowering its resistance to disease.

Both passages and diagrams may have unstated assumptions. Ask yourself: What does the writer or illustrator think I already know?

Put a check mark next to each fact that the writer takes for granted and does not state in the passage or show in the graph.

_____ a. Mild, routine stress is part of our everyday lives.

_____ b. The immune system fights disease-causing agents.

_____ c. Chronic stress increases your chance of catching cold.

_____ d. People suffering interpersonal chronic stress are twice as likely to catch cold as those suffering routine stress.

_____ e. Chronic stress is severe stress that lasts a long time.

_____ f. Work-related chronic stress has a greater effect on the risk of catching cold than interpersonal chronic stress.

You are correct if you chose *options a, b,* and *e.* These are facts that the writer assumes you know, so they are not actually stated. The other options are explained in the paragraph or shown in the graph.

GED Practice

Directions: Choose the one best answer to each question.

Questions 1 and 2 refer to the following paragraph and map.

The Food and Drug Administration (FDA) in the United States recently approved a vaccine against Lyme disease, a bacterial infection transmitted to humans through the bite of a deer tick. The three-dose vaccine is approved only for adults. It works by stimulating the immune system to produce antibodies that destroy the bacteria. In studies involving 11 000 people, the vaccine was shown to be about 78 percent effective. Scientists are advising people who work or play in wooded or overgrown areas where Lyme disease and deer ticks are common to get the vaccine.

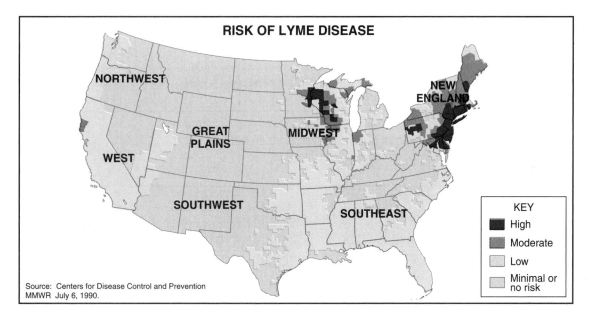

RISK OF LYME DISEASE

KEY
- ■ High
- ▨ Moderate
- ░ Low
- ▫ Minimal or no risk

Source: Centers for Disease Control and Prevention
MMWR July 6, 1990.

1. Based on the paragraph and the map, which of the following people would probably be advised to get vaccinated against Lyme disease?

   (1) a woman who lives in a wooded area of the Upper Midwest
   (2) a man who lives and works in a city in the Lower Midwest
   (3) a woman who lives on a ranch in the Great Plains region
   (4) a man who works on a cargo ship
   (5) a young child who lives in a wooded area of New England

2. Which of the following statements is supported by the information given in the paragraph?

   (1) Lyme disease is a viral infection whose incidence is on the increase.
   (2) Everyone who lives in an area with a high risk of Lyme disease should be vaccinated.
   (3) The FDA requires the vaccine be given in four doses.
   (4) People who have received the vaccine are completely safe from contracting Lyme disease.
   (5) The vaccine stimulates the immune system to make bacteria-killing antibodies.

When a question refers to a passage and a diagram, be alert for unstated assumptions in both.

Questions 3 through 6 refer to the following paragraph and chart.

The endocrine system consists of glands that secrete chemicals called hormones. Hormones travel throughout the entire body but affect only some parts of it.

Endocrine Gland	Hormone	Effect
Thyroid	Thyroxine	Controls how quickly food is converted to energy in cells
Parathyroid	Parathormone	Regulates body's use of calcium and phosphorus
Thymus	Thymosin	May affect the formation of antibodies in children
Adrenal	Adrenaline Cortisone	Prepares the body to meet emergencies Maintains salt balance
Pancreas	Insulin	Decreases level of sugar in the blood
Ovaries (female gonads)	Estrogen	Controls the development of secondary sex characteristics
Testes (male gonads)	Testosterone	Controls the development of secondary sex characteristics
Pituitary	Growth hormone Oxytocin ACTH, TSH, FSH, LH	Controls the growth of bones and muscles Causes uterine contractions in labour Regulates the secretions of the other endocrine glands

3. In an emergency, your heart rate and breathing quicken and you have a sudden burst of energy. Which endocrine gland causes this reaction?

   (1) adrenal
   (2) pituitary
   (3) thymus
   (4) parathyroid
   (5) pancreas

4. Which hormone causes the uterus to contract during childbirth?

   (1) glucagon
   (2) oxytocin
   (3) estrogen
   (4) testosterone
   (5) adrenaline

5. Which of the following is the unstated method by which hormones are carried throughout the body?

   (1) by the digestive system
   (2) by the nerves
   (3) by the blood
   (4) by the saliva
   (5) by the skin

6. A person with high levels of sugar in the blood has a disease called diabetes. One type of diabetes is caused by lack of a particular hormone. Which hormone would a person with this type of diabetes lack?

   (1) parathormone
   (2) adrenaline
   (3) insulin
   (4) oxytocin
   (5) thymosin

Answers start on page 780.

The Nervous System and Behaviour

Identifying Faulty Logic

Scientific reasoning is logical most of the time. Sometimes, however, scientists' reasoning breaks down, and they use **faulty logic.** You have to read carefully to identify faulty logic.

One type of faulty logic is **oversimplification.** This happens when the complexity of a topic is reduced so much that the discussion is no longer correct. Oversimplification often occurs in statements of cause and effect. For example, you may have heard that a high-fat diet causes heart disease. This is an oversimplification. A high-fat diet may contribute to the development of heart disease in many people.

Sometimes oversimplification takes the form of the **either-or error.** In the either-or error, only two choices are presented when other choices also exist. For example, suppose someone says, "Heart disease is caused by a high-fat diet or by smoking." In truth, both diet and smoking contribute to heart disease, but so do lack of exercise, heredity, and other factors.

Read the paragraph and answer the questions that follow.

For years, people have debated whether human behaviour is determined by nature (your genetic inheritance) or nurture (your experience in the environment). The ancient Greek Plato thought that personality is inborn. Another ancient Greek, Aristotle, thought that everything in the mind comes in through the senses. The debate continues: Are gender differences due to biology or experience? Is personality shaped by heredity or environment? Today scientists think both nature and nurture influence human behaviour.

1. Put a check mark next to the sentence that states what Plato thought about personality.

   _____ a. Personality is influenced by the environment.

   _____ b. Personality is inborn.

You are correct if you chose *option b*. Plato thought biology determines personality.

2. Put a check mark next to the reason Plato's view of personality is an oversimplification.

   _____ a. Personality is determined by many factors, both inborn and environmental.

   _____ b. Personality is really the result of experience.

You are correct if you chose *option a*. Personality is complex and determined by many factors. When you try to attribute personality to one cause, the result may be faulty logic.

---

faulty logic
errors in reasoning

oversimplification
reduction of the complexity of a concept or topic by so much that the presentation becomes incorrect

either-or error
when only two choices are presented although there are actually other possibilities

To identify faulty logic, go over the material step-by-step. Look for things that are too simple or too general. Look for things that don't make sense.

GED Practice

Directions: Choose the <u>one best answer</u> to each question.

<u>Questions 1 through 3</u> refer to the following passage and diagram.

Some human behaviour, like a simple reflex, is inborn. A simple reflex is an automatic response to a stimulus. For example, if a flame burns your finger, you automatically withdraw your hand.

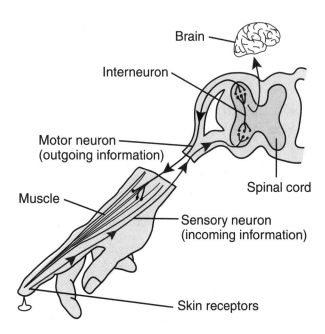

A simple reflex works this way: A sensory neuron carries information about a stimulus from your skin to your spinal cord. In your spinal cord, the information is passed to motor neurons that go to muscles in your arm and hand. You pull your hand away quickly. The reflex is so rapid that it takes place before information about the event has time to reach your brain. Once it reaches your brain, you experience pain.

However, much human behaviour is not innate. Instead, it is learned. You learn to associate events, such as the smell of cooking with the arrival of dinner. You learn to repeat behaviour that brings rewards and avoid behaviour that brings punishment. And by observation, you learn from the experiences and examples of others. Unlike simple reflexes, learning involves complex pathways in the brain.

1. "In a simple reflex, information is transmitted from a sensory neuron directly to a motor neuron." According to the diagram, in what way does this statement show faulty logic?

   (1) Only sensory neurons are involved in simple reflexes.
   (2) Only motor neurons are involved in simple reflexes.
   (3) Only interneurons are involved in simple reflexes.
   (4) Simple reflexes are processed by the brain, not the neurons.
   (5) Information is also passed by interneurons in the spinal cord.

2. Which of the following is an example of learning to repeat a behaviour because it brings rewards?

   (1) A child cringes when he sees lightning because he knows that thunder will follow.
   (2) A woman learns to drive within the speed limit because she gets a speeding ticket.
   (3) A child learns to say "please" because she then gets what she asked for.
   (4) A man burns his hand on a hot stove and pulls it away quickly.
   (5) A child watches his father perform a trick and then tries it himself.

3. What is a difference between a simple reflex and learned behaviour?

   (1) A simple reflex involves the brain, and learned behaviour involves the spinal cord.
   (2) A simple reflex involves the spinal cord, and learned behaviour involves the brain.
   (3) Both simple reflexes and learned behaviour involve the brain.
   (4) A simple reflex involves sensory neurons and learned behaviour does not.
   (5) A simple reflex involves motor neurons and learned behaviour does not.

Questions 4 through 6 refer to the following passage and diagram.

The human brain has three main parts: the cerebrum, the cerebellum, and the brain stem.

The cerebrum is the largest part of the brain. It is responsible for sensory perception, voluntary movement (motor control), language, memory, and thought. Different areas of the cerebrum control different functions.

The cerebellum controls movements you make automatically, such as those related to posture. It also coordinates information from the eyes, inner ears, and muscles to help you maintain balance.

The brain stem controls heartbeat, breathing, and other vital functions of the body.

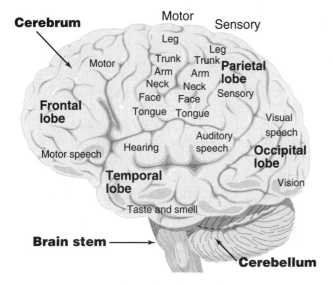

4. "The cerebellum is the part of the brain that controls movement." Which statement corrects the faulty logic of the previous sentence?

   (1) The cerebellum controls balance, not movement.
   (2) The cerebellum controls vital functions as well as movement.
   (3) Both the cerebellum and the cerebrum control movement.
   (4) The brain stem controls involuntary movement.
   (5) The brain stem controls heartbeat and breathing.

5. Which of the following functions is most likely to be affected by a blow to the back of the head?

   (1) taste
   (2) vision
   (3) heart rate
   (4) hearing
   (5) leg movement

6. What would be the best title for this passage and diagram?

   (1) The Human Nervous System
   (2) The Human Brain
   (3) The Cerebrum
   (4) The Brain
   (5) The Nervous System

7. At any given moment, your senses are bombarded by many stimuli. For example, you may hear passing traffic, people talking, and birds chirping; you may see cars whizzing by and neighbours strolling down the sidewalk; you might smell cut grass and brewing coffee; at the same time, you might feel an itch on your foot and taste a bite of your steaming, hot breakfast cereal. Selective attention is the process by which the brain chooses the stimuli to which it will pay attention.

In which situation would you be most likely to employ selective attention?

   (1) while watching an exciting movie in a movie theatre
   (2) when feeling sunlight strike your skin on a hot, humid summer day
   (3) when smelling the aroma of a simmering stew when you enter a restaurant
   (4) while tasting the sweetness of a sugary soft drink
   (5) while listening to one person's voice at a crowded party

Answers start on page 780.

Lesson 6

summarize
to briefly tell the
important points

When summarizing,
ask yourself, "Is this
point important?"
If the point is not
essential, leave it out.

Evolution
Summarizing Ideas

When you **summarize** something, you cover the main points briefly. For example, if you tell a friend what happened on a TV program, you don't take half an hour to describe each detail. Instead, you take a minute to tell only the most important things.

Summarizing is a skill you use when you read about science. When you summarize a passage, you look for the main ideas. The main idea is often stated in the topic sentence of a paragraph. All main ideas should be in a summary. Very important details should also be in a summary.

You can also summarize a diagram or chart. How? Study the title and labels or column heads. Ask yourself: What does this diagram or chart show? A complete but brief answer to that question is a summary.

Read the paragraph and answer the questions below.

Some scientists have hypothesized that dinosaurs are the ancestors of birds. As evidence, they cite many shared traits, such as wishbones. In the late 1990s, the first fossils, or remains, of ancient birdlike dinosaurs were found, providing further evidence that birds and dinosaurs are related. One such ancient species had long tail feathers. The other had feathers on its limbs, body, and tail. However, neither of these dinosaurs could fly. The feathers may have been for insulation, balance, or attracting a mate.

1. Write *M* next to the sentence that is the main idea of the paragraph.

   _____ a. Scientists have hypothesized that dinosaurs are the ancestors of birds.

   _____ b. Dinosaur feathers may have been used for balance.

   You are right if you chose *option a*. The main idea is that there may be a relationship between dinosaurs and birds.

2. Write *S* next to the sentence that is a summary of the paragraph.

   _____ a. Dinosaurs may be the ancestors of birds. Evidence for this includes shared traits, such as wishbones, and fossil evidence, such as feathered, birdlike dinosaurs.

   _____ b. Fossils of birdlike dinosaurs have been found. Dinosaur feathers may have been used to insulate, provide balance, or attract mates.

   You are correct if you chose *option a*. This option tells the main idea and the other important points very briefly.

GED Practice

Directions: Choose the <u>one best answer</u> to each question.

<u>Questions 1 through 4</u> refer to the following passage and diagram.

A species is a group of organisms whose members can mate with one another and produce fertile offspring. The development of a new species from an old one is called speciation. Speciation may occur when environments change or when groups separate, moving to different places. The result of speciation is two or more groups of organisms that can no longer reproduce with each other.

Sometimes many species evolve from one species, a process called adaptive radiation. Adaptive radiation occurs when small groups of individuals become separated from the rest of the population. This often happens on island chains or in areas bounded by mountains. For example, in Hawaii separated groups of honeycreepers became adapted to their different environments. Over time, each isolated group developed a beak shape ideally suited to exploiting the local food resources. Such an adaptation, or trait that helps individuals survive, is passed down to the offspring. Eventually the group develops into a new species.

ADAPTATIONS OF HONEYCREEPERS

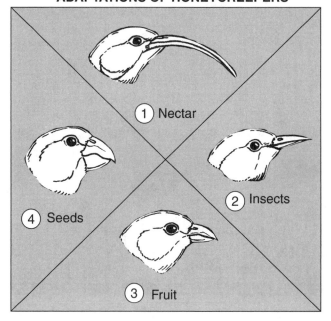

1. Which of the following is the <u>most likely</u> to contribute to speciation?

   (1) environmental changes
   (2) environmental stability
   (3) isolation of an entire species
   (4) no reproductive activity
   (5) plentiful food supply

2. How did the process of adaptive radiation affect honeycreepers?

   (1) They became more alike.
   (2) They reproduced with other species.
   (3) They became less alike.
   (4) There was little or no change.
   (5) There was rapid change within a year.

3. What might happen if an individual honeycreeper with a beak suited to eating nectar strayed into an environment in which nectar was scarce but insects were plentiful?

   (1) It would grow a beak for eating nectar.
   (2) It would grow a beak for eating insects.
   (3) Local birds would provide it with insects.
   (4) Local birds would provide it with nectar.
   (5) It would not be able to eat enough to live.

4. What effect has speciation had on the variety of animal and plant life over time?

   (1) created less variety
   (2) created more variety
   (3) not affected variety
   (4) slowed the formation of new varieties
   (5) stopped the formation of new varieties

Questions 5 through 7 refer to the following passage and diagram.

Darwin formulated the theory of natural selection in the 1850s, before genes and DNA were known. He based his theory on observations of similarities among different animals in body structure and early development. Recently scientists have begun to compare DNA sequences of different species. The more similar the sequences, the closer the evolutionary relationship.

New evidence from comparative DNA sequencing is overturning some long-held theories about relationships among species. Until 1800 all organisms were classified into two kingdoms—plants and animals. During the 1800s, scientists began to realize this division was too simple, and five kingdoms were eventually proposed: bacteria, protists, fungi, plants, and animals. Today, scientists divide organisms into three main groups: bacteria, archaea, and eukaryota. Plants, animals, and fungi are eukaryota.

For many years scientists thought that multicellular plants and animals evolved from single-celled eukarya at about the same time. New DNA evidence suggests that red plants evolved first, followed by brown and green plants about the same time. Later, animals and fungi evolved. These branching trees show old and new theories of how the eukaryota evolved.

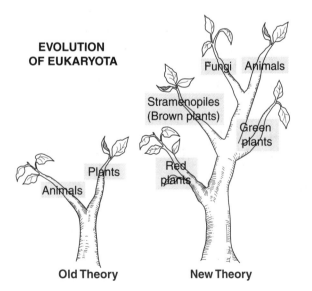

EVOLUTION OF EUKARYOTA

Fungi   Animals

Stramenopiles (Brown plants)

Green plants

Plants

Red plants

Animals

Old Theory   **New Theory**

5. According to the new branching tree, which group of organisms is most closely related to animals?

(1) plants
(2) red plants
(3) brown plants
(4) fungi
(5) green plants

6. For which of the following might comparative DNA sequencing be used?

(1) determining whether two people are related
(2) extracting DNA from fossils
(3) determining the age of an organism
(4) discovering the general structure of DNA
(5) estimating the age of Earth

7. Which of the following is the best summary of the passage and the diagram?

(1) DNA sequencing provides evidence for evolutionary relationships, sometimes overturning previously held views.
(2) By comparing the sequences of the DNA of two species, scientists can determine how closely related they are.
(3) It was once thought that plants and animals evolved at about the same time from single-celled organisms.
(4) The five major groups of multicellular organisms are red plants, brown plants, green plants, fungi, and animals.
(5) Darwin formulated the theory of evolution based on observations of similarities between species, before DNA had been discovered.

When summarizing a passage and a diagram, be sure to include the important points from both.

Answers start on page 781.

Energy Flow in Ecosystems
Distinguishing Conclusions from Supporting Details

Understanding what you read often involves telling the difference between conclusions and supporting statements. A **conclusion** is a logical result or generalization. **Supporting details** are observations, measurements, and other facts that help prove a conclusion is correct.

Telling the difference between conclusions and supporting statements draws on skills you have already learned. Sometimes you must distinguish between a main idea (conclusion) and the details that support it. Sometimes you must decide which facts support an opinion. And sometimes you must follow the logical thinking that leads from a group of details to a generalization, or conclusion.

conclusion
a logical result or generalization

supporting details
observations, measurements, and other facts that back up a conclusion

Read the passage and the chart and answer the question below.

To satisfy consumer demand, the fishing industry has overfished many species, causing sharp declines in some populations. For that reason, environmental groups have begun to offer consumers advice about which fish species are threatened and which are doing well. They hope consumers will change their eating habits to help restore fish populations.

FISH POPULATIONS	
Fish	**Status**
Atlantic cod, haddock, pollock	Years of overfishing caused populations to drop sharply
Wild Atlantic salmon	Healthy in the eastern North Atlantic, depleted elsewhere
Tuna	Bluefin tuna severely overfished
Striped bass	Restrictions on commercial fishing have brought this endangered species back

When you look for conclusions, pay attention to key words such as *for that reason, therefore, since, so,* and *thus.*

Write *SD* if the statement is a supporting detail. Write *C* if it is a conclusion.

_____ a. Striped bass were endangered before fishing was restricted.

_____ b. Atlantic cod and pollock populations are in sharp decline.

_____ c. Consumers can help restore the world's fisheries by changing their eating habits.

You are correct if you marked *option c* as the conclusion. *Options a and b* are details (SD) supporting the conclusion that consumers can help restore fish populations by not buying certain fish.

GED Practice

Directions: Choose the <u>one best answer</u> to each question.

Questions 1 through 4 refer to the following information.

There is usually at least one consumer of each plant and animal that serves to check its population growth. That is why numbers of plants and animals usually remain constant from year to year. When you take a species of plant or animal from its natural ecosystem and introduce it into another ecosystem, it might die out quickly. If it survives, the species may reproduce at an incredible rate.

How can a new species succeed so quickly? The food relationships in an ecosystem have evolved slowly, and they change very slowly. Just as many people are reluctant to eat an unfamiliar food, animals are unlikely to eat something they have never seen before. If there is no consumer willing to eat a new species, it will reproduce rapidly. For example, in 1859, 24 rabbits were imported to Australia from Europe. Without predators to keep them in check, the rabbits multiplied. Today, despite pest control measures, Australia has millions of rabbits that cause extensive damage to agricultural lands.

The best solution to overpopulation by an introduced species is to prevent its introduction in the first place. If new organisms do overrun an area, population growth can sometimes be controlled by importing another species that will prey on the first species.

1. Which of the following caused the overpopulation of rabbits in Australia?

   (1) the importing of predators
   (2) the continued importing of rabbits
   (3) an unstable ecosystem
   (4) the overpopulation of predators and slow reproduction of rabbits
   (5) the rapid reproduction of rabbits and lack of predators

2. What is the <u>best</u> way to avoid the problems associated with introducing new organisms into an ecosystem?

   (1) Introduce an animal to prey on the new organism.
   (2) Ensure that there will be something the new organism will eat.
   (3) Prevent the introduction of new organisms.
   (4) Ensure that the ecosystem has nothing the new organism will eat.
   (5) Prevent the introduction of predators that feed on the new organism.

3. Which of the following statements supports the conclusion that overpopulation of a new species can sometimes be controlled by the introduction of an animal that will prey on it?

   (1) The introduction of new organisms cannot always be prevented.
   (2) Rabbits were successfully wiped out in Australia.
   (3) In stable ecosystems, one consumer usually checks another's population growth.
   (4) In time, the population will decrease.
   (5) The overpopulated species cannot find anything to eat.

4. What can you assume about the ecosystem of Australia as it relates to rabbits?

   (1) It has neither food nor predators.
   (2) It has food that rabbits eat.
   (3) It has predators but no food.
   (4) It has many meat-eating animals.
   (5) It is very similar to Europe's ecosystem.

Science • Life Science

Questions 5 through 7 refer to the following information.

The spread of human populations has altered natural ecosystems and caused declines in many animal and plant populations throughout the world. However, in North America, even with the huge increase in the human population, coyotes have thrived. Five hundred years ago, they occupied only the western plains. Today, they inhabit almost the whole continent.

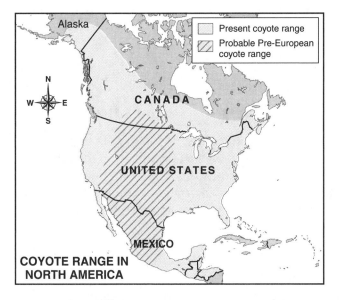

COYOTE RANGE IN NORTH AMERICA

In many areas, coyotes are the top predator because humans have eliminated the wolves, the coyotes' natural enemy. In packs, coyotes can bring down large animals such as deer. Hunting alone, they feed on small mammals such as mice; in the cities and suburbs, they eat cats and small dogs.

Coyotes will eat almost anything. An analysis of coyote waste showed about 100 types of food, from crickets to apples to shoe leather. Landfills and garbage cans provide a plentiful and varied diet.

The human-altered landscape is a good habitat for coyotes. They live in the small wooded areas common in suburbia. Coyotes are often safe from harm because they are frequently mistaken for dogs.

5. Why has the eradication of the wolf helped coyotes to thrive?

   (1) In many regions, coyotes now have no natural enemies.
   (2) Coyotes can hunt small mammals like mice and cats.
   (3) Coyotes live in small wooded areas common in suburbia.
   (4) Coyotes forage for food in landfills and garbage cans.
   (5) Wolves live in packs, and coyotes live in packs or on their own.

6. Which of the following is a conclusion, not a supporting detail?

   (1) People often mistake coyotes for dogs.
   (2) Coyotes have been found to feed on dozens of different items.
   (3) Hunting alone, coyotes prey upon small mammals.
   (4) In packs, coyotes can bring down large animals like deer.
   (5) The coyotes' adaptability in feeding and other behaviours has helped them enlarge their range.

7. Which statement about the coyotes in North America is supported by information in the map and the passage?

   (1) Coyotes prefer to live in urban areas rather than suburban areas.
   (2) Coyotes can live in many types of ecosystems and climates.
   (3) There are fewer coyotes now than there were five hundred years ago.
   (4) Over the years, humans have destroyed coyote habitats.
   (5) Coyotes spread from the eastern forests to other areas of North America.

Remember to use the title, key, labels, and compass rose of a map to answer map questions.

Answers start on page 782.

Lesson 8

applying ideas
taking information
learned in one
situation and using it
in another set of
circumstances

context
the situation within
which something is
said or done

Cycles in Ecosystems
Applying Ideas in New Contexts

When you put your knowledge to use in new situations, you are **applying ideas** to a new **context.** You are taking information you learned in one set of circumstances and using it in another set of circumstances.

When you read about a science topic, think about how the knowledge you gain might be used in other contexts. You can increase your ability to apply science knowledge to new situations by asking yourself these questions:

- What is being described or explained?
- What situations might this information relate to?
- How would this information be used in those situations?

Read the paragraph and answer the questions that follow.

One cause of the increase in carbon dioxide gas in the atmosphere is deforestation. Plants normally absorb carbon dioxide from the air for use in photosynthesis. But when large areas are cleared of trees, there are fewer plants to absorb carbon dioxide. Increased carbon dioxide gas in the atmosphere may cause global warming by trapping heat from the sun.

1. Put a check mark next to the statement that applies information about photosynthesis to a new situation.

_____ a. Clearing large areas of trees is called deforestation.

_____ b. Cutting down trees may contribute to global warming.

You are correct if you chose *option b.* The theory of a reduced level of photosynthesis helps explain how deforestation may contribute to global warming, a larger context.

2. Put a check mark next to a scenario that is similar to deforestation.

_____ a. The aquatic plants in a goldfish tank die.

_____ b. Some animals in a zoo have difficulty reproducing.

You are correct if you checked *option a.* Deforestation is similar to the death of plants in an aquarium. In both situations, there are fewer plants and a lower rate of photosynthesis.

 When you apply information to a new situation, ask yourself what you already know about the new situation. Then ask yourself how the information applies to the new context.

Science • Life Science

GED Practice

Directions: Choose the <u>one best answer</u> to each question.

<u>Questions 1 through 4</u> refer to the following passage.

When fog rolls into a redwood forest on the West Coast, the water droplets suspended in the fog condense on the tree's needles and then drip down the needles, branches, and trunk. Studies have shown that in one foggy night, a redwood tree can collect as much water as would fall during a heavy rainstorm. The redwoods' ability to capture water from fog is crucial to the other plants and animals in its habitat.

Scientists have measured the fog dripping off redwoods in forested areas and also the fog dripping off humanmade fog collectors in deforested areas. In deforested areas, the air warms up and dries out quickly; the water droplets evaporate before becoming heavy enough to fall to the ground. Thus, much less water is captured from fog in the deforested areas than in the redwood forests.

The fact that fog drip contributes to the water supply of an area is used by conservationists as an argument for saving stands of redwoods from logging. People whose wells and springs dwindle during the dry summers are beginning to realize the role redwoods play in maintaining their water supply.

1. How did scientists show that deforested areas collect less fog drip than redwood forests?

   (1) by observing that water drips down a redwood's needles, branches, and trunk
   (2) by comparing the amount of water dripping off redwoods to the amount collected in deforested areas
   (3) by observing whether streams dry up in deforested areas along the West Coast
   (4) by redirecting the fog from forested to deforested areas along the West Coast
   (5) by measuring the height of the redwood trees and comparing their height to the amount of water collected

2. Which of the following is most similar to redwoods capturing water for their habitats?

   (1) removing impurities from rainwater by filtering it
   (2) collecting rainwater and runoff in a large reservoir
   (3) removing salt from ocean water by evaporation and condensation
   (4) using fog collectors in dry coastal regions to collect water
   (5) using a system of gutters and tanks to collect rainwater

3. Which of the following supports the conclusion that redwoods contribute water to their habitat?

   (1) Fog rolls into the redwood forests from the Pacific Ocean.
   (2) Water droplets are suspended in fog and intercepted by redwood trees.
   (3) Water from fog drips down the needles, branches, and trunks of redwoods into the soil.
   (4) Other plants and animals rely on the water supply provided by the redwoods.
   (5) Only about 4 percent of the original redwood forest still stands.

4. Which of the following provides the greatest motivation for the majority of people who live in a region with redwoods to oppose the logging of these trees?

   (1) Over the years, humans have destroyed most of the redwood forests.
   (2) A single redwood tree may contain wood worth hundreds of thousands of dollars.
   (3) Homes made of redwood lumber are long-lasting and easy to care for.
   (4) The lumber industry provides jobs for people in the area.
   (5) Deforestation contributes to the drying up of local wells and springs.

Answers start on page 782.

Directions: Choose the one best answer to each question.

Questions 1 through 4 refer to the following passage and chart.

One point of view on what constitutes intelligence is the concept of multiple intelligences. According to this theory, people possess various forms of intelligence in varying degrees.

MULTIPLE INTELLIGENCES	
Type of Intelligence	**Description**
Linguistic	Language ability, especially the ability to understand shades of meaning
Logical-mathematical	The ability to reason
Spatial	The ability to perceive and draw spatial relationships
Musical	Musical ability, including singing, playing an instrument, and composing
Bodily-kinesthetic	The ability to control muscle movements gracefully
Interpersonal	The ability to understand and get along with others
Intrapersonal	The ability to understand oneself and use that knowledge to guide one's behaviour

1. Which of the following can be inferred from the concept of multiple intelligences?

   (1) Intelligence depends on the speed with which the brain processes information.
   (2) Intelligence is a single, general mental ability.
   (3) Multiple intelligences cannot be measured by standard verbal tests.
   (4) People who have strong bodily-kinesthetic intelligence often lack linguistic intelligence.
   (5) People who have strong spatial intelligence often lack interpersonal intelligence.

2. According to the theory, which forms of intelligence are you using while studying this book?

   (1) linguistic and logical-mathematical
   (2) logical-mathematical and spatial
   (3) spatial and bodily-kinesthetic
   (4) bodily-kinesthetic and interpersonal
   (5) interpersonal and intrapersonal

3. Which of the following people is most likely to use the concept of multiple intelligences in his or her work?

   (1) a lawyer
   (2) an elementary-school teacher
   (3) a sales person
   (4) an accountant
   (5) a doctor

4. Which of the following provides evidence to support the concept of multiple intelligences?

   (1) Specific brain areas specialize in different functions.
   (2) People who are good at one thing are usually good at other things.
   (3) The speed with which the brain processes information varies in each person.
   (4) People tend to sort common objects into broad categories.
   (5) People with high scores on tests of short-term memory tend to be intelligent.

Questions 5 through 8 refer to the following passage and diagram.

In a food chain, the position occupied by each species is called its trophic level. At each trophic level, energy is stored in the biomass (the total mass of the living organisms in a particular place) of living plants or animals. Most of the energy at any given trophic level is used by organisms for life processes or lost to the environment as heat. Thus, only about 10 percent of the energy taken in by one trophic level is available to the organisms in the next trophic level.

One way to show the loss of energy at each trophic level of a food chain is to construct an energy pyramid. Each section of the pyramid represents the energy available to the next higher level as well as the amount of biomass. Since only some of the energy at one level is usable by the level above it, each level supports less biomass and fewer organisms.

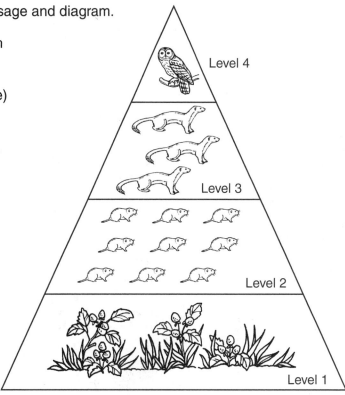

5. How is energy stored in a food chain?

   (1) as trophic levels
   (2) as sunlight
   (3) as heat
   (4) as biomass
   (5) as plants

6. Which of the following is a conclusion rather than a supporting detail?

   (1) Tawny owls occupy the fourth trophic level in this energy pyramid.
   (2) Berries and grasses form the base of the energy pyramid.
   (3) A food chain can support more primary consumers than secondary consumers.
   (4) About 10 percent of the energy in the third level is available to fourth level organisms.
   (5) Weasels provide energy to tawny owls in the food chain.

7. Which of the following statements is supported by the passage and the diagram?

   (1) The higher in the energy pyramid, the more biomass.
   (2) The most biomass is at the base of the energy pyramid.
   (3) There are more weasels than voles in the energy pyramid.
   (4) There are few tawny owls because they have been eaten by weasels.
   (5) As you rise in the energy pyramid, more energy is available.

8. An ocean energy pyramid consists of microscopic organisms called plankton at the base, then mussels, crabs, lobsters, and finally seals. Of which organism would you expect to find the fewest?

   (1) plankton
   (2) mussels
   (3) crabs
   (4) lobsters
   (5) seals

Answers start on page 783.

Life Science • Review

Earth and Space Science

Every day an Earth or space science story makes the news. There may be a story about a devastating earthquake. Perhaps there is a story about lives saved by the evacuation of a coastal town that lies in the path of a predicted hurricane. Or, you may read a story about a probe to Mars or new information about the size of the universe. Even if no natural disaster has occurred and no space story makes the news, there is always one Earth science story—the weather report!

Understanding Earth and space science is very important for success on the GED Science Test. Topics from these areas are the basis for about 20 percent of the questions on the test.

The Structures of Earth

Identifying Implications

implication
a fact or idea that is
suggested by stated
information

imply
to suggest something
is true without actually
stating it

When you take what is written and then figure out other things that are probably true, you are identifying **implications.** Implications are not directly expressed in words by the author. Rather, they are suggested by what is written. For example, suppose you read, "A surge in demand for heating oil has driven up the price of this fuel." One implication of this statement is that heating bills are going to rise. Implications are facts or ideas you can be reasonably sure are true because they follow from what is written.

You can increase your ability to identify implications by thinking about consequences. A consequence is an effect or result. If certain conditions exist, what effect does this have? For example, the fact that a tornado passed through a town **implies** the consequence that property was damaged.

 To determine whether a fact or an idea is implied by a passage, ask yourself whether the idea is based on something specific in the passage. If it is, the idea or fact is an implication.

GED Practice

Directions: Choose the <u>one best answer</u> to each question.

Questions 1 through 4 refer to the following information and diagram.

Sea floor spreading is caused by the upward movement of heated molten rock from the mantle through the crust. Where this material comes to the surface, the sea floor (Earth's crust) cracks, forming a ridge. The new material in the ridge pushes the sea floor on either side away from the ridge in each direction.

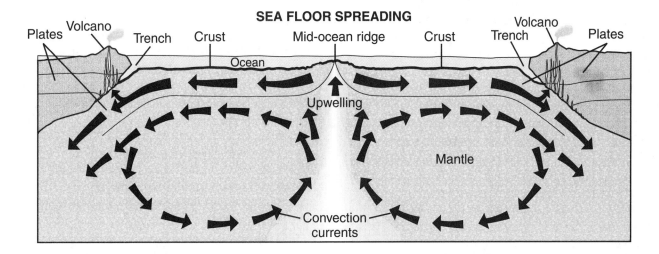

SEA FLOOR SPREADING

1. What causes sea floor spreading?

   (1) heat currents in the crust
   (2) heat currents in the mantle
   (3) the aging of the sea floor
   (4) volcanic activity along the coast
   (5) the drifting of the continents

2. Which of the following is implied by the diagram?

   (1) The farther from the ridge, the younger the sea floor.
   (2) The farther from the ridge, the older the sea floor.
   (3) Sea floor spreading occurs only in the Atlantic Ocean.
   (4) Sea floor spreading occurs only in the Pacific Ocean.
   (5) Sea floor spreading causes the ocean to dry up.

3. What causes the sea floor to descend back into the mantle?

   (1) It collides with a plate and dips below it.
   (2) It is lighter than the continental plates.
   (3) The mantle below it collapses.
   (4) It encounters earthquake action.
   (5) The mantle causes it to rise up.

4. Scientists have calculated that the sea floor in the North Atlantic is spreading about 3.5 cm per year. Which of the following conclusions does this evidence support?

   (1) Sea level will rise.
   (2) Sea level will fall.
   (3) The Atlantic Ocean will widen.
   (4) The Atlantic Ocean will narrow.
   (5) The width of the Atlantic Ocean will remain the same.

Questions 5 through 7 refer to the following passage.

The idea of continental drift was first set forth by German scientist Alfred Wegener in 1915. Wegener suggested that one supercontinent, which he called Pangaea, once existed. He also proposed that Pangaea began to break into smaller continents about 200 million years ago. These continents then drifted to their present positions. Wegener cited matching coastlines, fossil evidence, similar rock structures across continents, and evidence related to climate to support his idea.

Most of Wegener's contemporaries were very critical of his ideas. They thought that the evidence supporting continental drift was weak. More important, Wegener was unable to explain exactly how the continents moved. He proposed two ideas—either the gravity of the moon gave the continents a westward motion or the continents cut through the ocean floor. Both of these ideas were quickly dismissed as impossible.

For many years, little progress was made to explain how the continents could drift. Then in the 1950s and 1960s advances in technology permitted detailed mapping of the ocean floor. From this mapping came the discovery of a global ridge system under the oceans. In the early 1960s an American scientist, Harry Hess, proposed that the ocean ridges were above upwelling convection currents in the mantle. New crust was formed there, pushing older sea floor crust away and eventually back down into the mantle, forming trenches where the edges slip below other plates. Other evidence has since been found to support the idea of sea floor spreading. For the first time, there was a reasonable explanation for how portions of the crust move.

By 1968, the ideas of continental drift and sea floor spreading were united into the broader theory of plate tectonics. Canadian geophysicist J. Tuzo Wilson made major contributions to the theory of plate tectonics in the 1960s and 1970s. This theory is so encompassing that it provides a framework for understanding most geologic processes.

5. What was the main reason that Wegener's ideas were criticized?

   (1) He cited evidence that was very weak.
   (2) There were other explanations for the evidence he cited.
   (3) There was no evidence for continental drift.
   (4) He did not have a strong explanation for how the continents moved.
   (5) Pangaea was an imaginary supercontinent.

6. Which of the following is a conclusion rather than a supporting statement?

   (1) The coastlines of different continents match up.
   (2) Fossils of the same species have been found on different continents.
   (3) Millions of years ago, the climate was the same in now distant areas.
   (4) Rock structures on adjacent continents match up.
   (5) The continents originally formed one large land mass and then moved apart.

7. Which of the following natural phenomena can best be explained by the theory of plate tectonics?

   (1) the migration of modern land animals from one place to another
   (2) the recycling of water from the atmosphere to the land
   (3) the presence of sediment on large areas of the ocean floor
   (4) the presence of large cities along coastal plate boundaries
   (5) the occurrence of earthquakes along plate boundaries

Several types of evidence support the idea that the continents have drifted over hundreds of millions of years. First, some coastlines seem to match. For example, South America and Africa fit together as if they were once part of the same land mass. Second, rock types and structures found on one continent seem to continue in another. For example, rock types in eastern Brazil match those found in northwestern Africa. In addition, the Appalachian Mountains in eastern North America seem to continue into Greenland and Northern Europe.

Third, fossils of the same types of land plants and animals have been found in South America, Africa, Australia, and Antarctica. This suggests that at one time these continents may have been connected by land.

Fourth, there is evidence that ice sheets covered much of Africa, South America, Australia, and India about 220 million or 300 million years ago. If these land masses had formed a supercontinent closer to the South Pole, that would account for the colder climate.

CONTINENTAL DRIFT

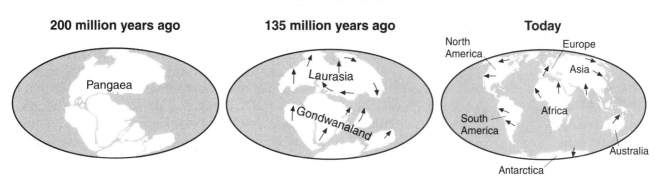

| 200 million years ago | 135 million years ago | Today |

8. If you were to draw a map of the world one hundred million years from now, which of the following would the map probably show?

    (1) Earth would look as it does today.
    (2) Earth would be covered by ocean.
    (3) Earth would be covered by continents.
    (4) The Atlantic Ocean would be narrower.
    (5) South America and Africa would be farther apart.

A series of illustrations that depicts how something developed over time may show a trend that is likely to continue.

9. Before the theory of continental drift was developed, which of the following hypotheses was used to explain the presence of fossils of the same species of land animals on different continents?

    (1) Adjacent rock structures in South America and Africa are the same.
    (2) The animals might have crossed the oceans on driftwood.
    (3) The animals might have swum from one continent to another.
    (4) The fossils may have been carried by ocean currents from one continent to another.
    (5) Ice sheets once covered portions of Africa, South America, Australia, and India.

Answers start on page 783.

The Changing Earth

Analyzing Cause and Effect

When you feel hungry, you probably eat. Here, hunger is a cause; eating is an effect. A **cause** is something that makes something else happen. An **effect** is what happens as a result of a cause. Causes always occur before effects. Situations in which one thing causes another are called **cause-and-effect relationships.**

Scientists often look for cause-and-effect relationships. They try to discover general laws that can help them predict what will result from specific causes. For example, they try to discover what causes volcanoes to erupt. They also try to discover effects. What happens as a result of a volcanic eruption?

cause
something that makes something else happen

effect
something that happens because something else happened

cause-and-effect relationship
a situation in which one thing (a cause) results in another (an effect)

Cause-and-effect relationships are sometimes signalled by words such as *because, since, thus, effect, affect, result, occurs when, led to,* and *due to.* Look for these words to identify cause-and-effect relationships.

Read the passage and answer the questions below.

From 1943 to 1952, scientists observed the formation of the volcano Paricutín. In February 1943, there was much underground activity near the village of Paricutín, Mexico. It caused many small Earth tremors that worried the villagers. On February 20, Dionisio and Paula Pulido noticed smoke rising from a small hole in their cornfield near the village. The hole had been there as long as the farmer and his wife could remember. That night hot rock fragments spewing from the hole looked like fireworks. By morning, the fragments had piled up into a cone about 40 m high. Within two years it was more than 400 m high. Ash from the volcano burned and covered the village of Paricutín. Lava flows buried another nearby village. After nine years, the volcanic activity stopped.

1. Write *C* next to the cause of the Earth tremors near Paricutín.

    _____ a. underground activity

    _____ b. smoke coming from a hole in the ground

You are correct if you chose *option a.* The underground activity in the area caused the Earth tremors. *Option b* is incorrect; the smoke was a result, not a cause, of the underground activity.

2. Write *E* next to each effect of the eruption of Paricutín. Mark all that apply.

    _____ a. A cone more than 400 m high was formed.

    _____ b. Ash buried the village of Paricutín.

    _____ c. People resumed their normal lives in the area.

    _____ d. Scientists learned a lot about how volcanoes form.

You are correct if you marked *options a, b,* and *d.* These are all results of the eruption of Paricutín. You can see that one cause may have several effects. Likewise, one effect may have many causes.

GED Practice

Directions: Choose the <u>one best answer</u> to each question.

<u>Questions 1 through 3</u> refer to the following information.

There are two main ways of predicting earthquakes. The first is to study the history of large earthquakes in an area. Based on past occurrences, scientists can determine the probability of another earthquake happening. However, these are long-term general forecasts. For example, scientists now forecast that there is a 67 percent chance of an earthquake measuring 6.8 or higher on the Richter scale in the San Francisco area during the next 30 years.

The second method of earthquake prediction relies on measurements of seismic waves and movement along faults. Scientists use seismic instruments to measure wave activity. In recent years, they have been using Global Positioning System (GPS) receivers installed along the San Andreas fault in California and faults in Turkey and Japan. Using signals from GPS satellites, the receivers give precise location data. Thus, scientists can now monitor how much movement occurs along a fault. Using this type of information and historical data, they can calculate the probability of an earthquake occurring.

Earthquakes tend to occur in clusters that strike a single area in a limited time. There are foreshocks, which occur before the large mainshock. Then there are aftershocks. So far, scientists are better at predicting aftershocks than foreshocks or mainshocks. Still, earthquake predictions in California have helped. For example, in June 1988, the San Francisco area experienced a foreshock measuring 5.1 on the Richter scale. Scientists predicted a mainshock would occur within five days. In response, local government emergency managers ran preparedness drills. Sixty-nine days later, the magnitude 7.1 Loma Prieta mainshock occurred. Local officials claim they were better able to respond than they would have been without the forecast. Still, there were 63 deaths and $6 billion in damage.

1. What are the two main methods of predicting earthquakes?

   (1) analyzing historical data and analyzing climatic data about an area
   (2) installing GPS receivers and measuring movement along faults
   (3) analyzing historical data and measuring seismic activity and movement along faults
   (4) using GPS satellites to directly measure seismic activity and analyzing historical data
   (5) analyzing historical data and waiting for a mainshock to occur

2. Why was the Loma Prieta forecast considered a partial success despite the fact that scientists were wrong about when the mainshock would occur?

   (1) It was the first use of historical data in predicting an earthquake.
   (2) It was the first use of the Global Positioning System in predicting an earthquake.
   (3) It was the first use of seismic activity data in predicting an earthquake.
   (4) Local officials practised their emergency responses and so were better prepared for the earthquake.
   (5) Many people ignored the warning when the shock did not occur in five days.

3. Governments fund much earthquake research. What benefit is the likely reason for such funding being awarded?

   (1) improved seismic instruments
   (2) improved ability to locate the focus of each earthquake
   (3) better records of historical data on earthquakes
   (4) improved ability to prevent earthquakes
   (5) reduced loss of life and property damage from future earthquakes

Questions 4 and 5 refer to the following passage.

Earthquakes and volcanoes can quickly change the landscape, but weathering usually produces gradual changes. Weathering is the process by which rocks are broken down as a result of exposure to sun, wind, rain, ice, and other elements of the environment.

There are two main types of weathering: mechanical and chemical. In mechanical weathering, rock breaks into bits but its composition remains the same. For example, when water freezes in the cracks of rock, it expands, widening the cracks. Eventually, this freeze-thaw weathering can crumble the rock. However, this crumbled rock is the same as the original rock. Chemical weathering occurs when substances, such as carbonic acid in rainwater, combine with the rock, dissolving certain minerals and changing the rock's chemical makeup.

Living organisms can cause both mechanical and chemical weathering. Roots from plants can grow into the cracks in a rock, making the cracks bigger. Lichens can grow on a rock, producing chemicals that break down the rock.

4. Which of the following is an example of mechanical weathering?

(1) A pebble rolls downhill.
(2) Groundwater dissolves limestone.
(3) The metal body of a car rusts.
(4) A jackhammer breaks apart a roadway surface.
(5) A rock breaks down into clay, salt, and silica.

5. Which of the following is an example of chemical weathering?

(1) Acid rain wears away marble.
(2) Potholes form during a cold winter.
(3) Roots widen the crack in a rock.
(4) Water freezes and cracks a pool's walls.
(5) Pipes freeze and burst during a cold spell.

Questions 6 and 7 refer to the following passage and diagram.

In erosion, water, ice, or wind wear away rock and soil and transport it elsewhere. Erosion usually produces a gradual change in the land.

The running water of a river has great power to erode rock and soil. The rocks and other debris carried by the river, called load, increase its power to wear away the banks and riverbed. Most erosion takes place at the outside of bends. The banks are undercut, often creating steep cliffs or bluffs down which more soil and rock fall.

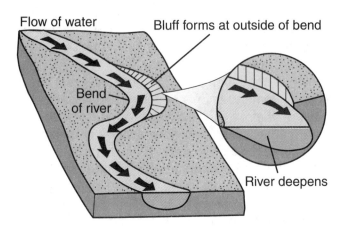

6. Which two processes are involved in erosion?

(1) wearing away and weathering
(2) wearing away and transporting
(3) transporting and depositing
(4) transporting and loading
(5) loading and diverging

7. Due to heavy rains upstream, there is a surge of water in a river. What is the likely effect on a bluff at the outside of a river bend?

(1) The bluff would be exposed to air.
(2) Erosion would decrease along the bluff.
(3) Erosion would increase along the bluff.
(4) The river would carry less load.
(5) Erosion would temporarily stop.

Answers start on page 784.

Weather and Climate
Assessing the Adequacy of Facts

Scientists present facts, measurements, and observations as support for their theories. When you read science materials, you must decide whether the facts support the conclusion being drawn.

You have already learned some skills that will help you **assess,** or evaluate, the **adequacy** of facts to support a conclusion. In Lesson 1 you learned to identify a main idea and the details that explain it. In Lesson 7 you learned to distinguish conclusions from supporting details. You will now apply these skills to evaluating the information you read.

When you assess whether a particular fact supports a conclusion, ask yourself, "Is this fact relevant? Does it have anything to do with this conclusion? Does it contribute logically to this conclusion?" When you assess whether a conclusion is supported by the information you are given, ask yourself, "Is there enough information to support this generalization or conclusion? Is additional information needed to prove this conclusion is correct?"

assess
to determine the importance, adequacy, or significance of something

adequacy
satisfactoriness; being sufficient for the purpose

Read the passage and answer the question below.

El Niño is a disruption in the currents and winds of the tropical Pacific. During El Niño, the ocean along the coast of Peru and Ecuador becomes unusually warm. The winds, which usually blow toward the west, blow toward the east instead. El Niño has many consequences. On the west coast of South America, the high temperature of the ocean disrupts the ecosystem, causing a decline in the commercial fish population. On Canada's west coast, El Niño caused a great increase in rainfall in 1998, more than double the annual average in some cases.

Put a check mark next to all the facts from the passage that support the conclusion that El Niño depresses the fishing industry on the Pacific Coast of South America.

_____ a. The commercial fish population declines because the ecosystem is disrupted.

_____ b. The anchovy cannot adapt to warmer water.

_____ c. Rainfall increases in the southern United States.

To assess the adequacy of facts, identify the conclusion and the supporting information in the passage. Then evaluate whether the information specifically supports and logically leads to the conclusion.

You are correct if you checked *option a.* According to the passage, the commercial fish population declines during an El Niño. That fact supports the conclusion that the fishing industry declines. *Option b* is incorrect because the passage gives no information about anchovies. It may be true, but you cannot evaluate it. *Option c* is true according to the passage, but it does not support the conclusion about the fishing industry.

GED Practice

Directions: Choose the one best answer to each question.

Questions 1 and 2 refer to the passage and the map below.

Weather changes from day to day, but climate refers to the long-term weather conditions of a region. Temperature and rainfall are the most important factors influencing climate. In addition, the distribution of ocean and land affects climate. Because land heats up and cools off rapidly, landlocked areas have more extreme climates than areas near the ocean. In addition, ocean currents carry heat from the tropics north to colder areas. Thus, oceans have a moderating effect on climate.

There are six main climate zones, as shown on the map below.

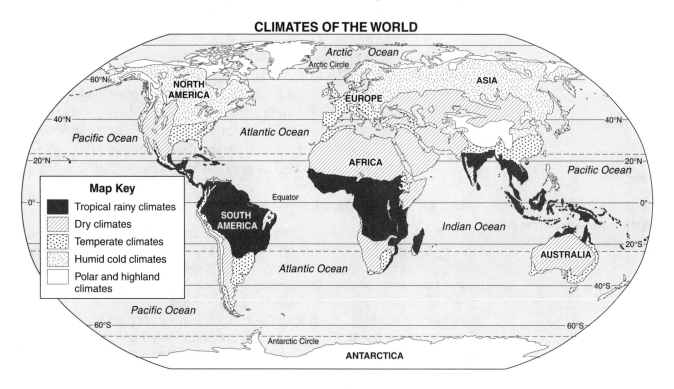

CLIMATES OF THE WORLD

1. What is climate?

   (1) the weather conditions in a particular place at a particular time
   (2) the temperature and rainfall of a particular area
   (3) the weather conditions of a region over a long time
   (4) the average annual rainfall of a region
   (5) the average annual temperature of a region

2. Suppose one of your friends likes living in a climate with four seasons and moderate weather. Which of the following locations would that person probably prefer?

   (1) Central America
   (2) South America
   (3) Europe
   (4) Africa
   (5) Australia

Science • Earth and Space Science

Questions 3 through 5 refer to the information below.

A hurricane is a large tropical storm with average wind speeds of at least 120 km/h, sometimes reaching 240 km/h. The winds spiral outward from a calm area of low pressure in the centre of the storm. The strong winds are usually accompanied by heavy rainfall and violent surges of ocean water. A hurricane can cause death as well as property damage from wind, rain, and floodwater.

The mission of the Tropical Prediction Center is to save lives and protect property by issuing storm watches, warnings, and forecasts to the general public, armed services, and mariners. It tracks storms over the Atlantic Ocean, Caribbean Sea, Gulf of Mexico, and eastern Pacific Ocean from May through November—prime hurricane season—each year.

Scientists at the centre collect data on tropical storms from satellites, reconnaissance aircraft, ocean buoys and vessels, and land-based radar. The data are analyzed by powerful computer models that use current and historical information to project the course that the storm will take. The centre issues predictions of the track, or path, of the storm as well as of its intensity.

An early warning of a coming tropical storm or hurricane can help reduce damage and loss of life. However, forecasters face several dilemmas. Should a storm warning be issued to a small area or to a wide area? If the prediction targets the wrong small area, a nearby area will face the storm unprepared. However, if a warning is issued to a wide area, great amounts of time and money may be spent on preparation that proves unnecessary. In spite of this, the Tropical Prediction Center usually issues a wide-area warning. That is because forecasts are not completely accurate, and forecasters would prefer to err on the side of caution.

3. During which of the following months should you schedule a vacation in the Caribbean if you want to avoid hurricanes?

   (1) March
   (2) May
   (3) July
   (4) September
   (5) November

4. Suppose that thousands of people are evacuated from their homes because of a wide-area hurricane warning that turns out to be wrong. What is a likely effect of such an event?

   (1) widespread property damage
   (2) many deaths
   (3) public skepticism about later hurricane warnings
   (4) a shift to small-area hurricane warnings
   (5) improved data collection techniques

5. Predictions of the path ("track") and intensity of the storm vary in accuracy. Predictions for the next three hours tend to be very accurate, and predictions for the next three days are often wrong. Which statement most adequately explains why short-term storm forecasts are more accurate than long-term forecasts?

   (1) Historical data provide trend patterns on which forecasters model current short-term predictions.
   (2) Historical data are useful, but forecasters cannot rely on these data completely when forecasting tropical storms.
   (3) In short-term forecasts, the current data are very similar to the projected data, increasing accuracy.
   (4) In short-term forecasts, the current data differ substantially from the data projected for three hours out.
   (5) In short-term forecasts, data are collected from a wide variety of land, air, and sea observation instruments.

Answers start on page 785.

Earth's Resources

Recognizing Values

Values are our deepest beliefs about what is important. For example, in Canada we share certain values such as freedom of expression, equality under the law, and civility. Individuals also have their own values. For example, some people value competitiveness. Others value cooperation.

Our values influence our actions, as individuals and as a society. Values also play an important role in science. A government may fund research likely to yield military technology. However, a government may not readily support areas of research such as fetal cell research that conflict with the religious, ethical, or moral beliefs of some of its citizens. A society may refrain from using some types of technology because of the values the society holds.

value
a belief that is prized as extremely important

Sometimes values are signalled by the same key words as those that signal an opinion, such as *believe, think, feel, accept,* and *embrace.*

Read the passage. Then answer the questions below.

In a nuclear power plant, a chain reaction of nuclear fission releases tremendous heat, which is used to generate electricity. Such plants are economical to run, but they also pose some risks to safety. An accident may release radiation, which can kill people close by, contaminate the environment, and cause long-term health problems. Also, no matter how securely radioactive waste is stored, it may leak out.

Some nations, like France, think that the economic benefits of nuclear power outweigh the risks. France gets almost 80 percent of its electricity from nuclear power. In contrast, public concern for safety has closed many nuclear power plants in the United States. The United States gets only 20 percent of its electricity from nuclear power.

1. Write *B* next to each benefit of nuclear power and *R* next to each risk.

   _____ a. Accidents may harm people and the environment.

   _____ b. Nuclear wastes may release radioactivity.

   _____ c. Nuclear energy produces a lot of electrical power.

   You are correct if you wrote *B* for *option c*. Nuclear power produces a lot of electricity. You are correct if you wrote *R* for *options a* and *b*. Nuclear power poses these risks.

2. Put a check mark next to the sentence that explains why the United States doesn't make more use of nuclear power.

   _____ a. U.S. citizens value safety and consider nuclear power risky.

   _____ b. The nation lacks sufficient nuclear fuel.

   You are correct if you checked *option a*. In the United States, public concern over safety has limited the use of nuclear power.

GED Practice

Directions: Choose the <u>one best answer</u> to each question.

<u>Questions 1 through 3</u> refer to the passage and diagram below.

Soil is the portion of the land surface that supports plant growth. It consists of minerals, organic matter, water, and air in varying proportions. About half the volume of a good soil consists of minerals and organic matter. The remaining half consists of space. The space is important because it allows air and water to circulate through the soil.

If you were to dig a deep hole in the soil, you would see horizontal layers of differing characteristics. These layers, called horizons, make up a particular soil's profile.

- The *A* horizon is the surface layer. It is the part of the soil with the greatest organic activity and living organisms.
- The *B* horizon is the subsoil. In it accumulate the materials that leach out of the *A* horizon through the action of water. Living organisms are plentiful in the *B* horizon.
- The *C* horizon is a layer of weathered, broken bedrock with little organic matter.

Below the *C* horizon is the solid bedrock, the material from which the soil is formed.

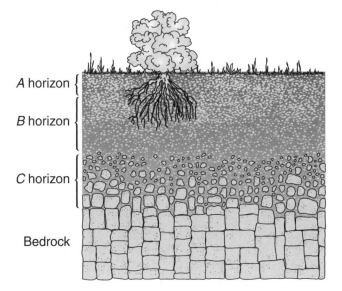

1. Why is a given volume of good soil less dense than the same volume of rock?

   (1) Soil is made of particles of mineral and organic matter.
   (2) About half the volume of soil consists of space, through which water and air circulate.
   (3) Both soil and rock contain mineral matter.
   (4) Soil contains organic matter, both living and dead.
   (5) The *C* horizon of soil consists of weathered bedrock.

2. Which of the following describes the exposed soil layer that would result if the *A* and *B* horizons were worn away by erosion?

   (1) The soil would be unable to support much plant and animal life.
   (2) The soil would have a finer consistency with greater mineral content.
   (3) The soil would be coarser with great amounts of organic activity.
   (4) The soil would be rich, consisting of about half water and air by volume.
   (5) There would be no soil, only a layer of solid bedrock with no organic activity.

3. A farmer for whom soil conservation is a very important value experiences a drought. The soil's *A* horizon is extremely dry and its top layers can blow away. In the spring the farmer needs to plant crops, but knows that tilling the soil can lead to greater water loss through evaporation. What would be the farmer's <u>most likely</u> response?

   (1) Make no changes in farming technique.
   (2) Till the soil aggressively so that water will evaporate.
   (3) Plant fewer, more drought-resistant crops.
   (4) Water the crops less frequently.
   (5) Stop farming until the drought is over.

Questions 4 through 6 refer to the information below.

The United States imports its entire supply of several minerals, including those in the chart.

Mineral	Major Uses
Bauxite	Aluminum production
Manganese	Steelmaking, batteries
Sheet mica	Electronic and electrical equipment
Strontium	Picture tubes, fireworks
Thallium	Superconductors, electronics

Source: U.S. Geological Survey

4. What is a good title for this information?

   (1) Minerals
   (2) Minerals and Their Uses
   (3) The Five Most Important Minerals
   (4) Some Imported Minerals and Their Uses
   (5) Mineral Resources of the United States

5. Which of the minerals listed in the chart are of most interest to the electronics industry?

   (1) bauxite and manganese
   (2) bauxite and strontium
   (3) manganese and strontium
   (4) strontium and thallium
   (5) sheet mica and thallium

6. Suppose a U.S. source of thallium were discovered, but recovering the mineral would be more expensive than importing it. What might be a reason for mining and processing thallium in the United States despite the extra cost?

   (1) Thallium is one of the minerals used in the production of superconductors.
   (2) Thallium is one of the minerals used in the production of electronic equipment.
   (3) The United States has always imported thallium from foreign nations.
   (4) The United States would reduce its dependence on foreign nations.
   (5) The United States would be the only source of thallium in the world.

7. In recent years, China has increased the amount of soft coal it burns in order to fuel its growing economy. As a result, China now leads the world in sulphur emissions, an air pollutant. A study of China's air pollution shows that the haze produced by burning soft coal acts as a filter, absorbing some of the sunlight that would normally be used by plants for photosynthesis.

Which of the following is a possible result of the air pollution in China?

   (1) increased wind speeds during storms
   (2) decreased agricultural production
   (3) decreased level of sulphur emissions
   (4) increased number of sunny days
   (5) increased supply of soft coal

8. A watershed is a drainage area, a land area that catches rainwater and drains it by means of surface runoff, streams, rivers, lakes, and groundwater. In 1997, the U.S. Environmental Protection Agency issued an analysis of the water quality of the watersheds in the continental United States. The results are shown below.

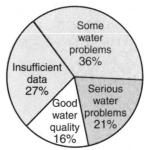

Source: U.S. Environmental Protection Agency

Which of the following statements is supported by the information given?

   (1) Most watersheds had good quality water.
   (2) Water pollution is not a major problem.
   (3) About one-fifth of the watersheds had serious quality problems.
   (4) More than half the watersheds had serious quality problems.
   (5) Three-quarters of the watersheds were not tested.

Answers start on page 786.

Earth in Space

Identifying Implications

As you learned in Lesson 9, an implication is a fact that is not stated directly. Rather, it is suggested by the author's words or by information in a diagram, graph, or other illustration.

When you identify an implication, you figure out something that is likely to be true based on the information that is stated or shown. For example, suppose on the day a space mission is scheduled to end you read, "The National Weather Service is forecasting a 70% probability of severe thunderstorms over the Kennedy Space Center." You can **infer,** or figure out, that the shuttle landing will be postponed or rescheduled to a different location because of the weather.

You can improve your ability to identify implications by using common sense. By using your common sense, looking for generalizations, and thinking about consequences, you can make reasonable **inferences** based on the information given.

infer
to figure out something that is suggested by stated information

inference
a fact or idea that you figure out based on stated information

Read the passage. Then answer the question below.

The National Aeronautics and Space Administration (NASA) has planned a series of robotic missions to explore Mars. These missions gather data to help plan piloted missions to the planet. *Global Surveyor* and *Pathfinder* were great successes. However, in 1999 both the *Mars Climate Orbiter* and *Polar Lander* missions failed. As a result, NASA is completely reviewing all its systems and mission plans.

1996–1997	1998–1999	2001–2002	2003–2008	2007–2013
Global Surveyor (mapping) *Pathfinder* (surface exploration)	*Climate Orbiter* (weather) *Polar Lander* (search for water)	*2001 Mars Odyssey* (surface survey)	Series of missions to gather samples	Additional sampling missions

Remember that implications are suggested by the information. They follow logically from what is stated.

Put a check mark next to the sentence that is implied by the fate of *Climate Orbiter* and *Polar Lander*.

_____ a. The United States lacks the technology to send robotic missions to Mars and other planets.

_____ b. Future Mars missions are likely to be delayed while NASA rechecks its systems and plans.

You are correct if you checked *option b*. Common sense tells you that two mission failures in a row will disrupt plans for the future. NASA is likely to take extra time and care with its future mission.

GED Practice

Directions: Choose the <u>one best answer</u> to each question.

<u>Questions 1 and 2</u> refer to the chart below.

Planet	Distance from Sun In Astronomical Units*
Mercury	0.39
Venus	0.72
Earth	1.0
Mars	1.5
Jupiter	5.2
Saturn	9.2
Uranus	19.2
Neptune	30.0
Pluto	39.4

*One astronomical unit is the distance from Earth to the sun.

1. If a planet is more than one astronomical unit from the sun, what does that imply?

    (1) It is closer to the sun than Earth is.
    (2) It is the same distance from the sun as Earth is.
    (3) It is farther from the sun than Earth is.
    (4) It is likely to receive more solar energy than Earth does.
    (5) It is likely to be a planet with no satellites.

2. It takes the sun's light 8 minutes to reach Earth. How long does it take the sun's light to reach Neptune?

    (1)   0.3 minutes
    (2)   8 minutes
    (3)   24 minutes
    (4)   30 minutes
    (5) 240 minutes

<u>Questions 3 and 4</u> refer to the following passage.

Optical telescopes use light to produce images of objects that are far away. In 1610, Galileo discovered four of Jupiter's moons by using an optical telescope. However, optical telescopes on Earth cannot produce large images of objects outside the solar system. No matter how powerful the telescope, stars are so distant that they look like points of light. In addition, the atmosphere distorts the light passing through it, making images fuzzy.

Today there are optical telescopes that orbit above Earth's atmosphere. The largest of these, the Hubble Space Telescope, was launched in 1990. It has provided stunning, clear images of planets and moons in the solar system as well as of distant stars and galaxies.

3. Which of the following is an unstated assumption important for understanding the passage?

    (1) Galileo discovered four of Jupiter's moons in 1610 using a telescope.
    (2) Optical telescopes magnify images of distant objects.
    (3) Stars are so far away that they appear only as points of light.
    (4) The atmosphere distorts images of heavenly bodies.
    (5) The Hubble Space Telescope orbits above the atmosphere.

4. Which is the best title for this passage?

    (1) The Hubble Space Telescope
    (2) Types of Telescopes
    (3) Optical Telescopes
    (4) Orbiting Telescopes
    (5) Radio Telescopes

Unifying Concepts and Processes

Questions 5 through 7 refer to the passage and the graph below.

Most astronomers believe that the universe began about 10 billion to 20 billion years ago in an explosion called the Big Bang. Just after the Big Bang, the universe was a small cloud of extremely hot and compressed hydrogen and helium. As the universe expanded, it cooled unevenly, and the gases began to form clumps. Because of the force of gravity, the clumps contracted and became galaxies. Today, the universe consists of about 100 billion galaxies that continue to move away from one another.

There is much evidence to support the Big Bang theory. Galaxies are moving away from Earth in every direction, as if they all once came from the same place. The farther away a galaxy is, the faster it appears to move, which is consistent with an expanding universe. In addition, cosmic background radiation (CBR), left over from the Big Bang, has been observed by radio telescopes in every direction in space. Ripples in the CBR indicate areas of density needed for the formation of galaxies.

However, there is much disagreement about what will happen to the universe. Its fate depends on the amount of mass it contains and its gravitational effect. Will it continue to expand? Will it stop at a certain size? Will it start to contract? Three different possibilities are shown below.

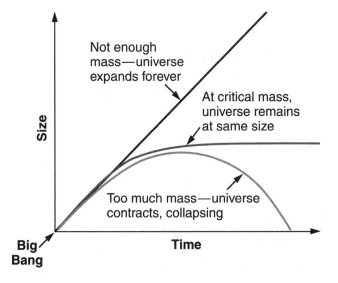

5. Which of the following situations most closely resembles the Big Bang?

   (1) A bonfire sends sparks and ashes up into the air.
   (2) Fireworks explode, sending sparks, ashes, and smoke in all directions.
   (3) Two cannonballs collide in midair, causing a fireball that quickly falls to the ground.
   (4) Several sparks fly as you light a match.
   (5) A candle burns until it is completely melted.

6. According to the graph, what is likely to happen if the universe contains enough matter to cause it to contract?

   (1) The universe would continue to expand.
   (2) The universe would collapse in on itself.
   (3) A parallel universe would begin elsewhere.
   (4) The universe would remain steady at a particular size.
   (5) Another Big Bang would take place in 10 billion years.

7. About 90 percent of the matter in the universe has mass and exerts gravity but cannot be seen. If this so-called dark matter is invisible, how can scientists know it is there?

   (1) They have observed it with orbiting space telescopes.
   (2) They have observed it from Earth.
   (3) They have observed its gravitational effects on visible objects.
   (4) They have observed distant galaxies moving away rapidly.
   (5) They have observed CBR in every direction.

Always study and understand the scales of a graph. Some graphs do not show specific quantities but rather show relationships—such as size, time, and mass.

Answers start on page 787.

Directions: Choose the one best answer to each question.

Questions 1 through 3 refer to the passage and diagram below.

The air around Earth is always moving. Moving air is called wind. Throughout history, people have used energy from wind to move ships, turn mill wheels, and pump water. In 1890, a windmill that could generate electricity was invented. Wind generators became a common sight on Canadian farms. However, most wind generators fell into disuse in the 1940s, when electricity from electric power plants became available to farmers.

The need to find energy sources other than fossil fuels such as coal, oil, and natural gas sparked new interest in wind energy. Since the 1970s, new materials and designs have been used to make aerodynamic, tough, and efficient wind generators. These machines adjust to changing wind conditions by moving the position of the blades and rotating into the wind. In some places, large wind farms consisting of thousands of linked wind generators can produce as much electricity as a fossil fuel power station. However, wind energy costs more than energy generated from fossil fuels; it accounts for only 0.1 percent of the electricity produced in Canada.

Today, an important use of wind energy is similar to that of the early 1900s—in places not connected to power plants where an independent and self-contained power generation system is needed. In such locations, wind power is economical.

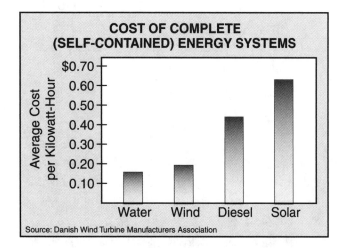

COST OF COMPLETE
(SELF-CONTAINED) ENERGY SYSTEMS

Source: Danish Wind Turbine Manufacturers Association

1. Which of the following would be most likely to use wind energy to produce electricity?

   (1) a huge metropolitan area
   (2) a factory
   (3) a wilderness research station
   (4) an industrial complex
   (5) a modern farm

2. Which is the greatest advantage to a farmer of having a wind generator even though electricity from a power plant is available?

   (1) Maintaining a wind generator is less work than getting electricity from a power plant.
   (2) Having a wind generator means having power if the main source of electricity fails.
   (3) Wind is a more reliable source of energy than a power plant.
   (4) Installing and running a wind generator is cheaper than getting energy from a power plant.
   (5) A wind generator uses a nonrenewable form of energy, unlike a power plant.

3. A rancher in western Canada for whom economy of operation is a major value wants to install an independent, self-contained energy system and selects wind power. What is the best explanation for this choice?

   (1) Wind is the cheapest source of power.
   (2) Diesel generators are expensive to run.
   (3) Solar energy costs more than wind energy.
   (4) A wind system is cheaper than diesel.
   (5) Water power is not available in that location.

Tip

Bar graphs usually compare amounts. For example, a bar graph may show the prices of different cars. The tallest (or longest) bar represents the highest price.

Questions 4 and 5 refer to the diagram below.

FORMATION OF CRATERS

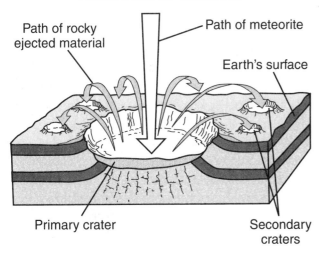

Path of rocky ejected material

Path of meteorite

Earth's surface

Primary crater

Secondary craters

4. According to the diagram, what causes the formation of secondary craters?

   (1) small meteorites hitting the surface near the larger meteorite
   (2) large meteorites breaking into many small meteorites before hitting the surface
   (3) a comet rather than a meteorite hitting the surface
   (4) debris thrown out of the large crater by the meteorite's impact
   (5) the sinking of small areas as the ground settles after the meteorite's impact

5. Most small objects burn up in the atmosphere and never hit the surface of Earth. Which of the following facts supports this conclusion?

   (1) Jupiter, which is a gas giant, has many storms in its atmosphere, including the Great Red Spot.
   (2) Saturn has a complex ring system consisting of particles of ice and rock.
   (3) Earth has fewer craters than the moon, which has no atmosphere.
   (4) Some craters on Earth are produced as a result of volcanic activity.
   (5) Craters on Earth are sometimes filled with water, forming round lakes.

Question 6 refers to the following paragraph and diagram.

A pair of stars viewed through a telescope may seem to be very close together because of the angles at which they are seen from Earth, even though in reality they are millions of light years apart.

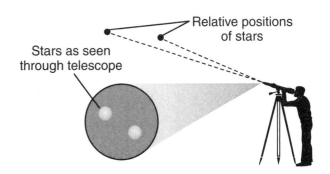

Relative positions of stars

Stars as seen through telescope

6. Which of the following people would probably be most interested in this information?

   (1) a planetary scientist
   (2) an amateur astronomer
   (3) an optician
   (4) a telescope manufacturer
   (5) a scientist who studies the sun

7. Some astronomers think the planet Pluto and its moon, Charon, may not be a planet and moon at all. Instead they hypothesize that Pluto and Charon are a double-planet system—two planets orbiting around a common point. This is because Pluto and Charon appear to be very similar in mass, whereas usually the planet is much larger than its moon(s). However, telescope images of Pluto are not good enough to determine the relative masses of the two bodies with any certainty.

Which type of evidence might provide enough information to determine whether Pluto and Charon are a double-planet system or a planet and a moon?

   (1) data from a space probe to Pluto
   (2) images from the Hubble Space Telescope
   (3) images from land-based telescopes
   (4) data from another double-planet system
   (5) data from the Earth-moon system

Answers start on page 787.

Physical Science

Physical scientists study the most basic questions about the universe. What is matter? What is energy? How are they related? The answers affect every area of science and technology, the workforce, and everyday life—from cooking and baking to understanding how atoms and molecules work, from designing cars, cosmetics, and nuclear power plants to daily laboratory tasks. Physical science is often divided into chemistry, the study of matter, and physics, the study of the relationship between matter and energy. Increasingly, however, knowledge from both chemistry and physics is required to make and use new scientific discoveries and innovations.

Understanding physical science is very important for success on the GED Science Test. Physical science topics are the basis for about 30 percent of the questions on the test.

Matter

Comparing and Contrasting

In science as well as in everyday life, you are often faced with looking at two items that appear alike. First you might **compare** them, or identify their similarities. As shown in the Venn diagram below, ethane and ethene are both hydrocarbons made from carbon and hydrogen. Next, you might **contrast** the two items to identify their differences. In this case, ethane is saturated and ethene is unsaturated. You can show these similarities and differences in a Venn diagram.

Comparing and contrasting are skills that can help you to understand science materials. To compare things, ask, "How are these things alike?" To contrast things, ask, "How are these things different?"

compare
to identify how things are alike

contrast
to identify how things are different

A Venn diagram may help you identify similarities and differences if you are having trouble comparing and contrasting two or more things.

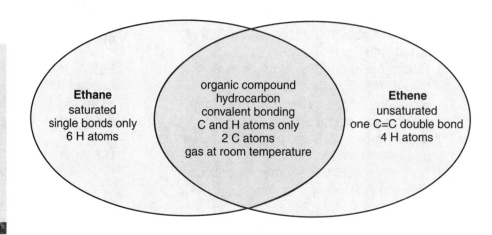

GED Practice

Directions: Choose the one best answer to each question.

Questions 1 through 3 refer to the following passage and diagrams.

Gases behave differently under different conditions of temperature, volume, and pressure (the force per unit area of the molecules' collisions with the container) because of the way their molecules move.

As shown in diagram A, the pressure of a gas doubles if the temperature doubles and the volume remains the same. The rise in temperature causes the molecules to move twice as fast in the same amount of space. This increases the pressure. The pressure of a gas also doubles if its volume is cut in half and its temperature remains constant, as shown in diagram B. This is because, in the smaller space, the molecules have twice the number of collisions. The pressure of a gas remains the same if the temperature and volume both double, as shown in diagram C. This is because the molecules move faster at higher temperatures, but, with the volume doubled, they have twice the space to move in.

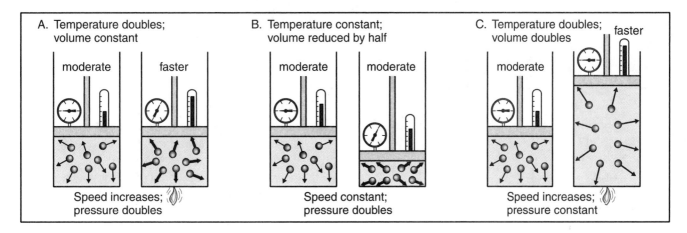

1. What is the pressure of a gas?

   (1) the heat energy of its molecules
   (2) the effect of molecules as they hit the sides of their container
   (3) the volume of the container multiplied by the temperature
   (4) the temperature of a given volume of gas
   (5) the volume of the gas compared to the size of the container

2. Under which conditions would a gas have the least pressure?

   (1) high temperature, large volume
   (2) high temperature, small volume
   (3) medium temperature, medium volume
   (4) low temperature, large volume
   (5) low temperature, small volume

3. Which of the following statements about gases is supported by the information given in the diagrams?

   (1) Pressure decreases when temperature and volume remain the same.
   (2) Pressure decreases when temperature increases and volume remains the same.
   (3) Pressure increases when volume decreases and temperature remains the same.
   (4) Pressure decreases when temperature and volume both double.
   (5) Pressure remains the same when temperature increases and volume decreases.

   If you hold a book in one hand and a comparably sized piece of foam packing material in the other, the book feels heavier. The book feels heavier because it has more mass in the same amount of space. This property of matter is referred to as density. Density is defined as the mass per unit volume of a material. It is an important property, one that when combined with other properties, helps distinguish one substance from another. In general, gases are less dense than liquids, which are less dense than solids. The bar graph shows the density of some common substances.

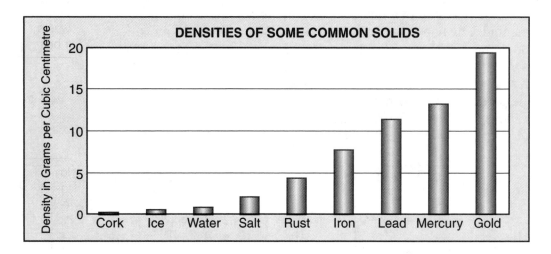

4. Which of the following substances is denser than lead?

   (1) water
   (2) salt
   (3) rust
   (4) iron
   (5) gold

5. According to the graph, if you melt ice, what is the effect on its density?

   (1) Its density increases.
   (2) Its density decreases.
   (3) Its density increases, then decreases.
   (4) Its density decreases, then increases.
   (5) Its density remains the same.

6. A materials scientist must identify a sample of matter. She measures its density at 7.9 grams per cubic centimetre. The sample is made of which of the following substances?

   (1) rust
   (2) iron
   (3) lead
   (4) mercury
   (5) Density alone cannot be used to identify a particular substance

Bar graphs are used to compare amounts. Usually, bars represent items in a category, and the length of each bar represents a measurable characteristic. Taller or longer bars have more of the characteristic than shorter bars.

Questions 7 through 10 refer to the following paragraph and table.

The ingredients of a mixture keep their own properties, and they can be separated from a mixture by physical means as described below.

Method	Description	Example
Sorting	Selecting the desired substance from the mixture	In coal mining, sorting coal from rock by hand
Magnetic separation	Using a magnet to separate a magnetic substance from the mixture	In iron ore processing, separating the magnetic iron from nonmagnetic waste rock using a magnetized conveyor belt
Distillation	Separating a solution by boiling and condensing; works because different substances have different boiling points	Removing the salt from seawater
Extraction	Dissolving an ingredient out of a mixture by using a specific solvent	Extracting vanilla flavouring from vanilla beans with alcohol
Gravitational separation	Sorting ingredients by the density of each	In panning for gold, the dense gold particles settle to the bottom of the pan and the lighter (less dense) rock particles wash away

7. Which of the following is the best title for the table?

   (1) Types of Mixtures
   (2) Sorting and Extraction
   (3) Industrial Uses of Mixture Separation
   (4) The Ingredients of Mixtures
   (5) Methods of Separating Mixtures

8. What do distillation and extraction have in common?

   (1) They both involve solutions.
   (2) They both involve magnetism.
   (3) They both involve density.
   (4) They both involve appearance.
   (5) They both remove salt from seawater.

9. Brittany used the chemical trichloroethylene to remove a salad dressing stain from a tablecloth. Which method of separating mixtures did Brittany use?

   (1) sorting
   (2) magnetic separation
   (3) distillation
   (4) extraction
   (5) gravitational separation

10. Petroleum is separated into products such as gasoline and kerosene by heating them to the boiling point and allowing them to cool again. Which method of separating mixtures is used to process petroleum?

   (1) sorting
   (2) magnetic separation
   (3) distillation
   (4) extraction
   (5) gravitational separation

Answers start on page 788.

Structure of Atoms and Molecules
Applying Ideas

One way we make sense of the world is by placing things in general categories, or groups. For example, we all know what a dog is. Even though we may not have seen every breed of dog that exists, when we see a new type of dog we still recognize that it is a dog. We apply what we know about dogs in general to the new dog.

In science, many things are defined in general terms. For example, any liquid is matter with a definite volume but no definite shape. When you see milk or motor oil, you recognize these specific types of matter as liquids because they too have a definite volume but no definite shape. They share the properties of liquids. In science, general ideas or categories, such as liquids, can be easier to understand if you apply them to specific examples such as milk or oil.

Read the passage and answer the questions below.

In the mid-1980s, it became possible to see atoms and molecules with new kinds of microscopes. One type is the scanning tunnelling microscope (STM). It uses a constant flow of electric current to scan a substance from a constant height. The STM can scan substances whose surfaces conduct electricity, such as many metals. It produces an image that shows the shapes of atoms. Another type is the atomic force microscope (AFM). The tip of the AFM flexes as the electric forces between the tip and the atoms push or pull. The AFM maps the atomic surface by keeping the force on its tip constant. It can be used to examine substances whose surfaces do not conduct electricity, such as biological samples.

To understand general ideas or categories in science, ask yourself these questions:

- What central idea or concept is being presented?
- What are its elements or characteristics?
- What are some specific examples?

1. Put a check mark next to the type of microscope that a scientist would use to measure the binding force between molecules of proteins.

    _____ a. STM   _____ b. AFM

You are correct if you checked *option b*. Proteins are biological samples, so the scientist would use the type of microscope that is suited to examine biological molecules—the AFM.

2. Put a check mark next to the type of microscope scientists probably used to distinguish between clusters of gold and silver atoms by measuring emitted light and voltage.

    _____ a. STM   _____ b. AFM

You are correct if you checked *option a*. The passage indicates that STMs can scan materials that conduct electricity, such as metals like gold and silver.

GED Practice

Directions: Choose the one best answer to each question.

Questions 1 through 3 refer to the following passage and chart.

All living things contain carbon. Compounds containing carbon and hydrogen are called organic compounds. An organic compound that contains only the two elements hydrogen and carbon is called a hydrocarbon. There are thousands of different hydrocarbons, including fossil fuels. Even though they contain just two elements, hydrocarbons vary greatly in their properties. Scientists classify hydrocarbons into subgroups called series.

Members of one group, called the alkane series, are the most abundant hydrocarbons. You're probably familiar with many of them. If you've been camping, you may have used propane or butane. These two gases are often sold in canisters for use in barbecue grills, camp stoves, and lanterns. The gasoline that fuels a car usually contains pentane, hexane, heptane, and octane. Some alkanes are listed below.

THE ALKANE SERIES			
Name	Formula	Physical State at Room Temperature	Boiling Point ($^\circ$ C)
Methane	CH_4	gas	−162
Ethane	C_2H_6	gas	−89
Propane	C_3H_8	gas	−42
Butane	C_4H_{10}	gas	−1
Pentane	C_5H_{12}	liquid	36
Hexane	C_6H_{14}	liquid	69
Heptane	C_7H_{16}	liquid	98
Octane	C_8H_{18}	liquid	126
Nonane	C_9H_{20}	liquid	151
Decane	$C_{10}H_{22}$	liquid	174
Eicosane	$C_{20}H_{42}$	solid	344

1. According to the passage and the chart, which of the following is a characteristic of all members of the alkane series?

    (1) They are living things because they contain hydrogen and carbon.
    (2) They are both organic compounds and hydrocarbons.
    (3) They are all liquid when they are at room temperature.
    (4) They all contain the same number of carbon atoms.
    (5) They are made up of helium atoms.

2. If you open the valve on the fuel tank of a gas barbecue grill, the fuel that escapes is in the gaseous state. Which of the following is likely to be the fuel in the grill?

    (1) C_3H_8
    (2) C_8H_{18}
    (3) C_9H_{20}
    (4) $C_{10}H_{22}$
    (5) $C_{20}H_{42}$

3. Which of the following conclusions can you draw based on the data in the chart?

    (1) Heptane boils at a lower temperature than hexane.
    (2) Butane boils at a higher temperature than ethane.
    (3) Butane melts at a lower temperature than ethane.
    (4) Eicosane contains the fewest carbon atoms.
    (5) Pentane contains fewer carbon and hydrogen atoms than butane does.

Questions 4 and 5 refer to the passage below.

Atoms of most elements can bond with other atoms. When atoms bond, they either transfer or share electrons. If electrons are transferred from one atom to another, each atom takes on a charge; charged atoms are called ions. A bond between ions is an ionic bond. Ionic bonds form only between two different elements; the substances that result are ionic compounds. Elements on opposite sides of the periodic table are most likely to join by ionic bonding.

Elements closer to each other in the periodic table tend to bond by sharing electrons. Bonds that result when electrons are shared are called covalent bonds. A single covalent bond requires a pair of electrons be shared; one electron comes from each atom. Two or more atoms joined by a covalent bond form a molecule.

Covalent bonds can form between atoms of the same element or between atoms of two or more different elements. When atoms of different elements are joined by covalent bonds, the result is a covalent compound.

4. Which situation involves ionic bonding?

   (1) two hydrogen atoms and an oxygen atom sharing two pairs of electrons
   (2) sugar and water mixed together
   (3) calcium giving up two electrons to two fluorine atoms
   (4) oxygen and nitrogen together in air
   (5) water and carbon dioxide in a soft drink

5. Which of the following is an unstated assumption suggested by the passage?

   (1) Compounds form from atoms of different elements.
   (2) Covalent bonds require electron sharing.
   (3) A molecule is made up of atoms bonded covalently.
   (4) Ions are atoms that carry a charge.
   (5) A molecule can have ionic bonds.

Question 6 refers to the following passage and diagram.

Compounds can be represented by chemical formulas, structural formulas, and diagrams. For example, the compound methane is shown by the chemical formula CH_4. The C stands for carbon, and H stands for hydrogen. The numbers tell you how many atoms are in one molecule of methane. When there is no number, that means there is one atom. Thus, a molecule of methane has one atom of carbon and four atoms of hydrogen.

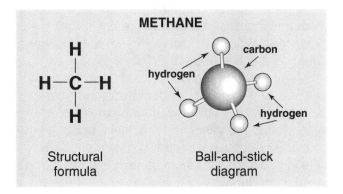

METHANE

Structural formula   Ball-and-stick diagram

6. The structural formula for propane is shown here.

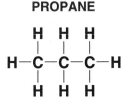

PROPANE

Which of the following statements is supported by the structural formula for propane?

   (1) Propane contains nitrogen atoms.
   (2) Propane has three atoms of carbon and three atoms of hydrogen.
   (3) Propane has three atoms of carbon and four atoms of oxygen.
   (4) The chemical formula for propane is C_3H_8.
   (5) The chemical formula for propane is C_3H_6.

Answers start on page 789.

Chemical Reactions

Assessing the Adequacy of Written Information

If you pay attention to science and health news, you know that scientists publish their data and conclusions in professional journals read by other scientists. For example, a new study may provide evidence that children who drink bottled water have more cavities than children who drink fluoridated tap water. Other scientists then examine or repeat the study to see whether new data support the conclusion that the authors reached.

Whenever you read anything factual, on a scientific topic or otherwise, you should examine whether the written information presented is adequate to support the conclusions. Ask yourself, "What conclusions are being reached? Which facts and observations are given to support these conclusions? Does this information give adequate support?"

evaluate
to examine something in order to judge its worth or significance

When you **evaluate** information, it helps to put aside what you already know about the topic. Focus on the supporting details and the conclusions that are presented. If a conclusion is not supported by adequate evidence, then it is not a sound conclusion.

Read the passage and answer the question below.

Think of a conclusion as a main idea. Then look for the details that support that main idea.

There are two main types of tea: green and black. With green tea, the leaves are quickly heated or steamed. This prevents the tea from reacting with air. Black tea is made by exposing the leaves to air, causing substances in the leaves to react with oxygen in the air, turning the leaves dark brown. This process, called oxidation, is a chemical reaction similar to the rusting of iron. In contrast to herbal teas, all teas made from the leaves of the tea plant contain caffeine, a chemical that stimulates the body, and polyphenols, chemicals that act as antioxidants, thought to prevent cell damage.

Put a check mark next to each fact from the passage that supports the conclusion that drinking tea has health benefits.

_____ a. Tea has been shown to reduce the likelihood of developing digestive tract cancer.

_____ b. Black tea is processed by exposure to the air, which causes oxidation.

_____ c. The polyphenols in tea act as antioxidants and help prevent cell damage.

You are correct if you checked *option c*. The last sentence of the passage describes the beneficial effects of polyphenols on cells. *Option a* might be true, but you can't tell because it is not discussed in the passage. *Option b* is true and is stated in the passage, but it does not support the conclusion that drinking tea benefits health.

GED Practice

Directions: Choose the <u>one best answer</u> to each question.

Questions 1 and 2 refer to the following passage.

Over the years, chemists have developed many ways to control chemical reactions. For example, they can vary temperature, pressure, concentration, acidity, and other factors to control the rate and outcome of a reaction. However, these techniques are often imprecise. They usually work by exciting the molecules, increasing their vibrations and causing the weakest bonds to break first.

There are situations in which more precise control is needed. For example, a chemist may want to break the strongest bonds first to ensure that a chemical reaction takes the desired course. In this type of situation, a new method holds promise.

In the new technique, interacting beams of light from two lasers are used to control a chemical reaction. By varying the intensity of the lasers' interactions, scientists can control which bonds in the molecules break apart first. This procedure gives scientists more control over the products of the reaction.

Although this method is experimental, it has the potential for practical application. Many chemical reactions proceed simultaneously along different pathways to yield a mixture of compounds. This can be a problem for drug manufacturers and others who are trying to produce one pure compound without other compounds in the product.

For example, some reactions produce chiral molecules. These are pairs of molecules that have the same chemical formula but are mirror-images in structure. One chiral molecule is designated the "right-handed" molecule and the other is designated the "left-handed" molecule. The left-handed and right-handed molecules often have very different properties. For example, the right-handed form of the drug thalidomide is a fairly safe sedative. The left-handed form, however, caused many birth defects in the 1960s. For the manufacture of such chemicals, the new laser technique may improve quality control.

1. Which is the most important way in which the laser technique for controlling chemical reactions differs from earlier methods?

   (1) It uses light beams.
   (2) It uses modern technology.
   (3) It is more precise.
   (4) It has practical applications.
   (5) It controls pressure and temperature.

2. Some chemical reactions can be controlled at the molecular level. According to the passage, which statement is evidence of this?

   (1) Scientists vary temperature, pressure, concentration, and other factors to control reactions.
   (2) Laser control of reactions allows scientists to break specific bonds between atoms.
   (3) Thalidomide manufacturers produced both left-handed and right-handed versions of the drug.
   (4) Control of chemical processes is possible using different forms of technology.
   (5) The laser technique may be used by drug and other manufacturers to ensure that they produce quality products.

When you are asked to identify evidence that supports a conclusion, look for logical relationships linking the evidence and the conclusion.

Questions 3 through 7 refer to the following passage and chart.

Labels on food often list amounts of saturated and unsaturated fats. A saturated molecule is one that contains only single bonds, in which one pair of electrons is shared in each bond. Unsaturated molecules contain other types of bonds, in which more than one pair of electrons are shared.

A saturated hydrocarbon is saturated with hydrogen. That is, it contains more hydrogen than an unsaturated hydrocarbon with the same number of carbon atoms. One example of a saturated hydrocarbon is ethane, C_2H_6. An example of an unsaturated molecule is ethene, C_2H_4. In the unsaturated hydrocarbon ethene, two electrons of one carbon atom are paired with two electrons of another carbon atom, forming a double bond.

In certain reactions, the double and triple bonds of an unsaturated hydrocarbon can be broken. Hydrogen can then be added to the molecule. A reaction in which hydrogen is added to an unsaturated hydrocarbon is called an addition reaction.

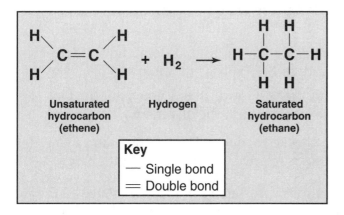

3. Which of the following elements is involved in an addition reaction involving hydrocarbons?

   (1) oxygen
   (2) nitrogen
   (3) lithium
   (4) neon
   (5) hydrogen

4. In contrast to a saturated molecule, what does an unsaturated molecule contain?

   (1) hydrogen atoms
   (2) only single bonds
   (3) shared electrons
   (4) double (or triple) bonds
   (5) carbon atoms

5. Which of the following is a fact stated about ethane?

   (1) It is an unsaturated hydrocarbon molecule.
   (2) Single bonding occurs between its carbon atoms.
   (3) Double bonding occurs between its carbon atoms.
   (4) Its atoms contain only two electrons.
   (5) It has four hydrogen atoms.

6. Which statement does the diagram support about the addition reaction shown?

   (1) One reactant is a saturated hydrocarbon.
   (2) Both reactants are hydrocarbons.
   (3) The reactants are H_2 and C_2H_6.
   (4) The product contains a double bond.
   (5) The product is C_2H_6.

7. Which of the following conclusions is supported by the information presented?

   (1) Saturated hydrocarbons can be produced from unsaturated hydrocarbons through addition reactions.
   (2) Unsaturated hydrocarbons can be produced from saturated hydrocarbons by means of addition reactions.
   (3) In addition reactions, the number of carbon atoms in the original molecule increases.
   (4) Ethene can be made from ethane by means of an addition reaction.
   (5) Under certain conditions, hydrocarbons react with chlorine to form compounds containing hydrogen, carbon, and chlorine.

Answers start on page 790.

Motion and Forces

Recognizing Unstated Assumptions

We bring our knowledge and experience of the world to bear on everything we do. For example, when a person writes a science article, he or she brings a lot of relevant knowledge to the task of writing. You bring a lot of relevant knowledge to the task of reading. Therefore, the writer does not explain everything in great detail. He or she assumes that you know a lot already. Thus, when you read, it's important to recognize the unstated assumptions of a passage. Recognizing unstated assumptions will help you to understand what you read.

Read the passage. Then answer the questions that follow.

When you are a passenger in a car, you are free to watch things whiz by on the side of the highway. Telephone poles, trees, houses, buildings all speed by you. In contrast, the car door and the driver don't seem to move at all. They stay right next to you.

Now, suppose you are standing on the side of the same road. The cars, with their drivers, move quickly past you, but the telephone poles, trees, houses, and buildings don't move an inch.

Tip

When looking for unstated assumptions, draw on the things you already know and your experiences of the world.

1. Put a check mark next to the unstated assumption related to the reason the car door and the driver do not seem to move when you are in the car.

_____ a. You are moving along with the car door and the driver and dashboard, so they appear stationary to you.

_____ b. Your view out the window distracts you from the fact that you, the car door, and the driver are all moving.

You are correct if you checked *option a*. The writer assumes you understand that all motion is relative to a person's point of view.

2. Put a check mark next to the unstated assumption related to the reason the cars appear to move when you are standing on the side of the road, but the trees and poles do not appear to move.

_____ a. The cars only appear to be moving, and the trees and poles are not actually moving.

_____ b. The cars are moving relative to your position, and the trees and poles are not.

You are correct if you checked *option b*. Again, the writer assumes you know that all motion is relative to your frame of reference. Thus, objects that are moving at the same rate you are appear to be motionless; you perceive motion only in objects whose motion differs from your own.

GED Practice

Directions: Choose the one best answer to each question.

Questions 1 and 2 refer to the following passage and diagram.

According to Newton's Third Law of Motion, if one object exerts a force on a second object, then the second object exerts an equal and opposite force, called the reaction force, on the first object.

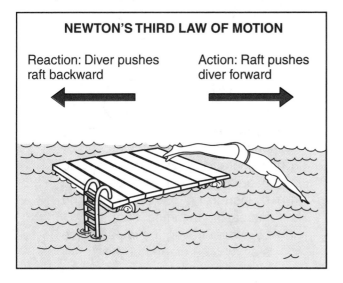

NEWTON'S THIRD LAW OF MOTION

Reaction: Diver pushes raft backward

Action: Raft pushes diver forward

You can feel the effects of Newton's Third Law if you dive off the side of an unanchored or lightly tethered raft. Your feet push off the raft; the raft pushes you forward at the same time that you are pushing the raft backward.

1. Which of the following is an example of a reaction force?

   (1) hot air rushes out of a balloon
   (2) wind blowing against a kite
   (3) a ball hitting a wall
   (4) the backward "kick" of a fired rifle
   (5) a swimmer's stroke against the water

When you are looking for a specific example of a general law in science, substitute the specific elements of the example for the general elements of the law to see whether they fit.

2. A rocket engine is designed to take advantage of Newton's Third Law of Motion. Which of the following causes a rocket engine to move forward?

   (1) air flowing through the engine from the front to the back
   (2) the lift caused by differences in air speed over the top and bottom of the engine
   (3) the force exerted by gases escaping the rear of the engine
   (4) the force of gravity pulling the rocket back to Earth
   (5) the force of friction exerted by the air past which the rocket travels

3. According to Isaac Newton, the momentum of an object can be found by multiplying its mass by its velocity (speed). For example, if someone taps your hand with a ruler, you barely feel it. However, if someone brings the ruler down fast on your hand, the blow hurts. The ruler has not gotten heavier, but its velocity has increased, increasing its momentum. Newton showed that to change an object's momentum you must apply a force. When the ruler hits your hand, you supply the force to stop the ruler, which is why the blow hurts.

Which of the following statements supports the idea that a speeding truck has more momentum than a small car moving at the same speed?

   (1) The truck has a larger mass than the car does.
   (2) The car has a larger mass than the truck does.
   (3) The truck has a larger velocity than the car does.
   (4) The car has a larger velocity than the truck does.
   (5) The truck and the car experience relative motion.

Questions 4 through 6 refer to the following passage.

According to Newton's First Law of Motion, a body in motion tends to stay in motion unless acted on by an outside force. Thus, when a car collides with a tree, it stops abruptly. Inside the car, however, the driver's inertia keeps him moving forward until his motion is stopped by the steering column, dashboard, or windshield— or his seatbelt.

Let's use a specific example to see how a seatbelt works. Suppose a car going 50 km/h collides with a tree and crumples 30 cm (that is, from point of impact to where the car stops is 30 cm). If the driver, who weighs 75 kg, is not wearing a seatbelt, he keeps moving forward rapidly and meets the windshield. His motion from point of impact until his body's motion stops is only a few centimetres because the windshield does not continue moving after the car stops. In this case the force of the impact on the driver is about 129 000 N (newtons), the same force as the driver would feel if sandwiched under a mass of 12.9 t (tonnes).

Now suppose this accident occurred while the driver was wearing a seatbelt. The seatbelt would restrain his forward motion after the collision. But from initial impact with the seatbelt he continues to move with the car and a little farther before stopping, about 45 cm. In this case, the force of the impact would be about 16 000 N. Wearing a seatbelt reduces the impact force dramatically.

What does an air bag do? The air bag does not affect the force of the impact. Instead, it distributes the impact force over a large area, decreasing the pressure on any given point of the driver's body.

4. Which of the following is an unstated assumption suggested by this passage?

   (1) Inertia keeps the driver moving forward when the car is stopped in a collision.
   (2) In a collision, a driver not wearing a seatbelt is stopped by a part of the car.
   (3) Air bags have caused as much harm as good in car crashes.
   (4) The less the impact force on the driver, the less serious his injuries are likely to be.
   (5) Air bags spread the impact force over a large area of the driver's body.

5. How does a seatbelt work?

   (1) by restraining forward motion and increasing the impact force
   (2) by restraining forward motion and decreasing the impact force
   (3) by increasing forward motion and decreasing the impact force
   (4) by increasing forward motion and increasing the impact force
   (5) by concentrating the impact force on a small area of the body

6. The principle by which an air bag works is most similar to which of the following?

   (1) a hot air balloon, which rises because the gases inside the balloon are less dense than the gases outside it
   (2) a jet engine, which moves an airplane forward with a force equal and opposite to that of the hot gases escaping out the back
   (3) a system of pulleys, which reduces the force needed to move a load a certain distance
   (4) ball bearings, which reduce the friction between the moving parts of a machine, increasing its efficiency
   (5) snowshoes, which spread the weight of a person over a large area, allowing her to walk on the surface of the snow

Answers start on page 791.

Science • Physical Science

Work and Energy

Assessing the Adequacy of Visual Information

In science, diagrams, charts, and drawings can help you understand objects, processes, and ideas. However, be careful about the conclusions you draw from this type of information. For example, a diagram may show the parts of a machine. You can figure out how the machine works by studying the diagram. But the diagram won't enable you to figure out how *well* the machine works. To do that, you would need more data. To assess the adequacy of data in visuals to support a generalization or conclusion, concentrate on what is actually shown rather than adding your own interpretation or drawing conclusions that are not supported by the information.

Study the passage and the diagrams. Then answer the questions that follow.

A group of scientists, design students, and people working in Antarctica are designing a bicycle suitable for polar conditions. The extreme cold and drifting snow make conventional mountain bikes useless there. The designs being tested include three types of wide-tread wheels and tires.

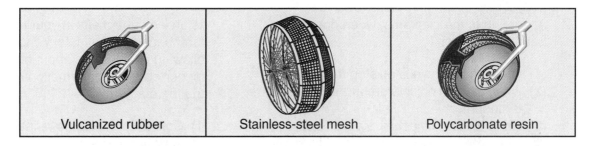

| Vulcanized rubber | Stainless-steel mesh | Polycarbonate resin |

1. Put a check mark next to the wheel type that is <u>most similar</u> to that of a regular bicycle.

    _____ a. wheel with vulcanized rubber tires

    _____ b. stainless steel mesh wheel

    _____ c. polycarbonate resin wheel

You are correct if you checked *option a*. The diagrams show that the wheel with rubber tires is <u>most similar</u> to those of a regular bicycle.

2. Put a check mark next to the information you would need to decide which wheel design works best.

    _____ a. detailed drawings of how the wheels look and work

    _____ b. results of the tests conducted on each wheel type

You are correct if you checked *option b.* Only data from an actual test can prove one wheel works better than the others.

Tip

When determining whether a conclusion is supported by a diagram, think of the diagram as a source of data. Ask yourself whether these data are sufficient to enable you to draw that conclusion.

GED Practice

Directions: Choose the one best answer to each question.

Questions 1 through 4 refer to the following paragraph and diagrams.

   The transfer of heat from one object to another can be explained in terms of moving molecules. The molecules in hot objects have more kinetic energy and move faster than the molecules in cold objects. When two objects come in contact with each other, the higher-energy molecules in the warmer object begin to collide with the molecules in the cooler object. Energy is transferred in the process. This process shows that coldness is actually the absence of heat. As heat energy leaves an object, the object becomes less warm, or cold.

HEAT TRANSFER BETWEEN TWO OBJECTS

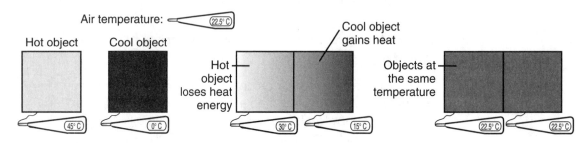

1. According to the diagrams, when does the heat transfer stop?

   (1) when all the molecules stop moving
   (2) when the two objects are at the same temperature
   (3) when the two objects are pulled apart
   (4) when the cold object loses heat to the hot object
   (5) when the cold object begins to warm up

2. Which of the following is most similar to the action of molecules in a heated substance?

   (1) a car travelling in a straight line
   (2) a ball rolling
   (3) popcorn popping
   (4) Earth rotating on its axis
   (5) a truck coming to a sudden stop

3. As an ice cube melts in your hand , your hand begins to feel cold. Which of the following conclusions about heat transfer is supported by the information in the passage and the diagram?

   (1) Cold from the ice flows into your hand.
   (2) Your hand's heat is absorbed by the ice.
   (3) The ice loses heat energy and melts.
   (4) Molecules in your hand gain energy.
   (5) Molecules in the ice lose energy.

4. What other heat transfer involving the objects in the diagrams is likely to take place?

   (1) The cold object transfers heat to the hot object.
   (2) The cold object transfers heat to the air.
   (3) The air transfers heat to the hot object.
   (4) The hot object transfers heat to the air.
   (5) No other heat transfer is likely to occur.

Additional practice material available on page 878.

Science • Physical Science

<u>Questions 5 through 7</u> refer to the following passage.

The automobile may be one of the best-loved machines on Earth, but it uses a great deal of an important nonrenewable resource: gasoline, refined from oil, a valuable fossil fuel. Autos also contribute to environmental problems, releasing many pollutants and waste heat into the air.

In a conventional automobile, gasoline burned in the engine provides heat energy, which is converted to mechanical energy to power the drive train. The battery is used simply to provide electrical energy to start the vehicle and to help power parts such as headlights. Almost all the energy in a traditional automobile comes from burning gasoline.

An all-electric car is much cleaner than a conventional car. It powers the engine with electrical energy produced by batteries. The main drawback of all-electric cars is their limited driving range. Most can drive only about 100 km before their batteries need recharging. And recharging the batteries is time-consuming— taking from three to eight hours.

A more practical design is a vehicle that combines a small gasoline engine with an electric motor powered by batteries that are recharged automatically by the running of the gasoline engine; so with the gasoline-electric hybrid car, the batteries do not need to be plugged in to be recharged. These hybrid vehicles are of two basic types. In a series hybrid, the gasoline engine provides heat energy to generate electrical energy that is stored as chemical energy in the batteries. The batteries, in turn, provide electrical energy to run the motor that produces mechanical energy to power the drive train. In a parallel hybrid, both the gasoline engine and electric motor can power the drive train directly.

Gasoline-electric hybrid cars use less gasoline than comparable conventional cars. Because they burn less gasoline, they produce less heat and air pollution as well. Auto manufacturers sold the first gasoline-electric hybrid cars in North America in 1999.

5. Which type of energy powers the drive train in a parallel gasoline-electric hybrid car?

   (1) heat energy only
   (2) electrical energy only
   (3) either heat or electrical energy
   (4) light energy
   (5) nuclear energy

6. Why are gasoline-electric hybrid cars more practical than all-electric cars?

   (1) They have a greater driving range and their batteries recharge automatically.
   (2) They get more kilometres per litre of gas than all-electric cars.
   (3) They give off less heat pollution than all-electric cars.
   (4) They give off less air pollution than electric cars.
   (5) In both types of cars, an electric motor can power the drive train.

7. The sales history of all-electric cars has been poor, even in places such as Europe and Japan, where gas costs several times what it costs in North America. What does this indicate that car buyers value the most?

   (1) contributing to a cleaner environment
   (2) conserving nonrenewable resources
   (3) the convenience of a conventional car
   (4) the lower operating costs of electric cars
   (5) setting trends with new technology

When things are being compared and contrasted, make a chart listing the characteristics of each thing. That will help you sort out their similarities and differences.

Answers start on page 791.

Electricity and Magnetism

Analyzing Cause and Effect

When you think about cause and effect, you are thinking about how one thing influences another. A cause is what makes something happen. An effect is what happens as a result of the cause.

When you flip on a light switch, you cause the lights to come on. This obvious action, or cause, produces an obvious result, or effect.

Cause-and-effect relationships are not always so obvious. What is really happening when you flip the light switch, for example, is that you are completing an electric circuit, allowing current to flow into the bulb and produce light.

Study the passage. Then answer the questions that follow.

A photocopier uses static electricity to produce copies of documents. Inside the photocopier is a metal drum that is given a negative electric charge. Lenses project an image of the document onto the drum. Where light strikes the metal drum, the electric charge disappears. Only the dark parts of the image on the drum remain negatively charged. The copier contains a dark powder called toner. The positively charged toner is attracted to the negatively charged dark parts of the image on the drum. Then a piece of paper rolls over the drum. The toner is transferred to the paper and sealed by heat. A warm photocopy comes out of the machine.

1. Put a check mark next to the statement that explains why toner forms an image of the document on the drum.

   _____ a. The positively charged toner is attracted to the negatively charged areas of the drum.

   _____ b. Heat from the machine causes the toner to form the image of the document.

You are correct if you checked *option a*. The dark parts of the image are negatively charged on the drum. They attract the positively charged particles of toner.

2. Put a check mark next to the statement that tells what would happen if just light were projected onto the drum when you were making a photocopy.

   _____ a. A blank sheet of copy paper would emerge.

   _____ b. A greyish-black sheet of copy paper would emerge.

You are correct if you checked *option a*. Since light would reach all areas of the drum, the negative charge would disappear, leaving nothing to attract the toner. Thus, the copy would be blank.

Tip

When evaluating cause-and-effect situations, read the passage carefully to discover possible causes and effects. Use definitions and equations in the passage to figure out these relationships.

GED Practice

Directions: Choose the <u>one best answer</u> to each question.

Questions 1 and 2 refer to the following paragraph and diagram.

In a simple electric motor, direct current from a battery flows through a coil inside a fixed magnet. When current flows through the coil, it becomes magnetic, with a north and south pole. Since like poles repel and unlike poles attract, the coil makes a half turn so its north pole faces the magnet's south pole. The flow of current through the coil is then reversed, reversing the magnetic field. The coil makes another half turn. As the current continues to reverse, the coil, which is attached to the shaft of the motor, keeps turning.

ELECTRIC MOTOR

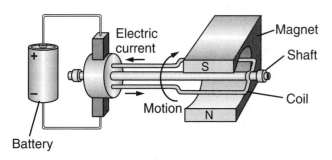

1. Based on the passage and the diagram, what turns the shaft of the motor?

   (1) the battery
   (2) the rotation of the coil
   (3) the rotation of the magnet
   (4) the poles of the magnet
   (5) the centre of the magnet

2. What would happen if current in the coil flowed continuously in the same direction?

   (1) The coil would stop turning.
   (2) The coil would turn more rapidly.
   (3) The magnetic field of the fixed magnet would reverse.
   (4) The magnetic field of the coil would reverse.
   (5) The battery would never run down.

3. Electromagnetic induction is the use of magnetism to produce electricity. A bar magnet is pushed through a wire coil, producing an electric current as long as the magnet keeps moving.

   Which of the following makes use of the principle of electromagnetic induction?

   (1) an electromagnet, which uses electricity to produce a magnetic field
   (2) a turbine, which is powered by fluid
   (3) an internal combustion engine, which burns fuel to produce heat energy
   (4) a battery, which uses chemical energy to produce electricity
   (5) a generator, which uses a magnetic field to produce electricity

Question 4 refers to the following chart.

FORCE	DESCRIPTION
Gravity	Force of attraction between a star, planet, or moon and the objects on and near it
Electro-magnetic	Force of attraction between negatively charged electrons and positively charged protons, which holds atoms together
Weak nuclear	Force that causes radioactive decay of atomic nuclei
Strong nuclear	Force that holds protons and neutrons together in atomic nuclei

4. Which of the following fundamental forces involves attraction between objects that can be easily seen every day in the world around you?

   (1) gravity
   (2) electromagnetism
   (3) the weak nuclear force
   (4) the strong nuclear force
   (5) all of the forces

Questions 5 through 7 refer to the following passage.

During a lecture in 1820, the Danish physicist Hans Oersted noticed that an electric current he produced changed the direction of a nearby compass needle. He concluded that an electric current could produce a magnetic field. Thus, Oersted was the first to demonstrate that electricity and magnetism are related—a discovery that changed human history because it made possible machines that employ electromagnetism.

Shortly afterward, a French scientist, André-Marie Ampère, proved that wires could behave like magnets when electrical current passed through them. He also showed that reversing the direction of the current reversed the polarity of the magnetic field.

In 1821, English scientist Michael Faraday showed the reverse of what Oersted had observed: that a magnet could cause a current-carrying wire to move. This phenomenon is the underlying principle of the electric motor, which converts electrical energy into mechanical energy. By 1840, several inventors had produced electric motors of varying designs and efficiency. Faraday also discovered that a moving magnetic field causes electric current to flow in a wire. This phenomenon underlies the production of electricity in generators.

5. Which important discovery did Oersted make?

   (1) An electric current flowing through a wire produces a magnetic field.
   (2) Earth has a magnetic field that causes compass needles to point north.
   (3) A magnetic field causes an electric current to flow.
   (4) A magnet causes a current-carrying wire to move.
   (5) An electric motor converts electrical energy to mechanical energy.

6. Which of the following is an unstated assumption based on the passage?

   (1) An electric current produces a magnetic field.
   (2) An electric motor is based on electromagnetism.
   (3) A compass needle is magnetic.
   (4) Electricity and magnetism are related.
   (5) Oersted discovered electromagnetism.

7. Which of the following was a result of the discovery of electromagnetism?

   (1) the use of fossil fuels to power internal combustion engines
   (2) the use of steam to power locomotives
   (3) the use of windmills to pump water
   (4) the large-scale generation of electricity by means of moving magnetic fields
   (5) the use of batteries to produce electrical energy

8. The ancient Chinese, Greeks, and Romans were familiar with magnetism as a natural property of certain rocks such as lodestones. However, magnetism had few practical uses until the 1200s when compasses were first used in navigation. However, with the discoveries of Oersted, Ampère, and Faraday in the 1800s, interest in magnetism increased sharply.

Which of the following most likely accounts for the increased interest in magnetism in the 1800s?

   (1) New uses for lodestones were found.
   (2) Navigation was much more accurate with magnetic compasses.
   (3) There were more scientists in the 1800s than in previous centuries.
   (4) A renewed interest in ancient civilizations sparked scientific discoveries.
   (5) Electromagnetism had many potentially valuable applications.

Answers start on page 792.

Waves

Identifying Faulty Logic

When you read science materials, you need to watch for instances of faulty logic. One type of faulty logic is called the **circular argument.** In a circular argument, the reasons supporting a conclusion simply restate the conclusion itself. Suppose Janna said that Lowell is handsome because he is good looking. This is a circular argument. The meaning of handsome is good looking, so Janna is not providing any evidence or reasons to conclude that Lowell is indeed good looking.

Another form of faulty logic is the **hasty generalization.** In a hasty generalization, a conclusion is based on insufficient evidence. If Janna sees Lowell once from afar and concludes he is handsome, that is a hasty generalization. Janna didn't see Lowell clearly enough to conclude that he was handsome.

circular argument
a form of faulty logic in which a conclusion is supported by reasons that simply restate the conclusion

hasty generalization
a form of faulty logic in which a conclusion is based on insufficient evidence

When reading, check the logic of the facts, ideas, and conclusions presented. Ask yourself, does this make sense? Is this conclusion what the facts show?

Study the passage. Then answer the questions that follow.

A tsunami is a wave caused by an undersea earthquake, landslide, or volcanic eruption. When the ocean floor is disturbed, it sets off a water wave that travels outward in circles. A tsunami can travel at speeds up to 800 km/h. Out at sea, the wave may be only half a metre high. When it reaches shallow coastal water, the wave rapidly grows much higher. By the time it reaches shore, a tsunami may be 15 m or higher. Such waves can wipe out coastal areas. From 1992 to 1997, tsunamis killed more than 1800 people around the Pacific Ocean.

1. Put a check mark next to the reason tsunamis are dangerous.

   _____ a. They pose many hazards.

   _____ b. They cause floods, kill people, and damage property.

You are correct if you checked *option b.* It cites specific reasons tsunamis are dangerous. *Option a* is incorrect because it's a circular argument. It is simply another way of saying tsunamis are dangerous.

2. Write *C* next to the conclusion that is supported by sufficient evidence from the passage.

   _____ a. Most tsunamis occur in the Pacific Ocean.

   _____ b. A tsunami is not very dangerous while it is out at sea.

You are correct if you chose *option b.* A half metre high wave is not dangerous. *Option a* is a hasty generalization. The Pacific death toll is not sufficient evidence to conclude that tsunamis usually occur there.

GED Practice

Directions: Choose the <u>one best answer</u> to each question.

<u>Questions 1 through 4</u> refer to the following passage and diagram.

Electromagnetic radiation is a wave motion of oscillating electric and magnetic fields. The electric and magnetic fields are perpendicular to one another and to the direction in which the wave is traveling.

Electromagnetic waves range from the very long wavelengths of radio waves to the extremely short wavelengths of gamma waves. The range of electromagnetic waves is called the electromagnetic spectrum. The only waves in the spectrum that we can see are visible light.

All electromagnetic waves travel at the same speed through a vacuum. This speed is 300 000 km/s.

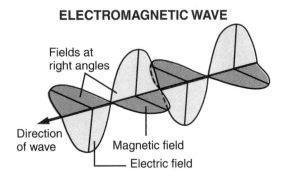

ELECTROMAGNETIC WAVE

Fields at right angles

Direction of wave

Magnetic field
Electric field

ELECTROMAGNETIC SPECTRUM

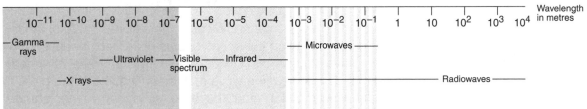

1. What is electromagnetic radiation?

   (1) electromagnetic waves of varying wavelengths
   (2) a wave with disturbance in one direction
   (3) a longitudinal wave with alternating compressions and rarefactions
   (4) electric and magnetic fields that oscillate in a wave
   (5) one type of visible light

2. In what direction is the disturbance in an electromagnetic wave?

   (1) parallel to the direction of motion
   (2) at right angles to the direction of motion
   (3) at 45° angles to the direction of motion
   (4) back and forth in the same direction as motion
   (5) in circles around the direction of motion

3. How do visible light waves differ from radiowaves?

   (1) Light waves consist only of moving magnetic fields.
   (2) Light waves consist only of moving electric fields.
   (3) Light waves have shorter wavelengths.
   (4) Radio waves must travel through air.
   (5) Radio waves are sound waves.

4. Based on the diagram and the passage, which of the following statements is true of infrared waves?

   (1) They are produced by X-ray machines.
   (2) They travel through a vacuum at 300 000 km/s.
   (3) They travel faster through space than radio waves do.
   (4) Some have a wavelength of 100 m.
   (5) They are not electromagnetic waves.

Questions 5 through 7 refer to the following passage.

Cellular phones give off low levels of electromagnetic radiation in the microwave range. High levels of this type of radiation can produce biological damage through heating—that's how a microwave oven works. But can the low levels emitted by cell phones cause health problems in humans? Of particular concern is a possible link between cell phones with built-in antennas, which are held close to the head, and brain cancer.

To date, there is no definitive judgment on the safety of cell phones. The scientific evidence from animal studies is conflicting. In one study, mice that had been genetically altered to be predisposed to develop a certain type of cancer did develop more cases of that cancer when exposed to low-level microwave radiation than did the control group. In other animal studies, the results have been inconclusive.

Studies of humans have not found any association between brain cancer and cell phone use. It is true that some people who use cell phones develop brain cancer. But people who do not use cell phones also develop brain cancer. About 9 500 000 people use cell phones in Canada today. As long-term use of cell phones increases, further studies, of both animals and humans, will be needed to clarify the relationship—if any—between cell phone use and the development of brain cancer.

Tip

When deciding whether you have enough information to support a conclusion, ask yourself, is the information adequate to support the conclusion or does it only suggest that it *might* be true?

5. Why do some people think cell phone use may lead to brain cancer?

   (1) Cell phones emit microwaves near the head.
   (2) Distance causes transmission to break up.
   (3) Mice exposed to operating cell phones have developed cancer.
   (4) Cell phone use has grown dramatically in the past five years.
   (5) Cell phones are wireless.

6. Which of the following steps could a cell phone user take to minimize exposure to microwave radiation?

   (1) Use the cell phone outdoors in wide open spaces.
   (2) Use a cell phone with a remote antenna to lessen microwave intensity near the head.
   (3) Alternate the side of the head to which the cell phone is held.
   (4) Use the cell phone to receive incoming calls only.
   (5) Use the cell phone to make outgoing calls only.

7. Which of the following conclusions is supported by the information in the passage?

   (1) In all studies, low levels of microwave emissions caused cancer in laboratory animals.
   (2) Cell phone use is associated with certain types of brain cancer in humans.
   (3) Low levels of microwaves are sufficient to heat foods in microwave ovens.
   (4) No definitive link has been found between cell phone use and brain cancer.
   (5) People who use cell phones have a higher risk of developing brain cancer.

Answers start on page 793.

Directions: Choose the <u>one best answer</u> to each question.

Questions 1 through 3 refer to the following paragraph.

A conductor is a substance that allows electric current to flow through it easily. Metals such as copper, gold, and aluminum are the best conductors. An insulator is a substance that resists the flow of electrons. Insulators tend to be nonmetals such as glass, plastic, and porcelain.

1. Which of the following is a good insulator?

   (1) aluminum
   (2) copper
   (3) gold
   (4) rubber
   (5) silver

2. Which of the following would be the best use for a conductor?

   (1) electrical wire for a lamp
   (2) an electrical outlet cover
   (3) shoe soles for electrical line repairers
   (4) decorative base for a lamp
   (5) the outside of a light bulb

3. Which of the following conclusions is supported by the information in the paragraph?

   (1) A silver pipe is likely to have a lower resistance than a plastic pipe.
   (2) How well a substance conducts electricity depends on its temperature.
   (3) Silver is a better insulator than porcelain.
   (4) A glass tube is likely to have a lower resistance than a copper tube.
   (5) Electrons move more readily through nonmetals than through metals.

Questions 4 and 5 refer to the following paragraph and diagrams.

In a series circuit, there is only one path for the electric current. When the circuit is broken, the current stops flowing. In a parallel circuit, the current flows in two or more separate paths. If the current in one path is interrupted, it still flows in the other branches.

Series circuit   **Parallel circuit**

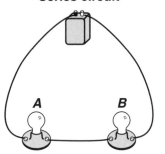 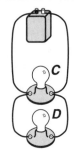

4. Look at the diagrams. Assume that the light bulbs labelled A and C have burned out. Which of the following will occur as a result?

   (1) The wire between A and B needs to be replaced.
   (2) Bulb B also will not light.
   (3) Bulb D also will not light.
   (4) The parallel circuit needs to be rewired.
   (5) Both circuits need a new battery.

5. One light bulb in a kitchen circuit burns out, but the other lights on the same circuit still work. Which statement supports the conclusion that the kitchen uses a single parallel circuit?

   (1) A power failure caused the light to go out.
   (2) The current stopped in the entire circuit.
   (3) The current continues in all but one path of the circuit.
   (4) A circuit breaker shut off the current.
   (5) The burned-out bulb was on its own series circuit.

Questions 6 through 8 refer to the following passage and diagram.

A colloid is a type of mixture in which particles of matter measuring from one-one-millionth to ten-one-millionths of a millimetre in diametre are scattered throughout a liquid or a gas. Examples of colloids include smoke (solid particles in a gas); cytoplasm (solid particles in a liquid); and foam (gas particles in a liquid or solid).

Colloids differ from solutions in that the colloidal particles are larger than the solute molecules of solutions. This can be shown with a semipermeable membrane, which allows small molecules such as those of water and the dissolved solute to pass through, but blocks larger colloidal particles, such as those of proteins. If you pour cream, a colloid, through a semipermeable membrane, the solid particles in the cream do not pass through the membrane, but the water does. In contrast, when you pour a food coloring solution through a semipermeable membrane, both the solute—the food coloring—and the solvent—water—pass through.

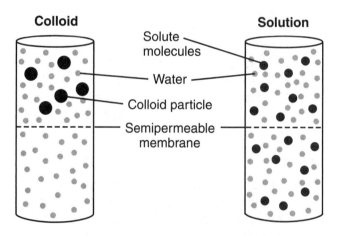

6. Based on the passage and the diagrams, how do colloids and solutions differ?

    (1) A colloid is a gas and a solution is a liquid.
    (2) The freezing point of a colloid is lower than the freezing point of a solution.
    (3) The molecules in solutions are smaller than the particles in colloids.
    (4) Colloid particles can pass through a semipermeable membrane and the solute molecules in a solution cannot.
    (5) Colloids are usually solids, and solutions are always liquids.

7. If you were to substitute wire mesh for the semipermeable membranes in the diagram, which of the following would be likely to occur?

    (1) Solid particles of the colloid would flow through, but molecules of the solute would not.
    (2) Solid particles of the colloid would not flow through, but molecules of the solute would.
    (3) Both the colloid particles and the solute molecules would flow through.
    (4) Neither particles of the colloid nor molecules of the solute would flow through.
    (5) Only water molecules would be able to flow through the mesh.

8. A suspension is a type of mixture, such as muddy water, whose particles are even larger than those of colloids. What is implied by this?

    (1) The particles of a suspension are larger than the molecules of a solution.
    (2) The particles of a suspension would flow through the semipermeable membrane.
    (3) Suspensions are always solids suspended in liquids.
    (4) A suspension can be identified by its color.
    (5) A suspension is the only type of mixture that can be separated into its ingredients.

9. The freezing point of water can be lowered a few degrees by adding a solute to form a solution. The molecules of solute spread through the solvent, in this case water. That makes it more difficult for the water to freeze and form crystals. Which of the following observations supports this information?

    (1) When it snows, calcium chloride (salt) is applied to roads to prevent the formation of ice.
    (2) Ice crystals form on windows when the temperature is below freezing.
    (3) A glass jar of soup cracks when the soup freezes.
    (4) When you place ice cubes in a glass of water, they melt.
    (5) When water freezes, it expands.

Answers start on page 794.

Directions: Choose the one best answer to each question.

Questions 1 through 3 refer to the following passage and diagram.

Factories, power stations, and cars produce waste gases such as sulphur dioxide and nitrogen oxides. These gases rise into the air and react with water vapour to form acids. Acid rain then falls, sometimes hundreds of kilometres away from its origin. Acid rain damages plants and pollutes streams and lakes.

1. What causes acid rain?

   (1) emissions from factories, power plants, and cars
   (2) condensation of water vapour in the air
   (3) pesticide runoff from agricultural areas
   (4) industrial discharges into streams and lakes
   (5) heavy metal residues in lake and stream bottoms

2. Provincial officials want to reduce the province's acid rain, so they place controls on industrial and vehicle emissions in the province. Why might this plan not reduce acid rain in the province?

   (1) It is difficult to reduce industrial and car emissions enough to reduce acid rain.
   (2) The province will not be able to enforce their controls on industrial and vehicle emissions.
   (3) It is possible to reduce industrial emissions but not vehicle emissions.
   (4) The emissions that cause acid rain in the province probably originate in some other place.
   (5) The amount of acid rain that falls depends mostly on climate, not emissions.

3. What is the likely effect of acid rain pollution of streams and lakes?

   (1) damage to aquatic organisms
   (2) increased industrial emissions
   (3) increased pollution upstream
   (4) reduced industrial emissions
   (5) reduced pollution upstream

4. When an organism dies, its complex organic compounds are broken down into simpler substances. Large decomposers such as earthworms break down large pieces of dead matter so that smaller decomposers such as fungi and bacteria can complete the process, releasing carbon dioxide, nitrates, phosphates, and other substances into the environment.

   Decomposition is most similar to which of the following human body processes?

   (1) respiration
   (2) urination
   (3) circulation
   (4) digestion
   (5) locomotion

Questions 5 and 6 refer to the following paragraph and diagram.

In a single-pulley system, the load moves the same distance as the rope that is pulled. A pulley does not increase the effort force, but it changes its direction. Instead of lifting something up, you are pulling something down.

HOW A SINGLE PULLEY WORKS

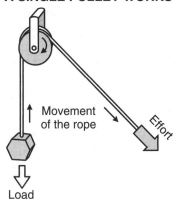

5. Which information would you need in order to calculate the distance the load moves in this pulley system?

    (1) size of the pulley wheel
    (2) distance the rope is pulled
    (3) weight of the load
    (4) effort force
    (5) total length of the rope

6. In an ideal single-pulley system, the effort equals the load. In real life, the effort is always slightly greater than the load. Why?

    (1) The distance pulled on the rope is equal to the distance the load moves.
    (2) The distance pulled on the rope is greater than the distance the load moves.
    (3) The distance pulled on the rope is less than the distance the load moves.
    (4) As the load moves up, it becomes heavier, so the rope puller exerts more effort.
    (5) The friction from the pulley wheel must be overcome by the effort used in pulling the rope.

7. Most of the heat energy from gasoline-powered engines is not converted to mechanical energy. Instead, it is wasted.

    Based on this information, why is the temperature on heavily travelled streets higher than the temperature on streets with less traffic?

    (1) The heavily travelled streets absorb more sunlight than the less travelled streets.
    (2) Heat released from many cars raises the temperature of heavily travelled streets.
    (3) The wearing away of road surfaces increases the heat on heavily travelled streets.
    (4) Heavily travelled streets have fewer trees to provide shade.
    (5) More heat-generating industries are near heavily travelled streets.

8. Power is the rate at which work is done. A 75 kg man is pulled down by gravity with a force of 750 N (newtons). If the man climbs a staircase that is 3 m high, he does $750 \times 3 = 2250$ J (joules) of work. If he can run up the stairs in only 3 s, then his power is $2250/3 = 750$ J/s, or 750 W (watts), which is almost exactly one horsepower.

    Horsepower is used to describe the power of an engine. In cars, engines that produce more horsepower can carry a greater load and can accelerate into traffic more easily. However, these engines use more fuel than lower-horsepower engines.

    Which of the following situations would be most likely to require you to replace a low-horsepower car with one that has a more powerful engine?

    (1) You changed jobs and now drive a longer distance to work.
    (2) You want to save money on fuel.
    (3) You are moving to a place that gets a lot of snow and are concerned about driving on slippery roads.
    (4) Your new job requires you to transport heavy supplies in your car.
    (5) You are concerned about air pollution.

Questions 9 through 11 refer to the following passage and diagram.

The major organ of the circulatory system is the heart, which pumps blood throughout the body. The right and left sides of the heart are divided by a wall called the septum. Each side is divided into two chambers called the atria and the ventricles.

Oxygen-poor blood from the body enters the right atrium through large veins called the venae cavae. When the atrium contracts, it forces the blood into the right ventricle. Next the right ventricle contracts, forcing the blood into the pulmonary arteries, which carry it to the lungs. In the lungs the blood picks up oxygen. The oxygen-rich blood then flows through the pulmonary veins and back to the heart where it enters the left atrium. The left atrium contracts and forces the blood into the left ventricle. As the left ventricle contracts, it forces the blood into a large artery called the aorta. From the aorta, blood flows into a system of blood vessels that carry it throughout the body.

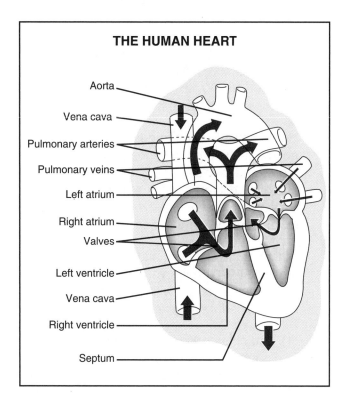

THE HUMAN HEART

Aorta

Vena cava

Pulmonary arteries

Pulmonary veins

Left atrium

Right atrium

Valves

Left ventricle

Vena cava

Right ventricle

Septum

9. Which chamber sends blood from the heart through the body?

(1) the right ventricle
(2) the right atrium
(3) the left ventricle
(4) the left atrium
(5) the venae cavae

10. What would be most likely to happen if the aorta were partially blocked?

(1) Too much blood would enter the left ventricle.
(2) Not enough oxygen-poor blood would enter the heart.
(3) Oxygen-poor blood would not be able to reach the lungs.
(4) The body would not get enough oxygen-rich blood.
(5) Oxygen-rich blood would enter the venae cavae.

11. Which of the following does the writer assume the reader already knows?

(1) The arteries and veins are blood vessels, and they are part of the circulatory system.
(2) The atria are the upper chambers of the heart, and the ventricles are the lower chambers.
(3) The pulmonary veins carry blood from the lungs to the left atrium of the heart.
(4) The septum separates the left and right sides of the heart.
(5) In the heart, blood flows from the atria to the ventricles.

When referring to information on a diagram, think about everything you know that may relate to the topic. Apply your own knowledge as you read the new information.

Question 12 refers to the following information and diagram.

In deserts, wind-blown sand is one of the main agents of erosion. Continuous "blasting" and battering by sand particles wears away the base of rocks, as shown in the diagram.

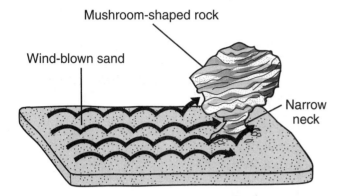

Mushroom-shaped rock

Wind-blown sand

Narrow neck

12. Why does the action of wind and sand affect the base of the rock rather than the top?

(1) Because of its weight, most sand is blown near the ground.
(2) The base of the rock is made of softer material than the top.
(3) Water has already partially eroded the base of the rock.
(4) The top of the rock is protected by rising warm air.
(5) The top of the rock may eventually topple off the base.

13. Igneous rock is a type of rock that forms when magma cools and solidifies. Which of the following conclusions is supported by this information?

(1) Limestone forms from the remains of shells and skeletons.
(2) Limestone turns to marble under great heat and pressure.
(3) Sandstone, formed from cemented sand particles, is an igneous rock.
(4) Rocks formed under great heat and pressure are igneous rocks.
(5) Rocks of volcanic origin are igneous rocks.

Questions 14 and 15 refer to the following map.

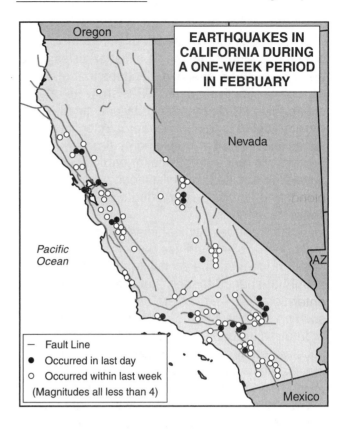

EARTHQUAKES IN CALIFORNIA DURING A ONE-WEEK PERIOD IN FEBRUARY

Oregon

Nevada

Pacific Ocean

AZ

— Fault Line
● Occurred in last day
○ Occurred within last week
(Magnitudes all less than 4)

Mexico

14. Based on the map, which part of California had the most earthquake activity in the last day of the period shown?

(1) the region bordering Oregon
(2) north central California
(3) south central California
(4) the region bordering Nevada
(5) the region bordering Mexico

15. Which of the following conclusions is supported by the information in the map?

(1) Earthquakes rarely occur during the winter in California.
(2) Some California earthquakes had a magnitude of 6 that week.
(3) Many earthquakes were not recorded by seismic stations.
(4) Earthquakes are a common occurrence in California.
(5) All the California earthquakes were felt by the general population.

Questions 16 through 18 refer to the following passage.

At the beginning of the twentieth century, scientists thought that the smallest particles were the protons, neutrons, and electrons that make up atoms. However, in the 1920s showers of subatomic particles produced by cosmic rays were detected in the atmosphere. Scientists soon realized that protons and neutrons were themselves made up of smaller particles named quarks. In addition, scientists found evidence of a category of force-carrying subatomic particles known as bosons.

To study subatomic particles such as quarks and bosons, scientists use particle accelerators. These huge machines consist of ring- or doughnut-shaped tunnels that are kilometres in circumference. An accelerator launches particles such as protons into the ring. As they travel the kilometres around the ring, the particles are accelerated almost to the speed of light. Then they arrive at the detector, where they collide with other particles. When particles collide, they release energy that immediately turns into new particles of matter. By analyzing the collisions that take place in particle accelerators, scientists help prove or disprove the latest theories about the structure of matter and the forces that bind matter.

Today, two of the largest particle accelerators are engaged in a race. Scientists at Fermi National Accelerator Laboratory (Fermilab) in Illinois and the European Laboratory for Particle Physics (CERN) in Switzerland all hope to be the first to prove the existence of the Higgs boson. Scientists have predicted that the interactions of Higgs bosons are what give matter its mass. A great deal of energy is required to produce a Higgs boson in a particle collision. So far neither accelerator has been able to generate sufficient energy to produce direct evidence that the Higgs boson exists.

16. Based on the passage, which subatomic particles are protons and neutrons made of?

(1) cosmic rays
(2) quarks
(3) bosons
(4) Higgs bosons
(5) electrons

17. Suppose that a collision in an accelerator briefly produces a subatomic particle that carries a force called a gluon. What type of particle is a gluon?

(1) cosmic ray
(2) quark
(3) boson
(4) neutron
(5) electron

18. Particle accelerators are huge, complex machines that are controversial because they are usually built with public funds. Which of the following arguments would be used by a person favouring the building of a new accelerator?

(1) An accelerator would occupy land better put to other uses.
(2) The collisions in an accelerator could pose a hazard to people in the area.
(3) The cost of an accelerator greatly outweighs its benefits.
(4) Scientists should be investigating matters with immediate practical applications.
(5) Understanding subatomic particles may lead to advances in technology.

Tip

Values are often reflected in fact-opinion and support-for-conclusion type questions. Values are often a clue to opinion.

Question 19 refers to the diagram and the paragraph below.

BACTERIAL CELL

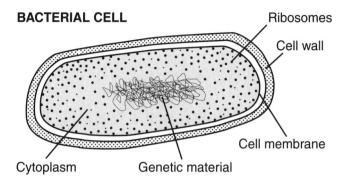

Bacteria are one-celled organisms. Bacterial cells are much smaller than animal and plant cells, and they do not have a nucleus. Like plant cells, bacterial cells have cell walls.

19. Which of the following statements is supported by information in both the diagram and the paragraph?

    (1) Plant and animal cells are smaller than bacterial cells.
    (2) There are no ribosomes in the cytoplasm of a bacterial cell.
    (3) Bacterial cells have a cell membrane but no cell wall.
    (4) Bacterial cells have genetic material but no nucleus.
    (5) Unlike plant and animal cells, bacterial cells do not have cytoplasm.

20. When organisms reproduce sexually, their reproductive cells have half the number of chromosomes found in nonreproductive cells.

    Reproductive cells have a reduced number of chromosomes to allow organisms to reproduce in which of the following ways?

    (1) by splitting in half
    (2) from a single reproductive cell
    (3) by combining its reproductive cell with that of another organism of the same species
    (4) by combining two reproductive cells with two from another organism of the same species
    (5) by combining nonreproductive cells

21. In normal cells, the tips of the chromosomes shrink a tiny bit each time the cell divides. In cancer cells, the tips of the chromosomes are longer than those of normal cells. Cancer is a disease in which cells divide in a rapid, chaotic way.

    What is the unstated main idea of this paragraph?

    (1) When normal cells divide, their chromosomes become shorter.
    (2) The tips of the chromosomes may play a role in the rate of cell division.
    (3) The structure of the chromosome does not influence the rate of cell division.
    (4) Cancer cells multiply very rapidly.
    (5) Normal cells multiply faster than cancer cells.

22. The drawings below show some types of cells in the human body. Which of the following cells is likely to line the passages inside your nose, using hair-like structures called cilia to filter out dust?

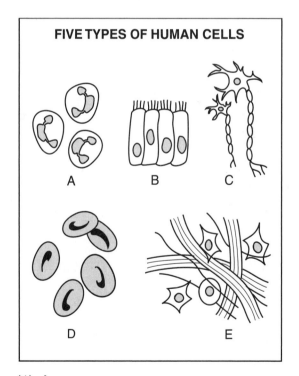

    (1) A
    (2) B
    (3) C
    (4) D
    (5) E

Answers start on page 795.

LANGUAGE ARTS, READING

The GED Language Arts, Reading Test will cover the following content and skills.

The Test

- 40 multiple-choice questions
- 65 minutes to complete

The Content

Literary texts including
- Poetry
- Drama
- Prose fiction before 1920
- Prose fiction 1920–1960
- Prose fiction after 1960

Nonfiction texts including
- Nonfiction prose
- Critical reviews
- Business documents

The Questions

- Comprehension
- Application
- Analysis
- Synthesis

Improving your reading skills is important preparation for meeting your future goals. When you read, you explore ideas expressed by others, whether you find these ideas in a novel, on a Web site, in a newspaper, or in a business document. Reading makes you think—it helps you to analyze ideas and encourages you to apply them. These are the same skills need for the Language Arts, Reading Test: understanding the text, analyzing and applying what you read, and formulating new ideas. As well, these are the skills that are essential for your success and vital for a lifetime of learning and exploration.

Study Tip

Review is a good way to build your confidence.

As you decide what you want to study and when, set aside some time for reviewing materials you have already studied.

- Build review time into your schedule.
- Prioritize material for review, based on when assignments are due and tests are scheduled.
- Gather everything that you need for the review, such as texts and class notes.
- Make note of concepts that seem difficult.
- Briefly go over material from earlier units.
- Create graphic aids such as tables and circle graphs to help you summarize material.
- Consider reviewing with others studying the same material.

Interpreting Nonfiction

You probably read several types of nonfiction materials on a regular basis. Nonfiction materials include newspapers, magazines, textbooks, biographies, TV and movie reviews, manuals, and business documents. Their purpose is to convey information. Writing that explains how to do something or gives information is one of the most common types of reading material. In the workplace, for instance, you may have to refer to an employee manual to help you understand a policy relating to your job. At home, you may have to read directions to use your new compact disc player.

The GED Language Arts, Reading Test will include several nonfiction passages to determine how well you understand these forms of writing. Overall, nonfiction materials are the basis for 25 percent of the questions on the GED Reading Test.

Finding the Main Idea and Supporting Details

When you understand the **main idea** of a piece of writing, you understand the most important point a writer makes. The main idea can be stated at the beginning, middle, or end of a paragraph or passage.

In many paragraphs, the main idea is stated in a single sentence, the **topic sentence.** The topic sentence is often located at the beginning or at the end of a paragraph. If it is at the beginning, the rest of the sentences in the paragraph add details that support or explain the main idea. If the topic sentence is at the end, the **supporting details** are given first and then summed up in the topic sentence.

In some forms of nonfiction, the main idea is not stated at all. The reader must **infer,** or figure out, the meaning by putting together the details the author provides.

main idea
the most important idea or point in a piece of writing

topic sentence
the sentence that contains the main idea

supporting details
information that supports or explains the main idea

infer
to figure out the meaning by using clues

 Tip Pay attention to headlines or titles; they usually contain key ideas.

GED Practice

Directions: Choose the one best answer to each question.

Questions 1 through 4 refer to the following excerpt from an article.

WHAT'S SO SPECIAL ABOUT NEWS MAGAZINES?

Beyond the bottom line, Wall Street doesn't much care about editorial quality; journalists do and others should. Not because journalism is perfect, but because
(5)   it isn't.
News magazines come at the end of the food chain of journalism. First radio reports the news hourly, then the evening television news repeats it and adds
(10)   pictures. Newspapers fill out the story in greater detail. Finally the news magazine comes along to summarize and analyze it. By that time the reader may be suffering an acute case of information glut. It takes
(15)   wit, reflection, a gift for compression, some fresh reporting or consultation with experts, and an original turn of mind to add something new. The real job of the news magazine is to help the reader to make
(20)   sense out of his times. Those who can do this, the best of them, form a shaggy group of contentious minds.

Thomas Griffith, "What's So Special About News Magazines?" *Newsweek.*

1. Which of the following is the best restatement of the phrase "Not because journalism is perfect, but because it isn't" (lines 3–5)?

   (1) Most journalists do not care about editorial quality.
   (2) Attention to editorial quality may help improve earnings.
   (3) Good journalists do not waste time trying to be perfect.
   (4) Attention to editorial quality may help improve journalism.
   (5) Good journalists pay attention to how many people buy magazines.

2. What is the main idea of the second paragraph of the excerpt (lines 6–22)?

   (1) It takes hard work to make a good news magazine.
   (2) Other media report stories before news magazines do.
   (3) News magazines are a collection of news reports.
   (4) News magazines often contain opposing points of view.
   (5) News magazines summarize and analyze the news.

3. Why is the statement "suffering an acute case of information glut" (lines 13–14) an effective use of figurative language?

   (1) It describes how the reader makes sense of the world.
   (2) It suggests that there is too much news on TV.
   (3) It reminds the reader of having an upset stomach from overeating.
   (4) It suggests that readers need to find new sources of information.
   (5) It implies that magazine readers should stop watching television news programs.

4. Which organizational pattern does the author use to describe the four news media that make up journalism (lines 6–12)?

   (1) chronological order—explaining the order in which the media cover the news
   (2) classification—grouping similar ideas together
   (3) comparison and contrast—finding similarities and differences among media
   (4) cause and effect—finding the connections between events and their causes
   (5) hierarchy—ranking media in terms of which is more important

Questions 5 through 8 refer to the following excerpt from an article.

WHAT GOES ON AT THE COUNTY FAIR?

The crafts judges form a sorority of expert peers, most from out of county. Several have been to the judging school at the Augusta Presbyterian Church, with
(5) cards to prove it. Unwary novice judges are assigned to cookies, jellies, and jams. Hundreds of sweet things are entered: platters of brownies, cakes, jams, and jellies. You'd think it would be fun tasting
(10) them, until you thought twice. The jelly judges did stay for lunch afterwards (thanks to the Highland Girl Scouts), but they hardly ate a thing.

Sewing judges sit at a table while
(15) assistants bring them garments to inspect for fabric grain lines, stitching, suitable thread, smooth darts, pleats, tucks, gathers, and facings. One lady holds up a black-and-white checked child's jumper.
(20) "Oh, look, she's covered the buttons."

The second judge turns a sundress pocket inside out to inspect the stitching. "What do you do when they're both nice?" The senior judge says, "You get to
(25) nitpicking," and she awards first prize to the jumper. "I don't know how it is other places, but in Highland County, covered buttons are *it*." …

The canned vegetable judges look for a
(30) perfect seal and a nice-looking ring and label. The liquid should be free of sediment and bubbles. The color should be natural, pieces must be uniform and of good quality. Mildred Detamore holds a jar of
(35) stewed tomatoes up to the light and sighs, "The tomatoes are so much seedier this year. It's because of the drought."

Donald McCaig, "The Best Four Days in Highland County," *An American Homeplace.*

5. The author uses the quote "You get to nitpicking" (lines 24–25) to suggest which of the following?

(1) The senior judge is a picky person.
(2) Covered buttons are an important feature of all garments.
(3) A judge may award a prize based upon some small point.
(4) The sewing judges often like two garments equally well.
(5) Small details are not the most important aspect of a garment.

6. What was most likely the deciding factor in awarding the first prize to the black-and-white child's jumper?

(1) its fine stitches
(2) its smooth darts
(3) its covered buttons
(4) its overall appearance
(5) the grain lines on its fabric

7. What does the author's use of the word "sighs" (line 35) suggest?

(1) The judge is tired of tasting samples.
(2) Judging is hard work and often boring.
(3) The judge thinks that the jar is defective.
(4) The judge is dissatisfied with this year's crop.
(5) The judge will not get paid for all her work.

8. Which of the following is the best description of the style in which this article is written?

(1) dry and scholarly
(2) informal and casual
(3) complex and technical
(4) formal and scientific
(5) lighthearted and comical

Answers start on page 799.

Summarizing Major Ideas

You read workplace documents and other types of nonfiction materials to find information that you need. When you **summarize** the important ideas in what you read, you are actively translating these ideas into information you can use. Summarizing is often called an "active reading strategy."

You have probably summarized the important ideas in informational material quite often without realizing it. Imagine, for example, that you receive a memo at work about new safety regulations. One of your co-workers asks you what the memo says. You might reply, "It says that we are now required to wear ear plugs whenever we are on the shop floor." You have effectively summarized the main points of the memo without giving all the details.

summarize
to express the main points of a piece of writing in your own words

Read the following excerpt from a memo and complete the exercise below.

Effective June 1, the ABC Company will offer all regular full-time employees medical and dental coverage. "Full time" constitutes a 37.5-hour work week. Coverage takes effect on the first day of the month following three months of continuous, active employment. Employees should select the coverage they want by filling out the attached form. Health coverage is for Single or Family. Dental coverage is Single, Couple, or Family. There is no deductible for the Health Plan, but the deductible for Dental is $25 per individual, $25 per family per calendar year for Major Services only. For more information, please read the attached material and contact Human Resources with any questions.

When you summarize what you read, try to answer these questions about the major points that were made: *Who? What? Where? When? Why?* and *How?*

Headings are often used to summarize the main points in informational materials. Put a check mark by the heading that would <u>better</u> summarize the major ideas of this memo.

_____ a. Two New Healthcare Plans Are Available for Full-Time Employees

_____ b. Annual Deductibles for Healthcare Plans for Individuals and Families

You are correct if you chose *option a*. This heading summarizes the main points of the memo. *Option b* contains details, but not the most important information.

GED Practice

Directions: Choose the one best answer to each question.

Questions 1 through 3 refer to the following excerpt from a company notice.

WHY IS THIS LAW IMPORTANT?

All employees must be informed of the law regarding health benefits for ex-employees.

(5) As an employer of more than 20 people, Jetstream Airways is required by law to let "qualified beneficiaries" keep their health insurance after separation from the company due to certain "qualifying events."

(10) A qualified beneficiary is a current or former employee covered under a group health plan, his or her spouse, dependent child, or a child born to or adopted by the employee when covered. For a covered employee, a "qualifying event" is voluntary

(15) or involuntary termination (except if fired for gross misconduct), reduction in hours of employment, or filing of bankruptcy by the employer. For a spouse or dependent child, it means the employee's loss of

(20) employment, the covered employee's death, a spouse's divorce or legal separation from the covered employee, a dependent's loss of dependent status, or the employer's filing of a bankruptcy

(25) proceeding.

Covered employees must be told of their rights when hired and upon leaving Jetstream Airways. Coverage can last up to 18 months for a termination or reduction in

(30) working hours, up to 29 months for certain qualified beneficiaries with disabilities, and up to 36 months for divorce or separation.

Once coverage is elected, qualified beneficiaries are required to pay a

(35) premium, which includes a nominal administration fee, on the first day of the month for which coverage applies.

1. Which of the following reasons would most likely disqualify an employee for coverage under this policy?

   (1) bankruptcy of the company
   (2) job loss due to downsizing
   (3) adoption of a child
   (4) quitting one's job
   (5) theft of a computer

2. Which statement best summarizes this excerpt?

   (1) The company has clear policies for dealing with ex-employees.
   (2) Ex-employees can often retain their health insurance after leaving.
   (3) Qualified ex-employees and their dependents can retain their health insurance.
   (4) Employees have rights, including the right to health insurance.
   (5) The government is concerned about the rising cost of medical care.

3. Which of the following inferences about health insurance laws is supported by the excerpt?

   (1) Dependents under age 21 who are not in school lose coverage.
   (2) Companies with fewer than 20 employees are exempt.
   (3) Covered employees cannot keep their insurance when they take a new job.
   (4) Ex-employees must pay enormous premiums to retain their coverage.
   (5) Illnesses occurring after an employee leaves a company are not covered.

Answers start on page 799.

Language Arts, Reading • Interpreting Nonfiction

Restating Information

You can show you understand something you read by **restating** it in your own words. This is an active reading strategy that you can use to deepen and reinforce your understanding of written materials. You use this skill often in daily life. For example, imagine that you are helping a friend assemble his new desk. You read "Insert dowel A into hole A." Your friend asks you to explain the directions more clearly, so you say, "Put the long peg in the hole that connects the desk top to the desk side." You have just restated information.

Read the following excerpt from an article and complete the exercise below.

Despite the flashiness of the Web, e-mail is and has always been the primary reason most people go online, followed by research, according to a survey by Louis Harris & Associates. More than 1.6 billion noncommercial e-mail messages are sent each day in the United States, which is nearly three times the number of first-class postal mailings, according to an analysis by eMarketer, an Internet market research firm in New York City.

It's easy to see why. E-mail is cheaper and faster than a letter, less intrusive than a phone call, and more flexible than a fax. You can e-mail at work, school, and home, 24 hours a day, exchanging not only text but also photos, voice messages, and even video.

Reid Goldsborough, "We've All Got E-Mail," *The Editorial Eye.*

1. Put a check mark next to one of the following statements that <u>better</u> restates the main idea of this excerpt?

    _____ a. E-mail is not being used to its fullest potential.

    _____ b. E-mail is superior to many other communication methods.

2. The second sentence of the second paragraph lists three reasons for the popularity of e-mail. Write each of the reasons next to its correct two-word restatement below.

    a. more efficient: _____

    b. more welcome: _____

    c. more adaptable: _____

You are correct if you chose *option b* for question 1. For question 2 the correct answers are: a. *cheaper and faster than a letter,* b. *less intrusive than a phone call,* and c. *more flexible than a fax.*

restating
showing that you understand something by putting it into your own words

To restate ideas, find the main idea of a piece of writing and then put it in words that make the most sense to you.

GED Practice

Directions: Choose the <u>one best answer</u> to each question.

Questions 1 through 4 refer to the following excerpt from an article.

WHAT IS A BILL GATES BILL?

Consider that Bill Gates, whose personal net worth has recently soared to over $40 billion, made this money in the twenty-two years or so since he founded
(5) Microsoft. If we presume that he has worked fourteen hours a day on every business day since then, that means he's been making money at a staggering $500,000 per hour, or about $150 per
(10) second. This, in turn, means that if Bill Gates saw or dropped a $500 bill on the ground, it wouldn't be worth his time to take the four seconds required to bend over and pick it up.
(15) The "Too-small-a-bill-for-Bill" index has risen dramatically over the years. When Microsoft went public in 1986, the new multimillionaire would have lost out by leaving behind anything but $5 bills. And I
(20) can remember speaking to him at a conference in 1993, thinking, "$31 per second, $31 per second" as we talked.
Another way to examine this staggering net worth is to compare it with that of an
(25) average American of reasonable but modest wealth. Perhaps she has a net worth of $100,000. Mr. Gates's net worth is 400,000 times larger. Which means that to Bill, $100,000 (her entire net worth) is
(30) like 25 cents. You can work out the right multiplier for your own net worth. So, a new Lamborghini Diablo, which we think of as costing $250,000, would be 63 cents in Bill Gates dollars. And that fully loaded,
(35) multimedia, active-matrix 233-MHz laptop with the 1024 × 768 screen? A penny. A nice home in a rich town like Palo Alto, California? $2. You might be able to buy a plane ticket on a Boeing 747 for $1,200,
(40) full-fare coach. In Bill bills, Mr. Gates could buy three 747s: one for him, one for his wife, Melinda, and one for young Jennifer Katharine.

Brad Templeton, "It's Net Worth It," "Bill Gates Wealth Index."

1. What does the author mean by the statement, "The 'Too-small-a-bill-for-Bill' index has risen dramatically over the years" (lines 15–16)?

   (1) Gates is worth more, so his time is more valuable.
   (2) Gates has to work more to earn more.
   (3) Gates has become more generous with his money.
   (4) Gates will probably earn less in the future.
   (5) Gates earns much more than the average North American earns.

2. What is the tone of this article?

   (1) congratulatory
   (2) envious
   (3) critical
   (4) disgusted
   (5) humorous

3. What does the author mean by the statement "her entire net worth is like 25 cents" (lines 29–30)?

   (1) Gates treats others as if they are not worth very much.
   (2) The average person cannot afford luxury items.
   (3) Gates spends fortunes without a second thought.
   (4) Modest wealth seems like pocket change to Gates.
   (5) Most people do not save enough money.

4. Based on the excerpt, which approach would the author <u>most likely</u> use to describe the distance from Earth to the moon?

   (1) He would use highly technical language.
   (2) He would make comparisons.
   (3) He would use exaggeration for emphasis.
   (4) He would describe different viewpoints.
   (5) He would state the information matter-of-factly.

Language Arts, Reading • Interpreting Nonfiction

Questions 5 through 8 refer to the following product warranty statement.

WHAT DOES THIS WARRANTY DO?

CYBERTECH COMPUTER TECHNOLOGIES, INC. warrants that this product is free from defective materials or
(5) defects in factory work and will replace or repair this unit or any part thereof, if it proves to be defective in normal use or service within one year from the date of original purchase. Our obligation under this
(10) warranty is the repair or replacement of the defective instrument or any part thereof. This warranty will be considered void if the unit is tampered with, improperly serviced, or subjected to misuse, negligence, or
(15) accidental damage. There are no other express warranties other than those stated herein.

EXCLUSIONS: This limited warranty does not apply to repairs or replacement necessitated by any cause beyond
(20) the control of Cybertech Computer Technologies including, but not limited to, any malfunction, defects, or failures that in the opinion of the Company are caused by or resulting from unauthorized service
(25) or parts, improper maintenance, operation contrary to furnished instructions, shipping or transit accidents, modification or repair by the user, abuse, misuse, neglect, accident, fire, flood or natural disasters,
(30) incorrect line voltage, cosmetic damages, defaced or removed parts, and normal wear and tear.

The limited warranty does not apply to damage that occurs during unpacking,
(35) setup, or installation; removal of the product for repair; or reinstallation of the product after repair.

At the Company's discretion, a labour charge may be assessed on products
(40) returned for Limited Warranty repairs in which no fault is found.

This warranty gives you specific legal rights, and you may also have other rights, which vary from province to province.

5. Which of the following best expresses the main idea of the second paragraph?

   (1) Any customer who breaks a computer must purchase it.
   (2) The warranty applies only to manufacturing defects.
   (3) The warranty is no good if the purchaser breaks the computer.
   (4) The warranty applies only to repairs beyond the control of Cybertech.
   (5) Purchasers must treat the computer with great care.

6. What is the purpose of this warranty statement?

   (1) to describe the conditions under which the company will replace or repair the product
   (2) to exempt the company from responsibility for replacing or repairing the product
   (3) to guarantee that purchasers will be completely satisfied
   (4) to serve as proof that the product passed a careful inspection before it was sold
   (5) to explain that the manufacturer will provide no refunds or exchanges

7. For the manufacturer to honour the warranty, which of the following criteria is the purchaser most likely to have to meet?

   (1) be a resident of Canada
   (2) furnish proof of the date of purchase
   (3) show that the product was defective
   (4) return the product to the place of purchase
   (5) complete a questionnaire about buying habits

8. Which words best describe the style of this document?

   (1) informal and conversational
   (2) vague and misleading
   (3) harsh and threatening
   (4) boring and repetitive
   (5) formal and legal

Answers start on page 800.

Applying Ideas

Applying ideas means taking information that you read and using it. For example, when you follow the steps of a recipe to make a certain dish, you are taking the words and putting them into action—in other words, you are applying ideas. A number of reading materials that you encounter in daily life require you to use this skill.

Read the following excerpt from an employee orientation manual and complete the exercise below.

One of the major benefit changes that takes effect on the first day of January is the company's match of employees' contributions to their RRSP account. The reason for this benefit is to encourage employees to contribute to their own retirement accounts beyond what the company contributes. Employees can do so by making elective deferrals from their paycheques to their RRSP accounts. For every dollar invested up to 1 percent of your base salary over the next year, the company will match it with a dollar. This represents an immediate 100 percent return on your investment. For every dollar that you invest up to the next 1 percent of your base salary the company will match it with 50 cents—a 50 percent return on your investment. All contributions are made on a pretax basis.

applying ideas
the ability to take information you read and transfer it to a new situation

1. Fill in the blanks with the correct word from the list below.

   bank   money   RRSP   paycheque

   On the basis of this excerpt, an elective deferral is

   _____ that is taken out of your

   _____ each pay period and deposited

   in your _____ account.

Applying ideas is a two-step process. Step 1: Make sure you understand the main idea or supporting details. Step 2: Apply that information to the new situation you are given.

2. Which of the following activities is similar to an elective deferral?
   _____ a. regular withdrawals from a savings account
   _____ b. regular meetings with an investment counsellor
   _____ c. regular deposits to a savings account

3. What other account would have the same purpose as an RRSP?
   _____ a. savings account
   _____ b. chequing account
   _____ c. government bonds
   _____ d. individual retirement account
   _____ e. stocks

You are correct if you wrote *money, paycheque,* and *RRSP* for question 1. The answer to question 2 is *option c* because both involve saving money regularly. The answer to question 3 is *option d;* both individual retirement accounts and RRSP accounts involve saving money for retirement.

GED Practice

Directions: Choose the <u>one best answer</u> to each question.

<u>Questions 1 through 4</u> refer to the following excerpt from an article.

WHY IS THE "WORLD WIDE WEB" A GOOD NAME FOR THE INTERNET?

The World Wide Web represents the greatest resource of information that the world has ever known. But without some preparation, Web searching can be a little

(5) like wandering in a library during a power outage—you know your answers are nearby, but you can't find them.

In order to fully utilize the search capacities of the Web, you've got to be

(10) familiar with the tools that are available, and you must have a solid understanding of how to prepare a search. Spending a few wise moments before you hit that "Submit" key can make all the difference.

(15) **The Search Engine**

Unlike your friendly neighborhood library, there's no Dewey Decimal System awaiting you on-line—just a collection of documents that experts say will soon

(20) reach 1 billion in number. The Web isn't indexed in any standard manner, either, so finding information can seem a daunting task. That's what makes the search engine such an essential tool. Search engines are

(25) the tools that find documents in response to a submitted query. Each engine maintains its own database created by computer programs or "robots." Also called "spiders," these programs travel along the

(30) Web (hence the nickname) locating new sites, updating old ones and removing obsolete ones from the database. In performing your search, they use both a title and a location technique: Pages

(35) containing your search-words (or keywords) in the title are considered most relevant.

Art Daudelin, "Keys to Effective Web Searching," *Physicians Financial News.*

1. Which of the following summarizes the main idea of this excerpt?

   (1) how the Web got its name
   (2) how to get a computer job
   (3) how to search the Web
   (4) how to create a search engine
   (5) how the Web is replacing the library

2. If you wanted information about jobs in cooking, which keywords would be the <u>most</u> helpful in getting results?

   (1) cooking techniques
   (2) job opportunities
   (3) food service opportunities
   (4) French cooking schools
   (5) catering services

3. Based on the information in this excerpt, which of the following inferences can you make about searching the Web?

   (1) The Web is a huge search engine.
   (2) No two search engines are alike.
   (3) The Web is an electronic library.
   (4) Updating Web sites is nearly impossible.
   (5) Word frequency is not an important searching technique.

4. Based on the information in the article, which of the following types of titles would attract the greatest number of interested searchers to a particular Web page?

   (1) a humorous title that makes readers laugh
   (2) a title consisting of a one-word summary of the page
   (3) a title containing a few important words from the page
   (4) a title with vivid, poetic words
   (5) a general, nonspecific title

Questions 5 through 7 refer to the following excerpt from an employee benefits guide.

WHAT ARE THE FEATURES OF THIS PLAN?

The Company is pleased and proud to announce the addition of vision benefits to our already exceptional benefits package. We pride ourselves on being one of the

(5) most progressive and employee-friendly companies to work for in Canada. Our motto is "We take care of our employees, and they take care of us!" With this in mind, we have added the following

(10) benefits. Please review these benefits carefully. If you have any questions, contact the Human Resources Department.

The Company will enroll in the EyeCare

(15) Vision Plan, one of the largest networks in the metropolitan area. All employees who are current enrollees in the Company's medical plan will automatically be covered. In order to accomplish this, the Company

(20) will be increasing each employee's health insurance premium by $10 per month, or $120 per year. The plan requires the payment of a $50 yearly deductible per family, after which the network pays

(25) 90 percent of the covered charges.

In order to receive the 90 percent co-insurance provision, employees must use the ophthalmologists, optometrists, or opticians who participate in the EyeCare

(30) network. Employees who elect to use nonparticipating eyecare professionals will be reimbursed at a 75 percent rate.

Under the plan, lens replacement (eyeglasses or contact lens) is allowed

(35) every 12 months, but only if necessary due to a change in prescription or damage to the lenses. Frames may be replaced every 24 months. Laser surgery for purely cosmetic purposes is not covered under

(40) the plan. Please contact Human Resources for an enrollment form, description of benefits, and list of participating vision professionals.

5. Based on the excerpt, which of the following defines a "co-insurance provision" (line 27)?

It is the amount that

(1) the insurance plan pays
(2) the employee's company pays
(3) a second insurer must pay
(4) the employee pays
(5) the optometrist must pay

6. Based on the description of the company in the first paragraph, which of the following is the most likely description of the company's policy on paternity leave (time off from work given to new fathers)?

(1) No paternity leave is granted other than taking accrued sick or personal days.
(2) Up to six months' leave is granted if the father is the primary caretaker.
(3) Paternity leave may be granted for an unlimited period of time.
(4) Paternity leave is granted for biological children only.
(5) Paternity leave is not granted other than as a leave of absence.

7. You can infer that the use of approved eyecare professionals is encouraged by the company for which of the following reasons?

(1) They are more qualified than out-of-network professionals.
(2) The company receives a fee from them for every employee referral.
(3) Their use helps to control insurance costs.
(4) They do not overcharge their patients.
(5) They have received high professional ratings by healthcare authorities.

When applying ideas, look for similarities between the information you read and the situation to which you must apply it.

Answers start on page 801.

Making Inferences

Sometimes when you read nonfiction, facts are only implied or suggested. In such cases you must figure out what the author is saying by using both stated and suggested information. This skill is called **making an inference.**

In Lesson 1, you learned that in some forms of nonfiction writing, the main idea is not directly stated. When the author does not directly state the main idea, you must make an inference to figure it out.

making an inference
using stated and
suggested information
to figure out an
unstated idea

Read the following excerpt from an article and complete the exercise below.

It was the early 1980s. … An expert interviewed for the news piece said that in 20 years, thanks to computers, the average workweek was going to be reduced to 20 hours. The United States was going to become a country of leisure and culture. We were going to have more time on our hands to fulfill our dreams. Computers were going to revolutionize medicine, business, communication, government, education, make our existence easier than we could imagine and rid us of the anxieties that plague us. …

Jump to the present, the year 2000. The personal computer has proliferated. PCs are saturating larger and larger chunks of U.S. households, and Internet companies are dominating the stock market. Computers have paved the way for extraordinary research in genetics and quantum physics and space exploration. And we work more hours, are more harried and more anxious than ever before.

So much for the 20-hour workweek. …

Víctor Landa, "My 20-Hour Workweek Never Arrived," © 2000 Hispanic Link News Service.

To infer the main
idea of a paragraph,
identify the topic
and the details that
support it. By seeing
how the topic and
details are related,
you will be able
to determine the
main idea.

1. Put a check mark next to the implied main idea of this excerpt.

   _____ a. Computers have revolutionized many areas of modern life.

   _____ b. Despite predictions to the contrary, computers have made life busier than ever.

2. Put a check mark next to each detail that helped you answer question 1. You should check more than one.

   _____ a. An expert predicted that computers would reduce the average workweek to 20 hours.

   _____ b. Internet companies play an important role in the stock market.

   _____ c. Today we work more hours than ever before.

You are correct if you chose *option b* for question 1. For question 2, the details that support the main idea are *options a* and *c*.

GED Practice

Directions: Choose the <u>one best answer</u> to each question.

<u>Questions 1 through 3</u> refer to the following excerpt from an opinion piece.

HOW CAN CANADIANS HATE BRIAN MULRONEY SO MUCH AND STILL LOVE JEAN CHRÉTIEN?

I remain puzzled, bewildered, and perplexed as to why Brian Mulroney is arguably the most universally loathed and reviled man in the country … while his
(5) successor, Jean Chrétien, records 60+ percent approval ratings month-in and month-out.

I never particularly warmed to Mulroney myself, but what in the name of Larry did
(10) the man ever do to make Canadians love to hate him with such passion, while conversely demonstrating a perverse willingness to forgive Chrétien virtually anything?

(15) Could it be the GST? In opposition and on the campaign trail, Chrétien vowed repeatedly to abolish the unpopular tax, but embraced it once in power. He even broadened its scope in three of the four
(20) Atlantic Provinces with the Harmonized Sales Tax.

Maybe Free Trade and NAFTA? Opposition Leader Chrétien denounced those too, but then enthusiastically
(25) adopted them as Prime Minister. …

It is a puzzlement.

Perhaps English-speaking Canada's baffling hatred of Mr. Mulroney and its infatuation with Mr. Chrétien is indeed
(30) attributable to the latter's carefully calculated "man-of-the-people" persona vs. public perception of Mulroney as having upper-crust pretensions. As the late American philosopher Richard Weaver
(35) observed, "the adulation of the regular fellow, the political seduction of the common man," is a dominant theme in North American politics, nowhere more so than in Canada. Notwithstanding that Brian
(40) Mulroney has more convincing proletarian roots than Chrétien, the latter is a master at playing the role, while Mulroney was always transparently honest about his personal aspirations. …

(45) I think I've got it. It was Mulroney's closet-full of Gucci shoes that turned the Canadian public against him. I trust that history will be more rational, kinder, and fairer.

© 1998 Charles W. Moore.

1. Which of the following best states the "puzzlement" felt by the author of this opinion piece?
   (1) Why do Canadians passionately love to hate Mulroney?
   (2) Why do Canadians loathe Mulroney yet forgive Chrétien for everything?
   (3) Why did Chrétien adopt Free Trade and NAFTA?
   (4) Why do English-speaking Canadians hate Mulroney, who speaks English well?
   (5) How did a man named Larry make Canadians hate Mulroney?

2. According to the author of this opinion piece, Jean Chrétien gained favour and approval with Canadians because
   (1) He was enthusiastic in adopting policies such as NAFTA.
   (2) He vowed to abolish unpopular policies before he was in power.
   (3) He was humbled at his 60+-percentage approval rating.
   (4) He was a master at role-playing the common-man, or "man-of-the-people."
   (5) He was honest about his goals before being elected.

3. Based on the opinion piece, which of the following can you infer is the author's own view of Brian Mulroney's situation?
   (1) Mulroney is from too much of an upper-crust background.
   (2) Mulroney has not been treated kindly or fairly by the public.
   (3) Mulroney's support of Free Trade and NAFTA made him very unpopular.
   (4) Mulroney has too many designer shoes to be considered a "man-of-the-people."
   (5) Mulroney's introduction of the GST made him very unpopular.

Questions 4 through 6 refer to the following excerpt from an editorial.

WHY ARE THESE BUILDINGS THREATENED?

The buildings in the Washington Square Park area provide a unique glimpse into our city's past.

(5) The tourist-drawing character of this and other downtown neighborhoods is under an increasing threat. Residential construction is booming in the South Loop, West Loop, and Near North Side. In general this is a great thing for our city.

(10) But what if a potential construction site is already occupied by beautiful buildings?

Sadly, this question is sometimes answered by the sound of a wrecking ball. Never mind that a piece of land may

(15) already be occupied by Victorian mansions or an attractive row of Italianate, three-story buildings from the 1870s. In response to such concerns, the new buildings often are made very enticing.

(20) "We'll even make it Art Deco," a developer might say. Or, "How about a Beaux Arts design?"

Given these options, we should keep the 1870s buildings every time. In such

(25) cases, no new building—no matter how elegant the design—can improve on what is already there.

This principle applies to a potential new project at the corner of Dearborn and

(30) Elm Streets in the Washington Square Park area.

One of the development-inducing buzzwords is "under-utilized." You might hear this word in reference to a piece of

(35) land that has not achieved its highest tax-generating potential.

Sure, a new high-rise structure will generate more real estate tax revenue. But when there is demand in the marketplace

(40) for such buildings, they should *first* be placed on *non-historic* sites.

… The rights of property owners should be balanced against the wider public good. This good includes preserving beauty and

(45) history, as well as achieving the related (though sometimes intangible) economic benefits of preservation.

Michael C. Moran, "Saving downtown's gems," *Chicago Tribune.*

4. Which of the following is the <u>best</u> restatement of the last sentence of the excerpt?

   (1) Preserving historic properties brings in sizable tourist dollars.
   (2) Historic preservation is directly related to a city's economic growth.
   (3) The public interest should come before private interests.
   (4) The benefits of preservation can't always be measured in dollars and cents.
   (5) There is no comparison between tax dollars realized and tourist dollars spent.

5. Based on the information in the excerpt, what is <u>most likely</u> the chief concern of real estate developers?

   (1) increasing the city's property tax rolls
   (2) increasing the office space available
   (3) making profits from new building projects
   (4) maintaining the character of the neighbourhoods
   (5) relieving the shortage in affordable housing

6. Which of the following is the overall purpose of this editorial?

   (1) to raise awareness about the importance of preserving historic buildings
   (2) to stimulate tourism by promoting the city's past
   (3) to criticize the city's zoning officials
   (4) to put a stop to all downtown construction
   (5) to impress readers with the author's knowledge of architectural styles

Tip

To figure out an implied main idea, read the entire excerpt. What does the author's attitude seem to be toward the topic? What is the author hinting at? Asking these questions may give you clues that help you determine the main idea.

Answers start on page 801.

Identifying Style and Tone

Style and tone are two important aspects of writing. **Style** is the way a writer writes—the kinds of words he or she chooses and the way the words are arranged to form sentences and paragraphs. Writers choose a style of writing that best fits the subject they are writing about. A writer's style sometimes indicates how he or she feels about the subject. **Tone** results from style. It is the feeling that a writer wants you to get from a piece of writing. It is revealed through word choice and it reflects the author's attitudes and feelings about a subject.

Read the following excerpt from a personal essay and complete the exercise below.

Until I moved to western South Dakota, I did not know about rain, that it could come too hard, too soft, too hot, too cold, too early, too late. That there could be too little at the right time, too much at the wrong time, and vice versa.

I did not know that a light rain coming at the end of a hot afternoon, with the temperature at 100 degrees or more, can literally burn wheat, steaming it on the stalk so it's not worth harvesting.

I had not seen a long, slow rain come at harvest, making grain lying in the swath begin to sprout again, ruining it as a cash crop.

Kathleen Norris, "Rain," from *Dakota.*

style
the way a writer writes—the words and sentence structure used to convey ideas

tone
the writer's attitude as revealed by the words he or she chooses

1. Which of the following characteristics describe the style of the first paragraph? Put a check mark next to all that apply.

_____ a. repetition of a key word

_____ b. short, simple sentences

_____ c. use of the first-person pronoun "I"

_____ d. use of a string of opposites

2. Put a check mark next to the two words that describe the style of this excerpt.

_____ a. technical

_____ b. simple

_____ c. informal

Tip

Listen to the way the words "sound" in your ear. What emotion do they communicate?

3. Which word best describes the tone of the excerpt?

_____ a. serious

_____ b. sarcastic

_____ c. sentimental

You are correct if you checked *options a, c,* and *d* for question 1. The correct answers to question 2 are *options b* and *c;* the correct answer for question 3 is *option a.*

GED Practice

Directions: Choose the <u>one best answer</u> to each question.

Questions 1 through 4 refer to the following excerpt from an essay.

HOW DOES A TEACHER AND POET GRADE HIS STUDENTS?

There are two ways of coming close to poetry. One is by writing poetry. And some people think I want people to write poetry, but I don't; that is, I don't necessarily. I only
(5) want people to write poetry if they want to write poetry. I have never encouraged anybody to write poetry that did not want to write it, and I have not always encouraged those who did want to write it. That ought
(10) to be one's own funeral. It is a hard, hard life, as they say. …
There is another way to come close to poetry, fortunately, and that is in the reading of it, not as linguistics, not as
(15) history, not as anything but poetry. It is one of the hard things for a teacher to know how close a man has come in reading poetry. How do I know whether a man has come close to Keats in reading Keats? It is
(20) hard for me to know. I have lived with some boys a whole year over some of the poets and I have not felt sure whether they have come near what it was all about. One remark sometimes told me.
(25) One remark was their mark for the year; had to be—it was all I got that told me what I wanted to know. And that is enough, if it is the right remark, if it came close enough. I think a man might make twenty
(30) fool remarks if he made one good one some time in the year. His mark would depend on that good remark.

Robert Frost, "Education by Poetry," *The Selected Prose of Robert Frost.*

Look at the types of sentences in an excerpt. Short sentences with strong verbs often indicate an urgent tone.

1. What does Frost mean when he talks about "coming close to poetry" (lines 1–2)?

   (1) being near great poets
   (2) leading a poetic life
   (3) being able to recite poetry
   (4) understanding poetry
   (5) translating poetry

2. On the basis of the excerpt, which of the following <u>best</u> describes what Frost thinks about teaching and understanding poetry?

   (1) Both are inexact and unscientific.
   (2) Both require historical knowledge.
   (3) Both benefit from religious faith.
   (4) Both are a waste of time.
   (5) Both are subjects for linguists.

3. Which of the following statements <u>best</u> sums up Frost's ideas about grading?

   (1) A student who doesn't wish to write poetry will not receive a good mark.
   (2) A student must be exact in his or her understanding of a poem.
   (3) Grading a student's understanding of poetry is difficult and circumstantial.
   (4) A student who makes more than 20 foolish remarks will fail.
   (5) Grading a student's understanding of poetry can sometimes take a whole year.

4. Which of the following phrases <u>best</u> describes the style in which the essay is written?

   (1) formal and informative
   (2) dry and complex
   (3) technical and scientific
   (4) emotional and artistic
   (5) serious and conversational

Answers start on page 802.

Drawing Conclusions

When you **draw conclusions,** you consider the facts presented in a given situation and then think of reasonable explanations for those facts. Consider the following situation: You put a slice of bread in the toaster and push down the lever to toast it. After a minute you come back to find your toaster cold and your bread unbrowned. You unplug the toaster and plug it into a different outlet. This time the toaster works perfectly. Based on the fact that the toaster worked in the second outlet, you conclude that there is a problem with the original outlet.

Read the following excerpt from an article and answer the questions below.

Perhaps we should give a hand to Linda Hamilton's arms. After the "Terminator 2" actress unveiled her buff biceps eight years ago, more and more women ventured where none dared go before, embracing weight lifting, boxing, rock climbing, martial arts and almost every other form of vigorous exercise once known only to man. "There is no gender difference in working out anymore," says Radu, a New York City trainer whose clients include Cindy Crawford. It's not just about vanity—although the possibility of banishing cellulite forever is certainly part of the lure of extreme exercise. Intense workouts also head off osteoporosis and depression and build self-esteem, says Dr. Miriam Nelson, author of "Strong Women Stay Young": "The whole mind-body connection is really there." And there's the lift that comes from knowing that whatever he can do, you can probably do better.

"Living Well," *Newsweek.*

drawing conclusions
making decisions
based on all the facts
provided in a given
situation

To draw a correct conclusion, list all of the available facts and then think of reasonable explanations for them.

1. Which of the following conclusions does this excerpt support?

   ____ a. Intense exercise is the most popular form of exercise among women today.

   ____ b. Intense exercise is good for everyone.

   ____ c. Intense exercise has several benefits for women.

2. Which two details from the excerpt support your choice for question 1?

   _____

   _____

You are correct if you chose *option c* for question 1. Details that you may have written for question 2 include *the possibility of banishing cellulite forever,* and *head off osteoporosis and depression and build self-esteem.*

GED Practice

Directions: Choose the <u>one best answer</u> to each question.

Questions 1 through 4 refer to the following
excerpt from an article.

WHAT IS HAPPENING AT THE ROOSEVELT HOTEL?

By seven o-clock I was dead tired and
soaked with rain and perspiration. I walked
to the Roosevelt, hoping to get a room for
a brief rest. Instead of taking guests,
(5) however, the hotel was busy evacuating
them. There were no lights, and the threat
of explosion from escaping gas had
increased throughout the demolished area.
Another warning of the possibility of a
(10) second tornado had been issued. Fearful
persons jammed the lobby in silent wait for
the next blow.
The Roosevelt switchboard had one
telephone circuit in operation. The operator
(15) called the Raleigh Hotel up the street and
reserved rooms for Roy Miller and me,
although I did not know Roy's whereabouts
at the time. Next time I saw him he said he
had driven to Hillsboro, about thirty-five
(20) miles away, to telephone his wife and
reassure her of his safety. He was fuming.
"I drive seventy miles to call my wife," he
said; "I says, 'Honey, I'm all right. I'm safe.
You don't need to worry any longer.' And
(25) what do I get? She says, 'Who's worried?
You always have been all right. Why do
you have to call me long distance to tell me
so? Roy Miller,' she says, 'what have you
been up to?'" Mrs. Miller had not heard of
(30) the storm.

Ira A. J. Baden as told to Robert H. Parham, "Forty-five
Seconds Inside a Tornado," *Man Against Nature.*

When drawing conclusions, eliminate
explanations that the facts do not support.

1. Which of the following conclusions most
accurately sums up the general situation
described in the excerpt?

    (1) Men worry about what their wives will
        think.
    (2) The Raleigh Hotel had a great deal of
        business during the storm.
    (3) People were reacting to the tornado's
        effects.
    (4) The tornado had shut down phone
        service near the town.
    (5) Tornadoes can cause gas leaks.

2. Why did Mrs. Miller respond to her
husband's phone call the way that she did?

    (1) She was not afraid of tornadoes.
    (2) She was too worried about the
        tornadoes near her to think about her
        husband.
    (3) She did not care about her husband.
    (4) She had slept through the tornado.
    (5) She did not understand why her
        husband had contacted her.

3. Which of the following <u>best</u> describes the
tone of this excerpt?

    (1) suspenseful
    (2) comical
    (3) tragic
    (4) mournful
    (5) playful

4. Which of the following describes the style in
which this excerpt is written?

    It is written in the style of

    (1) an urban legend
    (2) a newspaper article
    (3) an eyewitness account
    (4) a television interview
    (5) a police report

Questions 5 through 7 refer to the following excerpt from an article.

HOW IS THIS SHOW KEPT RUNNING?

Any visitor to the Burbank production offices of "E.R.," the NBC medical drama series, could quickly discern who is the guiding force behind the biggest network
(5) hit in several years.

It is not Michael Crichton, the novelist and screenwriter, who created the show, wrote its pilot episode—and departed almost immediately to write new novels.
(10) It is not Steven Spielberg, whose Amblin Television company took the project to a big studio, Warner Brothers. It is not Leslie Moonves, the president of Warner Brothers Television, which produces the
(15) show for NBC.

It is a man named John Wells, a veteran television scriptwriter, most notably for "China Beach."

At any one moment, Mr. Wells is
(20) supervising the content and execution of at least four one-hour episodes in various stages of development—from script to filming to editing to post-production. Future story lines of the series are also his
(25) responsibility. … In the terms of the trade, Mr. Wells is "E.R." 's show runner.

For the last 10 years at least, the person with that unofficial title has been the true auteur [creator] of series
(30) television. Day to day, a show runner makes all important decisions about the series' scripts, tone, attitude, look and direction. He or she oversees casting, production design and budget. This person
(35) chooses directors and guest stars, defends the show against meddling by the network or production company and, when necessary, changes its course.

Even in this notoriously collaborative
(40) medium, show runners are responsible for what viewers see on the screen. Yet the show runner's true position and influence are unknown to nearly everyone on the other side of the picture tube.

Andy Meisler, "The Man Who Keeps *E.R.'s* Heart Beating," *The New York Times.*

5. Based on this excerpt, which of the following conclusions can be made about producing a television series?

   (1) Show runners and screenwriters share responsibility for a show's success.
   (2) Production companies often interfere with a show's management.
   (3) Show runners are among the most important people in television.
   (4) The creation of a hit show is often a matter of luck.
   (5) Veteran scriptwriters are responsible for television shows.

6. Which of the following responsibilities might a show runner delegate to someone else?

   (1) writing the pilot for a related new show
   (2) hiring actors
   (3) approving the story line for an episode
   (4) reducing actors' salaries
   (5) changing the location of the set

7. Irony can be defined as the difference between what you expect to be true and what actually is true. Which of the following is most ironic in this excerpt?

   (1) The most important person on the set of a TV series is the director.
   (2) The guiding force behind *E.R.* is largely unknown to viewers.
   (3) Show runners do not like to collaborate.
   (4) The show runner supervises more than one show at a time.
   (5) *E.R.* remains one of the most highly watched shows on TV.

Answers start on page 802.

Comparing and Contrasting Ideas

When you **compare** ideas, you look for ways in which they are alike and different. When you **contrast** ideas, you only look for ways in which they are different. Writers often use comparison and contrast as a way to organize ideas based on similarities and differences. Certain words often signal when two things are being compared or contrasted.

Read the following paragraphs and complete the exercise below.

Commercial TV, once the undisputed king of entertainment and information, is facing a serious threat from cable television, and it appears to be losing the battle. With its seemingly endless number of channels, cable TV offers the viewing public an extensive menu of programming, while commercial TV is limited to the warmed-over fare served up by the "big four" networks.

In its effort to capture the interest of the Canadian public, cable TV has excelled at televising programs that are more imaginative, risk-taking, and thoughtful than the insipid, predictable, and insulting shows that commercial TV calls "entertainment." In a feeble effort to compete with a medium that clearly has found its audience, commercial TV has chosen to push the envelope further and further, resulting in shows that have reached new lows in good taste.

compare
to show how things are alike and different

contrast
to show how things are different

These clue words indicate similarities: *and, also, likewise, in addition to, similarly.* These clue words indicate differences: *although, however, yet, but, on the other hand, on the contrary, while, versus, in contrast to, either ... or.*

1. This passage contrasts _____ with

   _____ .

2. What word in the last sentence of the first paragraph signals that a

   contrast is being made? _____

3. List the three words in the second paragraph that describe cable TV and the three words that describe commercial TV.

cable TV	commercial TV
_____	_____
_____	_____
_____	_____

You are correct if you wrote the phrases *commercial TV* and *cable TV* for question 1. For question 2, the word that signals a contrast is *while.* For question 3, you were correct if you listed the words *imaginative, risk-taking,* and *thoughtful* under cable TV and the words *insipid, predictable,* and *insulting* under commercial TV.

GED Practice

Directions: Choose the <u>one best answer</u> for each question.

Questions 1 through 3 refer to the following excerpt from an opionion piece.

HOW DOES THIS MAN FEEL ABOUT THE WEST COAST?

I don't know, call me crazy, call me a coward, but what person in their right mind would live in Los Angeles?

(5) What comes to mind when you think of Los Angeles? Riots. Fires. Six cops beating a man within an inch of his life. Three guys dropping a rock on another guy's head. Four feet of water rush down your street while hellfire comes straight out of the

(10) ground, burning your car and house in under three minutes. And if that's not bad enough, apparently Liona Boyd lives there.

I'm from Newfoundland. People say, "Why do you live in Newfoundland?" We

(15) say, "Why do you live in Toronto?" But, c'mon, we all have our reasons why we prefer to be in one region of Canada over the others.

Really, God love Canada. How often do

(20) any of us here wake up with a nine-hundred-pound mahogany dresser-drawer heading towards our face at warp speed?

We've got it scald. We have every right in the world to be holier than thou when it

(25) comes to the flaky state of California. Except for the crowd in B.C., who, yes, even though the tulips come up in February, and the quality of life is apparently two thousand times greater

(30) than ours, they too are just sitting there eating sushi waiting for the Big One.

People have their priorities mixed up, and I think the events of the last little while have proven that everyone should stop

(35) moving west and move east. Sure, it's more tundra-like than Vancouver. And granted, we don't have celebrities walking the streets, but at least when we hear someone saying, "The Big One is coming"

(40) we know they're probably talking about the WWF show at the hockey arena. You might still want to run and hide, but you don't have to. The choice is yours.

So come east, young man and woman,

(45) come east. It mightn't be as warm, but at least it's not gonna kill you.

Rick Mercer, "Streeters: Rants and Raves," *This Hour Has 22 Minutes.*

1. What is the author's dominant argument for why everyone should stop moving west and move east instead?
   - (1) The quality of life is two thousand times greater.
   - (2) Easterners are "holier than thou."
   - (3) Liona Boyd lives in the West.
   - (4) People are just sitting around eating sushi in the West.
   - (5) The East won't kill you. "The Big One" in the West might.

2. The author does not say what "the Big One" refers to in the West. Which of the following phrases, as used in the excerpt, best infers what the "the Big One" is in the West?
   - (1) Three guys dropping a rock on another guy's head.
   - (2) The flaky state of California.
   - (3) Six cops beating a man.
   - (4) Four feet of water rush down your street while hellfire comes straight out of the ground. …
   - (5) Tulips come up in February.

3. Which of the following <u>best represents</u> the attitude of the author toward his main subject?
   - (1) He dislikes Liona Boyd.
   - (2) He does not like sitting around eating sushi.
   - (3) He is afraid of the riots, fires, and violence of Los Angeles.
   - (4) People in their right mind would not live in Los Angeles (or anywhere else in the West).
   - (5) The best thing about the East is the WWF show at the hockey arena.

To contrast two subjects, list adjectives used to describe them that are different or opposite.

Questions 4 through 7 refer to the following excerpt from a nonfiction book.

WHAT IS THE DEFINITION OF A BEAUTIFUL PHOTOGRAPH?

In photography's early decades, photographs were expected to be idealized images. This is still the aim of most amateur photographers, for whom
(5) a beautiful photograph is a photograph of something beautiful, like a woman, a sunset. In 1915 Edward Steichen photographed a milk bottle on a tenement fire escape, an early example of a quite
(10) different idea of the beautiful photograph. And since the 1920s, ambitious professionals, those whose work gets into museums, have steadily drifted away from lyrical subjects, conscientiously exploring
(15) plain, tawdry, or even vapid material. In recent decades, photography has succeeded in somewhat revising, for everybody, the definitions of what is beautiful and ugly—along the lines that
(20) Whitman had proposed. If (in Whitman's words) "each precise object or condition or combination or process exhibits a beauty," it becomes superficial to single out some things as beautiful and others as not.
(25) If "all that a person does or thinks is of consequence," it becomes arbitrary to treat some moments in life as important and most as trivial.

To photograph is to confer importance.
(30) There is probably no subject that cannot be beautified; moreover, there is no way to suppress the tendency inherent in all photographs to accord value to their subjects. But the meaning of value itself
(35) can be altered—as it has been in the contemporary culture of the photographic image which is a parody of Whitman's evangel. In the mansions of pre-democratic culture, someone who gets photographed
(40) is a celebrity. In the open fields of American experience, as catalogued with passion by Whitman and as sized up with a shrug by Warhol, everybody is a celebrity. No moment is more important than any other
(45) moment; no person is more interesting than any other person.

Susan Sontag, *On Photography.*

4. What is the tone of this excerpt?

   (1) argumentative
   (2) persuasive
   (3) descriptive
   (4) explanatory
   (5) analytical

5. According to this excerpt, what is the aim of many recent professional photographers?

   (1) to make beautiful and lyrical photographs
   (2) to photograph precise images of places
   (3) to photograph everyday subjects
   (4) to make ordinary and tasteless photographs
   (5) to make photographs that will get into museums

6. Based on the information given in lines 40–43 about Whitman and Warhol, which of the following comparisons is most accurate?

   Whitman is to Warhol as

   (1) a photograph is to a subject
   (2) a celebrity is to a non-celebrity
   (3) beauty is to ugliness
   (4) special is to ordinary
   (5) feeling is to indifference

7. Based on the information in the excerpt, with which of the following statements would Whitman most likely agree?

   (1) Every being has dignity and worth.
   (2) The best photographs are not in museums.
   (3) The ugliest subjects are frequently the most beautiful.
   (4) Art should be based on feeling rather than thought.
   (5) Many people are superficial.

Answers start on page 803.

Recognizing Author's Viewpoint

A writer's attitude, or **viewpoint,** toward a subject often influences how he or she treats it. For example, a movie critic might dislike comedies but love dramas. Such a critic might be likely to say more positive things about a dramatic movie than about a humorous one. Readers can identify an author's viewpoint based on clues about the writer's background or interests, the vocabulary used, and details that point to the writer's likes and dislikes.

Read the following excerpt from an article and complete the exercise below.

As an improviser, [Gregory] Hines's choices are *always* surprising and wild. He takes you in unpredictable directions, cutting into phrases in unexpected places, alternating rest periods with full-blown movement as he skitters over the surface of his soundstage. A tough, get-down tapper who hunches over his feet, Hines keeps his head low like a fighter, listening, focusing himself and us on the sound of his feet. Neither graceful nor light (although he makes his feet whisper sweet nothings when he wants to) Hines is something better and rarer in the tap dance world, a sexy and compelling performer. Of all the tappers I know, Hines is perhaps the most inventive because he is fearless. Almost single-handedly he is pushing tap's technology and is a true modernist in how he uses rhythms. Frequently, he'll wrench phrases out of rhythm to create tension. On the feet of a lesser performer it could be chaotic. On Hines, it is exhilarating.

Sally R. Sommer, "Superfeet," *The Village Voice.*

1. What is this critic's attitude toward Hines's tap dancing?

   _____ a. indifferent

   _____ b. unfavourable

   _____ c. admiring

2. List the words and phrases from the excerpt that are clues to the critic's point of view.

   _____

   _____

   _____

You are correct if you chose *option c* for question 1. For question 2, the clues include *surprising, wild, better, rarer, sexy, compelling, inventive, fearless, true modernist,* and *exhilarating.* Each of these says something very positive about Hines's dancing.

viewpoint
a writer's attitude or opinion about a subject

Tip

Look for positively or negatively charged words that indicate how a writer feels about a subject.

GED Practice

Directions: Choose the <u>one best answer</u> to each question.

Questions 1 through 3 refer to the following excerpt from a movie review.

IS *HENRY V* A SUCCESS?

Shakespeare's plays rarely translate into great cinema, because they're either made on low budgets or look like filmed stage plays. So it's quite a surprise that
(5) *Henry V,* not Shakespeare's best, is one of the few movies in which Shakespeare seems not only a great playwright, but a seasoned screenwriter.

A lot of it has to do with Kenneth
(10) Branagh, a little-known English actor whose identification with Henry V is like Laurence Olivier's with Hamlet. He plays the title role, directs and adapts this play dealing with his psychological transition
(15) from Prince Hal to King Henry during the ruler's heroic campaigns into France. Branagh is young enough that his face has a boyish fleshiness, but old enough to project the charisma of a king. Even if you
(20) gasp to keep up with the Elizabethan language, his natural, eloquent inflections and the details of his direction clearly convey what he—and the large cast—is talking about.
(25) The film is full of beautifully photographed images, but they're never just decorative. In fact, it has a rough, primitive medieval look in keeping with its 15th-century setting. Though the battle
(30) sequences are sweeping, their details show the suffering, sorrow, and pettiness of Henry's men. The film even inspires us with their battle heroism. After all, their wars were more a sport than a means of
(35) annihilation.

Henry V emerges a first-class epic film, so entertaining that it needs no apologies for being based on a 400-year-old play. The only disappointments: Paul Scofield, whose
(40) portrayal of the French king is surprisingly dour, and the last 10 minutes, which turn

needlessly cute as Henry courts his future wife, Katherine. But that's as much Shakespeare's fault as Branagh's.

David Patrick Stearns, "Majestic *Henry V* does justice to the bard," *USA Today.*

1. Which statement <u>best</u> expresses the reviewer's opinion of the movie *Henry V*?

   (1) It contains realistic action sequences.
   (2) It is as good as other movies based on Shakespeare's plays.
   (3) It is an entertaining film.
   (4) It is a poor translation of the original play.
   (5) It has a large cast.

2. Which of the following <u>most</u> accurately states the main idea of the second paragraph?

   (1) Branagh is as good an actor as Olivier.
   (2) Branagh is perfect for the role of Henry V.
   (3) Branagh will become a better-known actor as a result of the film.
   (4) Branagh is a director as well as an actor.
   (5) Branagh really looks the part of Henry V.

3. In which of the following ways are the first and last paragraphs of this review similar?

   (1) Shakespeare's play *Henry V* is criticized.
   (2) Scenes from the movie are summarized.
   (3) Branagh is credited with rescuing the movie.
   (4) Shakespeare's reputation is attacked.
   (5) The critic says his expectations were not fulfilled.

Directions: Choose the one best answer to each question.

Questions 1 through 6 refer to the following excerpt from a review.

WHAT DID THESE MEN TAKE TO WAR?

Only a handful of novels and short stories have managed to clarify, in any lasting way, the meaning of the war in Vietnam for America and for the soldiers

(5) who served there. With *The Things They Carried,* Tim O'Brien adds his second title to the short list of essential fiction about Vietnam. As he did in his novel *Going After Cacciato* (1978), which won a National

(10) Book Award, he captures the war's pulsating rhythms and nerve-racking dangers. But he goes much further. By moving beyond the horror of the fighting to examine with sensitivity and insight the

(15) nature of courage and fear, by questioning the role that imagination plays in helping to form our memories and our own versions of truth, he places *The Things They Carried* high up on the list of best fiction

(20) about any war.

The Things They Carried is a collection of interrelated stories. ...

In the title story, Mr. O'Brien juxtaposes the mundane and the deadly items that

(25) soldiers carry into battle. Can openers, pocketknives, wristwatches, mosquito repellent, chewing gum, candy, cigarettes, salt tablets, packets of Kool-Aid, matches, sewing kits, C rations are "humped" by the

(30) G.I.'s along with M-16 assault rifles, M-60 machine guns, M-79 grenade launchers. But the story is really about the other things the soldiers "carry": "grief, terror, love, longing ... shameful memories" and,

(35) what unifies all the stories, "the common secret of cowardice." These young men, Mr. O'Brien tells us, "carried the soldier's greatest fear, which was the fear of blushing. Men killed, and died, because

(40) they were embarrassed not to."

Embarrassment, the author reveals in "On the Rainy River," is why he, or rather the fictional version of himself, went to Vietnam. He almost went to Canada

(45) instead. What stopped him, ironically, was fear. "All those eyes on me," he writes, "and I couldn't risk the embarrassment. ... I couldn't endure the mockery, or the disgrace, or the patriotic ridicule. ... I was a

(50) coward. I went to the war." ...

Mr. O'Brien strives to get beyond literal descriptions of what these men went through and what they felt. He makes sense of the unreality of the war—makes

(55) sense of why he has distorted that unreality even further in his fiction—by turning back to explore the workings of the imagination, by probing his memory of the terror and fearlessly confronting the way

(60) he has dealt with it as both soldier and fiction writer. In doing all this, he not only crystallizes the Vietnam experience for us, he exposes the nature of all war stories.

Robert R. Harris, "Too Embarrassed Not to Kill," *New York Times Book Review.*

1. Why does the reviewer most likely discuss two stories from the book in detail?

   (1) to show off his extensive knowledge of the war
   (2) to show what the stories have in common
   (3) to give examples of the characters in the book
   (4) to relate those stories to his own experience
   (5) to demonstrate why the author disliked the war

2. Based on the information in the excerpt, what is the most important reason the reviewer thinks *The Things They Carried* is worth reading?

   (1) It describes the routines of men in war.
   (2) It is a collection of short stories.
   (3) It examines the soldiers' feelings.
   (4) It is not about just one person.
   (5) It describes battles in detail.

3. What does the author of *The Things They Carried* mean when he says that he "couldn't endure … the patriotic ridicule" (lines 48−49)?

   He did not want to

   (1) explain publicly his reasons for not going to war
   (2) be criticized for not going to war
   (3) be condemned for deciding to fight
   (4) feel embarrassed while wearing his uniform
   (5) receive a call from the president of the United States

4. How does the reviewer feel about the author's previous novel, *Going After Cacciato*?

   The reviewer thinks

   (1) it is better than *The Things They Carried*
   (2) it does not go far enough in examining the terror of war
   (3) it should be read in addition to *The Things They Carried*
   (4) it fails because it does not depict the typical war experience
   (5) it does not have enough exciting scenes

5. What is the overall tone of this article?

   (1) harsh
   (2) frustrated
   (3) indifferent
   (4) pleased
   (5) admiring

6. Based on the excerpt, what is *The Things They Carried* most likely to help the reader understand?

   (1) the author's life
   (2) the experience of war
   (3) certain battles in Vietnam
   (4) politics during the Vietnam war
   (5) the interrelation of stories

To identify the author's viewpoint, try to separate the facts in a piece of writing from the opinions. The relationship between facts and opinions can give you a good idea of the author's point of view.

Answers start on page 804.

Understanding Fiction

Fiction is a form of writing that tells a story. A fiction writer creates a world from imagination. The most common works of fiction are novels and short stories.

Understanding fiction is an important part of passing the GED Language Arts, Reading Test. Questions about fiction passages make up approximately 75 percent of the test questions.

Getting Meaning from Context

When writers present words or situations that are unfamiliar, you can rely on surrounding words and phrases, or **context,** to help find meaning. These words and phrases may be in the same sentence or in a group of nearby sentences. Study these words for clues to understand what you are reading.

context
the words or sentences that surround words

Even if you cannot figure out the exact meaning of a word or phrase, clues from the context will help you to make a good guess. For example, if you saw an unfamiliar item in a store, you would probably look around at the other items on the shelf for clues. Then, you can make a reasonable guess as to what the unfamiliar item is.

Read the following excerpt from a novel and complete the exercise below.

To figure out unfamiliar words in an excerpt, substitute words you know in their place. If the substituted words make sense within the context, you have made a good guess at the definition.

Mark went over the engine room slowly, double-checking everything. He washed the dishes in the galley, placing them carefully behind the little racks that held them tight in a gale. He checked the log, put away the charts, made up the berths, cleaned the refrigerator, and closed the portholes. When he was done, the sun was high in the sky, and he went out on deck to await the canoes.

Margaret Craven, *I Heard the Owl Call My Name.*

Based on the context clues in the excerpt, what is a *gale?*

_____ a. a gentle breeze

_____ b. a strong wind

You are correct if you chose *option b, a strong wind*. Dishes need to be held in place to keep them from breaking when a boat is rocked by strong winds.

GED Practice

Directions: Choose the <u>one best answer</u> for each question.

<u>Questions 1 through 7</u> refer to the following excerpt from a novel.

HOW DOES THIS MAN FIGHT COMMERCIAL TV?

Years before, he had invented a module that, when a television commercial appeared, automatically muted the sound. It wasn't at first a context-recognition
(5) device. Instead, it simply monitored the amplitude of the carrier wave. TV advertisers had taken to running their ads louder and with less audio clutter than the programs that were their nominal vehicles.
(10) News of Hadden's module spread by word of mouth. People reported a sense of relief, the lifting of a great burden, even a feeling of joy at being freed from the advertising barrage for the six to eight
(15) hours out of every day that the average American spent in front of the television set. Before there could be any coordinated response from the television advertising industry, Adnix had become wildly popular.
(20) It forced advertisers and networks into new choices of carrier-wave strategy, each of which Hadden countered with a new invention. Sometimes he invented circuits to defeat strategies which the agencies
(25) and the networks had not yet hit upon. He would say that he was saving them the trouble of making inventions, at great cost to their shareholders, which were at any rate doomed to failure. As his sales volume
(30) increased, he kept cutting prices. It was a kind of electronic warfare. And he was winning.

They tried to sue him—something about a conspiracy in restraint of trade.
(35) They had sufficient political muscle that his motion for summary dismissal was denied, but insufficient influence to actually win the case. The trial had forced Hadden to investigate the relevant legal codes. Soon
(40) after, he applied, through a well-known

Madison Avenue agency in which he was now a major silent partner, to advertise his own product on commercial television. After a few weeks of controversy his
(45) commercials were refused. He sued all three networks and in *this* trial was able to prove conspiracy in restraint of trade. He received a huge settlement, that was, at the time, a record for cases of this sort,
(50) and which contributed in its modest way to the demise of the original networks.

There had always been people who enjoyed the commercials, of course, and they had no need for Adnix. But they were
(55) a dwindling minority. Hadden made a great fortune by eviscerating[1] broadcast advertising. He also made many enemies. …

As he further developed context-
(60) recognition chips, it became obvious to him that they had much wider application—from education, science, and medicine, to military intelligence and industrial espionage. It was on this issue
(65) that lines were drawn for the famous suit *United States v. Hadden Cybernetics.* One of Hadden's chips was considered too good for civilian life, and on recommendation of the National Security
(70) Agency, the facilities and key personnel for the most advanced context-recognition chip production were taken over by the government. It was simply too important to read the Russian mail. God knows,
(75) they told him, what would happen if the Russians could read our mail.

---

[1] depriving of vital force or power

Carl Sagan, *Contact.*

1. What is suggested about Hadden's personality by the detail in lines 21–23 "each of which Hadden countered with a new invention"?

   (1) He likes to annoy people.
   (2) He is persistent.
   (3) He is devious.
   (4) He is lazy.
   (5) He is not trustworthy.

2. To what does the phrase "nominal vehicles" (line 9) refer?

   (1) television commercials
   (2) a type of car popular with TV advertisers
   (3) TV ads featuring cars and other vehicles
   (4) television programs
   (5) ads with less audio clutter

3. Based on this excerpt, what is "Adnix"?

   (1) a device that silences TV commercials
   (2) a machine that recognizes voices
   (3) a computer chip used to spy on enemies
   (4) a device to add audio clutter to commercials
   (5) a computer chip that causes commercials to short circuit

4. Based on this excerpt, which of these statements <u>most likely</u> describes Hadden's attitude toward television?

   (1) The quality of commercials needs to be improved.
   (2) Television networks should produce more educational programming.
   (3) Television networks do not have viewers' best interests at heart.
   (4) People are very careful about what they watch on television.
   (5) Viewers must tolerate commercials as a necessary evil.

5. Based on the details in this excerpt, what is its theme, or message?

   (1) the dangers of watching too much television
   (2) the undesirable nature of commercials
   (3) the superiority of public television over commercial television
   (4) the workings of the mind of an inventor
   (5) the benefits of commercial TV

6. Which of the following developments in commercial television might Hadden disapprove of most?

   (1) the increasing use of profanity during prime time
   (2) the scarcity of minorities in the prime-time lineup
   (3) the unnecessary sex and violence
   (4) the acceptance of "infomercials" to promote products
   (5) the blurring of the lines between news and entertainment

7. Based on the excerpt, what was the central issue of the suit *United States v. Hadden Cybernetics?*

   (1) Television networks refused to air Hadden's commercials.
   (2) Hadden wanted to use his chip to spy on his competitors.
   (3) The U.S. government wanted to prevent Hadden from using his chip to gather military information.
   (4) The U.S. government wanted to take over production and use of Hadden's chip.
   (5) The United States wanted Hadden to stop producing chips that blocked commercials.

Answers start on page 805.

Language Arts, Reading • Understanding Fiction

Identifying Plot Elements

Plot refers to what happens to characters in a story, the order in which those events take place, and how they can lead to, or cause, another. Through the plot, writers arrange events to create a believable and interesting story.

A plot has a beginning, middle, and end. The beginning, or exposition, introduces the characters, setting, and other details and hints at an unstable situation. The middle introduces complications that create conflict and increase the story's tension. Complications reach their highest intensity at the climax, after which the conflict is resolved and the end, or resolution, is reached.

Read the following plot summary and complete the exercise below.

A young man crashes a party and is attracted to a beautiful woman. Despite a feud between their families, they fall in love and are secretly married. The woman's cousin kills the young man's friend over an insult. Avenging his friend's death, the man kills his wife's cousin and flees. Meanwhile, the woman's family attempts to force her to marry another man. On her wedding day, she takes a drug that makes her appear to be dead. She is taken to the family tomb, where she is to meet her lover when she awakes. He arrives, thinks she is dead, and commits suicide by drinking poison. The woman awakens to find her lover dead and kills herself with his dagger. After discovering the lovers' fate, the grieving families end their feud.

Identify each plot element by writing *E* for exposition, *C* for complication, *Con* for conflict, *Cl* for climax, and *R* for resolution.

____ a. The young man and woman fall in love.

____ b. The woman's cousin kills her lover's friend.

____ c. The families agree to end their feud.

____ d. The woman commits suicide with a dagger.

____ e. The lovers' families hate each other.

You were correct if you chose *E* for *option a* because this is important information about the characters introduced in the beginning. The answer is *C* for *option b* because it is a complication that creates or heightens the conflict. *R* is the answer for *option c* because it is the outcome of the story. *Cl* is the answer for *option d* because it is the point where complications reach their highest intensity, and *Con* is the answer to *option e* because it is the underlying conflict that creates the tension in the story.

plot
the order of events in a story and the relationships among these events

When identifying plot elements, look for the important characters and any conflicts that may influence the outcome of events.

GED Practice

Directions: Choose the one best answer to each question.

Questions 1 through 4 refer to the following excerpt from a short story.

WHERE WILL THEY VACATION?

The grandmother didn't want to go to Florida. She wanted to visit some of her connections in east Tennessee and she was seizing at every chance to change
(5) Bailey's mind. Bailey was the son she lived with, her only boy. He was sitting on the edge of his chair at the table, bent over the orange sports section of the *Journal*. "Now look here, Bailey," she said, "see
(10) here, read this," and she stood with one hand on her thin hip and the other rattling the newspaper at his bald head. "Here this fellow that calls himself The Misfit is aloose from the Federal Pen and headed toward
(15) Florida and you read here what it says he did to these people. Just you read it. I wouldn't take my children in any direction with a criminal like that aloose in it. I couldn't answer to my conscience if I did."
(20) Bailey didn't look up from his reading so she wheeled around then and faced the children's mother, a young woman in slacks, whose face was as broad and innocent as a cabbage and was tied
(25) around with a green head-kerchief that had two points on the top like a rabbit's ears. She was sitting on the sofa, feeding the baby his apricots out of a jar. "The children have been to Florida before," the
(30) old lady said. "You all ought to take them somewhere else for a change so they would see different parts of the world and be broad. They never have been to east Tennessee."
(35) The children's mother didn't seem to hear her but the eight-year-old boy, John Wesley, a stocky child with glasses, said, "If you don't want to go to Florida, why dontcha stay at home?" He and the little
(40) girl, June Star, were reading the funny papers on the floor.

Flannery O'Connor, "A Good Man Is Hard to Find,"
A Good Man Is Hard to Find and Other Stories.

1. Based on this excerpt, which of the following words best describes the grandmother?

   (1) selfish
   (2) worried
   (3) innocent
   (4) timid
   (5) devoted

2. How do the other family members respond to the grandmother's behaviour?

   (1) They poke fun at her.
   (2) They ignore her for the most part.
   (3) They exclude her from their activities.
   (4) They let her have her way.
   (5) They openly defy her.

3. Which of the following situations is most similar to the situation in the excerpt?

   (1) a conference in which teachers discuss the best way to educate children
   (2) a meeting in which a boss tries to change his staff's mind about an issue
   (3) a gathering in which neighbours vote on how to curb crime in their community
   (4) a family reunion in which relatives express their love for one another
   (5) a classroom in which students share their views about current events

4. What is the main way in which the grandmother's character is revealed in this excerpt?

   (1) description of what she looks like
   (2) background about her Tennessee heritage
   (3) details about what she likes to read
   (4) explanations of what the other characters think of her
   (5) dialogue in which her manner of speaking is shown

Answers start on page 805.

Language Arts, Reading • Understanding Fiction

Lesson 12

apply
to take information
and transfer it to a
new situation

Applying Ideas

One way to show an understanding of what you read is to take information and **apply** it to a related situation. In fiction, writers develop characters that usually act consistently. Based on characters' actions, what motivates them, and how they react to events in a story, you can often predict how they might react in new situations. Applying information to a new context can help you better understand the characters and the plot of a story.

Read the following excerpt from a short story and complete the exercise below.

… My own talent was I could always make money. I had a touch for it, unusual in a Chippewa. From the first I was different that way, and everyone recognized it. I was the only kid they let in the American Legion Hall to shine shoes, for example, and one Christmas I sold spiritual bouquets for the mission door to door. The nuns let me keep a percentage. Once I started, it seemed the more money I made the easier the money came. Everyone encouraged it. When I was fifteen I got a job washing dishes at the Joliet Café, and that was where my first big break happened.

Louise Erdrich, "The Red Convertible," *Love Medicine.*

1. Based on the excerpt, for which job would the character be most suited if he were to volunteer at a homeless shelter?

_____ a. soup kitchen worker

_____ b. fundraiser

You were correct if you chose *option b, fundraiser.* The excerpt states that the character's talent is making money; therefore, he would likely be most suited for fundraising.

2. Based on this excerpt, which of the following phrases best describes the character's way with money?

_____ a. Money burns a hole in his pocket.

_____ b. Everything he touches turns to gold.

You are correct if you chose *option b, Everything he touches turns to gold.* The excerpt states that he could always make money—that he had a touch for it.

 Questions that ask you to predict what a character would say or do are usually application questions.

GED Practice

Directions: Choose the <u>one best answer</u> to each question.

Questions 1 through 3 refer to the following excerpt from a novel.

HOW WILL THEY CELEBRATE?

I raced down the block from where the number eight bus dropped me off, around the corner from our house. The fall was slowly settling into the trees on our block,
(5)   some of them had already turned slightly brown.

I could barely contain my excitement as I walked up the steps to the house, sprinting across the living room to the
(10)   kitchen.

Ma was leaning over the stove, the pots clanking as she hummed a song to herself.

"My passport should come in a month or so," I said, unfolding a photocopy of the
(15)   application for her to see.

She looked at it as though it contained boundless possibilities.

"We can celebrate with some strong bone soup," she said. "I am making some
(20)   right now."

In the pot on the stove were scraps of cow bones stewing in hot bubbling broth.

Ma believed that her bone soup could cure all kinds of ills. She even hoped that
(25)   it would perform the miracle of detaching Caroline from Eric, her Bahamian fiancé. Since Caroline had announced that she was engaged, we'd had bone soup with our supper every single night.
(30)   "Have you had some soup?" I asked, teasing Caroline when she came out of the bedroom.

"This soup is really getting on my nerves," Caroline whispered in my ear
(35)   as she walked by the stove to get some water from the kitchen faucet.

Edwidge Danticat, *Krik? Krak!*

1. On the basis of this excerpt, which of the following would be the mother's <u>most likely</u> reaction if Caroline were to break her engagement with her fiancé?

   She might

   (1) think the bone soup was responsible
   (2) go to the Bahamas to find a husband for Caroline
   (3) ask her other daughter to postpone her trip
   (4) cast a spell over the fiancé
   (5) scold Caroline for making a mistake

2. Why does the narrator ask Caroline if she has had some soup?

   (1) She worries that Caroline does not eat enough.
   (2) She hopes Caroline will break off her engagement.
   (3) They like to poke fun at their mother's beliefs.
   (4) She wants Caroline to celebrate.
   (5) They enjoy their mother's cooking.

3. Which of the following can you infer about the mother based on the way she responds to her daughters' plans?

   (1) She wants her daughters to stay at home.
   (2) She hopes her daughters will become good cooks like she is.
   (3) She supports her daughters' decisions.
   (4) She cares about her daughters' futures.
   (5) She wishes her daughters were more tolerant of other cultures.

Answers start on page 805.

Language Arts, Reading • Understanding Fiction

Lesson 13

cause
an action that makes
something else happen

effect
the result of an action

Tip

You can identify a
cause-and-effect
relationship by asking
why something
happened and what
its results were.

Identifying Cause and Effect

A **cause** is an initial action—a thought, word, or deed—that makes something else happen. An **effect** is the consequence, or result of that action. Often, a cause has more than one effect, or an effect may have more than one cause. Sometimes the link between a cause and effect is not obvious, and you need to think carefully about how the events are related.

A fiction writer uses causes and effects to create a story. Paying careful attention to the causes and effects in a story can give you a better understanding of its plot.

Read the following excerpt from a novel and complete the exercise below.

He was an old man who fished alone in a skiff in the Gulf Stream and he had gone eighty-four days now without taking a fish. In the first forty days a boy had been with him. But after forty days without a fish the boy's parents had told him that the old man was now definitely and finally *salao*, which is the worst form of unlucky, and the boy had gone at their orders in another boat which caught three good fish the first week. It made the boy sad to see the old man come in each day with his skiff empty and he always went down to help him carry either the coiled lines or the gaff and harpoon and the sail that was furled around the mast. The sail was patched with flour sacks and, furled, it looked like the flag of permanent defeat.

Ernest Hemingway, *The Old Man and the Sea.*

1. The boy's parents force him to go in another boat. What is the cause of this effect?

    _____ a. The first week the other boat caught three fish.

    _____ b. The old man goes forty days without catching a fish.

You are correct if you chose *option b.* The boy's parents feel the old man is unlucky, and they make the boy go to another boat.

2. The old man came in each day with his boat empty. What is the effect of this cause?

    _____ a. The old man was very unlucky.

    _____ b. The boy felt sad.

You are correct if you chose *option b.* The excerpt directly states that the boy is sad because the boat is empty.

GED Practice

Directions: Choose the <u>one best answer</u> for each question.

Questions 1 through 5 refer to the following excerpt from a novel.

HOW HAVE THESE PEOPLE CHANGED?

On the morning of the thirteenth sleep of sickness in the Lone Eater camp, Fools Crow and his father, Rides-at-the-door, walked through the village. They went from
(5) lodge to lodge and called to the people within. There were still many sick and dying, but the number of new victims had gone down. The rage of the white-scabs was subsiding. It seemed impossible that
(10) it would last such a short time and leave so many dead or scarred for life by the draining sores. Others were out walking listlessly in the warm sun or just sitting outside their lodges. There was none of
(15) the bustle that usually occurred on a morning of winter camp. The people did not greet each other. If they met on the path to the river, they would move off the path and circle warily until they were well
(20) beyond. If a child was caught playing with the children from a family hard hit by the bad spirit, he would be called inside and scolded. But it was one old woman, the only survivor of her lodge, who sat and
(25) wailed and dug at the frozen ground until her fingers were raw and bloody—it was this old woman who made the people realize the extent of their loss. Gradually they emerged from the deep void of
(30) sickness and death and saw that they had become a different people.

James Welch, *Fools Crow.*

1. What has happened to the people in the village?

   (1) They are dying of starvation.
   (2) They are victims of a natural disaster.
   (3) They have contracted a contagious disease.
   (4) They are afraid to leave their lodges.
   (5) They are at war with another village.

2. A villager walking far around another villager to avoid coming into contact with the bad spirit is most similar to which of the following situations?

   (1) a person catching a horrible disease
   (2) a person taking a new route to avoid someone he dislikes
   (3) a person wearing a face mask in the hospital to avoid germs
   (4) a person leaving a path to walk through the woods
   (5) a person sneezing on another person and giving her a cold

3. What do the people believe is causing their problems?

   (1) the white man's invasion of their territory
   (2) the presence of a bad spirit
   (3) punishment from the gods
   (4) pollution from the river
   (5) being forced to live close together

4. Lines 30–31 state that "they had become a different people." Which of the following is the most probable change?

   (1) They were disheartened and sad.
   (2) Their faces were scarred for life.
   (3) They were happy to have survived.
   (4) They decided to join a new camp.
   (5) They no longer cared what happened to them.

5. What is the effect of telling the story mainly from the villagers' point of view?

   (1) It distances readers from the events of the story.
   (2) It helps readers understand how the characters feel.
   (3) It suggests that the people like to gossip.
   (4) It biases readers against the white man.
   (5) It demonstrates the villagers' dislike of outsiders.

Questions 6 through 9 refer to the following excerpt from a short story.

WHAT HAS INVADED THE FARM?

She went out to join the old man, stepping carefully among the insects. They stood and watched. Overhead the sky was blue, blue and clear.

(5) "Pretty," said old Stephen with satisfaction.

Well, thought Margaret, we may be ruined, we may be bankrupt, but not everyone has seen an army of locusts
(10) fanning their wings at dawn.

Over the slopes, in the distance, a faint red smear showed in the sky, thickened and spread. "There they go," said old Stephen. "There goes the main army,
(15) off South."

And from the trees, from the earth all round them, the locusts were taking wing. They were like small aircraft, maneuvering for the take-off, trying their wings to see if
(20) they were dry enough. Off they went. A reddish brown stream was rising off the miles of bush, off the lands, the earth. Again the sunlight darkened.

And as the clotted branches lifted, the
(25) weight on them lightening, there was nothing but the black spines of branches, trees. No green left, nothing. All morning they watched, the three of them, as the brown crust thinned and broke and
(30) dissolved, flying up to mass with the main army, now a brownish-red smear in the Southern sky. The lands which had been filmed with green, the new tender mealie plants, were stark and bare. All the trees
(35) stripped. A devastated landscape. No green, no green anywhere.

Doris Lessing, "A Mild Attack of Locust," *The Habit of Loving.*

6. What effect did the locusts have on the land?

   (1) They left it bare of leaves.
   (2) They turned it brownish-red.
   (3) They stirred up clouds of dust.
   (4) They broke branches from the trees.
   (5) They littered it with their shells.

7. To what does the phrase "a faint red smear" (lines 11–12) refer?

   (1) the rosy colour of dawn
   (2) the dust raised by a group of soldiers
   (3) the colours of sunset
   (4) the swarm of locusts
   (5) the pesticides spread by crop dusters

8. Which of the following conflicts is highlighted in this excerpt?

   (1) people versus themselves
   (2) people versus society
   (3) people versus fate
   (4) people versus nature
   (5) people versus machines

9. Which of the following details is used most frequently throughout this excerpt?

   (1) colour
   (2) texture
   (3) size
   (4) shape
   (5) sound

Tip

Ask yourself, "What happened?" The answer is an effect. Then ask yourself, "Why did it happen?" The answer is the cause.

Answers start on page 806.

Lesson 14

characters
the people in a work
of fiction

Characters' actions
do not always match
their words. Just as
in real life, you will
have to judge whether
characters are honest
and reliable.

Analyzing Character

Fiction writers create people, or **characters,** to capture a reader's interest. There are several ways to find out about characters in literature. Writers develop characters by describing what the characters look like, how they behave, what they think and say, and what other characters say about them.

Read the following excerpt from a novel and complete the exercise below.

Mr. Chadband is a large yellow man, with a fat smile and a general appearance of having a good deal of train-oil[1] in his system. … Mr. Chadband moves softly and cumbrously,[2] not unlike a bear who has been taught to walk upright. He is very much embarrassed about the arms, as if they were inconvenient to him, and he wanted to grovel; is very much in a perspiration about the head; and never speaks without first putting up his great hand, as delivering a token to his hearers that he is going to edify[3] them.

"My friends," says Mr. Chadband, "peace be on this house! On the master thereof, on the mistress thereof, on the young maidens, and on the young men! My friends, why do I wish for peace? What is peace? Is it war? No. Is it strife? No. Is it lovely, and gentle, and beautiful, and pleasant, and serene, and joyful? Oh yes! Therefore, my friends, I wish for peace upon you and upon yours."

[1] oil from a marine animal, such as a whale   [2] moving with difficulty due to weight or size   [3] enlighten

Charles Dickens, *Bleak House.*

1. Put a check mark by all of the following that are true of Mr. Chadband.

    _____ a. He is a man of few words.

    _____ b. He is preachy.

    _____ c. He is self-important.

    _____ d. He frowns a lot.

2. Underline descriptive phrases in the excerpt that tell you something about Mr. Chadband's character.

You are correct if you chose *options b* and *c.* Mr. Chadband speaks as if he is giving a sermon and behaves as if he is going to enlighten his audience. Examples of phrases that you may have underlined are *a fat smile; a general appearance of having a good deal of train-oil in his system;* and *never speaks without first putting up his great hand.*

GED Practice

Directions: Choose the <u>one best answer</u> for each question.

<u>Questions 1 through 3</u> refer to the following excerpt from a short story.

WHAT KIND OF PERSON IS GRANNY WEATHERALL?

She flicked her wrist neatly out of Doctor Harry's pudgy careful fingers and pulled the sheet up to her chin. The brat ought to be in knee breeches. Doctoring
(5) around the country with spectacles on his nose! "Get along now, take your schoolbooks and go. There's nothing wrong with me."

Doctor Harry spread a warm paw like a
(10) cushion on her forehead where the forked green vein danced and made her eyelids twitch. "Now, now, be a good girl, and we'll have you up in no time."

"That's no way to speak to a woman
(15) nearly eighty years old just because she's down. I'd have you respect your elders, young man."

"Well, Missy, excuse me." Doctor Harry patted her cheek. "But I've got to warn you,
(20) haven't I? You're a marvel, but you must be careful or you're going to be good and sorry."

"Don't tell me what I'm going to be. I'm on my feet now, morally speaking.
(25) It's Cornelia. I had to go to bed to get rid of her."

Her bones felt loose, and floated around in her skin, and Doctor Harry floated like a balloon around the foot of
(30) the bed. He floated and pulled down his waistcoat and swung his glasses on a cord. "Well, stay where you are, it certainly can't hurt you."

"Get along and doctor your sick," said
(35) Granny Weatherall. "Leave a well woman alone. I'll call for you when I want you. … Where were you forty years ago when I pulled through milk-leg and double pneumonia? You weren't even born.
(40) Don't let Cornelia lead you on," she shouted, because Doctor Harry appeared to float up to the ceiling and out. "I pay my own bills, and I don't throw money away on nonsense!"

(45) She meant to wave good-by, but it was too much trouble. Her eyes closed of themselves, it was like a dark curtain drawn around the bed. The pillow rose and floated under her, pleasant as a
(50) hammock in a light wind. She listened to the leaves rustling outside the window. No, somebody was swishing newspapers: no, Cornelia and Doctor Harry were whispering together. She leaped broad
(55) awake, thinking they whispered in her ear.

"She was never like this, *never* like this!" "Well, what can we expect?" "Yes, eighty years old …"

Katherine Anne Porter, "The Jilting of Granny Weatherall," *Flowering Judas and Other Stories.*

1. Which of the following is probably true about Granny?

   (1) She is healthier now.
   (2) She is much sicker than she says she is.
   (3) She thinks doctors are invaluable.
   (4) She is able to get around easily.
   (5) She thinks Cornelia is a fine woman.

2. Which of the following <u>best</u> describes the doctor's tone?

   (1) understanding but firm
   (2) distant and scientific
   (3) gentle but unsure
   (4) serious and gloomy
   (5) bright and cheery

3. Which of the following reveals the <u>most</u> about Granny Weatherall's <u>character?</u>

   (1) what others say about her
   (2) what she says
   (3) what she thinks
   (4) what others do in her presence
   (5) what she feels

WHY DOES THIS WOMAN BUY POISON?

"I want some poison," she said to the druggist. She was over thirty then, still a slight woman, though thinner than usual, with cold, haughty black eyes in a face the

(5) flesh of which was strained across the temples and about the eyesockets as you imagine a lighthouse-keeper's face ought to look. "I want some poison," she said.

"Yes, Miss Emily. What kind? For rats

(10) and such? I'd recom—"

"I want the best you have. I don't care what kind."

The druggist named several. "They'll kill anything up to an elephant. But what you

(15) want is—"

"Arsenic," Miss Emily said. "Is that a good one?"

"Is … arsenic? Yes, ma'am. But what you want—"

(20) "I want arsenic."

The druggist looked down at her. She looked back at him, erect, her face like a strained flag. "Why, of course," the druggist said. "If that's what you want. But the law

(25) requires you to tell what you are going to use it for."

Miss Emily just stared at him, her head tilted back in order to look him eye for eye, until he looked away and went and got the

(30) arsenic and wrapped it up.

William Faulkner, "A Rose for Emily," *Collected Stories of William Faulkner.*

4. What is meant by the description of Miss Emily's face as being similar to a "strained flag" (line 23)?

(1) She is about to cry.
(2) She is very tense.
(3) She appears lonely.
(4) She seems quite fragile.
(5) She is strangely pale.

5. Based on this excerpt, how would Miss Emily most likely walk across a crowded room?

(1) carefully, trying not to bump into anyone
(2) energetically stomping with heavy footsteps
(3) shyly, with her head down and with small footsteps
(4) confidently, with her head held high
(5) clumsily, sometimes stumbling into people

6. Based on this excerpt, which of the following descriptions best characterizes Miss Emily?

(1) She cannot make up her mind.
(2) She is open about her life.
(3) She is embarrassed that her house has rats.
(4) She has a limited income.
(5) She intimidates other people.

7. Based on the dialogue in this excerpt, how is Miss Emily's demeanour different from that of the druggist?

(1) Miss Emily is grumpy, but the druggist is friendly.
(2) Miss Emily is talkative, but the druggist is brief.
(3) Miss Emily is forceful, but the druggist is accommodating.
(4) Miss Emily is calm, but the druggist is impatient.
(5) Miss Emily is rational, but the druggist is suspicious.

Answers start on page 806.

Analyzing Tone

When you talk, the **tone** of your voice reveals your attitude—how you feel about your subject and audience. A writer's tone also conveys how he or she feels about a subject. A writer's words may suggest emotions or attitudes such as seriousness, humour, anger, or sympathy. **Mood** is the emotional atmosphere of a piece of literature. Mood is the feeling the author wants the reader to experience. The mood can be the same as or different from the tone. A writer often uses description to help create these feelings. As you read, look for these clues: how an author uses descriptive words and how a story builds to its conclusion.

tone
the details present in a writer's work that suggest how he or she feels about a subject

mood
the emotional climate or atmosphere conveyed by the words a writer chooses

Read the following excerpt from a short story and complete the exercise below.

During the whole of a dull, dark, and soundless day in the autumn of the year, when the clouds hung oppressively low in the heavens, I had been passing alone, on horseback, through a singularly dreary tract of country; and at length found myself, as the shades of the evening drew on, within view of the melancholy House of Usher. I know not how it was—but, with the first glimpse of the building, a sense of insufferable gloom pervaded my spirit … There was an iciness, a sinking, a sickness of the heart. …

Edgar Allan Poe, "The Fall of the House of Usher," *The Fall of the House of Usher and Other Writings.*

1. Put a check mark by one of the following words that describes the tone of this excerpt.

    _____ a. puzzled

    _____ b. angry

    _____ c. gloomy

2. Underline the words in the first line of the excerpt that suggest the author's tone.

3. The excerpt takes place in early evening. How do you think the time of day contributes to the mood?

_____

_____

Tip

Word choice is a clue to determining the tone of a piece of fiction.

You are correct if you chose *option c* for question 1 and underlined *dull, dark,* and *soundless* for question 2. The time of day contributes to the mood because many people associate darkening skies with fear or sadness.

GED Practice

Directions: Choose the <u>one best answer</u> to each question.

Questions 1 through 10 refer to the following excerpt from a novel.

IS THIS FAMILY HAVING A SATISFYING MEAL?

"George is in town, Papa; and has gone to the Horse Guards, and will be back to dinner."

"Oh, he is, is he? I won't have the
(5) dinner kept waiting for *him,* Jane"; with which this worthy man lapsed into his particular chair, and then the utter silence in his genteel, well-furnished drawing-room was only interrupted by the alarmed ticking
(10) of the great French clock.

When [it] … tolled five in a heavy cathedral tone, Mr. Osborne pulled the bell at his right hand violently, and the butler rushed up.

(15) "Dinner!" roared Mr. Osborne.

"Mr. George isn't come in, sir," interposed the man.

"Damn Mr. George, sir. Am I master of the house? DINNER!" Mr. Osborne
(20) scowled. Amelia trembled. A telegraphic communication of eyes passed between the other three ladies. The obedient bell in the lower regions began ringing the announcement of the meal. The tolling
(25) over, the head of the family thrust his hands into the great tail-pockets of his great blue coat and brass buttons, and without waiting for a further announcement, strode downstairs
(30) alone, scowling over his shoulder at the four females.

"What's the matter now, my dear?" asked one of the other, as they rose and tripped gingerly behind the sire.
(35) "I suppose the funds are falling," whispered Miss Wirt; and so, trembling and in silence, this hushed female company followed their dark leader.

They took their places in silence. He
(40) growled out a blessing, which sounded as gruffly as a curse. The great silver dishcovers were removed. Amelia trembled in her place, for she was next to the awful Osborne, and alone on her side of the
(45) table—the gap being occasioned by the absence of George.

"Soup?" says Mr. Osborne, clutching the ladle, fixing his eyes on her, in a sepulchral[1] tone; and having helped her
(50) and the rest, did not speak for a while.

"Take Miss Sedley's plate away," at last he said. "She can't eat the soup—no more can I. It's beastly. Take away the soup, Hicks, and to-morrow turn the cook out of
(55) the house, Jane."

Having concluded his observations upon the soup, Mr. Osborne made a few curt remarks respecting the fish. …

---

[1] deathly

William Makepeace Thackeray, *Vanity Fair.*

1. Which of the following words <u>best</u> describes Mr. Osborne's daughters?

   (1) fearful
   (2) snobbish
   (3) considerate
   (4) friendly
   (5) obedient

2. To what does the phrase "tripped gingerly" in line 34 refer?

   (1) fell gracefully
   (2) whispered softly
   (3) stumbled clumsily
   (4) ran quickly
   (5) walked carefully

3. Based on the excerpt, which of the following is an explanation given by another character for Mr. Osborne's behaviour?

   (1) He is angry with George for being late.
   (2) He is dissatisfied with the food served at dinner.
   (3) His position in the household is challenged.
   (4) He may be losing money on his investments.
   (5) He is angry that he must wait for his dinner.

4. Based on this excerpt, how would Osborne react if one of his daughters were late for an important appointment with him?

   (1) He would pace the floor nervously.
   (2) He would dismiss her without seeing her.
   (3) He would lecture her on the importance of being punctual.
   (4) He would forgive her without a second thought.
   (5) He would wait patiently for her arrival.

5. Which of the following words best describes the mood of this excerpt?

   (1) cheerful
   (2) melancholy
   (3) comical
   (4) tense
   (5) cool

6. Based on the context, to what does the phrase "Mr. Osborne made a few curt remarks respecting the fish" (lines 57–58) likely refer?

   (1) Mr. Osborne was ordering his daughters to taste the fish.
   (2) Mr. Osborne was impressed by the way the cook had prepared the fish.
   (3) Mr. Osborne did not seem satisfied with the fish.
   (4) Mr. Osborne did not have much to say about the fish.
   (5) Mr. Osborne was trying to make dinner conversation.

7. Which of the following best indicates Mr. Osborne's lack of warmth?

   (1) the reference to Mr. Osborne as the "head of the family" (line 25)
   (2) Mr. Osborne's referring to himself as the "master of the house" (lines 18–19)
   (3) the reference to Amelia's fear when she sits next to him
   (4) Jane's referring to her father as "Papa" (line 1)
   (5) Osborne's refusal to address any of his daughters by name

8. What is suggested about Mr. Osborne's character when he tells his daughter to fire the cook?

   (1) He is extremely intolerant.
   (2) He is a former gourmet cook.
   (3) He has poor taste in food.
   (4) He is very alarmed.
   (5) He has a weakness for teasing.

9. Who is George?

   He is

   (1) a visiting family acquaintance
   (2) a general in the Horse Guards
   (3) the real master of the house
   (4) one of Jane's siblings
   (5) Mr. Osborne's business partner

10. Which of the following best describes the narrator's attitude toward Mr. Osborne?

   Mr. Osborne is

   (1) a serious man
   (2) an admirable man
   (3) a patient man
   (4) a grumpy man
   (5) a terrible man

Questions 11 through 14 refer to the following excerpt from a novel.

WHAT IS THE SIGNIFICANCE OF CARTER DRUSE'S DECISION?

The sleeping sentinel in the clump of laurel was a young Virginian named Carter Druse. He was the son of wealthy parents, an only child, and had known such ease
(5) and cultivation and high living as wealth and taste were able to command in the mountain country of western Virginia. His home was but a few miles from where he now lay. One morning he had risen from
(10) the breakfast-table and said, quietly but gravely: "Father, a Union regiment has arrived at Grafton. I am going to join it."

The father lifted his leonine head, looked at the son a moment in silence, and
(15) replied: "Well, go, sir, and whatever may occur do what you conceive to be your duty. Virginia, to which you are a traitor, must get on without you. Should we both live to the end of the war, we will speak
(20) further of the matter. Your mother, as the physician has informed you, is in a most critical condition; at the best she cannot be with us longer than a few weeks, but that time is precious. It would be better not to
(25) disturb her."

So Carter Druse, bowing reverently to his father, who returned the salute with a stately courtesy that masked a breaking heart, left the home of his childhood to go
(30) soldiering. By conscience and courage, by deeds of devotion and daring, he soon commended himself to his fellows and his officers; and it was to these qualities and to some knowledge of the country that he
(35) owed his selection for his present perilous duty at the extreme outpost.

Ambrose Bierce, *A Horseman in the Sky.*

11. Which of the following best describes Carter Druse's father?

(1) a hard-hearted man who cares little for his wife and son
(2) a demanding individual who wants his son to follow in his footsteps
(3) a coward who wants to avoid his responsibilities
(4) a man of honour who respects his son's beliefs
(5) a poor man with simple tastes and limited education

12. Which of the following actions would be in keeping with Carter Druse's character as described in the excerpt?

(1) running away from a battle
(2) lying to one of his officers
(3) keeping a difficult promise
(4) deserting to the Confederate Army
(5) stealing from his father

13. Which of the following best describes the tone of this excerpt?

(1) threatening
(2) formal
(3) envious
(4) comical
(5) chatty

14. Carter Druse's decision brings into sharp focus which of the following realities about the Civil War?

(1) The war led to western Virginia's secession from the state.
(2) The war resulted in more deaths than any war before it.
(3) The war divided even the closest families.
(4) The war produced unlikely heroes.
(5) The war was fought mainly in the South.

Answers start on page 807.

Identifying Figurative Language

Fiction writers often use words to create vivid images. This technique is called **figurative language.** Most figurative language is based on comparisons that make a point. A **simile** makes a comparison using *than, as,* or *like.* For instance, the statement "His hair was <u>like</u> a bad dream" is a simile. A **metaphor,** on the other hand, makes a comparison by simply stating that one thing is another—for example, "His hair was a nightmare."

A third type of figurative language is a **symbol**—a person, place, or thing that stands for some other, larger idea. For example, a character's cunning may be suggested by a frequent reference to a fox.

Figurative language is different from literal language. Literal language is factual; it is not exaggerated for effect. The description "Maria is very tall" is a literal statement; however, "Maria towers over everyone like a skyscraper" is a figurative statement.

Read the following excerpt from a short story and complete the exercise below.

His mother didn't know how to paint her face; she just put on all the makeup and probably didn't even know she looked like an old, tired clown. She had red tomatoes for cheeks and red strawberries for lips. The lines of her eyebrows were drawn with a black pencil, and she looked horrible. I never understood why she wore so much paint on her face.

Enedina Cásarez Vásquez, "The House of Quilts," *Daughters of the Fifth Sun.*

1. Place a check mark by the type of figurative language used in the line "she looked like an old, tired clown."

   _____ a. simile

   _____ b. symbol

   _____ c. metaphor

2. What clue helped you to answer question 1? _____

3. Write two metaphors from the excerpt.

   _____

   _____

You are correct if you chose *simile* for question 1. The clue word is *like.* Two metaphors are *red tomatoes for cheeks* and *red strawberries for lips.*

figurative language
words used imaginatively to create vivid pictures

simile
a comparison between two different people, places, or things signalled by the words *like, than, similar to,* or *as*

metaphor
a comparison that states one thing is another

symbol
a person, place, or thing that stands for a larger idea

To identify figurative language, look for comparisons between two different things. In what ways does the writer suggest they are alike?

GED Practice

Directions: Choose the <u>one best answer</u> to each question.

Questions 1 through 4 refer to the following excerpt from a short story.

HOW ARE INSECTS LIKE MEN?

Dr. Nahum Fischelson paced back and forth in his garret room in Market Street, Warsaw.[1] Dr. Fischelson was a short, hunched man with a grayish beard, and
(5) was quite bald except for a few wisps of hair remaining at the nape of the neck. His nose was as crooked as a beak and his eyes were large, dark, and fluttering like those of some huge bird. It was a hot
(10) summer evening, but Dr. Fischelson wore a black coat which reached to his knees, and he had on a stiff collar and a bow tie. From the door he paced slowly to the dormer window set high in the slanting
(15) room and back again. One had to mount several steps to look out. A candle in a brass holder was burning on the table and a variety of insects buzzed around the flame. Now and again one of the creatures
(20) would fly too close to the fire and sear its wings, or one would ignite and glow on the wick for an instant. At such moments Dr. Fischelson grimaced. His wrinkled face would twitch and beneath his disheveled[2]
(25) mustache he would bite his lips. Finally he took a handkerchief from his pocket and waved it at the insects.

"Away from there, fools and imbeciles," he scolded. "You won't get warm here;
(30) you'll only burn yourself."

The insects scattered but a second later returned and once more circled the trembling flame. Dr. Fischelson wiped the sweat from his wrinkled forehead
(35) and sighed, "Like men they desire nothing but the pleasure of the moment."

---

[1] the largest city in Poland   [2] disordered

Isaac Bashevis Singer, "The Spinoza of Market Street."

1. Based on the clues in this excerpt, what type of room is a garret?

   (1) a dining room
   (2) a basement
   (3) a room in a dormitory
   (4) a room in an attic
   (5) a penthouse suite

2. Based on this excerpt, how would Dr. Fischelson likely respond to a stray cat that appeared on his doorstep?

   (1) He would chase the cat away.
   (2) He would call the animal control centre.
   (3) He would care for the cat.
   (4) He would scold the cat.
   (5) He would try to kick the cat.

3. Which of Dr. Fischelson's features are compared to a bird's?

   (1) nose and eyes
   (2) head and feet
   (3) eyes and neck
   (4) nose and feet
   (5) feet and eyes

4. What is the tone of the excerpt?

   (1) frightened
   (2) violent
   (3) ominous
   (4) silly
   (5) painful

Tip

To create symbols, writers use words and images in original ways. Is an image or word repeated? If so, it usually has a larger meaning.

Answers start on page 808.

Making Inferences

In everyday life, you often encounter situations in which you do not have all the information you need. In such cases, you must make decisions based on the facts you do have, as well as your knowledge and experience. This skill is called **making an inference.** You can also make inferences when reading fiction. First, you find out what an author is suggesting, and then you make a decision based on your own understanding of what the writer said indirectly. Writers often imply information about characters, setting, atmosphere, and tone.

Read the following excerpt from a short story and complete the exercise below.

The big kids call me Mercury cause I'm the swiftest thing in the neighborhood. Everybody knows that—except two people who know better, my father and me. He can beat me to Amsterdam Avenue with me having a two fire-hydrant headstart and him running with his hands in his pockets and whistling. But that's private information. Cause can you imagine some thirty-five-year-old man stuffing himself into PAL shorts to race little kids? So as far as everyone's concerned, I'm the fastest and that goes for Gretchen, too, who has put out the tale that she is going to win the first-place medal this year. Ridiculous.

Toni Cade Bambara, "Raymond's Run," *Gorilla, My Love.*

making an inference putting together clues or details to reach a logical conclusion when facts are not stated directly

1. Write *F* by the statement that is a fact, and *I* by the statement that is an inference.

    _____ a. The narrator has a good sense of humour.

    _____ b. The narrator's father can run faster than she can.

2. Put a check mark by all of the statements that support the inference that the narrator has great confidence in her ability.

    _____ a. "He can beat me to Amsterdam Avenue"

    _____ b. "I'm the swiftest thing in the neighborhood"

    _____ c. "Ridiculous"

To make inferences, look for clue words in a passage and add to them what you already know from personal experience.

For question 1, you are correct if you chose *inference* for *option a.* The excerpt does not state this directly, but the narrator makes two humorous comments about her father, so you can infer that she has a good sense of humour. *Option b* is a *fact* mentioned by the narrator. For question 2, you should have checked *b* and *c.* Only someone with confidence in her ability would state that she was the fastest in the neighbourhood and that it was ridiculous that someone else thought she could be beaten.

GED Practice

Directions: Choose the <u>one best answer</u> to each question.

Questions 1 through 9 refer to the following excerpt from a short story.

WHO IS THE NEW CHOIR SOLOIST?

In the centre row of women singers stood Alma Way. All the people stared at her, and turned their ears critically. She was the new leading soprano. Candace
(5) Whitcomb, the old one, who had sung in the choir for forty years, had lately been given her dismissal. The audience considered that her voice had grown too cracked and uncertain on the upper notes.
(10) There had been much complaint, and after long deliberation the church-officers had made known their decision as mildly as possible to the old singer. She had sung for the last time the Sunday before, and
(15) Alma Way had been engaged to take her place. With the exception of the organist, the leading soprano was the only paid musician in the large choir. The salary was very modest, still the village people
(20) considered it large for a young woman. Alma was from the adjoining village of East Derby; she had quite a local reputation as a singer.

Now she fixed her large solemn blue
(25) eyes; her long, delicate face, which had been pretty, turned paler; the blue flowers on her bonnet trembled; her little thin gloved hands, clutching the singing-book, shook perceptibly; but she sang out
(30) bravely. That most formidable mountain-height of the world, self-distrust and timidity, arose before her, but her nerves were braced for its ascent. In the midst of the hymn she had a solo; her voice rang
(35) out piercingly sweet; the people nodded admiringly at each other; but suddenly there was a stir; all the faces turned toward the windows on the south side of the church. Above the din of the wind

(40) and the birds, above Alma Way's sweetly straining tones, arose another female voice, singing another hymn to another tune.

"It's her," the women whispered to each
(45) other; they were half aghast, half smiling.

Candace Whitcomb's cottage stood close to the south side of the church. She was playing on her parlor organ, and singing, to drown out the voice of her rival.
(50) Alma caught her breath; she almost stopped; the hymn-book waved like a fan; then she went on. But the long husky drone of the parlor organ and the shrill clamor of the other voice seemed louder
(55) than anything else.

When the hymn was finished, Alma sat down. She felt faint; the woman next to her slipped a peppermint into her hand. "It ain't worth minding," she whispered, vigorously.
(60) Alma tried to smile; down in the audience a young man was watching her with a kind of fierce pity.

In the last hymn Alma had another solo. Again the parlor organ droned above
(65) the carefully delicate accompaniment of the church organ, and again Candace Whitcomb's voice clamored forth in another tune.

Mary Wilkins Freeman, "A Village Singer."

1. Why did Candace Whitcomb stay home to play the organ and sing?

   (1) She did not feel well that day.
   (2) She had the day off so a new soloist could be auditioned.
   (3) She felt she needed the practice for the following Sunday.
   (4) She was envious of the new soloist.
   (5) She had decided to retire.

2. The sentence "That most formidable mountain-height of the world, self-distrust and timidity, arose before her, but her nerves were braced for its ascent" (lines 30–33) means which of the following?

   (1) Alma had climbed mountains before.
   (2) Alma was prepared to conquer her fear.
   (3) Alma did not trust her voice to hit the high notes.
   (4) Alma believed nervousness before a performance was normal.
   (5) Alma felt the walk to the singer's podium was like climbing a mountain.

3. Which of the following best explains the meaning of the phrase "half aghast" in line 45?

   (1) The women's mouths were half-open.
   (2) Half of the women were opposed to Alma.
   (3) The women were smiling weakly.
   (4) The women were trying to be quiet.
   (5) The women were partially horrified.

4. Why did Alma feel faint (line 57)?

   (1) She was exhausted after her incredible performance.
   (2) She was dizzy from the heat inside the church.
   (3) She was nervous because a young man in the audience was watching her.
   (4) She felt weak from the strain of having to compete with Candace's singing.
   (5) She was scared that Candace's singing might be better than her own.

5. If Alma were to quit singing with the choir, what would Candace most likely do?

   (1) try to convince Alma to return
   (2) try to get reinstated as the choir's soloist
   (3) ask Alma to sing duets with her
   (4) apologize for making Alma feel bad
   (5) continue to perform from her cottage

6. Which of the following details from the excerpt helps the reader to understand the emotional atmosphere in the church?

   (1) "her voice had grown too cracked and uncertain" (lines 8–9)
   (2) "the leading soprano was the only paid musician in the large choir" (lines 17–18)
   (3) "All the people stared at her, and turned their ears critically." (lines 2–3)
   (4) "she had quite a local reputation as a singer" (lines 22–23)
   (5) "She was the new leading soprano." (lines 3–4)

7. Which of the following can be learned about Alma's personality from this excerpt?

   (1) She is willing to face a challenge.
   (2) She is vain about her looks.
   (3) She resents competition.
   (4) She does not value her talent.
   (5) She is often pessimistic.

8. Which of the following descriptions best characterizes the style of writing in this excerpt?

   (1) dry and scholarly
   (2) flat and unemotional
   (3) ironic and joking
   (4) informal and serious
   (5) complex and confusing

9. Based on the excerpt, which of the following pairs shows the same relationship as that between Candace's voice and Alma's voice?

   (1) a crow's voice and an eagle's
   (2) an eagle's voice and a hummingbird's
   (3) a hummingbird's voice and a crow's
   (4) an owl's voice and a songbird's
   (5) a crow's voice and a canary's

Questions 10 through 13 refer to the following excerpt from a novel.

HOW DOES THE NARRATOR FEEL ABOUT THIS WOMAN?

… She put me in them new clothes again, and I couldn't do nothing but sweat and sweat, and feel all cramped up. Well, then, the old thing commenced again.
(5) The widow rung a bell for supper, and you had to come to time. When you got to the table you couldn't go right to eating, but you had to wait for the widow to tuck down her head and grumble a little over the
(10) victuals, though there warn't really anything the matter with them—that is, nothing only everything was cooked by itself. In a barrel of odds and ends it is different; things get mixed up, and the juice
(15) kind of swaps around, and the things go better.
　　After supper she got out her book and learned me about Moses and the Bulrushers, and I was in a sweat to find out
(20) all about him; but by and by she let it out that Moses had been dead a considerable long time; so then I didn't care no more about him, because I don't take no stock in dead people.
(25) 　　Pretty soon I wanted to smoke, and asked the widow to let me. But she wouldn't. She said it was a mean practice and wasn't clean, and I must try to not do it any more. That is just the way with some
(30) people. They get down on a thing when they don't know nothing about it. Here she was a-bothering about Moses, which was no kin to her, and no use to anybody, being gone, you see, yet finding a power of fault
(35) with me for doing a thing that had some good in it. And she took snuff, too; of course that was all right, because she done it herself.

Mark Twain, *The Adventures of Huckleberry Finn.*

10. What is the widow trying to do to the narrator?

　(1) adopt him
　(2) reform him
　(3) annoy him
　(4) poke fun at him
　(5) entertain him

11. Based on the information in this excerpt, the narrator would most enjoy eating which of the following?

　(1) a hotdog
　(2) mashed potatoes
　(3) a bowl of beef stew
　(4) cheese and crackers
　(5) a fresh green salad

12. Which of the following words best describes the tone of this excerpt?

　(1) suspenseful
　(2) formal
　(3) serious
　(4) cheerful
　(5) conversational

13. What is the main effect of the author's use of slang and nonstandard English?

　(1) It gives clues about the time and place.
　(2) It creates a contrast with the widow's speech.
　(3) It results in a likable character.
　(4) It creates a humorous situation.
　(5) It makes the excerpt easier to understand.

To check your skill in making inferences, ask yourself "Are there clues in this passage that support my inference? If so, what are they?"

Answers start on page 809.

Comparing and Contrasting

When you **compare** things, you show how they are alike and different. When you **contrast** them, you show only how they are different. One of the joys of reading fiction is in the development of the characters. Writers may compare or contrast the characters' personalities in a story to give the reader a vivid image. This character development can also provide insight into the conflict of the story.

When you read fiction, understanding the process of comparing and contrasting can help you better understand what you read.

compare
show how things
are alike and different

contrast
show how things
are different

Read the following excerpt from a novel and complete the exercise below.

Mr. Bennet was so odd a mixture of quick parts, sarcastic humour, reserve, and caprice,[1] that the experience of three and twenty years had been insufficient to make his wife understand his character. *Her* mind was less difficult to develop. She was a woman of mean[2] understanding, little information, and uncertain temper. When she was discontented she fancied herself nervous. The business of her life was to get her daughters married; its solace[3] was visiting and news.

——————
[1] impulsiveness   [2] limited   [3] comfort

Jane Austen, *Pride and Prejudice*.

Identify similarities by looking for clue words such as *like, likewise, also,* and *similarly.* To identify contrasts, look for clue words such as *unlike, however, but, on the other hand,* and *differently.*

1. Circle the correct underlined word in the sentence below.

   This paragraph <u>compares</u>/<u>contrasts</u> Mr. and Mrs. Bennet.

2. Put a check mark by the sentence that contrasts two things.

   _____ a. Mr. Bennet is more difficult to understand than his wife.

   _____ b. Mrs. Bennet thrives on gossip and visiting.

   _____ c. Mrs. Bennet is confused by her own feelings.

3. Underline the sentence in the excerpt that indicates that the characters will be contrasted.

You are correct if you circled *contrasts* for question 1. The excerpt shows only how the characters are different. In question 2, *option a* is the correct response. For question 3, you should have underlined *Her mind was less difficult to develop.* The emphasis of the word *her* combined with the word *less* tells you that she is being contrasted with Mr. Bennet.

GED Practice

Directions: Choose the <u>one best answer</u> to each question.

Questions 1 through 3 refer to the following excerpt from a novel.

WHERE ARE THESE TWO BOYS?

Ralph did a surface dive and swam under water with his eyes open; the sandy edge of the pool loomed up like a hillside. He turned over, holding his nose, and a
(5) golden light danced and shattered just over his face. Piggy was looking determined and began to take off his shorts. Presently he was palely and fatly naked. He tiptoed down the sandy side of the pool, and sat
(10) there up to his neck in water smiling proudly at Ralph.

"Aren't you going to swim?"

Piggy shook his head.

"I can't swim. I wasn't allowed. My
(15) asthma—"

"Sucks to your ass-mar!"

Piggy bore this with a sort of humble patience.

"You can't half swim well."

(20) Ralph paddled backwards down the slope, immersed his mouth and blew a jet of water into the air. Then he lifted his chin and spoke.

"I could swim when I was five. Daddy
(25) taught me. He's a commander in the Navy. When he gets leave he'll come and rescue us. What's your father?"

Piggy flushed suddenly.

"My dad's dead," he said quickly, "and
(30) my mum—"

He took off his glasses and looked vainly for something with which to clean them.

"I used to live with my auntie. She kept
(35) a candy store. I used to get ever so many candies. As many as I liked. When'll your dad rescue us?"

"Soon as he can."

Piggy rose dripping from the water and
(40) stood naked, cleaning his glasses with a sock. The only sound that reached them now through the heat of the morning was the long, grinding roar of the breakers on the reef.

William Golding, *Lord of the Flies.*

1. What has happened to the two boys in this excerpt?

   (1) They have been kidnapped.
   (2) They have run away from home.
   (3) They have been stranded.
   (4) They have gone to summer camp.
   (5) They have escaped from a reformatory.

2. Based on the details in this excerpt, what would Piggy likely do if he were teased for wearing glasses?

   (1) pick a fight with his tormentor
   (2) go and tell an adult
   (3) join in and laugh at himself
   (4) suffer in silence
   (5) walk away crying

3. How are Ralph and Piggy alike?

   (1) Both seem to envy each other.
   (2) Both have grown up without their mothers.
   (3) Both believe Ralph's father will rescue them.
   (4) Both learned to swim at a young age.
   (5) Both suffer from asthma.

Tip

To identify comparison and contrast patterns, underline the adjectives used to describe characters. Are the descriptive words about one character similar to and/or different from those used to describe another character? If they are both similar and different, a comparison is being made; if only dissimilar, a contrast is being made.

Answers start on page 810.

Language Arts, Reading • Understanding Fiction

Interpreting Theme

The **theme** is the general idea about life or human nature that a short story or novel reveals. Theme is sometimes compared to the **moral** of a story, a lesson meant to teach right from wrong. Morals are often stated at the end of a fable. However, the theme is usually not stated directly; you must infer it. Nor does a theme necessarily tell the reader how to behave. It simply expresses the author's views about the way life is.

Read the following excerpt from a short story and complete the exercise below.

> When it occurs to a man that nature does not regard him as important, and that she feels she would not maim the universe by disposing of him, he at first wishes to throw bricks at the temple, and he hates deeply the fact that there are no bricks and no
> (5) temples. Any visible expression of nature would surely be pelleted with his jeers.
> Then, if there be no tangible thing to hoot, he feels, perhaps, the desire to confront a personification[1] and indulge in pleas, bowed to one knee, and with hands supplicant,[2] saying, "Yes, but I love
> (10) myself."
> A high cold star on a winter's night is the word he feels that she says to him. Thereafter he knows the pathos[3] of his situation.
> The men in the dinghy had not discussed these matters, but each had, no doubt, reflected upon them in silence and according
> (15) to his mind. There was seldom any expression upon their faces save the general one of complete weariness. Speech was devoted to the business of the boat.

> ---
> [1] an object given human form   [2] begging   [3] tragic sorrow

> Stephen Crane, "The Open Boat," *The Portable.*

theme
the general idea about the way life is that you infer from a short story or novel

moral
a lesson that can be applied to your life

As you read, ask yourself "Is the author trying to give me advice or express a truth or insight?"

1. Put a check mark by how the man in this excerpt feels about nature.

   _____ a. indifferent

   _____ b. angry

2. Put a check mark by the best description of nature as it is portrayed in this excerpt.

   _____ a. nurturing

   _____ b. vengeful

   _____ c. indifferent

You are correct if you chose *option b* for question 1. The man is angry at nature. For question 2, the correct answer is *option c*. The phrase "nature does not regard him as important" should have helped you correctly answer question 2.

GED Practice

Directions: Choose the <u>one best answer</u> to each question.

Questions 1 through 10 refer to the following excerpt from a novel.

WHY DOES THE WAR STILL LIVE FOR THE NARRATOR?

Everyone has a moment in history which belongs particularly to him. It is the moment when his emotions achieve their most powerful sway over him, and
(5) afterward when you say to this person "the world today" or "life" or "reality" he will assume that you mean this moment, even if it is fifty years past. The world, through his unleashed emotions, imprinted itself
(10) upon him, and he carries the stamp of that passing moment forever.

For me, this moment—four years is a moment in history—was the war. The war was and is reality for me. I still instinctively
(15) live and think in its atmosphere. These are some of its characteristics: Franklin Delano Roosevelt is the President of the United States, and he always has been. The other two eternal world leaders are Winston
(20) Churchill and Josef Stalin. America is not, never has been, and never will be what the songs and poems call it, a land of plenty. Nylon, meat, gasoline, and steel are rare. There are too many jobs and not enough
(25) workers. Money is very easy to earn but rather hard to spend, because there isn't very much to buy. Trains are always late and always crowded with "servicemen." The war will always be fought very far from
(30) America, and it will never end. Nothing in America stands still for very long, including the people who are always either leaving or on leave. People in America cry often. Sixteen is the key and crucial and natural
(35) age for a human being to be, and people of all other ages are ranged in an orderly manner ahead of and behind you as a harmonious setting for the sixteen-year-olds of the world. When you are sixteen,

(40) adults are slightly impressed and almost intimidated by you. This is a puzzle finally solved by the realization that they foresee your military future, fighting for them.

You do not foresee it. To waste anything
(45) in America is immoral. String and tinfoil are treasures. Newspapers are always crowded with strange maps and names of towns, and every few months the earth seems to lurch from its path when you see
(50) something in the newspapers, such as the time Mussolini, who had almost seemed one of the eternal leaders, is photographed hanging upside down on a meathook. Everyone listens to news broadcasts five
(55) or six times every day. All pleasurable things, all travel and sports and entertainment and good food and fine clothes, are in the very shortest supply, always were and always will be. There are
(60) just tiny fragments of pleasure and luxury in the world, and there is something unpatriotic about enjoying them. All foreign lands are inaccessible except to servicemen; they are vague, distant, and
(65) sealed off as though behind a curtain of plastic. The prevailing color of life in America is a dull, dark green called olive drab. That color is always respectable and always important. Most other colors risk
(70) being unpatriotic.

John Knowles, *A Separate Peace.*

1. What is the main idea of the first paragraph?

   (1) Emotions may influence history.
   (2) People should not dwell on the past.
   (3) People should learn more about history.
   (4) Life in America is not all it is claimed to be.
   (5) A person's worldview is shaped by key events.

Language Arts, Reading • Understanding Fiction

2. Which of the following best restates lines 48 and 49: "every few months the earth seems to lurch from its path"?

   (1) Every few months the earth is shaken by earthquakes.
   (2) Every few months there is a bomb attack.
   (3) Every few months America attacks another country.
   (4) Every few months something shocking occurs.
   (5) Every few months there is another shortage of supplies.

3. With which of the following statements would the narrator be most likely to agree?

   (1) Politics makes strange bedfellows.
   (2) There is no time like the present.
   (3) Time is something we will never understand.
   (4) The historical era affects the individual.
   (5) Time stands still for no one.

4. How does the narrator help the reader understand how he feels about the war?

   (1) by explaining that adults were intimidated by soldiers
   (2) by talking about the war as if it were happening now
   (3) by referring to well-known world leaders
   (4) by specifically stating his emotions in clear terms
   (5) by making the war years sound romantic and appealing

5. What is the main purpose of the narrator's discussion of World War II?

   (1) to recall events that took place during his adolescence
   (2) to describe realities of war that remain with Americans
   (3) to criticize the state of affairs in the world
   (4) to call for a return to the "good old days"
   (5) to speak out against the horrors of war

6. Based on the excerpt, why did the war years affect the narrator as they did?

   (1) He was young and impressionable.
   (2) He admired Roosevelt's policies.
   (3) Money was easy to get.
   (4) Everyone was very sad.
   (5) He feared becoming a soldier.

7. Which of the following best describes the tone of this excerpt?

   (1) critical
   (2) upbeat
   (3) sentimental
   (4) expectant
   (5) serious

8. Which of the following best describes the style of writing in this excerpt?

   (1) formal and scholarly
   (2) witty and sarcastic
   (3) engaging and colourful
   (4) matter-of-fact and repetitive
   (5) flowery and inspiring

9. Which of the following is the main effect of the author's style in this excerpt?

   It helps to

   (1) appeal to the reader's sense of patriotism
   (2) convey the horrors of war
   (3) make the reader count his or her blessings
   (4) indicate the monotony imposed by war
   (5) reveal how a sixteen-year-old thinks

10. Which of the following statements best expresses the narrator's point of view?

   (1) Everyone has fifteen minutes of fame.
   (2) Those who do not remember the past are doomed to repeat it.
   (3) The "good old days" were not always good.
   (4) The world is too much with us.
   (5) There will always be wars and rumours of war.

   Answers start on page 810.

Directions: Choose the <u>one best answer</u> to each question.

Questions 1 through 7 refer to the following excerpt from a novel.

WHY DOES LEE CHONG MAKE A DEAL WITH MACK?

Lee Chong stiffened ever so slightly when Mack came in and his eyes glanced quickly about the store to make sure that Eddie or Hazel or Hughes or Jones had
(5) not come in too and drifted away among the groceries.

Mack laid out his cards with a winning honesty. "Lee," he said, "I and Eddie and the rest heard you own the Abbeville
(10) place."

Lee Chong nodded and waited.

"I and my friends thought we'd ask you if we could move in there. We'll keep up the property," he added quickly. "Wouldn't
(15) let anybody break in or hurt anything. Kids might knock out the windows, you know—" Mack suggested. "Place might burn down if somebody don't keep an eye on it."

Lee tilted his head back and looked into
(20) Mack's eyes through the half-glasses and Lee's tapping finger slowed its tempo as he thought deeply. In Mack's eyes there was good will and good fellowship and a desire to make everyone happy. Why then
(25) did Lee Chong feel slightly surrounded? Why did his mind pick its way as delicately as a cat through cactus? It had been sweetly done, almost in a spirit of philanthropy. Lee's mind leaped ahead
(30) at the possibilities—no, they were probabilities, and his finger tapping slowed still further. He saw himself refusing Mack's request and he saw the broken glass from the windows. Then Mack would offer a
(35) second time to watch over and preserve Lee's property—and at the second refusal, Lee could smell the smoke, could see the little flames creeping up the walls. Mack and his friends would try to help to put it
(40) out. Lee's finger came to a gentle rest on the change mat. He was beaten. He knew that. There was left to him only the possibility of saving face and Mack was likely to be very generous about that. Lee

(45) said, "You like pay lent my place? You like live there same hotel?"

Mack smiled broadly and he was generous. "Say—" he cried. "That's an idear. Sure. How much?"
(50) Lee considered. He knew it didn't matter what he charged. He wasn't going to get it anyway. He might just as well make it a really sturdy face-saving sum. "Fi' dolla' week," said Lee.
(55) Mack played it through to the end. "I'll have to talk to the boys about it," he said dubiously. "Couldn't you make that four dollars a week?"

"Fi' dolla'," said Lee firmly.
(60) "Well, I'll see what the boys say," said Mack.

And that was the way it was. Everyone was happy about it. And if it be thought that Lee Chong suffered a total loss, at
(65) least his mind did not work that way. The windows were not broken. Fire did not break out, and while no rent was ever paid, if the tenants ever had any money, and quite often they did have, it never occurred
(70) to them to spend it any place except at Lee Chong's grocery.

John Steinbeck, *Cannery Row*.

1. What is Mack's most likely motivation in offering to "keep up the property" (lines 13–14) and "keep an eye on it" (line 18)?

   (1) He is trying to strike up a friendship.
   (2) He is trying to improve the community.
   (3) He is asking Lee Chong for a job.
   (4) He is threatening Lee Chong.
   (5) He is trying to cheat his friends.

2. What would Mack and his friends most likely do if someone were to set fire to the Abbeville place?

   (1) move out
   (2) add fuel to the flames
   (3) try to help put out the fire
   (4) run away
   (5) steal the groceries before they burn

3. Which of the following words best describes the deal between Lee Chong and Mack?

   (1) useful
   (2) immoral
   (3) dangerous
   (4) pathetic
   (5) kind

4. If Lee Chong owned a car dealership, how would he most likely run his business?

   He would offer

   (1) discounted prices to his friends and family
   (2) fair prices to ensure many repeat customers
   (3) low prices to keep his inventory small
   (4) inflated prices by using pressure tactics
   (5) higher prices to customers who are difficult

5. Which of the following ideas are most clearly contrasted in this excerpt?

   (1) wealth and poverty
   (2) innovation and tradition
   (3) giving and receiving
   (4) power and practicality
   (5) anger and sympathy

6. Which of the following best states the theme of the excerpt?

   (1) Saving face is a weak approach.
   (2) True friends are helpful in times of trouble.
   (3) Weighing risks helps in making good decisions.
   (4) Good negotiating skills cannot always solve problems.
   (5) Being unfair to a neighbour brings no reward.

7. What is the overall tone of the excerpt?

   (1) casual
   (2) humorous
   (3) tense
   (4) angry
   (5) friendly

Tip

To answer application questions, read each answer choice and look for details such as behaviours or beliefs. Eliminate choices that contain details that do not fit the character.

Answers start on page 811.

Understanding Poetry

Lesson 20

Poetry is a special kind of writing in which descriptive language is used to create images or feelings. It appeals to the emotions, the senses, or the imagination of the reader. You read poems in books and magazines. You write poems to express your feelings or sometimes to tell a story. When you listen to music, you are hearing a kind of poetry in the song lyrics. Although fiction and nonfiction are written in sentences and paragraphs, poetry is written in lines or groups of lines called stanzas.

Understanding poetry will help you pass the GED Language Arts, Reading Test. Questions about literature make up about 75 percent of the GED Reading Test. Some of these questions will relate to poetry.

Identifying the Effects of Rhythm and Rhyme

rhythm
a pattern created by the rise and fall in the sounds of words as well as by the use of punctuation

rhyme
a similarity in the sounds at the ends of words that ties two or more words together

In poetry, sounds support meaning. The words of a poem communicate ideas; the sounds of those words communicate feelings connected to the ideas. Poets create "sound effects" by carefully choosing words and arranging them in patterns. Two word patterns are **rhythm** and **rhyme.**

All poems have rhythm, or a beat. This beat may be fast or slow, regular or irregular. Rhythm is primarily created by a pattern of stressed syllables. To understand how, slowly say the phrase "Once upon a midnight dreary." Notice that every other syllable is stressed. This creates rhythm.

Another way poets create rhythm in a poem is through punctuation. Commas, periods, or the absence of punctuation both within and at the ends of lines affect the poem's sound and rhythm.

Many poems also have rhyme. Rhyme is created by repeating the sounds at the ends of words, as in *struck* and *truck*. Sometimes word endings sound similar but do not rhyme completely, as in *house* and *bounce*. Both full and partial rhymes tie parts of a poem together in a pattern. Rhythm and rhyme create the shape and feel of a poem.

 Tip To become more aware of a poem's rhythm and rhyme, read it aloud. Do the lines move along slowly or quickly? Do any of the words have similar sounds? These patterns will help you tie ideas or feelings together.

GED Practice

Directions: Choose the <u>one best answer</u> to each question.

Questions 1 through 3 refer to the following poem.

WHERE DO THESE ROADS LEAD?

The Road Not Taken

Two roads diverged in a yellow wood,
And sorry I could not travel both
And be one traveler, long I stood
And looked down one as far as I could
(5)   To where it bent in the undergrowth;

Then took the other, as just as fair,
And having perhaps the better claim,
Because it was grassy and wanted wear;
Though as for that the passing there
(10)   Had worn them really about the same,

And both that morning equally lay
In leaves no step had trodden black.
Oh, I kept the first for another day!
Yet knowing how way leads on to way,
(15)   I doubted if I should ever come back.

I shall be telling this with a sigh
Somewhere ages and ages hence:
Two roads diverged in a wood, and I—
I took the one less traveled by,
(20)   And that has made all the difference.

Robert Frost, *The Poetry of Robert Frost.*

1. What is the <u>most likely</u> meaning of "diverged" in "Two roads diverged in a yellow wood" (line 1)?

   (1) ran parallel
   (2) separated
   (3) merged
   (4) overlapped
   (5) appeared

Poets often use rhythm to create the mood of a poem. Think of the way music uses rhythm to make us feel sad or romantic or joyful.

2. Which of the following <u>best</u> describes the theme of the poem?

   (1) regrets over choices not made
   (2) the ability to accomplish anything
   (3) how decisions define people's lives
   (4) traveling as a positive experience
   (5) how walking in nature can change you

3. What would the speaker in this poem <u>most likely</u> do if he had to decide where to <u>live</u>?

   (1) think carefully before committing himself
   (2) ask his friends for their opinions
   (3) choose the most popular neighbourhood
   (4) worry that he made the wrong choice
   (5) be unable to make up his mind

WHAT MADE THIS SPEAKER SO HAPPY?

I Wandered Lonely as a Cloud

I wandered lonely as a cloud
That floats on high o'er vales and hills,
When all at once I saw a crowd,
A host, of golden daffodils;
(5) Beside the lake, beneath the trees,
Fluttering and dancing in the breeze.

Continuous as the stars that shine
And twinkle on the milky way,
They stretched in never-ending line
(10) Along the margin of a bay:
Ten thousand saw I at a glance,
Tossing their heads in sprightly dance.

The waves beside them danced; but they
Outdid the sparkling waves in glee;
(15) A poet could not but be gay,
In such a jocund company;
I gazed—and gazed—but little thought
What wealth the show to me had brought:

For oft, when on my couch I lie
(20) In vacant or in pensive mood,
They flash upon that inward eye
Which is the bliss of solitude;
And then my heart with pleasure fills,
And dances with the daffodils.

William Wordsworth, "I Wandered Lonely As a Cloud."

4. Which of the following sentences best restates the main idea of the poem?

   (1) Unexpected sights can produce endless pleasure.
   (2) Daffodils are the speaker's favourite flower.
   (3) Flowers often seem to possess human qualities.
   (4) Certain images can be easily forgotten.
   (5) Wandering is a way for poets to find subject matter.

5. To what does the speaker compare the daffodils?

   (1) a lonely cloud
   (2) the stars of the milky way
   (3) a pensive mood
   (4) a heart filled with pleasure
   (5) dancing waves

6. Which of the following is the best restatement of "They flash upon that inward eye / Which is the bliss of solitude" (lines 21–22)?

   (1) The speaker often looks inward to his soul.
   (2) The daffodils remind the speaker of yellow lightning flashes.
   (3) The speaker sometimes pictures the flowers in his mind when he is alone.
   (4) Being alone brings the speaker great pleasure.
   (5) Having left the flowers, the speaker cannot picture them in his mind.

7. What is the best description of the rhythm of this poem?

   (1) pounding and insistent
   (2) sprightly and upbeat
   (3) fast-paced and energetic
   (4) slow and thoughtful
   (5) uneven and surprising

8. Based on the poem, which of the following would the speaker most likely do if he were caught in a rain shower?

   He would

   (1) feel annoyed that his clothes were getting wet
   (2) be relieved that the storm was not worse
   (3) notice all the details of how the rain looked and felt
   (4) think that the rain looked like sparkling waves
   (5) conclude that nature is predictable and kind

Answers start on page 811.

Interpreting Figurative Language

Poetry may sometimes seem difficult to understand. One reason for this is that poetry has a language all its own—that is, it uses words in a way different from most other types of writing. One way in which poets make their writing unique is through the use of **figurative language.** Figurative language involves the use of ordinary words in unusual ways. Poets use figurative language to make a particular point. For instance, exaggeration is one type of figurative language. If a poet states that the stars of the night sky are close enough to touch, he or she is exaggerating to emphasize how close the stars appear. Poets may also use **personification** and give human qualities to animals, objects, or ideas, as in the sentence "The trees danced in the wind."

Other types of figurative language include similes and metaphors, which you learned about in Lesson 16. Paying close attention to the figurative language in a poem can help you grasp the poem's meaning.

Read the following poem and answer the question below.

HARLEM

What happens to a dream deferred?

> Does it dry up
> like a raisin in the sun?
> Or fester like a sore—
> and then run?
> Does it stink like rotten meat?
> Or crust and sugar over
> like a syrupy sweet?
> Maybe it just sags
> like a heavy load.

Or does it explode?

Langston Hughes, *Collected Poems.*

What does the line "dry up / like a raisin in the sun" suggest about a dream deferred? Put a check mark next to your answer.

____ a. It can be preserved to enjoy later.

____ b. It shrinks and loses its strength.

You are correct if you chose *option b*. This line suggests that when a dream is put off, it can shrink and lose its power in the same way that a grape shrivels in the sun.

figurative language
language in which ordinary words are combined in new ways to make a point

personification
a type of figurative language that gives human qualities to non-human objects

If a description or comparison does not make literal sense, then it is probably figurative. Look for unusual descriptions and comparisons, then use your imagination to figure out what they mean.

GED Practice

Directions: Choose the <u>one best answer</u> to each question.

<u>Questions 1 through 3</u> refer to the following poem.

WHAT HAS THIS SPEAKER REALIZED?

Abel Melveny

I bought every kind of machine that's known—
Grinders, shellers, planters, mowers,
Mills and rakes and ploughs and threshers—
And all of them stood in the rain and sun,
(5)　Getting rusted, warped and battered,
For I had no sheds to store them in,
And no use for most of them.
And toward the last, when I thought it over,
There by my window, growing clearer
(10)　About myself, as my pulse slowed down,
And looked at one of the mills I bought—
Which I didn't have the slightest need of,
As things turned out, and I never ran—
A fine machine, once brightly varnished,
(15)　And eager to do its work,
Now with its paint washed off—
I saw myself as a good machine
That Life had never used.

Edgar Lee Masters, *The Spoon River Anthology.*

1. Which of these sentences <u>best</u> describes the similarities between the speaker and the machines?

   (1) Both must work hard before they break.
   (2) Both need constant attention to stay in good shape.
   (3) Both were meant to work hard but did not.
   (4) Both grow old gracefully.
   (5) Both are easily replaced.

2. Which of the following is the machinery in this poem <u>most</u> like?

   (1) an outdoor sculpture garden
   (2) a toaster that was never taken out of its box
   (3) useless junk piled in a landfill
   (4) objects with great sentimental value
   (5) a used car that needs a little work

3. Which of the following <u>best</u> suggests the central theme of this poem?

   The speaker

   (1) will live life to the fullest from now on
   (2) believes it is too late to live a full life
   (3) will take care of his material possessions from now on
   (4) will engage in courageous acts from now on
   (5) has moved from a life of wealth to one of poverty

Remember, poets often want to help their readers look at the world in a new way. To understand how they do this, look for ordinary words used in figurative ways.

Answers start on page 812.

Interpreting Symbols and Images

A **symbol** in a poem is a word or phrase that stands for an important idea, such as youth, age, life, death, or hope. A symbol is often difficult to recognize by itself. You need to look at the content of the poem to figure it out. A person, an object, an event, or anything else in a poem may be a symbol, and it may stand for one or several ideas.

An **image** appeals to the reader's senses. It recreates sensations of sight, taste, touch, smell, and hearing. A poet will create an image by using words that readers can associate with their own experience.

Read the following poem and answer the questions below.

Oread[1]

Whirl up, sea—
whirl your pointed pines,
splash your great pines
on our rocks,
hurl your green over us,
cover us with your pools of fir.

_____
[1] the mountain nymphs in Greek mythology

H. D. (Hilda Doolittle), *Collected Poems 1912–1944.*

symbol
a powerful image that represents a person, animal, place, or thing beyond the object it describes

image
a mental picture created by the imaginative use of words

1. What ideas do the images in this poem suggest? Put a check mark next to the correct answer.

   _____ a. energy and movement

   _____ b. peace and quiet

2. What feeling does the line "cover us with your pools of fir" create? Put a check mark next to the correct answer.

   _____ a. a sense of the struggle between humans and nature

   _____ b. a desire to be joined with the forces of nature

Option a is the correct answer to question 1. Everything about the poem—whirling, splashing, hurling—is full of energy. *Option b* is the correct answer for question 2. Although the poem gives a sense of wildness, there is no indication of battle or struggle. The image of being covered with trees gives the feeling of being one with nature.

 To identify symbols, look for repeated or closely related images. Repetition of an image often signals that the image is symbolic.

GED Practice

Directions: Choose the <u>one best answer</u> to each question.

<u>Questions 1 through 8</u> refer to the following poem.

WHAT GOES ON AT THE ZOO?

The Woman at the Washington Zoo

The saris go by me from the embassies.

Cloth from the moon. Cloth from another planet.
They look back at the leopard like the leopard.

And I. …
(5)   This print of mine, that has kept its color.
Alive through so many cleanings; this dull null
Navy I wear to work, and wear from work, and so
To my bed, so to my grave, with no
Complaints, no comment: neither from my chief,
(10) The Deputy Chief Assistant, nor his chief—
Only I complain … this serviceable
Body that no sunlight dyes, no hand suffuses
But, dome-shadowed, withering among columns,
Wavy beneath fountains—small, far-off, shining
(15) In the eyes of animals, these beings trapped
As I am trapped but not, themselves, the trap,
Aging, but without knowledge of their age,
Kept safe here, knowing not of death, for death—
Oh, bars of my own body, open, open!

(20) The world goes by my cage and never sees me.
And there come not to me, as come to these,
The wild beasts, sparrows pecking the llamas' grain,
Pigeons settling on the bears' bread, buzzards
Tearing the meat the flies have clouded. …
(25)   Vulture,
When you come for the white rat that the foxes left,
Take off the red helmet of your head, the black
Wings that have shadowed me, and step to me as man:
The wild brother at whose feet the white wolves fawn;
(30) To whose hand of power the great lioness
Stalks, purring. …
              You know what I was,
You see what I am: change me, change me!

Randall Jarrell, *The Woman at the Washington Zoo.*

1. What does the poem suggest about the speaker's job?

   (1) She is an office worker.
   (2) She is an animal keeper at a zoo.
   (3) She works for the military.
   (4) She is retired.
   (5) She works at an embassy.

2. Which of the following sentences best restates the meaning of the line "The world goes by my cage and never sees me" (line 20)?

   (1) She never has any visitors to her home.
   (2) She would like to travel more.
   (3) She feels as though her friends do not appreciate her.
   (4) She refuses to let others know her true self.
   (5) She sees life happening without her.

3. What does the speaker mean by "these beings trapped / As I am trapped but not, themselves, the trap" (lines 15–16)?

   (1) She and the animals are held captive for their own good.
   (2) She lives next to the zoo and seeing animals in cages upsets her.
   (3) She was once caught in an animal trap by accident.
   (4) She feels caged within herself just as the animals are penned in cages.
   (5) She feels as dangerous as a trapped animal.

4. Based on the information in the poem, which of the following is most likely the speaker's greatest wish?

   (1) to let the animals out of their cages
   (2) to have people notice her more often
   (3) to wear more interesting clothing
   (4) to break free of her life's routine
   (5) to get a promotion at work

5. Which of the following does the vulture mentioned in lines 25–33 most likely symbolize?

   (1) fear
   (2) life
   (3) nature
   (4) change
   (5) hunger

6. What two types of cloth are contrasted in the poem?

   (1) the colourful cloth of the saris and the dull cloth of the speaker's work clothes
   (2) cloth from the moon and cloth from another planet
   (3) the cloth that has kept its colour and the dull navy cloth
   (4) the cloth of the saris and the leopard-print cloth
   (5) the cloth of the speaker's work clothes and the cloth dyed by sunlight

7. Which of the following words best describes the tone of the poem?

   (1) furious
   (2) peaceful
   (3) despairing
   (4) patient
   (5) hopeful

8. Which of the following does the phrase "for death— / Oh, bars of my own body, open, open" (lines 18 and 19) most likely mean?

   The speaker

   (1) feels trapped by her physical limitations
   (2) feels that death will release her from captivity
   (3) deeply fears growing old
   (4) wishes she lived in a more exciting city
   (5) has a great fear of death

Answers start on page 813.

Making Inferences

Some poems are similar to puzzles—you need to figure out what the poet is suggesting in order to fully understand the poem. Then you make a decision based on your own understanding of what is indirectly stated. By considering the facts and information, you can make a logical decision about what the poem is about. But sometimes the facts are not spelled out. You must then make a decision based on stated and suggested information. This is called making an **inference.**

Of course, your inference may be reasonable and still not be correct. So, when reading a poem, be sure to make inferences using all the clues the poet provides; that is, the words the poet chooses and the images they create.

inference
an idea the reader figures out based on stated and suggested information

Read the following excerpt from a poem and complete the exercise below.

A Narrow Fellow in the Grass

A narrow Fellow in the Grass
Occasionally rides—
You may have met Him—did you not
His notice sudden is—

The Grass divides as with a Comb—
A spotted shaft is seen—
An then it closes at your feet
And opens further on—

Emily Dickinson, *The Poems of Emily Dickinson.*

1. What does this excerpt most resemble? Put a check mark by the correct answer.

       a. a riddle

       b. a joke

2. What can you infer is the subject of the poem? Put a check mark by the correct answer.

       a. a turtle

       b. a snake

3. Circle the clues from the poem that support your answer to question 2.

Option a is the correct answer to question 1. You must deduce the subject of the poem by using clues, which makes it similar to a riddle. *Option b* is the correct answer to question 2. Clues that you may have circled for question 3 include *narrow Fellow, Grass divides,* and *A spotted shaft.*

Tip

Take note of what is implied in the poem. Then add this to what is directly stated and make an inference based on both the direct and implied information.

GED Practice

Directions: Choose the one best answer to each question.

Questions 1 through 10 refer to the following poem.

HOW DOES THIS MAN FEEL ABOUT NATURE?

Earth and Rain, the Plants & Sun

Once near San Ysidro
on the way to Colorado,
I stopped and looked.

The sound of a meadowlark
(5)   through smell of fresh cut alfalfa.

Raho would say,
"Look, Dad." A hawk

sweeping
           its wings

(10)   clear through
               the blue
       of whole and pure
               the wind
                   the sky.

(15)   It is writhing
       overhead.
       Hear. The Bringer.
               The Thunderer.

       Sunlight falls
(20)   through cloud curtains,
       a straight bright shaft.

       It falls,
           it falls,
           down
(25)   to earth,
       a green plant.

Today, the Katzina[1] come.
The dancing prayers.

Many times, the Katzina.
(30)   The dancing prayers.
       It shall not end,
       son, it will not end,
       this love.
       Again and again,
(35)   the earth is new again.
       They come, listen, listen.
       Hold on to your mother's hand.
       They come

O great joy, they come.
(40)   The plants with bells.
       The stones with voices.
       Listen, son, hold my hand.

       ———————
       [1] Southwest Native American masked
       dancers who, during certain ceremonial
       rites, impersonate ancestral spirits

Simon J. Ortiz, *Woven Stone.*

1. Which of the following is the best
   restatement of lines 1–3?

   (1) You should always take time to stop and
       enjoy nature while traveling.
   (2) San Ysidro is the most beautiful area on
       the way to Colorado.
   (3) My schedule did not allow me to stop
       during my previous journey.
   (4) I stopped to look at the land around
       San Ysidro while travelling to Colorado.
   (5) The land around Colorado is worth
       stopping and looking at.

2. Which of the following phrases **best** describes the effect of the rhythm of lines 8–14?

It gives

(1) a quick and anxious feeling
(2) the feeling of gliding back and forth
(3) the peaceful feeling of a beautiful day
(4) a happy, excited feeling
(5) the feeling of a storm brewing in the distance

3. In which season does the poem <u>most likely</u> take place?

(1) spring
(2) summer
(3) winter
(4) fall
(5) harvest

4. Which of the following <u>best</u> describes the mood of the poem?

(1) joyful
(2) depressed
(3) angry
(4) surprised
(5) disinterested

5. Based on the context, who or what is "writhing / overhead" (lines 15–16)?

(1) a hawk and its prey
(2) the plants in the wind
(3) clouds filled with rain
(4) the Katzina dancers
(5) the falling sunlight

6. Based on the poem, what can be inferred about the speaker?

(1) He is leaving his wife and son.
(2) He is travelling with his family.
(3) He is making his journey alone.
(4) He is recalling a difficult journey.
(5) He is waiting to see a ceremonial dance.

7. To what or whom does the phrase "they come" in line 39 refer?

(1) the mother and son
(2) the hawks
(3) the plants with bells
(4) the renewal of the plants and earth
(5) the Katzina

8. What is the theme, or underlying message, of this poem?

(1) A day in the country goes by quickly.
(2) Travel with a child can be filled with pleasure.
(3) The earth is renewed by rainfall.
(4) The cycle of nature and plant life is wonderful.
(5) The Katzina dancers add ritual to our lives.

9. Based on the information in the poem, if the speaker could live anywhere he wanted, which of the following locations would he <u>most likely</u> choose?

(1) Toronto
(2) the suburbs
(3) the North Pole
(4) a space station
(5) a forest

10. To what do the lines "The plants with bells. / The stones with voices" (lines 40–41) <u>most likely</u> refer?

(1) The people have hung plants and stones with decorations.
(2) The plants and stones make music if you listen closely.
(3) The speaker is having a wonderful dream.
(4) The dancers seem as if they are a part of nature.
(5) The plants and stones have come to life.

Answers start on page 813.

Lesson 24

theme
the main idea in a work of literature, or a basic comment about life that the writer wants to share

To identify the theme of a poem, ask yourself, "What is the poet saying about life?" Try to sum up the theme in a single sentence.

Interpreting Theme

If a poem started with the words "Love will scar you," you could be fairly certain that its **theme,** or central idea, would have to do with the painful side of love. If, instead, you read "love is a rosebud," you would be guided toward a different theme. The theme of a poem expresses a specific opinion or belief about a larger topic. In the examples above, the topic is love, but the theme is what the poet has to say about love. For example, a theme might be that "love is a painful experience" (the scars) or "love is delicate and full of possibilities" (the rosebud).

Typically, the theme of a poem will not be directly stated. Therefore, you will have to infer it. You infer a theme by deciding what the poem is about (its topic) and then considering what the poet has to say about that topic. What figurative language and images does the poet use to describe the topic? What comparisons are made? What senses are involved? All of these are important clues to theme.

Read the following excerpt from a poem and answer the questions below.

The Wind in the Trees

> clears the morning of doves.
> You remember the loneliness,
> the loneliness you knew as a child
> when everyone in the house was busy.

Cathy Song, *Frameless Windows, Squares of Light: Poems.*

1. Put a check mark next to the main topic of this excerpt.

    _____ a. morning

    _____ b. loneliness

2. Put a check mark next to the theme of this excerpt.

    _____ a. Adults are too preoccupied to see the loneliness of childhood.

    _____ b. Childhood is a lonely and cruel time of life.

You are correct if you answered *option b* for question 1. The word *loneliness* is repeated twice in the short excerpt, giving it great emphasis. For question 2, *option a* is the correct answer. The theme is almost directly stated in the last two lines. *Option b* is incorrect because the poem does not indicate that all of childhood is lonely, nor that it is a cruel time of life.

GED Practice

Directions: Choose the <u>one best answer</u> to each question.

Questions 1 through 4 refer to the following poem.

WHY IS THE SPEAKER CALLING THE CHILD?

Calling the Child

From the third floor I beckon to the child
Flying over the grass. As if by chance
My signal catches her and stops her dance
Under the lilac tree;
(5)   And I have flung my net at something wild
And brought it down in all its loveliness.
She lifts her eyes to mine reluctantly,
Measuring in my look our twin distress.

Then from the garden she considers me
(10)   And gathering joy, breaks from the closing net
And races off like one who would forget
That there are nets and snares.
But she returns and stands beneath the tree
With great solemnity, with legs apart,
(15)   And wags her head at last and makes a start
And starts her humorous marching up the stairs.

Karl Shapiro, *Collected Poems 1940–1978.*

1. What is suggested by the child's "flying over the grass" (line 2)?

   (1) The child can actually fly.
   (2) The little girl has abundant energy.
   (3) The child is playing with a model airplane.
   (4) The girl is pretending to fly.
   (5) The girl is trying not to touch the grass.

2. Which of the following <u>best</u> describes what the speaker means by "Measuring in my look our twin distress" (line 8)?

   (1) The child looks like the speaker.
   (2) The speaker observes happiness in the child's eyes.
   (3) The child is a twin.
   (4) The speaker and the child have similar feelings of regret.
   (5) The speaker and the child are equally reluctant to stop their play.

3. What is the effect of the image of the net in the poem?

   (1) It emphasizes the child's untamed, free nature.
   (2) It shows that the speaker is a skilled hunter.
   (3) It shows that parents trap their children.
   (4) It shows that the speaker is heartless.
   (5) It shows how movement adds meaning to the poem.

4. Which of the following <u>best</u> states the theme of the poem?

   (1) Adults enjoy restricting a child's freedom.
   (2) There is the spirit of a child in everyone.
   (3) A natural, free spirit is eventually tamed by adulthood.
   (4) There should be no restrictions in life.
   (5) Children find humour in everything.

WHAT ARE THE TOURISTS DOING?

Fences

Mouths full of laughter,
the *turistas* come to the tall hotel
with suitcases full of dollars.

Every morning my brother makes
(5) the cool beach sand new for them.
With a wooden board he smooths
away all footprints.

I peek through the cactus fence
and watch the women rub oil
(10) sweeter than honey into their arms and legs
while their children jump waves
or sip drinks from long straws,
coconut white, mango yellow.

Once my little sister
(15) ran barefoot across the hot sand
for a taste.

My mother roared like the ocean,
"No. No. It's their beach.
It's their beach."

Pat Mora, *Communion.*

5. Which of the following <u>best</u> states the theme of the poem?

   (1) The tourists and the local people experience the beach differently.
   (2) Tourists pay such high prices that it is as if they own the beach.
   (3) Sometimes good fences are necessary to make good neighbours.
   (4) Small children are often disobedient.
   (5) A firm voice can help to control unruly children.

6. Which of the following ideas are <u>most</u> clearly contrasted in the poem?

   (1) beach and sea
   (2) freedom and restriction
   (3) maturity and childhood
   (4) misbehaviour and good manners
   (5) knowledge and ignorance

 Tip If the theme, or underlying message, of a poem is not stated directly, look for clues that tell you what the poem is about. A poet's tone and the images he or she chooses are two ways that the poem's theme can be expressed.

Answers start on page 814.

Directions: Choose the <u>one best answer</u> to each question.

Questions 1 through 6 refer to the following poem.

HOW DOES THIS WOMAN FEEL ABOUT HER NEW HOME?

Moving In

The telephone-installer was interested
In the students helping me.
He said he had a father of 93, plus a mother 77
And his wife kept running her heart out.
(5)   Students could help, what a good idea! Let me know
If at any time this telephone needs adjusting.

As he left, the upstairs apartment entered
With some slices of chocolate angel food cake
To make herself acquainted.
(10)   She was a retired librarian and it turned out
The one librarian I knew in the town I came from
Was an old friend of hers, they both came
From South Dakota mining country.

The telephone-installer returned to ask
(15)   If students were dependable? They can be.
Even more than a good chocolate cake, even more
Than a good telephone.
This could mean a new life for my wife and me, he said,
I think I'll bring you a longer cord for that phone.
(20)   Don't let this last piece of cake go begging, begged the upstairs apartment.

Josephine Miles, "Moving In," *Collected Poems 1930–83.*

1. Which of the following sentences best describes what the speaker and her new neighbour have in common?

   (1) Both are friends with the installer.
   (2) Both are from South Dakota.
   (3) Both have a librarian friend.
   (4) Both have just moved into the building.
   (5) Both enjoy talking with neighbours.

2. Which of the following best describes what the speaker means by "And his wife kept running her heart out" (line 4)?

   (1) The installer's wife likes to exercise.
   (2) The installer's wife is very busy.
   (3) The students like the installer's wife.
   (4) The installer cannot keep up with his wife.
   (5) The installer's wife has a medical condition.

3. What does the author mean by the phrase "the upstairs apartment" (line 7)?

   (1) the rental unit above the speaker's
   (2) the installer's elderly parents
   (3) the speaker's neighbour
   (4) the telephone installer
   (5) the students working nearby

4. What is the most likely reason the speaker states that students can be more dependable than cakes and telephones?

   (1) She has faith in humanity.
   (2) Cake disappears too quickly.
   (3) Her telephone is not working properly.
   (4) She has known the students for years.
   (5) She does not trust the installer.

5. In what way are the installer, the students, and the neighbour similar?

   They are

   (1) incompetent
   (2) unwanted
   (3) pushy
   (4) helpful
   (5) lonely

6. What is the tone of the poem?

   (1) conversational
   (2) celebratory
   (3) disapproving
   (4) forgiving
   (5) cautious

Paying extra attention to the punctuation within lines and at the end of lines can help you understand the rhythm and meaning of a poem.

Answers start on page 815.

Understanding Drama

In the following lessons, you will learn to analyze drama using both the spoken and the unspoken language of a play. The GED Language Arts, Reading Test will include drama selections to determine how well you understand this form of literature.

Understanding Plot

plot
the events in a play and the order in which they are arranged

Like a story, a play has a beginning, middle, and end. The events in a play, the order in which they occur, and how one thing leads to, or causes, another—from the opening of the play to the conclusion—is the **plot.**

In a typical plot, the exposition gives background information and introduces the setting and the characters. As the play develops, complications occur that create a conflict—a problem that needs to be resolved. The point at which the conflict reaches its peak is the climax. It represents the turning point of the play. Afterward, the tension decreases, and problems that were not resolved during the climax come to an end in the resolution.

Read the following summary of a play and complete the exercise below.

Two close friends, Valentine and Proteus, fall in love with Silvia, the daughter of the Duke of Milan. The duke, however, wants his daughter to marry a man named Thurio, whom Silvia does not love. Proteus betrays his friend Valentine and causes him to be banished from the kingdom. Silvia decides she wants to be with Valentine and escapes to the forest to join him. Proteus pursues Valentine and Silvia. He catches Silvia and is about to overpower her when Valentine rescues her. Valentine then forgives Proteus for his behaviour. Silvia's father arrives. The duke is impressed by Valentine's honourable conduct and gives his consent to a marriage between Silvia and Valentine. Proteus, meanwhile, realizes the error of his ways and becomes content to marry his former girlfriend, Julia.

1. Write a description of the climax of the play on the lines below.

   _____

   _____

For question 1, you may have written something such as *Valentine rescues Silvia from Proteus.*

To determine the complications in a plot, be alert to circumstances or events that make life more difficult for the characters. To identify conflicts, analyze the characters' reactions to the complications.

GED Practice

Directions: Choose the one best answer to each question.

Questions 1 through 4 refer to the following excerpt from a play.

WHAT HAS NORA DONE FOR HER HUSBAND?

MRS. LINDE: … A wife can't borrow without her husband's consent.

NORA: *(tossing her head)* Ah, but when it happens to be a wife with a bit of a (5) sense of business … a wife who knows her way about things, then …

MRS. LINDE: But, Nora, I just don't understand. …

NORA: You don't have to. I haven't said I (10) did borrow the money. I might have got it some other way. *(throws herself back on the sofa)* I might even have got it from some admirer. Anyone as reasonably attractive as I am …

(15) MRS. LINDE: Don't be so silly!

NORA: Now you must be dying of curiosity, Kristine.

MRS. LINDE: Listen to me now, Nora dear—you haven't done anything rash, (20) have you?

NORA: *(sitting up again)* Is it rash to save your husband's life?

MRS. LINDE: I think it was rash to do anything without telling him. …

(25) NORA: But the whole point was that he mustn't know anything. Good heavens, can't you see! He wasn't even supposed to know how desperately ill he was. It was me the doctors came (30) and told his life was in danger, that the only way to save him was to go South for a while. Do you think I didn't try talking him into it first? I began dropping hints about how nice it would (35) be if I could be taken on a little trip abroad, like other young wives. I wept, I pleaded, I told him he ought to show some consideration for my condition, and let me have a bit of my own way. (40) And then I suggested he might take out a loan. But at that he nearly lost his temper, Kristine. He said I was being frivolous, that it was his duty as a husband not to give in to all these (45) whims and fancies of mine—as I do believe he called them. All right, I thought, somehow you've got to be saved. And it was then I found a way.

Henrik Ibsen, *A Doll's House.*

1. Based on the dialogue in the scene, how can Nora's character best be described?

   (1) humble and obedient
   (2) hysterical and panicky
   (3) arrogant and evil
   (4) resourceful and determined
   (5) childish and impulsive

2. Which of the following words best describes the tone expressed in the excerpt?

   (1) frightened
   (2) secretive
   (3) hopeless
   (4) upbeat
   (5) humorous

3. Based on the excerpt, what would Mrs. Linde most likely do if a friend asked her to conceal an envelope containing important documents?

   (1) feel very offended
   (2) offer to help in some other way
   (3) feel honoured at the confidence
   (4) agree to the request enthusiastically
   (5) insist that her friend be straightforward

4. Why does Nora want to go South?

   (1) She wants to do some travelling.
   (2) She wants to do what is best for her husband's health.
   (3) She wants to take a break from her husband's temper.
   (4) She wants to save money.
   (5) She wants to leave her home and start a better life.

Answers start on page 815.

characters
the fictional people who participate in the events of the play

protagonist
the central character, who struggles to resolve one or more conflicts

To understand a character, examine what the character does and says. Look at the stage directions that refer to the character. Then look for clues in the dialogue of other characters; notice what they say about him or her.

Inferring Character

Characters in drama are fictional people who take part in a play's events. The main character is called the **protagonist.** The action and main conflict of the play centre on this character. The other characters that the protagonist encounters help bring about the climax.

How can you learn about a play's characters? First, you can learn about them from what they say in their dialogue with other characters. Dialogue may reveal what the characters feel or what they are thinking. It may also reveal details about the characters' backgrounds.

Second, you can learn about characters from their actions. The stage directions are words in parentheses that describe characters' gestures, movements, and expressions. Stage directions may also give details about costumes or the setting. For example, a description of a character wearing a wrinkled suit with one shoe untied helps you understand the type of person the character is.

Read the following excerpt from a play and complete the exercise below.

AUSTIN: I don't want to hear about it, okay? Go tell it to the executives! Tell it to somebody who's going to turn it into a package deal or something. A T.V. series. Don't tell it to me.
SAUL: But I want to continue with your project too, Austin. It's not as though we can't do both. We're big enough for that, aren't we?
AUSTIN: "We"? I can't do both! I don't know about "we."
LEE: *(to* SAUL*)* See, what'd I tell ya'. He's totally unsympathetic.
SAUL: Austin, there's no point in our going to another screenwriter for this. It just doesn't make sense. You're brothers. You know each other. There's a familiarity with the material that just wouldn't be possible otherwise.
AUSTIN: There's no familiarity with the material! None! I don't know what "Tornado Country" is. I don't know what a "gooseneck" is. And I don't want to know! *(pointing to* LEE*)* He's a hustler! He's a bigger hustler than you are! If you can't see that, then—

Sam Shepard, *True West.*

Put a check mark next to the answer that best describes Austin's attitude toward Saul in this excerpt.

_____ a. defiant

_____ b. cooperative

You are correct if you chose *option a.* Austin refuses to cooperate with Saul's plan for Austin to be part of this project.

GED Practice

Directions: Choose the <u>one best answer</u> to each question.

Questions 1 through 10 refer to the following excerpt from a play.

WHY DO TROY AND CORY DISAGREE?

TROY: I'm through with it now. You go on and get them boards. *(Pause.)* Your mama tells me you got recruited by a college football team? Is that right?

(5) CORY: Yeah. Coach Zellman say the recruiter gonna be coming by to talk to you. Get you to sign the permission papers.

TROY: I thought you supposed to be

(10)   working down there at the A&P. Ain't you suppose to be working down there after school?

CORY: Mr. Stawicki say he gonna hold my job for me until after the football

(15)   season. Say starting next week I can work weekends.

TROY: I thought we had an understanding about this football stuff? You suppose to keep up with your chores and hold

(20)   that job down at the A&P. Ain't been around here all day on a Saturday. Ain't none of your chores done … and now you telling me you done quit your job.

(25) CORY: I'm gonna be working weekends.

TROY: You damn right you are! And ain't no need for nobody coming around here to talk to me about signing nothing.

(30) CORY: Hey, Pop … you can't do that. He's coming all the way from North Carolina.

TROY: I don't care where he coming from. The white man ain't gonna let you get

(35)   nowhere with that football no way. You go on and get your book-learning so you can work yourself up in that A&P or learn how to fix cars or build houses or something, get you a trade. That

(40)   way you have something can't nobody take away from you.

You go on and learn how to put your hands to some good use. Besides hauling people's garbage.

(45) CORY: I get good grades, Pop. That's why the recruiter wants to talk with you. You got to keep up your grades to get recruited. This way I'll be going to college. I'll get a chance …

(50) TROY: First you gonna get your butt down there to the A&P and get your job back.

CORY: Mr. Stawicki done already hired somebody else 'cause I told him I was

(55)   playing football.

TROY: You a bigger fool than I thought … to let somebody take away your job so you can play some football. Where you gonna get your money to take out your

(60)   girlfriend and whatnot? What kind of foolishness is that to let somebody take away your job?

CORY: I'm still gonna be working weekends.

(65) TROY: Naw … naw. You getting your butt out of here and finding you another job.

CORY: Come on, Pop! I got to practice. I can't work after school and play football too. The team needs me.

(70)   That's what Coach Zellman say …

TROY: I don't care what nobody else say. I'm the boss … you understand? I'm the boss around here. I do the only saying what counts.

August Wilson, *Fences.*

1. Of what does Troy accuse Cory?

   (1) receiving failing grades in school
   (2) refusing to speak to the recruiter
   (3) spending too much money
   (4) not doing his chores
   (5) working too many hours at the A&P

2. How does Troy feel about Cory's decision?

   (1) Troy is quite pleased with Cory's choice.
   (2) Troy is happy for Cory but worries about his studies.
   (3) Troy is opposed to Cory's desire to play football.
   (4) Troy thinks Cory does not have enough money for college.
   (5) Troy believes Cory should quit school and work full time at the A&P.

3. Which of the following best describes what Cory wants?

   (1) to become the manager of the A&P
   (2) to go to college
   (3) to marry his girlfriend
   (4) to do whatever Troy thinks is best
   (5) to find another job

4. Which of the following phrases best describes the overall mood of the excerpt?

   (1) resigned and depressed
   (2) angry and bitter
   (3) forbidding and frightening
   (4) sorrowful and painful
   (5) tense and disharmonious

5. Based on the excerpt, which of the following is most likely to happen?

   (1) Cory's mother will tell the recruiter not to visit.
   (2) Mr. Stawicki will fire Cory from the A&P.
   (3) Corey will decide to stop doing his chores.
   (4) Troy will change his mind and talk to the recruiter.
   (5) Cory will try to reason with Troy.

6. Who is the central character in the excerpt?

   (1) Mr. Stawicki
   (2) Cory
   (3) Cory's coach
   (4) Cory's mother
   (5) Troy

7. Which of the following most likely causes Troy to make the statement, "The white man ain't gonna let you get nowhere with that football no way" (lines 34–35)?

   (1) Troy will say anything to persuade Cory to return to his job at the A&P.
   (2) Troy knows Coach Zellman and knows he is unfair.
   (3) Troy knows from experience that playing college sports gets students nowhere.
   (4) Troy has been treated unfairly in the past and is warning Cory.
   (5) Troy fears that Cory is not talented enough to make the team.

8. Which piece of advice is Troy most likely to give his son?

   (1) A parent must be hard on a child to avoid spoiling him or her.
   (2) A leader often does not know any more than the person following.
   (3) What is good for one person is good for everyone.
   (4) A true friend is always available to help you.
   (5) Seeking immediate gain can cost you later on.

9. What is the main reason Troy wants Cory to continue working at the A&P?

   (1) because he cannot afford Cory's tuition
   (2) so Cory can continue to do his chores
   (3) so Cory will have a job that cannot be taken away
   (4) so Cory will not waste time going to college
   (5) because football is a dangerous sport

10. Which of the following best describes Mr. Stawicki's attitude toward Cory?

   (1) amused
   (2) unappreciative
   (3) skeptical
   (4) displeased
   (5) supportive

Answers start on page 816.

Lesson 27

Understanding Motivation

Motivation is the reason a character behaves a certain way. A character's motivation tells who he or she really is. One way in which plays differ from novels and short stories is that plays are told entirely through dialogue and action. In a play, the characters' thoughts are not often directly revealed to the reader or audience. As a result, the motivations of the characters are sometimes more difficult to identify.

To understand what motivates the characters in a play, pay attention to what they say. Ask yourself why a character makes certain statements and what he or she hopes to achieve by making them. Characters' motivations can be found not only in what they say, however, but also in what they do. Stage directions, which may describe a character's actions, can also provide clues to motivation.

motivation
the reason a character does or says something

Discover a character's motivation by asking yourself, "Why is this character behaving this way?" Then try to figure out the true reason behind the character's words or actions.

Read the following excerpt from a play and complete the exercise below.

JESSIE *(Standing behind* MAMA *now, holding her shoulders):* Now, when you hear the shot, I don't want you to come in. First of all, you won't be able to get in by yourself, but I don't want you trying. Call Dawson, then call the police, and then call Agnes. And then you'll need something to do till somebody gets here, so wash the hot-chocolate pan. You wash that pan till you hear the doorbell ring and I don't care if it's an hour, you keep washing that pan.

MAMA: I'll make my calls and then I'll just sit. I won't need something to do. What will the police say?

Marsha Norman, *'night, Mother.*

1. Put a check mark next to the <u>most likely</u> motivation for the daughter to tell her mother to wash the pan.

   _____ a. She does not want her mother to hear the police arriving.

   _____ b. She does not want her mother to think about the shot.

   _____ c. She does not want her mother to get into trouble.

2. Put a check mark next to the statement that better describes the daughter's feelings toward her mother.

   _____ a. She cares about her mother.

   _____ b. She feels her mother is too nosy.

You are correct if you chose *option b* for question 1 and *option a* for question 2. The daughter seems to care about her mother. This is indicated both by her gesture of holding her mother's shoulders and by her words, which show concern for her mother's well-being.

GED Practice

Directions: Choose the <u>one best answer</u> to each question.

<u>Questions 1 through 5</u> refer to the following excerpt from a play.

WHAT DO THESE MEN HAVE IN COMMON?

LUKE: You play piano like I dreamed you would.

DAVID: I been finding out lately you was pretty good. Mama never let us keep a
(5) phonograph. I just didn't never hear any of your records—until here lately. You was right up there with the best, Jellyroll Morton and Louis Armstrong and cats like that. … You never come
(10) to look for us. Why?

LUKE: I started to. I wanted to. I thought of it lots of times.

DAVID: Why didn't you never do it? Did you think it was good riddance we was
(15) gone?

LUKE: I was hoping you wouldn't never think that, never.

DAVID: I wonder what you expected me to think. I remembered you, but couldn't
(20) never talk about you. I use to hear about you sometime, but I couldn't never say, That's my daddy. I was too ashamed. I remembered how you used to play for me sometimes. That was
(25) why I started playing the piano. I used to go to sleep dreaming about the way we'd play together one day, me with my piano and you with your trombone.

LUKE: David. David.

(30) DAVID: You never come. You never come when you could do us some good. You come now, now when you can't do nobody any good. Every time I think about it, think about *you,* I want to
(35) break down and cry like a baby. You make me—ah! You make me feel so bad.

LUKE: Son—don't try to get away from the things that hurt you. The things that
(40) hurt you—sometimes that's all you got. You got to learn to live with those things—and—use them.

James Baldwin, *The Amen Corner.*

1. What does David seem to want <u>most</u>?

    (1) to learn why his father became a musician
    (2) to forget about his father for good
    (3) to be a better musician than his father
    (4) to find out what his father thinks of him
    (5) to understand his father's absence

2. What does David <u>most likely</u> mean when he says, "You was right up there with the best" (line 7)?

    (1) Luke was one of David's heroes.
    (2) Luke lived in a good neighbourhood.
    (3) Luke was a great musician.
    (4) Mama hid Luke's records among the others.
    (5) Mama admired Luke a great deal.

3. What is the <u>most likely</u> reason that David started playing piano?

    (1) He had a natural talent for it.
    (2) He needed to occupy his free time.
    (3) He wanted to be a famous musician.
    (4) He was encouraged by his mother.
    (5) He wanted to be connected to his father.

4. Which of the following attitudes <u>best</u> describes David's feelings toward <u>his</u> father?

    (1) admiring and respectful
    (2) hurt and angry
    (3) indifferent and numb
    (4) hopeful and questioning
    (5) ashamed and embarrassed

5. What is the overall mood of this piece?

    (1) calm and comforting
    (2) violent and disruptive
    (3) gloomy and mournful
    (4) lighthearted and playful
    (5) emotional and earnest

Answers start on page 816.

Interpreting Theme

The central idea in a play is called the **theme.** The theme is the underlying meaning that the playwright wants the reader or audience to understand about the play. An example of a theme is "Friendship is based on understanding." It is not enough to say that the theme is friendship. You have to go one step further and answer the question, "What is it about friendship that the playwright is trying to say?" Usually, the playwright does not state the theme directly, so it is up to the reader or audience to decide what it is.

Remember, the theme is different from the general topic or a plot summary of the play. For example, imagine a play with two main characters—John, a Liberal, and Cynthia, a Conservative. The general topic might be a romance between the two characters. But the theme of this play might be "Love can overcome any differences."

Read the following excerpt from a play and complete the exercise below.

PETER: Are you in love?
SCOOP: Excuse me?
PETER: I like to think that when two people our age get married, they are in love.
HEIDI *(takes Peter's arm):* Peter's very romantic.
SCOOP: I see. Are you an item now?
HEIDI: No.
PETER *(louder):* Yes.
SCOOP: Makes sense. Lisa marries a nice Jewish lawyer; Heidi marries a warm Italian pediatrician. It's all interchangeable, isn't it? To answer your question am I in love, sure, why not?
HEIDI *(squeezes Peter's hand):* Why not?

Wendy Wasserstein, *The Heidi Chronicles.*

Put a check mark next to the statement that best identifies the theme of this excerpt.

_____ a. Scoop and Heidi are old friends.

_____ b. Peter is too outspoken.

_____ c. Reacting defensively with friends is not productive.

_____ d. Love is a delicate subject between some friends.

You are correct if you chose *option d*. The friends seem to want to talk about their love lives, but also seem cautious about revealing too much. This is the underlying message of the excerpt.

theme
the central idea in a piece of literature

To identify theme, ask yourself, "What does this play say about human nature? What is the most important point the playwright is trying to make?"

GED Practice

Directions: Choose the <u>one best answer</u> to each question.

Questions 1 through 11 refer to the following excerpt from a play.

DOES MEDVEDENKO LOVE MASHA?

MEDVEDENKO: Why do you always wear black?

MASHA: I am in mourning for my life. I'm unhappy.

(5) MEDVEDENKO: You unhappy? I can't understand it. Your health is good, and your father is not rich but he's well enough off. My life is much harder to bear than yours. I get twenty-three

(10) roubles a month, and that's all, and then out of that the pension fund has to be deducted, but I don't wear mourning. (They sit down.)

MASHA: It isn't a question of money. Even

(15) a beggar can be happy.

MEDVEDENKO: Yes, theoretically he can, but not when you come right down to it. Look at me, with my mother, my two sisters and my little brother, and my

(20) salary twenty-three roubles in all. Well, people have to eat and drink, don't they? Have to have tea and sugar? Have tobacco? So it just goes round and round.

(25) MASHA: (Glancing towards the stage) The play will begin soon.

MEDVEDENKO: Yes. The acting will be done by Nina Zaretchny and the play was written by Constantine

(30) Gavrilovitch. They are in love with each other, and today their souls are mingled in a longing to create some image both can share and true to both. But my soul and your soul can't find any

(35) ground to meet on. You see how it is. I love you; I can't stay at home because I keep wishing so for you; and so every day I walk four miles here and four miles back and meet with nothing but

(40) indifference on your side. That's only natural. I've got nothing, we're a big family. Who wants to marry a man who can't even feed himself?

MASHA: Fiddlesticks! (She takes snuff)

(45) Your love touches me, but I can't return it, that's all. (Offers him snuff) Help yourself.

MEDVEDENKO: I'd as soon not. (A pause.)

(50) MASHA: My, how close it is! It must be going to storm tonight. All you do is philosophise or talk about money. You think the worst misery we can have is poverty. But I think it's a thousand

(55) times easier to go ragged and beg for bread than—But you'd never understand that—

Anton Chekhov, *The Sea Gull.*

1. Which statement <u>best</u> describes Medvedenko's father?

   (1) He is usually at home with the family.
   (2) He is out of town on business.
   (3) He works hard all day.
   (4) He is sick at home.
   (5) He does not live with the family.

2. Which of the following phrases <u>best</u> describes Medvedenko?

   (1) sincere and lonely
   (2) moody and arrogant
   (3) lighthearted and sweet
   (4) dull and uneducated
   (5) pathetic and victimized

3. What does Masha mean when she says that Medvedenko's love touches her (line 45)?

   (1) She is beginning to love him back.
   (2) She appreciates his feelings.
   (3) She is angry that he will not leave her alone.
   (4) She is struggling to keep her love hidden.
   (5) She is trying to give him hope for their future.

4. Which of the following best describes the relationship between Masha and Medvedenko?

   (1) one-sided love
   (2) secret love
   (3) deep friendship
   (4) mutual respect
   (5) friendly acquaintanceship

5. Which of the following statements best describes the theme developed in the excerpt?

   (1) Happiness does not depend on money.
   (2) Love is often unexpected.
   (3) Persistence will win you the one you love.
   (4) Opposite personalities attract one another.
   (5) Money makes life easier.

6. How does the statement "It must be going to storm tonight" (lines 50–51) contribute to the mood of the excerpt?

   It suggests

   (1) restlessness
   (2) ease
   (3) danger
   (4) sudden freedom
   (5) unearthly power

7. Based on the excerpt, what is the most likely meaning of "I can't stay at home because I keep wishing so for you" (lines 36–37)?

   (1) Medvedenko is unhappy at home and has abandoned his family.
   (2) Medvedenko hates himself and feels he does not deserve his home.
   (3) Medvedenko feels compelled by love to visit Masha.
   (4) Medvedenko is so cheap he will not share his wealth with his family.
   (5) Medvedenko feels guilty for seeing Masha.

8. Which of the following reasons is the most likely motivation for Medvedenko's mentioning that the actress and the playwright are in love with each other?

   (1) He thinks it will give additional meaning to the play.
   (2) He hopes the information will change Masha's feelings.
   (3) He enjoys gossiping about wealthy and famous people.
   (4) He thinks Masha will enjoy the information.
   (5) He contrasts their relationship with his relationship with Masha.

9. Why does Medvedenko think Masha will not marry him?

   (1) because she dislikes him
   (2) because he is poor
   (3) because they have nothing in common
   (4) because she is too unhappy
   (5) because he worries too much

10. Which of the following is the most likely reason that Medvedenko refuses the snuff?

    (1) He does not like to use it.
    (2) He knows the play is about to begin.
    (3) He prefers to continue the conversation.
    (4) He is upset that Masha doesn't love him.
    (5) He doesn't want to appear to be a beggar.

11. If Medvedenko were a travelling shoe salesman, what kind would he most likely be?

    (1) He would be persistent and try to win over customers.
    (2) He would be shy and not want to bother people.
    (3) He would complain about the customers.
    (4) He would make more sales than anyone else.
    (5) He would refuse to travel long distances.

Answers start on page 817.

Directions: Choose the <u>one best answer</u> to each question.

Questions 1 through 6 refer to the following excerpt from a play.

WHAT KIND OF FRIEND IS MRS. X?

MRS. X.: Now you must see what I have bought for my little chicks. *(Takes out a doll.)* Look at this. That's for Lisa. Do you see how she can roll her eyes and (5) turn her head. Isn't she lovely? And here's a toy pistol for Maja.

(She loads the pistol and shoots it at MISS Y. who appears frightened.)

MRS. X.: Were you scared? Did you think I (10) was going to shoot you? Really, I didn't think you'd believe that of me. Now if *you* were to shoot me it wouldn't be so surprising, for after all I did get in your way, and I know you never forget it— (15) although I was entirely innocent. You still think I intrigued to get you out of the Grand Theatre, but I didn't. I didn't, however much you think I did. Well, it's no good talking, you will believe (20) it was me … *(Takes out a pair of embroidered slippers.)* And these are for my old man, with tulips on them that I embroidered myself. As a matter of fact I hate tulips, but he has to have (25) tulips on everything.

(MISS Y. looks up, irony and curiosity in her face.)

MRS. X: *(putting one hand in each slipper)* Look what small feet Bob has, hasn't (30) he? And you ought to see the charming way he walks—you've never seen him in slippers, have you?

(MISS Y. laughs.)

MRS. X.: Look, I'll show you.

(35) *(She makes the slippers walk across the table, and MISS Y. laughs again.)*

MRS. X.: But when he gets angry, look, he stamps his foot like this. "Those damn girls who can never learn how to make (40) coffee! Blast! That silly idiot hasn't trimmed the lamp properly!" Then there's a draught under the door and his feet get cold. "Hell, it's freezing, and the damn fools can't even keep (45) the stove going!"

(She rubs the sole of one slipper against the instep of the other. MISS Y. roars with laughter.)

MRS. X.: And then he comes home and (50) has to hunt for his slippers, which Mary has pushed under the bureau … Well, perhaps it's not right to make fun of one's husband like this. He's sweet anyhow, and a good, dear husband. (55) You ought to have had a husband like him, Amelia. What are you laughing at? What is it? Eh? And, you see, I know he is faithful to me. Yes, I know it. He told me himself—what *are* you (60) giggling at?—that while I was on tour in Norway that horrible Frederica came and tried to seduce him. Can you imagine anything more abominable?

August Strindberg, *The Stronger.*

1. Based on the information in the excerpt, how does Mrs. X. <u>most likely</u> feel about her husband?

   (1) She is angry that he is flirtatious.
   (2) She wishes he were less angry.
   (3) She thinks he is a silly old man.
   (4) She is thinking about a divorce.
   (5) She is glad that she married him.

2. Which of the following words <u>best</u> describes Mrs. X.?

   (1) friendly
   (2) grateful
   (3) vindictive
   (4) sinister
   (5) manipulative

3. Why does Mrs. X. say to Miss Y., "if *you* were to shoot me it wouldn't be so surprising" (lines 11–13)?

   (1) Miss Y. hates Mrs. X.
   (2) Miss Y. cannot be trusted.
   (3) Mrs. X. thinks Miss Y. resents her.
   (4) Mrs. X. and Miss Y. have long been enemies.
   (5) Miss Y. is emotionally unstable.

4. Which of the following words <u>best</u> describes the relationship between the two women?

   (1) warm
   (2) competitive
   (3) guarded
   (4) hostile
   (5) honest

5. If Miss Y. decided to speak her true feelings to Mrs. X., which of the following statements would she <u>most likely</u> make?

   (1) I never cared about the Grand Theatre.
   (2) That is a terrible imitation of your husband.
   (3) I know more about you than you think I do.
   (4) You are the funniest person I know.
   (5) Your husband is a lucky man.

6. Later in the play, Mrs. X. says, " You just sit there without moving—like a cat at a mouse-hole. You can't drag your prey out, you can't chase it, but you can out-stay it." Based on this information and the excerpt, which of the following <u>best</u> describes Miss Y.?

   (1) cunning
   (2) unintelligent
   (3) indifferent
   (4) mean
   (5) lazy

Tip

A character's motivation can be revealed by the way he or she treats the other characters. Does the character speak to the other characters respectfully? Or is he or she unfriendly?

Answers start on page 818.

Directions: Choose the <u>one best answer</u> to each question.

Questions 1 through 4 refer to the following excerpt from an essay.

WOULD YOU HIRE THIS MAN?

As for my own business, even that kind of surveying which I could do with most satisfaction my employers do not want. They would prefer that I should do my work
(5)   coarsely and not too well, ay, not well enough. When I observe that there are different ways of surveying, my employer commonly asks which will give him the most land, not which is most correct. I
(10) once invented a rule for measuring cordwood, and tried to introduce it in Boston; but the measurer there told me that the sellers did not wish to have their wood measured correctly—that he was
(15) already too accurate for them, and therefore they commonly got their wood measured in Charlestown before crossing the bridge.
The aim of the laborer should be, not to
(20) get his living, to get "a good job," but to perform well a certain work; and, even in a pecuniary sense, it would be economy for a town to pay its laborers so well that they would not feel that they were working for
(25) low ends, as for a livelihood merely, but for scientific, or even moral ends. Do not hire a man who does your work for money, but him who does it for love of it.

Henry David Thoreau, "Life Without Principle," from *Major Writers of America*.

1. Based on the excerpt, which of the following opinions does the author <u>most likely</u> hold about some of his clients?

   (1) They criticize his work too much.
   (2) They like Charlestown better than Boston.
   (3) They don't pay him enough.
   (4) They are a little dishonest.
   (5) They are very lazy.

2. Based on the excerpt, what would the author <u>most likely</u> do if he were offered a job doing something that he did not like?

   (1) accept the job for the money
   (2) turn down the job
   (3) accept it but do a bad job
   (4) demand more money
   (5) hire someone else to do the job

3. Based on the excerpt, which statement correctly contrasts Thoreau (the author) and his employers?

   (1) Thoreau is hardworking, and his employers are not.
   (2) Thoreau and his employers are both surveyers.
   (3) Thoreau loves his work, and his employers do not.
   (4) Thoreau prefers accuracy, and his employers prefer money.
   (5) Thoreau invents new rules, and his employers steal his ideas.

4. What is the main idea of the last paragraph?

   (1) Workers should not care about money or other material things.
   (2) Towns should pay workers very well.
   (3) Workers should do what they love and be paid well for it.
   (4) Workers who are paid well will love their jobs.
   (5) Towns should hire people with high morals.

WHY IS THIS BIRD SINGING?

Sympathy

I know what the caged bird feels, alas!
    When the sun is bright on the upland slopes;
When the wind stirs soft through the springing grass,
And the river flows like a stream of glass;
(5)   When the first bird sings and the first bud opes,
And the faint perfume from its chalice steals—
I know what the caged bird feels!

I know why the caged bird beats his wing
    Till its blood is red on the cruel bars;
(10) For he must fly back to his perch and cling
When he fain would be on the bough a-swing;
    And a pain still throbs in the old, old scars
And they pulse again with a keener sting—
I know why he beats his wing!

(15) I know why the caged bird sings, ah me,
    When his wing is bruised and his bosom sore,—
When he beats his bars and he would be free;
It is not a carol of joy or glee,
    But a prayer that he sends from his heart's deep core,
(20) But a plea, that upward to Heaven he flings—
I know why the caged bird sings!

Paul Laurence Dunbar, *The Complete Poems of Paul Laurence Dunbar.*

5. Which of the following statements best explains why the bird's wing is "bruised and his bosom sore" (line 16)?

  (1) The bird has accidentally flown into the cage's bars.
  (2) The bird has hurt himself while struggling to escape his cage.
  (3) The bird is injuring himself on purpose because he is unhappy.
  (4) The bird's cage is too small for a creature of his size.
  (5) The bird's cage contains no good place on which he can land.

6. What does the word "chalice" refer to in the phrase, "faint perfume from its chalice" (line 6)?

  (1) the bird
  (2) the cage
  (3) a flower
  (4) the river
  (5) a gentle breeze

7. Which of the following ideas are most clearly contrasted in the poem?

  (1) freedom and imprisonment
  (2) fear and joy
  (3) violence and peacefulness
  (4) life and death
  (5) truth and deception

Questions 8 through 10 refer to the following excerpt from a review.

IS THIS FILM A SLAM DUNK?

There are quite a few strong players in *Love and Basketball*, but for the most part they have to stay on the bench. Four talented actors (Alfre Woodard, Dennis

(5) Haysbert, Debbi Morgan and Harry J. Lennix) play the stars' parents, and every one of them turns out to be more interesting than the young lovers who are the focus of the movie.

(10) This is not to say that stars Sanaa Lathan and Omar Epps are less than adequate as hoopsters who take a long, long time to realize they love each other as much as they love the game. Lathan and

(15) Epps are appealing (though they seem rather short for the roles) as suburban kids who grow up so close that one can hear the other whispering through a bedroom window. The actors do what they can to

(20) give life to these glossy characters, but they have no rough edges and their struggles turn out to be far more predictable than the average basketball game.

Though writer/director Gina Prince-

(25) Bythewood's direction is smooth and slick (especially so considering that this is her first feature), her plot is awkwardly structured. The movie is divided into four periods, like a basketball game, but this

(30) attempt to impose structure on a meandering tale feels arbitrary. Childhood conflicts we were never told about suddenly become plot complications midway through the movie—then are

(35) resolved just as abruptly a few scenes later. A basketball game played strip poker-style looks exciting in the coming attractions trailer, but it lacks snap in the actual movie because the competitors are

(40) already lovers when they play the scene.

By the very nature of its subject, *Love and Basketball* holds some interest, and anyone curious about what basketball players go through in the college and pro

(45) years will learn a thing or two (though not a lot). But a love story with a basketball backdrop is by its very nature so unusual, so there's no excuse for this one to feel so pat and predictable. One wishes producer

(50) Spike Lee had stepped in to give the dialogue some sass. …

Andy Seiler, " 'Love and Basketball' misses the net," *USA Today.*

8. Which of the following statements expresses the reviewer's overall opinion of the movie?

   (1) It is an appealing, though flawed, love story.
   (2) It is based on a clichéd combination of sports and romance that does not work.
   (3) It fails miserably in its attempt to portray first love.
   (4) It successfully tells the story of the coming-of-age of a basketball player.
   (5) It is a believable, true-to-life story of young love.

9. What is the effect of the author's repetition of the word "long" in the phrase "hoopsters who take a long, long time to realize they love each other" (lines 12–13)?

   (1) It expresses the reviewer's enthusiasm for his subject.
   (2) It suggests that there is a slow, plodding pace to the movie.
   (3) It shows that the reviewer is very patient.
   (4) It implies that the movie is actually too short.
   (5) It suggests that the main characters are cautious about love.

10. Which of the following changes most likely would have caused the reviewer to react more favourably to the film?

   (1) if the lead actors were different
   (2) if the director were more experienced
   (3) if the subject matter did not involve basketball
   (4) if the setting were the inner city rather than the suburbs
   (5) if the plot were structured differently

Questions 11 through 15 refer to the following excerpt from a novel.

WHAT IS THIS MAN'S JOB?

It was a pleasure to burn.

It was a special pleasure to see things eaten, to see things blackened and *changed.* With the brass nozzle in his fists,
(5) with this great python spitting its venomous kerosene upon the world, the blood pounded in his head, and his hands were the hands of some amazing conductor playing all the symphonies of blazing and
(10) burning to bring down the tatters and charcoal ruins of history. With his symbolic helmet numbered 451 on his stolid head, and his eyes all orange flame with the thought of what came next, he flicked the
(15) igniter and the house jumped up in a gorging fire that burned the evening sky red and yellow and black. He strode in a swarm of fireflies. He wanted above all, like the old joke, to shove a marshmallow on a
(20) stick in the furnace, while the flapping pigeon-winged books died on the porch and lawn of the house. While the books went up in sparkling whirls and blew away on a wind turned dark with burning.

Ray Bradbury, *Fahrenheit 451.*

11. Based on the information in the excerpt, what is the character doing?

   (1) fighting a huge house fire
   (2) conducting a training session for firefighters
   (3) burning a pile of trash at the local dump
   (4) burning a house filled with books
   (5) supervising a display of fireworks

12. Which of the following jobs would the character in this excerpt most likely enjoy?

   (1) conductor
   (2) construction worker
   (3) demolition worker
   (4) librarian
   (5) chef

13. Which of the following techniques does the author use to bring the excerpt to life?

   (1) detailed imagery
   (2) realistic dialogue
   (3) first-person narration
   (4) conflict between characters
   (5) a sense of humour

14. What is the meaning of the statement "the house jumped up in a gorging fire" (lines 15–16)?

   (1) The flames descended from the top of the house.
   (2) The flames immediately engulfed the house.
   (3) The flames on the lawn suddenly illuminated the house.
   (4) The house collapsed as the fire turned it to ashes.
   (5) The house glowed in the weakening flames.

15. To what does the phrase "this great python spitting its venomous kerosene" (lines 5–6) refer?

   (1) the character, who feels like a poisonous snake getting ready to strike
   (2) a poisonous snake that will be let loose upon the world
   (3) a hose that is suggestive of a snake
   (4) the flames that curve upward like a snake about to strike
   (5) the stream of water being sprayed on the fire like a spitting snake

To figure out what is happening in a complex excerpt, try to ignore the descriptive words and phrases and focus on the action words (verbs) instead. These words can point to what a character is actually doing.

Questions 16 through 20 refer to the following excerpt from a play.

IS MRS. DUDGEON PLEASED?

MRS. DUDGEON: … Oh, it's you, is it, Mrs. Anderson?

JUDITH: *(very politely—almost patronizingly)* Yes. Can I do anything

(5) for you, Mrs. Dudgeon? Can I help to get the place ready before they come to read the will?

MRS. DUDGEON: *(stiffly)* Thank you, Mrs. Anderson, my house is always ready

(10) for anyone to come into.

JUDITH: *(with complacent amiability)* Yes, indeed it is. Perhaps you had rather I did not intrude on you just now.

MRS. DUDGEON: Oh, one more or less

(15) will make no difference this morning, Mrs. Anderson. Now that you're here, you'd better stay. If you wouldn't mind shutting that door! (JUDITH *smiles, implying "How stupid of me!" and shuts*

(20) *it with an exasperating air of doing something pretty and becoming.)* That's better. I must go and tidy myself a bit. I suppose you don't mind stopping here to receive anyone that

(25) comes in until I'm ready.

JUDITH: *(graciously giving her leave)* Oh yes, certainly. Leave that to me, Mrs. Dudgeon; and take your time. *(She hangs up her cloak and bonnet.)*

(30) MRS. DUDGEON: *(half sneering)* I thought that would be more in your way than getting the house ready.

George Bernard Shaw, *The Devil's Disciple.*

16. Based on this excerpt, what do Mrs. Dudgeon's words and actions indicate?

   (1) She is patient and long-suffering.
   (2) She is gentle and easygoing.
   (3) She is pure and high-minded.
   (4) She is stingy and tightfisted.
   (5) She is rude and touchy.

17. Based on the stage directions, which of the following is the best description of Judith?

   (1) sweet and self-sacrificing
   (2) smug and self-satisfied
   (3) high-strung and sensitive
   (4) depressed and withdrawn
   (5) angry and defensive

18. Which of the following best states the main idea of this excerpt?

   (1) Judith has arrived very early for a party at Mrs. Dudgeon's.
   (2) Judith is an unexpected guest for the reading of a will.
   (3) Judith and Mrs. Dudgeon are trying to become friends.
   (4) Judith's politeness has made an awkward meeting easier.
   (5) Mrs. Dudgeon is pleased that Judith has come to help.

19. Which of the following best describes the mood of this excerpt?

   (1) mournful
   (2) tense
   (3) lighthearted
   (4) suspenseful
   (5) tender

20. What is the most likely reason that Mrs. Dudgeon says, "I thought that would be more in your way than getting the house ready" (lines 30–32)?

   (1) She did not hear Judith's offer to help clean.
   (2) She thinks Judith is excellent at greeting people.
   (3) She believes Judith is untidy.
   (4) She thinks Judith was insincere about wanting to clean.
   (5) She wants to be kind to Judith.

Questions 21 through 24 refer to the following excerpt from a short story.

WHY DID THIS WOMAN'S SISTER LEAVE HOME?

I was getting along fine with Mama, Papa-Daddy, and Uncle Rondo until my sister Stella-Rondo just separated from her husband and came back home again.

(5) Mr. Whitaker! Of course I went with Mr. Whitaker first, when he first appeared here in China Grove, taking "Pose Yourself" photos, and Stella-Rondo broke us up. Told him I was one-sided. Bigger on one

(10) side than the other, which is a deliberate, calculated falsehood: I'm the same. Stella-Rondo is exactly twelve months to the day younger than I am and for that reason she's spoiled.

(15) She's always had anything in the world she wanted and then she'd throw it away. Papa-Daddy gave her this gorgeous Add-a-Pearl necklace when she was eight years old and she threw it away playing baseball

(20) when she was nine, with only two pearls.

So as soon as she got married and moved away from home the first thing she did was separate! From Mr. Whitaker! This photographer with the popeyes she said

(25) she trusted. Came home from one of those towns up in Illinois and to our complete surprise brought this child of two.

Mama said she like to make her drop dead for a second. "Here you had this

(30) marvelous blonde child and never so much as wrote your mother a word about it," says Mama. "I'm thoroughly ashamed of you." But of course she wasn't.

Stella-Rondo just calmly takes off this

(35) *hat,* I wish you could see it. She says, "Why, Mama, Shirley T.'s adopted, I can prove it."

"How?" says Mama, but all I says was, "H'm!" There I was over the hot stove,

(40) trying to stretch two chickens over five people and a completely unexpected child into the bargain, without one moment's notice.

Eudora Welty, "Why I Live at the P.O.," *A Curtain of Green and Other Stories.*

21. What does the narrator mean when she says she was "trying to stretch two chickens over five people" (lines 40–41)?

She did not have enough

(1) recipes to suit everyone's taste
(2) food to feed everyone
(3) time to go grocery shopping
(4) feather blankets for all the beds
(5) room in the kitchen to cook dinner

22. What would the narrator most likely do if Mr. Whitaker were to drop in?

She would

(1) scold him for running off with her younger sister
(2) refuse to let him in
(3) tell him how disappointed she is in him
(4) make room for a sixth person at the table
(5) ask him if Stella-Rondo is telling the truth about the child

23. Which of the following best describes the tone of this excerpt?

(1) dramatic
(2) suspenseful
(3) lighthearted
(4) serious
(5) irritable

24. Which of the following words best describes the narrator's attitude toward Stella-Rondo?

(1) protective
(2) resentful
(3) supportive
(4) suspicious
(5) concerned

To understand tone, try "hearing" how the characters in a story would speak their lines.

Answers start on page 819.

Unit 6

MATHEMATICS

The GED Mathematics Test will cover the following content and skills.

The Test

- Test of 80% multiple-choice questions, 20% alternative format questions
- Calculator allowed on Part 1
- 90 minutes to complete both parts

The Content

- Numbers and operations
- Measurement, data analysis, and probability
- Algebra
- Geometry

The Questions

- Conceptual understanding
- Procedural knowledge
- Problem solving

Government use of taxpayers' money, control of federal spending, and the reduction of the deficit are all problems faced by the Canadian federal and provincial governments. Our members of Parliament in Ottawa are responsible for the entire country, while their provincial counterparts are involved in projects and civic enterprises at a provincial level. All members of government study the complex problems confronting Canada. Once they understand an issue, they consider methods to handle the problem and work toward a solution.

Problem solving in math follows a similar path. First, you must understand the concept or problem; what is it that you want to know? Next, you consider ways to solve the problem: what information do you have? How can you use that information to find the solution? Finally, you use what you know to solve the problem. This unit shows you how to understand concepts, select procedures to solve problems, and find solutions.

When studying our country's problems, our government faces many challenges. Your own challenges are probably just as unique. One of the bonuses to earning your GED is that you will have fine-tuned your skills to meet your challenges with confidence and determination.

Which of the senses do you use to learn?

Not everyone learns the same way. Know which senses are most helpful as you learn, and use them when you study.

- If it's hearing, read lessons aloud.
- If it's sight, draw diagrams and pictures.
- If it's touch, create models.

Numbers and Operations

Lesson 1

Numbers are an important part of your daily life. Have you ever calculated the distance between where you are and where you want to go? When was the last time that you estimated whether you had enough cash to purchase items in a store? Have you ever paid part of a bill and then figured out how much you had left to pay?

All these everyday actions rely on your understanding of numbers, number sense, and basic math operations. This unit covers basic number sense and operations with whole numbers, fractions, decimals, and percents. Keep in mind that you will use the skills in this unit on 20 percent to 30 percent of the questions on the GED Mathematics Test.

Number and Operation Sense

Place Value

Whole numbers are made up of these ten digits: 0, 1, 2, 3, 4, 5, 6, 7, 8, and 9. The number 3820 has four digits; 1 000 000 is a seven-digit number, although six of the digits are the same.

Our number system is based on place value. Place value means that the value of a digit depends on its position, or place, in a number. This chart shows the names of the first 9 whole number places.

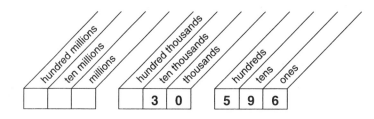

The total value of a number is the sum of the values of the digits in each place.

Example   What is the value of each digit in 30 596?
3 is in the ten thousands place. $3 \times 10\,000 =$ **30 000**
0 is in the thousands place. $0 \times 1\,000 =$ **0 000**
5 is in the hundreds place. $5 \times 100 =$ **500**
9 is in the tens place. $9 \times 10 =$ **90**
6 is in the ones place. $6 \times 1 =$ **6**

Reading and Writing Numbers

When writing a number, leave a space every three digits counting from the right. Each group of three digits is called a period and is named for the number place to the left of the space. Always read a number from left to right. Read each group of digits before a space; then say the name of the period the space represents.

Write a number in words exactly as you read it aloud. Do not say or write the word *and* or *ones* when reading or writing whole numbers.

Example   Read the number 12 950 068, and write it in words.

12 950 068
millions thousands [ones]

The number is read and written in words as **twelve million, nine hundred fifty thousand, sixty-eight.**

Tip

Four-digit numbers can be written with or without a space. The number four thousand five hundred twenty can be written as 4520 or 4 520. Both are correct.

Rounding Whole Numbers

Use rounding to make difficult calculations easier to perform. Round the numbers you are working with when you do not need an exact answer.

Example   Round the number 24 902 to the thousands place.

Step 1 Find the digit you want to round to. Circle it.	2④902
Step 2 Look at the digit to the right of the circled digit.	2④902
Step 3 If the digit to the right is 5 or more, add 1 to the circled digit. If the digit is less than 5, do not change the circled digit. Change all digits to the right of the circled digit to zeros.	2⑤000

Examples   Round to the nearest thousand.   ③499 rounds to **3 000**
                                                  1⑨930 rounds to **20 000**

A. Write the value of the underlined digit in words. Refer to the chart on page 458.

1. 5 5̲17 _____

2. 3̲ 742 691 _____

3. 4 7̲00 510 _____

4. 964 2̲51 _____

B. Round each number as directed. Refer to the chart on page 458.

5. Round 8 671 to the hundreds place. _____

6. Round 5 099 620 to the nearest million. _____

Answers start on page 822.

Comparing, Ordering, and Grouping

When shopping, you often compare prices to find the best buy. You can use the following rules when comparing whole numbers.

RULE 1 The whole number with the most digits is always greater.

Example Compare 7235 and 848. The number 7235 (4 digits) is greater than 848 (3 digits).

RULE 2 When two numbers have the same number of digits, compare the digits from left to right.

Example 646 is less than 690 because 40 is less than 90.

To write number comparisons, use the following symbols:

=	means *equals*	140 = 140	140 equals 140
>	means *is greater than*	25 > 23	25 is greater than 23
<	means *is less than*	4 < 5	4 is less than 5

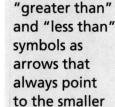

Tip

Think of the "greater than" and "less than" symbols as arrows that always point to the smaller number.

Using the same rules, you can put several numbers in order of value.

Example 1 An Internet company sells books, toys, and videos. Yesterday, the company recorded these sales in each category: books, 1247; toys, 1271; and videos, 990. Arrange the sales in order from least to greatest.

Step 1 Count the digits in the sales numbers. Since 990 has only 3 digits and the other numbers have 4 digits, 990 is less than the other two sales numbers.

Step 2 Compare the digits in 1247 and 1271, working from left to right. The digits in the thousands place and the hundreds place are the same in both numbers. So, look at the tens place in each. Since 40 is less than 70, the number 1247 is less than 1271.

From least to greatest, the sales are **990, 1247,** and **1271.**

Understanding place value can also help you find the range that contains a certain number.

Example 2 Samuel is looking for file #13496. A label on the front of each drawer tells the range of file numbers in the drawer. For example, Drawer A contains files numbered from 13090 to 13274. Which drawer contains file #13496?

Drawer A	Drawer B	Drawer C	Drawer D
#13090 to #13274	#13275 to #13490	#13491 to #13598	#13599 to #14701

Compare the number 13496 to the signs. File #13496 will be between the two numbers on the correct drawer. Since 13496 is greater than 13491 and less than 13598, the file is found in **Drawer C.**

Choosing the Operation

To solve math word problems, you must make several decisions. You need to decide what the question is asking and what information you require to solve the problem. You must also choose the operation needed to solve the problem: addition, subtraction, multiplication, or division.

Read the word problem carefully, and think about the information you are given in the problem and how you will solve it. Here are some guidelines that may help you choose an operation.

You	When You Need To
Add (+)	Combine quantities Find a total
Subtract (−)	Find a difference Take away a quantity Compare to find "how many more," "how much less," or "how much is left"
Multiply (×)	Put together equal amounts to find a total Add the same number repeatedly
Divide (÷)	Split a quantity into equal parts

Example 1   Victor has a grocery bill of $55 and a drugstore bill of $12. Which operation shows the total of the bills?

    (1) $55 + $12
    (2) $55 − $12
    (3) $12 × $55
    (4) $55 ÷ $12
    (5) $12 − $55

You need to find a total, so you add the amounts. The correct answer is **option (1).**

Example 2   Ahmed, Rita, and Lilia are sharing equally the $126 profit from their yard sale. Which operation shows how much each person will receive?

    (1) 3 + $126
    (2) $126 − 3
    (3) $126 × 3
    (4) $126 ÷ 3
    (5) 3 ÷ $126

To split $126 into equal amounts, divide. The correct answer is **option (4).**

Tip

Note: The order in which you write numbers in subtraction and division problems is important. The amount being subtracted from or being divided must come first.

GED Practice

Directions: Choose the one best answer to each question.

1. The Chang family pays a car loan payment of $269 a month. Which of the following operations shows how much they will pay on the loan in 12 months?

   (1) 12 + $269
   (2) $269 − 12
   (3) $269 × 12
   (4) $269 ÷ 12
   (5) 12 − $269

2. Last month Teresa paid $137 to heat her home. This month she paid $124. Which of the following operations shows the total cost of heating her home for the 2 months?

   (1) $137 + $124
   (2) $137 − $124
   (3) $124 × $137
   (4) $137 ÷ $124
   (5) $124 ÷ $137

3. Carl filled up the gas tank on his delivery truck. The total cost of the gas is shown on the pump below. If he paid for the gas with a fifty-dollar bill, which of the following operations shows how much money Carl should get back in change?

   (1) $50 + $28
   (2) $28 − $50
   (3) $28 × $50
   (4) $50 ÷ $28
   (5) $50 − $28

4. Kim needs to read a 348-page book for class. She has three weeks to read it, and she plans to read an equal number of pages each week. Which of the following operations shows how many pages Kim must read per week?

   (1) 3 + 348
   (2) 348 − 3
   (3) 348 × 3
   (4) 348 ÷ 3
   (5) 3 ÷ 348

5. Mark starts with $327 in his chequing account. If he writes a cheque for $189, which of the following operations shows how much will be left in his account?

   (1) $189 + $327
   (2) $327 − $189
   (3) $189 × $327
   (4) $327 ÷ $189
   (5) $189 ÷ $327

6. Four friends carpool to work together Monday through Friday. Each week they pay a total of $62 for gas, parking, and tolls. Which of the following operations shows how they could split the cost evenly?

   (1) 4 + $62
   (2) $62 − 4
   (3) 4 × $62
   (4) 4 ÷ $62
   (5) $62 ÷ 4

You need to read a problem carefully to find all the numbers. Sometimes a number appears as a word, such as "four" friends.

Answers start on page 822.

Operations with Whole Numbers

Adding and Subtracting Whole Numbers

Lesson 2

One key to success in math is knowing how to perform the basic operations accurately and when to use each operation. Use addition to combine quantities or to find a total or sum. Follow these steps to add whole numbers.

Step 1   Line up the numbers being added so that digits with the same place value are aligned. Start with the ones column. Working from right to left, add the numbers in each column.

Step 2   When a column of digits has a sum greater than 9, regroup, or carry, to the next column on the left.

Example 1   EZ Video rented 169 videos on Thursday and 683 videos on Friday. Find the total rentals for the two days.

Step 1   Add the ones column (9 + 3 = 12). Write 2 in the ones column; regroup 1 to the tens column.

Step 2   Continue adding the remaining columns, regrouping when necessary.

$$
\begin{array}{r} 1 \\ 169 \\ +683 \\ \hline 2 \end{array}
\qquad
\begin{array}{r} 1\,1 \\ 169 \\ +683 \\ \hline 852 \end{array}
$$

On your calculator, enter the numbers to be added.

   169 **+** **683** **=** **852.**

EZ Video rented a total of **852 videos** on Thursday and Friday.

Use subtraction to find the difference between two numbers or amounts. Follow these steps to subtract whole numbers.

Step 1   Write the number being subtracted below the other number, making sure to line up the place-value columns. Starting with the ones column, work from right to left, subtracting the numbers in each column.

Step 2   When a digit in the bottom number is greater than the digit above it, you must regroup, or borrow, to subtract the column.

Example 2   Jeff's Home Repair charges $5025 to remodel a kitchen and $2438 to paint a two-storey house. Find the difference in cost.

Step 1   Arrange the numbers in columns. Regroup 1 ten from the tens column to subtract the ones column (15 − 8 = 7).

$$
\begin{array}{r} 1\;15 \\ \$50\cancel{2}\cancel{5} \\ -\;2438 \\ \hline 7 \end{array}
$$

Step 2   Subtract the tens column. Regroup. Since there are no hundreds, borrow from the thousands. Now there are ten hundreds in the hundreds column.

$$
\begin{array}{r} 4\;10\,1\;\;15 \\ \$\cancel{5}\cancel{0}\cancel{2}\cancel{5} \\ -\;2438 \\ \hline 7 \end{array}
$$

<table>
<tr><td></td><td style="text-align:right">9 11</td></tr>
</table>

Step 3	Finally, regroup from the hundreds column and complete the subtraction.

$$\begin{array}{r} \overset{9\ 11}{4\ \cancel{10}\cancel{1}\ 15} \\ \$\cancel{5025} \\ -\ 2438 \\ \hline \$2587 \end{array}$$

Step 4	Check your answer by adding the result and the number you subtracted. The sum should equal the top number in the problem.

$$\begin{array}{r} \overset{1\ 1\ 1}{} \\ \$2587 \\ +\ 2438 \\ \hline \$5025 \end{array}$$

On your calculator, enter the larger number first.

5025 − **2438** = **2587.**

The remodelling job costs **$2587** more than the painting job.

Multiplying and Dividing Whole Numbers

Use multiplication when you need to add the same number many times. The answer to a multiplication problem is called the product. Follow these steps to multiply.

Step 1	Working from right to left, multiply the digits in the top number by the digit in the ones column of the bottom number to find a partial product. Then multiply the top number by the tens digit of the bottom number to find a partial product and so on.
Step 2	Line up each partial product under the digit you multiplied by. Then add the partial products together.

Example 1	A company spends $913 per week on advertising. How much will the company spend in 52 weeks?

Step 1	To multiply $913 by 52, first multiply $913 by the ones digit, 2. The partial product 1826 is lined up under the ones column.	$\begin{array}{r}\$913\\ \times\ \ 52\\ \hline 1\ 826\end{array}$
Step 2	Multiply $913 by the tens digit, 5. The partial product 4565 is lined up under the tens column. Use zero as a placeholder. Add the partial products to find the product.	$\begin{array}{r}45\ 650\\ \hline \$47\ 476\end{array}$

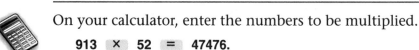

On your calculator, enter the numbers to be multiplied.

913 × **52** = **47476.**

The company will spend **$47 476** on advertising in a 52-week period.

Use division when you need to separate a whole (the dividend) into equal parts. The answer to a division problem is called a quotient. The example will help you understand the steps in long division. Put the dividend inside the bracket. Put the number you are dividing by (the divisor) outside the bracket on the left. Work from left to right.

Example 2   Elena is packaging glassware. She packs 18 juice glasses into each carton. If she has 7310 glasses to pack, how many cartons can she completely fill?

Step 1   Divide 7310 by 18. Since 18 does not go into 7, look at the first two digits: divide 18 into 73. Write 4 in the answer above the hundreds place. Multiply 18 by 4, and then subtract that amount from 73. Bring down the next digit.

$$\begin{array}{r} 4 \\ 18\overline{)7310} \\ 72 \\ \hline 11 \end{array}$$

Step 2   18 will not divide into 11. Write 0 above the tens place in the quotient and bring down the next digit (the ones digit). Divide 18 into 110. Write 6 in the answer above the ones place. Multiply 18 by 6 and then subtract that amount from 110. This result, 2, is called the remainder. Use the letter r to show the remainder.

$$\begin{array}{r} 406 \text{ r2} \\ 18\overline{)7310} \\ 72 \\ \hline 110 \\ 108 \\ \hline 2 \end{array}$$

Step 3   To check your answer, multiply it by the number you divided by. Then add the remainder. The result should be the number you were dividing.

$$\begin{array}{r} 406 \\ \times\ 18 \\ \hline 3248 \\ 4060 \\ \hline 7308 \\ +\ \ \ 2 \\ \hline 7310 \end{array}$$

To divide using a calculator, enter the numbers in the order shown below. On a calculator, the remainder is given as a decimal. You will learn more about decimal remainders in Lesson 9.

7310 ÷ 18 = 406.1111111

This answer tells us Elena can fill **406 cartons** and will have some glasses left over.

Solve these problems using paper and pencil.

1. $\begin{array}{r} 746 \\ \times\ \ 5 \end{array}$

2. $\begin{array}{r} 4862 \\ \times\ \ \ 9 \end{array}$

3. $\begin{array}{r} 36 \\ \times 23 \end{array}$

4. $\begin{array}{r} 5084 \\ \times\ \ 76 \end{array}$

5. $7\overline{)3206}$

6. $4\overline{)23\ 984}$

7. $12\overline{)76\ 402}$

8. $24\overline{)219\ 315}$

9. $2584 \times 2700 =$

10. Multiply 25 097 by 25.

11. $190 \times 2186 =$

12. Divide 139 400 by 205.

Answers start on page 822.

GED Practice

Directions: Choose the <u>one best answer</u> to each question. Use your calculator when indicated.

1. Last month the Lees paid $137 to heat their home. This month they paid $124. What is the total cost of heating their home for the two months?

   (1) $ 13
   (2) $130
   (3) $161
   (4) $251
   (5) $261

2. Maurice has $827 in his chequing account. He writes a cheque for $189. How much will be left in the account?

   (1) $1016
   (2) $ 762
   (3) $ 738
   (4) $ 648
   (5) $ 638

Question 3 refers to the following diagram.

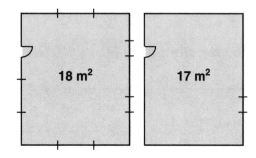

18 m²   17 m²

3. Alexa is buying carpet for her home. The diagram shows the amount of carpeting needed for each of two rooms. What is the total square metres of carpet that Alexa needs?

   (1) 35
   (2) 38
   (3) 32
   (4) 306
   (5) 40

4. The Valdez family pays $289 a month on a car loan. How much will the family spend on the car loan in a year?

   (1) $ 289
   (2) $ 360
   (3) $1200
   (4) $2890
   (5) $3468

 5. Six friends commute to work together. Each week, the gas, parking, and tolls cost $114. If they split the costs equally, how much does each friend pay per week toward the commuting costs?

   (1) $ 17
   (2) $ 18
   (3) $ 19
   (4) $108
   (5) $120

 6. Emiko worked 68 hours in 2 weeks. She earns $7 per hour. How much did she earn in the 2 weeks?

   (1) $ 51
   (2) $ 75
   (3) $435
   (4) $476
   (5) $952

On the GED Mathematics Test you will need to know common equivalencies such as
24 hours = 1 day; 7 days = 1 week
52 weeks = 12 months = 1 year

Answers start on page 823.

Mathematics • Numbers and Operations

Basic Calculator Functions

For Part I of the GED Mathematics Test, each testing centre will provide examinees with a CASIO *fx-260SOLAR* scientific calculator. Throughout this book, you will practise solving problems with calculators. Although various calculators may look different, the keys on the calculators function the same way. For more information about the calculator used on the GED Test, review the Calculator Handbook, pages 913–916.

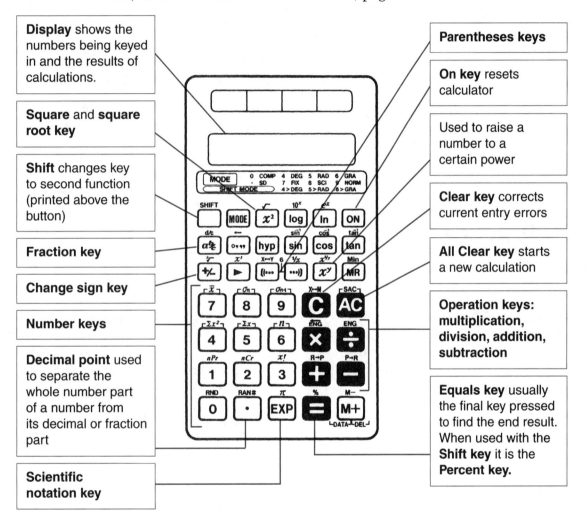

Display shows the numbers being keyed in and the results of calculations.

Square and **square root key**

Shift changes key to second function (printed above the button)

Fraction key

Change sign key

Number keys

Decimal point used to separate the whole number part of a number from its decimal or fraction part

Scientific notation key

Parentheses keys

On key resets calculator

Used to raise a number to a certain power

Clear key corrects current entry errors

All Clear key starts a new calculation

Operation keys: multiplication, division, addition, subtraction

Equals key usually the final key pressed to find the end result. When used with the **Shift key** it is the **Percent key.**

Here are some more important points about calculator use:

- Even though you may be only entering whole numbers, many calculators will automatically display a decimal point at the end of the whole number.
- When adding or multiplying, it doesn't matter in what order the numbers are entered. However, it is very important to enter the numbers in the correct order when subtracting or dividing.
  - **Subtraction problems**—the number being taken away must be entered second: 32 − 28
  - **Division problems**—the number being divided must be entered first: 24 ÷ 3

You can practise with the GED calculator at the testing centre before taking the test.

Example 1   Katie drove 236 km on Friday, 304 km on Saturday, and 271 km on Sunday. How many kilometres did she drive during the three days?

Add to find the total number of kilometres that Katie drove.

$$236 + 304 + 271$$

You can enter these numbers in a calculator in any order. It is very important, however, to make sure that the digits within a number stay in the same order. Any of the following entries will give you the same answer.

236 ＋ 304 ＋ 271 ＝   or 271 ＋ 304 ＋ 236 ＝

or 304 ＋ 271 ＋ 236 ＝

You should see the answer **811** in the display. It is not necessary to press the ＝ key until you finish entering all the numbers.

Example 2   Malik's workteam made 1056 widgets in 6 hours. How many widgets did they make per hour?

1056 ÷ 6 ＝   NOT 6 ÷ 1056 ＝

You should see the answer **176** in the calculator display.

GED Practice

Directions: Choose the <u>one best answer</u> to each question. You <u>may</u> use your calculator.

1. Scott changed the oil in his car when the odometer read 35 297 km. The next time he changed the oil, the odometer read 38 874 km. How many kilometres did he drive between oil changes?

   (1) 3377
   (2) 3477
   (3) 3577
   (4) 3677
   (5) 3777

2. Each month Carlos pays $595 in rent. How much rent does he pay in two years?

   (1) $ 1190
   (2) $ 5950
   (3) $ 7140
   (4) $14 280
   (5) $28 560

3. On Wednesday, J & R Electronics had total sales of $14 688 for its new stereo system. If each system sold for $459 (including tax), how many new stereo systems did J & R sell?

   (1) 31
   (2) 32
   (3) 33
   (4) 34
   (5) 35

4. Kim's bank statement listed a balance of $76 in her chequing account. Over the next month, she made deposits of $96, $873, and $98. What is the new balance in her account after all these transactions?

   (1) $ 603
   (2) $1047
   (3) $1067
   (4) $1134
   (5) $1143

Answers start on page 823.

Steps for Solving Word Problems

Estimating to Solve Problems

To estimate means to find an approximate value. Suppose you stop at the grocery store to buy a few items, but you have only $20. How do you know whether you have enough to pay for the items? You could estimate a total by rounding each price up to the nearest whole dollar and adding.

A good way to estimate an answer is to round the numbers in the problem to a convenient place value.

Example 1 The city of Lakewood has 13 968 registered voters. In a recent election, only 4787 people voted. Approximately how many registered voters did not vote?

    (1)   6500
    (2)   7500
    (3)   8000
    (4)   9000
    (5) 10 000

To find the difference between the number of registered voters and the number of people who voted, you need to subtract. The word *approximately* tells you to estimate the answer. To estimate the difference, round the numbers to the nearest thousand and subtract.

Estimate: 14 000 − 5000 = 9000. The correct answer is **option (4).**

You can also use estimation to see whether a computed answer makes sense. In the problem below, estimate first to see that your answer should be around 9000. You subtract and get 9181 as your answer. Your estimate confirms that this answer makes sense.

Example 2 Lakewood has 13 968 registered voters. In a recent election, only 4787 people voted. How many voters did not vote?

    (1)   2917
    (2)   4787
    (3)   8221
    (4)   9181
    (5) 18 755

Use the estimate from Example 1 to eliminate options (1), (2), and (5) as either too low or too high. Subtract: 13 968 − 4787 = 9181. **Option (4)** is correct. Your estimate tells you that it makes sense.

An estimate can help you check whether your answer makes sense. Estimating is also a quick check that you have pressed the correct calculator keys.

Another way to estimate is to work with compatible numbers. Numbers that divide exactly and are easy to work with are compatible. To estimate the answer to a division problem, find compatible numbers that are close to the numbers in the problem.

Example 3   Clarissa divides 1935 by 9. She uses her calculator, and the display reads 21.44444444. Is her answer reasonable?

The number 9 is close to 10, and 1935 is close to 2000. You know that $2000 \div 10 = 200$, so the correct answer should be close to 200. Clarissa's answer of a little more than 21 is too low. She may have pressed a wrong key on her calculator. She should rework the problem. The answer is **215.**

Choosing and Organizing Information

Some problems present more information than you need to solve a problem. Your first step is to organize the information, if necessary, and then to find the facts you need.

Tables and charts contain many items of data organized in columns and rows. To find the information you need, pay close attention to labels, titles, and headings. Don't be distracted by information that you do not need to solve the problem.

Example 1   The Fairfax Public Library kept the following records on the number of books checked out from January through April.

January	February	March	April
10 356	7542	7625	9436

How many more books were borrowed in April than in February?

(1)   83
(2)   820
(3)   1811
(4)   1894
(5) 16 978

You are asked to find the difference between February and April so you need only the numbers for those two months to solve the problem. Subtract to find the difference: $9436 - 7542 = 1894$. The correct answer is **option (4) 1894.**

Some problems may not give all the information you need. Read the problem carefully. What facts do you need to answer the question?

Tip

Don't use all the numbers given in a problem just because they are there. Always think about what you are asked to find and then use only those amounts that apply.

Writing in Answers in a Standard Grid

One type of special format question that appears on the GED Mathematics Test is the standard grid shown below. For this type of question, instead of choosing among five multiple-choice options, you write and mark in your answer on the grid.

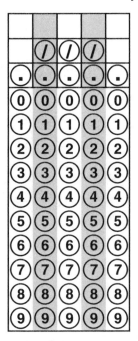

Here are some important points to keep in mind when using the standard grid:

- The grid is used to enter a single numerical answer.
- The row at the top is blank and is intended for you to write in your answer. Although you can actually leave this row blank, it is helpful to fill it in as a guide for marking in the circled numbers in the rows below.
- Your answer can start in any of the five columns, as long as your answer is complete.
- Any unused columns should be left blank.
- For answers that are whole numbers, you will not use the second row of fraction bars, $\oslash$, or the third row of decimal points, $\odot$.

Example   Mark drove 157 km on Saturday and 189 km on Sunday. How many kilometres did he drive during the two days?

The total number of kilometres for the two days is $157 + 189 = 346$.

First write the answer 346 in the blank first row. Then colour in the corresponding circled numbers in the standard grid below. Since the answer can start in any of the five columns, all three grids shown below are correctly filled in.

GED Practice

Directions: Solve the following problems and enter your answers on the grids provided.

1. Susan's weekly gross salary is $615. If $172 is taken out for taxes and $35 is taken out for other deductions, what is Susan's weekly take-home salary?

3. Six sisters send their family a total of $720 every month. If the contribution is divided equally among the sisters, how much does each sister contribute?

2. Alberto buys a computer and pays for it in 24 equal monthly installments. If each installment is $78, how much will Alberto pay in all for the computer?

4. This week Lourdes earned $620 in commissions on her sales. If this amount is $54 more than she earned last week, how much did she earn in commissions last week?

Answers start on page 823.

Steps for Solving Multi-Step Problems

Order of Operations

Multi-step problems require more than one calculation. Often, they involve more than one operation. Read the problem carefully, think about the situation, and do the operations in the order that gives the correct answer. Some questions on the GED Mathematics Test ask you to choose the correct method for solving a problem; others ask you to find the answer. In both situations, you need to know how to write and evaluate mathematical expressions that contain more than one operation.

The order in which you do operations in multi-step problems may affect your answer. Look at the problem $6 + 3 \times 5$. This problem uses both multiplication and addition. There are two ways to work the problem, and they give different results; only one is correct. Do you know which one?

Option 1   Multiply first (3×5), then add: $6 + 15 = 21$
Option 2   Add first ($6 + 3$), then multiply: $9 \times 5 = 45$

The answer could be 21 or 45 depending on the order in which the operations are performed. Mathematicians have agreed on an order of operations. With these rules, everyone gets the same solution to a problem. Following the order of operations, the correct answer is **21.**

Step 1   Do operations in parentheses.
Step 2   Do multiplication and division in order from left to right.
Step 3   Do addition and subtraction in order from left to right.

Example 1 $7 \times 4 + 15 \div 3 - 12 \times 2 = ?$

Step 1   There are no parentheses. Go on to the next step.
Step 2   Multiply and divide:

$$7 \times 4 + 15 \div 3 - 12 \times 2 = ?$$
$$28 \quad + \quad 5 \quad - \quad 24 \quad = ?$$

Step 3   Add and subtract:

$$33 \quad - \quad 24 \quad = 9$$

The correct solution is **9.**

Parentheses are used to change the order of operations. Always do an operation in parentheses first.

Example 2 $(12 + 8) \div 4 - 2 = ?$
Without the parentheses, you would begin by dividing 8 by 4, but the parentheses tell you to add first.

Step 1   Do the operation in parentheses: $(12 + 8) \div 4 - 2 = ?$
Step 2   Divide: $20 \quad \div 4 - 2 = ?$
Step 3   Subtract: $5 \quad - 2 = 3$

The correct solution is **3.**

Try remembering the order of operations using the acronym BEDMAS:

<u>B</u>rackets
<u>E</u>xponents
<u>D</u>ivision and
<u>M</u>ultiplication
<u>A</u>ddition and
<u>S</u>ubtraction

(More on exponents in Lesson 18)

There are other properties of numbers that will help you solve problems. The commutative property applies to both addition and multiplication. This property states that you can add or multiply numbers in any order and the result will be the same.

Examples $a + b = b + a$ $a \times b = b \times a$
$7 + 5 = 5 + 7$ $6 \times 3 = 3 \times 6$

The associative property also applies to both addition and multiplication. When adding or multiplying three or more numbers, the way in which you group the numbers does not affect the final result.

Examples $(a + b) + c = a + (b + c)$ $(a \times b) \times c = a \times (b \times c)$
$(15 + 2) + 8 = 15 + (2 + 8)$ $(18 \times 5) \times 20 = 18 \times (5 \times 20)$

Solving Multi-Step Problems

To solve a multi-step problem you perform more than one calculation. The key to solving multi-step problems is to think about the situation, identify the needed information, and identify each step and operation needed *before* you work the problem.

The examples below and on the next page are based on the following information.

Employee	Hourly Wage	Hours Worked				
		M	T	W	T	F
D. Suddeth	$8	8	7	8	8	6
S. Bartok	$9	7	5	6	5	5

Example 1 How much did Dillon Suddeth earn for the week?

(1) $259
(2) $296
(3) $320
(4) $333
(5) Not enough information is given.

There are two steps: Determine how many hours Dillon worked, and then multiply the number of hours by the hourly wage.

Step 1 Add the hours worked for each day: $8 + 7 + 8 + 8 + 6 = 37$
Step 2 Multiply by the hourly wage of $8: $37 \times \$8 = \$296$

The correct answer is **option (2) $296.**

There may be different ways to solve a problem. In Example 1 you could find the daily earnings (hours worked each day × the hourly wage). Then add the daily earnings to find the earnings for the week.

Example 2 Sharon Bartok set a goal of earning $342 per week. How many more hours would she have to work this week to reach her goal?

(1) 10
(2) 28
(3) 38
(4) 90
(5) 252

Compare the hours Sharon needs to work to earn $342 to the number of hours she already worked during the week shown in the table.

Step 1 Sharon earns $9 per hour. Divide to find how many hours she needs to work to earn $342. $342 \div 9 = 38$

Step 2 Add to find the hours she worked during the week shown. $7 + 5 + 6 + 5 + 5 = 28$

Step 3 Compare by subtracting. $38 - 28 = 10$

The correct answer is **option (1) 10.**

GED Practice

Directions: Choose the one best answer to each question.

1. West Freight held an awards banquet for its 65 employees. The company paid $350 for the use of a banquet room and $9 per person for food. Which expression shows how much the company paid for the room and the food?

   (1) $65 \times \$350$

   (2) $65 \times \$9$

   (3) $(\$350 + \$9)65$

   (4) $(65 \times \$9) + \$350$

   (5) $\frac{(\$350 + \$9)}{65}$

2. David can drive 300 km on 1 tank of gas. Which expression shows how many tanks of gas he will need to drive 1200 km?

   (1) $300 + 1200$

   (2) $1200 - 300$

   (3) 300×1200

   (4) $\frac{300}{1200}$

   (5) $\frac{1200}{300}$

3. A parking garage has spaces for 70 cars and charges each driver $6 per day for parking. If all the spaces are full, which expression shows how much more the garage owner could make if he charged $8 per day?

   (1) $70 + \$8 + \$6$

   (2) $70 \times \$8 \times \$6$

   (3) $70(\$8 - \$6)$

   (4) $70(\$6 + \$8)$

   (5) $\frac{(70 \times \$6)}{(70 \times \$8)}$

4. Arturo had $150 to spend on his university books. He bought 2 textbooks costing $35 each and 3 textbooks for $18 each. Which expression shows how much money he had left after his purchase?

   (1) $\$150 - (2 \times \$35) + (3 \times \$18)$

   (2) $\$150 - (2 \times \$35) - (3 \times \$18)$

   (3) $(2 \times \$35) - (3 \times \$18)$

   (4) $\$150 - \$35 - \$18$

   (5) $\$150 \times \$35 \times \$18$

Answers start on page 824.

Order of Operations

The order of operations also applies when using a calculator.

Step 1   Do operations in parentheses.
Step 2   Do multiplication and division in order from left to right.
Step 3   Do addition and subtraction in order from left to right.

You should always check to see whether the calculator you are using is programmed with the order of operations. You can perform this simple test. Key in the following expression:

$$3 \quad + \quad 4 \quad \times \quad 2 \quad =$$

If your calculator is programmed with the order of operations, it will perform the multiplication first ($4 \times 2 = 8$), and then the addition ($3 + 8$). The correct answer is **11.**

If your calculator does not have the order of operations programmed into it, it will perform the operations in the order that you enter the numbers, giving $3 + 4 = 7$ first, and then $7 \times 2 = 14$ as the answer. If your calculator does not perform the order of operations, you need to be very careful when using your calculator to help you solve problems.

Example 1   Constance, an office assistant, is buying 3 printer cartridges that cost $24 each. If she gives the cashier a $100 bill, how much change should she receive?

To solve this problem, you could key in the following expression on your calculator:

$$100 \quad - \quad 3 \quad \times \quad 24 \quad =$$

Remember, be careful if you are using a calculator that does not have the order of operations programmed into it. The calculator will display the wrong answer of 2328.

In order to get the correct answer with this calculator, follow the order of operations by keying in the multiplication first: $3 \times 24 = 72$. Then subtract the result from 100: $100 - 72 = 28$. The correct answer is **$28.**

Example 2   Anthony has already saved $272. If he saves $2 a day for 1 year, how much will he have saved in all?

First think of 1 year as 365 days. Solve by adding how much Anthony has now to how much he will save. Be sure the multiplication is performed first.

$$2 \quad \times \quad 365 \quad + \quad 272 \quad =$$

The final answer is **$1002.**

GED Practice

 Directions: Choose the <u>one best answer</u> to each item. You <u>may</u> use your calculator.

Questions 1 and 2 refer to the following information.

The tenants in two apartment buildings agree to hire a private trash collector to serve their buildings. The total yearly cost of the service will be $3096. There are 18 apartments in one building and 25 apartments in the other.

1. Which combination of operations would you need to perform to find out how much each apartment will pay per year for the service if each apartment pays an equal share of the cost?

   (1) addition and multiplication
   (2) addition and division
   (3) subtraction and division
   (4) multiplication and subtraction
   (5) multiplication and division

2. How much is each apartment's share of the yearly cost?

   (1) $ 7
   (2) $ 43
   (3) $ 72
   (4) $124
   (5) $172

3. What is the value of the expression 2184 + 1476 × 408?

   (1)   498 982
   (2)   499 982
   (3)   598 093
   (4)   604 392
   (5) 1 493 280

Questions 4 and 5 refer to the following table.

Stock Purchases	
Stock	Price per Share
Ampex	$58
Branton	$87
Comtex	$92

4. Marissa invests money for her clients. She purchased 112 shares of Ampex and 89 shares of Comtex. What was the total cost?

   (1) $ 201
   (2) $ 351
   (3) $ 6496
   (4) $ 8188
   (5) $14 684

5. Marissa also bought 68 shares of Branton stock for a different client. If this client had $6000 to invest, how much money still remains to be invested?

   (1) $ 84
   (2) $ 155
   (3) $ 5845
   (4) $ 5916
   (5) $516 084

6. Last month, Delta Computers had net sales of $685 170 for its laptop computers. If each laptop computer cost $1986, how many were sold?

(1) 694 700

(2)   3500

(3)   3450

(4)   345

(5)   35

7. Atlas Corp. gave each of its 1216 employees a $760 year-end bonus. What was the total amount of the year-end bonuses?

(1) $924 160

(2) $ 92 416

(3) $ 9242

(4) $ 9241

(5) Not enough information is given.

8. What is the value of 50 + 15 000 ÷ 25?

(1) 650

(2) 602

(3) 250

(4) 200

(5) 25

9. Last year, a bookstore sold 569 346 novels, 234 908 biographies, and 389 782 travel books. What was the total number of books sold in these three categories?

(1) 11 940 360

(2) 1 194 036

(3)   119 404

(4)   11 940

(5) Not enough information is given.

10. What is the value of $40(50 - 5 \times 2)$?

(1)   40

(2)   800

(3) 1600

(4) 3600

(5) 3990

11. In a recent election, the winner received 290 876 more votes than his opponent. If the winner received 3 898 705 votes, how many votes did his opponent receive?

(1) 4 189 581

(2) 4 089 581

(3) 3 707 829

(4) 3 608 829

(5) 3 607 829

Answers start on page 824.

Mathematics • Numbers and Operations

Introduction to Fractions

Facts About Fractions

To count, you use whole numbers. To show part of something, you use fractions. Fractions show part of a whole object or part of a group.

A fraction is two numbers, separated by a fraction bar. The bottom number, or denominator, tells the number of equal parts into which the whole object or group is divided. The top number, or numerator, tells the number of equal parts in the object or group being considered. The numerator and denominator are the terms of the fraction.

To use a fraction to show a part of a whole, imagine that the object is divided into equal parts. For example, the rectangle below is divided into 6 equal parts, or sixths. The entire rectangle represents $\frac{6}{6}$ or 1 whole. Any fraction with the same numerator and denominator is equal to 1.

When the numerator of a fraction has nearly the same value as the denominator, the value of the fraction is close to 1.

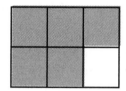

5 of the 6 parts are shaded.
The fraction $\frac{5}{6}$ represents the shaded part.

$\frac{5}{6}$ ← number of shaded parts (numerator)
   ← number of equal parts in the whole (denominator)

You can also use a fraction to show part of a group.

Example   Nicco received 18 orders on Wednesday. There were 11 phone orders. What fraction of the orders came by phone?

$\frac{11}{18}$ ← number of phone orders
   ← number of orders received on Wednesday

$\frac{11}{18}$ of Wednesday's orders came by phone.

The fractions $\frac{5}{6}$ and $\frac{11}{18}$ are examples of proper fractions. A proper fraction shows a quantity that is less than 1. The numerator of a proper fraction is always less than the denominator.

An improper fraction is used to show a quantity equal to or greater than 1. The numerator of an improper fraction is equal to or greater than the denominator.

The figure is divided into three equal parts, and three parts are shaded. The fraction $\frac{3}{3}$ represents the shaded part. $\frac{3}{3}$ is an improper fraction because it is equal to 1 whole.

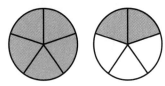

Each circle is divided into 5 equal parts, and 7 parts are shaded. The fraction $\frac{7}{5}$ represents the shaded part. $\frac{7}{5}$ is an improper fraction because the numerator is greater than the denominator. $\frac{7}{5}$ is greater than 1.

Changing Improper Fractions and Mixed Numbers

A mixed number is another way to show a fraction greater than 1. A mixed number consists of a whole number and a proper fraction.

Example 1   Write a mixed number for the shaded portion.

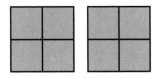

In the figure, each square is divided into 4 equal parts. Two of the squares are completely shaded, and $\frac{1}{4}$ of the last square is shaded. The shaded portion is $\mathbf{2\frac{1}{4}}$. The mixed number $2\frac{1}{4}$ means two and one-fourth or $2 + \frac{1}{4}$.

You have seen that the shaded portion above equals the improper fraction $\frac{9}{4}$. So, you can conclude that $\frac{9}{4} = 2\frac{1}{4}$. Any amount equal to or greater than 1 can be expressed as either an improper fraction or a mixed number. As you work with fractions, you will need to know how to change back and forth between improper fractions and mixed numbers.

Follow these steps to change an improper fraction to a mixed number or whole number.

Step 1   Think of the fraction bar as a division symbol. Divide the numerator of the improper fraction by the denominator. The whole number answer becomes the whole number part of the mixed number.

Step 2   Write the remainder over the original denominator. This is the fraction part of the mixed number.

Example 2   Change $\frac{14}{3}$ to a mixed number.

Step 1 $\frac{14}{3}$ means $14 \div 3$. Divide. The whole number is 4.

Step 2   Write the remainder as the numerator over the divisor as the denominator: 2 over 3.

$$\begin{array}{r} \mathbf{4} \leftarrow \text{whole} \\ \text{denominator} \rightarrow \mathbf{3}\overline{)14} \quad \text{number} \\ \underline{12} \\ \mathbf{2} \leftarrow \text{numerator} \end{array}$$

The improper fraction $\frac{14}{3}$ equals $\mathbf{4\frac{2}{3}}$.

A mixed number can also be changed to an improper fraction.

Step 1 Multiply the whole number part of the mixed number by the denominator of the fraction.

Step 2 Add the numerator of the fraction part.

Step 3 Write the total over the original denominator.

Example 3   Change $2\frac{3}{8}$ to an improper fraction.

whole number   denominator

Step 1 Multiply 2 by 8. $2 \times 8 = 16$

Step 2 Add the numerator, 3. $16 + 3 = 19$

Step 3 Write the total over the denominator, 8. $\frac{19}{8}$

The mixed number $2\frac{3}{8}$ equals $\frac{19}{8}$.

Choosing the Operation

Fraction problems can also appear as word problems. As always, read a problem carefully before you choose which operation to use. Identify what you are trying to find out. Below is an expanded version of the operations chart you used for whole numbers. Review these guidelines for choosing an operation.

You	When You Need To
Add (+)	Combine quantities Find a total
Subtract (−)	Find a difference Take away a quantity Compare to find "how many more," "how much less," or "how much is left"
Multiply (×)	Put together a number of equal amounts to find a total Add the same number repeatedly Find a "part of" a whole item or group
Divide (÷)	Split a quantity into equal parts Find how many equal parts are in a whole

Example 1   A worker at a coffee shop mixed $10\frac{3}{8}$ tins of gourmet coffee with $6\frac{3}{4}$ tins of regular grind coffee. How many more tins of the gourmet coffee were used than the regular grind coffee?

(1) $10\frac{3}{8} + 6\frac{3}{4}$

(2) $10\frac{3}{8} - 6\frac{3}{4}$

(3) $6\frac{3}{4} \times 10\frac{3}{8}$

(4) $10\frac{3}{8} \div 6\frac{3}{4}$

(5) $6\frac{3}{4} - 10\frac{3}{8}$

The correct answer is **option (2).** You subtract to find "how many more."

Tip

When solving a fraction problem that asks you to find a "part of" a whole or other fraction, you multiply.

Example 2 Of Ed's 128 employees, $\frac{3}{8}$ volunteered to work on Saturday. How many employees volunteered to work on Saturday?

(1) $\frac{3}{8} + 128$

(2) $128 - \frac{3}{8}$

(3) $128 \times \frac{3}{8}$

(4) $128 \div \frac{3}{8}$

(5) $\frac{3}{8} \div 128$

The correct answer is **option (3)**. You need to find "part of" a group.

GED Practice

Directions: Choose the <u>one best answer</u> to each question.

1. A recipe calls for $5\frac{3}{4}$ cups of flour. Brian has only $2\frac{3}{8}$ cups left in the bag. How much more does he need?

(1) $5\frac{3}{4} + 2\frac{3}{8}$

(2) $5\frac{3}{4} - 2\frac{3}{8}$

(3) $2\frac{3}{8} \times 5\frac{3}{4}$

(4) $5\frac{3}{4} \div 2\frac{3}{8}$

(5) $2\frac{3}{8} \div 5\frac{3}{4}$

2. If $6\frac{1}{4}$ bags of firewood are to be distributed among $2\frac{1}{2}$ groups of hikers, how many bags of firewood will each group receive?

(1) $6\frac{1}{4} + 2\frac{1}{2}$

(2) $6\frac{1}{4} - 2\frac{1}{2}$

(3) $2\frac{1}{2} \times 6\frac{1}{4}$

(4) $6\frac{1}{4} \div 2\frac{1}{2}$

(5) $2\frac{1}{2} \div 6\frac{1}{4}$

3. A restaurant ordered $15\frac{3}{4}$ cases of almonds. The nut supplier sent only $\frac{1}{2}$ the order. How many cases of almonds did the supplier send?

(1) $\frac{1}{2} + 15\frac{3}{4}$

(2) $15\frac{3}{4} - \frac{1}{2}$

(3) $15\frac{3}{4} \times \frac{1}{2}$

(4) $15\frac{3}{4} \div \frac{1}{2}$

(5) $\frac{1}{2} \div 15\frac{3}{4}$

4. Katya's driving class lasts $\frac{3}{4}$ of an hour. How many classes can she teach in $4\frac{1}{2}$ hours?

(1) $4\frac{1}{2} + \frac{3}{4}$

(2) $4\frac{1}{2} - \frac{3}{4}$

(3) $\frac{3}{4} \times 4\frac{1}{2}$

(4) $4\frac{1}{2} \div \frac{3}{4}$

(5) $\frac{3}{4} \div 4\frac{1}{2}$

Answers start on page 824.

Fractions, Ratios, and Proportions

Equal Fractions

You know from experience that different fractions can have the same value.

- Since there are 100 pennies in a dollar, 25 pennies is equal to $\frac{25}{100}$ of a dollar. The same amount also equals a quarter, or $\frac{1}{4}$ of a dollar.
- On a metre stick, $\frac{1}{2}$ m is the same amount as $\frac{2}{4}$ m.
- On an odometer, $\frac{5}{10}$ of a kilometre is the same as $\frac{1}{2}$ km.
- Out of a dozen doughnuts, six doughnuts equal $\frac{6}{12}$, or $\frac{1}{2}$ dozen.

Fractions that have the same value are called equivalent or equal fractions. You can tell whether two fractions are equal by finding cross products.

Example   Are $\frac{4}{8}$ and $\frac{3}{6}$ equal fractions?

Multiply diagonally as shown by the arrows below. If the cross products are equal, the fractions are equal.

$$\frac{4}{8} \diagup\!\!\!\!\diagdown \frac{3}{6} \qquad \begin{array}{l} 4 \times 6 = 24 \\ 8 \times 3 = 24 \end{array}$$

Since the cross products are equal, $\frac{4}{8} = \frac{3}{6}$.

Reducing Fractions

Reducing a fraction means finding an equal fraction with a smaller numerator and denominator. The fraction is reduced to lowest terms when there is no number other than 1 that will divide evenly into both the numerator and the denominator.

To reduce a fraction, divide both the numerator and the denominator by the same number, and write the new fraction.

If both the numbers in the fraction are even numbers, you can always divide by 2.

Example 1   In one hour, 10 customers visited Stuart's newsstand. Of those, 6 bought a magazine. What fraction of the customers purchased a magazine?

Write a fraction: $\frac{6}{10}$. Reduce the fraction to lowest terms by dividing both the numerator and denominator by 2.

$$\frac{6}{10} = \frac{6 \div 2}{10 \div 2} = \frac{3}{5} \qquad \frac{3}{5} \text{ of the customers purchased a magazine.}$$

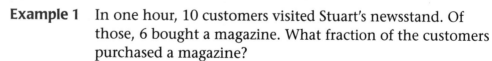

You may need to divide more than once to reduce a fraction to lowest terms. Remember, keep dividing until there is no number other than 1 that will divide evenly into both numerator and denominator.

Example 2   Write $\frac{24}{30}$ in lowest terms.

Step 1   First divide the numerator and denominator by 3. However, the fraction $\frac{8}{10}$ is not in lowest terms.

$$\frac{24}{30} = \frac{24 \div 3}{30 \div 3} = \frac{8}{10}$$

Step 2   Divide the numerator and denominator by 2. The fraction $\frac{4}{5}$ is in lowest terms.

$$\frac{8}{10} = \frac{8 \div 2}{10 \div 2} = \frac{4}{5}$$

Note: If you noticed that 6 divides evenly into both 24 and 30, you could reduce the fraction to lowest terms in one step.

A. Reduce each fraction to lowest terms.

1. $\frac{2}{4} =$ 4. $\frac{6}{8} =$ 7. $\frac{5}{20} =$ 10. $\frac{12}{30} =$

2. $\frac{6}{9} =$ 5. $\frac{6}{15} =$ 8. $\frac{12}{48} =$ 11. $\frac{7}{42} =$

3. $\frac{10}{25} =$ 6. $\frac{18}{27} =$ 9. $\frac{16}{20} =$ 12. $\frac{24}{36} =$

B. Circle the two equal fractions in each line. You may find it helpful to reduce each fraction to lowest terms.

13. $\frac{4}{6}$ $\frac{8}{12}$ $\frac{6}{10}$ $\frac{2}{4}$ $\frac{10}{12}$ 15. $\frac{3}{12}$ $\frac{8}{16}$ $\frac{2}{8}$ $\frac{4}{20}$ $\frac{2}{6}$

14. $\frac{8}{16}$ $\frac{2}{3}$ $\frac{5}{12}$ $\frac{3}{6}$ $\frac{3}{4}$ 16. $\frac{5}{8}$ $\frac{6}{8}$ $\frac{6}{10}$ $\frac{4}{16}$ $\frac{3}{5}$

C. Solve. Express each answer in lowest terms.

17. Sadrac worked 8 hours on Monday. If he worked 40 hours during the week, what fraction of the total time did he work on Monday?

18. Morley's Paint advertised its store sale in the newspaper. On Friday, the store had 50 customers. Of those, 15 saw the advertisement. What fraction of Friday's customers saw the advertisement?

19. Crown Manufacturing completed 1000 assemblies today. Of those, 50 were defective. What fraction of the assemblies was defective?

20. Jean withdrew $40 from her savings account. She spent $24 at the drugstore. What fraction of the withdrawal did she spend at the drugstore?

Answers start on page 825.

Raising Fractions to Higher Terms

Sometimes you need to find an equal fraction with higher terms. You raise a fraction to higher terms by multiplying both the numerator and the denominator by the same number (except 0).

$\frac{5}{8}$ and $\frac{20}{32}$ are equal fractions because $\frac{5 \times 4}{8 \times 4} = \frac{20}{32}$.

Often you will need to find an equal fraction with a specific denominator. To do this, think, "What number multiplied by the original denominator will result in the new denominator?" Then multiply the original numerator by the same number.

Example $\frac{3}{4} = \frac{?}{24}$

Since $4 \times 6 = 24$, multiply the numerator 3 by 6. $\frac{3 \times 6}{4 \times 6} = \frac{18}{24}$

The fractions $\frac{3}{4}$ **and** $\frac{18}{24}$ **are equal fractions.**

Comparing Fractions

When two fractions have the same number as the denominator, they are said to have a common denominator, and the fractions are called like fractions. When you compare like fractions, the fraction with the greater numerator is the greater fraction.

Example 1   Which fraction is greater, $\frac{3}{5}$ or $\frac{4}{5}$?

The fractions $\frac{3}{5}$ and $\frac{4}{5}$ are like fractions because they have a common denominator, 5. Compare the numerators.

Since 4 is greater than 3, $\frac{4}{5}$ **is greater than** $\frac{3}{5}$.

Fractions with different denominators are called unlike fractions. To compare unlike fractions, you must change them to fractions with a common denominator.

The common denominator will always be a multiple of both of the original denominators. The multiples of a number are found by going through the times tables for the number. For instance, the multiples of 3 are 3, 6, 9, 12, 15, 18, and so on.

You can often find a common denominator by using mental math. If not, try these methods:

1. See whether the larger denominator could be a common denominator. If the smaller denominator can divide into the larger denominator evenly, use the larger denominator as the common denominator.

2. Go through the multiples of the larger denominator. The first one that can be divided evenly by the smaller denominator is the lowest common denominator.

3. Multiply the denominators. This number is a common denominator, though not necessarily the lowest common denominator.

Tip

Finding common denominators is important to your success on the GED Mathematics Test. Practise writing the first 12 multiples of the numbers 2 through 12.

Example 2   Which is greater, $\frac{5}{6}$ or $\frac{3}{4}$?

Go through the multiples of the larger denominator: 6, 12, 18, 24, 30 . . .
Since 12 can be divided evenly by both 4 and 6, 12 is the lowest common
denominator.

Build equal fractions, each with the
denominator 12:
$$\frac{5 \times 2}{6 \times 2} = \frac{10}{12} \qquad \frac{3 \times 3}{4 \times 3} = \frac{9}{12}$$

Compare the like fractions. Since $\frac{10}{12} > \frac{9}{12}$, the fraction $\mathbf{\frac{5}{6}} > \mathbf{\frac{3}{4}}$.

A. Find an equal fraction with the given denominator.

1. $\frac{2}{3} = \frac{?}{12}$

2. $\frac{2}{7} = \frac{?}{21}$

3. $\frac{4}{5} = \frac{?}{25}$

4. $\frac{5}{8} = \frac{?}{32}$

5. $\frac{7}{9} = \frac{?}{63}$

6. $\frac{3}{10} = \frac{?}{120}$

7. $\frac{3}{4} = \frac{?}{36}$

8. $\frac{4}{9} = \frac{?}{81}$

9. $\frac{9}{50} = \frac{?}{150}$

B. Compare the fractions. Write >, < , or = between the fractions.

10. $\frac{1}{3}$ $\frac{1}{4}$

11. $\frac{3}{4}$ $\frac{7}{8}$

12. $\frac{3}{9}$ $\frac{1}{3}$

13. $\frac{2}{3}$ $\frac{1}{2}$

14. $\frac{5}{6}$ $\frac{15}{18}$

15. $\frac{9}{12}$ $\frac{3}{4}$

16. $\frac{7}{10}$ $\frac{2}{3}$

17. $\frac{7}{15}$ $\frac{2}{5}$

18. $\frac{9}{10}$ $\frac{3}{4}$

Working with Ratios

A ratio is a comparison of two numbers. A ratio can be written with the
word *to*, with a colon (:), or as a fraction. Always write the terms of
the ratio in the same order as the problem compares them.

Example 1   A painter mixes 4 L of white paint and 2 L of blue paint.
What is the ratio of white paint to blue paint?

The ratio of white paint to blue paint can be written as **4 to 2, 4:2,** or $\mathbf{\frac{4}{2}}$.

Just as you can reduce fractions to lowest terms, you can simplify ratios
to their lowest terms. The ratio $\frac{4}{2}$ can be simplified to $\frac{2}{1}$, which means for
every 2 L of white paint, there is 1 L of blue paint. Ratios are written as a
fraction even if the denominator is 1.

Ratios have much in common with fractions, but there is an important
difference. A ratio may look like an improper fraction, but it should not
be changed to a whole or mixed number because it is a comparison of
two items, not just a part of a whole.

Ratios often express rates. A ratio with the denominator 1 is called a
unit rate. Unit rates are often expressed using the word *per*.

Answers start on page 825.

Mathematics • Numbers and Operations

Writing the ratio in words will help you keep the numbers in the correct order. The words will also help you to remember the meaning of the numbers. Including labels in your final ratio is also helpful.

Example 2 If Jing-Mei earns $180 in 15 hours, how much does she earn per hour?

Write the ratio of earnings to hours. Then divide to find the unit rate.

$$\frac{\text{dollars earned}}{\text{hours}} = \frac{\$180}{15} = \frac{180 \div 15}{15 \div 15} = \frac{\$12}{1 \text{ hr}}$$

Jing-Mei earns $12 for every 1 hour she works. In other words, she earns **$12 per hour.**

Some ratio problems require more than one step. You may not be given both the numbers you need to write a ratio. Instead, you may have to solve for one number.

Example 3 Kimball Discount has 25 employees. Of those 25 employees, 15 are women. What is the ratio of the number of male to the number of female employees?

You need to write a ratio comparing the number of men to the number of women. You have been given the total number of employees and the number of female employees.

Step 1 Subtract to find the number of men. $25 - 15 = 10$ men

Step 2 Write the ratio of men to women. $\dfrac{\text{men}}{\text{women}} = \dfrac{10}{15}$

Step 3 Simplify the ratio. $\dfrac{10}{15} = \dfrac{10 \div 5}{15 \div 5} = \dfrac{2}{3}$

The ratio of men to women employees at Kimball Discount is $\frac{2}{3}$.

Solving Proportions

In a proportion, the terms in both ratios must be written in the same order. In this example, both ratios have dollars on the top and hours on the bottom. Use labels to keep track of the order.

When two ratios are written as equal ratios, the equation is called a proportion. Think about the following statement:

Example 1 If Paul earns $8 in 1 hour, then he will earn $56 in 7 hours.

From the information in the sentence, you can write a proportion. Use cross products to make sure the ratios are equal.

$$\frac{\text{dollars earned}}{\text{hours}} \qquad \frac{8}{1} \overset{?}{\times} \frac{56}{7} \qquad \text{Cross products: } 1 \times 56 = 8 \times 7$$
$$56 = 56$$

As you can see from the example above, every proportion has four terms. In a proportion problem, one of the four terms is missing. The proportion can be solved using this rule:

> **Cross-Product Rule:** To find the missing number in a proportion, cross multiply and divide the product by the third number.

Example 2 Gayla drove 165 km in 3 hours. At the same rate, how far can she drive in 5 hours?

In this problem, you are comparing kilometres to hours. Set up two equal ratios. Write x to stand for the missing term.

$$\frac{\text{kilometres}}{\text{hours}} = \frac{165}{3} = \frac{x}{5}$$

Step 1 Find the cross product. $165 \times 5 = 825$

Step 2 Divide by 3, the remaining term. $825 \div 3 = 275$

Gayla can drive **275 km** in 5 hours.

You can easily solve proportion problems using a calculator. Enter the numbers and operations in this order:

165 ✕ 5 ÷ 3 = 275.

Some proportion problems state a ratio using a colon. Read carefully to understand what the numbers in the ratio represent.

Example 3 At a school board meeting, the ratio of parents to teachers is 3:2. If there are 72 parents at the meeting, how many teachers are there?

Step 1 The ratio 3:2 compares parents to teachers. Write the second ratio in the same order.

$$\frac{\text{parents}}{\text{teachers}} = \frac{3}{2} = \frac{72}{x}$$

Step 2 Find the cross product, and divide by the remaining term.

$2 \times 72 = 144$
$144 \div 3 = 48$

There are **48 teachers** at the meeting.

A. Solve for the missing term in each proportion.

1. $\dfrac{2}{3} = \dfrac{x}{15}$

2. $\dfrac{28}{12} = \dfrac{14}{x}$

3. $\dfrac{9}{10} = \dfrac{x}{20}$

4. $\dfrac{5}{6} = \dfrac{x}{18}$

5. $\dfrac{15}{24} = \dfrac{5}{x}$

6. $\dfrac{12}{15} = \dfrac{24}{x}$

7. $\dfrac{14}{6} = \dfrac{7}{x}$

8. $\dfrac{115}{30} = \dfrac{x}{6}$

9. $\dfrac{49}{7} = \dfrac{x}{10}$

10. $\dfrac{32}{8} = \dfrac{x}{15}$

11. $\dfrac{18}{6} = \dfrac{3}{x}$

12. $\dfrac{6}{120} = \dfrac{5}{x}$

B. For each situation, the first ratio has been written for you. Write the second ratio to complete the proportion and solve.

13. A recipe that serves 8 people calls for 2 L of milk. How many litres of milk are needed for 36 servings?

$$\frac{\text{servings}}{\text{litres of milk}} \quad \frac{8}{2} = \frac{?}{?}$$

14. A person uses about 315 calories to jog 3 km. How many calories will be used in a 10-km jog?

$$\frac{\text{calories}}{\text{kilometres}} \quad \frac{315}{3} = \frac{?}{?}$$

Answers start on page 825.

Operations with Fractions

Adding and Subtracting Fractions

Lesson 7

Adding and subtracting can only be performed with the same kinds of objects. You can add dollars to dollars and metres to metres, but not dollars to metres. This is also true of fractions. You can add or subtract only like fractions, those with the same, or a common, denominator.

With like fractions, add or subtract the numerators and write the answer over the common denominator. If necessary, reduce the answer to lowest terms. Rewrite an improper fraction as a whole or mixed number.

Example 1   Add $\frac{3}{8}$ and $\frac{4}{8}$.

Step 1   Add the numerators. $3 + 4 = 7$

Step 2   Write the sum of the numerators over common denominator. $\frac{7}{8}$

The sum of $\frac{3}{8}$ and $\frac{4}{8}$ is $\frac{7}{8}$.

Example 2   Subtract $\frac{2}{12}$ from $\frac{11}{12}$.

Step 1   Remember the order of the numbers in subtraction. The fraction being subtracted <u>from</u> must be written first. Then subtract the numerators.
$$\frac{11}{12} - \frac{2}{12} = \frac{11 - 2}{12} = \frac{9}{12}$$

Step 2   Reduce to lowest terms.
$$\frac{9 \div 3}{12 \div 3} = \frac{3}{4}$$

The difference of $\frac{11}{12}$ and $\frac{2}{12}$ is $\frac{3}{4}$.

Unlike fractions have different denominators. Use these steps to add or subtract unlike fractions.

Step 1   Find a common denominator and change one or both of the fractions to make like fractions.

Step 2   Add or subtract the like fractions.

Step 3   Reduce the answer if necessary. If the answer is an improper fraction, rewrite it as a whole or mixed number.

Tip

Whenever possible, use the lowest common denominator. The numbers in the problem will be smaller and easier to work with.

Example 3   Jarod bought $\frac{1}{2}$ kg of dark chocolate and $\frac{3}{4}$ kg of white chocolate. How many kilograms of chocolate did he buy?

Step 1   The lowest common denominator for both fractions is 4. Raise $\frac{1}{2}$ to an equal fraction with a denominator of 4.
$$\frac{1}{2} = \frac{1 \times 2}{2 \times 2} = \frac{2}{4}$$

Step 2   Add $\frac{2}{4}$ and $\frac{3}{4}$.
$$\frac{2}{4} + \frac{3}{4} = \frac{5}{4}$$

Step 3   Reduce the improper fraction to lowest terms.
$$\frac{5}{4} = 1\frac{1}{4}$$

Jarod bought **$1\frac{1}{4}$ kg** of chocolate.

Adding and Subtracting Mixed Numbers

A mixed number is a whole number and a proper fraction. To add or subtract mixed numbers, work with each part separately and then combine the results.

If you can't decide which operation to use in a fraction word problem, think about how you would solve it using only whole numbers. Then use the same operation with the fractions.

Example 1   For a painting job, Leland spent $6\frac{1}{3}$ hours preparing the rooms to be painted and $4\frac{3}{4}$ hours doing the painting and cleanup. How many hours did he spend on the job?

Step 1   Write the fractions with common denominators.

$$6\frac{1}{3} = 6\frac{1 \times 4}{3 \times 4} = 6\frac{4}{12}$$
$$+4\frac{3}{4} = 4\frac{3 \times 3}{4 \times 3} = 4\frac{9}{12}$$

Step 2   Add the fractions first. Add the numerators and put the sum over the common denominator. Then add the whole numbers.

$$6\frac{4}{12}$$
$$+4\frac{9}{12}$$
$$\overline{10\frac{13}{12}}$$

Step 3   Change the improper fraction to a mixed number. Add this to the whole number answer.

$$\frac{13}{12} = 1\frac{1}{12}$$
$$10 + 1\frac{1}{12} = 11\frac{1}{12}$$

Leland spent **$11\frac{1}{12}$** hours on the job.

When subtracting mixed numbers, sometimes the fraction from which you are subtracting will be smaller than the fraction you are taking away. In this situation, you will need to regroup, or borrow, 1 from the whole number and rewrite it as a fraction. Remember: A fraction with the same numerator and denominator equals 1.

Example 2   If $3\frac{3}{4}$ cans of paint are used from a total of $5\frac{1}{8}$ cans of paint, how many cans of paint remain?

Step 1   Write the fractions with common denominators. The lowest common denominator is 8.

Step 2   Because $\frac{1}{8}$ is less than $\frac{6}{8}$, you need to regroup. Regroup 1 from the whole number 5, rewriting 5 as $4\frac{8}{8}$. Then add the fractional parts $\frac{1}{8}$ and $\frac{8}{8}$.

$$
\begin{array}{ccc}
\text{Step 1} & \text{Step 2} & \text{Step 3} \\
5\frac{1}{8} = & 5\frac{1}{8} = 4\frac{8}{8} + \frac{1}{8} = & 4\frac{9}{8} \\
-3\frac{3}{4} = & -3\frac{6}{8} & -3\frac{6}{8} \\
\hline
& & 1\frac{3}{8}
\end{array}
$$

Step 3   Subtract. The fraction is already reduced to lowest terms.

There are **$1\frac{3}{8}$** cans of paint remaining.

A. Add or subtract as directed. Reduce answers to lowest terms.

1. $3\frac{3}{4}$
   $+4\frac{1}{3}$

2. $1\frac{1}{2}$
   $+5\frac{5}{8}$

3. $2\frac{3}{10}$
   $+9\frac{4}{5}$

4. $22\frac{1}{9}$
   $+21\frac{2}{3}$

5. $6\frac{1}{2}$
   $-3\frac{1}{3}$

6. $8\frac{5}{6}$
   $-2\frac{1}{4}$

7. $20\frac{1}{3}$
   $-8\frac{2}{3}$

8. $5\frac{2}{3}$
   $-3\frac{3}{4}$

B. Solve. Reduce your answers.

9. Belinda kept records of how much candy her family ate. If they ate $8\frac{1}{2}$ bags one month, $9\frac{3}{10}$ bags the next month, and $8\frac{7}{10}$ bags the third month, how many bags of candy did they eat?

10. Three entertainers were on stage for $1\frac{2}{3}$ hours, $\frac{1}{2}$ of an hour, and $\frac{3}{4}$ of an hour, respectively. How long did the show run?

Multiplying Fractions and Mixed Numbers

To multiply fractions, you do not need to change the fractions to like fractions. Simply multiply the numerators, then the denominators, and reduce your answer.

Example 1 If $\frac{2}{3}$ of a cake is cut in half, what fraction of the cake is each new piece?

Step 1 Multiply one numerator by the other numerator. Then multiply one denominator by the other denominator.

$$\frac{2}{3} \times \frac{1}{2} = \frac{2 \times 1}{3 \times 2} = \frac{2}{6}$$

Step 2 Reduce the answer to lowest terms.

$$\frac{2 \div 2}{6 \div 2} = \frac{1}{3}$$

Each new piece is $\frac{1}{3}$ of the cake.

As you know, reducing a fraction means to divide the numerator and the denominator by the same number. You can use this principle to simplify before you work the problem. This process is called cancelling.

Example 2 Find $\frac{1}{6}$ of $\frac{2}{3}$.

Both the numerator of one fraction and the denominator of the other fraction can be divided by 2. Since $2 \div 2 = 1$, draw a slash through the numerator 2 and write 1. Since $6 \div 2 = 3$, draw a slash through the denominator 6 and write 3. Then multiply the simplified fractions.

$$\frac{1}{6} \times \frac{2}{3} = \frac{1 \times \overset{1}{\cancel{2}}}{\underset{3}{\cancel{6}} \times 3} = \frac{1}{9}$$

> **Tip**
>
> A fraction followed by the word "of" means that you should multiply by that fraction. For example, when you find $\frac{1}{6}$ of $\frac{2}{3}$, you multiply $\frac{1}{6} \times \frac{2}{3}$.

Answers start on page 826.

Since you used cancelling before multiplying, there is no need to reduce the answer: $\frac{1}{6}$ of $\frac{2}{3}$ is $\frac{1}{9}$. Notice that cancelling gives the same answer as in Example 1 above.

When you cancel, make sure you divide a numerator and a denominator by the same number. The cancelling shown here is incorrect. Although 6 and 3 can both be divided by 3, both numbers are in the denominator.

Incorrect:

$$\frac{1}{6} \times \frac{2}{3} = \frac{1 \times 2}{\underset{2}{\cancel{6}} \times \underset{1}{\cancel{3}}}$$

To multiply with mixed numbers, change the mixed numbers to improper fractions before you multiply.

Example 3 Multiply $1\frac{2}{3}$ by $7\frac{1}{2}$.

Step 1
Change to improper fractions.

$$1\frac{2}{3} \times 7\frac{1}{2} = \frac{5}{3} \times \frac{15}{2}$$

Step 2
Cancel and multiply.

$$\frac{5}{\underset{1}{\cancel{3}}} \times \frac{\overset{5}{\cancel{15}}}{2} =$$

Step 3
Write as a mixed number.

$$\frac{25}{2} = 12\frac{1}{2}$$

The product of $1\frac{2}{3}$ and $7\frac{1}{2}$ is **$12\frac{1}{2}$**.

GED Practice

Directions: Choose the <u>one best answer</u> to each question.

1. How much greater is the sum of $\frac{3}{5}$ and $\frac{4}{5}$ than 1?

   (1) $\frac{2}{5}$

   (2) $\frac{3}{5}$

   (3) $\frac{4}{5}$

   (4) $1\frac{2}{5}$

   (5) $2\frac{2}{5}$

2. Carolyn worked $7\frac{2}{3}$ hours yesterday and $6\frac{3}{5}$ hours today. How many hours did she work in the two days?

   (1) $13\frac{4}{15}$

   (2) $13\frac{5}{8}$

   (3) $14\frac{4}{15}$

   (4) $14\frac{5}{8}$

   (5) Not enough information is given.

Answers start on page 826.

Dividing Fractions and Mixed Numbers

Multiplication and division are inverse (opposite) operations. You use this relationship to divide fractions.

Example 1 $\frac{6}{8} \div \frac{1}{4} = ?$

To solve this problem, you need to find out how many $\frac{1}{4}$s there are in $\frac{6}{8}$. Follow these steps:

Step 1   Invert, or turn over, the divisor (the fraction you are dividing by) and change the operation to multiplication.

$$\frac{6}{8} \div \frac{1}{4} = \frac{6}{8} \times \frac{4}{1}$$

Step 2   Complete the problem as you would any multiplication problem. Always simplify your answer by reducing to lowest terms and changing improper fractions to mixed or whole numbers.

$$\frac{6}{8} \times \frac{4}{1} = \frac{6}{\underset{2}{8}} \times \frac{\overset{1}{4}}{1} = \frac{6}{2} = 3$$

The fraction $\frac{6}{8}$ divided by $\frac{1}{4}$ is **3**. In other words, there are three $\frac{1}{4}$s in $\frac{6}{8}$. This picture shows that this is true.

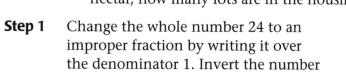

Many real-world situations involve dividing a mixed or whole number by a fraction.

Example 2   A housing subdivision has 24 ha of land available for sale. If this land is divided into home lots that are each $\frac{3}{4}$ of a hectar, how many lots are in the housing subdivision?

Step 1   Change the whole number 24 to an improper fraction by writing it over the denominator 1. Invert the number you're dividing by and change the operation to multiplication.

$$24 \div \frac{3}{4} = \frac{24}{1} \times \frac{4}{3}$$

Step 2   Multiply. Write your answer in lowest terms.

$$\frac{24}{1} \times \frac{4}{3} = \frac{\overset{8}{24}}{1} \times \frac{4}{\underset{1}{3}} = \frac{32}{1} = 32$$

The land will be divided into **32** home lots.

Always think about your answer to see whether it makes sense. You can always use multiplication to check a division problem.

Check: $32 \times \frac{3}{4} = \frac{\overset{8}{32}}{1} \times \frac{3}{\underset{1}{4}} = \frac{24}{1} = 24$

Tip

When you divide by a proper fraction, the answer will be greater than the number you divided. Knowing this can help you see whether your answer makes sense.

Tip

Remember, as in any division problem, the fraction you are dividing must be written first.

A. Divide. Write your answers in lowest terms.

1. $\dfrac{1}{3} \div \dfrac{5}{6} =$

2. $\dfrac{2}{3} \div \dfrac{2}{5} =$

3. $\dfrac{7}{10} \div 2 =$

4. $\dfrac{5}{6} \div \dfrac{5}{24} =$

5. $\dfrac{6}{7} \div 3 =$

6. $\dfrac{4}{9} \div \dfrac{2}{3} =$

7. $\dfrac{7}{8} \div \dfrac{1}{4} =$

8. $4\dfrac{1}{2} \div \dfrac{1}{8} =$

9. $12 \div 1\dfrac{1}{2} =$

10. $3\dfrac{3}{4} \div 1\dfrac{2}{3} =$

11. $6\dfrac{1}{2} \div \dfrac{1}{4} =$

12. $2\dfrac{1}{4} \div 1\dfrac{1}{2} =$

13. $18 \div \dfrac{2}{3} =$

14. $2\dfrac{2}{5} \div \dfrac{6}{25} =$

15. $4\dfrac{9}{10} \div 1\dfrac{1}{6} =$

16. $6\dfrac{1}{9} \div 1\dfrac{5}{6} =$

17. $2\dfrac{2}{3} \div \dfrac{1}{3} =$

18. $4 \div 1\dfrac{1}{4} =$

19. $9\dfrac{1}{8} \div 1\dfrac{2}{3} =$

20. $10 \div 1\dfrac{1}{5} =$

21. $8\dfrac{3}{4} \div \dfrac{1}{4} =$

22. $12 \div \dfrac{4}{9} =$

23. $16 \div \dfrac{4}{5} =$

24. $4 \div 2\dfrac{1}{5} =$

B. Solve. Simplify your answers.

25. If 12 hours of TV are divided into shows that are $\dfrac{3}{4}$ of an hour long, how many shows will air?

26. A cook uses a $\dfrac{1}{3}$ scoop of hamburger to make the lunch special. How many specials can he make from 15 scoops of hamburger?

27. A class of grade 10 students can read 24 books in $\dfrac{3}{4}$ days. How many books can they read in 1 day?

28. Carina works part-time at a toy store as a bike assembler. She can build a bicycle in $2\dfrac{1}{2}$ hours. If she works 25 hours in a week, how many bicycles can she assemble?

29. You have 10 cups of sugar. Your cookie recipe calls for $1\dfrac{1}{4}$ cups of sugar for one batch. How many batches of cookies can you make with the sugar that you have?

Answers start on page 826.

Mathematics • Numbers and Operations

Estimating with Fractions

Knowing the approximate value of fractions makes working with these numbers easier. Rounding fractions to the nearest whole number is a good way to estimate answers to problems that involve fractions. To round a fraction to the nearest whole number, compare the fraction to $\frac{1}{2}$.

Remember: The words *about* and *approximately* mean you should estimate the answer.

RULE If a fraction is less than $\frac{1}{2}$, round down the fraction to 0. In a mixed number, the whole number part stays the same.

Example   Round $5\frac{1}{3}$ to the nearest whole number. Compare $\frac{1}{3}$ and $\frac{1}{2}$. Change to like fractions with a common denominator of 6. $\frac{1}{3} = \frac{2}{6}$ and $\frac{1}{2} = \frac{3}{6}$

Since $\frac{2}{6}$ is less than $\frac{3}{6}$, $\frac{1}{3}$ is less than $\frac{1}{2}$. Round $5\frac{1}{3}$ down to **5**.

RULE If a fraction is $\frac{1}{2}$ or more, round up the fraction to 1. In a mixed number, add 1 to the whole number part.

Example   Round $8\frac{5}{8}$ to the nearest whole number. Change $\frac{1}{2}$ to a fraction with a denominator of 8 to compare $\frac{5}{8}$ and $\frac{1}{2}$. $\frac{1}{2} = \frac{4}{8}$

Since $\frac{5}{8}$ is greater than $\frac{4}{8}$, $\frac{5}{8}$ is greater than $\frac{1}{2}$. Round $8\frac{5}{8}$ up to **9**.

Estimation with fractions is more accurate in addition and subtraction than in multiplication and division.

If the numerator of a fraction is more than half its denominator, the fraction is more than $\frac{1}{2}$. If the numerator is less than half the denominator, the fraction is less than $\frac{1}{2}$.

- $\frac{3}{8}$ is less than $\frac{1}{2}$
- $\frac{5}{8}$ is more than $\frac{1}{2}$

Example   Kiko and Maria each jog twice a week. Kiko jogged $4\frac{3}{4}$ laps and $4\frac{1}{5}$ laps during the week. Maria jogged $3\frac{1}{4}$ laps and $3\frac{7}{8}$ laps during the week. <u>About</u> how many more laps did Kiko jog than Maria?

(1) 0
(2) 1
(3) 2
(4) 3
(5) 4

Step 1   Round the laps that Kiko jogged, then add. $5 + 4 = 9$
$4\frac{3}{4}$ rounds up to 5, and $4\frac{1}{5}$ rounds down to 4.

Step 2   Round the laps that Maria jogged, then add. $3 + 4 = 7$
$3\frac{1}{4}$ rounds down to 3, and $3\frac{7}{8}$ rounds up to 4.

Step 3   Compare the two amounts by subtracting. $9 - 7 = 2$

Option (3) is correct. Kiko jogged about **2 laps** more than Maria.

GED Practice

Directions: Choose the <u>one best answer</u> to each question.

<u>Questions 1 through 3</u> refer to the table.

Ace Repair: Monday Morning Sales

Paint	$14\frac{1}{3}$ cans red paint
	$6\frac{3}{4}$ cans green paint
	$9\frac{1}{4}$ cans white paint
Hardware	$12\frac{1}{6}$ boxes of nails
Lumber	$9\frac{5}{8}$ feet of 2-by-4 boards
	$27\frac{1}{4}$ feet of 2-by-8 boards
	$4\frac{2}{3}$ feet of 1-by-4 boards
	$36\frac{3}{8}$ feet of 1-by-6 boards

1. What is the best estimate for the number of cans of paint sold on Monday morning?

   (1) 26
   (2) 28
   (3) 30
   (4) 32
   (5) 34

2. About how many feet of lumber were sold?

   (1) 70
   (2) 74
   (3) 76
   (4) 78
   (5) 82

3. An additional $10\frac{2}{5}$ boxes of nails are sold Monday afternoon. Approximately how many boxes of nails were sold on Monday?

   (1) 20
   (2) 22
   (3) 24
   (4) 26
   (5) 28

<u>Questions 4 through 6</u> refer to the following information.

Walton Nut Company sells two mixtures.

Mix A: $2\frac{2}{3}$ scoops of cashews

$2\frac{3}{8}$ scoops of peanuts

$3\frac{1}{2}$ scoops of salted walnuts

$2\frac{1}{8}$ scoops of Brazil nuts

Mix B: $6\frac{1}{2}$ scoops of almonds

$3\frac{7}{8}$ scoops of black walnuts

$4\frac{1}{5}$ scoops of peanuts

4. Approximately how many more scoops of peanuts are in Mix B than in Mix A?

   (1) 2
   (2) 4
   (3) 6
   (4) 10
   (5) Not enough information is given.

5. Estimate the number of scoops of cashews and Brazil nuts in Mix A.

   (1) 1
   (2) 2
   (3) 3
   (4) 5
   (5) 15

6. Mix B contains approximately how many more scoops of nuts than Mix A?

   (1) 26
   (2) 15
   (3) 11
   (4) 4
   (5) Not enough information is given.

Answers start on page 827.

Writing Fractions in a Standard Grid

When using the standard grid to write fractional answers to problems, it is important to remember the following points:

- Write your answer at the top of the grid box.
- In the second row of the grid, the symbol $\oslash$ is the fraction bar.
- Your answer can start in any of the five columns, as long as your answer is complete. Any unused columns should be left blank.
- Mixed numbers cannot be entered on the grid. Therefore, change all mixed number answers to improper fractions.

Example 1   Felipe ran for $1\frac{1}{8}$ hours on Tuesday and for $\frac{1}{2}$ hour on Wednesday. How many more hours did he run on Tuesday than on Wednesday?

$$1\frac{1}{8} - \frac{1}{2} =$$
$$\frac{9}{8} - \frac{4}{8} = \frac{5}{8}$$

When answering in the grid, remember to write your answer in the top row, fill the correct circle below, and leave unused columns blank.

The difference between the number of hours Felipe ran on Tuesday and the number of hours he ran on Wednesday is $\frac{5}{8}$ **hour.** All three grids shown at right are filled in correctly.

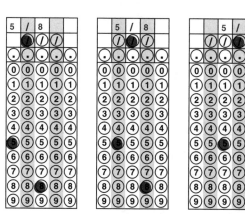

Example 2   Angie worked $5\frac{1}{2}$ hours on Monday and $4\frac{3}{4}$ hours on Tuesday. How many hours did Angie work in the two days?

$$5\frac{1}{2} + 4\frac{3}{4} =$$
$$5\frac{2}{4} + 4\frac{3}{4} = 9\frac{5}{4}$$
$$= 10\frac{1}{4}$$

The total number of hours Angie worked is $10\frac{1}{4}$. Since you cannot enter mixed numbers on the standard grid, first change $10\frac{1}{4}$ to the improper fraction $\frac{41}{4}$. Both grids shown at right are correct.

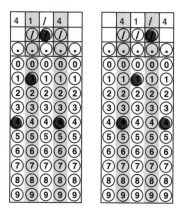

GED Practice

Directions: Solve the following problems. Write your answer in the top row of each grid, and then fill in the corresponding circles to match your answer.

1. In an election for club president, Naomi received 23 out of the 47 votes cast. What fraction of the votes did Naomi receive?

2. At dinner, Neil paid $17 and Sam paid $15. What is the ratio of the amount paid by Sam to the amount paid by Sam and Neil together?

3. An 18-m path is being built using a nail every 25 cm. What is the ratio of the number of nails to the number of metres of path?

4. Karen typed 7 pages in 21 minutes. What is the simplified ratio of minutes to typed pages?

Tip

Be sure to write your answer in the blank row at the top of each grid. This will help you fill in the circles in the correct order.

5. If $1\frac{3}{4}$ hours of a program are over and the program is $2\frac{7}{8}$ hours long, how much of the program is left?

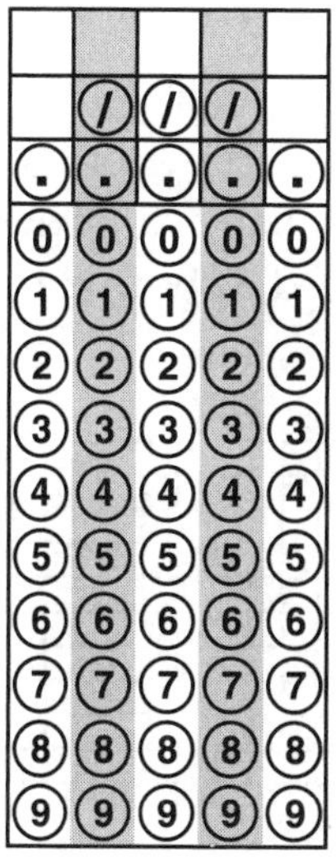

(grid with answer bubbles)

6. If $2\frac{3}{4}$ bars of chocolate are equally distributed among 3 friends, how many bars does each friend get?

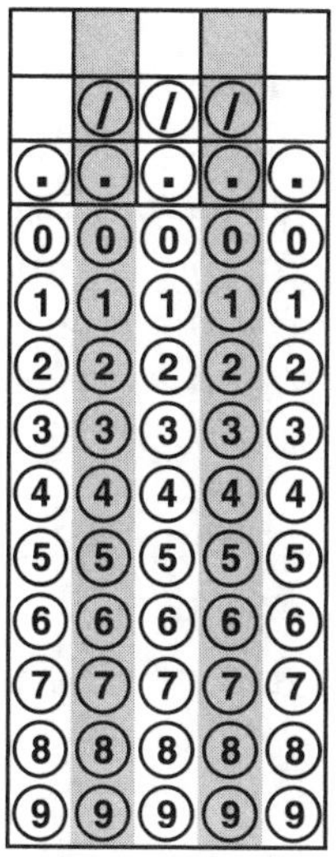

(grid with answer bubbles)

7. Rachel has 4 scoops of flour and uses $\frac{2}{3}$ of it for a recipe. How many scoops of flour are left?

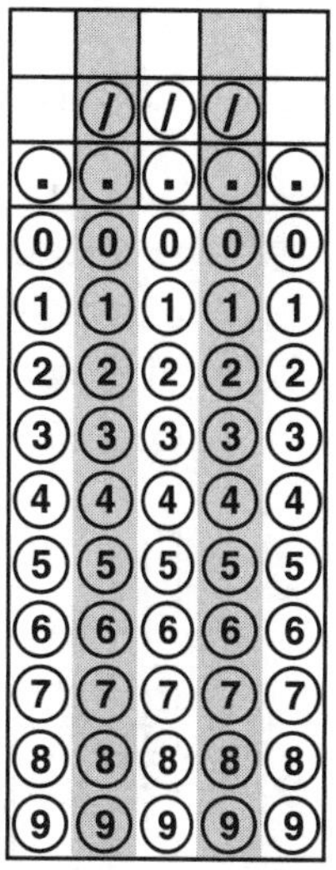

(grid with answer bubbles)

8. A map scale shows that $\frac{1}{3}$ cm on the map equals an actual distance of 3 km. If a distance on the map is $\frac{3}{4}$ cm, what is the actual distance in kilometres?

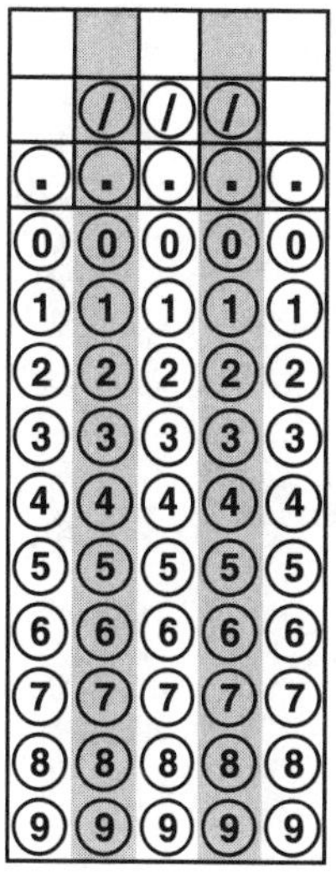

(grid with answer bubbles)

Be sure you are answering the question asked. When asked to find "how much is left," check to see what value you found. Did you find how much was used or how much was left?

There are different approaches to problem solving. For example, if a map scale is $\frac{1}{3}$ cm = 3 km, then 1 cm equals 9 km.
Thus, $\frac{1}{9} = \frac{\frac{3}{4}}{x}$ or $\frac{3}{4} \times 9 = x$.

Answers start on page 828.

Introduction to Decimals

Understanding Decimals

In Lessons 5 through 7, you used fractions to represent quantities of less than one. A decimal number is another way to express a fractional amount. A decimal is a fraction that uses the place value system. For each diagram below, the shaded portion is expressed as both a fraction and a decimal.

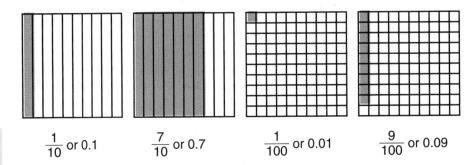

$\frac{1}{10}$ or 0.1 $\frac{7}{10}$ or 0.7 $\frac{1}{100}$ or 0.01 $\frac{9}{100}$ or 0.09

To show thousandths, imagine dividing each box on a hundredths chart into 10 equal pieces. To show ten-thousandths, imagine dividing each box into 100 equal pieces.

The chart shows the names of the first five decimal place values. Notice that the whole numbers are to the left of the decimal point and the decimals are to the right.

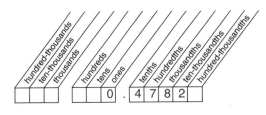

Compare the whole number and decimal place values. Do you see a pattern? Think of the ones column and decimal point as the centre of the chart. As you move out from the centre, the column names are related.

As you move to the left on the chart, each column is 10 times greater than the column to its right. As you move to the right, the value of the columns becomes smaller. Each column is $\frac{1}{10}$ the value of the column to its left.

The zero in the tenths place of 16.034 is a placeholder. Its only purpose is to fill the space between the whole number and the digits farther to the right.

As with whole numbers, the sum of the values of the digits equals the total value of the number.

Example 1 What is the value of each digit in 0.4782?

4 is in the **tenths** place.	4×0.1	$= \mathbf{0.4}$
7 is in the **hundredths** place.	7×0.01	$= \mathbf{0.07}$
8 is in the **thousandths** place.	8×0.001	$= \mathbf{0.008}$
2 is in the **ten-thousandths** place.	$+2 \times 0.0001$	$= \mathbf{0.0002}$
		$\mathbf{0.4782}$

Note: When a decimal number does not have a whole number part, a zero is often written to the left of the decimal point. The zero has no value.

Example 2   How do you write 16.034 in words?

Read the whole number part of the number. Say *and* to represent the decimal point. Read the digits to the right of the decimal point, and say the place name of the last digit on the right. Note that there are spaces setting off groups of three digits in the part of the number to the right of the decimal point (e.g., 3.141 592).

The number 16.034 is read as ***sixteen and thirty-four thousandths.***

Rounding, Comparing, and Ordering Decimals

The steps for rounding decimals are similar to those you used for rounding whole numbers. There is one important difference in **Step 3.**

Example 1   Round 5.362 to the nearest tenth.

Step 1	Find the digit you want to round to. It may help to circle it.	5.③62
Step 2	Look at the digit immediately to the right of the circled digit.	5.③62
Step 3	If the digit to the right is 5 or more, add 1 to the circled digit. If the digit to the right is less than 5, do not change the circled digit. *Drop the remaining digits.*	**5.4**

Examples   Round to the indicated place value.
Round 1.832 to the nearest hundredth.   1.8③2 rounds to **1.83**
Round 16.95 to the nearest tenth.   16.⑨5 rounds to **17.0**
Round 3.972 to the ones place.   ③.972 rounds to **4**

Remember that > means *is greater than* and < means *is less than*. The arrow points to the smaller number.

Comparing decimals uses an important mathematical concept. You can add zeros to the right of the last decimal digit without changing the value of the number. Study these examples.

RULE When comparing decimals with the same number of decimal places, compare them as though they were whole numbers.

Example   Which is greater, 0.364 or 0.329?
Both numbers have three decimal places. Since 364 is greater than 329, the decimal **0.364 > 0.329.**

The rule for comparing whole numbers in which the number with more digits is greater does not hold true for decimals. The decimal number with more decimal places is not necessarily the greater number.

RULE When decimals have a different number of digits, write zeros to the right of the decimal with fewer digits so the numbers have the same number of decimal places. Then compare.

Example Which is greater, 0.518 or 0.52?

Add a zero to 0.52.   0.518 ? 0.520

Since 520 > 518, the decimal **0.52 > 0.518.**

RULE When numbers have both whole number and decimal parts, compare the whole numbers first.

Example 1 Compare 32.001 and 31.999.

Since 32 is greater than 31, the number **32.001 is greater than 31.999.** It does not matter that 0.999 is greater than 0.001.

Using the same rules, you can put several numbers in order according to value. When you have several numbers to compare, write the numbers in a column and line up the decimal points. Then add zeros to the right until all the decimals have the same number of decimal digits.

Example 2 A digital scale displays weight to thousandths of a kilogram. Three packages weigh 0.094 kg, 0.91 kg, and 0.1 kg. Arrange the weights in order from greatest to least.

Step 1 Write the weights in a column, aligning the decimal point.	0.094
	0.91**0**
Step 2 Add zeros to fill out the columns.	0.1**00**
Step 3 Compare as you would whole numbers.	

In order from greatest to least, the weights are **0.91, 0.1,** and **0.094 kg.**

A. Round each number as directed. Refer to the chart on page 500.

1. Round 3.5719 to the tenths place. _____

2. Round 5.132 to the hundredths place. _____

3. Round 0.543 to the ones place. _____

4. Round 7.0813 to the tenths place. _____

5. Round 1.0699 to the thousandths place. _____

B. Compare the following numbers. Write >, <, or = between the numbers.

6. 0.32 ___ 0.3109   10. 1.075 ___ 1.57

7. 0.98 ___ 1.9   11. 0.18 ___ 0.108

8. 0.5 ___ 0.50   12. 2.38 ___ 2.83

9. 0.006 ___ 0.06   13. 3.60 ___ 3.600

Answers start on page 829.

Estimation and Money

Estimating with money can be a very useful skill. In many everyday situations involving money, you do not need exact amounts. For example, you can estimate when you want to know whether you have enough cash to buy the three things you want at the grocery store or about how much each person should contribute to split the cost of lunch. In such cases, you can use amounts rounded to the nearest dollar (the ones place).

Example 1 Using the price list, <u>about</u> how much would Pat pay for a steering wheel cover, a wide-angle mirror, and an oil drip pan?

(1) between $31 and $33
(2) between $33 and $35
(3) between $35 and $37
(4) between $37 and $39
(5) between $39 and $41

Auto Parts Price List	
Outside Wide-Angle Mirror	$13.45
Steering Wheel Cover	$15.95
Oil Drip Pan	$ 8.73
Windshield Washer Fluid	$ 2.85
Brake Fluid	$ 6.35

Round the cost of each item to the nearest dollar and find the total of the estimates.

Item	Cost	Estimate
Steering wheel cover	$15.95	$16
Wide-angle mirror	13.45	13
Oil drip pan	8.73	+ 9
Total:		$38

The best estimate is **option (4) between $37 and $39.**

GED Practice

Directions: Choose the <u>one best answer</u> to each question.

1. Hank's Hardware sells carbon monoxide detectors for $38.83 and smoke detectors for $12.39. Choose the best estimate for the cost of 4 smoke detectors.

   (1) $12
   (2) $24
   (3) $40
   (4) $48
   (5) $52

2. Twice a month, $27.50 is deducted from Petra's paycheque for RRSPs. About how much does she contribute per year to her RRSP?

   (1) $ 30
   (2) $ 60
   (3) $360
   (4) $600
   (5) $700

Answers start on page 829.

Operations with Decimals

Adding and Subtracting Decimals

Lesson 9

Example 1 Anna assembles machine parts. One part comes in two sections with lengths of 4.875 and 3.25 centimetres. Once assembled, what is the total length of the two sections?

Step 1 To add, write the numbers so that the decimal points are aligned. If necessary, write zeros to the right of the last digit so that all the numbers have the same number of decimal places.

$$\begin{array}{r} 4.875 \\ +3.25\mathbf{0} \end{array}$$

Step 2 Add as you would with whole numbers. Regroup as needed.

$$\begin{array}{r} {\scriptstyle 1\ \ 1} \\ 4.875 \\ +3.250 \\ \hline 8\ 125 \end{array}$$

Step 3 Align the decimal point in the answer with the decimal points in the problem.

$$\begin{array}{r} 4.875 \\ +3.250 \\ \hline 8.125 \end{array}$$

 When adding decimals with a calculator, be sure to enter the decimal points where they are needed.

$$4\ \boxed{\cdot}\ 875\ \boxed{+}\ 3\ \boxed{\cdot}\ 25\ \boxed{=}\ 8.125$$

The total length of the assembled parts is **8.125 centimetres.**

Example 2 Cesar has $213 in a chequing account. If he writes a cheque for $32.60, how much will be left in the account?

Step 1 To subtract, write the numbers so that the decimal points are aligned. Note that a number without a decimal point is understood to have one to the right of the ones place. If necessary, write zeros to the right of the last digit in a number.

$$\begin{array}{r} \$213.00 \\ -\ \ \ 32.60 \end{array}$$

Step 2 Subtract as you would with whole numbers. Regroup as needed.

$$\begin{array}{r} {\scriptstyle 1\ 11\ 2\ \ 10} \\ \$2\cancel{1}\cancel{3}.\cancel{0}0 \\ -\ \ \ 32.60 \\ \hline \$180\ 40 \end{array}$$

Step 3 Align the decimal point in the answer with the decimal points in the problem.

$$\begin{array}{r} \$213.00 \\ -\ \ \ 32.60 \\ \hline \$180.40 \end{array}$$

Cesar will have **$180.40** left in his chequing account.

> **Tip**
>
> When you work with money amounts on a calculator, be careful how you read the results. The sum of $5.55 and $3.75 would appear as 9.3 on the calculator display, but the answer is $9.30.

Mathematics • Numbers and Operations

A. Solve the decimal problems using paper and pencil. Align problems on decimal points.

1.　 0.03
　　 +2.60

2.　 1.35
　　 +4.05

3.　 6.90
　　 −1.353

4.　 5.075
　　 −2.15

5. 7.1 + 8.003

6. 10.3 − 6.125

7. 3.61 + 1.2

8. 16.05 − 4.27

9.　 1.85
　　 0.03
　　 19.007
　 +62

10.　 12.4
　　 11.08
　　 16.1
　 + 4.575

11.　 16 004.1
　　 − 6 972.1

12.　 3.8
　　 −1.006

13. 12.87 − 9.923

14. 23.07 − 5.965

15. 14.01 + 8.6 + 0.058

16. 56.8 − 24.95

 B. Use your calculator to solve these problems.

17. 0.95 + 1.843 + 3.008 + 0.9

18. 0.6 − 0.3407

19. 3.15 + 2.816 + 4.05 + 0.3

20. 39.05 − 15.7

21. 0.125 + 1.4 + 3.76 + 0.01

22. 25.6 − 12.85

Answers start on page 830.

Multiplying and Dividing Decimals

Example 1 In the deli department at a grocery store, a block of cheese weighs 1.6 kg and costs $1.79 per kilogram. To the nearest whole cent, what is the cost of the cheese?

To multiply by a power of 10 (10, 100, . . .), count the number of zeros and move the decimal point that number of places to the right.

$1.4 \times 100 = 140.$

Step 1 Multiply the weight of the cheese by the cost per kilogram. Multiply as you would with whole numbers. Note that there is no need to align the decimal points when multiplying.

$$
\begin{array}{r}
\$1.79 \\
\times\ \ 1.6 \\
\hline
1074 \\
+1790 \\
\hline
2864
\end{array}
$$

Step 2 Count the number of decimal places in the original problem to find how many decimal places are needed in the answer. Starting at the right of the answer, count decimal places. In this problem, count 3 decimal places. Place the decimal point in the answer.

$1.79 \leftarrow 2$ decimal places
$\times\ 1.6 \leftarrow 1$ decimal place
$2.\mathbf{864} \leftarrow 3$ decimal places

Step 3 The problem says to round your answer to the nearest whole cent. Therefore, round to the hundredths place.

2.864 rounds to **$2.86**

Enter the numbers to be multiplied. Notice that dollar signs are not entered into a calculator.

1.6 ✕ **1.79** = **2.864**

The block of cheese costs **$2.86.**

Example 2 Marvin bought a portable CD player for $74.55. He plans to pay for it in 6 equal payments. How much will each payment be? Round your answer to the nearest cent.

To divide by a power of 10, count the number of zeros and move the decimal point that number of places to the left.

$1.4 \div 100 = 0.014$

Step 1 Set up the problem. Place the decimal point in the answer directly above the decimal point in the problem.

Step 2 Divide as you would with whole numbers. If there is a remainder, write a zero to the right of the last decimal place in the number you are dividing. Continue this process until either there is no remainder or you reach one place to the right of the desired place value.

$$
\begin{array}{r}
\$12.425 \\
6)\overline{\$74.550} \\
\underline{6} \\
14 \\
\underline{12} \\
25 \\
\underline{24} \\
15 \\
\underline{12} \\
30 \\
\underline{30}
\end{array}
$$

Step 3 Round your answer to the nearest whole cent.

$12.425 rounds to $12.43

Enter the numbers to be divided. Remember that it's important to enter the number being divided *first*.

74.55 ÷ **6** = **12.425**

Mathematics • Numbers and Operations

Example 3   A pharmacist is preparing capsules with 0.007 g of aspirin each. How many capsules can be prepared with 14 g of aspirin?

Step 1   Set up the problem. To divide by a decimal, make the divisor (the number you are dividing by) a whole number. In this problem, move the decimal point three places to the right in the divisor. Write zeros to the right of the number you are dividing so that you can move the decimal point the same number of places: three.

$$0.007\overline{)14.000.}$$

Step 2   Place the decimal point in the answer directly above the decimal point in the number you are dividing. Divide as you would with whole numbers.

$$\begin{array}{r} 2\,000. \\ 7\overline{)14\,000.} \\ \underline{14} \end{array}$$

 Enter the numbers to be divided. Notice that you do not need to move the decimal point when working with a calculator.

14 ÷ 0.007 = 2000.

The pharmacist can prepare **2000 capsules.**

A. Place the decimal point in each answer. You may need to add zeros.

1. $8.5 \times 0.4 =$ 3 4 0
2. $0.04 \times 0.6 =$ 2 4
3. $5.6 \times 0.002 =$ 1 1 2
4. $12 \times 3.06 =$ 3 6 7 2
5. $21.1 \times 14.7 =$ 3 1 0 1 7
6. $0.008 \times 12 =$ 9 6

B. Solve the decimal problems using paper and pencil.

7. 1.07×12
8. 0.09×6.1
9. $8\overline{)20.48}$
10. $3\overline{)3.2916}$

11. 2.27×1.8
12. 5.04×15
13. $3.6\overline{)7.704}$
14. $1.05\overline{)6.3987}$

15. 0.008×2.5
16. 1.05×0.11
17. $6\overline{)0.021}$
18. $0.07\overline{)4.34}$

 C. Use your calculator to solve these problems. Round answers to the nearest hundredth.

19. 0.012×12
20. $7\overline{)2}$

21. 7.15×0.03
22. $11\overline{)3}$

23. 12.25×1.5
24. $6\overline{)5}$

Answers start on page 830.

Solving Multi-Step Problems

Example 1 Jeri buys an item that costs $5.24. She also pays $0.31 sales tax. If Jeri pays with a $20 bill, which expression shows how much change Jeri should receive?

(1) $20 + $5.24 + $0.31
(2) $5.24 + $0.31 − $20
(3) $20 − $5.24 + $0.31
(4) $5.24 − ($0.31 + $5.24)
(5) $20 − ($5.24 + $0.31)

Remember to use the order of operations:

1. First, do all operations in parentheses.
2. Next, do multiplication or division.
3. Then, do addition or subtraction.

Read the problem carefully. What do you need to know to solve the problem? You need to know the total cost (cost of the item plus sales tax). You also need to find the difference between the amount paid and the total cost. In other words, subtract the total cost from $20.

- Option (1) is incorrect because it adds the three amounts.
- In option (2), $20 is subtracted from the total of $5.24 and $0.31. Subtracting $20 from the total is not the same as subtracting the total from $20.
- Option (3) is incorrect because no parentheses means that only $5.24, rather than the sum of $5.24 and $0.31, is subtracted from $20.
- Option (4) is incorrect because the sum is subtracted from $5.24, not from $20.
- **Option (5) is correct.** Because of the parentheses, finding the total cost of the item is the first step ($5.24 + $0.31). Then the total cost is subtracted from $20.

GED Practice

Directions: Choose the one best answer to each question.

Question 1 refers to the following information.

The Computer Centre sells recordable CDs for $0.89 each. Computer Warehouse sells the same CDs for $1.05 each.

1. Which expression shows how much a customer will save by buying 25 recordable CDs at The Computer Centre?

(1) 25($1.05 − $0.89)
(2) 25($1.05 + $0.89)
(3) 25 − ($1.05 + $0.89)
(4) 25 + ($1.05 − $0.89)
(5) 25 ÷ ($1.05 − $0.89)

Question 2 refers to the following information.

Wanda has $35 in cash. She buys a blouse for $12.98, a belt for $10.67, and a poster for $5.98.

2. If Wanda pays $2.37 in sales tax, how much does she have left?

(1) $ 3.00
(2) $ 5.37
(3) $22.02
(4) $29.63
(5) $32.00

Answers start on page 831.

Mathematics • Numbers and Operations

Writing Decimals in a Standard Grid

Earlier in this book you learned how to use the standard grid with whole numbers and fractions. You'll be using the same grid when working with decimals.

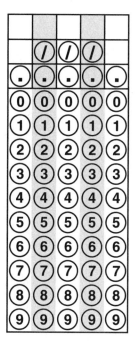

Points to remember

- Each grid is used to enter a single answer.
- When filling in a grid for a decimal answer, your answer can start in any of the columns as long as the final answer is complete.
- Note that the ⊙ stands for a decimal point.
- Leave any unused columns blank.
- Fill in only one value for each column.

Example   Sarah is responsible for tracking her time on a job. She spent 3.75 hours, 4.5 hours, and 1.25 hours getting a customer's computer system running. How many hours did she spend in all on this customer's computer problem?

The problem asks you to find the total number of hours Sarah spent on the customer's computer problem. Add together the hours she worked:

$$3.75 + 4.5 + 1.25 = \mathbf{9.5}$$

Fill in your answer on the grid. Note that all three grids are filled in correctly.

GED Practice

Directions: Solve the following problems. Enter your answers on the grids provided.

1. Marta rides her bike three times a week. She tries to ride a short distance farther each time. This week she rode 4.5 km, 5.25 km, and 6 km. What was her total distance for the week?

2. Manny's batting average was 0.275 last year. This year his batting average reached a career high of 0.340. By how much did his average increase?

3. A piece of copper tubing is 60 m long. Assuming there is no waste, how many pieces measuring 1.2 m in length can be cut from the piece of tubing?

4. Marita ordered 14 parts that cost $2.99 per part. How much was the total order?

Answers start on page 831.

Mathematics • Numbers and Operations

Decimals and Fractions

Changing Decimals to Fractions

Both decimals and fractions can be used to show part of a whole. Sometimes it is easier to calculate using fractions. At other times, decimals are more useful. If you know how to change from one form to the other, you can solve any problem using the form that is best for the situation.

Example 1   Josh is solving a problem using a calculator. The calculator display reads 0.375, but he needs to write the answer in the form of a fraction. Change 0.375 to a fraction.

Step 1   Write the number without the decimal point as the numerator of the fraction.

$$0.375 = \frac{375}{?}$$

Step 2   Write the place value for the last decimal digit as the denominator.

$$0.375 = \frac{375}{1000}$$

Step 3   Reduce the fraction to lowest terms.

$$\frac{375 \div 125}{1000 \div 125} = \frac{3}{8}$$

The decimal 0.375 is equal to the fraction $\frac{3}{8}$.

When you work with money, you will sometimes see decimals with a fraction part. This combination is commonly found as a unit price, the cost of one item or unit.

Example 2   On a grocery store shelf, Rita reads that the price per gram for a brand of shampoo is $0.33\frac{1}{3}$. What fraction of a dollar is the unit price?

Step 1   Write the fraction as you did in the example above.

$$0.33\frac{1}{3} = \frac{33\frac{1}{3}}{100}$$

Step 2   In your work with improper fractions, you learned that the fraction bar indicates division.

$$\frac{33\frac{1}{3}}{100} \text{ means}$$

$$33\frac{1}{3} \div 100$$

Step 3   Use the rules for dividing mixed numbers. Change both numbers to improper fractions, invert the number you are dividing by, and multiply.

$$33\frac{1}{3} \div 100 = \frac{100}{3} \div \frac{100}{1} = \frac{\overset{1}{\cancel{100}}}{3} \times \frac{1}{\underset{1}{\cancel{100}}} = \frac{1}{3}$$

The unit price is **$\frac{1}{3}$ of a dollar.**

Tip

To find the number of zeros you need in the denominator of a fraction, count the number of decimal places in the decimal you are converting. For example:

$$0.\underbrace{375}_{} = \frac{375}{\underbrace{1000}_{}}$$

3 decimal places   3 zeros

Changing Fractions to Decimals

To solve some problems, you may need to change a fraction to a decimal. To do so, you perform the division indicated by the fraction bar.

Example 1   Change $\frac{2}{5}$ to a decimal.

Step 1   Divide the numerator by the denominator:

$$5\overline{)2}$$

Step 2   Set the decimal point in the answer directly above the decimal point in the problem. Add zeros and continue dividing until the remainder is zero or until you reach the desired number of decimal places.

$$\begin{array}{r} 0.4 \\ 5\overline{)2.0} \\ 2\,0 \end{array}$$

The fraction $\frac{2}{5}$ equals the decimal **0.4.**

A few fractions have decimal equivalents that contain a digit or group of digits that repeats. Round repeating decimals to a certain decimal place or express the remainder as a fraction.

Example 2   Change $\frac{2}{9}$ to a decimal. Show the answer to the hundredths place with the remainder expressed as a fraction.

Step 1   Divide the numerator by the denominator:

$$9\overline{)2}$$

Step 2   You can see that the division will continue repeating because the subtraction is the same each time. Write the remainder as a fraction by writing the remainder, 2, over the divisor, 9.

$$\begin{array}{r} 0.22 \\ 9\overline{)2.00} \\ 1\,8 \\ \hline 20 \\ 18 \end{array}$$

The fraction $\frac{2}{9}$ equals the decimal **0.22$\frac{2}{9}$.**

As you may know, a unit price is often stated as a decimal with a fraction. The fraction expresses part of one cent.

Example 3   The unit price of a brand of fruit punch is $8\frac{1}{2}$ cents per gram. What is the cost of 32 g of the punch?

Multiply 32 by $8\frac{1}{2}$ or $\$0.08\frac{1}{2}$ to solve the problem. Change the fraction part of the decimal to a decimal digit. The fraction $\frac{1}{2}$ converts to 0.5 ($1 \div 2 = 0.5$). So $8\frac{1}{2}$ cents can be written as 8.5 cents or $0.085. Multiply.

$$\begin{array}{r} 32 \\ \times 0.085 \\ \hline 160 \\ +2\,560 \\ \hline 2.720 \end{array}$$

The cost of 32 g of fruit punch is **$2.72.**

Example 4   What is the cost per kilogram of a 20-kg bag of dog food that sells for $12.75?

Divide $12.75 by 20 to two decimal places. Write the remainder as a fraction and reduce to lowest terms. $\frac{15}{20} = \frac{3}{4}$

$$\begin{array}{r} 0.63 \\ 20\overline{)12.75} \\ 12\,0 \\ \hline 75 \\ 60 \\ \hline 15 \end{array}$$

The unit price of one kilogram of dog food is **$63\frac{3}{4}$ cents.**

Tip

If you prefer working with fractions, multiply 32 by $8\frac{1}{2}$. Then express your answer as 2 dollars and 72 cents. Always choose a method for solving a problem that makes the most sense to you.

A. Change these decimals to fractions. Reduce all fractions to lowest terms.

1. $0.25 =$

2. $0.4 =$

3. $0.35 =$

4. $0.128 =$

5. $0.05 =$

6. $0.31\frac{1}{4} =$

7. $0.26\frac{2}{3} =$

8. $0.06\frac{2}{3} =$

9. $0.23\frac{3}{4} =$

B. For each calculator display, write the decimal in fraction form. Then reduce each fraction to lowest terms if needed.

10. $0.9 = \frac{?}{10}$

11. $0.625 =$

12. $0.125 =$

13. $0.55 =$

14. $0.28 =$

15. $0.3125 =$

C. Change these fractions to decimals. Round to three decimal places.

16. $\frac{4}{5} =$

17. $\frac{3}{8} =$

18. $\frac{11}{20} =$

19. $\frac{5}{8} =$

20. $\frac{3}{5} =$

21. $\frac{7}{25} =$

D. Change these fractions to decimals. Divide to two decimal places and write the remainder as a fraction.

22. $\frac{5}{6} =$

23. $\frac{8}{9} =$

24. $\frac{1}{16} =$

25. $\frac{3}{11} =$

26. $\frac{7}{15} =$

27. $\frac{1}{3} =$

E. Solve. Simplify your answers. Remember to change all mixed numbers to improper fractions.

28. A brand of raspberry jam costs $\$0.43\frac{3}{4}$ per gram. What fraction of a dollar is the unit price?

29. A brand of frozen drink concentrate is $\$0.16\frac{2}{3}$ per gram of concentrate. Write the unit price as a fraction.

30. The unit price of a bagel is $37\frac{1}{2}$ cents. What fraction of a dollar is the unit price?

31. A company announces a unit price increase of $\$0.02\frac{1}{2}$ per kilogram. Write the decimal as a fraction.

Answers start on page 832.

GED Practice

Directions: Solve the following problems and enter your answers on the grids provided.

1. Jim runs $2\frac{1}{4}$ laps on Monday, 1.5 laps on Tuesday, and $3\frac{3}{4}$ laps on Wednesday. How many total laps did Jim run in the 3 days?

3. A can of green beans contains $40\frac{1}{2}$ g. If one serving is 3.75 g, how many servings are in 1 can?

2. If gasoline sells for $1.25 per litre, how much would $3\frac{3}{5}$ L cost?

4. Al has a board that is 9.375 m long. If Al cuts off a piece that is $3\frac{1}{8}$ m long, how many metres are left of the original board?

If the answer you need to enter on a grid contains an end zero after the decimal point, you can include it or leave it off. For example, 1.20 could be correctly filled in as 1.20 or 1.2.

Questions involving both fractions and decimals may ask for the answer to be in a certain form. Be sure your answer is in the form asked for, as either a fraction or a decimal.

Answers start on page 833.

Mathematics • Numbers and Operations

Fractions and Decimals

Most calculators use only decimal numbers and whole numbers. Even whole numbers entered in a calculator usually appear with a decimal point after the ones' place. For example, 32 entered on a calculator would probably be displayed as 32. with a decimal point. When using a calculator, you need to change a fraction to a decimal, for example, $\frac{3}{4}$ to 0.75.

Here are some important points to keep in mind when using fractions and decimals on the calculator.

- To change a fraction to a decimal, divide the numerator by the denominator.
  Example Change $\frac{3}{8}$ to a decimal by dividing 3 by 8 = 0.375.

- When working with a mixed number on a calculator, leave the whole number part as it is and change only the fraction to a decimal.
  Example $17\frac{1}{2}$ would become 17.5.

- All decimals that do not contain a whole number part will be displayed with a 0 as the whole number part, even if you do not key in a 0.
  Example The decimal .64, when keyed in, will appear as 0.64.

- When working with decimals, you do not need to key in zeros that are to the right of the last digit in the decimal part of the number.
  Example 24.600 can be keyed in as 24.6.

Example Sam bought a laptop computer for $1620 and made a down payment of $\frac{1}{4}$ of the cost. How much was the down payment?

(1) $ 25.00
(2) $ 40.00
(3) $ 64.80
(4) $ 405.00
(5) $1595.00

Since the problem asks you to find $\frac{1}{4}$ of $1620, you need to multiply. To do this problem on a calculator, you could change $\frac{1}{4}$ to .25. Then you would press the calculator keys in the sequence shown below.

Since $\frac{1}{4}$ also means 1 divided by 4, you could also use any of these sequences:

.25 ☒ 1620 ═   or   1 ÷ 4 ☒ 1620 ═

or   1 a b/c 4 ☒ 1620 ═

You should see the answer 405 in the display. **Option (4) $405** is correct.

GED Practice

 Directions: Choose the <u>one best answer</u> to each item. You <u>may</u> use your calculator.

1. Carolyn rode her bike 26.8 km on Thursday, $14\frac{3}{8}$ km on Friday, and $27\frac{3}{4}$ km on Saturday. How many kilometres did she ride in all for the 3 days?

   (1) 26.825
   (2) 67.05
   (3) 67.825
   (4) 68.925
   (5) 80.4

2. During a recent storm, snow fell at the rate of 1.24 cm per hour. At this rate, how many centimetres of snow would fall in $6\frac{1}{4}$ hours?

   (1) $5\frac{1}{10}$
   (2) $5\frac{2}{5}$
   (3) $7\frac{1}{4}$
   (4) $7\frac{61}{100}$
   (5) $7\frac{3}{4}$

3. Mikkel is paid at the rate of $9.50 per hour for the first 40 hours worked in a week, and $1\frac{1}{2}$ times that rate for all hours over 40. If he works for $52\frac{1}{4}$ hours in 1 week, what is his gross pay, rounded to the nearest cent?

   (1) $550.56
   (2) $552.56
   (3) $554.56
   (4) $557.56
   (5) $560.56

4. If gasoline sells for $1.39 per litre, how much would $16\frac{1}{8}$ L cost, rounded to the nearest cent?

   (1) $31.12
   (2) $22.49
   (3) $22.41
   (4) $22.24
   (5) $11.60

Questions 5 and 6 refer to the following table.

Kilometres Jogged	
Alicia	4.875
Brett	$3\frac{3}{5}$
Krystyna	$4\frac{3}{4}$

5. How many more kilometres did Alicia jog than Brett did?

   (1) 1.275
   (2) 1.375
   (3) 1.400
   (4) 1.500
   (5) 1.575

6. What was the total number of kilometres jogged by the three people listed?

   (1) 13.525
   (2) 13.425
   (3) 13.325
   (4) 13.225
   (5) 13.125

Answers start on page 834.

Mathematics • Numbers and Operations

The Meaning of Percent

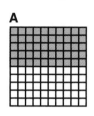

Percent is another way to show part of a whole. With fractions, the whole can be divided into any number of equal parts. With decimals, the number of parts must be 10, 100, 1000, or another power of 10. With percents, the whole is always divided into 100 equal parts.

A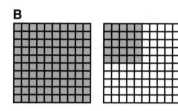

Drawing A is divided into 100 equal parts. The entire square represents 100%. Fifty parts, or one-half of the whole square, are shaded. The shaded part is 50% of the whole. The percent sign, %, means "out of 100." Fifty out of 100 parts are shaded. The drawing also represents the fraction $\frac{1}{2}$ and the decimal 0.5.

B

Percents can be greater than 100%. Drawing B represents 125%. One whole square and 25 parts of the second square are shaded. Since 100 parts equal 1 and 25 out of 100 parts is $\frac{1}{4}$, 125% equals $1\frac{1}{4}$ or 1.25.

Drawing C represents $\frac{1}{2}$%, or 0.5%. Only one-half of one part is shaded.

A percent that is less than 1% is less than $\frac{1}{100}$.

$$0.5\% = 0.005 = \frac{5}{1000} = \frac{1}{200}$$

C

Changing Percents to Decimals

To solve percent problems using pencil and paper, you need to change the percent to either a decimal or a fraction.

Example 1 Change 45% to a decimal.
Drop the percent sign, and insert a decimal point to the right of the ones digit. Then move the decimal point two places to the left.

45.%
0.45.

So 45% is equal to the decimal **0.45.**

Example 2 Change 7.5% to a decimal.
Drop the percent sign, and move the decimal point two places to the left. Write a zero in the tenths place as a placeholder.

7.5%
0.07.5

So 7.5% is equal to the decimal **0.075.**

To change a percent to a decimal using a calculator, enter the number of the percent and divide by 100.

7.5 ÷ 100 = 0.075

Changing a Decimal to a Percent

The examples below show how to change a decimal to a percent.

Example   Change 0.15 to a percent.
Move the decimal point two places to the
right, and write the percent sign. (Notice that
the zero placeholder is no longer needed.)

$$0.15. = 15\%$$

The decimal 0.15 is equal to **15%.**

Examples   Add a zero in order to move the
decimal point two places.

$$2.5 = 2.50. = 250\%$$

Do not show the decimal point
after a whole number or between
a whole number and a fraction.

$$0.33\tfrac{1}{3} = 0.33.\tfrac{1}{3} = 33\tfrac{1}{3}\%$$

 To change a decimal to a percent using a calculator, enter the
decimal and multiply by 100.

    0.15 ✕ **100** = **15.**

Changing a Fraction to a Percent

You can convert a fraction to a percent by first changing the fraction to
a decimal and then changing the decimal to a percent.

Example 1   Change $\tfrac{3}{4}$ to a percent.

Step 1   Divide the numerator by the denominator. $3 \div 4 = 0.75$
Step 2   Multiply the decimal by 100. Move the decimal $0.75 = 75\%$
    point two places to the right; write a percent sign.

The fraction $\tfrac{3}{4}$ is equal to **75%.**

You can also change a fraction or a mixed number directly to a percent.

Example 2   Change $\tfrac{3}{4}$ to a percent.

Step 1   Multiply the fraction by $\tfrac{100}{1}$.
Step 2   Change to a whole or mixed number and write $\dfrac{3}{\cancel{4}_{1}} \times \dfrac{\cancel{100}^{25}}{1} = 75\%$
    the percent sign.

The fraction $\tfrac{3}{4}$ is equal to **75%** by this method as well.

On the calculator
provided for the
GED Mathematics
Test, you need to
press (SHIFT) (=)
for the percent
key. See page 913
to learn more
about using
percent keys on
calculators.

Example 3   Change $3\frac{1}{4}$ to a percent.

Step 1   Change the mixed number to an improper fraction.

$$3\frac{1}{4} = \frac{13}{4}$$

Step 2   Multiply by $\frac{100}{1}$ and add the percent sign.

$$\frac{13}{\cancel{4}_{1}} \times \frac{\cancel{100}^{25}}{1} = 325\%$$

The mixed number $3\frac{1}{4}$ is equal to **325%.**

To change a fraction to a percent using a calculator, divide the numerator by the denominator and press the percent key.

Change $\frac{3}{4}$ to a percent.   **3** ÷ **4** **SHIFT** **=** **75.** or **75%**

Change $\frac{2}{5}$ to a percent.   **2** ÷ **5** **SHIFT** **=** **40.** or **40%**

Changing a Percent to a Fraction or Mixed Number

As you know, the word *percent* means "out of 100." To change a percent to a fraction or mixed number, drop the percent sign and write the number as a fraction with a denominator of 100. Then reduce.

Example 1   Change 35% to a fraction.
Write as a fraction with a denominator of 100 and reduce.

$$\frac{35}{100} = \frac{35 \div 5}{100 \div 5} = \frac{7}{20}$$

So 35% is equal to the fraction $\frac{7}{20}$.

Example 2   Change 150% to a mixed number.
Write as an improper fraction (denominator of 100); simplify.

$$\frac{150}{100} = \frac{150 \div 50}{100 \div 50} = \frac{3}{2} = 1\frac{1}{2}$$

So 150% is equal to the mixed number **$1\frac{1}{2}$**.

Converting percents with fraction or decimal parts requires extra steps.

Example 3   Change $41\frac{2}{3}\%$ to a fraction.
Write $41\frac{2}{3}$ over 100 and divide.

$$\frac{41\frac{2}{3}}{100} = 41\frac{2}{3} \div 100 = \frac{\cancel{125}^{5}}{3} \times \frac{1}{\cancel{100}_{4}} = \frac{5}{12}$$

So $41\frac{2}{3}\%$ is equal to the fraction **$\frac{5}{12}$**.

Example 4   Change 37.5% to a fraction.

Step 1   Change the percent to a decimal: move the decimal point 2 places left.

$$37.5\% = .37.5 = 0.375$$

Step 2   Change decimal to a fraction; reduce.

$$\frac{375 \div 125}{1000 \div 125} = \frac{3}{8}$$

So 37.5% is equal to the fraction **$\frac{3}{8}$**.

Some calculators have special keys to change percents to fractions.

To change 150% to a fraction: enter the percent number, press the fraction key, enter 100, then press = .

150 a b/c **100** = **1 ⌐1 ⌐2.**
This calculator display means $1\frac{1}{2}$.

Tip

Your calculator display may look different from the one shown here. Read the instructions that came with your calculator to learn how to use it to solve problems with fractions.

Change each percent to a fraction or mixed number.

1. 65%

2. 84%

3. 140%

4. 275%

5. 39%

6. 450%

Using Proportions with Percents

There are three basic elements in a percent problem: **part = base × rate.** Think about this statement:

Example   Of 200 applicants, 25% or 50 cannot work weekends.

- The **base** is the whole amount. In this statement, the base is 200.
- The **part** is a piece of the whole or base. In this statement, 50 tells what part of the 200 applicants (the base) cannot work weekends.
- The **rate** is always followed by a percent sign (%). The rate tells the relationship of the part to the base. In this statement, it is 25%.

In a percent problem, one of the three elements is missing. To find the missing element set up a proportion using the base, part, and rate. Substitute the known values, and solve for the missing element.

Tip

The base, or whole, is often an original amount such as an original price, starting balance, or total amount.

$$\frac{\textbf{Part}}{\textbf{Base}} = \frac{\textbf{Rate\%}}{\textbf{100\%}}$$ To find the missing element, cross multiply and divide by the third number.

Example 1   12 is 75% of what number?

(1) 1200
(2)   75
(3)   63
(4)   16
(5)   12

Here, you know the part and the rate. You need to solve for the base.

Step 1   Set up the proportion. $\frac{12}{?} = \frac{75}{100}$

Step 2   Cross multiply. $12 \times 100 = 1200$

Step 3   Divide by 75. $1200 \div 75 = 16$

So, 12 is 75% of 16. **Option (4)** is correct.

Answers start on page 834.

GED Practice

Directions: Choose the <u>one best answer</u> to each question. Use your calculator when indicated.

1. The sweater shown above is on sale for 20% off. If the price tag lists the original price, how much would you save by buying it on sale?

   (1) $ 7
   (2) $ 9
   (3) $12
   (4) $14
   (5) $15

2. Sidney's insurance paid 90% of the cost to fix his car. If the repair bill was $625, how much did the insurance pay?

   (1) $437.50
   (2) $468.75
   (3) $500.00
   (4) $562.50
   (5) $605.15

3. Aldora earns $1344 per month. If 2.5% of her earnings goes to income tax, how much does she pay per month in income tax?

   (1) $ 20.16
   (2) $ 26.88
   (3) $ 33.60
   (4) $ 42.20
   (5) $336.00

4. On a test, a student got 80% of the items correct. If the student got 56 items correct, how many items were on the test?

   (1) 64
   (2) 70
   (3) 72
   (4) 84
   (5) 90

5. The Bulldogs won 18 games out of 45. What percent of their games did the Bulldogs win?

   (1) 40%
   (2) 45%
   (3) 50%
   (4) 55%
   (5) 60%

6. Eighty percent of the Usagi Express Company's employees are drivers. If there are 300 drivers in the company, how many employees work for Usagi Express?

   (1) 320
   (2) 335
   (3) 342
   (4) 365
   (5) 375

Tip

To solve a percent problem use the formula **part = base × rate** or set up a proportion:

$$\frac{\text{Part}}{\text{Base}} = \frac{\text{Rate\%}}{100\%}$$

Determine which element is missing: the base, part, or rate; substitute the numbers into the proportion and solve.

Answers start on page 834.

Solving Percent Problems (Part 1)

The Elements of a Percent Problem

You now know that percent problems have three basic elements—the base, the part, and the rate. Think about this statement:

Kina spends $320, or 20%, of her monthly income of $1600 on groceries.

The base, $1600, is the whole amount. The other numbers in the problem are compared to the base. The part, $320, is a portion of the base. The rate, 20%, tells the relationship of the part to the base.

In a percent problem, one of the three elements is missing. You learned earlier how to solve a percent problem by using a proportion. You can also find the missing element using the percent formula:

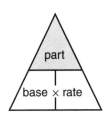

$$\textbf{part} = \textbf{base} \times \textbf{rate}$$

The triangle diagram shows the relationship among the three elements. You will learn how to use the diagram in the examples throughout this lesson.

Finding the Part

Example   Aretha puts 5% of her weekly paycheque in her savings account. If her weekly paycheque is $326, how much will she put into savings?

Step 1   Identify the elements you know. The base, or whole amount, is $326. Aretha puts a *part* of this amount in savings. The rate is 5%. You need to solve for the part.

Step 2   Use the diagram to find out which operation to perform. Cover the word *part*. The remaining elements are connected by the multiplication symbol. Multiply: **base × rate.**

Step 3   Change the rate to a decimal. $5\% = 0.05$
           Multiply. $326 \times 0.05 = \$16.30$

When you solve any word problem, take a moment to decide whether your answer makes sense. Since 5% is a small part of 100%, you know Aretha's savings should be a small part of her paycheque. The answer $16.30 is a reasonable amount.

Tip

If the rate is greater than 100%, the part will be greater than the base. 150% of 200 is 300.

You need to find 5% of $326. Multiply. Enter the base first.

    326 × **5** SHIFT =   **16.3**

(Remember: SHIFT = gives the % key on the GED calculators.)

Aretha will put **$16.30** of her weekly paycheque into savings.

Finding the Rate

Tip

To learn about using the percent key on the GED Test calculator, see page 913.

Example   Joel earns $1700 per month. He decides to take out a loan to buy a used car. His monthly loan payments are $204. What percent of his monthly income is the loan payment?

Step 1   Think about the problem. The whole amount Joel earns each month is the base. Part of these earnings is spent on the loan payment. You need to solve for the percent, or rate.

Step 2   Use the diagram to find out which operation to perform. Cover the word *rate*. The remaining elements are connected by the division symbol: **part ÷ base = rate.**

Step 3   Divide. 204 ÷ 1700 = 0.12.
Convert to a percent. 0.12 = 12%

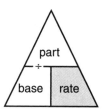

You can do both calculations in one step using your calculator's percent key or the SHIFT = keys on the GED Test calculator.

    204 ÷ **1700** % **12.**   or   **204** ÷ **1700** SHIFT = **12.**

Joel spends **12%** of his monthly earnings on the loan payment.

Finding Percent of Increase or Decrease

Some percent problems ask you to find the rate that an amount has changed over time. The change may be either an increase or a decrease. To solve these problems, follow these steps.

Step 1   Subtract to find the difference between the original amount and the new amount.

Step 2   Divide the difference from Step 1 by the original amount.

Step 3   Convert the decimal to a percent.

Tip

Look for clues in the words of the problem to help you identify the original amount. For example, "what percent of" is usually followed by the base.

Example   Brent works as a sales clerk in a clothing store. When he started the job, he was paid $7.50 an hour. Recently, he received a raise. He now earns $8.10 per hour. Find the rate of increase in his hourly pay.

Brent's pay started at $7.50 per hour (the original amount) and increased to $8.10, the new amount.

Step 1   Subtract to find the difference. $8.10 − $7.50 = $0.60

Step 2   Divide by the original hourly wage. $0.60 ÷ $7.50 = 0.08

Step 3   Convert the decimal to a percent.   0.08 = 8%

Brent's raise is an **8% increase.**

GED Practice

Directions: Choose the one best answer to each question.

1. The Gardner Public Library records the number of books borrowed each month. Of the 8520 books borrowed in May, 10% were children's books. How many children's books were borrowed in May?

   (1) 85
   (2) 170
   (3) 852
   (4) 1704
   (5) 2000

Question 2 refers to the diagram below.

2. Estelle works as a waitress. A customer left a 15% tip based on the total of the cheque shown above. How much was Estelle's tip?

   (1) $1.30
   (2) $1.60
   (3) $2.75
   (4) $3.90
   (5) $5.00

3. Martin bought some stereo equipment for $150 plus 5% sales tax. How much sales tax did he pay?

   (1) $155.00
   (2) $ 50.00
   (3) $ 30.00
   (4) $ 15.00
   (5) $ 7.50

4. Sara sold a radio/CD player originally priced at $70 and discounted 20%. How much was the discount?

   (1) $20.00
   (2) $14.00
   (3) $ 7.00
   (4) $ 1.40
   (5) $ 0.70

5. Zoila's take-home pay is $1500 a month. Of that amount, 25% goes toward paying rent. How much does she pay each month for rent?

   (1) $ 60
   (2) $150
   (3) $300
   (4) $375
   (5) $500

6. The Johnson Community Centre is selling tickets to its fundraising concert. They have sold 30% of the 1800 tickets. How many tickets have they sold?

   (1) 600
   (2) 540
   (3) 60
   (4) 54
   (5)   6

Remember that a whole number is understood to have a decimal point after the ones place. $40 = $40.00

Answers start on page 834.

Mathematics • Numbers and Operations

Solving Percent Problems (Part 2)

Finding the Base

Example 1 The employees at Galindo Printing are required to complete a safety course during their first year of work. Of the current employees, 90% have completed the course. If 63 employees have completed the course, how many employees work at Galindo Printing?

Step 1 Think about the problem. The base or whole amount is the total number of employees at Galindo Printing. The number 63 is part of the number of employees. The 63 employees are 90% of the total employees. You need to solve for the base.

You can also use a proportion to solve for the base:

$$\frac{63}{x} = \frac{90\%}{100\%}$$

Since the percent formula is not on the formula sheet, make sure you memorize your favourite way of calculating percents.

Step 2 Use the diagram to find out what operation to perform. Cover the word *base*. The remaining elements are connected by the division symbol. Divide: **part ÷ rate.**

Step 3 Convert the rate to a decimal. 90% = 0.9 Divide.

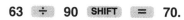

$$0.9\overline{)63.0.}$$
$$\underline{63}$$
$$00$$

gives 70.

There are **70** employees at Galindo Publishing.

You can perform the calculations in one step using your calculator. Divide.

63 ÷ 90 SHIFT = 70.

Galindo Printing has **70 employees.**

As you know, the part may be greater than the base. You can recognize these situations because the rate is greater than 100%.

Always read carefully. At first glance, this may seem to be a rate-of-increase problem. Make sure you know what you are solving for before you begin your calculations.

Example 2 Regina recently started a better-paying job. Her new weekly salary is 120% of the weekly earnings at her old job. If her new weekly salary is $326.40, how much did she earn per week at her old job?

Step 1 Analyze the situation. Regina's new salary is 120% of her old salary. The new salary, $326.40, is the part even though it is the greater amount. The old salary is the base.

Step 2 Convert the rate to a decimal and divide the part by the rate.

$$120\% = 1.2 \qquad \$326.40 \div 1.2 = \$272.00$$

Regina's old salary is **$272.00.**

Solving Interest Problems

Tip

See page 55 for a copy of the GED formulas page that you will be given for use on the GED Mathematics Test. Be familiar with these formulas and know how to use them before you take the test.

Interest is a fee charged for using someone else's money. When you borrow money for a purchase, you pay interest to the company that loans you the money. When you put your money into a savings account, the bank pays you interest for the use of your money.

If you have had a credit card or have borrowed money, you have had experience with paying interest. There are several different types of interest and ways to calculate it. On the GED Mathematics Test, you will be tested on your understanding of simple interest. Simple interest is based on the time of a loan in years.

The formula for finding simple interest is $i = prt$. This formula is similar to the percent formula you have been using. When the letters, or variables, in a formula are written next to each other, they are to be multiplied. This interest formula can also be written in a triangle.

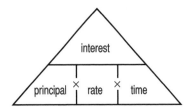

i = **interest**

p = **principal**, the amount borrowed or invested

r = **interest rate**, as a percent

t = **time** of the loan, in years

Example   Lynn Alvarez borrows $2500 for 6 months at a 12% rate of interest. How much interest will Lynn pay on the loan?

The principal (p) is $2500, the amount of the loan. The interest rate (r) is 12%. The time (t) is 6 months, or $\frac{1}{2}$ a year.

Step 1   Change the interest rate to a decimal. $12\% = 0.12$

Step 2   Write the time in years. $6 \text{ months} = \frac{6}{12} = \frac{1}{2} \text{ year.}$

(If the problem states the time in months, write the time as a fraction of a year. Write the number of months as the numerator and the number 12 as the denominator. Reduce the fraction to lowest terms.)

Tip

To solve interest problems using a calculator, change the fractional part of a year to a decimal. For example, 6 months equals 0.5 year.

Step 3   Multiply: **principal × rate × time.**
The result is the interest.
$$\$2500 \times 0.12 \times \frac{1}{2} =$$
$$\$300 \times \frac{1}{2} = \$150$$

Lynn will owe **$150** in interest.

Some problems ask you to find the amount paid back. This includes the principal and any interest owed. In the example above, Lynn borrowed $2500 and must pay $150 in interest. But this does not answer the question. To find the payback amount, add the principal and the interest: $2500 + $150 = $2650.

Lynn must pay back **$2650.**

GED Practice

Directions: Choose the one best answer to each question.

$$\begin{array}{|c|} \hline \text{\$\$} \quad \quad \text{\$\$} \\ \text{\$} \quad 15\% \text{ off} \quad \text{\$} \\ \textbf{\textit{everything}} \\ \textbf{\textit{in the store}} \\ \hline \end{array}$$

1. Murray's Bargain Basement is having a sale on household goods. What would be the sale price of a twin-size blanket originally priced at $20?

    (1) $ 3.00
    (2) $ 5.00
    (3) $ 7.50
    (4) $17.00
    (5) $18.67

2. Flora received a 6% raise on her hourly wage of $9.00. Choose the expression that shows Flora's new hourly wage.

    (1) $9 + 0.06
    (2) $9 + 0.06 × $9
    (3) $9 − 0.06 × $9
    (4) $9 × 0.06
    (5) $9(1 − 0.06)

3. Alfredo bought a used car for $1500. He replaced the engine and repaired the body. He sold the car for $4500. What was the rate of increase in the price of the car?

    (1) 67%
    (2) 133%
    (3) 200%
    (4) 300%
    (5) 400%

4. At a factory, Mitali supervises 30 employees. Next month, her staff will be increased by 40%. Which expression shows the number of employees Mitali will supervise next month?

    (1) 0.4(30) + 0.4
    (2) 0.4(30) + 30
    (3) 0.4(30) − 0.4
    (4) 0.04(30) + 0.4
    (5) 0.4(30) − 30

5. Lavina put on layaway a coat that costs $160. She paid 10% down and will pay the rest in 6 monthly installments. Which expression can be used to find the amount of each monthly payment?

    (1) $\dfrac{\$160 - (\$160 \times 0.1)}{6}$
    (2) $\dfrac{\$160}{6}$
    (3) $160 − ($160 × 0.1)
    (4) $160 × 0.1
    (5) $160 + ($160 × 0.1)

6. Grantsville Copper Mines employs 1400 workers. The company must lay off 5% of its workforce immediately and another 20% of the remaining workforce by the end of the year. How many workers will be laid off?

    (1) 350
    (2) 336
    (3) 280
    (4) 210
    (5) 70

Answers start on page 834.

Calculators and Percents

One of the most useful keys on a calculator is the percent key. When using this key, you won't have to change a percent to a decimal or a decimal to a percent—the calculator will do it for you automatically.

Example   Julia paid 32% of her monthly salary of $3540 for taxes. How much did she pay for taxes?

If you don't use the percent key, you would first have to change 32% to decimal form, or 0.32, before multiplying by $3540. This method for using a calculator is shown below.

3540 × **.32** =

You would see the answer 1132.8, or **$1132.80 in taxes,** in the display.

By using the percent key, you would not change the percent to a decimal, but simply key in the numbers as they appear in the problem. This is shown below. (Note that some calculators do not require the equals key at the end.)

3540 × **32** % =

Remember: There is no percent "key" on the calculator used for the GED Mathematics Test. You must press the **SHIFT** = keys to work with a percent.

3540 × **32** **SHIFT** = **1132.8**

Using the Percent Key

Here are some important points to keep in mind when using the percent key on the calculator.

- **When solving for the base or part, key in the percent exactly as it appears in the problem.** Do not move the decimal point. For example, if you want to find 8% of a number, do not change 8% to the decimal 0.08. Simply multiply the number by 8 and press the % key after the 8.
- **When solving for the rate, the answer you see in the display is the percent, not the decimal equivalent.** Do not move the decimal point. For example, divide the part (1) by the base (4) followed by the percent key. (If your calculator display shows 0.04, press the equals key.) The display shows 25, which is 25%. There is no need to move the decimal point.
- **Be careful about the order in which you key in numbers.** When solving for the part, you multiply the base by the percent. When solving for the percent or base, you divide. Be careful to key in the part first.

GED Practice

Directions: Choose the one best answer to each item. You may use your calculator.

1. At the end of the first quarter, the *Gazette* had 3450 employees. In the second quarter, 12% more employees were hired. How many new employees did the *Gazette* hire in the second quarter?

   (1)   41
   (2)   404
   (3)   414
   (4)   424
   (5) 4140

2. The Smith family went to dinner at a restaurant and had a total bill of $120. If they left a tip of $21.60, what percent of the total bill did they leave?

   (1) 15%
   (2) 16%
   (3) 17%
   (4) 18%
   (5) 19%

3. The vice president of a bank contributed $8\frac{3}{4}\%$ of her salary to a retirement plan. If she contributed $4375 to the plan in one year, what was her annual salary that year?

   (1) $42 000
   (2) $43 750
   (3) $49 383
   (4) $50 000
   (5) $50 383

4. The office expenses at Delta Products were reduced from $1400 last month to $1225 this month. What was the percent of reduction in office expenses?

   (1) 12.0%
   (2) 12.5%
   (3) 13.0%
   (4) 13.5%
   (5) 14.0%

5. Axelle bought a microwave oven regularly priced at $394. If the oven was on sale for 40% off the regular price, how much did she pay for the microwave?

   (1) $226.95
   (2) $232.60
   (3) $236.40
   (4) $240.25
   (5) $250.00

Question 6 refers to the following table.

Daly's Pharmacy		
Item	April Sales	May Sales
Toothpaste	$4200	$4956
Soap	$3980	$4293
Shampoo	$3420	$3290

6. Toothpaste sales in May were what percent higher than the toothpaste sales in April?

   (1) 15%
   (2) 16%
   (3) 17%
   (4) 18%
   (5) 19%

Questions 7 and 8 refer to the following table.

Company Sales (Millions of Dollars)	
Month	Sales
Jan.	$ 2
Feb.	$ 6
Mar.	$ 8
Apr.	$ 8
May	$14
June	$18

7. The sales in February were what percent of the total sales for the six months listed? Round to the nearest whole percent.

   (1) 10%

   (2) 11%

   (3) 12%

   (4) 13%

   (5) 14%

8. Between which two consecutive months was the percent of increase in company sales the greatest?

   (1) January to February

   (2) February to March

   (3) March to April

   (4) April to May

   (5) May to June

9. Larry borrows $12 500 at 16% simple annual interest for $3\frac{1}{2}$ years. How much interest will he owe on the loan at the end of that period?

   (1) $2 000

   (2) $3 000

   (3) $4 000

   (4) $5 000

   (5) $7 000

10. Lars has a current annual salary of $38 650. If he gets a raise of $3280, what percent is the raise of his current annual salary? Round to the nearest whole percent.

    (1) 6%

    (2) 7%

    (3) 8%

    (4) 9%

    (5) 10%

11. Jim buys a coat for $136 and pays sales tax of $8\frac{1}{4}$%. Which expression shows the amount that Jim paid for the coat, including the sales tax?

    (1) $136 + 0.0825

    (2) $136 × 0.0825

    (3) ($136 × 0.0825) + $136

    (4) ($136 + $136)0.0825

    (5) $\frac{\$136}{0.0825}$

12. Attendance at a craft show dropped from 1420 last year to 1209 this year. What was the percent of decrease in attendance, rounded to the nearest percent?

    (1) 15%

    (2) 16%

    (3) 17%

    (4) 18%

    (5) 19%

13. In October, the circulation of the local newspaper was 247 624. The circulation of the newspaper in September was 238 100. What is the percent of change in circulation from September to October?

    (1) increase of 3%

    (2) decrease of 3%

    (3) increase of 4%

    (4) decrease of 4%

    (5) increase of 5%

Answers start on page 835.

GED Review Numbers and Operations

Directions: Choose the one best answer to each question. You may use a calculator.

1. What is the value of 6000 − 2784?

   (1) 8784
   (2) 4785
   (3) 4784
   (4) 4216
   (5) 3216

2. What is the value of 3024 ÷ 6?

   (1)   54
   (2)   504
   (3)   540
   (4) 5004
   (5) 5040

3. Karin needs $3220 for a used car. If she saves $230 each month, how many months will it take her to save the entire amount?

   (1) 11
   (2) 12
   (3) 13
   (4) 14
   (5) 15

4. Yvonne pays $480 for rent each month. How much rent does she pay in one year?

   (1) $14 400
   (2) $ 5 760
   (3) $ 4 800
   (4) $ 576
   (5) $ 480

Questions 5 through 7 refer to the following table.

Number of Videotapes Rented	
January	4320
February	5980
March	4987
April	6007
May	7985

5. What was the total number of videotapes rented in February and March?

   (1) 10 300
   (2) 10 400
   (3) 10 967
   (4) 11 067
   (5) 15 287

6. How many more videotapes were rented in May than in April?

   (1)   993
   (2) 1 070
   (3) 1 978
   (4) 1 988
   (5) 13 992

7. Twice as many videotapes were rented in June as in January. How many videotapes were rented in June?

   (1) 15 970
   (2) 12 014
   (3)   9974
   (4)   8640
   (5)   2160

8. Last year, Anne paid $13 600 in taxes, which was 32% of her gross annual salary. What was her gross annual salary?

(1) $30 000

(2) $34 500

(3) $36 000

(4) $38 500

(5) $42 500

9. In its current catalogue, Sheridan Office Supplies lists an electric stapler for $69.95. If it offers a discount of 35%, what is the price after the discount, rounded to the nearest cent?

(1) $24.48

(2) $34.47

(3) $42.43

(4) $45.47

(5) $94.43

10. The value of the inventory at Sam's Sporting Goods store increased from $46 400 to $52 200 during the first quarter of the year. What is the percent of increase in the value of the inventory?

(1) 10.5%

(2) 12.0%

(3) 12.5%

(4) 58.3%

(5) Not enough information is given.

11. In a recent company survey, $\frac{3}{4}$ of the employees said they drove to work. Of those who drive to work, $\frac{3}{5}$ said they drive in a carpool. What fraction of the employees drives in a carpool?

Question 12 refers to the following table.

Monthly Budget	
Expense	**Fraction Budgeted**
Rent	$\frac{3}{8}$
Salaries	$\frac{1}{4}$
Advertising	$\frac{1}{5}$
Supplies	$\frac{1}{8}$
Miscellaneous	$\frac{1}{20}$

12. Which of the expenses received the highest amount of the monthly budget?

(1) Rent

(2) Salaries

(3) Advertising

(4) Supplies

(5) Miscellaneous

Questions 13 through 15 refer to the following table.

Company Profit	
Region	**Fraction of Profit**
Northeast	$\frac{1}{8}$
Southeast	$\frac{1}{4}$
Northwest	$\frac{1}{8}$
Southwest	$\frac{1}{5}$
Central	$\frac{3}{10}$

13. Which region had the highest fraction of the company's profit?

    (1) Northeast
    (2) Southeast
    (3) Northwest
    (4) Southwest
    (5) Central

14. The fraction of combined profit from the Northeast and Northwest regions is how much greater than the fraction of profit from the Southwest region?

    (1) $\frac{1}{20}$
    (2) $\frac{3}{20}$
    (3) $\frac{1}{5}$
    (4) $\frac{1}{4}$
    (5) $\frac{2}{5}$

15. If the total company profit last year was $1 987 865, how much profit came from the Southwest region?

    (1) $ 248 483
    (2) $ 397 573
    (3) $ 496 966
    (4) $ 596 966
    (5) $9 939 325

16. Which of the following decimals has the same value as the fraction $\frac{3}{7}$, rounded to the nearest hundredth?

    (1) 0.04
    (2) 0.42
    (3) 0.43
    (4) 0.44
    (5) 0.45

17. For the first five months of the year Menchu had electric bills of $64.16, $78.92, $63.94, $50.17, and $42.87. What was the total amount of these bills?

    (1) $287.86
    (2) $298.06
    (3) $299.06
    (4) $300.06
    (5) Not enough information is given.

18. Stuart purchased three items at Rite Pharmacy priced at $17.60, $9.25, and $3.68. If the tax was $2.40, and he gave the salesperson a $50 bill, how much change did he receive?

    (1) $17.07
    (2) $17.93
    (3) $18.07
    (4) $18.93
    (5) $19.07

Remember there can be more than one way to write some expressions.
40(7 − 5) is (40 × 7) − (40 × 5)

Part 2

Directions: Choose the one best answer to each question. You may not use your calculator.

19. Cooper's Fashions has 2100 employees working at 14 branches. After 200 new employees are hired, what is the total number of employees?

    (1) 214
    (2) 2114
    (3) 2300
    (4) 2314
    (5) 4900

20. R.J. Landscaping buys supplies at wholesale. To do the landscaping for a model home, the company spent $560 for bushes and $638 for river rock. The company also purchased paving blocks at $3 each. If 250 blocks are needed, which expression shows how much the paving blocks will cost?

    (1) $\frac{(\$560 + \$638 + \$3)}{250}$
    (2) ($560 + $638 + $3)250
    (3) $560 + $638 + $3 − 250
    (4) 250 × $3
    (5) $\frac{250}{\$3}$

21. Marcus buys a computer on credit. He makes a down payment of $720. He also agrees to pay $85 per month on the remaining balance. What is the total cost of the computer?

    (1) $ 720
    (2) $ 765
    (3) $1020
    (4) $1275
    (5) Not enough information is given.

22. John paid $1224.96 in 12 equal monthly installments. Estimate the amount of each monthly installment.

    (1) $1200
    (2) $1000
    (3) $ 120
    (4) $ 100
    (5) $ 12

23. Yaffa has $175. She spends $54.25 and $30.50. Which of the following expressions shows how much money Yaffa has left after the two purchases?

    (1) $175 + $54.25 + $30.50
    (2) $175 − ($54.25 + $30.50)
    (3) ($175 + $54.25) − ($175 + $30.50)
    (4) $175 + $54.25 − $30.50
    (5) $175 − $54.25 + $30.50

Question 24 refers to the following table.

Paul's Plants Price List	
7-cm Potted Plant	$1.79
10-cm Potted Plant	$2.89
13-cm Potted Plant	$3.69
Bag of Potting Soil	$3.19
Watering Can	$1.89

24. What is the greatest number of 7-cm potted plants that Mohammed can buy with $10?

    (1) 2
    (2) 3
    (3) 5
    (4) 8
    (5) 10

25. Net sales in August were reported as 120% of net sales in February. If February's net sales were $13 985, what were the net sales in August?

   (1) $11 188
   (2) $11 654
   (3) $14 782
   (4) $16 782
   (5) $17 481

26. During a sale, an office furniture store marks down the price of a swivel chair by 30%. If the regular price of the chair is $180, what is the price after the markdown?

   (1) $ 54
   (2) $120
   (3) $126
   (4) $184
   (5) $234

Question 27 refers to the following table.

Expense Budget Total: $60 000	
Category	% of Budget
Advertising	16%
Salaries	35%
Supplies	25%
Rent	24%

27. How much more is budgeted for supplies than for advertising?

   (1) $5000
   (2) $5400
   (3) $6400
   (4) $7400
   (5) $9000

28. Debra invested $5000 in an account that paid 8% simple annual interest. At the end of 3 years, how much money was in the account, including the interest earned?

   (1) $ 400
   (2) $1200
   (3) $5400
   (4) $5800
   (5) $6200

29. During the holiday season, the price of a particular toy rose from $1 to $3. What is the percent of increase in the price of the toy?

   (1) 100%
   (2) 200%
   (3) 300%
   (4) 400%
   (5) 500%

30. Sam bought a new television for $440. If he paid 20% of this amount as a down payment, and paid the rest in 8 equal monthly installments, how much was the amount of each installment?

   (1) $43
   (2) $44
   (3) $45
   (4) $46
   (5) $47

31. Meg borrowed $2500 from her employer for 2 years at $2\frac{1}{2}$% interest. What is the total amount she will pay back?

   (1) $2625
   (2) $3137
   (3) $3426
   (4) $5000
   (5) $6150

Answers start on page 835.

Measurement and Data Analysis

Measurement and data analysis are important areas of math that we use every day. We use measurement when we make things. Sometimes we measure items such as litres of paint or grams of chocolate chips. At other times we measure length or space, such as the perimeter or area of a floor, wall, or garden or the volume of a container. Data analysis is becoming an increasingly important activity in our lives. The increasing use of computers has accelerated the collection, display, and analysis of data, especially information in numerical form. Most often, we see such data presented in tables, charts, and graphs.

Questions related to measurement and data analysis will account for more than 25 percent of the GED Mathematics Test. Additionally, you will find that you can use many of the skills in this unit in your personal life and on the job.

The Metric System of Measurement

The metric system is used throughout most of the world. It uses these basic metric units:

> **metre (m)** unit of length
> **gram (g)** unit of weight or mass
> **litre (L)** unit of volume

Other units of measure are made by adding the prefixes shown below to the basic units listed above.

milli-	means $\frac{1}{1000}$	A milligram (mg) is $\frac{1}{1000}$ of a gram.	
centi-	means $\frac{1}{100}$	A centimetre (cm) is $\frac{1}{100}$ of a metre.	
deci-	means $\frac{1}{10}$	A decilitre (dL) is $\frac{1}{10}$ of a litre.	
deca-	means 10	A decagram (dag) is 10 grams.	
hecto-	means 100	A hectolitre (hL) is 100 litres.	
kilo-	means 1000	A kilometre (km) is 1000 metres.	

The metric system is based on the powers of ten. Convert metric units by moving the decimal point. Use this chart to make metric conversions.

To convert to smaller units, move the decimal point right. --------->

kilo- 1000	hecto- 100	deca- 10	metre gram litre	deci- $\frac{1}{10}$	centi- $\frac{1}{100}$	milli- $\frac{1}{1000}$

◄-------------- To convert to larger units, move the decimal point left.

Measuring Common Figures

Perimeter

Lesson 15

Perimeter is a measure of the distance around the edge of any flat shape. To find the perimeter of any figure, add the lengths of its sides.

Example 1 The county supervisor plans to fence in the area shown at the left for a playground. How much fencing is needed?

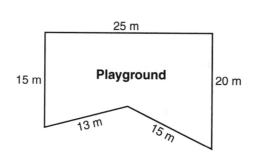

The fence will go around the perimeter of the playground. Find the perimeter by adding the lengths of the sides.

$$15 + 13 + 15 + 20 + 25 = 88$$

It will take **88 m** of fencing to enclose the playground.

Sometimes not all sides of a figure in a problem are labelled. To find the missing lengths, you will need to apply your knowledge of the properties of that figure.

A rectangle has 4 sides, 4 square corners or right angles, and opposite sides of equal length. Opposite sides are directly across from each other.

Example 2 Monica needs to glue yarn around the perimeter of a rectangular piece of poster board that is 18 cm long and 15 cm wide. How much yarn does she need?

Step 1 Fill in the measures of the opposite sides.
Step 2 Add the measurements. $18 + 18 + 15 + 15 = 66$ cm

Another way to approach the problem is to double the length and the width and add the results. $(18 \times 2) + (15 \times 2) = 36 + 30 = 66$ cm

---

If your calculator is programmed with the order of operations (like the one provided on the GED Mathematics Test), you can enter the second method without parentheses. The calculator automatically does the multiplication operations before it adds.

18 ✕ **2** ＋ **15** ✕ **2** ＝ **66.**

The perimeter of the poster board is **66 cm.**

A square has 4 equal sides and 4 square corners. If you know the length of one side, you can find the perimeter of the square by multiplying by 4.

> **Tip**
> If you use a calculator that is not programmed with the order of operations, you must enter the calculation as an addition problem: $18 + 18 + 15 + 15 = 66$.

Area of Squares and Rectangles

Area is a measure of the surface of a flat figure. Area is measured in square units. Area tells how many square units it takes to cover the space inside the figure.

5 cm
6 cm

Example 1   A rectangle is 6 cm by 5 cm. What is the area of the rectangle in square centimetres?

Step 1   The rectangle is 6 cm along the bottom, so 6 squares, each 1 cm by 1 cm, can be lined up on the bottom row. It will take 5 of these rows to fill the rectangle.

5 rows
6 columns

Step 2   The area is the number of squares inside the rectangle. A quick way to count the squares is to multiply the number of columns by the number of rows. $6 \text{ cm} \times 5 \text{ cm} = 30 \text{ cm}^2$

The area of the rectangle is **30 cm².**

Laundry Room

11 m

Example 2   Kim's laundry room floor has the shape of a square. He wants to tile the room. If one side of the room measures 11 m, what is the area of the floor in square metres (m²)?

A square is actually a special kind of rectangle. To find the area of a rectangle, you multiply length by width. Use the same method to find the area of a square. The room is 11 m by 11 m. To find the area, multiply the length by the width. $11 \text{ m} \times 11 \text{ m} = 121 \text{ m}^2$

When you multiply a number by itself, you square the number. On a calculator, square a number by multiplying or using the x^2 key. This key multiplies any number, x, by itself. The raised 2 in x^2 (an exponent) tells how many times the number should appear in the multiplication problem.

    11 ✕ 11 = 121.   **11 x² 121.**

The area of the laundry room is **121 m².**

Tip

Practise all kinds of problems with and without a calculator. Use the official GED calculator if possible. You will be issued a GED calculator at the test site and will be allowed to use it on the first part of the GED Mathematics Test.

Some complex shapes are actually a combination of squares and rectangles. To find the area of these shapes, break the figure into smaller pieces, find the area of each piece, and add to find the total area.

Example 3   An office suite has the shape shown below. What is the area in square metres of the office suite?

Step 1   Break the shape into squares and rectangles. There may be more than one way to do this. Choose the way that makes sense to you. No matter how the shape is broken up, the area remains the same.

21 m
21 m   Office Suite   35 m
49 m

Step 2   Find the area of each piece.
Square: The dimensions are 21 m by 21 m.
Multiply to find the area. $21 \text{ m} \times 21 \text{ m} = 441 \text{ m}^2$

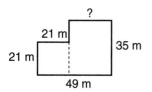

?

21 m

21 m

35 m

49 m

Rectangle: One side measures 35 m. The other measurement is not given. However, you know that the side of the square is 21 m and the length of the entire figure is 49 m. Subtract to find the missing measurement.   49 m − 21 m = 28 m

Multiply the rectangle's dimensions.   35 m × 28 m = 980 m²

Step 3   Add the areas of the square and rectangle to find the total area.   441 m + 980 m = 1421 m²

Key in the problem in one step using the parentheses keys on a calculator not programmed with the order of operations.

(21 × 21) + (35 × 28) = 1421.

The area of the office suite is **1421 m²**.

GED Practice

Directions: Choose the one best answer to each question.

Questions 1 and 2 refer to the following diagram.

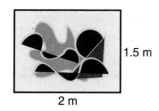

1.5 m

2 m

1. Cherise wants to frame the painting in the diagram. How many metres of wood will she need to frame the picture?

    (1) 3

    (2) $3\frac{1}{2}$

    (3) 5

    (4) 7

    (5) 9

2. Cherise plans to cover the painting with glass. How many square centimetres of glass will it take to cover the surface?

    (1)   3

    (2)   30

    (3)   300

    (4)   3000

    (5) 30 000

3. The perimeter of a rectangle is 48 m. The length of the rectangle is 3 times the width. What is the width in metres of the rectangle?

    (1)   4

    (2)   6

    (3)   8

    (4) 12

    (5) 16

4. What is the perimeter of the figure?

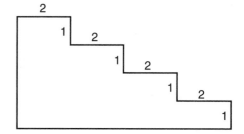

    (1) 10

    (2) 12

    (3) 20

    (4) 24

    (5) 30

Answers start on page 837.

Lesson 15 • Measuring Common Figures

Volume

Measures of length can be used to calculate area—the space inside a two-dimensional figure. Area is the square units that cover the space.

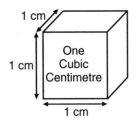

Measures of length are also used to calculate volume. Volume is a measure of the amount of space inside a three-dimensional object. Volume is measured in three-dimensional units or cubic units—cubic centimetres (cm^3), cubic metres (m^3), and other metric units. Each of these units is a cube with identical square sides.

One of the most common three-dimensional objects is the rectangular container. Boxes, crates, and rooms are examples of rectangular containers. To find the volume of these objects, multiply the length times the width times the height.

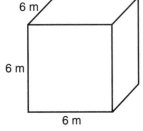

Example 1 What is the volume of a rectangular container that is 14 cm long, 8 cm wide, and 4 cm high?

Multiply: length times width times height.

$$14 \text{ cm} \times 8 \text{ cm} \times 4 \text{ cm} = 448 \text{ cubic cm}$$

Multiply the numbers as shown.

 14 ✕ 8 ✕ 4 = 448.

The volume of the container is **448 cubic cm.** In other words, you could fit 448 one-centimetre cubes inside the container.

A cube is a special rectangular container, so you can find the volume in the same way. However, since each side has the same measure, you are multiplying the same number three times, or "cubing" the number.

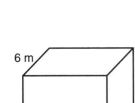

Example 2 A shipping crate has the shape of a cube that is 6 m long on each edge. What is its volume in cubic metres?

$$\text{Volume} = \text{length} \times \text{width} \times \text{height}$$
$$= 6 \text{ m} \times 6 \text{ m} \times 6 \text{ m} = 216 \text{ m}^3$$

The GED calculator also has a **x^3** key.

Enter the number you want to multiply, press **SHIFT**, and then press **►**. The answer will appear.

6 SHIFT ► 216.

The volume of the shipping crate is **216 cubic m.**

Using other scientific calculators, you can cube a number using the **x^y** key. Enter the number you want to multiply, press **x^y**, enter the exponent 3, and press the **=** key. Remember, the exponent is the number of times the number is used in the multiplication problem, $x \times x \times x$. Try both methods to see that you get the same answer.

6 ✕ 6 ✕ 6 = 216.   **6 x^y 3 = 216.**

GED Practice

Directions: Choose the one best answer to each question.

1. A rectangular school playground measures 100 m by 75 m. There is a square blacktop area in the centre of the playground with sides that measure 40 m. The rest of the playground is seeded with grass. What is the area in square metres of the grassy portion of the playground?

   (1) 9100
   (2) 7660
   (3) 7500
   (4) 5900
   (5) 1600

2. One side of the square base of a milk carton measures 4 cm. If the carton can be filled to a height of 8 cm, how many cubic centimetres can the carton hold?

   (1) 112
   (2) 128
   (3) 132
   (4) 138
   (5) 146

3. A quilt is 4 squares wide and 6 squares long. A tassel is sewn on each point where 4 squares touch. How many tassels are needed to complete the quilt?

   (1) 10
   (2) 15
   (3) 20
   (4) 24
   (5) 35

4. Janice is trying to find her way to a job interview downtown. She starts at a parking garage and walks 4 blocks north, 5 blocks east, 2 blocks south, 2 blocks west, and 2 blocks farther south. How many blocks east of the parking garage does she end up?

   (1) 1
   (2) 2
   (3) 3
   (4) 4
   (5) Not enough information is given.

5. A new game is played on a rectangular field that is 150 m by 60 m. A chalk line is drawn on the field exactly 2 m inside the outer rectangle at all points. What is the total length in metres of the chalk line?

   (1) 112
   (2) 202
   (3) 210
   (4) 292
   (5) 404

6. Cathy wants to install an air conditioner in her office, which measures 10 m by 8 m by 7 m. Which expression could be used to find the measure of the office space in cubic metres?

   (1) 8 + 10 + 8 + 10
   (2) (7 + 8 + 10)2
   (3) 8 × 7
   (4) 10 × 8
   (5) 10 × 8 × 7

7. The length of a rectangle is 36 cm. What is its area in square centimetres?

   (1) 324

   (2) 432

   (3) 504

   (4) 576

   (5) Not enough information is given.

8. What is the perimeter in centimetres of the figure below?

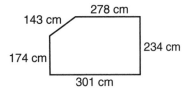

   (1) 829

   (2) 852

   (3) 956

   (4) 987

   (5) 1130

9. Boxes A and B are cubes. Each side of Box A measures 2 m. The sides of Box B are twice the length of the sides of Box A. Which of the following is a true statement about the volume of the boxes?

   (1) The volume of Box A is $\frac{1}{6}$ the volume of Box B.

   (2) The volume of Box A is $\frac{1}{2}$ the volume of Box B.

   (3) The volumes of the boxes are equal.

   (4) The volume of Box B is four times the volume of Box A.

   (5) The volume of Box B is eight times the volume of Box A.

Questions 10 and 11 refer to the figure below.

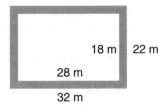

10. The figure is formed by two rectangles. What is the area, in square metres, of the shaded part?

    (1) 100

    (2) 200

    (3) 504

    (4) 704

    (5) 1208

11. How many more metres is the perimeter of the larger rectangle than the perimeter of the smaller rectangle?

    (1)   8

    (2) 16

    (3) 56

    (4) 92

    (5) 108

12. One litre of paint covers 200 m². How many litres are needed to paint a rectangular floor that is 40 m by 60 m?

    (1) 12

    (2) 24

    (3) 40

    (4) 60

    (5) 120

Answers start on page 837.

Mathematics • Measurement and Data Analysis

Measures of Central Tendency and Probability

Mean, Median, and Mode

Finding the "centre" of a group of numbers helps us to make comparisons with numbers. There are three ways to measure the centre of a group of numerical data: mean, median, and mode. Each measure adds to our understanding of the data.

You may know the mean as the average. The average is generally thought of as typical or normal. To find the mean of a group of numbers, add the values and divide the sum by the number of items in the list. Remember: average means the mean.

Example 1 David had scores of 82, 92, 75, 82, and 84 on five tests. What was his average score?

Step 1 Add the data values. $82 + 92 + 75 + 82 + 84 = 415$
Step 2 Divide by 5, the number of scores. $415 \div 5 = 83$

Scientific calculators perform multiplication or division steps before addition steps. To make sure your calculator does the addition step first when calculating means, press ▣ before you divide.

82 ⊞ 92 ⊞ 75 ⊞ 82 ⊞ 84 ▣ ÷ 5 ▣ 83.

David's average test score is **83**.

The median is the middle value in a set of numbers. To find the median, arrange the data in order from lowest to highest or highest to lowest and find the middle number. The median value is often used when one value would dramatically affect the average of a group of values.

Example 2 Find the median of David's scores.

Step 1 Arrange the test scores in order. 92, 84, 82, 82, 75
Step 2 Find the middle value. 92, 84, **82,** 82, 75

David's median score is **82**.

If there is an even number of data items, the median is the average (mean) of the two middle numbers.

Example 3 Ami's point totals for six games of basketball were 24, 16, 19, 22, 6, and 12 points. Find the median of her point totals.

Step 1 Arrange the data in order. 24, 22, **19, 16,** 12, 6
Step 2 The two middle numbers are 19 and 16. $19 + 16 = 35$
Average these to find the median. $35 \div 2 = 17.5$

Ami's median point total is **17.5 points.**

Tip

Always ask yourself whether your answer makes sense. For example, when solving for the mean, median, or mode, the answer must be between the highest and lowest values in the group of numbers.

The mode of a group of numbers is the number that occurs most often. In Example 1, the mode of David's test scores is 82, the only score that occurs twice in the data. In Example 3, since every item of data occurs only once, there is no mode. A set of data may have no mode, one mode, or several modes. Mode is often used in business to find out which size, price, or style is most popular. (Note: The MODE key on the GED calculator is *not* used to find the mode of data.)

Another measure that can help us understand data is range. To find the range, subtract the lowest number in the set from the greatest number. If the range is a small number, you know that the data values are grouped close together. If the range is large, you know the data values are spread out.

Examples: The range of David's test scores: $92 - 75 = 17$
The range of Ami's point totals: $24 - 6 = 18$

GED Strategy • Using Your Calculator

Finding the Mean

To calculate the mean (average) of a set of numbers, first add the numbers and then divide the sum by the number of values in the set.

Example 1 During the past semester, Pat's test scores in her history class were 86, 76, 82, and 92. What was her mean test score?

Step 1 First add Pat's test scores. $86 + 76 + 82 + 92 = 336$
Step 2 Then divide the sum by 4, the number of test scores. $336 \div 4 = 84$

(The number of test scores is the number of items or values in the set.) Pat's average, or mean, test score was **84.**

Check how your calculator solves this type of problem.

86 + 76 + 82 + 92 ÷ 4 =

If your calculator is not programmed with the order of operations, it will give you the correct answer, 84.

However, if a calculator uses the order of operations, as the calculator used on the GED Test does, it will first perform all multiplication and division before it performs any addition and subtraction. This results in the wrong answer of 267.

To obtain the correct answer on a calculator that uses the order of operations, press the equals key after entering the last score to be added. This will total all the scores before dividing. Complete the problem by dividing by the number of values.

86 + 76 + 82 + 92 = ÷ 4 = 84.

GED Practice

 Directions: Choose the one best answer to each item. You may use your calculator.

Question 1 refers to the table below.

Game	Score
1	94
2	73
3	86
4	102
5	96
6	71

1. What was the average (mean) score for the six games listed?

   (1) 94.0

   (2) 90.0

   (3) 87.0

   (4) 86.5

   (5) 86.0

2. For the past five days the high temperatures in Winnipeg were 18.0° C, 15.2° C, 20.0° C, 9.3° C, and 12.0° C. What was the average (mean) high temperature for those days?

   (1) 14.9° C

   (2) 15.2° C

   (3) 16.7° C

   (4) 18.0° C

   (5) 20.4° C

Questions 3 and 4 refer to the table below.

Rainfall in Union City	
Month	**Centimetres**
June	6.3
July	4.5
August	3.8
September	10.2

3. What was the average (mean) rainfall in Union City during the months shown in the table, rounded to the nearest centimetre?

   (1) 4

   (2) 5

   (3) 6

   (4) 7

   (5) 10

4. What was the median rainfall in Union City during the months shown in the table, rounded to the nearest centimetre?

   (1) 4

   (2) 5

   (3) 6

   (4) 7

   (5) 10

5. Karen's electric bills for six months were $28.84, $18.96, $29.32, $16.22, $17.98, and $21.80. What was the median bill for these months?

   (1) $ 6.79

   (2) $16.22

   (3) $18.96

   (4) $20.38

   (5) $21.80

Answers start on page 838.

Simple Probability

Probability is the study of chance. Probability tells how likely it is that an event will happen. For instance, you may hear on the news that there is a 10% chance of rain tomorrow. From the report, you know that it is unlikely to rain tomorrow, but there is a small chance it might. Probability doesn't tell you what will happen, only the chance that an event will happen.

Probability is often expressed as a percent from 0%, meaning the event cannot occur, to 100%, meaning the event is certain to occur.

You can also express probability as a ratio, fraction, or decimal. For example, the chance of tossing a coin and getting heads can be expressed as a

ratio: 1 out of 2, or 1:2   **fraction:** $\frac{1}{2}$

decimal: 0.5   **percent:** 50%

In any probability situation, there are two numbers to consider:

1. the number of favourable outcomes (events you want to happen)

2. the total number of possible outcomes or trials

To find probability (P), write the ratio of favourable outcomes to possible outcomes.

$$P = \frac{\text{favourable outcomes}}{\text{total possible outcomes}}$$

Example 1   Aaron bought 4 raffle tickets at a community fundraiser. If 200 tickets are sold, what is the probability that one of Aaron's tickets will be the winner?

Step 1   Use the information from the problem to write the probability ratio.

$$P = \frac{\text{favourable outcomes}}{\text{total possible outcomes}} = \frac{4}{200}$$

Step 2   The ratio has been written as a fraction. Reduce the fraction and convert it to a decimal and percent.

$$\frac{4}{200} = \frac{1}{50} = 0.02 = 2\%$$

The probability that one of Aaron's tickets will win is $\frac{1}{50}$, or **1 out of 50.** This converts to **0.02,** or **2%.**

Sometimes probability is based on the results of an experiment. The experiment is repeated a certain number of times. Each repetition is called a trial. The results of the experiment are recorded. Experimental probability is the ratio of favourable outcomes to the total number of trials.

Tip

To change a decimal to a percent, move the decimal point two places to the right. For example, $0.25 = 25\%$

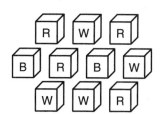

Example 2   A bag holds red, white, and blue cubes of the same size. A cube is drawn at random from the bag, the colour is recorded, and the cube is replaced. The results of 10 trials are shown to the left. What is the experimental probability, expressed as a percent, of drawing a red cube?

Step 1   Write the ratio of favourable outcomes (red cubes) to the number of trials (10).

$\dfrac{4}{10}$

Step 2   Reduce and convert to a percent.

$\dfrac{4}{10} = \dfrac{2}{5} = 0.4 = 40\%$

There is a **40%** experimental probability of drawing a red cube.

Express each probability as a fraction, decimal, and percent.

Questions 1 through 4 refer to the spinner below.

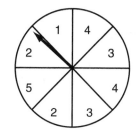

1. The spinner has 8 equal sections. What is the probability of spinning an even number?

2. Evan spins the spinner once. What is the probability of spinning 3 or greater?

3. Jan needs either a 1 or a 2 to win the game. What is the probability that Jan will win on her next spin?

4. What is the probability of spinning a number other than 4? (*Hint:* The favourable outcomes are all numbers that are not 4.)

Independent and Dependent Probability

The probability of heads turning up when you flip a coin is $\frac{1}{2}$, but what is the probability of heads turning up on two coins? To find the combined probability of more than one event, make a chart or use multiplication.

Example 1   A dime and nickel are tossed in the air. What is the probability that both will land heads up?

One way to solve the problem is to make an organized list of all the possible outcomes. There are 4 possible outcomes. Only 1 outcome shows both coins as heads. In other words, $\frac{1}{4}$ of the possibilities shows two heads.

Nickel	Dime
H	**H** ←
H	T
T	H
T	T

There are 4 possible outcomes. Only 1 outcome shows both coins as heads. In other words, $\frac{1}{4}$ of the possibilities shows two heads.

You can also find the probability that two events will both occur by multiplying the probabilities of each event occurring alone.

Answers start on page 838.

Tip

To figure out whether events are dependent, ask yourself, "Do the conditions change after the first event?"

The probability that the nickel will land heads up: $\frac{1}{2}$

The probability that the dime will land heads up: $\frac{1}{2}$

The probability that both will land heads up: $\frac{1}{2} \times \frac{1}{2} = \frac{1}{4}$

Using either method, the probability that both coins will land heads up is $\frac{1}{4}$, **0.25, 25%,** or **1 out of 4** (which is sometimes shown as 1:4).

In Example 1, the two events are **independent.** The first event does not affect the second event. The position of the first coin does nothing to change the probability of getting heads on the second coin.

Two events are **dependent** if the result of the first event does affect the result of the second event.

Example 2   Three white socks and two brown socks are in a drawer. Gloria removes one sock at **random,** without looking. Then, without replacing the first sock, she takes out a second sock. What is the probability that both socks are white?

Step 1   To find the probability that both socks are white, assume that the first sock Gloria selects is white. With 5 socks in the drawer, of which 3 are white, her chance of selecting white is $\frac{3}{5}$.

Step 2   Now there are 4 socks left in the drawer, and 2 are white. Gloria's chance of selecting white the second time is $\frac{2}{4}$, or $\frac{1}{2}$.

Step 3   Multiply to find the combined probability. $\frac{3}{5} \times \frac{1}{2} = \frac{3}{10}$

Tip

Problems with dependent events often involve selecting an object and not replacing it, that is, removing it from the set.

The probability that both socks will be white is $\frac{3}{10}$, **0.3,** or **30%.** These events are dependent. The first event, taking the first sock, affects the second event by changing the number of socks in the drawer.

Solve.

Refer to the following information to answer Questions 1 and 2.

A game is played by spinning a spinner and then, without looking, drawing a card. After each turn, the card is replaced and the cards are shuffled.

1. What is the percent chance that a player will spin red and then draw a 4 or higher?

2. Rounded to the nearest percent, what is the chance that a player will spin either red or blue and then draw a 5?

Refer to the following information to answer Questions 3 and 4.

A company decides to select two workers at random to attend a computer class. Stephanie and Yuki both hope to be chosen. The names of ten workers are put in a box. Two names will be drawn randomly from the box.

3. What is the probability, expressed as a decimal, that the first name drawn is either Stephanie or Yuki?

4. Suppose Stephanie's name is chosen first. What is the chance, expressed as a fraction, that Yuki's name will be chosen second?

Answers start on page 838.

Mathematics • Measurement and Data Analysis

Tables, Charts, and Graphs

Tables and Charts

Tables and charts organize information or data in columns and rows. Specific items of data are found where columns and rows intersect, or meet. To use a table to find information, first read all titles and labels carefully. Then find the column and row that relate to the information you need.

Example 1 Greg uses distance tables in his work as a driver. He needs to drive from Lamesa to Canyon and from Canyon to Guthrie. Use the table below. How many kilometres will he drive?

Kilometres Between Cities

	Lubbock	**Lamesa**	Plainview	**Canyon**	Guthrie
Lubbock		61.4	48.0	8.0	92.8
Lamesa	61.4		108.6	67.1	140.5
Plainview	48.0	108.6		46.3	109.1
Canyon	8.0	67.1	46.3		87.6
Guthrie	92.8	140.5	109.1	87.6	

Tables usually contain more information than you need. Double-check to make sure you are using the correct data items for your calculations.

Step 1 Find the distance from Lamesa to Canyon. Locate Lamesa in the second row and go across to the column for Canyon. Or locate Canyon in the fourth row and go across to the column for Lamesa. Both methods give the same answer. 67.1 km

Step 2 Find the distance from Canyon to Guthrie. Locate Canyon and find where it intersects with Guthrie. 87.6 km

Step 3 Add to find the total kilometres. $67.1 + 87.6 = 154.7$

The total distance of Greg's trip is **154.7 km.**

A frequency table tracks how often certain events occur.

Example 2 A software company wants to know the reasons customers call customer support. Alli used a frequency table to track the calls he received. How many more callers placed orders than needed tech support?

Frequency Table: Reason for Call

Placed order	┼┼┼┼ ┼┼┼┼ ┼┼┼┼ ┼┼┼┼ ┼┼┼┼ ┼┼┼┼ ‖
Exchanged product	┼┼┼┼ ‖‖
Returned product for refund	┼┼┼┼ ┼┼┼┼ ‖
Needed technical support	┼┼┼┼ ┼┼┼┼ ┼┼┼┼ ┼┼┼┼ ┼┼┼┼ │

Step 1 Count the tally marks for "Placed order" (32). Count the tally marks for "Needed technical support" (26).

Step 2 Subtract to find the difference. $32 - 26 = 6$

There were **6 more calls** from customers placing orders than from those needing technical support.

Bar and Line Graphs

Graphs represent data visually to compare data from different sources, show change over time, and make projections about the future. This bar graph was created to show the difference in staffing levels for each of a company's three shifts. Notice these parts of the graph:

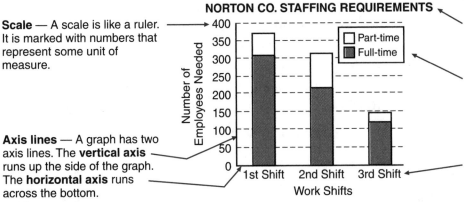

Scale — A scale is like a ruler. It is marked with numbers that represent some unit of measure.

Axis lines — A graph has two axis lines. The **vertical axis** runs up the side of the graph. The **horizontal axis** runs across the bottom.

Title — The title tells what kind of information is found on the graph.

Key — A key, or legend, gives any additional information needed to read the graph.

Bar Labels — Labels tell what individual parts of the graph describe.

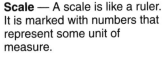

Often bar graph bars show two items of data: the height of the top portion is the height of the entire bar minus the bottom portion.

A graph key is needed only when data about more than one category are shown. Each axis line is labelled. Graphs may have scales on one or both axis lines. A bar graph has only one scale. Each bar has a label. These labels replace the second scale. Always read all labels carefully.

Example 1 About how many full-time and part-time employees work during the 2nd shift?

Step 1 Find the bar for the 2nd shift. The entire bar represents the total of part-time and full-time workers.

Step 2 Follow the top of the bar to the scale at the left. The bar ends between 300 and 350. A good estimate for the bar value is 320.

About 320 employees work during the 2nd shift.

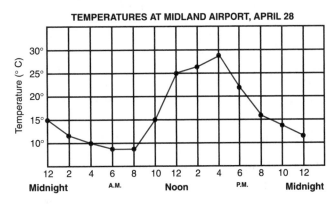

Line graphs often show changes over time with some measure on the vertical scale and time on the horizontal scale. Line graphs have two scales and often have a key as well (when the graph shows more than one line). Points plotted on the graph connect the two scales. On this graph each point represents the temperature at a specific time.

The points are then connected by a line. The line shows a trend or a pattern of change over time. For example, this line graph shows a warming trend from 8 A.M. until 4 P.M. Then the temperature cools steadily until midnight. We can use trends to make predictions of how data may change in the near future.

Example 2 What was the temperature at 10 A.M. on April 28?

Step 1 Find the dot directly above 10 A.M. on the horizontal scale.

Step 2 Follow across from the dot to the temperature scale.

It was **15° C** at 10 A.M. on April 28.

Circle Graphs

Circle graphs show how parts of an amount are related to the whole amount; the entire circle equals 100%. Most circle graphs show percents, but fractions, decimals, or whole numbers can also be used.

Example 1 Cliff has a budget of $400 to plan a day trip for 50 children. The circle graph on the left shows how he plans to spend the money. On which item will he spend about $\frac{1}{3}$ of his budget?

DAY TRIP BUDGET: $400

The sections of the graph are labelled with the name of the budget item and the percentage that will be spent on the item. The size of each section represents a fraction of the budget. For instance, a half-circle represents $\frac{1}{2}$ of the budget, or 50%. A quarter-circle represents $\frac{1}{4}$, or 25%, of the total budget. Since $\frac{1}{3}$ equals $33\frac{1}{3}\%$, the section labelled "Lunches 34%" is about $\frac{1}{3}$ of the circle.

Cliff will spend about $\frac{1}{3}$ of the budget on **lunches.**

You can also use the graph to find the dollar amount that is budgeted for an item.

Example 2 How much does Cliff plan to spend on the bus?

Step 1 **Read the graph.** Cliff will spend 47% of his total budget of $400 to pay for the bus. Find 47% of $400.

Step 2 **Use a proportion.** $\frac{47}{100} = \frac{x}{\$400}$, $47 \times \$400 \div 100 = \$188$

 Using a calculator:

400 ✕ **47** % **188.**   or   **400** ✕ **4 7** SHIFT = **188.**

Cliff will spend **$188** of the $400 budget to pay for the bus.

MARTINEZ FAMILY MONTHLY BUDGET

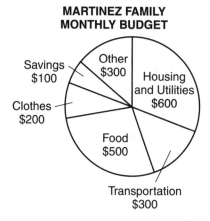

The circle graph to the left is labelled with dollar amounts. You can still use the size of the sections to understand how each part compares to the whole.

Example 3 Which item requires $\frac{1}{4}$ of the family's entire budget?

Step 1 **Find the total** value of the circle.
$600 + $300 + $500 + $200 + $100 + $300 = $2000

Step 2 **Find the fraction** closest to $\frac{1}{4}$. $\frac{\$500}{\$2000} = \frac{1}{4}$

The amount budgeted for **food** is $\frac{1}{4}$ of $2000, or $500.

> **Tip** A circle graph represents the whole. In a circle graph using percents, the sections total 100%. In circle graphs using fractions or decimals, the sections total 1.

GED Practice

Directions: Choose the <u>one best answer</u> to each question. You <u>may</u> use your calculator.

Questions 1 and 2 refer to the graph.

THE PRICE OF GOLD
(Dollars per ounce)

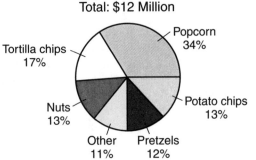

Price on the Last Day of the Month

1. By how much did the price of gold increase, in dollars per ounce, from July to September?

   (1) $100
   (2) $200
   (3) $400
   (4) $500
   (5) $600

2. What was the ratio of the price of gold in September to the price of gold in July?

   (1) 1:3
   (2) 1:2
   (3) 2:1
   (4) 3:1
   (5) 6:1

Question 3 refers to the graph below.

SNACK SALES IN MAY
Total: $12 Million

Popcorn 34%

Tortilla chips 17%

Potato chips 13%

Nuts 13%

Other 11%

Pretzels 12%

3. What was the total amount, in millions of dollars, spent on nuts, pretzels, and tortilla chips in May?

   (1) $ 1.44
   (2) $ 1.56
   (3) $ 5.04
   (4) $10.56
   (5) $15.60

Question 4 refers to the following information.

AVERAGE DAILY PARK ATTENDANCE

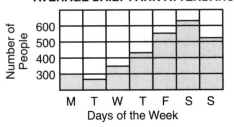

Days of the Week

4. Approximately how many more people visit the park on Saturdays than on Mondays?

   (1) 210
   (2) 320
   (3) 410
   (4) 620
   (5) 920

Additional practice material available on page 878.

Answers start on page 838.

Mathematics • Measurement and Data Analysis

GED Review Measurement and Data Analysis

Part 1

Directions: Choose the one best answer to each question. You may use your calculator.

Questions 1 and 2 refer to the following information.

Five Acme employees have salaries of $27 560, $30 050, $22 750, $42 800, and $28 900.

1. What is the average (mean) salary of the employees at Acme?

   (1) $20 050
   (2) $27 560
   (3) $28 900
   (4) $29 475
   (5) $30 412

2. What is the median salary of the employees at Acme?

   (1) $20 050
   (2) $27 560
   (3) $28 900
   (4) $29 475
   (5) $30 412

3. A dresser drawer contains 2 red socks, 4 blue socks, and 8 black socks. What is the probability that a sock chosen at random from the drawer is not a black sock?

   (1) $\frac{4}{7}$
   (2) $\frac{3}{7}$
   (3) $\frac{2}{7}$
   (4) $\frac{1}{7}$
   (5) $\frac{1}{14}$

Question 4 refers to the figure below.

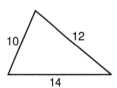

4. What is the perimeter of the figure?

   (1) 22
   (2) 24
   (3) 26
   (4) 36
   (5) Not enough information is given.

5. The length of one side of a square is 16 cm. What is the distance around the entire square in centimetres?

   (1) 64
   (2) 20
   (3) 32
   (4) 60
   (5) 48

6. The area of a rectangle is the same as the area of a square with a side of 8 cm. If the length of the rectangle is 16 cm, what is its width in centimetres?

(1) 4
(2) 8
(3) 16
(4) 24
(5) 64

7. How many cubes, each having an edge of 2 cm, will fit exactly inside a larger cube with an edge of 4 cm?

(1) 2
(2) 8
(3) 12
(4) 16
(5) 48

8. The sides of a triangle measure 10 m, 12 m, and 13 m. What is the distance around the triangle, in centimetres?

(1)   35
(2) 3500
(3) 350
(4) 1560
(5) Not enough information is given.

9. A rectangular frame is 8 m long. If its width is 2 m more than half its length, what is the perimeter of the frame, in metres?

(1) 6
(2) 8
(3) 14
(4) 28
(5) 48

Questions 10 and 11 refer to the figure below.

A kitchen and dining room have the dimensions as shown below, in metres. All corner angles are right angles.

10. How many metres of border are needed to go around the edge of the rooms?

(1) 72
(2) 70
(3) 66
(4) 60
(5) 57

11. How many square metres of tile are needed for flooring?

(1) 378
(2) 306
(3) 234
(4) 162
(5) 144

12. A computer was left on for 10 weeks in a row. For how many hours was the computer left on?

(1)   70
(2) 168
(3) 240
(4) 1680
(5) 2400

Mathematics • Measurement and Data Analysis

Part 2

Directions: Choose the one best answer to each question. You may not use your calculator.

Questions 13 and 14 refer to the following information.

Last week, Karla exercised every day for the following number of minutes each day: 42, 54, 62, 40, 57, 50, and 38.

13. What was the average number of minutes that Karla exercised per day last week?

    (1) 45
    (2) 46
    (3) 47
    (4) 48
    (5) 49

14. What was the median number of minutes that Karla exercised last week?

    (1) 42
    (2) 50
    (3) 54
    (4) 57
    (5) 62

Question 15 refers to the following information.

A bag contains 20 table tennis balls, each one painted with a different number from 1 to 20.

15. If a ball is chosen at random from the bag, what is the probability that it is painted with a number greater than 15?

    (1) $\frac{1}{20}$
    (2) $\frac{1}{5}$
    (3) $\frac{1}{4}$
    (4) $\frac{1}{2}$
    (5) $\frac{3}{4}$

Questions 16 through 18 refer to the following graph.

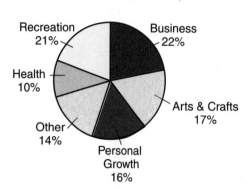

ADULT EDUCATION COURSES
(Total: 500 Courses Offered)

16. How many Personal Growth courses are offered?

    (1)   8
    (2) 16
    (3) 64
    (4) 80
    (5) 100

17. What is the ratio of Business courses offered to Health courses offered?

    (1) 5:7
    (2) 21:22
    (3) 17:10
    (4) 11:8
    (5) 11:5

18. How many more Business courses are offered than Recreation courses?

    (1)   1
    (2)   5
    (3) 10
    (4) 12
    (5) 50

19. Which expression can be used to find the perimeter of the figure below?

18
21

(1) 21 + 21 + 12 + 12

(2) 21 + 21 + 18 + 18

(3) 2(12 + 18)

(4) 12 + 18

(5) 21 × 18

20. What is the distance in metres around a rectangular flower bed that measures 25 m by 3 m?

(1) 56

(2) 60

(3) 65

(4) 66

(5) 75

21. A photograph is $3\frac{3}{4}$ units wide and $5\frac{1}{4}$ units long. If the dimensions of the photograph are doubled, how many inches wide will the photograph be?

(1) $10\frac{1}{2}$

(2) $10\frac{1}{4}$

(3) $7\frac{3}{4}$

(4) $7\frac{1}{2}$

(5) $6\frac{3}{4}$

22. A rectangular box measures 5 m long, 4 m wide, and 2 m high. What is the volume of the box in cubic centimetres?

(1)   4000

(2)   20 000

(3)   40 000

(4)   400 000

(5) 40 000 000

Question 23 refers to the following graph.

PERSONS EMPLOYED IN VARIOUS OCCUPATIONS
Total: 25 000 People

Other
3%

Business, Legal, Prof.
22%

Wholesale
20%

Entertainment
1%

Health and
Education
12%

Retail
42%

23. How many more people were employed in a business, legal, or professional occupation than in an entertainment occupation?

(1) 4000

(2) 4350

(3) 5000

(4) 5250

(5) 5500

Questions 24 refers to the following chart.

Lamp Style	Wholesale Price	Retail Price
A	$32.00	$45.00
B	$16.80	$24.90
C	$34.00	$41.80
D	$23.00	$28.90
E	$56.50	$74.50

24. Which style of lamp has the greatest percent of increase from the wholesale price to the retail price?

(1) A

(2) B

(3) C

(4) D

(5) E

Answers start on page 838.

Algebra

Algebra is one of the most important areas of mathematics. It involves translating everyday situations into mathematical symbols and language. We can use algebra to solve problems and to learn to think logically. Understanding algebra is also an important springboard into the advanced areas of mathematics that are required for jobs in science and technology.

Questions related to algebra will account for more than 25 percent of the GED Mathematics Test. Additionally, you will find that you can use many of the skills in this unit to solve problems in arithmetic and geometry.

Integers and Algebraic Expressions

Understanding Integers

Integers, also called signed numbers, are positive whole numbers, their negatives, and zero. To show the complete set of numbers called integers, we extend the positive number line to the left of zero (0) to include negative numbers.

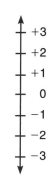

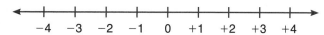

Positive numbers show an increase, a gain, or an upward movement (on a vertical number line). A positive number can be written with or without a plus sign. Negative numbers show the opposite: a decrease, a loss, or a downward movement. A negative number is always written with a minus sign. Note that the number zero is neither positive nor negative.

Adding and Subtracting Integers

Tip

The order of operations is always the same. But you must also apply the rules for signed numbers as you perform each operation.

We can show the addition of integers on a number line. Move to the right for positive numbers and to the left for negative numbers.

Example 1 Add: $(+6) + (-4)$.

Step 1 Start at 0 and move 6 units to the right.

Step 2 Start at +6; move 4 units left.

The number line shows $(+6) + (-4) = $ **+2.**

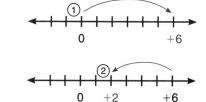

Use these rules to add integers:

RULE 1   If the integers have like signs, add $(+3) + (+5) = +8$
the numbers and keep the same sign. $(-2) + (-6) = -8$

RULE 2   If the integers have unlike signs, find the $(-9) + (+3) = \quad?$
difference between the numbers without $9 - 3 = \quad 6$
the signs (the absolute values) and give   9 is negative
the answer the sign of the larger number. $(-9) + (+3) = -6$

Since the larger number (-9) is negative, the answer is negative, **−6.**

To add more than two integers find the sum of the positive numbers and the sum of the negative numbers. Then use Rule 2 to find the total.

Example 2 $(+30) + (-8) + (-15) + (+3) + (-20) = ?$

Step 1   Add the positive numbers. Add the $(+30) + (+3) = +33$
negative numbers. (Rule 1) $(-8) + (-15) + (-20) = -43$
Step 2   Add the unlike sums. (Rule 2) $(+33) + (-43) = \mathbf{-10}$

Do not confuse the sign of the operation with the sign of the integer. For example, $(+5) - (-2)$ is "five minus negative 2."

Subtracting signed integers requires additional steps: **(1)** first rewrite the subtraction operation as addition, **(2)** then change the sign of the number to be subtracted, **(3)** add as usual.

Example 3   Subtract: $(+5) - (-2)$

Step 1   Change subtraction to
addition. $(+5) - (-2) = (+5) + (\quad)$
Step 2   Change the sign of the
number being subtracted. $(+5) - (-2) = (+5) + (+2)$
Step 3   Add. $(+5) + (+2) = +7$

The answer to $(+5) - (-2)$ is **+7.**

___

To subtract integers on a calculator, enter the expression without rewriting it as an addition problem. To enter negative numbers on a calculator, simply enter the number first, then press ⁺⁄₋ to change the sign of the number to negative. **5 − 2 ⁺⁄₋ = 7.**

___

A. Solve.

1. $(+7) + (+5)$ 2. $(-10) + (-6)$ 3. $(-1) - (+5)$ 4. $(+6) + (-8)$

B. Solve each problem. You may use a calculator.

5. $(-118) - (-628)$ 8. $(-6) - (+9) + (+10) - (+1)$

6. $(+315) - (+456)$ 9. $(-5) - (-4) - (-8)$

7. $(+7) + (-5) + (-4) + (+9)$ 10. $(+13) - (+34) + (-12)$

Answers start on page 839.

Multiplying and Dividing Integers

Multiply and divide integers as you would whole numbers. Then use the rule below to determine whether the answer is negative or positive.

> **Multiplication/Division Rule**
> If the signs are the same, the answer is positive.
> If the signs are different, the answer is negative.

Examples

$(3)(5) = +15$ $\qquad$ $-3(5) = -15$ $\qquad$ $3(-5) = -15$ $\qquad$ $(-3)(-5) = 15$

$\dfrac{24}{6} = 4$ $\qquad\qquad$ $\dfrac{-24}{6} = -4$ $\qquad\qquad$ $\dfrac{24}{-6} = -4$ $\qquad\qquad$ $\dfrac{-24}{-6} = 4$

Applying the Order of Operations

When an algebraic expression contains several operations, you must follow the order of operations. Use parentheses to change the order in which operations are performed.

> **Order of Operations—BEDMAS**
>
> **Step 1** Perform all work inside grouping symbols such as parentheses or brackets: multiply and divide first; then add and subtract. The fraction bar is also a grouping symbol.
> **Step 2** Find the values of powers (exponents) and roots. (See Lesson 20.)
> **Step 3** Multiply and divide, working from left to right.
> **Step 4** Add and subtract, working from left to right.

Example 1 $\quad 3^2 + (-4)(2) - (4 + 6 \times 3)$

Step 1 Begin with the operations grouped $\qquad$ $3^2 + (-4)(2) - (4 + 6 \times 3)$
in parentheses. Multiply. (6×3) $\qquad$ $3^2 + (-4)(2) - (4 +\ \mathbf{18})$
Then add. $(4 + 18)$ $\qquad\qquad\qquad$ $3^2 + (-4)(2) -\ \quad \mathbf{22}$

Step 2 Find the value of the power. (3×3) $\quad$ $\mathbf{9} + (-4)(2) -\ \quad 22$

Step 3 Perform the remaining operations
in order: multiply, then add and $\qquad$ $9 +\ \ (\mathbf{-8}) -\ \quad 22$
subtract from left to right. Apply $\qquad\qquad$ $\mathbf{1} \qquad\quad -(+22)$
the rules for signed numbers. $\qquad\qquad$ $1 \qquad\quad +(-22) = -21$

The answer is **−21.**

The division bar groups the top numbers and the bottom numbers as if they were in parentheses. Apply the order of operations to the numerator and denominator separately. Then do the final division.

Example 2 $\quad \dfrac{3 + 5}{2 - 4}$

$$\frac{3 + 5}{2 - 4} = \frac{8}{-2} = -4$$

This is the same as $(3 + 5) \div (2 - 4) = 8 \div -2 = -4.$
Since the signs are different, the answer is **−4.**

A. Multiply or divide.

1. $(-2)(+3)$

2. $(-4)(-7)$

3. $(+6)(-5)$

4. $(+12)(+3)$

5. $(-6)(-1)(+2)$

6. $(+9)(-2)(-3)$

7. $(-64) \div (+4)$

8. $(+15) \div (-3)$

9. $(+20) \div (+5)$

10. $(-36) \div (-12)$

11. $\frac{-132}{11}$

12. $\frac{-4}{-1}$

B. Solve each expression.

13. $6 + 8 \times 2^2$

14. $\frac{-2 - (+8)}{(6) \div (-6)}$

15. $(-9 \times 4) - (-3 \times 2)$

16. $(-25) - 4 \times 3^2$

17. $6 - (4 \times 8 + (-1))$

18. $\frac{(-4) + (-6)}{(+4) - (-1)}$

Variables and Algebraic Expressions

An algebraic expression is a group of numbers, operation signs, and variables.

Examples $\quad 2x + 3 \qquad 4x + \frac{1}{3} \qquad 3x - 4 \qquad 3(6x)$

Expressions such as these are formed by translating number relationships into symbols. Analyze the following expressions carefully.

In words	In symbols
4 times a number	$4x$
6 more than a number	$x + 6$
2 less than a number	$x - 2$
one-half a number is then increased by 7	$\frac{1}{2}x + 7$ or $\frac{x}{2} + 7$
the product of 6 and a number	$6x$
the quotient of x and 5	$\frac{x}{5}$ or $x \div 5$
a number times itself or a number squared	x^2
the product of x and 8 added to the sum of 2 and x	$8x + (2 + x)$

An algebraic expression always contains variables. Variables are letters that are used to represent numbers. Whenever the value of x changes, the expression also changes in value.

This table shows how the value of the expression $2x + 1$ changes as the value of x changes.

x	$2x + 1$
3	$2(3) + 1 = \;\;\;$ **7**
0	$2(0) + 1 = \;\;\;$ **1**
−2	$2(-2) + 1 =$ **−3**
−4	$2(-4) + 1 =$ **−7**

An algebraic expression has a value only when all the variables are replaced by numbers. Finding the value of an expression when the variables are known is called evaluating an expression.

Tip

Remember that order is critical in subtraction and division: "The difference between 4 and 2" means $4 - 2$. But, "4 less than 2" means $2 - 4$. "The quotient of 4 and 2" means $\frac{4}{2}$.

Answers start on page 840.

Example Find the value of $x^2 - 3y$, when $x = -4$ and $y = 2$.

Step 1	Substitute the given values for the variables.	$x^2 - 3y$ $(-4)^2 - 3(2)$
Step 2	Follow the order of operations. Raise -4 to the second power. Multiply. Subtract.	$16 - 3(2)$ $16 - 6$ 10

After substituting the values for the variables in Step 1, you can use your calculator to find the value of the expression.

$\boxed{4}$ $\boxed{+/-}$ $\boxed{x^2}$ $\boxed{-}$ $\boxed{[(\text{---}}$ $\boxed{3}$ $\boxed{\times}$ $\boxed{2}$ $\boxed{\text{---})]}$ $\boxed{=}$ **10.**

Note: The GED calculator does not require the $\boxed{[(\text{---}}$ $\boxed{\text{---})]}$ keys. The value of the expression is **10,** when $x = -4$ and $y = 2$.

Simplifying Expressions

Tip

A number next to a letter means multiplication; all these mean "2 multiplied by y":
$2y$ $2 \times y$
$2 \bullet y$ $2(y)$

Simplifying an expression means combining like terms. A term is a number or the combination of a number and one or more variables or a variable raised to a power. The factors of a number are the values that, when multiplied together, result in that number.

Examples	5	x	$2x$	xy	$4x^2$
Factors	5 and 1	1 and x	2 and x	x and y	4 and x^2

In an algebraic expression, a positive or negative sign is part of the term that follows it: the term "owns" the sign that comes before it. An addition sign is understood in front of the negative sign.

Example The expression $3x^2 - 7x + 14$ has three terms.

This expression can also be written as **$3x^2 + (-7x) + (+14)$.**

Like terms have the same variable or variables raised to the same power. Study these examples to identify like terms.

Examples $4x$ and $9x$ are like terms. Both terms contain x.
     $7xy$ and $8xy$ are like terms. Both terms contain xy.
     4 and $6y$ are not like terms. An integer and y are different.
     $3x$ and $3y$ are not like terms. Variables x and y are different.
     $5y^2$ and $6y$ are not like terms. The powers are different.

We combine like terms in an expression so that there is only one term containing that variable. Simplified expressions are easier to evaluate.

Example 1 Simplify $4x + 6y - 3x - 4y$.

Step 1	Group the like terms. Group the x terms and group the y terms. (The sign travels with the term.)	$4x + 6y - 3x - 4y =$ $4x + 6y + -3x + -4y =$ $(4x + -3x) + (6y + -4y) =$
Step 2	Combine like terms.	$(4x - 3x) + (6y - 4y) =$ $x \quad + \quad 2y$

In simplified form, $4x + 6y - 3x - 4y$ is equal to **$x + 2y$.**

The order of operations says to perform operations in parentheses first. However, in algebraic expressions parentheses often contain unlike terms that cannot be combined. To simplify an expression that contains parentheses, use the distributive property to remove the parentheses.

Distributive Property	To multiply a factor by a sum of terms, multiply the factor by each term in parentheses. Then combine the products. $5(x + y) = 5x + 5y$

Example 2 Simplify $2x(3x - 6) + 5x$.

Step 1 To remove parentheses multiply each term in the parentheses by the factor.

Step 2 Combine like terms.

$2x(3x - 6) + 5x$ is equal to $\mathbf{6x^2 - 7x}$.

$$2x(3x + -6) \quad + 5x$$
$$2x(3x) + 2x(-6) + 5x$$

$$6x^2 - \quad 12x \quad + 5x$$
$$6x^2 - \quad \quad 7x$$

A. Evaluate these expressions as directed.

1. What is the value of $3(x - 6) + 2y$
   a. when $x = -7$ and $y = 10$?
   b. when $x = 5$ and $y = -2$?
   c. when $x = 0$ and $y = 6$?
   d. when $x = 3$ and $y = 3$?

2. What is the value of $x^2 - y^2$
   a. when $x = 0$ and $y = 2$?
   b. when $x = -2$ and $y = 1$?
   c. when $x = 5$ and $y = -5$?
   d. when $x = -1$ and $y = -2$?

3. What is the value of $\frac{(6 + x)^2}{y}$
   a. when $x = 4$ and $y = -1$?
   b. when $x = 0$ and $y = 6$?
   c. when $x = 0$ and $y = -6$?
   d. when $x = 2$ and $y = 2$?

4. What is the value of $x^2 + 2x - 6$
   a. when $x = -3$?
   b. when $x = 2$?
   c. when $x = 4$?
   d. when $x = 8$?

B. Simplify each expression.

5. $7x - 8y + 9x$

6. $5y^2 - 4y - 2y^2$

7. $4m - 9n - 3 + 6n$

8. $-5x + 16 - 8x - 14 + 10x$

9. $9x - 6 + 8x^2 + 13$

10. $25 - 3n + 16n$

11. $12(x + 3y)$

12. $5x(-y + 9)$

13. $4(2x + y) - 3(x - 5)$

14. $15 + 6(x - 4) + 8x$

15. $3m + 2(m - n) - 5(m + n)$

16. $x - 2(xy - y) + 4xy - x(3 + y)$

C. Simplify. Then evaluate each expression as directed.

17. Find the value of $3x + 5(x + 9) - 4x$, when $x = -5$.

18. Find the value of $2m - 3(m + 5) - 15$, when $m = 10$.

19. Find the value of $3y(2xz + 2) - 6xyz$, when $x = -4$, $y = -3$, and $z = 7$.

20. Find the value of $4(2x - y) - 3x + 2y$, when $x = 0$ and $y = -2$.

Answers start on page 840.

GED Practice

Directions: Choose the one best answer for each question.

1. In a card game, Rita loses 1 point, gains 5 points, and loses 8 points. Jerry has 6 points. What is the difference in their scores?

   (1) 4
   (2) 6
   (3) 8
   (4) 10
   (5) 12

2. On a number line, Max places a mark 3 units to the left of the point halfway between 1 and -3. On what point is Max's mark?

   (1) 2
   (2) 0
   (3) -1
   (4) -3
   (5) -4

3. At 10 A.M., it is 5° C below zero. By 11 A.M., the temperature rises 6° C. If it drops 3° C by 1 P.M., what is the temperature at 1 P.M.?

   (1) $-4°$ C
   (2) $-2°$ C
   (3) 0° C
   (4) 2° C
   (5) 14° C

4. Which of the following expressions is equal to the expression $-m(2m + 2n) + 3mn + 2m^2$?

   (1) mn
   (2) $5mn$
   (3) $-4m^2 + mn$
   (4) $4m^2 + mn$
   (5) $4m^2 + 5mn$

5. The expression $3(-4b) - 2(a - b - c)$ is equal to which of the following expressions?

   (1) $-2a - 10b - 2c$
   (2) $-2a - 10b + 2c$
   (3) $-2a - 5b + 2c$
   (4) $-2a - 4b - 2c$
   (5) $2a - 4b - 2c$

Question 6 refers to the following information.

Aaron's Dice Rolls

Round	Red Die	Green Die
3	4	6
4	2	1
5	6	4

6. In a dice game, each player rolls two dice, one red and one green. The number on the red die is added to the player's score from the previous round. The number on the green die is subtracted from the player's score. If Aaron had +4 points after the first two rounds, how many points does he have after five rounds?

   (1) -5
   (2) -3
   (3) 1
   (4) 3
   (5) 5

Answers start on page 841.

Lesson 18 • Integers and Algebraic Expressions   563

Equations

Solving One-Step Equations

An equation is a mathematical statement that shows that two quantities are equal. When an equation contains a variable, we use algebra to find the value of the variable. To solve an equation means to find the number that makes the statement true.

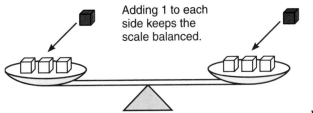

Adding 1 to each side keeps the scale balanced.

Solve the equation. $2x - 1 = 9$
When x equals 5, $2(5) - 1 = 9$
the statement is true. $10 - 1 = 9$
                              $9 = 9$

To solve an equation, you must keep the two sides of the equation equal. Think of an equation as a balance scale. Whatever you do to one side of the scale, you must also do to the other side to keep the scale balanced.

The basic strategy in solving an equation is to isolate the variable, that is, get the variable alone on one side of the equation by performing inverse, or opposite, operations to both sides of the equation.

Remember: • Addition and subtraction are inverse operations.
          • Multiplication and division are inverse operations.

Example 1   Solve: $x - 13 = 25$.

Step 1	**Think about the meaning** of the equation, the operation, and its inverse: here, the operation is subtraction; the inverse operation is addition.	$x - 13 = 25$
Step 2	**Perform the inverse operation to both sides of the equation** to isolate the variable and keep the equation balanced. Here, add 13 to both sides.	$x - 13 + 13 = 25 + 13$ $x = 38$
Step 3	**Check.** Substitute your solution, 38, into the original equation for the variable x.	$38 - 13 = 25$ $25 = 25$

The value **38** makes the equation true.

Example 2   Solve: $5x = -35$.

Step 1	The operation is multiplication; the inverse of multiplication is division.	$5x = -35$
Step 2	Divide both sides by 5.	$\dfrac{5x}{5} = \dfrac{-35}{5}$
Step 3	Substitute and check.	$x = -7$ $5(-7) = -35$ $-35 = -35$

The value **−7** makes the equation true.

Tip

You may be able to solve simple equations using mental math. However, writing out each step will improve your understanding of algebra and make it easier to check your work.

Solving Multi-Step Equations

Some equations involve more than one operation. Remember: your goal is to isolate the variable on one side of the equation. Also, when solving multi-step equations, use the reverse order of operations.

Example 1 $5x - 10 = 35$

Step 1   Perform the inverse operations for addition and subtraction first.
Add 10 to both sides.

$$5x - 10 + 10 = 35 + 10$$
$$5x = 45$$

Step 2   Perform the inverse operations for multiplication and division second.
Divide both sides by 5.

$$\frac{5x}{5} = \frac{45}{5}$$

$$x = 9$$

Step 3   Check. Substitute the value for x.

$$5(9) - 10 = 35$$
$$45 - 10 = 35$$
$$35 = 35$$

The solution is **x = 9.**

Some equations may have variable terms on both sides. If so, you need to group all of the variable terms on one side of the equation.

Example 2 $12x + 9 = 10x + 1$

> **Tip**
>
> There is often more than one way to solve equations, such as first adding or subtracting the integer and then the variable. But, you must always follow the basic rules for solving equations: always add or subtract first; then multiply or divide.

Step 1   Group the variable.
Subtract 10x from both sides.

$$12x - 10x + 9 = 10x - 10x + 1$$
$$2x + 9 = 1$$

Step 2   Subtract 9 from both sides.

$$2x + 9 - 9 = 1 - 9$$
$$2x = -8$$

Step 3   Divide both sides by 2.

$$\frac{2x}{2} = \frac{-8}{2}$$

$$x = -4$$

Step 4   Check.

$$12(-4) + 9 = 10(-4) + 1$$
$$-48 + 9 = -40 + 1$$
$$-39 = -39$$

The solution is **x = -4.**

Some equations contain parentheses. Remove the parentheses by multiplying each term within the parentheses by the factor.

Example 3 $3(x + 1) = -12$

Step 1   Multiply both terms inside the parentheses by 3.

$$3(x + 1) = -12$$
$$3x + 3 = -12$$

Step 2   Subtract 3 from both sides.

$$3x + 3 - 3 = -12 - 3$$
$$3x = -15$$

Step 3   Divide both sides by 3.

$$\frac{3x}{3} = \frac{-15}{3}$$
$$x = -5$$

Step 4   Check.

$$3(-5 + 1) = -12$$
$$3(-4) = -12$$
$$-12 = -12$$

The solution is **x = -5.**

The first step in solving some equations is to combine like terms. Always simplify each side of the equation before solving.

The integer for a lone variable is understood to be 1: $x = 1x$ and $-x = -1x$.

Example 4 $2x + 5 - 3x = 8 + 2$

Step 1	**Simplify by combining like terms.** $2x - 3x = -x$; $8 + 2 = 10$	$2x + 5 - 3x = 8 + 2$ $-x + 5 = 10$
Step 2	**Isolate the variable.** Here, subtract 5 from each side.	$-x + 5 - 5 = 10 - 5$ $-x = 5$
Step 3	**Solve for x.** Multiply each side by -1 so that you solve for x, not $-x$.	$-x(-1) = 5(-1)$ $x = -5$
Step 4	**Check.**	$2(-5) + 5 - 3(-5) = 8 + 2$ $-10 + 5 - (-15) = 10$ $-10 + 5 + 15 = 10$ $10 = 10$

The solution is **−5.**

A. Solve. Do not use a calculator.

1. $x - 15 = 4$

2. $x - 7 = 3$

3. $x - 8 = -10$

4. $\dfrac{x}{-3} = 18$

B. Solve. You may use a calculator for these items.

5. $x - 94 = 52$

6. $6.5 + x = 12.25$

7. $-69 + x = 124$

8. $-3.6x = -17.28$

C. Translate each question into an algebraic equation and solve.

9. -13 added to what number equals 20? (*Hint:* $-13 + x = 20$)

10. What number multiplied by 10 equals 900?

11. What number divided by 4 equals 60?

12. What number divided by 4 is 32?

13. What number multiplied by -6 equals 48?

14. 52 added to what number equals 100?

D. Solve each equation.

15. $6x + 7 = 37$

16. $4x + 5x - 10 = 35$

17. $3x - 6x + 2 = -4x$

18. $6 - x + 12 = 10x + 7$

19. $5x + 7 - 4x = 6$

20. $9x + 6x - 12x = -7x + 2x - 12 + 5x$

21. $7x + 3 = 31$

22. $6(2 + x) = 5x + 15$

23. $4x + 5 = 21$

24. $2x - 5x + 11 = 38$

25. $3x - 8 = x + 4$

26. $7(x - 2) = 21$

27. $5x - 13x + 2x = -70 + x$

28. $8x + 12 = 44 + 4x$

Answers start on page 842.

Mathematics • Algebra

Translating Problems into Equations

To solve word problems translate the information in the problem into algebraic symbols and write an algebraic equation relating the information. Read the problem carefully to figure out which quantities or numbers are unknown. Label all other quantities in terms of one unknown amount.

Tip

As a general rule, let *x* equal the quantity you know the least about; this is usually the amount to which the other amount is compared or related.

Example 1   During lunch one day, a café sold 8 more turkey sandwiches than ham sandwiches. If 32 sandwiches were sold in all, how many were ham sandwiches?

Step 1   **Identify the unknown amount(s); assign the variable.** There are 2 unknown amounts: the number of ham sandwiches and the number of turkey sandwiches. Pick one to be the unknown *x*. Here, let *x* = the number of ham sandwiches.

Step 2   **Label the other quantities in terms of *x*.** Since there were 8 more turkey sandwiches than ham, let *x* + 8 equal the number of turkey sandwiches. If you had let *x* = the number of turkey sandwiches, then the number of ham sandwiches would be *x* − 8.

Step 3   **Write an equation.** You know 32 sandwiches in all were sold. Thus, the sum of the number of turkey sandwiches (*x* + 8) and the number of ham sandwiches (*x*) is 32: $(x + 8) + x = 32$. The equation **$(x + 8) + x = 32$** can be used to solve the problem.

Some algebra items on the GED Mathematics Test are set-up problems. Instead of solving the equation, you choose a correct method to solve the problem. To work with these items, analyze the situation and write an equation. Then compare your equation to the answer choices.

Solving Algebraic Equations

Algebra word problems describe the relationship among the numbers in a situation. To solve an algebra problem, translate the information into algebraic symbols, write and solve an equation, and check your answer.

Example 1   The total of three **consecutive numbers** is 189. What is the greatest of the three numbers?

Step 1   **Identify the unknown amounts; assign *x*.** Let *x* represent the smallest number.

Step 2   **Label the other quantities in terms of *x*.** If *x* is the smallest number, the next two numbers are *x* + 1 and *x* + 2.

Tip

Make sure that you answer the question that is asked in the problem. The value of *x* may not be the answer to the question.

Step 3   **Write an equation.** The sum of the three numbers is 189.

$$x + (x + 1) + (x + 2) = 189$$
$$x + x + 1 + x + 2 = 189$$

Step 4   **Combine like terms and solve for *x*.**

$$3x + 3 = 189$$
$$3x = 186$$
$$x = 62$$

Step 5   **Solve the problem.** The value of *x* represents the smallest of three consecutive numbers: the three numbers are 62, 63, and 64. Because you are looking for the greatest number, the correct answer is **64.**

Step 6   **Check your answer.** Since 62 + 63 + 64 = 189, the answer makes sense.

GED Practice

Directions: Choose the one best answer to each question.

1. Birnham Mills has 360 employees. The number of production employees is twelve more than three times the number of employees who work in management. Which equation could be used to find the number of management employees?

   (1) $3x + 12 = 360$

   (2) $4x = 360$

   (3) $3x - 12 + x = 360$

   (4) $(3x + 12) - x = 360$

   (5) $x + (3x + 12) = 360$

2. At a gym Filipe did a certain number of pushups. Tom did 12 more than Filipe. The total number both men did was 66. Which equation could be used to find the number of pushups Filipe did?

   (1) $x(x + 12) = 66$

   (2) $x + 12x = 66$

   (3) $2x + 12 = 66$

   (4) $2x = 66 + 12$

   (5) $x + 12 = 66 + x$

3. Eva got two parking tickets. The fine for the second ticket was $4 less than twice the fine for the first ticket. If the fines total $65, which equation could be used to find the amount of the first fine?

   (1) $3x = 65 - 4$

   (2) $2(x - 4) = 65$

   (3) $x(x - 4) = 65$

   (4) $x + (2x - 4) = 65$

   (5) $2(2x - 4) = 65$

4. Eight times a number, divided by 4, equals two times that number. Which of the following equations could be used to find the number?

   (1) $\frac{8y}{4} = 2y$

   (2) $8\left(\frac{4}{y}\right) = 2y$

   (3) $\frac{8}{4y} = 2y$

   (4) $8y(4) = 2$

   (5) $\frac{8y}{4y} = 2y$

5. The number of girls signed up for a sports program is 12 fewer than twice the number of boys (x). If 60 children are signed up for the program, which of the following equations could be used to find the number of boys?

   (1) $2x - 12 = 60$

   (2) $2(x + x - 12) = 60$

   (3) $x + 2x = 60 - 12$

   (4) $x + 2(x - 12) = 60$

   (5) $3x = 60 + 12$

6. An adult ticket is twice the cost of a child's ticket. Angela paid $28 for two adult tickets and three children's tickets. Which of the following equations could be used to find the price of a child's ticket?

   (1) $x + 2x = 28$

   (2) $3x + 2(2x) = 28$

   (3) $2(x + 2x) = 28$

   (4) $3(2x) + 2x = 28$

   (5) $3x + 2x = 28$

 Tip To use any calculator, break an expression into parts, work each part, and write down the result from each operation; then perform the final operations.

Answers start on page 843.

Mathematics • Algebra

Using Distance and Cost Formulas

Tip

The variables in a formula use related units of measure: if the rate is in *kilometres per hour*, the distance will be in *kilometres*, and the time will be in *hours*.

A formula is a special type of equation. A formula relates information to solve a certain kind of problem. When you take the GED Mathematics Test, you will be given a page of formulas to use in solving problems. The GED formulas page is on page 55.

Two important formulas are the distance and cost formulas.

Distance   distance = rate × time or $d = rt$

Total Cost   total cost = (number of units) × (cost per unit) or $c = nr$

To use formulas, first choose the formula that shows how the facts in the problem are related. Then substitute the known quantities and solve.

Example 1   A plane travels at an average speed of 525 km per hour for 4 hours. How many kilometres does it travel?

    (1)   60.0
    (2)   131.25
    (3)   240.0
    (4)   525.0
    (5) 2 100.0

Tip

You can use a formula to solve for any of its variables. Using $c = nr$, you can also find $n = \frac{c}{r}$ or $r = \frac{c}{n}$.

Step 1   **Use** the distance formula where d = distance, r = rate (average speed), and t = time. $d = rt$

Step 2   **Substitute** the known quantities. $d = 525 \times 4$

Step 3   **Solve** for d. $d = 2100$

The plane travelled **2100 km.**

You can solve for any variable in a formula if you know the values of the other variables. Substitute the values you know for the variables in the problem. Then use inverse operations to solve for the unknown variable.

Example 2   The total cost of a shipment of chairs is $2250. If each chair costs $75, how many chairs are in the shipment?

    (1)   30
    (2)   75
    (3)   225
    (4)   2 250
    (5) 168 750

Tip

The following formulas all work the same way:
$d = r \times t$ (distance)
$c = n \times r$ (cost)
$p = b \times r$ (percent)
$i = p \times r \times t$ (interest)

Step 1   Use the cost formula, where c = total cost, n = number of units, and r = cost per unit, to solve for n, the number of chairs. $c = nr$

Step 2   Substitute the known quantities. $\$2250 = n(\$75)$

Step 3   Solve for n. Divide both sides of the equation by $75. $\dfrac{\$2250}{\$75} = \dfrac{n(\$75)}{\$75}$
              $30 = n$

There are **option (1) 30 chairs** in the shipment.

GED Practice

Directions: Choose the one best answer to each question.

1. A hardware store purchased 6 dozen hammers for a total cost of $345.60. What was the cost of one dozen hammers?

   (1) $ 4.80
   (2) $ 9.60
   (3) $ 28.80
   (4) $ 57.60
   (5) $115.20

2. Marta bought 3 m of fabric at $6.98 per metre and 4 m of a different fabric for $4.50 per metre. Which of the following expressions could be used to find the amount of her purchase? (*Hint*: You would need to find the total cost of each type of fabric and then find the sum.)

   (1) 7($6.98)($4.50)
   (2) 7($6.98 + $4.50)
   (3) 3($6.98) + 4($4.50)
   (4) 4($6.98) + 3($4.50)
   (5) (3 + 4)($6.98 + $4.50)

3. Steve drove for 6 hours and travelled 312 km. Which of the following expressions could be used to find his average speed during the trip?

   (1) 6 + 312
   (2) $\frac{312}{6}$
   (3) $\frac{6}{312}$
   (4) 6(312)
   (5) 6(6)(312)

4. A label on the grocery store shelf states that the store brand of shampoo sells for 1.45 cents per millilitre. What is the cost of a 240 mL bottle of the shampoo?

   (1) $0.60
   (2) $1.66
   (3) $3.48
   (4) $6.00
   (5) $7.65

5. Kate drove $2\frac{1}{2}$ hours at an average speed of 55 km per hour and $1\frac{1}{2}$ hours at an average speed of 65 km per hour. How many kilometres did she travel?

   (1) 260
   (2) 235
   (3) 220
   (4) $137\frac{1}{2}$
   (5) $97\frac{1}{2}$

Question 6 refers to the following information.

Bakery Goods Price List	
Party Tray	$ 9.99
Party Platter	$13.99
Half Sheet Cake	$26.99

6. Rodrigo is organizing a party for his office. He orders three party trays, two party platters, and a half sheet cake. How much will he spend for the order?

   (1) $ 29.97
   (2) $ 50.97
   (3) $ 80.94
   (4) $ 84.94
   (5) $305.82

Answers start on page 843.

Mathematics • Algebra

Exponents and Roots

Exponents

Exponents are used to simplify problems that call for repeated multiplication. The expression 5^3, which is read "five to the third power" or "five cubed," has a base of 5 and an exponent of 3. The exponent tells how many times the base should appear in the multiplication problem.

Examples
$$5^3 = 5 \times 5 \times 5 = 125$$
$$12^2 = 12 \times 12 = 144$$
$$2^5 = 2 \times 2 \times 2 \times 2 \times 2 = 32$$

To raise a number to the second power, use the x^2 key.
Find the value of 13^2. **13** $\boxed{x^2}$ **169.** or **13** $\boxed{\times}$ **13** $\boxed{=}$

To raise a number to a higher power, use the x^y key.
Find the value of 5^3. **5** $\boxed{x^y}$ **3 = 125.** or **5** $\boxed{\times}$ **5** $\boxed{\times}$ **5** $\boxed{=}$

Tip

The exponent for a power of 10 is the same as the number of zeros in the product.
$10^6 = 1\ 000\ 000$

An exponent can also be 1, 0, or a negative number.

Remember: • Any number with an exponent of 1 equals itself.
• Any number (except 0) with an exponent of 0 equals 1.

Examples

$2^1 = 2$	$9^1 = 9$	$7^1 = 7$
$4^0 = 1$	$3^0 = 1$	$10^0 = 1$

Our number system is based on the idea of grouping by tens. Powers of 10 are especially important.

$$10^1 = 10$$
$$10^2 = 10 \times 10 = 100$$
$$10^3 = 10 \times 10 \times 10 = 1000$$
$$10^4 = 10 \times 10 \times 10 \times 10 = 10\ 000$$

Negative powers of 10 are useful for writing very small numbers. Any number to a negative power represents a fraction or decimal.

Tip

The negative exponent for a power of 10 and the number of decimal places are the same.
$10^{-4} = 0.0001$

$$10^{-1} = \frac{1}{10} = 0.1$$

$$10^{-2} = \frac{1}{10} \times \frac{1}{10} = 0.01$$

$$10^{-3} = \frac{1}{10} \times \frac{1}{10} \times \frac{1}{10} = 0.001$$

Scientific notation is a method that uses powers of ten to write very small and very large numbers. A number in scientific notation is expressed as a product of a number between one and ten and a power of ten.

Example 1   The distance to the sun is about 149 000 000 km. Write the distance in scientific notation.

Step 1   Move the decimal point to the left until the last digit on the left is in the ones column.   1.49000000

Step 2   Drop the zeros and multiply by 10 raised to a power equal to the number of places the decimal point was moved, here, 8. $149\ 000\ 000 = \mathbf{1.49 \times 10^8}$

Example 2   In a scientific experiment, the mass of a sample is 2×10^{-5} kg. Write the mass in standard notation.

Step 1   Write the given number with a string of zeros in front of it. You haven't changed the value.   0000002.

Step 2   Move the decimal point to the left by the number of places shown in the exponent. Discard extra zeros.   00.00002.

$2 \times 10^{-5} = \mathbf{0.00002}$

If you perform operations that result in a very large or very small number, your calculator may display the solution in scientific notation. Enter this operation: $30\ 000 \times 5\ 000\ 000 =$

Your display may read: $\mathbf{1.5^{11}}$ or **1.5 11**, which equals $\mathbf{1.5 \times 10^{11}}$.

A. Find each value. Do not use a calculator.

1. 2^4

2. 4^3

3. 16^1

4. 1^6

5. 5^0

6. 3^4

7. 3^3

8. 7^2

9. 3^{-2}

10. 8^2

11. 5^{-3}

12. 12^0

 B. Find each value. Use a calculator for these problems.

13. 6^4

14. 9^5

15. 3^6

16. 8^{-2}

17. 12^5

18. 5^7

19. 2^{-5}

20. 7^4

C. Solve.

21. The Smith family used 518 000 L of water. Which of the following expressions represents that amount in scientific notation?

   (1) 5.18×10^{-5}

   (2) 5.18×10^{-4}

   (3) 5.18×10^3

   (4) 5.18×10^5

   (5) 5.18×10^6

22. In which of the following are the numbers arranged in order from least to greatest?

   (1) 2.43×10^2, 5.2×10^2, 4.7×10^{-1}

   (2) 2.34×10^2, 4.7×10^{-1}, 5.2×10^2

   (3) 4.7×10^{-1}, 5.2×10^2, 2.34×10^2

   (4) 4.7×10^{-1}, 2.34×10^2, 5.2×10^2

   (5) 5.2×10^2, 4.7×10^{-1}, 2.34×10^2

Answers start on page 843.

Mathematics • Algebra

Square Roots

Raising a number to the second power is also called squaring the number. You have already seen that to find the area of a square, you multiply the length of one side of the square by itself. In other words, you square the length of one side to find the area.

The square root of a number is the number that when multiplied by itself equals the given number. The symbol for square root is $\sqrt{\ }$. To find the square root of a certain number, ask yourself: "What number times itself equals this number?"

Example 1   What is the measure of a side of a square if the area of the square is 25 square centimetres?

Step 1   The area of the square is found by multiplying the length of one side by itself. Ask: What number times itself equals 25?

Step 2   Since $5 \times 5 = 25$, the square root of 25 is 5.

Each side of the square measures **5 cm.**

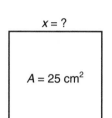

$x = ?$

$A = 25 \text{ cm}^2$

Memorize the following list of squares to help you find square roots.

$1^2 = 1$	$4^2 = 16$	$7^2 = 49$	$10^2 = 100$
$2^2 = 4$	$5^2 = 25$	$8^2 = 64$	$11^2 = 121$
$3^2 = 9$	$6^2 = 36$	$9^2 = 81$	$12^2 = 144$

It is always a good idea to estimate an answer. A good estimate can help you decide whether the number in your calculator's display makes sense.

Example 2   What is $\sqrt{81}$?
The problem asks, "What is the square root of 81?"
Since $9^2 = 81$, $\sqrt{81} = $ **9.**

Most square roots are not whole numbers. You can use the list of common squares above to help you estimate an answer, or you can find a more exact answer using your calculator.

Example 3   What is $\sqrt{55}$?
What number times itself equals 55? You know that 7^2 equals 49 and 8^2 equals 64. Therefore, the square root of 55 must be **between 7 and 8** because 55 is between 49 and 64.

To find the square root of 55 using a calculator, use the square root key. You may need to press **SHIFT** or **2ndF** to access the square root function.

The key sequence on your calculator may be:

55 $\boxed{\sqrt{\ }}$ **7.416198487**   or   **55** $\boxed{\sqrt{x}}$

On your GED calculator: **55** $\boxed{\text{SHIFT}}$ $\boxed{x^2}$ **7.416198487**

Some square roots are whole numbers or have a limited number of decimal digits. Some are repeating decimals. Others continue without repeating a pattern of digits. Read problems carefully to see whether you should round to a particular decimal digit.

A. Write the square roots. Do not use a calculator.

1. $\sqrt{16}$ 3. $\sqrt{9}$ 5. $\sqrt{25}$

2. $\sqrt{0}$ 4. $\sqrt{49}$ 6. $\sqrt{1}$

B. Find the length of the side of each square.

7. $x = ?$
$A = 36$ cm²

8. $x = ?$
$A = 16$ m²

9. $x = ?$
$A = 81$ m²

C. Use a calculator to find the square roots. Round your answers to the nearest hundredth.

10. $\sqrt{28}$ 11. $\sqrt{95}$ 12. $\sqrt{6}$ 13. $\sqrt{324}$ 14. $\sqrt{130}$ 15. $\sqrt{169}$

Working Backward

Each multiple-choice question on the GED Mathematics Test has five answer options. You must choose the best answer for each question.

For most questions, it is faster to solve the problem directly. Read the problem carefully, decide what the question asks, choose the operations to use, and solve. Always make sure your answer makes sense. Then, look at the five options to see whether your answer is among them.

For some algebra problems, however, working backward from the answer choices may save time. Most algebra problems ask you to solve for a particular variable. Ordinarily, you would write an equation and solve it. However, it may be faster to try each answer choice in the given situation to see which one is true.

Tip

Use your knowledge of averages to solve problems asking for consecutive numbers. If the sum of 3 consecutive numbers is 30, the average is 10. Look for a choice with a middle value of 10.

Example 1   The sum of three consecutive numbers is 30. What are the numbers?

(1)   6, 7, and 8
(2)   8, 9, and 10
(3)   9, 10, and 11
(4)   11, 12, and 13
(5)   14, 15, and 16

It is not necessary to write an equation to solve this problem. You know the numbers add up to 30, so simply add the numbers for each option. You can quickly eliminate options (4) and (5) since $10 + 10 + 10 = 30$ and all the numbers in these options are greater than 10. Clearly, options (4) and (5) total more than 30. Quickly add the numbers for the first three options.

Option (1): $6 + 7 + 8 = 21$
Option (2): $8 + 9 + 10 = 27$
Option (3): $9 + 10 + 11 = 30$

Option (3) 9, 10 , and 11 is the correct answer.

Answers start on page 844.

Applying Patterns and Functions

A mathematical **pattern** is an arrangement of numbers or terms formed by following a particular rule. If you know the rule, you can find other terms in the pattern.

Example 1 Find the eighth term in the sequence: 1, 7, 13, 19, 25, . . .

Step 1 **Identify the rule used to make the pattern.** Study the sequence. Each number in the sequence is six more than the preceding number. The rule is "add 6."

Step 2 **Apply the rule to continue the pattern.** The number 25 is the 5th term in the pattern. You need to find the 8th term.

1st	2nd	3rd	4th	5th	6th	7th	8th
1	7	13	19	25	31	37	43

$$+6 \quad +6 \quad +6 \quad +6 \quad +6 \quad +6 \quad +6$$

The correct answer is **43.**

To identify a mathematical pattern, find how one term became the one following it. That is, what function is applied to the first term to obtain the next? Then test your function on the rest of the pattern.

An algebraic rule is sometimes called a **function.** You can think of a function as a machine that performs certain operations. For each number that enters the machine (x), there will be only one number that comes out (y). The function shown here multiplies a number by 3 and then subtracts 4. We can write the function as an equation: $y = 3x - 4$.

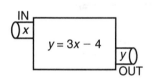

Example 2 For the function, $y = 3x - 4$, what numbers are needed to complete the table below?

x	−3	−2	−1	0	1	2
y	−13	−10	−7		−1	

(1) −6 and 2
(2) −5 and 2
(3) −5 and 3
(4) −4 and 2
(5) −4 and 4

Use substitution to find the value of y. Replace x with 0 and 2. Solve for y.

$$y = 3x - 4 \qquad\qquad y = 3x - 4$$
$$y = 3(0) - 4 \qquad\quad y = 3(2) - 4$$
$$y = 0 - 4 \qquad\qquad y = 6 - 4$$
$$y = -4 \qquad\qquad\quad y = 2$$

The missing numbers are **−4** and **2.** Check your work by testing the pattern. Each value for y is 3 more than the number before it. Continue the pattern to make sure −4 and 2 are correct.

GED Practice

Directions: Choose the one best answer to each question.

1. The sum of three consecutive numbers is 45. What are the three numbers?

   (1) 10, 11, and 12
   (2) 12, 13, and 14
   (3) 13, 14, and 15
   (4) 14, 15, and 16
   (5) 15, 16, and 17

2. Jess and David took an 800-km driving trip. Jess drove 200 km more than David did on the trip. How many kilometres did David drive?

   (1) 200
   (2) 250
   (3) 300
   (4) 400
   (5) 500

3. The sum of two consecutive numbers is 95. What are the two numbers?

   (1) 40 and 41
   (2) 42 and 43
   (3) 47 and 48
   (4) 52 and 53
   (5) 57 and 58

4. Four consecutive numbers total 38. What are the four numbers?

   (1) 7, 8, 9, and 10
   (2) 8, 9, 10, and 11
   (3) 9, 10, 11, and 12
   (4) 10, 11, 12, and 13
   (5) 11, 12, 13, and 14

Question 5 refers to the following diagram.

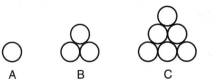 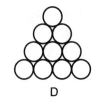

5. If you were to continue the pattern above, how many circles would be in figure E?

   (1) 12
   (2) 15
   (3) 20
   (4) 21
   (5) Not enough information is given.

6. What is the 8th term in the sequence below?

   3, 6, 12, 24, 48, . . .

   (1) 96
   (2) 144
   (3) 192
   (4) 288
   (5) 384

7. For the function $y = \frac{x}{4}$, which of the following values for x results in a fractional value of y (that is, y is not a whole number)?

   (1) 42
   (2) 32
   (3) 28
   (4) 12
   (5) 8

Answers start on page 844.

Mathematics • Algebra

Factoring and Inequalities

Multiplying Factors with Two Terms

You have already learned how to use the distributive property to multiply a single term, here 2, by a factor that has two terms, here $(x + 5)$: $2(x + 5) = 2x + 10$. Each term inside the parentheses is multiplied by the integer 2 outside the parentheses.

You can also use the distributive property to multiply two factors when each has two terms. Each term in the first factor is multiplied by each term in the second factor. To make sure you remember each step of the process, use the FOIL method shown in the example below.

Example 1 Multiply: $(x + 7)(x - 3)$.

Step 1 **Multiply the terms.** The letters in the word FOIL stand for First, Outer, Inner, and Last. If you multiply the terms in this order, you can be sure that you have multiplied every possible combination of terms. Remember that a term owns the operation sign that precedes it.

F	first	$(x + 7)(x - 3)$	$x(x) = x^2$
O	outer	$(x + 7)(x - 3)$	$x(-3) = -3x$
I	inner	$(x + 7)(x - 3)$	$7(x) = 7x$
L	last	$(x + 7)(x - 3)$	$7(-3) = -21$

Step 2 **Find the sum of the products from each FOIL step.** Simplify the expression.
$$x^2 + (-3x) + (7x) + (-21) = x^2 + 4x - 21$$

The product of $x + 7$ and $x - 3$ is $\boldsymbol{x^2 + 4x - 21}$.

Tip

Remember, when simplifying an expression, you can only combine like terms.

When using the FOIL method, your answer could have two, three, or four terms. In Example 2, the solution has only two terms.

Example 2 Multiply: $(x + 4)(x - 4)$.

Step 1 Use the FOIL method to multiply the terms.

F	$x(x) = x^2$
O	$x(-4) = -4x$
I	$4(x) = 4x$
L	$4(-4) = -16$

Step 2 Find the sum of the products.

$$x^2 + (-4x) + 4x + (-16)$$
$$x^2 \qquad\qquad\quad - 16$$

Since the sum of $-4x$ and $4x$ is 0, the answer has only two terms. The product of $x + 4$ and $x - 4$ is $\boldsymbol{x^2 - 16}$.

Factoring

Factors are numbers that are multiplied together. In the algebraic term $7x$, 7 and x are factors. An expression of more than one term can sometimes be factored. To factor an expression, look for a number or a variable that divides evenly into each term in the expression.

Example 1   Factor the expression $6x + 10$.

Step 1   Find a factor that divides evenly into both terms. Both $6x$ and 10 can be divided by 2.   One of the factors is the number 2.

Step 2   Divide to find the other factor. $\dfrac{6x + 10}{2} = \dfrac{6x}{2} + \dfrac{10}{2}$

$(3x + 5)$

Step 3   Check by multiplying the factors. $2(3x + 5) = 6x + 10$

The factors of $6x + 10$ are **2** and **$3x + 5$.**

A quadratic expression is one that contains a variable raised to the second power, or "squared," as in $x^2 + 2x$. Both factors of quadratic expressions will always contain the variable.

Example 2   Factor $x^2 + 2x$.

Step 1   Both terms divide evenly by x.   One factor is x.

Step 2   Divide by one factor (x) $\dfrac{x^2 + 2x}{x} = \dfrac{x^2}{x} + \dfrac{2x}{x}$
to find the other factor.

$(x + 2)$

Step 3   Check by multiplying the two factors. $x(x + 2) = x^2 + 2x$

The factors are **x** and **$x + 2$.**

A quadratic expression in this form, $x^2 - 3x - 4$, results when you multiply two expressions, each with a variable and an integer. To factor quadratic expressions with three terms, work backward.

Example 3   Factor $x^2 - 3x - 4$.

Step 1   **Find all the possible factors for the third term.**
The third term in this example is -4.
The possible factors are $(-4)(1)$, $(4)(-1)$, $(-2)(2)$, and $(2)(-2)$

Step 2   **Find the two factors from Step 1 that when added give the integer part of the middle term,** here, $-3x$.
The sum of only the factors -4 and 1 equals -3. $-4 + 1 = -3$
None of the other possible factors equal -3 when
added together: $4 + (-1) = 3$, $-2 + 2 = 0$, and $2 + -2 = 0$.

Step 3   **Write the two factors using the variable as the first term in each factor and the integers from Step 2 as the second term.**   The factors are $(x - 4)$ and $(x + 1)$.

Step 4   **Check.** Multiply using the FOIL method.

$$(x - 4)\,(x + 1) = x^2 + 1x - 4x - 4 = x^2 - 3x - 4$$

The factors are **$(x - 4)$** and **$(x + 1)$.**

Find the product of each pair of factors.

1. $(x + 1)(x + 4)$ 3. $(x - 5)(2x - 7)$ 5. $(x - 4)(y + 6)$

2. $(x + 6)(x + 3)$ 4. $(x + 2)(x - 2)$ 6. $(2x + 8)(3x + 9)$

Solving Quadratic Equations

As you have learned, a quadratic expression contains a variable that is raised to the second power, or squared. When an equation contains a squared variable, it is called a **quadratic equation.** Quadratic equations usually have two different solutions. In other words, there are two values for the variable that will make the equation true. Follow these steps to solve a quadratic equation.

Example 1 If $x^2 + 3x = 10$, then what values of x make the equation true?

Step 1	**Rewrite the equation to set the quadratic expression equal to 0.** In this case, subtract 10 from both sides of the equation.	$x^2 + 3x = 10$ $x^2 + 3x - 10 = 10 - 10$ $x^2 + 3x - 10 = 0$
Step 2	**Factor the quadratic expression.**	$x^2 + 3x - 10 = 0$ $(x + 5)(x - 2) = 0$
Step 3	**For each factor, determine the value of x that will make that factor equal to 0.** Since any number multiplied by 0 equals 0, if either factor equals 0, the entire expression will equal 0.	If $x + 5 = 0$ or $x - 2 = 0$ then, $x = -5$ or $x = 2$
Step 4	**Check** both values by substituting them into the original equation.	

$$x^2 + 3x = 10 \qquad\qquad x^2 + 3x = 10$$
$$(-5)^2 + 3(-5) = 10 \qquad\qquad (2)^2 + 3(2) = 10$$
$$25 + (-15) = 10 \qquad\qquad 4 + 6 = 10$$
$$10 = 10 \qquad\qquad 10 = 10$$

The two solutions for the equation $x^2 + 3x = 10$ are **−5** and **2.**

When a quadratic equation is presented in a multiple-choice question, you may be able to solve the problem more quickly by working backward from the answer choices.

Example 2 What are the possible values for x if $x^2 - 7x = 60$?

    (1) -20 and 3
    (2) -12 and 5
    (3) -10 and 6
    (4) -6 and 10
    (5) -5 and 12

Substitute one of the numbers from each option into the equation. You may find it easier to work with the positive number from each option.

Tip

Often working backward is a good test-taking strategy for any multiple-choice problem that involves lengthy computations.

Answers start on page 844.

Option 1	Option 2	Option 3	Option 4	Option 5
$x^2 - 7x = 60$	$x^2 - 7x = 60$	$x^2 - 7x = 60$	$x^2 - 7x = 60$	$x^2 - 7x = 60$
$3^2 - 7(3) = 60$	$5^2 - 7(5) = 60$	$6^2 - 7(6) = 60$	$10^2 - 7(10) = 60$	$12^2 - 7(12) = 60$
$9 - 21 = 60$	$25 - 35 = 60$	$36 - 42 = 60$	$100 - 70 = 60$	$144 - 84 = 60$
$-12 \neq 60$	$-10 \neq 60$	$-6 \neq 60$	$30 \neq 60$	$60 = 60$
false	**false**	**false**	**false**	**true**

Note: The symbol $\neq$ means "is not equal to."

Option (5) is the correct answer. If you have time, you could substitute -5, the other value from option 5, to check your work.

$$(-5)^2 - 7(-5) = 60 \qquad 25 + 35 = 60 \qquad 60 = 60 \qquad \text{true}$$

GED Practice

Directions: Choose the <u>one best answer</u> for each question.

1. In the equation $x^2 + 72 = 18x$, what are the possible values for x?

   (1) -9 and -8
   (2) -9 and 8
   (3) -6 and 12
   (4) 8 and 9
   (5) 12 and 6

2. If $2x^2 - 10x + 12 = 0$, what is one possible value for x?

   (1) -4
   (2) -3
   (3) 3
   (4) 6
   (5) 12

3. In the equation $x^2 - x = 12$, what are the possible values for x?

   (1) 6 and -2
   (2) 4 and -3
   (3) 3 and -4
   (4) 2 and -6
   (5) -3 and -4

4. If $x^2 + 13x = -40$, what are the possible values for x?

   (1) 10 and 4
   (2) 8 and 5
   (3) -4 and -10
   (4) -5 and -8
   (5) -6 and -7

5. In the quadratic equation $9x^2 - 36 = 0$, which pair of solutions makes the equation true?

   (1) 9 and -4
   (2) 6 and -6
   (3) 4 and -9
   (4) 3 and -12
   (5) 2 and -2

6. In the equation $2x^2 - x = 45$, what is one possible value of x?

   (1) 9
   (2) 5
   (3) 3
   (4) -5
   (5) -9

Answers start on page 845.

Mathematics • Algebra

Solving and Graphing Inequalities

An inequality means two algebraic expressions are not equal. Other inequality symbols in addition to greater than and less than symbols are

≥ means "is greater than or equal to" $4 \geq 2$
≤ means "is less than or equal to" $7 \leq 9$

In an inequality, a variable may have many values that make the statement true. Consider $x < 5$. The numbers 4, 3, 2, 1, and so on are all possible values for x. We can graph the possible solutions to an inequality.

Example 1   Graph the solution set of the inequality $x < 5$.

On a number line, every number to the left of 5 is a solution. Graph the solution by drawing a solid line on the number line. An empty circle at the number 5 shows that 5 itself is not included as a solution. Five is not "less than" 5.

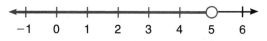

Example 2   Graph the solution set of the inequality $x \geq -3$.

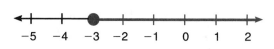

The solution set of the inequality $x \geq -3$ includes the number -3 and all numbers to the right of -3. The circle at -3 is filled in to show that -3 is included as a solution.

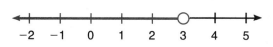

An inequality can be solved much like an equation. The same number can be added to or subtracted from both sides of an inequality.

Example 3   Solve $2x + 7 < x + 10$.

Step 1	Subtract x from both sides.	$x + 7 < 10$
Step 2	Subtract 7 from both sides.	$x < 3$
Step 3	Check using a number less than 3 (such as 2).	$2(2) + 7 < 2 + 10$
		$11 < 12$ is true

The solution to the inequality is **$x < 3$.**

Both sides of an inequality can also be multiplied or divided by the same number to simplify the inequality. But there is an important rule to remember: If you multiply or divide an inequality by a negative number, the inequality sign must be <u>reversed</u>.

Example 4   Solve: $3x - 4 < 5x$.

Step 1	Subtract $5x$ from both sides.	$-2x - 4 < 0$
Step 2	Add 4 to both sides.	$-2x - 4 + 4 < 0 + 4$
Step 3	Divide by -2, and reverse the inequality sign.	$\dfrac{-2x}{-2} < \dfrac{4}{-2}$
		$x > -2$
Step 4	Check using a number greater than -2.	$3(2) - 4 < 5(2)$

The solution to the inequality is **$x > -2$.** $2 < 10$ is true

The Coordinate Plane

Coordinate Graphs

Imagine a blank sheet of paper with one dot on it. How could you describe the exact location of the dot? You might use the edges of the paper to give directions. For example, you could say that the dot was four centimetres from the top edge and three centimetres from the left edge. A coordinate graph works the same way.

A coordinate graph is a system for finding the location of a point on a flat surface called a plane. A coordinate graph is formed from two axis lines that cross at a point called the origin. The horizontal line is the x-axis and the vertical line is the y-axis. Both lines are marked as number lines with the origin at zero. The axes divide the graph into four quadrants.

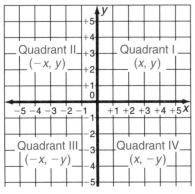

Each point on the grid is named by two numbers, an x-coordinate and a y-coordinate. The x-coordinate is always written first; the y-coordinate is always written second. Together, the coordinates are called an ordered pair and are enclosed in parentheses, separated by a comma.

Example 1 Plot the point (5,3) on a coordinate grid.

Step 1 **Start at the origin**—coordinates (0,0). **Move the number of units of the x-coordinate in the appropriate direction,** here 5 units to the right, the positive x direction.

Step 2 **From that point, move the number of units of the y-coordinate in the appropriate direction,** here 3 units upward, the positive y direction.

The location of point (5,3) is shown by **the dot** on the grid.

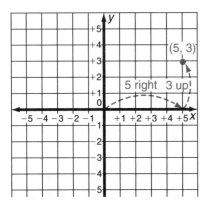

You may be asked to use coordinates to draw a line segment or a figure on a coordinate system.

Example 2 Draw a line segment on the coordinate grid connecting points (0,−4) and (−3,2).

Step 1 Plot point (0,−4). Start at the origin. The 0 indicates that no move along the x-axis is required. Move −4 on the y-axis (down from the origin), and plot the point.

Step 2 Plot point (−3,2). Start at the origin; move 3 units to the left on the x-axis, then 2 units up; plot the point.

Step 3 Connect the points by drawing a line segment.

The location of the points and segment are shown on the grid.

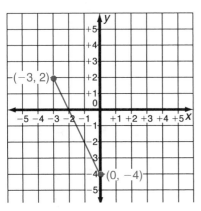

GED Strategy • Working with Special Formats

Plotting Ordered Pairs

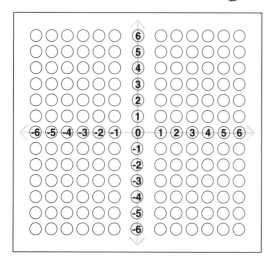

Some questions on the GED Mathematics Test ask you to show the location of a point on a coordinate grid. A special coordinate grid will be provided on the answer sheet to record your answers. This grid uses circles to represent each ordered pair on the coordinate plane.

The answer grid shown to the left is a sample of this GED answer format. Since positive and negative numbers are shown on the axis lines, there are no circles for points that lie directly on either the *x*- or *y*-axis. The origin (0,0) is not labelled, but you know that it lies at the intersection of the *x*- and *y*-axes.

To use the grid to record an answer, carefully colour in the circle at the correct location. Be careful not to make stray marks on the grid.

Tip

The *x*- and *y*-axes on a graph may not be labelled with numbers. Remember that the origin on either scale (the point where the axes cross) is always 0.

Most questions that test your understanding of the coordinate grid will refer to a diagram or graph.

Example   Jesse has graphed three points on the coordinate grid at right. The points will become three corners of a rectangle. Where must he place the fourth point to complete the rectangle? Graph your answer on the coordinate grid.

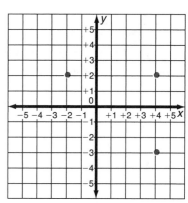

Step 1   Complete the rectangle to find the location of the fourth point. You know that a rectangle has four sides. The opposite sides must be the same length. From the three points already shown on the graph, you know the length and the width of the rectangle. The remaining point must be located at point **(−2,−3).**

Step 2   Colour in your answer on the coordinate grid. Starting at the origin, count two units left and three down. Fill in the circle neatly and completely.

The grid to the left shows the correct location of the fourth point.

GED Practice

<u>Directions:</u> Grid in the answer to each question on the answer grid provided.

1. A point has an *x*-coordinate of 4 and a *y*-coordinate of −1. Show the location of the point on the coordinate grid.

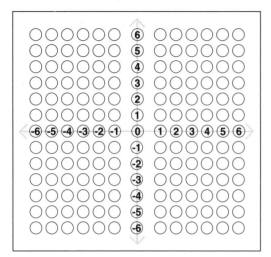

2. On the coordinate plane below, three points are drawn to mark the corners of a square. Graph the location of the fourth corner needed to complete the square.

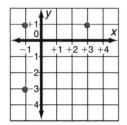

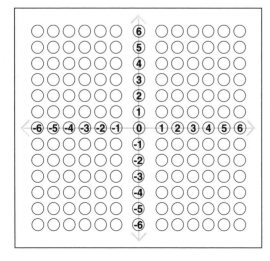

3. A point has an *x*-coordinate of −5 and a *y*-coordinate of 3. Show the location of the point on the coordinate grid.

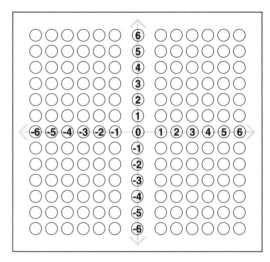

4. On the coordinate plane below, three points are drawn to mark the corners of a rectangle. Graph the location of the fourth corner needed to complete the figure.

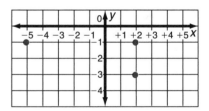

Answers start on page 845.

Mathematics • Algebra

Graphing Equations

You know that some equations have two different variables. For example, the equation $y = 2x - 4$ has two variables, x and y. For each specific value substituted for x, there is a unique value of y. One way to show the possible solutions for such an equation is to draw the graph of the equation on a coordinate grid.

The equation $y = 2x - 4$ is called a linear equation because its graph forms a straight line. To draw the line, you need to know at least two points on the line.

Example 1   Graph the equation $y = 2x - 4$.

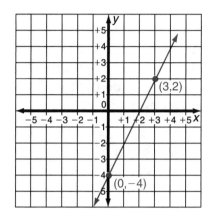

Step 1	Identify a point on the line. Choose any value for x; 0 is usually ideal. Substitute x into the equation. Solve for y. This ordered pair makes the equation true.	Let $x = 0$ $y = 2(0) - 4$ $y = 0 - 4 = -4$ $(0, -4)$
Step 2	Find another point on the line. Choose another value for x and solve for the new y. Write the coordinates.	Let $x = 3$ $y = 2(3) - 4$ $y = 6 - 4 = 2$ $(3, 2)$
Step 3	Locate both ordered pairs on a grid and draw a line through them.	

The graph of the equation is shown to the left. Every point on the line satisfies, or solves, the equation.

Tip

Although you only need two points to draw the graph of a line, it is always a good idea to find a third point to check your work.

Some questions refer to the graph of an equation, but they can be solved without drawing the graph.

Example 2   Which of the following points lies on a graph of the equation $x = 3 + y$?

(1) $(4, -1)$
(2) $(3, 1)$
(3) $(2, -1)$
(4) $(1, 2)$
(5) $(0, -4)$

Instead of drawing the graph, substitute the coordinates from each answer choice for x and y in the equation. The correct option is the ordered pair that makes the equation true.

Only **option (3) (2, −1)** makes the equation true. $2 = 3 + (-1)$
$2 = 2$

Graph each equation on a coordinate grid.

1. $y = 3x - 4$

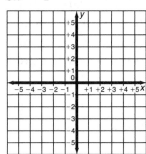

2. $x - 2y = 1$

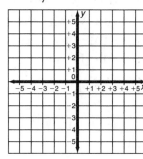

3. $-x = y + 2$

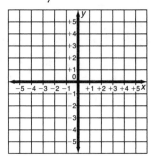

Finding the Slope of a Line

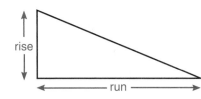

Slope is a number that measures the steepness of a line. In everyday life, we use slope to calculate the steepness of a ramp or flight of stairs. We may determine the slope of a roof or a roadway. Slope is the ratio of rise to run, where rise is a measurement of vertical distance and run is a measurement of horizontal distance.

Slope can be positive or negative. All lines that rise as they move from left to right have a positive slope. All lines that fall as they move from left to right have a negative slope. If you have a graph of a line, you can find its slope by examining the line and counting grid units to find the rise and run.

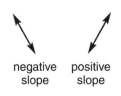

Example 1 Find the slope of Line A.

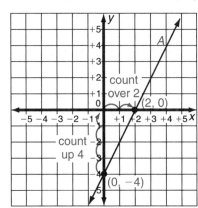

Step 1 **Select two points on the line.** Starting at either point, **count the number of units** up or down to reach the level of the second point. This is the rise of the line. Here, start at $(0, -4)$ and count up 4.

Step 2 **From this intermediate point, count the units** left or right to reach the second point. This is the run of the line. Here, count 2 to the right.

Step 3 **Write the slope as the fraction rise over run.** $\frac{4}{2} = 2$

Step 4 **Decide whether the slope is positive or negative.** Here, the slope is positive since the line rises as it moves from left to right.

The slope of Line A is **+2.**

You can also find the slope of a line by using an algebraic formula. It will be listed on the page of formulas you will be given when you take the GED Mathematics Test.

slope (m) of a line $= \dfrac{\text{rise}}{\text{run}} = m = \dfrac{y_2 - y_1}{x_2 - x_1}$, where (x_1, y_1) and (x_2, y_2) are two points on the line

Answers start on page 845.

Mathematics • Algebra

Example 2   Find the slope of Line B with points $(-1,2)$ and $(1,-4)$.

Step 1   Let one point be (x_1,y_1) and the other be (x_2,y_2). In this case, let $(-1,2) = (x_1,y_1)$ and $(1,-4) = (x_2,y_2)$.

Step 2   Substitute into the formula and solve.

$$m = \frac{y_2 - y_1}{x_2 - x_1} = \frac{-4 - 2}{1 - (-1)} = \frac{-6}{2} = -3$$

The slope of the line is **−3.**

Some unique features of slope to remember include the following:

- The slope of any horizontal line, including the x-axis, is 0.
- A vertical line, including the y-axis, has no slope.
- All lines with the same slope are parallel.

A. Find the slope of each line.

1.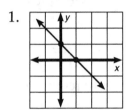

2.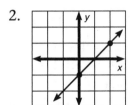

3.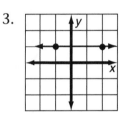

B. Find the slope of the line that passes through each pair of points.

4. $(1,-3)$ and $(0,1)$

5. $(4,5)$ and $(3,-4)$

6. $(-3,-3)$ and $(-2,0)$

Finding the Distance Between Points

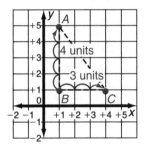

It is sometimes necessary to find the distance between two points on a coordinate grid. You can easily find the distance between points on a vertical or a horizontal line by counting. For example, on the grid at left, point A is 4 units from point B, and point B is 3 units from point C. Note that points ABC form a right triangle.

To find the distance between two points that are not on the same grid line such as points A and C, you can use a formula. This formula is on the GED formulas page that you will be given when you take the GED Mathematics Test.

$$\text{distance between points} = \sqrt{(x_2 - x_1)^2 + (y_2 - y_1)^2}$$

To use the formula, you need to know the coordinates for the two points. Assign one point to be (x_1,y_1) and the other point to be (x_2,y_2). Then substitute the values into the formula and solve. It does not matter which point you choose to be (x_1,y_1).

Answers start on page 846.

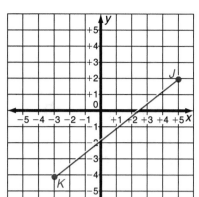

Example 1 In the coordinate grid at left, what is the distance between points *J* and *K?*

Step 1 **Find the coordinates of the points.**

Point $J = (5,2)$; $K = (-3,-4)$

Step 2 **Assign the variables.**

Let $J\,(5,2) = (x_1,y_1)$
Let $K\,(-3,-4) = (x_2,y_2)$

Step 3 **Substitute the coordinates into the formula and solve.**

$$d = \sqrt{(x_2 - x_1)^2 + (y_2 - y_1)^2}$$
$$= \sqrt{(-3 - 5)^2 + (-4 - 2)^2}$$
$$= \sqrt{(-8)^2 + (-6)^2}$$
$$= \sqrt{64 + 36}$$
$$= \sqrt{100}$$
$$= 10$$

The distance between points *J* and *K* is **10 units.**

Finding the Equation of a Line

You know how to graph an equation by finding ordered pairs that make the equation true and drawing a line through those points. You may be asked to work backward from points to determine the equation of a line.

On the GED Mathematics Test the answer choices to such questions are written in a format called the slope-intercept form of a line. The variable *m* is the slope of the line. The variable *b* is the *y*-intercept, the point at which the line crosses the *y*-axis.

$$y = mx + b, \text{ where } m = \text{slope and } b = y\text{-intercept}$$

Example 1 What is the equation of the line shown on the graph?

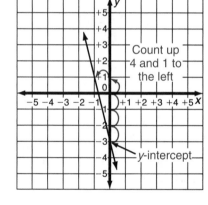

(1) $y = -2x - 3$
(2) $y = -3x + 2$
(3) $y = -4x + 2$
(4) $y = -4x - 3$
(5) $y = -4x + 3$

Tip

You can check your work by substituting the coordinates of a point on the line for *x* and *y* in the equation. If the equation is true, your answer is correct.

Step 1 **Find the *y*-intercept of the line.** The line shown crosses the *y*-axis at $(0,-3)$. Therefore:

the *y*-intercept is -3

Step 2 **Find the slope of the line using the grid-unit counting method.** Count from the *y*-intercept to another point on the line with whole numbers as the ordered pair, here, $(-1,1)$. The line rises 4 units for every 1 unit of run to the left (a negative direction).

$$\text{slope} = \frac{\text{rise}}{\text{run}} = \frac{4}{-1} = -4$$

Step 3 **Use the slope-intercept form** to write the equation.

$$y = mx + b \qquad y = -4x + (-3) \text{ or } y = -4x - 3$$

The correct answer is **option (4) $y = -4x - 3$.**

GED Practice

Directions: Choose the <u>one best answer</u> to each question.

1. What are the coordinates of the *y*-intercept of the line $y = -3x - 2$?

   (1) $(0,-5)$
   (2) $(0,-3)$
   (3) $(0,-2)$
   (4) $(-2,0)$
   (5) $(-3,0)$

4. The point $(0,-5)$ is the *y*-intercept of which of the following lines?

   (1) $y = 2x$
   (2) $y = -x + 5$
   (3) $y = 3x - 5$
   (4) $y = -2x - 3$
   (5) Not enough information is given.

Questions 2 and 3 refer to the following graph.

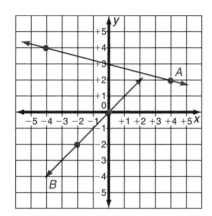

Questions 5 and 6 refer to the following graph.

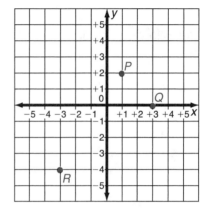

2. What is the equation of Line *A*?

   (1) $y - 4x = 3$
   (2) $y - \frac{1}{4}x = -2$
   (3) $y = 4x$
   (4) $y + \frac{1}{4}x = -2$
   (5) $y + \frac{1}{4}x = 3$

5. What would be the equation of a line drawn through points *P* and *Q*?

   (1) $y = -x + 3$
   (2) $y = -x - 3$
   (3) $y = 2x - 3$
   (4) $y = 3x + 2$
   (5) $y = 3x + 3$

3. What is the equation of Line *B*?

   (1) $y = -x$
   (2) $y = x$
   (3) $y = 2x$
   (4) $y = -2x$
   (5) $y = x + 1$

6. Which of the following is the *y*-intercept of a line drawn through points *R* and *Q*?

   (1) $(-3,-4)$
   (2) $(0,-2)$
   (3) $(0,-3)$
   (4) $(0,-4)$
   (5) $(3,-4)$

Answers start on page 846.

GED Review Algebra

1. Which of the following expressions shows the product of 9 and x, subtracted from the quotient of 2 and x?

   (1) $\frac{2}{x} - 9x$

   (2) $-9x - \frac{2}{x}$

   (3) $2x(-9x)$

   (4) $9 - x - \frac{2}{x}$

   (5) $(2 + x) - 9x$

2. Which of the following expressions has the greatest value?

   (1) $(-2) + (-7)$

   (2) $(-6) + (+8)$

   (3) $(-3) - (-4)$

   (4) $(+4) - (+10)$

   (5) $(-8) + (+9)$

3. When 13 is subtracted from the sum of two consecutive numbers, the answer is 18. What are the two consecutive numbers?

   (1) 6 and 7

   (2) 9 and 10

   (3) 10 and 11

   (4) 15 and 16

   (5) 31 and 32

4. Ten less than a number is equal to the same number divided by 2. What is the number?

   (1) 8

   (2) 10

   (3) 14

   (4) 20

   (5) 28

5. Bill is one year less than twice as old as his sister Caroline. The total of their ages is 26. How old is Bill?

   (1) 9

   (2) 12

   (3) 17

   (4) 19

   (5) 24

6. Eunsook drives an average speed of 62 km per hour for $4\frac{1}{2}$ hours. How many kilometres does she travel?

   (1) 67

   (2) 137

   (3) 248

   (4) 279

   (5) 725

 Tip Remember, subtracting a positive number is the same as adding a negative number. For example,

$$-3 - 5 = -3 + (-5) \qquad -4 - 2 = -4 + (-2)$$

7. Which of the following rules can be used to form the following sequence?

$$-19, -15, -11, -7, -3, \ldots$$

(1) Add -5.

(2) Add -4.

(3) Subtract 4.

(4) Subtract 6.

(5) Add 4.

8. What is the 5th term in the sequence below?

$$64, -32, 16, -8, \underline{\hspace{2em}}$$

(1) 8

(2) 4

(3) 2

(4) -2

(5) -4

9. The function $y = 10x - 5$ has been used to create the following table. Which numbers are missing from the table?

x	-2	0	2	4	6
y	-25	-5			55

(1) 5 and 25

(2) 10 and 30

(3) 15 and 35

(4) 20 and 40

(5) 25 and 45

10. Bill works two jobs. Last week, he worked 30 hours in all. If he worked two hours more at one job than he worked at the other, how many hours did he work at each job?

(1) 9 and 11

(2) 13 and 15

(3) 14 and 16

(4) 19 and 21

(5) 24 and 26

11. Marta scored a total of 93 points on her English test. She scored 5 points lower on the writing part of the test than on the reading part. What were her scores on each part of the test?

(1) 43 and 48

(2) 44 and 49

(3) 45 and 50

(4) 47 and 52

(5) 54 and 59

12. Evelyn drove a total of 334 km on Monday and Tuesday. She drove 50 km farther on Tuesday than she did on Monday. How many kilometres did she drive each day?

(1) 92 and 142

(2) 125 and 175

(3) 142 and 192

(4) 234 and 284

(5) 284 and 334

There is often more than one way to write an equation:
$x + (x + 8) = 32$ and $2x + 8 = 32$ are the same as $(x + 8) + x = 32$.

Part 2

Directions: Choose the <u>one best answer</u> to each question. You may <u>not</u> use your calculator.

13. If $x^2 + x = 20$, what are the values for x that will make the equation true?

    (1) -5 and 4

    (2) -5 and -4

    (3) 5 and 4

    (4) 5 and -4

    (5) Not enough information is given.

14. Aaron's weekly pay (p) can be represented by $p = \$200 + \$6s$, where s is the number of sales he makes in a week. How much will Aaron earn in a week if he makes 32 sales?

    (1) $192

    (2) $232

    (3) $238

    (4) $384

    (5) $392

15. Which ordered pair is a solution of $4x - y = 3$?

    (1) $(-5,2)$

    (2) $(-1,1)$

    (3) $(0,3)$

    (4) $(1,-1)$

    (5) $(2,5)$

16. A square mural has an area of about 240 m². What is the approximate length of one side of the mural?

    (1) between 18 and 19 m

    (2) between 17 and 18 m

    (3) between 16 and 17 m

    (4) between 15 and 16 m

    (5) between 14 and 15 m

Question 17 refers to the following figures.

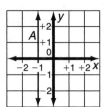 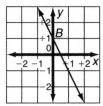 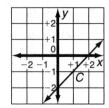

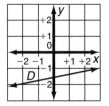 

17. Which of the lines shown above has a negative slope?

    (1) A

    (2) B

    (3) C

    (4) D

    (5) E

18. Which of the following is equal to the expression $\frac{x + 4x}{x^2 - 2x}$?

    (1) 2

    (2) $\frac{5}{x - 2}$

    (3) $x + 2$

    (4) $1 + 2x$

    (5) $2x$

19. Which point is <u>not</u> on a graph of the line $2x - y = -1$?

    (1) $(-3,-5)$

    (2) $(-1,-1)$

    (3) $(1,3)$

    (4) $(2,5)$

    (5) $(3,6)$

Question 20 refers to the following figure.

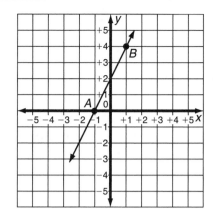

20. What is the equation of the line shown on the graph?

    (1) $y = 2x + 2$

    (2) $y = 2x - 1$

    (3) $y = x + 2$

    (4) $y = x - 1$

    (5) $y = \frac{1}{2}x + 2$

21. A repair company charges a flat fee of $40 plus $30 for each hour ($h$) spent making a repair. Which of the following equations could be used to find the charge (c) for any service call?

    (1) $c = \$30h$

    (2) $c = \$40h$

    (3) $c = \$40 + \$30h$

    (4) $c = \$40h + \$30h$

    (5) $c = \$30 + \$40h$

22. What is the slope of a line that passes through points at $(-2, -2)$ and $(-4, 4)$?

    (1) -3

    (2) -1

    (3) $-\frac{1}{3}$

    (4) $\frac{1}{3}$

    (5) 3

23. The following amounts were deposited in a savings account each month.

    | January | $20 | March | $44 |
    | February | $32 | April | $56 |

    If the pattern continues, how much will be deposited in December?

    (1) $112

    (2) $140

    (3) $144

    (4) $152

    (5) $164

Questions 24 and 25 refer to the following graph.

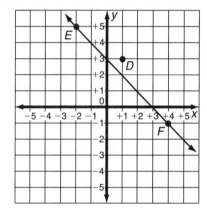

24. What is the equation of the line that passes through points E and F?

    (1) $y = -3x - 3$

    (2) $y = 3x + 3$

    (3) $y = x + 3$

    (4) $y = -x + 3$

    (5) $y = -x - 3$

25. What is the distance in units from point F to point D?

    (1) 3

    (2) 4

    (3) 5

    (4) 6

    (5) 7

Answers start on page 846.

Geometry

Geometry is the area of mathematics that deals with points, lines, angles, two-dimensional shapes, and three-dimensional figures and is used to solve many everyday problems. Geometric shapes are everywhere. You can see them indoors in rooms, furniture, clothing, and household objects and outside in buildings, streets, and bridges. One of the most important parts of geometry is learning to use formulas, such as those for perimeter, area, and volume, and the Pythagorean Relationship.

The principles of geometry show how the measurements of a shape or figure are related to its characteristics and how two-dimensional shapes and three-dimensional figures are related. Geometry is a very important topic on the GED Mathematics Test. Questions related to geometry will account for about 25 percent of the test.

Applying Formulas

Triangles and Parallelograms

Two common shapes are triangles and parallelograms. A triangle has three sides and three angles. The sides of triangles can have different lengths, and their angles can have different measures.

A parallelogram is a four-sided figure whose opposite sides are parallel. *Parallel* means the extended lines never intersect, or meet. Rectangles and squares are special parallelograms, although we usually think of a parallelogram as a rectangle leaning to one side.

The perimeter of geometric figure is the distance around a figure found by adding the lengths of all the sides of a figure, regardless of the number or lengths of the sides.

Area is the measure of the surface of a two-dimensional shape. The area of a parallelogram is the product of the base and the height. The base can be any side. The height is the distance from a point on the opposite side straight down to the base. The height and base form a 90° angle.

Triangles

Parallelograms

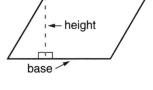

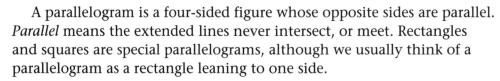

Area of a parallelogram = base × height
or $A = bh$, where b = base and h = height

The "base" is the side that forms a 90° angle with the height. Any side of the figure can be the base, not just the side the figure is "sitting" on.

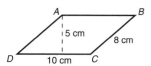

A ——————— B
5 cm
8 cm
D ——10 cm—— C

Example 1 Find the perimeter and area of parallelogram *ABCD*.

Step 1 Find the perimeter. Add the
lengths of the sides. $10 + 10 + 8 + 8 = 36$ cm

Step 2 Find the area. **Choose the formula.** $A = bh$
Substitute the measures. $A = 10(5)$
Solve. $A = 50$ cm^2

The perimeter is **36 cm**; the area is **50 cm^2**.

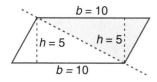

$b = 10$
$h = 5$ $h = 5$
$b = 10$

A diagonal line drawn through the opposite corners divides the parallelogram into two identical triangles. Each triangle is one-half of the parallelogram. The formula for the area of a triangle is based on this fact.

Area of a triangle = $\frac{1}{2} \times$ base $\times$ height or $A = \frac{1}{2}bh$

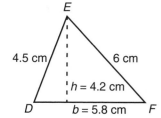

E
4.5 cm   6 cm
$h = 4.2$ cm
D $b = 5.8$ cm   F

Example 2 Find the perimeter and area of triangle *DEF*.

Step 1 Find the perimeter. Add the $6 + 4.5 + 5.8 = 16.3$ cm
lengths of the sides.

Step 2 Find the area. Choose the formula. $A = \frac{1}{2}bh$

Substitute the measures. $A = \frac{1}{2}(5.8)(4.2)$

Solve. $A = 12.18$ cm^2

Use the decimal 0.5 for the $\frac{1}{2}$ in the area formula when using a calculator to solve problems.

area: 0.5 ✕ 5.8 ✕ 4.2 = 12.18

The perimeter of triangle *DEF* is **16.3 cm**;
the area is **12.18 cm^2**.

Find the perimeter and area of each figure. You may use your calculator.

1.
10 cm   16.2 cm
6 cm
23 cm

3.
12 m
4 m   4.5 m

5.
7.1 cm
7 cm
4 cm   7.6 cm

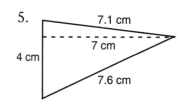

2.
10 cm
8.7 cm
10 cm   10 cm

4.
3 cm   4.2 cm
8 cm

6.
10 cm
4 cm   5 cm

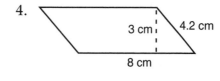
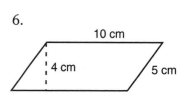

Answers start on page 848.

Circles

Most shapes have straight sides. A circle, on the other hand, has a curved edge. The perimeter, or the distance around a circle, is called the circumference. To find the circumference of a circle, you need to know either the diameter or radius of the circle.

The diameter of a circle is a line segment drawn through the centre of the circle with endpoints on the circle. The radius is a line segment connecting the circle's centre to a point on the circle. The length of the radius is one-half the length of the diameter.

$$r = \frac{1}{2}d = \frac{d}{2} \quad \text{or} \quad 2r = d$$

For any circle, the ratio of the circumference to the diameter $\left(\frac{C}{d}\right)$ is always the same value. This value is represented by the Greek letter π (pi). The value of π is about $\frac{22}{7}$ or 3.14. The GED Mathematics Test uses 3.14 as the value for pi.

Thus, since $\frac{C}{d} = \pi$, then the formula for finding circumference (C) is $C = \pi \times d$, where d = diameter, or, in words, pi times diameter.

Tip

Estimate the circumference of a circle by multiplying its diameter by 3.

Example 1   Flo plans to put a railing around a circular pool. The diameter of the pool is 20 m. What will be the length of the railing?

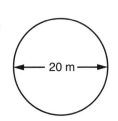

Step 1   Choose the formula.
Step 2   Substitute the values.
Step 3   Solve.

$C = \pi d$
$C = 3.14(20)$
$C = 62.8$ m

The railing will be about **62.8 m** long.

The formula for finding the area of a circle is $A = \pi r^2$, where r is the radius. In other words, the area of a circle is found by multiplying π (3.14) by the square of the radius.

Example 2   Paul wants to paint a circle on a wall of his store as part of a sign. What is the area of the circle in square metres if the diameter is 12 m?

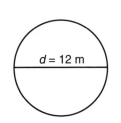

Step 1   Choose the formula.

$A = \pi r^2$

Step 2   Find the radius.

$r = \frac{1}{2}d$

$r = \frac{1}{2}(12) = 6$ m

Step 3   Substitute the values.
Step 4   Solve.

$A = 3.14 \times 6 \times 6$
$A = 113.04$ m^2

Solve. Remember to use 3.14 for π.

1. The diameter of a circle is 7 cm. What is the circumference to the nearest centimetre?

2. If the radius of a circle is 2 m, what is the area of the circle in square metres?

3. A circle has a radius of 3 m. What is its area to the nearest square metre?

4. What is the circumference to the nearest centimetre of a circle with a radius of 7 cm?

Answers start on page 848.

Volume

Volume is a measure in cubic units of the amount of space inside a three-dimensional (or "solid") object. Each cubic unit is a cube made up of 6 identical square sides (called *faces*). For example, a cubic centimetre is a cube with 1-cm edges on each face. Imagine filling a space with neat layers of ice cubes. The volume of the space equals the number of cubes.

Three common solid shapes are a rectangular solid, a cube, and a cylinder. The volume (*V*) of these shapes is the area (*A*) of the base (the side making a 90° angle to the height) multiplied by the height of the object. The general formula is $V = Ah$. This general formula is rewritten for each type of shape. Note that the base of each solid figure is a shape you already know.

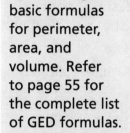

Tip

Save time by memorizing the basic formulas for perimeter, area, and volume. Refer to page 55 for the complete list of GED formulas.

Rectangular Solid	Cube	Cylinder
V = (area of rectangle)h = (length × width) × height = lwh	V = (area of square)h = (edge × edge) × edge = s^3 (edge = side)	V = (area of circle)h = (pi × radius²) × height

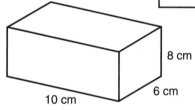

Example 1 What is the volume of the block shown at left?

Step 1 Choose the formula. $\qquad$ $V = lwh$
Step 2 Substitute and solve. $\qquad$ $V = 10 \times 6 \times 8 = 480 \text{ cm}^3$

The volume of the block is **480 cm³**.

A cube is a special rectangular solid. The volume formula is still the product of length, width, and height, but the formula is written differently.

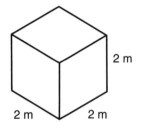

Example 2 What is the volume of a cube that is 2 m long on each side?

Step 1 Choose the formula. $\qquad$ $V = s^3$
Step 2 Substitute. $\qquad$ $V = 2^3$
Step 3 Solve. $\qquad$ $V = 2 \times 2 \times 2 = 8 \text{ m}^3$

Use the $\boxed{x^y}$ or $\boxed{x^3}$ key to cube a number.

$2 \boxed{x^y} 3 \boxed{=} 8.$ $\qquad$ or $\qquad$ $2 \boxed{\text{SHIFT}} \boxed{\blacktriangleright} 8.$

The volume of the cube is **8 m³**.

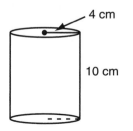

The base of a cylinder is a circle. To find the volume of the cylinder, find the area of the circle (πr^2) and multiply this area by the height (*h*).

Example 3 What is the volume of the cylinder shown at left?

Step 1 Choose the formula. $\qquad$ V = (area of a circle) × $h = \pi r^2 h$
Step 2 Substitute. $\qquad$ $V = 3.14 \times 4^2 \times 10$
Step 3 Solve. $\qquad$ $V = 3.14 \times 16 \times 10 = 502.4 \text{ cm}^3$

Pyramids and Cones

The three-dimensional solids studied so far—rectangular containers, cubes, and cylinders—all have two identical bases. You may think of these bases as the top and bottom sides of the figure. Pyramids and cones are also three-dimensional solids, but they have only one base.

Pyramid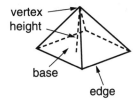

A pyramid has one base with sides of the same length. A pyramid can have either a square or triangular base. However, the volume formula used on the GED Mathematics Test is for only a pyramid with a square base. The base is connected to a single point, called a vertex, by triangular faces (sides).

A cone has one circular base and one vertex. A curved surface connects the base and vertex.

Cone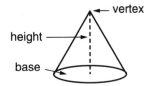

The volume of a pyramid or a cone is $\frac{1}{3}$ of the area of its base multiplied by its height.

$$V = \frac{1}{3} \times \text{Area of base} \times \text{height} \qquad V = \frac{1}{3}Ah$$

pyramid   Volume $= \frac{1}{3} \times$ (area of square) $\times$ height

$= \frac{1}{3} \times$ (base edge)$^2 \times$ height $\qquad V = \frac{1}{3}s^2h$

cone   Volume $= \frac{1}{3} \times$ (area of circle) $\times$ height

$= \frac{1}{3} \times \pi \times$ radius$^2 \times$ height $\qquad V = \frac{1}{3}\pi r^2h$

Example 1   Find the volume of the pyramid in cubic centimetres.

Step 1   **Find the area of the base** (a square).
 Choose the formula.
 Substitute and solve.

$A = s^2$
$A = 6^2 = 36 \text{ cm}^2$

Step 2   **Choose the volume formula.**
 Substitute.
 Solve.

$V = \frac{1}{3}Ah$

$V = \frac{1}{3}(36)(5)$

$V = 60 \text{ cm}^3$

You can use the fraction key to multiply by a fraction.
Or multiply the area and height and divide by 3.

1 [a b/c] 3 [×] 36 [×] 5 [=] 60. or 36 [×] 5 [÷] 3 [=] 60.

The volume of the pyramid is **60 cm³.**

Example 2   Find the volume of the cone to the nearest cubic centimetre.

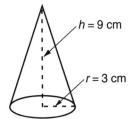

Step 1   Use the formula for finding the volume of a cone.

$V = \frac{1}{3}\pi r^2h$

Step 2   Substitute.

$V = \frac{1}{3}(3.14)(3^2)(9)$

Step 3   Solve.

$V = \frac{1}{3}(3.14)(9)(9) = 84.78,$
which rounds to 85 cm³

The volume of the cone is about **85 cm³.**

GED Practice

Directions: Choose the <u>one best answer</u> to each question.

1. The area of a rectangular mural is 180 square metres. If the mural is 15 m in length, what is its width in metres?

   (1)   6
   (2)   12
   (3) 165
   (4) 2700
   (5) Not enough information is given.

Question 2 refers to the following diagram.

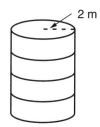

2 m

2. A storage barrel has the shape of a cylinder. The volume of the barrel is about 81.64 cubic metres. Which of the following expressions could be used to find its height in metres?

   (1) $\dfrac{81.64}{(3.14)(2^2)}$

   (2) $\dfrac{(3.14)(2^2)}{81.64}$

   (3) $\dfrac{81.64(2^2)}{(3.14)}$

   (4) $81.64(3.14)(2^2)$

   (5) $81.64 - (3.14)(2^2)$

3. A small section of a roof has the shape of a triangle. The total area of the section is 10.5 square metres. If the height of the section is 3.5 m, what is the measure of the base in metres?

   (1) 3
   (2) 6
   (3) 7
   (4) 14
   (5) 36.75

4. What is the approximate volume in <u>cubic units</u> of a box with a length of $2\frac{1}{2}$ units, a width of $1\frac{1}{2}$ units, and a height of $1\frac{3}{4}$ units?

   (1) between 3 and 4
   (2) between 4 and 5
   (3) between 5 and 6
   (4) between 6 and 7
   (5) between 7 and 8

Question 5 refers to the following diagram.

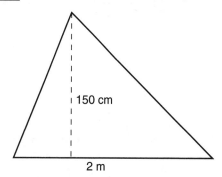

150 cm

2 m

5. What is the area in <u>square centimetres</u> of the triangle in the figure?
   (*Hint:* 1 m = 100 cm)

   (1) 12 000
   (2) 12 500
   (3) 15 000
   (4) 20 000
   (5) 22 500

6. A cone has a height of 1.5 m and a base with an area of 200 cm². What is the volume of the cone in <u>cubic centimetres</u>?

   (1) 15 000
   (2) 10 000
   (3) 1 000
   (4) 30 000
   (5) 3 000

Answers start on page 848.

Lines and Angles

Kinds of Angles

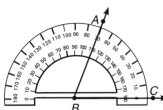

An angle is the space or opening between a pair of lines, called rays, that extend from a common point, the vertex. Angles can be named using three letters: a point on one ray, the vertex, and a point on the other ray. They can also be named by the letter of the vertex alone or by a number written inside the angle. The symbol for angle is $\angle$. This angle can be named $\angle ABC$, $\angle B$, or $\angle 1$.

Angles are measured in degrees (°) using a protractor. When ray BC is placed along the bottom of the protractor, the measure of the angle is read along the scale that starts at 0. The measure (m) of angle ABC equals 70° or in symbols, $m\angle ABC = 70°$.

Angles are classified by their measures. These measures are based on the fact that a circle contains 360°. When measuring an angle, you are actually measuring the number of degrees (or part of the circle) contained in the opening between two rays.

A **right angle** measures exactly 90°.	An **acute angle** measures less than 90°.	An **obtuse angle** measures more than 90° but less than 180°.	A **straight angle** measures exactly 180°.	A **reflex angle** measures more than 180° but less than 360°.
This symbol means the angle measures 90°.				

Angles are also related based on the sum of their measures.

- If the sum of the measures of two angles equals 90°, the angles are called complementary angles.
- If the sum of the measures of two angles equals 180°, the angles are called supplementary angles.

Here's a memory aid: 90 comes before 180; c comes before s.

Example 1 If the measure of $\angle BXC$ is 25°, what is the measure of $\angle AXB$?

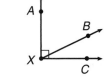

The angles are complementary because $\angle AXC$ has a right angle symbol, and a right angle measures 90°.

Step 1 **Write an equation.**	$m\angle AXB + m\angle BXC = 90°$
Step 2 **Substitute the known measures.**	$m\angle AXB + 25° = 90°$
Step 3 **Solve.** Subtract 25 from both sides.	$m\angle AXB = 65°$

The measure of $\angle AXB$ is **65°**.

Mathematics • Geometry

Congruent and Vertical Angles

Angles can be related in other ways. Angles that have equal measures are congruent angles. In the figure below, angle *ABC* is congruent to angle *XYZ*. The angles are congruent even though they are not turned in the same direction. The symbol ≅ means "is congruent to."

∠*ABC* ≅ ∠*XYZ*

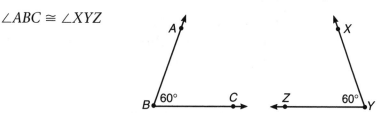

Some angles have a special relationship because of their location with respect to each other. When two lines intersect, or cross, four angles are formed. The angles that are across from each other are called opposite angles, or vertical angles. Each pair of vertical angles is congruent.

∠5 ≅ ∠6   *m*∠5 = *m*∠6

∠7 ≅ ∠8   *m*∠7 = *m*∠8

Angles can also be described as adjacent or non-adjacent. Adjacent angles have a common vertex and a common ray.

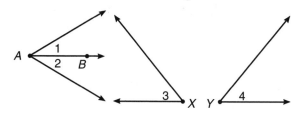

∠1 and ∠2 are adjacent. They share vertex *A* and ray *AB* (also written as $\overrightarrow{AB}$).

∠3 and ∠4 are non-adjacent angles.

Many geometry problems require you to apply logical reasoning to find congruent angles. Use your understanding of the properties of angles to solve geometry problems.

Example   In the figure, angle 1 measures 30°. Find the measures of angles 2, 3, and 4.

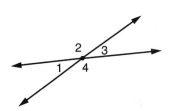

Step 1	**Assign the known values.**	*m*∠1 = 30°
Step 2	**Identify known relationships.**	
	(a) supplementary angles	*m*∠1 + *m*∠2 = 180°
	(b) vertical angles	*m*∠1 = *m*∠3; *m*∠2 = *m*∠4
Step 3	**Solve for unknown values.**	

(a) *m*∠1 + *m*∠2 = 30° + *m*∠2 = 180°; *m*∠2 = 150°

(b) *m*∠3 = 30°; *m*∠4 = 150°

The angle measures are ***m*∠2 = 150°, *m*∠3 = 30°**, and ***m*∠4 = 150°**.

Lines and Angles

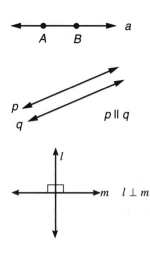

In geometry, arrows are drawn at both ends of a line to show that the line extends indefinitely in both directions. A line can be named by two points on the line. The line shown here is "line AB" ($\overleftrightarrow{AB}$). The line can also be named by a lower-case letter (line a).

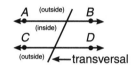

Two lines in the same plane (flat surface) either intersect (cross) or are parallel. Parallel lines never intersect. They have exactly the same slope. The symbol $\parallel$ means "is parallel to."

As you have seen, intersecting lines form vertical angles. When two lines intersect to form right angles, the lines are perpendicular. The symbol for perpendicular lines is $\perp$.

Special pairs of angles are formed when a line, called a transversal, crosses two or more parallel lines. In the figure at left, the transversal intersects line AB and line CD. Notice that some of the angles formed are inside the parallel lines and some are outside.

You already know that vertical angles are equal in measure ($\angle a$ and $\angle d$; $\angle b$ and $\angle c$; $\angle e$ and $\angle h$; $\angle f$ and $\angle g$). The following pairs of angles are also always equal in measure (congruent).

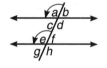

Corresponding angles are in the same position with respect to the transversal. That is, they are on the same side of the transversal and either both above or both below the parallel lines

$\angle a$ and $\angle e$ $\angle b$ and $\angle f$ $\angle c$ and $\angle g$ $\angle d$ and $\angle h$

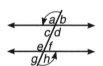

Alternate exterior angles are always outside the parallel lines and on opposite sides of the transversal.

$\angle a$ and $\angle h$ $\angle b$ and $\angle g$

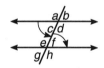

Alternate interior angles are always inside the parallel lines and on opposite sides of the transversal.

$\angle c$ and $\angle f$ $\angle d$ and $\angle e$

If you know the measure of one angle, you can find the measures of the others. There are often several ways to determine the other angles.

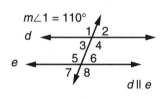

Example   If the measure of $\angle 1$ is 110°, what is the measure of $\angle 6$?

Step 1   **Identify an angle that is related to both the known and unknown angles.**

Angles 1 and 5 are corresponding (congruent) angles. $m\angle 1 = m\angle 5$
Angles 5 and 6 are supplementary angles. $m\angle 5 + m\angle 6 = 180°$

Step 2   **Find the measure of the angle identified in Step 1.**

Since $m\angle 1 = 110°$, and $m\angle 1 = m\angle 5$, $m\angle 5 = 110°$

Step 3   **Find the measure of the unknown angle.**

$m\angle 5 + m\angle 6 = 180°$; $m\angle 5 = 110°$ $m\angle 6 = 180° - 110° = 70°$

The measure of $\angle 6$ is **70°.**

GED Practice

Directions: Choose the <u>one best answer</u> to each question.

Question 1 is based on the following figure.

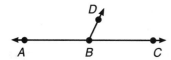

1. Angle *ABC* is a straight angle. Which of the following statements is true?

   (1) $m\angle DBC = 90°$
   (2) $\angle ABD$ and $\angle DBC$ are supplementary.
   (3) $m\angle ABD = 90°$
   (4) $\angle ABD$ and $\angle DBC$ are complementary.
   (5) $m\angle ABC = 90°$

2. Angle 1 is congruent to $\angle 5$. Which of the following pairs of angles is also congruent?

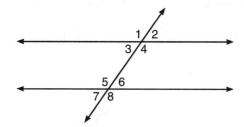

   (1) $\angle 1$ and $\angle 2$
   (2) $\angle 3$ and $\angle 4$
   (3) $\angle 3$ and $\angle 7$
   (4) $\angle 3$ and $\angle 8$
   (5) $\angle 7$ and $\angle 8$

3. One angle is 12° less than its complement. If the measure of the larger angle is *x*, which of the following statements must be true?

   (1) $x + (x - 12°) = 180°$
   (2) $x + (x - 12°) = 90°$
   (3) $x + (12° - x) = 90°$
   (4) $x + (x + 12°) = 180°$
   (5) $x - 90° = x + 12°$

4. The measure of $\angle 7$ is 116°. Which of the following is a true statement?

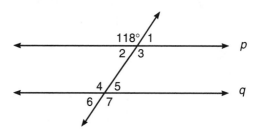

   (1) $\angle 1$ and $\angle 5$ are congruent.
   (2) $\angle 1$ and $\angle 4$ are supplementary.
   (3) $m\angle 1 + m\angle 4 = 180°$
   (4) Lines *p* and *q* are not parallel.
   (5) Lines *p* and *q* are perpendicular.

5. Which conclusion is true?

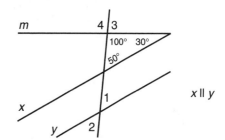

   (1) $m\angle 1 = 50°$
   (2) $m\angle 2 = 80°$
   (3) $m\angle 3 = 50°$
   (4) $m\angle 4 = 80°$
   (5) $m\angle 4 = m\angle 3$

6. What is the measure of $\angle AXB$ if it is four times the measure of its supplement, $\angle BXC$?

   (1) 36°
   (2) 45°
   (3) 72°
   (4) 135°
   (5) 144°

Answers start on page 849.

Triangles and Quadrilaterals

Triangles

A triangle has three sides and three angles and is named by its vertices (in any order). Identify a side of a triangle by the two letters that name the vertices at the ends of the side. In △ABC, the sides are $\overline{AB}$, $\overline{BC}$, and $\overline{AC}$.

A triangle is named by the lengths of its sides and the measures of its angles. The triangles below are named by the lengths of their sides.

Equilateral Triangle
All sides and angles are congruent; each angle measures 60°.

Isosceles Triangle
Two sides and the two angles opposite these sides are congruent.

Scalene Triangle
No sides and no angles are congruent.

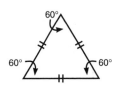
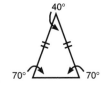

The following triangles are named by the measures of their angles.

Right Triangle
One angle is a right angle (equal to 90°).

Acute Triangle
All three angles are acute (less than 90°).

Obtuse Triangle
One angle is obtuse (greater than 90°).

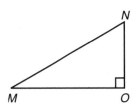
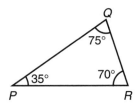
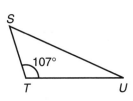

In any triangle, the sum of the measures of the angles is 180°. (Note: A triangle can have only one right or obtuse angle. The other two angles must be acute.)

Example In a right triangle, one acute angle is twice the measure of the other acute angle. What is the measure of the larger angle?

Step 1 **Make a sketch.** A right triangle has one right angle ($m = 90°$).

Step 2 **Assign the unknowns.**

Let x = the measure of the smaller acute angle.
Let $2x$ = the measure of the larger acute angle.

Step 3 **Write an equation.** $\qquad x + 2x + 90° = 180°$
Step 4 **Solve.** $\qquad\qquad\qquad\qquad 3x + 90° = 180°$
$$3x = 90°; \text{ so } x = 30° \text{ and } 2x = 60°$$

The larger acute angle measures **60°**.

> **Tip**
>
> The symbols |, ||, and ||| marked on a side show which sides are congruent. Remember: Congruent means equal.

Quadrilaterals

A quadrilateral is any polygon with four (*quad*) sides (*lateral*). A figure with four sides also has four angles, and the sum of these four angle measures always equals 360°.

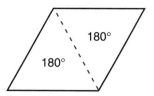

To prove this relationship, draw any quadrilateral and draw a line segment called a diagonal between the vertices of two opposite angles. The diagonal divides the quadrilateral into two triangles. You know that the sum of the three angles in a triangle is 180°. Since there are two triangles, the sum of the angles in the quadrilateral must be 180° + 180° = 360°.

The following quadrilaterals may appear on the GED Mathematics Test.

Parallelogram
Opposite sides are parallel and congruent; opposite angles are of equal measure.

Rectangle
A special parallelogram that has four right angles.

Rhombus
A special parallelogram that has four sides of equal length.

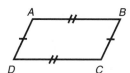

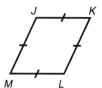

Square
A special parallelogram/rhombus/rectangle that has four sides of equal length and four right angles.

Trapezoid
A figure with only one pair of parallel sides (called bases).

Tip

Write algebraic expressions on the drawing to remember what the variables represent.

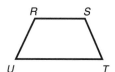

On the GED Mathematics Test, you must combine your knowledge of algebra and geometric principles to solve problems.

Example   Angle B of the rhombus shown at the left measures **40°**. What is the measure of $\angle C$?

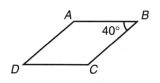

Step 1	**Identify known values.**	$m\angle B = 40°$
Step 2	**Identify known relationships.**	sum of angles = 360°
	Opposite angles are equal.	$m\angle D = 40°$; $m\angle C = m\angle A$
Step 3	**Assign the unknown values.**	Let $x = m\angle C$ (and $m\angle A$)
Step 4	**Write an equation.**	$m\angle A + m\angle B + m\angle C + m\angle D = 360°$
Step 5	**Substitute known values.**	$x + 40° + x + 40° = 360°$
		$2(40°) + 2x = 360°$
Step 6	**Solve for unknown values.**	$80° + 2x = 360°$
		$2x = 280°$; $x = 140°$

The measure of $\angle C$ is **140°**.

Congruent Figures

Congruent figures are the same shape and size. One way to find out whether two figures are congruent is to place one figure on top of the other to see whether the sides and angles align perfectly. You may even be able to tell whether figures are congruent simply by looking at them. However, on the GED Mathematics Test, you need to be able to do more than identify which figures "look" congruent; you must be able to prove that the two figures are congruent.

Let's look at triangles. Congruent triangles are exactly the same shape and size. They have matching or corresponding vertices, sides, and angles. Marks are used to show which parts correspond.

There are three rules used to prove that two triangles are congruent. Two triangles are congruent if any one of the following rules is true:

RULE 1 Three sides (SSS) are congruent.

RULE 2 Two sides and the angle between them (SAS) are congruent.

RULE 3 Two angles and the side between them (ASA) are congruent.

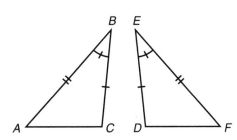

Example 1   Are triangles *ABC* and *FED* congruent?

Step 1   **Identify the given corresponding congruent parts.** $\overline{AB} \cong \overline{FE}, \overline{BC} \cong \overline{ED}$
$\angle B \cong \angle E$

Step 2   **Identify what relationships are known.**
There are two pairs of corresponding congruent sides. The angles between the congruent sides are also congruent. (SAS)

Step 3   **Identify additional information needed.**
None.

Step 4   **Draw a conclusion.**   Rule 2 is true; the triangles are congruent.

The triangles are congruent. **△ABC ≅ △FED**

Similar Figures

Two figures are similar (~) if their corresponding angles have equal measure and the corresponding sides are in proportion. Similar figures have the same shape, but they are *not necessarily* the same size.

If the measures of two angles of one triangle are equal to two angle measures in another triangle, the measures of the third angles will also be equal (AAA) and the triangles are similar.

Example 1   Is △ABC similar to △DEF?

In △ABC, $m\angle A = 60°$. In △DEF, $m\angle D = 60°$.
In △ABC, $m\angle C = 70°$. In △DEF, $m\angle F = 70°$.

Since the measures of two angles of △ABC are equal to two angle measures in △DEF, the triangles are similar. **△ABC ~ △DEF**

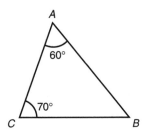
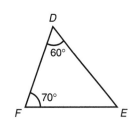

Mathematics • Geometry

Similar triangles are often used to solve problems when it is not possible to find a distance by measuring.

Example 2   At 4 p.m., a flagpole casts a 20-m shadow. At the same time, a person 2 m tall casts a 4-m shadow. What is the height of the flagpole?

The sun strikes the person and flagpole at the same angle (since measurements are taken at the same place and same time). So, the objects and shadows form similar triangles.

Set up a proportion. $\dfrac{\text{person's height}}{\text{flagpole's height}}$ $\dfrac{2}{x} = \dfrac{4}{20}$ $\dfrac{\text{person's shadow}}{\text{flagpole's shadow}}$

Solve.
$$4x = 2(20)$$
$$x = 40 \div 4$$
$$x = 10$$

The height of the flagpole is **10 m.**

Using Proportion in Geometry

Many measurement and geometry problems involve indirect measurement. Instead of making actual measurements, use proportions and knowledge of corresponding parts to find the answer. Finding a missing measurement when working with similar triangles is an example of indirect measurement. A scale drawing is another measurement situation that can be solved using indirect measurement.

A scale drawing is a sketch of an object with all distances proportional to corresponding distances on the actual object. The scale gives the ratio of the sketch measurements to the actual measurements. A map is an example of a scale drawing.

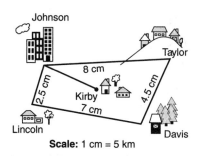

Scale: 1 cm = 5 km

Example 1   The distance on the map between Taylor and Davis is 4.5 cm. What is the actual distance between the two towns?

Step 1   **Read the map scale.** According to the scale 1 cm on the map equals 5 km of actual distance.

Step 2   **Write a proportion.** $\dfrac{\text{map distance}}{\text{actual distance}}$ $\dfrac{1 \text{ cm}}{5 \text{ km}} = \dfrac{4.5 \text{ cm}}{x \text{ km}}$

Step 3   **Solve.** $x = 5(4.5) = 22.5 \text{ km}$

The actual distance is **22.5 kilometers.**

 Tip   With real-life situations, use experience to decide whether your answers make sense.

GED Practice

Directions: Choose the <u>one best answer</u> to each question.

Questions 1 and 2 refer to the following drawing.

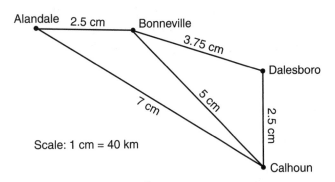

Scale: 1 cm = 40 km

1. The map distances between cities are shown on the map. What is the actual distance in kilometres between Bonneville and Dalesboro?

    (1) 120
    (2) 150
    (3) 160
    (4) 180
    (5) 200

2. Susan drove from Calhoun to Alandale, then from Alandale to Bonneville, and back to Calhoun. How many kilometres did she drive?

    (1) 460
    (2) 480
    (3) 540
    (4) 580
    (5) 620

3. Hillsboro is 50 km from Merville. On a map these towns are 2.5 cm apart. What is the scale of this map?

    (1) 1 cm = $\frac{1}{5}$ km
    (2) 1 cm = 2 km
    (3) 1 cm = 2.5 km
    (4) 1 cm = 20 km
    (5) 1 cm = 25 km

4. A portion of a metal sculpture includes an isosceles triangle. The equal sides measure 15 cm each. What is the perimeter of the triangle, in centimetres, if all angles are acute angles?

    (1) 15
    (2) 30
    (3) 45
    (4) 60
    (5) Not enough information is given.

Questions 5 and 6 refer to the following figure.

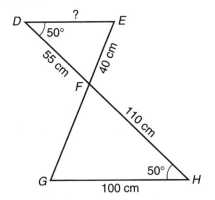

5. If triangles *DEF* and *FGH* are similar, which of the following are corresponding sides?

    (1) sides *DF* and *FG*
    (2) sides *EF* and *FH*
    (3) sides *DE* and *DF*
    (4) sides *DF* and *GH*
    (5) sides *DF* and *FH*

6. What is the length in centimetres of side *DE* in the figure?

    (1) 20
    (2) 33
    (3) 40
    (4) 50
    (5) 55

Answers start on page 849.

Mathematics • Geometry

Irregular Figures
Area and Volume

A figure may be made up of several shapes. To find the area or volume of a combined figure, find the area or volume of each part and add the results.

Example 1   Marcus is making a raised flower bed. He needs to know the area of the flower bed in order to know how much soil he will need. What is the area of the flower bed to the nearest square metre?

Step 1   **Divide the figure into simple shapes.** Think of each end as a half-circle attached to a rectangle.

Step 2   **Find the area of each part.** The two half-circles can be combined to make one whole circle.

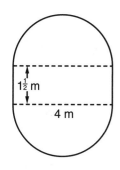

Find the area of the circle. $A = \pi \times radius^2 = \pi r^2$

Remember: $r = \dfrac{d}{2}$.

$$r = 4 \div 2 = 2$$
$$A = \pi r^2$$
$$= 3.14(2^2)$$
$$= 3.14(4) = 12.56 \text{ square metres}$$

Find the area of the rectangle. $A = lw$
$$= 4\left(1\tfrac{1}{2}\right) = 6 \text{ square metres}$$

Step 3   **Add the areas.**

$$12.56 + 6 = 18.56,$$
which rounds to 19 square metres

The area of the flower bed is about **19 square metres.**

Irregular figures can also be made up of common solid shapes.

Example 2   Find the volume of the object shown at left.

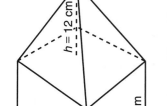

Step 1   **Divide the figure into simple figures.** This figure is made up of a pyramid and a rectangular solid.

Step 2   **Find the volume of each part.**
Find the volume of the pyramid. $V = \tfrac{1}{3} \times A \times h$
Since the base is a square, $A = s^2$, where s = base edge.

$$V = \tfrac{1}{3} \times (\text{base edge})^2 \times \text{height}$$
$$= \tfrac{1}{3}(11^2)(12) = \tfrac{1}{3}(121)(12)$$
$$= 484 \text{ cubic centimetres}$$

Find the volume of the rectangular solid. $V = l \times w \times h$
$$= 11 \times 11 \times 10 = 1210 \text{ cubic centimetres}$$

Step 3   **Add to find the total volume.**
$$484 + 1210 = 1694 \text{ cubic centimetres}$$

The volume of the object is **1694 cubic centimetres.**

Approaching Multi-Step Problems

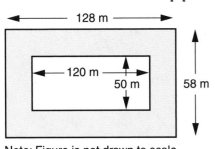

128 m

120 m

50 m

58 m

Note: Figure is not drawn to scale.

Some problems involving irregular figures test your ability to use logical reasoning to find the solution. In these problems, you need to figure out how to use the information you have been given to find the area or volume of an unusual shape.

Example An apartment complex has a central recreation area as shown in the diagram. The tenants vote to pave a 4-metre walkway around the lawn. What is the area of the walkway?

Addition method:

Sections 2 & 4:
$A = lw = 128(4) = 512$

Sections 1 & 3:
$A = lw = 50(4) = 200$

Sections $1 + 2 + 3 + 4 =$
$200 + 512 + 200 + 512 =$
1424 m^2

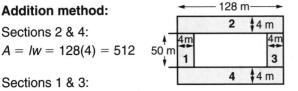

128 m

2   4 m

4m   4m

50 m

1   3

4   4 m

Addition Method: One way to solve the problem is to divide the walkway into four rectangles, find the area of each rectangle, and add to find the total area.

Subtraction Method: The total area equals the area of the walkway plus the area of the lawn. Find the total area and then subtract the area of the lawn. The difference is equal to the area of the walkway.

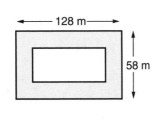

128 m

58 m

120 m

50 m

Step 1 Find the area of the larger (outer) rectangle. The outer rectangle measures 128 by 58 m.

$A = lw$
$= 128(58)$
$= 7424 \text{ m}^2$

Step 2 Find the area of the smaller rectangle. The smaller rectangle measures 120 by 50 m.

$A = lw$
$= 120(50)$
$= 6000 \text{ m}^2$

Step 3 Find the difference.

$7424 - 6000 = 1424 \text{ m}^2$

Another method involves the use of the memory keys on your calculator. Use this key sequence on the GED calculator.

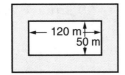

AC SHIFT MR	To clear the memory.
128 × 58 = 7424. M+	M+ means "add to memory."
120 × 50 = 6000. SHIFT M+	SHIFT M+ = M− means "subtract from memory."
MR 1424.	MR means "memory recall."

The area of the walkway is **1424 m²**.

GED Practice

Directions: Choose the one best answer to each question.

Question 1 refers to the following figure.

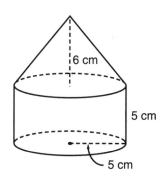

1. What is the volume to the nearest cubic centimetre of the object shown above?

   (1) 79
   (2) 157
   (3) 393
   (4) 471
   (5) 550

Question 2 refers to the following figure.

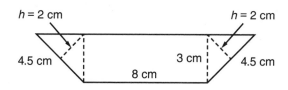

2. What is the area in square centimetres of the figure shown?

   (1) 27
   (2) 28.5
   (3) 33
   (4) 37.5
   (5) 42

Question 3 refers to the following figure.

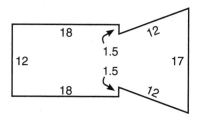

3. What is the perimeter of the figure?

   (1) 72
   (2) 75
   (3) 90
   (4) 92
   (5) 101

Question 4 refers to the following figure.

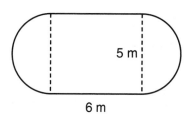

4. A flower bed has the measurements shown in the figure. If the ends of the flower bed are half-circles, what is the approximate area of the flower bed in square metres?

   (1) 110
   (2) 80
   (3) 50
   (4) 40
   (5) 25

Answers start on page 850.

Working with Right Triangles

The Pythagorean Relationship

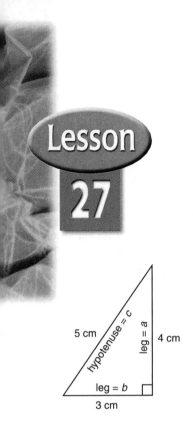

The ancient Egyptians discovered a special property of triangles whose sides measure 3, 4, and 5 units. They learned that the angle opposite the longest side is <u>always</u> a right angle. The ancient Greeks learned why this relationship exists and named it the Pythagorean Relationship after the Greek mathematician Pythagoras.

The Pythagorean Relationship explains the special relationship between the legs (the two shorter sides) and the hypotenuse (the longest side) of a right triangle. It states that in a right triangle, the sum of the squares of the lengths of the legs is equal to the square of the length of the hypotenuse. Note that a 3-4-5 triangle is always a right triangle, but a right triangle is not always a 3-4-5 triangle.

Pythagorean Relationship $\quad a^2 + b^2 = c^2$, where a and b are the legs and c is the hypotenuse of a right triangle

You can use the Pythagorean Relationship to find a missing length of a right triangle.

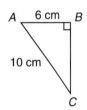

Example 1 What is the length of side BC of the triangle shown to the left?

Step 1 **Identify the legs and the hypotenuse.** Sides AB and BC are the legs. Side AC is the hypotenuse. The hypotenuse is always opposite the right angle.

Step 2 **Assign a variable.** Let b represent the measure of side BC, a leg, the missing measure.

Step 3 **Use the Pythagorean Relationship.**

$$a^2 + b^2 = c^2$$
$$6^2 + b^2 = 10^2$$
$$36 + b^2 = 100$$
$$b^2 = 64$$
$$b = \sqrt{64}$$
$$b = 8$$

Tip

Watch for 3-4-5 right triangles in problems on the GED Math Test. Multiples are also commonly used: 6-8-10, 9-12-15, and 1.5-2-2.5.

To find the length of a side b using a calculator, rewrite the Pythagorean Relationship as $c^2 - a^2 = b^2$. Then input as follows:

10 $\boxed{x^2}$ $\boxed{-}$ 6 $\boxed{x^2}$ $\boxed{=}$ $\boxed{\text{SHIFT}}$ $\boxed{x^2}$ 8.

The length of the missing side is **8 cm.**

Given the lengths of the sides of a triangle, you can use the Pythagorean Relationship to determine whether the triangle is a right triangle.

Mathematics • Geometry

GED Practice

Directions: Choose the <u>one best answer</u> to each question.

Question 1 refers to the following diagram.

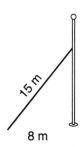

8 m

1. A support wire 15 m long is attached to the ground 8 m from the base of a pole. The pole and the ground form a right angle. How high up the pole will the other end of the wire reach (to the nearest metre)?

   (1)   12
   (2)   13
   (3)   17
   (4)   23
   (5)   161

Question 2 refers to the following diagram.

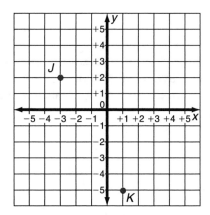

2. What is the distance between points *J* and *K* to the nearest tenth unit?

   (1)   6.5
   (2)   7.7
   (3)   8.1
   (4)   8.6
   (5)   11.0

Question 3 refers to the following diagram.

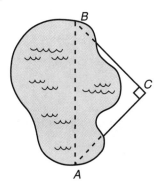

3. Dushan wants to find the width of the pond. He places stakes at *A* and *B* and then finds *C* so that *C* is a right angle. This makes △*ABC* a right triangle. If $\overline{AC}$ = 60 m and $\overline{BC}$ = 80 m, about how far is it from *A* to *B*?

   (1)   less than 85 m
   (2)   from 85 to 95 m
   (3)   from 95 to 105 m
   (4)   from 105 to 115 m
   (5)   more than 115 m

Question 4 refers to the following diagram.

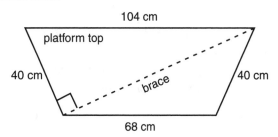

4. Jan builds a platform with a top in the shape of a trapezoid. The plans call for a diagonal brace to be added. What is the length of the brace to the nearest centimetre?

   (1)   64
   (2)   88
   (3)   96
   (4)   111
   (5)   Not enough information is given.

5. On a map with a scale of 1.5 cm = 60 km, 4.7 cm on the map represents how many actual kilometres?

    (1)   40

    (2) 117

    (3) 188

    (4) 282

    (5) 423

Question 6 refers to the following diagram.

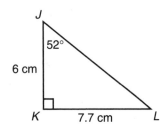

6. If △JKL is a right triangle, what is the measure of ∠L?

    (1)   26°

    (2)   38°

    (3)   52°

    (4)   90°

    (5) 128°

7. A 3-m post casts a $4\frac{1}{2}$-m shadow at the same time that a telephone pole casts a shadow of 33 m. What is the length in metres of the telephone pole?

    (1) 18

    (2) 22

    (3) 28

    (4) 33

    (5) 99

8. Which of the following is a right triangle?

    (1) a triangle with sides of 4, 5, and 6

    (2) a triangle with sides of 5, 7, and 9

    (3) a triangle with sides of 6, 8, and 11

    (4) a triangle with sides of 7, 9, and 12

    (5) a triangle with sides of 7, 24, and 25

9. To the nearest metre, how long will the ladder need to be to reach a third floor window?

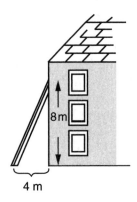

    (1) 6

    (2) 7

    (3) 8

    (4) 9

    (5) 11

10. A circular pool, 20 m in diameter, has a 2-m wide gravel walk around it. What is the approximate area of the walk in square metres?

    (1) 100

    (2) 138

    (3) 144

    (4) 314

    (5) 452

Answers start on page 850.

Part 1

Directions: Choose the <u>one best answer</u> to each question. You <u>may</u> use your calculator.

<u>Questions 1 through 3</u> refer to the figure.

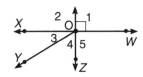

1. Which of the following angles is supplementary, but not adjacent, to ∠2?

   (1) ∠1
   (2) ∠3
   (3) ∠4
   (4) ∠5
   (5) Not enough information is given.

2. The measure of ∠3 is 25°. What is the measure of ∠WOY?

   (1) 65°
   (2) 115°
   (3) 135°
   (4) 155°
   (5) 165°

3. If an angle is supplementary to ∠XOZ, the angle must also be which of the following?

   (1) an acute angle
   (2) a right angle
   (3) an obtuse angle
   (4) a vertical angle
   (5) congruent to ∠3

4. A circular pool has a circumference of about 40 m. Which of the following expressions could be used to find the diameter of the pool in metres?

   (1) 40π
   (2) $\frac{40}{\pi}$
   (3) $\frac{\pi}{40}$
   (4) $\frac{2(40)}{\pi}$
   (5) $\frac{\pi}{2(40)}$

5. One side of the square base of a box measures 4 cm. If the box can be filled to a height of 4 cm, how many cubic centimetres of liquid can the box hold?

   (1) 12
   (2) 16
   (3) 20
   (4) 32
   (5) 64

6. A rectangular frame is $2\frac{1}{2}$ m by 50 cm. What is the frame's perimeter in <u>metres</u>?

   (1) 10
   (2) $8\frac{1}{2}$
   (3) $5\frac{1}{2}$
   (4) 6
   (5) 100

Question 7 refers to the following diagram.

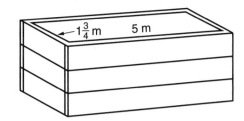

7. Mike plans to build a wooden flower box similar to the one shown in the diagram. He wants the box to have a volume of $17\frac{1}{2}$ cubic metres. If the base of the box has the dimensions shown above, what should the height of the box measure in metres?

(1) 2

(2) $2\frac{1}{2}$

(3) $3\frac{1}{2}$

(4) 10

(5) Not enough information is given.

Solve Questions 8 and 9 and enter your answers on the grids provided.

8. A parallelogram has a base of 32 cm and a height of 8 cm. How many centimetres is the side of a square with the same area as the parallelogram?

Question 9 refers to the following graph.

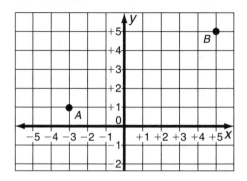

9. To the nearest whole unit, what is the distance between points A and B?

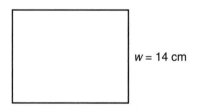

Question 10 refers to the following figure.

$w = 14$ cm

10. The perimeter of the rectangle is 64 cm. Which of the following expressions could be used to find the length of the rectangle?

(1) $\frac{64}{14}$

(2) $\frac{64}{2(14)}$

(3) $64 - 14$

(4) $\frac{64 - 2(14)}{2}$

(5) $\frac{64 + 2(14)}{2}$

Part 2

Directions: Choose the <u>one best answer</u> to each question. You may <u>not</u> use your calculator.

Questions 11 and 12 refer to the following figure.

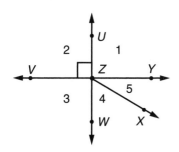

11. Line *UW* intersects line *VY* at point *Z*. The measure of ∠4 is 60°. What is the measure of ∠*UZX*?

    (1) 30°
    (2) 100°
    (3) 120°
    (4) 150°
    (5) 180°

12. If *m*∠4 = 60°, what is the measure of ∠5?

    (1) 30°
    (2) 100°
    (3) 120°
    (4) 150°
    (5) 180°

13. Susan has a ring box with the following measurements: length = 10 cm, width = 3 cm, and height = 4 cm. What is the volume of the ring box in cubic centimetres?

    (1) 60
    (2) 80
    (3) 100
    (4) 120
    (5) 160

Questions 14 through 16 refer to the following figure.

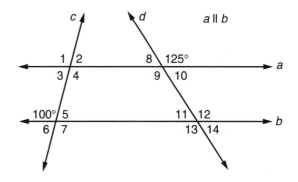

14. Which of the following statements is true?

    (1) ∠3 is complementary to ∠4.
    (2) ∠12 is supplementary to ∠13.
    (3) ∠4 and ∠10 are congruent angles.
    (4) ∠1 is a right angle.
    (5) ∠5 is supplementary to ∠1.

15. Which of these groups contains only angles that are congruent to ∠4?

    (1) ∠1, ∠2, and ∠3
    (2) ∠1 and ∠7
    (3) ∠1, ∠8, and ∠10
    (4) ∠2 and ∠7
    (5) ∠7, ∠10, and ∠14

16. What is the measure of ∠12?

    (1)   55°
    (2)   65°
    (3)   80°
    (4) 100°
    (5) 125°

Do not consider lines parallel or perpendicular unless the problem gives the information in either words or symbols.

17. A four-sided figure has sides, in order, of 6, 10, 6, and 10. There are no right angles. What is the figure?

    (1) triangle
    (2) square
    (3) trapezoid
    (4) rhombus
    (5) parallelogram

Question 18 refers to the following figure.

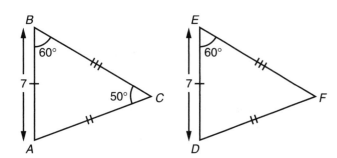

18. The two triangles are congruent. What is the measure of ∠D?

    (1) 50°
    (2) 70°
    (3) 110°
    (4) 180°
    (5) Not enough information is given.

19. The three sides of triangle ABC measure 12 cm, 16 cm, and 20 cm. Triangle DEF is similar to △ABC. The shortest side of △DEF measures 15 cm. What are the lengths in centimetres of the other two sides of △DEF?

    (1) 18 and 23
    (2) 18 and 25
    (3) 19 and 23
    (4) 20 and 24
    (5) 20 and 25

20. What is the measure of ∠L?

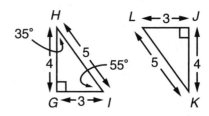

    (1) 35°
    (2) 45°
    (3) 55°
    (4) 90°
    (5) Not enough information is given.

21. Sides AB and BC of △ABC each measure 10 cm. If $m\angle A = 60°$ and $m\angle B = 60°$, what is the length in centimetres of side AC?

    (1) 5
    (2) 6
    (3) 10
    (4) 14
    (5) Not enough information is given.

22. To prove that △ACE ≅ △BCD by SSS, it is necessary to know which of the following?

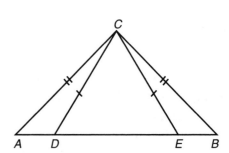

    (1) $\overline{AD} \cong \overline{BC}$
    (2) $\overline{AE} \cong \overline{BD}$
    (3) ∠DAC ≅ ∠EBC
    (4) ∠CDE ≅ ∠CED
    (5) $\overline{DE} \cong \overline{EB}$

Answers start on page 851.

Mathematics • Geometry

Part 1

Directions: Choose the one best answer to each question. You may use your calculator.

1. Ralph is building a bookcase and uses 4 boards, each 350 cm in length. What is the total length of the boards?

   (1)   700 cm
   (2)   354 cm
   (3) 1400 cm
   (4) 1000 cm
   (5)   850 cm

2. The three sides of a triangle measure 16.52 cm, 17.24 cm, and 22.19 cm. What is the perimeter of the triangle, in centimetres?

   (1) 53.95
   (2) 54.45
   (3) 54.95
   (4) 55.45
   (5) 55.95

Question 3 refers to the figure below.

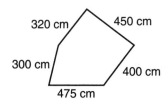

3. Anthony has an odd-shaped plot of grass that he would like to border with a hedge. How many metres long is the border of the plot, rounded to the nearest metre?

   (1) 18
   (2) 19
   (3) 15
   (4) 14
   (5) 20

4. What is the volume, in cubic metres, of a cube that measures 3.5 m on one side?

   (1) 12.250
   (2) 22.875
   (3) 32.875
   (4) 42.250
   (5) 42.875

5. A swimming pool having the shape of a rectangular solid has a length of 30 m, a width of 10 m, and a depth of 3 m. If the pool is $\frac{3}{4}$ full with water, how many cubic metres of water are in the pool?

   (1) 1 000
   (2)   800
   (3)   675
   (4)   430
   (5)   780

Question 6 refers to the rectangle below.

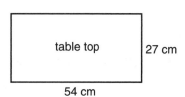

6. Anna wants to protect the top of her coffee table with a piece of glass. How many square centimetres of glass would she need to cover the top of her coffee table?

   (1)   81
   (2)   100
   (3)   162
   (4)   200
   (5) 1 458

Action Athletics	
Department	**Net Sales**
Footwear	$20 897
Outerwear	$57 941
Sporting Goods	$31 009
Exercise Equipment	$28 987
Skiing Equipment	$18 883

7. What were the total net sales for the five departments listed?

(1) $137 717

(2) $147 707

(3) $147 717

(4) $157 717

(5) Not enough information is given.

8. Combined net sales for Footwear and Sporting Goods were how much less than the net sales for Outerwear?

(1) $ 6 000

(2) $ 6 035

(3) $20 897

(4) $68 053

(5) Not enough information is given.

9. What was the difference in net sales between the department with the largest net sales and the department with the smallest net sales?

(1) $76 828

(2) $57 941

(3) $39 058

(4) $37 644

(5) $28 954

10. A car travels 406 km at an average speed of 58 km per hour. How many hours does it take the car to travel this distance?

(1) 4

(2) 5

(3) 6

(4) 7

(5) 8

11. Brittany bought 5 plastic storage bins to help her organize her closets. After adding sales tax of $2.06, the total cost of the bins was $31.51. Which of the following equations could be used to find the price of one bin (x)?

(1) $5 + x = \$31.51 - \$2.06$

(2) $5(x + \$2.06) = \$31.51$

(3) $5x = \$31.51$

(4) $5x - \$2.06 = \$31.51$

(5) $5x + \$2.06 = \$31.51$

12. The expression $-5(x - 6) - 2(x + 8)$ is equal to which of the following expressions?

(1) $7x + 14$

(2) $7x + 2$

(3) $-7x - 5$

(4) $-7x + 14$

(5) $-7x + 46$

13. In a certain game, points you win are positive numbers and points you lose are negative numbers. What is the value of this series of plays: win 8, lose 6, lose 7, win 11, lose 2?

(1) -15

(2) -4

(3) 4

(4) 12

(5) 19

Questions 14 through 16 refer to the following graph.

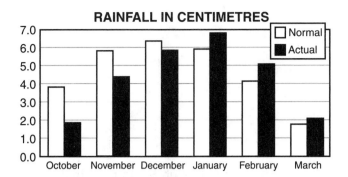

RAINFALL IN CENTIMETRES

14. For which months was the actual rainfall less than normal?

    (1) October, November, and December

    (2) October, November, and January

    (3) October, December, and March

    (4) October, February, and March

    (5) January, February, and March

15. For how many months was the actual rainfall greater than 5.0 cm?

    (1) 2

    (2) 3

    (3) 4

    (4) 5

    (5) 6

16. How many more centimetres of rain fell in January than in March?

    (1) 2.2

    (2) 3.5

    (3) 4.0

    (4) 4.6

    (5) 5.8

Question 17 refers to the following diagram.

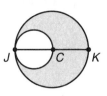

17. Two circles intersect at point J. If C is the centre of the larger circle, and the diameter of the larger circle is 28 cm, what is the radius of the smaller circle in centimetres?

    (1) 1.75

    (2) 3.5

    (3) 7

    (4) 14

    (5) Not enough information is given.

18. What is the volume in <u>cubic metres</u> of a rectangular crate that is $3\frac{1}{2}$ m by $1\frac{3}{4}$ m by 2 m?

    (1) $6\frac{1}{2}$

    (2) $7\frac{1}{4}$

    (3) $12\frac{1}{4}$

    (4) $13\frac{1}{3}$

    (5) 147

Question 19 refers to the following figure.

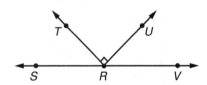

19. If $m\angle URV = 53°$, what is the measure of $\angle TRS$?

    (1) 37°

    (2) 53°

    (3) 106°

    (4) 127°

    (5) 143°

Solve Questions 20 and 21 and enter your answers on the grids provided.

20. Show the location of the *x*-intercept for the line $-2x + 3y = 6$.

21. Grid in the value of the following expression:
$\sqrt{81} + 2^4 - \sqrt{169} + 5^2$

22. In the equation $-2(x + 4) = 5x + 6$, what is the value of *x*?

(1) -2

(2) $-\dfrac{1}{2}$

(3) 1

(4) $\dfrac{1}{2}$

(5) 2

23. Sybil is taking her Cub Scout pack to the zoo. Each adult ticket is $2 more than the price of a children's ticket. Sybil pays $78 to buy 12 children's tickets and 5 adult tickets. What is the price of a children's ticket?

(1) $3.00

(2) $3.50

(3) $4.00

(4) $5.00

(5) $6.00

Question 24 refers to the following number line.

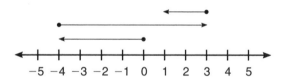

24. Which of the following expressions represents the changes shown on the number line?

(1) $-4 + 3 + (-1)$

(2) $-4 + 7 + (-2)$

(3) $-4 + 7 - (-2)$

(4) $4 + (-7) + 2$

(5) $4 - (-7) - 2$

Mathematics • Unit Review

25. A wooden rectangular frame is 6 units by 8 units. A diagonal brace will be added to the back of the frame. What is the length in units of the brace?

(1) 5

(2) 7

(3) 8

(4) 10

(5) 13

26. A circle has a radius of 7 cm. Which of the following is the best estimate of the circumference of the circle in centimetres?

(1) 15

(2) 25

(3) 40

(4) 50

(5) 150

27. Triangle *ABC* has sides measuring 2.9, 4.6, and 4.9 cm. Its angle measures are 78°, 36°, and 66°. Triangle *ABC* can be classified as which of the following two kinds of triangles?

(1) equilateral and acute

(2) isosceles and acute

(3) isosceles and obtuse

(4) scalene and acute

(5) scalene and obtuse

28. In a right triangle, the measure of one acute angle is five times larger than the measure of the other acute angle. Which of the following equations can be used to find the measure of the smaller angle?

(1) $x + 5x + 90° = 180°$

(2) $x + (5 + x) + 90° = 180°$

(3) $x + 5x = 180°$

(4) $90x + 5x = 180°$

(5) $180° - 90° = 5x$

Question 29 refers to the following figures.

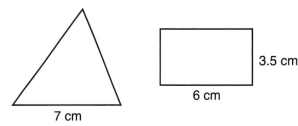

7 cm

6 cm

3.5 cm

29. A rectangle and triangle have the same area. What is the height of the triangle in centimetres?

(1) 3

(2) 3.5

(3) 6

(4) 12

(5) 21

Question 30 refers to the following figure.

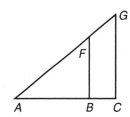

30. If $\triangle ABF \sim \triangle ACG$, then which of the following is a true proportion?

(1) $\dfrac{\overline{AF}}{\overline{AB}} = \dfrac{\overline{AB}}{\overline{AC}}$

(2) $\dfrac{\overline{AB}}{\overline{AC}} = \dfrac{\overline{FB}}{\overline{GC}}$

(3) $\dfrac{\overline{AF}}{\overline{AC}} = \dfrac{\overline{AC}}{\overline{AB}}$

(4) $\dfrac{\overline{AB}}{\overline{GC}} = \dfrac{\overline{AC}}{\overline{FB}}$

(5) $\dfrac{\overline{AG}}{\overline{AC}} = \dfrac{\overline{AB}}{\overline{AF}}$

Part 2

Directions: Choose the <u>one best answer</u> to each question. You <u>may not</u> use a calculator.

31. Which of the following represents
    two hundred three thousand, forty-nine?

    (1)   2 349
    (2) 203 049
    (3) 203 490
    (4) 230 049
    (5) 230 490

32. Which of the following is the value of 39 462
    rounded to the nearest thousand?

    (1) 39 000
    (2) 39 400
    (3) 39 460
    (4) 39 500
    (5) 40 000

33. Tarik pays $387 a month on a school loan.
    Which of the following operations represents
    how much he pays in 12 months?

    (1) 12 + $387
    (2) $387 − 12
    (3) $387 × 12
    (4) $387 ÷ 12
    (5) 12 ÷ $387

34. Three friends rent an apartment for a total
    of $972 per month. If they share the rent
    equally, which of the following operations
    represents the amount each one pays
    per month?

    (1) 3 + $972
    (2) $972 − 3
    (3) $972 × 3
    (4) $972 ÷ 3
    (5) 3 ÷ $972

35. Empire Clothing Company presented a
    training seminar to 35 employees. If the
    company paid $12 per person for lunch,
    how much did the company pay to feed
    the employees?

    (1) $700
    (2) $420
    (3) $350
    (4) $336
    (5) $ 70

36. Cynthia works 4 hours each day, 6 days a
    week. How many hours does she work in
    3 weeks?

    (1) 12
    (2) 18
    (3) 24
    (4) 48
    (5) 72

37. Alfredo has $1200 in his bank account.
    If he takes out $140, what is the balance left
    in his account?

    (1) $1340
    (2) $1160
    (3) $1140
    (4) $1060
    (5) $ 200

38. A computer system costs $1050. If Roberto
    has $985 saved, how much more does he
    need to purchase the system?

    (1) $ 65
    (2) $ 75
    (3) $ 165
    (4) $ 985
    (5) $1050

Mathematics • Unit Review

Directions: Solve the following questions and enter your answers on the grids provided.

Question 39 refers to the following figure.

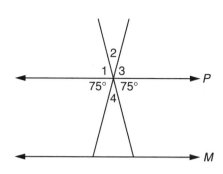

39. Lines *P* and *M* are parallel, and ∠2 and ∠4 are vertical angles. What is the measure of ∠4 in degrees?

40. The height of a triangle is 40 cm. If the area of the triangle is 200 cm², what is the length of the base in centimetres?

Question 41 refers to the following figure.

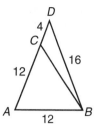

41. The measure of ∠*DAB* is 70°. What is the measure of ∠*D* in degrees?

42. A sign 4 m tall casts a shadow 5 m long. At the same time, a tree casts a shadow 30 m long. What is the height of the tree in metres?

43. The points graphed on the grid below satisfy which of the following equations?

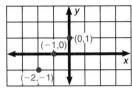

(1) $x - y = 1$

(2) $x - y = -1$

(3) $2y - x = 0$

(4) $x = 0$

(5) $y = 0$

44. Which ordered pair is a solution of $x - y = 1$?

(1) $(-3, -4)$

(2) $(-3, -2)$

(3) $(-1, 0)$

(4) $(0, 1)$

(5) $(1, -2)$

45. What is the missing x-value if $(?, 1)$ is a solution of $-4x + 7y = 15$?

(1) $\dfrac{-11}{2}$

(2) -2

(3) 2

(4) $\dfrac{19}{7}$

(5) $\dfrac{11}{2}$

46. Sarah jogs at an average rate of $\dfrac{2}{15}$ laps per minute. At this rate, how many laps will she jog in 30 minutes?

(1) 2

(2) 4

(3) $4\dfrac{1}{2}$

(4) $7\dfrac{1}{2}$

(5) 15

47. A scale on a map shows that $\dfrac{3}{4}$ cm on the map equals an actual distance of 5 km. If the actual distance between two cities is 45 km, how many centimetres apart are they on the map?

(1) $6\dfrac{3}{4}$

(2) 9

(3) $9\dfrac{3}{4}$

(4) 12

(5) $12\dfrac{3}{4}$

Questions 48 and 49 refer to the following table.

Monthly Budget	
Expense	**Fraction Budgeted**
Rent	$\dfrac{3}{8}$
Salaries	$\dfrac{1}{4}$
Advertising	$\dfrac{1}{5}$
Supplies	$\dfrac{1}{8}$
Miscellaneous	$\dfrac{1}{20}$

48. Which of the expenses received the highest amount of the monthly budget?

(1) Rent

(2) Salaries

(3) Advertising

(4) Supplies

(5) Miscellaneous

49. If the total amount of the budget for March was $16 000, how much was budgeted for Salaries and Supplies combined?

(1) $ 2 000

(2) $ 4 000

(3) $ 6 000

(4) $ 8 000

(5) $10 000

Questions 50 through 52 refer to the following graph.

NUMBER OF NEW SUBSCRIBERS TO THE *DAILY GAZETTE*
(in thousands)

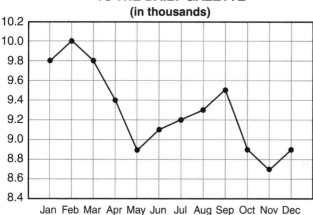

Questions 53 through 55 refer to the following graph.

D & T DEPARTMENT STORE
(Daily net sales in thousands of dollars)

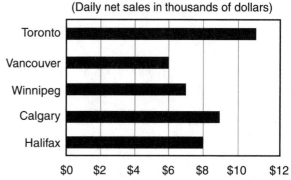

50. What is the range of new subscribers per month, from lowest to highest?

   (1) 8 400 to 10 200

   (2) 8 700 to 9 800

   (3) 8 700 to 10 000

   (4) 8 800 to 10 000

   (5) 9 800 to 10 000

51. A turn-around is a point on the graph where the direction of the line changes. How many turn-arounds are shown on this graph?

   (1) two

   (2) three

   (3) four

   (4) five

   (5) six

52. Which of the following periods showed an increase in new subscribers?

   (1) February to March

   (2) March to April

   (3) September to October

   (4) October to November

   (5) November to December

53. Approximately how much more were net sales for the Toronto store than net sales for the Winnipeg store?

   (1) $2000

   (2) $2500

   (3) $3000

   (4) $4000

   (5) $5000

54. What is the ratio of the net sales of the Vancouver store to the net sales of the Calgary store?

   (1) 1:2

   (2) 2:3

   (3) 6:7

   (4) 3:2

   (5) 7:6

55. What is the average (mean) net sales of the five stores shown, in thousands of dollars?

   (1) $ 6.0

   (2) $ 7.2

   (3) $ 8.2

   (4) $10.5

   (5) $41.0

Answers start on page 852.

LANGUAGE ARTS, WRITING, PART I

Directions

The Language Arts, Writing Simulated Test is intended to measure your ability to use English clearly and effectively. It is a test of English as it should be written, not as it might be spoken.

This test consists of paragraphs with numbered sentences. Some sentences have errors in sentence structure, organization, usage, or mechanics (spelling, punctuation, and capitalization). Read the sentences and answer the multiple-choice questions that follow. Some questions refer to sentences that are written correctly. The best answer for these questions is the one that leaves the sentence as originally written. The best answer for some questions is the one that creates a sentence that is consistent with the verb tense and point of view used throughout the paragraph.

You should spend no more than 75 minutes answering the 50 questions on this test. Work carefully, but do not spend too much time on any one question. Do not skip any items. Make a reasonable guess when you are not sure of an answer. You will not be penalized for incorrect answers.

When time is up, note the last item you finished. This will tell you whether you can finish the real GED Test in the time allowed. Then complete the Simulated Test.

Record your answers to the questions on a copy of the answer sheet on page 917. Be sure that all required information is properly recorded on the answer sheet.

To record your answers, mark the numbered circle on the answer sheet that corresponds to the answer you choose for each question on the test.

Example

Sentence 1: **We were all honoured to meet lieutenant governor Phillips.**

Which correction should be made to sentence 1?

(1) change honoured to honouring
(2) insert a comma after honoured
(3) change meet to met
(4) change lieutenant governor to Lieutenant Governor
(5) no correction is necessary

In this example, the words lieutenant governor should be capitalized; therefore, answer space 4 would be marked on the answer sheet.

Do not rest the point of your pencil on the answer sheet while thinking about your answer. Do not make any stray or unnecessary marks. If you change an answer, erase your first mark completely. Mark only one answer space for each question; multiple answers will be scored as incorrect. Do not fold or crease your answer sheet.

When you finish the test, use the Performance Analysis Chart on page 642 to determine whether you are ready to take the real GED Test and, if not, which skill areas need additional review.

Directions: Choose the *one best answer* to each question.

Questions 1 through 8 refer to the following information.

Drive-in Movies

(1) The drive-in movie was one of the ultimate expressions of North Americans love of cars. (2) It was invented by Richard M. Hollingshead an auto parts salesman. (3) Hollingshead attached a projector to the hood of his car and nailed a screen to trees in his backyard. (4) The first drive-in theatre opened in 1933, but it wasn't until the 1950s that drive-ins really take off. (5) In the heyday of the drive-in, families packed snacks and blankets, piled into the car, and would head for a movie under the stars. (6) The car of choice was the station wagon with a fold-down back gate. (7) Some families brought the entire makings of a picnic the barbecue grill, charcoal, cooler, and lawn chairs all were packed in with the kids. (8) Most theatres had concession stands, and many also had playgrounds. (9) The largest theatre was the All-Weather Drive-In in Copiague, New York. (10) The All-Weather held 2500 cars and offered a playground, a restaurant, and a shuttle train. (11) Not even pesky mosquitoes, rowdy teenagers or scratchy speakers dimmed the drive-in's appeal. (12) Nowadays, most families go to large multiplexes. (13) Only a few open-air cinemas survives. (14) In fact, today drive-ins hold more nostalgia than customers.

1. Sentence 1: **The drive-in movie was one of the ultimate expressions of North Americans love of cars.**

   Which correction should be made to sentence 1?

   (1) change drive-in to drive in
   (2) change was to had been
   (3) change North Americans to North Americans'
   (4) remove ultimate
   (5) no correction is necessary

2. Sentence 2: **It was invented by Richard M. Hollingshead an auto parts salesman.**

   Which is the best way to write the underlined portion of this sentence? If the original is the best way, choose option (1).

   (1) Hollingshead an
   (2) Hollingshead, an
   (3) Hollingshead. An
   (4) Hollingshead who had been an
   (5) Hollingshead being

The article has been repeated for your use in answering the remaining questions.

Drive-in Movies

(1) The drive-in movie was one of the ultimate expressions of North Americans love of cars. (2) It was invented by Richard M. Hollingshead an auto parts salesman. (3) Hollingshead attached a projector to the hood of his car and nailed a screen to trees in his backyard. (4) The first drive-in theatre opened in 1933, but it wasn't until the 1950s that drive-ins really take off. (5) In the heyday of the drive-in, families packed snacks and blankets, piled into the car, and would head for a movie under the stars. (6) The car of choice was the station wagon with a fold-down back gate. (7) Some families brought the entire makings of a picnic the barbecue grill, charcoal, cooler, and lawn chairs all were packed in with the kids. (8) Most theatres had concession stands, and many also had playgrounds. (9) The largest theatre was the All-Weather Drive-In in Copiague, New York. (10) The All-Weather held 2500 cars and offered a playground, a restaurant, and a shuttle train. (11) Not even pesky mosquitoes, rowdy teenagers or scratchy speakers dimmed the drive-in's appeal. (12) Nowadays, most families go to large multiplexes. (13) Only a few open-air cinemas survives. (14) In fact, today drive-ins hold more nostalgia than customers.

3. Sentence 4: **The first drive-in theatre opened in 1933, but it wasn't until the 1950s that drive-ins really take off.**

Which correction should be made to sentence 4?

(1) change take off to took off
(2) remove the comma after 1933
(3) replace but with so
(4) insert a comma after 1950s
(5) no correction is necessary

4. Sentence 5: **In the heyday of the drive-in, families packed snacks and blankets, piled into the car, and would head for a movie under the stars.**

Which correction should be made to sentence 5?

(1) change packed to would pack
(2) remove the comma after blankets
(3) change piled to piling
(4) change would head to headed
(5) no correction is necessary

5. Sentence 7: **Some families brought the entire makings of a <u>picnic the</u> barbecue grill, charcoal, cooler, and lawn chairs all were packed in with the kids.**

Which is the best way to write the underlined portion of this sentence? If the original is the best way, choose option (1).

(1) picnic the
(2) picnic, the
(3) picnic, even the
(4) picnic and the
(5) picnic. The

6. Sentence 10: **The All-Weather <u>held 2500 cars and offered</u> a playground, a restaurant, and a shuttle train.**

Which is the best way to write the underlined portion of this sentence? If the original is the best way, choose option (1).

(1) held 2500 cars and offered
(2) was holding 2500 cars and offered
(3) holds 2500 cars and offered
(4) held 2500 cars and offers
(5) held 2500 cars and offering

7. Sentence 11: **Not even pesky mosquitoes, rowdy teenagers or scratchy speakers dimmed the drive-in's appeal.**

Which correction should be made to sentence 11?

(1) replace <u>Not even</u> with <u>However</u>
(2) insert a comma after <u>teenagers</u>
(3) insert <u>listening to</u> after <u>or</u>
(4) change <u>dimmed</u> to <u>dimming</u>
(5) no correction is necessary

8. Sentence 13: **Only a few open-air cinemas survives.**

Which correction should be made to sentence 13?

(1) change <u>open-air cinemas</u> to <u>Open-air Cinemas</u>
(2) change <u>survives</u> to <u>had survived</u>
(3) change <u>survives</u> to <u>survive</u>
(4) insert a comma after <u>few</u>
(5) no correction is necessary

Kwam Sanford
Accounting Director
KraftMade, Inc.
200 Blue Mound Road
Winnipeg, MB R3H 0J9

Dear Mr. Sanford:

(A)

(1) Please consider my application recently advertised in the *Winnipeg Free Press* for the entry-level bookkeeping position. (2) I check the help-wanted ads every week. (3) I believe that my skills fit the position well.

(B)

(4) After obtaining my GED last March with the highest math test score recorded at Maplewood Night School, I taken three bookkeeping courses there. (5) In order to pay for my tuition, I worked in the night school office. (6) I gained valuable practical experience. (7) The office manager, Anita Cusamano, even let me help prepare the school's annual budget. (8) They told me I did a great job.

(C)

(9) In January, I was accepted at red river community college. (10) Currently taking two courses at night in advanced math and basic accounting. (11) I plan to be an Accounting major. (12) I look forward to meeting you and discussing the position further. (13) As you will see, I am very serious about becoming a successful bookkeeper. (14) I believe my skills, experience, and determination will be a valuable asset to your company.

Respectfully,

Joshua Rice

9. Sentence 1: **Please consider my application recently advertised in the *Winnipeg Free Press* for the entry-level bookkeeping position.**

Which correction should be made to sentence 1?

(1) insert a comma after application
(2) move recently advertised in the *Winnipeg Free Press* to the end of the sentence
(3) change bookkeeping position to Bookkeeping Position
(4) change consider to considering
(5) no correction is necessary

10. Which revision should be made to paragraph A?

(1) move sentence 1 to the end of the paragraph
(2) remove sentence 1
(3) begin a new paragraph after sentence 2
(4) remove sentence 2
(5) no revision is necessary

11. Sentence 4: **After obtaining my GED last March with the highest math test score recorded at Maplewood Night School, I taken three bookkeeping courses there.**

Which correction should be made to sentence 4?

(1) change I taken to I took
(2) change I taken to I would take
(3) change I taken to I had taken
(4) remove the comma after School
(5) no correction is necessary

12. Sentence 6: **I gained valuable practical experience.**

The most effective revision of sentence 6 would begin with which group of words?

(1) Valuable practical experience
(2) Gaining valuable practical experience
(3) For instance, I gained
(4) Even though I gained
(5) As a result of my work, I

13. Sentence 8: <u>**They told**</u> **me I did a great job.**

Which is the best way to write the underlined portion of the sentence? If the original is the best way, choose option (1).

(1) They told
(2) She told
(3) He told
(4) They tell
(5) He tells

14. Sentence 9: **In January, I was accepted at <u>red river community college.</u>**

Which is the best way to write the underlined portion of the sentence? If the original is the best way, choose option (1).

(1) red river community college
(2) Red River community college
(3) red river Community College
(4) Red River Community College
(5) Red River Community college

15. Sentence 10: **<u>Currently taking</u> two courses at night in advanced math and basic accounting.**

Which is the best way to write the underlined portion of this sentence? If the original is the best way, choose option (1).

(1) Currently taking
(2) Currently, taking
(3) Currently while taking
(4) Currently I am taking
(5) Currently take

16. Which revision would improve the effectiveness of paragraph C?

(1) move sentence 9 to the end of paragraph B
(2) remove sentence 10
(3) begin a new paragraph with sentence 12
(4) move sentence 13 to the end of the paragraph
(5) remove sentence 14

Using the Library

(A)

(1) A popular misconception about libraries is that its hard to find information in them. (2) In fact, finding information in libraries is easier than ever. (3) You can use a computer terminal to search the library's catalogue and get call numbers for the books, CDs, or videos you need. (4) Most libraries have directories that show you where to look to find each call number, and librarians are glad to help.

(B)

(5) In addition to circulating books, libraries hold an enormous number of reference books. (6) These books are kept together in a special section. (7) It is filled with books used to find facts. (8) Reference librarians are trained to find any kind of information you might could want. (9) Suppose you want to find the address of an organization, perhaps you want information on buying a home. (10) A reference librarian can help but you have to ask.

(C)

(11) Some libraries provide typewriters and computers for the use of their patrons that don't have other access to these devices. (12) Many libraries have special programs for children. (13) Libraries must be viewed as one of our greatest public resources, they provide so many services.

17. Sentence 1: **A popular misconception about libraries is that its hard to find information in them.**

    Which is the best way to write the underlined portion of the sentence? If the original is the best way, choose option (1).

    (1) its
    (2) it's
    (3) it was
    (4) it would be
    (5) it has

18. Sentences 6 and 7: **These books are kept together in a special section. It is filled with books used to find facts.**

    The most effective combination of sentences 6 and 7 would include which group of words?

    (1) section, so it is
    (2) section and filled
    (3) section, yet filled
    (4) section being filled
    (5) section that is filled

19. Sentence 8: **Reference librarians are trained to find any kind of information you might could want.**

Which is the best way to write the underlined portion of this sentence? If the original is the best way, choose option (1).

(1) might could want
(2) may could want
(3) would want
(4) might want
(5) could be wanting

20. Sentence 9: **Suppose you want to find the address of an organization, perhaps you want information on buying a home.**

Which correction should be made to sentence 9?

(1) remove the comma
(2) insert or after the comma
(3) insert a comma after perhaps
(4) replace perhaps with likewise
(5) no correction is necessary

21. Sentence 10: **A reference librarian can help but you have to ask.**

Which correction should be made to sentence 10?

(1) insert a comma after help
(2) change help but to help. But
(3) insert a comma after but
(4) change have to got
(5) no correction is necessary

22. Sentence 11: **Some libraries provide typewriters and computers for the use of their patrons that don't have other access to these devices.**

Which correction should be made to sentence 11?

(1) change provide to provides
(2) replace these with those
(3) insert a comma after typewriters
(4) replace that with who
(5) no correction is necessary

23. Sentence 13: **Libraries must be viewed as one of our greatest public resources, they provide so many services.**

Which correction should be made to sentence 13?

(1) remove must be
(2) insert a comma after viewed
(3) remove the comma
(4) replace the comma with because
(5) no correction is necessary

24. Which sentence would be most effective if inserted at the beginning of paragraph C?

(1) Knowing how to use reference books is an important skill.
(2) You must be quiet when you visit the library.
(3) Libraries have more to offer than just books.
(4) Books are grouped together according to subject.
(5) Libraries are really great.

Local Express Airlines
411 Wiley Post Avenue
Thunder Bay, ON P7B 6E6

To Whom It May Concern:

(A)

(1) I often flies Local Express Airlines. (2) Recently, had an experience that is an example of the excellent service I always receive from Local Express Airlines. (3) On my last flight, I left a book on my seat. (4) It was a library book. (5) I know I shouldn't travel with library books, but unfortunately I did. (6) As I was waiting at the baggage carousel, I had remembered the book and told a clerk at the baggage desk. (7) Phoned the clerks at the gate and asked them to check the plane. (8) Sadly, they didn't find my book. (9) I called the library on Monday to say the book was lost. (10) The librarian said the book had come in the male that morning!

(B)

(11) Bravo to your airline staff! (12) I will continue to recommend your Airline.

Sincerely,

Milan Fajir

---

25. Sentence 1: **I often flies Local Express Airlines.**

    Which is the best way to write the underlined portion of the sentence? If the original is the best way, choose option (1).

    (1) I often flies
    (2) I usually flies
    (3) I often fly
    (4) I often am flying
    (5) I often did fly

26. Sentences 3 and 4: **On my last flight, I left a book on my seat. It was a library book.**

    The most effective combination of sentences 3 and 4 would include which group of words?

    (1) which was
    (2) which I had gotten
    (3) a book from the library
    (4) a library book
    (5) belonging to the library

27. Sentence 6: **As I was waiting at the baggage carousel, I <u>had remembered</u> the book and told a clerk at the baggage desk.**

    Which is the best way to write the underlined portion of the text? If the original is the best way, choose option (1).

    (1) had remembered
    (2) remember
    (3) remembered
    (4) was remembering
    (5) have remembered

28. Sentence 7: **Phoned the clerks at the gate and asked them to check the plane.**

    What correction should be made to sentence 7?

    (1) insert She before <u>Phoned</u>
    (2) change <u>asking</u> to <u>asked</u>
    (3) replace <u>gate and asked</u> with <u>gate. Asking</u>
    (4) replace <u>Phoned</u> with <u>Phoning</u>
    (5) no correction is necessary

29. Sentence 9: **I <u>called the library</u> on Monday to say the book was lost.**

    Which is the best way to write the underlined portion of the sentence? If the original is the best way, choose option (1).

    (1) I called the library
    (2) I am calling the library
    (3) I call the library
    (4) I was calling the library
    (5) I have called the library

30. Sentence 10: **The librarian said the book had come in the male that morning!**

    What correction should be made to sentence 10?

    (1) replace <u>The librarian</u> with <u>They</u>
    (2) replace <u>the book</u> with <u>it</u>
    (3) change <u>had come</u> to <u>had came</u>
    (4) change <u>male</u> to <u>mail</u>
    (5) no correction is necessary

31. Which revision would improve the effectiveness of paragraph A?

    (1) move sentence 1 to the end of the paragraph
    (2) remove sentence 2
    (3) remove sentence 5
    (4) move sentence 5 after sentence 2
    (5) move sentence 8 to the end of the paragraph

32. Sentence 12: **I will continue to recommend your Airline.**

    Which correction should be made to sentence 12?

    (1) change <u>will continue</u> to <u>will be continuing</u>
    (2) insert a comma after <u>continue</u>
    (3) replace <u>will</u> with <u>might</u>
    (4) change <u>Airline</u> to <u>airline</u>
    (5) no correction is necessary

Island of the Sharks

(A)

(1) Out in the Pacific Ocean is an island of unmatched beauty called Cocos. (2) It is also called "Island of the Sharks." (3) Its abundance of life are famous throughout the world. (4) Jewel-like fish circle the island's underwater reef, while hundreds of sharks have hunted them in schools. (5) Divers also can see huge manta rays octopuses green turtles and giant eels.

(B)

(6) Today, the island is uninhabited. (7) It was once frequented by pirates. (8) Some people believe that there is still treasure buried on the island. (9) Hundreds of expeditions have been formed to search for buried gold, but none has been found. (10) The real treasure of Cocos Island is its balanced, healthy ecosystem.

(C)

(11) Cocos Island is actually the peek of an extinct volcano. (12) When deep ocean currents reach the volcano, they have been forced upward. (13) These currents bring cold water that is rich in plant life and food to the surface. (14) Minute plants and animals, collectively known as plankton, grows when they are exposed to sunlight and food. (15) The plankton attract small fish. (16) The small fish attract larger fish. (17) Finally, the largest fish in the chain attract the sharks that give Cocos its nickname.

33. Sentences 1 and 2: **Out in the Pacific Ocean is an island of unmatched beauty called Cocos. It is also called "Island of the Sharks."**

    The most effective combination of sentences 1 and 2 would include which group of words?

    (1) Cocos, "Island of the Sharks"
    (2) that is also called
    (3) an island of sharks
    (4) ("Island of the Sharks")
    (5) Out in Cocos

34. Sentence 3: **Its abundance of life are famous throughout the world.**

    Which is the best way to write the underlined portion of this sentence? If the original is the best way, choose option (1).

    (1) are
    (2) is
    (3) has been
    (4) have been
    (5) being

35. Sentence 4: **Jewel-like fish circle the island's underwater reef, while hundreds of sharks have hunted them in schools.**

    Which correction should be made to sentence 4?

    (1) change circle to circled
    (2) change reef, while to reef. While
    (3) change have hunted to hunting
    (4) change have hunted to hunt
    (5) no correction is necessary

36. Sentence 5: **Divers also can see huge manta rays octopuses green turtles and giant eels.**

    Which is the best way to write the underlined portion of this sentence? If the original is the best way, choose option (1)

    (1) manta rays octopuses green turtles and giant eels
    (2) manta rays octopuses green turtles also giant eels
    (3) manta rays octopuses green turtles, and giant eels
    (4) manta rays plus octopuses green turtles and giant eels
    (5) manta rays, octopuses, green turtles, and giant eels

37. Sentences 6 and 7: **Today, the island is uninhabited. It was once frequented by pirates.**

    Which is the most effective combination of sentences 6 and 7?

    (1) Today, the island frequented by pirates is uninhabited.
    (2) Once frequented by pirates, today, it is uninhabited.
    (3) Today, the island is uninhabited, but it was once frequented by pirates.
    (4) Today, the island is uninhabited it was once frequented by pirates.
    (5) Today, the island is uninhabited and it was once frequented by pirates.

38. Sentence 11: **Cocos Island is actually the peek of an extinct volcano.**

    Which correction should be made to sentence 11?

    (1) change Island to island
    (2) replace peek with peak
    (3) move actually to the end of the sentence
    (4) change is to are
    (5) no correction is necessary

39. Sentence 12: **When deep ocean currents reach the volcano, they have been forced upward.**

    Which is the best way to write the underlined portion of this sentence? If the original is the best way, choose option (1).

    (1) have been
    (2) are
    (3) were
    (4) will be
    (5) been

40. Sentence 14: **Minute plants and animals, collectively known as plankton, grows when they are exposed to sunlight and food.**

    Which correction should be made to sentence 14?

    (1) change grows to grow
    (2) replace they are with it is
    (3) change are to be
    (4) change exposed to being exposed
    (5) no correction is necessary

41. Sentences 15 and 16: **The plankton attract small fish. The small fish attract larger fish.**

    The most effective combination of sentences 15 and 16 would include which group of words?

    (1) fish, and it, in turn, attracts
    (2) fish, and them, in turn, attract
    (3) fish, and one, in turn, attracts
    (4) fish, and those there, in turn, attract
    (5) fish, and they, in turn, attract

42. Which revision would improve the effectiveness of the article?

    (1) join paragraphs A and B
    (2) join paragraphs B and C
    (3) move paragraph B after paragraph C
    (4) begin a new paragraph at sentence 14
    (5) no revision is necessary

Questions 43 through 50 refer to the following passage.

Childproofing Your Home

(A)

(1) Every year, millions of children are injured by hazards in their homes. (2) Fortunately, you don't need a class in home economics 101 to help prevent these injuries. (3) You can simply install child safety devices such as safety locks, latches, gates, and anti-scald devices.

(B)

(4) You can put safety locks and latches on cabinets and drawers. (5) They keep children from pulling drawers down on their heads and to scatter objects that might cause them to trip. (6) They also keep knives and sharp tools out of reach. (7) A lock or latch can prevent children from getting into household cleaners or medicines, too.

(C)

(8) Safety gates also help childproof a home. (9) Gates can keep a child out of unsafe spaces placed between rooms. (10) The gates should also be installed at the top of stairs to prevent tumbles. (11) Gates that screw into the wall are more secure than pressure gates.

(D)

(12) Anti-scald devices regulate water temperature in your home, and can prevent burns. (13) A plumber can install it in showers and faucets. (14) Set the temperature to 50 degrees Celcius, which is hot enough for washing but won't burn the skin.

(E)

(15) To find out about the reliability and cost of childproofing devices, talk to friends or look at consumer-related magazines. (16) Consumer magazines cover safety subjects. (17) Ranging from alarm systems to liability insurance. (18) Once you done installed these safety devices, you can enjoy a new kind of security in your home.

43. Sentence 2: **Fortunately, you don't need a class in home economics 101 to help prevent these injuries.**

Which correction should be made to sentence 2?

(1) remove the comma after <u>fortunately</u>
(2) change <u>prevent</u> to <u>preventing</u>
(3) change <u>home economics</u> to <u>Home Economics</u>
(4) replace <u>these</u> with <u>those</u>
(5) no correction is necessary

44. Sentence 4: **You can put safety locks and latches on cabinets and drawers.**

Which revision would improve the effectiveness of sentence 4?

(1) replace sentence 4 with <u>Safety locks and latches protect children in several ways.</u>
(2) replace sentence 4 with <u>Install safety locks on drawers.</u>
(3) move sentence 4 to the end of paragraph A
(4) remove sentence 4
(5) no revision is necessary

45. Sentence 5: **They keep children from pulling drawers down on their heads and to scatter objects that might cause them to trip.**

Which is the best way to write the underlined portion of this sentence? If the original is the best way, choose option (1).

(1) and to scatter
(2) and scattering
(3) and to have scattered
(4) but scattering
(5) but to scatter

46. Sentence 9: **Gates can keep a child out of unsafe spaces placed between rooms.**

Which correction should be made to sentence 8?

(1) insert a comma after spaces
(2) change keep to kept
(3) move placed between rooms after Gates
(4) replace between with among
(5) no correction is necessary

47. Sentence 12: **Anti-scald devices regulate water temperature in your home, and can prevent burns.**

Which is the best way to write the underlined portion of this sentence? If the original is the best way, choose option (1).

(1) home, and can
(2) home and can
(3) home, yet can
(4) home and also can
(5) home, and might

48. Sentence 13: **A plumber can install it in showers and faucets.**

Which correction should be made to sentence 12?

(1) change A plumber to Plumbers
(2) change can to could
(3) insert the before showers
(4) replace it with them
(5) no correction is necessary

49. Sentences 16 and 17: **Consumer magazines cover safety subjects. Ranging from alarm systems to liability insurance.**

Which is the best way to write the underlined portion of these sentences? If the original is the best way, choose option (1).

(1) subjects. Ranging from
(2) subjects; ranging from
(3) subjects ranging from
(4) subjects. Having a range from
(5) subjects and range from

50. Sentence 18: **Once you done installed these safety devices, you can enjoy a new kind of security in your home.**

Which is the best way to write the underlined portion of this sentence? If the original is the best way, choose option (1).

(1) you done installed
(2) one done installed
(3) you installed
(4) you would install
(5) you have installed

Simulated Test Performance Analysis Chart
Language Arts, Writing

This chart can help you determine your strengths and weaknesses on the content and skill areas of the Language Arts, Writing Test. Use the Answers and Explanations starting on page 856 to check your answers to the test. Then circle on the chart the numbers of the test items you answered correctly. Put the total number correct for each content area and skill area in each row and column. If you answered fewer than 50 questions correctly, look at the total items correct in each column and row and decide which areas need more study. Use the page references to study those areas.

Item Type / Content Area	Correction	Revision	Construction Shift	Number Correct	Page References
Sentence Structure					**68/95**
Sentences/Sentence Fragments	28	15, 49		____/3	68/71
Compound Sentences/ Combining Ideas			18, 37	____/2	72/75
Subordinating Ideas	23		26, 33	____/3	76/79
Run-ons/Comma Splices	20	5		____/2	80/83
Modifiers	9, 46			____/2	84/86
Parallel Structure	4	6, 45		____/3	87/89
Organization					**96/113**
Paragraph Structure/ Unity and Coherence	10, 31		42	____/3	96/99
Topic Sentences			24, 44	____/2	100/102
Paragraph Divisions			16	____/1	103/105
Transitions			12	____/1	106/108
Usage					**114/131**
Subject-Verb Agreement	8, 40	25, 34		____/4	114/117
Verb Forms	11	19, 29, 50		____/4	118/120
Verb Tenses	3, 35	27, 39		____/4	121/123
Pronouns	22, 48	13, 41		____/4	124/127
Mechanics					**132/144**
Capitalization	32, 43	14		____/3	132/134
Commas	7, 21	2, 36, 47		____/5	135/137
Spelling	1, 30, 38	17		____/4	138/141

1–40 → You need more review.
41–50 → Congratulations! You're ready to write the official Language Arts Writing Part I

LANGUAGE ARTS, WRITING, PART II

Essay Directions and Topic

Look at the box on the next page for your assigned topic and the letter of that topic.

You must write on the assigned topic **only**.

You will have 45 minutes to write on your assigned essay topic. Return to the multiple-choice section after you complete your essay, if you have time remaining in this test period. Do not return the Language Arts, Writing booklet until you finish both Parts I and II of the Language Arts, Writing Test.

Two evaluators will score your essay according to its overall effectiveness. Their evaluation will be based on the following features:

- Well-focused main points
- Clear organization
- Specific development of your ideas
- Control of sentence structure, punctuation, grammar, word choice, and spelling

Remember, you must complete both the multiple-choice questions (Part I) and the essay (Part II) to receive a score on the Language Arts, Writing Test. To avoid having to repeat both parts of the test, be sure to do the following:

- Do not leave the pages blank.
- Write legibly in ink so that the evaluators will be able to read your writing.
- Write on the assigned topic. If you write on a topic other than the one assigned, you will not receive a score for the Language Arts, Writing Test.
- Write your essay on the lined pages of the separate answer sheet booklet. Only the writing on these pages will be scored.

Part II is a test to determine how well you can use written language to explain your ideas.

In preparing your essay, you should take the following steps:

- Read the **directions** and the **topic** carefully.
- Plan your essay before you write. Use the scratch paper provided to make notes and a brief outline. These notes will be collected but not scored.
- Before you turn in your essay, reread what you have written and make any changes that will improve your essay.

Your essay should be long enough to develop the topic adequately.

When you finish your essay, see page 860 of the Answers and Explanations to evaluate and score your essay.

SOCIAL STUDIES

Directions

This Social Studies GED Simulated Test is intended to measure your knowledge of general social studies concepts.

The questions are based on short readings or on graphs, maps, charts, cartoons, or illustrations. Study the information given and then answer the questions that follow. Refer to the information as often as necessary in answering the questions.

Spend no more than 70 minutes answering the 50 questions on this test. Work carefully, but do not spend too much time on any one item. Do not skip any items. Make a reasonable guess when you are unsure of an answer. You will not be penalized for incorrect answers.

When time is up, note the last item you finished. This will tell you whether you can finish the real GED Test in the time allowed. Then complete the Simulated Test.

Record your answers to the questions on a copy of the answer sheet on page 918. Be sure that all required information is recorded on the answer sheet.

To record your answers, fill in the numbered circle on the answer sheet that corresponds to the answer you choose for each item on the test.

Example

Early pioneers of the western frontier looked to settle on land that had adequate access to water. To ensure access to water, many early pioneers settled on land near which type of geographic feature?

(1) forests
(2) grasslands
(3) rivers
(4) glaciers
(5) oceans

The correct answer is <u>rivers</u>; therefore, answer circle 3 should be filled in on the answer sheet.

Do not rest the point of your pencil on the answer sheet while considering your answer. Do not make any stray or unnecessary marks. If you change an answer, erase your first mark completely. Mark only one answer for each question; multiple answers will be scored as incorrect. Do not fold or crease your answer sheet.

When you finish the test, use the Performance Analysis Chart on page 664 to determine whether you are ready to take the real GED Test and, if not, which skill areas need additional review.

Directions: Choose the one best answer to each question.

Questions 1 through 3 refer to the following paragraph and graph.

The amount of money that consumers, businesses, and the government have available to spend is known as the money supply. Rapid changes in the money supply can cause economic problems, so it is important to keep it under control. This responsibility is among the duties of the Bank of Canada. The graph illustrates the money supply's importance by tracking prices, production, and the money supply over a 20-year period.

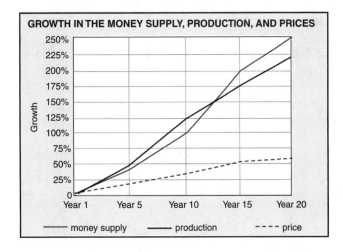

GROWTH IN THE MONEY SUPPLY, PRODUCTION, AND PRICES

— money supply   — production   ---- price

1. During the first 10 years shown on the graph, what happened to prices when the amount of money in the economy increased?

   (1) They rose sharply.
   (2) They rose but more slowly than the increase in the money supply.
   (3) They rose at the same rate as the increase in the money supply.
   (4) They fell.
   (5) They did not change.

2. When the supply of money grows faster than the rate at which the economy produces goods and services, what happens to prices?

   (1) Inflation causes prices to rise.
   (2) Prices fall.
   (3) Prices rise, then fall, and then rise again.
   (4) Prices are not affected.
   (5) The relationship cannot be determined.

3. What conclusion about the relationship among the money supply, production, and prices do the data in the graph support?

   (1) An increase in the money supply will cause a decrease in production.
   (2) An increase in production will cause an increase in the money supply.
   (3) An increase in prices will cause a decrease in production.
   (4) A decrease in production will cause an increase in the money supply.
   (5) There is not enough information to determine the relationship.

Question 4 refers to the following table.

AVERAGE ANNUAL EARNINGS FOR SELECTED OCCUPATIONS—1890	
Farm labourers	$233
Public school teachers	256
Bituminous coal miners	406
Manufacturing employees	439
Street railway employees	557
Steam railroad employees	560
Gas & electricity workers	687
Ministers	794
Clerical workers in manufacturing & steam RR	848
Postal employees	878

4. Based on the table, what was one probable cause of people moving from the rural areas to cities in 1890?

   (1) Railroads did not go into the country.
   (2) There was little need for farm labourers.
   (3) City jobs generally paid better wages.
   (4) Schoolteachers were needed in cities.
   (5) Many government jobs were available.

Question 5 refers to the following passage.

Christopher Columbus believed that he could reach the Indies—the name Europeans gave to the lands and islands of East Asia—by sailing west across the Atlantic Ocean. He persuaded the king and queen of Spain to finance such a voyage.

On October 12, 1492, after several weeks at sea, Columbus reached an island in what is now called the Bahamas, which he claimed for Spain and named San Salvador. Because Columbus was certain he had reached the Indies, he called natives who greeted him "Indians." Before returning to Spain, he established a colony on another island, which he named Hispaniola.

When Columbus returned to Hispaniola in 1493, he discovered that the colony had been destroyed. He founded a new colony nearby and left to search for China and Japan. While Columbus was away, the natives revolted over the colonists' constant demands for gold and food. The colonists also fought over land and Aboriginal labour. Some returned to Spain and complained about Columbus. From that point on, his reputation suffered. It became more difficult for Columbus to obtain money and people for his voyages. But he was able to return to America two more times before his death in 1506. He died still believing that he had reached Asia.

Many people consider Columbus a hero because of his voyages. However, some people view his activities as the beginning of the terrible destruction of Aboriginal peoples and their culture. Whatever view one holds, it is clear that Columbus's voyages were a turning point in history.

5. What title best expresses the main idea of this passage?

   (1) Conflict in the Americas
   (2) How Aboriginals Got the Name "Indians"
   (3) Christopher Columbus and His Work
   (4) The Search for China and Japan
   (5) The Spanish Exploration of America

Question 6 refers to the following passage.

During the 1300s, many Italian merchants became rich by selling Asian goods in Europe. In the leisure their new wealth made possible, the merchants became interested in the art and culture of their ancestors. Their curiosity inspired the Renaissance, a 300-year period of advances in art, literature, and science throughout Europe. Italian scholars called humanists studied ancient Greek and Roman writings. They applied the ideas from these writings to their own world.

Humanism taught that involvement with the arts was an important part of life. So, wealthy merchants began providing financial support to artists. This help made it possible for Italian painters and sculptors like Leonardo da Vinci and Michelangelo to create masterpieces.

Literature and learning were encouraged when German printer Johann Gutenberg perfected his printing press in 1455. Because the printing press made books easier to produce, they increased in number. This development helped the ideas of the Renaissance spread across Europe.

6. Which modern-day event has had an effect most like that of the printing press in the 1400s?

   (1) the popularity of cartoon art
   (2) the invention of the video tape recorder
   (3) the creation of the Internet
   (4) the growing number of shopping malls
   (5) the performance of Renaissance music

Question 7 refers to the following passage and photograph.

The twentieth century was a time of great tension in the world. World War I, which lasted from 1914 to 1918, was supposed to be "the war to end all wars." It was soon followed by even greater devastation in World War II, waged from 1939 to 1945. For much of the rest of the century, people worried about nuclear annihilation as the United States and the Soviet Union faced off in the Cold War.

When World War II ended, so did the uneasy cooperation between the United States and the Soviet Union, who had been wartime allies. The world soon divided into three camps. The United States led the West, which included the major democracies—Great Britain, France, Canada, and their allies. The Soviet Union emerged as leader of the communist bloc, which included its satellite nations in Eastern Europe as well as China and North Korea. Much of the rest of the world formed a third group of nonaligned nations.

In the early 1980s, it seemed as if the Cold War between the Soviet Union and the West would never end. But by 1989, Soviet political control began to break down. Nowhere were these events more dramatic than in Berlin, a city surrounded by communist East Germany. Since 1961, a wall erected by the East German government had separated the people of East Berlin and West Berlin.

At midnight on November 9, 1989, thousands of Germans stormed the wall that separated East and West Berlin. East Berliners tore at the Berlin Wall, venting their rage at decades of oppression. At the same time, West Berliners pounded out the tensions that had resulted from fear that they too might someday lose their freedom. By morning, the world's most notorious reminder that millions of people lacked basic human rights was coming down.

The destruction of the Berlin Wall marked the end of the Cold War and the threat of world communism.

7. Why did the people of West Berlin fear and hate the Berlin Wall as much as the people of East Berlin?

(1) It prevented them from travelling to and from East Berlin.
(2) The wall was unstable and presented a safety hazard.
(3) They feared that communism would spread to West Berlin.
(4) It hampered trade and hurt business in West Berlin.
(5) The wall divided Germany into communist East Berlin and capitalist West Berlin.

Simulated Test • Social Studies

Question 8 refers to the following passage.

Special leaders can emerge in any one of the basic forms of government. These leaders have a rare quality known as "charisma," which is the ability to arouse extreme devotion and enthusiasm among their followers. The force of their personalities is enough to inspire entire nations to follow their lead. Revolutionary movements sometimes form around charismatic figures who appear to represent or symbolize the principles and ideas they advocate.

Two of the most famous charismatic leaders in history are the visionary Joan of Arc and, later, France's great military leader and ruler Napoleon Bonaparte. In more recent times, notable charismatic figures have included the Nazi dictator Adolf Hitler, India's brilliant Mohandas Gandhi, China's Mao Zedong, Great Britain's Winston Churchill, and Cuba's Fidel Castro.

The nature of Canadian democracy hinders the development of such powerful and popular figures. Nonetheless, Canadians have elected four hugely popular politicians who governed the nation for more than half of its history. W. L. Mackenzie King was in power for 22 years, and Canada's first prime minister, Sir John A. Macdonald, held office for 20 years. Sir Wilfrid Laurier and Pierre Trudeau each served for 15 years.

8. Which of the following is an opinion stated in or implied by the passage?

(1) Joan of Arc claimed to have visions.
(2) Pierre Trudeau was a popular prime minister.
(3) Adolf Hitler was a Nazi.
(4) Mohandas Gandhi was a brilliant person.
(5) Fidel Castro is a dictator.

Question 9 refers to the following cartoon.

"The meek will inherit the earth, but NEVER the market."

Cartoon by Dean Vietor. Copyright 1989 Dean Vietor.

9. What does the creator of this cartoon assume readers know about "the market"?

(1) It is a grocery store.
(2) It is the stock market.
(3) It refers to natural resources.
(4) It refers to an advertising promotion.
(5) It refers to inherited property.

Question 10 refers to this excerpt from the eulogy of Justin Trudeau at the funeral of his father, on Tuesday, October 2, 2000.

Pierre Elliott Trudeau. The very words convey so many things to so many people. Statesman, intellectual, professor, adversary, outdoorsman, lawyer, journalist, author, prime minister. … He taught us to believe in ourselves, to stand up for ourselves, to know ourselves, and to accept responsibility for ourselves. … As I guess it is for most kids, it was always a real treat to visit my dad at work. … including lunch at the parliamentary restaurant. But at eight, I was becoming politically aware. And I recognized one whom I recognized to be one of my father's chief rivals. Thinking of pleasing him, I told a joke about him—a generic, silly little grade school thing.

My father looked at me sternly with that look I would learn to know so well, and said: "Justin, never attack the individual. One can be in total disagreement with someone without denigrating him as a consequence."

Saying that, he stood up and took me by the hand and brought me over to introduce me to this man. …

My father's adversary spoke to me in a friendly manner and it was then that I understood that having different opinions from those of another person in no way precluded holding this person in the highest respect.

Because mere tolerance is not enough: we must have true and deep respect for every human being, regardless of his beliefs, his origins, and his values. That is what my father demanded of his sons and that is what he demanded of our country. He demanded it out of love—love of his sons, love of his country.

1. In what way did Pierre Elliott Trudeau articulate a national identity for Canada and Canadians in the world?

   (1) He proclaimed that Canadians were better than other people.
   (2) He personified qualities of character such as intelligence and tolerance that people all over the world could respect.
   (3) He expected all Canadians to cheer loudly for their country.
   (4) He showed that Canada couldn't be pushed around by the United States
   (5) He was a demanding father and a demanding political leader.

Question 11 refers to the following passage and reproduction of a painting.

When I [Canadian painter Charles Pachter] did the image of the Queen on the moose, it was 30 years ago, and only 20 years into her reign. It was done with mischief, but affection. It was an investigation of the post-colonial tie with the monarchy. I had this childhood confusion with the monarch and the moose; I remembered in school they called the moose the "Monarch of the North," and it just came to me to do this juxtaposition.

By putting her on a moose I was just trying to reaffirm that she was Queen of Canada. But … in our culture that kind of gentle satire couldn't be abided. … I've been told, "You've touched an Achilles heel in Canadian consciousness with this image, but don't expect you'll ever be invited to meet her." I met Prince Charles and told him, "Thanks to your mother, I made a living for 20 years," and he cracked up.

1. What value probably motivated the painter Charles Pachter to portray the Queen on a moose?

   (1) An intense hatred of the monarchy.
   (2) A desire to represent part of Canada's historical connection with Britain in a light-hearted way.
   (3) A deep love of Canadian wild animals.
   (4) An intention to protest against the continuing domination of England in Canada's affairs.
   (5) A belief in the supremacy of constitutional monarchy over a republican system of government.

Simulated Test • Social Studies

Questions 12 through 14 refer to the following paragraph and table.

Canadian provinces have embraced lotteries and other gaming activities as a source of revenue. Since changes were made to the Criminal Code of Canada in 1969, provincial governments have recognized lotteries as an essential means of meeting their budgets. Many Canadians agree that these lotteries are preferential to a raise in personal taxes.

Gross and Net Revenues (1994–1995) for Canada's Five Main Lottery Corporations		
Lottery Corporation LC	Revenue from Ticket Sales (in millions of dollars)	Proceeds After Prizes and Expenses (in millions of dollars)
British Columbia LC	780.8	234.5
Western Canadian LC	612.1	241.2
Ontario LC	1900	626.6
Loto-Quebec	1500	480.6
Atlantic LC	655.9	239.8

Source: Canadian Centre on Substance Abuse, <www.ccsa.ca/ncw/gamcont.htm>.

12. How much money did Ontario's lottery provide in 1994–1995 to fund the province's operations and programs?

   (1) $626 600
   (2) $1 900 000
   (3) $6 266 000
   (4) $626 600 000
   (5) $1 900 000 000

13. Which statement is supported by the information provided about lotteries?

   (1) Lotteries provide enough revenue for the provinces that use them.
   (2) Lotteries can supply millions of dollars in revenue.
   (3) Government-run lotteries have been in operation since the beginning of the twentieth century.
   (4) BC has the best lottery system in the nation.
   (5) Provinces rely only on lotteries for revenues.

14. Which of these lotteries is the least efficient in providing operating money for the province(s)?

   (1) British Columbia Lottery Corporation
   (2) Ontario Lottery Corporation
   (3) Loto-Quebec
   (4) Atlantic Lottery Corporation
   (5) Western Canadian Lottery Corporation

Question 15 refers to the following paragraph and chart.

Canadians' constitutional rights and freedoms have evolved since the *British North America Act* in 1867. In the *Statute of Westminster* in 1931, Britain no longer created legislation for Canada unless requested by the Canadian government. In 1961, Parliament passed the *Canadian Bill of Rights*. Finally, Canadians' rights were further entrenched in the *Constitutional Act* of 1982. The following chart illustrates Canada's constitutional rights and freedoms.

Fundamental Freedoms

"Everyone has the following fundamental freedoms:
a) freedom of conscience and religion
b) freedom of thought, belief, opinion and expression, including freedom of the press and other means of communication."

Mobility Rights

"Every citizen of Canada has the right to enter, remain in, and leave Canada. Every citizen of Canada and every person who has the status of a permanent resident of Canada has the right
a) to move and take up residence in any province; and
b) to pursue the gaining of livelihood in any province."

Legal Rights

"Everyone has the right to life, liberty and security of the person and the right not to be deprived thereof except in accordance with the principles of fundamental justice. Everyone has the right to be secure against unreasonable search or seizure."

Equality Rights

"Every individual is equal before and under the law and has the right to the equal protection and equal benefit of the law without discrimination and, in particular, without discrimination based on race, national or ethnic origin, colour, religion, sex, age or mental or physical disability."

Minority Language Educational Rights

"Citizens of Canada of whom any child has received or is receiving primary or secondary school instruction in English or French in Canada, have the right to have all their children receive primary and secondary school instruction in the same language."

---

15. If the majority of judicial cases concerning the *Charter of Rights and Freedoms* has involved the conduct of Canadian police officers, which clause of the Constitution has been affected by this trend?

(1) Minority Language Educational Rights
(2) Equality Rights
(3) Mobility Rights
(4) Legal Rights
(5) Fundamental Freedoms

Question 16 refers to the following table.

Unemployment as a Percentage of the Labour Force 1930–1941 and 1992–2001			
Year	**Unemployment**	**Year**	**Unemployment**
1930	13.1	1992	11.2
1933	32.4	1995	9.5
1934	26.5	1998	8.3
1938	15.8	2000	6.8
1941	3.2	2001	7.2

Source: Statistics Canada.

16. Workers' wages were higher in 1930 than they were in 1938. Which principle of economics does the table suggest was responsible for this difference in wages?

(1) the relationship of supply and demand
(2) the operation of the barter system
(3) the forces of inflation
(4) the occurrence of equilibrium
(5) the operation of the money economy

17. "For democracy to function, voters need to be well-informed decision-makers." Based on this opinion, which of the following should be most highly valued in a democracy?

(1) tradition
(2) wealth
(3) neighbourliness
(4) individuality
(5) education

Simulated Test • Social Studies

Marco Polo became a world explorer at age 17. In 1271, he set out for China with his father and uncle, who were Venetian merchants. After three years of travel across central Asia by ship and camels, the Polos arrived in Shang-tu at the summer palace of Kublai Khan, the Mongol emperor of China. Marco quickly became a favourite of the khan and for 17 years travelled throughout China as the khan's representative.

Near the end of this time, the Polos were ready to return home. At first, the khan was unwilling to let them leave. But in 1292, he agreed and allowed them to sail to Persia. From there they were finally able to reach Venice in 1295—24 years later.

Shortly after Marco Polo's return to Italy, he gave a detailed account of his experiences to a writer. The book that resulted is known today as *The Travels of Marco Polo.* For more than 300 years, it remained the only published description of East Asia available in Europe.

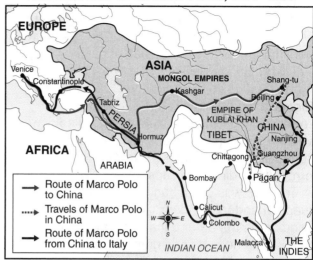

THE TRAVELS OF MARCO POLO, 1271–1295

18. Why did Kublai Khan not want the Polos to return to Italy?

   (1) He feared they were spies.
   (2) He did not want Marco Polo to publish his book.
   (3) He was afraid for their safety.
   (4) He thought the trip home would take too long.
   (5) He did not want to lose his trusted representative, Marco Polo.

19. Which unstated assumption is suggested about Marco Polo and Kublai Khan?

   (1) Kublai Khan feared Marco Polo.
   (2) They enjoyed travelling together.
   (3) Kublai Khan admired and trusted Marco Polo.
   (4) Marco Polo feared Kublai Khan.
   (5) The khan helped Marco Polo write his book.

20. The Polos' trips to China and back each took three years. What map information supports the idea that they took less time on their return trip?

   (1) On the trip to China they travelled through Persia.
   (2) The trip home was along a more direct route than was the trip to China.
   (3) The trip to China covered a much greater distance than did the trip home.
   (4) The trip home required the Polos to cross Tibet.
   (5) The trip home was mainly over water, while the trip to China was mainly over land.

Questions 21 and 22 refer to the following passage.

The FLQ kidnappings in Quebec in October 1970 provoked a major political crisis in Canada. Newspapers covered the events closely and in many cases fanned the flames of panic.

Television journalists also covered the events. In one famous confrontation, a CBC reporter cornered the prime minister outside the Parliament buildings in Ottawa and asked him whether it was really necessary to send armed Canadian soldiers into the streets, thus terrorizing ordinary citizens.

Trudeau was clearly agitated by the reporter's question and responded: "Well, there's a lot of bleeding hearts around that just don't like to see people with helmets and guns. All I can say is: go ahead and bleed."

The reporter then asked how far he was prepared to go in this unprecedented situation. Trudeau replied, "Just watch me!"

21. What did Pierre Trudeau mean when he referred to some people as "bleeding hearts"?

   (1) Some Canadians had severe medical problems.
   (2) Some people thought that sending in the army was a sign of weakness.
   (3) Those who thought he should do nothing were weak and cowardly.
   (4) The "bleeding hearts" should be praised for their kindness and sympathy for the FLQ.
   (5) Television reporters always sided with the underdog.

22. What did Pierre Trudeau's comments suggest was most important to him?

   (1) personal popularity
   (2) fanning the flames of panic
   (3) negotiating with the terrorists
   (4) pleasing television journalists
   (5) maintaining order in the country

Questions 23 and 24 refer to the following passage.

Beginning in the mid-800s, a series of powerful clans gained control of Japan's government. The emperor remained the symbolic ruler, but the currently dominant clan's members held all the important government jobs. The family member who headed the clan was the true head of Japan's government.

The Fujiwara family controlled the government from 857 to 1160. When two other clans challenged its power, a long civil war broke out. In 1192, the emperor named the head of the victorious clan shogun, or military ruler of Japan. Shogun was a hereditary title, but when a shogun died, a power struggle usually followed. Because of these rivalries, the government's authority seldom extended very far beyond the shogun's home city.

From the 1400s to the early 1600s, the real power in Japan was held by wealthy landowners called daimyos. Each daimyo hired professional warriors called samurai to protect his lands and the peasants who worked in his fields. When Tokugawa Ieyasu became shogun in 1600, the government began to reestablish control over the daimyos. Tokugawa shoguns ruled for more than 250 years. By 1868, when the last shogun was overthrown and the emperor's power restored, the modern nation of Japan emerged.

23. Samurai were most like which Europeans?

   (1) merchants
   (2) nobles
   (3) kings
   (4) knights
   (5) serfs

24. Which conclusion is best supported by the information in the passage?

   (1) Japan's emperors had great power.
   (2) The Tokugawa became emperors of Japan.
   (3) A system similar to European feudalism existed in Japan.
   (4) Japan had no emperor for about a thousand years.
   (5) The daimyos still control Japan today.

Questions 25 and 26 refer to the following information.

The economy of Canada grew throughout the 1920s, but when the Great Depression began in 1929, Canada was hit especially hard. The principal reason was that the country's economy was based on staple products such as wheat and other agricultural crops, lumber, and minerals from mines. Most of these staples were for export to the United States, already Canada's most important trading partner, or for markets overseas. In addition, American investors supplied a lot of the money used to finance Canadian economic development, so any downturn in the economy of the United States would immediately affect Canada.

But in the autumn of 1929 most Canadians were unaware of how vulnerable their economy was. Bankers and company presidents thought the prosperity of the 1920s would never end. They persuaded investors to believe their rosy economic forecasts and to continue to invest or speculate on the stock market.

The bubble of optimism burst, however, as American share prices began a downward slide. Canadian stocks quickly followed suit. Worried investors began to lose confidence in the companies whose shares they had bought and many began to sell their shares. Soon there was panic.

As stock prices plummeted, wheat prices dropped so much that the Winnipeg Grain Exchange collapsed in October. Thousands of investors lost everything. Then, on Tuesday, October 29, the stock markets in New York, Toronto, and Montreal crashed. On the Toronto Stock Exchange, the value of 16 important shares dropped $1 million per minute. Even shares in such respected and stable companies as the Ford Motor Company and International Nickel lost half of their value. Many investors were ruined, and even though few ordinary Canadians actually owned stock, they felt the after-effects of the stock market crash when the world economy began to collapse. This was the beginning of the Great Depression.

25. What was the mood of investors and bankers as the American and Canadian economies began to collapse?

   (1) contentment
   (2) puzzlement
   (3) mild concern
   (4) optimism
   (5) panic

26. According to the passage, what was the principal problem with an economy such as Canada's, which was based primarily on staple products?

   (1) If exports fell sharply for any reason, the economy went into a serious decline.
   (2) If the weather was bad, the production of lumber declined.
   (3) Panicky investors didn't like to invest in agricultural companies.
   (4) Canada had only a few natural resources.
   (5) All of Canada's staple products could be bought more cheaply from Argentina and Japan.

Question 27 refers to the following map.

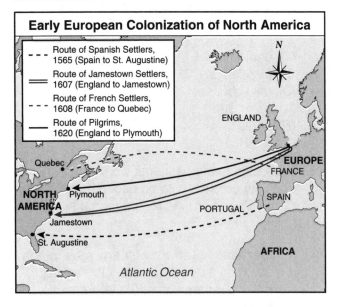

Early European Colonization of North America

- - - Route of Spanish Settlers,
1565 (Spain to St. Augustine)

═══ Route of Jamestown Settlers,
1607 (England to Jamestown)

- - - Route of French Settlers,
1608 (France to Quebec)

——— Route of Pilgrims,
1620 (England to Plymouth)

Quebec

Plymouth

NORTH
AMERICA

Jamestown

St. Augustine

Atlantic Ocean

ENGLAND

EUROPE
FRANCE

SPAIN

PORTUGAL

AFRICA

N

27. Which of the following is a conclusion supported by information from the map?

(1) Spanish colonists settled in what we now call the southern United States in the late sixteenth century.
(2) English colonists founded Jamestown.
(3) French colonists established a settlement in what we now call Canada in the early seventeenth century.
(4) France, England, and Spain were major European colonizers of eastern North America.
(5) Portugal was the major European colonizer of the eastern part of South America.

Question 28 refers to the following paragraph.

The main purpose of a special interest group is to promote the concerns of its members. One method such groups use to achieve this goal is a practice called "lobbying." This means trying to convince government leaders to support or favor certain causes. Many special interest groups employ paid lobbyists. These professionals work at all levels of government, all across the country.

28. Which of the following actions is most like lobbying?

(1) a TV newscaster reporting on the activities of government officials
(2) writing a letter to a government official that presents your position on a controversial issue
(3) writing a letter to the editor of your local newspaper about a controversial issue
(4) a newspaper editor writing a column that takes a position on a controversial issue
(5) joining a special interest group

29. Although the Canadian women's movement made advances in the early twentieth century, Quebec was the last province to allow women the right to vote. After lobbying politicians at the Legislative Assembly for many years, Quebec women were granted the vote by 1940.

Which of the following was the most likely reason that Quebec trailed other Canadian provinces in women's suffrage?

(1) The female population was lower in Quebec than in other provinces.
(2) Quebec women had a variety of social interests.
(3) Cultural values in Quebec society discouraged women from voting.
(4) Québécois were not politically active.
(5) English Canada discriminated against Quebec.

Questions 30 through 32 refer to the following political cartoon.

This cartoon first appeared in 1990 and shows U.S. President George Bush, Sr. and Canadian Prime Minister Brian Mulroney.

Source: Reprinted with permission from *The Globe and Mail*.

30. Which fact does the cartoonist assume you know in order to understand the cartoon?

   (1) Canadian politics is known for its regional diversity.
   (2) The American president exerts great political power in international politics.
   (3) The Canadian prime minister often visits the American president at the White House.
   (4) North American leaders need to focus on international issues.
   (5) Americans need to stay out of political issues in the Middle East.

31. What is the main message of the cartoon?

   (1) Canadian and American leaders enjoy each other's company.
   (2) The Canadian prime minister is like a toy for the American president.
   (3) The United States is more powerful than Canada.
   (4) Canadian and American leaders like to play electronic games.
   (5) The United States controls Canadian foreign policy.

32. Which of the following is an opinion with which the cartoonist would disagree?

   (1) The American president has too much influence on Canadian politics.
   (2) U.S. political leaders force weaker nations to comply with American views.
   (3) Canada plays a leading role in international politics.
   (4) Canada is dependent on the United States in foreign affairs.
   (5) Canada lacks political power when dealing with the United States.

Governments have five basic functions in a social system. First, a government represents the people of a society in dealing with other governments. Second, a government makes laws and enforces them. The laws of a society reflect the general way people are expected to behave. For example, a law against theft means that stealing is regarded as unacceptable behaviour in that society. Third, government protects the society against dangers and threats that come from both within and outside the nation. Fourth, a government settles disputes between conflicting interests within a society. It sets up systems, such as courts, and processes, such as elections, that help resolve differences and promote systematic methods of decision-making. Finally, government coordinates and develops goals for society and carries them out. In a democracy, many of these goals come from groups in the society. Sometimes it is not possible for people to achieve these goals alone, so they ask for government help. The following ad is an example of this process.

RAISE THE LEGAL DRIVING AGE TO 21

This ad paid for by

Citizens for Safer Streets & Highways

- Studies show that teen drivers have a high accident rate.

- Teen drivers are reckless and careless.

- Raising the driving age will end speeding on our streets and highways.

ASK YOUR MEMBER OF PARLIAMENT TO SUPPORT THIS PROPOSAL.

33. Which of the following is an opinion related to the passage and newspaper advertisement?

 (1) Governments have five basic functions in a social system.
 (2) The goals of society are developed and coordinated by the government.
 (3) Theft is acceptable in some situations.
 (4) The government takes responsibility for making laws and enforcing them.
 (5) Laws reflect the general way people are expected to behave.

34. Which of the following is an opinion held by the sponsor of the advertisement?

 (1) Teenage drivers have a large number of accidents.
 (2) Teenage drivers are unsafe and a menace on the highways.
 (3) The legal driving age is not 21 years old.
 (4) The sponsors want the readers to contact their legislator to support this proposal.
 (5) Citizens for Safer Streets and Highways paid for this advertisement.

The immense diversity of Canada's geography offers many wonderful vacation spots. In British Columbia, many are drawn to the slopes of Whistler and Blackcomb in winter; in summer, one may enjoy the breathtaking view of Shuswap Lake while vacationing in Sicamous, Canada's houseboat capital. In Alberta, tourists flock to Banff and Jasper in the scenic Canadian Rockies for a variety of outdoor activities such as skiing, biking, hiking, and horseback riding. Going east one observes the vast expanse of the Canadian Prairies, with its diverse geography ranging from farms and ranches to wide river valleys, numerous lakes, and rolling hills. In Ontario, tourists are invariably drawn to the natural wonder of Niagara Falls, located at the Canadian–U.S. border. Further east, one is awestruck at the serenity and natural beauty of Quebec. Its multitude of lakes, rivers, and streams invites people to fish and go rafting on La Rivière Rouge in the Laurentian Mountains. In the Maritimes, the Cabot Trail on Cape Breton Island attracts sightseers to its rugged and majestic coastline, and the rusty red soil of Prince Edward Island produces some of the most delicious potatoes in the world. Finally, Nordic travellers can bundle up and go dog-sledding on the glaciers of Baffin Island in the Canadian north.

35. Which statement is the best summary of the paragraph?

    (1) The varied landscapes of Canada provide vacations for everyone.
    (2) People eat better in the Maritimes than in British Columbia.
    (3) Canada is known for its snow and ice.
    (4) Vacations can be taken throughout the year.
    (5) Most Canadians prefer skiing and hiking to fishing and houseboating.

36. What can you conclude from the paragraph about Canada's physical geography?

    (1) Canada's coastlines are beautiful.
    (2) Canada does not have a lot of fresh water.
    (3) Canada has a lot of mountains.
    (4) Canada has a limited number of outdoor pursuits.
    (5) Canadians like to ski.

37. Which of the following states a fact?

    (1) Hiking is a wonderful experience.
    (2) Fresh water activities are most popular.
    (3) In general, Canadians dislike summer sports.
    (4) Cape Breton Island is more beautiful than the Laurentian Mountains.
    (5) Canada has many lakes, rivers, and mountains.

Question 38 refers to the following table.

POPULATION GROWTH IN CANADA Figures are in thousands			
Period	Total Population Growth	Births	Immigration
1941–1951	2 141	3 186	548
1961–1966	1 777	2 249	539
1986–1991	1 930	946	1 199
1991–1996	1 641	1 024	1 137

Source: Statistics Canada, <www.statcan.ca>.

38. What conclusion is supported by the table?

    (1) Life expectancy is longer in the 1990s compared with the 1940s and the 1960s.
    (2) Population has declined since 1941.
    (3) Population growth derived more from immigration than births in the 1990s compared with the 1940s and 1960s.
    (4) Life expectancy is shorter in the 1940s and the 1960s than in the 1990s.
    (5) More babies are born from immigrants in the 1990s compared to the 1940s.

Questions 39 through 42 refer to the following cartoon.

"We plan to bargain all night until an agreement is reached."

From *The Wall Street Journal*—Permission, Cartoon Features Syndicate.

39. What is the main idea of this cartoon?

  (1) Collective bargaining is a long, hard, and exhausting process.
  (2) Employers always lie to the media to make it appear that they are bargaining hard.
  (3) Union leaders always lie to the media to make it appear that they are bargaining hard.
  (4) The public and the media have a right to know the facts in an important labour dispute.
  (5) Negotiators falsely maintain the image of marathon negotiations.

40. Based on the details of the cartoon, which of the following is most likely happening in the negotiations shown?

  The negotiators

  (1) are not making progress.
  (2) have fallen ill.
  (3) are near an agreement.
  (4) are taking a lunch break.
  (5) have just signed a contract.

41. What does the cartoonist assume the reader will recognize?

  (1) which company is negotiating with the union
  (2) which union is negotiating with the company
  (3) that the man with the notebook is a reporter
  (4) the identity of the speaker with the pillow
  (5) the issue being negotiated

42. The cartoon's message is intended to have an effect on the public. Which of the following is the message most like in terms of its intent?

  (1) crying "Fire" in a crowded theatre
  (2) saying, "The cheque is in the mail."
  (3) publicly criticizing a popular politician
  (4) a suspected criminal saying, "No comment."
  (5) admitting that no agreement is possible

43. Work stoppages in the last half of the twentieth century peaked in 1986. That year almost 224 000 workers stopped work or went on strike. In 2001, only 86 000 were involved in work stoppages.

  What is implied by this information?

  (1) There were more work stoppages in 1980 than in 1986.
  (2) The number of workers involved in work stoppages has remained steady.
  (3) There has been a decline in the number of work stoppages since 1986.
  (4) Workers usually have good reasons for stopping work.
  (5) People do not get paid during work stoppages.

Canada's first constitution, the *British North America Act*, was introduced in the British Parliament on March 1, 1867 and passed with little debate. The new country would be a confederation of four provinces, with a central government organized like its British model, and four provincial governments.

In the minds of the Fathers of Confederation, railways would link the provinces; railways were the symbol of the progressive spirit of the age. The Fathers had visions of everexpanding factories and natural resources whose products would move by rail to every corner of the new Dominion. Of course, Canada's continuing ties to the mother country would cement these bonds.

In recent times, Confederation has been described as a "top-down" exercise. There was no election or referendum where the people said "yes" or "no" to it, except in tiny New Brunswick. There was also no constitutional convention, following the American example. In short, Confederation followed the traditional British North American way of little democracy. Although it is true that the old oligarchies of British North America were forced to accept more openness in both government and the economy, the government actually remained in the hands of a very small group of men. Women played no role at all in the constitutional discussions, so perhaps it is not surprising that the *BNA Act* was silent on issues related to gender. Patriarchy was just assumed to be the natural law. Aboriginal people were also excluded from the deliberations. The *BNA Act* recognized their existence only to the extent that their welfare was a federal government responsibility.

44. What is meant by the claim that Confederation was a "top-down" exercise?

   (1) The *British North America Act* was signed in a railway car open to the air.
   (2) Queen Victoria forced her will on the Canadian delegates to the British Parliament.
   (3) It was imposed on the rest of the population by a small, exclusive group of men, without consultation or a vote.
   (4) It was a free and democratic process.
   (5) It came about as a result of civil war.

45. The railway was the dominant symbol of progress in the age of Confederation. At the close of the twentieth century, what technological symbol seemed to represent progress, not only in Canada, but around the world?

   (1) wind power
   (2) cable television
   (3) microwave ovens
   (4) computers and the Internet
   (5) cars

Question 46 refers to the following passage.

In the early 1500s, soldier-explorers called conquistadors defeated the native Aztec people in Mexico and established Spain's first colony in North America. As Spanish settlement slowly spread north, Catholic priests founded missions. Each mission consisted of a town built around a church. The Spanish founded about 150 missions in what is now the United States. Most missions were in the present-day states of Florida, Texas, New Mexico, Arizona, and California.

The purpose of a mission was to develop the surrounding region and convert its Aboriginal peoples to Christianity. Gradually, large Aboriginal villages developed around missions. Most of the mission's work was done by these village residents. The lives of the "mission Indians" were harsh. They worked in shops, weaving cloth and making other products. In nearby fields, they tended cattle and raised a variety of crops. They were forced to obey the priests' orders and also to give up their religions. Those who resisted often were whipped.

46. The passage suggests that the lives of "mission Indians" were most like the lives of which other group?

   (1) factory workers
   (2) farmers
   (3) Catholic priests
   (4) Spanish colonists
   (5) slaves

Questions 47 and 48 refer to the following cartoon and paragraph.

"Have you given any thought to what you'll do with your Saturdays when the world's fossil fuels are used up?"

Fossil fuels include all fuels derived from underground deposits of coal, oil, and natural gas. Fossil fuels have been formed over millions of years from the buried remains of plants and animals. The burning of fossil fuels provides most of the world's energy. Less than 10 percent of the energy used is produced by other methods. The increasing demand for energy has begun to exhaust the supply of fossil fuels. Some experts estimate that coal will be gone in 250 years, and that the world's known oil reserves may last only another 30.

47. What fact does the cartoonist assume you know to understand the point of the cartoon?

(1) Washing cars depletes water resources.
(2) Most Canadians use commercial car washes.
(3) Most Canadians do not work on Saturdays.
(4) Gasoline, which powers automobiles, is a fossil fuel.
(5) Coal supplies most of the world's energy.

48. Which conclusion is supported by the information in the paragraph and the cartoon?

(1) We are too dependent on fossil fuels.
(2) People should conserve water resources.
(3) Fossil fuels will not run out soon.
(4) New forms of transportation will be invented.
(5) People will walk more in the future.

49. Temperatures of places are affected by their latitude and elevation. Latitude is the distance of a place from the equator. The sun's heat is strongest at the equator. Elevation affects temperature because the higher a place is, the cooler it will be.

Which of these places would be the coldest?

(1) close to the equator with a high elevation
(2) far from the equator with a low elevation
(3) close to the equator with a low elevation
(4) far from the equator with a high elevation
(5) on the equator with a high elevation

Question 50 refers to the following passage and cartoon.

For nearly a century after the Union of South Africa was created in 1910, the nation was controlled by its white minority. Black South Africans, who made up the vast majority of the population, were denied the right to vote.

After World War II, the government introduced a policy of apartheid, meaning "apartness," that regulated nearly every aspect of black South Africans' lives. When the African National Congress (ANC), a black-rights organization, protested the government's policies, it was banned. Its leader, Nelson Mandela, was sentenced to life in prison in 1962.

Despite these actions, opposition to apartheid grew during the following decades. The South African government responded with increased violence. In the 1980s, people around the world, as well as growing numbers of white South Africans, called for an end to apartheid.

By 1990, many apartheid laws had been relaxed or repealed. The ban on the ANC was lifted, and Mandela was freed. However, black South Africans continued to press for full and equal rights. The government finally agreed to South Africa's first all-race elections.

In April 1994, millions of black South Africans waited patiently in long lines to take part in their first national election. Nelson Mandela was elected South Africa's first black president, winning an overwhelming majority of the votes.

Jack Higgins, courtesy of the *Chicago Sun-Times*.

50. What does the wrist iron and chain symbolize in the cartoon?

   (1) black South Africans
   (2) low wages
   (3) violent change
   (4) the ANC
   (5) apartheid

Simulated Test Performance Analysis Chart
Social Studies

   This chart can help you determine your strengths and weaknesses on the content and skill areas of the GED Social Studies Simulated Test. Use the Answers and Explanations on page 861 to check your answers to the test. Then circle on the chart the numbers of the test items you answered correctly. Put the total number correct for each content area and skill area in each row and column. Look at the total items correct in each column and row and decide which areas are difficult for you. Use the lesson references to study those areas.

Thinking Skill / Content Area	Comprehension (Lessons 1, 2, 7, 16, 18)	Analysis (Lessons 3, 4, 6, 9, 10, 11, 12, 19)	Application (Lessons 14, 15)	Evaluation (Lessons 5, 8, 13, 17, 20)	Total Correct
Canadian History (*Lessons 1–6*)	5, 25	**4**, 22, 26, **27, 44**	10, 45, 46	**11**, 21	____/12
World History (*Lessons 7–10*)	7, **50**	**18, 19**	6, 23	**20**, 24	____/8
Civics and Government (*Lessons 11–14*)	**12, 31**	8, **14**, 29, **30, 32, 33, 34**	**15**, 28	**13**, 17	____/13
Economics (*Lessons 15–17*)	**1, 39**, 43	**2, 9, 16, 41**	**42**	**3, 40**	____/10
Geography (*Lessons 18–20*)	35	36, 37, **47**	49	**38, 48**	____/7
Total Correct	____/10	____/20	____/10	____/10	____/50

> 1–40 → You need more review.
> 41–50 → Congratulations! You're ready for the GED!

Boldfaced numbers indicate questions based on charts, graphs, diagrams, photos, and drawings.

SCIENCE

Directions

The Science Simulated Test consists of multiple-choice questions intended to measure your understanding of general science concepts. The questions are based on short readings, graphs, charts, or diagrams. Study the information given, and then answer the questions that follow. Refer to the information as often as necessary in answering the questions.

Spend no more than 80 minutes answering the 50 questions on the Science Simulated Test. Work carefully, but do not spend too much time on any one question. Do not skip any items. Make a reasonable guess when you are unsure of an answer. You will not be penalized for incorrect answers.

When time is up, note the last item you finished. This will tell you whether you can finish the real GED Test in the time allowed. Then complete the Simulated Test.

Record your answers to the questions on a copy of the answer sheet on page 919. Be sure that all required information is properly recorded on the answer sheet.

To record your answers, mark the numbered circle on the answer sheet that corresponds to the answer you choose for each question on the test.

Example

Which of the following is the smallest unit in a living thing?

(1) tissue
(2) organ
(3) cell
(4) muscle
(5) capillary

The correct answer is "cell"; therefore, answer circle 3 should be marked on the answer sheet.

Do not rest the point of your pencil on the answer sheet while considering your answer. Do not make any stray or unnecessary marks. If you change an answer, erase your first mark completely. Mark only one answer circle for each question; multiple answers will be scored as incorrect. Do not fold or crease your answer sheet.

When you finish the test, use the Performance Analysis Chart on page 684 to determine whether you are ready to take the real GED Test and, if not, which skill areas need additional review.

Directions: Choose the one best answer to each question.

Questions 1 through 5 refer to the information below.

Scientists have developed a geologic timeline to record the history of Earth. Geological time is often described in terms of four eras.

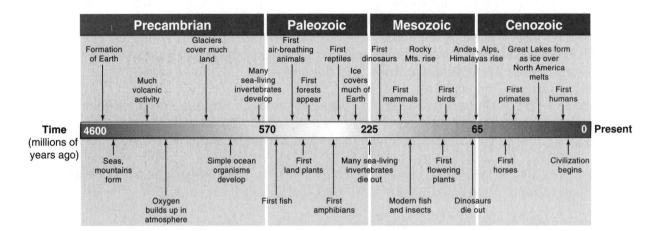

1. Which of the following statements is a conclusion rather than a supporting detail?

    (1) Primates appeared about 50 million years ago.
    (2) Humans appeared in the late Cenozoic.
    (3) Horses appeared in the Cenozoic.
    (4) Humans did not exist for most of geologic time.
    (5) The Great Lakes formed during the Cenozoic.

2. Which of the following kinds of fossils would most likely be found in Mesozoic rocks?

    (1) only simple ocean organisms
    (2) land plants, dinosaurs, and horses
    (3) fish, land plants, and dinosaurs
    (4) primates and humans
    (5) flowering plants and primates

3. About how long did dinosaurs exist?

    (1)   65 million years
    (2)   160 million years
    (3)   225 million years
    (4) 4535 million years
    (5)   1 billion years

4. Which of the following might have been eaten by the first fish?

    (1) flowering plants
    (2) sea-living invertebrates
    (3) insects
    (4) amphibians
    (5) land plants

5. Which of the following statements is supported by the information in the timeline?

    (1) The first air-breathing animals were amphibians.
    (2) Dinosaurs were the chief form of life during the Paleozoic Era.
    (3) The Great Lakes are younger than the Rocky Mountains.
    (4) Dinosaurs died out five million years ago.
    (5) The first forms of life originated on land and then developed in the sea.

Question 6 refers to the following paragraph and structural formulas.

Two compounds whose molecules have the same number and kind of atoms but different arrangements of atoms are called isomers. Compare the isomers of the hydrocarbon butane shown below. Although these isomers have the same chemical formula, they are different compounds with different properties. For example, the straight-chain butane has a higher boiling point than the branched-chain butane. The more carbon atoms contained in a hydrocarbon molecule, the more isomers that molecule can form.

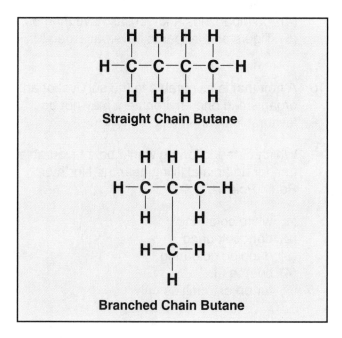

Straight Chain Butane

Branched Chain Butane

6. Pentane (C_5H_{12}), a member of the alkane series of hydrocarbons, has three isomers. Based on information from the paragraph, how does another member of this series, decane ($C_{10}H_{22}$), contrast with pentane?

   (1) Decane has fewer hydrogen atoms.
   (2) Decane has no isomers.
   (3) Decane has fewer isomers.
   (4) Decane has the same number of isomers.
   (5) Decane has more isomers.

Question 7 refers to the information below.

A mineral is a substance that has five basic characteristics, or properties:

   1. It is found naturally on Earth.
   2. It is a solid.
   3. It was never alive.
   4. It is made of particular elements.
   5. Its particles are arranged in a definite pattern called a crystal.

Minerals are often found mixed together in rocks. Rock deposits that contain certain minerals are called ores. Removing a mineral from ore involves mining the ore and then smelting it. During smelting, the ore is heated in such a way that the particular mineral separates from the other substances in the rock.

7. One piece of granite was formed from tiny particles of three different colours. Another piece of granite was formed from particles of four different colours. Which of the following statements best supports the conclusion that granite is merely a rock, not a mineral?

   (1) Granite occurs naturally on Earth.
   (2) Granite is one of the most common rocks on Earth's surface.
   (3) There are different types of granite, each made of different minerals.
   (4) Granite forms from cooling magma.
   (5) Granite is a solid.

EARTH'S ATMOSPHERE

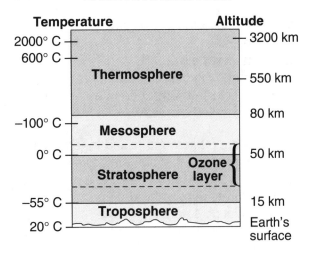

8. As you go higher in the troposphere, the air becomes "thinner," or less dense. There is much less oxygen in a given volume of air than there is at sea level. Which of the following experiences gives adequate evidence to confirm this statement?

(1) A runner from Halifax, which is at sea level, has trouble breathing while jogging in the Rocky Mountains.
(2) A person exposed to the ultraviolet rays of the sun is much likelier to get burned at higher altitudes than at sea level.
(3) A hiker in the mountains is much more likely to experience cold temperatures than a hiker at sea level.
(4) A person who climbs high mountains trains for an expedition by re-creating atmospheric conditions at sea level.
(5) Before opening a parachute, a skydiver experiences free-fall from 3600 m to about 750 m above the ground.

9. Convergence occurs when species that are not closely related evolve similar traits independently. These traits are adaptations to a similar environment. For example, sharks and dolphins have similarly shaped bodies and fins, but they are not closely related. Sharks are fish and dolphins are mammals.

Which of the following is another example of convergence?

(1) Bluebirds and butterflies have wings.
(2) Dolphins and whales have blowholes.
(3) Dogs and wolves have sharp canine teeth.
(4) Chimpanzees and gorillas have thumbs.
(5) Tigers and leopards have patterned fur.

10. A trait that is favourable to the survival of an organism in one environment may not be favourable in another.

Which of the following would be a favourable trait for an animal living near the North or South Pole?

(1) white colouring
(2) dark colouring
(3) dappled colouring
(4) sparse fur
(5) fur on extremities only

Question 11 refers to the following information.

After years of decline, the water bird population of a city harbour is increasing because of cleaner water. Population trends for two species are shown.

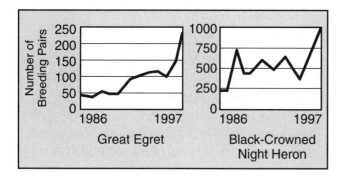

11. Which of the following is supported by the information given?

(1) Water birds lost harbour island habitats to apartment developments.
(2) New laws in 1970 reduced the release of pollutants from cars.
(3) There are more herons and egrets because clean water means more fish to eat.
(4) Water bird populations are increasing because they have no predators.
(5) Heron and egret females lay only one or two eggs per year.

Question 12 refers to the following passage.

You may not think of the kitchen as being a chemistry lab, but many chemicals can be found right on your kitchen shelf. One substance that contains several interesting chemicals is baking powder, which is used to make cake batter rise.

The principal ingredient in baking powder is sodium bicarbonate, $NaHCO_3$. When sodium bicarbonate reacts with an acid, it produces water and the gas carbon dioxide (CO_2). When sodium bicarbonate is heated to baking temperatures, it breaks down to form carbon dioxide and sodium carbonate (Na_2CO_3), a bland-tasting salt. Baking powder also contains a compound, such as a tartrate, that will react with water to form acids.

12. When baking powder is added to batter, which substance causes the cake to rise?

(1) salt
(2) oxygen gas
(3) water
(4) tartrate
(5) carbon dioxide gas

13. The fossil record consists of the preserved remains of long-dead organisms that have been studied by scientists. The fossil record provides clues about how and when organisms evolved.

For which of the following would the fossil record be useful?

(1) predicting which modern species will eventually die out
(2) plotting the evolutionary relationships among extinct organisms
(3) determining the life span of an individual member of a modern species
(4) calculating how long ago Earth first formed
(5) measuring the number of species on Earth today

14. Parasitism is a relationship in which one species benefits at the expense of another. Which of the following is an example of parasitism?

(1) Cowbirds lay their eggs in the nests of songbirds, which incubate and raise cowbird chicks.
(2) The remora fish obtains food by picking parasitic organisms off the skin of a shark.
(3) Plants with nitrogen-fixing bacteria on their roots gain nitrogen compounds while the bacteria gain food.
(4) The crocodile bird obtains food from the crocodile's teeth while cleaning them.
(5) Sea anemones get food from hermit crabs while protecting the crabs from predators.

15. Friction between two solid objects can be reduced by lubricating them—inserting a layer of fluid between them. Because the molecules in fluids such as oil flow freely, they allow easier movement between the two surfaces.

What would be the result of running an engine that is low on oil?

(1) decreased friction on the moving parts
(2) increased friction on the moving parts
(3) decreased friction on the stationary parts
(4) increased friction on the stationary parts
(5) easier movement of the engine's parts

16. The thyroid gland produces a substance containing iodine that helps regulate growth. Goiter is an enlargement of the thyroid gland caused by a lack of iodine in the diet. Goiter is uncommon in coastal areas where people eat seafood that contains a form of iodine. It is more common inland, where people eat food that has been grown in soil lacking iodine.

Which phrase restates the cause of the disease goiter, as given in the passage?

(1) eating too much fish
(2) eating too little of foods high in iodine
(3) exposure to a bacterium found in iodine
(4) fertilizing the soil with iodine
(5) inheriting a defective thyroid gene

Questions 17 and 18 refer to the following passage and diagram.

Three important groups of chemical compounds are acids, bases, and salts. When dissolved in water, these compounds produce ions. Ions are atoms or molecules with an electric charge. In water, acids produce hydrogen, or H^+ ions. In water, bases produce hydroxide, or OH^- ions.

There are many commonly used acids and bases. Citric acid is found in citrus fruits. Vitamin C is ascorbic acid. Magnesium hydroxide is a base that is the active ingredient in many stomach remedies. Sodium bicarbonate is a base in baking soda and baking powder.

A strong acid, such as sulphuric acid, or a strong base, such as sodium hydroxide, is poisonous and can burn the skin. Yet a weak acid, such as citric acid, or a weak base, such as magnesium hydroxide, can be safely handled and even ingested (eaten).

The strength of an acid or base is measured on a scale called the pH scale. The pH scale generally ranges from 0 to 14. The number 7 is the neutral point. Substances with a pH below 7 are acidic, and substances with a pH above 7 are basic. Extremely strong acids have a pH of 0; extremely strong bases have a pH of 14.

pH Scale

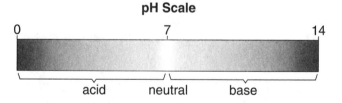

When an acid and a base combine chemically, the results are two neutral compounds: water and a salt. One familiar salt is sodium chloride, table salt.

17. Which of the following is correctly ordered from lowest to highest pH?

(1) magnesium hydroxide, citric acid, pure water, sulphuric acid, sodium hydroxide
(2) pure water, sulphuric acid, citric acid, sodium hydroxide, magnesium hydroxide
(3) sulphuric acid, sodium hydroxide, citric acid, magnesium hydroxide, pure water
(4) sulphuric acid, citric acid, pure water, magnesium hydroxide, sodium hydroxide
(5) sodium hydroxide, magnesium hydroxide, pure water, citric acid, sulphuric acid

18. When calcium hydroxide, a base, reacts with citric acid, the reaction produces calcium citrate and water. What is calcium citrate?

(1) a strong acid
(2) a weak acid
(3) a salt
(4) a weak base
(5) a strong base

Question 19 refers to the following passage and diagram.

Protein synthesis occurs in the cytoplasm of the cell and uses instructions from the DNA in the cell's nucleus. During the first stage of protein synthesis, the two sides of the DNA strands unzip, exposing a section of the molecule. The exposed bases on the DNA segment act as a template to make messenger RNA. Bases on messenger RNA nucleotides sequence themselves to pair correctly with the bases on the DNA segment. This template for the original DNA segment, called messenger RNA, then passes from the nucleus into the cytoplasm.

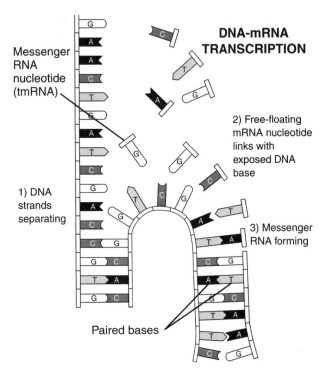

The messenger RNA attaches itself to a ribosome in the cytoplasm, which reads the sequence of bases. Each group of three base pairs, called a codon, specifies a particular amino acid. In the ribosome, the codons are matched with the correct amino acids, the building blocks of proteins. A protein may contain 100 to 500 amino acids linked in a chain.

19. A mutation occurs when one DNA base is substituted for another in error, causing a change in a codon. What is the most likely result of such a mutation?

(1) a change in the sequence of amino acids in a protein
(2) a change in the cytoplasm of the organism's cells
(3) a change in the nuclei of the organism's cells
(4) a change in the ribosomes of the organism's cells
(5) the death of the organism

Question 20 refers to the following information and diagram.

A shield volcano results from quiet, often slow, flows of lava. The lava from a shield volcano spreads over a large area, forming a gently sloping dome-shaped mountain.

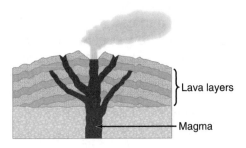

20. Which of the following volcanoes is a shield volcano?

(1) Mt. Vesuvius, which erupted violently in 79 C.E., burying Pompeii in three days
(2) Mt. Fujiyama, a steep-sided, symmetrical cone in Japan
(3) Mt. Pelee, which erupted with a fiery cloud that destroyed St. Pierre in ten minutes
(4) Paricutín, a volcano built of lava fragments and ash, which grew to a height of 40 m overnight
(5) Kilauea Iki, whose lava spread over Hawaii during several months

Questions 21 and 22 refer to the following passage.

The genetic code of an organism is called its genome. It is determined by the sequence in which four chemicals (called nitrogen bases and abbreviated A, T, C, and G) appear in the DNA molecules that make up genes. Variations in the sequence of these four nitrogen bases account for the unique genetic code of each organism.

The Human Genome Project began in 1990. This was an effort to identify individual genes, map their locations along the chromosomes, and identify the sequence of nitrogen bases within them. Scientists have approached this project in several steps. First they have worked on mapping the location of genes along large portions of DNA; next they have been sequencing the nitrogen bases that make up each gene. Because the human genome has about 3 billion nitrogen-base pairs, the project was expected to take about 15 years.

However, in 1998, a private company developed a new technology, enabling them to sequence all the nitrogen bases in the entire human genome in a few years, before identifying and mapping the gene locations. Millions of fragments of human DNA were run through high-speed sequencing machines. Then they were reassembled by powerful supercomputers. The company completed the sequencing in 2000. Early in 2000 details were published on the mapping of the human genome.

Some scientists argue that this procedure may have led to errors in reassembling the DNA fragments, so that individual genes cannot be accurately identified and mapped. Supporters say the results will be adequate for use in a variety of research.

21. Which of the following is an opinion rather than a fact?

(1) The Human Genome Project was expected to take 15 years.
(2) The human genome consists of about 3 billion nitrogen-base pairs.
(3) Each organism has a genetic code called a genome.
(4) A private company developed sequencers that analyzed the human genome in a few years.
(5) The results of the private company's sequencing and mapping are of poor quality.

22. In which of the following areas should scientists' ability to "read" the human genome be of greatest advantage?

(1) designing and producing more efficient gene-sequencing machines
(2) improving the course of study in medical schools
(3) preventing and treating hereditary diseases
(4) preventing and treating bacterial diseases
(5) improving the quality of genetically engineered agricultural products

23. Each person has a unique pattern of DNA that can be analyzed. Because the results of such an analysis are unique to each individual, they are often called a "DNA fingerprint."

Which of the following would be the most useful application of DNA fingerprinting?

(1) identifying criminals
(2) typing blood
(3) analyzing the nutrients in food
(4) doing laser surgery
(5) treating disease

24. A transplant is the placing of organs or grafting of tissue from one person or animal into another or from one part of the body to another part. The success of a transplant depends on compatibility between donor and recipient. If the donor organ or tissue is not compatible, the recipient's immune system may reject it.

Which of the following transplants is most likely to succeed?

(1) A man receives a heart from a baboon.
(2) A boy receives a kidney from a cousin.
(3) A girl receives a lung from an unrelated woman.
(4) Healthy sections of a man's intestine are used to replace diseased sections.
(5) A leukemia patient receives a bone marrow transplant from her aunt.

Question 25 refers to the following passage.

Herbicides are chemicals that kill plants. When herbicides are used on crops, it is important that the herbicide kill only the weeds and not the crops. Through genetic engineering, scientists have been developing crops that are not affected by specific herbicides. These resistant crops enable farmers to use herbicides to control weeds. For example, scientists have developed a strain of corn that is resistant to the herbicide glyphosate. When this herbicide is used, it kills weeds but not the resistant corn plants. Other crops that have varieties resistant to certain herbicides are soybeans, tobacco, tomatoes, sugar beets, and cotton.

Some environmental groups are opposed to the development of herbicide-resistant crops. They say that these crops encourage farmers to continue to use chemicals that pollute the environment for long periods and that may be unsafe. These groups favour methods such as improved cultivation techniques and creative planting plans that make the use of chemicals unnecessary.

25. Based on the passage, which of the following is an opinion rather than a fact?

(1) Chemical herbicides are used to kill weeds.
(2) Some varieties of soybean and tobacco plants are resistant to certain herbicides.
(3) Glyphosate is a type of chemical herbicide.
(4) Improved cultivation techniques are preferable to herbicide use.
(5) Scientists have developed strains of herbicide-resistant crops.

Question 26 refers to the following passage and diagram.

The tide is the periodic rise and fall of the sea. High and low tides occur about twice a day. In areas in which the water rises and falls more than 4.6 m, the water flow can be used to generate electricity.

A tidal power station is part of a dam built across the mouth of a river. Channels in the dam allow water to flow through when the tide rises and flow back out when the tide falls. The water flow turns turbines that operate generators that produce electricity.

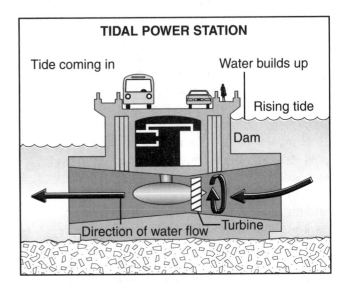

TIDAL POWER STATION

Tide coming in — Water builds up — Rising tide — Dam — Direction of water flow — Turbine

The energy harnessed by tidal power is very clean in that no pollutants are given off. However, tidal power plants disrupt the ecology of the river system they block.

26. Which of the following locations would be most suitable for a tidal power station?

(1) the source of the Assiniboine River in central Saskatchewan
(2) the mouth of the Moose River at Moosonee, with moderate variation in high and low tides
(3) the mouth of the Annapolis River, Nova Scotia, with large variation in high and low tides
(4) the falls of the Missouri River, in the Great Plains of the United States
(5) the Kemano Dam on the Nechako River, British Columbia

Question 27 refers to the following passage.

A force that slows down or prevents objects from moving is friction. One example of friction is air resistance, which you can feel if you stick your hand out the window of a moving car.

A more exciting way to experience air resistance is the sport of skydiving. When a skydiver first jumps from a plane, the only force affecting her is gravity, which pulls her downward. As she falls faster, friction from the passing air increases, slowing her acceleration. Eventually, at about 160 km/h to 240 km/h, the force of friction balances the force of gravity, and she stops accelerating. This is called her terminal velocity. Terminal velocity depends mainly on the skydiver's mass and the body position she holds.

When the skydiver opens her parachute, she increases the area affected by air resistance. She slows to about 40 km/h, a much safer terminal velocity for a landing.

27. To calculate the time it would take for a skydiver to reach Earth, you need to know the distance she must fall and the surface area and mass of her parachute. What other information are you likely to need?

(1) her mass
(2) her volume
(3) her height
(4) speed of airplane
(5) type of airplane

Question 28 refers to the following paragraph and diagram.

In a microwave oven, a magnetron produces a beam of microwaves, a type of electromagnetic radiation. The microwaves strike molecules of water in food, causing the water molecules to align and reverse alignment. The rapid and repeated twisting of the water molecules produces heat.

Microwaves

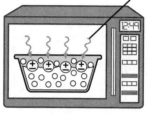 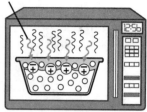

1. Water molecules align

2. Water molecules reverse alignment

28. Which of the following conclusions is supported by information in the passage and diagram?

(1) All types of electromagnetic radiation can cause water molecules to twist.
(2) A microwave oven converts heat energy to electromagnetic energy.
(3) A microwave oven heats food using the same principle as a conventional oven.
(4) Food with a high water content heats more rapidly in a microwave oven than dry food does.
(5) Microwave ovens pose a radiation hazard to people near them.

Questions 29 through 32 refer to the following passage and map.

In the early twentieth century, grey wolves were eradicated throughout the West and in most of the rest of the United States. In 1995 and 1996, grey wolves from Canada were reintroduced to two areas of the western United States—central Idaho and Yellowstone National Park in Wyoming. Natural immigration of wolves from Canada resulted in a third population in northern Montana.

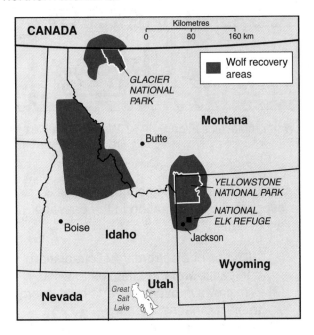

One reason the wolves were imported was to help control the native elk population of Yellowstone, which had grown huge. One wolf pack in Yellowstone has learned how to attack and kill bison as well. They also have killed domesticated animals in their range. During the first three years after their reintroduction in the West, wolves killed 80 cattle, 190 sheep, and 12 dogs. The owners of these animals were compensated for their losses, and the offending wolves were either moved or killed.

Despite the fact that about 10 percent of the wolves die each year, the three populations have increased substantially. There are now several hundred wolves in more than 30 packs. In at least two known instances, wolves from different populations have mated. Eventually there may be a single large population throughout the Rocky Mountain area. Some people argue that the grey wolf should now be removed from the list of endangered species.

29. According to the map, which state has the most scattered areas of wolf population?

(1) Idaho
(2) Montana
(3) Nevada
(4) Utah
(5) Wyoming

30. Which of the following is a title that gives the main idea of the map?

(1) Yellowstone National Park
(2) Idaho, Montana, and Wyoming
(3) National Parks of the Rockies
(4) The Range of the Grey Wolf
(5) Grey Wolves in the National Parks

31. Which of the following is an opinion rather than a fact?

(1) Wolves have learned to hunt bison.
(2) There are more than 30 packs of wolves in the U.S. Rockies.
(3) About 10 percent of the wolves in the western United States die each year.
(4) Owners were paid for livestock killed by wolves.
(5) The grey wolf should no longer be considered endangered.

32. Which of the following is most similar to the reintroduction of grey wolves in the United States?

(1) building passways in dams so salmon can migrate upstream
(2) limiting hunting of certain species of game animals to certain times of year
(3) restoring tallgrass varieties to small portions of the Prairies
(4) introducing a nonnative species to wipe out a pest
(5) preventing nonnative species from entering an area

Sound waves travel best through solids, because the molecules are packed tightly together. Elastic solids, such as nickel, steel, and iron, carry sound especially well; inelastic solids, such as sound-proofing materials, carry sound less well. Liquids are second-best in carrying sound, and gases are least effective.

33. Which of the following expressions relates to the fact that sound waves travel fastest through solids?

    (1) The hills are alive with the sound of music.
    (2) It's music to my ears.
    (3) If a tree falls where no one hears it, does it make a sound?
    (4) Put your ear to the ground.
    (5) Children should be seen and not heard.

34. A virus is a molecule of genetic material covered by a protective protein coat. It shows no sign of life when outside a living cell. To become active, a virus invades a living cell and uses this host cell to duplicate its own genetic material.

    Which is the best restatement of this information?

    (1) A virus is a molecule of genetic material surrounded by a protein coat.
    (2) The protein coat of a virus protects it from threats in the environment.
    (3) A virus is genetic material that appears lifeless until it takes over a cell to reproduce.
    (4) There are about a hundred viruses that cause the common cold.
    (5) Viral diseases are hard to treat because viruses don't respond to antibiotics.

35. Brownian motion occurs when the smaller molecules of a fluid hit the larger particles suspended in it, causing the larger particles to move randomly.

    Which of the following is an unstated assumption important for understanding the information above?

    (1) Brownian motion occurs in a fluid.
    (2) A fluid is a liquid or a gas.
    (3) The fluid's molecules are small.
    (4) Small particles bombard large ones.
    (5) Brownian motion is random.

36. In the process of photosynthesis, green plants use water, carbon dioxide, and the energy from light to make their own food. Researchers have demonstrated that tomato plants grow bigger and produce more tomatoes when the soil is covered with sheets of silver-coloured reflective plastic. According to the researchers, when this plastic is used, more photosynthesis takes place and the plants grow larger.

    Which property of the plastic is likely to cause the increase in photosynthesis?

    (1) its thickness
    (2) its weight
    (3) its reflectivity
    (4) its length
    (5) its flatness

Question 37 refers to the paragraph and the map below.

Most earthquakes and volcanic activity occur along the boundaries of Earth's tectonic plates. In these areas, the plates are crunching together, pulling apart, or sliding past one another.

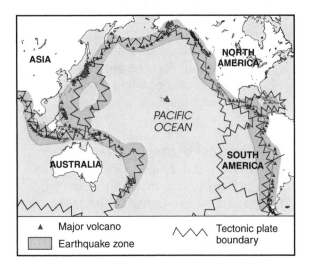

Major volcano

Earthquake zone

Tectonic plate boundary

37. In 1994, a robot named Dante II was sent into the crater of an active volcano to collect data for scientists. In which location was this expedition most likely to have taken place?

(1) the east coast of North America
(2) an island in the southern Pacific
(3) northern Asia
(4) an island in the northern Pacific
(5) northern Australia

Question 38 refers to the following paragraph and diagrams.

The friction created when objects move in air is called drag. Drag acts to slow down a moving object. The amount of drag depends on the shape of the object. Air flows more smoothly around objects with a tapered shape.

AIRFLOW AROUND OBJECTS

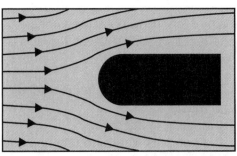

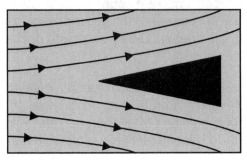

38. Which of the following would result if the drag acting on a moving object were increased?

(1) decreased speed
(2) increased speed
(3) smoother airflow
(4) increased airflow
(5) decreased friction

Question 39 refers to the following passage and diagram.

A polymer consists of large molecules made of many small, repeating units called monomers, which are joined together by covalent bonds. Most of the organic compounds found in living things are polymers. These include cellulose, carbohydrates, fats, and proteins. Many synthetic materials are also polymers. Plastics, nylon and other synthetic fibres, and adhesives are all polymers.

Polymers form structures that take several shapes. A linear polymer consists of long chains of monomers. A branched polymer consists of a long chain molecule with side chains. A cross-linked polymer consists of two or more chains joined together by side chains.

STRUCTURES OF POLYMERS

```
        – M – M – M – M – M – M – M –
                Linear polymer

        |                   |
        M                   M
        |                   |
        M                   M
        |                   |
    – M – M – M – M – M – M – M –
                    |
                    M
                    |
                    M
                    |
                Branched polymer

    – M – M – M – M – M – M – M – M –
        |       |       |       |
        M       M       M       M
        |       |       |       |
        M       M       M       M
        |       |       |       |
    – M – M – M – M – M – M – M – M –
              Cross-linked polymer
```

M = monomer unit

39. Based on the passage, which of the following is characteristic of the monomers that make up polymers?

   Monomers in polymers are

   (1) repetitive.
   (2) large.
   (3) ionic.
   (4) metallic.
   (5) gaseous.

Question 40 refers to the following passage and diagram.

Gravity is a force of attraction that affects all matter. The force of gravity between any two objects depends on their mass and the distance between them.

For example, Earth exerts gravity on objects near its surface, pulling them toward its centre. When you release an object such as a ball, it falls straight down. Earth also exerts gravity on distant objects such as the moon. Because the moon is far away, the force of Earth's gravity is weaker. Earth's gravity is too weak to cause the moon to fall to Earth. However, it is strong enough to exert a pull on it. If Earth were not exerting gravity, the moon would travel in a straight line according to Newton's First Law of Motion. Instead, it travels in an orbit around Earth.

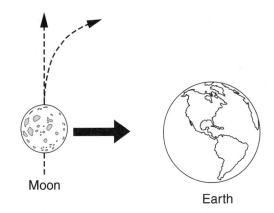

Moon

Earth

40. Which of the following is an unstated assumption about mass that is important for understanding the passage?

   (1) Mass is the volume of an object.
   (2) Mass is the amount of matter in an object.
   (3) The force of gravity is related to an object's mass.
   (4) Some objects do not have any mass.
   (5) The mass of objects cannot be measured.

41. During a baseball game, a spectator sitting in the farthest bleachers sees the ball in the air well before hearing the crack of the bat. Which statement offers the best explanation for this?

(1) The person's ears are plugged up.
(2) The player hit the ball more slowly than usual.
(3) The player hit the ball more quickly than usual.
(4) The baseball is made of elastic materials.
(5) Sound waves travel more slowly than light waves do.

42. A protein in the mucus in your nasal passages can break down the cell walls of bacteria, many of which cause disease. Which of the following is the most likely result of this action?

(1) Bacteria will not be able to enter your nose.
(2) Bacteria that enter your nose will be killed.
(3) Bacteria will enter your nose more easily.
(4) Bacteria in your nose will grow more rapidly.
(5) Bacteria in your nose will not be able to change shape.

43. Transpiration is the process by which plants lose water vapour to the air through pores in their leaves. Where are you most likely to observe evidence of transpiration?

(1) in a desert
(2) at the North Pole
(3) in the ocean
(4) in a greenhouse
(5) in a field of vegetables

44. A longitudinal wave travelling through a medium disturbs the molecules as it passes, causing them to move back and forth in the same direction as the wave moves. Which of the following would make the best model of a longitudinal wave?

(1) Grasp a jump rope and shake the end vigorously up and down.
(2) Turn a jump rope in time to a peppy song.
(3) Pull a few coils of a loose spring toward you and then quickly release them.
(4) Skip a stone across a pond.
(5) Throw a bounce pass during a basketball game.

Question 45 refers to the following paragraph.

Resistance is a material's opposition to the flow of electric current. Some materials provide more resistance to current flow than others do and can be used as insulators. Resistance depends on many factors, including the material, its size, shape, and temperature. Resistance is measured in ohms. Resistance, voltage, and current are related in a formula called Ohm's Law:

$$\text{Resistance} = \frac{\text{Voltage}}{\text{Current}}$$

45. Gold has a lower resistance than copper, and copper has a lower resistance than steel. The thicker the wire, the lower the resistance.

    Which of the following changes would increase the current, assuming that the voltage remains the same? (Hint: Rearrange the formula to determine how resistance must change to increase current.)

    (1) Replace a thick gold wire with a thin gold wire.
    (2) Replace a thin copper wire with a thin steel wire.
    (3) Replace a thick steel wire with a thin steel wire.
    (4) Replace a thick gold wire with a thick copper wire.
    (5) Replace a thin steel wire with a thick copper wire.

46. The law of reflection states that the angle at which a light ray strikes a surface (the angle of incidence) is equal to the angle at which the ray is reflected (the angle of reflection). Both angles are measured in relation to the normal, the line perpendicular to the surface.

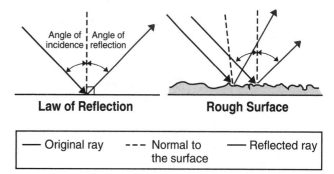

Which statement do the diagrams support?

    (1) A rough surface cannot reflect light, if the original rays come in parallel.
    (2) A rough surface reflects parallel light rays at different angles.
    (3) The law of reflection does not hold for rough surfaces.
    (4) Reflection of one light ray is not normal.
    (5) Reflection of many light rays is not normal.

Question 47 refers to the following passage and diagram.

Great amounts of energy are released by atoms when their nuclei rearrange themselves. In a nuclear fission reaction, an atomic nucleus splits into two smaller, approximately equal-sized nuclei, releasing a great deal of energy. The rapid splitting of many nuclei is a nuclear fission chain reaction.

A NUCLEAR FISSION REACTION

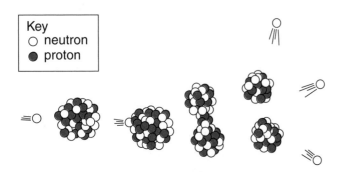

Key
○ neutron
● proton

Nuclear fission can occur naturally or be forced. The first sustained and controlled fission reaction was engineered in 1942. In July 1945, a team of physicists at Los Alamos, New Mexico, created the first nuclear explosion. The following month, the United States dropped two atomic bombs on Japan, devastating two cities and ending World War II. In the years after the war, many of the physicists came to feel they had been wrong to develop a weapon of such mass destruction. They opposed the continued spread of nuclear weapons.

47. Which was probably a primary value of the physicists working on the atomic bomb?

(1) the opportunity to work independently
(2) nonviolent means of conflict resolution
(3) scientific and technical challenge
(4) large monetary reward
(5) the power to destroy

48. Lipids, which include fats, are one class of the organic compounds that make up living things. Cells store energy in lipids for later use.

Which of the following is an example of an organism's use of lipids?

(1) During the winter, a hibernating bear lives on the energy stored as fat.
(2) In the absence of light energy, a green plant stops photosynthesizing.
(3) A student eats an apple for some quick energy.
(4) Enzymes in saliva break down starches into sugars.
(5) Lipids are made up of the elements carbon, hydrogen, and oxygen.

Question 49 refers to the following chart.

Blood Type	A	B	AB	O
Canadian	41.0%	10.0%	4.0%	45.0%
British	26.0%	21.0%	3.7%	49.3%
Aboriginal	7.7%	1.0%	0.0%	91.3%
Swedish	46.7%	10.3%	5.1%	37.9%
Japanese	38.4%	21.8%	8.6%	31.2%
Polynesian	60.8%	2.2%	0.5%	36.5%
Chinese	25.0%	35.0%	10.0%	30.0%

49. Which of the following would be the best title for this chart?

(1) Blood Type Frequency in Selected Populations
(2) Human Blood Types Around the World
(3) Receiving and Giving Blood in Selected Populations
(4) The Genotypes of Each Blood Type
(5) Blood Type Frequency in Canada

50. The leaf is the plant structure in which most photosynthesis takes place. Which characteristic of most leaves maximizes the amount of light energy that can be captured for photosynthesis?

   (1) pores on the underside
   (2) broad, flat shape
   (3) main stalk
   (4) network of veins
   (5) root system

Simulated Test Performance Analysis Chart
Science

This chart can help you determine your strengths and weaknesses on the content and reading skill areas of the Simulated GED Science Test. Use the Answers and Explanations starting on page 866 to check your answers to the test. Then, on the chart, circle the numbers of the test questions you answered correctly. Put the total number correct for each content area and skill area in each row and column. Look at the total questions correct in each column and row and decide which areas are difficult for you. Use the lesson references to study those areas.

Thinking Skill / Content Area	Comprehension (Lessons 1, 2, 6, 9, 13)	Application (Lessons 8, 15)	Analysis (Lessons 3, 4, 7, 10, 14, 17, 19)	Evaluation (Lessons 5, 11, 12, 16, 18, 20)	Total Correct
Life Science (Lessons 1–8)	16, **29**, **30**, 34, **49**	9, 10, 14, 23, 24, **32**, 43, 48	**19**, 21, 22, 25, **31**, 36, 42, 50	**11**, 13	____/23
Earth and Space Science (Lessons 9–13)	2, 3	**20, 26, 37**	**1, 4**	**5**, 7, **8**	____/10
Physical Science (Lessons 14–20)	**17, 39**	**18**, 33, 44, 45	**6**, 12, 15, 35, **38, 40**	27, **28**, 41, **46, 47**	____/17
Total Correct	____/9	____/15	____/16	____/10	____/50

1–40 → You need more review.
41–50 → Congratulations! You're ready for the GED!

Boldfaced numbers indicate questions based on charts, graphs, diagrams, or drawings.

LANGUAGE ARTS, READING
Directions

The Language Arts, Reading Simulated Test consists of excerpts from fiction, nonfiction, poetry, and drama. Each excerpt is followed by multiple-choice questions about the reading material.

Read each excerpt first and then answer the questions that follow. Refer to the reading material as often as necessary in answering the questions.

A "purpose question" precedes each excerpt. The purpose question gives a reason for reading the material. Use these purpose questions to help focus your reading. You do not have to answer the purpose questions. They are given only to help you concentrate on the ideas presented in the reading material.

Spend no more than 65 minutes answering the 40 questions on this test. Work carefully, but do not spend too much time on any one question. Do not skip any items. Make a reasonable guess when you are not sure of an answer. You will not be penalized for incorrect answers.

When time is up, make a note of the last item you finished. This will tell you whether you can finish the real GED Test in the time allowed. Then complete the Simulated Test.

Record your answers to the questions on a copy of the answer sheet on page 920. Record all required information properly on the answer sheet.

To record your answers, fill in the numbered circle on the answer sheet that corresponds to the answer you choose for each question on the test.

Example

It was Susan's dream machine. The metallic blue paint gleamed, and the sporty wheels were highly polished. Under the hood, the engine was no less carefully cleaned. Inside, flashy lights illuminated the instruments on the dashboard, and the seats were covered by rich leather upholstery.

What does "It" most likely refer to in this excerpt?

(1) an airplane
(2) a stereo system
(3) an automobile
(4) a boat
(5) a motorcycle

The correct answer is "an automobile"; therefore, answer circle 3 would be filled in on the answer sheet.

Do not rest the point of your pencil on the answer sheet while you are considering your answer. Do not make any stray or unnecessary marks. If you change an answer, erase your first mark completely. Mark only one answer circle for each question; multiple answers will be scored as incorrect. Do not fold or crease your answer sheet.

When you finish the test, use the Performance Analysis Chart on page 700 to determine whether you are ready to take the real GED Test and, if not, which skill areas need additional review.

Directions: Choose the one best answer to each question.

Questions 1 through 7 refer to the following excerpt from a novel.

ARE THESE TWO SISTERS HAVING THE SAME LUCK AT LOVE?

Yet the misery, for which years of happiness were to offer no compensation, received soon afterwards material relief, from observing how much the beauty of
(5)   her sister re-kindled the admiration of her former lover. When first he came in, he had spoken to her but little; but every five minutes seemed to be giving her more of his attention. He found her as
(10) handsome as she had been last year; as good natured, and as unaffected, though not quite so chatty. Jane was anxious that no difference should be perceived in her at all, and was really persuaded that she
(15) talked as much as ever. But her mind was so busily engaged, that she did not always know when she was silent.

When the gentlemen rose to go away, Mrs. Bennet was mindful of her intended
(20) civility, and they were invited and engaged to dine at Longbourn in a few days time. …

As soon as they were gone, Elizabeth walked out to recover her spirits; or in other words, to dwell without interruption
(25) on those subjects that must deaden them more. Mr. Darcy's behaviour astonished and vexed her.

"Why, if he came only to be silent, grave, and indifferent," said she, "did he
(30) come at all?"

She could settle it in no way that gave her pleasure.

"He could be still amiable, still pleasing, to my uncle and aunt, when he was in
(35) town; and why not to me? If he fears me, why come hither? If he no longer cares for me, why silent? Teasing, teasing man! I will think no more about him."

Her resolution was for a short time
(40) involuntarily kept by the approach of her sister who joined her with a cheerful look, which showed her better satisfied with their visitors, than Elizabeth.

"Now," said she, "That this first meeting
(45) is over, I feel perfectly easy. I know my own strength, and I shall never be embarrassed again by his coming. I am glad he dines here on Tuesday. It will then be publicly seen, that on both sides, we meet only as
(50) common and indifferent acquaintance."

"Yes, very indifferent indeed," said Elizabeth, laughingly. "Oh Jane, take care."

"My dear Lizzy, you cannot think me so weak, as to be in danger now."

(55) "I think you are in very great danger of making him as much in love with you as ever."

Jane Austen, *Pride and Prejudice.*

1. Which of the following words best describes what Elizabeth feels toward Mr. Darcy?

   (1) attraction
   (2) envy
   (3) gratitude
   (4) respect
   (5) suspicion

2. Why is Elizabeth upset?

   (1) Her sister flirts with Mr. Darcy.
   (2) Mr. Darcy has ignored her.
   (3) Mr. Darcy fusses over her too much.
   (4) Her mother intrudes on the men's visit.
   (5) Mr. Darcy has been rude to her relatives.

3. Based on the excerpt, what is Elizabeth most likely to do in the future?

   (1) She will apologize to Mr. Darcy for her rude behaviour.
   (2) She will be preoccupied with thoughts about Mr. Darcy.
   (3) She will try to convince Jane to drop her boyfriend.
   (4) She will stop speaking to her aunt and uncle.
   (5) She will give up all hope of romance.

4. Based on the excerpt, which description best characterizes the relationship between Elizabeth and Jane?

   (1) critical and competitive
   (2) distant but polite
   (3) close and affectionate
   (4) turbulent and troubled
   (5) fragile but deepening

5. Which of the following best describes what Elizabeth means when she says "very indifferent indeed" (line 51)?

   (1) She is commending Jane for her behaviour.
   (2) She is describing Mr. Darcy's attitude.
   (3) She is questioning Jane's claims of indifference.
   (4) She is giving her opinion of the planned dinner.
   (5) She is sharing her observations about Mrs. Bennet.

6. Of the characters in this excerpt, whose inner thoughts are hidden from the reader?

   (1) Elizabeth's
   (2) Jane's
   (3) Jane's visitor's
   (4) Mr. Darcy's
   (5) Mrs. Bennet's

7. In which of the following ways are Jane and Mr. Darcy alike?

   (1) Neither is very talkative on the day of the visit.
   (2) Both question Elizabeth about her behaviour.
   (3) Neither has any desire to go to Longbourn.
   (4) Both seem especially cheerful after the visit.
   (5) Both appear to enjoy teasing Elizabeth.

CAN THIS CHILD BE TRUSTED?

MARY: *(without looking up)* I'm not lying. I went out walking and I saw the flowers and they looked pretty and I didn't know it was so late.

(5) KAREN: *(impatiently)* Stop it, Mary! I'm not interested in hearing that foolish story again. I *know* you got the flowers out of the garbage can. What I do want to know is why you feel you have to lie

(10) out of it.

MARY: *(beginning to whimper)* I *did* pick the flowers near Conway's. You never believe me. You believe everybody but me. It's always like that. Everything I

(15) say you fuss at me about. Everything I do is wrong.

KAREN: You know that isn't true. *(Goes to MARY, puts her arm around her, waits until the sobbing has stopped)* Look,

(20) Mary, look at me. *(Raises MARY'S face with her hand)* Let's try to understand each other. If you feel that you *have* to take a walk, or that you just *can't* come to class, or that you'd

(25) like to go into the village by yourself, come and tell me—I'll try and understand. *(smiles)* I don't say that I'll always agree that you should do exactly what you want to do, but I've

(30) had feelings like that, too—everybody has—and I won't be unreasonable about yours. But this way, this kind of lying you do, makes everything wrong.

MARY: *(looking steadily at KAREN)* I got

(35) the flowers near Conway's cornfield.

KAREN: *(looks at MARY, sighs, moves back toward desk and stands there for a moment)* Well, there doesn't seem to be any other way with you; you'll have

(40) to be punished. Take your recreation periods alone for the next two weeks.

No horseback-riding and no hockey. Don't leave the school grounds for any reason whatsoever. Is that clear?

(45) MARY: *(carefully)* Saturday, too?

KAREN: Yes.

MARY: But you said I could go to the boat races.

KAREN: I'm sorry, but you can't go.

(50) MARY: I'll tell my grandmother. I'll tell her how everybody treats me here and the way I get punished for every little thing I do. I'll tell her. I'll—

MRS. MORTAR: Why, I'd slap her

(55) hands! . . .

KAREN: *(turning back from door, ignoring MRS. MORTAR'S speech. To MARY)* Go upstairs, Mary.

MARY: I don't feel well.

(60) KAREN: *(wearily)* Go upstairs now.

MARY: I've got a pain. I've had it all morning. It hurts right here. *(pointing vaguely in the direction of her heart)* Really it does.

(65) KAREN: Ask Miss Dobie to give you some hot water and bicarbonate of soda.

MARY: It's a bad pain. I've never had it before.

KAREN: I don't think it can be very

(70) serious.

MARY: My heart! It's my heart! It's stopping or something. I can't breathe. *(She takes a long breath and falls awkwardly to the floor.)*

Lillian Hellman, *The Children's Hour.*

8. Which of the following phrases best describes Mary?

   (1) lonely and misunderstood
   (2) pathetic and victimized
   (3) friendly and open
   (4) slow-witted and dull
   (5) sneaky and uncooperative

9. Based on the information in this excerpt, how would Mary most likely behave on the job?

   She would

   (1) make excuses for turning in work late
   (2) be too frightened to voice her opinion
   (3) quit after only a few days
   (4) work hard to get promoted
   (5) be able to communicate well with co-workers

10. Which of the following best describes the mood created in this scene?

    (1) harmonious
    (2) suspenseful
    (3) tense
    (4) sorrowful
    (5) lighthearted

11. Which of the following is the most likely reason that Mary falls to the floor?

    (1) She is upset and has fainted.
    (2) She has a heart ailment.
    (3) She does not like what Karen said.
    (4) She does not want Mrs. Mortar to slap her.
    (5) She exhausted herself on her long walk.

12. Based on the excerpt, what can be inferred about Karen's relationship with Mrs. Mortar?

    (1) Karen does not value Mrs. Mortar's opinions.
    (2) Mrs. Mortar is Karen's close and trusted friend.
    (3) Karen is careful not to hurt Mrs. Mortar's feelings.
    (4) Karen ultimately has respect for Mrs. Mortar.
    (5) Mrs. Mortar was once Karen's teacher.

13. Based on the excerpt, which of the following is Karen most likely to do next?

    (1) call Mary's grandmother
    (2) call a doctor
    (3) scold Mrs. Mortar
    (4) wait for Mary to decide to get up
    (5) ask someone to take Mary to her room

WHAT DID GRANDPA BLAKESLEE'S WILL SAY?

"Now I want my burying to remind folks that death aint always awful. God invented death. Its in God's plan for it to happen. So when my time comes I do not want no trip
(5) to Birdsong's Emporium or any other. Dressing somebody up to look alive don't make it so. …

"I don't want no casket. Its a waste of money. What I would really like is to be
(10) wrapped up in two or three feed sacks and laid right in the ground. But that would bother you all, so use the pine box upstairs at the store that Miss Mattie Lou's coffin come in. I been saving it. And tho I just as
(15) soon be planted in the vegetable patch as anywhere, I don't think anybody would ever eat what growed there, after. Anyhow, take me right from home to the cemetery.

"Aint no use paying Birdsong for that
(20) hearse. Get Loomis to use his wagon. Specially if it is hot weather, my advisement is dont waste no time."

Mama, scandalized, had both hands up to her mouth. Mary Toy had turned white
(25) as a sheet. I held her tight. Aunt Loma seemed excited, like when watching a spooky stage play. I felt excited myself. I wondered was this Grandpa's idea of a practical joke or was it a sermon.
(30) Maybe after he made his point, he'd put a postscript saying that when he was dead it really wouldn't matter to him what kind of funeral he had. But I doubted it. …

Papa read on. "I want Loomis and them
(35) to dig my grave right next to Miss Mattie Lou. I don't want no other preacher there but him, but don't let him give a sermon. It would go on for hours. Just let him pray for God to comfort my family. …"

(40) Papa read on. "I don't want nobody at the burial except you all and them at the store that want to come. Don't put *Not Dead But Sleeping* on my stone. Write it *Dead, Not Sleeping.* Being dead under six
(45) foot of dirt wont bother me a-tall, but I hate for it to sound like I been buried alive. …"

Olive Ann Burns, *Cold Sassy Tree.*

14. Based on the excerpt, what does Grandpa Blakeslee probably think about death?

He thinks death is

(1) the end of everything
(2) the beginning of the afterlife
(3) a waste of money
(4) normal and natural
(5) a little frightening

15. Which of the following best expresses the main idea of the excerpt?

(1) Grandpa Blakeslee does not want a fuss made at his funeral.
(2) Death eventually happens to everyone.
(3) Birdsong's Emporium is too expensive.
(4) Funerals should be simple and dignified.
(5) The writer of the will does not want to be dressed up after he dies.

16. Which of the following is the best description of Grandpa Blakeslee's last will and testament?

(1) a slap in the face to his heirs
(2) an attack on organized religion
(3) an endorsement of the back-to-nature movement
(4) the last gasp of a practical joker
(5) a humorous criticism of the funeral industry

17. What is the main effect of the author's use of phrases such as "Aint no use" (line 19) and "dont waste no time" (line 22)?

(1) It shows that Grandpa Blakeslee was an unintelligent man.
(2) It creates the impression that Grandpa Blakeslee likes to talk.
(3) It creates the impression that Grandpa Blakeslee wrote his will in a hurry.
(4) It makes it seem as though Grandpa Blakeslee is actually speaking.
(5) It creates the impression that Grandpa Blakeslee is a practical man.

HOW DOES THIS YOUNG WIFE FEEL?

The River Merchant's Wife: A Letter

While my hair was still cut straight across my forehead
I played about the front gate, pulling flowers.
You came by on bamboo stilts, playing horse,
You walked about my seat, playing with blue plums.
(5)   And we went on living in the village of Chokan:
Two small people, without dislike or suspicion.

At fourteen I married My Lord you.
I never laughed, being bashful.
Lowering my head, I looked at the wall.
(10) Called to, a thousand times, I never looked back.

At fifteen I stopped scowling.
I desired my dust to be mingled with yours
Forever and forever and forever.
Why should I climb the look out?

(15) At sixteen you departed,
You went into far Ku-to-yen, by the river of swirling eddies,
And you have been gone five months.
The monkeys make sorrowful noise overhead.

You dragged your feet when you went out.
(20) By the gate now, the moss is grown, the different mosses,
Too deep to clear them away!
The leaves fall early this autumn, in wind.

The paired butterflies are already yellow with August
Over the grass in the West garden;
(25) They hurt me. I grow older.
If you are coming down through the narrows of the river Kiang,
Please let me know beforehand,
And I will come out to meet you
As far as Cho-fu-sa. (by Rihaku)

Ezra Pound, *Personae.*

18. At the beginning of the poem, what is the relationship between the couple?

(1) They are schoolmates.
(2) They are enemies.
(3) They are sweethearts.
(4) They are rivals.
(5) They are playmates.

19. Which of the following phrases best describes the overall mood of the poem?

(1) wistful longing
(2) lighthearted playfulness
(3) stormy anger
(4) dreadful suspense
(5) romantic passion

20. Which of the following is the most likely explanation of why the yellow, paired butterflies "hurt" the woman (lines 23–25)?

(1) They remind her that winter is on the way.
(2) They warn her that her husband is in danger.
(3) They symbolize her happy childhood.
(4) They remind her that life is short and she is alone.
(5) They taunt her because she has no children.

21. Which of the following can you infer about the couple's youthful marriage?

(1) They fell in love with each other at age fourteen.
(2) The girl was a servant in her husband's home.
(3) The marriage was arranged by their two families.
(4) No one else suitable lived in the village of Chokan.
(5) They were desperate to marry before they got too old.

22 If the woman in this poem could give a lesson about life to a young girl, which of the following would she be most likely to say?

(1) The course of life is unpredictable.
(2) Always be joyful, no matter what happens.
(3) Life is painful from beginning to end.
(4) Marry when you are very young.
(5) Always obey your parents.

23. Which of the following best describes the woman's emotions over the course of the poem?

(1) sorrow to devotion to obedience to joy
(2) playfulness to obedience to devotion to longing
(3) obedience to sorrow to playfulness to devotion
(4) sorrow to melancholy to peacefulness to joy
(5) playfulness to longing to hopelessness to despair

WHAT IS THE VALUE OF THIS PROGRAM?

Most personal problems do not disappear between the hours of 9 and 5. When employees experience difficulties at home, the problems usually follow them to
(5) work. In some instances, employees face additional problems at the workplace, such as deadline pressures and conflicts with co-workers. Situations like these can impede an employee's ability to perform
(10) well at work or in other activities.

Several types of problems can affect an employee's job performance. These problems can be emotional, marital, family related, occupational, financial, or
(15) substance-abuse related. How can an employee address problems such as these? Often, short-term counselling is all that is necessary to help the employee resolve the problem before it begins to
(20) affect job performance seriously. That's where Employees' Advisory and Referral Service (EARS) comes in. EARS can help employees resolve many types of personal problems.

(25) EARS is staffed by highly trained counsellors and is offered through the current medical insurance program. There is no cost for this benefit to employees and their immediate family members. However,
(30) employees are responsible for costs incurred if they are referred to a professional outside the EARS program. Under this circumstance, the group medical insurance will pay the same
(35) reasonable and customary charges that would be paid if an employee were being treated by a medical professional.

EARS counsellors maintain strict confidentiality. No one, including the
(40) employer, will be informed of an employee's participation in the program unless the employee reveals it. Nor will participation in the program jeopardize an employee's job.

(45) The EARS program is based on self-referral, meaning that the employee refers himself or herself. He or she will discuss the problem with an EARS counsellor, who will help determine what kind of help is
(50) needed. EARS is staffed 24 hours a day. If the problem cannot be resolved by one of the staff's counsellors, the employee will be referred to a qualified professional outside the program.

(55) During the course of participation, the employee's EARS counsellor will maintain support and follow-up. In the event that an outside referral becomes necessary, the employee's financial circumstances and
(60) geographical location will be taken into consideration.

At EARS we strive to offer you the best service that we can. We listen. We care. After all, we're all EARS.

24. Which of the following best restates the phrase "Situations like these can impede an employee's ability to perform well" (lines 8–10)?

Situations like these can

(1) make it impossible to do a good job
(2) make medical intervention necessary
(3) make the employee not care about job performance
(4) make it difficult to excel at work
(5) make it necessary to fire an employee

25. Based on the excerpt, which of the following can be inferred about the directors of the company that offers EARS to employees?

(1) They place little value on employee benefits.
(2) They think this benefit will help to attract high-quality employees.
(3) They want their employees to function well.
(4) They require their employees to leave their problems at home.
(5) They want to refer employees with problems to outside professionals.

26. Which of the following problems could be helped through the EARS program?

(1) a problem with repetitive motion injury
(2) a shortage of adequate child care
(3) having too much work
(4) feeling overwhelmed by a project
(5) a desire to retire early

27. Imagine that EARS is available at your workplace. Which of these people could meet with an EARS counsellor at no cost to you?

(1) your friend who has emotional difficulties
(2) your son who is depressed
(3) your spouse who has a broken arm
(4) your neighbour who has credit problems
(5) your sister-in-law's mother who needs counselling

28. Which of the following best describes the style in which this excerpt is written?

(1) straightforward and matter-of-fact
(2) dry and scholarly
(3) technical and challenging
(4) lighthearted and amusing
(5) detailed and clinical

29. Which of the following best describes the way in which the excerpt is organized?

(1) by giving a sequence of events
(2) by comparing
(3) by listing information in order of importance
(4) by introducing a problem and offering a solution
(5) by discussing familiar items first, then moving to unfamiliar items

DOES THIS WOMAN LIVE IN A DREAM WORLD?

The windows of the drawing-room opened on to a balcony overlooking the garden. At the far end, against the wall, there was a tall, slender pear tree in fullest,
(5) richest bloom; it stood perfect, as though becalmed against the jade-green sky. Bertha couldn't help feeling, even from this distance, that it had not a single bud or a faded petal. Down below, in the garden
(10) beds, the red and yellow tulips, heavy with flowers, seemed to lean upon the dusk. A grey cat, dragging its belly, crept across the lawn, and a black one, its shadow, trailed after. The sight of them, so intent
(15) and so quick, gave Bertha a curious shiver.

"What creepy things cats are!" she stammered, and she turned away from the window and began walking up and down. …
(20) How strong the jonquils smelled in the warm room. Too strong? Oh, no. And yet, as though overcome, she flung down on a couch and pressed her hands to her eyes.

"I'm too happy—too happy!" she
(25) murmured.

And she seemed to see on her eyelids the lovely pear tree with its wide open blossoms as a symbol of her own life.

Really—really—she had everything.
(30) She was young. Harry and she were as much in love as ever, and they got on together splendidly and were really good pals. She had an adorable baby. They didn't have to worry about money. They
(35) had this absolutely satisfactory house and garden. And friends—modern, thrilling friends, writers and painters and poets or people keen on social questions—just the kind of friends they wanted. And then there
(40) were books, and there was music, and she had found a wonderful little dressmaker, and they were going abroad in the summer, and their new cook made the most superb omelettes. …
(45) "I'm absurd! Absurd!" She sat up; but she felt quite dizzy, quite drunk. It must have been the spring.

Yes, it was the spring. Now she was so tired she could not drag herself upstairs
(50) to dress.

A white dress, a string of jade beads, green shoes and stockings. It wasn't intentional. She had thought of this scheme hours before she stood at the
(55) drawing-room window.

Katherine Mansfield, "Bliss," *The Short Stories of Katherine Mansfield.*

30. When does the scene in this excerpt take place?

    (1) early morning
    (2) noontime
    (3) afternoon
    (4) early evening
    (5) night

31. Based on the information in this excerpt, Bertha would most likely participate in which of the following activities?

    (1) visiting art galleries
    (2) going on fox hunts
    (3) grooming cats
    (4) cleaning the house
    (5) cooking gourmet meals

32. Why does Bertha see the pear tree as a symbol of her life?

    (1) It seems perfect, just as her circumstances do.
    (2) It is tall and slender, just as she is.
    (3) It will soon be bearing fruit, and she is pregnant.
    (4) It is growing and changing, just as she is.
    (5) It projects a sense of calmness, and she is calm.

33. What is the most likely meaning of lines 52–55: "It wasn't intentional. She had thought of this scheme hours before she stood at the drawing-room window"?

    (1) The colours she planned to wear matched her surroundings.
    (2) The colours she planned to wear matched her mood.
    (3) Bertha did not believe in coincidences.
    (4) Bertha was rehearsing what she would tell those who commented on her attire.
    (5) Bertha was plotting to do something evil.

34. What effect does the season in which it is set (spring) have on the mood of the story?

    (1) It contributes to a fresh, new feeling.
    (2) It contributes to the feeling of unreality.
    (3) It contributes to a joyous, playful feeling.
    (4) It enables the pear tree to be a more effective symbol.
    (5) It gives the feeling of a new beginning for Bertha.

35. Based on the excerpt, which of the following words would the narrator most likely use to describe Bertha?

    (1) intelligent
    (2) naive
    (3) careless
    (4) sensible
    (5) hateful

HOW DOES THIS AUTHOR READ *TV GUIDE*?

The first thing I do upon picking up *TV Guide* at the supermarket is to tear out the superabundance of commercial inserts. It's not the advertisements I mind but that
(5) they're printed on heavy stock which makes locating desired pages annoyingly difficult. After removing the obstacles, I settle down to scanning the schedule and noting which programs are to be viewed
(10) and/or video taped for subsequent retrieval. Owing to the numbers of channels chronicled, this too can prove frustrating especially when attempting to compile a list of movies other than those
(15) offered exclusively on premium cable channels. It would be far more advantageous for discerning film and, indeed, sport fans if *TV Guide* provided separate and complete schedules catering
(20) to both interests. Considering the diversity of special interest programs, they might adopt a similar scheme for listing children's, news and special events.

Through no fault of its own, *TV Guide*
(25) lists little else but the title of programs broadcast by the A&E Network, The Discovery Channel, The Disney Channel and absolutely nothing for C-Span. With the exception of The Disney Channel, each
(30) sells its own monthly program guide for anywhere between $15.00 and $30.00 annually (The Disney Channel Magazine is included with the monthly cable fee). ...

Programs on The Discovery Channel
(35) are continually interesting. Notable among them is Gus MacDonald's engrossing series on the archaeology and evolution of still photography and his very stimulating history on early cinema both here and
(40) abroad; in addition to a variety of foreign documentaries including those exploring all aspects of the life and times of the British Empire. Yet they hardly warrant the extra expenditure for a program guide as so
(45) many are repeats. The same is true of A&E but even more so. Repeats, for example, far exceed new programs. While the occasional foreign language film is a bonus to be sure, what isn't welcomed is the
(50) frequency of movies shown where scenes have been deleted for time's sake. ...

Some of the most significant programming on television is supplied by the combined C-Span channels and as
(55) such ought to be listed in *TV Guide* and all daily newspapers, but it is not. Hence, C-Span's monthly guide is invaluable save only for inevitable late hour changes in the schedule.
(60) What is needed is a comprehensive weekly teleguide encompassing, in depth, programs on all the channels in any given area; one whose information is arranged for the viewer to gain access to it with a
(65) minimum of difficulty.

Chris Buchman, "The Television Scene," *Films in Review.*

36. Which of the following is the main idea of the excerpt?

The author

(1) thinks that the programming on C-Span is very significant
(2) would like more interest-focused, detailed program guides
(3) doesn't like the programming choices or the number of repeats on A&E
(4) wants people to buy *TV Guide*
(5) wishes more people shared his reading and viewing habits

37. Which of the following best expresses the author's opinion of A&E?

(1) Its programming is much better than what is offered on C-Span.
(2) It is necessary to have a special program guide for its broadcasts.
(3) Its program guide is a waste of money.
(4) It shows some of the best programs on television.
(5) It should never be watched.

38. Which of the following best describes the tone of this excerpt?

(1) informative
(2) angry
(3) humorous
(4) overwhelmed
(5) pleased

39. Which of the following best describes the style in which this review is written?

(1) technical
(2) casual
(3) methodical
(4) ornate
(5) economical

40. According to the author, which of the following words best describes *TV Guide*?

(1) thoughtful
(2) detailed
(3) superficial
(4) confusing
(5) biased

Simulated Test Performance Analysis Chart

Language Arts, Reading

This chart can help you determine your strengths and weaknesses on the content and skill areas of the GED Language Arts, Reading Simulated Test. Use the Answers and Explanations starting on page 871 to check your answers to the test. Then circle on the chart the numbers of the test items you answered correctly. Put the total number correct for each content area and skill area in each row and column. Look at the total items correct in each column and row and decide which areas need more study and work.

Thinking Skill / Content Area	Comprehension	Application	Analysis	Synthesis	Total Correct
Nonfiction (Lessons 1–9)	24, 36, 40	26, 27	25, 37	28, 29, 38, 39	_____/11
Fiction (Lessons 10–19)	1, 2, 14, 15, 30	3, 31	4, 5, 6, 32, 33	7, 16, 17, 34, 35	_____/17
Poetry (Lessons 20–24)	18	22	20, 21	19, 23	_____/6
Drama (Lessons 25–28)	8	9	11, 12, 13	10	_____/6
Total Correct	_____/10	_____/6	_____/12	_____/12	_____/40

1–32 → You need more review.
33–40 → Congratulations! You're ready for the GED!

MATHEMATICS
Part I

Directions

The Mathematics Simulated Test consists of multiple-choice and alternate format questions intended to measure your general mathematical skills and problem-solving ability. The questions are based on short readings that often include a graph, chart, or diagram.

You will have 45 minutes to complete the 25 questions in Part I. Work carefully, but do not spend too much time on any one question. Be sure to answer every question. You will not be penalized for incorrect answers. When time is up, mark the last item you finished. This will tell you whether you can finish the real GED Test in the time allowed. Then complete the Simulated Test.

Formulas you may need are given on page 704. Only some questions will require a formula. Not all the formulas given will be needed.

Some questions contain more information than you will need to solve the problem; other questions do not give enough information. If the question does not give enough information to solve the problem, the correct answer choice is "Not enough information is given."

You may use a calculator in Part I. Calculator directions for the CASIO *fx-260SOLAR* scientific calculator can be found on page 703.

Record your answers on a copy of the separate answer sheet provided on page 922. Be sure all required information is properly recorded on the answer sheet.

To record your answers, mark the numbered circle on the answer sheet that corresponds to the answer you select for each question on the test.

Example: If a grocery bill totalling $15.75 is paid with a $20.00 bill, how much change should be returned?

(1) $5.25
(2) $4.75
(3) $4.25
(4) $3.75
(5) $3.25

The correct answer is $4.25; therefore, answer space 3 would be marked on the answer sheet.

Do not rest the point of your pencil on the answer sheet while you are considering your answer. Make no stray or unnecessary marks. If you change an answer, erase your first mark completely. Mark only one answer for each question; multiple answers will be scored as incorrect. Do not fold or crease your answer sheet.

When you finish the test, use the Performance Analysis Chart on page 717 to determine whether you are ready to take the real GED Test and, if not, which skill areas need additional review.

Mixed numbers, such as $3\frac{1}{2}$, cannot be entered in the alternate format grid. Instead, represent them as decimal numbers (in this case, 3.5) or fractions (in this case, 7/2). No answer can be a negative number, such as -8.

To record your answer for an alternate format question

- begin in any column that will allow your answer to be entered.
- write your answer in the boxes on the top row.
- in the column beneath a fraction bar or decimal point (if any) and each number in your answer, fill in the circle representing that character.
- leave blank any unused column.

Example

The scale on a map indicates that $\frac{1}{2}$ cm represents an actual distance of 120 km. In centimetres, how far apart on the map will two towns be if the actual distance between them is 180 km?

The answer to the above example is 3/4, or 0.75, cm. The answer could be gridded using any of the methods below.

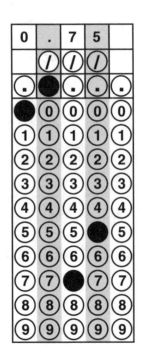

Points to remember

- The answer sheet will be machine scored. **The circles must be filled in correctly.**
- Mark no more than one circle in any column.
- Grid only one answer even if there is more than one correct answer.
- Mixed numbers, such as $3\frac{1}{2}$, must be gridded as a decimal (3.5) or fraction (7/2).
- No answer can be a negative number.

CALCULATOR DIRECTIONS

To prepare the calculator for use the **first** time, press the ⟨ON⟩ (upper-rightmost) key. "DEG" will appear at the top-centre of the screen and "0." at the right. This indicates the calculator is in the proper format for all your calculations.

To prepare the calculator for **another** question, press the ⟨ON⟩ or the red ⟨AC⟩ key. This clears any entries made previously.

To do any arithmetic, enter the expression as it is written. Press ⟨=⟩ (equal sign) when finished.

EXAMPLE A: $8 - 3 + 9$

First press ⟨ON⟩ or ⟨AC⟩.
Enter the following:

8 ⟨−⟩ 3 ⟨+⟩ 9 ⟨=⟩

The correct answer is 14.

If an expression in parentheses is to be multiplied by a number, press ⟨×⟩ (multiplication sign) between the number and the parenthesis sign.

EXAMPLE B: $6(8 + 5)$

First press ⟨ON⟩ or ⟨AC⟩.
Enter the following:

6 ⟨×⟩ ⟨((---⟩ 8 ⟨+⟩ 5 ⟨---)⟩ ⟨=⟩

The correct answer is 78.

To find the square root of a number

- enter the number.
- press ⟨SHIFT⟩ (upper-leftmost) key ("SHIFT" appears at the top-left of the screen).
- press ⟨x²⟩ (third from the left on top row) to access its second function: square root.
  DO NOT press ⟨SHIFT⟩ and ⟨x²⟩ at the same time.

EXAMPLE C: $\sqrt{64}$

First press ⟨ON⟩ or ⟨AC⟩.
Enter the following:

64 ⟨SHIFT⟩ ⟨x²⟩

The correct answer is 8.

To enter a negative number such as −8

- enter the number without the negative sign (enter 8).
- press the "change sign" (⟨+/−⟩) key, which is directly above the 7 key.

All arithmetic can be done with positive or negative numbers.

EXAMPLE D: $-8 - -5$

First press ⟨ON⟩ or ⟨AC⟩.
Enter the following:

8 ⟨+/−⟩ ⟨−⟩ 5 ⟨+/−⟩ ⟨=⟩

The correct answer is −3.

FORMULAS

AREA of a

square	Area = side^2
rectangle	Area = length × width
parallelogram	Area = base × height
triangle	Area = $\frac{1}{2}$ × base × height
trapezoid	Area = $\frac{1}{2}$ × (base$_1$ + base$_2$) × height
circle	Area = π × radius^2; π is approximately equal to 3.14

PERIMETER of a

square	Perimeter = 4 × side
rectangle	Perimeter = 2 × length + 2 × width
triangle	Perimeter = side$_1$ + side$_2$ + side$_3$

CIRCUMFERENCE of a circle   Circumference = π × diameter; π is approximately equal to 3.14

VOLUME of a

cube	Volume = edge^3
rectangular container	Volume = length × width × height
square pyramid	Volume = $\frac{1}{3}$ × (base edge)^2 × height
cylinder	Volume = π × radius^2 × height; π is approximately equal to 3.14
cone	Volume = $\frac{1}{3}$ × π × radius^2 × height; π is approximately equal to 3.14

COORDINATE GEOMETRY

distance between points = $\sqrt{(x_2 - x_1)^2 + (y_2 - y_1)^2}$; (x_1, y_1) and (x_2, y_2) are two points in a plane

slope of a line = $\frac{y_2 - y_1}{x_2 - x_1}$; (x_1, y_1) and (x_2, y_2) are two points on a line

PYTHAGOREAN RELATIONSHIP

$a^2 + b^2 = c^2$; a and b are legs and c the hypotenuse of a right triangle

MEASURES OF CENTRAL TENDENCY

mean = $\frac{x_1 + x_2 + \ldots + x_n}{n}$, where the x's are the values for which a mean is desired and n is the total number of values for x

median = the middle value of an odd number of ordered scores, and halfway between the two middle values of an even number of ordered scores

SIMPLE INTEREST   interest = principal × rate × time

DISTANCE   distance = rate × time

TOTAL COST   total cost = (number of units) × (price per unit)

Questions 1 and 2 refer to the following graph.

PERSONS EMPLOYED IN VARIOUS OCCUPATIONS
Total: 25 000 People

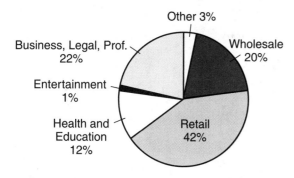

1. What was the total number of people employed in a wholesale occupation or a health and education occupation?

   (1) 2000

   (2) 3000

   (3) 5000

   (4) 7000

   (5) 8000

2. How many more people were employed in a business, legal, or professional occupation than in an entertainment occupation?

   (1) 4000

   (2) 4350

   (3) 5000

   (4) 5250

   (5) 5500

3. A business has $15 000 in its chequing account. The company deposits cheques in the amount of $1800, $3000, and $900. It also writes cheques for $3600 and $2800 to pay bills. How much is in the account after these transactions?

   (1) $27 100

   (2) $16 800

   (3) $14 300

   (4) $ 3 800

   (5) Not enough information is given.

Question 4 refers to the following figure.

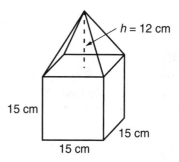

4. What is the volume of the figure in cubic centimetres?

   Mark your answer in the circles in the grid on your answer sheet.

5. What is the value of the expression $(908 + 23 \times 48) \div 2 + 687$?

   Mark your answer in the circles in the grid on your answer sheet.

6. From January to February the price of Argon stock rose from $2 per share to $8 per share. What was the percent of increase?

   (1)　 6%

   (2)　40%

   (3)　75%

   (4) 300%

   (5) Not enough information is given.

7. Sarah buys 6 raffle tickets. If a total of 300 raffle tickets is sold, what is the probability that one of Sarah's tickets will win?

   (1) $\frac{1}{4}$

   (2) $\frac{1}{20}$

   (3) $\frac{1}{25}$

   (4) $\frac{1}{50}$

   (5) $\frac{1}{300}$

Questions 8 and 9 refer to the following figure.

310 m

120 m

8. The city parks committee plans to fence in the rectangular driving range shown in the drawing. How many metres of fencing will it take to enclose the driving range?

(1) 240
(2) 430
(3) 620
(4) 860
(5) 980

9. The city needs to buy grass seed to cover the driving range. If one bag of grass seed covers 75 square metres, how many bags will the city need to buy to seed the driving range?

(1) 160
(2) 357
(3) 496
(4) 653
(5) 744

10. The price of a stereo system on Friday was $272, a discount of 15% from its price on Thursday. What was the price of the stereo system on Thursday?

(1) $231.20
(2) $312.80
(3) $318.20
(4) $320.00
(5) $328.00

11. For its standard chequing account, a bank charges a monthly fee of $2.50 plus $0.10 per cheque. The function used to determine total monthly charges is $C = \$2.50 + \$0.10n$, where C = monthly charges and n = the number of cheques. If a customer writes 24 cheques during a month, how much will the customer be charged?

(1) $ 2.40
(2) $ 2.50
(3) $ 4.90
(4) $ 6.00
(5) $26.50

12. Albert is five times as old as Timothy. In five years, Albert will be four times as old as Timothy. How old will Timothy be in five years?

Mark your answer in the circles in the grid on your answer sheet.

Question 13 refers to the following figure.

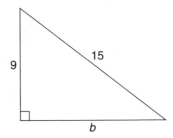

13. In a right triangle, the short leg is 9 and the hypotenuse is 15. What is the measure of the other leg?

Mark your answer in the circles in the grid on your answer sheet.

14. Roberto borrows $14 000 and agrees to pay $9\frac{3}{4}$% simple annual interest. Which of the following expressions shows how much interest he will pay if he borrows the amount for $3\frac{1}{2}$ years?

    (1) $14 000 + 0.0975 + 3.5

    (2) $14 000 × 9.75 × 3.5

    (3) $14 000 × 0.0975 × 3.5

    (4) $14 000 × $\frac{0.0975}{3.5}$

    (5) $\$\frac{14\ 000}{3.5}$ × 0.0975

Question 15 refers to the following figure.

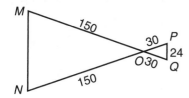

15. If $\overline{PQ}$ and $\overline{MN}$ are parallel, what is the length of $\overline{MN}$?

    (1) 48

    (2) 60

    (3) 90

    (4) 120

    (5) 150

Question 16 refers to the following diagram.

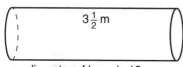

diameter of base is 12 cm

16. Which of the following expressions can be used to find the volume of the cylinder in cubic centimetres?

    (1) 350(6)

    (2) 3.14(6)(350)

    (3) 3.14(6^2)(350)

    (4) 3.14(6^3)(35)

    (5) (6^2)(350)

17. Show the location of the point whose coordinates are (3, −4).

Mark your answer on the coordinate plane grid on your answer sheet.

18. Which of the following graphs shows the solution set for the inequality?

$$6 - 5x < 7x - 6$$

(1)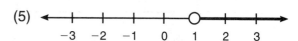

(2)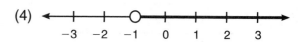

(3)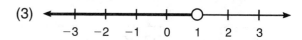

(4)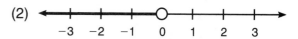

(5)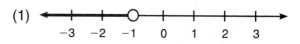

Question 19 refers to the table below.

UTILITY PAYMENTS	
Period	**Amount**
Jan−Feb	$89.36
Mar−Apr	$90.12
May−Jun	$74.47
Jul−Aug	$63.15
Sept−Oct	$59.76
Nov−Dec	$84.31

19. What is the median of the amounts in the table?

    (1) $84.31

    (2) $79.39

    (3) $74.47

    (4) $63.15

    (5) Not enough information is given.

20. Which equation of a line is shown on the graph?

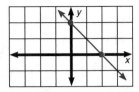

   (1) $x + y = -4$

   (2) $x + y = -2$

   (3) $x + y = 0$

   (4) $x + y = 2$

   (5) $x + y = 4$

Question 21 refers to the table below.

COMEDY CLUB TICKET SALES					
Week	1	2	3	4	5
Sales	184	176	202	178	190

21. A comedy club had the following ticket sales: 184, 176, 202, 178, and 190. What was the average (mean) number of tickets sold?

Mark your answer in the circles in the grid on your answer sheet.

22. Areta borrowed $42.48 from Julia on Monday and another $64.76 on Friday. On Saturday she paid back $\frac{1}{4}$ of the total amount she owed. How much did she still owe?

Mark your answer in the circles in the grid on your answer sheet.

23. A 5-km race has three checkpoints between the start and finish line. Checkpoint 1 is 1.8 km from the starting point. Checkpoint 3 is 1.2 km from the finish line. Checkpoint 2 is halfway between checkpoints 1 and 3. How far in kilometres is Checkpoint 2 from the finish line?

   (1) 1.2

   (2) 1.5

   (3) 1.8

   (4) 2.0

   (5) 2.2

Question 24 refers to the following figure.

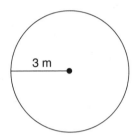

24. To the nearest tenth of a metre, what is the circumference of a circle with a radius of 3 m?

   (1) 4.7

   (2) 7.1

   (3) 9.4

   (4) 18.8

   (5) 28.2

25. Which of the following expresses the product of 6000 and 14 000 in scientific notation?

   (1) 8.4×10^8

   (2) 8.4×10^7

   (3) 8.4×10^6

   (4) 84×10^8

   (5) 84×10^7

MATHEMATICS
Part II

Directions

The Mathematics Simulated GED Test consists of multiple-choice and alternate format questions intended to measure your general mathematical skills and problem-solving ability. The questions are based on short readings that often include a graph, chart, or diagram.

You will have 45 minutes to complete the 25 questions in Part II. Work carefully, but do not spend too much time on any one question. Be sure to answer every question. You will not be penalized for incorrect answers. When time is up, mark the last item you finished. This will tell you whether you can finish the real GED Test in the time allowed. Then complete the Simulated Test.

Formulas you may need are given on page 711. Only some questions will require a formula. Not all the formulas given will be needed.

Some questions contain more information than you will need to solve the problem; other questions do not give enough information. If the question does not give enough information to solve the problem, the correct answer choice is "Not enough information is given."

The use of calculators is not allowed in Part II.

Record your answers on a copy of the separate answer sheet provided on page 923. Be sure all required information is properly recorded on the answer sheet.

To record your answers, mark the numbered circle on the answer sheet that corresponds to the answer you select for each question on the test.

Example: If a grocery bill totalling $15.75 is paid with a $20.00 bill, how much change should be returned?

(1) $5.25
(2) $4.75
(3) $4.25
(4) $3.75
(5) $3.25

The correct answer is $4.25; therefore, answer space 3 would be marked on the answer sheet.

Do not rest the point of your pencil on the answer sheet while you are considering your answer. Make no stray or unnecessary marks. If you change an answer, erase your first mark completely. Mark only one answer for each question; multiple answers will be scored as incorrect. Do not fold or crease your answer sheet.

When you finish the test, use the Performance Analysis Chart on page 717 to determine whether you are ready to take the real GED Test and, if not, which skill areas need additional review.

MATHEMATICS

Mixed numbers, such as $3\frac{1}{2}$, cannot be entered in the alternate format grid. Instead, represent them as decimal numbers (in this case, 3.5) or fractions (in this case, 7/2). No answer can be a negative number, such as -8.

To record your answer for an alternate format question

- begin in any column that will allow your answer to be entered.
- write your answer in the boxes on the top row.
- in the column beneath a fraction bar or decimal point (if any) and each number in your answer, fill in the circle representing that character.
- leave blank any unused column.

Example

The scale on a map indicates that $\frac{1}{2}$ cm represents an actual distance of 120 km. In centimetres, how far apart on the map will two towns be if the actual distance between them is 180 km?

The answer to the above example is 3/4, or 0.75, cm. The answer could be gridded using any of the methods below.

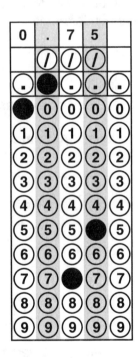

Points to remember

- The answer sheet will be machine scored. **The circles must be filled in correctly.**
- Mark no more than one circle in any column.
- Grid only one answer even if there is more than one correct answer.
- Mixed numbers, such as $3\frac{1}{2}$, must be gridded as a decimal (3.5) or fraction (7/2).
- No answer can be a negative number.

Simulated Test • Mathematics

FORMULAS

AREA of a

square	Area = side²
rectangle	Area = length × width
parallelogram	Area = base × height
triangle	Area = $\frac{1}{2}$ × base × height
trapezoid	Area = $\frac{1}{2}$ × (base₁ + base₂) × height
circle	Area = π × radius²; π is approximately equal to 3.14

PERIMETER of a

square	Perimeter = 4 × side
rectangle	Perimeter = 2 × length + 2 × width
triangle	Perimeter = side₁ + side₂ + side₃
CIRCUMFERENCE of a circle	Circumference = π × diameter; π is approximately equal to 3.14

VOLUME of a

cube	Volume = edge³
rectangular container	Volume = length × width × height
square pyramid	Volume = $\frac{1}{3}$ × (base edge)² × height
cylinder	Volume = π × radius² × height; π is approximately equal to 3.14
cone	Volume = $\frac{1}{3}$ × π × radius² × height; π is approximately equal to 3.14

COORDINATE GEOMETRY

distance between points = $\sqrt{(x_2 - x_1)^2 + (y_2 - y_1)^2}$; (x_1, y_1) and (x_2, y_2) are two points in a plane

slope of a line = $\frac{y_2 - y_1}{x_2 - x_1}$; (x_1, y_1) and (x_2, y_2) are two points on a line

PYTHAGOREAN RELATIONSHIP

$a^2 + b^2 = c^2$; a and b are legs and c the hypotenuse of a right triangle.

MEASURES OF CENTRAL TENDENCY

mean = $\frac{x_1 + x_2 + \ldots + x_n}{n}$, where the x's are the values for which a mean is desired and n is the total number of values for x

median = the middle value of an odd number of ordered scores, and halfway between the two middle values of an even number of ordered scores

SIMPLE INTEREST

interest = principal × rate × time

DISTANCE

distance = rate × time

TOTAL COST

total cost = (number of units) × (price per unit)

26. Which of the following is the value of 2.1374 rounded to the nearest hundredth?

    (1) 2.10
    (2) 2.13
    (3) 2.14
    (4) 2.17
    (5) 2.20

Question 27 refers to the following figure.

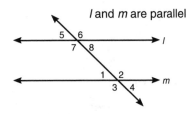

l and *m* are parallel

27. If ∠8 measures 50°, which two angles measure 130°?

    (1) ∠1 and ∠7
    (2) ∠2 and ∠6
    (3) ∠4 and ∠6
    (4) ∠4 and ∠7
    (5) ∠5 and ∠7

28. A box of cereal costs $1.59. If a case holds 8 boxes, how much would $3\frac{1}{2}$ cases cost?

    (1) $ 5.57
    (2) $12.72
    (3) $28.00
    (4) $38.92
    (5) $44.52

Questions 29 and 30 refer to the figure below.

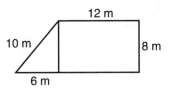

A homeowner is having a new deck built in the shape shown above. The longest side of the deck will attach to the house.

29. How many metres of railing are needed if the side attached to the house will not have a railing?

    (1) 30
    (2) 36
    (3) 40
    (4) 48
    (5) 56

30. After the wood has aged and weathered, it can be stained. The surface of the rectangular section is four times the size of the triangular section. Which expression could be used to find the surface area of the deck?

    (1) $12 \times 8 + 6$
    (2) $(12 \times 8) + (10 \times 8)$
    (3) $\frac{1}{4}(12 \times 8)$
    (4) $(12 \times 8) + \frac{1}{4}(12 \times 8)$
    (5) $4 \times 12 \times 8$

31. What is the value of the following expression if $x = 2$ and $y = -2$?

$$6x^2 - 5xy - 4y^2$$

Mark your answer in the circles in the grid on your answer sheet.

Questions 32 and 33 refer to the following graph.

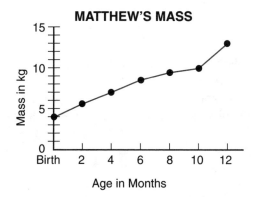

32. Over which two-month period did Matthew have the greatest gain in mass?

   (1) birth to 2 months

   (2) 4 to 6 months

   (3) 6 to 8 months

   (4) 8 to 10 months

   (5) 10 to 12 months

33. The average mass for a male infant at one year of age is 10.5 kg. About how many more kilograms than average was Matthew's mass at one year?

   (1) 0.5

   (2) 0.8

   (3) 1.1

   (4) 1.3

   (5) 2.5

Question 34 refers to the information below.

A box contains 15 cards, each one numbered with a different whole number from 1 to 15.

34. If a card is chosen at random from the box, what is the probability that it is less than 4?

   (1) $\frac{1}{15}$

   (2) $\frac{1}{5}$

   (3) $\frac{4}{15}$

   (4) $\frac{1}{2}$

   (5) $\frac{11}{15}$

Question 35 refers to the following figure.

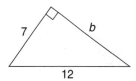

35. The hypotenuse of a right triangle measures 12 cm. If one leg measures 7 cm, which of the following expressions could be used to find the length of the other leg?

   (1) $12^2 + 7^2$

   (2) $\sqrt{12^2 + 7^2}$

   (3) $12^2 - 7^2$

   (4) $\sqrt{12^2 - 7^2}$

   (5) $(12 + 7)^2$

36. Which of the following shows the product of -6 and x, decreased by the sum of -6 and y?

   (1) $-6x - (-6 + y)$

   (2) $-6y - (-6x)$

   (3) $(-6 + x) - (-6y)$

   (4) $(-6 + y) - (-6x)$

   (5) $(-6 + x) - (-6 + y)$

37. Show the location of the *y*-intercept for the line $2x - y = 4$.

Mark your answer on the coordinate plane grid on your answer sheet.

38. Twice a number, added to 3, is equal to the negative of the number. What is the number?

   (1) -3

   (2) -1

   (3) $-\frac{1}{3}$

   (4) 1

   (5) 3

Question 39 refers to the information below.

DUE DATE	GRADE
9/7	60
9/14	85
9/21	95
9/28	80
10/5	95
10/12	95

Mohammed took a writing workshop and received the following grades on papers he wrote for the course: 60, 85, 95, 80, 95, 95.

39. What was the mean score for the papers?

   (1) 95

   (2) 90

   (3) 85

   (4) 80

   (5) 60

40. If *C* equals circumference, *d* = diameter, and *r* = radius, which of the following formulas is not valid?

   (1) $d = 2r$

   (2) $C = \pi d$

   (3) $C = 2\pi r$

   (4) $\frac{C}{d} = \pi$

   (5) $\pi = \frac{C}{r}$

41. Chi Ho drives to work and back five days each week. If her job is 14.82 km from her home, approximately how many kilometres does she drive to work and back each week?

   (1) 15

   (2) 30

   (3) 50

   (4) 75

   (5) 150

42. An 8-kg turkey costs $15.92. Which of the following could be used to find how much a 10-kg turkey would cost at the same price per kilogram?

   (1) $\frac{8}{\$15.92} = \frac{10}{?}$

   (2) $\frac{\$15.92}{8} = \frac{10}{?}$

   (3) $\frac{8}{\$15.92} = \frac{?}{10}$

   (4) $\frac{8}{10} = \frac{?}{\$15.92}$

   (5) $\frac{10}{8} = \frac{\$15.92}{?}$

43. Shanti drove 78 km in $1\frac{1}{2}$ hours. At the same rate, how many kilometres could she drive in 2.5 hours?

Mark your answer in the circles in the grid on your answer sheet.

Question 44 refers to the following figure.

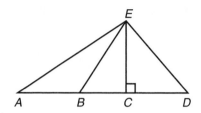

44. Triangle *ECD* is a right triangle. Which of the following must be an obtuse angle?

   (1) $\angle ABE$

   (2) $\angle ACE$

   (3) $\angle BCE$

   (4) $\angle DAE$

   (5) Not enough information is given.

Question 45 refers to the following graph.

45. Which inequality is graphed on the number line?

   (1) $-2 > x$

   (2) $x < -2$

   (3) $-2 \leq x$

   (4) $x \leq -2$

   (5) $2 = x$

46. The length of a rectangle is 6 times its width. The perimeter must be more than 110 m. Which inequality can be solved to find the width (*x*)?

   (1) $7x > 110$

   (2) $6x^2 > 110$

   (3) $x + 6x > 110$

   (4) $2(6x) + x > 110$

   (5) $x + 6x + x + 6x > 110$

Question 47 refers to the following figure.

Line *a* is parallel to line *b*.
$m\angle 3 = m\angle 4$

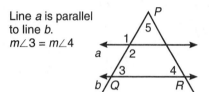

47. Which statement is true if $m\angle 3 = 60°$?

   (1) $m\angle 5 = 45°$

   (2) $m\angle 4 = 120°$

   (3) $m\angle 2 = 60°$

   (4) $m\angle 5 = 60°$

   (5) $m\angle 1 = 135°$

48. Sonia can pick 14.5 baskets of strawberries per hour. At this rate, how many baskets can she pick in $5\frac{1}{2}$ hours?

   (1) 70

   (2) $72\frac{1}{2}$

   (3) $79\frac{3}{4}$

   (4) $82\frac{1}{2}$

   (5) 87

Question 49 refers to the following diagram.

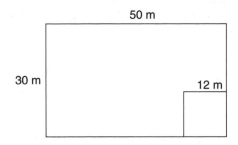

49. The Grahams' rectangular yard measures 50 by 30 m. They plan to plant a square vegetable garden, measuring 12 m per side, in one corner of the yard. The remaining area will be grass. What is the area in square metres of the grass portion of the yard?

(1) 900
(2) 1140
(3) 1356
(4) 1500
(5) 1644

50. Carrie has three projects. The first project will take 20 minutes, the second project will take the same amount of time as the first project, and the third project will take 30 minutes. What is the latest time she can start to work in order to finish all three projects by 12 noon?

(1) 10:10 A.M.
(2) 10:50 A.M.
(3) 10:53 A.M.
(4) 11:07 A.M.
(5) 11:10 A.M.

Simulated Test • Mathematics

Simulated Test Performance Analysis Charts
Mathematics

The following charts can help you determine your strengths and weaknesses in the content and skill areas of the GED Mathematics Test. Use the Answers and Explanations starting on page 874 to check your answers to the test. Then circle on the charts for Part I and Part II the numbers of the test items you answered correctly. Put the total number correct for each content area and skill area in each row and column. Look at the total items correct in each column to determine which areas are difficult for you. Use the lesson references to study those skills.

Part I

Content Area	Concept	Procedure	Application	Total Correct
Numbers and Operations *(Lessons 1–13)*	5	14	3, 6, 10, 22	_____/6
Measurement *(Lessons 14–15)*			**8**, 23	_____/2
Data Analysis *(Lessons 16–17)*	**1, 21**	**2, 19**	7	_____/5
Algebra *(Lessons 18–22)*	17, **20**, 25	**9**, 11	12, **18**	_____/7
Geometry *(Lessons 23–27)*	**13**	**16**	**4, 15, 24**	_____/5
Total Correct	_____/7	_____/6	_____/12	_____/25

Part II

Content Area	Concept	Procedure	Application	Total Correct
Numbers and Operations *(Lessons 1–13)*	26	42	28, 41, 43, 48, 50	_____/7
Measurement *(Lessons 14–15)*		**30**	**29**	_____/2
Data Analysis *(Lessons 16–17)*	**32**	**39**	**33**, 34	_____/4
Algebra *(Lessons 18–22)*	31, **45**	36, **46**	37, 38	_____/6
Geometry *(Lessons 23–27)*	**27, 44**	**35**, 40	**47, 49**	_____/6
Total Correct	_____/6	_____/7	_____/12	_____/25

The item numbers in **bold** are based on graphics.

> 1–40 → You need more review.
> 41–50 → Congratulations! You're ready for the GED!

Answers and Explanations

Entry Tests

Language Arts, Writing Part I
(pages 13–20)

1. **(3) Smithville Children's Hospital**
(Capitalization) Option (3) is correct because Smithville Children's Hospital is a proper name and should be capitalized. Option (1) is not correct because it does not capitalize the proper name. Options (2) and (4) are not correct because they capitalize only one part of the proper name. Option (5) is not correct because it contains an incorrectly formed possessive.

2. **(5) remove sentence 2** (Unity and coherence) Option (5) is correct because sentence 2 gives information that can be inferred from sentence 1. Options (1), (2), (3), and (4) are not correct because moving the sentence does not relate it to the rest of the paragraph.

3. **(1) begin a new paragraph with sentence 4** (Paragraph divisions) Option (1) correctly creates a second paragraph when the main idea shifts to wrapping the presents. Options (2) and (3) begin the new paragraph at inappropriate places, separating details that belong together. Option (4) incorrectly makes one long paragraph out of three distinct main ideas and their supporting details. A new paragraph is needed, so option (5) is incorrect.

4. **(1) to wrap the presents** (Subordinating ideas) Option (1) is correct because it smoothly combines the ideas in the two sentences. Options (2), (3), (4) and (5) do not combine the sentences smoothly.

5. **(4) replace sentence 8 with On Tuesday, we will need help delivering the presents.**
(Topic sentences) Option (4) is correct because it replaces an ineffective topic sentence with an effective one. Option (1) is not a good topic sentence because it doesn't tell what help is needed. Option (2) is not a good topic sentence because it doesn't tell what will happen on Tuesday. Option (3) is not a good topic sentence because it is a question. Option (5) is not a good topic sentence because it doesn't tell when the presents will be delivered or who will make the deliveries.

6. **(2) station wagons, vans, or trucks**
(Commas) Option (2) is correct because it places commas between each word in the series.

Option (1) is not correct because it does not place commas between the words in the series. Option (3) is not correct because it places a comma between only two of the words in the series. Option (4) incorrectly links the words in the series with *or*. Option (5) incorrectly places a comma after *or*.

7. **(3) replace his with their** (Pronouns) Option (3) replaces the incorrect pronoun with a pronoun that agrees with its antecedent *they*. Option (1) replaces one incorrect pronoun with another incorrect pronoun. Option (2) replaces the correct pronoun *they* with the incorrect pronoun *he*. *He* is incorrect because it does not agree with the antecedent *kids'*. Option (4) removes the necessary comma after the introductory phrase. Option (5) is not correct because the pronoun *his* does not agree with its antecedent *they*.

8. **(1) change wouldn't to won't** (Verb forms) Option (1) is correct because it replaces the verb in the conditional tense (*wouldn't*) with a verb in the future tense (*won't*). The future tense, not the conditional tense, should follow the present tense verb *is*. Option (2) replaces *is* with the incorrect verb form *was*. Since the memo is encouraging people who have never been to the hospital to go, the past tense (*was*) is not correct. Option (3) adds an incorrect comma between the subject and verb. Option (4) incorrectly changes the tense of the verb from present participle to present perfect participle. Option (5) is not true because the sentence contains an incorrect verb tense sequence (*is* followed by *wouldn't*).

9. **(2) Friday so we can** (Comma splice) Option (2) is correct because it fixes the comma splice by adding the coordinating conjunction *so*. Option (1) is incorrect because it does not fix the comma splice. Option (3) changes the comma splice to a run-on sentence. Option (4) adds a coordinating conjunction, *and*, that does not make sense in the sentence. Option (5) is not correct because it does not tell what signing up by Friday has to do with assigning people to car pools.

10. **(4) rose** (Verb forms) Option (4) is correct because the verb *became* agrees in tense with the preceding verb, *taught*. The other options are not correct because they do not agree in tense with the preceding verb *taught*. *Taught* is in the past tense, while option (1) is in present progressive

tense, option (2) is in past progressive tense, option (3) is in future tense, and option (5) is in present tense.

11. **(1) replace <u>husband bedridden</u> with <u>husband was bedridden</u>.** (Sentence fragments) Option (1) is correct because it fixes the sentence fragment by adding a necessary verb (*was*). Option (2) introduces an unnecessary comma. Option (3) unnecessarily capitalizes a common noun. Option (4) does not add a necessary verb, so it does not fix the sentence fragment. Option (5) is not true because the sentence is a fragment.

12. **(3) change <u>were accepting</u> to <u>was accepting</u>** (Subject-verb agreement) Option (3) is correct because it changes the plural *were* to the singular verb *was* to agree with *college*. Option 1 would not be correct because *she* clearly refers to Stowe in the previous sentence. Option (2) incorrectly changes the verb tense from past to present. Option (4) adds incorrect capitalization. Option (5) is not true because the subject does not agree with the verb.

13. **(2) a student** (Parallel structure) Option (2) is correct because it is in the same form as <u>a caregiver</u> and <u>a parent</u>. None of the other options is in the same form as these.

14. **(2) did not prohibit** (Subject-verb Agreement) Option (2) is correct because the singular subject *it* needs a singular verb (*prohibit*). The other options are incorrectly plural. Options 3, 4, and 5 also introduce shifts in tense.

15. **(5) no correction is necessary** (Verb forms) Option 5 leaves the sentence correctly written. Options (1), (2), (3), and (4) use incorrect verb forms.

16. **(1) replace <u>Their</u> with <u>There</u>** (Spelling) Option (1) replaces the incorrect homonym with the third person plural possessive pronoun. Option (2) replaces one incorrect homonym with another incorrect one. Option (3) replaces the correct spelling of *Medal* with the incorrect homonym *Meddle*. Option (4) replaces the correct spelling of *posthumously* with an incorrect spelling. Option (5) is not correct because the homonym *There* is used in place of the third person plural possessive, *Their*.

17. **(3) Sentence 17** (Paragraph divisions) Option (3) is correct because it splits the paragraph between two topics: *Stowe's determination to become a doctor* and *the posthumous recognition that Stowe received*. Options (1) and (2) split the paragraph in the middle of the information about Stowe's determination, and options (4) and (5) split the paragraph in the middle of the information about Stowe's posthumous recognition.

18. **(3) used cars** (Spelling) Option (3) is correct because it replaces the possessive form with the plural form. Option (1) is a possessive form. Option (2) is a possessive form with an incorrect hyphen. Option (4) is the plural possessive form. Option (5) is the plural possessive form with an incorrect hyphen.

19. **(2) insert a comma after <u>models</u>** (Commas) Option (2) is correct because it inserts a comma after the introductory phrase. Option (1) replaces a correct verb form with one that does not agree with the noun *you*. Option (3) incorrectly capitalizes a common noun. Option (4) replaces a correct conjunction with one that does not make sense in the sentence. Option (5) does not correct the comma error.

20. **(3) No matter how you shop, you** (Pronouns) Option (3) is correct because it replaces the pronoun *it* with one that agrees with the antecedent *you*. Option (1) does not make sense in the sentence. Option (2) leaves the sentence without a subject. Options (4) and (5) use the pronoun *it*, which does not agree with the implied antecedent *you*.

21. **(2) or show** (Verb tenses) Option (2) is correct because *show* agrees with the preceding verb *are* in tense and number. Option (1) is not correct because *shows* is singular, while the preceding verb *are* is plural. Option (3) replaces the conjunction *or* with a conjunction that does not make sense in the sentence (*yet*). Option (4) replaces the verb *shows* with a possessive noun (*show's*). Option (5) replaces the correct conjunction *or* with an incorrect coordinating conjunction *nor*. *Nor* is used only after *neither*.

22. **(1) change <u>pedals, that</u> to <u>pedals. That</u>** (Comma splice) Option (1) is correct because it fixes the comma splice by splitting it into two complete sentences. Option (2) turns the comma splice into a run-on sentence. Option (3) creates an incorrect verb form (*can tells*). Option (4) does not make sense in the sentence. Option (5) does not correct the comma splice.

23. **(4) move <u>on the engine</u> after <u>oil</u>** (Misplaced modifiers) Option (4) is correct because it moves the modifier *on the engine* directly after the noun it modifies (*oil*). Option (1) does not make sense in the sentence. Option (2) replaces the correct

verb form with one that does not agree in number with the noun *oil*. Option (3) does not fix the misplaced modifier. Option (5) is not true because the modifier is misplaced.

24. **(3) insert a comma after <u>kilometrage</u>** (Commas) Option (3) is correct because a comma is needed after the introductory phrase. Options (1) and (2) are incorrect verb forms. Option (4) removes the subject. Option (5) is a run-on sentence.

25. **(4) the engine. Make sure** (Run-on sentences) Option (4) correctly divides a wordy run-on sentence into two complete sentences. Option (1) is a run-on sentence. Option (2) adds a coordinating conjunction, *and*, but leaves the sentence too wordy and long. Options (3) and (5) do not make sense.

Language Arts, Writing Part II, Essay
(pages 22–23)

Evaluating and scoring your essay can be done by you or by someone else. If you are taking a class, have your teacher evaluate your essay. If you are working independently, ask a friend or relative to read your essay. If this is not possible, evaluate your writing yourself. After finishing an essay, put it aside for a day. Then read it as objectively as possible. No matter who checks your writing, make sure that person follows the Essay Scoring Guide on page 185 and uses the checklist on page 187 as scoring evaluation guides.

Write the date on your completed essays and keep them together in a folder or notebook. Use the Essay Self-Assessment form on page 896 to track your progress, note your strengths, and determine areas in which you want to improve.

Social Studies
(pages 24–32)

1. **(4) to promote world peace** (Comprehension) This is a restatement of the point that the UN was created in the hope of preventing future wars. Option (1) is incorrect because, as the passage states, the UN was created just as World War II was drawing to a close; so the UN could not have ended the war. Options (2) and (3) are UN activities that promote peace, but they are not the reason that the UN was formed. Option (5) was a mission that the UN later undertook, but it was not the reason that the UN was formed.

2. **(2) The Christians were attacking the Muslims.** (Analysis) According to the passage, the reason the UN's peacekeeping force was sent to Bosnia was to protect the Muslim population

from attacks by the Christian Serbs. Option (1) is incorrect because, although the French and Canadians were a part of the UN's peacekeeping force in Bosnia, they were not fighting each other. Option (3) is incorrect because the Muslims were not attacking the Christian Serbs; the passage explains that the opposite was happening. Options (4) and (5) are not supported by the passage.

3. **(3) hearing a teacher threaten to suspend a bully but not following through** (Application) This is another example of hot air, that is, making threats but not following through. The other options are not examples of empty threats.

4. **(4) The UN should be able to enforce its missions.** (Evaluation) Both the passage and the cartoon support this conclusion. The passage explains that some UN peacekeeping missions are not effective, and the cartoon shows the UN peacekeepers as bluffing but not really threatening the Serbs. Options (1), (2), and (3) are incorrect because nothing in the cartoon or passage suggests that the UN should be disbanded, have its own army, or get out of Bosnia. Option (5) is incorrect because there is no discussion of Bosnian refugees.

5. **(4) Individual freedom is protected by law.** (Evaluation) This right gives freedom to individuals, because no one cannot be detained without reason or for an indefinite time. Option (1) is incorrect as it goes against this right. Option (2) is incorrect because lawyers can obtain writs but cannot issue them. Option (3) is true, British law has influenced Canadian law, but this does not demonstrate an important value of our judicial system. Some democratic principles are enshrined in the *Constitution Act of 1982,* though it is more general than the right of *habeas corpus.* Therefore, option (5) does not answer the question.

6. **(2) a restraining order** (Application) As a writ of *habeas corpus* allows for the arrest and detention of an individual, a restraining order keeps an individual from doing something. Both involve court-issued orders that direct human behaviour. Option (1), a credit card, gives a person credit. Option (3), a marriage certificate, provides a record of marriage. Option (4), a constitutional amendment, has broader influence than a writ. Option (5), a certificate of insurance, proves that an individual has coverage for a particular insurance product; it does not relate to a legal document like the writ of *habeas corpus.*

7. **(2) The province was ripe for political and social change.** (Analysis) Violence in a society is usually caused by a deep-seated problem. The period after World War II was a period of rapid change and modernization in most of Canada. The inward orientation and conservatism of Duplessis were at odds with this trend. The passage contradicts option (1), and there is no evidence in the paragraph to support options (3), (4), or (5).

8. **(3) Maurice Duplessis allied himself with the church, big business, and the police.** (Application) The photograph clearly reveals the presence of a political leader in close quarters with both the church hierarchy and the police. There is no evidence to support option (1). Although option (2) may be true, the mere presence of the clergy in the photo does not support this assertion. The information in the passage does not provide any support for options (4) or (5).

9. **(5) The teachers' union would bargain with the school board.** (Application) By law, the teachers' union must negotiate before it can strike, so option (1) is incorrect. It would also try negotiations before agreeing to option (2) or pursuing option (3). Because a school board would not want to close one of its schools, the school board would likely try negotiation before turning to option (4).

10. **(1) They are too powerful.** (Analysis) This is an opinion with which not everyone will agree. A worker whose union has lost a strike, for example, would not share this view. Option (2) is supported by evidence of higher wages, improved working conditions, and other benefits that unions have won for workers. Options (3), (4), and (5) are facts that are stated in the passage.

11. **(4) compromise** (Evaluation) The passage indicates that collective bargaining is a negotiation in which each side often has to give up something it wants so that the process can continue. This shows a strong commitment to the principle of compromise. The process wouldn't work if option (1), (3), or (5) were most important, for in a union contract each side gives up the ability to act independently on issues related to work and the workplace. Although money issues are always among the most important in a labour-management negotiation, nothing in the process or the passage suggests that option (2) is valued above compromise in successful collective bargaining.

12. **(3) Sulphur dioxide emission is caused mostly by industrial sources in Canada and by electrical utilities in the United States.** (Comprehension) Emissions from Canadian industrial source show a 74 percent rate and American electrical utilities show a 67 percent rate; thus, these are the major sources of emissions. Option (1) is incorrect because the chart measures sulphur dioxide emissions, not transportation figures. Option (2) is incorrect because the chart does not indicate the relative successes of each industry. Options (4) and (5) are incorrect because the chart deals with percentages, not with gross amounts of emission.

13. **(2) 1933** (Comprehension) The highest figure for unemployment was 32.4 percent in 1933. The figures for options (1), (3), (4), and (5) are all lower.

14. **(4) The rates in the 1990s are lower than the rates during the 1930s.** (Analysis) The table shows that unemployment rates were greater than 13 percent in the 1930s compared to less than 12 percent in the 1990s. This relationship means options (3) and (5) are incorrect. The rates for 1930 and 1941 make option (1) incorrect. The rates for each year in the 1930s make option (2) incorrect.

15. **(2) The history of early Canada was primarily written from a European point of view.** (Comprehension) This is a restatement of the second sentence, which is the focus of the passage. Option (1) is incorrect because the passage concerns only Canadian history. There is no support to prove option (3). Options (4) and (5), while true, are details about Canadian history, not the main idea of the passage.

16. **(5) It gives us an incomplete picture of what really happened and why.** (Analysis) The passage explains that a Eurocentric understanding leaves out important details about Aboriginal cultures and is thus incomplete. There is no support in the passage for option (1). Options (2) and (3) are contradicted by the information. Option (4) may be true but is not stated in the passage.

17. **(3) St. John's is expecting near-freezing temperatures and rain.** (Analysis) St. John's shows a temperature of 2° C, which is near the freezing point, and rain, not snow, for precipitation. Option (1) is not supported by the map because, though Regina is –19° C, there is no indication that this results in icy roads and accidents.

Option (2) is incorrect because Vancouver is cloudy but not expecting snow. Option (4) is incorrect because, as shown on the map, Ottawa is the coldest (not the warmest) city in Ontario. Option (5) does not relate to the map because what is "usual" is not indicated.

18. **(1) Heavy snowfall in Toronto will delay traffic.** (Application) Because the map shows a heavy snowfall for Toronto, a likely effect is that it will slow traffic. Option (2) cannot be substantiated because the map shows that Vancouver will be cloudy, weather that is not likely to affect the city's electrical power. Option (3) cannot be verified by the map because the map does not show wind. Option (4) is incorrect because the map does not indicate average temperatures or information on tourism. Option (5) is incorrect because the map shows that Montreal is cloudy and has snow.

19. **(1) Provincial premiers have little influence on federal healthcare policies.** (Analysis) The cartoonist is using a T-shirt saying to satirize the lack of power that provincial premiers have on federal healthcare policies. Option (2) does not relate to the cartoon, because the cartoon indicates that the provincial governments have little say in these policies. Option (3) is close to the correct response, but only healthcare policies are mentioned in the cartoon. Options (4) and (5) are humorous responses but do not express the opinions shown in the cartoon.

20. **(3) Grant Aboriginals self-government** (Analysis) Aboriginal self-government is an "important matter of public interest" and therefore could be a recommendation of a royal commission. Option (1) is most unlikely as it would probably be seen as self-interest on the part of the members of a commission. Option (2) is incorrect because recommending higher salaries for politicians is not a matter of investigation. Option (4) is incorrect because royal commissions deal with issues within Canada only. Option (5) is incorrect because having a ballot recount does not require the investigation of a royal commission.

21. **(4) If Allan provided money to the Conservatives, his company would be guaranteed the lucrative charter to build the railway** (Analysis) There is an implied "quid pro quo" (you help us and we'll help you)

in the Conservatives' request for money from Sir Hugh Allan. Option (1) implies that the money was a loan and would be paid back, rather than a bribe. Options (2), (3), and (5) have no support in the passage.

22. **(2) that he was cynical and corrupt** (Evaluation) The cartoonist portrays Sir John A. Macdonald as someone who is surprised that anyone would think that bribery is a sign of corruption. Option (1) is the opposite of what the cartoon implies about Macdonald. The cartoonist clearly means that a corrupt politician is not truthful, the opposite of option (3). Neither option (4) nor option (5) can be deduced from the cartoon.

23. **(5) In recent years, the federal government has not been overspending.** (Comprehension) The graph indicates that the federal government decreased its spending in recent years, in contrast to 1993–1994, when it overspent its revenues by 36.2 percent. Options (1) and (2) are correct for 1993–1994 only. Option (3) is incorrect because the graph does not show how much the government earned or spent, only the ratio between the two. Option (4) is not supported by the graph, as it shows a healthy ratio between revenues and expenditures in recent years.

24. **(4) The media wields too much power in Canadian politics.** (Analysis) The words "too much" are not definable and therefore express an opinion. Options (1), (2), (3), and (5) are facts that are stated in the passage.

25. **(5) More Japanese live on Honshu than on any of the other islands.** (Evaluation) The map shows that Honshu is the largest island and that it contains most of the nation's major cities, so this is a reasonable conclusion from the evidence provided. The map does not label Japan's highest mountains, so option (1) cannot be concluded from the map. Option (2) is contradicted by the evidence on the map; the island of Shikoku is clearly smaller than the island of Kyushu. Major cities are found on both the eastern and western coasts of Japan's major islands and farm regions are not shown, so option (3) cannot be concluded from the information on the map. Option (4) is incorrect because the map provides no information about Japan's economy.

Science

(pages 34–40)

1. **(2) the process by which an immature form changes into a different adult form** (Comprehension) Option (2) restates the process of metamorphosis as described in the passage. Option (1) is incorrect because metamorphosis does not refer to reproduction. Option (3) is incorrect because metamorphosis is not merely growth; it applies only to organisms whose form changes at different stages of development. Option (4) describes aging, not metamorphosis. Option (5) refers to respiration through gills, not metamorphosis.

2. **(4) development of a caterpillar into a butterfly** (Application) The development of a caterpillar into a butterfly, like the tadpole and frog, involves a change of form during growth. Options (1), (2), (3), and (5) involve only growth; there is no complete change of the organism's form from one stage to another.

3. **(3) Different body structures are suitable for different environments.** (Analysis) The diagram shows the tadpole's structures, suitable for underwater swimming, and the frog's structures, suitable for land dwelling. The passage mentions lungs and gills and also mentions that tadpoles live in water and adult frogs live on land. But the author assumes you know that different structures are adapted to different environments. Options (1) and (2) are incorrect since few animals and no plants undergo metamorphosis. Options (4) and (5) are not true and are not closely related to the subject of the passage.

4. **(2) There are almost as many women as men with colon cancer.** (Evaluation) The graph shows that women get colon cancer at almost the same rate as men. For example, at age 70, about 250 out of 100 000 women get colon cancer, and about 350 out of 100 000 men get colon cancer. Therefore, saying colon cancer is a man's disease is a generalization that is not true. Option (1) is true, but it does not explain what is wrong with the statement. Options (3) and (4) are not true, as indicated by the graph. No information about option (5) is included in the graph and this information, whether true or not, does not directly explain why the statement is illogical.

5. **(1) The position of the moon is also a factor in the occurrence of a lunar eclipse.** (Evaluation) The position of all three bodies—sun, Earth, and moon—is critical in determining when a lunar eclipse occurs. Option (2) is incorrect because the season does not affect whether a lunar eclipse occurs. Option (3) is not true; Earth is always revolving around the sun. Option (4) is true but it does not explain why considering only the positions of the sun and Earth is an oversimplification. Option (5) is not true; Earth's position is one factor in determining the occurrence of a lunar eclipse.

6. **(4) eight** (Application) The diagram shows the covalent bonds: the two hydrogen atoms and the oxygen atom are sharing two pairs of electrons. Since covalent bonding involves each atom contributing one electron to form the bond, each unbonded hydrogen atom must have had a single electron. The oxygen atom also must have contributed one atom to each of the two bonds. So, before the bonding occurred, the oxygen atom must have had the two electrons in the inner shell, plus the four free electrons in the outer shell, plus two of the electrons (out of four) now being shared in the two covalent bonds. This adds up to a total of eight electrons. Option (1) is incorrect; only the hydrogen atoms have one electron. Option (2) is incorrect; there are two electrons in the oxygen atom's inner shell, but that is not the total number. Option (3) is incorrect because there are six electrons in an oxygen atom's outer shell, but that is not the total number. Option (5) is incorrect because ten is the total number of electrons the oxygen atom and the two hydrogen atoms have altogether.

7. **(5) SETI projects are based on dreams rather than realistic possibilities about space.** (Analysis) The scientific value of SETI projects is debated in the scientific community. Some think looking for aliens is an activity best left for science fiction; others think it is a worthwhile scientific endeavour. Options (1), (2), (3), and (4) are facts about radio waves and SETI.

8. **(5) The world's deepest trenches are in the Pacific Ocean.** (Evaluation) Because, as the passage indicates, the table shows the deepest trenches in each ocean, the deepest trenches are in the Pacific—they are the deepest trenches in the table. Options (1), (3), and (4) contradict the information given in the table. Option (2) is incorrect because trenches are depressions, not spreading sea floor.

9. **(4) The rate of cellular respiration goes up during exercise to give additional energy to the body.** (Analysis) Options (1) and (2) are incorrect because they do not pertain to Jason's experiment. Option (3) is incorrect because more energy is needed for exercise, not less. Option (5) is incorrect because the amount of carbon dioxide in exhaled breath is not directly related to lung capacity.

10. **(2) a dropper** (Analysis) A dropper would be useful for adding drops of sodium hydroxide solution to the water. Option (1) is incorrect because no heating is involved. Option (3) is incorrect because nothing needs to be measured with a spoon. Options (4) and (5) are also unnecessary for this procedure.

11. **(2) The cells of plant roots absorb water from the surrounding soil.** (Application) Water flows across the cell membrane of root cells into the plant when there is more water in the soil than in the root cells. Option (1) describes cell division, not osmosis. Option (3) involves diffusion of oxygen and carbon dioxide, not water, across a membrane. Option (4) describes the movement of water through a pore (a small hole) out of a leaf, not across any membrane. Option (5) describes a method by which proteins, not water, enter cells.

12. **(2) move toward the equator** (Application) Because ice would be moving south from the North Pole, residents of North America would tend to move south, toward the equator. Option (1) would not help because ice would be spreading north in the Southern Hemisphere. Option (3) is incorrect because the ice sheets in the northern part of the continent would make the region difficult to live in. Option (4) is not likely because human beings are very adaptable and have survived previous ice ages. Option (5) is the opposite of what happens during an ice age.

13. **(4) age 70–90 after one introduction** (Comprehension) According to the graph, the group that did most poorly was the oldest group after just one introduction; they recalled only about 12% of the names. Options (1), (2), (3), and (5) are incorrect because they show percentages greater than 12%.

14. **(3) Vestigial structures are the remains of well-developed and functional structures.** (Analysis) This is the conclusion to which scientists came after examining the evidence for vestigial structures. Options (1), (2), (4), and (5) are details, stated in the paragraph or shown in the diagram, that support the conclusion.

15. **(4) less energy available for living things** (Analysis) A decrease in photosynthesis means less chemical energy available in the food web. Options (1), (2), and (3) are incorrect because the sun would continue to produce the same amount of energy regardless of what happened on Earth. Option (5) is incorrect because the amount of chemical energy available to living things would be less if there were less photosynthesis.

16. **(4) number of cycles that pass a given point and unit of time** (Comprehension) Frequency is defined in the first sentence of the passage as the number of waves that pass a given point in a specific unit of time. Options (1), (2), and (3) are incorrect because neither height (another word for amplitude) nor distance between crests or troughs is directly related to frequency. Option (5) is incorrect because calculating frequency does not involve distance.

17. **(3) the pull of Earth's gravity on a space station** (Application) The ball swung on a string is pulled to the centre of the circle by centripetal force, and a space station is held in its circular orbit because it is pulled toward Earth by the force of gravity. None of the remaining options describe circular motion, the key element here.

18. **(5) biosphere** (Application) A large, self-sustaining environment that includes organisms and their physical surroundings is a biosphere. The key here is the word "self-sustaining," that is, containing everything needed to sustain life, like Earth. Options (1) to (4) are incorrect because the level of complexity is too low in each of them.

19. **(5) The common ancestor of fish, birds, and humans was probably a water animal.** (Evaluation) The statement is supported by the existence of gill slits in early stages of the three embryos. Options (1), (2), and (4) may or may not be true, but there is not enough information given to tell. The diagram contradicts option (3).

20. **(2) Methane provides the most heat.** (Evaluation) According to the table, methane provides the most heat per gram combusted: 55.9 kilojoules. Option (1) is incorrect because natural gas releases more heat than oil. Option (3) is incorrect because wood gives off less than half the heat of oil. Option (4) is incorrect because wood gives off less heat than coal. Option (5) is incorrect because coal gives off less heat than oil.

21. **(5) Causes and Effects of Glaciers**
(Comprehension) The passage explains how mountain glaciers are formed (causes) and the changes they make on the landscape (effects). Option (1) is incorrect because the passage does not discuss the history of glaciers. Option (2) is too general. Options (3) and (4) are too specific.

22. **(3) its electromagnetic fields** (Analysis) Because infrared waves are a form of electromagnetic radiation, they produce electric and magnetic fields that affect the ability of the sensor to conduct electricity. Options (1) and (2) are incorrect because these are properties of matter, not of waves. Options (4) and (5) are wave properties, but they are not the cause of changes in conductivity in the thermometer's sensor.

23. **(5) a car whose speedometer reads 100 km/h** (Application) A speedometer indicates the speed of a vehicle at any given moment. It is the only example of instantaneous speed among the options. Options (1) and (4) are examples in which the speed is changing. Options (2) and (3) are examples that allow you to calculate average, not instantaneous, speed.

24. **(5) 20 m north at 5 m/s** (Application) Velocity includes both direction and speed. It is the only option that mentions a direction, north. The remaining options are examples of speed; they give information about distance over time, but no information about direction.

25. **(4) screening for genetic diseases** (Application) The DNA profiles of Icelanders would be very useful in conducting tests for genetic diseases. Options (1) and (2) are incorrect because HIV/AIDS and bacterial infections are infectious diseases that are not related to genetics. Option (3) is incorrect because diet is not related to genetics. Option (5) is incorrect because DNA profiles have nothing to do with infant vaccinations.

Language Arts, Reading
(pages 42–51)

1. **(4) He did not follow in his father's footsteps.** (Comprehension) In lines 24–26, the narrator says that "Business was just as much out of the question for me as politics had been for my father." The excerpt also says that the family still had a few political connections. You can infer from this that someone, likely the narrator's grandfather, was in politics and that the narrator's father didn't go into it. This implies that neither the narrator nor his father before him followed their father's career paths. There is not enough evidence in the excerpt to support options (1), (2), (3), and (5).

2. **(1) It emphasizes that the narrator wanted to escape into a safer world.** (Analysis) The narrator notes that business could cause suffering and alludes to negative family history that makes an ivory tower appealing. The image of an ivory tower is one of being raised up above it all, something like an escape. There is no evidence for option (2). The reference is not to Jack, so options (3) and (4) are incorrect. Option (5) is incorrect because the excerpt shows how little the father and son have in common.

3. **(5) He would do his best to accept Jack's views.** (Application) Based on the tone of the excerpt, it is apparent that the father seeks to reconcile with his son. This suggests that he would try to accept his son's views even if he did not share them. Option (1) is incorrect because it does not describe the behaviour of a father seeking to make friends with a son. There is no support for options (2), (3), and (4).

4. **(3) well-known slavery opponents** (Comprehension) Lines 29–30 refer to Garrison, Lovejoy, and others agitating for freedom. This suggests that the two men were abolitionists seeking to overthrow the institution of slavery. There is no evidence in the excerpt to support options (1), (2), (4), and (5).

5. **(3) a person-to-person means of transmitting information** (Analysis) Lines 35–42 refer to "late-at-night whispered discussions" that the author heard his mother and other slaves indulge in, indicating that they "understood the situation." This suggests that " 'grape-vine' telegraph" is another term for word-of-mouth communication. None of the other options makes sense in the context of the term.

6. **(4) the author's deep interest in education** (Synthesis) Lines 5–8 state, "The picture of several dozen boys and girls in a schoolroom engaged in study made a deep impression upon me." This suggests that the impression was long lasting and very likely motivated him to pursue a career in education. Options (1) and (5) would have no bearing on the author's pursuit of a career in education. There is no support in the excerpt for option (2). Option (3) might inspire a desire for learning but would not necessarily correlate with the pursuit of a career in education.

7. **(3) the wind (Comprehension)** In the first line of each stanza, the poet compares the kite metaphorically to each of the items in options (1), (2), (4), and (5). He says in option (1), for example, "the kite is a fish you've already caught" meaning it is *like* a fish that's already caught. The poet does not relate the kite and the wind in this way. Although the word *wind* is mentioned in three instances (in lines 14, 16, and 23), he does not make a comparison between the kite and the wind.

8. **(2) to a desperate trained falcon (Comprehension)** The comparison of the kite to option (2) is directly stated here. In lines 5 and 6, the poet says it (the kite) lives *like* a desperate trained falcon. Options (1) and (3) are other images in the poem to which the kite is not compared. Options (4) and (5) are images that are not included in the poem.

9. **(1) cordless (Synthesis)** The poet's use of the word *cordless* allows the reader to infer a link between the kite and the moon. They are both in the sky "travelling," and yet different in that the kite is "corded," and the moon is "cordless." This one word therefore links the two but at the same time stresses a difference (or contrast). Option (2) only points to a similarity—not a contrast—in that both the kite and the moon are "travelling" in the sky. Options (3), (4), and (5) do not relate to either the kite or the moon.

10. **(1) replacement cost coverage renters insurance** (Application) The excerpt states that this type of insurance will pay to replace the lost property "with comparable new property" (line 23). Option (2) is incorrect because this type of coverage pays replacement cost minus depreciation. The fact that the dolls are collectibles might mean that this type of

insurance would pay very little for their loss. Option (3) is incorrect because a deductible is a feature of many types of insurance, not a type of policy itself. Option (4) is incorrect because this type of insurance is for claims brought against the insured, not losses incurred by the insured. Option (5) covers only a single type of peril.

11. **(2) informative and direct** (Synthesis) The excerpt defines terms commonly used in renters insurance policies and explains the different types of coverage in a straightforward manner. None of the other options accurately describes the style in which it is written.

12. **(4) John is being pressured to become a preacher.** (Comprehension) The word "altar" is used figuratively in the excerpt to stand for the church. Therefore, the phrase implies that both the church and his parents were pushing him toward becoming a preacher. Options (1) and (5) are incorrect because there is no evidence to support them. Options (2) and (3) are incorrect because it is clear that John is already a member of the church.

13. **(1) use of many descriptive words** (Synthesis) The author uses many descriptive words to describe John's admiration of Elisha such as "deeper," "manlier," "leanness," "grace," "strength," and "darkness." None of the other options are true of this excerpt.

14. **(2) Bad things can result even when someone means well.** (Analysis) Mr. Brooks may mean well, but his wife is quite unhappy. This is why she brings up her grandmother's saying. The issue of trust is not present in this excerpt, so option (1) is incorrect. There is no evidence suggesting what Mr. Brooks was like earlier in his life, so option (3) is incorrect. There is no evidence to support options (4) and (5).

15. **(1) She has thought for a long time about leaving Mr. Brooks.** (Comprehension) Mrs. Brooks refers to "the last straw," implying that this decision had been building up over time. There is no evidence for options (2), (3), or (5). Although Ruby tries to persuade Mrs. Brooks not to leave her husband, there is no evidence that Mrs. Brooks will change her mind; therefore, option (4) is incorrect.

Answers and Explanations • Entry Tests

16. (3) Disagreements over money can affect relationships. (Synthesis) The Brooks' marriage is affected by how they both react to money. Mr. Brooks may feel that his wife complains unnecessarily, option (1), but this is not supported in the excerpt. Option (2) is a generalization that is probably false. Although Ruby may not be as supportive as Mrs. Brooks would like, option (4), this is not the focus of the excerpt. There is no support in this excerpt for option (5).

17. (3) She was dressed as a widow in mourning. (Analysis) Widow's dress is appropriate for a woman who has lost her husband, not her child, so this would be an indication that the character is becoming mentally imbalanced. Options (1) and (2) do not suggest mental instability. Option (4) is incorrect because the fact that her child was killed is not evidence that she had lost her mind. Option (5) is incorrect because although the flag and medals insult rather than comfort her, this reaction is not unusual enough to be evidence that she was losing her mind.

18. (2) refuse to attend the ceremony (Application) Doña Ernestina's response of "*no gracias*" to the military's offer to give her son a military funeral suggests that she would not attend the ceremony. Option (1) is incorrect because the excerpt makes it clear that she would not attend. Option (3) is incorrect because she does not discuss the war in the excerpt. Option (4) is incorrect because it is not characteristic of her based on the way she is described in the excerpt. Option (5) is incorrect because it is the opposite of her feelings toward the president and the military.

19. (4) She had a wild look in her eyes. (Analysis) This description of Doña Ernestina is the best clue to her state of mind. Option (1) might suggest her state of mind but it is not as telling as her physical description. Options (2) and (3) are descriptions that do not reflect mental instability. Option (5) indicates her sense of pride more than mental instability.

20. (4) Spanish phrases (Synthesis) The excerpt features the use of such Spanish words and phrases such as "*lato,*" "*Ya no vive aqui,*" and "*No, gracias.*" Although the author does use third-person narration, this technique does not add to the excerpt's authenticity, so option (1) is incorrect. Options (2), (3), and (5) are not true of the style of this excerpt.

Mathematics
(pages 52–65)
Part 1

1. **(4) $89.16** Set up a proportion using the ratio of the cost of insurance to the amount of insurance. Cross multiply and solve. $\frac{\$7.43}{\$2500} = \frac{?}{\$30\,000}$
   $\$7.43 \times \$30\,000 \div \$2500 = \$89.16$

2. **(1) 10** Find the area of a triangle.
   $A = \frac{1}{2}bh = \frac{1}{2}(5.2)(4) = 10.4$, round to 10 cm²

3. **(4) (2 + 3)$35** First find the number of camera sales made (2 + 3). Then multiply that amount by the commission she earns. The price of each camera is not needed.

4. **(4) −4 and 0** Find each pair of points on a number line and locate the midpoint.

   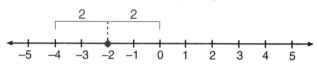

5. **(2) 50°** The sum of the angles in a triangle is 180°, so $m\angle RPQ = 180° − 90° − 40° = 50°$.

6. **12.3** You know two sides of a right triangle. Use the Pythagorean Relationship to find the missing side.
   $10.2^2 + b^2 = 16^2$
   $b^2 = 16^2 − 10.2^2$
   $b^2 = 151.96$
   $b = \sqrt{151.96} = 12.3272$
   Round to 12.3
   Using your GED calculator:
   16 **x²** **−** 10.2 **x²** **=**
   SHIFT **x²** 12.32720568
   Round to 12.3

7. **(5) $4.08** Multiply the percent spent on popcorn by the total amount spent.
   $0.34 \times \$12$ million $= \$4.08$ million
   Using your GED calculator:
   12 **×** .34 **SHIFT** **=** 4.08

8. **(2) 2:1** Write a ratio of the percent spent on popcorn to the percent spent on tortilla chips.
   34:17 Reduce the ratio. 34:17 = 2:1

9. **(4) 3x + 7y** $4(x + 2y) − (x + y)$
   $4x + 8y − x − y$
   $3x + 7y$

10. **3300** Convert 1 m to centimetres.
    $1 \times 100 = 100$ cm. Use the formula for finding the area of a rectangle.
    $A = lw$
    $A = 33(100)$
    $A = 3300$ cm²

11. (1) 50 $A = \pi r^2$
$A = 3.14(4^2)$
$A = 50.24 \text{ m}^2$
Round to 50 m²

12. (−3,2) Start at the origin (0,0). Move 3 units to the left and 2 units up. The point is in Quadrant II.

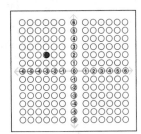

Part 2

13. (3) 48 Let x, $x + 2$, and $x + 4$ represent the consecutive even numbers. Write an equation and solve.
$$x + (x + 2) + (x + 4) = 138$$
$$3x + 6 = 138$$
$$3x = 132$$
$$x = 44$$
The numbers are 44, 46, and 48.

14. (2) 37 Find the perimeter of the top of the carton. The measurements of the top are the same as those of the bottom, so the top is 8.5 cm by 10 cm. Add the sides.
$8.5 + 8.5 + 10 + 10 = 37$ cm

15. (4) 8.5 × 12 To find the area of the rectangular front of the carton, multiply the length × width.

16. (2) −x − 5 Think of the subtraction operation as multiplying the contents of the parentheses by −1.
$2 - (x + 7) = 2 + (-1)(x + 7) = 2 - x - 7 = -x - 5$

17. (4) $7100 Multiply the amount borrowed by the interest rate, and then multiply the result by the number of years. $5000 × 0.14 × 3 = $2100 Add the interest to the amount borrowed.
$5000 + $2100 = $7100

18. 4.9 Divide the total length of the board by 4. $19.6 ÷ 4 = 4.9$
or $\dfrac{49}{10}$

$\dfrac{196}{10} ÷ 4 = \dfrac{196}{10} ÷ \dfrac{4}{1} =$

$\dfrac{\overset{49}{\cancel{196}}}{10} × \dfrac{1}{\underset{1}{\cancel{4}}} = \dfrac{49}{10}$

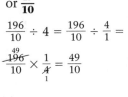

19. (1) 16 + 2π The sum of the three straight sides is $6 + 4 + 6 = 16$. The circumference of the half-circle is $\frac{1}{2}\pi(4)$, which equals 2π. The perimeter of the whole figure is $16 + 2\pi$.

20. (2) 21 + 21 + 18 + 18 Add the four sides of the figure to find the perimeter. $21 + 21 + 18 + 18$

21. (2) 90.0 Write the 6 scores in increasing or decreasing order. 71, 73, 86, 94, 96, 102 Since there is an even number of games, there is no middle number. Find the average (mean) of the two middle numbers, 86 and 94.
$(86 + 94) ÷ 2 = 90$

22. (3) A, D, and F One way to solve the problem is to find the coordinates of some of the points on the graph and substitute them in the given equation. If you choose this method, remember that it isn't necessary to try every point. Choose points that appear in only one or two choices in order to eliminate as many choices as possible.

Another way to solve the problem is to graph the equation on the grid. Notice that the equation is written in slope-intercept form, or $y = mx + b$, where m = slope and b = y-intercept. The y-intercept is (0,3), the location of point D. The slope is $-\frac{3}{2}$. To find another point on the line, start at point D and count down 3 and 2 to the right. You are now at point A. The correct option passes through points A, D, and F.

23. (1) $\dfrac{(\$1800 - \$300)}{\$150}$ First subtract the $300 payment from the $1800 debt ($1800 − $300). Then divide the remaining debt by the amount to be paid each month ($150).

24. (2) $\dfrac{7}{15}$ There are 7 cards numbered with an even number: 2, 4, 6, 8, 10, 12, and 14. Write a fraction with the total number of favourable outcomes, 7, over the total number of possible outcomes, 15. $\dfrac{7}{15}$

25. (3) 4200 5 weeks $5 × 7 = 35$ days; $35 × 4 = 140$ hours; $140 ÷ 2 = 70$ hours for each exam, or 4200 minutes

UNIT 1: LANGUAGE ARTS, WRITING

Sentence Structure
Lesson 1: Sentences and Sentence Fragments
GED Practice (pages 70–71)

All items in this practice are related to sentence fragments.

1. **(5) no correction is necessary** The sentence is complete as is. Option (1) repeats the subject. Options (2), (3), and (4) create fragments.

2. **(2) cooking, which is one** Option (2) is correct because it joins the fragment (sentence 4) to a complete thought. Option (1) is incorrect because sentence 4 is a fragment. Options (3) and (5) do not correct the fragment. Option (4) does not make sense.

3. **(1) replace Less with Microwaves are less** Option (1) is correct because it gives this fragment both a subject and a verb. Options (2), (3), and (5) do not fix the fragment. Option (4) creates a new fragment.

4. **(4) are not worried because most** This option is correct because it provides the correct verb and the connecting word *because* to join the fragment to the complete sentence. Options (1), (2), and (5) do not have complete predicates. Option (3) repeats the subject.

5. **(3) us, such as your** Option (3) is correct because it joins a sentence fragment to a complete sentence. Option (1) is incorrect because it contains a fragment. Option (2) runs ideas together without correct punctuation. Options (4) and (5) use inappropriate words to connect the thoughts.

6. **(5) no correction is necessary** Options (1), (2), and (3) all create fragments in a sentence that is already a complete thought. Option (4) misspells a word.

7. **(2) when you want to download** Option (2) correctly joins a fragment to a complete thought and supplies a subject and a predicate. Options (1), (3), (4), and (5) would create awkwardly worded sentences or change the meaning of the text.

8. **(1) insert can be before updated** Option (1) correctly completes the predicate to eliminate the fragment. Option (2) is incorrect because it fails to complete the verb and eliminate the fragment. Option (3) creates another fragment. Option (4) does not correct the fragment. Option (5) does not complete the main verb of the sentence.

Lesson 2: Compound Sentences
GED Practice (pages 74–75)

All items in this practice are related to compound sentences.

1. **(2) designs such as maps** Option (2) corrects the fragment by combining it with the previous sentence. Option (1) connects the fragment as if it were an independent clause. Options (3), (4), and (5) do not connect the fragment and do not keep the meaning of the original text.

2. **(1) patches, or they** The sentence is correct because two complete, related thoughts are joined by a comma and an appropriate coordinating conjunction. Option (2) is missing the necessary comma. Option (3) creates a fragment. Option (4) misplaces the comma. Option (5) has a second, unnecessary comma.

3. **(5) uniform, yet** Option (5) is correct because two complete, related thoughts are correctly joined by a comma and a contrasting coordinating conjunction. Option (1) lacks the necessary comma. Option (2) uses an inappropriate conjunctive adverb and is incorrectly punctuated. Option (3) creates a fragment. Option (4) misplaces the comma.

4. **(2) change Became to It became** Option (2) corrects the fragment by adding a subject. Option (1) incorrectly changes the form of the verb and does not add a subject. Option (3) inserts an unnecessary comma. Option (4) capitalizes a word unnecessarily. Option (5) is a sentence fragment.

5. **(1) Internet, so your** Option (1) is correct because two complete, related thoughts are correctly joined by a comma and an appropriate coordinating conjunction. Option (2) is incorrect because the two sentences are only joined by a comma without a coordinating conjunction. In option (3), the comma should be before *so*. In option (4), *so* is not preceded by a comma. Option (5) creates a fragment.

6. **(3) insert a comma after information** Option (3) is correct because compound sentences must be joined by a coordinating conjunction preceded by a comma. Option (1) removes the coordinating conjunction and forms a run-on sentence. Option (2) places the comma after, instead of before, the coordinating conjunction *and*. Option (4) removes the subject of the second sentence.

7. **(5) rejected, but the** Option (5) is correct because it correctly combines the two sentences with a comma followed by the appropriate

coordinating conjunction. Option (1) does not contain a coordinating conjunction for the compound sentence. Option (2) uses incorrect punctuation. Option (3) contains no punctuation and an inappropriate connecting word. Option (4) contains the correct coordinating conjunction but is missing a comma.

8. **(2) insert or after the comma** Option (2) is correct because it provides an appropriate coordinating conjunction for the two clauses in the compound sentence. Options (1) and (5) are incorrect because the compound sentence needs a coordinating conjunction. Option (3) is incorrect because a conjunctive adverb needs a semicolon before it and a comma after it. Option (4) is incorrect because a comma is not needed.

Lesson 3: Subordinating Ideas
GED Practice (pages 78–79)
All items in this practice are related to subordinating ideas.

1. **(3) country, moving** Option (3) is correct because it fixes a subordinate-clause fragment by attaching it to the independent clause that follows it and includes a comma after the subordinate clause. Option (1) creates a fragment. Option (2) omits the comma after the introductory subordinate clause. Option (4) is incorrect because it uses an inappropriate coordinating conjunction. Option (5) uses an inappropriate subordinating conjunction before the independent clause, making a sentence fragment.

2. **(2) insert a comma after time** Option (2) is correct because it inserts a comma after the introductory subordinate clause. Option (1) uses an inappropriate subordinating conjunction and does not include the comma after the clause. Option (3) incorrectly changes the verb to the past tense. Option (4) inserts an unnecessary comma. Option (5) is a run-on sentence.

3. **(5) address and** Option (5) is correct because it combines related details smoothly and reduces repetition. Option (1) creates choppy sentences. Option (2) joins two independent clauses without a coordinating conjunction. Option (3) is incorrect because it doesn't combine the details smoothly. Option (4) creates a fragment.

4. **(3) survival kit containing** Option (3) is correct because it smoothly combines the details into one sentence. Option (1) does not combine the details smoothly and repeats words. Option (2) uses an inappropriate connecting

term between *kit* and the listed items. Option (4) leaves out necessary information about the kit. Option (5) creates a sentence fragment with an incomplete predicate.

5. **(2) books and commercial exercise programs are** Option (2) is correct because it combines the subjects into one sentence. Option (1) omits the coordinating conjunction needed for a compound sentence. Option (3) does not combine the ideas smoothly. Option (4) uses an inappropriate coordinating conjunction. Option (5) omits a verb.

6. **(3) insert a comma after shape** Option (3) is correct because a comma is needed after an introductory subordinate clause. Option (1) creates a compound sentence with no coordinating conjunction. Option (2) inserts the comma in the middle of the subordinate clause. Option (4) creates a fragment out of the subordinate clause. Option (5) is incorrect because a comma should follow the subordinate clause.

7. **(5) a good pair of walking shoes** Option (5) combines the detail from the second clause into the first. The revised sentence would be *You can simply buy a good pair of walking shoes and take a brisk walk in them several times a week.* Options (1) and (4) do not combine the details as smoothly. Options (2) and (3) do not keep the meaning of the original text.

8. **(3) feel since you've** Option (3) fixes the subordinate-clause fragment, shown in option (1), by attaching it to the independent thought before it. Option (2) inserts an unnecessary comma and coordinating conjunction; the relationship between the two thoughts is subordinate, not equal. Option (4) uses an inappropriate subordinating conjunction. Option (5) removes the connecting word that shows how the ideas in the two clauses are related.

Lesson 4: Run-Ons and Comma Splices
GED Practice (pages 82–83)
All items in this practice are related to run-on sentences.

1. **(5) application, and everything** Option (5) fixes the run-on, shown in option (1), by separating the independent clauses with a comma and an appropriate coordinating conjunction. Option (2) creates a comma splice. Option (3) uses an inappropriate conjunctive adverb and incorrect punctuation. Option (4) omits the necessary comma in a compound sentence.

2. **(3) change the comma to a period** Option (3) is correct because it fixes the comma splice by making the two clauses into two sentences. Option (1) is incorrect because it separates an idea from the clause it belongs with. Option (2) creates a run-on sentence. Option (4) uses an inappropriate coordinating conjunction. Option (5) connects the ideas inappropriately.

3. **(1) insert I can after the comma** Option (1) correctly adds a subject to fix the sentence fragment. Option (2) does not fix the fragment; it only changes the form of the verb. Option (3) adds an inappropriate subject and removes the verb. Option (4) inserts an unnecessary comma because *or* is not separating two independent clauses in this sentence. Option (5) is a sentence fragment.

4. **(4) letter and include my name,** Option (4) is correct because it fixes the lack of a comma between the independent clauses and removes unnecessary words by combining two verbs in one main clause. The other options do not lead to smoothly combined ideas in one sentence.

5. **(5) equipment. Some** Option (5) is correct because it uses a period to separate the independent clauses of the comma splice into two sentences. Options (1) and (2) are incorrect because they create run-on sentences. Option (3) uses an inappropriate conjunctive adverb with incorrect punctuation. Option (4) uses an inappropriate subordinating conjunction.

6. **(3) syndrome. Their** Option (3) is correct because it uses a period to separate the independent clauses of the run-on into two sentences. Option (1) is a run-on sentence. Option (2) is a comma splice. Options (4) and (5) create compound sentences with coordinating conjunctions that are not preceded by commas.

7. **(5) no correction is necessary** Option (1) creates a fragment. Option (2) inserts an unnecessary comma because *and* is not separating two independent clauses in this sentence; it is joining two subjects in a compound sentence. Option (3) removes the necessary word *and*. Option (4) creates a fragment by taking away the verb of the sentence.

8. **(4) jobs; for example,** Option (4) is correct because it separates the two clauses of the comma splice with an appropriate connecting word and punctuation. Option (1) creates a compound sentence, but with an inappropriate coordinating conjunction. Option (2) creates a subordinate clause from the first independent clause, but with an inappropriate subordinating conjunction. Option (3) creates a subordinate clause from the second independent clause, but with an inappropriate subordinating conjunction. Option (5) omits information from the original text.

9. **(4) change common workers to common. Workers** Option (4) correctly separates the two independent clauses into two sentences. Option (1) creates a subordinate clause from the first independent clause, but with an inappropriate subordinating conjunction and without the necessary comma after the introductory clause. Option (2) creates a comma splice. Option (3) creates a compound sentence without the necessary comma between the two clauses. Option (5) does not correct the run-on sentence.

Lesson 5: Misplaced and Dangling Modifiers
GED Practice (pages 85–86)
All items in this practice are related to misplaced and dangling modifiers.

1. **(1) replace By installing with If you install** Option (1) is correct because it inserts a subject and verb into the dangling modifier, transforming the phrase into a subordinating clause. Option (2) removes a comma needed after an introductory phrase and does not fix the dangling modifier. Option (3) treats the sentence as if it were compound, with two independent clauses, but it is not. Option (4) merely changes the verb form in the main clause and does not fix the dangling modifier. Option (5) is incorrect because the sentence lacks the subject that the modifier is describing.

2. **(1) Costing about $20,** Option (1) is correct because it moves the wrongly placed phrase near the word it modifies, *way*. The revised sentence would be *Costing about $20, the best way to save money is by etching your vehicle identification number into the windows*. The other options do not create a sentence in which the modifier is placed correctly and the meaning of the original text is kept.

3. **(4) hard for car thieves to break** Option (4) is correct because it moves the wrongly placed phrase near the word it modifies, *hard*. The revised sentence would be *Etched windows make it hard for car thieves to break down a car into sellable pieces*. The other options do not create a sentence in which all modifiers are placed correctly.

4. **(5) no correction is necessary** The sentence is correct because all the modifiers are placed correctly. Option (1) unnecessarily replaces the introductory subordinate clause. Option (2) removes the comma needed after an introductory subordinate clause. Option (3) replaces the subject of the main clause with a subject and a verb. Option (4) inserts an unnecessary comma because the *and* is not separating two independent clauses in this sentence.

5. **(1) As senior crew supervisor, Erica Ortiz** Option (1) is correct because the modifying phrase is placed correctly in the sentence. Option (2) creates a fragment. Option (3) creates a sentence with two verbs—*is* and *supervises*. Option (4) is wordy and requires commas around the modifying phrase. Option (5) creates a sentence with two subjects—*Erica Ortiz* and *she*.

6. **(4) sure that the crews have their job assignments and tools when** Option (4) is correct because it moves the modifying clause near the noun it modifies—*crews*. Option (1) would not create an effective revision or keep all the information in the sentence. Option (2) makes the clause modify *Erica*, not *crew*. Options (3) and (5) change the meaning of the sentence.

7. **(3) Landscapers in 1998 and quickly gained the respect of crew members** Option (3) is correct because it moves the wrongly placed phrase *in 1998* closer to the idea it modifies and removes wordiness by giving the sentence two verbs—*started* and *gained*. Options (1) and (4) do not move the phrase *in 1998* to the best location in the sentence. Neither does Option (5), which also creates a comma splice. Option (2) is a run-on sentence.

8. **(1) Erica also has** Option (1) is correct because it gives the opening modifying phrase the correct subject to modify—*Erica*. The revised sentence would be *Proudly representing Strong Landscapers, Erica also has a great reputation among our customers in the community.* Options (2), (3), and (4) create a dangling modifier by not supplying the correct subject. Option (5) leaves out the verb to be used in the main clause.

9. **(2) change Erica Oriz is recommended to I recommend Erica Ortiz** Option (2) is correct because it uses the subject that the phrase *With pleasure* modifies—*I*. Option (1) creates a fragment. Option (3) creates a fragment by making the verb incomplete. Option (4) inserts an unnecessary comma because the word *for* is not a coordinating conjunction in this sentence. Option (5) creates a dangling modifier.

Lesson 6: Parallel Structure
GED Practice (pages 88–89)
All items in this practice are related to parallel structure.

1. **(3) replace <u>with a lot of</u> with <u>having</u>** Option (3) is correct because it matches the other *-ing* endings in the series. Option (1) changes the parallel form to a non-parallel form *(to)*. Option (2) removes a necessary comma between items in the series. Option (4) changes a parallel form to a non-parallel form. Option (5) inserts an unnecessary comma.

2. **(4) and apologizing loudly** Option (4) is correct because the phrases are parallel when each contains an *-ing* word and an adverb. Option (1) contains no *-ing* word. Option (2) uses a subordinate clause. Option (3) uses the *to* form of the verb. Option (5) uses a phrase.

3. **(1) and sneakers** Option (1) is correct because the three nouns—*jeans, sweatshirt,* and *sneakers*—are in parallel structure. Options (2) and (3) are incorrect because they use phrases. Option (4) unnecessarily repeats *wearing*. Option (5) uses a phrase after the noun. All these create non-parallel structures.

4. **(5) remove <u>look</u>** Option (5) is correct because it removes the verb and allows *serious* to match the other adjectives in this series. Options (1) and (2) create fragments. Option (3) removes the comma that is needed between items in a series. Option (4) inserts an unnecessary coordinating conjunction. The comma is all that is necessary to separate the items.

5. **(5) replace <u>and we can recognize it</u> with <u>and recognizable</u>** Option (5) is correct because it changes a clause into a single-word adjective, like the others in the series—*soft, vague, recognizable*. Option (1) changes the form of the verb but does not correct the error in parallel structure. Options (2) and (3) change the other adjectives in the series to further the error in parallel structure. Option (4) changes the subordinate conjunction but does not keep the meaning of the original text.

6. **(4) change <u>reducing</u> to <u>reduce</u>** Option (4) is correct because it puts all the verbs in the series in the same form—*calm, lower, reduce.* Options (1) and (5) do not correct the non-parallel structure. Option (2) furthers the non-parallel structure by changing the middle verb to a different form. Option (3) changes the meaning of the original sentence.

7. **(4) in stores, at work, and in stressful situations** Option (4) is correct because it creates a series of parallel prepositional phrases. In options (1) and (3), the third phrase in each series is not parallel. In options (2) and (5), all the phrases are in different forms.

8. **(3) insert a comma after absenteeism** Option (3) is correct because a comma is necessary between the items in a series. Option (1) inserts an unnecessary comma. Option (2) creates a fragment with an incomplete verb. Option (4) creates a non-parallel structure. Option (5) creates a run-on sentence.

9. **(5) no correction is necessary** Option (5) is correct because three words ending in *-ing* are in parallel structure. Option (1) is incorrect because the comma is needed after the introductory subordinate clause. Option (2) is incorrect because it changes the parallel *-ing* form to a non-parallel form. Option (3) is incorrect because leaving *earplugs* alone would create non-parallel structure. Option (4) is incorrect because replacing the *-ing* form with a clause would create non-parallel structure.

GED Review Sentence Structure
(pages 90–95)

1. **(3) instead, which** (Sentence fragments) Option (3) is correct because it joins a fragment to a complete thought. Option (1) is a fragment. Option (2) changes only the end punctuation; it does not eliminate the fragment. In option (4), the word *and* does not fit the meaning of the sentence. In option (5), the combination of *and* and *which* does not eliminate the fragment.

2. **(5) no correction is necessary** (Sentence fragments) Options (1), (2), and (3) are incorrect because each creates a fragment. Option (4) creates two complete sentences without end punctuation.

3. **(1) insert It has been before 15** (Sentence fragments) Option (1) is correct because it provides the fragment with a subject and verb. Options (2), (3), (4), and (5) do not correct the fragment.

4. **(2) insert is after This** (Sentence fragments) Option (2) corrects the fragments by inserting the missing verb. Option (1) removes the subject and does not eliminate the fragment. Option (3) creates an additional fragment. Options (4) and (5) do not eliminate the fragment.

5. **(3) account unless I receive an** (Sentence fragments) Option (3) is correct because it provides the appropriate connecting word and a subject and verb for the fragment. Options (1), (2), (4), and (5) do not make sense.

6. **(3) insert so after the comma** (Compound sentences) Option (3) is correct because it provides the appropriate coordinating conjunction. Option (1) is incorrect because *Two months are combined* is not a complete independent clause. Option (2) contains an inappropriate conjunctive adverb punctuated incorrectly. Option (4) is incorrect because both a comma and a coordinating conjunction are needed to combine two sentences. Option (5) creates a comma splice.

7. **(5) month, but it** (Compound sentences) Option (5) is correct because it joins two complete sentences with a comma and an appropriate coordinating conjunction. Options (1) and (3) contain an inappropriate conjunctive adverb punctuated incorrectly. Option (2) lacks a comma. Option (4) uses an inappropriate coordinating conjunction and is punctuated incorrectly.

8. **(1) change pickup and, to pickup, and** (Compound sentences) Option (1) moves the comma to its correct place before the coordinating conjunction. Option (2) uses an inappropriate connecting word and is punctuated incorrectly. Option (3) removes the necessary coordinating conjunction. Option (4) removes the comma from the wrong place but does not reinsert it correctly. Option (5) puts the punctuation in the wrong place.

9. **(2) calls, but** (Compound sentences) Option (2) is correct because it joins two complete sentences with a comma and an appropriate coordinating conjunction. Option (1) lacks a comma. Option (3) requires a semicolon before the conjunctive adverb *however*. Option (4) lacks a comma. Option (5) is incorrect because it separates the related clauses into two sentences.

10. **(5) no correction is necessary** (Compound sentences) The clauses in the sentence are correctly combined and punctuated. Option (1) uses an inappropriate contrasting conjunctive adverb. Option (2) uses an inappropriate coordinating conjunction and is incorrectly punctuated. Option (3) removes a necessary comma. Option (4) uses an unnecessary comma because the coordinating conjunction *and* is not linking two independent clauses.

11. **(4) City Hospital. You are correct** (Run-on sentences) Option (4) is correct because it uses a period to separate the independent clauses of the run-on into two sentences. Option (1) is a run-on sentence. Option (2) is a comma splice and capitalizes incorrectly. Option (3) is also a comma splice. Option (5) omits the necessary comma in a compound sentence.

12. **(5) no correction is necessary** (Run-on sentences) Option (1) inserts an unnecessary comma because *for* is not a coordinating conjunction in this sentence. Option (2) removes the comma needed in a compound sentence. Option (3) inserts a second, unnecessary coordinating conjunction. Option (4) creates a comma splice.

13. **(5) insert but after the comma** (Run-on sentences) Option (5) adds the necessary coordinating conjunction to fix the comma splice. Option (1) makes the first clause subordinate, but with an inappropriate subordinating conjunction. Option (2) creates a run-on sentence. Option (3) creates a compound sentence without the necessary comma. Option (4) inserts an appropriate conjunctive adverb but without the semicolon and comma it requires.

14. **(1) programs, and almost all fail to comply in one or more areas. Total** (Run-on sentences) Option (1) is correct because it creates a compound sentence and a simple sentence. Options (2), (3), (4), and (5) do not clearly separate the clauses and keep the meaning of the original text.

15. **(3) replace how easy it is to use with ease of use** (Parallel structure) Option (3) is correct because it creates a phrase that matches the other phrases in the series. Option (1) removes the comma needed between items in a series. Option (2) changes a parallel word into a non-parallel phrase. Option (4) merely changes the verb in the clause that is causing the non-parallel structure. Option (5) does not correct the non-parallel structure.

16. **(3) insert a comma after crashing** (Compound sentences) Option (3) inserts the comma needed between independent clauses in a compound sentence. Option (1) makes the verb in the first clause incomplete. Option (2) incorrectly changes a verb form. Option (4) incorrectly replaces a needed coordinating conjunction *and*. Option (5) incorrectly changes the verb in the second independent clause from *does not* to *do not*.

17. **(4) drive, reconnect my mouse three times, and reinstall** (Subordination—Combining details) Option (4) combines the information in the three independent clauses into one sentence: *I had to change my hard drive, reconnect my mouse three times, and reinstall my Internet connection twice.* The other options do not eliminate the wordiness or repetition. Furthermore, option (2) leaves out important information.

18. **(5) complicated, and the** (Run-on sentences) Option (5) fixes the run-on by inserting the comma and coordinating conjunction needed between the independent clauses. Option (1) is a run-on sentence. Option (2) omits the necessary comma. Option (3) uses an inappropriate conjunctive adverb without correct punctuation. Option (4) creates a comma splice.

19. **(2) insert a comma after enter** (Subordinating ideas) Option (2) is correct because an introductory subordinate clause is always followed by a comma. Option (1) is incorrect because it uses an inappropriate subordinating conjunction. Option (3) creates a fragment. Options (4) and (5) insert unnecessary commas.

20. **(3) buys such as magazines, candy, and** (Subordinating ideas) Option (3) combines all the details into one smooth sentence by listing them. Option (1) would not produce a sentence or keep the meaning of the original text. Option (2) combines the subjects but not all the other details. Option (4) creates a compound sentence missing a coordinating conjunction. Option (5) repeats a form of the verb *see* and does not combine the details.

21. **(5) milk, we'll** (Subordinating ideas) Option (5) fixes the subordinate-clause fragment, in option (1), by attaching it to the beginning of an independent clause and adding a comma. Options (2) and (3) make compound sentences with inappropriate coordinating conjunctions. Option (4) omits the necessary comma.

22. **(4) if we understand** (Subordinating ideas) Option (4) combines the thoughts into a complex sentence by making the second sentence a subordinate clause. Options (1) and (2) create compound sentences but use inappropriate coordinating conjunctions. Options (3) and (5) create complex sentences but do not keep the meaning of the original text.

Unit 1

23. **(3) residents in certain provinces** (Misplaced modifiers) Option (3) is correct because it moves the misplaced phrase near the word it modifies. The other options do not lead to sentences that smoothly and clearly state the information.

24. **(3) replace left with residents leave these items** (Dangling modifiers) Option (3) is correct because it inserts a subject and verb into the dangling modifier, transforming the phrase into a subordinating clause. Options (1) and (2) do not fix the dangling modifier. Option (4) removes the comma needed after the introductory phrase and does not fix the dangling modifier. Option (5) merely changes the verb form in the main clause and does not fix the dangling modifier.

25. **(3) insert are after future** (Sentence fragments) Option (3) is correct because it fixes the fragment by completing the verb. Option (1) merely rearranges the modifying phrase and the word it modifies. By inserting a verb into the first part of the sentence, option (2) creates another misplaced modifier. Option (4) inserts an unnecessary comma. Option (5) is missing a complete verb.

26. **(5) makes soles for athletic shoes using worn-out tires** (Run-on sentences) Option (5) is correct because it combines all the details in the three independent clauses into one clause and places them correctly. The other options lead to sentences that are wordy or repetitive or that contain misplaced modifiers.

Organization
Lesson 7: Effective Paragraphs
GED Practice (pages 98–99)
All items in this practice are related to paragraph unity and coherence.

1. **(1) remove sentence 4** Option (1) correctly eliminates a sentence that does not support the main idea. Options (2) and (3) move this information but do not eliminate it. Option (4) suggests that a supporting detail is the topic of the paragraph. Paragraph A could be more effective with the elimination of sentence 4, so option (5) is incorrect.

2. **(3) move sentence 8 to follow sentence 10** Option (3) is correct because it reorders the sentences more logically. It puts the mention of Weir's "left-handedness" after the description of the problems that arise from learning to golf in a colder climate. Option (1) is incorrect because it removes an important piece of information.

Option (2) is incorrect because it places information about Weir's left-handedness before the complete description of why learning to golf in a colder climate is more difficult. Option (4) is incorrect because it suggests that sentence 8 is the topic sentence of paragraph C. Reordering the sentences improves the article, so option (5) is incorrect.

3. **(4) move sentence 13 to the beginning of paragraph C** Option (4) is correct because it moves a concluding remark from paragraph B to introduce the final, concluding paragraph. Option (1) incorrectly places the remark as the topic sentence of the whole letter. Option (2) incorrectly moves the concluding remark to the introductory paragraph. Option (3) incorrectly removes an effective introductory sentence for paragraph C. Paragraph C becomes more effective with the inclusion of sentence 13, so option (5) is incorrect.

4. **(5) no correction is necessary** The sentence is correct as written. Option (1) inserts a second, unnecessary subject. Option (2) creates a fragment. Option (3) removes a comma needed in a parallel series. Option (4) creates an error in parallel structure.

5. **(2) remove sentence 10** Option (2) correctly eliminates a sentence that doesn't support the main idea of the paragraph. Options (1) and (4) eliminate supporting details. Option (3) incorrectly moves a supporting detail out of logical order. A correction is necessary, so option (5) is incorrect.

6. **(3) remove sentence 2** Option (3) correctly eliminates a sentence that doesn't support the main idea. Option (1) incorrectly removes a topic sentence. Option (2) would misplace the topic sentence at the end of the paragraph. Option (4) incorrectly removes a supporting detail from the paragraph. Option (5) does not improve the passage.

Lesson 8: Topic Sentences
GED Practice (pages 101–102)
All items in this practice are related to topic sentences.

1. **(2) To keep receiving mail when you move, notify the post office of your new address.** Option (2) is correct because it introduces the main idea of the paragraph and provides a topic to which all the sentences that follow relate. Options (1), (3), (4), and (5) are too general to be effective topic sentences.

2. **(1) insert at the beginning of the paragraph <u>The post office will forward your personal mail and most packages.</u>** Option (1) inserts a clear, effective topic sentence for the paragraph. Option (2) removes a supporting detail. Option (3) moves the sentence to an illogical place. Option (4) substitutes a general, unclear statement for a clear statement. Since a new topic sentence makes paragraph B more effective, option (5) is incorrect.

3. **(5) Don't forget to notify businesses you deal with that you have moved.** Option (5) is correct because it introduces the main idea of the paragraph and provides a topic to which all the sentences that follow relate. Options (1) and (2) are too general. Option (3) is an irrelevant detail. Option (4) does not effectively state the main idea of the paragraph.

4. **(3) Changes in the natural colour of your nails can warn you of disease.** Option (3) is correct because it introduces the main idea of the paragraph and provides a topic to which all the sentences that follow relate. Options (1) and (2) are too general. Option (4) makes an inaccurate, misleading statement. Option (5) does not clearly and effectively state the main idea of the paragraph.

5. **(4) remove sentence 7** Option (4) correctly eliminates a sentence that is irrelevant and does not support the main idea. Option (1) removes an important supporting detail. Options (2) and (3) incorrectly move supporting details out of logical order. Option (5) moves an irrelevant sentence that should be eliminated.

6. **(1) The grade seven students will visit the Science Museum on Monday, October 5.** Option (1) is the best topic sentence because it introduces the main idea of the paragraph. Options (2), (4), and (5) are too general to be effective topic sentences. Option (3) is too specific to be an effective topic sentence.

7. **(3) The cost of the trip is $8.00 payable by cash or cheque.** Option (3) introduces the main idea of the paragraph and provides essential information to which all the sentences that follow relate. Option (1) provides inaccurate information. Option (2) does not provide specific enough information. Option (4) provides unnecessary information. Option (5) is too vague.

Lesson 9: Paragraphing
GED Practice (pages 104–105)
All items in this practice are related to paragraph divisions.

1. **(2) begin a new paragraph with sentence 6** Option (2) is correct because the sentence shifts to a new idea about what happens after you have purchased a permit. Option (1) breaks apart the first paragraph, about buying a permit. Options (3) and (4) remove important supporting details. Option (5) incorrectly suggests that a detail from one paragraph should become part of another paragraph.

2. **(2) with sentence 3** Option (2) is correct because the sentence shifts from the introduction to a new idea. Option (1) breaks apart the introductory paragraph. Options (3), (4), and (5) break apart the second paragraph, about the events at the hospital.

3. **(2) with sentence 3** Option (2) is correct because the sentence shifts from the introduction to a new idea. Option (1) breaks apart the introductory paragraph. Option (3) separates a topic sentence about novice writers from the details about that main idea. Options (4) and (5) break apart what should be the second paragraph, about novice writers.

4. **(1) with sentence 7** Option (1) is correct because the sentence shifts to the second of three ideas about proficient student writing. Options (2), (3), and (4) break apart what should be the third paragraph. Option (5) is incorrect because sentence 7 introduces a new idea.

5. **(4) with sentence 15** Option (4) is correct because the sentence shifts to the conclusion. Option (1) separates a topic sentence about superior writers from the details about that main idea. Options (2) and (3) break apart what should be the fourth paragraph. Option (5) breaks apart what should be the concluding paragraph.

Lesson 10: Clear Transitions
GED Practice (pages 107–108)
All items in this practice are related to transitions.

1. **(1) replace <u>The</u> with <u>Unfortunately, the</u>** Option (1) is correct because it inserts a transition that suggests the idea in sentence 4 contrasts with the idea in sentence 3. Options (2), (3), and (4) insert the transition in places where the relationship between the ideas is not clearly shown; in addition, they are incorrectly punctuated. Option (5) is incorrect because a transition is needed.

2. **(3) Fortunately, you can keep varnished wood looking good if you follow this advice.** Option (3) is correct because it provides an effective topic sentence for paragraph B and includes a transition between the main ideas in paragraphs A and B. Options (1), (2), (4), and (5) use inappropriate transitions that do not contain the main idea of paragraph B.

3. **(2) and, in addition,** Option (2) is correct because it suggests combining two related sentences with a transition that shows the addition of a detail. Option (1) does not show this relationship. Option (3) suggests that the idea in sentence 6 is a result of the idea in sentence 5. Option (4) suggests that the idea in sentence 6 is an example of the idea in sentence 5. Option (5) suggests that the idea in sentence 6 is a contrast to the idea in sentence 5.

4. **(4) furniture. In fact, polish** Option (4) correctly combines a sentence and a supporting detail with an appropriate transition. Options (1) and (2) are incorrect because they fail to show the relationship between the ideas in the two sentences. Option (2) also creates a comma splice. Option (3) incorrectly suggests that the idea in sentence 9 causes the idea in sentence 10. Option (5) incorrectly suggests that the idea in sentence 10 is the same as the idea in sentence 9.

5. **(4) Start by exercising your right,** Option (4) is correct because it adds a transition at the beginning of the sentence that explains the relationship between the ideas in sentences 2 and 3. It also has the correct tone. Options (1) and (5) create awkwardly worded sentences. Options (2) and (3) do not lead to effective sentences that accurately restate the meaning of the original text.

6. **(1) so, request** The original is the best way to express the idea because it uses an appropriate transitional phrase and is correctly punctuated. Options (2) and (3) create fragments. Options (4) and (5) insert unnecessary and inappropriate transitions. Option (5) is also incorrectly punctuated.

7. **(1) insert <u>however,</u> after the comma** Option (1) is correct because it adds a transition showing contrast between the ideas in sentences 1 and 2. Options (2), (3), (4), and (5) insert the transition in places where the relationship between the ideas is not clearly shown. They are also incorrectly punctuated.

8. **(1) replace Lateness with Consequently, <u>lateness</u>** Option (1) is correct because it adds a

transition that shows the idea in sentence 6 is a result of the idea in sentence 5. Options (2), (3), and (4) insert the transition in places where the relationship between the ideas is not clearly shown. Option (5) is incorrect because a transition is needed.

GED Review Organization
(pages 109–113)

1. **(4) move sentence 3 to the end of the paragraph** (Unity and coherence) Option (4) correctly moves a supporting detail to its logical place in the paragraph. Option (1) moves a topic sentence from its most effective position. Options (2) and (3) remove important supporting details. Option (5) moves a detail supporting the main idea of paragraph A to paragraph B.

2. **(2) remove sentence 7** (Unity and coherence) Option (2) is correct because it removes an irrelevant detail. Options (1) and (3) merely move the irrelevant detail. Option (4) replaces the irrelevant detail with another irrelevant detail. Since sentence 7 is irrelevant and should be removed, option (5) is incorrect.

3. **(5) no revision is necessary** (Unity and coherence) This sentence is an appropriate conclusion to the paragraph and the passage. Options (1), (2), and (3) move the sentence to where it would make no sense. Option (4) removes the conclusion to the passage.

4. **(4) remove sentence 4** (Unity and coherence) Option (4) correctly eliminates a sentence that does not support the main idea of the paragraph. Option (1) removes the topic sentence. Option (2) moves a detail to an illogical place in the paragraph. Option (3) removes an important supporting detail. Option (5) is incorrect because sentence 4 is irrelevant and should be removed.

5. **(2) combine paragraphs B and C** (Paragraph divisions) Option (2) correctly combines two short paragraphs that contain details and information about one main idea. Options (1), (3), and (4) incorrectly move supporting details out of logical order. Option (5) removes an important piece of information.

6. **(2) combine paragraphs A and B** (Paragraph structure) Option (2) correctly combines two paragraphs that contain details on one main idea. Option (1) moves only one of the details to the first paragraph and leaves a one-sentence paragraph. Options (3) and (5) remove important supporting details. Option (4)

incorrectly moves a topic sentence from the paragraph it introduces.

7. **(4) with sentence 8** (Paragraph divisions) Option (4) is correct because sentence 8 shifts to a new main idea and so should begin a new paragraph. Options (1), (2), and (3) involve sentences that are details about the main idea of paragraph B. Option (5) is a detail that relates to the idea in sentence 8, so *it* should follow it in the new paragraph.

8. **(2) Charting your family's health history may help save a life because heredity plays a role in many illnesses.** (Topic sentences) Option (2) is the best choice for a topic sentence because it introduces the overall subject of the paragraph and tells the main idea about that topic. Options (1), (4), and (5) are too general; they don't address the main point of the paragraph. Option (3) is too specific.

9. **(2) remove sentence 6** (Unity and coherence) Option (2) correctly eliminates a sentence that does not support the main idea. Option (1) incorrectly moves a supporting detail to an illogical place. Option (3) merely moves the irrelevant information. Options (4) and (5) remove important supporting details.

10. **(1) Like most things, however, daydreaming can have a negative side as well.** (Topic sentences) Option (1) is the best topic sentence because it introduces the main idea of the paragraph. Option (2) is too general and does not closely relate to the details in the paragraph. Options (3), (4), and (5) are too specific and do not address the main point of the paragraph.

11. **(4) move sentence 12 to the end of paragraph C** (Unity and coherence) Option (4) is correct because it places a detail in the most logical position in the paragraph. Option (1) moves a detail out of the paragraph where it belongs. Options (2) and (5) are incorrect because they remove important details. Option (3) moves a detail to an illogical position in the paragraph.

12. **(5) no revision is necessary** (Unity and coherence) Option (5) correctly keeps the topic sentence at the beginning of the paragraph, where it belongs. Options (1), (3), and (4) move it to inappropriate positions. Option (2) removes the topic sentence.

Usage
Lesson 11: Subject–Verb Agreement
GED Practice (page 117)
All items in this practice are related to subject-verb agreement.

1. **(2) change guarantee to guarantees** Option (2) is correct because *guarantees* agrees with the singular subject *Fair Point Company*. Option (1) incorrectly changes the verb tense. Options (3) and (4) insert unnecessary commas. Since the subject *Fair Point Company* and the verb must agree, option (5) is incorrect.

2. **(3) has** Option (3) is correct because *has* needs to agree with the singular subject *company*, not the interrupting phrase between the subject and the verb. Option (1) is incorrect because *company* and *have* do not agree. Option (2) creates a sentence fragment because the verb is incomplete. Option (4) repeats the subject. Option (5) is an incorrect verb form for the sentence.

3. **(4) is caused** Option (4) is correct because the verb agrees with the last subject after *or*. Option (1) is incorrect because it is a plural verb and the subject is singular. Options (2), (3), and (5) are incorrect verb forms for the sentence.

4. **(2) change cover to covers** Option (2) is correct because the singular verb *covers* agrees with the singular subject *warranty*. Option (1) inserts an unnecessary transition. Option (3) creates a sentence fragment with an incomplete verb. Option (4) inserts an unnecessary comma. The subject and verb must agree, so option (5) is incorrect.

Lesson 12: Verb Forms
GED Practice (page 120)
All items in this practice relate to verb forms.

1. **(2) have changed** Option (2) is correct because *have* is the correct helping verb to go with the past participle *changed*. Option (1) uses an incorrect helping verb. Option (3) is a singular verb with a plural subject. Option (4) creates a sentence fragment with an incomplete verb. Option (5) uses an incorrect helping verb.

2. **(4) change thinking to think** Option (4) is correct because the present participle *thinking* requires a helping verb. *Think* is the correct verb form to use with *teens*. Option (1) inserts an unnecessary comma. Option (2) creates a sentence fragment with an incomplete verb. Option (3) is an incorrect verb form. Option (5)

would break the subject-verb agreement *50 percent . . . carry*.

3. **(5) feel** Option (5) is the correct form of the verb *feel*. Option (1) is a present participle without the needed helping verb. Option (2) is a singular verb with a plural subject. Options (3) and (4) are incorrect verb forms.

4. **(4) have not spoken** Option (4) supplies the correct form of the helping verb and past participle of *speak*. Options (1), (2), and (5) are incorrect verb forms. Option (3) does not accurately restate the meaning of the original sentence and is an incorrect verb form.

Lesson 13: Verb Tenses

GED Practice (page 123)

All items in this practice relate to verb tenses.

1. **(2) change have been to are** Option (2) is correct because it fixes an unnecessary verb tense shift; the present tense is consistent with the rest of the paragraph. Option (1) incorrectly changes the verb to the past perfect tense, which is inconsistent with the rest of the paragraph. Option (3) incorrectly changes another verb in the sentence to the present perfect. Option (4) inserts an unnecessary comma. Option (5) uses the wrong verb tense.

2. **(1) will ship** Option (1) is correct because *within the next thirty days* indicates that the verb should be in the future tense. Options (2) and (4) are past tenses. Option (3) is the present tense. Option (5) is missing the helping verb *will* and so creates a sentence fragment.

3. **(3) arrives** Option (3) is correct because *as soon as* is a clue that the simple present tense is needed. Option (1) is the future perfect. Option (2) is a plural past tense, so it does not agree in time or in number with the subject. Option (4) is incorrect because *is arriving* suggests the action is going on now. Option (5) is an incomplete verb form and would create a fragment.

4. **(4) change be calling to call** Option (4) correctly uses a present tense verb in the second clause because the verb in the first clause is in the present tense. Option (1) uses an incorrect present tense because the action is not ongoing. Option (2) removes a necessary comma after an introductory dependent clause. Option (3) creates a fragment out of the clause. The verb tenses within a sentence must be consistent, so option (5) is incorrect.

5. **(5) appreciate** Option (5) is correct because the present tense is consistent with the other verb in the sentence, *look*. Options (1), (2), (3), and (4) are all incorrect shifts in verb tense.

Lesson 14: Pronouns

GED Practice (page 127)

All the items in this practice relate to pronouns.

1. **(4) replace it with the disease** Option (4) is correct because it makes the antecedent of *it* clear; it could have referred to *disease, bite,* or *tick*. Option (1) is incorrect because the plural subject *things* requires a plural verb, *are*. Options (2) and (3) are incorrect because they are pronoun shifts. Option (5) has an unclear antecedent.

2. **(2) You should tuck** Option (2) corrects the vague antecedent of the original, option (1). Option (3) uses another pronoun with a vague antecedent. Options (4) and (5) create pronoun shifts from the second person pronoun *you* used in the passage.

3. **(4) replace see them with see the ticks** Option (4) is correct because it makes the antecedent of *them* clear; it could have referred to *ticks* or *colours*. Option (1) creates a pronoun shift from *you* to *one*. Option (2) removes the necessary comma after an introductory clause. Option (3) inserts an unnecessary comma. Option (5) creates a pronoun shift from *them* to *it*.

4. **(1) replace They with Tick collars** Option (1) is correct because it makes the antecedent of *They* clear; it could refer to *tick collars* or *pets*. Option (2) replaces a noun with an unclear pronoun. Option (3) creates a sentence fragment. Option (4) replaces a correct present tense verb with an incomplete verb form. Option (5) has an unclear antecedent.

GED Review Usage

(pages 128–131)

1. **(4) change holded to held** (Verb forms) Option (4) is correct because the past participle of *hold* is *held*. Option (1) is incorrect because the helping verb *have* is needed before *driven*. Option (2) is incorrect because a past participle is required with the helping verb *have*. Option (3) is incorrect because a comma is needed when two independent clauses are joined with a coordinating conjunction. Option (5) inserts an unnecessary comma.

2. **(4) change growed to grew** (Verb forms) Option (4) is correct because *grew* is the past form of *grow*. Option (1) creates a sentence

fragment because the independent clause would lack a subject. Options (2) and (5) use incorrect verb forms. Option (3) creates a run-on sentence.

3. **(2) drove** (Verb forms) Option (2) correctly supplies the past form of *drive*. Options (1), (3), and (5) are incorrect verb forms. Option (4) is a past participle without a helping verb.

4. **(1) have been** (Verb forms) Option (1) is correct because the original, *have been,* is the correct past participle form of the verb *be*. Option (2) does not agree with the subject *I*. Options (3), (4), and (5) are not correct verb forms.

5. **(2) change I to me** (Pronouns) Option (2) is correct because an object pronoun is needed for a direct object of the verb *informed*. Option (1) inserts an unneeded subject pronoun after the noun subject. Option (3) incorrectly changes the verb tense from present to past. Option (4) incorrectly uses a verb that does not agree with the subject of the clause. Option (5) incorrectly uses a subject pronoun.

6. **(5) Rick and I** (Pronouns) Option (5) is correct because *I* is a subject pronoun. Options (1) and (2) are incorrect because *me* is an object pronoun regardless of the order it appears in a compound subject. Option (3) is incorrect because *him* is an object pronoun. Option (4) is incorrect because it is unclear who *he* refers to and *me* is an object pronoun.

7. **(4) replace them with car pool groups** (Pronouns) Option (4) is correct because it makes the antecedent of *them* clear; *them* could refer to *car pool groups* or *employees*. Options (1) and (5) create unclear antecedents. Option (2) is incorrect because it inserts an unnecessary subject pronoun after a noun subject. A pronoun that follows immediately after its antecedent is unnecessarily repetitive. Option (3) incorrectly changes the tense of the verb.

8. **(5) no correction is necessary** (Pronouns) Option (1) is incorrect because it would create a pronoun shift. Option (2) replaces a correct helping verb with an incorrect one. Option (3) inserts an unnecessary comma. Option (4) removes a necessary comma after an introductory clause.

9. **(3) give the information to me, and I will compile it** (Pronouns) Option (3) is correct because it makes the antecedent of *it* clear by switching the order of the pronoun and its antecedent in the sentence. None of the other options leads to a smooth, effective sentence that makes the antecedent clear and accurately restates the meaning of the original sentence.

10. **(2) change are to is** (Subject-verb agreement) Option (2) is correct because *is* agrees with the singular subject *advice*. Option (1) is incorrect because it creates a fragment without a verb. Option (3) is incorrect because dependent clauses following independent clauses generally do not need a comma. Option (4) makes the subject and verb disagree in the dependent clause. Option (5) inserts an unnecessary comma.

11. **(4) change lasts to last** (Subject-verb agreement) Option (4) is correct because *last* agrees with the plural subject *houseplants*. Options (1) and (2) insert unnecessary commas. Option (3) creates a sentence fragment because the verb is incomplete. Option (5) is incorrect because the verb *lasts* does not agree with the subject *houseplants*.

12. **(3) change survive to survives** (Subject-verb agreement) Option (3) is correct because *survives* agrees with the singular subject *nothing*. Option (1) is incorrect because it removes an important transition. Options (2) and (5) do not correct the subject-verb disagreement. Option (4) creates a sentence fragment because the verb is incomplete.

13. **(2) protect** (Subject-verb agreement) Option (2) is correct because the plural verb *protect* agrees with the subject *Layers*. Options (1) and (4) are incorrect because they are singular verbs. Option (3) creates a sentence fragment because the verb is incomplete. Option (5) is incorrect because only the plural verb *protect* is needed in the sentence.

14. **(2) are covered** (Subject-verb agreement) Option (2) is correct because the plural verb *are covered* is needed with the plural subject *bricks*. Option (1) is incorrect because it is a singular verb. Options (3) and (5) are incorrect verb forms for the sentence. Option (4) creates a sentence fragment because the verb is incomplete.

15. **(5) have known** (Verb tenses) Option (5) is correct because the time phrase *for many years* indicates a past action that continues into the present, which requires the present perfect tense. Option (1) is the simple present tense. Option (2) is the past participle without a helping verb. Option (3) is an incorrect verb form for the past tense. Option (4) is the future tense.

16. (2) change become to became (Verb tenses)
Option (2) is correct because the phrase *a number of years ago* is a clue that the simple past is needed. Option (1) removes a necessary comma. Option (3) inserts an unnecessary comma. Option (4) changes a correct past tense verb to the past perfect. Option (5) changes the verb to the past perfect when the simple past is needed.

17. (4) looks (Verb tenses) Option (4) is correct because the words *today* and *often choose* are clues that the simple present tense is needed. Options (1), (2), (3), and (5) are incorrect shifts in verb tense.

18. (3) will focus (Verb tenses) Option (3) is correct because the simple future tense is needed in the second, main clause. The introductory clause *(As consumer demand . . . increases)* sets up a condition that continues into the future. Options (1), (2), and (4) are incorrect shifts in verb tense. Option (5) is an incomplete verb form.

Mechanics
Lesson 15: Capitalization
GED Practice (page 134)
All items in this practice are related to capitalization.

1. **(4) change mother's day to Mother's Day**
Option (4) is correct because holidays are capitalized. Option (1) incorrectly changes the verb tense. Option (2) is incorrect because *Easter* is a holiday and should be capitalized. Options (3) and (5) insert unnecessary commas.

2. **(2) change foundation to Foundation**
Option (2) is correct because *foundation* is part of the name of a specific organization and should be capitalized. For the same reason, option (1) incorrectly makes a proper name lowercase. Option (3) is incorrect because the verb *claim* does not agree with the singular subject *Foundation*. Option (4) incorrectly uses a pronoun with an unclear antecedent. Option (5) incorrectly changes the verb form.

3. **(5) change mid-june to mid-June** Option (5) is correct because months of the year should be capitalized. Option (1) is incorrect because *northern* is a direction and does not name a specific region of the country. Option (2) incorrectly changes the verb tense. Option (3) inserts an unnecessary comma. Option (4) incorrectly capitalizes the wrong part of the phrase *mid-June*.

4. **(1) change Summer to summer** Option (1) is correct because seasons are not capitalized.

Option (2) removes a comma after an introductory clause. Option (3) creates a sentence fragment out of the introductory clause. Option (4) is incorrect because there is no reason to capitalize the adjective *pine*. Since seasons are not capitalized, option (5) is incorrect.

Lesson 16: Commas
GED Practice (page 137)
All items in this practice are related to commas.

1. **(5) Friday, Saturday, and Sunday,** Option (5) is correct because *Friday* is the first item in a series of three days. Options (1), (2), (3), and (4) do not correctly punctuate the series.

2. **(1) insert a comma after In addition**
Option (1) correctly inserts a comma after an introductory phrase, so option (5) is incorrect. Option (2) incorrectly removes a comma in a series. Option (3) inserts an unnecessary comma at the end of the series. Option (4) incorrectly changes the verb tense.

3. **(2) insert a comma after Tan** Option (2) is correct because *Jin Tan* is a nonessential appositive that identifies the noun *manager* and should be set off by commas before and after. Option (1) is incorrect because *manager* is not a proper noun. Option (3) inserts an unnecessary comma. Option (4) incorrectly changes the verb tense. Option (5) uses a pronoun with a vague antecedent.

4. **(3) remove the comma after friends**
Option (3) is correct because a comma is not needed between two items. Option (1) incorrectly creates a pronoun shift. Option (2) uses an incorrect verb form. Option (4) inserts an unnecessary comma. The unnecessary comma should be removed, so option (5) is incorrect.

Lesson 17: Spelling
GED Practice (page 141)
All items in this practice are related to spelling.
1. **(4) replace weakly with weekly** Option (4) is correct because the homonym meaning "once every seven days" is needed in the sentence. Option (1) incorrectly creates a pronoun shift. Option (2) incorrectly removes a comma after an introductory clause. Option (3) incorrectly changes the verb tense. Option (5) replaces a correctly spelled word with its homonym.

2. **(1) change magazines' to magazine's**
Option (1) is correct because the possessive is singular, not plural. Option (2) is incorrect because *provides* agrees with the singular subject

coverage. Option (3) incorrectly creates a pronoun shift. Option (4) replaces a correctly spelled word with its homonym. Option (5) is incorrect because the possessive is singular, not plural.

3. **(3) replace well with we'll** Option (3) is correct because the contraction of *we will* needs an apostrophe. Option (1) incorrectly replaces the possessive pronoun *your* with the contraction of *you are*. Option (2) incorrectly removes a comma after the introductory phrase. Option (4) is incorrect because *special reports* is not a proper noun. Option (5) is incorrect because contractions use apostrophes.

4. **(5) no correction is necessary** The sentence is correct as written. Option (1) replaces a correctly spelled word with its homonym. Option (2) inserts an unnecessary comma. Option (3) is incorrect because a title followed by a name should be capitalized. Option (4) incorrectly replaces a possessive with a plural.

GED Review Mechanics
(pages 142–144)

1. **(5) no correction is necessary** (Commas) The sentence is correct as written. Option (1) inserts an unnecessary comma. Option (2) incorrectly removes a comma after an introductory phrase. Options (3) and (4) replace correctly spelled words with their homonyms.

2. **(5) change customer's to customers'** (Spelling) Option (5) corrects the misspelled plural possessive. Options (1) and (3) replace correctly spelled words with their homonyms. Option (2) is incorrect because *is* does not agree with the plural subject *tips*. Option (4) inserts an unnecessary comma.

3. **(1) replace Its with It's** (Contractions) Option (1) is correct because the contraction of *It is* is needed in the sentence. Option (2) incorrectly replaces a plural with a plural possessive. Option (3) creates a comma splice. Option (4) inserts an unnecessary comma. Option (5) misspells a contraction.

4. **(1) replace Than with Then** (Spelling) Option (1) is correct because the homonym meaning "at that time" is needed in the sentence. Option (2) replaces a correctly spelled word with its homonym. Option (3) replaces a correctly spelled singular possessive with a plural. Option (4) removes a necessary comma in a series. Option (5) inserts an unnecessary comma at the end of the series.

5. **(3) remove the comma after lasting** (Commas) Option (3) is correct because it removes an unnecessary comma at the end of a series. Option (1) incorrectly changes the verb tense. Options (2) and (4) insert unnecessary commas. Option (5) is incorrect because the unnecessary comma should be removed.

6. **(3) insert a comma after pills** (Commas) Option (3) is correct because it inserts a comma after the introductory clause. Option (1) incorrectly changes the verb tense. Option (2) inserts an unnecessary comma. Option (4) incorrectly capitalizes a noun that is not proper. Option (5) is incorrect because there should be a comma after the introductory clause.

7. **(4) calcium, and** (Commas) Option (4) is correct because it inserts a comma before the coordinating conjunction that connects two independent clauses in a compound sentence. Options (1), (2), (3), and (5) do not use the correct combination of commas and conjunctions.

8. **(2) insert a comma after milk** (Commas) Option (2) is correct because it inserts a comma after the introductory phrase. Option (1) is incorrect because it inserts the comma too early in the sentence; *digesting milk* is part of the introductory phrase. Option (3) incorrectly changes the verb. Option (4) is incorrect because *is* does not agree with the plural subject *alternatives*. Option (5) is incorrect because the sentence needs a comma after the introductory phrase.

9. **(3) remove the comma after calcium** (Commas) Option (3) is correct because it removes an unnecessary comma separating the subject from the verb. Option (1) incorrectly replaces *that* with a pronoun. Option (2) incorrectly changes the verb tense. Option (4) removes a comma needed in a series. Option (5) inserts an unnecessary comma because the pair *bread and cereals* is the last item in the series.

10. **(1) change Fall to fall** (Capitalization) Option (1) is correct because seasons of the year are not capitalized. Option (2) is incorrect because *goes* does not agree with the subject *Americans*. Option (3) incorrectly changes the verb tense. Option (4) is incorrect because a title is not capitalized unless it is followed by a name. *Fall* should not be capitalized, so option (5) is not correct.

11. **(2) change State to state** (Capitalization)
Option (2) is correct because *state* is not a proper noun and therefore should not be capitalized. For the same reason, option (1) is incorrect; *Nation's* should not be capitalized. Option (3) is incorrect because the verb *have* does not agree with the subject *state*. Option (4) creates a comma splice. Option (5) is incorrect because a title is not capitalized unless it is followed by a name.

12. **(5) change vice president to Vice President** (Capitalization) Option (5) is correct because a title is capitalized when it is followed by a name. Option (1) incorrectly removes a comma after an introductory phrase. Option (2) is incorrect because *White House* is a proper noun naming a specific building. Option (3) incorrectly removes a comma after an introductory clause. Option (4) capitalizes only part of the title.

13. **(4) change congress to Congress** (Capitalization) Option (4) is correct because *Congress* is a proper noun naming a specific organization. Options (1) and (2) incorrectly change the verb tense. Option (3) incorrectly capitalizes a title that is not followed by a name. Option (5) is incorrect because *Midwest* is a proper noun naming a specific region of the country.

GED Unit Review Language Arts, Writing
(pages 145–155)

1. **(4) replace you're with your** (Mechanics/Spelling possessives and homonyms) Option (4) is correct because the possessive pronoun *your*, not the contraction for *you are* as in the original, is needed in the sentence. Options (1) and (2) incorrectly shift the verb tenses in the two clauses of the sentence. Option (3) inserts an unnecessary comma. Option (5) is incorrect because *you're* should be replaced.

2. **(2) When you need a cracked or broken windshield replaced,** (Sentence structure/Modifiers) Option (2) correctly inserts a subordinating conjunction and a subject and verb into the dangling modifier, changing the phrase into a subordinating clause. Options (1), (3), (4), and (5) do not correct the error.

3. **(5) no correction is necessary** (Usage/Subject-verb agreement) Option (1) incorrectly shifts the verb tense to the future. Option (2) is incorrect because the singular verb *looks* agrees with the singular subject *Everyone*. Option (3) supplies an incorrect verb form. Option (4) inserts an unnecessary comma.

4. **(1) change Spring to spring** (Mechanics/Capitalization) Option (1) is correct because seasons of the year are not capitalized. Option (2) removes a necessary comma after an introductory phrase. Option (3) incorrectly capitalizes the common noun *province*. Option (4) incorrectly shifts the verb tense to the future. Option (5) removes a necessary comma in a series.

5. **(5) change are to is** (Usage/Subject-verb agreement) Option (5) is correct because the singular verb *is* agrees with the singular subject *person*, not the interrupting phrase *digging with hand tools*. Option (1) incorrectly makes the verb *is digging*. Options (2) and (4) insert unnecessary commas. Option (3) incorrectly makes a plural noun possessive.

6. **(4) The building department** (Usage/Pronouns) Option (4) correctly replaces a vague pronoun with its antecedent. Option (1) is the pronoun with a vague antecedent. Options (2) and (3) are incorrect pronouns. Option (5) provides an incorrect antecedent.

7. **(1) move sentence 8 to the end of paragraph B** (Organization/Unity and coherence) Option (1) correctly moves a detail to the paragraph it supports. Sentence 9 begins a whole new topic. Options (2) and (4) remove important details. Option (3) moves a supporting detail out of logical order. Moving sentence 8 improves paragraph C, so option (5) is incorrect.

8. **(2) remove the comma after signs** (Mechanics/Unnecessary commas) Option (2) correctly removes an unnecessary comma between a subject and verb. Option (1) removes a necessary comma in a series. Option (3) is an incomplete verb form. Option (4) incorrectly changes the verb from plural to singular; the verb should agree with *signs*. Option (5) leaves in an unnecessary comma.

9. **(3) change are to is** (Usage/Subject-verb agreement) Option (3) is correct because the singular verb *is* agrees with the singular subject *merchandise*. When a compound subject is joined by *or*, the verb should agree with the last subject. Option (1) incorrectly changes a plural to a possessive. Option (2) inserts an unnecessary comma. Option (4) replaces a correctly spelled word with its homonym. The preposition *for* is needed in the sentence, not the number word *four*. The plural verb *are* does not agree with the singular subject *merchandise*, so option (5) is incorrect.

10. **(2) Another questionable tactic, called a kickback,** (Sentence structure/Modifiers) Option (2) places the modifier next to the noun it is modifying. Options (1), (3), (4), and (5) do not reconstruct the sentence so that the modifier is clear and the sentence accurately restates the meaning of the original text.

11. **(1) change Do'nt to Don't** (Mechanics/ Spelling contractions) Option (1) correctly places the apostrophe so that it takes the place of the missing *o* in the contraction for *do not*. Option (2) incorrectly shifts the tense from present to present perfect. Options (3) and (4) replace correctly spelled words with their homonyms. Option (5) does not correct the contraction.

12. **(3) change fitness centres' to Fitness Centres'** (Mechanics/Capitalization) Option (3) is correct because all elements of the name of a specific organization should be capitalized and by reading the entire piece you see that there are 36 fitness centres. Option (1) incorrectly replaces a singular possessive with a plural. Option (2) is incorrect because it lower-cases part of a name. Option (4) incorrectly replaces a plural possessive with a singular possessive. Option (5) is incorrect because the sentence does not have correct capitalization.

13. **(1) more than one half of the temporary hires create** (Sentence structure/Modifiers) Option (1) has the correct subject (*one half of temporary hires*) next to the modifier (*Because they have . . .*). Options (2), (3), (4), and (5) do not lead to sentences in which it is clear what the modifier is modifying.

14. **(5) replace I with me** (Usage/Pronouns) Option (5) is correct because it provides the correct objective pronoun *me* as an object of the verb *contact*. Option (1) leads to a disagreement between subject and verb. Option (2) misspells the homonym *to*. Option (3) removes the comma needed after the introductory clause. Option (4) inserts an unnecessary connecting word.

15. **(1) UGO, whose cereal** (Sentence structure/ Subordination) Option (1) correctly combines the details of the two sentences by subordinating the information in the second sentence and eliminating repetition. Options (2), (3), (4), and (5) do not lead to smooth, effective sentences and change the meaning of the original text.

16. **(4) year, despite** (Sentence structure/ Subordination) Option (4) effectively subordinates the information in the second independent clause to the first and removes repetition. Option (1) is the original wordy and awkward sentence. Option (2) removes a necessary comma. Options (3) and (5) create fragments.

17. **(5) replace their with its** (Usage/Pronouns) Option (5) is correct because the singular possessive pronoun *its* matches the antecedent *United Seed Company*. Option (1) removes the comma needed after an introductory element. Option (2) is incorrect because *Company* is part of the organization's name and should be capitalized. Option (3) is incorrect because the singular verb *continues* agrees with the singular subject *United Seed Company*. Option (4) replaces a correctly spelled word with its homonym.

18. **(1) with sentence 5** (Organization/Paragraph divisions) Option (1) correctly begins a new paragraph when the main idea shifts to other divisions in the corporation. Options (2), (3), (4), and (5) are details related to that main idea.

19. **(5) change academy to Academy** (Mechanics/Capitalization) Option (5) is correct because all elements in the name of a specific organization are capitalized. For the same reason, option (4) is incorrect. Option (1) is incorrect because a common noun like *nominee* is not capitalized. Option (2) incorrectly removes the comma needed before a nonessential appositive. Option (3) incorrectly inserts an unnecessary comma between two items.

20. **(2) awards, yet it** (Sentence structure/ Fragments) Option (2) corrects the fragment by inserting a subject and making a compound sentence with an appropriate conjunction and comma. Option (1) is the original fragment. Option (3) creates a comma splice. Options (4) and (5) do not lead to smooth, effectively structured sentences.

21. **(1) Oscars are awarded in many film categories.** (Organization/Topic sentences) Option (1) is the best choice of topic sentence because it is a general statement of the main idea of the paragraph. Options (2), (3), and (4) do not relate to the main idea. Option (5) is too specific to be a topic sentence.

22. **(5) change West to west** (Mechanics/ Capitalization) Option (5) is correct because directions should not be capitalized. Option (1)

removes a necessary comma after an introductory element. Option (2) is incorrect because the name of a specific organization such as Pony Express should be capitalized. Option (3) uses an incomplete verb form. Option (4) inserts an unnecessary comma.

23. **(2) change rose to risen** (Usage/Verb forms) Option (2) uses the correct past participle form of the verb *rise*. Option (1) incorrectly uses a plural helping verb for the singular subject *cost*. Option (3) inserts an unnecessary comma. Option (4) is incorrect because *colonial* is not a proper adjective and should therefore not be capitalized. Option (5) uses an incorrect verb form.

24. **(5) postage, yet it costs** (Sentence structure/ Fragments) Option (5) corrects the fragment by giving it a subject and joining it to an independent clause to make a compound sentence. Options (1), (2), (3), and (4) do not show the relationship between the ideas in the sentence and fragment, nor do they fix the fragment with correct punctuation.

25. **(5) does** (Usage/Subject-verb agreement) Option (5) is correct because the third person singular verb *does* agrees with the third person singular subject *U.S. Postal Service.* Option (1) is not a third person verb form. Option (2) is a plural verb form. Option (3) is a plural verb form and shifts the tense. Option (4) also incorrectly shifts the tense.

26. **(2) quarters, and** (Mechanics/Commas in compound sentences) Option (2) correctly puts a comma before the coordinating conjunction *and* that joins the independent clauses in this compound sentence. Option (1) lacks the comma before *and*. Option (3) incorrectly puts the comma after *and*. Option (4) creates a sentence fragment. Option (5) incorrectly places commas both before and after *and*.

27. **(1) change is to are** (Usage/Subject-verb agreement) Option (1) is correct because the plural verb *are* agrees with the plural subject *tips*. Option (2) inserts an unnecessary comma. Option (3) uses an incorrect verb form. Option (4) incorrectly changes a singular possessive to a plural possessive. Option (5) incorrectly changes the singular possessive to a plural.

28. **(3) If this label is missing,** (Sentence structure/Modifiers) Option (3) correctly changes the dangling modifier at the beginning of the

sentence into an introductory dependent clause. Options (1), (2), (4), and (5) do not lead to smooth, effective sentences that fix the problem of the dangling modifier and restate the meaning of the original sentence.

29. **(2) replace You with If that's the case, you** (Organization/Transitions) Option (2) is correct because it supplies a transition that relates the meaning between sentences 7 and 8. Option (1) moves a supporting detail to an illogical place. Option (3) supplies an inappropriate transition. Option (4) moves a detail out of the paragraph in which it belongs. Option (5) removes an important detail.

30. **(5) will see** (Usage/Verb forms) Option (5) corrects the verb form and uses the future tense, which is appropriate in the sentence because it is describing an action that will come. Option (1) is the original incorrect verb form. Options (2), (3), and (4) are correct verb forms but incorrect tenses for the sentence.

31. **(3) remove sentence 4** (Organization/Unity and coherence) Option (3) correctly eliminates a sentence that does not support the main idea, therefore option (5) is incorrect. Option (1) moves the topic sentence from the beginning of the paragraph to an ineffective position at the end. Option (2) removes an important detail that leads into the main idea expressed in the second paragraph. Option (4) incorrectly moves the topic sentence from the second paragraph into the first paragraph.

32. **(3) change hospital to Hospital** (Mechanics/ Capitalization) Option (3) is correct because *hospital* is part of a proper noun—the name of a specific hospital—and should be capitalized. Option (1) removes the comma needed after the introductory transitional element. Option (2) inserts an unnecessary comma. Option (4) is incorrect because the singular verb *requires* agrees with the singular subject *job*. Option (5) incorrectly replaces a plural with a singular possessive.

33. **(5) went** (Usage/Verb tenses) Option (5) is the correct tense; the phrase "Yesterday morning" is a clue the simple past tense is needed. Option (1) is a present perfect tense. Option (2) is an incorrect verb form. Option (3) does not agree with the subject and is a present perfect tense. Option (4) is a continuous past tense, not the simple past required by the sentence.

34. **(1) Joe Forest, the supervisor, who said** (Sentence structure/Subordination) Option (1) eliminates repetition and wordiness by subordinating the detail about Joe Forest and making it an appositive. Options (2), (3), (4), and (5) do not eliminate the repetition or wordiness.

35. **(3) insert a comma after me** (Mechanics/ Commas after introductory elements) Option (3) is correct because a comma is needed after an introductory clause. Option (1) would create a run-on sentence. Option (2) misspells the contraction for *had not*. Option (4) uses an incorrect verb form. Option (5) needlessly replaces a clearly understood pronoun.

36. **(3) change johannes gutenberg to Johannes Gutenberg** (Mechanics/ Capitalization) Option (3) is correct because all proper names are capitalized. Option (1) inserts an unnecessary comma. Option (2) is incorrect because there is no reason to capitalize *century*. Option (4) incorrectly shifts the verb tense. Option (5) contains an error in capitalization.

37. **(3) replace All with Before the invention of the printing press, all** (Organization/ Transitions) Option (3) is correct because it shows the time-order transition between ideas in the first paragraph and the second paragraph. Option (1) incorrectly moves a detail out of the paragraph it belongs with. Option (2) uses an inappropriate term to introduce the transition between paragraphs. Option (4) removes an important piece of information. A transition is needed, so option (5) is incorrect.

38. **(4) made except, perhaps, for the personal computer** (Sentence structure/Run-ons) Option (4) combines the ideas in the series of clauses into a clear, simple sentence without wordiness or repetition. Options (1), (2), (3), and (5) do not eliminate the run-on and wordiness.

39. **(3) felt** (Usage/Verb tenses) Option (3) corrects a tense shift because only the simple past is needed in the sentence. Options (1), (2), and (4) are perfect, not simple, forms of the past tense. Option (5) incorrectly uses the present tense.

UNIT 2: ESSAY

Lesson 1: Planning
GED Practice (page 159)
Topic 1 describes
Kind of information: discuss the qualities of something

Topic 2 state your point of view
Kind of information: tell what you think about an issue and why

Topic 3 explaining both the advantages and disadvantages
Kind of information: write about effects

Topic 4 explains why
Kind of information: write about causes or reasons

Topic 5 tell your point of view
Kind of information: tell what you think about an issue and why

GED Practice (page 161)
Many answers are possible. Here are some sample answers.
Topic 1
violent shows can make children violent
causes people to be less physically active
educational shows can teach
provides world, national, and local news
entertains; provides relaxation

Topic 2
may place too much emphasis on sports
may ignore family or other important areas of life
encourages supportiveness and team loyalty
brings fun and entertainment to your life
may cause you to spend money that is needed for other things

Topic 3
employers expect employees to have enough education to handle job tasks
helps you compete with other employees who are educated
best jobs go to the best qualified
GED or diploma shows you have ability to learn
GED or diploma shows you can persevere

Topic 4
teens identify with their music
brings young people together
violent lyrics may harm young people
some lyrics promote drug use
loud music can damage hearing

GED Practice (page 163)
A. **Topic 1.** Possible main idea statement: There are many different reasons people become homeless.

   Topic 2. Possible main idea statement: It is easy to make a trip affordable.

B. Your answers will depend on what you wrote on page 161. Ask your instructor or another student to compare your main idea statements with your lists and idea maps.

C. There are many possible answers. Have your instructor or another student evaluate your idea maps or lists and your main idea statements.

GED Review Planning
(page 164)
1. explain your point of view

2. tell what you think about the topic and why

3. list ideas or make an idea map

4. write a main idea statement

Lesson 2: Organizing
GED Practice (page 170)
Topic 1: Organization: Order of importance
Possible order of ideas: 1 Little Equipment, 2 Ease and Convenience, 3 Benefits

Topic 2: Main idea statement (sample): Passing the GED Test would give a person many advantages.
Organization: Order of importance
Possible order of ideas: 1 Educational Reasons, 2 Job-Related Reasons, 3 Personal Reasons

Topic 3: Main idea statement (sample): Society's emphasis on being thin has positive as well as seriously negative effects.
Organization: Contrast
Possible order of ideas: 1 Good Effects on Health, 2 Bad Effects on Individuals, 3 Bad Effects on Society

GED Review Organizing
(page 171)
1. You should group ideas that have something in common and then label the groups. Try to make three groups.

2. To think of more ideas, you can reread the topic, your main idea, and your groups of ideas. Ask yourself *who, what, when, where,* and *why* about the topic; think how the topic affects you or the people you know; and try to think of things that you have read or heard about the topic.

3. Because the essay contrasts life in a city with life in a small town, the best method of organization is contrast.

4. Your order will depend on your ideas and how you feel about them. Have your instructor or another student evaluate your groups.

Lesson 3: Writing
GED Practice (page 175)
1. **a.** good work habits
   b. A good worker is someone who understands how important it is not to be absent too often and who gets the job done.
   c. people lose jobs because they don't show up for work or don't work hard enough; managers need workers they can count on; employers don't tolerate workers who sit around visiting

Sample answers:
2. Smoking is costly to your health and your wallet.

3. Getting out of debt may be difficult, but there are ways to do it.

GED Practice (page 177)
Sample answer for Topic 1:
   Some people complain that professional athletes make too much money. However, these athletes deserve every penny they get. Athletes work extremely hard, make many sacrifices, and perform important services for the community.

Topics 2 and 3:
There is more than one appropriate and effective way to write each introductory paragraph. Share your work with your instructor or another student.

GED Practice (page 179)
There is more than one appropriate and effective way to write each set of body paragraphs. Share your work with your instructor or another student.

GED Practice (page 182)
There is more than one appropriate and effective way to write each concluding paragraph. Share your work with your instructor or another student.

GED Review Writing
(page 183)
Your answers may be worded differently, but they should be similar to the following:
1. I would include an introduction, body, and conclusion.

2. The introductory paragraph includes a thesis statement that tells the topic of the essay and the main idea. It includes a preview of the essay and sometimes background information.

3. I would write one body paragraph for each group of ideas I've listed. I would try to have three body paragraphs in all.

4. I would use the label of each group to write the topic sentence for that paragraph. I would use the ideas in each group to develop supporting details.

5. Like the introductory paragraph, the concluding paragraph states the topic and reviews the supporting details. However, the perspective is different. Instead of looking ahead to these ideas, it looks back at them.

Lesson 4: Evaluating
GED Practice (pages 188–190)
Here are likely scores and explanations.
Essay 1: A likely score is 2. The writer states a point of view and provides support for a main idea, but there is insufficient paragraph development for an essay because there are too few details. The sentence structure contains errors.

Essay 2: A likely score is 4. The essay has effective organization with a clear thesis statement and topic sentences. Several examples are given to support the topic sentences of the paragraphs. There are random errors in the conventions of English, but they do not distract the reader significantly. They would not detract from its score with GED evaluators.

GED Review Evaluating
(page 191)
Compare your answers to the evaluation checklist. Note the criteria that you missed.

Lesson 5: Revising
GED Practice (page 197)
Run-on sentences: The last sentence in paragraph 2 could be corrected this way: "In addition, they usually offer short menus. You can make a quick, easy decision about what you want to order."

The second sentence in paragraph 4 could be corrected this way: "The husband and wife are tired when they come home and don't want to cook. Instead, they want to spend time with their kids."

Sentence fragment: The second sentence in paragraph 3 could be corrected this way: "Hamburgers cost just a couple of dollars."

Verb use: The verb in the first sentence of paragraph 4 should be plural: "more and more families *are* made up of working couples."

Punctuation: Delete the unnecessary comma in the second sentence in paragraph 2: "near companies and along highways."

Spelling: The following words are misspelled:
It's (paragraph 1), *finally* (paragraph 4), *therefore*
(paragraph 4), *popularity* (paragraph 5).

GED Review Revising
(page 198)
Your answers may be worded differently, but they
should be similar to these:

1. I should first revise the ideas and then proofread
   for the use of conventions of English. As I revise,
   I will probably cross some sentences out and
   rewrite others. It's more efficient to proofread
   when the text is in a more final form.

2. I can make changes by writing between the lines
   or in the margin, using a caret to show where
   additions belong, and crossing out any unwanted
   words or phrases.

3. I can use the checklists on pages 192 and 195
   to help me decide what to change. I should also
   memorize the checklists so that I can apply them
   when I take the GED Test.

4. I can look back at my plan and check to see
   whether I included all the ideas in my essay.

GED Unit Review Essay
(page 199)
Topics 1–5
Share your work with your instructor or another
student.

Use the Essay Self-Assessment form on page 896
to track your progress, note your strengths, and
determine areas in which you want to improve.

UNIT 3: SOCIAL STUDIES

Canadian History
Lesson 1: European Colonization of North America

GED Practice (pages 203–205)

1. **(4) Aboriginal peoples had well-ordered societies that included a set of spiritual beliefs.** (Analysis) The passage describes the accepted standards of behaviour and the commonly held beliefs that are characteristic of a stable society. Option (1) is incorrect because the information in the passage contradicts it, and there is no mention of the information provided in option (2). Option (3) is just one example of the beliefs of Aboriginal peoples, and although option (5) may be true, it is not supported by evidence in the passage.

2. **(3) There should be respect for all forms of life—both in society and in nature.** (Evaluation) The passage highlights the principles for a peaceful community life and the need to revere the natural world. Option (1) is incorrect because Aboriginal societies constrained the behaviour of individuals. Although option (2) may be true, it is not mentioned in the passage. Both options (4) and (5) are contradicted by the information in the passage.

3. **(2) The group's survival depended on conformity and cooperative behaviour.** (Analysis) Survival in difficult climatic conditions and against warlike neighbours would demand collaboration. There is no evidence to support option (1). Option (3) contradicts the values described in the passage. The passage does not support either options (4) or (5).

4. **(5) Public statues and carved figures often represented religious figures in Christian European societies.** (Evaluation) Europeans would have been accustomed to seeing statues of religious figures in public places. Option (1) is incorrect, since Christianity was not an Aboriginal religion. Although option (2) may be correct, it does not imply a religious meaning for totem poles. Option (3) identifies the material used for totem poles, not their significance. Option (4) would exclude the use of artistic products for decoration or aesthetic enjoyment, so it is not correct.

5. **(4) To identify the variety of activities that the Huron people people engaged in during the year** (Comprehension) The

calendar organizes the subsistence activities to identify which activities were done by whom and at what time of the year. Option (1) is incorrect because the calendar shows that the tasks were about equally divided between men and women. Option (2) is incorrect because the calendar does not focus only on fishing and agriculture. Options (3) and (5) have no support in the table.

6. **(3) The Huron people produced tools and other implements for their daily use.** (Evaluation) Although it is probably true that the Hurons made tools, the table does not reveal this activity. The table demonstrates that the activities cited in options (1), (2), (4), and (5) were part of the yearly cycle of subsistence activity in Huron society.

7. **(3) The Impact of European Goods on Aboriginal Life** (Comprehension) The passage identifies many European goods acquired by trading and used by Aboriginal people. Option (1) reflects only one aspect of Aboriginal life and is not the main idea of the passage. Options (2) and (4) provide details about only two European goods. Option (5) is incorrect because survival is not the focus of the passage.

8. **(4) kettles** (Comprehension) This is clearly stated in the very first sentence of the passage. Scissors, option (2) are mentioned as making women's tasks easier but are not described as having the greatest impact on daily life. Glass beads, option (2), are mentioned as having an impact on only one aspect of Aboriginal life, decorative beadwork on clothing. Options (3) and (5) are incorrect because they are not mentioned at all in the passage.

9. **(2) Fur pelts worn for a year dropped their thick outer hairs and left more usable, soft fur.** (Analysis) The wearing of beaver pelts helped to prepare the furs for later commercial use in making felt. Option (1) is incorrect because the passage does not refer to children's activities. Options (3) and (4) are not supported by evidence in the passage. Although option (5) was undoubtedly true, the wearing of fur satisfied personal needs and was not motivated by the fur trade.

10. **(1) approximately 14 000** (Comprehension) The population graph indicates a steady population of about 14 000 from 1530 until 1570. None of the other options are supported by the graph.

11. **(5) The Aboriginal population fell dramatically after contact with the Europeans.** (Analysis) The graph reveals a sharp decline in the Aboriginal population beginning in 1570, at the precise time that Europeans were setting up the fur trade and exploring the continent. There is no mention of option (1) in the passage. Neither the graph nor the passage offers support for options (2) through (4).

12. **(4) Aboriginal peoples did not see the need to respond to European economic demand with an increased supply of furs.** (Evaluation) Since Aboriginal populations had survived for milennia without a strong capitalist economic system, there was little inclination to adopt a new values system. There is no evidence in the material to support option (1). Option (2) is incorrect because trade among Aboriginal peoples was well-established long before contact with the Europeans. Option (3) is the opposite of the truth. Option (5) may have been true, but there is no support in the passage for it.

Lesson 2: New France and the British Conquest
GED Practice (pages 207–208)

1. **(5) the Great Lakes** (Evaluation) The western border of Champlain's map does not contain any large lakes and likely means that he was not yet aware of their existence. Options (1), (2), and (3) are clearly present on his map. Option (5), the Fraser River, is in British Columbia, undiscovered by any Europeans in 1612.

2. **(3) The system of lakes and rivers allowed easy access to the interior of the continent.** (Comprehension) As Champlain's map shows, the waterway system connected the interior of the continent with the established settlements in New France, allowing exploration. Option (1) is incorrect, since some rivers ran to Hudson Bay, and later discoverers found rivers running to the Arctic Ocean and the Gulf of Mexico. Option (2) is not correct because much of the eastern continent is hilly and even contains low mountain ranges, making passage difficult. Option (4) is incorrect because the Rocky Mountains are not in eastern North America. Option (5) is also incorrect because, although frozen lakes and rivers would allow easy travel in winter, the waterways were still accessible in the warm seasons, allowing exploration.

3. **(1) The expulsion of the Huguenots from New France was probably a serious mistake.** (Analysis) The passage describes the positive contributions provided to New France by the Huguenots, leading to the conclusion that the loss of these qualities was detrimental to the colony's future. Option (2) is simply a restatement of information in the passage, not a conclusion. Option (3) expresses an opinion contrary to the information in the passage. There is no support for option (4), and option (5) is not mentioned in the material.

4. **(4) The Americans resented having to pay for Britain's wars through taxes in which they had no say.** (Analysis) The issue of British taxation on the Thirteen Colonies was one of the main causes of the American Revolution. Although option (1) may be true, there is no evidence in the passage for it. Option (2) is not supported by the passage. There is no mention of Spain in the passage, so option (3) is incorrect. There is no support for option (5) in the passage.

5. **(4) to allow English settlers to move west unhindered** (Comprehension) The English colonists in the Thirteen Colonies needed more land, but their westward expansion was blocked by the French. Although option (1) was a factor in English-French struggles, the main issue was control of territory, not religion. At the time, Washington was a loyal British army officer, so option (2) is incorrect. The passage does not support option (3). Option (5) is incorrect because French-Aboriginal alliances are not mentioned in the passage.

6. **(1) The *Canadiens* would be easily assimilated** (Analysis) The passage claims that the English thought the French would willingly accept English rule in New France. There is no evidence to support option (2) in the passage. Option (3) is not validated in the passage. Option (4) is the opposite of the English intentions in North America, and so is not correct. The passage supports the opposite view of what the English assumed, so option (5) is incorrect.

Lesson 3: Building a Country

GED Practice (pages 210–211)

1. **(4) Simcoe's administration was a period of dynamic growth and development in Upper Canada.** (Comprehension) The passage describes the many initiatives taken by Simcoe to develop the colony. Options (1) and (2) are examples of the changes brought about by Simcoe, not the main idea. Option (3) is a single fact of history. The evidence provided in the passage negates option (5) as the main idea.

2. **(5) There would be trouble between the United States and Upper Canada.** (Analysis) The last sentence of the passage strongly suggests this development. Option (1) is a stated fact in the passage, not an assumption. Options (2) and (4) are contradicted by information in the passage. Option (3) may have been true but is not supported in the passage.

3. **(4) British North America would one day become its own country—Canada.** (Analysis) The passage makes clear that the defeat of the American invasion raised the pride of Upper and Lower Canadians who had cooperated to repulse a formidable foe. Adversity brought them together, suggesting the beginnings of a nation. Option (1) is contradicted by information in the passage. Option (2) is a statement of fact, not an assumption. Options (3) and (5) may have been true, but are not supported by information in the passage.

4. **(5) Canada's independence was achieved with the stroke of a pen, whereas America's was achieved by a revolution.** The signing of the *British North America Act* in 1867 was a peaceful event. Option (1) is not mentioned, and option (2) is not supported by information in the passage. Option (3) is incorrect because, though Britain supported the move to confederation, there is no evidence that Canada was forced to become an independent country. Option (4) is incorrect since Americans did not sit in the British House of Commons.

5. **(3) defence** (Analysis) Since national defence is a concern of the entire country, not just of individual provinces, this power was assigned to the federal government. All the other powers are not of a national concern, so they became the responsibility of the provincial governments. Therefore, options (1), (2), (4), and (5) are incorrect.

6. **(1) If the new country faltered, the United States might decide to "help out" by annexing Canada and making it part of the United States** (Evaluation) The cartoon and caption reveal that Britain appears happy to be relieved of the responsibility for its infant colony, while Uncle Sam declares that he is ready to "catch" the new country if it falls. Hidden in Uncle Sam's offer is an implied desire to annex the defenceless country to the north. There is no support for options (2) and (4), since Britain strongly favoured Confederation. Option (3) is incorrect because it is not reasonable to assume that tiny Canada would attack either its giant neighbour or its mother country. Although it is possible that any newly created country might be initially vulnerable, there was nothing in Canada's past to suggest self-destruction, so option (5) is not a viable assumption.

Lesson 4: Settling the West

GED Practice (pages 213–214)

1. **(2) He decided that if Canada didn't act quickly, the Americans might annex all of western North America.** (Analysis) American settlers were already moving onto the vast Prairie lands and beginning to settle, and at the same time the U.S. government was buying land in the west. There is no support for option (1) or option (3) in the passage. Option (4) is incorrect because Macdonald's goal was to join Canada from sea to sea. Option (5) is incorrect because recent American policies showed that they wanted to expand, not abandon lands.

2. **(2) The British courts often sided with the provinces.** (Comprehension) The passage explains that the judgments of the British Courts often curbed the power of the federal government, in favour of the provinces. There is no support for option (1) in the passage. The court results contradict option (3). Option (4) is not supported by the information, and there is no mention of option (5) in the passage.

3. **(4) There were different opinions about how Confederation should operate.** (Analysis) It is often assumed that once the *BNA*

Act was passed, the organization and government of Canada would be clear; this passage indicates that right from the beginning there were different theories about the meaning of Confederation. Option (1) cannot be supported either by the passage or by history. Although option (2) might be suggested by some, there is no support for it in the passage. Canada's history of federal-provincial power struggles renders option (3) unsupportable. The fact that Canada still exists contradicts option (5).

4. **(3) renewed hope for economic security and happiness** (Application) The pictures and information on the poster portrayed a land of prosperity and contentment. Option (1) is unlikely, since prospective immigrants knew that they would be farming. Option (2) is incorrect because the advertising portrays a rural life. Option (4) is incorrect because English readers would see that there was little resemblance between rural England and the western Canadian landscape. There is nothing in the information to support option (5).

5. **(1) Troops could be sent to crush the rebellion and the transcontinental railway could be completed**.
(Comprehension) If the railroad could be quickly finished, troops could be sent to put down the uprising in six days rather than trekking overland for three months. Option (2) is incorrect because vestiges of English-French resentments still exist today. The passage does not support option (3). Option (4) was not an outcome sought by Macdonald. There is no evidence that Quebec would renounce Louis Riel; in fact, he became a rallying symbol for Quebec, so option (5) is not correct.

Lesson 5: Turmoil and Triumph
GED Practice (pages 216–217)

1. **(4) maintaining peace and civil order** (Evaluation) All governments were nervous about the potential for civil unrest when workers or others challenged the existing authority. As a result, they quickly applied force to quell any signs of disorder. Option (1) is not supported in the passage. There is no mention of option (2) or option (3) in the passage. Although option (5) may have been a goal of civic leaders, their first priority was maintaining law and order.

2. **(2) collective bargaining** (Comprehension) Paragraph 4 provides the context for understanding the meaning of the term when it refers to groups of workers negotiating rather than single workers. Although options (1), (3), and (5) may have been a part of organized labour's actions, none of these options explains the term. Option (4) is not supported in the passage.

3. **(1) It drew attention to poor social and economic conditions and caused workers and others to become more politically active.** (Application) News of the Winnipeg General Strike travelled all across the country and prompted people to form new political parties and groups advocating social justice. Option (2) did not happen in Canada. Options (3) and (4) are not supported by information in the passage. Although option (5) is true, it is only an example of one local event.

4. **(5) The civil authorities used mounted police to break up labour demonstrations.** (Evaluation) The photograph shows mounted police swinging baseball bats as they charge the crowd. Although option (1) is true, it is not revealed in the photograph, and neither are options (2), (3), and (4).

5. **(5) trust in the integrity of the capitalist economic system** (Evaluation) As the passage points out, most economic leaders believed that falling stock prices were simply a natural part of business operations and would rebound in the normal workings of the stock market. In this way, they displayed a faith in the soundness of the system. Option (1) is incorrect because most capitalists in North America did not either believe in or support the ideas of socialism, in which governments participate actively in the economy, controlling and even owning parts of it. Option (2) is not supported in the passage. Option (3) is not mentioned in the passage, and option (4) is not consistent with the values system of capitalism, which relies on the participation of banks in the workings of the economy.

6. **(1) All parts of the economy were interrelated.** (Analysis) Paragraph 2 explains the cause and effect relationship of the series of events, revealing that every part of the economy was related to other parts. Option (2) is not an explanation of the widespread effects of the Depression. Although options (3), (4), and (5) identify events, they do not explain the interrelationship of events.

7. **(4) J. S. Woodsworth voted against the war.** (Analysis) The passage identifies Woodsworth as a pacifist, someone who morally

objects to all war, and his vote against war clearly shows his commitment to pacifist values. Neither option (1) nor option (2) is supported in the passage. Option (3) indicates that the passing of the statute was important to Britain, but it is not the best reflection of values among the options. Although option (5) reflects revolutionary values, it is not based on information in the passage.

8. **(2) Before the Statute of Westminster was passed, Canada was still a colony.** (Analysis) Having the power to control both internal and external affairs is a sign of a country's complete independence. Option (1) expresses a passing thought, not a proposal to change a long-established national holiday. Option (3) is not supported in the passage, and option (4) is not mentioned. Option (5) is not correct because it contradicts what the passage means.

Lesson 6: Canada and the Modern World
GED Practice (pages 219–220)

1. **(2) A national consensus in favour of social programs for all Canadians emerged in Canada.** (Analysis) Many of the steps that led to a national medicare program are described in the passage. Option (1) contradicts the information in the passage, so it is not correct. The passage does not present information to support option (3). The information in the passage does not support options (4) and (5).

2. **(1) The people of Quebec preferred to solve their political issues peacefully.** (Analysis) The fact that even the separatist Parti Québécois began to soften its radical stance indicated that violence had been rejected as a method of solving political differences in Quebec. Trudeau's actions contradict option (2). Option (3) is a generalization that has no support in the passage. There is no evidence in the passage to support option (4). The fact that few violent political events have happened since in Canada shows that option (5) is incorrect.

3. **(3) The courts bear the burden of interpreting the Charter.** (Evaluation) There is clear support for this conclusion in the details provided in the second paragraph. Option (1) is incorrect because, although there is mention of "thousands of court cases," this situation is not characterized as a "glut." Option (2) contradicts what is stated in the first paragraph. Although option (4) may be true, this is not stated in the passage. There is no support in the passage for option (5).

4. **(2) The police don't inform you that you have the right to speak to a lawyer when they arrest you.** (Application) The police are agents of the government. Options (1), (3), (4), and (5) are incorrect because they all refer to private issues, some of which may result in people going to court, but none of which involves actions of the government or any of its agents.

5. **(4) the supremacy of God and the rule of law** (Comprehension) The preamble of the Charter specifies these two fundamental bases on which the rest of the document rests. There is no support in the passage or the document for options (1), (2), (3), or (5).

GED Review Canadian History
(pages 221–223)

1. **(5) They would find the report both insulting and threatening.** (Comprehension) Since Durham made no secret of his recommendation that the French be assimilated by the English, it is not surprising that the French found his recommendations both a threat and an insult. Option (1) is incorrect because it is the opposite of what the French would have felt. There is no evidence in the passage to support option (2) or option (3). It is difficult to imagine that a report recommending the disappearance of one's own culture and heritage would be met with indifference, so option (4) is not reasonable.

2. **(5) He used effective tactics to delay and ultimately kill a morally repugnant bill.** (Analysis) The passage describes Simcoe's tactic of stalling debate to stop a bill in the Assembly that would have reinstituted slavery in Upper Canada. Options (1) and (2) and are not supported in the paragraph, even though Simcoe may have criticized slave owners and encouraged them to sell their slaves. Option (3) is incorrect because, although Simcoe did maintain law and order, this is not related to the issue of slavery. There is no mention of option (4) in the passage.

3. **(4) A strong individual can set the moral standard for a whole continent, if not the world.** (Application) The fact that Simcoe forced the passage of the *Slave Act* is proof that behind his convictions lay a determination to do the morally right thing even when many people opposed him. The information in the passage contradicts option (1). Option (2) is an opinion that cannot be defended. Option (3) is a historical fact and not a general principle. There is no support in the passage for option (5).

4. (2) There was a large rural-to-urban shift.
(Analysis) The inset information on Canada's population reveals that in 1901 the rural component was 62.5 percent, but in 1998 it was only 22.1 percent, a decline of more than 40 percent. Option (1) cannot be deduced from the population statistics inset in the map. There is no support for option (3). Option (4) is incorrect because the population statistics reveal that Canada's population grew from 1901 to 1998. Option (5) is incorrect because the passage explains that only 20 percent indicated this.

5. (1) Canadians can write in their ethnic background(s) rather than just select from a limited number. (Comprehension) The passage explicitly states this innovation in the recent census form. Multiculturalism implies many cultures and languages, not just English and French, so option (2) is not correct. There is no mention in the passage of option (3) or option (4), which, in any event, is not related to Canada's multicultural status. Option (5) is refuted by the information in the passage.

6. (3) They wanted to express a new identity.
(Analysis) Their actions indicate a strong intention to assert their Canadianness over other identities. Option (1) is not supported by the passage. Option (2) is not mentioned in the passage. Option (4) is an opinion that cannot be supported by the passage. Although some people may hold the feeling expressed in option (5), it cannot account for 20 percent of the total responses, and is thus incorrect.

7. (4) the territory of Nunavut (Analysis) The dates shown on the map reveal the entry of provinces and territories into Confederation. Options (1) and (3) have earlier entry dates than Nunavut and so are incorrect. There are no dates provided for Edmonton or the Greater Toronto Area and both are cities, so both option (2) and option (5) are incorrect.

8. (1) make strong efforts to ensure pay equity for men and women (Application) Canada ranked fourth in the gender-related index, part of which is concerned with equality of opportunity for both men and women. Option (2) is incorrect as military spending is not related to the definition of human development. There is no support for options (3), (4), or (5) in the passage.

9. (2) Poverty also exists in the so-called "best" country in the world. (Analysis) The cartoonist is intending to call into question the validity of Canada's ranking by revealing that poverty also exists here; street begging, for example, is increasingly a feature of urban Canadian life. Option (1) implies that Canada has no social problems and this is decidedly not the case. The cartoon implies the opposite of option (3). Although option (4) is true, it is a fact, not an opinion. Option (5) is not correct because the cartoonist intends to call Canada's high ranking into question, not suggest that poor countries should follow Canada's lead.

World History
Lesson 7: Ancient Empires of the World
GED Practice (pages 225–227)

1. (2) The English word *democracy* comes from the Greek term meaning "the people." (Comprehension) By providing the Greek term *demos* and its meaning as a lead-in to discussing Greek democracy, the author hints at the word's origin rather than directly stating the connection. Nothing in the passage suggests that option (1) is true. The passage does not touch on the size of the city-states, so option (3) is incorrect. Option (4) is a judgment, and the passage does not hint that this is the writer's opinion. Option (5) is contradicted by information in the passage.

2. (5) The early Greeks influenced modern science. (Analysis) The chart states the important scientific contributions of Democritus and Hippocrates. Option (1) is wrong because the chart does not tell where the playwrights came from. Nothing in the chart suggests or supports option (2), (3), or (4).

3. (3) its democratic form of government (Comprehension) The writer hints at this relationship by connecting Athens as the greatest Greek democracy and Athens as the centre of the Golden Age. There is nothing to suggest that options (1), (2), or (5) are true. Option (4) is incorrect because the passage states that such rivalries helped to end Athens's leadership rather than promote it.

4. (3) Farming was important in each culture. (Analysis) Farming is the only topic in the passage that is common to all three cultures. Option (1) is incorrect because it was only noted about the Maya. The passage states that the Moche had an extensive system of roads and implies that Maya may have had roads, because they had extensive trade. But nothing about Nazca roads is stated or implied, so option (2) is incorrect. Option (4) is contradicted by

Unit 3

information in the passage because the Mayan civilization existed in Central America, not South America. Option (5) is not the correct answer, because no information about the decline and disappearance of the Nazca and Moche is given in the passage.

5. **(2) The Aztec and Inca empires existed at the same time.** (Evaluation) The map key shows that the Aztec and Inca empires were both in existence in 1500 C.E. Option (1) is incorrect because there is no evidence on the map that there were roads between the cities or that trade went on among them. Option (3) is incorrect because the Moche roads were in South America only, while Copán was in Central America. Option (4) is not correct because the map shows that the Aztec Empire was north of Tikal. The map key shows that the Maya were active in 400 C.E., while the date for the Aztec is 1500 C.E., so option (5) is incorrect.

6. **(5) trade** (Evaluation) Roads would have made it easier for the Moche to conduct trade, so their road building shows that trade was important to them. No connection exists between roads or road building and the importance of options (1), (3), and (4) in a culture. Roads might have encouraged people to move to cities, but neither the passage nor the map suggest that large cities were a feature of Moche culture, so option (2) is incorrect.

7. **(1) It was located in North Africa.** (Comprehension) The statement that Rome gained control of North Africa by defeating Carthage suggests the city's location. Option (2) is incorrect because it is directly stated in the passage. Nothing in the passage suggests option (3). Option (4) is incorrect because the passage suggests that the conquests in Greece, Spain, and present-day Turkey were even more responsible for this outcome. The passage directly contradicts option (5).

8. **(4) the justices of the Supreme Court, who determine whether laws agree with the Constitution** (Application) The chart states that the praetors interpreted questions about the law. None of the officials described in options (1), (2), (3), and (5) perform this type of legal function: the consuls were most like the prime minister; the Senate and popular assemblies were most like Parliament; and there were no officials in Rome like the members of the provincial legislatures or premiers.

9. **(2) political and military power** (Evaluation) The information in the chart and passage leads to the conclusion that control of their leaders and creation of an empire were important to Romans. No information supports options (1) and (4). Option (3) is contradicted by the passage. Although it is true that the Romans did value Greek art and culture, nothing in the chart or passage supports option (5).

Lesson 8: How Nations Arose
GED Practice (pages 229–230)

1. **(2) The Growth and Spread of Islam, 650–1550** (Comprehension) The passage documents the growth and spread of Islam, establishing that Arab and Ottoman Muslims controlled the Middle East, North Africa, Spain, part of India, and eastern Europe at various times between the mid-seventh century and 1550. Option (1) is incorrect because the passage is about political domination and mentions only one religion, Islam. Options (3) and (4) are incorrect because the Arabs and Ottomans are both covered in the passage. Option (5) is incorrect because a larger geographical region than North Africa was involved.

2. **(4) The arts flourished in the Ottoman Empire.** (Evaluation) The passage talks about how important the arts, science, and learning were to Muslim culture. Because the Ottomans were Muslims, it follows that the arts flourished in the Ottoman Empire. The passage does not mention how the Turks treated the Arabs and Christians, so options (1) and (5) are incorrect. Option (2) is incorrect because the passage indicates that the Ottoman Empire did not stretch to Spain and that Arab Muslims ruled Spain centuries before the Ottoman Empire came into being. Option (3) is incorrect because the passage does not mention the Renaissance in Europe.

3. **(1) human rights** (Evaluation) This value could not have been very important because the passage indicates that the people of Songhay traded in slaves. Options (2) and (5) are incorrect because Timbuktu contained many Islamic schools and three Islamic universities that offered religious training. Option (3) is wrong because the passage implies that Songhay was a wealthy trading empire. Option (4) is incorrect because poetry is listed as one of the subjects taught at the universities in Timbuktu under the Songhay.

Unit 3

4. (3) the growth of the Mongol Empire
(Comprehension) The passage describes the growth of the Mongol Empire, and the map illustrates its huge span. Options (1), (4), and (5) are details that support the main idea of the passage and map. Option (2) is incorrect because the map shows the empire and makes no mention of the leaders.

5. (4) A Mongol invasion of Japan did not succeed. (Analysis) The passage indicates an attack on Japan, but the map shows that Japan was not part of the Mongol Empire. This leads to the assumption that the attack failed. No evidence on the map supports option (1), (2), or (3). Nothing in the passage or on the map suggests that option (5) is true.

6. (5) The Mongols had a major impact on world history. (Evaluation) The Mongols ruled much of Asia and all of Russia, so their influence on history was immense in its scope. Option (1) is incorrect because the size of the empire suggests that, if anything, the Mongols were good at government. Option (2) is wrong because while the passage establishes their ferocity, it does not prove that they were the fiercest of all time. Nothing in the passage suggests that the Mongols had superior technology, so option (3) is wrong. Option (4) is incorrect because the empire grew after Genghis Khan's death.

Lesson 9: Global Expansion

GED Practice (pages 232–233)

1. (2) to show how imperialism affected Central America (Comprehension) The passage is a general discussion of imperialism in Central America. Option (1) is a detail that explains one of the causes of imperialism in the region. Option (3) is a major part of the passage, but is not the main point. Option (4) is incorrect because North American investment is mentioned only briefly and is also not the cause of imperialism. Although civil war and unrest is mentioned as one effect of imperialism, describing it is not the main purpose of the passage, so option (5) is also incorrect.

2. (5) the ultimate failure of the communists in Nicaragua (Analysis) The passage states that U.S. involvement with the contras eventually forced the communists to hold new elections, which they lost. The death of innocent citizens was an effect of events in El Salvador and Guatemala, and the passage does not provide any information about the fate of civilians in Nicaragua, so option (1) is not correct. Option

(2) was a result of the Nicaraguan communists' actions, not those of the United States. The passage contains no information about options (3) and (4).

3. (1) concern for Panama Canal security (Analysis) The passage states that U.S. concern over the canal increased after the 1977 agreement to turn control of it over to Panama—at about the same time that communist revolutions gained strength in the region. Nothing in the passage suggests option (2) as a cause. Option (3) is incorrect because the passage suggests that bananas and coffee are important to North American companies with investments there, not to consumers. The passage implies that the nations of Central America are weak, but the passage does not suggest that as a reason for U.S. involvement there, so option (4) is incorrect. There is no support in the passage for option (5).

4. (3) Cuba and the United States (Application) Imperialism occurs when one nation extends its control over another one. When Cuba and the United States intervened in revolutions in independent nations in Central America, both were practising imperialism. A nation that puts down internal rebellion against its own legitimate government, such as what occurred in El Salvador and Nicaragua, is not acting imperialistically, so options (1), (2), (4), and (5) are incorrect.

5. (4) strengthening democracy in Central America (Evaluation) The passage points out that the United States supported governments in Central America in the 1970s and before that were not democratic. The passage suggests that ensuring stable governments in Central America, whether or not they were democratic, in order to protect American investments and the Panama Canal was the major goal of U.S. policy in the region. Thus, options (1), (2), (3), and (5) are incorrect because these factors were important to the U.S. government.

6. (4) Industrialized countries became more powerful than nonindustrial countries. (Analysis) This is suggested by Britain's victory over China in the Opium War and by China's subsequent domination by the industrial powers. There is no support in the passage for option (1), (2), (3), or (5).

7. (2) Germany (Comprehension) This can be determined by studying the map. Options (1), (3), and (5) are incorrect because the map shows that France, Great Britain, and Russia had the three largest spheres of influence. Option (4) is incorrect because the map shows that Japan's two combined spheres of influence accounted for more territory than Germany's sphere.

8. **(3) controlling trade coming into China** (Evaluation) The passage suggests that the cause of the Opium War was Britain's refusal to stop selling opium in China. Option (1) is incorrect because the passage does not suggest that China wanted or received any profits from the drug trade. Option (2) is incorrect because Japan is not mentioned in the passage, and there is no reason to believe that China was trying to prove anything to Japan. Option (4) is incorrect because the passage does not suggest that China wanted all trade with India stopped. Option (5) cannot be true because the spheres of influence were established in the decades following the Opium War, not preceding it.

9. **(5) Japan was an industrial nation in 1912.** (Evaluation) Spheres of influence met the needs of the industrialized nations for additional markets and sources of raw materials for their industries. That Japan had such a sphere in 1912, as shown on the map, suggests that it had become an industrial nation. Option (1) cannot be determined from the map and passage; in fact, although Japan was not the enemy of England and France during this period, no formal alliance existed. Option (2) also cannot be determined from the map and the passage, although Japan had recently defeated Russia in a war that ended in 1905. Also, nothing on the map or in the passage supports options (3) and (4), although Japan did have these foreign policy goals.

Lesson 10: The Post–Cold War World
GED Practice (pages 235–236)

1. **(1) to express the view that agreements between the two sides have been shaky** (Comprehension) If you know, as the passage indicates, that the other agreements between the two sides have collapsed, the cartoon's symbolic reference to a "house of cards" becomes clear. There is no evidence in the passage or clue in the cartoon to imply that option (2) is true. Option (3) is incorrect because nothing in the cartoon connects the cards to gambling. There are also no clues in the cartoon to imply that the cards are visual symbols for options (4) and (5), so they are also incorrect.

2. **(3) They both lay claim to the same land.** (Comprehension) The passage states that since ancient times, Arabs and Jews have been competing intermittently for the land called Palestine. Option (1) is incorrect because religious differences are not mentioned in the passage. Although it is true that some Arab rulers supported the Germans during World War II, option (2) is not given as a reason in the passage either. Option (4) is incorrect because the passage makes no mention of the Ottomans stirring up conflict and, in fact, states that conflicts were not common during the rule of the Ottoman Turks. Although the British did aggravate the conflict between the Arabs and Jews, they did not cause it, so option (5) is also incorrect.

3. **(4) Most agreements between Israel and the PLO have not been fully carried out.** (Analysis) Without this knowledge, the significance of the symbol of the "house of cards" and caption will be more difficult to recognize. It is important to understand who each character represents, but knowing their names is not important to interpreting the cartoon, so options (1) and (2) are incorrect. The information contained in option (3) also does not help make sense of the cartoon. Option (5) is incorrect because knowing the name of Israel's parliament is not necessary to understand this cartoon.

4. **(4) A communist government controlled East Berlin.** (Analysis) This assumption can be made because of the statement that East Berlin was separated from democratic West Berlin. No information supports option (1), (2), or (5) as an assumption. In fact, the information about the collapse of European communism in general—and the wall in particular—strongly suggests that all three statements are untrue. Option (3) is incorrect because this information is contained in the passage.

5. **(3) North Korea and South Korea** (Application) Like East and West Germany, North and South Korea had been part of one country that was divided after World War II, restricting travel from one part of the country to the other and splitting up families. Option (1) is incorrect because, although the United States and Canada are neighbouring countries, they were not formerly one country as were East and West Germany. Option (2) is not correct because Great Britain and the United States had a relationship of colonizer and colony, not the same relationship as East and West Germany. Options (4) and (5) are incorrect because there is free movement between all states, including between North Carolina and South Carolina and

between West Virginia and Virginia, while there was not free movement between the two parts of Germany.

6. **(1) The dinosaur represents European communism under Soviet leadership.** (Analysis) The hammer and sickle appears on the Soviet flag, and the Soviets dominated Eastern Europe, installing harsh communist governments there and influencing them as satellite nations. Since the hammer and sickle appears on the dinosaur's side and because the tail of the dinosaur is the Berlin Wall (in Europe), it is implied that the dinosaur represents Soviet-supported communism in Europe. Since West Berlin was not under a communist government, option (2) is incorrect. Options (3) and (5) are incorrect because they are contradicted by the passage. Option (4) is true but doesn't help you understand the message of the cartoon.

7. **(3) European Communism Becomes Extinct** (Comprehension) This is why the cartoonist has chosen to depict communism in Europe as a dinosaur. Option (1) is incorrect because the Berlin Wall was torn down, not moved. Option (2) is incorrect because although the wall is represented by the dinosaur's tail, the tail is only an element of the cartoon, not its central focus. Option (4) is not correct because the cartoon deals with the wall as related to the fall of Soviet-supported communism in Europe; the fall of the Soviet Union came slightly later. Option (5) is incorrect because the extinct dinosaur symbolizes that European communism is dead.

GED Review World History
(pages 237–239)

1. **(5) imperialism in world history** (Comprehension) The passage summarizes the causes and effects of imperialism. Options (1), (2), and (4) are incorrect because they are details that provide examples of imperialism. Option (3) is incorrect because it is a detail that states a cause of increased European imperialism in the nineteenth century.

2. **(2) Europeans felt superior to other peoples.** (Analysis) This connection is suggested by the placement of these two ideas in the paragraph. Option (1) is incorrect because nothing in the passage suggests that the Europeans spread their culture because the Greeks and Romans had done so. Imperialism does not require culture to be spread, and many forms of imperialism do not involve the spread

of culture, so option (3) is incorrect. Option (4) has to do with the effects of the Industrial Revolution, not with spreading culture and religion. Option (5) is incorrect because nothing in the passage suggests the people the Europeans met had no culture, and in fact they all had their own cultures.

3. **(1) Spanish soldiers conquer the Inca Empire in the sixteenth century.** (Application) This fits the definition of imperialism that is stated in the passage. Outright conquest is the most extreme form of imperialism. Options (2) and (4) are incorrect because declaring independence and protecting the economic power of one's country do not qualify as imperialism. Option (3) is not an attempt to take over weaker nations, but instead to join with them. Option (5) is incorrect because the United States and its allies freed Kuwait and allowed it to return to its self-governing status.

4. **(2) the Industrial Revolution and the need for more markets to sell goods** (Analysis) The passage establishes that the Industrial Revolution created a need for more markets, which, in turn, encouraged further imperialism. Options (1) and (5) are incorrect because nothing in the passage indicates that the other nations were lacking armies or religion. (In fact, they were lacking neither.) Option (3) is incorrect because the subjugation of Africans was an effect, not a cause, of imperialism. The European nations did not have an excess of raw materials but instead needed them, so option (4) is incorrect.

5. **(5) The Pro-Democracy Movement in China** (Comprehension) Both the cartoon and most of the passage are devoted to this topic. Option (1) is incorrect because this information is historical background that explains the development of the movement for democracy and the government's reaction to it. Option (2) is incorrect because only a minor reference is made to it in the passage. Option (3) is incorrect because it is not described in the passage or depicted in the cartoon. Option (4) is incorrect because it helps explain why the pro-democracy movement developed; it is not the central focus of the material.

6. **(3) The world community criticized China.** (Analysis) The cartoon symbolizes China's use of the army against the protesters. The passage indicates that this and other actions against the pro-democracy movement caused the world to condemn China for violating the human

rights of its people. The cartoonist's use of irony in the obvious lie coming from the government soldier also implies criticism of the Chinese government. Options (1) and (5) were among the causes that led to the event illustrated in the cartoon, not effects of it. Option (2) is incorrect because the passage states that Mao died before the pro-democracy movement began. The passage contradicts option (4).

7. **(4) the protesters who demanded democracy** (Comprehension) The passage states that the army attacked and killed the pro-democracy protesters, and the cartoon shows a dead figure clutching a flag labeled democracy. Options (1) and (3) are incorrect because it is clear from the information in the passage that the Chinese army did not kill Mao or China's leaders at the time of the unrest. Although the flag in the cartoon resembles a U.S. flag, nothing in the passage suggests that option (2) could be correct. Neither the passage nor the cartoon provides any reason to believe that option (5) is the case.

8. **(1) control** (Evaluation) Using the army to crush a protest and continuing political suppression of the Chinese people despite world condemnation of their actions establishes that China's leaders value control of China more than the other options. The fact that the soldier in the cartoon is telling a lie disproves option (2). The dead Chinese protester as well as information in the passage about other government acts of oppression make options (3), (4), and (5) incorrect as well.

9. **(2) The desire for democracy is alive in China.** (Comprehension) The content of the text balloon over the flag implies that the soldier's claim about the protester actually applies to democracy in China after the army's attack on the pro-democracy movement. The caption over the flag does not support option (1) as the correct answer. Nothing in the cartoon suggests that option (3) or (5) is true. Option (4) is contradicted by the blood shown coming from the protester's head, flowing out on the ground at the feet of the soldier.

10. **(2) cultural imperialism** (Application) Introducing a religion fits the definition of cultural imperialism. Neoimperialism is economic imperialism, so option (1) is incorrect. Since Hawaii did not become part of the United States until much later, option (3) is also incorrect. Options (4) and (5) are incorrect because the information indicates that Hawaii

was then an independent kingdom and not an official colony of the United States.

11. **(5) military intervention** (Application) The chart indicates that this involves sending troops to influence the internal affairs of another nation, which is what Cuba did. Since Angola did not become part of Cuba, options (1) and (2) are incorrect. Since the situation does not fit the chart's description of formation of a protectorate, option (3) is also incorrect. Also, the information contains no suggestion of cultural imperialism, so option (4) is incorrect.

12. **(3) colonialism and cultural imperialism** (Application) According to the chart, one country's rule over another is colonialism. The information about the religious and government systems suggests cultural imperialism as well. The information does not indicate which type of colonies the Chinese established there, so options (1) and (5) cannot be correct. No information establishes that military intervention took place, so option (2) is not correct. Because economic imperialism is not discussed, option (4) is also incorrect.

13. **(4) neoimperialism and settlement colony** (Application) The trade treaty is evidence of economic imperialism, and the large number of Japanese who relocated to Korea suggests settlement colonies there. The Japanese settlement eliminates option (1) as the answer, because dependent colonies involve rule by the colonizer over a predominantly native people, without large numbers of colonists. Although a protectorate may have been formed and cultural imperialism may have occurred, the information does not indicate them, so options (2), (3), and (5) are incorrect.

Civics and Government
Lesson 11: Modern Government
GED Practice (pages 241–243)

1. **(1) freedom of speech** (Application) Like freedom of religion and conscience, freedom of speech is an example of a fundamental freedom. Option (2) is incorrect because a public trial is a civil right, not a fundamental freedom. Option (3) is incorrect because people need to meet certain requirements to obtain a licence to practise medicine, so obtaining such a licence is not a natural right. Option (4) is incorrect because paying tax is required of certain people by law and so is not a right. Option (5) is incorrect because it is an example of an entitlement.

2. **(3) a government-guaranteed student loan** (Application) This is a benefit provided by the government to people who meet the requirements of a loan, and it can be taken away by the government. Options (1), (4), and (5) involve personal freedom and thus are part of fundamental freedoms. Option (2) is a procedural process and is a civil right guaranteed to all Canadians in the *Charter of Rights and Freedoms.*

3. **(5) John Locke was a great political thinker.** (Analysis) This is the only opinion found in the passage or supported by other information in it. Nothing in the passage suggests that the writer holds option (1), (2), or (4) as an opinion. Option (3) is a fact, not an opinion.

4. **(2) Rights and freedoms are protected in the Canadian Charter.** (Comprehension) The fact that rights and freedoms are entrenched in the Charter and entitlements are not indicates that they are more important to Canadians. Option (1) is incorrect because many people do need the benefits to which they are entitled. Option (3) is the opposite of what the passage states about what is protected by the government. Option (4) is incorrect because it is the opposite of what is true, though the passage speaks only of citizens and not of other residents in Canada. Option (5) is true of the passage, though it does not answer the question asked.

5. **(4) to be limited in where you could travel** (Application) Under a government that controls every aspect of your life, freedom of movement would be restricted. Options (1), (2), and (3) would be unlikely because individual freedoms are extremely limited under this form of government. There is no support in the passage for option (5).

6. **(4) the legislature** (Comprehension) This is illustrated by the diagram and implied in the second paragraph of the passage. Option (1) is incorrect because the president is the chief executive in the presidential system. Option (2) is incorrect because the diagram shows that the voters select the legislature, not the prime minister. The diagram also shows that the prime minister and legislature choose the cabinet, which then chooses the judges, so options (3) and (5) are not correct.

7. **(3) The parliamentary system is a better form of government than the presidential system.** (Analysis) This statement is a judgment that does not have any direct support from the information in the passage or diagram. Option (1) is incorrect because the legislature in a parliamentary system has the power to choose the chief executive, while the legislature in a presidential system does not have this power, so the statement is a fact. Options (2), (4), and (5) are also statements of fact that are proven by information in the passage and diagram.

8. **(1) the cabinet** (Comprehension) This is established by the diagram. The diagram shows that options (2), (3), (4), and (5) are not true in a parliamentary system.

9. **(2) The prime minister must resign if he or she loses an important vote in the legislature.** (Evaluation) This is the best evidence that the prime minister is less independent, because the president is not required to resign if a proposal he or she supports is defeated in Congress. Options (1) and (5) are incorrect because, although they are accurate statements, they have nothing to do with the prime minister's level of independence. Option (3) is incorrect because the diagram shows that the president, with the input of Congress, also appoints a cabinet. Option (4) is incorrect because the prime minister is directly responsible to the legislature, not to the voters.

10. **(1) that it has accompanying restrictions** (Analysis) This opinion is expressed in the last paragraph of the passage. There is no evidence in the passage for option (2), (3), or (4). Because the passage indicates that freedom comes with responsibility, option (5) is incorrect.

11. **(4) It is built on respect for individual differences.** (Comprehension) The chart points out the importance of respect for the individual. Option (1) is incorrect because absolute rule by the majority with no attention to other views would lead to tyranny, and the chart points out the importance of compromise. Option (2) is contradicted by the chart. There is no information in the chart or passage to support the opinion expressed in option (3) that any one principle is the most important. The passage expresses the opinion that option (5) is not necessarily true.

12. **(2) In a democracy no person's rights can be allowed to interfere with the rights of others.** (Evaluation) The quote means that each person's rights stop where another person's rights begin. The information in the first row of the chart expresses the principle on which La Forest's statement is based. Option (1) is incorrect

because the chart indicates that individual freedom is important in a democracy. Option (3) is a democratic value, but equal opportunity has nothing to do with La Forest's statement. Nothing in the passage supports option (4) as an explanation of La Forest's statement. Option (5) is incorrect because the need for compromise is one of the pillars of democracy, which indicates that differences of opinion are expected and protected in a democracy.

Lesson 12: Structure of the Canadian Government

GED Practice (pages 245–246)

1. **(4) a way of dividing powers between federal and provincial governments** (Comprehension) The passage indicates that the federal and provincial governments have divided, or shared, powers. The cartoon further emphasizes this difference. The passage indicates that the role of the federal government has changed over the years from a more central governing authority, option (1), to a more shared system. Options (1) and (2) are therefore not correct. Option (3) goes too far in the other direction to be correct. The passage and cartoon clearly show that provinces do not rule in Ottawa. Option (5) is not indicated by the passage.

2. **(3) The federal government is exercising too much power.** (Evaluation) The cartoon shows that the federal government (a sketch of Parliament in Ottawa) is one power that sits above the rest of Canada. Option (1) is incorrect because the cartoon shows that it is the federal government, not the provinces, that is too strong. Options (2), (4), and (5) are not indicated by the cartoon.

3. **(5) a family** (Application) The federal government is similar to the parents in a family. All people in a family are important, though some have more control or power than others. Option (1) is incorrect because a dictatorship has one person in control and all others follow. Option (2) is incorrect because a king or queen would be in control and the power would not be shared. Options (3) and (4) are incorrect because these systems are hierarchical in nature, and power is not shared.

4. **(1) democratic rights** (Comprehension) The election of politicians is a democratic right every Canadian holds. This power of democracy ensures that a government cannot hold power

indefinitely and that an election must be called at least every five years. The passage does not reflect the rights outlined in options (2) through (5), which are therefore incorrect.

5. **(5) making decisions in a direct democracy** (Application) The residents are acting directly to handle their affairs themselves rather than through elected representatives. Option (1) is incorrect because no mention of partisanship is mentioned in relation to the neighbourhood group, whereas writing a platform for a political party is by nature a partisan activity. Options (2) and (3) are incorrect because they relate to representative democracy and representative government, and the people in a neighbourhood association do not elect representatives to vote for them. Option (4) would not be true unless the group formally voted on changing a resolution, proposal, or bylaw of the group.

6. **(3) It was one step toward Canadian autonomy from Britain.** (Analysis) The main idea of the passage is that Canada has progressively gained more freedom from Britain. The effect of the 1931 statute was one step toward that realization. Option (1) is not accurate according to the passage. The statute did not abolish British power; it only limited it. Option (2) is not correct since the Charter was created more than 50 years after the *Statute of Westminster*. Options (4) and (5) represent the opposite of what actually happened.

7. **(5) increasing provincial power** (Evaluation) The fact that amendments need provincial approval is proof of this answer. There is no mention of the judiciary or the prime minister, so options (1) and (3) are clearly wrong. Option (4) is true, but it does not answer the specific question relating to the formulas. Option (2) is too general a statement to have any logical reference to the question asked.

8. **(3) Any province can veto a proposed constitutional amendment.** (Analysis) The fact that an amendment must be approved by every legislature gives any province the power to veto or forbid the constitutional change. Options (1) and (4) are clearly facts and are not logical implications as asked by the question. There is no evidence to suggest that options (2) and (5) are correct.

Lesson 13: Canadian Politics in Action

GED Practice (pages 248–249)

1. **(3) They have been influential in politics.** (Comprehension) The passage indicates that third parties have been important in dealing with social issues and social reform that the governments and oppositions of the time did not seem to address. Option (1) is the opposite of what is mentioned in the passage. Option (2) is not mentioned in the passage. Canadians have been and are interested in the issues of third parties, thus, option (4) is not correct. Third parties have contributed much to federal politics and have helped the nation to keep its politicians focused on the issues at hand; option (5) is therefore incorrect.

2. **(5) Regional differences have led to the creation of more parties.** (Comprehension) Paragraph three speaks of the origins of third parties as emanating from discord in Western Canada and Quebec. Though options (1) and (3) are correct, they do not indicate the main idea of paragraph three. Option (2) is incorrect because this is not the purpose of third parties, though it was the main goal of the Bloc Québécois. Option (4) shows an opinion, which is not relevant in this paragraph.

3. **(4) Voters feel that the major parties are not addressing important problems.** (Analysis) The passage says, "Often, third parties begin because established parties fail to address some important social issues." This indicates that Canadians support the change that third parties and their candidates provide. Option (1) is incorrect because the passage speaks about how Canadians want change and how they do take a stand on political issues. Option (2) indicates an opinion ("more exciting") that the passage does not support. Option (3) states a desire by Canadians that is not upheld by the passage. Option (5) shows the opposite of what the passage indicates, that is, that Canadians are interested in changing politics.

4. **(5) a two-party system** (Application) If the Progressive Conservative party (PC) regains its former popularity, and the Bloc Québécois and the Reform parties decline in power, then the system would return to the PC and Liberal parties being the governing party and the Official Opposition. Option (1), a democracy, and option (2), a republic, are not types of party systems, therefore they do not answer the question. The prefix "multi" indicates more than two, thus option (3) is not correct. Option (4) cannot be correct if there are only two main parties.

5. **(3) A PQ election victory will destroy the Canadian union.** (Comprehension) The cartoonist is showing that this particular election victory (as the oversized character on the luge) would wipe out the Canadian union (shown as the undersized beaver in the direct path of the luge). As option (1) states, the cartoon does show that the PQ could be overpowering; however, it is showing what would happen *if* the PQ won the election. Option (2) does not represent the characters in the cartoon. Option (4) does not show the significance of the cartoon, which relates to the province of Quebec. Option (5) is not indicated by the action of the cartoon—the Québécois are not in control, but this election could diminish the importance of the union of Canada.

6. **(5) By-election results in a constituency measure the probable outcome of a provincial or national election.** (Comprehension) The reader needs to know that by-elections often predict the outcome of general elections. Option (1) is incorrect because it does not refer to the issue of by-elections asked by the question. Option (2) does not make sense, as political parties do not participate in the Olympics. Options (3) and (4) are logically wrong, since one election in one constituency cannot be more important or have more power than a general election.

7. **(2) They form relationships with powerful members of government.** (Evaluation) This states a conclusion as it relates to many different types of interests that people have. Option (1) does not relate to the question. Options (3) and (4) are mentioned in the passage, though they are not the conclusion that the paragraph is making. The paragraph states that interest groups are influential even after elections; thus, option (5) does not conclude the paragraph either.

8. **(4) influencing legislation** (Analysis) The impact that interest groups have on legislation (for example, free trade) is stated in the passage. Option (1) is not the purpose of interest groups, though at times how sports and cultural events are promoted does affect these groups. Option (2) was not mentioned. Although options (3) and (5) are concerns of interest groups, they do not accurately reflect on their main purpose.

9. **(5) democratic politics** (Analysis) The people have a say in how the government is run. Their involvement directly influences the government's choices. Option (1) does not answer the question because "bureaucracy" is

the administrative aspect of the government. Option (2) cannot be the correct response because the passage talks of groups, not individuals. "Competition" does not relate to the government so much as it does to free enterprise, thus option (3) is incorrect. Option (4) is incorrect because the interest groups themselves are not representative government.

Lesson 14: The Canadian Government and Its Citizens

GED Practice (pages 251–252)

1. **(2) The smallest portion of the budget was spent on Crown corporations.** (Comprehension) This response is obvious when one looks at the pie chart and sees the 2 percent spent on Crown corporations. Option (1) is incorrect as the passage talks about income taxes that citizens pay. Option (3) is incorrect because the passage indicates that the greatest amount of monies collected by the government come from taxes, though it also borrows money to pay for its expenses. Option (4) is incorrect because it is not the interest on the national debt but the borrowed monies that helps pay for programs. Option (5) is not correct because the government spends 6 percent on defence and 12 percent on other transfers.

2. **(3) Taxes will increase.** (Analysis) Because the government gets most of its income from taxes, if it spends more than it collects, a likely conclusion would be that it needs to increase its income from taxes. Options (1) and (2) are the opposite of what is likely to occur. Option (4) does not make sense as the government would need to make more money in a short time. Option (5) may be true in that Canadians would then pay more tax; however, this is impossible to dictate.

3. **(2) transfers to persons** (Application) Employment Insurance benefits are transfer payments that are made directly to persons, without other government agencies involved. Options (1), (3), (4), and (5) all include other aspects of government.

4. **(3) Ontario and Alberta** (Comprehension) Ontario and Alberta (particularly Alberta) show a noticeable increase and then decrease in debt. New Brunswick's debt per capita increases in each consecutive year. Quebec has a relatively insignificant decrease in the final year. Thus, options (1), (2), (4), and (5) do not answer the question.

5. **(4) Alberta is the only province with an overall decline in its per capita provincial debt.** (Evaluation) From the information in the table, it is evident that Alberta shows a decline from 1989 ($6400) until 2002 ($1957), though it did increase for 1993–94. All other provinces increased their debt per capita from the initial amounts shown in 1989. Option (1) does not work because Alberta did not increase. Option (2) is incorrect because Ontario had the lowest per capita provincial debt in 1989–90. New Brunswick has shown a steady increase in its per capita provincial debt, thus making option (3) incorrect. The table does not talk about overall debt, but debt per capita, so based on the table, there is no way of knowing which province has the largest debt. Option (5) is therefore, incorrect.

6. **(1) $24** (Application) One must subtract New Brunswick's per capita debt from Ontario's for the year 1993–94 ($7431–$7407 = $24). All other options show incorrect responses.

7. **(5) Alberta would have a negative provincial debt per capita**. (Application) The table indicates that Alberta's debt has decreased over the past eight years, thus, if it continued in such a manner, it would likely be eliminated and actually have a surplus. Option (1) does not correspond to the chart, because Quebec's debt has been only marginally reduced in the last four years. Option (2) does not agree with the data because Ontario's debt has decreased over the past four years. Option (3) contradicts the facts shown in the table for the past eight years. New Brunswick has not shown any decreases; thus, option (4) is not supported by the table.

8. **(1) Many Canadians have become cynical about politics.** (Evaluation) A lack of voter turnout indicates an apathetic attitude toward politics. Option (2) is incorrect, because a general statement was made without any indication as to the demographics of those eligible voters. If political parties were more popular than ever, as stated in option (3), then more people would have voted; thus, this response is incorrect. The passage does not mention anything about particular reasons for the low voter turnout; therefore, option (4) cannot be the answer. Option (5), though it may be true, does not indicate a reason for low voter turnout.

GED Review Civics and Government
(pages 253–255)

1. **(3) Legitimate power results in better government than does illegitimate power.** (Analysis) This is a judgment by the writer and therefore an opinion that may or may not be true. Options (1), (2), (4), and (5) are all statements of fact that are established by the information in the passage.

2. **(4) authority** (Application) In a monarchy, the royal family is recognized as having the legitimate power to rule. Having the eldest child become the ruler when the monarch dies is a recognized method for the legitimate transfer of power in a monarchy. Options (1) and (3) are incorrect because the king rules by virtue of his position, not from personal influence or persuasion. Option (2) is incorrect because Albert did not come to power by force. Option (5) is incorrect because elections are not mentioned in the passage, and monarchs are not generally elected.

3. **(2) People's support is necessary for power to be legitimate.** (Comprehension) The passage states that the people must accept their leaders' power as proper in order for that power to be legitimate. Therefore, the support of the people is necessary for government to be legitimate. Thus, option (1) is not correct. There is no support in the passage for option (3) or (5) as an explanation of why people's opinions are important to the exercise of power. Behaviour can be influenced by force, but the passage implies that it does not change opinions, so option (4) is incorrect.

4. **(5) It makes people behave in ways that government leaders desire.** (Comprehension) The passage states that force or fear of it can change behaviour, so option (1) is incorrect. Option (2) is incorrect because people's support must be willingly given for power to be legitimate. There is no information in the passage to suggest that option (3) or (4) is true.

5. **(3) to describe Canada's governing institutions** (Comprehension) Each paragraph is a description of the various branches of government. Option (1) is incorrect as there was only one item mentioned about the American president (terms of office). Option (2) is the main idea of the last paragraph, not the entire passage. Option (4) is shown in the second paragraph, but it is not the main purpose of that paragraph nor the entire passage. Option (5), the governor general's role in government, is discussed, but it is not the main idea.

6. **(4) The Senate exercises too much power in the Canadian government.** (Analysis) The words "too much" indicate that an opinion is being stated: Who is it that thinks this? Options (1), (2), (3), and (5) are facts that are mentioned in the passage.

7. **(2) No Canadian citizen or institution is above the law.** (Analysis) This is a conclusion from the section in the *Charter of Rights and Freedoms* that recognizes the "rule of law." The governor general is the Crown's representative, not the people's; therefore option (1) is incorrect. Option (3) is not supported by the passage. Option (4) does not reflect a conclusion from the passage because more than one hundred years of discussion about the role of the Senate has yet to change it. The Supreme Court is responsible for mediating and interpreting, not drafting, laws; thus option (5) is incorrect.

8. **(4) a parliamentary government** (Application) Canada is a parliamentary government because, ultimately, power is vested in the legislative process since it can even override the Canadian constitution. Option (1) is incorrect since one person is not responsible for the entire government. Options (2) and (3) do not relate because of the role of the Crown (governor general) in Canadian politics. Option (5) states a fact—Canada does have a bicameral legislature—but this does not reflect the entirety of Canada's governmental system.

9. **(2) a merchant** (Application) A merchant has a vested interest in the sale of alcohol because he or she can directly benefit from it. A preacher in 1898, option (1), would likely be opposed to the sale of alcohol because of the "ills" associated with it. A prohibitionist, option (3), is against alcohol consumption and would oppose its sale. A doctor, option (4), and a farmer, option (5), may or may not vote in favour of this referendum.

10. **(4) Quebec separating from Canada** (Analysis) Sovereignty-association with a federal government indicates that Quebec would no longer be ruled by the Canadian federal government, but would be independent. Option (1) does not work because the referendum would eliminate federal power in Quebec. Option (2) is not stated. The purpose of the legislature of Quebec would have changed, as stated in option

(3), but the referendum did not directly state how. Option (5) is incorrect as voters did not face an abuse of democratic privileges in this referendum.

11. **(3) Some would welcome the use of a referendum; others would criticize.**
(Application) The passage indicates that referendums can help people to be "drawn together" or can "subvert power," depending on which opinion one holds. The passage states "the will of minority groups is unfairly sacrificed" so option (1) is a possibility. However, it is not the "most likely reaction." Politicians are not indifferent to referendums—though the passage does not mention the reaction of politicians to referendums, which means that option (2) is incorrect. Option (4) is incorrect since the passage does not mention new immigrants, who cannot participate in such a vote anyway. Option (5) is difficult to verify as, depending on the issue, Canadian nationalists may or may not praise the advantages of a national referendum.

12. **(4) an 18-year-old male** (Evaluation) This man would be the one conscripted, thus interest in the referendum would be greatest. A retired butcher, mentioned in option (1) would not be conscripted, thus he or she would not have a personal interest in the result of the referendum. Options (2), (3), and (5) may or may not be directly related to this referendum, depending on the age and gender of the people.

Economics
Lesson 15: General Economic Principles
GED Practice (pages 257–258)

1. **(5) police officer and nurse** (Analysis) The graph shows that the average starting pay for these occupations is $36 000 a year. Option (1) is incorrect because there is a $13 000 difference in the starting pay of teachers ($38 000) and dental hygienists ($25 000). Option (2) is incorrect because there is a $20 000 difference in the starting pay of nurses ($36 000) and sales clerks ($16 000). Option (3) is incorrect because there is a $10 000 difference between a messenger ($16 000) and computer operator ($26 000). Option (4) cannot be determined because neither the passage nor the graph indicates the earnings of doctor's office receptionists.

2. **(5) Nurses require more training than messengers.** (Analysis) Nurses must have specialized and expensive training at a college or university level, lasting from two to four years. The profession of nursing requires a high degree of knowledge and skill in academic subjects, especially the sciences, and technical training on sophisticated medical equipment. Messengers, on the other hand, may pursue their occupation with very little or no specialized training and education. Option (1) is incorrect, since although there are some dangers in nursing, messengers have a high incidence of accidents. If the demand for nurses were less than for messengers they might in fact earn less. Option (3) is an opinion or a matter of preference and would not explain the earnings differential. Option (4) is not an explanation because what sets a job's wages is the demand for people to fill a job compared to the supply of people willing and able to do it, not the number of people in absolute terms. Option (5) does not explain nurses' higher earnings.

3. **(1) The job of police officer is dangerous.** (Application) Supply is the basic principle that applies here. The passage indicates that danger makes certain jobs difficult or undesirable, which limits the supply of available workers, thereby raising pay. When there is a shortage of workers, employers offer higher wages in order to attract more job seekers. Nothing in the passage suggests option (2), which, if true, would cause pay to be lower since the supply of potential officers would be higher than the demand for them. Option (3) is incorrect because some training is required for most jobs, many of which do not pay as well as police officer. Neither the passage nor the graph discusses the effect of gender on salary, so option (4) is incorrect. Option (5) is incorrect because there is no evidence in the passage or chart comparing the salaries and service to society of police officers and doctors.

4. **(4) It was better in the past than it is today.** (Evaluation) The passage indicates that when there was a shortage of lawyers, pay was high, and now that there is a lawyer surplus, wages are subject to the forces of supply and demand. This information supports the idea that starting salaries might have fallen for lawyers. There is not enough information in the passage and graph to support option (1) or (5). The passage indicates that the trend would be the opposite of option (2). Option (3) is true, but it cannot be concluded from the information provided in the passage and graph.

5. **(5) The owners of each get the profits.** (Comprehension) According to the passage, the sole owner gets the profits in a proprietorship, and owners share the profits in a partnership.

There is no support for option (1) or (2). Option (3) is incorrect because management in a partnership is shared. Option (4) is the opposite of what the passage describes.

6. **(3) responsibility for business debt** (Analysis) According to the passage, partners are liable for the company's debts, but the owners of a corporation have no personal liability. Option (1) is incorrect because the passage does not compare the sizes of partnerships and corporations. Option (2) is incorrect because in both cases profits are divided among the owner-investors according to how much of the company they own. Option (4) cannot be determined from the information in the passage. Option (5) is incorrect because both partnerships and corporations can have more than one owner.

7. **(4) They will agree about business decisions.** (Analysis) Because Ann and Dan's business arrangement is a partnership, neither Ann nor Dan can make decisions alone. If they are unable to agree, nothing can get done. Option (1) is incorrect because, unless Ann and Dan agree to another arrangement, profits in a partnership are split according to the percentage of ownership. Option (2) is an opinion, and there is no support for it. Option (3) is incorrect because in a partnership all partners are legally liable for the company's debts. Option (5) would be true only if both partners agreed to it.

8. **(2) People borrow more money.** (Comprehension) The paragraph states that lower interest rates encourage people to borrow more money and spend it. Options (1) and (3) are incorrect because they state the opposite of what would be true in this situation. Nothing in the paragraph suggests option (4) or (5), the opposite of which would likely be true in this situation.

9. **(3) He will have fewer customers.** (Analysis) The paragraph establishes that when unemployment rises, people have less money to spend. It also implies that when people feel financially pinched, they tend to buy fewer nonessentials. This would likely mean fewer meals in restaurants. As the paragraph indicates, option (1) is the opposite of what is generally true when unemployment rises. Nothing in the paragraph suggests a relationship between unemployment rates and interest rates or prices, so options (2) and (4) are incorrect. Option (5) is unlikely when unemployment is rising.

Lesson 16: The Government and the Economy
GED Practice (pages 260–261)

1. **(3) Small businesses can compete.** (Analysis) This is correct because the passage states that socialism allows some competition. The writer assumes that you know that competition is an aspect of capitalism's "free enterprise." Options (1) and (2) are incorrect because they are features of socialism and communism, not of capitalism. Although providing people with everything they need is part of the theory of communism, the passage does not claim that any system—neither capitalism, nor socialism, nor communism—does this, so option (4) is incorrect. Option (5) refers only to capitalism.

2. **(4) They are economic systems.** (Analysis) This is the only thing they have in common. In almost every way, communism and capitalism are vastly different systems. Option (1) applies only to capitalism. Option (2) is true, in theory, only of communist systems, not capitalist systems. Option (3) is true of capitalism but not of communism, which, because it depends heavily on central planning, works best in a dictatorship. Option (5) is true in communist systems but not in capitalist ones.

3. **(1) Individual freedom is associated with capitalism.** (Evaluation) According to the passage, private ownership and economic freedom are the main features of capitalism, so individual freedom must be part of it as well. Option (2) is incorrect because the passage has nothing to say about the success or failure of socialism. Option (3) is not supported by the passage, which says only that, in theory, everyone gets what they need under communism. Option (4) is contradicted by information that capitalism is linked with democracy. Option (5) is incorrect because the last paragraph outlines some links between economic and political systems.

4. **(3) what the reality of communism is** (Evaluation) Information about the reality of communism, which is not given in the passage, is needed to draw a conclusion about how it differs from theory as presented in the passage. So option (1) is incorrect. Option (2) is not enough to allow the contrast between reality and theory. Some details of theory are included in the passage, but the passage does not provide any information about reality, so option (4) is incorrect. Option (5) would not lead to a conclusion about communist theory and practice.

5. **(2) consumer protection** (Application) A warranty protects the buyer in case the product does not work right or something else is wrong with it. Warranties are not related to economic systems, so options (1) and (5) are incorrect. Warranties do not relate to national economics or to market forces, so options (3) and (4) are incorrect.

6. **(5) If consumers didn't have government protections, companies might knowingly sell products that harm people.** (Comprehension) This is implied by the last statement in the first paragraph of the passage. The passage's focus on government consumer protection agencies suggests that the writer disagrees with options (1) and (4). Option (2) is incorrect because neither the passage nor the chart compares the effectiveness of Health Canada to that of Transport Canada in protecting consumers. Option (3) is incorrect because, although toys are mentioned in the chart, nothing in the chart suggests that the writer views toys as the most serious product safety issue.

7. **(3) consumers** (Application) This can be determined by applying the information that grocers figure the anticipated cost of their losses from "bad" food when they set their prices, thus passing the cost of these losses on to the consumer. Nothing in the passage or chart suggests option (1), (4), or (5) is the correct answer. Option (2) is incorrect because of the information in the passage about costs being passed to consumers.

8. **(5) to ensure that Canadian consumers can purchase safe goods and services and be able to deal effectively with problems** (Analysis) Each agency and department listed in the chart sets and enforces quality, safety, and labelling regulations and standards that perform this function for some category of goods or services. Options (1), (3), and (4) are incorrect because they are not common goals of all the agencies and departments. Option (2) is not a function of the agencies and departments listed, so it is incorrect.

Lesson 17: Labour and the Economy
GED Practice (pages 263–264)

1. **(1) when the company being bought does not want to be purchased** (Comprehension) This is implied by the last sentence in the first paragraph. Nothing in the passage or table suggests that option (2), (3), or (4) is necessary to a hostile takeover. Option (5) has nothing to do with whether a takeover is hostile or not.

2. **(3) Consumers will have fewer product choices.** (Analysis) This is because the buyer-company will likely eliminate products of its own, or of its former rival company, that are similar and that used to compete against each other. This will result in fewer product choices. No information suggests that option (1), (4), or (5) would occur. The passage suggests that the opposite of option (2) will be more likely to occur.

3. **(5) only the information in the table** (Evaluation) The merger and acquisition numbers in the table and the trend they establish are all the evidence needed to support the statement that mergers and acquisitions have become facts of Canadian economic life. Options (1) and (2) are incorrect because knowing the names of companies involved in mergers or knowing how many takeovers were hostile isn't necessary to support this conclusion. The conclusion does not mention job loss, so option (3) is incorrect. Option (4) by itself would not provide enough data to support the conclusion. The table is valuable as evidence without it.

4. **(2) the information in paragraph three** (Evaluation) This is the best evidence because it gives statistics of similar past events against which such employees can measure the probability of keeping their jobs. Options (1) and (3) are not as useful because they deal with what might happen and what sometimes happens without hard data to provide a sense of how often these things *do* happen. Option (4) provides hard data, but not the type that gives information about what happens to employees of the companies involved in mergers. Option (5) is incorrect because it does not mention the effect of mergers on workers.

5. **(5) more about what becomes of teenagers who drop out of school** (Evaluation) The statistic that 16 percent of teenage dropouts are unemployed indicates a problem but does not support the judgment that it is a cause for alarm. Data comparing the current dropout rate to the past rates, tying dropout rates to crime rates, or more nonstatistical information about the dropouts' lifestyles, connection to the cycle of poverty, and so on, are needed to assign the problem the status of "alarming." Option (1) provides information that touches on only

one part of the problem—that is, earnings. Option (2) lays out the problem, but does not provide enough specific information to label the problem as alarming. Option (3) also only relates to some teenagers and then to only one aspect of life that could cause financial concern for some teenage dropouts. Option (4) is incorrect since this information touches on only some aspects of possible problems related to the teenage dropout rate.

6. **(3) level of education** (Evaluation) The graph supports this conclusion by showing that the income level rises as the education level rises. No evidence is cited in the passage or graph to support option (1), (2), or (4). Option (5) cannot be concluded because the graph shows that although not graduating limits one's earning potential, people who go beyond high school earn much more money than those who stop their education when they earn their high-school diploma.

7. **(2) more children in poverty** (Analysis) The passage implies that the children of high-school dropouts are less likely to have adequate financial support. The passage implies that option (1) is a cause of the problem, not an effect of it. Nothing in the passage supports option (3) as an effect of teenagers dropping out. The passage indicates that the opposite of options (4) and (5) is true.

8. **(4) Adult education is popular in Canada.** (Evaluation) This can be concluded from the high levels of enrollment the data indicate. The information does not include material on motivations or lifestyles, so options (1) and (5) are incorrect. Option (2) cannot be determined without knowing the population figures for each group. There is no data or other information to support option (3).

GED Review Economics
(pages 265–267)

1. **(4) the GDP adjusted for price increases that are due to inflation** (Comprehension) This definition is given in the final paragraph of the passage. Option (1) is defined in the passage as the actual GDP. Nothing in the passage states or implies option (2), (3), or (5) as a definition of the real GDP.

2. **(3) an ear of corn grown in Manitoba** (Application) The passage defines goods as physical products and states that the GDP is the value of all goods and services produced in Canada during a year. The ear of corn is a

physical object that was produced and is thus a good. It is also a food—one of the things cited as types of goods. Option (1) is a good but, as a used car, it would have been counted in the GDP for the year in which it was produced. Options (2) and (4) are services rather than goods because they are not physical objects. Option (5) would not be included because it was produced in Japan rather than in Canada.

3. **(2) The nation's economy grew steadily.** (Comprehension) This can be seen in the steady rise of the lines for both the actual GDP and the real GDP on the graph. None of the other options, even if they are true, can be inferred from the information on the graph.

4. **(1) If growth continued at the same rate, Canada's GDP would have reached one trillion dollars by 2002.** (Evaluation) This projection can be seen by extending the graph upward along its present course. Options (2) and (3) are incorrect as no GDP figures are shown in the 1980s. Option (4) is not correct as the chart shows the growth of GDP, which is made up of both goods and services. The chart does not differentiate between goods and services. Option (5) is incorrect as unemployment is not represented on the chart.

5. **(3) Ontario** (Comprehension) The table shows that except for 1980, when British Columbia had the lowest level of family poverty, Ontario's percentage of families living in poverty was consistently lower than the rest of Canada. Options (1) and (4), Quebec and the Atlantic provinces, were, overall, the provinces having the highest levels of family poverty in the 15 years recorded. Options (2) and (5), the Prairie provinces and British Columbia, were higher than Ontario, but lower than Quebec and the Atlantic provinces.

6. **(1) All people would spend similar proportions of their income on food and housing.** (Application) These two items are necessities of life on which everyone spends money. If everyone had about the same amount of money, the proportion of their income they would devote to these necessities would be similar. This contrasts with Canada, where people with less money spend a higher proportion of their income on necessities than people with more money do. Options (2) and (5) are not necessities, so there would be more difference in people's spending in these areas, depending on their tastes, preferences, and

values. Options (3) and (4) are incorrect because neither family size nor education level is directly tied to the amount of money that a person has.

7. **(2) Most families in poverty have more children than wealthy families do.** (Analysis) For the mathematical analysis of the percentage of families living in poverty, the family is considered one unit. For the mathematical analysis of the percentage of children living in poverty, each child is considered a unit. If most families in poverty have more than one child, this would explain why the percentage of children in poverty is higher than the percentage of families in poverty. Option (1) would not account for this result because it applies to almost all children regardless of economic level. Options (3) and (4) may be true, but neither explains the difference in poverty rates between children and families. Most children do not work at all, so option (5) cannot be the reason.

8. **(3) Yes, because the passage shows that the distribution of income has become more unequal.** (Evaluation) The passage clearly indicates that family poverty levels continue to rise and that the gap between rich and poor is also widening. Option (1) is incorrect because poverty levels have not actually risen, according to the table. Option (2) is not correct, because the passage does relate rising prices to rising family poverty. Option (4) is incorrect because the table does not show that family poverty levels have declined. Option (5) is incorrect, since the passage indicates that 25 percent of children were poor in 1995 but does not show that poverty rates are rising.

9. **(3) changing** (Comprehension) The pattern is one of change—from much business activity, to little activity, and back to increased business activity. Options (1) and (2) are opinions about the cycle that are not supported by the passage. Option (4) is the opposite of what the passage describes. Nothing in the passage suggests option (5).

10. **(3) trough** (Analysis) The chart suggests that recession and depression are both economic low points that vary in degree of severity. This indicates that they would occur at the bottom of a business cycle. Option (1) is incorrect because neither the chart nor the passage links inflation with depression or recession. Options (2), (4), and (5) relate to prosperous economic periods, the opposite of recession and depression.

11. **(1) inflation** (Application) This is the only option that results in higher prices. Options (2) and (3) are related to economic downturns, in which people have less money, making price increases unlikely. Options (4) and (5) do not correlate definitively to what happens to prices of particular goods.

12. **(5) It is not seriously affected by minor variations in the pattern.** (Analysis) The passage indicates that the business cycle—and with it, the Canadian economy—continues in its overall pattern despite frequent upswings and downswings. There is no discussion in the passage of the current state of the economy or the effect inflation has on it, so options (1) and (2) are incorrect. Option (3) is an opinion. Nothing in the paragraph suggests option (4), the opposite of which would likely be true in this situation.

Geography
Lesson 18: Places and Regions
GED Practice (pages 269–271)

1. **(3) The Transantarctic Mountains divide it into eastern and western regions.** (Comprehension) The map shows that these mountains form the border between the two regions, which are identified on the map. Nothing on the map suggests option (1), which is incorrect. Options (2) and (4) are contradicted by the map. Option (5) is incorrect because the map shows that the South Pole is not located in one of Antarctica's mountainous areas.

2. **(5) Places with little precipitation are deserts.** (Comprehension) The passage implies that Antarctica is a desert because very little precipitation falls there each year. This suggests that a low level of precipitation is the defining characteristic of a desert. Nothing in the passage suggests that option (1), (3), or (4) is true. Option (2) is incorrect, because it is contradicted by the passage; precipitation level, not temperature, defines a desert.

3. **(4) The interior has no good food source.** (Analysis) The passage states that only a few plants exist in Antarctica, and only a few insects live beyond the edges of the continent, so large animals would not have a source of food. Large animals are able to survive in other cold polar regions and in rugged mountains, so options (1) and (2) are incorrect. Option (3) does not explain why large animals don't live inland, since the passage states and the map shows that most of the continent is covered with a thick layer of ice. There is no information to support option (5).

4. **(1) curiosity—to learn more about the continent** (Evaluation) The map provides the information that the settlements in Antarctica are research stations. This indicates that the nations that sponsor them want to learn more about the continent. Option (2) might be a motive for individuals to live in Antarctica but not for a nation to set up research stations there. Option (3) is incorrect because, as the passage indicates, there never were permanent settlers in Antarctica. Option (4) is incorrect because Antarctica's animals are not endangered and nothing in the passage or map indicates that they are. Option (5) is incorrect because the settlements are research stations, not industrial sites, which would be difficult to operate in the extremely cold environment.

5. **(2) Nova Scotia and PEI** (Comprehension) This response shows that these two provinces are very small in land area and are almost completely in the "moderately populated" zone. Option (1), British Columbia and Yukon, and option (5), Alberta and Saskatchewan, have a variety of moderate, sparse, and isolated settlements over large areas of land. Option (3), Ontario and Quebec, has a combination of dense, moderate, and sparse populations, but they are also spread over considerably large areas of land. Option (4), the Northwest Territories and Nunavut, show isolated settlements almost exclusively.

6. **(1) Most Canadians live near the American border.** (Comprehension) The more densely populated areas are shown in the darkest blue and are the most southerly regions in Canada. Options (2) and (4) are not shown on the map because the information provided shows density, not exact numbers. In option (3), a statement using "more" indicates a comparison, which is not being explained with the information on this map. The United States immigration patterns are now shown, so (5) is incorrect.

7. **(5) Major cities are located in these areas.** (Analysis) The response that best relates to this map is option (5) because all Canada's major cities are located in the densely or moderately populated zones. Cities are obviously more densely populated than rural areas. Option(1) is incorrect because tourists are not included in population counts. Option (2) is not reinforced by the map because, although major lakes may draw people to live near them, there are just as many lakes in the lesser populated areas as in the heavily populated areas. Option (3) highlights

soil fertility, which is a good thing for farming but not a necessity for population density. Option (4) does not work because, although climates in these areas are often warmer than their more northerly counterparts, some of the cities (Toronto, Regina, Montreal, etc.) are still cold in winter.

8. **(3) Ontario** (Application) Based on the map, Ontario has the largest section of dense population, indicating that it has more cities and people to support restaurants than option (1), Yukon, which has isolated settlements; option (2), Newfoundland and Labrador, which is moderately and sparely populated; Manitoba (4), which is moderately and sparely populated with isolated settlements; and option (5), Nunavut, which has only isolated settlements.

9. **(2) Geographic latitude and oceans affect climate.** (Comprehension) The passage covers two major factors in climate: latitude and ocean currents. Option (1), on the unpredictability of weather and climate, is not mentioned in the passage. Option (3) may be true but is not mentioned in the passage. Option (4) is correct but does not provide a complete summary of the passage. Though true, Option (5) does not reflect the main ideas in the passage.

10. **(5) Much of Canada's climate is either Subarctic or Arctic.** (Comprehension) The map shows that the majority of Canada's area is in these two zones. Option (1) cannot be seen on the map, as there are no descriptions of what the climate zones mean. No population is shown on this map, making option (2) incorrect. Option (3) cannot be ascertained as the Canadian lakes shown on this map are in three different climate zones. Option (4) cannot be assumed by this map because, again, details of what the climate zones mean are not given.

11. **(3) Winters would be colder and summers warmer.** (Application) As indicated in the passage, the oceans have a moderating effect on the climates of their regions. Thus, if Canada were bordered on the east and west by land, their climates would be more like that of the interior of the country. Option(1) is incorrect because, if Canada changed as stated, the seasonal temperatures would become more extreme and less consistent. Option (2) is incorrect because it is the opposite of what now happens in the interior of the country. Option (4) has no bearing on the information in the passage. Option (5) is incorrect because there would be a significant change if the oceans were not there.

12. **(4) roads** (Application) Physical maps are maps that show landforms and other features of physical geography. This is the only option that is human made. Options (1) and (2) are landforms. Options (3) and (5) are types of physical regions.

Lesson 19: Resources Affect Where People Live
GED Practice (pages 273–274)

1. **(4) The flooding allowed farmers to produce more crops.** (Analysis) This effect is suggested by the last sentence in the second paragraph. Nothing in the passage suggests that option (1) or (3) resulted from the flooding. Options (2) and (5) are contradicted by the passage.

2. **(5) Farmers along the Nile have had to enrich their soil with expensive chemical fertilizers.** (Evaluation) This detail provides an example of how changing the Nile by damming it has affected some people. Options (1), (2), and (3) state ways a river can change but they provide no information about how such changes affect people. Option (4) describes the river and the way people lived before the change. It does not support the conclusion that changes in the river changed people's lives.

3. **(2) Rivers are economically important.** (Evaluation) Farmers, fishers, and other Egyptians depend on the Nile for electricity and their livelihoods. There is no evidence in the passage that supports options (1) and (3). Option (4) cannot be determined from the passage. Option (5) is contradicted by the passage.

4. **(3) Changes in Earth are caused by nature and by people.** (Comprehension) This is the general idea of the paragraph. Options (1), (2), and (5) are details that support the main idea. Option (4) is incorrect because it is not stated in the paragraph and it is not true.

5. **(2) Therefore, small industries (such as sawmills) blossomed in towns and cities in close proximity to a lake or river.** (Comprehension) This response is the correct one because one can see that many of the settlements in Ontario are located close to water. Option (1), though factual, is not the main idea of either the map or the passage. Option (3), though stated in the passage, is not shown on the map. Option(4) is factual but only partly restates information on the map. Option (5) is only partly correct because the map shows more than just the "Golden Horseshoe" trend.

6. **(3) Access to water was a critical aspect of the development of industry and urbanization in southern Ontario.** (Comprehension) The area known as the "Golden Horseshoe" was important because industries relied on the availability of water for power and transportation. Without it, the development of industry and, in turn, urbanization would not have occurred here. Option(1) is incorrect because the soil of the area is not mentioned. Option (2) is not implied by the passage because it is actually stated that one of the reasons for the growth of the area is people moving to look for work. Option (4) is incorrect because pollution is not mentioned. Option (5) is not correct because the actual economics of Ontario is not discussed.

7. **(5) Water resources created most of the major cities in southern Ontario.** (Analysis) As stated in the passage, water was central to the development of industry in southern Ontario. Option(1) is not a conclusion because, though automobile manufacturing is mentioned in the passage, it is not the sole industry. Option (2) is not correct because, although Toronto is the largest city in the province, it is not the focus of the passage. Option (3) is incorrect because it does not thoroughly summarize the passage: water did more than just "help"; it was essential to Ontario's manufacturing industry. Option (4) is not an accurate conclusion because, though people did and still do migrate to cities for employment, the passage is not mainly about this migration.

Lesson 20: How People Change the Environment
GED Practice (pages 276–277)

1. **(4) A fisherman has caught a fish that has eaten people's trash.** (Comprehension) This description covers the important point of the cartoon. Options (1) and (2) are not supported by the cartoon. Option (3) does not describe the main action shown in the cartoon. Option (5) is incorrect because fish are not used to clean up the oceans.

2. **(2) The world's oceans are polluted.** (Analysis) The cartoonist portrays the fish spitting out a big pile of trash, which the fish presumably ate off the ocean floor. There is no evidence in the cartoon to support the opinions expressed in option (1), (3), (4), or (5).

3. (3) It is all right to litter if people cannot see it. (Evaluation) This is a common attitude among people who toss empty bottles, cans, and other trash into the water, and trash in the water is the subject of this cartoon. Options (1), (4), and (5) are also values that some people hold, but none of them is suggested by the cartoon. There is also nothing in the cartoon to suggest option (2).

4. (5) Pollution affects the ocean's animals. (Evaluation) The cartoon shows that fish are affected by people dumping garbage in the ocean. Nothing in the cartoon suggests option (1) or (2). The cartoon is not critical of fishing methods or of fishing itself, so options (3) and (4) are incorrect.

5. (3) a window (Application) Like windows, communications satellites allow things going on in one place to be seen and heard in another. Option (1) is incorrect because it is a barrier like an ocean or desert that blocks communication and movement from one place to another. Options (2), (3), and (4) are incorrect because these structures generally block rather than facilitate communication and movement between people in different parts of a building.

6. (3) trap the sand (Comprehension) The diagram shows that jetties trap sand that the waves that form the longshore current would otherwise carry away. Option (1) is incorrect because it describes the effect of a breakwater, as shown by the waves being turned back from the shore. Option (2) is incorrect because the diagram shows that the jetties change the angle of incoming waves not stop them. Option (4) is incorrect because, as the passage indicates, longshore currents are caused by the waves that hit the shore at an angle, not by jetties. Option (5) is incorrect because, according to the passage, sandbars are created by waves that strike land directly, which is unrelated to the action of a jetty.

7. (1) Protecting property is important. (Evaluation) The passage makes it clear that the primary reason for preventing beach erosion is to protect homes, businesses, and other development along coastlines. This development and the efforts to protect it makes option (2) incorrect. The construction of the devices contradicts option (3). Option (4) is incorrect because the devices change the coastline and can be considered eyesores. Nothing in the passage suggests that option (5) is a value related to the construction of these devices.

8. (4) a guardrail along a highway (Application) Both are protective devices that redirect the energy of incoming substances or objects. The diagram shows that a breakwater stops the waves that are coming toward the beach and redirects them back out to sea. A highway guardrail prevents vehicles from going off the road by changing their direction when they hit it. Options (1) and (2) are incorrect because they are not protective devices but transportation devices solely intended to move something from one place to another. Option (3) is not a protective device. Option (5) is a protective device but it does not accomplish its mission by redirecting energy as do a breakwater and a highway guardrail.

9. (5) Breakwaters and jetties accelerate erosion. (Analysis) The phrase "some experts believe" in the passage indicates that this information is an opinion. In addition, the other information suggests that breakwaters and jetties have the opposite effect. The passage and diagrams establish that options (1), (2), (3), and (4) are facts rather than opinions.

GED Review Geography
(pages 278–280)

1. (3) Water pollution is a widespread problem. (Comprehension) This expresses the main idea of the passage. Options (1) and (2) are details, not the main idea. Option (4) is not suggested in the passage. Option (5) is an opinion related to a specific circumstance and not the main idea of the passage.

2. (4) People who get their drinking water from wells should have it periodically tested. (Evaluation) The passage states that harmful chemicals can get into groundwater and then into well water, which can be hazardous to human health if the water is consumed. Option (1) is contradicted by information in the first paragraph of the passage. Options (2) and (3) are incorrect because the passage makes no judgment about which water source is more polluted. Option (5) cannot be concluded because the passage states that the effects of lead poisoning occur over time and that only some older homes present potential lead-poisoning problems.

3. (1) their health (Evaluation) The passage indicates that the motive behind drinking bottled water is to avoid polluted drinking water, which may contain substances harmful to human health. Nothing in the passage suggests that option (2) is correct. Although lead pipes in

Unit 3

old houses are mentioned as a source of pollution of household drinking water, option (3) is incorrect because the passage indicates that many people decide to drink bottled water because of concerns about the groundwater. So concern about lead from pipes in old homes is not the only reason to drink bottled water. Options (4) and (5) are incorrect because drinking bottled water does not conserve water resources or help to clean up the environment.

4. **(5) Yes, because seepage from rainwater could carry these chemicals into the groundwater.** (Analysis) This cause-and-effect relationship can be inferred from the discussion of groundwater and its sources. The information given in options (1), (3), and (4) may be true, but this information has nothing to do with whether or not buried chemicals are a source of water pollution. Option (2) contradicts the passage.

5. **(4) the west coast of the United States** (Comprehension) This is the only other area indicated by the map legend as a winter home for the butterflies. The map shows that option (1) is part of their warm-weather range. The map does not indicate that option (2) or (3) has anything to do with the monarchs. Option (5) is the first land reached by monarchs crossing the Gulf of Mexico, but the map does not indicate that they stay there.

6. **(5) A monarch has orange-and-black wings.** (Analysis) This knowledge is necessary to understand the writer's reference to an orange-and-black sky. The butterflies' relation to birds provides no useful information, so options (1) and (4) are incorrect. Option (2) is directly stated in the passage. Nothing in the passage suggests that option (3) is true.

7. **(2) a wildlife refuge** (Application) This is land set aside by government to protect plants and animals, as Mexico's preserve is intended to do. Option (1) is incorrect because the monarchs would not be held in captivity. Nothing in the passage suggests any farming on the Mexican preserve, so option (3) is not correct. Although there are tourists in the preserve, nothing in the passage indicates that the preserve was set up to be a resort or that it provides recreational facilities or activities, which eliminates options (4) and (5) as answers.

8. **(1) Logging the forest threatens the well-being of the monarchs.** (Analysis) The passage indicates that the monarchs stay on the trunks and branches of trees. Cutting down trees in their forest would harm them by destroying their habitat. Option (2) is incorrect because the passage gives no evidence the Mexican government created the monarch preserve at the request of the tourists. The passage implies that the government created the preserve to stop the logging, so option (3) is incorrect. Nothing in the passage implies that option (4) is true. Option (5) is contradicted by the information the passage presents about the continued logging of the preserve.

9. **(5) Most Canadians live in urban areas, which are part of the environment.** (Comprehension) The paragraph discusses cities as being part of the environment and indicates that most Canadians live in urban areas. Option (1) is incorrect because it is a detail that supports the main idea of the paragraph. Option (2) is incorrect because the passage does not compare the number of people who live in suburbs with the number who live in cities. Option (3) is incorrect because the paragraph does not compare the amount of space taken up by cities and by farms, only the relative populations of urban and rural areas. Option (4) is incorrect because the passage indicates that all land is part of the environment, not only urban and suburban land.

10. **(3) The problems that cities face result from many people being concentrated in a small area.** (Analysis) This conclusion is given in paragraph 2. Options (1), (2), and (4) are details that support this conclusion. Option (5) is a detail that is related to but does not directly support the conclusion.

11. **(2) too many people** (Analysis) If a city has too many people for the amount of water that is available, a water supply problem results. Options (1) and (3) could result in water supply problems, but they do not occur in all cities and thus are not the general cause of such problems. Options (4) and (5) could be problems in some cities and at certain times, but they would not have a negative effect on the supply of water.

12. **(3) Urban growth has not been well planned.** (Analysis) Despite the urban problems cited in the passage, the quality of the nation's preparations for urban growth is the author's opinion, with which some experts might disagree. Options (1) and (2) are established facts stated in the passage. Option (4) is a fact that can be confirmed by noting legislation and urban

programs some politicians have worked to put in place. Option (5) is a fact that can be demonstrated by confirming the existence of such laws.

13. **(3) As Canadians have become more aware of urban problems, government has come under more pressure to improve cities.** (Analysis) The passage suggests that as more voters have come to live in cities and have become aware of urban problems, elected officials have grown more sensitive to those concerns and more willing to do something about them. Although the passage states that the amount of land occupied by cities is small, nothing suggests that option (1) is correct. No information supports option (2) or (5). Nothing in the passage suggests that city dwellers are unhappy, so option (4) is also incorrect.

14. **(1) The oil spill was an environmental disaster.** (Evaluation) The information that it was the worst oil spill in North America and the statistics indicating its size and consequences support this conclusion. Option (2) cannot be supported on the basis of this single incident alone. Not enough details are provided to prove that option (3) or (4) is true. Nothing in the paragraph supports option (5) as a conclusion.

GED Unit Review Social Studies
(pages 281–287)

1. **(1) a gradual rise in the sea level** (Analysis) Slow warming will gradually melt the polar ice, thereby gradually raising the sea level. Option (2) is incorrect because slow warming will not produce a sudden increase in sea level. Options (3) and (5) are the opposite of the likely result. Option (4) is not an effect of global warming or the level of the sea.

2. **(3) North America and Africa** (Analysis) The map shows that both these continents are threatened by flooding at numerous sites along most of their coastlines. Options (1), (2), (4), and (5) are incorrect because the coastlines of South America and Australia have fewer affected areas, and the threat of coastal flooding is concentrated on only one side of each continent.

3. **(2) coastal cities** (Application) As the map shows, many areas along the coastlines all over the world are likely to be flooded when the sea level rises. Options (1) and (3) are incorrect because the map shows that fewer places are threatened in Europe and Australia than on other continents. Option (4) is incorrect because the west coast of South America does not have any

areas that are likely to be affected. Option (5) is incorrect because seas will rise all over the world, and although people who live in some places along the Arctic coast near the North Pole will be affected, they will not be affected any more than people along the coasts of other oceans.

4. **(4) Trade increased in anticipation of the introduction of NAFTA.** (Analysis) The passage describes the introduction of NAFTA and its primary intention to remove tariffs and, by so doing, to increase trade generally. It is logical to assume that exporters in the countries that signed the agreement would begin to increase their trade in anticipation of the agreement. Options (1) and (2) are tourism-related and not about the trade in products. Option (3) is incorrect, since trade does not increase from a previous period without a reason. Option (5) is incorrect, since an increase in the value of the Canadian dollar would tend to have the opposite effect, that is, to decrease trade.

5. **(4) Canadian exports to the United States sharply increased in the first year under NAFTA.** (Evaluation) The bar graph shows an approximate 20 percent increase of trade between the two countries, far greater than previous changes indicated in the graph. Options (1), (2), and (3) are incorrect, as they are not supported by information in the passage or in the bar graph. Option (5) is incorrect because specific products are not mentioned.

6. **(3) U.S. exports to Canada and imports from Canada have both increased.** (Application) The graph shows that overall Canadian trade with the United States—imports as well as exports—has increased since 1994, when NAFTA began to remove trade barriers between the two countries. Nothing in the graph or paragraph suggests that the direction of change of imports and exports differs, so options (1) and (2) are incorrect. The graph information suggests that the opposite of option (4) would likely be true of U.S. trade with Canada. There is no support for option (5) in either the paragraph or the graph.

7. **(4) a limited war in Korea to drive communist invaders of South Korea back into North Korea** (Application) The United States and its allies were content to keep communism contained in North Korea rather than attempting to overthrow it there. Options (1), (2), and (3) do not illustrate the element of containment. Option (5) illustrates the spread of communism, not the containment of it.

8. **(2) The French president appeared to support the separatist movement in Quebec.** (Analysis) By calling for a free Quebec, de Gaulle implied that the province and its French-speaking majority were somehow not free; in so doing he was expressing a view held by separatists in Quebec. Option (1) is not supported in the passage. Option (3) did not happen, so it is incorrect. There is no mention in the passage of option (4). Although there are elements of the continental French culture in Quebec culture, its history and heritage are firmly North American, so option (5) is incorrect.

9. **(4) Many Canadians had died to help liberate France.** (Comprehension) Pearson reminded the French president that during World War II, thousands of Canadians had died in the struggle to liberate France from the Nazis. The excerpt of Lester B. Pearson's telegram does not mention option (1). There is no support for option (2), which is not correct. Quebec had the same freedoms as all other Canadian provinces, so option (3) is incorrect. The passage does not mention the opinion suggested by option (5).

10. **(3) Canada's multicultural society** (Application) Since World War II, the ethnic makeup of Canadian society has changed greatly, and now represents more than a hundred national origins, with dozens of religious traditions and different ethnicities from around the globe. None of options (1), (2), or (4) is suggested by the description in the passage, since the speaker was referring to the people of the proposed new Confederation rather than economic or political systems or technology. The rainbow is not a part of the British heritage already present in many of Canada's symbols, so option (5) is not likely.

11. **(5) Voters elected twice the number of women to Parliament than in the previous election.** (Comprehension) From observing the graph, it is obvious that in 1993 there were 53 women elected, in contrast to only 27 in 1984 (almost double the number). Option (1) is incorrect as there is no mention of the numbers of women who ran as candidates. Option (2) is incorrect as the passage and the graph do not speak of discrimination. Option (3) is correct but is not the <u>best</u> answer. Option (4) is misleading because Campbell was not elected while running for prime minister; she replaced Mulroney, who resigned.

12. **(5) Over time, women have gained more power in federal politics.** (Analysis) The graph and the passage support this claim as there has been a steady increase in the number of women elected to the House of Commons, as well as an increase in those serving other positions (Speaker of the House, governor general, and prime minister). Options (1) and (3) are the opposite of what is indicated by the information given. Option (2) is not mentioned in the information that is given. Option (4) shows an opinion that does not conclude the passage or the bar graph.

13. **(4) Women should not run in federal elections.** (Evaluation) Before 1921, women's roles were considerably different from what they are now. Most often women worked in the home and were not actively involved in the political arena. Option (1), the media, is not mentioned, but it is unlikely that something as unusual as a woman running for office would have been ignored by the media. Options (2), (3), and (5) are likely the opposite of what occurred, as the cultural perspective of the time did not allow women to participate in these sorts of "public" activities.

14. **(4) the *Canadian Charter of Rights and Freedoms*.** (Application) The United Nations declaration was, in fact, a model for the *Canadian Charter of Human Rights and Freedoms*. There is no support in the passage for any of options (1), (2), and (5).

15. **(3) He has worked as a bookkeeper.** (Application) Of his qualifications, this experience is the most directly related to what the employer is looking for in the person to be hired. Option (1) is incorrect because the advertisement does not mention the need to speak a second language. Options (2) and (4) have nothing to do with the job requirements. Although a high-school diploma is required, the advertisement says nothing about grades, so option (5) is incorrect.

16. **(4) A person without payroll experience probably won't be hired.** (Analysis) The word *probably* marks this as an opinion. Also, the advertisement indicates that payroll experience is helpful, but not required. Options (1), (2), (3), and (5) are facts that can be verified by reading the ad.

17. **(2) There are regionalized tensions in Canada.** (Comprehension) Not only is Canada upset, but each area of the country also shows a different degree of tension. Option (1) is not information provided by the map. Option (3) is incorrect because the cartoon does not indicate that anyone wants to separate from Canada. Option (4) states a fact but the cartoon does not show it. Option (5) closely relates to the theme of the cartoon, though the separations between the regions further indicates that response (2) is the better of the two correct responses.

18. **(1) The price of a taxi ride is high.** (Comprehension) The taxi company is a monopoly, a business with no competition and therefore with complete control over the selling of its service. Since there is no transportation alternative to take away business by offering lower prices and/or better service, ABC can keep its prices high. Options (2) and (3) are incorrect because there is no incentive for the company to provide low prices or good service when there is no competition. Options (4) and (5) are very unlikely given the monopoly that ABC enjoys.

19. **(4) the Canadian North** (Comprehension) As indicated on the chart, the Canadian North accounts for only 0.01 percent of the representation in the House of Commons. Options (1), (2), (3), and (5) each show between 11 percent and 35 percent representation.

20. **(2) They contrast early handwork with later mechanized production.** (Evaluation) The illustrations depict the increase in productivity between handcrafted shoe production and mechanized work. Option (1) is incorrect because the illustrations do not reveal anything about workers' craft unions. Option (3) is not correct because any differences in quality of the product cannot be deduced from the illustrations. Although industrial production may have been less interesting work than farming, the illustrations do not support that opinion, so option (4) is incorrect. Option (5) is an opinion and does not answer the question.

21. **(4) The rate of unemployment among women declined overall between 1984 and 1996.** (Analysis) This is clearly shown on the graph, which indicates a general decline from 8 percent to 5.5 percent. Option (1) is incorrect; the lowest rate was in 1990. Option (2) is not correct, since the decline was not steady—an increase occurred between 1990 and 1992. Option (3) is incorrect, since the rate *is* the same but is actually 7 percent. The employment rate among women has declined, so option (5) is incorrect.

22. **(3) Discrimination against non-Europeans was acceptable.** No Chinese workers were invited to the important occasion shown in the photograph. The passage makes clear that Chinese labourers were systematically discriminated against in wages and assigned highly dangerous work. Moreover, the company and the government reneged on their promise of passage back to China. There is no support in the passage for option (1) or (2). The passage does not mention option (4), and option (5) is not supported in the paragraph.

UNIT 4: SCIENCE

Life Science
Lesson 1: Cell Structures and Functions
GED Practice (pages 291–293)

1. **(3) The Process of Mitosis** (Comprehension) This title describes the main topic of the passage. Options (1), (2), and (4) are incorrect because they focus on details relating to interphase or mitosis. Option (5) is incorrect because the passage does not explain why cell division is important.

2. **(1) The nuclear membrane dissolves during prophase.** (Evaluation) Option (1) is correct because the second frame of the diagram shows the nuclear membrane disappearing during prophase. Option (2) is incorrect because the diagram does not show the spindle fibres as they form during prophase. Option (3) is incorrect because the diagram does not indicate what happens if spindle fibres are cut. Option (4) is incorrect, because the diagram does not indicate anything about the protein content of the cell. Option (5) is incorrect because the diagram does not indicate the duration of each phase.

3. **(3) 6** (Comprehension) According to the passage, each daughter cell will have the same number of chromosomes as the parent cell after cell division. So if the parent cell has 6 chromosomes at the beginning of interphase (before cell division begins to take place), each daughter cell it eventually produces will also have 6 chromosomes.

4. **(4) Cell biologists have succeeded in growing blood vessels from living cells.** (Comprehension) The passage and diagram describe growing blood vessels using other types of cells. Option (1) is incorrect because it is too general. Option (2) is not true. Option (3) is not mentioned in the passage or diagrams, and whether true or not, it is only a detail. Option (5) also is only a detail.

5. **(2) Scientists may someday be able to form replacement body parts from living cells.** (Analysis) Scientists are pursuing research of this type because they may someday be able to use the blood vessels to repair damage to the human circulatory system. Option (1) is incorrect because if artificial parts were superior, people would not bother to try to make parts from living cells. Option (3) is incorrect because it is only recently that scientists have succeeded in doing this. Option (4) is incorrect because the diagram gives the amount of time for blood vessel formation (eight weeks) without making a judgment about this length of time. Option (5) is incorrect because it is a fact stated in the diagram.

6. **(3) to provide a physical support for the growing nerve cells** (Application) The plastic would be likely to serve the same purpose in growing nerve cells as it does in growing blood vessels. Option (1) is incorrect because the plastic is placed between the cut nerves. Option (2) is incorrect because the plastic cannot provide living nerve cells. Option (4) is incorrect because the plastic does not function to take away wastes. Option (5) is incorrect because no muscle cells are present with the nerve cells and the plastic does not cause the nerve cells to grow.

7. **(1) Plant Cell Structures and Their Functions** (Comprehension) The diagram shows the structures of a plant cell, and the passage describes their functions. Option (2) is incorrect because the diagram and passage do not cover cellular reproduction. Option (3) is incorrect because the passage does not mention similarities between plant and animal cells. Option (4) is incorrect because it is a detail, not the main idea, of the passage and diagram. Option (5) is incorrect because only plant cells, not parts of plants, are discussed and shown.

8. **(4) chromoplasts** (Application) Chromoplasts contain yellow, orange, and red pigments that give daffodil and rose petals their colour. Options (1), (2), (3), and (5) are incorrect because they are structures not involved with colour in plants.

9. **(2) The vacuoles shrank as their water was used up.** (Analysis) Vacuoles help support the plant when they are full of water, so when they empty out, that support decreases and the plants wilt. Options (1), (3), (4), and (5) are incorrect because they are consequences that do not involve water.

Lesson 2: Cells and Energy
GED Practice (pages 295–296)

1. **(4) mitochondrion** (Comprehension) According to the passage, the bulk of the energy is released in the mitochondrion, not in the other cell structures listed in options (1), (2), (3), and (5).

2. **(5) Glucose and oxygen combine to yield carbon dioxide, water, and energy.** (Comprehension) Option (5) correctly restates

the chemical formula for cellular respiration.
Option (1) is incorrect because it is a restatement
of the chemical formula for photosynthesis.
Option (2) is incorrect because water and oxygen
have been reversed as an ingredient and a
product of respiration. Option (3) is incorrect
because carbon dioxide is a product and oxygen
is an ingredient of respiration. Option (4) is
incorrect because energy is released as a product,
not absorbed as an ingredient, of respiration.

3. **(1) Less energy is released.** (Analysis) Both
the diagram and the passage show that oxygen is
one of the ingredients for cellular respiration;
when the supply of oxygen is reduced, cellular
respiration slows, and less energy will be released.
Option (2) is incorrect because it is the opposite
of what would happen. Option (3) is incorrect
because with less oxygen, respiration slows
down. Option (4) is incorrect because less cellular
respiration means less, not more, of its product,
carbon dioxide, is released. Option (5) is
incorrect because the supply of oxygen does
affect cellular respiration.

4. **(2) More green plants means more oxygen
in the air.** (Evaluation) Since oxygen is a
product of photosynthesis, more green plants
means more oxygen released into the
atmosphere. Option (1) is incorrect because it
is the opposite of what is true. Option (3) is
incorrect because with less photosynthesis taking
place, carbon dioxide in the air would increase,
not decrease. Fewer green plants making glucose
means less glucose is produced, and so less
energy is stored in glucose, not more, as stated
in option (4). Option (5) may or may not be true,
but the passage does not provide enough
information to support it.

5. **(2) the sum of all the chemical processes
carried out by a cell** (Comprehension) As
defined in the first sentence of the passage,
metabolism is the total of all chemical reactions
in a cell. Option (1) is the definition of
photosynthesis, not of metabolism. Option (3)
is the definition of cellular respiration, not of
metabolism. Option (4) is incorrect because it
is only a partial definition of metabolism.
Option (5) is incorrect because metabolism is
related to cell processes, not to the amount of
raw material.

6. **(5) sunburst** (Comprehension) The arrows,
option (1), represents processes. Option (2), the
circles, represents amino acids. Option (3), the
chained circles, represents protein chains.
Option (4), the hexagons, represents glucose.

7. **(4) There are fewer catabolic reactions.**
(Analysis) Since glucose is a raw material of the
catabolic reactions, less glucose means less
catabolism. Option (1) is incorrect because light
energy is not affected by the amount of glucose
entering a cell. Option (2) is incorrect because
the amount of glucose entering a cell would not
affect the amount of amino acids that enter.
Option (3) is incorrect because less glucose would
mean less energy to make proteins. Option (5)
is incorrect because the cell would produce less
(not more) energy with less glucose.

8. **(2) increased catabolic reactions**
(Application) More exercise means more energy
will be needed, and catabolism will increase.
Options (1) and (4) are incorrect because
photosynthesis takes place only in green plants,
not in the human body. Option (3) is incorrect
because increased use of energy would not
necessarily affect the rate of anabolism.
Option (5) is the opposite of what would
have happened.

Lesson 3: Genetics
GED Practice (pages 298–299)

1. **(1) controlling the production of proteins
in the cell** (Comprehension) According to the
passage, this is a function of DNA. Options (2)
and (3) are incorrect because different cell
structures perform these functions. Option (4)
is not a function of DNA but of other chemicals
in the cell. Option (5) does not state the pairs
correctly.

2. **(4) TACAGTCG** (Comprehension) Since A
always pairs with T and G always pairs with C,
the match for ATGTCAGC is TACAGTCG. The
other options include incorrect pairing sequences.

3. **(5) The sidepieces of DNA are formed of
alternating units of sugar and phosphate.**
(Evaluation) The diagram shows option (5) to
be correct. Option (1) is incorrect because, as
the diagram shows, the crosspieces are made
of nitrogen bases. Option (2) is incorrect because
sidepieces of DNA contain both sugars and
phosphates. Option (3) is incorrect because
thymine is always paired with adenine.
Option (4) is incorrect because the diagram
shows all four of the nucleotide bases attaching
to the two sidepieces.

4. **(2) 1** (Comprehension) All the people
represented in the Punnett square have cleft
chins, because each has at least one copy of the
dominant gene. Because of this, the other
options are incorrect.

5. **(1) the phenotype of her chin** (Evaluation) All you can tell with any accuracy is the girl's appearance, or phenotype. Options (2) and (3) are incorrect because you can't tell whether the girl has a recessive gene or not simply by looking at her. Options (4) and (5) are incorrect because you cannot tell by looking at the girl whether one or both parents have a cleft chin, and if only one parent has a cleft chin, which one it is.

6. **(5) 4 out of 4** (Analysis) According to the information, the red plant has the genotype RR and the white plant has the genotype rr. So all the offspring would inherit the genotype Rr, which results in pink flowers. The Punnett square, below, shows how this works.

	R	R
r	Rr	Rr
r	Rr	Rr

RR = red
rr = white
Rr = pink

Lesson 4: Human Body Systems
GED Practice (pages 301–302)

1. **(1) a woman who lives in a wooded area of the Upper Midwest** (Application) According to the map and passage, people living in the Upper Midwest have a high risk of contracting Lyme disease if they live, work, or play in wooded areas. Option (2) is incorrect because people who live and work in large cities in the Lower Midwest are not likely to come into contact with deer ticks. Option (3) is incorrect because the map shows that the Great Plains is a low-risk area. Option (4) is incorrect because a man who works at sea is not likely to come into contact with deer ticks. Option (5) is incorrect because the vaccine is not approved for use with children.

2. **(5) The vaccine stimulates the immune system to make bacteria-killing antibodies.** (Evaluation) This statement is supported by the description of how the vaccine works. Options (1), (2), (3), and (4) are incorrect because the information in the passage contradicts them.

3. **(1) adrenal** (Analysis) According to the chart, adrenaline secreted by the adrenal glands prepares the body for emergencies. The reactions stated in the question are reactions to emergency situations and are caused by adrenaline. Options (2), (3), (4), and (5) are incorrect because they name other endocrine glands with other functions.

4. **(2) oxytocin** (Comprehension) According to the chart, oxytocin is the hormone that causes uterine contractions during labour, or childbirth. Option (1) is not mentioned in the chart. Options (3) and (4) are sex hormones, produced by the ovaries and the testes, respectively. Option (5) is the hormone secreted in emergencies.

5. **(3) by the blood** (Analysis) The function of the blood is to carry substances throughout the body. Options (1), (2), (4), and (5) are incorrect because they list systems or substances that do not transport hormones throughout the body; they each have other functions.

6. **(3) insulin** (Comprehension) According to the chart, insulin secreted by the pancreas lowers the level of sugar in the blood. Therefore, a high level of sugar may indicate inadequate amounts of the hormone insulin. Options (1), (2), (4), and (5) are incorrect because these hormones do not affect blood-sugar levels.

Lesson 5: The Nervous System and Behaviour
GED Practice (pages 304–305)

1. **(5) Information is also passed by interneurons in the spinal cord.** (Evaluation) According to the diagram, interneurons, as well as sensory and motor neurons, are involved in simple reflexes. Options (1), (2), (3), and (4) are untrue. Simple reflexes involve all three types of neurons and involve the spinal cord, not the brain.

2. **(3) A child learns to say "please" because she then gets what she asked for.** (Application) Saying "please" (a learned behaviour) gets the child what she wants (a reward). Options (1) and (2) are incorrect because the behaviour is followed by something that is not a reward. Option (4) is an example of a simple reflex, not a learned behaviour. Option (5) is an example of learning by observing.

3. **(2) A simple reflex involves the spinal cord, and learned behaviour involves the brain.** (Analysis) A simple reflex is automatically processed in the spinal cord, but learned behaviour is processed in the brain. Option (1) is the opposite of what occurs. Option (3) is incorrect because simple reflexes do not involve the brain. Options (4) and (5) are incorrect because sensory and motor neurons can be involved in both reflexes and learning.

4. **(3) Both the cerebellum and the cerebrum control movement.** (Evaluation) The sentence given in the question stem is an oversimplification, as more than one part of the brain is involved in controlling movement. Options (1), (2), and (4) are not true. Option (5) is true, but it has nothing to do with the function of the cerebellum.

5. **(2) vision** (Analysis) Since the perception of vision is located in the occipital lobe, a blow to the back of the head is likely to affect it. Options (1) and (4) are located at the side of the head. Option (3) is controlled by the brain stem at the base of the brain. Option (5) is controlled in the upper part of the cerebrum.

6. **(2) The Human Brain** (Comprehension) The passage and diagram focus on the structure of the human brain. The passage does not describe the entire nervous system, making options (1) and (5) incorrect. It describes more than just the cerebrum, making option (3) incorrect. It describes the human brain, not brains in general, making option (4) incorrect.

7. **(5) while listening to one person's voice at a crowded party** (Application) In this situation, you are picking out one voice from a babble of voices, an example of selective attention. The other situations involve one main stimulus and thus do not involve picking out one stimulus from many.

Lesson 6: Evolution
GED Practice (pages 307–308)

1. **(1) environmental changes** (Comprehension) According to the passage, environmental changes are a cause of speciation. Option (2) is incorrect because environmental stability would promote species stability. Option (3) is incorrect because the entire species would continue to evolve as a group. Option (4) is incorrect because when a species stops reproducing it dies out. Option (5) is incorrect because a large food supply suggests a stable environment, which is not likely to lead to speciation.

2. **(3) They became less alike.** (Analysis) As the honeycreepers were dispersed into different environments, they adapted differently to fit their different habitats. Options (1) and (4) are not true. Option (2) is incorrect because species cannot reproduce with one another. Option (5) is incorrect because evolutionary change among animals such as birds does not generally happen within such a short period.

3. **(5) It would not be able to eat enough to live.** (Analysis) Since its beak is not suited for catching insects, it is likely the honeycreeper would starve. Options (1) and (2) are incorrect because adaptations are inherited traits that occur from one generation to the next, not in a single individual. Options (3) and (4) are not likely to happen since different species do not usually share their resources.

4. **(2) created more variety** (Comprehension) Speciation leads to more diversity, or variety in plant and animal life. Option (1) is the opposite of what speciation does. Options (3) and (5) are incorrect because speciation increases variety. Option (4) is incorrect because speciation does not affect the rate of formation of new varieties.

5. **(4) fungi** (Comprehension) On the branching tree, animals and fungi originate from one offshoot and are closer to one another than to the other types of organisms. The diagram indicates that the remaining options are organisms more distantly related to animals than fungi.

6. **(1) determining whether two people are related** (Application) Just as comparative DNA sequencing can be used to determine whether two species are related, so too can it be used to determine whether two individuals are related. Note that the word *comparative* in the question is a clue: the answer should refer to a comparison of the DNA of two different individuals or species. Option (2) is incorrect because extracting DNA from fossils is a separate process. Options (3) and (5) are incorrect because comparative gene sequencing does not reveal age. Option (4) is incorrect because the general structure of the DNA molecule was discovered decades ago, in the 1950s, and comparative sequencing could not be done without a previous understanding of DNA's general structure.

7. **(1) DNA sequencing provides evidence for evolutionary relationships, sometimes overturning previously held views.** (Comprehension) This provides an overall summary of the passage and diagram. Options (2), (3), (4), and (5), while true, are details, not important points, of the passage and diagram.

Lesson 7: Energy Flow in Ecosystems
GED Practice (pages 310–311)

1. **(5) the rapid reproduction of rabbits and lack of predators** (Analysis) The rapid reproduction of rabbits unchecked by predators led to the overpopulation of rabbits in Australia. Option (1) is incorrect since it is likely to be a solution to overpopulation. Option (2) is incorrect because continued imports would not, if predators were available, result in overpopulation. Option (3) is a result of overpopulation. Option (4) would result in the opposite of what actually happened.

2. **(3) Prevent the introduction of new organisms.** (Comprehension) According to the passage, preventing the introduction of new species is the best solution. Option (1) is a solution but not the best one. Options (2) and (5) would increase, not solve, the problem. Option (4) is generally not controllable by humans and overall, may have a harmful effect on the ecosystem.

3. **(3) In stable ecosystems, one consumer usually checks another's population growth.** (Evaluation) Application of this principle leads to the conclusion that introducing a predator may control the organism that is overrunning its new environment. Option (1) is true but it does not support the conclusion in the question stem. Option (2) is not true. Option (4) is incorrect because there is nothing to indicate that time will eventually solve the overpopulation problem. Option (5) may end up being true in the long run, but it does not support the conclusion stated in the question stem.

4. **(2) It has food that rabbits eat.** (Analysis) Since rabbits thrived in Australia, you can assume they found plenty to eat. Options (1) and (3) are incorrect because without food, rabbits would have starved. Option (4) is incorrect because if there were many meat-eating animals, it is likely that the rabbits would have been eaten. Option (5) cannot be true, because if the ecosystem were similar to Europe's, the rabbit population would not have gotten out of control.

5. **(1) In many regions, coyotes now have no natural enemies.** (Comprehension) Wolves prey on coyotes, so after wolves were killed off in many areas, the coyotes had no predator. Options (2) through (5) are all true, but they do not explain why the absence of wolves has helped coyotes thrive.

6. **(5) The coyotes' adaptability in feeding and other behaviours has helped them enlarge their range.** (Analysis) This is a conclusion. Options (1), (2), (3), and (4) are details that support the conclusion that coyotes are adaptable in feeding and other behaviours.

7. **(2) Coyotes can live in many types of ecosystems and climates.** (Evaluation) Since their range is so extensive, as indicated by the map and the passage, you can infer that coyotes can adapt to hot, temperate, and cold climates and various types of terrain among various types of animals. Option (1) is incorrect because the map shows that coyotes live in all types of areas. Option (3) is incorrect because it's likely the coyote population is much higher now, since their range is so much bigger. Option (4) is incorrect because the passage states that coyotes are comfortable living among humans. Option (5) is incorrect because the passage states that coyotes spread not from the eastern forests but from the western plains to other areas of the continent.

Lesson 8: Cycles in Ecosystems
GED Practice (page 313)

1. **(2) by comparing the amount of water dripping off redwoods to the amount collected in deforested areas** (Comprehension) To prove that one quantity is greater than another, both must be measured, which is what the scientists did. Option (1) does not yield enough information for comparison. Option (3) is not directly related to measuring the amount of water collected from fog. Option (4) is not directly related to measuring the amount of water collected from fog and also is not something that scientists are likely to be able to do. Option (5) is incorrect because it involves comparing the wrong factors.

2. **(4) using fog collectors in dry coastal regions to collect water** (Application) Like the redwood trees, fog collectors capture water from fog. Options (1), (2), and (5) are incorrect because they involve rainwater, not fog. Option (3) is incorrect because it involves removing a dissolved substance from water.

3. **(3) Water from fog drips down the needles, branches, and trunks of redwoods into the soil.** (Evaluation) The water drips from the tree into the soil, where it is available to other plants and animals of the habitat. Option (1) is incorrect because it does not explain how redwoods contribute water to

Unit 4

their habitats. Option (2) is incorrect because it does not explain how the water gets from the redwoods to the rest of the habitat. Option (4) is incorrect because it restates the conclusion. Option (5) is incorrect because the amount of forested land is not relevant to whether redwoods provide water to the habitats that still exist.

4. **(5) Deforestation contributes to the drying up of local wells and springs.** (Evaluation) Since people often act in their own interests, when their personal water supply is threatened, they are more likely to support redwood conservation measures. Option (1) deals with past practices that cannot be changed and is not, in itself, a motivation for stopping logging. Options (2), (3), and (4) give motivation to log, not to conserve.

GED Review Life Science
(pages 314–315)

1. **(3) Multiple intelligences cannot be measured by standard verbal tests.** (Comprehension) A standard verbal test would measure only linguistic and logical-mathematical ability. Options (1) and (2) are incorrect because both ideas contradict the theory of multiple intelligences. Options (4) and (5) are generalizations that do not follow from the theory of multiple intelligences.

2. **(1) linguistic and logical-mathematical** (Comprehension) Studying this book involves language and reasoning, the abilities involved in linguistic and logical-mathematical intelligence. Options (2), (3), (4), and (5) are incorrect because they do not involve language and reasoning ability.

3. **(2) an elementary-school teacher** (Application) A teacher can use this theory to tailor lessons to the specific abilities of each student. Options (1), (3), (4), and (5) involve work that does not necessarily involve helping other people learn and so would not require a person to use the theory of multiple intelligences. However, a person doing the kind of work listed in each of these options might employ different intelligences on the job.

4. **(1) Specific brain areas specialize in different functions.** (Evaluation) This tends to support the theory of multiple intelligences, because in different people, different areas of the brain might work better. Options (2) and (3) would support the theory that intelligence is a single general ability. Options (4) and (5) do not provide evidence for multiple intelligences.

5. **(4) as biomass** (Comprehension) As stated in the first paragraph of the passage, energy is stored as organic matter, or biomass, in a food chain. Option (1) is incorrect because a trophic level is a concept defined by feeding level, not an energy storage medium. Option (2) is incorrect because sunlight is the source of energy, not a place to store it, for a food chain. Option (3) is incorrect because energy in a food chain is lost, not stored, as heat. Option (5) is only partially correct, since animals are also part of the food chain and they store energy in their tissues.

6. **(3) A food chain can support more primary consumers than secondary consumers.** (Analysis) This is a conclusion supported by the information in the passage and diagram. Options (1), (2), (4), and (5) are all details from the passage and diagram.

7. **(2) The most biomass is at the base of the energy pyramid.** (Evaluation) As indicated in the second paragraph and by the energy pyramid diagram, the section at the base of the pyramid is the largest, representing the amount of biomass at that level. Option (1) is incorrect because the illustration and passage indicate that the higher in an energy pyramid you go, the less biomass there is. Option (3) is incorrect because, according to the illustration, there are more voles than weasels in the energy pyramid. Option (4) is incorrect because, as indicated by the illustration, weasels do not eat tawny owls. Option (5) is incorrect because, according to the passage, the higher you go in the energy pyramid, the less energy is available.

8. **(5) seals** (Application) Since the seals are at the top of the energy pyramid, you would expect to find the fewest seals. Options (1), (2), (3), and (4) are incorrect because, as the question text indicates, they are organisms lower in the energy pyramid.

Earth and Space Science
Lesson 9: The Structures of Earth
GED Practice (pages 317–319)

1. **(2) heat currents in the mantle** (Comprehension) According to the diagram and the passage, heated rock circulates in the mantle, pushing up through the crust and causing the sea floor to spread. Option (1) is incorrect because the diagram shows that the heat currents are in the mantle, not in the crust. Option (3) is incorrect because the aging of the sea floor occurs with the passage of time and is not a cause of sea floor spreading. Options (4) and (5)

result from sea floor spreading, as shown in the diagram or explained in the previous passage.

2. **(2) The farther from the ridge, the older the sea floor.** (Comprehension) New crust formed at the ridge pushes the older sea floor crust outward. It follows that the farther from the ridge, the older the sea floor. Option (1) is incorrect because it is the opposite of what the diagram implies. Options (3) and (4) are incorrect because the diagram does not label a specific ocean and because sea floor spreading occurs in all the oceans. Option (5) is not implied by the diagram and in fact is not true.

3. **(1) It collides with a plate and dips below it.** (Analysis) As shown in the diagram, when the sea floor meets another plate, the sea floor dips beneath this plate, forming a trench. Option (2) is incorrect because if the sea floor were lighter than the continental plates, it would rise above them or push them up from below, but not form a deep trench where it meets them. Option (3) is incorrect because the mantle does not collapse; the material in it circulates due to convection currents. Option (4), earthquake action, is a result, not a cause, of the plate movement, including the sea floor dipping below a continental plate. Option (5) is incorrect because the sea floor is descending, not rising up, at this point.

4. **(3) The Atlantic Ocean will widen.** (Evaluation) Since scientists have estimated the actual rate of spreading, this supports the conclusion that the ocean is getting wider. Options (1) and (2) are incorrect because the depth of the ocean depends on factors other than sea floor spreading. Option (4) is the opposite of what will happen, because spreading implies widening of the ocean. Option (5) is incorrect because the spreading of the sea floor indicates that the width of the ocean is changing.

5. **(4) He did not have a strong explanation for how the continents moved.** (Comprehension) Without a good explanation for what caused the continents to move, Wegener's idea was quite weak, and it was with this that his critics found most fault. Options (1) and (2) were also sources of criticism, but not as important as Wegener's inability to explain how the continents moved. Option (3) is not true—there is evidence that the continents were once joined. Option (5) is incorrect because Pangaea was not imaginary but part of the hypothesis. However, as with options (1) and (2), Wegener's

critics did not debate smaller details of Wegener's theories but whether he could explain what he proposed.

6. **(5) The continents originally formed one large land mass and then moved apart.** (Analysis) This was the conclusion Wegener drew. Options (1), (2), (3), and (4) are all supporting details that he cited to support this conclusion.

7. **(5) the occurrence of earthquakes along plate boundaries** (Application) Because plate boundaries are areas where a lot of geologic activity occurs, it follows that earthquakes would occur along plate boundaries. Options (1), (2), and (4) have nothing to do with plate tectonics. Option (3) is a result of erosion and the deposition of sediment on the ocean floor, not plate tectonics.

8. **(5) South America and Africa would be farther apart.** (Comprehension) The maps show that South America is moving away from Africa, widening the Atlantic. This implies that South America and Africa will continue to move farther apart. Option (1) is incorrect because, since the world has always changed, it is likely that it will continue to change over the next hundred million years. Options (2) and (3) are unlikely to occur, given that the relative areas of the oceans and of the continents have stayed stable over time. Option (4) is the opposite of what the map would show—the map series shows the continents on either side of the Atlantic increasingly drifting apart and thus the ocean is widening.

9. **(2) The animals might have crossed the oceans on driftwood.** (Evaluation) Before the idea of continental drift was widely accepted, this was one of the explanations proposed for the presence of the same fossils on widely separated continents. Option (1) is incorrect because it does not explain why the same fossils are found on both continents. Option (3) is highly unlikely because species of land animals probably could not swim thousands of miles across the ocean and survive. Since fossils are imbedded in rock, option (4) is not likely. Option (5) has nothing to do with fossils.

Lesson 10: The Changing Earth
GED Practice (pages 321–322)

1. **(3) analyzing historical data and measuring seismic activity and movement along faults** (Comprehension) According to the passage, these are the two main methods.

Option (1) is incorrect because climatic data are not relevant to earthquake prediction. Option (2) is a monitoring technique, not a main method of predicting earthquakes. Option (4) is incorrect because although GPS data can be used to infer seismic activity, the GPS satellites actually record location, not seismic activity. Option (5) is incorrect because waiting for a mainshock is not a prediction method.

2. **(4) Local officials practised their emergency responses and so were better prepared for the earthquake.** (Analysis) Even though the prediction was wrong about the timing of the mainshock, it did prompt government officials to run emergency drills. Thus, when the mainshock occurred, they were better prepared to respond. Options (1), (2), and (3) are not mentioned in the passage and also are not true; each method had been used before the Loma Prieta earthquake. Option (5) is an indicator of failure, not success.

3. **(5) reduced loss of life and property damage from future earthquakes** (Evaluation) Government funding is often awarded when there is a possible benefit to society as a result of the research. Options (1), (2), and (3) are scientific or technical benefits, which play a lesser role in decision making about funding research. Option (4) is not a likely result of earthquake research.

4. **(4) A jackhammer breaks apart a roadway surface**. (Application) According to the passage, mechanical weathering involves a physical breaking down of rock. This is the only example of a physical breakdown among the choices. Option (1) is incorrect because weathering involves physical breakdown, not physical movement. Options (2), (3), and (5) are all examples or results of chemical weathering.

5. **(1) Acid rain wears away marble.** (Application) According to the passage, chemical weathering involves changes in the weathered substance through reaction with substances in the environment. Options (2) and (3) are examples of mechanical weathering. Options (4) and (5) have nothing to do with the weathering of rock.

6. **(2) wearing away and transporting** (Comprehension) According to the first sentence of the passage, erosion consists of two processes, the wearing away of rock and soil and its transport elsewhere. Option (1) is incorrect because transporting is necessary for erosion

to take place. Option (3) is incorrect because erosion involves wearing away material, not depositing it. Options (4) and (5) are incorrect, because both involve an inappropriate use of the verb *load* and because, for option (5), erosion does not involve things diverging.

7. **(3) Erosion would increase along the bluff.** (Analysis) With more water in the river exerting more force on its channel, erosion would increase. Option (1) is unlikely; the river will rise and the bluff would be exposed to less, not more, air. Option (2) is incorrect because more water means more erosion, not less. Option (4) is incorrect because there would be more eroded material in the river during a surge. Option (5) is not true; erosion would continue and, in fact, increase.

Lesson 11: Weather and Climate
GED Practice (pages 324–325)

1. **(3) the weather conditions of a region over a long time** (Comprehension) The difference between weather and climate is explained in the first sentence of the passage. Option (1) describes weather, not climate. Option (2) is too specific. Options (4) and (5) are aspects of climate, but do not explain what climate is.

2. **(3) Europe** (Application) A person who liked moderate weather and four seasons would most enjoy living in Europe, the only place listed that has a temperate climate. Options (1), (2), (4), and (5) have primarily a tropical rainy climate, which does not result in four distinct seasons.

3. **(1) March** (Application) The centre tracks storms from May through November, which implies that storms are not as much of a problem during the rest of the year. The only month listed that is not in this hurricane season is March. Options (2), (3), (4), and (5) are incorrect because those months are in prime hurricane season, during which the centre does track storms, as stated in the passage.

4. **(3) public skepticism about later hurricane warnings** (Analysis) A warning that results in an unnecessary evacuation is likely to make people think that warnings in the future will also turn out to be wrong. Options (1) and (2) are incorrect because damage and deaths are likely to be reduced as a result of the warning in areas the hurricane did hit and would not occur in areas where it didn't. Option (4) is not likely to result, because, as the passage states, for safety reasons, the Tropical Prediction Centre prefers to

issue wide-area warnings even if they turn out to be inaccurate. Option (5) is not a likely result of such an error.

5. **(3) In short-term forecasts, the current data are very similar to the projected data, increasing accuracy.** (Evaluation) When the time frame is very short, conditions are not likely to change that much, so predictions can be more accurate. Options (1) and (2) are incorrect because historical data are equally applicable to short- and long-term forecasts, and so they do not explain why short-term forecasts tend to be more accurate. Option (4) is incorrect because it is the opposite of what actually happens. Option (5) is true of both short- and long-term forecasts, so it does not explain why short-term forecasts are more accurate than long-term forecasts.

Lesson 12: Earth's Resources
GED Practice (pages 327–328)

1. **(2) About half the volume of soil consists of space, through which water and air circulate.** (Comprehension) The spaces in soil make the soil less dense than rock. Options (1), (3), (4), and (5) are true, but they do not explain the difference in density between soil and rock.

2. **(1) The soil would be unable to support much plant and animal life.** (Analysis) The top two layers of soil contain the bulk of soil's plant and animal life. Once that is gone, the remaining layer is not suitable for sustaining much life. Option (2) is incorrect because the diagram shows that C horizon soil is coarser, not finer. Option (3) is incorrect because the passage indicates that C horizon soil does not contain much organic matter. Option (4) is incorrect because C horizon soil is not rich. Option (5) is incorrect because the bedrock is below the remaining C horizon layer.

3. **(3) plant fewer, more drought-resistant crops** (Application) A farmer who values soil conservation highly would most likely try to protect the soil while still growing crops. Option (1) is incorrect because the drought would require the farmer to make some changes to protect the soil from drying up and blowing away. Options (2) and (4) would both result in further loss of water in the A horizon, which would increase the amount of soil that would dry up and blow away. Option (5) is not likely, since the farmer must grow some crops to make a living.

4. **(4) Some Imported Minerals and Their Uses** (Comprehension) This title covers the information in the passage and chart. Options (1) and (2) are too general since the chart covers only imported minerals. Option (3) is incorrect because the chart shows five imported minerals, not the five most important minerals. Option (5) is incorrect because the chart lists minerals that are not resources of the United States.

5. **(5) sheet mica and thallium** (Comprehension) According to the chart, these two minerals are used in the electronics industry. Options (1), (2), (3), and (4) are incorrect because the chart indicates that one or both of the minerals listed are used mainly for purposes other than electronics.

6. **(4) The United States would reduce its dependence on foreign nations.** (Evaluation) Nations usually want to be as self-sufficient as possible so that politics does not interrupt the supply of a critical resource. Thus, they may be willing to spend more on extracting the resource than on importing it. Options (1), (2), and (3) are all true but do not explain why a nation would spend more to develop its own supply of thallium. Option (5) is not true.

7. **(2) decreased agricultural production** (Analysis) With reduced photosynthesis caused by haze from air pollution, agricultural crops will not grow as well, reducing output. Option (1) is incorrect because there is no indication that the air pollution affects wind speeds. Options (3) and (5) are the opposite of what would occur, based on the information in the passage. Option (4) is incorrect because the haze from the air pollution is likely to reduce the number of sunny days, not increase them.

8. **(3) About one-fifth of the watersheds had serious quality problems.** (Evaluation) According to the circle graph, 21%, or about one-fifth, of the watersheds had serious quality problems. Options (1) and (2) are incorrect because more than half the watersheds had some degree of water quality problems. Option (4) is incorrect because only 21% had serious quality problems. Option (5) is not true because the graph does not show the percentage of watersheds not tested, and only 27%, or about one-quarter, had insufficient data.

Lesson 13: Earth in Space
GED Practice (pages 330–331)

1. **(3) It is farther from the sun than Earth is.** (Comprehension) Since the distance from Earth to the sun is one astronomical unit, it follows that a planet more than one astronomical unit from the sun will be farther from the sun than Earth is. Options (1) and (2) are therefore incorrect. Option (4) is incorrect because a planet farther from the sun than Earth is likely to receive less solar energy than Earth does. Option (5) has nothing to do with distance from the sun.

2. **(5) 240 minutes** (Application) It takes the sun's light 8 minutes to travel one astronomical unit. Therefore, it would take 30×8, or 240 minutes, to travel 30 astronomical units—the distance from the sun to Neptune.

3. **(2) Optical telescopes magnify images of distant objects.** (Analysis) It is assumed that you understand that optical telescopes magnify images. Options (1), (3), (4), and (5) are stated directly in the passage.

4. **(3) Optical Telescopes** (Comprehension) The passage covers optical telescopes, from the land-based telescope used by Galileo to the Hubble Space Telescope. Options (1) and (4) are too specific. Option (2) is too general because the passage discusses only optical telescopes, not other types of telescopes. Option (5) is incorrect because radio telescopes are not discussed.

5. **(2) Fireworks explode, sending sparks, ashes, and smoke in all directions.** (Application) This is the only option that describes an instantaneous explosion that results in material flying in all directions similar to the Big Bang. Option (1) is incorrect because it does not describe an explosive event with material flying off in all directions. Option (3) is incorrect because the Big Bang was not the result of a collision. Options (4) and (5) are incorrect because neither describes an instantaneous explosion.

6. **(2) The universe would collapse in on itself.** (Analysis) The graph shows that if the universe has too much mass, it will begin to contract, eventually collapsing in on itself. Scientists have named this scenario the "Big Crunch." According to the graph, option (1) is the opposite of what would happen. Options (3) and (5) are incorrect because the graph gives no evidence that a contracting universe would cause a parallel universe to exist or that another Big Bang would occur. According to the graph, option (4) describes a universe that is neither expanding nor contracting.

7. **(3) They have observed its gravitational effects on visible objects.** (Evaluation) The evidence for dark matter is indirect. The existence of dark matter is inferred from the behaviour of the visible objects around it. Options (1) and (2) are incorrect because dark matter is not visible. Options (4) and (5) are evidence for the Big Bang theory, not dark matter.

GED Review Earth and Space Science
(pages 332–333)

1. **(3) a wilderness research station** (Application) Of the options given, the research station is the only one distant enough not to be served by a power plant, so it is the most likely to use wind power as a source of energy. Options (1), (2), (4), and (5) are all likely to be connected to power plants.

2. **(2) Having a wind generator means having power if the main source of electricity fails.** (Evaluation) Having a backup power source would be a good reason to have a wind generator on a modern farm. Option (1) is incorrect because having to maintain your own equipment is more work than simply plugging into the power grid. Option (3) is incorrect because in most locations, wind is not as reliable as a power plant. Option (4) is incorrect, because, as the passage indicates, wind energy is still relatively expensive compared with getting power from a power plant. Option (5) is not true and, in any case, would bestow no benefit to the farmer.

3. **(5) Water power is not available in that location.** (Evaluation) According to the graph, water is the cheapest source of power. A person considering cost over other factors would choose water if it were available. Option (1) is not true; water is cheaper than wind. Options (2), (3), and (4) are all true but they are not reasons for choosing wind over an even cheaper alternative.

4. **(4) debris thrown out of the large crater by the meteorite's impact** (Analysis) If you examine the diagram, you will see that the secondary craters are formed as a result of debris being blasted out of the large crater by the meteor's impact. Options (1) and (2) are incorrect because the diagram indicates there is only one meteorite and not several of them. Option (3) is incorrect because the diagram labels indicate

that a meteorite, not a comet, formed the crater. Option (5) is incorrect because the diagram shows the holes being punched from above; it indicates nothing about the ground settling after impact.

5. **(3) Earth has fewer craters than the moon, which has no atmosphere.** (Evaluation) The fact that Earth, with a thick atmosphere, has few craters and the moon, with no atmosphere, has many, supports the conclusion that many objects burn up in the atmosphere and so never reach the surface of Earth. Options (1) and (2) are true, but they have nothing to do with crater formation on Earth. Options (4) and (5) are true, but they do not concern the formation of craters by objects from space.

6. **(2) an amateur astronomer** (Application) The diagram shows a situation in which an amateur astronomer would find himself or herself. Option (1) is incorrect because planetary scientists study the planets, not the stars. Option (3) has nothing to do with astronomy. Option (4) is incorrect because a manufacturer is more interested in the object manufactured than in what can be seen with it and because it is not possible to make a telescope that can avoid this type of optical illusion. Option (5) is incorrect because such a scientist would be interested in the sun, not in optical double stars.

7. **(1) data from a space probe to Pluto** (Evaluation) A space probe that actually got close to Pluto would be able to get better information about the mass of Pluto and Charon than we can from telescopes on Earth or above Earth. Options (2) and (3) are incorrect because, as the question text states, telescopes cannot get good enough images to determine the relative mass of Pluto and Charon. Options (4) and (5) would provide general data about the two types of systems. However, these data would not specifically be applicable to Pluto and Charon.

Physical Science
Lesson 14: Matter
GED Practice (pages 335–337)

1. **(2) the effect of molecules as they hit the sides of their container** (Comprehension) According to the passage, pressure is the force with which the molecules of gas hit the sides of the container. Option (1) is related to the pressure of a gas, but it is not the definition of pressure. Option (3) is incorrect because pressure

is related to molecular motion, not to the product of volume and temperature. Option (4) refers to the amount of heat held by a gas, not the pressure it exerts. Option (5) is incorrect because it does not relate to pressure but to volume of a gas; it is nonsensical, as well, because gases always quickly come to fill the volume of their container, so the volume of the gas and of the container (its "size") are the same.

2. **(4) low temperature, large volume** (Analysis) According to the passage and diagrams, pressure increases when temperature increases or volume decreases. Therefore, pressure would decrease when temperature was low and the volume was large. Option (1) is incorrect because high temperature would increase pressure. Option (2) is incorrect because high temperature and small volume would increase pressure. Option (3) is incorrect because the pressure would not be least under "medium" conditions. Option (5) is incorrect because the small volume would increase pressure.

3. **(3) Pressure increases when volume decreases and temperature remains the same.** (Evaluation) This statement is supported by diagram B, which shows pressure increasing as volume decreases and temperature remains constant. Option (1) is not shown in the diagrams and is incorrect because pressure would remain constant (not change) if temperature and volume remained the same (constant). Option (2) is incorrect because pressure would increase when temperature increases and volume remains the same, as shown in A. Option (4) is incorrect because pressure would remain the same if temperature and volume both doubled, as shown in C. Option (5) is not shown in the diagrams, and it is incorrect because pressure would increase if temperature increased and volume decreased since each change alone causes pressure to increase.

4. **(5) gold** (Comprehension) According to the graph, the density of lead is 11.3 grams per cubic centimetre. Of the options listed, only gold has a higher density—19.3 grams per cubic centimetre. All the other substances offered as options (1), (2), (3), and (4) are less dense than lead.

5. **(1) Its density increases.** (Analysis) When ice melts, it becomes liquid water. According to the graph, the density of ice is 0.9 grams per cubic centimetre and the density of water is 1.0 gram

per cubic centimetre. Therefore, the density of ice increases when it melts. Note that water is unusual in this respect. When most solids melt, their densities decrease.

6. **(5) Density alone cannot be used to identify a particular substance.** (Application) Although iron has a density of about 7.9 grams per cubic centimetre, more information about the unknown substance is needed to definitively identify it. Therefore, option (2) is incorrect. Options (1), (3), and (4) are incorrect because their densities are 4.5, 11.3, and 13.6 grams per cubic centimetre, respectively—all different from 7.9.

7. **(5) Methods of Separating Mixtures** (Comprehension) The table lists, describes, and gives examples of different ways to separate mixtures, so this title covers the content. Options (1) and (4) are incorrect because the table covers separation methods, not types or ingredients of mixtures. Options (2) and (3) are incorrect because they are too specific.

8. **(1) They both involve solutions.** (Analysis) In distillation, a solution is boiled to separate out ingredients; in extraction, a solvent is used to create a solution of one of the mixture's ingredients. Options (2), (3), and (4) are incorrect because neither distillation nor extraction involves magnetism, density, or appearance. Option (5) is incorrect because only distillation would be used to remove salt from seawater.

9. **(4) extraction** (Application) The trichloroethylene is a solvent that dissolved the stain and removed it, a process known as extraction. Option (1) is incorrect because you cannot sort a stain from a fabric. Option (2) is incorrect because salad dressing stains are not magnetic. Option (3) is incorrect because the tablecloth was not boiled. Option (5) is incorrect since using a chemical solvent does not involve differences in density.

10. **(3) distillation** (Application) Boiling crude petroleum yields different products as various ingredients reach their boiling points, boil off, and then condense, in a process called distillation. Options (1) and (2) are incorrect because the ingredients of petroleum cannot be separated by sorting or by using magnetism. Option (4) is incorrect because boiling and condensing are not part of the extraction process. Option (5) is incorrect because density is not used to separate petroleum.

Lesson 15: Structure of Atoms and Molecules
GED Practice (pages 339–340)

1. **(2) They are both organic compounds and hydrocarbons.** (Comprehension) The passage describes the alkane series as the most abundant of the hydrocarbons. Since a hydrocarbon is a special kind of organic compound, the members of the alkane series must be organic compounds also. Option (1) is incorrect because members of the alkane series are organic compounds, not living things. The term *organic* means carbon-based. All living things on Earth contain organic compounds, but organic compounds themselves are not living. Option (3) is incorrect because the chart lists members that are gases and a solid at room temperature. Option (4) is incorrect because the chart lists formulas for members having different numbers of carbon atoms. Option (5) is incorrect because members of the alkane series are made up of only carbon and hydrogen, not helium.

2. **(1) C_3H_8** (Application) The fuel that escapes from the container is a gas, and propane, C_3H_8, is a gas at room temperature. Options (2), (3), (4), and (5) are incorrect because these compounds are not gases at room temperature.

3. **(2) Butane boils at a higher temperature than ethane.** (Evaluation) The chart lists boiling points in order from lowest to highest temperature. The boiling point of butane (–1° C) is higher than that of ethane (–89° C). Option (1) is incorrect because heptane boils at a higher temperature than hexane. Option (3) is incorrect because melting points are not provided. Option (4) is incorrect because, of the series members listed, eicosane contains the most carbon atoms. Option (5) is incorrect because pentane contains five carbon atoms and twelve hydrogen atoms, as compared to four carbon atoms and ten hydrogen atoms for butane.

4. **(3) calcium giving up two electrons to two fluorine atoms** (Application) As the passage states, ionic bonds involve the transfer of electrons between two or more atoms. Calcium gives up, or transfers, two of its electrons to two fluorine atoms, forming ionic bonds. The result is the ionic compound, CaF_2. Option (1) is an example of covalent bonding, since the electrons are shared between the hydrogen and oxygen atoms; this results in the covalent compound H_2O—or water. Options (2), (4), and (5) are each examples of mixtures, not ionic compounds.

5. **(1) Compounds form from atoms of different elements.** (Analysis) The first paragraph of the passage states that ionic bonds form only between two different elements, resulting in ionic compounds. The third paragraph of the passage states that covalent compounds form from atoms of two or more different elements bonding covalently. Since both ionic and covalent compounds involve the joining of atoms of two or more different elements, the passage assumes but does not state that all compounds form from atoms of two or more elements; it differentiates compounds from molecules, which can be formed from atoms of a single element or atoms of different elements. Options (2), (3), and (4) are stated directly in the passage. Option (5) is contradicted by the passage; molecules, by definition, have covalent, not ionic, bonds.

6. **(4) The chemical formula for propane is C_3H_8.** (Evaluation) The structural formula for propane shows that a propane molecule is made up of three atoms of carbon and eight atoms of hydrogen. Option (1) is incorrect because propane has no nitrogen atoms. Option (2) is incorrect because propane has eight atoms of hydrogen, not three. Option (3) is incorrect because propane has no oxygen atoms. Option (5) is incorrect because propane has eight hydrogen atoms, not six.

Lesson 16: Chemical Reactions

GED Practice (pages 342–243)

1. **(3) It is more precise.** (Analysis) The significance of the laser method of controlling reactions is that it allows scientists to control reactions more precisely, to the point that particular molecular bonds can be targeted. Options (1) and (2) are both differences from earlier techniques, but they are not significant differences. Option (4) is true of earlier techniques as well. Option (5) is a description of two earlier techniques.

2. **(2) Laser control of reactions allows scientists to break specific bonds between atoms.** (Evaluation) The fact that lasers can target particular molecular bonds is evidence that some chemical reactions can be controlled at the molecular level. Option (1) describes imprecise forms of control that do not target molecules. Options (3), (4), and (5) are true, but they do not provide evidence that some chemical reactions can be controlled at the molecular level.

3. **(5) hydrogen** (Comprehension) According to the passage and diagram, hydrogen is the element added during an addition reaction. Options (1), (2), (3), and (4) are incorrect because these elements are not mentioned in connection with addition reactions.

4. **(4) double (or triple) bonds** (Comprehension) The passage states that unsaturated molecules contain bonds other than single bonds and saturated molecules contain only single bonds. Option (1) is incorrect because both kinds of molecules can contain hydrogen atoms. Option (2) is only true of saturated molecules. Option (3) is not true because both kinds of molecules contain shared electrons. Option (5) is incorrect because both kinds of molecules can contain carbon atoms.

5. **(2) Single bonding occurs between its carbon atoms.** (Comprehension) The passage states that ethane is a saturated hydrocarbon, in which only one electron of each carbon atom is paired with one electron of another carbon atom to form a single bond; the other electrons are shared with hydrogen atoms. Option (1) is incorrect because ethane is saturated. Option (3) is incorrect because according to the passage, double bonding does not occur between the carbon atoms of ethane. Option (4) is not stated in the passage and it is not true. Option (5) is incorrect because ethane's chemical formula is given in the passage as C_2H_6, which indicates that it has six hydrogen atoms.

6. **(5) The product is C_2H_6.** (Evaluation) The product contains two carbon atoms and six hydrogen atoms, so it can be restated as C_2H_6. Option (1) is incorrect since the only saturated hydrocarbon is the product. Option (2) is incorrect because the reactant H_2 is not a hydrocarbon. Option (3) is incorrect since C_2H_6 is the product, not a reactant. Option (4) is incorrect since the product only contains single bonds.

7. **(1) Saturated hydrocarbons can be produced from unsaturated hydrocarbons through addition reactions.** (Evaluation) The chemical equation shows an addition reaction in which a saturated hydrocarbon is produced from an unsaturated hydrocarbon. Option (2) is incorrect because addition reactions yield saturated, not unsaturated, hydrocarbons. Option (3) is incorrect because the number of carbon atoms in the hydrocarbon remains the same after an addition reaction; it is the number of hydrogen atoms that increases. Option (4)

is incorrect because ethane can be made from ethene by an addition reaction, not the other way around. Option (5) is true but is not supported by the information presented.

Lesson 17: Motion and Forces
GED Practice (pages 345–346)

1. **(4) the backward "kick" of a fired rifle** (Application) When the bullet is fired out the barrel of a rifle, this action force causes a reaction that pushes the rifle back, causing a "kick." Because a person is so much larger than a bullet, the kick does not move the person very far. All the other options describe an action force rather than a reaction force: hot air rushes out of a balloon, wind pushes against a kite, the force of the ball pushes against the wall, the swimmer's arm and hand push against the water.

2. **(3) the force exerted by gases escaping the rear of the engine** (Analysis) As the hot gases escape the rear of the engine, they exert a force against the engine, pushing it forward. Option (1) is incorrect because air flowing through the engine doesn't have anything to do with how a rocket moves or with Newton's Third Law; in fact, there is no air in space to flow through the rocket engine. Option (2) explains how lift works, the principle behind airplane flight, not rocket propulsion. Option (4) is incorrect because gravity pulls the rocket downward, back to Earth, working against its forward acceleration. Option (5) is incorrect because air flow would exert friction, which would tend to slow the rocket, not move it forward and, in fact, there is no air in space to have any effect at all on the rocket.

3. **(1) The truck has a larger mass than the car does.** (Evaluation) Momentum is defined as mass times velocity. That the truck and the car are moving at the same speed, and thus have the same velocity, is given. Since the truck has more mass than the small car, option (1) supports the idea that the truck has more momentum than the car does. Option (2) is the opposite of what is true. Options (3) and (4) are incorrect, because the car and truck have the same velocity, as stated in the question text. Option (5) is true but irrelevant to determining momentum.

4. **(4) The less the impact force on the driver, the less serious his injuries are likely to be.** (Analysis) This is an assumption underlying the passage: seatbelts reduce impact force and thus reduce injuries. Options (1), (2), and (5) are incorrect because they are actually stated in the passage. Option (3) is incorrect because nothing

in the passage indicates that the writer assumes that air bags have serious drawbacks; the passage simply describes how air bags work.

5. **(2) by restraining forward motion and decreasing the impact force** (Comprehension) According to the passage, a seatbelt decreases the forward motion of the person wearing it. Decreasing the forward motion in a collision decreases the impact force. Option (1) is incorrect because seatbelts decrease the impact force. Option (3) is incorrect because seatbelts decrease the forward motion. Option (4) is incorrect because seatbelts reduce the impact force, not increase it. Option (5) is incorrect because that is not the principle by which seatbelts work, although seatbelts do indeed concentrate the impact force more than air bags, which spread it out.

6. **(5) snowshoes, which spread the weight of a person over a large area, allowing her to walk on the surface of the snow** (Application) Like an air bag distributing the impact force over a large area of the driver's body, reducing the pressure on any one point, snowshoes distribute a person's weight over a large area so that there is not enough pressure at any one point to break through the surface of the snow. Option (1) is incorrect because the rising of a hot air balloon has to do with differing densities, not with spreading force over a large area. Option (2) is incorrect because it is an application of Newton's Third Law of Motion, not of the idea of force, area, and pressure. Option (3) is incorrect because it does not involve the spreading of force over a large area. Option (4) is incorrect because ball bearings actually work by concentrating the force of friction on a very small area.

Lesson 18: Work and Energy
GED Practice (pages 348–349)

1. **(2) when the two objects are at the same temperature** (Comprehension) According to the third part of the diagram, the heat transfer stops when the hot object has transferred enough energy to the cold object so that their temperatures are equal. Option (1) is incorrect because molecules are always moving, even in cold objects. Option (3) is incorrect because the diagram does not show the two objects being pulled apart. Option (4) is incorrect because the cold object does not lose heat, it gains heat from the hot object. Option (5) is incorrect because it indicates when the heat transfer starts, not when it stops.

2. **(3) popcorn popping** (Application) As popcorn pops, the kernels move and collide with one another. This is most similar to the movement of molecules in a heated substance. Options (1), (2), and (4) are steady movements not typical of heated molecules. Option (5) is the opposite of what happens to a heated molecule.

3. **(2) Your hand's heat is absorbed by the ice.** (Evaluation) According to the passage and diagrams, heat moves from a hot object to a cold object; in this case, from your warm hand to the cold ice. Option (1) is incorrect because, according to the passage, cold is the absence of heat, not something that can flow. Option (3) is incorrect because the ice gains heat energy and then melts. Options (4) and (5) are incorrect because they state the opposite of what is actually happening—the molecules in your hand are losing energy to the molecules in the ice, which are gaining energy.

4. **(4) The hot object transfers heat to the air.** (Analysis) Not only are the two objects in contact with one another and thus transferring heat from the hot object to the cold object, they are also in contact with the air. Since the hot object is hotter than the air, as shown by the thermometer in the diagram, there will be heat transfer from the hot object to the air. Options (1) and (2) are incorrect because heat is transferred from hot to cold objects or substances, not the other way around. Option (3) is incorrect because the air absorbs heat from the hot object, since, as indicated in the diagrams, it is cooler than the hot object. Option (5) is incorrect because the two objects are in contact with substances other than just one another, so other heat transfers among all these substances are taking place.

5. **(3) either heat or electrical energy** (Comprehension) According to the passage, both the gasoline engine, which gives off heat energy, and the electric motor, which gives off electrical energy, can power the drive train. Since both can power the drive train, options (1) and (2) are incorrect. Options (4) and (5), light energy and nuclear energy, are not used to power the drive train of a parallel gasoline-electric car.

6. **(1) They have a greater driving range and their batteries recharge automatically.** (Analysis) All-electric cars cannot be driven more than 100 km or so before they need recharging, which takes three to eight hours. Therefore, they are not practical vehicles for most people. In contrast, gasoline-electric hybrid vehicles are about as practical as conventional cars, with a much longer driving range and no need for battery recharging. Option (2) is not a viable comparison of practicality since all-electric cars don't use gasoline at all. Options (3) and (4) are not true; because the hybrid car uses gasoline, it gives off more heat and air pollution than an all-electric car. Option (5) is true but not related to the cars' practicality.

7. **(3) the convenience of a conventional car** (Evaluation) The low operating cost of an all-electric vehicle is apparently not enough to compensate for the inconvenience of the short driving range and the time needed for battery recharging. Consumers value convenience highly. Options (1), (2), (4), and (5) are incorrect because if consumers valued a cleaner environment, conservation of resources, low operating costs, or being trendsetters more than convenience, they would have bought more all-electric cars.

Lesson 19: Electricity and Magnetism
GED Practice (pages 351–352)
1. **(2) the rotation of the coil** (Comprehension) According to the passage and the diagram, the turning coil turns the shaft of the motor. Option (1) is incorrect because the battery provides energy. Options (3), (4), and (5) are incorrect because the magnet is stationary and thus it cannot turn a shaft.

2. **(1) The coil would stop turning.** (Analysis) If the current flowed only in one direction, the coil would have a stationary magnetic field. Thus, once the south pole of the moving coil was attracted to the north pole of the stationary magnet, the coil would stop turning. Option (2) would occur only if the current changed direction more frequently. Option (3) is incorrect because the magnet doesn't move and it is a natural magnet, not an electromagnet; therefore, its magnetic field doesn't reverse. Option (4) is incorrect because the magnetic field of the coil reverses only when the current reverses. Option (5) is incorrect because the battery continues to provide electrical energy and thus would eventually run down, whether the current is flowing in one direction or two.

3. **(5) a generator, which uses a magnetic field to produce electricity** (Application) In a generator, a moving magnet produces current in a coil of wire, an application of the principle of electromagnetic induction. Option (1) is an example of a machine that uses

Unit 4

electricity to produce magnetism, not the other way around. Options (2) and (3) do not involve electromagnetism. Option (4) is incorrect because a battery generates electric current by a chemical reaction, not by magnetism.

4. **(1) gravity** (Comprehension) According to the table, only gravity involves attraction between objects larger than atoms. Gravitational attraction causes such common occurrences as objects feeling heavy and objects falling. Option (2) is incorrect because static electricity is the only visible effect of the electromagnetic force that you see acting between objects and this is less common than the effects of gravity listed above. Even though the results of electromagnetic force can be seen, the force actually operates at the subatomic level—as do the forces listed in options (3) and (4). Option (5) is incorrect because not all these forces are easily seen every day.

5. **(1) An electric current flowing through a wire produces a magnetic field.** (Comprehension) Oersted discovered this when the electric current he had produced caused a nearby compass needle to move. Option (2) was known before Oersted's time, as indicated by the fact that Oersted had a compass. Option (3) is the opposite of what Oersted discovered. Option (4) is a discovery that the passage indicates Faraday made. Option (5) is incorrect because, as the passage indicates, electric motors were a later invention by people other than Oersted.

6. **(3) A compass needle is magnetic.** (Analysis) The author does not explain that the compass needle was magnetic; he assumes you know that this is why the compass needle moved when the nearby electric current produced a magnetic field. All the other options are actually stated in the passage.

7. **(4) the large-scale generation of electricity by means of moving magnetic fields** (Analysis) Once the principles of electromagnetism were understood, the large-scale generation of electricity using moving magnetic fields became possible. Options (1), (2), (3) and (5) are incorrect because an internal combustion engine, a locomotive engine, windmill powering a mechanical pump, and batteries do not involve electromagnetism.

8. **(5) Electromagnetism had many potentially valuable applications.** (Evaluation) The interest in magnetism increased once its relationship to electricity was better

understood because the interaction between electricity and magnetism could be put to practical uses. Option (1) is incorrect; nothing in the passage indicates that lodestones had many uses. Option (2) is true, but it is not the correct choice because compasses had been used in navigation since the 1200s. Option (3) is true, but it does not explain why the scientists should focus so much attention on magnetism rather than on other phenomena. Option (4) is not true as related to the understanding of magnetism because as the question indicates it was the discoveries of the nineteenth-century scientists Oersted, Ampère, and Faraday that sparked new interest in magnetism, not a renewed interest in ancient civilizations.

Lesson 20: Waves
GED Practice (pages 354–355)

1. **(4) electric and magnetic fields that oscillate in a wave** (Comprehension) This is a restatement of the definition given in the passage. Option (1) is incorrect because it's circular reasoning: it is simply another way of describing electromagnetic radiation. Option (2) is incorrect because the disturbances in electromagnetic radiation are in two directions. Option (3) is incorrect because electromagnetic radiation consists of transverse, not longitudinal, waves. Option (5) is incorrect because visible light is a form of electromagnetic radiation, not the other way around.

2. **(2) at right angles to the direction of motion** (Comprehension) According to the diagram and the passage, the electric and magnetic fields oscillate perpendicular to the direction of motion. Options (1) and (4) are incorrect because they describe the disturbance in a longitudinal wave, not in a transverse wave such as an electromagnetic wave. Option (3) is incorrect because the angles are 90° angles, not 45° angles. Option (5) is incorrect because the motion is perpendicular to the direction of motion, not circular.

3. **(3) Light waves have shorter wavelengths.** (Analysis) According to the diagram of the electromagnetic spectrum, visible light waves have shorter wave lengths than radio waves. Options (1) and (2) are incorrect because both the diagram and the passage indicate that all types of electromagnetic waves consist of both magnetic and electric fields. Option (4) is incorrect because the passage states that electromagnetic waves can travel through a

vacuum, so neither needs a medium through which to travel. Option (5) is incorrect because the diagram indicates and the passage states that radio waves are part of the electromagnetic spectrum; they are not sound waves.

4. **(2) They travel through a vacuum at 300 000 km/s.** (Evaluation) According to the diagram of the electromagnetic spectrum, infrared waves are electromagnetic waves. According to the passage, all electromagnetic waves travel at the same speed through a vacuum, at 300 000 km/s. Option (1) is incorrect because X-ray machines produce X rays, not infrared waves. Option (3) is incorrect because all electromagnetic waves travel at the same speed through space, which is a vacuum. Option (4) is incorrect because infrared waves have wavelengths from about 10^{-4} to about 10^{-6} metres. Option (5) is incorrect because the diagram shows that infrared waves are a type of electromagnetic wave.

5. **(1) Cell phones emit microwaves near the head.** (Comprehension) According to the passage, cell phone use has become a matter of concern because the phones emit this type of electromagnetic radiation right near the brain. People are concerned because the phones may pose a health risk to users. Options (2) and (4) are incorrect because they focus on aspects of cell phones not relevant to the risk of developing brain cancer. Option (3) is incorrect; the mice were exposed to similar radiation but not specifically to cell phones, and the type of cancer they developed is not specified. Option (5) is incorrect because the fact that cell phones are wireless does not make people suspect them of possibly causing increased risk for brain cancer.

6. **(2) Use a cell phone with a remote antenna to lessen microwave intensity near the head.** (Application) Increasing the distance between the source of microwave emissions (the antenna) and the user's head will reduce the bombardment of microwaves on the brain, thereby decreasing whatever risk, if any, exists. Option (1) is incorrect because using the cell phone outdoors does not affect the distance between the cell phone's antenna and the person's head. Option (3) is incorrect because even if the user alternates sides of the head, the brain is still being hit by microwaves. Options (4) and (5) are incorrect because the antenna is in use whether the calls are incoming or outgoing.

7. **(4) No definitive link has been found between cell phone use and brain cancer.** (Evaluation) According to the passage, neither the animal studies nor the human studies has offered conclusive evidence that cell phones are associated with higher than normal risks of developing brain cancer. Options (1), (2), and (5) are incorrect because they are hasty generalizations that are not supported by the information presented in the passage; to date, there is not enough evidence to reach any of these conclusions. Option (3) is incorrect because the passage states that high levels of microwaves are needed to heat food in microwave ovens, not low levels.

GED Review Physical Science
(pages 356–357)

1. **(4) rubber** (Comprehension) The paragraph indicates that rubber is a good insulator, so option (4) is correct. The paragraph also states that metals are good conductors and thus are the opposite of good insulators. Since options (1), (2), (3), and (5) are metals, they would not be good insulators.

2. **(1) electrical wire for a lamp** (Application) Since a conductor allows electrical current to flow easily through it, it would make a good electrical wire. Options (2) and (3) are objects in which insulators are used to prevent electric shock. Options (4) and (5) are also objects for which insulators are more appropriate materials than conductors.

3. **(1) A silver pipe is likely to have a lower resistance than a plastic pipe.** (Evaluation) Since conductors allow electric current to flow easily through them, they would also tend to have low resistance. Also, since metals tend to be better conductors than nonmetals, silver would be likely to have a lower resistance than plastic. Although option (2) is true, it is an incorrect answer, because the paragraph does not mention the effect of temperature or how well a substance conducts electricity. Option (3) is incorrect because the paragraph indicates that porcelain (a nonmetal) is a better insulator than silver (a metal). Option (4) is incorrect because the paragraph indicates that glass has a higher resistance than copper. Option (5) is incorrect because the paragraph implies that electrons move more readily through metals than through nonmetals.

4. **(2) Bulb *B* also will not light.** (Analysis)
Since bulb *A* is in a series circuit, when the circuit
is broken because of burned-out bulb *A*, bulb *B*
also will not light. Option (1) will not fix the
circuit, since it is the burned-out bulb that has
stopped the current flow in the circuit, not a
defective wire. Option (3) is incorrect, because
bulb *C* is in a parallel circuit, and when the
current flow is interrupted by this burned-out
bulb (bulb *C*), current continues to flow through
the other path, keeping bulb *D* lit. Option (4) is
incorrect, because replacing bulb *C*, not rewiring
the circuit, will restore current flow throughout
the circuit. Option (5) is incorrect because the
burning out of a single light bulb in each circuit
does not indicate that the batteries need to be
replaced.

5. **(3) The current continues in all but one
path of the circuit.** (Evaluation) The fact that
the other lights still work after the bulb burned
out indicates that the circuit must be a parallel
circuit. Options (1) and (4) are incorrect because
power failures and circuit breakers would stop the
flow of current in both parallel and series circuits.
Option (2) is incorrect because it would occur
only if the circuit were a series circuit. Option (5)
contradicts the information given in the
question, that the kitchen is on a single circuit.

6. **(3) The molecules in solutions are
smaller than the particles in colloids.**
(Comprehension) The first sentence of the
second paragraph highlights the key difference
between colloids and solutions: the particles of
colloids are much bigger than the molecules of
solutions. Option (1) is not true; some colloids
are liquids and some solutions are gases.
Option (2) may or may not be true, depending
on the specific colloid and solution involved,
but the passage and diagram do not discuss
the freezing points of colloids and solutions.
Option (4) is contradicted by the passage and
diagram, which shows that particles of a colloid
cannot pass through the semipermeable
membrane. Option (5) is incorrect because the
passage and the diagram do not support it; the
passage gives examples of gases and liquids that
are colloids, not solids; the passage doesn't list
examples of solutions nor say that solutions are
always liquids (they aren't).

7. **(3) Both the colloid particles and the
solute molecules would flow through.**
(Analysis) A wire mesh has much larger, visible
openings through which both the particles of a
colloid and the molecules of a solution would
be able to pass. Option (1) is incorrect because if
the molecules of a solution could flow through
the semipermeable membrane, with its tiny
openings, then they could also flow through
a wire mesh, with much larger openings.
Option (2) is incorrect because the wire mesh
openings would be large enough for the colloid
particles to pass through. Option (4) is incorrect
because the wire mesh would let more pass than
the semipermeable membrane would. Option (5)
is incorrect because all the particles would be
able to flow through the wire mesh, not just
water molecules.

8. **(1) The particles of a suspension are
larger than the molecules of a solution.**
(Comprehension) Since the particles of
suspensions are larger than those of colloids
and the particles of colloids are larger than
the molecules of solutions, it follows that the
particles of suspensions are larger than the
molecules of solutions. Option (2) is incorrect
because the particles of a suspension, being larger
than those of a colloid, will not flow through
something that a colloid could not flow through.
Option (3) does not follow from the information
given; a suspension could be a gas. Option (4)
also does not follow from the information in
the passage and diagram, which do not discuss
colour as a property of colloids and suspensions.
Option (5) is not true; by definition, any type of
mixture can be separated into its ingredients.

9. **(1) When it snows, calcium chloride
(salt) is applied to roads to prevent the
formation of ice.** (Evaluation) According to
the passage, adding a solute (like calcium
chloride) to a solvent (snow or water), lowers the
freezing point; that's the purpose of salting icy
roads. Option (2) is incorrect because it does not
involve a solute. Option (3) is incorrect because
it focuses on the expansion of water when it
freezes, not on changes in the freezing point.
Options (4) and (5) are both true, but they do not
describe the effect of a solute.

GED Unit Review Science
(pages 358–363)

1. **(1) emissions from factories, power plants,
and cars** (Comprehension) According to the
passage and the diagram, waste gases from
industrial and vehicular sources mix with water

vapour in the air, making the resulting rain acidic. Option (2) describes the usual formation of rain without indicating the source of the acid. Options (3), (4), and (5) are incorrect because they reflect pollution problems in water on Earth, not in rain.

2. **(4) The emissions that cause acid rain in the province probably originate in some other place.** (Evaluation) Since the waste gases from emissions often travel great distances before mixing with water vapour and causing acid rain, controlling emissions within the province is not likely to help that province reduce its acid rainfall. Option (1) may be true, but it is not the reason that the officials' plan is faulty. Option (2) is incorrect because the province can enforce controls if it chooses to. Options (3) and (5) are not true.

3. **(1) damage to aquatic organisms** (Analysis) Since acid rain causes the water in streams and lakes to become acidic, the most likely effect is damage to organisms that live in them. Option (2) would be a cause of pollution, not an effect. Option (3) is incorrect because acid rain pollution of a stream or lake is not likely to move upstream. Options (4) and (5) are not results of acid rain pollution.

4. **(4) digestion** (Application) Like decomposition, digestion is a process in which large complex substances are broken down in stages into simple substances. Options (1), (2), (3), and (5) are incorrect because they have nothing to do with the breakdown of complex substances into simpler, more usable components.

5. **(2) distance the rope is pulled** (Evaluation) According to the passage and diagram, the distance the rope is pulled is equal to the distance the load travels. Therefore, if you know the distance the rope is pulled, you can figure out the distance the load moves. Options (1), (3), and (4) are not needed in order to figure out the distance the load moved. Option (5), the total length of the rope, gives you the maximum distance the load can travel, but it is not adequate to figure out how far the load actually moved.

6. **(5) The friction from the pulley wheel must be overcome by the effort used in pulling the rope.** (Analysis) Although in theory the effort force equals the load in a single pulley system, in reality, the person pulling on the rope must expend a little extra force (effort) to overcome the friction of the pulley wheel.

Option (1) is true but it does not explain why the person pulling on the rope must exert a little extra effort. Options (2) and (3) are incorrect because in a simple pulley system the distance pulled on the rope is equal to the distance the load moves. Option (4) is incorrect because the load does not change in weight as it moves up.

7. **(2) Heat released from many cars raises the temperature of heavily travelled streets.** (Analysis) Since car engines waste most of the heat they produce, it is absorbed by their surroundings. Thus the more traffic, the warmer the street from heat pollution of vehicles. Option (1) is incorrect because the heavily travelled streets and lightly travelled streets are likely to absorb about the same amount of sunlight, if shadiness and street orientation are the same. Option (3) may increase the friction of travelling on worn-away streets, but this is not as significant as waste heat from vehicle engines. Options (4) and (5) may or may not be true in specific instances; not enough information has been provided to evaluate their significance.

8. **(4) Your new job requires you to transport heavy supplies in your car.** (Application) Increasing the horsepower of the car's engine will help you carry a heavier load, such as the heavy supplies. Options (1) and (3) are not related to a car's horsepower. Options (2) and (5) would be good reasons to buy a car with a lower-horsepower engine, not a higher-horsepower engine, since the latter would burn more fuel and add more pollutants to the atmosphere.

9. **(3) the left ventricle** (Comprehension) The left ventricle forces blood through the aorta, which leads to blood vessels throughout the body. Option (1), the right ventricle, sends oxygen-poor blood to the lungs. Option (2), the right atrium, collects oxygen-poor blood from the body. Option (4), the left atrium, receives oxygen-rich blood from the lungs. Option (5) is a pair of blood vessels, not a chamber of the heart.

10. **(4) The body would not get enough oxygen-rich blood.** (Analysis) Since the aorta sends oxygen-rich blood throughout the body, if it were partially blocked, the flow of this blood would be reduced. Option (1) is incorrect because blood doesn't enter the left ventricle through the aorta. Option (2) is incorrect because oxygen-poor blood enters the heart through the venae cavae, not through the aorta. Option (3) is incorrect because the oxygen-poor blood passes to the lungs through the pulmonary arteries,

not through the aorta. Option (5) is incorrect because oxygen-rich blood does not enter the venae cavae.

11. **(1) The arteries and veins are blood vessels, and they are part of the circulatory system.** (Analysis) The writer gives information about veins and arteries and their functions, but does not state explicitly that they are blood vessels and part of the circulatory system. Options (2) through (5) are all true, but they are stated in the passage or shown in the diagram.

12. **(1) Because of its weight, most sand is blown near the ground.** (Analysis) The diagram shows wind-blown sand bouncing along near the ground, wearing away the base of the rock. Nothing in the information given suggests that options (2), (3), or (4) is true. Option (5) may happen eventually, but it does not explain the low-to-the-ground action of sand and wind.

13. **(5) Rocks of volcanic origin are igneous rocks.** (Evaluation) Since volcanoes occur where magma reaches the surface and eventually cools, it follows that rocks resulting from volcanic activity are igneous rocks. Options (1), (2), (3), and (4) make no mention of magma being involved in the formation. In fact, options (1) and (3) describe the formation of sedimentary rocks, and options (2) and (4) describe the conditions under which metamorphic rocks form.

14. **(3) south central California** (Comprehension) By consulting the key and looking for a cluster of earthquakes that occurred in the last day, you can see that the earthquakes in the last day occurred mostly in south central California. Options (1), (2), (4), and (5) are areas that do not show large numbers of earthquakes within the last day.

15. **(4) Earthquakes are a common occurrence in California.** (Evaluation) With so many minor quakes occurring during a one-week period, you can conclude that earthquake activity is frequent in California. Option (1) is not true since the map shows a week in February with lots of earthquake activity. Option (2) is incorrect because none of the earthquakes had a magnitude as great as 6 that week. Option (3) may or may not be true, but there is no way to tell from the map. Option (5) is incorrect because most of the earthquakes were of very low magnitude and probably went unnoticed by most people.

16. **(2) quarks** (Comprehension) According to the passage, protons and neutrons are made up of subatomic particles called quarks. Option (1) is incorrect; cosmic rays are not subatomic particles, but they contain many types of subatomic particles. Options (3) and (4) are incorrect because bosons are force-carrying particles, and the passage does not say that they are found in protons and neutrons. Option (5) is incorrect because electrons are negatively charged particles different from protons and neutrons.

17. **(3) boson** (Application) According to the passage, bosons are force-carrying particles. If the gluon, a force-carrying particle, is produced by a collision in an accelerator, then it is likely to be a boson. None of the other options is a force-carrying particle.

18. **(5) Understanding subatomic particles may lead to advances in technology.** (Evaluation) Advances in technology are valued by many people, because such advances often lead to economic growth. Thus the potential for technological applications would be an argument that could be used in favour of the building of a new accelerator. All the other options are arguments that people would use if they opposed the building of a new accelerator.

19. **(4) Bacterial cells have genetic material but no nucleus.** (Evaluation) According to the paragraph, bacterial cells have no nucleus, but the diagram shows the genetic material of a bacterial cell suspended in the cytoplasm. Option (1) is incorrect because the paragraph states that bacterial cells are smaller. Options (2), (3), and (5) are incorrect because the diagram shows that bacterial cells have ribosomes, a cell wall and a cell membrane, and cytoplasm.

20. **(3) by combining its reproductive cell with that of another organism of the same species** (Analysis) Since each of the reproductive cells has half the normal number of chromosomes, combining two reproductive cells—one each from a male and a female—produces an offspring with the normal number of chromosomes. Option (1) is incorrect because this manner of reproduction does not require reproductive cells. Option (2) is incorrect because the resulting offspring would have only half the chromosomes it needed. Option (4) is incorrect because the result would be twice the number of chromosomes as needed. Option (5) is incorrect because organisms that reproduce sexually do so by means of their reproductive cells, not by combining nonreproductive cells.

21. **(2) The tips of the chromosomes may play a role in the rate of cell division.** (Comprehension) Since the tips of the chromosomes differ in healthy (normal cell division) and cancerous (rapid cell division) cells, the tips of the chromosomes are involved in the rate of cell division. This expresses the main idea of the paragraph. Options (1) and (4) are incorrect because they are details of the paragraph, not the main idea. Option (3) is incorrect because the structure of the chromosome does affect the rate of cell division. Option (5) is not true; according to the paragraph, cancer cells multiply faster than normal cells.

22. **(2) B** (Comprehension) Of the cells shown here, only those in option (2) have hair-like structures (cilia) that can filter out dust. Options (1), (3), (4), and (5) show (1) white blood cells, (3) nerve cells, (4) red blood cells, and (5) cells in connective tissue, none of which have cilia.

Unit 4

UNIT 5: LANGUAGE ARTS, READING

Interpreting Nonfiction
Lesson 1: Finding the Main Idea and Supporting Details
GED Practice (pages 367–368)

1. **(4) Attention to editorial quality may help improve journalism.** (Comprehension) The lines preceding the quote in the question are "Wall Street doesn't care much about editorial quality; journalists do and others should" (lines 1–3). The quotation in the question is a continuation of this thought—that people should care about editorial quality because journalism is not perfect. This implies that attention to quality can help improve journalism. Option (1) is the opposite of what is stated in the excerpt. Option (2) may be true but is not discussed in the excerpt. There is no support in the excerpt for options (3) and (5).

2. **(5) News magazines summarize and analyze the news.** (Analysis) The paragraph discusses the place and function of news magazines in "the food chain of journalism" (lines 6–7). It says that the "news magazine comes along to summarize and analyze" (lines 11–12) and describes what it takes to do this. Options (1), (3), and (4) may be true but are not discussed in the excerpt. Option (2) is a detail from the paragraph, not the main idea.

3. **(3) It reminds the reader of having an upset stomach from overeating.** (Analysis) The figurative suggestion compares receiving too much information to the discomfort of overeating. Option (1) has no support. Option (2) might be true in general, but other media besides television are part of the problem discussed. Option (4) would only add to the problem. Option (5) is not suggested.

4. **(1) time order—explaining the order in which the media cover the news** (Synthesis) In the second paragraph, when describing the "food chain," the author uses the words "first" when discussing radio news, "then" when referring to television news, and "finally" when referring to the news magazine. This indicates the use of a sequence, or chronological order, pattern.

5. **(3) A judge may award a prize based upon some small point.** (Comprehension) The preceding paragraph raises the question of how to choose between two good entries. This paragraph containing the quote explains how the judge makes that choice: She focuses on a detail in one of the garments that the other does not have—the covered buttons. There is no evidence that the senior judge is, in general, a picky person, so option (1) is incorrect. Option (2) is incorrect because there is no evidence that all garments need covered buttons. They only became important when everything else was equal. Option (4) is true, but is not suggested by the word "nitpicking," so it is incorrect. "Nitpicking" suggests the opposite of option (5), so it is incorrect.

6. **(3) its covered buttons** (Analysis) The fact that the judge states that "in Highland County, covered buttons are *it*" (lines 27–28) suggests that the buttons are an important factor in the decision. There is no evidence that options (1), (2), and (5) are outstanding features of the jumper, so they are incorrect. The fact that the judges get nitpicky, or look at very small details, suggests option (4) is incorrect.

7. **(4) The judge is dissatisfied with this year's crop.** (Analysis) A sigh can show regret or displeasure. Option (1) may be true but has no support in the excerpt. Options (2) and (5) may be true, but the excerpt does not indicate that the judge is sighing because she is bored or because she is not being paid. There is no evidence for option (3).

8. **(2) informal and casual** (Synthesis) The dialogue in the excerpt as well as the subject of the article, a county fair, both support the description of the writing as informal and casual. None of the other options accurately describe the style of the writing.

Lesson 2: Summarizing Major Ideas
GED Practice (page 370)

1. **(5) theft of a computer** (Comprehension) The excerpt states that terminated employees are eligible for coverage under most circumstances except "gross misconduct" (line 16). Options (1) and (2) are problems with the company, not with the employee's conduct, and therefore would not disqualify the employee. Options (3) and (4) are described in the excerpt as situations in which the employee would qualify for benefits; therefore, they are incorrect.

2. **(3) Qualified ex-employees and their dependents can retain their health insurance.** (Comprehension) Option (1) is too general to describe the main idea of the excerpt and therefore is incorrect. Option (2) is true but

is incomplete because the excerpt also describes how the dependents of ex-employees can retain insurance. Option (4) is too general. Option (5) is not covered in the excerpt.

3. **(2) Companies with fewer than 20 employees are exempt.** (Analysis) The excerpt states that Jetstream Airways is required by law to provide the coverage described because it is "an employer of more than 20 people" (line 4). You can infer from this statement that companies with fewer than 20 employees are not required to provide this coverage. There is no support in the excerpt for the other options.

Lesson 3: Restating Information
GED Practice (pages 372–373)

1. **(1) Gates is worth more, so his time is more valuable.** (Comprehension) The excerpt describes how, in 1986, it was not worth Bill Gates' time to pick up a $5 bill, whereas now it is not worth his time to pick up a $500 bill. The excerpt does not indicate that Bill Gates will have to work more; therefore, option (2) is incorrect. Option (3) may be true, but is not suggested by the excerpt. There is no support in the excerpt for option (4). Option (5) is true, but it does not restate the lines given in the question and therefore is not the correct choice.

2. **(5) humorous** (Synthesis) The author uses humour to describe the immense amount of money that Bill Gates earns. For instance, he creates an image of Bill Gates wasting his time by picking up a $500 bill. The author does not seem to be congratulating Bill Gates, nor does he seem envious or critical of him; therefore, options (1), (2), and (3) are incorrect. There is also no evidence that the author is disgusted by Gates's wealth, option (4).

3. **(4) Modest wealth seems like pocket change to Gates.** (Analysis) This section of the excerpt is devoted to comparing what money means to an average American with what that same amount of money means to Bill Gates. There is no support in the excerpt for option (1). Although options (2) and (5) may be true, they do not restate the lines from the excerpt. The author suggests that Gates could spend fortunes without a second thought, but there is not evidence that he does so.

4. **(2) He would make comparisons.** (Application) The author uses comparisons throughout the excerpt to emphasize both how much money Bill Gates makes as well as how his earning power has increased over the years.

Therefore, he would probably use comparisons to describe a great distance, such as that from Earth to the moon. The author does use technical language to describe a top-of-the-line computer, but most of the language in the excerpt is nontechnical; therefore, option (1) is incorrect. The author does not exaggerate Gates' wealth, option (3), nor does he describe different viewpoints, option (4). The author does not simply state facts about Gates's wealth; instead he goes out of his way to make sure the reader understands just how large Gates's fortune is. Therefore, option (5) is not the best choice.

5. **(2) The warranty applies only to manufacturing defects.** (Comprehension) The paragraph describes in detail all the circumstances under which the company is not responsible for defects or damage; these include anything that happens after manufacturing, including damage incurred during shipping. A person with this warranty would already have bought the item in question, so option (1) is incorrect. Option (3) is true, but is only a detail from the paragraph and so is incorrect. Option (4) is the opposite of what the paragraph states, so it is incorrect. Option (5) is a matter of opinion, not an idea given in the paragraph, and so is incorrect.

6. **(1) to describe the conditions under which the company will replace or repair the product** (Comprehension) The purpose of the warranty is stated in the first sentence of the first paragraph. Option (2) is true only in certain circumstances. Options (3) and (5) are not stated in the warranty. Option (4) is stated in the warranty statement but is not the main purpose of the warranty.

7. **(2) furnish proof of the date of purchase** (Analysis) The warranty applies only up to one year after the original purchase. Therefore, although it is not specified in the warranty statement, it is reasonable to expect the purchaser to provide proof of the date of purchase for the company to comply with the terms of the warranty agreement. Options (1), (3), and (5) would not likely be criteria that a purchaser should meet for a manufacturer to honour a warranty agreement. Option (4) could be a criterion, but there is no reference made to such a requirement in the excerpt.

8. **(5) formal and legal** (Analysis) The agreement uses legal terminology such as "thereof," "herein," and "exclusions." The sentences are long and complex. Whether the style is boring is

Unit 5

a matter of opinion, so option (4) is not the best answer. None of the other options is supported by the details in the warranty statement.

Lesson 4: Applying Ideas
GED Practice (pages 375–376)

1. **(3) how to search the Web** (Comprehension) The excerpt describes how confusing it can be to try to find information on the Web and gives some hints and information about using search engines. Option (1) is a detail from the excerpt but does not describe the main idea and so is incorrect. Options (2) and (5) are not supported by the excerpt and so are incorrect. Option (4) is incorrect because the excerpt tells how to use a search engine, not how to create one.

2. **(3) food service opportunities** (Application) The words *food service* indicate that this option has to do with cooking, and the word *opportunities* suggests jobs. Options (1) and (4) would give information about cooking and learning to cook, but not about jobs; therefore, they are incorrect. Option (2) would give you information about all types of jobs. Because this information would not be specific to cooking, this is not the best option. Option (5) would give information about businesses that provide food, not about jobs, and so is incorrect.

3. **(3) The Web is an electronic library.** (Analysis) The excerpt describes the Web as "the greatest resource of information the world has ever known" (lines 2–3), which suggests that it is an enormous electronic library. Option (1) is not a true statement and so is incorrect. Options (2) and (4) are not supported by the excerpt and so are incorrect. Option (5) is the opposite of what is stated in the article and so is incorrect.

4. **(3) a title containing a few important words from the page** (Application) The excerpt states that in doing a search, search engines try to find documents that contain the searchers' keywords in the title (lines 34–37). Options (1), (2), and (5) would not enable search engines to find the document effectively; therefore, they are incorrect. Option (2) would attract some interested searchers, but using only one word would limit the number of searchers who would find the page.

5. **(1) the insurance plan pays** (Comprehension) The last sentence of the second paragraph defines the co-insurance provision as 90 percent of the covered charges that the network (to which the insurance plan belongs) pays.

6. **(2) Up to six months' leave is granted if the father is to be the primary caretaker.** (Application) The excerpt states that the company is progressive and employee friendly. This would be consistent with a generous paternity leave. Options (1), (4), and (5) are not generous and so are incorrect. Option (3) is far too generous; it would be impractical for any company to offer an unlimited amount of time.

7. **(3) Their use helps to control insurance costs.** (Analysis) Cost containment is a compelling reason for employers to encourage the use of certain healthcare providers. There is nothing in the excerpt to suggest that approved eyecare professionals are more qualified than those that are not approved. Therefore, option (1) is incorrect. Option (4) implies that out-of-network eyecare professionals overcharge their patients, a generalization that is unfounded. Options (2) and (5) are not supported by the facts in the excerpt.

Lesson 5: Making Inferences
GED Practice (pages 378–379)

1. **(2) Why do Canadians loath Mulroney yet forgive Chrétien for everything?** (Comprehension) The second paragraph of the excerpt (lines 5–8) expresses the two sides of the question that puzzles the author. (This puzzlement is also presented in the title.) Option (1) presents only one aspect of the author's "puzzlement." Option (3) presents one specific puzzling *example* of what people forgave Chrétien for. Options (4) and (5) are misreadings and/or exaggerations of details in the opinion piece.

2. **(4) He was a master at role-playing the common man, or "man of the people."** (Comprehension) In the sixth paragraph of the excerpt (lines 16–25), the author suggests that the public's infatuation with Chrétien is attributed to his "man-of-the people" persona. Later, in the same paragraph, the author also stresses that Chrétien was a master of role-playing, while Mulroney was more honest. Options (1) and (2) may be supported by the piece, but they are not presented as reasons for Chrétien's public favour. Options (3) and (5) are not factually supported by this excerpt.

3. **(2) He has not been treated kindly or fairly by the public.** (Analysis) In the last line of this opinion piece, the author suggests ("I trust. …") that in time the public perception of Mulroney might be "more rational, kinder, and fairer," thus inferring that he has not been

viewed kindly or fairly. All the other options are presented as perceptions of the public, they are not the author's opinions.

4. **(4) The benefits of preservation can't always be measured in dollars and cents.** (Comprehension) The phrase "economic benefits" pertains to making money. From the context of the sentence, you can infer that the word *intangible* means "not measurable by money." None of the other options make sense in the context of the excerpt.

5. **(3) making profits from new building projects** (Analysis) The writer states that developers are often willing to duplicate a certain style and implies that they describe some historic buildings as not achieving their "highest tax-generating potential" (lines 35–36). This suggests that developers are more concerned about making money than preserving historic neighbourhoods. Option (1) might be true, but would not be real estate developers' chief concern. They are trying to make a profit and do not work for the city. Options (2) and (5) are not mentioned in the excerpt. Option (4) is the concern of the author of the editorial, not the real estate developers.

6. **(1) to raise awareness about the importance of preserving historic buildings** (Synthesis) The entire editorial focuses on the importance of preserving historic buildings that serve as a unique glimpse into the city's past. None of the other options reflect the overall purpose of the editorial.

Lesson 6: Identifying Style and Tone
GED Practice (page 381)

1. **(4) understanding poetry** (Comprehension) For Frost, "coming close to poetry" means understanding "what it [is] all about" (line 23). There is no evidence for options (1), (2), (3), and (5).

2. **(1) Both are inexact and unscientific.** (Comprehension) The fact that, for Frost, the best indication of a student's grasp of poetry is a "right remark" (line 28) shows how inexact and unscientific both teaching it and understanding it are. There is no evidence for options (2), (3), (4), and (5).

3. **(3) Grading a student's understanding of poetry is difficult and circumstantial.** (Analysis) From the excerpt, you can conclude that Frost believes that grading a person's understanding of poetry is not a simple task.

Frost says that a passing grade may depend on only one remark, providing it is a good one. Option (1) is incorrect because Frost says he doesn't believe everyone should write poetry. Option (2) is incorrect because it can be inferred that, for Frost, grading a student's understanding of poetry is neither exact nor simple. Option (4) is a misreading of the excerpt. Option (5) is true of Frost's grading system, but it is not the best summary of his ideas.

4. **(5) serious and conversational** (Synthesis) The subject, understanding poetry, is serious, but the author writes about it as though he is having a conversation with the reader, frequently referring to himself, using "I." Option (1) is incorrect because the language used is not formal. Options (2), (3), and (4) do not characterize the style in which the excerpt is written.

Lesson 7: Drawing Conclusions
GED Practice (pages 383–384)

1. **(3) People were reacting to the tornado's effects.** (Comprehension) This option includes the actions of all the people in the excerpt. Options (1), (2), (4), and (5) refer to details in the excerpt, not to the general situation.

2. **(5) She did not understand why her husband had contacted her.** (Comprehension) Mrs. Miller had not worried about her husband because she did not realize there was anything to worry about. Option (1) is highly unlikely. Most people find tornadoes very frightening. There is no evidence to support options (2) and (3). Although Mrs. Miller clearly did not know about the tornado, there is no evidence that she slept through it, option (4).

3. **(1) suspenseful** (Synthesis) The first paragraph describes the after-effects of the tornado and ends with the anticipation of a possible second tornado, creating suspense. The suspense is sustained in the second paragraph when the narrator says that he did not know his companion's whereabouts. Options (2) and (5) are inappropriate to describe the tone of such a devastating event. Option (3) is incorrect because although the tornado was unfortunate, it is not described as a tragedy. Option (4) is incorrect because there is no mention of death resulting from the tornado.

4. **(3) an eyewitness account** (Synthesis) The excerpt is narrated in the first person and relates the events from one person's perspective. This is similar to an eyewitness account. Option (1) is

incorrect because there is no evidence that the events described in the excerpt are exaggerated or untrue. A newspaper article would not be written in the first person, so option (2) is incorrect. A television interview would consist of questions and answers; therefore option (4) is incorrect. There is no evidence in the excerpt that suggests the speaker is relating his story to the police, so option (5) is also incorrect.

5. **(3) Show runners are among the most important people in television.** (Analysis) The author states that the show runner is more influential than screenwriters or heads of production companies; therefore, option (1) is incorrect. Because the excerpt does not state that production companies often intrude, option (2) is incorrect. Option (4) is the opposite of what is implied in the excerpt. There is no support in the excerpt for option (5).

6. **(1) writing the pilot for a related new show** (Application) The excerpt defines the responsibilities of the show runner for a series that is already in production. It does not suggest that the show runner is responsible for a new show based on an existing series; therefore, it is probable that this is something the show runner would delegate to someone else. All the other options are responsibilities described as belonging to the show runner.

7. **(2) The guiding force behind *E.R.* is largely unknown to viewers.** (Synthesis) One would expect that the most influential person involved in the production of a popular TV series would be a high-profile person such as the producer or director; in reality, however, it is a person whom most viewers have never heard of. Option (1) is not true based on the excerpt. Option (3) is neither stated nor implied in the excerpt. Options (4) and (5) do not illustrate irony.

Lesson 8: Comparing and Contrasting Ideas
GED Practice (pages 386–387)

1. **(5) The East won't kill you. "The Big One" in the West might.** (Comprehension) The last two sentences in the excerpt invite the reader to come East because it is not going to kill you. "The Big One" is the dominant and only option that suggests the capability of killing. Options (2), (3), and (4) are secondary reasons for choosing the East over the West. Option (1) is a reason for living in the West, not the East.

2. **(4) Four feet of water rush down your street while hellfire comes straight out of the ground. ...** (Analysis) This phrase infers that "the Big One" is a severe disruption in nature, such as an earthquake. Options (1), (2), and (3) simply characterize sights and happenings in Los Angeles, and option (5) characterizes B.C.

3. **(4) People in their right mind would not live in Los Angeles (or anywhere else in the West).** (Analysis) The author presents this view, or attitude toward his main subject, in the opening sentence and continues to cite in the rest of the excerpt the details to support his thinking. Options (1), (2), and (3) merely support this attitude. Option (5) is not stated or inferred in the excerpt.

4. **(5) analytical** (Synthesis) The author examines the changing perception of beauty in the recent history of photography in an intellectual and analytical manner. She is not argumentative; therefore, option (1) is incorrect. She does express opinions and offers evidence to support them; however, she does not seem to be trying to persuade readers. Therefore, option (2) is incorrect. She describes her perception of how ideas of beauty have changed; however, her discussion goes much deeper than a mere description; therefore, option (3) is not the best choice. Although she does explain certain ideas, option (4), this is not her main focus.

5. **(3) to photograph everyday subjects** (Comprehension) The excerpt states that ambitious photographers "conscientiously [explore] plain, tawdry, or even vapid material" (lines 13–15). The photographs resulting from this exploration may be beautiful or lyrical, but beauty or lyricism is not the photographers' main goal; therefore, option (1) is incorrect. There is no support for option (2). The excerpt states that these photographers explore plain and vapid subjects but not that the resulting photographs are themselves plain and vapid; therefore, option (4) is incorrect. The photographers probably do want their photographs to get into museums, but the excerpt does not indicate that this is their primary aim; therefore, option (5) is incorrect.

6. **(5) feeling is to indifference** (Synthesis) The excerpt describes American experience "as catalogued with passion by Whitman and as sized up with a shrug by Warhol" (lines 41–43). The two important words in this statement are

"passion" and "shrug"; they suggest the idea that Whitman is filled with feeling and Warhol is indifferent. The other options contain words that relate to ideas in the excerpt but not to descriptions of the two men.

7. **(1) Every being has dignity and worth.** (Application) The excerpt mentions Whitman's beliefs that every subject has beauty and that each person's actions and ideas are important. Therefore, he is likely to believe that all things and beings have dignity and are valuable. There is no evidence in the excerpt to support the other options.

Lesson 9: Recognizing Author's Viewpoint
GED Practice (page 389)

1. **(3) It is an entertaining film.** (Analysis) The reviewer's opinion can be found in lines 36–38. Although option (1) is an opinion expressed by the reviewer, option (3) better describes his opinion of the movie as a whole. Options (2) and (4) are opinions not held by the reviewer. Option (5) is a fact, not an opinion.

2. **(2) Branagh is perfect for the role of Henry V.** (Analysis) The paragraph describes how Branagh identifies with the role, is involved in many aspects of the movie, and looks and sounds perfect for the part. Options (1) and (3) are not supported by the paragraph. Options (4) and (5) are details from the paragraph but not the main idea.

3. **(1) Shakespeare's play *Henry V* is criticized.** (Synthesis) In the first paragraph, the reviewer refers to *Henry V* as not one of Shakespeare's best. In the last paragraph, he describes the last 10 minutes of the movie in which Henry courts his future wife as needlessly cute, assigning part of the fault for the weakness to Shakespeare. Option (2) is incorrect because only the final paragraph summarizes a scene from the movie. Options (3), (4), and (5) are not true of the review.

GED Review Interpreting Nonfiction
(pages 390–391)

1. **(2) to show what the stories have in common** (Analysis) The stories in the book are interrelated and illustrate some important effects of the war on soldiers. To give a sense of these effects, the reviewer discusses more than one story. In particular, he mentions two stories in which embarrassment plays a role in motivating soldiers. The reviewer is not the focus of this review, so options (1) and (4) are incorrect. There

is no evidence to support option (3). Although the book's author appears to have disliked the war, option (5) does not explain the structure of the review.

2. **(3) It examines the soldiers' feelings.** (Comprehension) The reviewer indicates that this book is unique because it discusses not only the horror of war, but also the soldiers' courage, fear, and shame. The review does not describe soldiers' routines, so option (1) is incorrect. The fact that the book comprises short stories is not emphasized as one of its particular strengths, so option (2) is incorrect. There is no evidence to support option (4). The review does not focus on the author's description of battles; therefore, option (5) is incorrect.

3. **(2) be criticized for not going to war** (Comprehension) The book describes embarrassment as the reason that the author, and perhaps others, served in the war—specifically embarrassment that they would be thought of as unpatriotic. There is no evidence to support the other options.

4. **(3) it should be read in addition to *The Things They Carried*** (Comprehension) The reviewer applauds this novel, too. He describes both of O'Brien's books as "essential fiction about Vietnam" (lines 7–8). He does not indicate that it is better than *The Things They Carried*, so option (1) is incorrect. There is no evidence to support options (2), (4), or (5).

5. **(5) admiring** (Synthesis) The reviewer states that the book is "high up on the list of best fiction about any war" (lines 19–20) and that the author examines the soldiers' feelings about the war "with sensitivity and insight" (line 14). Although the subject of the book is harsh, the review of the book is not; therefore, option (1) is incorrect. There is no evidence to support options (2) or (3). The author is very enthusiastic about O'Brien's book; therefore, option (4) is not strong enough to be the best description of the review's tone.

6. **(2) the experience of war** (Synthesis) The majority of the review describes the specifics of the war experience as written about in O'Brien's book. Although some of the stories may be based on the author's experiences, the review states that the stories are fictional; therefore, option (1) is incorrect. Particular battles are not discussed, so option (3) is incorrect. There is no evidence to support options (4) or (5).

Understanding Fiction
Lesson 10: Getting Meaning from Context
GED Practice (pages 393–394)

1. **(2) He is persistent.** (Synthesis) Although the networks may have found Hadden annoying, there is nothing in the excerpt to support options (1) and (3). There is also nothing in the excerpt to support option (5), and option (4) is the opposite of how he is portrayed.

2. **(4) television programs** (Comprehension) The excerpt states "the programs that were their nominal vehicles." This phrase clearly shows that the programs and the nominal vehicles are the same thing. Option (1) is incorrect because the ads were louder than the nominal vehicles, so they could not be the nominal vehicles. Options (2) and (3) are incorrect because there is no mention of anything to do with cars in the excerpt, indicating that "vehicle" has more than one meaning. Option (5) is the opposite of what the excerpt states.

3. **(1) a device that silences TV commercials** (Analysis) The first sentence says that Hadden had invented a module that automatically muted the sound when a commercial appeared. This information tells you that the product Adnix silences TV commercials. None of the other options support this conclusion.

4. **(3) Television networks do not have viewers' best interests at heart.** (Synthesis) Hadden kept attempting to thwart the networks' advertisements, which indicates that he believed the networks did not have viewers' best interests at heart. If Hadden believed in options (1), (4), or (5), he probably would not have built his device. Option (2) is not supported by the excerpt.

5. **(2) the undesirable nature of commercials** (Synthesis) The excerpt describes a character who invents a device that renders TV commercials mute. Based on this fact and the fact that people felt a sense of relief when freed from commercials, you can infer that the theme concerns the negative effects of commercial television. Option (1) is too broad a statement; option (3) is not implied by the information in the excerpt; option (4), though it may be inferred from the excerpt, is not the theme; and option (5) is the opposite of what the excerpt portrays.

6. **(4) the acceptance of "infomercials" to promote products** (Application) Of the options listed, only option (4) concerns commercials, the target of Hadden's inventions.

7. **(4) The U.S. government wanted to take over production and use of Hadden's chip.** (Analysis) Option (1) refers to an earlier trial. Options (2) and (3) are incorrect because the excerpt does not say that Hadden was involved in industrial espionage and military intelligence. Option (5) is incorrect because there is no mention of the U.S. government's wanting Hadden's muting device.

Lesson 11: Identifying Plot Elements
GED Practice (page 396)

1. **(1) selfish** (Analysis) *Selfish* means putting your own desires ahead of everyone else's. The grandmother does not want to go to Florida, so she tries to manipulate the family into doing what she wants. Option (2) is incorrect because she is mentioning The Misfit not because she is worried but because she doesn't want to go to Florida. There is no support in the excerpt for options (3), (4), or (5).

2. **(2) They ignore her for the most part.** (Analysis) When her son doesn't answer her, the grandmother addresses her daughter-in-law, who acts as if she does not hear her. The little boy is the only one to make a comment, and he merely suggests that she stay home. There is no support in the excerpt for the other options.

3. **(2) a meeting in which a boss tries to change his staff's mind about an issue** (Application) The grandmother is trying very hard to change her family's mind about where to vacation. None of the other options are supported by the excerpt.

4. **(5) dialogue in which her manner of speaking is shown** (Analysis) The dialogue reveals the grandmother to be a pushy and self-centred woman. The excerpt contains very little information about what she looks like, and no details about her heritage or her preferred reading matter; therefore, options (1), (2), and (3) are incorrect. The excerpt implies that the other characters find the grandmother tiresome, but there is no actual explanation of this; therefore, option (4) is incorrect.

Lesson 12: Applying Ideas
GED Practice (page 398)

1. **(1) think the bone soup was responsible** (Application) Lines 24–26 state that the mother hoped that the bone soup would perform the miracle of detaching Caroline from her Bahamian fiancé. This suggests that the mother believed

that it had special powers. None of the other options are supported by the details in the excerpt.

2. **(3) They like to poke fun at their mother's beliefs.** (Analysis) The excerpt states that the narrator was teasing when she asked Caroline whether she had had some soup; this indicates that the narrator was making fun of their mother's belief that the soup could cure all kinds of ills. There is no support in the excerpt for options (1) and (2). Options (4) and (5) may be true but are not why the narrator asked the question.

3. **(4) She cares about her daughters' futures.** (Synthesis) The mother is excited about the passport and the possibilities it holds; she is also worried about Caroline's engagement. These details show that she is quite concerned about her daughters' futures. There is no evidence in the excerpt to support options (1), (2), or (5). Option (3) is incorrect because the mother clearly does not support Caroline's decision to marry.

Lesson 13: Identifying Cause and Effect
GED Practice (pages 400–401)

1. **(3) They have contracted a contagious disease.** (Comprehension) Lines 6–8 state that there were many sick and dying but that the number of new victims had gone down. This, and the reference to the "rage of the white-scabs," indicates that the people have contracted a contagious disease. The excerpt does not support options (1) and (5). Option (2) is incorrect because the phrase "thirteenth sleep of sickness" means the thirteenth day that the sickness had set in. Option (4) is incorrect because the people did leave their lodges to walk in the sun or to sit.

2. **(3) a person wearing a face mask in the hospital to avoid germs** (Application) The villagers are avoiding one another in order to keep from getting sick; a person wearing a face mask to avoid germs is also trying to keep from getting sick. Options (1) and (5) concern people actually getting sick, so these are incorrect. The excerpt does not mention villagers disliking each other, so option (2) is incorrect. Option (4) is incorrect because the villagers leave the path to avoid other villagers, not because they want to walk in the woods.

3. **(2) the presence of a bad spirit** (Analysis) Lines 20–22 mention families hit hard by the bad spirit. This implies that the people believed a bad

spirit caused the epidemic. The other options are not supported by the details in the excerpt.

4. **(1) They were disheartened and sad.** (Analysis) Several clues in the excerpt point to this answer. The people do not greet each other, there was none of the usual bustle, and the wailing old woman made the people realize how much they had lost. All these things point to sadness. Option (2) may be correct, but it wouldn't cause them to be a different people. There is no support for options (3), (4), or (5).

5. **(2) It helps readers understand how the characters feel.** (Synthesis) This approach gives the reader a sense of being inside the situation and can therefore help give the reader a fuller understanding of the views and feelings of the villagers. Option (1) is incorrect because it is the opposite of what occurs. There is no support in the excerpt for option (3). Options (4) and (5) are incorrect because there is no mention in the excerpt of either the white man or outsiders.

6. **(1) They left it bare of leaves.** (Analysis) The result is described in the last paragraph. The colour in option (2) refers to a swarm of locusts, not the land. Options (3), (4), and (5) are not mentioned in the excerpt.

7. **(4) the swarm of locusts** (Analysis) The locusts are referred to in line 9 as an army; after Stephen sees the red smear, which thickens and spreads, he says, "There goes the main army" (line 14). The excerpt states that the sky is blue, so options (1) and (3) are incorrect. There is no mention of either actual soldiers or crop dusters, so options (2) and (5) are incorrect.

8. **(4) people versus nature** (Synthesis) Old Stephen and Margaret's farm has been ruined by locusts, which are a part of nature. None of the other options are supported by the excerpt.

9. **(1) colour** (Synthesis) The author mentions several colours in the excerpt to describe the attack: blue, green, red, reddish brown, brownish red, black.

Lesson 14: Analyzing Character
GED Practice (pages 403–404)

1. **(2) She is much sicker than she says she is.** (Analysis) The description of how her bones felt and how her vision was affected suggests that she is very ill, as does the conversation between Cornelia and Doctor Harry. Therefore, options (1) and (4) are incorrect. There is no evidence to support option (3), and option (5) is incorrect

because she has nothing good to say about Cornelia.

2. **(1) understanding but firm** (Analysis) The effect of the doctor's words is soothing but carries a hint of warning. The words he uses are informal and simple, so option (2) is incorrect. Although "gentle" might be an appropriate description, the doctor is sure of himself, so option (3) is incorrect. Option (4) is too extreme, even though the doctor warns Granny. Because of the warning, option (5) is also incorrect.

3. **(2) what she says** (Synthesis) Granny Weatherall's words, option (2), are featured throughout the excerpt. What she has to say effectively shows her proud and somewhat cantankerous character. Each of the other options names something that actually does give some information about Granny Weatherall's character, but not nearly as much as option (2). Therefore, none of the remaining options is the best choice.

4. **(2) She is very tense.** (Comprehension) A strained flag is one that is stretched tight by the wind or held tense and taut. The excerpt does not support the other options.

5. **(4) confidently, with her head held high** (Application) Miss Emily speaks straightforwardly and holds her head erect. This shows that she is a confident, proud woman. There is no evidence in the excerpt to support options (1), (2), (3), or (5).

6. **(5) She intimidates other people.** (Synthesis) Miss Emily does not state the purpose for which the arsenic will be used and stares at the druggist until he wraps it up. This indicates that she intimidates him. In addition, she also constantly interrupts the druggist, which can also be a method of intimidation. Her insistence on buying arsenic rules out option (1), that she cannot make up her mind. There is no evidence in the excerpt to support options (2), (3), and (4).

7. **(3) Miss Emily is forceful, but the druggist is accommodating.** (Synthesis) Option (1) is incorrect because Miss Emily does not seem terribly grumpy, although she does seem determined. The druggist can be said to be accommodating because he gives Miss Emily the arsenic without making her say why she wants it. Options (2), (4), and (5) are not supported by the excerpt.

Lesson 15: Analyzing Tone
GED Practice (pages 406–408)

1. **(1) fearful** (Comprehension) Lines 36–37 describe the daughters as "trembling and in silence," which shows their fear. There is no support for options (2), (3), or (4). Option (5) may be true of the women, but there is no direct evidence in this excerpt to support this option.

2. **(5) walked carefully** (Comprehension) In the previous paragraph, Mr. Osborne walked (strode) downstairs. In the following paragraph, the seemingly frightened women are quietly following him. From this you can infer that they are walking carefully and quietly behind Mr. Osborne. There is no evidence that the women are falling; therefore, options (1) and (3) are incorrect. Although the women are whispering, the phrase "tripped gingerly" refers to the way they are moving, not the way they are speaking; therefore, option (2) is incorrect. There is no support for option (4).

3. **(4) He may be losing money on his investments.** (Comprehension) Although all of the answer options may be possible explanations for Mr. Osborne's behaviour, only option (4) is specifically mentioned by one of the characters. In line 35, Miss Wirt says, "I suppose the funds are falling," suggesting that Mr. Osborne is losing money.

4. **(2) He would dismiss her without seeing her.** (Application) Mr. Osborne's rash decision to fire the cook and his impatience with George's tardiness for dinner support the idea that he would dismiss one of his daughters for failing to keep an appointment. Options (1), (4), and (5) are incorrect because Mr. Osborne is not characterized as being nervous, forgiving, or patient. There is not enough evidence in the excerpt to support option (3).

5. **(4) tense** (Synthesis) The words "scowling," "roared," "violently," "growled," "gruffly," and "trembled" establish a tense mood. Mr. Osborne's words and actions put everyone on edge. There is no support for the other options.

6. **(3) Mr. Osborne did not seem satisfied with the fish.** (Analysis) The word "curt" (line 58) means "sharp" or "annoyed," so Mr. Osborne was not happy with the fish. Additionally, he had already stated his strong dissatisfaction with the cook's soup, so he was probably not happy with her cooking in general. The excerpt implies that Mr. Osborne's remarks

are criticisms of the fish, not commands that it should be eaten; therefore, option (1) is incorrect. There is no evidence in the excerpt to support options (2) and (4). Mr. Osborne does not appear to be the sort of man who would try to make conversation, so option (5) is incorrect.

7. **(3) the reference to Amelia's fear when she sits next to him** (Analysis) Mr. Osborne does not show any warmth toward anyone, and everyone seems frightened by him. Options (1) and (2) refer to his position in the family, a role traditionally given to fathers in the past. Option (4) does not indicate lack of warmth. Option (5) is incorrect because he does refer to Jane, one of his daughters, by name.

8. **(1) He is extremely intolerant.** (Analysis) This behaviour is suggestive of a person who is intolerant of others' shortcomings. It is not a good example of alarm, rendering option (4) incorrect. Options (2), (3), and (5) are not supported by the text.

9. **(4) one of Jane's siblings** (Analysis) The way Jane speaks of George, using his first name and saying he'll be back to dinner, as well as the way the butler calls him "Mr. George" (line 16), indicates that he is a family member. This familiarity rules out options (1), (2), and (5). There is no support in the excerpt for option (3).

10. **(5) a terrible man** (Synthesis) Lines 42–44, "for she was next to the awful Osborne," reveal the narrator's attitude toward Mr. Osborne. Mr. Osborne is depicted as cruel and violent, so option (1) is not the best choice. Mr. Osborne is depicted as neither admirable nor patient, so options (2) and (3) are incorrect. Although Mr. Osborne is certainly grumpy, this word is too mild to capture his cruelty, so option (4) is not the best choice.

11. **(4) a man of honour who respects his son's beliefs** (Comprehension) His response illustrates that he respects Carter's decision, even though he does not agree with it; therefore, option (2) is incorrect. Option (1) is incorrect because the excerpt indicates the father's stated concern for his wife and his unstated concern for his son. There is no evidence for option (3). The first paragraph states that Carter is the son of wealthy parents, so option (5) is incorrect.

12. **(3) keeping a difficult promise** (Application) Carter is clearly an honest and honourable man, so if he made a promise, he would keep it. It is

not in his character as described in the excerpt to do what is suggested by options (1), (2), and (5). Because he has made the decision to enter the Union Army in the face of opposition, option (4) is unlikely.

13. **(2) formal** (Analysis) The father and son address each other in a formal manner, and the author uses formal language such as "cultivation," "leonine," and "perilous" in his descriptions. Options (1), (3), (4), and (5) are not supported by the details in the excerpt.

14. **(3) The war divided even the closest families.** (Synthesis) One of the tragedies of the Civil War was that family members sometimes fought on opposing sides. The father's statement that Druse is a traitor to Virginia when he joins the Union regiment emphasizes this fact. Options (1), (2), (4), and (5) are all true but do not involve Druse's decision.

Lesson 16: Identifying Figurative Language
GED Practice (page 410)

1. **(4) a room in an attic** (Comprehension) The excerpt refers to a "dormer window set high in the slanting room" (lines 14–15). This is a description of an attic, a room immediately below a slanting roof. There is no support for the other options.

2. **(3) He would care for the cat.** (Application) The excerpt shows Dr. Fischelson's concern for insects when he waves them away from the candle. If he shows such concern for insects, it can be inferred that he would show similar concern for a stray cat. The other options do not reflect his concern for living creatures.

3. **(1) nose and eyes** (Comprehension) The excerpt describes his nose as crooked as a beak and his eyes as being large, dark, and fluttering like those of some huge bird. His head, feet, and neck are not compared to a bird, so the other options are incorrect.

4. **(3) ominous** (Synthesis) Dr. Fischelson is dressed uncomfortably and is pacing back and forth. The insects are burning in the candle flame, and Dr. Fischelson finds this troubling. These details give the reader the feeling that something bad is going to happen. There is no support for options (1), (2), and (4). In option (5), although the insects die a painful and violent death, this detail does not characterize the overall tone of the excerpt.

Lesson 17: Making Inferences

GED Practice (pages 412–414)

1. **(4) She was envious of the new soloist.** (Comprehension) This answer is suggested by the fourth paragraph. There is no evidence for option (1). Option (2) is incorrect because the church has already hired a new soloist. Option (3) is incorrect because Candace no longer sings at church. Option (5) is incorrect because she is forced to retire against her will.

2. **(2) Alma was prepared to conquer her fear.** (Comprehension) The sentence describes her lack of confidence and fear in a figurative way—as a mountain—and says that her nerves were braced for its ascent. This means she was prepared to conquer her fear. There is no evidence in the excerpt to support options (1), (3), (4), and (5).

3. **(5) The women were partially horrified.** (Comprehension) The sentence says that they were "half aghast, half smiling." This suggests that *aghast* is being contrasted with, and is therefore the opposite of, *smiling* and *amused*, so option (3) is incorrect. There is no support for options (1), (2), and (4).

4. **(4) She felt weak from the strain of having to compete with Candace's singing.** (Analysis) The fifth and sixth paragraphs describe Alma's reaction to Candace's interruption; therefore, options (1) and (2) are incorrect. The man looked at her after she felt faint, so option (3) is incorrect. Candace was removed from her job as soloist because of her flawed voice, so option (5) is incorrect.

5. **(2) try to get reinstated as the choir's soloist** (Application) The reasons for Candace's removal from the choir and her jealousy toward Alma indicate that she is unwilling to give up her status as soloist; therefore, option (1) is incorrect. Option (3) is incorrect because it is obvious that Candace considers Alma a rival and would probably not want to sing with her. There is no clear support for options (4) and (5).

6. **(3) "All the people stared at her, and turned their ears critically." (lines 2–3)** (Analysis) Only option (3) contributes to the atmosphere, or general feeling, in the church. Options (1), (2), (4), and (5) are details that describe the characters and not the setting of the story.

7. **(1) She is willing to face a challenge.** (Analysis) Alma is nervous, but she sings well anyway. Option (2) is incorrect because she is not thinking about her looks. There is no support for the other options.

8. **(4) informal and serious** (Analysis) The language is not technical, so option (1) is incorrect. Option (2) is incorrect because the author describes the emotions of the characters. There is little suggestion of humour, so option (3) is incorrect. The language is direct and informative, so option (5) is incorrect.

9. **(5) a crow's voice and a canary's** (Synthesis) Candace's voice is described as being cracked, shrill, and clamouring, which could be seen as comparable to a crow's caw. Alma's voice is described as being "piercingly sweet" (line 35) and canaries are noted for their sweet and beautiful song. The cry of an eagle, the near silence of a hummingbird, and the hoot of an owl are not comparable to either Candace's voice or Alma's voice as described in the excerpt; therefore, options (1), (2), (3), and (4) are incorrect.

10. **(2) reform him** (Comprehension) The excerpt refers to the widow putting the narrator into new clothes, having him say grace before eating, teaching him about Moses, and refusing to let him smoke. These are all efforts to reform him. There is no support in the excerpt for options (1), (3), (4), and (5).

11. **(3) a bowl of beef stew** (Application) The narrator says, "In a barrel of odds and ends it is different; things get mixed up, and the juice kinds of swaps around, and the things go better" (lines 13–16). Of the choices, a bowl of stew is the only food that fits that description.

12. **(5) conversational** (Analysis) The narrator of the story relates his experiences as if he were talking to another person; therefore, the tone is conversational. The excerpt supports none of the other options.

13. **(1) It gives clues about the time and place.** (Synthesis) The use of slang and nonstandard English is true to the era and place where this story takes place—the South in the early nineteenth century. Option (2) is incorrect because the widow's speech is not revealed. Options (3) and (4) might be true but are not the main reasons that it is effective. Option (5) is an opinion and cannot be supported by the excerpt.

Lesson 18: Comparing and Contrasting

GED Practice (page 416)

1. **(3) They have been stranded.**
   (Comprehension) In lines 36–37, Piggy asks, "When'll your dad rescue us?" This suggests that the boys are stranded. There is no evidence to support the other options.

2. **(4) suffer in silence** (Application) In lines 17–18, Piggy responds to Ralph's comment about his asthma "with a sort of humble patience." This supports option (4). There is nothing in the excerpt that would support options (1), (2), (3), and (5).

3. **(3) Both believe Ralph's father will rescue them.** (Synthesis) Ralph directly states that his father will come get them. Piggy asks when this will happen, suggesting that he believes what Ralph says. Options (2) and (5) are only true of Piggy, and option (4) is true only of Ralph. There is no evidence that either boy envies the other, so option (1) is also incorrect.

Lesson 19: Interpreting Theme

GED Practice (pages 418–419)

1. **(5) A person's worldview is shaped by key events.** (Comprehension) This idea is stated in the last sentence of the first paragraph. There is no evidence for options (1) and (4). Options (2) and (3) may be true but are not supported by the excerpt.

2. **(4) Every few months something shocking occurs.** (Comprehension) The narrator gives the example of Mussolini's death, which was a shocking event because he "had almost seemed one of the eternal leaders" (lines 51–52). There is no support in the excerpt for options (1), (2), and (3). Although the narrator refers to a shortage of supplies, there is no mention that this occurs every few months, so option (5) is incorrect.

3. **(4) The historical era affects the individual.** (Application) The statement is similar to the author's belief that a person is affected by certain events in life. People's experiences are directly affected by the time and place in history during which they live; therefore, individuals' understanding of how the world works will be affected by this as well. Option (1) is not suggested by the excerpt. Option (2) suggests that the present is more important than the past, but the author is talking about the importance of the past. Option (3) is too general, and option (5) has nothing to do with what the author is saying.

4. **(2) by talking about the war as if it were happening now** (Analysis) The present tense makes the war seem more immediate, as close as it seems to the author. Options (1) and (3) are mentioned but do not help to explain the author's feelings. Options (4) and (5) are false.

5. **(1) to recall events that took place during his adolescence** (Analysis) From the perspective of a sixteen-year-old, the narrator describes in detail the effects the war had on Americans. Option (2) is incorrect because not all of the realities that the narrator experienced affect Americans today. Option (3) is incorrect because the excerpt does not address the present. Option (4) is incorrect because the narrator does not recall many pleasant times during the war; and option (5) is incorrect because the excerpt describes the American way of life during the war, not the horrors of war.

6. **(1) He was young and impressionable.** (Analysis) He seems to have seen the events from a youthful point of view; sixteen is an age when emotions are easily influenced. Option (2) may be true but is not supported. Options (3) and (4) are mentioned, but they were not the cause of the narrator's feelings. Option (5) is incorrect because the narrator says that he did not foresee himself becoming a soldier.

7. **(5) serious** (Analysis) The entire excerpt describes the difficult realities of living through the war years. This description is presented in a serious manner. Option (1) is incorrect because the narrator doesn't criticize; he presents the realities as they were. Option (2) is the opposite of the tone of the excerpt. Option (3) is incorrect because it implies warm feelings that the narrator does not express, and option (4) is incorrect because the focus is on the past and not the future.

8. **(4) matter-of-fact and repetitive** (Synthesis) The narrator describes the effect of the war primarily in short sentences with very little description, and he repeatedly uses the word "always" (lines 18–33). None of the other options accurately describe the style in which the excerpt is written.

9. **(4) indicate the monotony imposed by war** (Synthesis) The style of the excerpt is characterized mainly by short sentences presented in a repetitive pattern that reflect the monotony and regimentation of wartime. Option (1) is incorrect because the excerpt does not promote patriotism. Option (2) is incorrect

because it does not discuss the war directly. Option (3) may be a result of reading about the hardships of war but would not affect the style in which the author chose to write. Option (5) is incorrect because it was written by an adult and does not truly reflect the mindset of a sixteen-year-old.

10. **(3) The "good old days" were not always good.** (Synthesis) The narrator is critical of the America he knew during his youth, recounting the negative effects that the war had on American life. None of the other statements are supported by the details in the excerpt.

GED Review Understanding Fiction
(pages 420–421)

1. **(4) He is threatening Lee Chong.** (Analysis) These are veiled statements that indicate to Lee Chong that Mack and his friends might harm Lee's property if Lee does not allow them to move in. There is no evidence to support options (1), (2), (3), or (5).

2. **(3) try to help put out the fire** (Application) Mack's deal with Lee allows him and his friends to live in the Abbeville place. Therefore, it is in their best interest to protect the place and put out the fire. If fire destroyed the house, they would have to move out, option (1). However, since they would not move out unless they had to, option (1) is not the best choice. Mack implies that he and his friends would burn the place only if he does not get what he wants; since he is getting what he wants, option (2) is incorrect. There is no support for option (4). Although there is some indication that Lee Chong thinks Mack and his friends are capable of theft, they do not actually steal anything in the excerpt; therefore, option (5) is not the best choice.

3. **(1) useful** (Analysis) Both parties get what they need: Mack and his friends have a place to live, and Lee Chong is assured that his place will not be destroyed. Although Mack's behaviour may be considered immoral, option (2), Lee Chong's behaviour probably would not be. The situation might have become dangerous only if Lee Chong did not agree to let Mack live in the place, so option (3) is incorrect. There is no evidence to support options (4) and (5).

4. **(2) fair prices to ensure many repeat customers** (Application) Judging from his behaviour in the excerpt, Lee Chong is a practical man who keeps an eye on the long-term benefit more than short-term gain; therefore, he would

probably choose an approach that would be the most likely to benefit him in the long run. There is no evidence that he shows favouritism to his friends; friendship is not part of the deal that he and Mack make; therefore, option (1) is incorrect. There is no evidence to support option (3). He does not seem to be unfair to customers at the grocery store; therefore, options (4) and (5) are incorrect.

5. **(4) power and practicality** (Synthesis) The group exerts its power over Lee Chong by threatening his property, so Lee Chong responds with a practical approach to protecting it. There is no support for options (1), (2), or (5). Although Mack and his friends do receive the benefit of living in the Abbeville place, the granting of that favour is not entirely voluntary on Lee's part. Therefore, option (3) is not the best answer.

6. **(3) Weighing risks helps in making good decisions.** (Synthesis) Lee Chong thinks carefully about the negative and positive consequences before deciding to agree to Mack's proposal. Lee decides to work with the group rather than risk danger to his house. Since Lee Chong's saving face was the result of taking the path that would cause the least amount of damage to his property, it is not a weak approach. Therefore, option (1) is not the best choice. Mack and Lee are not friends; in fact, Mack is forcing Lee Chong to let him use the property, so option (2) is incorrect. Lee Chong does use negotiation skills to protect his interests; therefore, option (4) is incorrect. Mack is gaining a place to live by being unfair to Lee Chong; therefore, option (5) is also incorrect.

7. **(3) tense** (Synthesis) Lee Chong is not pleased with his visit from Mack, and the conversation between the two men is tense. There is no evidence to support options (1) or (2). Neither Mack nor Lee Chong expresses anger; therefore, option (4) is incorrect. There may be a superficial friendliness, option (5), but this choice does not address the underlying conflict of the situation.

Understanding Poetry
Lesson 20: Identifying the Effects of Rhythm and Rhyme
GED Practice (pages 423–424)

1. **(2) separated** (Comprehension) Option (1) is incorrect because line 4 states that one road bends. Options (3) and (4) are the opposite of what the poet describes. There is no direct evidence for option (5).

2. **(3) how decisions define people's lives** (Analysis) In lines 16–20, the speaker indicates the effects of his decisions on his life. The speaker does not express regret regarding his choices; therefore, option (1) is incorrect. Options (2) and (4) are not supported by the poem. The changes the speaker experiences occur as a result of his decisions in life rather than as a result of a literal walk in the woods. For this reason, option (5) is incorrect.

3. **(1) think carefully before committing himself** (Application) The speaker is likely to make a decision about where to live in the same way that he chooses a road in the woods. In the poem, the speaker thought for a while and then made a confident decision. The speaker clearly makes the decision by himself without relying on friends; therefore, option (2) is incorrect. The speaker does not choose the road that is more popular; therefore, option (3) is incorrect. Option (4) is incorrect because there is no evidence that the speaker worries about his decision. The speaker took some time to make his decision, but he made a definite choice and followed it; therefore, option (5) is incorrect.

4. **(1) Unexpected sights can produce endless pleasure.** (Comprehension) The sight of the daffodils was unexpected and the memory of this sight often brings pleasure to the speaker. There is no evidence to support options (2) and (5). Although the speaker does describe the flowers as "dancing" (line 6) and "Tossing their heads" (line 12), these are details, not the main idea. Therefore, option (3) is incorrect. Option (4) is the opposite of what is implied by the poem.

5. **(2) the stars of the milky way** (Analysis) It is the speaker who wanders lonely as a cloud, the speaker who experiences a pensive mood, and the speaker whose heart is filled with pleasure; therefore, options (1), (3), and (4) are incorrect. Option (5) is incorrect because the speaker contrasts the flowers with the sparkling waves; he emphasizes the difference between the two.

6. **(3) The speaker sometimes pictures the flowers in his mind when he is alone.** (Analysis) The phrase "inward eye" makes reference to what the author can see inside his head, or in his imagination. There is no support for option (2). There is no direct evidence for option (1). Option (4) does not mention flowers. Option (5) is the opposite of what occurs in the poem and therefore is incorrect.

7. **(2) sprightly and upbeat** (Synthesis) The rhythm of the poem gives a happy feeling of flowers dancing. Option (1) overstates the regular rhythm of the poem; therefore, it is incorrect. This steady but active rhythm is thoughtful but not slow; nor could it be called fast-paced; therefore, options (3) and (4) are incorrect. The rhythm is fairly even; therefore, option (5) is incorrect.

8. **(3) notice all the details of how the rain looked and felt** (Application) The speaker notices so many details about the daffodils that he can replay them in his mind's eye. Therefore, he is likely to remember the details of a rain shower. There is no support in the poem for option (1). Options (2) and (4) might be true, but there is no evidence in the poem to support them. The speaker does not seem to feel that nature is predictable; therefore, option (5) is incorrect.

Lesson 21: Interpreting Figurative Language
GED Practice (page 426)

1. **(3) Both were meant to work hard but did not.** (Analysis) The speaker describes the machines that sit idle outside his window. He then compares himself to a good machine that once was "eager to do its work" (line 15) but had never been used. Option (1) is incorrect because there is no evidence that the machines break or are broken. There is no evidence that the machines or the speaker needs constant attention—perhaps just regular use; therefore, option (2) is incorrect. Option (4) is contradicted by information in the poem. There is no evidence to support option (5).

2. **(2) a toaster that was never taken out of its box** (Application) The machinery was never used, much like a toaster that was never removed from its box. There is no support in the poem for options (1) and (4). The machinery may be useless junk now, but it was once potentially useful; therefore, option (3) is incorrect. The machinery was never used and may be beyond repair at this point; therefore, option (5) is incorrect.

3. **(2) believes it is too late to live a full life** (Synthesis) The poet is expressing sadness at realizing his life is almost over and he has done so little with it. There is no support for options (1), (4), and (5). Option (3) is too literal and therefore is incorrect.

Lesson 22: Interpreting Symbols and Images
GED Practice (pages 428–429)

1. **(1) She is an office worker.** (Comprehension) She wears conservative clothing and works for a boss who also has a boss—this sounds as though she likely has an office job. Options (2) and (3) are possible answers, but there is more support for option (1) in the context of the poem. There is no support for option (4); it is contradicted by the statement "I wear to work" (line 7). Option (5) is incorrect. It is not the speaker who has any connection with an embassy but the people who wear saris.

2. **(5) She sees life happening without her.** (Comprehension) The caged animals are visited by other animals and also the human visitors to the zoo. Even though they are caged, life is happening to them and around them. This is not the way the speaker feels about her life. Options (1) and (2) may be true but are not supported in the poem. Option (3) is incorrect because there is no mention of the woman's friends in the poem. Option (4) is incorrect because there is no evidence that the speaker is refusing to let others know her. Instead, the poem suggests that others ignore her.

3. **(4) She feels caged within herself just as the animals are penned in cages.** (Analysis) Her own life is the trap, not something done to her by someone else. There is no evidence for the other options.

4. **(4) to break free of her life's routine** (Synthesis) The speaker is stuck and unhappy in her current life; nothing new ever happens to her. There is no support for options (1) and (5). Options (2) and (3) may be true but do not have as much support as option (4).

5. **(4) change** (Analysis) The woman pleads with the vulture to change her. Earlier in the poem, she asks to be freed from her body; in other words, she wishes to be transformed by death. Therefore, the vulture is a symbol of change in this poem (specifically change from life to death). A further clue to the meaning of this symbol is the fact that vultures sometimes are associated with death because they eat dead animals. There is no evidence that the woman is afraid; therefore, option (1) is incorrect. There is no support in the poem for options (2) and (5). Although vultures are certainly a part of nature, this connection to nature is not heavily emphasized; therefore, option (3) is incorrect.

6. **(1) the colourful cloth of the saris and the dull cloth of the speaker's work clothes** (Analysis) These are the only two types of cloth mentioned in the poem, and they create a vivid contrast. The cloths mentioned in option (2) are both figurative references to the cloth of the saris. The descriptions in option (3) both pertain to the cloth of the speaker's work clothes and so do not create a contrast. Options (4) and (5) include cloth not mentioned in the poem and therefore are incorrect.

7. **(3) despairing** (Synthesis) The speaker seems lonely, sad, and almost hopeless; even the animals in the zoo have more visitors. There is no support for the other options.

8. **(2) feels that death will release her from captivity** (Analysis) The speaker brings up the topic of death in the previous line when she comments on how the animals are ignorant of it. The speaker also indicates that she feels trapped by her life. Therefore, when the speaker asks for release from the cage of her body, the most direct interpretation of this request is that she desires release from her body and her life through death. There is no support in the poem for options (1), (3), and (5). Option (4) may be true but does not explain the phrase or the reference to the speaker's body and therefore is incorrect.

Lesson 23: Making Inferences
GED Practice (pages 431–432)

1. **(4) I stopped to look at the land around San Ysidro while travelling to Colorado.** (Comprehension) The poem specifically states that this is in fact what the speaker did. Although option (1) may be true, it cannot be inferred from the lines. There is not enough evidence in the poem to support option (2). Option (3) is incorrect because the lines indicate that the speaker did stop. Option (5) may be true, but this is not where the speaker stopped.

2. **(2) the feeling of gliding back and forth** (Analysis) The rhythm of these lines glides and then pauses, much like the swooping hawk described in these lines. The rhythm is not quick or strong enough for options (1), (4), or (5) to be correct. There is too much movement in these lines to support option (3).

3. **(1) spring** (Comprehension) The earth is described as "new again," so spring is the season in which the events of the poem are most likely to occur. Therefore, options (2), (3), and (4) are incorrect. Option (5) is incorrect because the harvest season would be in the fall.

Unit 5

4. **(1) joyful** (Analysis) Lines 34–42 indicate the happiness that the speaker feels about the plants and earth. There is no direct evidence for options (2), (3), (4), and (5).

5. **(3) clouds filled with rain** (Analysis) The word "overhead" indicates that the lines refer to something in the sky, and the words "The Thunderer" later in the stanza suggest the idea of rain coming. There is no mention of the hawk's prey; therefore, option (1) is incorrect. Options (2) and (4) do not refer to something overhead and so are incorrect. The sunlight falls in a straight shaft; therefore, option (5) does not fit the definition of the word "writhing" and so is incorrect.

6. **(5) He is waiting to see a ceremonial dance.** (Comprehension) There is a time shift in the poem at line 27. The first part of the poem describes his recollection of a stop on a journey when he appreciated the beauty of Earth, and the last part describes his eager anticipation of the Katzina and their ceremony of Earth's renewal. There is no support for options (1) and (4). Options (2) and (3) make sense only if the speaker is still travelling, and it is not clear that he is.

7. **(5) the Katzina** (Comprehension) Line 27 states that "Today, the Katzina come." This is what the speaker is referring to. There is no support for options (1) or (2). Option (3) has some support because the bells refer to the Katzina, but it is not as complete an answer as option (5). The Katzina are coming to do a ceremonial dance about the renewal of the plants and earth, so there is also some support for option (4). However, the "plants with bells" and "stones with voices" in lines 40–41 refer to the masked dancers, not to literal plants and stones. Therefore, when the speaker uses the word "they" in the previous line, he is referring to the Katzina, not to the arrival of spring.

8. **(4) The cycle of nature and plant life is wonderful.** (Synthesis) This is the essence of the speaker's observations about the land. There is no evidence to support options (1) and (2). Option (3) may be true, but rainfall is not the central focus of the poem. Option (5) is incorrect because the speaker is less concerned with the ritual itself than with what that ritual represents—the celebration of the Earth's renewal.

9. **(5) a forest** (Application) The speaker feels joy in nature and in the growth of plants. New York City is large with relatively little plant life and

natural surroundings; therefore, option (1) is incorrect. Although suburbs are not big cities, they are still further from nature than a forest, so option (2) is incorrect. Option (3) is a natural environment but too barren to provide much, if any, plant growth; therefore, it is not the best option. Option (4) is not a natural environment and therefore is incorrect.

10. **(4) The dancers seem as if they are a part of nature.** (Analysis) The dancers are celebrating nature in a ceremonial dance; therefore, this option makes the most sense. There is no support in the poem for the other options.

Lesson 24: Interpreting Theme
GED Practice (pages 434–435)

1. **(2) The little girl has abundant energy.** (Analysis) The word "flying" suggests that the girl is running and leaping. Options (1), (3), and (4) assume the word is meant literally. Option (5) is incorrect because it suggests the girl was trying to avoid the grass, which is not mentioned.

2. **(4) The speaker and the child have similar feelings of regret.** (Analysis) The speaker's use of "twin distress" indicates both his regret at interrupting the child's play and the child's regret at being interrupted. There is no mention of an actual twin or a resemblance to the speaker; therefore, options (1) and (3) are incorrect. The child is observing the speaker's eyes, not the reverse; therefore, option (2) is incorrect. Option (5) is incorrect because the speaker does not say he was playing.

3. **(1) It emphasizes the child's untamed, free nature.** (Analysis) A net is usually used to catch butterflies. Options (2) and (4) would be correct only if you take the image literally, but it is figurative language. Option (3) is clearly not what is meant. Option (5) has nothing to do with the image of the net.

4. **(3) A natural, free spirit is eventually tamed by adulthood.** (Comprehension) The child is running free, unencumbered by restrictions. The speaker remembers how it feels to be a child even though he no longer behaves that way. He regretfully signals the child that it is time to stop playing and come inside. The other options are not supported by the poem.

5. **(1) The tourists and the local people experience the beach differently.** (Comprehension) The tourists and their children are having a wonderful time, while the speaker is

not even allowed to go on the beach. Option (2) may be the attitude of the local people, but it expresses only a part of the whole poem and so is incorrect. The fence is not keeping everyone happy as implied in option (3). Options (4) and (5) may be true, but these are generalizations without adequate support in the poem.

6. **(2) freedom and restriction** (Synthesis) The tourists are free to enjoy the beach while the speaker and her family are not. It is not the beach and sea that are contrasted in this poem but the people on either side of the fence; therefore, option (1) is incorrect. Childhood is mentioned in the poem, but maturity is not emphasized, so option (3) is incorrect. Good manners are not emphasized in this poem, so option (4) is incorrect. There is no support for option (5).

GED Review Understanding Poetry
(pages 436–437)

1. **(3) Both have a librarian friend.**
(Comprehension) The upstairs neighbour was a librarian, and she was friends with the librarian in the speaker's former town. There is no evidence to support option (1). The upstairs neighbour and the librarian friend are from South Dakota; the speaker, however, is not, so option (2) is incorrect. There is no evidence that the upstairs neighbour has just moved in; therefore, option (4) is incorrect. There is some support for option (5), in that the upstairs neighbour would not have come down to visit if she did not like talking. In addition, the speaker does not seem to dislike talking to the people in her apartment. However, there is little direct evidence that the speaker enjoys talking to neighbours in general; therefore, option (5) is not the best choice.

2. **(2) The installer's wife is very busy.**
(Analysis) The installer indicates he has elderly parents and that his wife could use some help in caring for them. Therefore, the line is an expression meaning that the installer's wife works hard. There is no evidence to support the other options.

3. **(3) the speaker's neighbour** (Comprehension) The speaker mentions that the upstairs apartment brought cake. Therefore, she is referring to the person who lives in the apartment, not the apartment itself. Option (1) is a literal interpretation of figurative language; therefore, it is incorrect. None of the people mentioned in options (2), (4), and (5) brought cake; therefore, these options also are incorrect.

4. **(1) She has faith in humanity.** (Analysis) The speaker's statement suggests that people are more dependable than objects. There is no evidence to support the other options.

5. **(4) helpful** (Synthesis) The installer is generous with his offers to help, the students are helping the speaker move in, and the neighbour brings cake. Therefore, options (1) and (2) are incorrect. There is no evidence to support options (3) or (5).

6. **(1) conversational** (Synthesis) The speaker seems to be almost chatting about her experiences moving into her new apartment. Although she does seem happy, celebratory is too strong a word to describe the tone of this poem; therefore, option (2) is not the best choice. The speaker acts pleased and friendly; therefore, options (3) and (5) are incorrect. There is no support in the poem for option (4).

Understanding Drama
Lesson 25: Understanding Plot
GED Practice (page 439)

1. **(4) resourceful and determined**
(Comprehension) Nora is not humble and obedient, option (1); hysterical, option (2); or evil, option (3). Although she may have an impulsive streak, option (5), her determination and resourcefulness are her most obvious qualities.

2. **(2) secretive** (Synthesis) The two are engaged in a conversation about the secrets Nora is keeping from her husband. Mrs. Linde seems uncomfortable and Nora seems worried about her husband, but neither is especially frightened; therefore, option (1) is incorrect. Nora has hope that she can change things, so option (3) is incorrect. Although Nora does seem in good spirits, the seriousness of the situation means that options (4) and (5) are not the best answer.

3. **(5) insist that her friend be straightforward** (Application) Mrs. Linde wants to ensure that Nora makes a reasonable and honest decision. Therefore, she would probably want a friend facing a similar situation to be straightforward as well. Mrs. Linde does not react to the situation in the excerpt by taking offence, so option (1) is incorrect. Neither does Mrs. Linde offer to help, option (2); she just expresses a lack of understanding. There is no evidence to support options (3) or (4).

4. **(2) She wants to do what is best for her husband's health.** (Comprehension) Nora tells Mrs. Linde that this is the way to save her husband's life. Option (1) is one way Nora tries to

get him to go South but is not her real reason for wanting to go. Options (3), (4), and (5) are not supported by the excerpt.

Lesson 26: Inferring Character
GED Practice (pages 441–442)

1. **(4) not doing his chores** (Comprehension) Troy believes that football is taking Cory away from his responsibilities. There is no support for options (1) and (3). It is Troy who refuses to speak to the recruiter, so option (2) is incorrect. Option (5) is incorrect because Cory is cutting back his hours at the A&P.

2. **(3) Troy is opposed to Cory's desire to play football.** (Comprehension) Troy makes a number of arguments trying to change Cory's mind; therefore, options (1) and (2) are incorrect. There is no support for option (4). Option (5) is incorrect because Troy doesn't ask Cory to quit school.

3. **(2) to go to college** (Comprehension) Cory states that he wants to play football because he sees it as an opportunity to go to college. Options (1) and (5) are Troy's desires, not Cory's. There is no evidence for option (3). Although option (4) may be correct, there is no support for it in the excerpt.

4. **(5) tense and disharmonious** (Synthesis) The conflict between Troy and Cory over football and Cory's job produces an air of tension. No evidence is present for options (1) and (3), so they are incorrect. Although there may be elements of options (2) and (4), each overstates the overall mood.

5. **(5) Cory will try to reason with Troy.** (Application) Throughout the excerpt, Cory tries to reason with his father. There is no evidence in the excerpt that Cory's mother will have any further involvement, option (1). Mr. Stawicki works with Cory to arrange a new schedule, and there is no indication Mr. Stawicki is unhappy with Cory's work, option (2). Cory has not demonstrated that he wants to spite his father, option (3). Troy shows no evidence of changing his mind, option (4).

6. **(2) Cory** (Comprehension) It is Cory who faces the major dilemma of whether to follow his father's wishes or disregard them. Mr. Stawicki, option (1); Cory's coach, option (3); and Cory's mother, option (4), are secondary characters who do not appear directly in this excerpt. Although Troy, option (5), plays a major part, it is Cory who has to solve the central problem.

7. **(4) Troy has been treated unfairly in the past and is warning Cory.** (Analysis) The reference to "white man" implies a racial concern that suggests Troy is aware of unfair treatment. Troy wants Cory to keep his A&P job, but there is no real indication that he would lie or manipulate in order to get Cory to do this; therefore, option (1) is incorrect. There is no evidence to support options (2), (3), or (5).

8. **(5) Seeking immediate gain can cost you later on.** (Analysis) Troy believes that steady work at the A&P is the right choice and does not seem to believe that his son will achieve anything in football. He is ignoring the fact that football could be his son's ticket to a college education and a bright future; he is looking at short-term economic gain and ignoring the long-term benefits. There is no evidence that Troy's main focus is on trying to avoid spoiling Cory, option (1). Troy does not seem to be leading Cory. Instead, Cory seems to be trying to make his own decisions; therefore, option (2) is incorrect. Troy wants Cory to be obedient, but not necessarily to live the same life as he does; therefore, option (3) is incorrect. There is no support for option (4).

9. **(3) so Cory will have a job that cannot be taken away** (Analysis) Troy says in lines 40–41 that he wants Cory to have a job that can't be taken away. There is no evidence to support options (1) or (5). Troy wants Cory to do his chores whether he works at the A&P or not, so option (2) is incorrect. Troy approves of college but doesn't want Cory to go to college because of football—especially because this means giving up a solid job at the A&P; therefore, option (4) is incorrect.

10. **(5) supportive** (Analysis) Mr. Stawicki agrees to adjust Cory's hours to fit Cory's football schedule. Therefore, options (2) and (4) are incorrect. There is no evidence to support options (1) or (3).

Lesson 27: Understanding Motivation
GED Practice (page 444)

1. **(5) to understand his father's absence** (Analysis) This point is made by David's frequent questions on this topic. Option (1) is not supported. Options (2) and (3) may be true, but there is no evidence to support them. Option (4) is true but only supports David's main motivation.

2. **(3) Luke was a great musician.**
(Comprehension) After making this statement, David lists two famous musicians, which implies that he is putting his father in the same category. Option (1) is incorrect because David states he was hurt by his father and felt ashamed of him. There is no mention of where Luke lived; therefore, option (2) is incorrect. David does not say that his mother hid Luke's records, only that she did not allow them to have a phonograph; therefore, option (4) is incorrect. There is no support for option (5).

3. **(5) He wanted to be connected to his father.** (Analysis) Lines 21–28 explain David's desire to be connected to his father and his dreams of playing piano with him. Although David may be talented, option (1), that is not the central reason for his playing piano. There is no evidence to support option (2). Option (3) may be true, but only because his father was a musician. David's mother discourages him by not letting him listen to his father's music, so option (4) is incorrect.

4. **(2) hurt and angry** (Comprehension) The last part of the excerpt reveals David's hurt and anger at Luke for being absent. Option (1) may be true for Luke's musical talent but not for his role as father. There is no evidence for options (3) or (4). Although option (5) is true, these emotions are not David's strongest feelings about Luke as a father.

5. **(5) emotional and earnest** (Synthesis) This excerpt conveys the sincerity of both father and son as they discuss the painful issue of the father's absence. Option (1) is incorrect because there is no peace for either father or son yet. There is no evidence to support options (2) or (4). Though the son is sad, other emotions such as anger and shame are also important in this excerpt; therefore, option (3) is not the best answer.

Lesson 28: Interpreting Theme
GED Practice (pages 446–447)
1. **(5) He does not live with the family.**
(Analysis) There is no mention of Medvedenko's father in the excerpt; additionally, if the father were present, Mevedenko would probably not be completely responsible for supporting his mother and siblings. Therefore, it is a logical inference to conclude that he is not present. There is no support for the other options.

2. **(1) sincere and lonely** (Analysis)
Medvedenko's statements to Masha are sincere, and he would like to have a wife. There is no evidence to suggest that Medvedenko is arrogant, option (2); lighthearted, option (3); or uneducated, option (4). Although his character may be somewhat pathetic and victimized, option (5), the focus of this excerpt is on his sincerity and love for Masha.

3. **(2) She appreciates his feelings.** (Analysis) Masha understands that Medvedenko has strong feelings for her, but she does not love him. This makes option (1) incorrect. She does not express anger at his visiting her, option (3). There is no evidence to support options (4) and (5).

4. **(1) one-sided love** (Comprehension)
Medvedenko says that he loves Masha even though she appears to be indifferent toward him. Masha does not indicate that she has a secret love for Medvedenko; therefore, option (2) is incorrect. Although they may have a friendship, there is no evidence that their friendship is deep; therefore, option (3) is incorrect. Because Masha does not seem to respect Medvedenko's view of what it means to be poor, option (4) is incorrect. Medvedenko's love for Masha brings their relationship to a level beyond simple acquaintanceship; therefore, option (5) is also incorrect.

5. **(1) Happiness does not depend on money.**
(Synthesis) The central conflict between Masha and Medvedenko is whether the lack of financial wealth is due cause for unhappiness. There is no support for option (2). Options (3) and (4) are the opposite of what is exhibited by the characters in this excerpt. Although Medvedenko may believe that option (5) is true, this is not the author's main point.

6. **(1) restlessness** (Analysis) Masha expresses that she feels stifled and unhappy with Medvedenko's discussion. Her restlessness is mirrored in the weather. She certainly is not at ease; therefore, option (2) is incorrect. There is no evidence to suggest danger, option (3); sudden freedom, option (4); or unearthly power, option (5).

7. **(3) Medvedenko feels compelled by love to visit Masha.** (Analysis) Medvedenko states that he walks four miles to see her even though she is indifferent toward him. Medvedenko has not abandoned his family, option (1). He may feel that he does not deserve Masha, but there is no

evidence that he feels he doesn't deserve his home and family; in fact, he feels responsible for supporting them, option (2). The opposite of option (4) is true. Medvedenko is not doing anything wrong; he is a single man who responsibly supports his mother and siblings. Therefore, he has no reason to feel guilty for seeing Masha, option (5).

8. **(5) He contrasts their relationship with his relationship with Masha.** (Analysis) Medvedenko states that there is no common point between himself and Masha, unlike the couple he mentions. Although this statement does give additional meaning to the play, option (1), Medvedenko does not make the statement for that reason. There is no evidence that Medvedenko thinks Masha's feelings will change, so option (2) is incorrect. There is no support for options (3) or (4).

9. **(2) because he is poor** (Analysis) Medvedenko says, "Who wants to marry a man who can't even feed himself?" (lines 42–43). Masha is willing to attend the play with him, so she does not entirely dislike him, option (1). There is no evidence to support options (3) or (5). Although Medvedenko does not understand Masha's sadness, option (4), he does not seem to consider it sufficient reason for her refusal.

10. **(4) He is upset that Masha doesn't love him.** (Comprehension) Masha offers the snuff immediately after saying that she doesn't love Medvedenko. There is no evidence to support option (1). Though the play is about to begin, or may have already begun, there is no evidence that this is the reason he refuses snuff; so, option (2) is incorrect. He may prefer to continue talking, but there is no reason that taking the snuff would stop him from saying what he wants to say; so, option (3) is incorrect. Masha already knows his financial situation, so option (5) is also incorrect.

11. **(1) He would be persistent and try to win over customers.** (Application) Medvedenko continues to visit Masha even though she doesn't return his affections, so it is likely that Medevedenko would approach customers in a similar way. He is not shy because he continues to visit Masha, so option (2) is incorrect. He complains about his own situation but not about other people, so option (3) is incorrect. There is no evidence to support option (4). He walks four miles to see Masha, who has lukewarm feelings for him, so option (5) is incorrect.

GED Review Understanding Drama
(pages 448–449)

1. **(5) She is glad that she married him.** (Comprehension) Mrs. X. states that he is "a good, dear husband" (line 54). The excerpt mentions that a woman tried to seduce Mrs. X.'s husband, but there is no evidence that he was flirting with her, so option (1) is incorrect. Although Mrs. X. mentions her husband's anger, she does not complain about it; therefore, option (2) is incorrect. There is no evidence to support options (3) or (4).

2. **(5) manipulative** (Analysis) Mrs. X. claims she did not "intrigue" Miss Y. out of the Grand Theatre, but her protestations are not quite believable. Mrs. X. may appear friendly, but she frightens Miss Y. with the gun and makes fun of her husband, indicating that the friendliness is not genuine. Therefore, option (1) is not the best answer. There is no evidence to support option (2). Mrs. X. does seem somewhat threatening, but her behaviour is not extreme enough to call her "vindictive" or "sinister"; therefore, options (3) and (4) are not the best choices.

3. **(3) Mrs. X. thinks Miss Y. resents her.** (Comprehension) According to Mrs. X., Miss Y. thinks that Mrs. X. tried to remove her from the Grand Theatre. For this reason, Mrs. X. believes that Miss Y. resents her. Miss Y. may actually hate Mrs. X., option (1), but there is no direct evidence in the excerpt to support this. There is no evidence in the excerpt to support options (2) or (5). Mrs. X. and Miss Y. may be enemies, but even if they are, there is no evidence that their rivalry is longstanding; therefore, option (4) is not the best answer.

4. **(3) guarded** (Analysis) Miss Y. is very cautious about being direct with Mrs. X.; Mrs. X. is convinced that Miss Y. holds a grudge against her. Any warmth between the two is purely superficial, so option (1) is incorrect. Mrs. X. does seem to want to show off in front of Miss Y. However, since Miss Y. does not demonstrate similar behaviour, option (2) is incorrect. Neither woman is openly unfriendly to the other, but both appear to be hiding something; therefore, options (4) and (5) are incorrect.

5. **(3) I know more about you than you think I do.** (Application) Miss Y. knows that Mrs. X. likely forced her out of the Grand Theatre. In addition, Miss Y. laughs when Mrs. X. says her husband has been faithful, as if she

knows something Mrs. X. does not. There is reason to believe that Miss Y. cared about the Grand Theatre, so option (1) is incorrect. Miss Y. laughs at the imitation of Mr. X., so option (2) is incorrect. Miss Y.'s feelings seem to go beyond mere amusement, so option (4) is not the best choice. There is no evidence to support option (5).

6. **(1) cunning** (Synthesis) A cat at a mouse hole is sly enough to wait silently for its prey to emerge. Similarly, Miss Y. sits silently in the excerpt, allowing Mrs. X. to talk and reveal information. There is no support in the excerpt for options (2), (4), or (5). Miss Y. is not indifferent, as evidenced by the attention she pays Mrs. X. and by her laughter at Mrs. X.'s jokes. Therefore, option (3) is incorrect.

GED Unit Review Language Arts, Reading
(pages 450–455)

1. **(4) They are a little dishonest.** (Analysis) The author says that his employer "commonly asks which will give him the most land, not which is most correct" (lines 8–9). Employers do not criticize his work, option (1), or underpay him, option (3). Options (2) and (5) are not supported by the excerpt.

2. **(2) turn down the job** (Application) Based on his statements in lines 26–28, the narrator would refuse to do a job before doing work he didn't love. Money is apparently not the primary concern for the narrator, so option (1) is incorrect. Option (3) is incorrect because the narrator is obviously proud of his work. There is no support for options (4) and (5).

3. **(4) Thoreau prefers accuracy, and his employers prefer money.** (Synthesis) Thoreau seems to want to do the type of surveying that is "most correct" (line 9); also, he invented a rule for measuring wood, but it was rejected because it was too accurate. One of Thoreau's employers, however, wants the type of surveying "which will give him the most land" (lines 8–9), a signal that the employer is most interested in personal gain. Options (1), (3), and (5) are incorrect because there is no evidence in the excerpt that Thoreau's employers are not hardworking, do not like their work, or steal Thoreau's ideas. Option (2) is incorrect because it does not make a contrast.

4. **(3) Workers should do what they love and be paid well for it.** (Comprehension) The last paragraph of the excerpt states that the best worker to hire is one who "does it for love of it" (line 28). It also states that towns should pay labourers well. Option (1) is not clearly stated in the excerpt and so is incorrect. Option (2) is a detail in the paragraph but not the complete main idea and so is incorrect. Option (4) may be somewhat suggested by the paragraph but is not the main idea. Option (5) is not suggested by the paragraph; the word "moral" is used to refer to the feeling a well-paid worker might have toward his or her job.

5. **(2) The bird has hurt himself while struggling to escape his cage.** (Comprehension) The focus of this poem is on the bird's struggle and inability to escape the bonds of its cage. Although options (1) and (4) may be true, these are not the best explanations of this line. There is no support in the poem for options (3) and (5).

6. **(3) a flower** (Comprehension) The "its" from line 6 refers to the flower bud of line 5; therefore, the flower's perfume would be its smell. There is no support in the poem for option (4). Although details of options (1), (2), and (5) appear in the poem, they are not discussed with regard to their smell.

7. **(1) freedom and imprisonment** (Synthesis) The bird struggles with being held captive in a cage and wanting to be free. Although joy is expressed at the idea of freedom, there is no mention of fear in the poem; therefore, option (2) is incorrect. Although the bird does injure itself on its cage and the scene outside the cage does seem peaceful, the contrast between violence and peacefulness is not the central idea of the poem; therefore, option (3) is incorrect. The issues in the poem are of freedom and lack of freedom, not life and death. Death is not discussed in this poem; therefore, option (4) is incorrect. There is no support for option (5) in the poem.

8. **(1) It is an appealing, though flawed, love story.** (Comprehension) The reviewer points out several appealing elements of the movie, including the strong cast, the smooth direction, and the interesting subject. However, he also indicates several failings, such as its glossy characters, their predictable struggles, and the awkward plot structure. Taken together, these points suggest that the film, though appealing, is flawed. Option (2) is not stated or implied by the reviewer. Option (3) is not true; the reviewer does not imply that the movie is a complete failure. Options (4) and (5) are too positive; neither takes into account the many flaws mentioned in the review.

9. **(2) It suggests that there is a slow, plodding pace to the movie.** (Analysis) By emphasizing how long it took for the lovers to get together, the reviewer suggests that the pace of the movie is too slow. Option (1) is incorrect because the reviewer is not that enthusiastic about the film. There is no support in the excerpt for options (3) and (5). Option (4) indicates an effect opposite to the one intended.

10. **(5) if the plot were structured differently** (Application) One of the reviewer's main criticisms of the film is that the plot is awkwardly structured. This suggests that the film might have been improved if the plot had been structured differently. None of the other options are supported by the details in the review.

11. **(4) burning a house filled with books** (Comprehension) The excerpt describes the man burning a home (lines 14–16), and describes the books that are burning (lines 20–24). Option (1) is incorrect because the hose sprays kerosene, not water. Options (2), (3), and (5) have no support in the excerpt.

12. **(3) demolition worker** (Application) The man enjoys destroying things by burning them. A demolition worker also destroys things. Options (1) and (5) are not related in any way to the excerpt. Option (2) relates to construction or repair—the opposite of destruction. Option (4) is not supported and refers only to the mention of books in the excerpt.

13. **(1) detailed imagery** (Analysis) The author paints a picture of the man, the house, and the books. Options (2), (3), (4), and (5) do not occur in the excerpt.

14. **(2) The flames immediately engulfed the house.** (Comprehension) The kerosene-soaked house has been ignited. Option (1) is incorrect because the flames are rising, not descending. Option (3) is incorrect because the house itself, not just the lawn, is on fire. The fire has just started, so options (4) and (5) are also incorrect.

15. **(3) a hose that is suggestive of a snake** (Comprehension) The word "nozzle" points to the conclusion that this is a figurative way of describing a hose. Options (1) and (2) are incorrect because the phrase "in his fists" shows that the character is holding the "great python." Option (4) is not supported; it merely mentions fire. Option (5) is incorrect because the hose contains kerosene, not water.

16. **(5) She is rude and touchy.** (Analysis) Mrs. Dudgeon's actions and statements toward Judith reveal these traits. Options (1), (2), and (3) are incorrect based on her behaviour. Though she may be stingy, option (4), there is no evidence of that trait in this excerpt.

17. **(2) smug and self-satisfied** (Analysis) Although her words are sweet, the stage directions suggest that Judith has a very high opinion of herself. If the reader had only the characters' speeches to rely on, option (1) would be correct. There is no support for options (3), (4), or (5).

18. **(2) Judith is an unexpected guest for the reading of a will.** (Comprehension) Mrs. Dudgeon is surprised to see Judith but says, not very nicely, that she can stay. The occasion is stated in lines 5–7. Option (1) has no support. Options (3) and (5) are the opposite of what is suggested. Option (4) might be true, but it is too general to be the main idea and does not best describe the situation.

19. **(2) tense** (Synthesis) These two women can barely manage to be polite to each other. Option (1) is incorrect because there is no evidence of sadness even though someone has died. Options (3) and (5) both suggest a pleasantness not found in this excerpt. Option (4) has no support.

20. **(4) She thinks Judith was insincere about wanting to clean.** (Analysis) Mrs. Dudgeon is unhappy with her unexpected guest's arrival. In addition, Mrs. Dudgeon has already gotten the house ready so there is no need for Judith to offer to help with this. These facts suggest that Mrs. Dudgeon thinks Judith was offering to help ready the house only to appear polite and was actually insincere. There is no support for option (1). There is no evidence that Mrs. Dudgeon thinks Judith would be especially good at greeting people, option (2). Mrs. Dudgeon may think that Judith is untidy for leaving the door open, but this is not enough evidence to support option (3). Mrs. Dudgeon doesn't express any truly kind feelings toward Judith (in fact, she speaks "half sneering" to her), so option (5) is incorrect.

21. **(2) food to feed everyone** (Comprehension) The narrator has been surprised by the unexpected guests and does not have enough food. The context clue "hot stove" indicates that option (4) is incorrect. The narrator does not

Unit 5

seem particularly concerned with pleasing other people, so option (1) is also incorrect. Although options (3) and (5) may be true, the phrase in the question is referring to the food, not space or time.

22. **(4) make room for a sixth person at the table** (Application) Based on the details in the excerpt, it is clear that the narrator still has feelings for Mr. Whitaker; also, she stretches the chickens to feed everyone who has shown up, so she probably would do the same for Mr. Whitaker. There is not enough evidence in the excerpt to support the other options.

23. **(5) irritable** (Analysis) The narrator's comments show that she is annoyed and irritated with her sister; therefore, option (5) is correct. None of the other options are supported by the details in the excerpt.

24. **(2) resentful** (Synthesis) In the first line, the narrator says that the family was getting along fine until Stella-Rondo came back home. This indicates her resentment. Options (1), (3), (4), and (5) are the opposite of how the narrator feels toward her sister.

Unit 5

UNIT 6: MATHEMATICS

Numbers and Operations
Lesson 1: Number and Operation Sense
(page 459)

1. **five hundred**

2. **three million**

3. **seven hundred thousand**

4. **fifty**

5. **8700**

6. **5 000 000**

GED Practice (page 462)

1. **(3) $269 × 12** You need to combine the same amount, $269, 12 times. Multiply.

2. **(1) $137 + $124** You are finding the total of two costs. Add.

3. **(5) $50 − $28** You are finding how much is left. Subtract. Be sure the total amount comes before the amount you subtract.

4. **(4) 348 ÷ 3** You need to break 348 pages into 3 equal parts. Divide. Be sure the amount being divided is written first.

5. **(2) $327 − $189** You are finding out how much is left. Subtract. Be sure the total amount comes before the amount you subtract.

6. **(5) $62 ÷ 4** You need to break an amount into equal parts. Divide. Be sure the whole amount being divided is written first.

Lesson 2: Operations with Whole Numbers
(page 465)

1. **3730**

$$
\begin{array}{r}
{}^{2\ 3} \\
746 \\
\times\ \ \ 5 \\
\hline
3730
\end{array}
$$

2. **43 758**

$$
\begin{array}{r}
{}^{7\ 5\ 1} \\
4\ 862 \\
\times\ \ \ \ \ 9 \\
\hline
43\ 758
\end{array}
$$

3. **828**

$$
\begin{array}{r}
36 \\
\times 23 \\
\hline
108 \\
+720 \\
\hline
828
\end{array}
$$

4. **386 384**

$$
\begin{array}{r}
5\ 084 \\
\times\ \ \ \ 76 \\
\hline
30\ 504 \\
+355\ 880 \\
\hline
386\ 384
\end{array}
$$

5. **458**

$$
\begin{array}{r}
458 \\
7\overline{)3206} \\
-28 \\
\hline
40 \\
-35 \\
\hline
56 \\
-56 \\
\hline
0
\end{array}
$$

6. **5996**

$$
\begin{array}{r}
5\ 996 \\
4\overline{)23\ 984} \\
-20 \\
\hline
3\ 9 \\
-3\ 6 \\
\hline
38 \\
-36 \\
\hline
24 \\
-24 \\
\hline
0
\end{array}
$$

7. **6366 r10**

$$
\begin{array}{r}
6\ 366\ r10 \\
12\overline{)76\ 402} \\
-72 \\
\hline
4\ 4 \\
-3\ 6 \\
\hline
80 \\
-72 \\
\hline
82 \\
-72 \\
\hline
10
\end{array}
$$

8. **9138 r3**

$$
\begin{array}{r}
9\ 138\ r3 \\
24\overline{)219\ 315} \\
-216 \\
\hline
3\ 3 \\
-2\ 4 \\
\hline
91 \\
-72 \\
\hline
195 \\
-192 \\
\hline
3
\end{array}
$$

9. **6 976 800**

$$
\begin{array}{r}
2\ 584 \\
\times 2\ 700 \\
\hline
0\ 000 \\
00\ 000 \\
1\ 808\ 800 \\
+5\ 168\ 000 \\
\hline
6\ 976\ 800
\end{array}
$$

Add zeros as placeholders.

Answers and Explanations • Unit 6

Unit 6

10. 627 425

$$
\begin{array}{r}
25\ 097 \\
\times\quad 25 \\
\hline
125\ 485 \\
501\ 940 \\
\hline
627\ 425
\end{array}
$$

11. 415 340

$$
\begin{array}{r}
2\ 186 \\
\times\quad 190 \\
\hline
0\ 000 \\
196\ 740 \\
218\ 600 \\
\hline
415\ 340
\end{array}
$$

12. 680

$$
\begin{array}{r}
680 \\
205\overline{)139\ 400} \\
123\ 0 \\
\hline
16\ 40 \\
16\ 40 \\
\hline
00
\end{array}
$$

GED Practice (page 466)

1. (5) $261

$$
\begin{array}{r}
{\scriptstyle 1} \\
\$137 \\
+124 \\
\hline
\$261
\end{array}
$$

2. (5) $638

$$
\begin{array}{r}
{\scriptstyle 7\ 11\ 17} \\
\$8\cancel{2}\cancel{7} \\
-189 \\
\hline
\$638
\end{array}
$$

3. (1) 35

$$
\begin{array}{r}
{\scriptstyle 1} \\
18 \\
+17 \\
\hline
35
\end{array}
$$

4. (5) $3468 1 year = 12 months; Multiply the monthly payment by 12 to find the amount for 1 year. $289 × 12 = $3468

$$
\begin{array}{r}
{\scriptstyle 1\ 1} \\
289 \\
\times\ 12 \\
\hline
{\scriptstyle 1} \\
578 \\
2890 \\
\hline
3468
\end{array}
$$

5. (3) $19   114 ÷ 6 = 19.

6. (4) $476   68 × 7 = 476.

GED Practice (page 468)

1. (3) 3577 Subtract the lower odometer reading from the higher reading.
38 874 − 35 297 = 3 577

2. (4) $14 280 Multiply the monthly rent by the number of months in two years.
$595 × 24 = $14 280

3. (2) 32 Divide the total sales of new stereo systems by the price of each system.
$14 688 ÷ $459 = 32

4. (5) $1143 Add the three deposits to the initial balance. $76 + $96 + $873 + $98 = $1143

Lesson 3: Steps for Solving Word Problems

GED Practice (page 472)
NOTE: The placement of your answer could be left, centre, or right. Just remember to leave unused columns blank. Enter only the numbers on the grid; there is no place for the dollar sign on the grid.

1. 408 $615 − $172 − $35 = $408

2. 1872 $78 × 24 = $1872

3. 120 $720 ÷ 6 = $120

Unit 6

Answers and Explanations • Unit 6

4. 566 $620 − $54 = $566

Lesson 4: Steps for Solving Multi-Step Problems

GED Practice (page 475)

1. **(4) (65 × $9) + $350** Find the amount paid for food by multiplying the number of employees by the cost of the food per person (65 × $9). Then add the cost of renting the banquet room ($350).

2. **(5) $\frac{1200}{300}$** To find the number of tanks of gas needed to drive 1200 km, divide that amount by the number of kilometres David can drive on one tank of gas (300 km).

3. **(3) 70($8 − $6)** To find how much more the garage owner could make by raising rates, first find the difference in the rates ($8 − $6). Then multiply by the number of parking spaces in the garage (70).

4. **(2) $150 − (2 × $35) − (3 × $18)** First find the costs of the textbooks. 2 for $35 (2 × $35) and 3 for $18 (3 × $18). Then subtract both amounts from $150.

GED Practice (pages 477–478)

1. **(2) addition and division** Add to find the total number of apartments. Then divide the cost of the service by the number of apartments.

2. **(3) $72** There are 43 apartments (18 + 25). Divide the yearly cost by the number of apartments.

   Using your GED calculator:

   3096 ÷ [(--- 18 + 25 ---)] = 72

3. **(4) 604 392** Multiply first, then add.
   2184 + (1476 × 408)
   1476 × 408 = 602 208
   2184 +   602 208 = 604 392

   Using your GED calculator:

   2184 + 1476 × 408 = 604392

4. **(5) $14 684** For each company's shares, multiply the cost per share by the number of shares purchased, then add the two products.
   (112 × 58) + (89 × 92) = 6496 + 8188 = 14 684

   Using your GED calculator:

   112 × 58 + 89 × 92 = 14684

5. **(1) $84** Multiply the cost per share by the number of shares. 68 × 87 = 5916 Then subtract from the starting amount. 6000 − 5916 = 84

   Using your GED calculator:

   6000 − 68 × 87 = 84

6. **(4) 345** Divide the total net sales by the cost of each laptop. $685 170 ÷ $1986 = 345

7. **(1) $924 160** Multiply the number of employees by the year-end bonus. 1216 × $760 = 924 160

8. **(1) 650** Follow the order of operations. First divide. Then add.
   50 + 15 000 ÷ 25
         15 000 ÷ 25 = 600
   50 +   600   = 650

   Using your GED calculator:

   50 + 15000 ÷ 25 = 650

9. **(2) 1 194 036** Add the number of books sold in each of the three categories.
   569 346 + 234 908 + 389 782 = 1 194 036

10. **(3) 1600** Follow the order of operations. First solve within the parentheses. Then multiply.
    40 (50 − 5 × 2)
       (50 −   10)   = 40
    40   (40)   = 1600

    Using your GED calculator:

    40 × [(--- 50 − 5 × 2 ---)] = 1600

11. **(5) 3 607 829** Subtract the difference in the votes from the number of votes received by the winner. 3 898 705 − 290 876 = 3 607 829

Lesson 5: Introduction to Fractions

GED Practice (page 482)

1. **(2) $5\frac{3}{4} − 2\frac{3}{8}$** You are comparing two quantities and finding the difference ("how much more").

2. **(4) $6\frac{1}{4} ÷ 2\frac{1}{2}$** You are finding how many equal parts $\left(2\frac{1}{2}\right)$ are in the whole $\left(6\frac{1}{4}\right)$.

3. **(3) $15\frac{3}{4} × \frac{1}{2}$** You are finding a fractional part "of" a whole amount.

4. **(4) $4\frac{1}{2} ÷ \frac{3}{4}$** You are finding how many equal parts $\left(\frac{3}{4}\right)$ are in the whole $\left(4\frac{1}{2}\right)$.

Lesson 6: Fractions, Ratios, and Proportions

(page 484)

1. $\frac{1}{2}$ Divide both the numerator (2) and denominator (4) by 2.

2. $\frac{2}{3}$ Divide both the numerator (6) and denominator (9) by 3.

3. $\frac{2}{5}$ Divide both the numerator (10) and denominator (25) by 5.

4. $\frac{3}{4}$ Divide both the numerator (6) and denominator (8) by 2.

5. $\frac{2}{5}$ Divide both the numerator (6) and denominator (15) by 3.

6. $\frac{2}{3}$ Divide both the numerator (18) and denominator (27) by 9.

7. $\frac{1}{4}$ Divide both the numerator (5) and denominator (20) by 5.

8. $\frac{1}{4}$ Divide both the numerator (12) and denominator (48) by 12.

9. $\frac{4}{5}$ Divide both the numerator (16) and denominator (20) by 4.

10. $\frac{2}{5}$ Divide both the numerator (12) and denominator (30) by 6.

11. $\frac{1}{6}$ Divide both the numerator (7) and denominator (42) by 7.

12. $\frac{2}{3}$ Divide both the numerator (24) and denominator (36) by 12.

13. $\frac{4}{6}$ **and** $\frac{8}{12}$ Both equal $\frac{2}{3}$. The other fractions reduce to $\frac{3}{5}$, $\frac{1}{2}$, and $\frac{5}{6}$.

14. $\frac{8}{16}$ **and** $\frac{3}{6}$ Both equal $\frac{1}{2}$. The other fractions do not reduce and none equals $\frac{1}{2}$.

15. $\frac{3}{12}$ **and** $\frac{2}{8}$ Both equal $\frac{1}{4}$. The other fractions reduce to $\frac{1}{2}$, $\frac{1}{5}$, and $\frac{1}{3}$.

16. $\frac{6}{10}$ **and** $\frac{3}{5}$ The fraction $\frac{6}{10}$ reduces to $\frac{3}{5}$. The other fractions equal or reduce to $\frac{5}{8}$, $\frac{3}{4}$, and $\frac{1}{4}$.

17. $\frac{1}{5}$ $\frac{8 \div 8}{40 \div 8} = \frac{1}{5}$

18. $\frac{3}{10}$ $\frac{15 \div 5}{50 \div 5} = \frac{3}{10}$

19. $\frac{1}{20}$ $\frac{50 \div 50}{1000 \div 50} = \frac{1}{20}$

20. $\frac{3}{5}$ $\frac{\$24 \div 8}{\$40 \div 8} = \frac{3}{5}$

(page 486)

1. $\frac{8}{12}$ Multiply the numerator of the first fraction by the same number the denominator is multiplied by to get the desired new denominator. $3 \times 4 = 12$; so $2 \times 4 = 8$

2. $\frac{6}{21}$
   $7 \times 3 = 21$ so $2 \times 3 = 6$

3. $\frac{20}{25}$
   $5 \times 5 = 25$ so $4 \times 5 = 20$

4. $\frac{20}{32}$
   $8 \times 4 = 32$ so $5 \times 4 = 20$

5. $\frac{49}{63}$
   $9 \times 7 = 63$ so $7 \times 7 = 49$

6. $\frac{36}{120}$
   $10 \times 12 = 120$ so $3 \times 12 = 36$

7. $\frac{27}{36}$
   $4 \times 9 = 36$ so $3 \times 9 = 27$

8. $\frac{36}{81}$
   $9 \times 9 = 81$ so $4 \times 9 = 36$

9. $\frac{27}{150}$
   $50 \times 3 = 150$ so $9 \times 3 = 27$

10. $\frac{1}{3} > \frac{1}{4}$ Convert each fraction to a common denominator. $\frac{1}{3} \times \frac{4}{4} = \frac{4}{12}$; $\frac{1}{4} \times \frac{3}{3} = \frac{3}{12}$ $\frac{4}{12} > \frac{3}{12}$ so $\frac{1}{3} > \frac{1}{4}$

11. $\frac{3}{4} < \frac{7}{8}$ because $\frac{6}{8} < \frac{7}{8}$

12. $\frac{3}{9} = \frac{1}{3}$ because $\frac{3}{9}$ reduces to $\frac{1}{3}$

13. $\frac{2}{3} > \frac{1}{2}$ because $\frac{4}{6} > \frac{3}{6}$

14. $\frac{5}{6} = \frac{15}{18}$ because $\frac{15}{18}$ reduces to $\frac{5}{6}$

15. $\frac{9}{12} = \frac{3}{4}$ because $\frac{9}{12}$ reduces to $\frac{3}{4}$

16. $\frac{7}{10} > \frac{2}{3}$ because $\frac{21}{30} > \frac{20}{30}$

17. $\frac{7}{15} > \frac{2}{5}$ because $\frac{7}{15} > \frac{6}{15}$

18. $\frac{9}{10} > \frac{3}{4}$ because $\frac{18}{20} > \frac{15}{20}$

(page 488)

1. **10** Cross multiply and solve. $2 \times 15 \div 3 = 10$

2. **6** $12 \times 14 \div 28 = 6$

3. **18** $9 \times 20 \div 10 = 18$

4. **15** $5 \times 18 \div 6 = 15$

5. **8** $24 \times 5 \div 15 = 8$

6. **30** $15 \times 24 \div 12 = 30$

7. **3** $6 \times 7 \div 14 = 3$

8. **23** $115 \times 6 \div 30 = 23$

9. **70** $49 \times 10 \div 7 = 70$

10. **60** $32 \times 15 \div 8 = 60$

11. **1** $6 \times 3 \div 18 = 1$

12. **100** $120 \times 5 \div 6 = 100$

13. **9 L** Write a proportion; cross multiply
    and solve. $\frac{8}{2} = \frac{36}{?}$

    $2 \times 36 \div 8 = 9$

14. **1050 calories** $\frac{315}{3} = \frac{?}{10}$

    $315 \times 10 \div 3 = 1050$

Lesson 7: Operations with Fractions

(page 491)

1. **$8\frac{1}{12}$**
$$3\frac{3}{4} = \quad 3\frac{9}{12}$$
$$+4\frac{1}{3} = +4\frac{4}{12}$$
$$\overline{\quad\quad 7\frac{13}{12}}$$

   Simplify. $7\frac{13}{12} = 7 + 1\frac{1}{12} = 8\frac{1}{12}$

2. **$7\frac{1}{8}$**
$$1\frac{1}{2} = \quad 1\frac{4}{8}$$
$$+5\frac{5}{8} = +5\frac{5}{8}$$
$$\overline{\quad\quad 6\frac{9}{8}}$$

   Simplify. $6\frac{9}{8} = 6 + 1\frac{1}{8} = 7\frac{1}{8}$

3. **$12\frac{1}{10}$**
$$2\frac{3}{10} = \quad 2\frac{3}{10}$$
$$+9\frac{4}{5} = +9\frac{8}{10}$$
$$\overline{\quad\quad 11\frac{11}{10}}$$

   Simplify. $11\frac{11}{10} = 11 + 1\frac{1}{10} = 12\frac{1}{10}$

4. **$43\frac{7}{9}$**
$$22\frac{1}{9} = \quad 22\frac{1}{9}$$
$$+21\frac{2}{3} = +21\frac{6}{9}$$
$$\overline{\quad\quad 43\frac{7}{9}}$$

5. **$3\frac{1}{6}$**
$$6\frac{1}{2} = \quad 6\frac{3}{6}$$
$$-3\frac{1}{3} = -3\frac{2}{6}$$
$$\overline{\quad\quad 3\frac{1}{6}}$$

6. **$6\frac{7}{12}$**
$$8\frac{5}{6} = \quad 8\frac{10}{12}$$
$$-2\frac{1}{4} = -2\frac{3}{12}$$
$$\overline{\quad\quad 6\frac{7}{12}}$$

7. **$11\frac{2}{3}$**
$$20\frac{1}{3} = 19\frac{3}{3} + \frac{1}{3} = \quad 19\frac{4}{3}$$
$$-8\frac{2}{3} = \quad\quad\quad\quad\quad -8\frac{2}{3}$$
$$\overline{\quad\quad\quad\quad\quad\quad\quad 11\frac{2}{3}}$$

8. **$1\frac{11}{12}$**
$$5\frac{2}{3} = \quad 5\frac{8}{12} = 4\frac{12}{12} + \frac{8}{12} = \quad 4\frac{20}{12}$$
$$-3\frac{3}{4} = -3\frac{9}{12} = \quad\quad\quad\quad\quad -3\frac{9}{12}$$
$$\overline{\quad\quad\quad\quad\quad\quad\quad\quad\quad 1\frac{11}{12}}$$

9. **$26\frac{1}{2}$ bags of candy** Add the amounts of candy
   bags to find the total candy bags for the month.
$$8\frac{1}{2} = \quad 8\frac{5}{10}$$
$$9\frac{3}{10} = \quad 9\frac{3}{10}$$
$$+8\frac{7}{10} = +8\frac{7}{10}$$
$$\overline{\quad\quad 25\frac{15}{10}}$$

   Simplify. $25\frac{15}{10} = 25 + 1\frac{5}{10} = 26\frac{5}{10} = 26\frac{1}{2}$

10. **$2\frac{11}{12}$ hours** Add the time for each entertainer
    to find the total length of the show.
$$1\frac{2}{3} = \quad 1\frac{8}{12}$$
$$\frac{1}{2} = \quad \frac{6}{12}$$
$$+\frac{3}{4} = + \frac{9}{12}$$
$$\overline{\quad\quad 1\frac{23}{12}}$$

   Simplify. $1\frac{23}{12} = 1 + 1\frac{11}{12} = 2\frac{11}{12}$

GED Practice (page 492)

1. **(1) $\frac{2}{5}$** $\frac{3}{5} + \frac{4}{5} = \frac{7}{5}$; $\frac{7}{5} - 1 = \frac{2}{5}$

2. **(3) $14\frac{4}{15}$** Rewrite the fractions with a common
   denominator and add the mixed numbers.
   $7\frac{2}{3} + 6\frac{3}{5} = 7\frac{10}{15} + 6\frac{9}{15} = 13\frac{19}{15} = 14\frac{4}{15}$

(page 494)

1. **$\frac{2}{5}$** $\frac{1}{3} \div \frac{5}{6} = \frac{1}{\underset{1}{\cancel{3}}} \times \frac{\overset{2}{\cancel{6}}}{5} = \frac{2}{5}$

2. **$1\frac{2}{3}$** $\frac{2}{3} \div \frac{2}{5} = \frac{\overset{1}{\cancel{2}}}{3} \times \frac{5}{\underset{1}{\cancel{2}}} = \frac{5}{3} = 1\frac{2}{3}$

3. **$\frac{7}{20}$** $\frac{7}{10} \div 2 = \frac{7}{10} \div \frac{2}{1} = \frac{7}{10} \times \frac{1}{2} = \frac{7}{20}$

4. **4** $\frac{5}{6} \div \frac{5}{24} = \frac{\overset{1}{\cancel{5}}}{\underset{1}{\cancel{6}}} \times \frac{\overset{4}{\cancel{24}}}{\underset{1}{\cancel{5}}} = \frac{4}{1} = 4$

5. $\frac{2}{7}$ $\frac{6}{7} \div 3 = \frac{6}{7} \div \frac{3}{1} = \frac{\cancel{6}^{2}}{7} \times \frac{1}{\cancel{3}_{1}} = \frac{2}{7}$

6. $\frac{2}{3}$ $\frac{4}{9} \div \frac{2}{3} = \frac{\cancel{4}^{2}}{\cancel{9}_{3}} \times \frac{\cancel{3}^{1}}{\cancel{2}_{1}} = \frac{2}{3}$

7. $3\frac{1}{2}$ $\frac{7}{8} \div \frac{1}{4} = \frac{7}{\cancel{8}_{2}} \times \frac{\cancel{4}^{1}}{1} = \frac{7}{2} = 3\frac{1}{2}$

8. **36** $4\frac{1}{2} \div \frac{1}{8} = \frac{9}{2} \div \frac{1}{8} =$
$\frac{9}{\cancel{2}_{1}} \times \frac{\cancel{8}^{4}}{1} = \frac{36}{1} = 36$

9. **8** $12 \div 1\frac{1}{2} = \frac{12}{1} \div \frac{3}{2} =$
$\frac{\cancel{12}^{4}}{1} \times \frac{2}{\cancel{3}_{1}} = \frac{8}{1} = 8$

10. $2\frac{1}{4}$ $3\frac{3}{4} \div 1\frac{2}{3} = \frac{15}{4} \div \frac{5}{3} =$
$\frac{\cancel{15}^{3}}{4} \times \frac{3}{\cancel{5}_{1}} = \frac{9}{4} = 2\frac{1}{4}$

11. **26** $6\frac{1}{2} \div \frac{1}{4} = \frac{13}{2} \div \frac{1}{4} =$
$\frac{13}{\cancel{2}_{1}} \times \frac{\cancel{4}^{2}}{1} = \frac{26}{1} = 26$

12. $1\frac{1}{2}$ $2\frac{1}{4} \div 1\frac{1}{2} = \frac{9}{4} \div \frac{3}{2} =$
$\frac{\cancel{9}^{3}}{\cancel{4}_{2}} \times \frac{\cancel{2}^{1}}{\cancel{3}_{1}} = \frac{3}{2} = 1\frac{1}{2}$

13. **27** $18 \div \frac{2}{3} = \frac{18}{1} \div \frac{2}{3} =$
$\frac{\cancel{18}^{9}}{1} \times \frac{3}{\cancel{2}_{1}} = \frac{27}{1} = 27$

14. **10** $2\frac{2}{5} \div \frac{6}{25} = \frac{12}{5} \div \frac{6}{25} =$
$\frac{\cancel{12}^{2}}{\cancel{5}_{1}} \times \frac{\cancel{25}^{5}}{\cancel{6}_{1}} = \frac{10}{1} = 10$

15. $4\frac{1}{5}$ $4\frac{9}{10} \div 1\frac{1}{6} = \frac{49}{10} \div \frac{7}{6} =$
$\frac{\cancel{49}^{7}}{\cancel{10}_{5}} \times \frac{\cancel{6}^{3}}{\cancel{7}_{1}} = \frac{21}{5} = 4\frac{1}{5}$

16. $3\frac{1}{3}$ $6\frac{1}{9} \div 1\frac{5}{6} = \frac{55}{9} \div \frac{11}{6} =$
$\frac{\cancel{55}^{5}}{\cancel{9}_{3}} \times \frac{\cancel{6}^{2}}{\cancel{11}_{1}} = \frac{10}{3} = 3\frac{1}{3}$

17. **8** $2\frac{2}{3} \div \frac{1}{3} = \frac{8}{3} \div \frac{1}{3} = \frac{8}{\cancel{3}} \times \frac{\cancel{3}^{1}}{1} = \frac{8}{1} = 8$

18. $3\frac{1}{5}$ $4 \div 1\frac{1}{4} = \frac{4}{1} \div \frac{5}{4} = \frac{4}{1} \times \frac{4}{5} =$
$\frac{16}{5} = 3\frac{1}{5}$

19. $5\frac{19}{40}$ $9\frac{1}{8} \div 1\frac{2}{3} = \frac{73}{8} \div \frac{5}{3} =$
$\frac{73}{8} \times \frac{3}{5} = \frac{219}{40} = 5\frac{19}{40}$

20. $8\frac{1}{3}$ $10 \div 1\frac{1}{5} = \frac{10}{1} \div \frac{6}{5} =$
$\frac{\cancel{10}^{5}}{1} \times \frac{5}{\cancel{6}_{3}} = \frac{25}{3} = 8\frac{1}{3}$

21. **35** $8\frac{3}{4} \div \frac{1}{4} = \frac{35}{4} \div \frac{1}{4} =$
$\frac{35}{\cancel{4}_{1}} \times \frac{\cancel{4}^{1}}{1} = \frac{35}{1} = 35$

22. **27** $12 \div \frac{4}{9} = \frac{12}{1} \div \frac{4}{9} =$
$\frac{\cancel{12}^{3}}{1} \times \frac{9}{\cancel{4}_{1}} = \frac{27}{1} = 27$

23. **20** $16 \div \frac{4}{5} = \frac{16}{1} \div \frac{4}{5} =$
$\frac{\cancel{16}^{4}}{1} \times \frac{5}{\cancel{4}_{1}} = \frac{20}{1} = 20$

24. $1\frac{9}{11}$ $4 \div 2\frac{1}{5} = \frac{4}{1} \div \frac{11}{5} = \frac{4}{1} \times \frac{5}{11} = \frac{20}{11} = 1\frac{9}{11}$

25. **16 shows** Divide 12 hours by $\frac{3}{4}$.
$12 \div \frac{3}{4} = \frac{12}{1} \div \frac{3}{4} = \frac{\cancel{12}^{4}}{1} \times \frac{4}{\cancel{3}_{1}} = \frac{16}{1} = 16$

26. **45 specials** Divide the total number of scoops, 15, by the amount used in each special, $\frac{1}{3}$ scoop.
$15 \div \frac{1}{3} = \frac{15}{1} \div \frac{1}{3} = \frac{15}{1} \times \frac{3}{1} = \frac{45}{1} = 45$

27. **32 books** Divide the number of books by $\frac{3}{4}$ days.
$24 \div \frac{3}{4} = \frac{24}{1} \div \frac{3}{4} = \frac{\cancel{24}^{8}}{1} \times \frac{4}{\cancel{3}_{1}} = \frac{32}{1} = 32$

28. **10 bicycles** Divide the number of hours, 25, by the time it takes Carina to build one bicycle, $2\frac{1}{2}$ hours.
$25 \div 2\frac{1}{2} = \frac{25}{1} \div \frac{5}{2} = \frac{\cancel{25}^{5}}{1} \times \frac{2}{\cancel{5}_{1}} = \frac{10}{1} = 10$

29. **8 batches** Divide the amount of sugar on hand, 10 cups, by the amount needed for 1 batch, $1\frac{1}{4}$ cups.
$10 \div 1\frac{1}{4} = \frac{10}{1} \div \frac{5}{4} = \frac{\cancel{10}^{2}}{1} \times \frac{4}{\cancel{5}_{1}} = \frac{8}{1} = 8$

GED Practice (page 496)

1. **(3) 30** Round the amounts. $14\frac{1}{3}$ rounds to 14

$6\frac{3}{4}$ rounds to 7

$9\frac{1}{4}$ rounds to 9

Add the rounded amounts. $14 + 7 + 9 = 30$

Unit 6

2. (4) 78 Round the amounts. $9\frac{5}{8}$ rounds to 10

$27\frac{1}{4}$ rounds to 27

$4\frac{2}{3}$ rounds to 5

$36\frac{3}{8}$ rounds to 36

Add the rounded amounts.
$10 + 27 + 5 + 36 = 78$

3. (2) 22 Round the amounts. $10\frac{2}{5}$ rounds to 10

$12\frac{1}{6}$ rounds to 12

Add the rounded amounts. $10 + 12 = 22$

4. (1) 2 Round the amounts.
peanuts in Mix B: $4\frac{1}{5}$ rounds to 4

peanuts in Mix A: $2\frac{3}{8}$ rounds to 2
Subtract the amounts. $4 - 2 = 2$

5. (4) 5 Round the amounts.
cashews: $2\frac{2}{3}$ rounds to 3

Brazil nuts: $2\frac{1}{8}$ rounds to 2
Add the rounded amounts. $3 + 2 = 5$

6. (4) 4 Round the amounts in Mix A.

$2\frac{2}{3}$ rounds to 3

$2\frac{3}{8}$ rounds to 2

$3\frac{1}{2}$ rounds to 4

$2\frac{1}{8}$ rounds to 2

Add the rounded amounts. $3 + 2 + 4 + 2 = 11$
Round the amounts in Mix B.

$6\frac{1}{2}$ rounds to 7

$3\frac{7}{8}$ rounds to 4

$4\frac{1}{5}$ rounds to 4

Add the rounded amounts. $7 + 4 + 4 = 15$
Subtract to find the difference. $15 - 11 = 4$

GED Practice (pages 498–499)

1. $\frac{23}{47}$

2. $\frac{15}{32}$

3. $\frac{4}{1}$

$\frac{72}{18} = \frac{4}{1}$

4. $\frac{3}{1}$

$\frac{21}{7} = \frac{3}{1}$

5. $\frac{9}{8}$

$2\frac{7}{8} = \quad 2\frac{7}{8}$
$-1\frac{3}{4} = -1\frac{6}{8}$
$\overline{\qquad\qquad 1\frac{1}{8} = \frac{9}{8}}$

Unit 6

6. $\dfrac{11}{12}$ $2\dfrac{3}{4} \div 3 = \dfrac{11}{4} \div \dfrac{3}{1} = \dfrac{11}{4} \times \dfrac{1}{3} = \dfrac{11}{12}$

7. $\dfrac{4}{3}$ If Rachel uses $\dfrac{2}{3}$ of the flour, $\dfrac{1}{3}$ is left.
Find $\dfrac{1}{3}$ of 4 scoops. $\dfrac{1}{3} \times 4 = \dfrac{1}{3} \times \dfrac{4}{1} = \dfrac{4}{3}$

8. $\dfrac{27}{4}$ Set up a proportion and solve.

$$\dfrac{\text{centimetres}}{\text{kilometres}} \quad \dfrac{\frac{1}{3}}{3} \quad \dfrac{\frac{3}{4}}{x}$$

$$\left(3 \times \dfrac{3}{4}\right) \div \dfrac{1}{3} = \left(\dfrac{3}{1} \times \dfrac{3}{4}\right) \times \dfrac{3}{1} = \dfrac{9}{4} \times \dfrac{3}{1} = \dfrac{27}{4}$$

Lesson 8: Introduction to Decimals
(page 502)

1. **3.6** The number to the right of the tenths place is 5 or more: 3.5719. Add 1 to the tenths place and drop the remaining digits to the right.

2. **5.13** The number to the right of the hundredths place is less than 5: 5.132. Drop the remaining digit to the right.

3. **1** The number to the right of the ones place is 5 or more: 0.543. Add 1 to the ones place and drop the remaining digits to the right.

4. **7.1** The number to the right of the tenths place is 5 or more: 7.0813. Add 1 to the tenths place and drop the remaining digits to the right.

5. **1.070** or **1.07** The number to the right of the thousandths place is 5 or more: 1.0699. Add 1 to the thousandths place. This affects the hundredths place. (69 + 1 = 70). Drop the remaining digits.

6. **0.32 > 0.3109** Add zeros, then compare. Since 3200 is greater than 3109, then 0.3200 > 0.3109.

7. **0.98 < 1.9** The first number, 0.98, does not have a whole number part; the second number, 1.9, has a whole number part of 1, so it is greater.

8. **0.5 = 0.50** The 0 after the 5 in 0.50 does not change the value of the number. Both have the same value: five tenths.

9. **0.006 < 0.06** Add zero to the second number: 0.060. The first number, 0.006, is less because 6 is less than 60.

10. **1.075 < 1.57** Both have the same whole number part. Add a zero to the second number: 1.570. The first number, 1.075, is smaller because 75 is less than 570.

11. **0.18 > 0.108** Add a zero to the first number: 0.180. The first number, 0.18, is greater because 180 is greater than 108.

12. **2.38 < 2.83** Both have the same whole number part. The first number is less because 38 is less than 83.

13. **3.60 = 3.600** Both have the same whole number part. The zeros after the 6 in both numbers do not change the value. Both have the same value.

GED Practice (page 503)

1. **(4) $48** Estimate the cost of one smoke detector. $12.39 rounds to $12. Multiply the estimate by 4. $12 × 4 = $48

2. **(5) $700** Estimate the amount deducted for RRSPs per paycheque. $27.50 rounds to $30. Since the amount is deducted twice a month, multiply the estimate by 2 to find the monthly deduction. 2 × $30 = $60. Multiply by 12 to find the estimated yearly amount. $60 × 12 = $720. The best estimate listed in the choices is $700.

Lesson 9: Operations with Decimals

(page 505)

1. 2.63

```
  0.03
+2.60
 2.63
```

2. 5.4

```
   1
 1.35
+4.05
 5.40
```

3. 5.547

```
   9 10
  8 10
6.900̸0̸
-1.353
 5.547
```

4. 2.925

```
 4 10
5̸.0̸75
-2.150
 2.925
```

5. 15.103

```
  7.100
 +8.003
 15.103
```

6. 4.175

```
      9 10
   2 10
10.3̸0̸0̸0̸
- 6.125
  4.175
```

7. 4.81

```
  3.61
+1.20
 4.81
```

8. 11.78

```
    9 15
  5 10
16.0̸5̸
- 4.27
 11.78
```

9. 82.887

```
  1.850
 ₁0.030
 19.007
+62.000
 82.887
```

10. 44.155

```
  1 1  1
 12.400
 11.080
 16.100
+ 4.575
 44.155
```

11. 9032

```
        9 10
     15 10
 1̸6̸ 0̸0̸4.1
 - 6 972.1
   9 032.0
```

12. 2.794

```
     9 10
    7 1̸0̸
 3.8̸0̸0̸
-1.006
 2.794
```

13. 2.947

```
 11 18
      6 10
12.8̸7̸0̸
- 9.923
 2.947
```

14. 17.105

```
 1 12 10
        6 10
23.0̸7̸0̸
- 5.965
 17.105
```

15. 22.668

```
   1
 14.010
  8.600
+ 0.058
 22.668
```

16. 31.85

```
     5 17
    7̸ 10
 5̸.6̸.8̸0̸
-24.95
 31.85
```

17. 6.701

18. 0.2593

19. 10.316

20. 23.35

21. 5.295

22. 12.75

(page 507)

1. **3.40 or 3.4** $8.5 \times 0.4 = 3.40$. There are 2 decimal places in the problem. Once the decimal point is placed, you can drop the zero in the hundredths place.

2. **0.024** $0.04 \times 0.6 = 0.024$. There are 3 decimal places in the problem. You need to write a zero in the tenths place as a placeholder.

3. **0.0112** $5.6 \times 0.002 = 0.0112$. There are 4 decimal places in the problem. You need to write a zero in the tenths place as a placeholder.

4. **36.72** $12 \times 3.06 = 36.72$. There are 2 decimal places in the problem.

5. **310.17** $21.1 \times 14.7 = 310.17$. There are 2 decimal places in the problem.

6. **0.096** $0.008 \times 12 = 0.096$. There are 3 decimal places in the problem. You need to write a zero in the tenths place as a placeholder.

7. **12.84**

```
    1.07
 ×    12
    214
   1070
  12.84
```
There are 2 decimal places in the problem.

8. **0.549**

```
    0.09
 ×   6.1
    009
    540
  0.549
```
There are 3 decimal places in the problem.

9. **2.56**

```
       2.56
   8)20.48
     16
      4 4
      4 0
        48
        48
```

10. **1.0972**

```
       1.0972
   3)3.2916
     3
     2
     0
     29
     27
      21
      21
      06
       6
```

11. **4.086**

```
    2.27
 ×   1.8
  1 816
  2 270
  4.086
```
There are 3 decimal places in the problem.

12. **75.6**

```
    5.04
 ×    15
  25 20
  50 40
  75.60
```
There are 2 decimal places in the problem.

13. **2.14**

```
          2.14
   3.6.)7.7.04
        7 2
         5 0
         3 6
         1 44
         1 44
```

14. 6.094

```
            6.094
1.05.)6.39.870
       6 30
         9 8
          0
         9 87
         9 45
          420
          420
```

15. 0.02

```
     0.008
  ×   2.5      There are 4 decimal places
     0040      in the problem.
   0 0160
   0.0200
```

16. 0.1155

```
     1.05
  ×0.11      There are 4 decimal places
     105      in the problem.
    1050
   00000
   0.1155
```

17. 0.0035

```
     0.0035
  6)0.0210
     18
      30
      30
```

18. 62

```
          62.
  0.07.)4.34.
        4 2
         14
         14
```

19. 0.14 0.144 rounds to 0.14

20. 0.29 0.285 rounds to 0.29

21. 0.21 0.2145 rounds to 0.21

22. 0.27 0.272 rounds to 0.27

23. 18.38 18.375 rounds to 18.38

24. 0.83 0.8333 rounds to 0.83

GED Practice (page 508)

1. **(1) 25($1.05 − $0.89)** One way to work the problem is to find the difference between the two prices for one recordable CD. Then multiply the difference by 25 to find the total savings. (You can also get the same answer by multiplying each price by 25 and finding the difference [25($1.05) − 25($0.89)], but this is not one of the answer options.)

2. **(1) $3.00** Carry out the operations:
$35 − ($12.98 + $10.67 + $5.98 + $2.37) =
$35 − $32.00 = $3.00

GED Practice (page 510)

1. **15.75** Add to find the total kilometres.
4.5 + 5.25 + 6 = 15.75

2. **0.065** Subtract to find the difference.
0.340 − 0.275 = 0.065

3. **50** Divide to find the number of equally sized pieces.
60 ÷ 1.2 = 50

4. **$41.86** Multiply the number of parts by the cost per part.
$2.99 × 14 = $41.86

Lesson 10: Decimals and Fractions
(page 513)

1. $\frac{1}{4}$ Write 25 over 100 and reduce to lowest terms.

$$\frac{25 \div 25}{100 \div 25} = \frac{1}{4}$$

2. $\frac{2}{5}$ Write 4 over 10 and reduce to lowest terms.

$$\frac{4 \div 2}{10 \div 2} = \frac{2}{5}$$

3. $\frac{7}{20}$ Write 35 over 100 and reduce to lowest terms.

$$\frac{35 \div 5}{100 \div 5} = \frac{7}{20}$$

4. $\frac{16}{125}$ Write 128 over 1000 and reduce to lowest terms.

$$\frac{128 \div 8}{1000 \div 8} = \frac{16}{125}$$

5. $\frac{1}{20}$ Write 5 over 100 and reduce to lowest terms.

$$\frac{5 \div 5}{100 \div 5} = \frac{1}{20}$$

6. $\frac{5}{16}$ $\quad \frac{31\frac{1}{4}}{100} = 31\frac{1}{4} \div 100 = \frac{\overset{5}{\cancel{125}}}{4} \times \frac{1}{\underset{4}{\cancel{100}}} = \frac{5}{16}$

7. $\frac{4}{15}$ $\quad \frac{26\frac{2}{3}}{100} = 26\frac{2}{3} \div 100 = \frac{\overset{4}{\cancel{80}}}{3} \times \frac{1}{\underset{5}{\cancel{100}}} = \frac{4}{15}$

8. $\frac{1}{15}$ $\quad \frac{6\frac{2}{3}}{100} = 6\frac{2}{3} \div 100 = \frac{\overset{1}{\cancel{20}}}{3} \times \frac{1}{\underset{5}{\cancel{100}}} = \frac{1}{15}$

9. $\frac{19}{80}$ $\quad \frac{23\frac{3}{4}}{100} = 23\frac{3}{4} \div 100 = \frac{\overset{19}{\cancel{95}}}{4} \times \frac{1}{\underset{20}{\cancel{100}}} = \frac{19}{80}$

10. $\frac{9}{10}$ Write 9 over 10. The fraction is reduced to lowest terms.

11. $\frac{5}{8}$ Write 625 over 1000 and reduce to lowest terms.

$$\frac{625 \div 125}{1000 \div 125} = \frac{5}{8}$$

12. $\frac{1}{8}$ Write 125 over 1000 and reduce to lowest terms.

$$\frac{125 \div 125}{1000 \div 125} = \frac{1}{8}$$

13. $\frac{11}{20}$ Write 55 over 100 and reduce to lowest terms.

$$\frac{55 \div 5}{100 \div 5} = \frac{11}{20}$$

14. $\frac{7}{25}$ Write 28 over 100 and reduce to lowest terms.

$$\frac{28 \div 4}{100 \div 4} = \frac{7}{25}$$

15. $\frac{5}{16}$ Write 3 125 over 10 000 and reduce to lowest terms.

$$\frac{3\,125 \div 625}{10\,000 \div 625} = \frac{5}{16}$$

16. **0.8** Divide 4 by 5.

$$\begin{array}{r} 0.8 \\ 5)\overline{4.0} \\ \underline{4\,0} \end{array}$$

17. **0.375** Divide 3 by 8.

$$\begin{array}{r} 0.375 \\ 8)\overline{3.000} \\ \underline{2\,4} \\ 60 \\ \underline{56} \\ 40 \\ \underline{40} \end{array}$$

18. **0.55** Divide 11 by 20.

$$\begin{array}{r} 0.55 \\ 20)\overline{11.00} \\ \underline{10\,0} \\ 1\,00 \\ \underline{1\,00} \end{array}$$

19. **0.625** Divide 5 by 8.

$$\begin{array}{r} 0.625 \\ 8)\overline{5.000} \\ \underline{4\,8} \\ 20 \\ \underline{16} \\ 40 \\ \underline{40} \end{array}$$

20. **0.6** Divide 3 by 5.

$$\begin{array}{r} 0.6 \\ 5)\overline{3.0} \\ \underline{3\,0} \end{array}$$

21. **0.28** Divide 7 by 25.

$$\begin{array}{r} 0.28 \\ 25)\overline{7.00} \\ \underline{5\,0} \\ 2\,00 \\ \underline{2\,00} \end{array}$$

22. $0.83\frac{1}{3}$

$$0.83\frac{2}{6} = 0.83\frac{1}{3}$$

$$6\overline{)5.00}$$
$$\underline{4\,8}$$
$$20$$
$$\underline{18}$$
$$2$$

23. $0.88\frac{8}{9}$

$$0.88\frac{8}{9}$$
$$9\overline{)8.00}$$
$$\underline{7\,2}$$
$$80$$
$$\underline{72}$$
$$8$$

24. $0.06\frac{1}{4}$

$$0.06\frac{4}{16} = 0.06\frac{1}{4}$$
$$16\overline{)1.00}$$
$$\underline{96}$$
$$4$$

25. $0.27\frac{3}{11}$

$$0.27\frac{3}{11}$$
$$11\overline{)3.00}$$
$$\underline{2\,2}$$
$$80$$
$$\underline{77}$$
$$3$$

26. $0.46\frac{2}{3}$

$$0.46\frac{10}{15} = 0.46\frac{2}{3}$$
$$15\overline{)7.00}$$
$$\underline{6\,0}$$
$$1\,00$$
$$\underline{90}$$
$$10$$

27. $0.33\frac{1}{3}$

$$0.33\frac{1}{3}$$
$$3\overline{)1.00}$$
$$\underline{9}$$
$$10$$
$$\underline{9}$$
$$1$$

28. $\frac{7}{16}$ $43\frac{3}{4} \div 100 = \frac{175}{4} \div \frac{100}{1} = \frac{\overset{7}{\cancel{175}}}{4} \times \frac{1}{\underset{4}{\cancel{100}}} = \frac{7}{16}$

29. $\frac{1}{6}$ $16\frac{2}{3} \div 100 = \frac{50}{3} \div \frac{100}{1} = \frac{\overset{1}{\cancel{50}}}{3} \times \frac{1}{\underset{2}{\cancel{100}}} = \frac{1}{6}$

30. $\frac{3}{8}$ $37\frac{1}{2} \div 100 = \frac{75}{2} \div \frac{100}{1} = \frac{\overset{3}{\cancel{75}}}{2} \times \frac{1}{\underset{4}{\cancel{100}}} = \frac{3}{8}$

31. $\frac{1}{40}$ $2\frac{1}{2} \div 100 = \frac{5}{2} \div \frac{100}{1} = \frac{\overset{1}{\cancel{5}}}{2} \times \frac{1}{\underset{20}{\cancel{100}}} = \frac{1}{40}$

GED Practice (page 514)
NOTE: The answers below were entered in the grid as decimals. Each could also be entered as an improper fraction. You cannot enter a mixed number in the grid.

1. 7.5 Change all the fractions to decimals and add the laps.
$2.25 + 1.5 + 3.75 = 7.5$
or $\frac{15}{2}$

$2\frac{1}{4} + 1\frac{1}{2} + 3\frac{3}{4} =$

$2\frac{1}{4} + 1\frac{2}{4} + 3\frac{3}{4} = 6\frac{6}{4}$

$6\frac{6}{4} = \frac{30}{4} = \frac{15}{2}$

2. \$4.50 Multiply the cost per litre of gasoline by the number of litres of gasoline.
$\$1.25 \times 3.6 = \$4.50$

3. 10.8 Divide the total weight of the can of green beans by the weight per serving.
$40.5 \div 3.75 = 10.8$
or $\frac{54}{5}$

$40\frac{1}{2} \div 3\frac{3}{4} =$

$\frac{81}{2} \div \frac{15}{4} =$

$\frac{81}{2} \times \frac{4}{15} = \frac{324}{30} = \frac{54}{5}$

4. 6.25 Subtract the length of the piece from the total length of the wooden board.
$9.375 - 3.125 = 6.25$
or $\frac{25}{4}$

$9.375 = 9\frac{3}{8}$

$9\frac{3}{8} - 3\frac{1}{8} = 6\frac{2}{8} = 6\frac{1}{4} = \frac{25}{4}$

---

1. **(4) 68.925** Change the fractions to decimals and add the kilometres ridden. $26.8 + 14.375 + 27.75$

   Using your GED calculator:

   26.8 `+` 14 `a b/c` 3 `a b/c` 8 `+` 27 `a b/c` 3 `a b/c` 4 `=` 68.925

2. **(5) $7\frac{3}{4}$** Multiply the rate at which snow fell by the number of hours. $1.24 \times 6.25 = 7.75$, or $7\frac{3}{4}$

3. **(3) $554.56** Multiply the regular rate per hour by 40 hours. $9.50 \times 40 = \$380$ Subtract 40 from the actual time worked to find the number of overtime hours. $52.25 - 40 = 12.25$ Multiply the overtime hours by the rate per hour by 1.5. $12.25 \times \$9.50 \times 1.5 = \$174.5625$, or $174.56 rounded to the nearest cent. Add the two amounts earned. $380 + \$174.56 = \$554.56$

4. **(3) $22.41** Multiply the price per litre by the number of litres.

   $\$1.39 \times 16\frac{1}{8} = \$1.39 \times 16.125 = \$22.41375$, or $22.41 rounded to the nearest cent.

   Using your GED calculator:

   1.39 `×` 16 `a b/c` 1 `a b/c` 8 `=` 22.41375 Round to $22.41.

5. **(1) 1.275** Subtract the number of kilometres jogged by Brett from the number of kilometres jogged by Alicia.

   $4.875 - 3\frac{3}{5} = 4.875 - 3.6 = 1.275$

   Using your GED calculator:

   4.875 `−` 3 `a b/c` 3 `a b/c` 5 `=` 1.275

6. **(4) 13.225** Add the number of kilometres jogged by the three people.

   $4.875 + 3\frac{3}{5} + 4\frac{3}{4} = 4.875 + 3.6 + 4.75 = 13.225$

   Using your GED calculator:

   4.875 `+` 3 `a b/c` 3 `a b/c` 5 `+` 4 `a b/c` 3 `a b/c` 4 `=` 13.225

Lesson 11: The Meaning of Percent

(page 520)

1. $\frac{13}{20}$ $\frac{65 \div 5}{100 \div 5} = \frac{13}{20}$

2. $\frac{21}{25}$ $\frac{84 \div 4}{100 \div 4} = \frac{21}{25}$

3. $1\frac{2}{5}$ $\frac{140 \div 20}{100 \div 20} = \frac{7}{5} = 1\frac{2}{5}$

4. $2\frac{3}{4}$ $\frac{275 \div 25}{100 \div 25} = \frac{11}{4} = 2\frac{3}{4}$

5. $\frac{39}{100}$ $\frac{39}{100}$ This fraction cannot be reduced.

6. $4\frac{1}{2}$ $\frac{450 \div 50}{100 \div 50} = \frac{9}{2} = 4\frac{1}{2}$

GED Practice (page 521)

1. **(1) $7** Write a proportion. $\frac{?}{\$35} = \frac{20}{100}$

   Cross multiply and solve. $\$35 \times 20 \div 100 = \$7$

2. **(4) $562.50** $\frac{?}{\$625} = \frac{90}{100}$

$625 \times 90 \div 100 = \$562.50$

3. **(3) $33.60** $\frac{?}{\$1344} = \frac{2.5}{100}$

   $\$1344 \times 2.5 \div 100 = \$33.60$

4. **(2) 70** $\frac{56}{?} = \frac{80}{100}$

   $56 \times 100 \div 80 = 70$

5. **(1) 40%** $\frac{18}{45} = \frac{?}{100}$

   $18 \times 100 \div 45 = 40$

6. **(5) 375** $\frac{300}{?} = \frac{80}{100}$

   $300 \times 100 \div 80 = 375$

Lesson 12: Solving Percent Problems (Part 1)

GED Practice (page 524)

1. **(3) 852** Find 10% of 8520 by moving the decimal point one place to the left. $8520. \to 852.$ This is the same as dividing by 10 or multiplying by 0.1. $8520 \times 0.1 = 852$

2. **(4) $3.90** Find 10% by moving the decimal point one place to the left. $\$26.00 \to \$2.60$ Divide $2.60 by 2 to find 5%. $\$2.60 \div 2 = \$1.30$ Add to find 15%. $\$2.60 + \$1.30 = \$3.90$ This is the same as multiplying by 0.15. $0.15 \times \$26 = \$3.90$

3. **(5) $7.50** Find 10% by moving the decimal point one place to the left. $\$150.00 \to \$15$ Divide by 2 to find 5%. $\$15.00 \div 2 = \$7.50$ Or multiply. $0.05 \times \$150 = \$7.50$

4. **(2) $14.00** Find 10% by moving the decimal point one place to the left. $\$70.00 \to \$7$ Multiply by 2 to find 20%. $\$7.00 \times 2 = \$14.00$ or $\$70 \times 0.2 = \$14.00$

5. **(4) $375** Find 10% by moving the decimal point one place to the left. $\$1500. = \$150$ Multiply $150 by 2 to find 20%. $\$150 \times 2 = \$300$ Divide $150 by 2 to find 5%. $\$150 \div 2 = \$75$ Add 20% + 5% = 25%. $\$300 + \$75 = \$375$ or $\$1500 \times 0.25 = \$375$

6. **(2) 540** Find 10% by moving the decimal point one place to the left. $1800. = 180.$ Multiply 180 by 3 to find 30%. $180 \times 3 = 540$ or $1800 \times 0.3 = 540$

Lesson 13: Solving Percent Problems (Part 2)

GED Practice (page 527)

1. **(4) $17.00** Find the amount of the discount. $\$20 \times 0.15 = \$3$ Subtract to find the sale price. $\$20 - \$3 = \$17$

2. **(2) $9 + 0.06 × $9** Find the raise $(0.06 \times \$9)$, and then add that amount to her current wage to find her new hourly wage. $\$9 + 0.06 \times \$9$

Unit 6

3. **(3) 200%** Find the difference in the two amounts. $4500 − $1500 = $3000 Divide by the original amount. $3000 ÷ $1500 = 2.00 = 200%

4. **(2) 0.4(30) + 30** You need to find the increase by multiplying 0.4 by 30. Then add the increase to the original amount.

5. **(1)** $\frac{\$160 - (\$160 \times 0.1)}{6}$ Subtract the amount of the down payment from the cost of the coat. $160 − ($160 × 0.1) Then divide that amount by the number of monthly payments, 6.

6. **(2) 336** Find the number of workers to be laid off first. 1400 × 0.05 = 70 Subtract from the original. 1400 − 70 = 1330 Find the number of workers in the second layoff. 1330 × 0.20 = 266 Add the number of workers in both layoffs. 70 + 266 = 336

GED Practice (pages 529–530)

1. **(3) 414** Multiply the total number of employees at the end of the first quarter by the percent of increase in the second quarter.

    3450 × 0.12 = 414 or 3450 [×] 12 [SHIFT]
    [=] 414

2. **(4) 18%** Divide the amount of the tip by the total bill. $21.60 ÷ $120 = 0.18 = 18%

    or 21.60 [÷] 120 [SHIFT] [=] 18

3. **(4) $50 000** Divide the amount of the contribution by the percent of the salary. $4375 ÷ 0.0875 = $50 000

    or 4375 [÷] 8 [a b/c] 3 [a b/c] 4 [SHIFT]
    [=] 50000

4. **(2) 12.5%** Subtract the office expenses for this month from the office expenses for last month. $1400 − $1225 = $175 Divide the result by the amount of expenses for last month. $175 ÷ $1400 = 0.125 = 12.5%

    or 175 [÷] 1400 [SHIFT] [=] 12.5

5. **(3) $236.40** Multiply the regular price of the microwave oven by the percent of discount.

    $394 × 0.4 = $157.60 or 394 [×] 40 [SHIFT]

    [=] 157.60 Subtract the result from the regular price. $394 − $157.60 = $236.40 Another approach: Since the discount is 40% off, the sale price is 60% of the original price (100% − 40%). 0.6 × $394 = $236.40

    or 394 [×] 60 [SHIFT] [=] 236.40

6. **(4) 18%** Subtract the sales of toothpaste in April from the sales of toothpaste in May. $4956 − $4200 = $756 Divide the result by the sales of toothpaste in April. $756 ÷ $4200 = 0.18, or 18%

    or 756 [÷] 4200 [SHIFT] [=] 18

7. **(2) 11%** Add the sales for the 6 months listed. $2 + $6 + $8 + $8 + $14 + $18 = $56 Divide the sales in February by this total.

    6 [÷] 56 [SHIFT] [=] 10.7 = 11%,

    rounded to the nearest whole percent

8. **(1) January to February** The percent of increase for each pair of consecutive months is the increase in sales from one month to the next divided by the sales in the first month in the pair. From January to February the percent of increase is ($6 − $2) ÷ $2 = $4 ÷ $2 = 200%. For each of the other pairs of consecutive months the percent of increase is less than 100%.

9. **(5) $7000** Multiply the amount borrowed by the annual interest rate by the number of years of the loan. $12 500 × 0.16 × 3.5

    or 12500 [×] 3.5 [×] 16 [SHIFT] [=] 7000

10. **(3) 8%** Divide the amount of the raise by the current annual salary.

    3280 ÷ 38650 [SHIFT] [=] 8.4 = 8%,

    rounded to the nearest whole percent.

11. **(3) ($136 × 0.0825) + $136** Multiply the price of the coat by the sales tax percent, and add the result (the amount of sales tax) to the price of the coat. ($136 × .0825) + $136

12. **(1) 15%** Subtract the attendance for this year from the attendance for last year. 1420 − 1209 = 211 Divide the result by the attendance for last year.

    211 [÷] 1420 [SHIFT] [=] 14.8 = 15%,

    rounded to the nearest whole percent.

13. **(3) increase of 4%** Subtract the circulation in September ("original") from the circulation in October ("new"). 247 624 − 238 100 = 9524 Then divide the difference by the circulation in September. 9524 ÷ 238 100 = 0.04 = 4% Since the circulation in October is greater than that in September, the change is an increase.

    $$\frac{247\ 624 - 238\ 100}{238\ 100} \times 100\% = 4\%$$

    Another way to look at this problem:
    $$\frac{(\text{new amount} - \text{original amount})}{\text{original amount}} \times 100\% = \%\ \text{of}$$

    change. $\frac{\frac{(247\ 624 - 238\ 100)}{238\ 100}}{} \times 100\% = 4\%$

    or [[(---] 247624 [−] 238100 [---)]]
    [÷] 238100 [SHIFT] [=] 4

GED Review Numbers and Operations
(pages 531–535)
Part 1
1. **(5) 3216**

2. **(2) 504**

3. **(4) 14** Divide the total amount needed by the amount saved per month. $3220 ÷ $230 = 14

4. **(2) $5760** Multiply the monthly rent by 12, the number of months in a year. $480 × 12 = $5760

5. **(3) 10 967** Add the number of videotapes rented in February and March. 5980 + 4987 = 10 967

6. **(3) 1978** Subtract the number of videotapes rented in April from the number rented in May. 7985 − 6007 = 1978

7. **(4) 8640** Multiply the number of tapes rented in January by 2. 4320 × 2 = 8640

8. **(5) $42 500** Divide the amount paid for taxes by the percent paid for taxes. $13 600 ÷ 0.32 = $42 500 or
13600 ÷ 32 SHIFT = 42500

9. **(4) $45.47** Multiply the list price of the stapler by the percent of discount.
$69.95 × 0.35 = $24.48 or 69.95 × 35
SHIFT = 24.48, rounded to the nearest cent. Subtract the result from the list price. $69.95 − $24.48 = $45.47

10. **(3) 12.5%** Subtract the original value of the inventory from the value at the end of the first quarter to get the increase.
$52 200 − $46 400 = $5800
Divide the result by the original value.
$5800 ÷ $46 400 = 0.125 = 12.5% increase

11. $\frac{9}{20}$ Find a fraction of a fraction. Multiply the fraction of employees that drive to work by the fraction of employees that drive in a carpool.
$\frac{3}{4} × \frac{3}{5} = \frac{9}{20}$

12. **(1) Rent** To compare the fractions, convert them to like fractions.

Rent: $\frac{3}{8} = \frac{15}{40}$

Salaries: $\frac{1}{4} = \frac{10}{40}$

Advertising: $\frac{1}{5} = \frac{8}{40}$

Supplies: $\frac{1}{8} = \frac{5}{40}$

Miscellaneous: $\frac{1}{20} = \frac{2}{40}$

The fraction $\frac{3}{8}$ is the largest of the fractions.

13. **(5) Central** Change all of the fractions to like fractions.

Northeast: $\frac{1}{8} = \frac{5}{40}$

Southeast: $\frac{1}{4} = \frac{10}{40}$

Northwest: $\frac{1}{8} = \frac{5}{40}$

Southwest: $\frac{1}{5} = \frac{8}{40}$

Central: $\frac{3}{10} = \frac{12}{40}$

The fraction $\frac{3}{10}$ is the largest.

14. **(1) $\frac{1}{20}$** Add the fractions of profit from the Northeast and Northwest regions, and then subtract the fraction from the Southwest region.
$\frac{5}{40} + \frac{5}{40} − \frac{8}{40} = \frac{10}{40} − \frac{8}{40} = \frac{2}{40} = \frac{1}{20}$

15. **(2) $397 573** Multiply the total company profit by the fraction that came from the Southwest region. $1 987 865 × $\frac{1}{5}$ = $397 573 or
1987865 × 1 a b/c 5 = 397573

16. **(3) 0.43** Divide 3 by 7. 3 ÷ 7 = 0.428 or 0.43, rounded to the nearest hundredth.

17. **(4) $300.06** Add the five electric bills.
$64.16 + $78.92 + $63.94 + $50.17 + $42.87 = $300.06

18. **(1) $17.07** Add the cost of the three items and the total tax.
$17.60 + $9.25 + $3.68 + $2.40 = $32.93
Subtract the result from the amount given in payment. $50 − $32.93 = $17.07

Part 2

19. **(3) 2300** Add the number of new employees hired to the original number of employees. 2100 + 200 = 2300

20. **(4) 250 × $3** This expression shows that you multiply the number of paving blocks (250) by the cost of each block ($3).

21. **(5) Not enough information is given.** You do not know the number of months Marcus pays for the computer.

22. **(4) $100** Round the amount paid back to $1200, a number easily divided by 12.
$1200 ÷ 12 = $100

23. **(2) $175 − ($54.25 + $30.50)** You would add the amounts of the purchases and subtract the total from $175.

24. **(3) 5** Divide $10 by the price of one 7-cm potted plant. $10 ÷ $1.79 = 5.59 Therefore, the greatest number of plants that Mohammed can buy is 5.

25. **(4) $16 782** Multiply February's net sales by 120%. $13 985 × 1.2 = $16 782

26. **(3) $126** Multiply the regular price of the chair by the percent of mark down. $180 × 0.3 = $54
Subtract the result from the regular price of the chair. $180 − $54 = $126

27. **(2) $5400** Subtract the percent budgeted for advertising from the percent budgeted for supplies. 25% − 16% = 9% Multiply the total amount of the budget by the resulting percent.
$60 000 × 0.09 = $5400

28. **(5) $6200** Use the formula $i = prt$. Multiply the amount of the investment by the annual interest rate by the number of years. $5000 × 0.08 × 3 = 1200 Add the resulting interest earned to the original amount invested. $5000 + $1200 = $6200

29. **(2) 200%** Find the change in price. $3 − $1 = $2 Find the percent of increase. $2 ÷ $1 = 2 = 200%

30. **(2) $44** After paying 20% as a down payment, 80% remains. Multiply the original price of the television by 80%. $440 × 0.8 = $352 Divide the result by 8. $352 ÷ 8 = $44

31. **(1) $2625** Use the formula $i = prt$. Find the interest. $2500 × 0.025 × 2 = $125 Add interest to principal. $125 + $2500 = $2625

Lesson 15: Measuring Common Figures

GED Practice (page 539)

1. **(4) 7**
$$P = l + l + w + w = 2 + 2 + 1.5 + 1.5 = 7$$

2. **(5) 30 000** Work in centimetres.
2 m = 200 cm; 1.5 m = 150 cm
$A = l × w = 200 × 150 = 30\ 000$ cm²

3. **(2) 6** Let the width $= w$ and the length $= 3w$. Use the formula for the perimeter of a rectangle. Perimeter $= 2 ×$ length $+ 2 ×$ width
$$48 = 2(3w) + 2w$$
$$48 = 6w + 2w$$
$$48 = 8w$$
$$6 = w$$

4. **(4) 24** The height of the figure is 4 units (4 × 1) and the base is 8 units (4 × 2). The perimeter is the sum of all the measurements.
$2 + 1 + 2 + 1 + 2 + 1 + 2 + 1 + 8 + 4 = $
24 units

GED Practice (pages 541–542)

1. **(4) 5900** The area of the rectangular playground is $100 × 75 = 7500$ m². The area of the square blacktop: $40 × 40 = 1600$ m². Subtract the area of the blacktop from the area of the playground to find the area of the grassy portion.
$7500 − 1600 = 5900$ m²

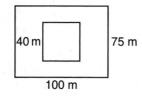

2. **(2) 128** Since the base is square, the length and width both measure 4 cm. The height is 8 cm. Volume = length × width × height
$V = 4 × 4 × 8 = 128$ cm²

3. **(2) 15** Sketch the quilt and count the points where four squares meet.

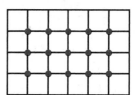

4. **(3) 3** Janice has gone north 4 blocks and south 4 blocks so she is back in line with the place where she began. She walked 5 blocks east and only 2 blocks west, so she is 3 blocks east of the place where she started.

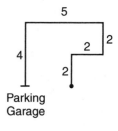

5. **(5) 404** The chalk line forms a rectangle two metres inside the other rectangle in all directions. Thus, the measurements of the new rectangle are 146 m by 56 m. (Subtract 2 m from both ends of each side, or 4 m from each measurement.) The perimeter of the chalk rectangle is the sum of the sides. $146 + 146 + 56 + 56 = 404$ m

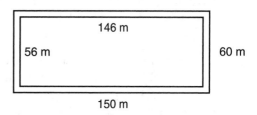

6. **(5) 10 × 8 × 7** The space inside the room is the volume. Volume = length × width × height

7. **(5) Not enough information is given.** Without knowing the width of the rectangle, its area cannot be computed.

8. **(5) 1130** Add the lengths of all the sides.
$278 + 234 + 301 + 174 + 143 = 1130$ cm

9. **(5) The volume of Box B is eight times the volume of Box A.** Find the volume of Box A (side = 2 m). $V = s³ = 2 × 2 × 2 = 8$ m³ Each side of Box B measures twice the length of each side of Box A, so each side of Box B measures $2 × 2 = 4$ m. Volume of Box B = $V = s³ = 4 × 4 × 4 = 64$ m³ Thus, the volume of Box B is 8 times the volume of Box A. $64 ÷ 8 = 8$
OR side of A = s, so $V = s³$. Side of B = $2s$, so volume of Box B = $V = (2s)² = 2s × 2s × 2s = 8s³$.

10. **(2) 200** Find the area of the larger rectangle. Area = length × width $A = 32 × 22 = 704$ m² Find the area of the smaller rectangle. $A = 28 × 18 = 504$ m² Subtract the area of the smaller rectangle from the area of the larger rectangle. $704 − 504 = 200$ m²

Unit 6

11. **(2) 16** Perimeter is the sum of the lengths of the four sides.
Larger rectangle: $P = 32 + 32 + 22 + 22 = 108$ m
Smaller rectangle: $P = 28 + 28 + 18 + 18 = 92$ m
Subtract the perimeter of the smaller rectangle from the perimeter of the larger rectangle.
$108 - 92 = 16$ m

12. **(1) 12** Area of the floor = length × width
$A = 60 \times 40 = 2400$ m². Divide the area of the floor by the area covered by one litre of paint.
$2400 \div 200 = 12$ L

Lesson 16: Measures of Central Tendency and Probability
GED Practice (page 545)

1. **(3) 87.0** On your GED calculator:
94 **+** 73 **+** 86 **+** 102 **+** 96 **+**
71 **=** 522 **÷** 6 **=** 87

2. **(1) 14.9° C** Add the temperatures and divide by five.

$$\frac{18.0°\,C + 15.2°\,C + 20.0°\,C + 9.3°\,C + 12.0°\,C}{5} = \frac{74.5°\,C}{5}$$

$= 14.9°$ C

On your GED calculator:
18.0 **+** 15.2 **+** 20.0 **+** 9.3
+ 12.0 **=** 74.5 **÷** 5 = 14.9

3. **(3) 6** Add the rainfall for the four months. Divide the result by the number of months.
On your GED calculator:
6.3 **+** 4.5 **+** 3.8 **+** 10.2 **=** 24.8 **÷** 4
= 6.2, or 6 rounded to the nearest centimetre.

4. **(2) 5** Write the values in order. 3.8, 4.5, 6.3, 10.2
Find the mean of the two middle values.
$(4.5 + 6.3) \div 2 = 10.8 \div 2 = 5.4$, or 5 rounded to the nearest centimetre. On your GED calculator:
[(--- 4.5 **+** 6.3 **---)]** **÷** 2 = 5.4

5. **(4) $20.38** Write the values in order. $16.22, $17.98, $18.96, $21.80, $28.84, $29.32
Find the mean of the two middle values.
$(\$18.96 + \$21.80) \div 2 = \$40.76 \div 2 = \$20.38$
On your GED calculator:
[(--- 18.96 **+** 21.80 **---)]** **÷** 2 **=** 20.38

(page 547)

1. $\frac{1}{2}$, **0.5, 50%** There are 4 even numbers out of 8 total numbers. P = $\frac{\text{favourable outcomes}}{\text{total outcomes}} = \frac{4}{8} = \frac{1}{2}$

2. $\frac{5}{8}$, **0.625, $62\frac{1}{2}$% or 62.5%** Five numbers are 3 or greater out of 8 total numbers. $\frac{5}{8} = 0.625$

3. $\frac{3}{8}$, **0.375, $37\frac{1}{2}$% or 37.5%** There are 3 sections marked 1 or 2 out of 8 total sections. $\frac{3}{8} = 0.375$

4. $\frac{3}{4}$, **0.75, 75%** 6 sections marked with a number other than 4, out of a total of 8 sections $\frac{6}{8} = \frac{3}{4}$

(page 548)

1. **25%** Chance of spinning red = $\frac{2}{4} = \frac{1}{2}$
Chance of drawing 4 or higher = $\frac{3}{6} = \frac{1}{2}$
Chance of both = $\frac{1}{2} \times \frac{1}{2} = \frac{1}{4} = 25\%$

2. **17%** There are four sections and all four are either red or blue. There is one 5 in the six cards.
Chance of spinning either red or blue = $\frac{4}{4}$
Chance of drawing a 5 = $\frac{1}{6}$
Chance of both = $\frac{4}{4} \times \frac{1}{6} = \frac{4}{24} = \frac{1}{6} = 0.166 = $
16.6%, which rounds to 17%

3. **0.2** Two out of ten names are favourable outcomes. $P = \frac{2}{10} = 0.2$

4. $\frac{1}{9}$ The events are dependent. After the first name is drawn, only nine names remain in the box.
Probability = 1 out of 9 = $\frac{1}{9}$

Lesson 17: Tables, Charts, and Graphs
GED Practice (page 552)

1. **(3) $400** Subtract the price of gold in July from the price in September. $600 − $200 = $400

2. **(4) 3:1** Form a ratio of the price of gold in September to the price of gold in July. Reduce.
$600:$200 = 3:1

3. **(3) $5.04** Add the three percents spent on nuts, pretzels, and chips. 13% + 12% + 17% = 42%
Multiply the resulting percent by the total amount spent. 0.42 × $12 million =
$5.04 million or 12 **×** 42 **SHIFT** **=** 5.04

4. **(2) 320** The average attendance is 300 on Mondays and about 620 on Saturdays. Subtract.
620 − 300 = 320

GED Review Measurement and Data Analysis
(pages 553–556)
Part 1

1. **(5) $30 412** Add the five annual salaries. Divide the result by the number of salaries.
$27 560 + $30 050 + $22 750 + $42 800 +
$28 900 = $152 060 ÷ 5 = $30 412

2. **(3) $28 900** List the salaries in order.
$22 750, $27 560, $28 900, $30 050, $42 800
The median is the middle number in the list.

3. **(2) $\frac{3}{7}$** Find the total number of possibilities that is not a black sock by adding the number of red socks and the number of blue socks. 2 + 4 = 6
Write a fraction by placing the result over the total number of outcomes, 14. Reduce the fraction to lowest terms. $\frac{6}{14} = \frac{3}{7}$

4. **(4) 36** Add the three sides of the triangle to find the perimeter. $10 + 12 + 14 = 36$

5. **(1) 64** Since a square has four equal sides, multiply the length of one side by 4.
$16\text{ cm} \times 4 = 64\text{ cm}$

6. **(1) 4** Find the area of the square by multiplying the side of the square by itself. $8 \times 8 = 64\text{ cm}^2$ Divide the resulting area by the length of the rectangle to find the width. $64 \div 16 = 4\text{ cm}$

7. **(2) 8** Find the volume of the larger cube: cube the length of its edge. $4 \times 4 \times 4 = 64\text{ cm}^3$ Find the volume of the smaller cube by cubing the length of its edge. $2 \times 2 \times 2 = 8\text{ cm}^3$ Divide the volume of the larger cube by the volume of the smaller cube. $64 \div 8 = 8$ cubes

8. **(2) 3500** Add the lengths of the sides to find the perimeter. $10 + 12 + 13 = 35\text{ m}$ The answer must be in centimetres. Since 1 metre = 100 cm, multiply the perimeter measured in metres by 100. $35 \times 100 = 3500\text{ cm}$

9. **(4) 28** Find the width of the rectangle by taking half its length and adding 2. $\frac{1}{2} \times 8 + 2 = 6\text{ m}$
Add the two lengths and the two widths.
$8 + 8 + 6 + 6 = 28\text{ m}$

10. **(2) 70** There are two missing measurements in the figure. To find the left side, add the two opposite lengths. $5 + 12 = 17\text{ m}$
To find the short missing side, subtract the two lengths at opposite ends of the figure.
$18 - 12 = 6\text{ m}$
Fill in the missing sides of the figure and add to find the perimeter.
$18 + 5 + 6 + 12 + 12 + 17 = 70\text{ m}$

11. **(3) 234** Divide the figure into two rectangles. Find the area of the top rectangle by multiplying its length by its width. $18 \times 5 = 90\text{ m}^2$
Find the area of the bottom rectangle by multiplying its length by its width.
$12 \times 12 = 144\text{ m}^2$
Add the two areas. $90 + 144 = 234\text{ m}^2$

12. **(4) 1680** Multiply the number of weeks times the number of days in a week, 7, times the number of hours in a day, 24.
$10 \times 7 \times 24 = 1680\text{ hr}$

Part 2

13. **(5) 49** Add the number of minutes for all the days. Divide the result by the number of days, 7.
$\frac{42 + 54 + 62 + 40 + 57 + 50 + 38}{7} = 343 \div 7 = 49$

14. **(2) 50** List the numbers in order.
38, 40, 42, 50, 54, 57, 62.
The median is the middle number in the list.

15. **(3) $\frac{1}{4}$** The total number of possible outcomes is 20. The total number of favourable outcomes (the numbers 16, 17, 18, 19, or 20) is 5. Write a fraction with the total number of favourable outcomes over the total number of outcomes. $\frac{5}{20}$
Reduce the fraction to lowest terms. $\frac{5}{20} = \frac{1}{4}$

16. **(4) 80** Multiply the total number of courses offered by the percent of Personal Growth courses. $500 \times 0.16 = 80$

17. **(5) 11:5** Compare the percent of Business courses offered to Health courses offered: 22%:10%. Reduce. $22\%{:}10\% = 11{:}5$

18. **(2) 5** Subtract the percent of Recreation courses from the percent of Business courses.
$22\% - 21\% = 1\%$ Multiply the result by the total number of courses. $500 \times 0.01 = 5$

19. **(2) 21 + 21 + 18 + 18** Add the four sides of the figure to find the perimeter. $21 + 21 + 18 + 18$

20. **(1) 56** Add the two lengths and the two widths.
$25 + 25 + 3 + 3 = 56\text{ m}$

21. **(4) $7\frac{1}{2}$** One method is to change the fraction to a decimal. $3\frac{3}{4} = 3.75$ To double the width, multiply by 2. $3.75 \times 2 = 7.5$ Change the decimal to a fraction. $7.5 = 7\frac{5}{10} = 7\frac{1}{2}$ units

22. **(5) 40 000 000** Change each measurement to centimetres. 5 m = 500 cm; 4 m = 400 cm; 2 m = 200 cm
Volume = length $\times$ width $\times$ height
$V = 500 \times 400 \times 200 = 40\,000\,000\text{ cm}^3$

23. **(4) 5250** Subtract the percent employed in an entertainment occupation from the percent employed in a business, legal, or professional occupation. $22\% - 1\% = 21\%$
Multiply the result by the total number of people. $25\,000 \times 21\% = 25\,000 \times 0.21 = 5250$

24. **(2) B** Find the percent of increase for each style: subtract to find the difference between the two prices, then divide by the original amount (the wholesale price). $24.90 - 16.80 = 8.1 \div 16.80 = 0.482 = 48\%$

The percent increase for the other options are:
A: $\$45.00 - \$32.00 = \$13.00 \div \$32.00 = 0.406 = 41\%$
C: $\$41.80 - \$34.00 = \$7.80 \div \$34.00 = 0.229 = 23\%$
D: $\$28.90 - \$23.00 = \$5.90 \div \$23.00 = 0.256 = 26\%$
E: $\$74.50 - \$56.50 = \$18.00 \div \$56.50 = 0.318 = 32\%$

Algebra
Lesson 18: Integers and Algebraic Expressions
(page 558)

1. **12** $(+7) + (+5) = +12$

2. **−16** $(-10) + (-6) = -16$

3. **−6** $\quad (-1) - (+5) = -6$

4. **−2** $\quad (+6) + (-8) = -2$

5. **510** $\quad (-118) - (-628) = +510$

On your GED calculator:

118 +/− − 628 +/− = 510

6. **−141** $\quad (+315) - (+456) = -141$

On your GED calculator:

315 − 456 = −141

7. **7** $\quad (+7) + (-5) + (-4) + (+9) =$
$\quad\quad (+7) + (+9) + (-5) + (-4) =$
$\quad\quad\quad (+16) \quad + \quad (-9) \quad = 7$

On your GED calculator:

7 **+** 5 **+/−** **+** 4 **+/−** **+** 9 **=** 7

8. **−6** $\quad (-6) - (+9) + (+10) - (+1) =$
$\quad\quad (-6) + (-9) + (-1) + (+10) =$
$\quad\quad\quad (-15) \quad\quad + (+19) = -6$

On your GED calculator:

6 **+/−** **−** 9 **+** 10 **−** 1 **=** −6

9. **7** $\quad (-5) - (-4) - (-8) =$
$\quad\quad (-5) + (+4) + (+8) =$
$\quad\quad (-5) + \quad (+12) \quad = 7$

On your GED calculator:

5 **+/−** **−** 4 **+/−** **−** 8 **+/−** **=** 7

10. **−33** $\quad (+13) - (+34) + (-12) =$
$\quad\quad (+13) + (-34) + (-12) =$
$\quad\quad (+13) + \quad (-46) \quad = -33$

On your GED calculator:

13 **−** 34 **+** 12 **+/−** **=** −33

(page 560)

1. **−6** $\quad (-2)(+3) = -6$

2. **28** $\quad (-4)(-7) = +28$

3. **−30** $\quad (+6)(-5) = -30$

4. **36** $\quad (+12)(+3) = +36$

5. **12** $\quad (-6)(-1)(+2) = (+6)(+2) = +12$

6. **54** $\quad (+9)(-2)(-3) = (-18)(-3) = +54$

7. **−16** $\quad (-64) \div (+4) = -16$

8. **−5** $\quad (+15) \div (-3) = -5$

9. **4** $\quad (+20) \div (+5) = +4$

10. **3** $\quad (-36) \div (-12) = +3$

11. **−12** $\quad \dfrac{-132}{11} = -12$

12. **4** $\quad \dfrac{-4}{-1} = +4$

13. **38** $\quad 6 + 8 \times 2^2 = 6 + 8 \times 4 = 6 + 32 = 38$

14. **10** $\quad \dfrac{-2 - (+8)}{(6) \div (-6)} = \dfrac{-10}{-1} = 10$

15. **−30** $\quad (-9 \times 4) - (-3 \times 2) =$
$\quad\quad -36 \quad - \quad (-6) \quad = -36 + 6 = -30$

16. **−61** $\quad (-25) - 4 \times 3^2 =$
$\quad\quad (-25) - 4 \times 9 =$
$\quad\quad (-25) \quad - \quad 36 \quad = -61$

17. **−25** $\quad 6 - (4 \times 8 + (-1)) =$
$\quad\quad 6 - (\quad 32 \quad + (-1)) =$
$\quad\quad 6 - \quad\quad 31 \quad\quad = -25$

18. **−2** $\quad \dfrac{(-4) + (-6)}{(+4) - (-1)} = \dfrac{-10}{5} = -2$

(page 562)

1. **a.** **−19** $\quad 3(-7 - 6) + 2(10) =$
$\quad\quad 3 \quad (-13) + \quad 20 =$
$\quad\quad\quad -39 + \quad 20 = -19$

b. **−7** $\quad 3(5 - 6) + 2(-2) =$
$\quad\quad 3 \;(-1) + \quad (-4) =$
$\quad\quad -3 \quad + \quad (-4) = -7$

c. **−6** $\quad 3(0 - 6) + 2(6) =$
$\quad\quad 3 \;(-6) + \quad 12 =$
$\quad\quad -18 \quad + \quad 12 = -6$

d. **−3** $\quad 3(3 - 6) + 2(3) =$
$\quad\quad 3 \;(-3) + \quad 6 =$
$\quad\quad -9 \quad + \quad 6 = -3$

2. **a.** **−4** $\quad 0^2 - 2^2 = 0 - 4 = -4$

b. **3** $\quad (-2)^2 - 1^2 = 4 - 1 = 3$

c. **0** $\quad 5^2 - (-5)^2 = 25 - 25 = 0$

d. **−3** $\quad (-1)^2 - (-2)^2 =$
$\quad\quad 1 - 4 = -3$

3. **a.** **−100** $\dfrac{(6 + 4)^2}{-1} =$
$\quad\quad \dfrac{10^2}{-1} \quad =$
$\quad\quad \dfrac{100}{-1} \quad = -100$

b. **6** $\dfrac{(6 + 0)^2}{6} =$
$\quad\quad \dfrac{6^2}{6} \quad =$
$\quad\quad \dfrac{36}{6} \quad = 6$

c. **−6** $\dfrac{(6 + 0)^2}{-6} =$
$\quad\quad \dfrac{6^2}{-6} \quad =$
$\quad\quad \dfrac{36}{-6} \quad = -6$

d. **32** $\dfrac{(6 + 2)^2}{2} =$
$\quad\quad \dfrac{8^2}{2} \quad =$
$\quad\quad \dfrac{64}{2} \quad = 32$

4. a. −3 $(-3)^2 + 2(-3) - 6 =$
          $9\ +\ (-6) - 6 =$
          $3\ \ \ \ \ \ \ \ \ \ -6 = -3$

b. 2 $2^2 + 2(2) - 6 =$
        $4 +\ \ 4\ \ - 6 =$
        $8\ \ \ \ \ \ \ - 6 = 2$

c. 18 $4^2 + 2(4) - 6 =$
        $16 +\ \ 8\ \ - 6 =$
        $24\ \ \ \ \ \ - 6 = 18$

d. 74 $8^2 + 2(8) - 6 =$
        $64 + 16\ - 6 =$
        $80\ \ \ \ \ \ - 6 = 74$

NOTE: You may have written terms in a different order. Your answer is correct if all terms are included and each has the correct sign. Remember, the term owns the sign that comes before it.

5. $16x − 8y$ $7x - 8y + 9x$
                $16x - 8y$

6. $3y^2 − 4y$ $5y^2 - 4y - 2y^2$
               $3y^2 - 4y$

7. $4m − 3n − 3$ $4m - 9n - 3 + 6n$
                 $4m - 3n - 3$

8. $−3x + 2$ $-5x + 16 - 8x - 14 + 10x$
              $-13x + 2 + 10x$
              $-3x + 2$

9. $8x^2 + 9x + 7$ $9x - 6 + 8x^2 + 13$
                 $8x^2 + 9x + 7$

10. $13n + 25$ $25 - 3n + 16n$
              $13n + 25$

11. $12x + 36y$ $12(x + 3y)$
              $12x + 36y$

12. $−5xy + 45x$ $5x(-y + 9)$
               $-5xy + 45x$

13. $5x + 4y + 15$ $4(2x + y) - 3(x - 5)$
               $8x + 4y - 3x + 15$
               $5x + 4y + 15$

14. $14x − 9$ $15 + 6(x - 4) + 8x$
           $15 + 6x - 24 + 8x$
           $14x - 9$

15. $−7n$ $3m + 2(m - n) - 5(m + n)$
           $3m + 2m - 2n - 5m - 5n$
           $- 7n$

16. $−2x + xy + 2y$ $x - 2(xy - y) + 4xy - x(3 + y)$
               $x - 2xy + 2y + 4xy - 3x - xy$
               $-2x + xy + 2y$

17. 25 $3x + 5(x + 9) - 4x$
          $3x + 5x + 45 - 4x$
          $4x + 45$
          $4(-5) + 45 = -20 + 45 = 25$

18. −40 $2m - 3(m + 5) - 15$
              $2m - 3m - 15 - 15$
              $-m - 30$
              $-10 - 30 = -40$

19. −18 $3y(2xz + 2) - 6xyz$
              $6xyz + 6y - 6xyz$
              $6y$
              $6(-3) = -18$

20. 4 $4(2x - y) - 3x + 2y$
           $8x - 4y - 3x + 2y$
           $5x - 2y$
           $5(0) - 2(-2) = 0 + 4 = 4$

GED Practice (page 563)

1. (4) 10 Start at zero, add −1, add 5, and add −8. $0 + (-1) + 5 + (-8) = -4$ Rita has −4 points, which is 10 points less than Jerry's score of +6.

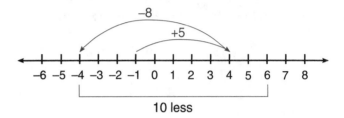

2. (5) −4 The point halfway between 1 and −3 is −1. Counting 3 units to the left is the same as adding −3. $-1 + (-3) = -4$.

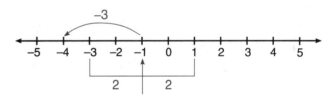

3. (2) −2° C Start at −5; then go up 6 and down 3. The temperature at 1 P.M. is −2° C.

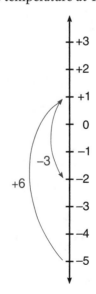

Unit 6

4. (1) *mn*
$$-m(2m + 2n) + 3mn + 2m^2 =$$
$$-2m^2 - 2mn + 3mn + 2m^2 =$$
$$mn$$

5. (2) **$-2a - 10b + 2c$** $3(-4b) - 2(a - b - c) =$
$$-12b - 2a + 2b + 2c =$$
$$-2a - 10b + 2c$$

6. (5) 5 To solve the problem on a number line, start at +4. Move right for the red die scores and left for the green die scores.

You can also add integers to find the answer.
$(+4) + (+4) + (+2) + (+6) + (-6) + (-1) +$
$(-4) = +5$

Lesson 19: Equations

(page 566)

1. 19
$$x - 15 = 4$$
$$x - 15 + 15 = 4 + 15$$
$$x = 19$$

2. 10
$$x - 7 = 3$$
$$x - 7 + 7 = 3 + 7$$
$$x = 10$$

3. −2
$$x - 8 = -10$$
$$x - 8 + 8 = -10 + 8$$
$$x = -2$$

4. −54
$$\frac{x}{-3} = 18$$
$$\frac{-3x}{-3} = 18(-3)$$
$$x = -54$$

5. 146
$$x - 94 = 52$$
$$x - 94 + 94 = 52 + 94$$
$$x = 146$$

6. 5.75
$$6.5 + x = 12.25$$
$$6.5 - 6.5 + x = 12.25 - 6.5$$
$$x = 5.75$$

7. 193
$$-69 + x = 124$$
$$-69 + 69 + x = 124 + 69$$
$$x = 193$$

8. 4.8
$$-3.6x = -17.28$$
$$\frac{-3.6x}{-3.6} = \frac{-17.28}{-3.6}$$
$$x = 4.8$$

9. 33
$$-13 + x = 20$$
$$-13 + 13 + x = 20 + 13$$
$$x = 33$$

10. 90
$$10x = 900$$
$$\frac{10x}{10} = \frac{900}{10}$$
$$x = 90$$

11. 240
$$\frac{x}{4} = 60$$
$$\frac{4x}{4} = 60(4)$$
$$x = 240$$

12. 128
$$\frac{x}{4} = 32$$
$$\frac{4x}{4} = 32(4)$$
$$x = 128$$

13. −8
$$-6x = 48$$
$$\frac{-6x}{-6} = \frac{48}{-6}$$
$$x = -8$$

14. 48
$$52 + x = 100$$
$$52 - 52 + x = 100 - 52$$
$$x = 48$$

15. 5
$$6x + 7 = 37$$
$$6x = 30$$
$$x = 5$$

16. 5
$$4x + 5x - 10 = 35$$
$$9x - 10 = 35$$
$$9x = 45$$
$$x = 5$$

17. −2
$$3x - 6x + 2 = -4x$$
$$-3x + 2 = -4x$$
$$2 = -x$$
$$-2 = x$$

18. 1
$$6 - x + 12 = 10x + 7$$
$$18 - x = 10x + 7$$
$$18 = 11x + 7$$
$$11 = 11x$$
$$1 = x$$

19. −1
$$5x + 7 - 4x = 6$$
$$x + 7 = 6$$
$$x = -1$$

20. −4
$$9x + 6x - 12x = -7x + 2x - 12 + 5x$$
$$3x = -12$$
$$x = -4$$

21. 4
$$7x + 3 = 31$$
$$7x = 28$$
$$x = 4$$

22. 3
$$6(2 + x) = 5x + 15$$
$$12 + 6x = 5x + 15$$
$$12 + x = 15$$
$$x = 3$$

Answers and Explanations • Unit 6

23. 4
$$4x + 5 = 21$$
$$4x = 16$$
$$x = 4$$

24. −9
$$2x - 5x + 11 = 38$$
$$-3x + 11 = 38$$
$$-3x = 27$$
$$x = -9$$

25. 6
$$3x - 8 = x + 4$$
$$2x - 8 = 4$$
$$2x = 12$$
$$x = 6$$

26. 5
$$7(x - 2) = 21$$
$$7x - 14 = 21$$
$$7x = 35$$
$$x = 5$$

27. 10
$$5x - 13x + 2x = -70 + x$$
$$-6x = -70 + x$$
$$-7x = -70$$
$$x = 10$$

28. 8
$$8x + 12 = 44 + 4x$$
$$4x + 12 = 44$$
$$4x = 32$$
$$x = 8$$

GED Practice (page 568)

1. **(5) $x + (3x + 12) = 360$** Let x = the number of employees in management. Let $3x + 12$ = the number of employees in production. The sum of these expressions is equal to the total number of workers, so $x + (3x + 12) = 360$

2. **(3) $2x + 12 = 66$** Let x equal the number of pushups Frank did and $x + 12$ equal the number of pushups Tom did. The sum of these expressions is equal to 66. So $x + (x + 12) = 66$ or $2x + 12 = 66$.

3. **(4) $x + (2x - 4) = 65$** Let x = the fine for the first ticket. The second fine is $4 less than twice the first fine: $2x - 4$. The sum of the fines is equal to $65, so $x + (2x - 4) = 65$.

4. **(1) $\frac{8y}{4} = 2y$** Eight times a number, y, is divided by 4: $\frac{8y}{4}$ This expression equals two times the number, or $2y$. Only option (1) shows that these expressions are equal.

5. **(5) $3x = 60 + 12$** Let x = the number of boys. Let $2x - 12$ = the number of girls. Add the expressions and set them equal to 60.
$$x + (2x - 12) = 60$$
Combine like terms. $3x - 12 = 60$
Simplify. $3x \quad = 60 + 12$

6. **(2) $3x + 2(2x) = 28$** Let x = the cost of a children's ticket. Let $2x$ = the cost of an adult ticket. Angela bought 2 adult tickets and 3 children's tickets: $2(2x)$ and $3x$. The total cost (sum of the expressions) is $28; the equation is $3x + 2(2x) = 28$

GED Practice (page 570)

1. **(4) $57.60** Use the cost formula.
$$c = nr$$
$$\$345.60 = 6r$$
$$\frac{\$345.60}{6} = \frac{6r}{6}$$
$$\$57.60 = r$$

2. **(3) $3(\$6.98) + 4(\$4.50)$** For each type of fabric, the total cost can be found using $c = nr$. The total cost of the first fabric is $3(\$6.98)$. The total cost of the second fabric is $4(\$4.50)$. Only option (3) shows the sum of these expressions.

3. **(2) $\frac{312}{6}$** Substitute the distance and time and solve for the rate, r.
$$d = rt$$
$$312 = 6r$$
$$\frac{312}{6} = r$$

4. **(3) $3.48** Remember, 1.45 cents = $0.0145.
$$c = nr$$
$$c = 240(0.0145)$$
$$c = 3.48$$

5. **(2) 235** Find the distance for each part of the journey and add. $d = rt$
Part one: $d = 55(2.5) = 137.5$ km
Part two: $d = 65(1.5) = 97.5$ km
$$137.5 + 97.5 = 235 \text{ km}$$

6. **(4) $84.94** For each item, use $c = nr$. The number of items multiplied by the unit price or rate (r) is the cost for that item. Add the costs.
$$3(\$9.99) + 2(\$13.99) + \$26.99 =$$
$$\$29.97 + \$27.98 + \$26.99 = \$84.94$$

Lesson 20: Exponents and Roots
(page 572)

1. **16** $2^4 = 2 \times 2 \times 2 \times 2 = 16$

2. **64** $4^3 = 4 \times 4 \times 4 = 64$

3. **16** A number to the first power is equal to itself.

4. **1** $1^6 = 1 \times 1 \times 1 \times 1 \times 1 \times 1 = 1$

5. **1** Any number (except 0) to the zero power is equal to 1.

6. **81** $3^4 = 3 \times 3 \times 3 \times 3 = 81$

7. **27** $3^3 = 3 \times 3 \times 3 = 27$

8. **49** $7^2 = 7 \times 7 = 49$

9. **$\frac{1}{9}$** $3^{-2} = \frac{1}{3 \times 3} = \frac{1}{9}$

10. **64** $8^2 = 8 \times 8 = 64$

11. **$\frac{1}{125}$ or 0.008** $5^{-3} = \frac{1}{5 \times 5 \times 5} = \frac{1}{125}$

12. **1** Any number (except 0) to the zero power is equal to 1.

13. **1296** 6 [x^y] 4 [=] 1296

14. **59 049** 9 [x^y] 5 [=] 59049

15. **729** 3 x^y 6 = 729

16. **0.015 625 or $\frac{1}{64}$** 8 x^y 2 +/− = 0.015625

17. **248 832** 12 x^y 5 = 248832

18. **78 125** 5 x^y 7 = 78125

19. **0.031 25 or $\frac{1}{32}$** 2 x^y 5 +/− = 0.03125

20. **2401** 7 x^y 4 = 2401

21. **(4) 5.18×10^5** To write a number in scientific notation, move the decimal point until only one digit is to the left of the decimal point. In this case, you have to move the decimal point 5 places to the left, so the power of ten is 10^5.

22. **(4) 4.7×10^{-1}, 2.34×10^2, 5.2×10^2** Find the value of each expression.
$4.7 \times 10^{-1} = 0.47$ Move decimal 1 place left.
$2.34 \times 10^2 = 234$ Move decimal 2 places right.
$5.2 \times 10^2 = 520$ Move decimal 2 places right.
Compare the resulting values and put the original expressions in order from least to greatest.

(page 574)
1. **4** $4 \times 4 = 16$

2. **0** $0 \times 0 = 0$

3. **3** $3 \times 3 = 9$

4. **7** $7 \times 7 = 49$

5. **5** $5 \times 5 = 25$

6. **1** $1 \times 1 = 1$

7. **6 cm**
Since $6^2 = 36$, the length of each side is 6 cm.

8. **4 m**
Since $4^2 = 16$, the length of each side is 4 m.

9. **9 m** Since $9^2 = 81$, the length of each side is 9 m.

10. **5.29** 28 SHIFT x^2

11. **9.75** 95 SHIFT x^2

12. **2.45** 6 SHIFT x^2

13. **18** 324 SHIFT x^2

14. **11.40** Since you are rounding to the hundredths place, show the 0 in the hundredths column.
130 SHIFT x^2

15. **13** 169 SHIFT x^2

GED Practice (page 576)
1. **(4) 14, 15, and 16** Quickly add the numbers in each option. Only option (4) has a sum of 45.

2. **(3) 300** You know that Jess drove 200 km more than David. Add 200 to each answer choice (to

get Jess's distance), then add the answer choice to that sum (to get the total distance). Look for a total sum of 800 km.
If David drove 300 km, Jess drove 500.
$300 + 500 = 800$ km,
or subtract 200 from 800 and divide by 2.
$\frac{(800 - 200)}{2} = 300$

3. **(3) 47 and 48** Add the numbers for each option.
$47 + 48 = 95$

4. **(2) 8, 9, 10, and 11** Add the numbers for each option. You may be able to add more quickly if you pair up the numbers.
$8 + 10 = 18$ and $9 + 11 = 20$; $18 + 20 = 38$

5. **(2) 15** Each new figure adds a row consisting of the number of circles in the bottom row of the preceding figure plus 1. There are 4 circles in the bottom row of figure D, and 10 circles in all. Figure E should look like figure D with an additional bottom row of 5 circles for a total of 15 circles.

6. **(5) 384** Each term is two times the number before it. This is a good problem to solve with a calculator.
The 6th term is $48 \times 2 = 96$.
The 7th term is $96 \times 2 = 192$.
The 8th term is $192 \times 2 = 384$.

7. **(1) 42** For y to be a whole number, x must be evenly divisible by 4. The numbers 8, 12, 28, and 32 are multiples of 4. If 42 is equal to x, y will not be a whole number; therefore, option (1) is the correct choice.

Lesson 21: Factoring and Inequalities
(page 579)
1. **$x^2 + 5x + 4$**
$x^2 + 4x + x + 4 = x^2 + 5x + 4$

2. **$x^2 + 9x + 18$**
$x^2 + 3x + 6x + 18 = x^2 + 9x + 18$

3. **$2x^2 - 17x + 35$**
$2x^2 - 7x - 10x + 35 = 2x^2 - 17x + 35$

4. **$x^2 - 4$**
$x^2 - 2x + 2x - 4 = x^2 - 4$

5. **$xy + 6x - 4y - 24$** This expression cannot be simplified. Note: The terms in expressions are generally written so that the variables are in alphabetical order. Your answer is still correct if the terms are in a different order; however, you must make sure that each term has the correct sign.

6. **$6x^2 + 42x + 72$**
$6x^2 + 18x + 24x + 72 = 6x^2 + 42x + 72$

1. **(5) 12 and 6** Rewrite the equation in standard quadratic form so that the quadratic expression is equal to 0. $x^2 - 18x + 72 = 0$
   Factor the equation. $(x - 12)(x - 6) = 0$
   Determine the value for x for each factor that will make the factor equal to 0:

$x - 12 = 0$	$x - 6 = 0$
$x = 12$	$x = 6$

   Check:

$x^2 + 72 = 18x$	$x^2 + 72 = 18x$
$12^2 + 72 = 18(12)$	$6^2 + 72 = 18(6)$
$144 + 72 = 216$	$36 + 72 = 108$
$216 = 216$	$108 = 108$

2. **(3) 3** When the squared variable is multiplied by a number (such as $2x^2$), it is often faster and easier to test the answer choices rather than to factor the equation. Only option (3) makes the equation true.
$$2x^2 - 10x + 12 = 0$$
$$2(3^2) - 10(3) + 12 = 0$$
$$2(9) - 30 + 12 = 0$$
$$18 - 30 + 12 = 0$$
$$0 = 0$$

3. **(2) 4 and −3** Rewrite: $x^2 - x - 12 = 0$
   Factor: $(x - 4)(x + 3) = 0$
   The values for x must be 4 and −3.

4. **(4) −5 and −8** Rewrite: $x^2 + 13x + 40 = 0$
   Factor: $(x + 5)(x + 8) = 0$
   The values for x must be −5 and −8.

5. **(5) 2 and −2** Substitute the numbers from each option into the equation. To save time, start with the first number in each pair. Only option (5) makes the equation true.

$x = 2$	$x = -2$
$9x^2 - 36 = 0$	$9x^2 - 36 = 0$
$9(2^2) - 36 = 0$	$9(-2^2) - 36 = 0$
$9(4) - 36 = 0$	$9(4) - 36 = 0$
$36 - 36 = 0$	$36 - 36 = 0$
$0 = 0$	$0 = 0$

6. **(2) 5** Substitute the answer choices. Only option (2) makes the equation true.
$$2x^2 - x = 45$$
$$2(5^2) - 5 = 45$$
$$2(25) - 5 = 45$$
$$50 - 5 = 45$$
$$45 = 45$$

Lesson 22: The Coordinate Plane

GED Practice (page 584)

1. **(4,−1)** Count 4 to the right along the x-axis (horizontal line) and 1 down along the y-axis (vertical line).

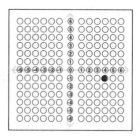

2. **(3,−3)** A square has 4 sides of equal lengths. From the graph in the problem, you can see that each side of the square is 4 units long. By counting, you can see that the missing corner must be placed at $(3,-3)$.

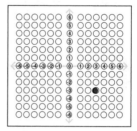

3. **(−5, 3)** Count 5 to the left along the x-axis and 3 up along the y-axis.

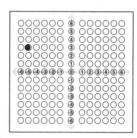

4. **(−5,−3)** A rectangle has four sides, with opposite sides of equal length. From the graph in the problem, you can see that the missing corner must be located at $(-5,-3)$.

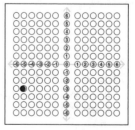

(page 586)
For questions 1–3, two ordered pairs on the line are given. You may have found other ordered pairs in order to draw your line. Your answer is correct if it passes through the points given here.

Unit 6

1. (0,−4), (1,−1)

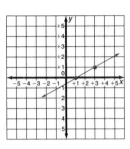

2. (1,0), (3,1)

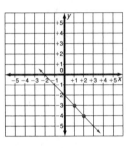

3. (2,−4), (1,−3)

(page 587)

1. **−1** The line goes downward 1 unit as it moves 1 unit to the right. $\frac{-1}{1} = -1$

2. **1** The line rises 2 units as it moves 2 units to the right. $\frac{2}{2} = 1$

3. **0** A horizontal line has a slope of 0.

For questions 4–6, use the slope formula: $m = \frac{y_2 - y_1}{x_2 - x_1}$

4. **−4** $m = \frac{1 - (-3)}{0 - 1} = \frac{4}{-1} = -4$

5. **9** $m = \frac{-4 - 5}{3 - 4} = \frac{-9}{-1} = 9$

6. **3** $m = \frac{0 - (-3)}{-2 - (-3)} = \frac{3}{1} = 3$

GED Practice (page 589)

1. **(3) (0,−2)** In the slope-intercept form of a line, the y-intercept is added to or subtracted from the product of the slope (*m*) and *x*. The *x*-coordinate of the *y*-intercept is always 0.

2. **(5) $y + \frac{1}{4}x = 3$** Line *A* rises 1 unit for every 4 units it moves to the left (a negative direction), so the slope is $-\frac{1}{4}$. The *y*-intercept is 3. In slope-intercept form, the equation of Line *A* is $y = -\frac{1}{4}x + 3$. Only option (5) is equal to this equation.

3. **(2) $y = x$** Line *B* rises 2 units for every 2 units it moves to the right, so the slope is $\frac{2}{2} = 1$. The line crosses the *y*-axis at the origin (0,0), so its *y*-intercept is 0. In slope-intercept form, the equation is $y = 1x + 0$, which equals $y = x$.

4. **(3) $y = 3x − 5$** Only option (3) subtracts 5 from the product of *x* and a number.

5. **(1) $y = −x + 3$** Find the slope using the coordinates of points *P* and *Q*. The line must rise 2 units for every 2 units it moves to the left: $\frac{2}{-2} = -1$. If you continue the line at a slope of −1, it will cross the *y*-axis at point (0,3). Using the slope-intercept form, the equation must be $y = -x + 3$.

6. **(2) (0,−2)** The line described must have a slope of $\frac{2}{3}$, meaning it rises 2 units for every 3 units it moves to the right. From Point *R*, count up 2 units and 3 to the right. You are at coordinates (0,−2), the *y*-intercept of the line.

GED Review Algebra

(pages 590–593)

Part 1

1. **(1) $\frac{2}{x} − 9x$** The product of 9 and *x* is 9 times *x* or 9*x*. The quotient of 2 and *x* means $2 \div x$ or $\frac{2}{x}$. Only option (1) shows 9*x* subtracted from $\frac{2}{x}$.

2. **(2) (−6) + (+8)** Evaluate each expression.
$(-2) + (-7) = -9$
$(-6) + (+8) = +2$
$(-3) - (-4) = -3 + 4 = +1$
$(+4) - (+10) = -6$
$(-8) + (+9) = +1$
Of the results, +2 is greatest.

Using your GED calculator:

2	+/−	+	7	+/−	=	−9
6	+/−	+	8	=	2	
3	+/−	−	4	+/−	=	1
4	−	10	=	−6		
8	+/−	+	9	=	1	

3. **(4) 15 and 16** Let *x* and *x* + 1 represent the consecutive numbers. Write an equation and solve.
$$x + (x + 1) - 13 = 18$$
$$2x - 12 = 18$$
$$2x = 30$$
$$x = 15 \text{ and } x + 1 = 16$$

4. **(4) 20** Write an equation and solve.
$$x - 10 = \frac{x}{2}$$
$$2(x - 10) = \frac{2x}{2}$$
$$2x - 20 = x$$
$$-20 = -x$$
$$(-1)(-20) = (-1)(-x)$$
$$20 = x$$

5. (3) 17 Let x equal Caroline's age. Bill's age is $2x - 1$. Write an equation and solve.
$$x + (2x - 1) = 26$$
$$3x - 1 = 26$$
$$3x = 27$$
$$x = 9$$

Caroline is 9 years old, and Bill is $2(9) - 1$, or 17.

6. (4) 279 Use the formula *distance = rate × time*.
$$d = rt$$
$$d = 62 \times 4.5$$
$$d = 279 \text{ km}$$

7. (5) Add 4. Each number in the sequence is 4 more than the number preceding it.

8. (2) 4 Each term in the sequence is found by dividing the term before it by -2. $-8 \div -2 = 4$

9. (3) 15 and 35 Substitute 2 and 4 into the function to find the two values for y.
$$y = 10(2) - 5 \qquad y = 10(4) - 5$$
$$y = 20 - 5 = 15 \qquad y = 40 - 5 = 35$$

10. (3) 14 and 16 All the choices show a difference of 2 hours. Add the numbers in each option to find a sum of 30 hours. $14 + 16 = 30$ hours

11. (2) 44 and 49 All the choices show a difference of 5 points. Add the numbers in each option to find a sum of 93 points. $44 + 49 = 93$

12. (3) 142 and 192 All the choices show a difference of 50 km. Add the numbers in each option to find a sum of 334 km. $142 + 192 = 334$

Part 2

13. (1) −5 and 4 This is a quadratic equation. Either use factoring or simply substitute each answer choice into the equation until you find the correct one.

To use the factoring method, rewrite the equation so that the quadratic expression equals 0. Then factor.
$$x^2 + x = 20$$
$$x^2 + x - 20 = 0$$
$$(x + 5)(x - 4) = 0$$

Then find the value of x for each factor that will make that factor equal to 0.
$$x + 5 = 0 \qquad x - 4 = 0$$
$$x = -5 \qquad x = 4$$

14. (5) $392 Substitute 32 for s in the function and solve for p.
$$p = \$200 + \$6(32)$$
$$p = \$200 + \$192$$
$$p = \$392$$

15. (5) (2,5) Substitute the answer choices into the equation. Only option (5) makes the equation true.

$$4x - y = 3$$
$$4(2) - 5 = 3$$
$$8 - 5 = 3$$
$$3 = 3$$

16. (4) between 15 and 16 m
Because the area of a square equals the side squared, the side of a square equals the square root of the area. Try squaring the numbers in the answer choices to find the approximate square root of 240.

You know $12 \times 12 = 144$ and $20 \times 20 = 400$, so start with values between these two.
$$14 \times 14 = 196 \quad 15 \times 15 = 225 \quad 16 \times 16 = 256$$
$$\sqrt{240} \text{ is between 15 and 16.}$$

17. (2) *B* A line with a negative slope moves downward as it goes from left to right. The slope of Line A is undefined. Lines C and D have positive slopes, and the slope of Line E is 0.

18. (2) $\dfrac{5}{x - 2}$ Factor each expression. Then simplify.
$$\frac{x + 4x}{x^2 - 2x} = \frac{x(1 + 4)}{x(x - 2)} = \frac{5}{x - 2}$$

Note: You can cancel x from the numerator and the denominator in the second step since $\frac{x}{x} = 1$.

19. (5) (3,6) Substitute the ordered pairs in the answer options until you find the one that does not make the equation true.
$$2x - y = -1$$
$$2(3) - 6 \neq -1$$

20. (1) $y = 2x + 2$ The answer choices are written in slope-intercept form $y = mx + b$, where m = slope and b = y-intercept. Remember, slope is the ratio of *rise over run*. Notice that the line rises 4 units and runs 2 units as it goes from Point A to Point B; therefore, the slope is $\frac{4}{2} = +2$. The y-intercept of the line, the point where the line crosses the y-axis, is $+2$. Therefore, the correct equation of the line is $y = 2x + 2$.

You could also solve the problem by finding the coordinates of two points on the line and substituting to find the correct equation. Always use two points since more than one line could pass through only one point.

21. (3) $c = \$40 + \$30h$ The charge for a service call is the sum of $40 (the flat fee) and the number of hours multiplied by $30. Only option (3) shows this sequence of operations.

22. (1) −3 Use the slope formula. Let $(-2, -2) = (x_1, y_1)$ and $(-4, 4) = (x_2, y_2)$
$$m = \frac{y_2 - y_1}{x_2 - x_1}$$
$$m = \frac{4 - (-2)}{-4 - (-2)}$$
$$m = \frac{6}{-2} = -3$$

23. (4) $152 Each month an additional $12 is deposited. Continue adding $12 until you reach December, the 12th month. You can also solve the problem by multiplying $12 by 11, the number of increases, and adding $20, the beginning deposit. 11($12) + $20 = $152

24. (4) $y = -x + 3$ The line moves downward 1 unit each time it goes to the right 1 unit for a slope of $\frac{-1}{1} = -1$. The y-intercept is +3. Use the slope-intercept form to write the equation of the line. $y = mx + b$, where m = slope and b = y-intercept.
$$y = -1x + 3, \text{ or } y = -x + 3$$

25. (3) 5 Use the formula for finding the distance between two points. Let $D(1,3) = (x_1, y_1)$ and $F(4,-1) = (x_2, y_2)$.

$$\text{distance} = \sqrt{(x_2 - x_1)^2 + (y_2 - y_1)^2}$$
$$= \sqrt{(4 - 1)^2 + (-1 - 3)^2}$$
$$= \sqrt{3^2 + (-4)^2}$$
$$= \sqrt{9 + 16}$$
$$= \sqrt{25} = 5$$

Geometry
Lesson 23: Applying Formulas
(page 595)

1. $P = 49.2$ cm; $A = 69$ cm²
To find perimeter, add the lengths of the sides.
$$10 + 23 + 16.2 = 49.2 \text{ cm}$$
To find area, use the formula for the area of a triangle. $A = \frac{1}{2}bh$
$$A = \frac{1}{2}(23)(6) = 69 \text{ cm}^2$$

2. $P = 30$ cm; $A = 43.5$ cm² or $43\frac{1}{2}$ cm² The base is the side that forms a 90° angle with the dotted line indicating the height. In this case, the base is 10 cm, since all sides have the same measure. To find perimeter, add the lengths of the sides. 10 + 10 + 10 = 30 cm
To find area, use the formula, for the area of a triangle. $A = \frac{1}{2}bh$
$$A = \frac{1}{2}(10)(8.7) = 43.5 \text{ cm}^2$$

3. $P = 33$ m; $A = 48$ m² Opposite sides of a parallelogram are equal. Therefore, the top and bottom sides both measure 12 m and the left and right sides each measure 4.5 m. The height is 4 m. To find perimeter, add the lengths of the sides. 12 + 12 + 4.5 + 4.5 = 33 m
To find area, use the formula for the area of a parallelogram. $A = bh$
$$A = 12(4) = 48 \text{ m}^2$$

4. $P = 24.4$ cm; $A = 24$ cm² Remember that the opposite sides of a parallelogram are equal. Therefore, the top and bottom sides both measure 8 cm and the sides on the left and right

each measure 4.2 cm. The height is 3 cm. To find perimeter, add the lengths of the sides.
$$8 + 8 + 4.2 + 4.2 = 24.4 \text{ cm}$$
Then use the area formula.
$$A = bh$$
$$A = 8(3) = 24 \text{ cm}^2$$

5. $P = 18.7$ cm; $A = 14$ sq cm
To find perimeter, add the lengths of the sides.
$$7.1 + 7.6 + 4 = 18.7 \text{ cm}$$
Then use the area formula.
$$A = \frac{1}{2}bh$$
$$A = \frac{1}{2}(4)(7) = 14 \text{ sq cm}$$

6. $P = 30$ cm; $A = 40$ cm²
To find perimeter, add the lengths of the sides.
$$10 + 10 + 5 + 5 = 30 \text{ cm}$$
Then use the area formula.
$$A = bh$$
$$A = 10(4) = 40 \text{ cm}^2$$

(page 596)

1. 22 cm $C = \pi d = 3.14(7) = 21.98$, round to 22 cm

2. 12.56 m²
$$A = \pi r^2$$
$$A = 3.14(2^2)$$
$$A = 3.14(4)$$
$$A = 12.56 \text{ m}^2$$

3. 28 m²
$$A = \pi r^2$$
$$A = 3.14(3^2)$$
$$A = 3.14(9)$$
$$A = 28.26, \text{ round to } 28 \text{ m}^2$$

4. 44 cm The radius of the circle is 7 cm; the diameter is twice the radius, or $7 \times 2 = 14$ cm.
$$C = \pi d$$
$$C = 3.14(14)$$
$$C = 43.96, \text{ round to } 44 \text{ cm}$$

GED Practice (page 599)

1. (2) 12 Use the formula. $A = lw$
Substitute. $\quad\quad 180 = 15w$
Solve. $\quad\quad \frac{180}{15} = \frac{15w}{15}$
$\quad\quad\quad\quad\quad 12 = w$

2. (1) $\frac{81.64}{3.14(2^2)}$ Use the formula. $V = \pi r^2 h$, where r = the radius of the base of the cylinder and h = height. Rewrite the formula to solve for height. Divide both sides of the formula by πr^2 and substitute the known measurements into the equation.

$$\frac{V}{\pi r^2} = h$$

$$\frac{81.64}{3.14(2^2)} = h$$

Only option 1 matches this setup.

3. (2) 6 Use the formula. $A = \frac{1}{2}bh$, where b = base

and h = height. $A = \frac{1}{2}bh$

Substitute. $10.5 = \frac{1}{2}(b)(3.5)$

Multiply both sides by 2. $21 = 3.5b$

Divide both sides by 3.5. $\frac{21}{3.5} = \frac{3.5b}{3.5}$

$\qquad\qquad\qquad\qquad\qquad 6 = b$

4. (4) between 6 and 7

$V = lwh$

$V = 2\frac{1}{2}\left(1\frac{1}{2}\right)\left(1\frac{3}{4}\right)$

$V = \frac{5}{2} \times \frac{3}{2} \times \frac{7}{4}$

$V = \frac{105}{16}$

$V = 6\frac{9}{16}$ cubic units, which is between 6 and 7 cubic units

5. (3) 15 000 Convert the base measurement to

centimetres. $\frac{\text{metre}}{\text{centimetres}} \quad \frac{1}{100} = \frac{2}{x}$

$x = 100(2) = 200$ cm

$A = \frac{1}{2}bh$

$A = \frac{1}{2}(200)(150)$

$A = 15\ 000$ cm^2

6. (2) 10 000

Find the volume of the cone.

$V = \frac{1}{3}Ah$

$V = \frac{1}{3}(200)(150)$

$V = 10\ 000$ cm^3

Lesson 24: Lines and Angles

GED Practice (page 603)

1. (2) $\angle ABD$ and $\angle DBC$ are supplementary.
$m\angle ABD + m\angle DBC = m\angle ABC$; $\angle ABC$ is a straight angle, which measures 180°. When the sum of the measures of two angles is 180°, they are supplementary.

2. (3) $\angle 3$ and $\angle 7$ Because $\angle 1$ is congruent to $\angle 5$, the figure shows two parallel lines crossed by a transversal. Angles 3 and 7 are congruent because they are corresponding angles. In other words, they are both in the same position with regard to the transversal.

3. (2) $x + (x - 12°) = 90°$ The larger angle is represented by x. The measure of the smaller angle must be 12° less than x, or $x - 12°$. Since they are complementary, their sum is 90°. Only option (2) correctly sets the sum of the expressions equal to 90°.

4. (4) Lines p and q are not parallel. Although the lines look parallel, neither the figure nor the

text gives this information. If the lines were parallel, the measure of $\angle 7$ would equal 118° because $\angle 7$ corresponds to $\angle 3$, which is a vertical angle to the angle measuring 118°.

5. (1) $m\angle 1 = 50°$ Angle 1 corresponds to the angle that measures 50°. Since corresponding angles are congruent, angle 1 also measures 50°.

6. (5) 144° Let the measure of $\angle BXC = x$ and the measure of $\angle AXB = 4x$. Since the angles are supplementary, their sum is equal to 180°. Write an equation and solve.

$x + 4x = 180°$

$\quad\ 5x = 180°$

$\quad\ \ x = \ \ 36°$

The measure of $\angle BXC$ is 36° and the measure of $\angle AXB$ is 4(36) = 144°.

Lesson 25: Triangles and Quadrilaterals

GED Practice (page 608)
NOTE: Throughout this section, decimal values have been used for fractions. However, you can solve the same proportions using fractions. When using a calculator to solve problems, use decimals for common fractions such as

$\frac{1}{4} = 0.25 \qquad \frac{1}{2} = 0.5 \qquad \frac{3}{4} = 0.75$

1. (2) 150 Write a proportion and solve.

$\frac{1\ \text{cm}}{40\ \text{km}} = \frac{3.75\ \text{cm}}{x\ \text{km}}$

$\quad 1x = 40(3.75)$

$\quad\ \ x = 150$ km

2. (4) 580 Add the distances on the map between the cities. 7 cm + 2.5 cm + 5 cm = 14.5 cm. Write a proportion and solve.

$\frac{1\ \text{cm}}{40\ \text{km}} = \frac{14.5\ \text{cm}}{x\ \text{km}}$

$\quad 1x = 40(14.5)$

$\quad\ \ x = 580$ km

3. (4) 1 cm = 20 km Write a proportion and solve.

$\frac{2.5\ \text{cm}}{50\ \text{km}} = \frac{1\ \text{cm}}{x\ \text{km}}$

$\quad 2.5x = 50(1)$

$\quad\ \ \ \ x = 20$ km

4. (5) Not enough information is given. The perimeter of a triangle is the sum of the lengths of the three sides. Even knowing 2 of these lengths is not enough information. You must know either the third length or the measure of at least one angle.

5. (5) sides DF and FH Mentally rotate $\triangle DEF$ so that angles D and H are in the same position (lower right). The corresponding sides are $\overline{DF}$ and $\overline{FH}$, $\overline{DE}$ and $\overline{GH}$, and $\overline{EF}$ and $\overline{FG}$ or redraw one of the triangles so it is in the same position as the other.

6. (4) 50 Write a proportion using the two known corresponding sides, DF and FH.

$$\frac{\overline{DF}}{\overline{FH}} = \frac{\overline{DE}}{\overline{GH}}$$

$$\frac{55}{110} = \frac{x}{100}$$

$$x = 50 \text{ cm}$$

Lesson 26: Irregular Figures

GED Practice (page 611)

1. (5) 550 This irregular figure combines a cylinder and a cone. Find separate volumes and combine.
Cylinder: $V = \pi r^2 h = 3.14(5^2)(5) = 392.5 \text{ cm}^3$

Cone: $V = \frac{1}{3}\pi r^2 h = \frac{1}{3}(3.14)(5^2)(6) = 157 \text{ cm}^3$

Add. $392.5 + 157 = 549.5 \text{ cm}^3$, round to 550 cm^3

2. (3) 33 Find the area of the rectangle and triangles separately. Then add to find total area. NOTE: The triangles are congruent. Find the area of one and multiply by 2.

Triangle: $A = \frac{1}{2}bh$

$$= \frac{1}{2} \times 4.5 \times 2$$

$$= 4.5 \text{ sq cm}$$

Multiply by 2. $4.5 \times 2 = 9 \text{ sq cm}$

Rectangle: $A = lw$
$$= 8 \times 3$$
$$= 24 \text{ sq cm}$$
Add. $24 + 9 = 33 \text{ sq cm}$

3. (4) 92 Find the sum of all the sides.
$12 + 18 + 1.5 + 12 + 17 + 12 + 1.5 + 18 = 92$

4. (3) 50 Think of the figure as a rectangle and two half-circles. The two half-circles make one whole circle. Find the area of the rectangle and the area of the circle and add the results.
Rectangle: $A = lw$
$$A = 6 \times 5$$
$$A = 30 \text{ m}^2$$
Circle: $A = \pi r^2$
$$A = 3.14 \times 2.5^2$$
$$A = 19.625 \text{ m}^2$$
Add. $30 + 19.625 = 49.625$, round to 50 m^2

Lesson 27: Working with Right Triangles

GED Practice (pages 613–614)

1. (2) 13 The wire is the hypotenuse. Let the distance from the pole (8 m) equal a. Solve for b.
$$a^2 + b^2 = c^2$$
$$8^2 + b^2 = 15^2$$
$$64 + b^2 = 225$$
$$b^2 = 161$$
$$b = \sqrt{161} \approx 12.6, \text{ round to } 13$$

2. (3) 8.1 Draw a right triangle so that the distance from J to K forms the hypotenuse. The legs of the triangle measure 7 and 4 units. Solve for the hypotenuse.
$$c^2 = a^2 + b^2$$
$$c^2 = 7^2 + 4^2$$
$$c^2 = 49 + 16$$
$$c^2 = 65$$
$$c = \sqrt{65} \approx 8.06, \text{ round to } 8.1$$

3. (3) from 95 to 105 m The distance from A to B is the hypotenuse of a right triangle. Solve for the hypotenuse.
$$a^2 + b^2 = c^2$$
$$60^2 + 80^2 = c^2$$
$$3600 + 6400 = c^2$$
$$10\,000 = c^2$$
$$c = \sqrt{10\,000} = 100$$
Also: This is a multiple of the 3-4-5 right triangle. Since $3 \times 20 = 60$ and $4 \times 20 = 80$, the hypotenuse must be $5 \times 20 = 100$.

4. (3) 96 The brace is one of the legs of a right triangle. The side measuring 104 cm is actually the hypotenuse. Don't be distracted by the orientation of the triangle. Always look for the right angle, locate the hypotenuse (which is always opposite the right angle), and then determine which sides are the legs. Solve for b, the second leg.
$$a^2 + b^2 = c^2$$
$$40^2 + b^2 = 104^2$$
$$1600 + b^2 = 10\,816$$
$$b^2 = 9216$$
$$b = \sqrt{9216} = 96$$

5. (3) 188 Write a proportion and solve.
$$\frac{1.5 \text{ cm}}{60 \text{ km}} = \frac{4.7 \text{ cm}}{x \text{ km}}$$
$$1.5x = 4.7(60)$$
$$1.5x = 282$$
$$x = 188 \text{ km}$$

6. (2) 38° The sum of the angles in a triangle equals 180°. To find the missing measure, subtract.
$180° - 90° - 52° = 38°$

7. (2) 22
$$\frac{3 \text{ m}}{x} = \frac{4.5 \text{ m}}{33 \text{ m}}$$
$$4.5x = 3(33)$$
$$4.5x = 99$$
$$x = 22 \text{ m}$$

8. (5) a triangle with sides 7, 24, and 25 Use the Pythagorean Relationship to evaluate each of the answer choices. Only the sides listed in option (5) make the equation true.
$$c^2 = a^2 + b^2$$
$$c^2 = 7^2 + 24^2$$
$$c^2 = 49 + 576$$
$$c^2 = 625$$
$$c = \sqrt{625} = 25$$

9. (4) 9 Solve for the hypotenuse.
$$c^2 = a^2 + b^2$$
$$c^2 = 4^2 + 8^2$$
$$c^2 = 16 + 64$$
$$c^2 = 80$$
$$c = \sqrt{80} \approx 8.94, \text{ round to 9 m}$$

10. (2) 138 First find the area of the pool. The diameter of the pool is 20 m, so the radius is half of 20, or 10 m.
$$A = \pi r^2$$
$$= 3.14(10^2)$$
$$= 3.14(100)$$
$$= 314 \text{ m}^2$$
Next find the area of the pool and walkway combined. The walkway adds 4 m to the diameter, or 2 m to the radius. $10 + 2 = 12$ m
$$A = \pi r^2$$
$$= 3.14(12^2)$$
$$= 3.14(144)$$
$$= 452.16 \text{ m}^2$$
Finally, subtract the area of the pool from the area of the pool and walkway combined.
$452.16 - 314 = 138.16$, round to 138 m^2

GED Review Geometry

(pages 615–618)
Part 1

1. (4) ∠5 ∠1 is a right angle, and ∠1 is supplementary to both ∠2 and ∠5. ∠1 is supplementary, but also adjacent, to ∠2. Only ∠5 is supplementary to ∠2, but not adjacent.

2. (4) 155° ∠WOY and ∠3 are supplementary. $m\angle 3 = 25°$, thus, $m\angle WOY = 180° - 25° = 155°$

3. (2) a right angle ∠XOZ is a vertical angle to ∠1, which is a right angle; therefore, ∠XOZ must be a right angle. Since the sum of two supplementary angles is 180°, any angle supplementary to ∠XOZ must measure $180° - 90° = 90°$, a right angle.

4. (2) $\frac{40}{\pi}$ Use the formula for finding the circumference of a circle: $\quad C = \pi d$
Substitute known value for C: $\quad 40 = \pi d$
Solve for d: $\quad \frac{40}{\pi} = d$

5. (5) 64 The container has a square base, with each side measuring 4 cm. If the container is filled to a depth of 4 cm, the liquid fills a cube shape 4 cm on each side. Use the formula for finding the volume of a cube.
$V = s^3 = 4^3 = 64$ cm^3

6. (4) 6 Since you need to express the answer in metres, convert 50 cm to metres. Use the conversion factor 100 cm = 1 m. Therefore, 50 cm = $\frac{1}{2}$ m To find the perimeter of a rectangle, either add the measures of the four sides or use the formula.

$$P = 2l + 2w$$
$$= 2\left(2\frac{1}{2}\right) + 2\left(\frac{1}{2}\right)$$
$$= 5 + 1$$
$$= 6 \text{ m}$$

7. (1) 2 Use the formula. $V = lwh$, where l = length, w = width, and h = height. Substitute, changing fractions to decimals.
$$V = lwh$$
$$17.5 = 5(1.75)h$$
Solve for h. $\quad 17.5 = 8.75h$
$$\frac{17.5}{8.75} = \frac{8.75h}{8.75}$$
$$2 = h$$

8. 16 The area of a parallelogram is equal to base × height, so $A = 32 \times 8$, or 256 cm^2. The area of a square is equal to a side squared. If the area of the square is 256 cm^2, you can find the measure of the side by finding the square root of 256, which is 16 cm.

9. 9 Draw a right triangle so that side AB is the hypotenuse. The legs of the triangle are 8 and 4 units.
$$c^2 = a^2 + b^2$$
$$c^2 = 8^2 + 4^2$$
$$c^2 = 64 + 16$$
$$c^2 = 80$$
$$c = \sqrt{80} \approx 8.9, \text{ round to 9 units}$$

10. (4) $\frac{64 - 2(14)}{2}$ Use the formula. $P = 2l + 2w$, where l = length and w = width. Rewrite the formula to solve for length. Begin by subtracting $2w$ from both sides. Then divide both sides by 2. Substitute the known measurements.

Unit 6

$$P = 2l + 2w$$
$$P - 2w = 2l$$
$$\frac{P - 2w}{2} = l$$
$$\frac{64 - 2(14)}{2} = l$$

Part 2

11. **(3) 120°** $\angle UZX$ is supplementary to $\angle 4$. Subtract to find its measure. $m\angle UZX$ $180° - 60° = 120°$

12. **(1) 30°** The symbol in $\angle 2$ indicates that $\angle 2$ is a right angle and that lines UW and VY are perpendicular. So, $m\angle WZY$ is also $= 90°$ since it is a vertical angle to $\angle 2$. Thus, $\angle 4$ and $\angle 5$ are complementary, so the sum of their measures is $90°$. Find the measure of $\angle 5$ by subtracting the given measure of $\angle 4$. $90° - 60° = 30°$

13. **(4) 120** The ring box is a rectangular solid. $V = lwh = 4(3)(10) = 120$ cm³

14. **(5) $\angle 5$ is supplementary to $\angle 1$.** The figure shows two sets of angles formed by parallel lines and a transversal. Each set must be addressed independently; they are not related to each other. Use logical reasoning to eliminate incorrect answer choices. Option (1) is false. Angles 3 and 4 are supplementary, not complementary. Option (2) is false because angles 12 and 13 are vertical angles, each measuring 125°. They are not supplementary since their sum does not equal 180°. Option (3) is false because $\angle 4$ and $\angle 10$ are not corresponding angles. They are not in the same position in relation to the *same* transversal. Option (4) is false because $\angle 1$ corresponds to an angle measuring 100°; therefore, its measure is also 100°, not 90°. Option (5) is true because $\angle 5$ is supplementary to an angle measuring 100°; therefore, its measure is $180° - 100° = 80°$. Since $\angle 1$ measures 100°, the sum of the measures of $\angle 5$ and $\angle 1$ is 180°, and the angles are supplementary.

15. **(2) $\angle 1$ and $\angle 7$** Angles 1 and 4 are vertical angles and are congruent. Angles 4 and 7 are corresponding angles and are congruent. Angles 2 and 3 are each supplementary to angle 4; supplementary angles are not congruent unless they are each right angles, so options (1) and (4) are incorrect. Angles 8, 10, and 14 are on a different transversal from angle 4 and thus cannot be compared. So options (3) and (5) can be eliminated as incorrect.

16. **(5) 125°** Angle 12 and the angle marked as measuring 125° are corresponding angles. Both are in the same position in relation to the transversal d; therefore, their measures are equal.

17. **(5) parallelogram** Although the problem does not state that the opposite sides are parallel, they must be so in order for the side measures to appear in the order given. There is no other possible option.

18. **(2) 70°** The triangles are congruent, so angles A and D must be congruent. You can find the measure of $\angle A$ by subtracting. $180° - 60° - 50° = 70°$ Angle D must have the same measure.

19. **(5) 20 and 25** There are several ways to solve this problem. One way is to write proportions to solve for each of the missing sides. Or notice that the 12–16–20 triangle is a multiple of the common 3–4–5 triangle. Therefore, $\triangle DEF$ must also be similar to a 3–4–5 triangle, which means that the remaining sides must be 20 and 25 cm.

20. **(3) 55°** Since the corresponding sides of the triangles are equal, the triangles are congruent. Mentally rotate the second triangle so that the corresponding sides are oriented the same way. You may find it helpful to redraw the second triangle. Since $\angle L$ is congruent to $\angle I$, the measure of $\angle L$ is 55°.

21. **(3) 10** Since the measures of $\angle A$ and $\angle B$ are each 60°, then the measure of $\angle C$ must also measure 60°. Therefore, the triangle is an equilateral triangle. By definition, an equilateral triangle has three sides of the same length; therefore, side AC must measure 10 cm.

22. **(2) $\overline{AE} \cong \overline{BD}$** You know that sides AC and CB are congruent; you also know that sides CE and CD are congruent. To know that the triangles have three pairs of congruent sides, you need to know that the measure of side AE equals the measure of side BD.

Unit Review Mathematics

(pages 619–627)
Part 1

1. **(3) 1400 cm** Multiply the length of one board by the number of boards.
300 cm $\times 4 = 1400$ cm

2. **(5) 55.95** Add the three sides of the figure to find the perimeter. $16.52 + 17.24 + 22.19 = 55.95$

3. **(3) 19 m** Add all the sides of the figure.
$320 + 300 + 475 + 400 + 450 = 1945$ cm
Reduce; round to the nearest metre.
$1900 + 45$ or 19 m

4. **(5) 42.875** All sides of a cube are equal.
Volume = length $\times$ width $\times$ height
$V = 3.5 \times 3.5 \times 3.5 = 42.875$ m³

Using your GED calculator:
3.5 x^y 3 $=$ 42.875

5. **(3) 675** Volume = length $\times$ width $\times$ height
$V = 30 \times 10 \times 3 = 900$ m³
Multiply the volume by $\frac{3}{4}$, or 0.75.
$900 \times 0.75 = 675$ m³

6. **(5) 1458** Multiply the length of the coffee table by its width to find the area of its surface.
$54 \times 27 = 1458$ cm²

7. **(4) \$157 717** Add the net sales of the five departments listed in the table. \$20 897 + \$57 941 + \$31 009 + \$28 987 + \$18 883

8. **(2) \$6035** Add the net sales for Footwear and Sporting Goods. \$20 897 + \$31 009 = \$51 906 Subtract the result from the net sales of Outerwear. \$57 941 − \$51 906 = \$6035

9. **(3) \$39 058** Subtract the net sales of Skiing Equipment from the net sales of Outerwear. \$57 941 − \$18 883 = \$39 058

10. **(4) 7** Use the formula *distance = rate × time.*
$$d = rt$$
$$406 = 58t$$
$$\frac{406}{58} = t$$
$$7 \text{ hours} = t$$

11. **(5) 5x + \$2.06 = \$31.51** Using the formula *total cost = number of units × cost per unit*, or $c = nr$, you know that 5 times the cost per one bin is the total cost of the bins before tax. The problem states that \$2.06 in sales tax has been added for a total bill of \$31.51. If x represents the cost of one bin, only option (5) shows the correct sequence of operations.

12. **(4) −7x + 14** Simplify the expression.
$$-5(x - 6) - 2(x + 8)$$
$$-5x + 30 - 2x - 16$$
$$-7x + 14$$

13. **(3) 4** Write integers and find their sum.
$(+8) + (-6) + (-7) + (+11) + (-2) = 4$

Using your GED calculator:

8 [+] 6 [+/−] [+] 7 [+/−] [+] 11 [+]
2 [+/−] [=] 4

14. **(1) October, November, and December** In October, November, and December, the shaded bars, representing the actual rainfall amounts, are lower than the unshaded bars, representing the normal rainfall amounts.

15. **(2) 3** The shaded bars representing December, January, and February are all above 5.0 cm.

16. **(4) 4.6** Subtract the actual rainfall in March from the actual rainfall in January. 6.8 − 2.2 = 4.6 cm

17. **(3) 7** The radius of the larger circle is equal to the diameter of the smaller circle. Since the diameter of the larger circle is 28 cm, its radius is 14 cm. The radius of the smaller circle is half its diameter. Since the diameter of the smaller circle is 14 cm, its radius is 7 cm.

18. **(3) $12\frac{1}{4}$** The dimensions of the crate are $3\frac{1}{2}$ m, $1\frac{3}{4}$ m, and 2 m. Use the formula for the volume of a rectangular solid.
$$V = lwh$$
$$= \left(3\tfrac{1}{2}\right)\left(1\tfrac{3}{4}\right)(2) \quad \text{OR} \quad = (3.5)(1.75)(2)$$
$$= \left(\tfrac{7}{2}\right)\left(\tfrac{7}{4}\right)(2)$$
$$= 12\tfrac{1}{4} \text{ m}^3 \qquad \text{OR} \quad = 12.25 = 12\tfrac{1}{4}$$

Using your GED calculator:

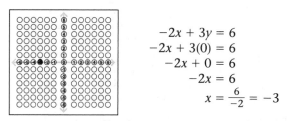

Although the answer options are all expressed as mixed numbers, sometimes it is easier to do your calculations with decimals and convert your answer to the mixed number.

19. **(1) 37°** The sum of the measures of angles *TRS*, *TRU*, and *URV* is 180°. $m\angle TRU = 90°$ Since $m\angle URV = 53°$, find the measure of the missing angle by subtracting. 180° − 90° − 53° = 37°

20. **(−3, 0)** Substitute $y = 0$ for the *x*-intercept. Solve.

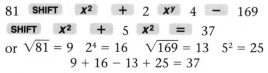

$$-2x + 3y = 6$$
$$-2x + 3(0) = 6$$
$$-2x + 0 = 6$$
$$-2x = 6$$
$$x = \frac{6}{-2} = -3$$

21. **37** Use your GED calculator.

81 [SHIFT] [x²] [+] 2 [xʸ] 4 [−] 169
[SHIFT] [x²] [+] 5 [x²] [=] 37
or $\sqrt{81} = 9$ $2^4 = 16$ $\sqrt{169} = 13$ $5^2 = 25$
$$9 + 16 - 13 + 25 = 37$$

Unit 6

22. (1) −2 Solve the equation.
$$-2(x + 4) = 5x + 6$$
$$-2x - 8 = 5x + 6$$
$$-7x - 8 = 6$$
$$-7x = 14$$
$$x = -2$$

23. (3) $4.00 Let x equal the cost of a children's ticket and $x + 2$ equal the cost of an adult's ticket. Write an equation and solve.
$$5(x + 2) + 12x = 78$$
$$5x + 10 + 12x = 78$$
$$17x + 10 = 78$$
$$17x = 68$$
$$x = 4$$

24. (2) −4 + 7 + (−2) The series of operations begins at 0 and moves 4 in a negative direction. Then the arrow moves 7 in a positive direction, followed by 2 in a negative direction. Only option (2) shows this series of changes.

25. (4) 10
$$c^2 = a^2 + b^2$$
$$c^2 = 6^2 + 8^2$$
$$c^2 = 36 + 64$$
$$c^2 = 100$$
$$c = \sqrt{100} = 10 \text{ units}$$

26. (3) 40 The formula for finding the circumference of a circle is $C = \pi d$, where d = diameter. The diameter is twice the length of the radius. $2(7) = 14$ cm. To estimate the circumference, use 3 for the value of pi. $C = 3(14) = 42$ cm. The best estimate is option (3).

27. (4) scalene and acute A triangle with three sides of different lengths is a scalene triangle. A triangle with three acute angles is an acute triangle.

28. (1) $x + 5x + 90° = 180°$ The sum of the measures of the three angles is 180°. If you let x equal the measure of the smaller acute angle, then $5x$ equals the measure of the larger angle. The third angle is the right angle measuring 90°. To write the equation, set the sum of the three angle measures equal to 180°.

29. (3) 6 Find the area of the rectangle.
$$A = lw = 6(3.5) = 21 \text{ cm}^2$$
Use the formula for finding the area of a triangle to solve for h (the height).
$$A = \frac{1}{2}bh$$
$$21 = \frac{1}{2}(7)h; \quad h = 6 \text{ cm}$$

30. (2) $\dfrac{\overline{AB}}{\overline{AC}} = \dfrac{\overline{FB}}{\overline{GC}}$ Two pairs of corresponding sides in these triangles are $\overline{AB}$ and $\overline{AC}$ and $\overline{FB}$ and $\overline{GC}$. Since corresponding sides of similar triangles have equal ratios, this is a true proportion.

Part 2

31. (2) 203 049 Remember, the comma between the words matches the space between the numbers—there is no "hundreds" in the words.

32. (1) 39 000 The digit to the right of the thousands place is 4. Since 4 is less than 5, leave the 9 as the thousands digit, and replace the digits to the right of the thousands place with zeros.

33. (3) $387 × 12 Multiply the amount of the monthly payment by the number of months. $387 × 12

34. (4) $972 ÷ 3 Divide the total rent per month by the number of friends sharing the rent. $972 ÷ 3

35. (2) $420 Multiply the price of food per person by the number of employees. $12 × 35 = $420

36. (5) 72 Multiply the number of hours Cynthia works per day by the number of days she works per week. $4 × 6 = 24$ Multiply the result by the number of weeks she works. $24 × 3 = 72$

37. (4) $1060 Subtract the amount taken out of the account from the beginning amount in the account. $1200 − $140 = $1060

38. (1) $65 Subtract the amount Roberto saved from the cost of the computer system. $1050 − $985 = $65

39. 30 You don't need to know that angles 2 and 4 are vertical angles. You know that the sum of the two angles measuring 75° and $\angle 4$ must be 180° because the sum of these three angles is a straight line. $180° − 75° − 75° = 30°$

40. **10** Use the formula for finding the area of a triangle.

$$A = \tfrac{1}{2}bh, \text{ where } b = \text{base and } h = \text{height.}$$

$$200 = \tfrac{1}{2} \times b \times 40$$
$$200 = 20 \times b$$
$$\tfrac{200}{20} = b$$
$$10 = b$$

43. **(2)** $x - y = -1$ Choose an ordered pair from the graph and substitute the x- and y-values into each equation in the answer choices. If the ordered pair makes more than one equation true, use another ordered pair from the graph. Remember, each point on the line is a solution for the equation of the line.

44. **(1)** $(-3, -4)$ Substitute the ordered pairs in the answer choices in the given equation. Only option (1) makes the equation true.

$$x - y = -1$$
$$-3 - (-4) = 1$$
$$-3 + 4 = 1$$
$$1 = 1$$

45. **(2)** -2 Although you could graph the equation in order to solve the problem, the easiest way is to substitute the value 1 for y in the equation and solve for x.

$$-4x + 7y = 15$$
$$-4x + 7(1) = 15$$
$$-4x + 7 = 15$$
$$-4x = 8$$
$$x = -2$$

46. **(2)** **4** Multiply the fraction of a lap jogged per minute by the total number of minutes.

$$\tfrac{2}{15} \times 30 = \tfrac{2}{15} \times \tfrac{30}{1} = 4$$

41. **40** By adding the lengths of $\overline{AC}$ and $\overline{CD}$, you can see that $\triangle ABD$ is an isosceles triangle. By definition, an isosceles triangle has two equal sides and two equal angles. The equal angles are opposite the equal sides. Since $\angle DAB$ measures 70°, $\angle ABD$ must have the same measure. Since the sum of the angles in a triangle must equal 180°, $m\angle D = 180° - 70° - 70° = 40°$

47. **(1)** $6\tfrac{3}{4}$ Set up a proportion using the ratio of the number of centimetres on the map to the number of kilometres. Solve for the unknown number of kilometres.

$$\frac{\frac{3}{4}}{5} = \frac{?}{45}$$

$$\tfrac{3}{4} \times 45 \div 5 = \tfrac{3}{4} \times \tfrac{45}{1} \div \tfrac{5}{1} =$$

$$\tfrac{3}{4} \times \tfrac{\overset{9}{\cancel{45}}}{1} \times \tfrac{1}{\underset{1}{\cancel{5}}} = \tfrac{27}{4} = 6\tfrac{3}{4}$$

42. **24** At any given time, the ratio of all objects to their shadows is the same. Write the ratios in the same order and solve the proportion.

$$\tfrac{4}{5} = \tfrac{x}{30}$$
$$5x = 120$$
$$x = 24 \text{ m}$$

48. **(1) Rent** To compare the fractions, convert them to like fractions.

Rent:	$\tfrac{3}{8}$	$= \tfrac{15}{40}$
Salaries:	$\tfrac{1}{4}$	$= \tfrac{10}{40}$
Advertising:	$\tfrac{1}{5}$	$= \tfrac{8}{40}$
Supplies:	$\tfrac{1}{8}$	$= \tfrac{5}{40}$
Miscellaneous:	$\tfrac{1}{20}$	$= \tfrac{2}{40}$

The fraction $\tfrac{3}{8}$ is the largest of the fractions.

49. (3) $6000 Add the fractions for Salaries and Supplies, and multiply the result by the total amount of the budget for March.

$$\left(\frac{1}{4} + \frac{1}{8}\right) \times \$16\,000 =$$

$$\left(\frac{10}{40} + \frac{5}{40}\right) \times \$16\,000 =$$

$$\frac{15}{40} \times \$16\,000 =$$

$$\frac{3}{8} \times \$16\,000 = \$6000$$

50. (3) 8700 to 10 000 The lowest value is in November (8700) and the highest value is in February (10 000).

51. (3) four The graph makes a turnaround in February, May, September, and November.

52. (5) November to December Of the months listed, only from November to December was there an increase in new subscribers.

53. (4) $4000 Subtract the net sales of the Winnipeg store from the net sales of the Toronto store. $11.0 − $7.0 = $4.0 The scale lists sales in thousands of dollars, so $4.0 represents $4000.

54. (2) 2:3 Write a ratio of the net sales of the Vancouver store to the net sales of the Calgary store. 6:9 Reduce the ratio. 6:9 = 2:3

55. (3) $8.2 Add the five net sales in the graph. $11 + $6 + $7 + $9 + $8 = $41 Divide the result by the number of stores, 5. $41 ÷ 5 = $8.2

Simulated Tests

Language Arts, Writing Part I
(pages 629–641)

1. **(3) change North American's to North Americans'** (Possessives) Option (3) is correct because it changes the plural *North Americans* to the plural possessive *North Americans'*. Option (1) is not correct because it removes a needed hyphen from a compound adjective. Option (2) is not correct because the verb form *had been* does not make sense in the sentence. Options (4) and (5) do not correct the spelling error.

2. **(2) Hollinghead, an** (Commas) Option (2) is correct because it uses a comma to set off an appositive phrase. Option (1) omits the comma before the appositive phrase. Option (3) creates a sentence fragment. Option (4) does not result in a smooth sentence. Option (5) adds an incorrect participle.

3. **(1) change take off to took off** (Verb tenses) Option (1) replaces the present tense verb with the correct past tense form. Option (2) removes a necessary comma in the compound sentence. Option (3) does not make sense in the sentence. Option (4) inserts an unnecessary comma. Option (5) does not correct the verb tense error.

4. **(4) change would head to headed** (Parallel structure) Option (4) is correct because *headed* is the same tense as *packed* and *piled*. Option (1) is not correct because only two of the verbs are in the same tense. Option (2) removes a needed comma between phrases in a series. Option (3) is not in the same form as *packed*. Option (5) does not correct the non-parallel structure.

5. **(5) picnic. The** (Run-on sentences) Option (5) is correct because it fixes the run-on sentence by separating it into two complete sentences. Option (1) is not correct because it does not fix the run-on sentence. Options (2) and (3) turn the run-on sentence into a comma splice. Option (4) omits the comma necessary to turn the run-on sentence into a compound sentence.

6. **(1) held 2500 cars and offered** (Parallel structure) Option (1) is a correct and parallel sentence. Options (2), (3), (4), and (5) do not have parallel structure.

7. **(2) insert a comma after teenagers** (Commas) Option (2) correctly places a comma between the items in the series. Option (1) changes the meaning of the sentence and is incorrectly punctuated. Option (3) removes the

parallel structure. Option (4) creates a fragment without a complete verb. Option (5) omits the needed comma in the series.

8. **(3) change survives to survive** (Subject-verb agreement) Option (3) is correct because *survive* is plural and its subject *cinemas* is also plural. Option (1) incorrectly capitalizes common nouns. Option (2) changes the verb to a tense (past perfect) that does not make sense in the sentence. Option (4) inserts an unnecessary comma. Option (5) is not true because the sentence's verb does not agree with its subject.

9. **(2) move recently advertised in the *Winnipeg Free Press* to the end of the sentence** (Misplaced modifiers) Option (2) is correct because *advertised in the Winnipeg Free Press* modifies *position*, not *application*. Option (1) inserts an unnecessary comma. Option (3) capitalizes common nouns. Option (4) replaces a correct verb form with one that does not make sense in the sentence. Option (5) is not true because the sentence contains a misplaced modifier.

10. **(4) remove sentence 2** (Unity and coherence) Option (4) correctly eliminates a sentence that does not support the main idea. Option (1) moves the topic sentence, creating a lack of coherence. Option (2) removes the topic sentence. Option (3) puts a supporting detail in the wrong paragraph. Option (5) does not remove the sentence that does not support the main idea.

11. **(1) change I taken to I took** (Verb forms) Option (1) is correct because it replaces an incorrect verb form with a correct one. Options (2) and (3) are not correct because they replace the incorrect verb form with one that does not make sense in the sentence. Option (4) removes a necessary comma after the introductory phrase. Option (5) is not true because *I taken* is not a correct verb form.

12. **(5) As a result of my work, I** (Transitions) Option (5) is correct because *As a result of my work* links the applicant's experience with the job in the night school office. Option (1) is not correct because the sentence would have to use a passive verb construction such as *Valuable practical experience was gained by me*. Option (2) would create a sentence fragment. Option (3) uses a transitional phrase, *for instance*, that does not make sense in the sentence. Option (4) does not make sense in the sentence.

13. **(3) She told** (Pronouns) Option (2) is correct because *she* agrees with its antecedent in the previous sentence, *Anita Cusamano*. Options (1) and (3) do not agree with the antecedent. Option (4) does not agree with the antecedent and uses a verb form that does not make sense in the sentence. Option (5) uses a verb form that does not make sense in the sentence.

14. **(4) Red River Community College** (Capitalization) Option (4) is correct because it capitalizes all the words that make up the proper name. Option (1) is not correct because it does not capitalize any of the words that make up the proper name. Options (2), (3), and (5) are incorrect because they do not capitalize all of the words that make up the proper name.

15. **(4) Currently I am taking** (Sentence fragments) Option (4) is correct because it supplies the missing subject needed to complete the sentence. Options (1), (2), (3), and (5) are not correct because they leave the sentence without a subject.

16. **(3) begin a new paragraph with sentence 12** (Paragraph divisions) Option (3) is correct because it splits the paragraph between two different subjects, the applicant's current enrollment at the community college and the applicant's desire for an interview. Option (1) is incorrect because the reader needs the information in sentence 9 to understand the rest of paragraph C. Option (2) removes a supporting detail. Option (4) moves a supporting detail to a place where it makes no sense. Option (5) removes an effective concluding statement.

17. **(2) it's** (Homonyms) Option (2) is correct because *it's* stands for *it is*. Option (1) is not correct because the word *its* is possessive. Options (3), (4), and (5) are incorrect because the verb tenses do not make sense in the sentence.

18. **(5) section that is filled** (Combining ideas) Option (5) is correct because it combines the sentences smoothly using a relative clause. Option (1) is not correct because the coordinating conjunction *so* does not make sense in the sentence. Option (2) is not correct because the subject of the verb *filled* would be *books*, which does not make sense. Option (3) is incorrect because the coordinating conjunction *yet* does not make sense and the second clause of the compound sentence has no subject. Option (4) is incorrect because the verb tense does not make sense in the sentence.

19. **(4) might want** (Verb forms) Option (4) is correct because the verb form is correct and the tense makes sense in the sentence. Options (1), (2), and (5) are not correct verb forms. Option (3) is not correct because the verb tense does not make sense in the sentence.

20. **(2) insert or after the comma** (Comma splices) Option (2) is correct because the coordinating conjunction *or* makes the comma splice a compound sentence. Option (1) makes the comma splice a run-on sentence. Option (3) inserts an unnecessary comma and does not fix the comma splice. Option (4) does not fix the comma splice and does not make sense in the sentence. Option (5) is a comma splice.

21. **(1) insert a comma after help** (Commas) Option (1) is correct because compound sentences require a comma before the coordinating conjunction. Option (2) is not correct because the second sentence is a fragment (sentences beginning with *but* are considered fragments). Option (3) inserts an unnecessary comma. Option (4) replaces a correct verb form with an incorrect one. Option (5) is not true because the compound sentence needs a comma before the coordinating conjunction.

22. **(4) replace that with who** (Pronouns) Option (4) is correct because *who* agrees with the antecedent *patrons*. Option (1) changes a plural verb form that agrees with its subject to a singular verb form (*provides*) that does not agree with its subject (*libraries*). Option (2) is not correct because it replaces the pronoun for something just mentioned (*these*) with the pronoun for something mentioned at an earlier time (*those*). Option (3) adds an unnecessary comma and, like option (5), does not fix the pronoun agreement.

23. **(4) replace the comma with because** (Subordinating ideas) Option (4) adds an appropriate and necessary subordinating conjunction to join the two sentences. Option (1) creates a fragment by removing part of the verb. Option (2) adds an unnecessary comma. Option (3) removes a comma but does not add the subordinating conjunction needed to separate the clauses in the compound sentence. Option (5) is a comma splice.

24. **(3) Libraries have more to offer than just books.** (Topic sentences) Option (3) is correct because the sentence introduces the information given in the rest of the paragraph. Option (1) is not correct because it belongs with the information about reference books in paragraph B, not with paragraph C. Options (2) and (4) are not correct because they do not relate to the information in paragraph C. Option (5) is not correct because it is too general to be a good topic sentence.

25. **(3) I often fly** (Subject-verb agreement) Option (3) is correct because the singular verb *fly* agrees with the singular subject *I*. Options (1) and (2) are incorrect because *flies* is plural and does not agree with *I*. Options (4) and (5) are not correct because the verb tenses do not make sense in the sentence.

26. **(4) a library book** (Subordinating ideas) Option (4) is correct because the most effective combination of sentences 3 and 4 is *On my last flight, I left a library book on my seat.* Option (1) is not correct because it would repeat *book* (*a book which was a library book*). Options (2), (3), and (5) are unnecessarily wordy.

27. **(3) remembered** (Verb tenses) Option (3) is correct because the past tense of *remember* should follow the past progressive (*was waiting*). Option (1) is not correct because the past perfect tense means that the subject of the sentence remembered the book before he was waiting at the baggage carousel. Option (2) is not correct because the present tense should not follow the past progressive. Option (4) is not correct because the past progressive indicates that remembering the book was an ongoing process rather than a sudden thought. Option (5) is not correct because the present perfect should not follow the past progressive.

28. **(1) insert She before Phoned** (Sentence fragments) Option (1) is correct because it adds a subject and completes the sentence. Option (2) replaces a correct verb form with an incorrect one. Option (3) creates two sentence fragments. Option (4) replaces a correct verb form with an incorrect one. Option (5) is not true because the sentence is a fragment.

29. **(1) I called the library** (Verb forms) Option (1) is correct as written. The other options use incorrect verb forms that do not make sense.

30. **(4) change male to mail** (Homonyms) Option (4) is correct because the word for *postal service* is needed in this context. Options (1) and (2) create vague pronoun references. Option (3) incorrectly uses the present tense when the past tense is needed. Option (5) uses an incorrect homonym.

31. **(3) remove sentence 5** (Unity and coherence) Option (3) is correct because sentence 5 does not relate directly to the subject of the paragraph (the airline's excellent customer service). Option (1) is not correct because the information in the sentence is needed to understand the rest of the paragraph. Option (2) is not correct because sentence 2 introduces the information about the airline's service. Option (4) is not correct because sentence 5 does not tell about the airline's service. Option (5) is not correct because the change would not follow the sequence of events.

32. **(4) change Airline to airline** (Capitalization) Option (4) is correct because *airline* is a common noun rather than a proper noun. A name of a particular airline would be a proper name and would be capitalized. Option (1) is not correct because the verb *continue* already describes an ongoing action. The progressive tense is redundant. Option (2) inserts an unnecessary comma. Option (3) does not make sense in the context of the paragraph. Since the writer is very pleased with the airline, he is certain to recommend it. Option (5) is not true because *Airline* is incorrectly capitalized.

33. **(1) Cocos, "Island of the Sharks"** (Subordinating ideas) Option (1) is correct because it uses an appositive to smoothly combine the ideas in the two sentences. Option (2) is not correct because it repeats words unnecessarily. Option (3) is not correct because it changes the ideas in the original sentences. Option (4) is not correct because the parentheses are not necessary. Option (5) is not correct because it changes the ideas in the original sentences.

34. **(2) is** (Subject-verb agreement) Option (2) is correct because *is* agrees with the singular subject *abundance*. Options (1) and (4) are plural verbs. Option (3) is singular but the wrong tense. Option (5) is an incomplete verb.

35. **(4) change have hunted to hunt** (Verb tenses) Option (4) is correct because the present tense, *hunt*, should follow the present tense of the preceding verb, *circle*. Option (1) is not correct because the rest of the selection is in the present tense. Option (2) is not correct because it creates a sentence fragment. Option (3) is not correct because *hunting* is not a correct verb form. Option (5) is not true because the sentence contains an unnecessary shift in verb tense.

36. **(5) manta rays, octopuses, green turtles, and giant eels** (Commas) Option (5) is correct because it places commas between all the words in the series. Options (1), (2), and (4) are not correct because they do not place commas between the words in the series. Option (3) is not correct because it places a comma between only two of the words in the series.

37. **(3) Today, the island is uninhabited, but it was once frequented by pirates.** (Compound sentences) Option (3) is correct because it combines sentences 6 and 7 in a correct compound sentence. Option (1) is not correct because it does not make sense (the island cannot be both uninhabited and frequented by pirates). Option (2) is not correct because there is no antecedent for the pronoun *it*. Option (4) creates a run-on sentence. Option (5) is not correct because the sentence needs a comma after *uninhabited* and the coordinating conjunction *and* does not make sense in the sentence.

38. **(2) replace peek with peak** (Homonyms) Option (1) is correct because it replaces the homonym *peek* (look at) with *peak* (the top of a mountain). Option (1) is not correct because *Island* is part of a proper name and should be capitalized. Option (3) is not correct because it would move the adverb *actually* away from the verb it modifies (*is*). Option (4) is not correct because *are* is plural and does not agree with the subject, *Island*. Option (5) is not true because the word *peek* does not make sense in the sentence.

39. **(2) are** (Verb tenses) Option (2) corrects a tense shift so that *are* is consistent with the other simple present tense verb in the sentence, *reach*. Options (1), (3), and (4) would make the verb tense inconsistent with *reach*. Option (5) is an incomplete verb form.

40. **(1) change grows to grow** (Subject-verb agreement) Option (1) is correct because the plural verb *grow* agrees with its subject, *plants and animals*. Option (2) is not correct because the singular pronoun *it* and the singular verb *is* do not agree with their antecedent, *plants and animals*. Option (3) replaces a correct verb form (*are*) with an incorrect one (*be*). Option (4) is incorrect because the progressive tense does not make sense in the sentence. Option (5) is incorrect because the singular verb *grows* does not agree with the plural subject *plants and animals*.

41. **(5) fish, and they, in turn, attract** (Pronouns) Option (5) is correct because it combines the sentences smoothly to make one compound sentence and replaces the repetitive *small fish* with the correct plural pronoun *they*.

Options (1), (2), (3), and (4) use incorrect pronouns for the antecedent *fish*.

42. **(3) move paragraph B after paragraph C** (Unity and coherence) Option (3) is correct because paragraph C continues the discussion of the island's physical geography and animal life from paragraph A. Option (1) is not correct because paragraphs A and B discuss different subjects. Option (2) is not correct because paragraphs B and C discuss different subjects. Option (4) is not correct because sentence 14 does not begin a new subject. Option (5) is not true because the paragraphs are not in logical order.

43. **(3) change home economics to Home Economics** (Capitalization) Option (3) is correct because *Home Economics* is the name of a specific school course. Option (1) is not correct because a comma is needed after the introductory adverb. Option (2) is not correct because *to help preventing* is not a correct verb form. Option (4) is not correct because *these* refers to the injuries just mentioned. Option (5) is not true because *home economics* is a proper name and should be capitalized.

44. **(1) replace sentence 4 with Safety locks and latches protect children in several ways.** (Topic sentences) Option (1) is correct because the new sentence introduces the information in paragraph B. Option (2) is not correct because it does not effectively introduce the information in paragraph B. Options (3) and (4) are not correct because the information in sentence 4 is necessary to understand the rest of paragraph B. Option (5) is not true because sentence 4 is not an effective topic sentence.

45. **(2) and scattering** (Parallel structure) Option (2) is correct because *scattering* agrees with the previous verb *pulling*. Option (1) is not correct because *to scatter* does not agree with *pulling*. Option (3) is not correct because *to have scattered* does not agree with *pulling*. Option (4) is not correct because the conjunction *but* does not make sense in the sentence. Option (5) is not correct because the conjunction *but* does not make sense in the sentence and *to scatter* does not agree with *pulling*.

46. **(3) move placed between rooms after Gates** (Misplaced modifiers) Option (3) is correct because *placed between rooms* should modify *Gates*, not *spaces*. Option (1) inserts an unnecessary comma. Option (2) creates an

incorrect verb form, *can kept*. Option (4) is not correct because each gate can be placed between two rooms. *Among* implies that a gate can be placed between more than two rooms at once. Option (5) is not true because the sentence contains a misplaced modifier.

47. **(2) home and can** (Commas) Option (2) is correct because the subject of the sentence, *devices*, has two verbs, *regulate* and *can prevent*. Option (1) is not correct because no comma is needed between the verb phrases. Option (3) keeps the unnecessary comma and adds a conjunction, *yet*, that does not make sense in the sentence. Option (4) is wrong because *also* repeats the same idea as *and*. Option (5) changes the verb *can prevent* to *might prevent*, which does not make sense in the sentence.

48. **(4) replace it with them** (Pronouns) Option (4) is correct because the pronoun *them* agrees with its antecedent in sentence 12, *devices*. Option (1) is not correct because only one plumber is needed to install the devices. Option (2) introduces a verb tense that does not make sense in the sentence. Option (3) is not correct because the sentence is not referring to any specific showers. Option (5) is not true because the pronoun *it* does not agree with its antecedent *devices*.

49. **(3) subjects ranging from** (Sentence fragments) Option (3) joins the fragment to the complete sentence before it. Options (1) and (4) are sentence fragments. Option (2) incorrectly uses a semicolon. Option (5) creates a compound sentence but uses an inappropriate coordinating conjunction and changes the meaning.

50. **(5) you have installed** (Verb forms) Option (5) is correct because *have installed* is a correct verb form which makes sense in the sentence. Options (1) and (2) are not correct because the verb form *done installed* is not correct. Option (3) is not correct because *Once* indicates that the verb should be in the present perfect tense to refer to the time after something has happened. Option (4) is not correct because the verb form does not make sense in the sentence.

Language Arts, Writing Part II, Essay
(pages 643–644)
Evaluating and scoring your essay can be done by you or by someone else. If you are taking a class, have your teacher evaluate your essay. If you are working independently, ask a friend or relative to read your essay. If this is not possible, evaluate your writing yourself. After finishing an essay, put it aside for a day.

Then read it as objectively as possible. No matter who checks your writing, make sure that person follows the Essay Scoring Guide on page 185 and uses the checklist on page 187 as scoring evaluation guides.

Write the date on your completed essays and keep them together in a folder or notebook. Use the Essay Self-Assessment form on page 896 to track your progress, note your strengths, and determine areas in which you want to improve.

Social Studies
(pages 645–664)

1. **(2) They rose but more slowly than the increase in the money supply.** (Comprehension) This relationship is shown by the solid and dotted lines. The graph shows that prices increased by about 25 percent between years 1 and 10, but the money supply grew by almost 100 percent during that same period. The relationships suggested in options (1), (3), (4), and (5) are all contradicted by the graph.

2. **(1) Inflation causes prices to rise.** (Analysis) The lines on the graph show that between years 10 and 15, the money supply grew much faster than production—from less than 100 percent to almost 200 percent for the money supply, compared to a growth in production from 125 percent to only 175 percent—these are the conditions under which inflation occurs. At the same time, the price line shows prices rising (the definition of inflation) during that 5-year period almost as much as they did during the previous 10 years on the graph. The graph data contradict options (2), (3), and (4). Option (5) is incorrect because there is sufficient information to determine how changes in production, money supply, and prices are related. This is the focus of the graph.

3. **(5) There is not enough information to determine the relationship.** (Evaluation) Although the graph data show how each of these three factors changes as the others do, the data do not provide adequate information to determine which changes are causes and which are effects. Therefore, options (1), (2), (3), and (4) cannot be determined from the data provided. More information is needed.

4. **(3) City jobs generally paid better wages.** (Analysis) Most of the jobs listed are in the city and pay more than farm labour. There is no support in the table for options (1) and (2). The table does not indicate whether the teacher wages are for urban or rural teachers, so there is no evidence for option (4). Option (5) is incorrect because the table does not suggest how many postal positions (the only government job listed) were available.

5. **(3) Christopher Columbus and His Work** (Comprehension) This title sums up the main idea of these paragraphs. Options (1) and (5) are incorrect because they are too broad to be the title of this passage. Options (2) and (4) are minor points of information that are not the focus of the passage.

6. **(3) the creation of the Internet** (Application) The main effect of the printing press was to spread ideas and information. Options (1) and (2) can also spread ideas and information, but not with anywhere near the scope and effect of the printing press and the Internet. Options (4) and (5) do not have this effect: shopping malls do not spread ideas, but rather make products available, and the performance of Renaissance music provides entertainment for a select audience.

7. **(3) They feared that communism would spread to West Berlin.** (Comprehension) Information from the photograph and passage suggests that West Berliners hated the wall as much as East Berliners because they feared the spread of communism to West Berlin. Although options (1) and (5) are true, there is no evidence in the photograph or passage to support these answer choices. There is no evidence to support either option (2) or option (4) as the answer.

8. **(4) Mohandas Gandhi was a brilliant person.** (Analysis) This is a judgment that cannot be incontestably proven. The other options are all facts that can be proven to be true. Options (1), (3), and (5) are matters of historical record. Option (2) can be demonstrated by the polls conducted while Trudeau was prime minister.

9. **(2) It is the stock market.** (Analysis) The term *the stock market* is often shortened to *the market*. The two men are clearly businesspeople talking in an office, so this choice would make sense. Neither option (1) nor option (4) makes sense in the context of this cartoon. There is no support for option (3). Option (5) is based on looking at the word *inherit* rather than at the cartoon as a whole.

10. **(2) He personified qualities of character such as intelligence and tolerance that people all over the world could respect.** (Application) Trudeau was both loved and reviled by Canadians, but there is general agreement that he was one of the most respected political

figures in Canadian history and throughout the world. Option (1) is the opposite of what is stated and implied in the passage. There is no evidence that option (3) is true. Although some interpret Trudeau's independence of thought as anti-American, the passage does not support option (4). Option (5) may be true, but it does not articulate a national identity for Canada.

11. **(2) A desire to represent part of Canada's historical connection with Britain in a light-hearted way.** (Evaluation) As the painter makes clear, he meant no disrespect to the Queen by his painting, but simply expressed a child-like and nostalgic bit of whimsy that tied together two distinctly Canadian symbols. Option (1) cannot be supported by information in the passage. There is no evidence that option (2) motivated the painter. The painter makes clear that his painting was not a political protest, so option (4) is incorrect. Nothing in the passage suggests that the painter believed option (5).

12. **(4) $626 600 000** (Comprehension) The table indicates that the amounts are in millions of dollars. It shows that Ontario has 626.6 million dollars to spend after prizes and expenses. Options (1) and (3) involve misreading the meaning of "millions of dollars." Both option (2) and option (5) involve misreading the meaning of "revenue from ticket sales," which is not the same as what is left after the expenses have been paid out. Option (2) is also a misreading of the meaning of "millions of dollars."

13. **(2) Lotteries can supply millions of dollars in revenue.** (Evaluation) The data in the third column of the table support this statement. Options (1) and (4) are not supported by the table nor the passage because "enough" and "best" are not defined. Option (3) is incorrect because the passage indicates that they have been in operation since 1969. Option (5) does not relate to the information because lottery revenues are one source of income, not the only source.

14. **(1) British Columbia Lottery Corporation** (Analysis) This is demonstrated by the fact that B.C. has the lowest percentage of proceeds after prizes and expenses (just under 30 percent). Options (2) through (5) show between 32 percent and 39 percent proceeds.

15. **(4) Legal Rights** (Application) Under Legal Rights it is stated: "Everyone has the right to be secure against unreasonable search or seizure."

Thus, it is this clause that would be cited when claiming a violation by a police officer. Options (1), (2), (3), and (5) do not suggest a violation of the process of justice.

16. **(1) the relationship of supply and demand** (Analysis) The table's unemployment figures indicate that, compared with the number of jobs, the supply of available workers was higher in 1938 than it was in 1930. Options (2), (4), and (5) are economics concepts that have nothing to do with wage levels. Option (3) is contradicted by the information given in the question; if option (3) were true, workers' wages would have been higher in 1938 than in 1930, but instead they were lower.

17. **(5) education** (Evaluation) Being a well-informed decision-maker requires that people be educated on issues, be able to engage in critical thinking, and have strong decision-making skills, which are also often linked to education. The values listed in options (1), (2), (3), and (4), although they may be important or helpful for other aspects of life, do not necessarily lead people to be well-informed or good decision-makers.

18. **(5) He did not want to lose his trusted representative, Marco Polo.** (Analysis) We can assume that the khan would not want his friend and trusted employee to leave. Marco Polo would not have been a favourite if the khan thought the Polos were spies, so option (1) is incorrect. The passage does not support option (2). Since the Polos had already survived a long and dangerous trip to get to China, options (3) and (4) are incorrect.

19. **(3) Kublai Khan admired and trusted Marco Polo.** (Analysis) This can be assumed from the information that the khan appointed Polo to represent him. Option (1) is incorrect because if the khan had feared Polo, it is unlikely that he would have made Polo his representative. There is no evidence in the passage to support option (2) or (4). Option (5) is incorrect because the passage states that Polo's book was written while he was in Italy, not China.

20. **(5) The trip home was mainly over water, while the trip to China was mainly over land.** (Evaluation) Because ships travel faster than people who are walking or riding on animals or in wagons, travelling over water would have allowed the Polos to travel much faster on their return trip than on their trip to China, which was mainly over land. Option (1)

Answers and Explanations • Simulated Tests

Simulated Tests

does not support the idea because the Polos travelled through Persia on both trips. Option (2) is incorrect because the map shows that the trip home was not along a more direct route. Option (3) is incorrect because the trip to China did not cover a greater distance than the return trip. The Polos did not cross Tibet on their return trip, so option (4) is incorrect.

21. **(3) Those who thought he should do nothing were weak and cowardly** (Analysis) Trudeau's rebuke of the reporter showed that he had disdain for people who would just stand by and watch while terrorist actions seemed to threaten the stability of the country. Option (1) is a misreading of the expression "bleeding hearts," which means people who are all sympathy and no backbone. The passage does not support either option (2) or (4). Although Trudeau may have agreed with the feeling expressed in option (5), there is no support for the statement in the passage.

22. **(5) maintaining order in the country** (Evaluation) Implied in Trudeau's comment, "Just watch me!" is a steely determination to take strong action against the kidnappings and murders by the FLQ using whatever means were at his disposal. The passage does not support the choice of option (1), as Trudeau was prepared to risk unpopularity to achieve his goal. Since he was trying to reduce the panic, option (2) is incorrect. He had no intention of negotiating with terrorists, so option (3) cannot be concluded. His sharp rebuke to the journalist proves that option (4) is incorrect.

23. **(4) knights** (Application) Like samurai, knights were feudal warriors who fought for their lords. Options (1) and (3) are incorrect because merchants and kings were not professional warriors. Option (2) is incorrect because the daimyos, not samurai, were the landowning nobles in Japan. Option (5) is incorrect because although, like samurai, serfs were required to fight for their lord, samurai were not peasants.

24. **(3) A system similar to European feudalism existed in Japan.** (Evaluation) The information in the passage supports the conclusion that Japan had a feudal-like system of government. Option (1) is wrong because the information in the passage shows it to be clearly untrue. The passage establishes that the Tokugawa rulers were shoguns not emperors, so option (2) would not be a correct conclusion to draw. No information in the passage supports option (4). The passage says that the

government began establishing authority over the daimyos after 1600 and that the emperor was restored to leadership by 1868, implying that the daimyos lost power, so option (5) is not a valid conclusion.

25. **(5) panic** (Comprehension) The passage makes it clear that, as share prices plunged, investors and bankers realized that not only that their own worth would be reduced, but also that the under-pinnings of the whole economy might be threatened. Although many were puzzled by the rapid course of events, the overwhelming feeling was one of great alarm, so option (2) is not correct. The information in the passage does not validate options (1), (3), or (4).

26. **(1) If exports fell sharply for any reason, the economy went into a serious decline.** (Analysis) Because staple products were the source of much of Canada's income as a country, any drop in exports meant a serious problem with inward cash flow. The passage does not mention the effect of weather on lumber exports, so option (2) is not supported. Option (3) does not refer to the role of staple products in Canada's economy. Option (4) is not correct; Canada is rich in natural resources. There is no proof offered in the passage for the claim in option (5).

27. **(4) France, England, and Spain were major European colonizers of eastern North America.** (Analysis) The map shows that these three nations established colonies in eastern North America in the late sixteenth century and the early seventeenth century, supporting the conclusion that these nations were major colonizers of the region. Options (1), (2), and (3) are not conclusions but are facts that support the conclusion in option (4). Option (5) is a conclusion that cannot be supported from the information given on the map.

28. **(2) writing a letter to a government official that presents your position on a controversial issue** (Application) In trying to convince the official of your position, you are acting like a lobbyist. Option (1) is not lobbying because it merely reports on government activities and does not try to influence leaders. Options (3) and (4) state a position but do not involve a contact with a government official. Option (5) is incorrect because the mere act of joining an interest group does not constitute lobbying.

29. **(3) Cultural values in Quebec society discouraged women from voting.** (Analysis)

The politicians in Quebec represent the people of Quebec, therefore their opinions should have been in line with the cultural values held by the people. Option (1) is not mentioned and would not have been a factor even if it were true. Option (2), a variety of social interests, does not negate an interest in the right to vote. Option (4) is the opposite of what actually took place because the passage indicates that Quebec women worked at lobbying the government for years for the right to vote. Option (5) has nothing to do with the issues within Quebec.

30. **(2) The American president exerts great political power in international politics.** (Analysis) The cartoon shows President Bush controlling Prime Minister Mulroney by remote control, as if he were a toy car. Option (1) is not indicated by the characters nor actions of the cartoon. Option (3) is a humorous, albeit insignificant, response. Options (4) and (5) use the words "need to," which indicate an opinion, not a fact.

31. **(5) The United States controls Canadian foreign policy.** (Comprehension) The cartoon is showing, as revealed by the remote control toy, that the United States controls Canada's foreign policy, even though it is in our hands. Options (1) and (4) are humorously misleading, even though they partly reflect details in the cartoon. Though the prime minister is being shown as a toy, option (2) does not encompass the entire message of the cartoon—that of foreign policy. Option (3) is not correct because the cartoon deals with foreign policy only, not with all the issues between the two countries.

32. **(3) Canada plays a leading role in international politics.** (Analysis) Portraying the Canadian prime minister as a toy indicates that the cartoonist seriously questions the importance of Canada's role in international politics. Options (1) and (4) are likely the opinions of the cartoonist, as they directly relate to what the cartoon is expressing. Option (2) could be an opinion of the cartoonist, though the only country that the cartoon is dealing with is Canada. Therefore, one cannot presume how he feels about the American response to other countries. Option (5) also is a likely opinion of the cartoonist, though one cannot assume this as the cartoon relates to foreign policy and not to other aspects of the relationship between the United States and Canada.

33. **(3) Theft is acceptable in some situations.** (Analysis) The passage states that a law against theft means that stealing is regarded as unacceptable behaviour in that society. That theft is acceptable in some situations is an opinion. Options (1), (2), (4), and (5) are all facts stated in the passage.

34. **(2) Teenage drivers are unsafe and a menace on the highways.** (Analysis) The ad indicates that the sponsors feel that teen drivers are reckless and careless. It is not a fact that all teenage drivers are unsafe. The ad states that studies have shown that teen drivers have a high accident rate, so option (1) is not an opinion. Options (3), (4), and (5) are all facts stated in the newspaper ad.

35. **(1) The varied landscapes of Canada provide vacations for everyone.** (Comprehension) This sentence best summarizes the passage because the main points of the passage all have to do with what Canadians and visitors can do in the varied landscapes of the country. Option (2) is incorrect because the main idea of the passage is not about what people eat. Option (3) indicates a popular opinion, but the passage does not focus on this idea. Option (4) does not work because is it too vague. Option (5) is not correct because the passage does not address trends in Canadian recreational activity.

36. **(3) Canada has a lot of mountains.** (Analysis) The passage talks about the mountains of Whistler/Blackcomb, the Rockies, and the Laurentians, as well as the rolling hills of Saskatchewan. Option (1) states an opinion that is not mentioned in the passage. Option (2) is incorrect, not only because Canada does have a lot of fresh water, but also because the point it makes is not a conclusion of the paragraph. Option (4) states the opposite of what the paragraph focuses on. Option (5) has nothing to do with physical geography.

37. **(5) Canada has many lakes, rivers, and mountains.** (Analysis) This response is the correct one because it is the only one that does not include words that state opinions, like "wonderful" in option (1), "most popular" in option (2), "dislike" in option (3), and "more beautiful" in option (4). These words indicate opinions and thus make these responses incorrect.

38. **(3) Population growth derived more from immigration than births in the 1990s compared with the 1940s and 1960s.**

Answers and Explanations • Simulated Tests

(Evaluation) This response is the correct one because the map indicates that the nineties is the only decade that showed a marked increase in population growth by immigration (1 137 000) compared with by birth (1 024 000). Options (1) and (4) are incorrect because the table does not show life expectancy. Option (2) is incorrect because total population is not expressed, only population *growth*. Option (5) is incorrect because this information is not shown on the table.

39. **(5) Negotiators falsely maintain the image of marathon negotiations.** (Comprehension) To identify the main idea, try to bring all the information together. In this cartoon, labour, management, and the press are all involved. Options (1) and (4) are concerned with details. Options (2) and (3) are not suggested in the cartoon.

40. **(1) are not making progress.** (Evaluation) They have been negotiating a long time without results and are tired. But they don't want to share their lack of progress with the public, which is why they are not telling the press the truth. Options (2) and (4) are contradicted by the details of the cartoon. Option (3) is unlikely because they would be eager to continue and to tell the press if they were about to reach an agreement. Option (5) is incorrect because it is contradicted by the cartoon's caption.

41. **(3) that the man with the notebook is a reporter** (Analysis) The man outside the room is writing on a notepad and has clearly asked a question, as reporters do. The lack of labels in the cartoon indicates that it refers to general union-management negotiations and not to a specific situation, so options (1), (2), (4), and (5) are incorrect.

42. **(2) saying "The cheque is in the mail."** (Application) Both messages are intended to reassure the listener while buying a little time for the speaker. Option (1) would cause panic. Option (3) could start an argument. Option (4) would make the listener doubt the speaker's innocence. Option (5) is the opposite of the intended message.

43. **(3) There has been a decline in the number of work stoppages since 1986.** (Comprehension) Since stoppages were at their highest in 1986 and were much lower in 2001, the general trend must have been downward. Option (1) is incorrect because the paragraph states that 1986 was the peak year. Option (2) is contradicted by the data. Options (4) and (5) cannot be concluded from the paragraph.

44. **(3) It was imposed on the rest of the population by a small, exclusive group of men, without consultation or a vote.** (Analysis) The passage describes the achievement of Confederation as the decision of an oligarchy or elite without much reference to common people. There is no evidence to support option (1). Option (2) is incorrect because, in the British parliamentary system, the monarch does not impose anything on anybody. Neither option (4) nor option (5) is true.

45. **(4) computers and the Internet** (Application) Computers and the Internet are examples of a technology that has revolutionized communication, economics, and daily life around the world. Although wind power is becoming increasingly important as a non-polluting source of energy, it has yet to match the impact of computers, so option (1) is not correct. The same might be said for options (2) and (3). Cars were not a technological innovation of the late twentieth century, so option (5) is incorrect.

46. **(5) slaves** (Application) The whippings and forced obedience are clues that "mission Indians" were treated like slaves. This description would not apply to any of the other options.

47. **(4) Gasoline, which powers automobiles, is a fossil fuel.** (Analysis) Unless you know this, you cannot appreciate the meaning of the cartoon's caption. The cartoon's focus is not on water resources, so options (1) and (2) are incorrect. (In addition, option (1) is untrue because water is not a fossil fuel.) Options (3) and (5) may or may not be true, but they do not aid understanding of the cartoon.

48. **(1) We are too dependent on fossil fuels.** (Evaluation) This is supported by the information that so little energy comes from other sources, even though some experts believe that fossil fuels may fairly soon be exhausted, and by the scene and caption of the cartoon. Even though option (2) may be a good idea, no facts provided in the paragraph or opinions expressed in the cartoon lead to this conclusion. Option (3) contradicts the paragraph. No information is provided that would lead to the conclusions stated in options (4) and (5).

49. (4) far from the equator with a high elevation (Application) According to the paragraph, the higher a place is, the colder it is, and the closer a place is to the equator, the hotter it is. Therefore, moving away from the equator would make a place colder. The combination of distance from the equator and a high elevation would produce the coldest place. Options (1), (2), (3), and (5) do not provide the right combination for the coldest temperature.

50. (5) apartheid (Comprehension) The wrist iron and chain is a symbol of control or bondage, and it represents the control of black South Africans by the policy of apartheid. Option (1) is incorrect because black South Africans are represented by the hand that is breaking free of the chain. Option (2) is incorrect because low wages were only one of the types of oppression under apartheid. Option (3) is incorrect because the subject of the cartoon, people standing in line to vote, shows peaceful, not violent, change. Option (4) is incorrect because the ANC is not portrayed or symbolized in the cartoon.

Science
(pages 666–683)

1. (4) Humans did not exist for most of geologic time. (Analysis) This statement is a conclusion reached by comparing the amount of time humans have existed with all the geological time preceding our development. Options (1), (2), (3), and (5) are all details regarding the era during which humans appeared, the Cenozoic.

2. (3) fish, land plants, and dinosaurs (Comprehension) By the Mesozoic, fish and land plants had already evolved. Dinosaurs first appeared during the Mesozoic. Because these organisms existed at that time, it follows that their fossils could occur in rocks of the Mesozoic Era. Option (1) is incorrect since many other organisms besides simple ocean organisms had appeared by the Mesozoic Era. Options (2), (4), and (5) are incorrect because horses, primates, and humans did not appear until after the Mesozoic Era, and so they would not be found in Mesozoic fossils.

3. (2) 160 million years (Comprehension) The timeline is measured in millions of years. Dinosaurs appeared slightly less than 225 million years ago and died out about 65 million years ago. Subtracting 65 million from 225 million gives 160 million years. Option (1) gives the time when dinosaurs died out. Option (3) gives the time when dinosaurs first appeared. Options (4) and (5) are longer than the period that dinosaurs existed.

4. (2) sea-living invertebrates (Analysis) Options (1), (3), and (4) are incorrect because the timeline shows that these organisms appeared after the first fish. Option (5) is incorrect for the same reason, and even if land plants had existed, the fish would not have been able to leave the water to eat them.

5.(3) The Great Lakes are younger than the Rocky Mountains. (Evaluation) The timeline shows that the Rocky Mountains appeared before the Great Lakes. Option (1) is incorrect because according to the timeline, air-breathing animals appeared in the early Paleozoic and amphibians did not appear until the late Paleozoic. Option (2) is incorrect because the timeline shows that dinosaurs lived during the Mesozoic Era. Option (4) is incorrect because the timeline shows that dinosaurs died out about 65 million years ago. Option (5) is incorrect because the timeline shows that the first life forms developed in the oceans.

6. (5) Decane has more isomers. (Analysis) The passage states that the more carbon atoms in a hydrocarbon molecule, the more isomers it can form. Decane has more carbon atoms than pentane does, so it will form more isomers. In fact, decane has 75 isomers compared to pentane's 3 isomers. Therefore, options (2), (3), and (4) are incorrect. Option (1) is incorrect because, as the chemical formula shows, decane has more hydrogen atoms than pentane.

7. (3) There are different types of granite, each made of different minerals. (Evaluation) The fact that there are different types of granite, each formed from different minerals, supports the idea that granite is not made of particular elements but can be made of an assortment of different elements. Thus, granite is made of different minerals but is not itself a mineral. All other options are true, but options (1) and (5) could be used to contradict the conclusion; options (2) and (4) are irrelevant to the conclusion.

8. (1) A runner from Halifax, which is at sea level, has trouble breathing while jogging in the Rocky Mountains. (Evaluation) A runner from a sea-level location gets less oxygen per breath than he or she is accustomed to when running at a higher altitude. Thus, the runner has trouble breathing. Options (2) and (3) may be true, but they do not provide evidence that less oxygen is available at higher altitudes. Option (4) makes no sense; a mountain climber needs to re-create atmospheric conditions at a high altitude, not at sea level. Option (5) is true; but it has nothing to do with the amount of oxygen in the air.

9. **(1) Bluebirds and butterflies have wings.** (Application) The wings are adaptations to life in the air, but bluebirds are birds and butterflies are insects, so they are not closely related. In the remaining options, the adaptations belong to closely related species and so are not examples of convergence.

10. **(1) white colouring** (Application) White colouring is camouflage in a snowy polar region. The remaining traits would not be useful in a polar environment.

11. **(3) There are more herons and egrets because clean water means more fish to eat.** (Evaluation) As the water became cleaner, fish populations increased, which meant more food for water birds. The information in the passage and graphs does not support options (1), (2), (4), and (5).

12. **(5) carbon dioxide gas** (Analysis) It is gas bubbles that cause the cake to rise, and the passage states that carbon dioxide gas, not oxygen, is produced. Options (1), (3), and (4) are incorrect because they are not gases, and options (1) and (4) are not produced when sodium bicarbonate reacts. Option (2) is a gas, but there is no mention of oxygen in the passage.

13. **(2) plotting the evolutionary relationships among extinct organisms** (Evaluation) By studying fossils, scientists can figure out evolutionary relationships. Options (1) and (5) are incorrect because fossils tell about the past, not the present or the future. Option (3) is incorrect because fossils are of ancient, not modern, organisms. Option (4) is incorrect because the fossil record does not go back as far as the formation of Earth.

14. **(1) Cowbirds lay their eggs in the nests of songbirds, which incubate and raise cowbird chicks.** (Application) In this case, cowbirds benefit by not having to use up energy hatching and feeding offspring, and songbirds use up energy they could otherwise use to hatch and raise their own chicks. Options (2) through (5) are incorrect because they are all symbiotic relationships—relationships in which both species benefit.

15. **(2) increased friction on the moving parts** (Analysis) An engine low on oil is not well-lubricated, and its moving parts will have increased friction and thus increased wear. Option (1) is incorrect because insufficient oil means increased, not decreased, friction. Options (3) and (4) are incorrect because friction does not affect stationary parts. Option (5) is incorrect because low oil means more friction, which means more difficult movement of the engine's parts.

16. **(2) eating too little of foods high in iodine** (Comprehension) According to the question text, goiter is caused by a lack of iodine in the diet. Option (1) is incorrect because, as indicated by the question text, fish contains iodine, which prevents goiter. Option (4) is incorrect because fertilizing the soil with iodine, if it does anything, would prevent goiter in people who eat food grown in the soil. Options (3) and (5) are incorrect because goiter is caused by a diet deficiency, not by a germ or a gene.

17. **(4) sulphuric acid, citric acid, pure water, magnesium hydroxide, sodium hydroxide** (Comprehension) This is correct because the pH scale starts low with strong acids, has neutral substances in the middle, and ends high with the strong bases; the substances in option (4) have been identified in the passage as a strong acid, a weak acid, a neutral substance, a weak base, and a strong base, following the order of the pH scale from lowest to highest. Options (1), (2), and (3) are not in order. In option (5) the correct order is exactly reversed and reads from highest to lowest.

18. **(3) a salt** (Application) The passage states that the reaction between an acid and a base produces water and a salt. Options (1), (2), (4), and (5) are incorrect because such a reaction would not produce either an acid or a base.

19. **(1) a change in the sequence of amino acids in a protein** (Analysis) Since the base sequence of DNA codes for protein synthesis, a mutation that changes one base in the DNA is likely to cause a change in the sequence of amino acids in a protein. Options (2), (3), (4), and (5) are all possibilities, depending on the nature of the protein affected by the mutation, but they are much less likely to occur.

20. **(5) Kilauea Iki, whose lava spread over Hawaii during several months** (Application)

This is the only volcano that fits the description of a shield volcano, with slow, relatively gentle lava flows. Options (1), (2), (3), and (4) have characteristics that are opposite to those of a shield volcano.

21. **(5) The results of the private company's sequencing and mapping are of poor quality.** (Analysis) Based on the passage, that is the opinion of some scientists. The clue here is the phrase *poor quality*, since assessments of quality generally involve opinion, and are not strictly related to fact. Options (1), (2), (3), and (4) are incorrect because they are facts stated in or implied by the passage.

22. **(3) preventing and treating hereditary diseases** (Analysis) The more that is known about the human genome, the better medical scientists will be able to understand hereditary diseases and develop treatments for them. Option (1) is incorrect because the fast and efficient sequencers were designed before the genome was "read." Option (2) is not directly related to knowledge of the human genome. Options (4) and (5) are incorrect because they would involve study of the genomes of other species (bacteria or plants).

23. **(1) identifying criminals** (Application) By matching a DNA "fingerprint" taken from a suspect's blood or other tissue to blood or tissue found at a crime scene, investigators can identify possible criminals. Option (2) is incorrect because blood typing does not require identifying DNA. Option (3) is incorrect because it does not refer to human DNA at all. Option (4) is incorrect because DNA is not needed to do laser surgery. Option (5) is incorrect because DNA fingerprints are not needed for treating disease.

24. **(4) Healthy sections of a man's intestine are used to replace diseased sections.** (Application) Of the choices given, this one involves the greatest compatibility between donor and recipient, since they are the same person. The closer the compatibility, the greater the chance of a successful transplant. Options (1), (2), (3), and (5) are incorrect because they involve donors and recipients who are more distantly related than the man described in option (4). Therefore, these transplants are less likely to be compatible and less likely to succeed.

25. **(4) Improved cultivation techniques are preferable to herbicide use.** (Analysis) This statement reflects the opinion of some environmental groups. The clue word here is *preferable*. Not everyone shares this point of view. Options (1), (2), (3), and (5) are statements of fact presented in the passage.

26. **(3) the mouth of the Annapolis River, Nova Scotia, with large variation in high and low tides** (Application) One requirement for a tidal power station is a great difference in the water level at high and low tide, so this location is the best of those listed. Options (1), (4), and (5) are incorrect because to take advantage of the tides, tidal power stations must be at the mouth of a river, where it meets the sea, not inland. Option (2) is not a good location because the tidal difference is too low.

27. **(1) her mass** (Evaluation) The body mass of the skydiver will affect the duration of the jump because it affects the point at which terminal velocity is reached. Options (2) and (3) are incorrect because the volume and height of the skydiver are not critical factors. Options (4) and (5) are incorrect because the speed and type of airplane do not affect the length of time the jump takes.

28. **(4) Food with a high water content heats more rapidly in a microwave oven than dry food does.** (Evaluation) Since microwaves act on water molecules, causing them to twist back and forth, producing heat, you can conclude that food with a high water content will heat up more rapidly than dry food. Option (1) is incorrect because nothing in the passage or diagram indicates that other types of electromagnetic radiation have that effect on water molecules. Option (2) is incorrect because a microwave oven converts electromagnetic energy to heat energy, not the other way around. Option (3) is incorrect because a conventional oven does not use microwaves; it conducts heat from a heat source to cook food. Option (5) may or may not be true, but nothing in the passage or diagram provides information to support this conclusion.

29. **(2) Montana** (Comprehension) The map shows that the state of Montana includes portions of all three ranges in different parts of the state. Option (1) is incorrect because Idaho includes only one of the populations. Options (3) and (4) are incorrect because no wolf population is shown in either of these states. Option (5) is incorrect because Wyoming has only one wolf population, in and around Yellowstone.

30. (4) The Range of the Grey Wolf
(Comprehension) The subject of the map is the locations where grey wolves can be found today. Option (1) is incorrect because the map shows far more than Yellowstone National Park. Option (2) is incorrect because the map shows more than these three states; it also shows portions of Nevada, Utah, and Canada. Option (3) is incorrect because the map's primary purpose is not to show national parks but to show where wolves live. Option (5) is incorrect because the map shows that wolves live outside national parks as well as inside them.

31. (5) The grey wolf should no longer be considered endangered. (Analysis) This is an opinion because it is a belief held by some people, but not by others. The key word is *should*. Options (1), (2), (3), and (4) are facts stated in or implied by the passage.

32. (3) restoring tallgrass varieties to small portions of the Prairies (Application) Restoring once-native plant species to an ecosystem is similar to restoring an animal species to its former ecosystem. Options (1), (2), (4), and (5) are incorrect because they do not involve the restoration of a species to its former ecosystem. Option (1) is incorrect, because it involves changing an altered ecosystem so it is more like its natural state, not returning a once native species to its ecosystem. Options (2) and (5) are ways of protecting native species, not returning them to their ecosystem. Option (4) deals with the introduction of a nonnative species, not the return of a native species.

33. (4) Put your ear to the ground.
(Application) Since sound waves travel faster through solid ground than they do through air, putting your ear to the ground means you will hear a distant sound sooner. The other options all have to do with sound and hearing, but not with the fact that sound waves travel fastest through solids.

34. (3) A virus is genetic material that appears lifeless until it takes over a cell to reproduce. (Comprehension) This sentence restates the points of the paragraph. Options (1) and (2) are incorrect because they restate only portions of the information. Options (4) and (5) are incorrect because there is no discussion of the common cold or of treating viral diseases in the information given.

35. (2) A fluid is a liquid or a gas. (Analysis) The writer assumes that you understand that a fluid is either a liquid or a gas—any substance whose molecules can move freely and randomly. The other options are incorrect because they are all stated in the passage.

36. (3) its reflectivity (Analysis) Reflective plastic will cast more light on the plants, increasing the rate of photosynthesis. The other properties of the plastic will not affect the rate of photosynthesis. Therefore, options (1), (2), (4), and (5) are incorrect.

37. (4) an island in the northern Pacific
(Application) Of the locations listed, only the northern Pacific has many volcanoes. In fact, Dante explored a volcano on one of Alaska's Aleutian Islands in the northern Pacific.

38. (1) decreased speed (Analysis) Since drag slows down moving objects, increasing drag would decrease an object's speed. Option (2) is the opposite of what would occur. Option (3) is incorrect because, as the paragraph implies and the diagrams show, streamlining causes decreased drag and smoother airflow, so increased drag means rougher airflow. Option (4) is incorrect because increasing the drag means the rate at which air flows over the object decreases. Option (5) is incorrect because drag is a kind of friction, so increasing drag means increasing friction.

39. (1) repetitive. (Comprehension) According to the passage and diagram, monomers are repeating units that make up polymers. Option (2) is incorrect because the passage indicates that monomers are small. Option (3) is incorrect because monomers are joined by covalent bonds, not ionic bonds. Options (4) and (5) are not true; none of the examples cited in the passage are metals or gases.

40. (2) Mass is the amount of matter in an object. (Analysis) The passage does not include a definition of mass, although you need to know what mass is to understand the information presented. Option (1) is not true; mass is not the volume of an object. Option (3) is true, but it is stated directly in the passage and not assumed. Options (4) and (5) are not true; all objects have mass, and mass can be measured.

41. (5) Sound waves travel more slowly than light waves do. (Evaluation) There is a time lag between seeing the ball hit and hearing the sound because sound waves travel much more slowly than light waves do. Options (1) and (4) would not affect the timing at which a person would hear the sound. Options (2) and (3) would not affect the speed at which the sound travelled.

42. **(2) Bacteria that enter your nose will be killed.** (Analysis) By destroying the cell wall, the protein kills the bacteria. Option (1) is incorrect because the protein cannot prevent bacteria from entering the nose when you breathe. Option (3) is incorrect because the protein cannot affect bacteria outside the nose. Option (4) is incorrect because if the cell wall is destroyed, the bacteria is destroyed and cannot reproduce. Option (5) is incorrect because the bacteria will change shape when the cell wall is broken down.

43. **(4) in a greenhouse** (Application) In a greenhouse full of plants, evidence of transpiration can be found in the humid air and condensation on the inner glass. Options (1) and (2) are incorrect because there are few plants and little transpiration in either type of environment. Option (3) is incorrect because ocean plants do not transpire since they are underwater. Option (5) is incorrect because the water vapour from the plants in the field would disperse into the air and would be difficult to detect.

44. **(3) Pull a few coils of a loose spring toward you and then quickly release them.** (Application) The key characteristic of a longitudinal wave is that the direction of the wave's motion and the direction of the disturbance the wave causes are the same. This can be modelled by plucking and releasing the coils of a loose spring. Option (1) is incorrect because the up-and-down motion of the rope is perpendicular to the motion of the wave; this pattern of motion is characteristic of a transverse rather than a longitudinal wave. Option (2) is incorrect because the rotation of a jump rope does not model the linear disturbance of a longitudinal wave. Options (4) and (5) are incorrect because skipping a stone and throwing a bounce pass are more similar to the motion caused by a transverse wave than a longitudinal wave, since the up-and-down motion is perpendicular to the direction both the stone and the ball travel.

45. **(5) Replace a thin steel wire with a thick copper wire.** (Application) If the voltage remains the same, any change that decreases the resistance increases the current. A thicker wire has a lower resistance than a thinner wire, and copper has a lower resistance than steel, so replacing a thin steel wire with a thick copper wire decreases the resistance, which increases the current. Options (1), (2), (3), and (4) all are changes that would increase the resistance, which would decrease the current.

46. **(2) A rough surface reflects parallel light rays at different angles.** (Evaluation) The right diagram shows that when parallel rays hit a rough surface, light is reflected but the reflected rays bounce off at different angles. Option (1) is incorrect because the diagram shows that parallel incoming rays can be reflected. Option (3) is incorrect because the law of reflection does hold for rough surfaces: the angle of incidence is always equal to the angle of reflection. The parallel light rays are reflected off a rough surface at different angles because they hit the rough surface at different angles. Options (4) and (5) are incorrect because they are based on a misunderstanding of the word *normal*, which in the diagrams refers to the line perpendicular to the surface.

47. **(3) scientific and technical challenge** (Evaluation) To go from the first controlled nuclear fission reaction in 1942 to a working bomb in three years was a great scientific and technological challenge, the sort of challenge likely to motivate the physicists. Option (1) is not likely to be correct because developing the bomb, as the passage indicates, was a team effort. Option (2) is unlikely because developing weapons of mass destruction is the opposite of developing nonviolent means of conflict resolution. Option (4) is incorrect because nothing in the passage indicates that the physicists were expecting a large monetary reward. Option (5) is incorrect because the passage indicates that after the war, many of the scientists came to regret the destruction caused by their work and tried to stop the spread of nuclear weapons.

48. **(1) During the winter, a hibernating bear lives on the energy stored as fat.** (Application) The hibernating bear is an example of the later use of energy stored in lipids in the bear's body. Options (2) and (4) do not involve lipids. Option (3) involves eating something for quick, not stored, energy. Option (5) is true, but it discusses the composition of lipids, not their use.

Answers and Explanations • Simulated Tests

49. **(1) Blood Type Frequency in Selected Populations** (Comprehension) The chart provides information on the percentage of people who have each blood type in several population groups. Option (2) is too general. Options (3) and (4) have nothing to do with the subject of the chart. Option (5) is too specific, since groups other than Americans are represented.

50. **(2) broad, flat shape** (Analysis) The shape of a leaf gives it a large surface area, so it can absorb lots of light energy. Option (1) is incorrect because the pores allow substances like carbon dioxide or water vapor to flow in and out. Option (3) is incorrect because the stalk provides support. Option (4) is incorrect because the veins allow transport of water and minerals. Option (5) is incorrect because the root system of the plant is not characteristic of the leaf.

Language Arts, Reading
(pages 685–700)

1. **(1) attraction** (Comprehension) Elizabeth's disappointment over Mr. Darcy's inattention to her (lines 26–38) suggests that she is attracted to him. There is no support for the other options.

2. **(2) Mr. Darcy has ignored her.** (Comprehension) Elizabeth's thoughts supply this information. There is no evidence in the excerpt for options (1), (3), and (4). Only Elizabeth is disappointed; thus option (5) is incorrect.

3. **(2) She will be preoccupied with thoughts about Mr. Darcy.** (Application) She tells herself not to think about him, suggesting that she will anyway. She feels that Mr. Darcy is the one who acted rudely, so option (1) is incorrect. There is no support for the other options.

4. **(3) close and affectionate** (Analysis) The dialogue between the sisters shows their close and loving relationship; additionally, at the beginning of the excerpt, Elizabeth found relief from her misery by seeing her sister's good fortune. This shows that the two are close and want the best for each other. There is no support for options (1), (4), and (5). Option (2) is only partially correct—the sisters are polite but not distant.

5. **(3) She is questioning Jane's claims of indifference.** (Analysis) Elizabeth suggests that Jane is not indifferent when she continues by warning Jane to be careful. Although Elizabeth seems to be agreeing with Jane, her meaning is quite the opposite; therefore, option (1) is incorrect. Since Elizabeth is commenting on Jane's behaviour, options (2), (4), and (5) are incorrect.

6. **(4) Mr. Darcy's** (Analysis) In paragraphs 3–7, the author shares Elizabeth's thoughts as she reflects on Mr. Darcy's behaviour. In the first paragraph, the author shares Jane's and her visitor's thoughts, describing their impressions of each other. In the second paragraph, the author shares Mrs. Bennet's thoughts when she mentions her intent to invite the men to dinner. Therefore, options (1), (2), (3), and (5) are incorrect. Mr. Darcy is the only character whose thoughts are hidden from the reader.

7. **(1) Neither is very talkative on the day of the visit.** (Synthesis) Elizabeth comments on Mr. Darcy's silence, and Jane is described as talking less than usual. Although Jane is cheerful after the visit, the reader does not learn of Mr. Darcy's reaction, so option (4) is incorrect. Only Mr. Darcy's behaviour is described as teasing, and this does not seem intentional, so option (5) is also incorrect. There is no support for options (2) and (3).

8. **(5) sneaky and uncooperative** (Comprehension) Mary's tears and tantrums, threats, and refusal to tell the truth tell us that she is hard to control. She may be lonely and misunderstood as well, option (1), but those are not her chief traits. There is no evidence for options (2), (3), and (4).

9. **(1) make excuses for turning in work late** (Application) Mary does not want to take responsibility for her actions, so as a worker she would probably make excuses or try to blame others. There is no evidence that Mary is timid around others, so option (2) is incorrect. She seems unhappy, but she does not say anything about quitting school; therefore, there is not enough evidence to conclude that she would quit a job right away, option (3). She does not seem to be successful or a good communicator; therefore, options (4) and (5) are incorrect.

10. **(3) tense** (Synthesis) The clash of wills between Mary and Karen makes this a scene full of conflict. There is no evidence for options (1), (2), (4), or (5).

11. **(3) She does not like what Karen said.**
(Analysis) Mary is upset that Karen has punished her and so dramatically falls to the floor to express herself. Because Mary seems to be falling in reaction to Karen's words, it seems unlikely that she is really fainting; therefore, option (1) is incorrect. The appearance of Mary's pain, which she points to vaguely, seems too coincidental to be genuine, so option (2) is incorrect. There is no support for option (4) or (5).

12. **(1) Karen does not value Mrs. Mortar's opinions.** (Analysis) The stage directions show that Karen ignores Mrs. Mortar. This implies that Karen does not value her opinions. The fact that Karen openly ignores her shows that the two women are not close friends, option (2). It also shows that Karen is not careful to protect Mrs. Mortar's feelings, option (3), nor does she respect her, option (4). There is no evidence for option (5) in the excerpt.

13. **(4) wait for Mary to decide to get up**
(Analysis) Karen does not appear worried when Mary says she feels ill, so options (1), (2), and (5) are unlikely. Option (3) is incorrect because Karen ignores Mrs. Mortar earlier in the excerpt.

14. **(4) normal and natural** (Comprehension) Grandpa Blakeslee says that death is not always awful and that it is part of God's plan. He also wants no fuss made over his death. These facts support the idea that he thinks death is normal and natural. There is no evidence to support options (1) and (2). Option (3) is incorrect because he thinks that funerals, not death, are a waste of money. Option (5) is the opposite of what Grandpa Blakeslee thinks.

15. **(1) Grandpa Blakeslee does not want a fuss made at his funeral.** (Comprehension) All the details of the will are about avoiding anything fancy at the burial. Options (2), (3), and (5) are details that help to suggest that idea. Grandpa Blakeslee may believe funerals should be simple but does not care about dignity, so option (4) is incorrect.

16. **(5) a humorous criticism of the funeral industry** (Synthesis) Grandpa Blakeslee makes comments about not wanting a trip to Birdsong's Emporium, dressing the dead to look alive, wanting to be taken straight from home to the cemetery, and not wanting a tombstone with the word "sleeping." All of these suggest that funerals make death into something artificial and are an unnecessary expense. None of the other options are supported by the details in the excerpt.

17. **(4) It makes it seem as though Grandpa Blakeslee is actually speaking.** (Synthesis) The tone of his will is so conversational that it seems as though Grandpa Blakeslee is there. Grandpa Blakeslee seems to be a thoughtful and perceptive man, so option (1) is incorrect. There is no support in the excerpt for options (2) and (3). Although he does seem to be practical, his nonstandard English does not give this impression, so option (5) is incorrect.

18. **(5) They are playmates.** (Comprehension) School is not mentioned, so option (1) is incorrect. Lines 2–6 describe a happy, friendly relationship, so options (2) and (4) are incorrect. There is no evidence for option (3).

19. **(1) wistful longing** (Synthesis) The references to past happiness and passing seasons give the poem a sense of longing. There is no support for options (2), (3), and (4). Although the speaker expresses her love, most of the poem is not romantic or passionate, so option (5) is incorrect.

20. **(4) They remind her that life is short and she is alone.** (Analysis) The appearance of the paired butterflies reminds her that time is passing, she is getting older, and she is by herself. Option (1) is incorrect because it doesn't address the fact that the butterflies are paired. There is no support in the poem for options (2), (3), or (5).

21. **(3) The marriage was arranged by their two families.** (Analysis) She was fourteen when they married and bashful around her husband; therefore it's logical that the marriage between the two was arranged. The woman was not in love when she married, so option (1) is incorrect. There is no support for options (2), (4), or (5).

22. **(1) The course of life is unpredictable.** (Application) She might say this because of her own unpredictable life. She is sorrowful, so she would be unlikely to support option (2). She has had joy in her life, so option (3) is also unlikely. Although the woman did marry young, the poem does not suggest that she would recommend this to someone else. Therefore, option (4) is incorrect. There is no support for option (5).

23. **(2) playfulness to obedience to devotion to longing** (Synthesis) She was playful as a child (lines 1–3), obediently married (lines 6–10), then became devoted to her husband (lines 11–14), and finally longed for him while he was gone. The poem does not support the other options.

24. **(4) make it difficult to excel at work**
(Comprehension) The first paragraph suggests that unresolved difficulties at home can prevent the employee from performing well. Option (1) is too strong in the context of this statement. Option (3) cannot be inferred from the statement. Options (2) and (5) are not supported by the information in the excerpt.

25. **(3) They want their employees to function well.** (Analysis) The excerpt states that outside problems can interfere with "an employee's ability to perform well" (lines 9–10). The excerpt suggests the opposite of option (1). Option (2) may be true but is not stated or implied in the excerpt. Option (4) is incorrect because the excerpt states that the company knows that this is often not possible. Option (5) is the opposite of the company's recommendation.

26. **(4) feeling overwhelmed by a project**
(Application) The program as described is set up to deal with emotional problems, such as feeling overwhelmed. Options (1), (2), and (3) do not involve emotions and so are incorrect. Option (5) is not necessarily a problem and so is incorrect.

27. **(2) your son who is depressed** (Application) Option (2) is correct because your son is an immediate relative and depression is a personal problem. Options (1), (4), and (5) are incorrect because they are not members of your immediate family. Option (3) is incorrect because a broken arm is a physical problem, not a personal problem.

28. **(1) straightforward and matter-of-fact**
(Synthesis) The excerpt is written in clear, frank, straightforward language that the average employee can understand. None of the other options accurately describes the excerpt's style.

29. **(4) by introducing a problem and offering a solution** (Synthesis) The excerpt begins by introducing the topic of personal problems and then offers a solution to help employees resolve them. Although the excerpt does discuss the steps involved in EARS counselling, this is just one small part of the excerpt and so option (1) is incorrect. Option (2) is not supported by the information in the excerpt. The help available is as important as the problems themselves; therefore, option (3) is incorrect. Option (5) does not effectively describe the organizational pattern of the excerpt.

30. **(4) early evening** (Comprehension) The excerpt describes the sky as being a dark colour—jade-green—and mentions flowers that "seemed to lean upon the dusk" (line 11). These are clues that the scene takes place in the early evening. The excerpt does not support the other options.

31. **(1) visiting art galleries** (Application) Among the things that make her happy, Bertha's mention of friends who are painters indicates that she would likely visit art galleries. Option (2) is not supported by the details in the excerpt, and option (3) is incorrect because she reacts negatively to cats. Option (4) is incorrect because she is quite well off and unlikely to do her own housework, and option (5) is incorrect because she has a cook.

32. **(1) It seems perfect, just as her circumstances do.** (Analysis) The pear tree is described as being "in fullest, richest bloom" (lines 4–5). Bertha compares the tree to her life, which she also sees as being in its fullest perfection. Option (2) is incorrect because the excerpt does not mention Bertha's physical attributes. Option (3) is incorrect because there is no indication in the excerpt that Bertha will be giving birth. Bertha makes no reference to growing and changing, so option (4) is incorrect. Option (5) is incorrect because Bertha is not described as being calm.

33. **(1) The colours she planned to wear matched her surroundings.** (Analysis) Before she went upstairs to dress, Bertha realized that the colours she had chosen to wear were the same as those reflected in the garden, the pear tree, and the sky. The statement indicates that the correlation was coincidental and not planned. None of the other options is supported by details from the excerpt.

34. **(2) It contributes to the feeling of unreality.** (Synthesis) The setting of the story in spring, when growing things are usually new, perfect, and unblemished, contributes to the story's mood of unreal, almost surreal, perfection. The excerpt does not discuss newness or new beginnings, so options (1) and (5) are incorrect. The excerpt is not particularly joyous or playful, so option (3) is incorrect. Option (4) refers to a detail from the excerpt and not the overall mood.

35. **(2) naive** (Synthesis) The character's statement that she is too happy, her reflection on her good fortune, and her dizzy and drunken feelings, all suggest an emotional state that is not likely to last. The character's apparent ignorance of her true feelings suggests her naiveté. The author's choice of words does not support the other four options.

36. (2) would like more interest-focused, detailed program guides (Comprehension) The commentary discusses the limitations of most program guides and the need for a more "encompassing" (line 61) guide. Options (1) and (3) are details in the excerpt, not the most important ideas, and so are incorrect. There is no support for option (4). Option (5) is incorrect because the author discusses his own habits in order to make his point; he is not trying to convince others to copy his behaviour.

37. (3) Its program guide is a waste of money. (Analysis) Lines 43–47 discuss how the large number of repeats on A&E means that its A&E program guide is not worth the extra price. Option (2) is the opposite of this idea; therefore, it is incorrect. Option (1) is incorrect because it contradicts what is implied by the excerpt. There is no support for option (4). Although the author is critical of A&E, option (5) cannot be inferred from the excerpt.

38. (1) informative (Synthesis) The author supplies the information in a straightforward and informative manner. Option (2) is incorrect because the author seems frustrated but not angry. The author does not use humour in his discussion; therefore, option (3) is incorrect. Option (4) is incorrect because the author is annoyed rather than overwhelmed. The author is not pleased by the available television listings, so option (5) is incorrect.

39. (3) methodical (Synthesis) The author sets forth his argument by explaining methodically how he uses *TV Guide*. He describes the different channels and the programs that they air and the way in which these programs are listed. His word choice in describing the process and the careful way in which he addresses the subject help to categorize his writing style as serious and methodical. None of the other options accurately describe the style in which the commentary is written.

40. (3) superficial (Comprehension) The author states that *TV Guide* merely lists the titles of programs for many channels. This is a superficial, or shallow, treatment of listings. There is no support in the excerpt for options (1) and (5). Option (2) is the opposite of what is suggested in the excerpt. Option (4) may be true but is not the focus of the discussion in the excerpt.

Mathematics
(pages 701–717)
Part 1

1. **(5) 8000** Add the percent employed in a wholesale occupation to the percent employed in a health or education occupation.
20% + 12% = 32%
Multiply the result by the total number of people. 25 000 × 0.32 = 8000

Using your GED calculator:
25000 ⎯X⎯ 32 SHIFT = 8000

2. **(4) 5250** Subtract the percent employed in an entertainment occupation from the percent employed in a business, legal, or professional occupation. 22% − 1% = 21%
Multiply the result by the total number of people. 25 000 × 21% = 25 000 × 0.21 = 5250

Using your GED calculator:
25000 ⎯X⎯ 21 SHIFT = 5250

3. **(3) $14 300** Add all the deposits to the current balance; then subtract both checks from the result.
$15 000 + $1800 + $3000 + $900 = $20 700
$20 700 − $3600 − $2800 = $14 300

4. **4275** Think of the figure as a cube and a pyramid. Find the volumes separately and add the results.
Cube: $V = s^3$
$V = 15^3 = 3375$ cubic centimetres

Square pyramid: $V = \frac{1}{3} \times$ (base edge)^2 × height

$V = \frac{1}{3} \times 15^2 \times 12 = 900$ cm³

Add. $3375 + 900 = 4275$ cm³

5. **1693** Do the operations in the parentheses first, starting with the multiplication, then the addition. Then divide and add.
(908 + 23 × 48) ÷ 2 + 687
(908 + 1104) ÷ 2 + 687
2012 ÷ 2 + 687
1006 + 687 = 1693

Using your GED calculator:
⟦(⎯⎯ 908 + 23 ⎯X⎯ 48 ⎯⎯)⟧ ÷ 2
+ 687 = 1693

6.(4) 300% Subtract the original amount from the new amount and divide by the original amount. ($8 − $2) ÷ $2 = 3 Change the result to a percent by multiplying by 100. 3 × 100 = 300% Using your GED calculator:

[(--- 8 − 2 ---)] ÷ 2 SHIFT = 300

7. (4) $\frac{1}{50}$ Write a fraction with the total number of successful outcomes over the total number of possible outcomes. Reduce the fraction. $\frac{6}{300} = \frac{1}{50}$

8. (4) 860 Find the perimeter of the figure. Add the two lengths and the two widths.
310 + 310 + 120 + 120 = 860 m

9. (3) 496 Find the area. Multiply the length of the driving range by its width. 310 × 120 = 37 200 Divide the resulting area by the area covered by one bag of grass seed. 37 200 ÷ 75 = 496

10. (4) $320.00 The price of the stereo system after the discount is 85% of the original price (100% − 15%). Divide the discounted price of the stereo system by this percent. $272 ÷ 0.85 = $320

11. (3) $4.90 Substitute 24 for n and solve for C.
$$C = \$2.50 + \$0.10(24)$$
$$C = \$2.50 + \$2.40$$
$$C = \$4.90$$

12. 20 Let Timothy's age now = x and Albert's age now = $5x$. In 5 years, Timothy will be $x + 5$ and Albert will be $5x + 5$. At that time, Albert's age will be 4 times Timothy's age. Write an equation and solve.

$$4(x + 5) = 5x + 5$$
$$4x + 20 = 5x + 5$$
$$-x + 20 = 5$$
$$-x = -15$$
$$x = 15$$

Timothy is 15 now. In five years, he will be 20 years old.

13. 12 Use the Pythagorean Relationship to solve for b.
$$a^2 + b^2 = c^2$$
$$9^2 + b^2 = 15^2$$
$$81 + b^2 = 225$$
$$b^2 = 144$$
$$b = \sqrt{144} = 12$$

You may have recognized that 9 and 15 are multiples of 3 and 5. This triangle is related to the common 3-4-5 triangle. Since 3 × 3 = 9 and 3 × 5 = 15, the missing leg is 3 × 4 = 12.

14. (3) $14 000 × 0.0975 × 3.5 Change the rate of interest to a decimal. $9\frac{3}{4}\% = 0.0975$ Change the amount of time to a decimal. $3\frac{1}{2} = 3.5$
Use the interest formula. $i = prt = \$14\,000 \times 0.0975 \times 3.5$

15. (4) 120 $\triangle MON$ and $\triangle POQ$ are similar isosceles triangles. Therefore, the corresponding sides are proportional.
$$\frac{x}{24} = \frac{150}{30}$$
$$30x = 3600$$
$$x = 120$$

16. (3) (3.14)(6²)(350)

The first step in finding the volume is to find the area of the base. Remember, the radius is $\frac{1}{2}$ the diameter. Substitute the known values in the formula for finding the volume of a cylinder.
$$A = \pi r^2 \qquad V = Ah$$
$$A = 3.14\left(\frac{12}{2}\right)^2 \qquad V = 3.14(6^2)(350)$$
$$A = 3.14(6^2)$$

17. (3,−4) Start at the origin (0,0). Move 3 units to the right and 4 units down. The point is in quadrant IV.

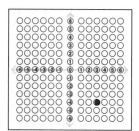

18. (5)

Solve the inequality for x. $6 − 5x < 7x − 6$
Add 6 to both sides. $12 − 5x < 7x$
Add $5x$ to both sides. $12 < 12x$
Divide both sides by 12. $1 < x$ or $x > 1$
Only option (5) shows the integer 1 circled and all values greater than 1 shaded.

19. (2) $79.39 List the amounts in the table in increasing or decreasing order.
$59.76, $63.15, $74.47, $84.31, $89.36, $90.12.

Since there are 6 amounts, find the average (mean) of the two middle numbers. ($74.47 + $84.31) ÷ 2 = $158.78 ÷ 2 = $79.39

20. **(4) $x + y = 2$** Find the ordered pair from a point on the graph: (2,0) or (0,2). Try the values for both of the points in each equation. If the point lies on the line, it will make the equation true.

21. **186** Add the five scores. Divide the result by the number of scores, 5.
$184 + 176 + 202 + 178 + 190 = 930 ÷ 5 = 186$

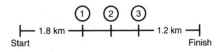

22. **$80.43** Add the two amounts that Areta borrowed.
$42.48 + $64.76 = $107.24

After she paid back $\frac{1}{4}$ of this amount, she still owed $\frac{3}{4}$ of this amount. Change $\frac{3}{4}$ to a decimal and multiply by thetotal amount.
$107.24 × 0.75 = $80.43

23. **(5) 2.2** Make a sketch and label the distance from the start to Checkpoint 1 (1.8 km) and the distance from Checkpoint 3 to the finish (1.2 km). Subtract the distances you know (1.8 + 1.2 = 3 km) from the total length of the race to find the distance from Checkpoint 1 to Checkpoint 3 (5 km − 3 km = 2 km). Since Checkpoint 2 is at the midpoint of this distance, Checkpoint 2 is 1 km from Checkpoint 1 and 1 km from Checkpoint 3. Add to find the distance from Checkpoint 2 to the finish line.
$1.0 + 1.2 = 2.2$

```
          ①   ②   ③
 ├ 1.8 km ┼──┼──┼ 1.2 km ┤
 Start                Finish
```

24. **(4) 18.8** The formula for finding the circumference of a circle is $C = \pi d$. Remember: diameter (d) = 2 × radius (r). Since the radius of the circle is 3 m, the diameter is 6 m. The circumference is 3.14 × 6, which equals 18.84 m. 18.84 rounds to 18.8 m.

25. **(2) $8.4 × 10^7$** You may want to use your calculator to perform the multiplication.
$$6000 × 14\,000 = 84\,000\,000$$
To write the number in scientific notation, you must place the decimal point after the first digit. To do so, you will move the decimal point 7 places to the left. The product is $8.4 × 10^7$.

Part 2

26. **(3) 2.14** Since the 7 in the thousandths place is greater than 5, increase the digit in the hundredths place by 1 and drop all the remaining digits to its right.

27. **(2) ∠2 and ∠6** If $m∠8 = 50°$, then $m∠6 = 130°$ because ∠6 and ∠8 are supplementary angles. The measure of ∠7 is also 130° because ∠6 and ∠7 are vertical angles. Since ∠2 corresponds to ∠6 and ∠3 corresponds to ∠7, these must also measure 130°. Only option (1) names two angles from those that measure 130°.

28. **(5) $44.52** Multiply the number of boxes in a case by the number of cases. 8 × 3.5 = 28 Multiply the result by the price of each box. $1.59 × 28 = $44.52

29. **(1) 30** Add the three outer edges that do not attach to the house. 10 + 12 + 8 = 30 m

30. **(4) $(12 × 8) + \frac{1}{4}(12 × 8)$** To find the area of the rectangle, multiply length by width (12 × 8). Since the area of the rectangle is four times the area of the triangle, the triangle is $\frac{1}{4}$ the area of the rectangle: $\frac{1}{4}(12 × 8)$. Add the two areas.

31. **28** Substitute the given values and evaluate the expression.
$$6x^2 \quad - \quad 5xy \quad - \quad 4y^2$$
$$6(2)(2) - 5(2)(-2) - 4(-2)(-2)$$
$$24 \quad + \quad 20 \quad - \quad 16 \quad = 28$$

32. **(5) 10 to 12 months** The line is the steepest (increases the most) from 10 months to 12 months.

33. **(5) 2.5** Matthew's mass after 1 year, or 12 months, is approximately 13 kg. Subtract the average mass of 10.5 kg from this amount.
$13 − 10.5 = 2.5$

34. **(2) $\frac{1}{5}$** Three of the 15 cards are less than 4: 3, 2, 1. The probability of drawing one of those three cards is $\frac{3}{15}$. Reduce. $\frac{3}{15} = \frac{1}{5}$

35. **(4) $\sqrt{12^2 - 7^2}$**
Since $c^2 - a^2 = b^2$, then $12^2 - 7^2 = b^2$. To set the left side of the equation equal to b, find the square root of both sides of the equation. $\sqrt{12^2 - 7^2} = b$

36. **(1) $-6x - (-6 + y)$** The product of −6 and x can be expressed as $-6x$. The sum of −6 and y can be written $(-6 + y)$. Only option (1) subtracts the sum from the product.

37. **(0, −4)** Substitute $x = 0$ for the y-intercept. Solve.

$$2x - y = 4$$
$$2(0) - y = 4$$
$$-y = 4$$
$$y = -4$$

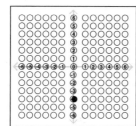

38. **(2) −1** Write an equation and solve.

$$2x + 3 = -x$$

Add x to both sides. $3x + 3 = 0$
Subtract 3 from both sides. $3x = -3$
Divide both sides by 3. $x = -1$

39. **(3) 85** Add all the grades. Divide the result by the number of grades.

$$\frac{60 + 85 + 95 + 80 + 95 + 95}{6} = 510 \div 6 = 85$$

40. **(5)** $\pi = \frac{C}{r}$ This formula gives $C = \pi r$ which is false. The correct formula is $C = \pi d$.

41. **(5) 150** The question asks for an approximate answer. Round 14.82 to 15. Multiply by 2 to find the distance going to and from work. $15 \times 2 = 30$ Multiply the distance by 5 days per week. $30 \times 5 = 150$

42. **(1)** $\frac{8}{\$15.92} = \frac{10}{?}$ Choose the proportion with ratios that compare the number of kilograms of turkey to the cost. $\frac{\text{kilograms}}{\$ \text{ cost}} = \frac{\text{kilograms}}{\$ \text{ cost}}$

43. **130** Change the mixed number to a decimal. $1\frac{1}{2} = 1.5$
Set up a proportion using the ratio of the number of kilometres to the number of hours. Solve for the unknown number of kilometres.
$\frac{78}{1.5} = \frac{?}{2.5}$; $78 \times 2.5 \div 1.5 = 130$

44. **(1)** $\angle ABE$ If $\angle ECD$ is a right angle, then its supplement, $\angle ECB$, must also be a right angle. If $\angle ECB$ measures 90°, then $\triangle ECB$ is a right triangle and $\angle CBE$ and $\angle BEC$ must be acute angles. If $\angle EBC$ is acute (less than 90°), then its supplement, $\angle ABE$, must be obtuse (greater than 90°).

45. **(4)** $x \leq -2$ The closed dot on -2 indicates that -2 is part of the solution set. The line is darkened to the left of -2 indicating that all values less than -2 are included in the solution set.

46. **(5)** $x + 6x + x + 6x > 110$ Make a sketch of a rectangle. Let x = the width and $6x$ = the length. The perimeter is equal to the sum of the lengths of the four sides: $x + 6x + x + 6x$. Only option (5) sets this sum as greater than 110.

47. **(4)** $m\angle 5 = 60°$ The problem gives the information $m\angle 3 = m\angle 4$. If $m\angle 3 = 60°$, then $m\angle 4 = 60°$. Since the sum of the angles in a triangle equals 180°, $m\angle 5$ must be 60° also. $180° - 60° - 60° = 60°$

48. **(3)** $79\frac{3}{4}$ Change $5\frac{1}{2}$ to 5.5 Multiply the number of baskets picked per hour by the number of hours. $14.5 \times 5.5 = 79.75$ Since answer choices are fractions, change 79.75 to $79\frac{3}{4}$.

49. **(3) 1356** Find the area of the rectangle and the area of the square. Then subtract the area of the square.

Rectangle: $A = lw$
            $A = 50 \times 30$
            $A = 1500 \text{ m}^2$
Square: $A = s^2$
            $A = 12^2$
            $A = 144 \text{ m}^2$
Subtract. $1500 - 144 = 1356$ square metres

50. **(2) 10:50 A.M.** Add the times of the three projects. $20 + 20 + 30 = 70$ min, or 1 hr 10 min Subtract the result from 12 noon, or 12 hr.

$$\begin{array}{lcl} 12 \text{ hr} & = & 11 \text{ hr } 60 \text{ min} \\ - \; 1 \text{ hr } 10 \text{ min} & = & - \; 1 \text{ hr } 10 \text{ min} \\ \hline & & 10 \text{ hr } 50 \text{ min} \end{array}$$

Simulated Tests

Tables, Graphs, Maps, and Diagrams

An Overview

Tables, graphs and charts, maps, and diagrams conveniently communicate information visually. They are widely used in newspapers, magazines, and businesses to convey complicated information or to impress a reader. The skills you will practise here transfer to many subjects. We recommend examining any charts, graphs, maps, and diagrams you come across in your daily life.

To understand a graph, table, map, or diagram follow these steps:

1. Read the title to determine what's being presented.
2. Read headings or labels.
3. Read any legend or key.
4. Read the units of measure (such as percent, centimetres, degrees, dollars) and note how they are marked.
5. Locate a fact and read the relationship of this fact to any other on the diagram.

Do a few questions and then check your answers. If you get something wrong—or even a lot of questions wrong—don't be discouraged. Here are some learning strategies:

- Redo the question and reflect on the book answer.
- Talk it over with a friend. Verbalizing helps learning.
- Sleep on the problem then come back to it with a clear mind.

Practice with Tables and Charts

A table is an arrangement of information or data usually in columns and rows. The simplest table is called a "two-column frequency table." The first column lists the classes into which the numerical data are grouped; the second column lists the frequency of occurrence for each class.

A chart is an effective way to visually communicate what numbers in a spreadsheet are saying. They are great for making comparisons, analyzing data, and showing trends. Charts depict only one set of mathematical or numerical data.

For more on tables and charts, see page 553.

Directions: Choose the one best answer to each question.

Question 1 refers to the following bus schedule.

5 Fairview / 6 Harewood Combo — Mon.–Sat. Nights / Sundays

City Centre Exch. to Harewood, the Univ. College & Jingle Pot

Monday – Saturday Night

Lv. City Centre Exch.	Lv. 4th at Howard	Lv. 8th at Park	Lv. 5th at Harewood Plaza	Lv. The College	Ar. Abbot at Westwood	Lv. Ashlee at Holland	Lv. The College	Ar. 5th at Harewood Plaza	Lv. 8th at Park	Ar. City Centre Exch.
-----	-----	-----	-----	-----	-----	-----	6:57	7:00	7:06	7:13
7:20	7:30	7:34	7:40	7:43	7:51	7:54	8:03	8:06	8:12	8:19
8:20	8:30	8:34	8:40	8:43	8:51	8:54	9:03	9:06	9:12	9:19
9:20	9:30	9:34	9:40	9:43	9:51	9:54	10:03	10:06	10:12	10:19
10:20	10:30	10:34	10:40	10:43	10:51	10:54	11:03	11:06	11:12	11:19
11:20	11:30	11:34	11:40	11:43	11:51	11:54	-----	-----	-----	-----

Sunday

Lv. City Centre Exch.	Lv. 4th at Howard	Lv. 8th at Park	Lv. 5th at Harewood Plaza	Lv. The College	Ar. Abbot at Westwood	Lv. Ashlee at Holland	Lv. The College	Ar. 5th at Harewood Plaza	Lv. 8th at Park	Ar. City Centre Exch.
9:17	9:27	9:31	9:37	9:40	9:48	9:51	10:00	10:03	10:09	10:16
10:17	10:27	10:31	10:37	10:40	10:48	10:51	11:00	11:03	11:09	11:16
11:17	11:27	11:31	11:37	11:40	11:48	11:51	12:00	12:03	12:09	12:16
12:17	12:27	12:31	12:37	12:40	12:48	12:51	1:00	1:03	1:09	1:16
1:17	1:27	1:31	1:37	1:40	1:48	1:51	2:00	2:03	2:09	2:16
2:17	2:27	2:31	2:37	2:40	2:48	2:51	3:00	3:03	3:09	3:16
3:17	3:27	3:31	3:37	3:40	3:48	3:51	4:00	4:03	4:09	4:16
4:17	4:27	4:31	4:37	4:40	4:48	4:51	5:00	5:03	5:09	5:16
5:17	5:27	5:31	5:37	5:40	5:48	5:51	6:00	6:03	6:09	6:16
6:17	6:27	6:31	6:37	6:40	6:48	6:51	7:00	7:03	7:09	7:16

All trips are accessible to persons with disabilities

1. You want to arrive at Ashlee/Holland just before noon on a Sunday morning. What time should you leave from 4th at Howard?

   (1) 11:17
   (2) 11:27
   (3) 11:30
   (4) 11:31
   (5) 11:51

Question 2 refers to the following distance chart.

DISTANCES IN KILOMETRES BETWEEN SOME CITIES

	Calgary	Edmonton	Halifax	Kitchener	Oshawa	Saskatoon	Sudbury	Vancouver
Calgary		299	4973	3543	3354	620	3057	1057
Edmonton	299		5013	3564	3375	528	3078	1244
Halifax	4973	5013		1897	1708	4485	1935	6050
Kitchener	3343	3564	1897		189	3036	463	4601
Oshawa	3354	3375	1708	189		2847	380	4412
Saskatoon	620	528	4485	3036	2847		2538	1677
Sudbury	3057	3078	1935	463	380	2538		4102
Vancouver	1057	1244	6050	4601	4412	1677	4102	

2. According to the chart, what is the distance between Halifax and Kitchener?

   (1) 5013 km
   (2) 4973 km
   (3) 3375 km
   (4) 1897 km
   (5) 299 km

Question 3 refers to the following table.

The Trans Canada Trail is a shared-use recreational trail that winds its way through every province and territory, linking more than 800 communities along its route. The Trans Canada Trail is the longest recreational trail in the world. Currently, 62 percent of the trail is "registered," meaning that landowners have given permission to have their land be part of the Trail.

TRANS CANADA TRAIL

REGISTERED TRAIL		
Province / Territory	Total Length (km)	% Registered
Alberta	2 200	51
British Columbia	2 700	40
Manitoba	1 188	92
New Brunswick	820	77
Newfoundland	900	98
Northwest Territories	640	92
Nova Scotia	700	77
Nunavut	180	100
Ontario	4 000	56
Prince Edward Island	350	100
Quebec	1 400	87
Saskatchewan	1 400	46
Yukon	1 600	45
National Total	**18 078**	**62**

3. When completed, what will be the total length of the Trans Canada Trail?

   (1) 18 078 km

   (2) 10 078 km

   (3)   2700 km

   (4)   2200 km

   (5) None of the above

Question 4 refers to the following table.

Town / City	Population — 2001 Census
Churchill, Town	963
Flin Flon, City	6 000
Gillam, Town	1 178
Grand Rapids, Town	355
Leaf Rapids, Town	1 309
Lynn Lake, Town	699
Snow Lake, Town	1 207
The Pas, Town	5 795

4. Tables can be converted to line, bar, or circle graphs depending on which is most effective. The information in the above table would best suit which type of graph?

   (1) a circle graph because circles look nice on paper

   (2) a line graph because the populations increase from 355 to 13 256

   (3) a pictograph because one symbol could represent 500 people

   (4) a bar graph because it shows differences clearly

   (5) a circle graph, but put the population numbers inside the circle

Answers start on page 892.

Appendix A: Tables, Graphs, Maps, and Diagrams

Practice with Graphs

Graphs present numerical facts and allow the viewer to compare and draw quick conclusions.

Directions: Choose the one best answer to each question.

Line Graphs

Line graphs show the relationship between two sets of information and are represented by a straight, broken, or curved line. Line graphs illustrate changes such as an increase or decrease in quantity by the rising or falling of the line. For more information on line graphs, see page 554.

Questions 5 and 6 refer to the following graph.

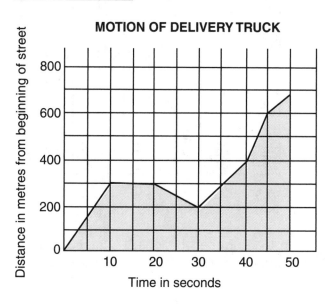

5. The graph shows the motion of a delivery truck whose driver is trying to find a particular house on a long, dark street. How far is the truck from its starting point after 35 seconds?

   (1) 100 m
   (2) 200 m
   (3) 300 m
   (4) 400 m
   (5) 500 m

6. How long does it take the truck to travel 600 m?

   (1) 50 seconds
   (2) 45 seconds
   (3) 40 seconds
   (4) 30 seconds
   (5) 25 seconds

Question 7 refers to the following two line graphs.

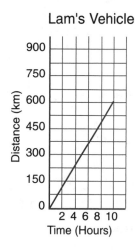 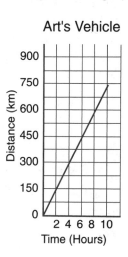

7. The line graphs model the distance Lam's and Art's vehicles travelled over time. Both vehicles started off at the same time and with the same amount of gas in their tanks. Based on the charts what can be concluded?

   (1) Lam's vehicle has a bigger engine.
   (2) Art drove his vehicle faster.
   (3) Art's vehicle gets better gas kilometrage.
   (4) Art's vehicle is a sports car.
   (5) Lam and Art travelled the same distance.

Question 8 refers to the following graph.

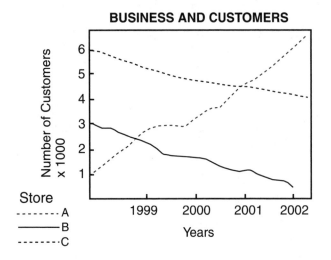

BUSINESS AND CUSTOMERS

Store
------- A
——— B
-------C

Bar Graphs

Bar graphs represent the relationship or comparison between two or more sets of data. The bars may be horizontal or vertical. Component bar graphs have several coloured or shaded areas on one bar. These differently shaded areas show different sub-classifications. For more on bar graphs, see page 554.

Question 9 refers to the following bar graph.

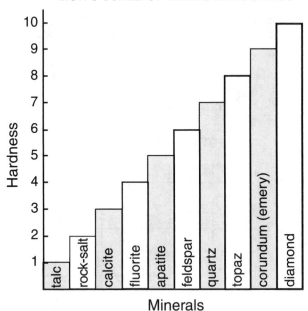

MOH'S SCALE OF MINERAL HARDNESS

8. Word of mouth can affect the competitive environment. Customers who are happy with the quality of service they receive will often tell other potential customers about their experience. What trend in the above graph might suggest that store A has quality service?

   (1) Store B and C had a decline in customers.

   (2) The economy is improving.

   (3) The graph of store A shows an increasing number of customers.

   (4) People will continue to shop at store A.

   (5) Store B is going broke.

9. In 1812, Frederich Mohs (1773–1839), a German mineralogist, created a scale of mineral hardness based on ten common minerals. What number is quartz on Moh's Scale of Mineral Hardness?

   (1) 4

   (2) 5

   (3) 6

   (4) 7

   (5) 8

Questions 10 and 11 refer to the following bar graph.

FUEL COST COMPARISON (PER YEAR)

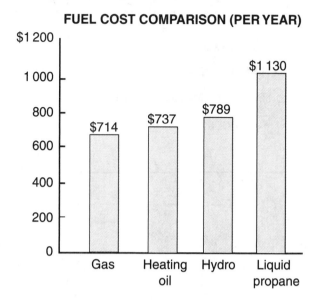

10. According to the graph, what is the difference in cost between the two highest priced fuels?

    (1) $416
    (2) $393
    (3) $341
    (4) $143
    (5) $23

11. The above graph was part of an advertisement that was mailed out to people's homes. Based on this graph, what type of company is <u>least</u> likely to have sent out this ad?

    (1) a liquid propane company
    (2) a hydro company
    (3) a heating oil company
    (4) a gas company
    (5) cannot be determined

Questions 12 and 13 refer to the following bar graph.

A survey at a correctional centre was conducted among 132 inmates. This graph represents the response to the question, "What was your reason for leaving high school?"

REASONS FOR LEAVING HIGH SCHOOL

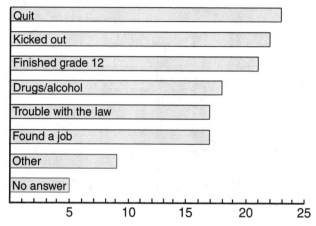

12. What is the ratio of those who quit to the entire group?

    (1) 23/109
    (2) 23/132
    (3) 109/23
    (4) 132/23
    (5) 23/25

13. What is the main reason for using a bar graph rather than a pie graph to show this data?

    (1) It more clearly shows how people view education.
    (2) It provides a better understanding of the source of the information.
    (3) It more clearly compares data for which small differences exist.
    (4) It illustrates more clearly why people are in correction centres.
    (5) It shows the information in a more attractive manner.

The following graph shows the points scored by five different teams in their practice and playoff basketball games.

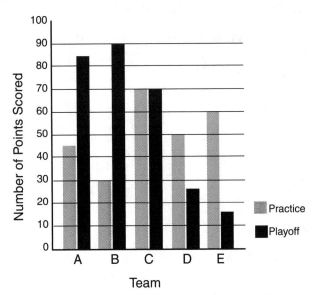

14. Which team scored the fewest points in the practice game?

    (1) Team A
    (2) Team B
    (3) Team C
    (4) Team D
    (5) Team E

15. Which team improved the most between the practice game and the playoff game?

    (1) Team A
    (2) Team B
    (3) Team C
    (4) Team D
    (5) Team E

SAMPLING OF MEN AND WOMEN WHO PREFER CLASSIC ROCK TO OTHER MUSIC

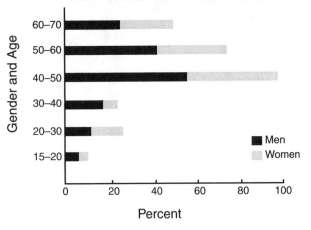

16. The above graph represents a sampling of vacationers of different age groups at Long Beach, B.C., who were asked whether they preferred classic rock to other music. This component bar chart shows different subclassifications: men and women. The total length of each bar is 100 percent of the total target population. Based on this information, what may one conclude?

    (1) The 15–20 age group prefer rap.
    (2) Men in the 30–40 age group do not like classic rock.
    (3) Women in the 60–70 age group like classic rock while men do not.
    (4) Most men and women in the 40–50 age group prefer classic rock.
    (5) Nothing can be concluded.

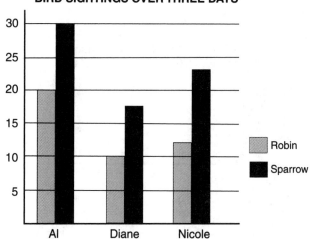

BIRD SIGHTINGS OVER THREE DAYS

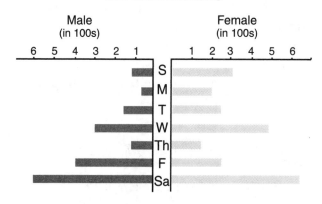

XYZ MALL PATRONS

Legend: S=Sunday, M=Monday, T=Tuesday, W=Wednesday
Th=Thursday, F=Friday, Sa=Saturday

17. Al lives on the west coast, Nicole lives on the east coast, and Diane lives in Northern Ontario. The three friends are bird watchers who communicate regularly by e-mail. They recorded their bird sightings over a three-day period, and recorded the results on the above graph. Based on this graph, how many more robins did Al see than Diane?

   (1) Al saw three times as many robins as Diane.

   (2) Diane saw fewer robins than Nicole.

   (3) Al saw more sparrows than either Diane or Nicole.

   (4) Nicole saw more sparrows than Diane.

   (5) Al saw twice as many robins as Diane.

18. Which of the following best summarizes the information in the graph?

   (1) Females are most likely to shop on Sunday, and males are least likely to shop on Monday.

   (2) Female and males are equally likely to shop on Wednesday.

   (3) Males are least likely to shop on Monday and more likely to shop on Saturday, while females are least likely to shop on Thursday and most likely to shop on Saturday.

   (4) Females will shop on Monday and Friday.

   (5) Males like to shop on their day off.

Circle (Pie) Graphs

Circle (or pie) graphs show how a part of something relates to the whole. A circle is divided into wedge-like sections. Each section is a percentage (or fraction) of the entire circle. The entire circle represents 100 percent (or the total) of the data. For more on circle graphs, see page 555.

Question 19 refers to the following pie graph.

WHICH TAX UPSETS YOU THE MOST?

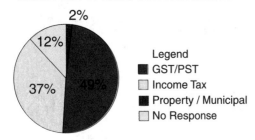

Legend
■ GST/PST
☐ Income Tax
■ Property / Municipal
☐ No Response

19. A teacher at a large school took a poll of her colleagues to find out which tax upset each of them the most. She recorded the responses in the above graph. According to the poll, which tax did the teachers find the least upsetting?

   (1) all are upsetting
   (2) income tax
   (3) GST/sales tax
   (4) no tax is upsetting
   (5) property/municipal taxes

Questions 20 and 21 refer to the following graph.

The following pie graph represents a city's budget.

HOW THE CITY SPENDS ITS SHARE OF YOUR PROPERTY TAX DOLLARS

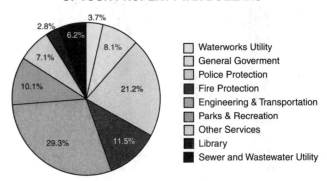

☐ Waterworks Utility
☐ General Goverment
☐ Police Protection
■ Fire Protection
▨ Engineering & Transportation
▨ Parks & Recreation
☐ Other Services
■ Library
■ Sewer and Wastewater Utility

20. Municipal spending is funded by property taxes. Didi's property tax is $1200. How much of her tax money goes toward Sewer and Wastewater utility?

   (1) $33.60
   (2) $44.40
   (3) $74.40
   (4) $97.20
   (5) $744.00

21. Approximately what fraction of the entire budget goes toward Parks and Recreation?

   (1) 1/10
   (2) 1/50
   (3) 7/100
   (4) 3/10
   (5) cannot be determined

Questions 22 and 23 refer to the following pie graph.

**$500 MILLION IN
TRANSPORTATION IMPROVEMENTS**

Amounts in Millions

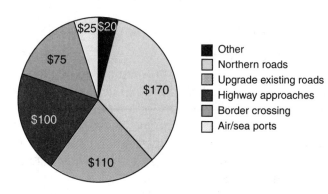

- ■ Other
- ☐ Northern roads
- ▨ Upgrade existing roads
- ■ Highway approaches
- ▨ Border crossing
- ☐ Air/sea ports

Question 24 refers to the following pie graphs.

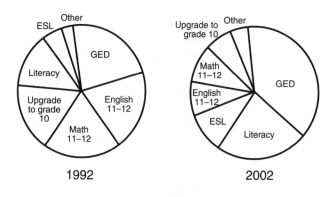

1992   2002

22. What is total amount of money spent on the two largest transportation sectors?

   (1) $170 million

   (2) $220 million

   (3) $280 million

   (4) $380 million

   (5) $500 million

23. How much more money is reserved for border crossing than for air/sea ports?

   (1) $25 million

   (2) $50 million

   (3) $75 million

   (4) $100 million

   (5) $500 million

24. Statistics can be helpful in projecting future trends. At a local education centre, trends in education were captured in the pie charts. Which statement is supported by the pie graphs?

   (1) The education centre should decrease its budget for literacy books.

   (2) Many people will graduate from college or university.

   (3) Most people over the age of 25 are working on the GED.

   (4) The number of GED candidates will increase.

   (5) ESL students will soon take the GED.

Questions 25 and 26 refer to the following circle graph.

The following circle graph shows the food content of one kilogram of a no-name cheese.

FOOD CONTENT OF A CHEESE

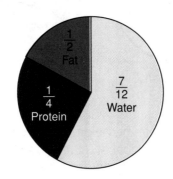

25. If you purchase 6 kg of this no-name cheese, how much of it is water content?

   (1) 5 kg
   (2) 3.5 kg
   (3) 2.5 kg
   (4) 2 kg
   (5) 1 kg

26. If you converted each of the fractions in the chart to a percent, what should the sum of the percents be?

   (1) 25 percent
   (2) 50 percent
   (3) 75 percent
   (4) 100 percent
   (5) cannot be determined

Pictographs

Pictographs use a series of small identifying pictures (or symbols) to present the data. Each symbol represents a particular number of units. Pictographs may be horizontal or vertical.

Question 27 refers to the following pictograph.

The Three Sisters
Indigenous people of North America would plant squash, beans, and corn in a mound together. The corn provided support for the beans while the squash covered the ground, preventing water evaporation. This tradition of "companion planting" is based on the idea that all living things rely on each other for survival.

DWAYNE'S GARDEN

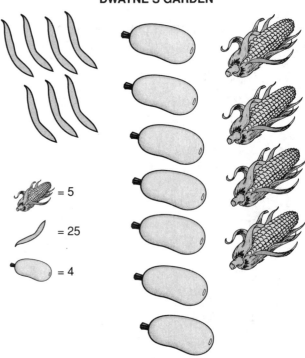

27. Dwayne was proud of his small garden's yield as a result of companion planting. How many more green beans than squash did his garden produce?

   (1) 20
   (2) 26
   (3) 147
   (4) 179
   (5) cannot be determined

Answers start on page 892.

Practice with Maps

A <u>map</u> is a representation of part of the Earth's surface. Maps can show locations of places and show patterns of distribution. Maps and globes help you visualize location and distance. For more on maps, see page 268

Directions: Choose the <u>one best answer</u> to each question.

Questions 28 to 31 refer to the following contour map and chart:

Map Legend: In the following contour map, Highway 238 travels through a park and crosses over the Coldwater River. The arrow in the top lefthand corner indicates north and the contour intervals are at 100-m increments.	‖ Bridge **X** Fire Tower	Scale 1 unit = 1 km 0 1 2 3 4 5

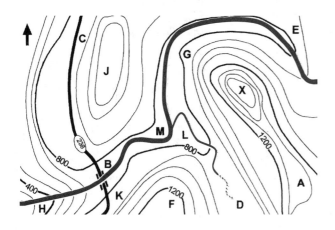

28. What is the highest point of elevation on the map?

(1) A
(2) F
(3) H
(4) X
(5) J

29. If you wanted to a hike from point C to point A, which route of travel would be the least difficult and less likely to get you wet?

(1) C to J to G to X to A
(2) C to B to M to L to D to A
(3) C to B to K to L to D to A
(4) C to B to K to F to D to A
(5) C to G to E to A

30. In what general direction does the Coldwater River flow?

(1) northeast to southwest
(2) southeast to northwest
(3) northwest to southeast
(4) southwest to northeast
(5) south to north

31. Near what point is the river most likely to have rapids or a waterfall?

(1) B
(2) C
(3) E
(4) H
(5) M

Answers start on page 893.

Practice with Diagrams

A <u>diagram</u> is a plan or figure drawn to explain a machine or idea. Diagrams show how something works and contain data in picture form. When you look at a diagram, concentrate on what is actually shown rather than adding your own interpretation.

<u>Directions:</u> Choose the <u>one best answer</u> to each question.

<u>Questions 32 and 33</u> refer to the following passages and diagrams.

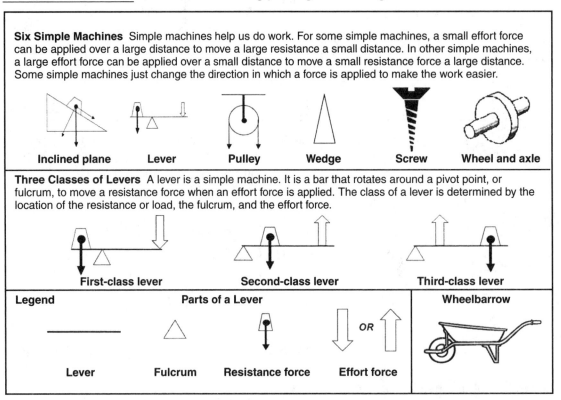

Six Simple Machines Simple machines help us do work. For some simple machines, a small effort force can be applied over a large distance to move a large resistance a small distance. In other simple machines, a large effort force can be applied over a small distance to move a small resistance force a large distance. Some simple machines just change the direction in which a force is applied to make the work easier.

Inclined plane   Lever   Pulley   Wedge   Screw   Wheel and axle

Three Classes of Levers A lever is a simple machine. It is a bar that rotates around a pivot point, or fulcrum, to move a resistance force when an effort force is applied. The class of a lever is determined by the location of the resistance or load, the fulcrum, and the effort force.

First-class lever   Second-class lever   Third-class lever

Legend   Parts of a Lever   Wheelbarrow

Lever   Fulcrum   Resistance force   Effort force   OR

32. What is the point of rotation for a lever?

    (1) the wheel and axle

    (2) the wedge

    (3) a second-class lever

    (4) the effort force

    (5) the fulcrum

33. How would the pulley shown in the diagram make it easier to do work?

    (1) A small effort force is applied over a large distance to move a large resistance a small distance.

    (2) A large effort force is applied over a small distance to move a small resistance force a large distance.

    (3) The direction of the effort force required to move the resistance force is changed.

    (4) 1 and 3 are correct

    (5) 2 and 3 are correct

Questions 34 to 37 refer to the following passage and diagrams.

An object placed on three inclined planes exerts a downward force or weight indicated by the arrow labelled **W**. For each inclined plane, this force can be resolved or separated into two forces: F_p and F_n. F_p represents the force parallel to the inclined plane, and F_n represents the force normal to, or perpendicular to, the inclined plane.

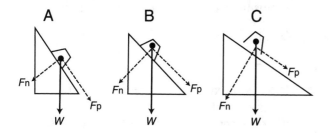

34. Which statement or statements are true for inclined plane A?

    (1) The force parallel to the inclined plane F_p is larger than that for the other inclined planes.

    (2) An object pushed up this inclined plane would require more force than the others.

    (3) A force is applied over the longest distance when pushing an object up this inclined plane.

    (4) (1) and (2) are true.

    (5) (1), (2), and (3) are true.

35. Which of the following is true for inclined plane B with a height and length that are the same?

    (1) The weight is less than the normal and parallel forces.

    (2) The normal force is the same as the parallel force.

    (3) The normal force is greater than the parallel force.

    (4) The normal force is less than the parallel force.

    (5) The normal force and the parallel force are perpendicular to the weight.

36. What would happen to the normal force if the weight of an object on inclined plane C were increased?

    (1) It increases and the parallel force would remain the same.

    (2) It remains the same and the parallel force would decrease.

    (3) It decreases and the parallel force would increase.

    (4) It increases and the parallel force would increase.

    (5) It increases and the parallel force would decrease.

37. Which statement is true when comparing the inclined plane C to A and B?

    (1) Inclined plane C requires the largest effort force applied over the longest distance.

    (2) Inclined plane C requires the largest effort force applied over the shortest distance.

    (3) Inclined plane C requires the same effort force applied over the longest distance.

    (4) Inclined plane C requires the least effort force applied over the longest distance.

    (5) None of the statements are true.

Answers start on page 894.

Answers to Appendix A

Practice with Tables and Charts
(pages 879–880)

1. **(2) 11:27** Locate Ashlee/Holland then move down the row past the "Sunday" line to the time closest to noon (11:51). From here move left along that row until you get to the 4th at Howard column. You should be on 11:27.

2. **(4) 1897 km** Using the top row of city names locate Halifax then move down the column until you get to the Kitchener row. You will see 1897, which is the distance in kilometres.

3. **(1) 18 078 km** A reminder to read all sections of a graph, table or chart. The bottom line says "National Total" and by reading across you see 18 078.

4. **(4) a bar graph because it shows differences clearly** Option (4) is the best because you can put the actual numbers on top or inside the bar clearly. Option (1) is not correct, because it's important for a graph to look nice, appearance is not the primary concern. Option (2) is not a good answer because the line graph would be very tall or the scale difficult to read. Option (3) is not a good answer because numbers are varied and there is no easy multiple of them all. Option (5), a circle graph, would be too cluttered.

Practice with Graphs
(pages 881–888)

5. **(3) 300 m** Read the time line to 35 seconds, and then move up to where the 35 second line intersects the graph line. This intersection point is on the horizontal 300-m line.

6. **(2) 45 seconds** Read the vertical (distance in metres) axis to 600 m. Read across to where it intersects the graph. The intersection point is on the vertical 45 seconds line.

7. **(2) Art drove his vehicle faster.** Art drove his vehicle faster because, as shown on the graph, at the end of 10 hours Art had travelled 750 km while Lam had travelled only 600 km. Whether the engine is stronger, faster or has better kilometrage or even if it's a sport car has nothing to do with the question. Art could have an old car that he drove faster.

8. **(3) The graph of store A shows an increasing number of customers.** Options (1) and (5) are true, but they don't address the question. Option (2) doesn't relate to the question. Option (4) may be true, but we cannot say this from the information in the graph.

9. **(4) 7** Start at the minerals (horizontal) axis, find quartz and read up to where it intersects the hardness axis, at 7.

10. **(3) $341** the two highest fuels are liquid propane at $1130 and hydro at $789. Find the difference between the two: $1130 – $789 = $341.

11. **(1) a liquid propane company** The company least likely to have sent out this ad would be one with the highest cost associated with its product, since this would not be good advertising for the company.

12. **(2) 23/132** This is a ratio/proportion question. Read the graph to find the number who quit, which is 23 people. The question tells you there are 132 in the entire group. So, ratio of the number who quit over the entire group is 23 over 132.

13. **(3) It more clearly compares data for which small differences exist.** Options (1), (2), and (4) have no bearing on the graph. Option (5) may be true, but is not the main reason for using a bar graph.

14. **(2) Team B** Using the key locate the practice bar. Compare all practice bars to find the lowest one. Team B scored 30 points, which is lower than all the rest.

15. **(2) Team B** Team B had both the lowest score in practice and the highest score in the playoff; therefore, it made the greatest improvement.

16. **(4) Most men and women in the 40–50 age group prefer classic rock.** Option (1) can't be supported in the graph. Options (2) and (3) are false, since the graph shows they do like classic rock. Option (5) isn't supported by the graph.

17. **(5) Al saw twice as many robins as Diane.** Option (1) is incorrect since Al didn't see 30 robins, or three times as many. Option (2) is wrong. Diane did see fewer than Nicole, but this

doesn't answer the question. Options (3) and (5) are true but don't address the question.

18. **(3) Males are least likely to shop on Monday and more likely to shop on Saturday, while females are least likely to shop on Thursday and most likely to shop on Saturday.** This is the only statement that addresses both male and female <u>and</u> when they most and least likely to shop. Options (1), (2), and (4) give only part of the answer. Option (5) is not supported by the graph.

19. **(5) property/municipal taxes** Option (1) is not correct because the question asks for <u>least</u> <u>upsetting</u>. In option (2) income tax is 37 percent. In option (3) GST/PST is 49 percent. Option (4) is not true for obviously some taxes are upsetting. So, option (5) property/municipal taxes at 12 percent is least upsetting.

20. **(3) $74.40** This is a percent problem. The whole (all of Didi's taxes) is $1200. Sewer and water utility is 6.2%. One way to find the part is to use the formula:

    Let P = Part and W = Whole

    $P = W \times \%$ (i.e. Part = Whole multiplied by Percent)

    $P = 1200 \times 6.2\%$

    $P = 1200 \times 0.062$ (remember, 6.2% = 0.062)

    $P = 74.40$

21. **(1) $\frac{1}{10}$** Parks and Recreation is 10.1% of the whole (100%) of the budget. Write that in fraction form, $\frac{10.1\%}{100\%}$, which reduces to about $\frac{1}{10}$.

22. **(3) $280 million** The two greatest sectors are Northern roads and Upgrade existing roads. $170 million + $110 million = $280 million.

23. **(2) $50 million** Border crossing, which is $75 million, minus $25 million air/sea ports, equals $50 million.

24. **(4) The number of GED candidates will increase.** The GED sector gets larger from 1992 to 2002. Options (1), (2), and (5) don't relate to the question asked. Option (3) isn't supported on the graphs.

25. **(2) 3.5 kg** The graph shows $\frac{7}{12}$ of the cheese, at any weight, is water. You purchase 6 kg. So $6 \text{ kg} \times \frac{7}{12} = \frac{42}{12} = 3\frac{6}{12}$ (or 3.5)

26. **(4) 100%** Since all circle graphs represent the whole, the total percentage is 100%.

27. **(3) 147.** According to the legend, each bean image is equal to 25 beans. Seven bean drawings are shown, or $7 \times 25 = 175$ beans. Each squash

image represents 4 squash. Seven squash drawings are shown, so there are $7 \times 4 = 28$ squash. One hundred and seventy-five beans minus 28 squash equal 147.

Practice with Maps
(page 889)

28. **(4) X** (Comprehension) The contour intervals range from 300 m to 1500 m. The contour interval for 1500 m surrounds the point X on the map. All other points are at a lower elevation. Option (1) is for point A, which is between the contour intervals for 1300 m and 1400 m and is the second highest point on the map. Option (2) is for point F, which is within the contour interval for 1200 m, the third highest point on the map. Option (3) is for point H, which is between the contour intervals for 300 m and 400 m, the lowest point on the map. Option (5) is for point J, which is within the contour interval for 1100 m.

29. **(3) C to B to K to L to D to A** (Analysis) This route would be the least difficult as it follows a relatively level route until the final part of the hike in which you would travel uphill from D to A. This route would allow you to stay dry, as you would use the bridge to cross the river. Option (1) is incorrect as you would walk over a hill and get wet crossing the river travelling from C to J to G, and then you travel up the steep hill to the Fire Tower at X, only then to descent to A. Option (2) is incorrect as you would get wet as you cross the river travelling between points M and L. Option (4) is incorrect as you would travel over a hill as you travel from K to F to D. Option (5) is incorrect as you would travel over a hill and get wet as you cross the river twice travelling from C to G to E.

30. **(1) northeast to southwest** (Analysis) The passage mentions that the arrow on the upper-left side of the map indicates the direction of north for the map. The contour intervals crossed by the Coldwater River indicate a general decrease in elevation and a river flows downhill from the northeast to southwest. Options (2) and (3) are incorrect as the map symbols do not indicate a river flowing between these directions. Option (4) is incorrect as this would suggest a flow of water uphill according to the elevations indicated by the contour intervals. Option (5) is incorrect as the map symbols do not indicate a river flowing between these directions. The passage and the north-south thick black line with route symbol 238 indicate a highway, not a river.

31. **(4) H** (Evaluation) Considering the contour intervals near point H and the distance scale of the map legend, the elevation of the river decreases from more than 700 m to less than 300 m over a distance of only 3 km to 4 km. This is a considerable decrease in elevation over a relatively short distance, suggesting the presence of rapids or waterfalls. Options (1), (3), and (5) are incorrect as the contour lines near points B, M, and G indicate that the river is relatively level and less likely to have rapids or waterfalls. Option (2) is incorrect as point C is near Highway 238, not the river.

Practice with Diagrams
(pages 890–891)

32. **(5) the fulcrum** (Comprehension) The second passage describes the fulcrum as the pivot point of a lever. The first row of the diagram shows a lever as one of the six simple machines while the second row shows the three classes of levers. The third row shows symbols used to represent the parts of a lever in the first two rows of the diagram. Options (1) and (2) are incorrect as the wheel and axle and the wedge are shown in the first row of the diagram as examples of other simple machines. Option (3) is incorrect as the second row of the diagram shows the second-class lever as one of the three classes of levers. Option (4) is incorrect as the effort force is described in the passage and shown in the third row of the diagram not to be the fulcrum.

33. **(3) The direction of the effort force required to move the resistance force is changed.** (Analysis) An object that needs to be lifted has a weight or downward resistance force that could only be moved by an upward force. The pulley in the diagram would change the direction of the effort force downward rather than upward. Options (1) and (2) and therefore (4) and (5) are incorrect as the pulley does not alter the size of the effort and resistance forces or the distances through which they are applied. Only the direction of the effort force is changed.

34. **(4) 1 and 2 are true.** (Analysis) Both options (1) and (2) are correct since inclined plane A has the steepest slope that resolves the weight of the object to be moved into two forces with the parallel force being larger than that for the other inclined planes. To overcome this larger parallel force a greater effort force would be required to move the object up the slope. Option (3) is incorrect as the length of the slope for inclined plane A is shorter than the slopes of the other inclined planes. This would make the individual choices for options (1) and (2) incorrect as both are true.

35. **(2) The normal force is the same as the parallel force.** (Analysis) The length and height of the inclined plane are equal. Therefore, the weight would resolve into a parallel force and a normal force that are equal. Options (1), (2), and (3) are incorrect as the parallel and normal forces can only be different if the length and height of the inclined plane are different.

36. **(4) It would increase and the parallel force would increase.** (Comprehension) The weight is a force that can be resolved into parallel and normal forces when placed on an inclined plane. If the weight increases then the resolved parallel and normal forces increase as well. Options (1), (2), (3), and (5) are incorrect as the resolved parallel and normal forces can only increase if the weight increases.

37. **(4) Inclined plane C requires the least effort force applied over the longest distance.** (Analysis) Inclined plane C has the least slope of the three inclined planes. Therefore, the weight of an object placed on inclined plane C would resolve into a parallel force that is smaller than the normal force, and also the smallest of the three inclined planes. However, the effort force would be applied over a greater distance than for the other inclined planes. Options (1), (2), and (3) are incorrect, as the parallel force would resolve to be the smallest parallel force being applied over the greatest distance. Option (5) is incorrect since option (4) is true.

GED Study Planner

Skill to be mastered: _____

Content area	
Lesson or project	
Special instructions	
Materials needed	
Date started	
Date completed	

What did you learn from this lesson? _____

_____

_____

_____

_____

What is one thing you need to work on to improve your skills in this area?

_____

_____

_____

_____

Essay Self-Assessment

Select your best writing samples. List them below.

Title or Topic

Date Written

_____   _____

_____   _____

_____   _____

_____   _____

_____   _____

(Continue the list on a separate piece of paper and attach.)

Choose the piece that you think is your best work.

Title or Topic:

_____

Explain why you think this is your best work to date.

_____

_____

_____

_____

_____

_____

What is one thing you need to work on to improve your writing?

_____

_____

_____

_____

Idea Map Form

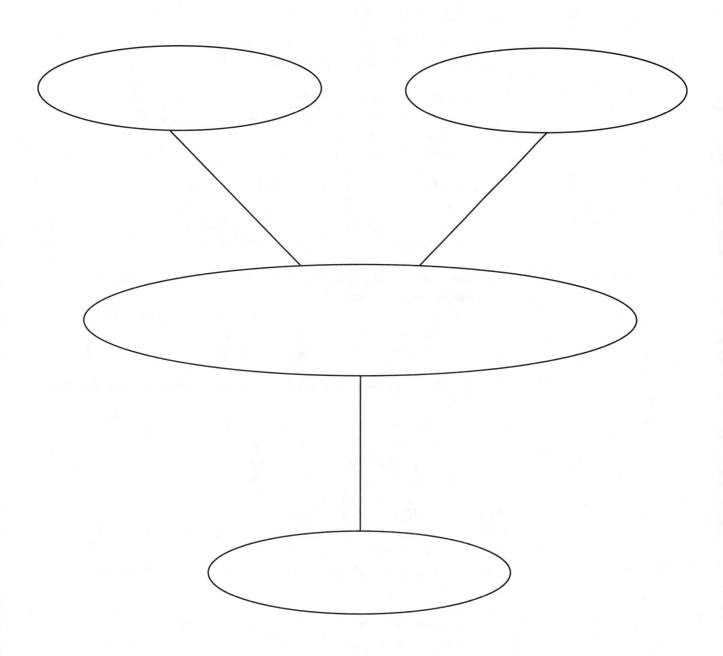

Writer's Checklist

Sentence Structure

When you edit your own writing or a passage on the GED Language Arts, Writing Test, ask yourself these questions:

❏ **Are all sentences complete?**
Each sentence has a subject and verb and expresses a complete thought.
Example: *Sarah had a good day.*

❏ **Are all sentences correctly punctuated?**
There are no run-on sentences and no comma splices. Each sentence has correct end punctuation.
Example: *Sarah had a good day at work.*

❏ **Are ideas combined smoothly and effectively in compound sentences?**
Equal ideas in independent clauses are connected with an appropriate coordinating conjunction and a comma.
Example: *She had written a memo, and her boss complimented her.*

❏ **Are ideas combined smoothly and effectively in complex sentences?**
A main idea is connected with additional information by an appropriate subordinating conjunction.
Example: *Because her meeting was running late, she had to skip lunch.*

❏ **Are details combined smoothly and effectively?**
Sentences vary in amount of detail and structure, without a series of short, choppy sentences.
Example: *Sarah works in a downtown real estate office five days a week.*

❏ **Do items in series have parallel structure?**
Items in series are expressed in the same form and separated by commas.
Example: *Her duties are to handle incoming calls, place print ads, and write televised listings.*

❏ **Are modifiers clear and understandable?**
Modifying words and phrases are placed near the words they describe.
Example: *Going home, she felt good about her day's work.*

Organization

When you edit your own writing or a passage on the GED Language Arts, Writing Test, ask yourself these questions:

❑ **Is the text divided into paragraphs where appropriate?**
Each paragraph has a main idea and supporting details that explain that idea.

❑ **Is each paragraph unified and coherent?**
The ideas in each sentence of a paragraph clearly support and relate to the main idea, and the ideas are presented in a logical order.

❑ **Does each paragraph have a topic sentence?**
The topic sentence states the main idea of the paragraph.

❑ **Do transitions show how ideas are related?**
Clue words and phrases connect one sentence to the next related sentence and one paragraph to the next related paragraph.

Example:

Many people want to own their homes, but owning can be expensive and stressful. **For one thing,** you need to come up with a down payment. **For another,** repairs can be costly, and repair companies can be unreliable. ~~Our teenaged babysitter is pretty unreliable, too.~~ **Finally,** property taxes are another hidden expense. **All told,** home ownership can be worrisome and costly.

The topic sentence is circled. Transitions are identified in bold text. A sentence that is irrelevant to the main idea is crossed out.

Usage

When you edit your own writing or a passage on the GED Language Arts, Writing Test, ask yourself these questions:

❏ **Do all subjects and verbs agree?**

Singular subjects have singular verbs.
Example: *Baseball is a popular sport.*

Compound and plural subjects have plural verbs.
Example: *Football and basketball are popular, too.*

Subjects and verbs agree, regardless of interrupting phrases or inverted order.
Example: *A very popular sport at the Olympics is figure skating.*

❏ **Are verb tenses consistent and correct?**

The past, present, and future tenses of verbs correctly show the timing of actions.
Example: *I go to Wood County Community College.*
Example: *Last fall I enrolled in a GED course.*
Example: *Next spring I will pass the GED Test.*

❏ **Are verb forms correct?**

The past and past participle forms of verbs, especially of irregular verbs, are used correctly.
Example: *My 90-year-old grandmother has seen some strange things in her lifetime.*

❏ **Are pronouns used correctly?**

Pronouns agree with their antecedents in person, number, and gender.
Example: *Anwar takes the bus to his job every day.*

Subject pronouns are used as subjects.
Example: *He likes the company that he works for.*

Object pronouns are used as objects of verbs or prepositions.
Example: *Anwar's boss has promised him a raise.*

The antecedent of each pronoun is clear.
Example: *Anwar and his boss are talking about Anwar's idea for improving customer service.*

Mechanics

When you edit your own writing or a passage on the GED Language Arts, Writing Test, ask yourself these questions:

❑ **Are words capitalized correctly?**

Proper nouns and adjectives are capitalized. Common nouns are not.

Example: *The Sands family is going to Mexico this fall.*

❑ **Are commas used correctly?**

Commas separate independent clauses in a compound sentence. They set off an introductory clause or phrase. They separate items in a series. They appear before and after a nonessential appositive. They are not used where there is no clear need for them.

Example: *They are leaving on September 10, and they won't return for two weeks.*

❑ **Are words spelled correctly?**

The apostrophe is placed correctly in each contraction and possessive. Contractions and possessives that sound alike are not confused. Other homonyms are not confused.

Example: *They can't wait to go there.*

Spelling Demons

Here are some homonyms and other commonly confused words. You may want to write each word in a sentence and then compare the spelling you used with the meaning given here. Check the words that give you trouble. Then work on learning to spell them.

❑ accept (to receive)
❑ except (to exclude)

❑ advice (words that try to help or tell what to do)
❑ advise (to tell what to do)

❑ affect (to influence)
❑ effect (a result)

❑ ate (past tense of *eat*)
❑ eight (the number 8)

❑ be (to exist)
❑ bee (an insect)

❑ board (piece of wood)
❑ bored (uninterested)

- brake (to stop)
- break (rest period; to damage or destroy)

- capital (city that is seat of government; very important; money to invest)
- capitol (building where an American legislature meets)

- check (to make sure; to inspect)
- cheque (a bank form)

- complement (to go with)
- compliment (flattering words)

- council (group or committee)
- counsel (to advise)

- course (path, track)
- coarse (rough, textured)

- feet (plural of foot)
- feat (achievement)

- for (to be used as; in favour of; meant to belong to)
- four (the number 4)

- grate (shred)
- great (very good)

- hear (to listen)
- here (in this place)

- hour (60 minutes)
- our (belonging to us)

- its (possessive of *it*)
- it's (it is)

- knew (to be certain of)
- new (latest, additional)

- know (to have information)
- no (negative; not; opposite of *yes*)

- lessen (to decrease)
- lesson (something taught)

- license (to grant a permit)
- licence (a permit)

- ❑ lose (to fail to win or keep)
- ❑ loose (not tight)

- ❑ made (created)
- ❑ maid (cleaning person)

- ❑ meat (flesh of an animal that is eaten)
- ❑ meet (to get together)

- ❑ one (the number 1)
- ❑ won (past tense of *win*)

- ❑ pane (window glass)
- ❑ pain (hurt)

- ❑ passed (went by)
- ❑ past (a time before)

- ❑ patience (ability to wait)
- ❑ patients (plural of *patient*)

- ❑ peace (calm)
- ❑ piece (a part of something)

- ❑ plane (flat surface; airplane)
- ❑ plain (simple, ordinary)

- ❑ poll (a vote)
- ❑ pole (a long piece of wood or other material)

- ❑ practice (custom; habit)
- ❑ practise (to do repeatedly)

- ❑ principal (main, head of a school)
- ❑ principle (rule, belief)

- ❑ quiet (still, silent)
- ❑ quite (completely; to a great extent)

- ❑ right (correct; opposite of *left*)
- ❑ write (to form words)

- ❑ roll (to turn over; a type of bread)
- ❑ role (a part played)

- ❑ scene (a view; part of a play or movie)
- ❑ seen (past participle of *see*)

- ❏ sight (the ability to see)
- ❏ site (place, location)

- ❏ sit (to rest one's body)
- ❏ set (to put something down)

- ❏ some (a few)
- ❏ sum (total amount)

- ❏ stationary (not moving)
- ❏ stationery (writing paper)

- ❏ their (belonging to them)
- ❏ there (at or in that place; toward)
- ❏ they're (they are)

- ❏ too (also, very)
- ❏ two (the number 2)
- ❏ to (part of infinitive verb form; in the direction of)

- ❏ wait (to stay around for someone or something)
- ❏ weight (how heavy something is)

- ❏ way (path, direction)
- ❏ weigh (to measure the heaviness of something)

- ❏ weak (opposite of strong)
- ❏ week (seven days)

- ❏ where (what place)
- ❏ wear (to have clothing)
- ❏ we're (we are)

- ❏ whether (if)
- ❏ weather (climate)

- ❏ whole (entire)
- ❏ hole (opening)

- ❏ who's (who is, who has)
- ❏ whose (possessive of *who*)

- ❏ wood (what trees are made of)
- ❏ would (verb expressing a wish)

- ❏ you're (you are)
- ❏ your (belonging to you)

Spelling List

With practice and concentration, you can improve your spelling ability. Here is a list of the most commonly misspelled words. Write the words as someone reads them to you. Make a list of the ones you spelled incorrectly. You may find it easier to master the ones you missed if you learn them ten to twelve words at a time.

a lot ☐	American ☐	auxiliary ☐	capital ☐
ability ☐	among ☐	available ☐	capitol ☐
absence ☐	amount ☐	avenue ☐	captain ☐
absent ☐	analysis ☐	awful ☐	career ☐
abundance ☐	analyze ☐	awkward ☐	careful ☐
accept ☐	angel ☐		careless ☐
acceptable ☐	angle ☐	bachelor ☐	carriage ☐
accident ☐	annual ☐	balance ☐	carrying ☐
accommodate ☐	another ☐	balloon ☐	category ☐
accompanied ☐	answer ☐	bargain ☐	ceiling ☐
accomplish ☐	antiseptic ☐	basic ☐	cemetery ☐
accumulation ☐	anxious ☐	beautiful ☐	centre ☐
accuse ☐	apologize ☐	because ☐	cereal ☐
accustomed ☐	apparatus ☐	become ☐	certain ☐
ache ☐	apparent ☐	before ☐	changeable ☐
achieve ☐	appear ☐	beginning ☐	characteristic ☐
achievement ☐	appearance ☐	being ☐	charity ☐
acknowledge ☐	appetite ☐	believe ☐	chief ☐
acquaintance ☐	apply ☐	benefit ☐	choose ☐
acquainted ☐	appreciate ☐	benefited ☐	chose ☐
acquire ☐	appreciation ☐	between ☐	cigarette ☐
address ☐	approach ☐	bicycle ☐	circumstance ☐
addressed ☐	appropriate ☐	board ☐	citizen ☐
adequate ☐	approval ☐	bored ☐	clothes ☐
advantage ☐	approve ☐	borrow ☐	clothing ☐
advantageous ☐	approximate ☐	bottle ☐	coarse ☐
advertise ☐	argue ☐	bottom ☐	coffee ☐
advertisement ☐	arguing ☐	boundary ☐	collect ☐
advice ☐	argument ☐	brake ☐	college ☐
advisable ☐	arouse ☐	breadth ☐	column ☐
advise ☐	arrange ☐	break ☐	comedy ☐
aerial ☐	arrangement ☐	breath ☐	comfortable ☐
affect ☐	article ☐	breathe ☐	commitment ☐
affectionate ☐	artificial ☐	brilliant ☐	committed ☐
again ☐	ascend ☐	building ☐	committee ☐
against ☐	assistance ☐	bulletin ☐	communicate ☐
aggravate ☐	assistant ☐	bureau ☐	company ☐
aggressive ☐	associate ☐	burial ☐	comparative ☐
agree ☐	association ☐	buried ☐	compel ☐
aisle ☐	attempt ☐	bury ☐	competent ☐
all right ☐	attendance ☐	bushes ☐	competition ☐
almost ☐	attention ☐	business ☐	complement ☐
already ☐	audience ☐		compliment ☐
although ☐	August ☐	cafeteria ☐	conceal ☐
altogether ☐	author ☐	calculator ☐	conceit ☐
always ☐	automobile ☐	calendar ☐	conceivable ☐
amateur ☐	autumn ☐	campaign ☐	conceive ☐

concentration ☐	description ☐	emphasis ☐	friend ☐
conception ☐	desert ☐	emphasize ☐	frightening ☐
condition ☐	desirable ☐	enclosure ☐	fundamental ☐
conference ☐	despair ☐	encouraging ☐	further ☐
confident ☐	desperate ☐	endeavour ☐	
congratulate ☐	dessert ☐	engineer ☐	garden ☐
conquer ☐	destruction ☐	English ☐	gardener ☐
conscience ☐	determine ☐	enormous ☐	general ☐
conscientious ☐	develop ☐	enough ☐	genius ☐
conscious ☐	development ☐	entrance ☐	government ☐
consequence ☐	device ☐	envelope ☐	governor ☐
consequently ☐	devise ☐	environment ☐	grammar ☐
considerable ☐	dictator ☐	equipment ☐	grateful ☐
consistency ☐	died ☐	equipped ☐	great ☐
consistent ☐	difference ☐	especially ☐	grey ☐
continual ☐	different ☐	essential ☐	grievance ☐
continuous ☐	dilemma ☐	evening ☐	grievous ☐
controlled ☐	dinner ☐	evident ☐	grocery ☐
controversy ☐	direction ☐	exaggerate ☐	guarantee ☐
convenience ☐	disappear ☐	exaggeration ☐	guard ☐
convenient ☐	disappoint ☐	examine ☐	guess ☐
conversation ☐	disappointment ☐	exceed ☐	guidance ☐
corporal ☐	disapproval ☐	excellent ☐	
corroborate ☐	disapprove ☐	except ☐	half ☐
council ☐	disastrous ☐	exceptional ☐	hammer ☐
counsel ☐	discipline ☐	exercise ☐	handkerchief ☐
counsellor ☐	discover ☐	exhausted ☐	happiness ☐
courage ☐	discriminate ☐	exhaustion ☐	healthy ☐
courageous ☐	disease ☐	exhilaration ☐	heard ☐
course ☐	dissatisfied ☐	existence ☐	heavy ☐
courteous ☐	dissection ☐	exorbitant ☐	height ☐
courtesy ☐	dissipate ☐	expense ☐	herd ☐
criticism ☐	distance ☐	experience ☐	heroes ☐
criticize ☐	distinction ☐	experiment ☐	heroine ☐
crystal ☐	division ☐	explanation ☐	hideous ☐
curiosity ☐	doctor ☐	extreme ☐	himself ☐
cylinder ☐	dollar ☐		hoarse ☐
	doubt ☐		holiday ☐
daily ☐	dozen ☐	facility ☐	hopeless ☐
daughter ☐	dyed ☐	factory ☐	horse ☐
daybreak ☐		familiar ☐	hospital ☐
death ☐		farther ☐	humorous ☐
deceive ☐	earnest ☐	fascinate ☐	hurried ☐
December ☐	easy ☐	fascinating ☐	hurrying ☐
deception ☐	ecstasy ☐	fatigue ☐	
decide ☐	ecstatic ☐	February ☐	ignorance ☐
decision ☐	education ☐	financial ☐	imaginary ☐
decisive ☐	effect ☐	financier ☐	imbecile ☐
deed ☐	efficiency ☐	flourish ☐	imitation ☐
definite ☐	efficient ☐	forcibly ☐	immediately ☐
delicious ☐	eight ☐	forehead ☐	incidental ☐
dependent ☐	either ☐	foreign ☐	increase ☐
deposit ☐	eligibility ☐	formal ☐	independence ☐
derelict ☐	eligible ☐	former ☐	independent ☐
descend ☐	eliminate ☐	fortunate ☐	indispensable ☐
descent ☐	embarrass ☐	fourteen ☐	inevitable ☐
describe ☐	embarrassment ☐	fourth ☐	influence ☐
	emergency ☐	frequent ☐	

influential ☐	livelihood ☐	occasional ☐	pertain ☐
initiate ☐	loaf ☐	occur ☐	picture ☐
innocence ☐	loneliness ☐	occurred ☐	piece ☐
inoculate ☐	loose ☐	occurrence ☐	plain ☐
inquiry ☐	lose ☐	ocean ☐	plane ☐
insistent ☐	losing ☐	offer ☐	playwright ☐
instead ☐	loyal ☐	often ☐	pleasant ☐
instinct ☐	loyalty ☐	omission ☐	please ☐
integrity ☐		omit ☐	pleasure ☐
intellectual ☐	magazine ☐	once ☐	pocket ☐
intelligence ☐	maintenance ☐	operate ☐	poison ☐
intercede ☐	manoeuvre ☐	opinion ☐	policeman ☐
interest ☐	marriage ☐	opportune ☐	political ☐
interfere ☐	married ☐	opportunity ☐	population ☐
interference ☐	marry ☐	optimist ☐	portrayal ☐
interpreted ☐	match ☐	optimistic ☐	positive ☐
interrupt ☐	mathematics ☐	origin ☐	possess ☐
invitation ☐	measure ☐	original ☐	possession ☐
irrelevant ☐	medicine ☐	oscillate ☐	possessive ☐
irresistible ☐	metre ☐	ought ☐	possible ☐
irritable ☐	million ☐	overcoat ☐	post office ☐
island ☐	miniature ☐		potatoes ☐
its ☐	minimum ☐	paid ☐	practical ☐
it's ☐	miracle ☐	pamphlet ☐	prairie ☐
	miscellaneous ☐	panicky ☐	precede ☐
January ☐	mischief ☐	parallel ☐	preceding ☐
jealous ☐	mischievous ☐	parallelism ☐	precise ☐
jewellery ☐	misspelled ☐	pare ☐	predictable ☐
journal ☐	mistake ☐	particular ☐	prefer ☐
judgment ☐	momentous ☐	partner ☐	preference ☐
	monkey ☐	pastime ☐	preferential ☐
kindergarten ☐	monotonous ☐	patience ☐	preferred ☐
kitchen ☐	moral ☐	patients ☐	prejudice ☐
knew ☐	morale ☐	peace ☐	preparation ☐
knock ☐	mortgage ☐	peaceable ☐	prepare ☐
know ☐	mountain ☐	pear ☐	prescription ☐
knowledge ☐	mournful ☐	peculiar ☐	presence ☐
	muscle ☐	pencil ☐	president ☐
labour ☐	mysterious ☐	people ☐	prevalent ☐
laboratory ☐	mystery ☐	perceive ☐	primitive ☐
laid ☐		perception ☐	principal ☐
language ☐	narrative ☐	perfect ☐	principle ☐
later ☐	natural ☐	perform ☐	privilege ☐
latter ☐	necessary ☐	performance ☐	probably ☐
laugh ☐	needle ☐	perhaps ☐	procedure ☐
leisure ☐	negligence ☐	period ☐	proceed ☐
length ☐	neighbour ☐	permanence ☐	produce ☐
lesson ☐	neither ☐	permanent ☐	professional ☐
library ☐	newspaper ☐	perpendicular ☐	professor ☐
licence ☐	newsstand ☐	perseverance ☐	profit ☐
license ☐	niece ☐	persevere ☐	profitable ☐
light ☐	noticeable ☐	persistent ☐	prominent ☐
lightning ☐		personal ☐	promise ☐
likelihood ☐	o'clock ☐	personality ☐	pronounce ☐
likely ☐	obedient ☐	personnel ☐	pronunciation ☐
literal ☐	obstacle ☐	persuade ☐	propeller ☐
literature ☐	occasion ☐	persuasion ☐	prophet ☐

prospect ☐	schedule ☐	suppress ☐	versatile ☐
psychology ☐	science ☐	surely ☐	vicinity ☐
pursue ☐	scientific ☐	surprise ☐	vicious ☐
pursuit ☐	scissors ☐	suspense ☐	view ☐
	season ☐	sweat ☐	village ☐
quality ☐	secretary ☐	sweet ☐	villain ☐
quantity ☐	seize ☐	syllable ☐	visitor ☐
quarrelling ☐	seminar ☐	symmetrical ☐	voice ☐
quart ☐	sense ☐	sympathy ☐	volume ☐
quarter ☐	separate ☐	synonym ☐	
quiet ☐	service ☐		waist ☐
quite ☐	several ☐	technical ☐	ware ☐
	severely ☐	telegram ☐	waste ☐
raise ☐	shepherd ☐	telephone ☐	weak ☐
realistic ☐	sheriff ☐	temperament ☐	wear ☐
realize ☐	shining ☐	temperature ☐	weather ☐
reason ☐	shoulder ☐	tenant ☐	Wednesday ☐
rebellion ☐	shriek ☐	tendency ☐	week ☐
recede ☐	siege ☐	tenement ☐	weigh ☐
receipt ☐	sight ☐	theatre ☐	weird ☐
receive ☐	signal ☐	therefore ☐	whether ☐
recipe ☐	significance ☐	thorough ☐	which ☐
recognize ☐	significant ☐	through ☐	while ☐
recommend ☐	similar ☐	title ☐	whole ☐
recuperate ☐	similarity ☐	together ☐	wholly ☐
referred ☐	since ☐	tomorrow ☐	whose ☐
rehearsal ☐	sincerely ☐	tongue ☐	witch ☐
reign ☐	site ☐	toward ☐	wretched ☐
relevant ☐	soldier ☐	tragedy ☐	
relieve ☐	solemn ☐	transferred ☐	
remedy ☐	sophomore ☐	treasury ☐	
renovate ☐	soul ☐	tremendous ☐	
repeat ☐	source ☐	tries ☐	
repetition ☐	souvenir ☐	truly ☐	
representative ☐	special ☐	twelfth ☐	
requirements ☐	specified ☐	twelve ☐	
resemblance ☐	specimen ☐	tyranny ☐	
resistance ☐	speech ☐		
resource ☐	stationary ☐	undoubtedly ☐	
respectability ☐	stationery ☐	United States ☐	
responsibility ☐	statue ☐	university ☐	
restaurant ☐	stockings ☐	unnecessary ☐	
rhythm ☐	stomach ☐	unusual ☐	
rhythmical ☐	straight ☐	useful ☐	
ridiculous ☐	strength ☐	usual ☐	
right ☐	strenuous ☐		
role ☐	stretch ☐	vacuum ☐	
roll ☐	striking ☐	vain ☐	
roommate ☐	studying ☐	valley ☐	
	substantial ☐	valuable ☐	
sandwich ☐	succeed ☐	variety ☐	
Saturday ☐	successful ☐	vegetable ☐	
scarcely ☐	sudden ☐	vein ☐	
scene ☐	superintendent ☐	vengeance ☐	

Your Personal Writing Strategy

You have learned several techniques to help you with the writing process. Different techniques are presented because every writer is different. To write your best GED essay, you need to determine the techniques that work best for you. Then you can create your own writing strategy for scoring high on the GED essay.

Gathering Ideas

Which of these techniques was most useful for you in gathering ideas? Which seemed the second best way? Number the techniques below 1 and 2.

_____ making a list

_____ drawing an idea map

_____ brainstorming

_____ asking questions

_____ using an idea circle

Organizing Ideas

Which of these techniques was most helpful to you in grouping and ordering ideas?

_____ circling and labelling in groups on the list

_____ rewriting the ideas in lists; labelling the lists

_____ drawing an idea map

_____ outlining

Writing

Which of these tips do you have the most trouble remembering?

_____ stick to my organizational plan

_____ add more ideas to the first ones I write down

_____ write neatly and legibly

_____ leave space between lines and in the margins for corrections

Evaluating and Revising

Which of these areas do you need to pay attention to when you evaluate and revise? Check any that you want to be sure to remember.

Presentation of Ideas

____ stating the thesis clearly in the introductory paragraph

____ writing preview sentences in the introductory paragraph

____ sticking to the topic

____ writing topic sentences for each body paragraph

____ including details, examples, facts, and opinions as support

____ expressing ideas clearly with precise words and transitions

____ restating the topic in the concluding paragraph

____ reviewing the ideas in the concluding paragraph

Conventions of English

____ using correct sentence structure

____ using a variety of sentence structures

____ making sure that subjects and verbs agree

____ making sure that verbs are in the correct tense and form

____ checking the punctuation

____ looking over the spelling

____ checking the capitalization

____ checking word choice

Using Your Time

Each of the five steps in the writing process takes a certain amount of time. This chart suggests an appropriate amount of time to spend on each step:

Planning:	5 minutes	
Organizing:	5 minutes	
Writing:	25 minutes	45 minutes total
Evaluating:	5 minutes	
Revising:	5 minutes	

However, the time frame that works best for you may be different. Perhaps you need less time to think of ideas but more time to organize them. Or you may need less time to write your essay and more time to revise it.

My Writing Strategy	Time

Planning ___ min.

The technique I will use to gather ideas is _____

_____ .

If I have trouble thinking of ideas, I'll also try _____

_____ .

Organizing ___ min.

The technique I will use to group and order my ideas is _____

_____

_____

_____ .

Writing ___ min.

I will follow my organizational plan to write an introductory paragraph, three body paragraphs, and a concluding paragraph.

When I write, I'll make sure I _____

_____

_____ .

Evaluating and Revising My Presentation of Ideas ___ min.

I will pay close attention to these areas when I evaluate and revise:

_____

_____

_____ .

Evaluating and Revising the Conventions of English ___ min.

I will pay close attention to these areas when I evaluate and revise:

_____

_____

_____ . **Total 45 min.**

Writing Checklist

The sample essay topics that you worked on throughout the Essay unit helped you to develop some basic writing skills. These skills will be necessary for writing an effective GED Essay on Part II of the Writing Test. When you write—either personal writing or more general writing—ask yourself these questions:

❏ Does the writing have a clear introduction, middle, and conclusion?

❏ Does each new main idea have its own paragraph?

❏ Are all sentences complete and clear?

❏ Are there interesting and specific details and examples?

❏ Are there vivid, specific modifiers that will help a reader understand what I am describing?

❏ Are there specific action verbs?

❏ Is the point of view consistent throughout the writing?

❏ Does the writing stay on topic? Are all ideas related to the topic?

❏ Is the use of sentence structure correct and appropriate? (See checklist on page 898.)

❏ Is the organization effective and clear? (See checklist on page 899.)

❏ Is the usage of English correct? (See checklist on page 900.)

❏ Are the mechanics of writing—capitalization, punctuation, and spelling—correct? (See checklist on page 901.)

Calculator Handbook

CASIO *fx-260SOLAR* Calculator Reference Handbook

When you take the GED Mathematics Test, you will be allowed to use a calculator on Part I of the test. This calculator, which will be provided by the testing centre, is the CASIO *fx-260SOLAR*. The information in this handbook is provided to help you use this calculator effectively.

The CASIO *fx-260SOLAR* is a scientific calculator. It has many more keys and functions than you need for the test. The keys that will be most helpful to you are labelled in the diagram below. Throughout this book you have learned basic operations that you can perform with most calculators. This handbook focuses on special features of the GED Test calculator.

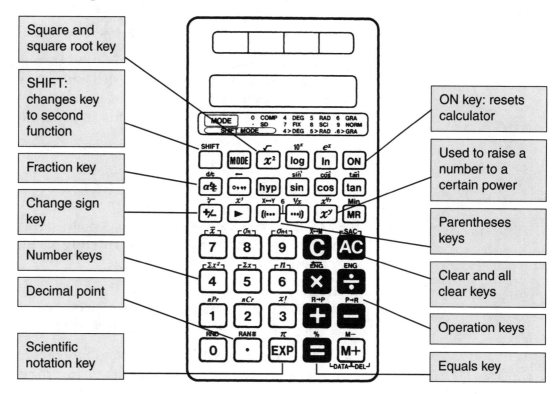

Square and square root key

SHIFT: changes key to second function

Fraction key

Change sign key

Number keys

Decimal point

Scientific notation key

ON key: resets calculator

Used to raise a number to a certain power

Parentheses keys

Clear and all clear keys

Operation keys

Equals key

Getting Started

ON Press the ON key to begin using the calculator. The ON key clears the memory and sets the display to 0. You will see the letters "DEG" at the top of the display window.

AC The "all clear" key clears all numbers and operations from the display. Always press AC or ON when you are ready to start a new problem.

C The "clear" key erases only the last number or operation that you entered. Use this key when you know that you have entered a number incorrectly. Press C, then enter the correct number.

Working with Signed Numbers

Use the +/- key to change the sign of a number. To enter a negative number, enter the digits of the number first, then press +/- .

Examples

Solve: $6 + (-9)$ Enter: 6 **+** 9 **+/-** **=** -3.

Solve: $-5 \times 4 \div (-2)$ Enter: 5 **+/-** **×** 4 **÷** 2 **+/-** **=** 10.

Working with Parentheses

Use the parentheses keys **[(---** and **---)]** to enter grouping symbols when an expression contains more than one operation. Put grouping symbols around the operation that must be performed first. Without parentheses, the calculator will always perform the multiplication and division steps first (following the order of operations).

Examples

Solve: $\dfrac{-4 + 6}{-2}$ Enter: **[(---** 4 **+/-** **+** 6 **---)]** **÷** 2 **+/-** **=** -1.

Solve: $5(4 + 7)$ Enter: 5 **×** **[(---** 4 **+** 7 **---)]** **=** 55.

In the last example, the algebraic expression shows the number 5 next to an operation in parentheses. Remember that this means multiply. To evaluate the expression using a calculator, you must press **×** before entering the operation in parentheses.

Other Features

π Use the second function of the **EXP** key to evaluate an expression containing pi. Notice that the symbol π is printed above the EXP key. Press the **SHIFT** key to access any of the functions printed above the calculator keys. Note that entering 3.14 for pi also results in the correct answer.

Example

Solve: Find 4π.   Enter: 4 **×** **SHIFT** **EXP** **=** 12.56637061

                          Enter: 4 **×** 3.14 **=** 12.56

% The percent function is the second function of the **=** key. You can enter a percent as written instead of converting it to a decimal.

Example

Solve: Find 45% of 200.   Enter: 200 **×** 45 **SHIFT** **=** 90.

Squares and Square Roots

To find the square of a number, you multiply the number by itself. For example, $6^2 = 6 \times 6 = 36$. You can square numbers quickly using the **x²** key on your calculator. You can also perform operations using squares. You will find this feature useful when solving problems involving the Pythagorean Relationship.

Examples

Solve: $8^2 = ?$ Enter: 8 **x²** 64.

Solve: $12^2 - 7^2 = ?$ Enter: 12 **x²** **−** 7 **x²** **=** 95.

The square root function is the second operation assigned to the square key **x²**. To find the square root of a number, enter the number, then press SHIFT and the square key.

Examples

Solve: What is the square root of 225?   Enter: 225 **SHIFT** **x²** 15.

Solve: $\sqrt{256} + \sqrt{81} = ?$

Enter: 256 **SHIFT** **x²** **+** 81 **SHIFT** **x²** **=** 25.

Exponents and Scientific Notation

To raise a number to a power other than 2, use the **xʸ** key, where x is the base and y is the exponent. Enter the base, press the **xʸ** key, and enter the exponent.

Examples

Solve: $5^4 = ?$ Enter: 5 **xʸ** 4 **=** 625.

Solve: $6^3 + 3^5 = ?$ Enter: 6 **xʸ** 3 **+** 3 **xʸ** 5 **=** 459.

In scientific notation, a number greater than or equal to one and less than ten is multiplied by a power of ten. Use the **EXP** key to enter a number written in scientific notation.

Examples

Solve: Express 3.2×10^6 in standard notation.

Enter: 3.2 **EXP** 6 **=** 3200000.

Solve: Express 4.89×10^5 in standard notation.

Enter: 4.89 **EXP** 5 **=** 489000.

Basic Key Functions of the CASIO *fx-260SOLAR* Calculator

[ON]	Power On	[AC]	All Clear
[C]	Clear	[▶]	Backspace
[.]	Decimal point	[3]	Digit or number
[SHIFT]	Use in conjunction with another key to change function		

Basic Calculations

[+]	Addition	[−]	Subtraction
[×]	Multiplication	[÷]	Division
[=]	Equal		

Special Keys

[a b/c]	Fraction key	[+/−]	Sign change key
%	Percent = [SHIFT] + [=]	√	Square root = [SHIFT] + [x^2]
[EXP]	Exponent key	[x^2]	Square key
[((---]	Open parentheses key	[---))]	Close parentheses key
π	Pi or 3.1415926536 = [SHIFT] + [EXP]		

Answer Sheet

GED Language Arts, Writing, Part I Test

Name: _____   Class: _____   Date: _____

Time started: _____
Time finished: _____

○ Entry Test   ○ Simulated Test

1 ① ② ③ ④ ⑤	11 ① ② ③ ④ ⑤	21 ① ② ③ ④ ⑤	31 ① ② ③ ④ ⑤	41 ① ② ③ ④ ⑤
2 ① ② ③ ④ ⑤	12 ① ② ③ ④ ⑤	22 ① ② ③ ④ ⑤	32 ① ② ③ ④ ⑤	42 ① ② ③ ④ ⑤
3 ① ② ③ ④ ⑤	13 ① ② ③ ④ ⑤	23 ① ② ③ ④ ⑤	33 ① ② ③ ④ ⑤	43 ① ② ③ ④ ⑤
4 ① ② ③ ④ ⑤	14 ① ② ③ ④ ⑤	24 ① ② ③ ④ ⑤	34 ① ② ③ ④ ⑤	44 ① ② ③ ④ ⑤
5 ① ② ③ ④ ⑤	15 ① ② ③ ④ ⑤	25 ① ② ③ ④ ⑤	35 ① ② ③ ④ ⑤	45 ① ② ③ ④ ⑤
6 ① ② ③ ④ ⑤	16 ① ② ③ ④ ⑤	26 ① ② ③ ④ ⑤	36 ① ② ③ ④ ⑤	46 ① ② ③ ④ ⑤
7 ① ② ③ ④ ⑤	17 ① ② ③ ④ ⑤	27 ① ② ③ ④ ⑤	37 ① ② ③ ④ ⑤	47 ① ② ③ ④ ⑤
8 ① ② ③ ④ ⑤	18 ① ② ③ ④ ⑤	28 ① ② ③ ④ ⑤	38 ① ② ③ ④ ⑤	48 ① ② ③ ④ ⑤
9 ① ② ③ ④ ⑤	19 ① ② ③ ④ ⑤	29 ① ② ③ ④ ⑤	39 ① ② ③ ④ ⑤	49 ① ② ③ ④ ⑤
10 ① ② ③ ④ ⑤	20 ① ② ③ ④ ⑤	30 ① ② ③ ④ ⑤	40 ① ② ③ ④ ⑤	50 ① ② ③ ④ ⑤

Answer Sheet

GED Social Studies Test

Name: _____ **Class:** _____ **Date:** _____

Time started: _____
Time finished: _____

○ Entry Test   ○ Simulated Test

1 ① ② ③ ④ ⑤	11 ① ② ③ ④ ⑤	21 ① ② ③ ④ ⑤	31 ① ② ③ ④ ⑤	41 ① ② ③ ④ ⑤
2 ① ② ③ ④ ⑤	12 ① ② ③ ④ ⑤	22 ① ② ③ ④ ⑤	32 ① ② ③ ④ ⑤	42 ① ② ③ ④ ⑤
3 ① ② ③ ④ ⑤	13 ① ② ③ ④ ⑤	23 ① ② ③ ④ ⑤	33 ① ② ③ ④ ⑤	43 ① ② ③ ④ ⑤
4 ① ② ③ ④ ⑤	14 ① ② ③ ④ ⑤	24 ① ② ③ ④ ⑤	34 ① ② ③ ④ ⑤	44 ① ② ③ ④ ⑤
5 ① ② ③ ④ ⑤	15 ① ② ③ ④ ⑤	25 ① ② ③ ④ ⑤	35 ① ② ③ ④ ⑤	45 ① ② ③ ④ ⑤
6 ① ② ③ ④ ⑤	16 ① ② ③ ④ ⑤	26 ① ② ③ ④ ⑤	36 ① ② ③ ④ ⑤	46 ① ② ③ ④ ⑤
7 ① ② ③ ④ ⑤	17 ① ② ③ ④ ⑤	27 ① ② ③ ④ ⑤	37 ① ② ③ ④ ⑤	47 ① ② ③ ④ ⑤
8 ① ② ③ ④ ⑤	18 ① ② ③ ④ ⑤	28 ① ② ③ ④ ⑤	38 ① ② ③ ④ ⑤	48 ① ② ③ ④ ⑤
9 ① ② ③ ④ ⑤	19 ① ② ③ ④ ⑤	29 ① ② ③ ④ ⑤	39 ① ② ③ ④ ⑤	49 ① ② ③ ④ ⑤
10 ① ② ③ ④ ⑤	20 ① ② ③ ④ ⑤	30 ① ② ③ ④ ⑤	40 ① ② ③ ④ ⑤	50 ① ② ③ ④ ⑤

Answer Sheet

GED Science Test

Name: _____ Class: _____ Date: _____

Time started: _____

Time finished: _____

○ Entry Test   ○ Simulated Test

1 ① ② ③ ④ ⑤	**11** ① ② ③ ④ ⑤	**21** ① ② ③ ④ ⑤	**31** ① ② ③ ④ ⑤	**41** ① ② ③ ④ ⑤
2 ① ② ③ ④ ⑤	**12** ① ② ③ ④ ⑤	**22** ① ② ③ ④ ⑤	**32** ① ② ③ ④ ⑤	**42** ① ② ③ ④ ⑤
3 ① ② ③ ④ ⑤	**13** ① ② ③ ④ ⑤	**23** ① ② ③ ④ ⑤	**33** ① ② ③ ④ ⑤	**43** ① ② ③ ④ ⑤
4 ① ② ③ ④ ⑤	**14** ① ② ③ ④ ⑤	**24** ① ② ③ ④ ⑤	**34** ① ② ③ ④ ⑤	**44** ① ② ③ ④ ⑤
5 ① ② ③ ④ ⑤	**15** ① ② ③ ④ ⑤	**25** ① ② ③ ④ ⑤	**35** ① ② ③ ④ ⑤	**45** ① ② ③ ④ ⑤
6 ① ② ③ ④ ⑤	**16** ① ② ③ ④ ⑤	**26** ① ② ③ ④ ⑤	**36** ① ② ③ ④ ⑤	**46** ① ② ③ ④ ⑤
7 ① ② ③ ④ ⑤	**17** ① ② ③ ④ ⑤	**27** ① ② ③ ④ ⑤	**37** ① ② ③ ④ ⑤	**47** ① ② ③ ④ ⑤
8 ① ② ③ ④ ⑤	**18** ① ② ③ ④ ⑤	**28** ① ② ③ ④ ⑤	**38** ① ② ③ ④ ⑤	**48** ① ② ③ ④ ⑤
9 ① ② ③ ④ ⑤	**19** ① ② ③ ④ ⑤	**29** ① ② ③ ④ ⑤	**39** ① ② ③ ④ ⑤	**49** ① ② ③ ④ ⑤
10 ① ② ③ ④ ⑤	**20** ① ② ③ ④ ⑤	**30** ① ② ③ ④ ⑤	**40** ① ② ③ ④ ⑤	**50** ① ② ③ ④ ⑤

Answer Sheet

GED Language Arts, Reading Test

Name: _____   Class: _____   Date: _____

Time started: _____
Time finished: _____

○ Entry Test   ○ Simulated Test

1 ① ② ③ ④ ⑤	11 ① ② ③ ④ ⑤	21 ① ② ③ ④ ⑤	31 ① ② ③ ④ ⑤	41 ① ② ③ ④ ⑤
2 ① ② ③ ④ ⑤	12 ① ② ③ ④ ⑤	22 ① ② ③ ④ ⑤	32 ① ② ③ ④ ⑤	42 ① ② ③ ④ ⑤
3 ① ② ③ ④ ⑤	13 ① ② ③ ④ ⑤	23 ① ② ③ ④ ⑤	33 ① ② ③ ④ ⑤	43 ① ② ③ ④ ⑤
4 ① ② ③ ④ ⑤	14 ① ② ③ ④ ⑤	24 ① ② ③ ④ ⑤	34 ① ② ③ ④ ⑤	44 ① ② ③ ④ ⑤
5 ① ② ③ ④ ⑤	15 ① ② ③ ④ ⑤	25 ① ② ③ ④ ⑤	35 ① ② ③ ④ ⑤	45 ① ② ③ ④ ⑤
6 ① ② ③ ④ ⑤	16 ① ② ③ ④ ⑤	26 ① ② ③ ④ ⑤	36 ① ② ③ ④ ⑤	46 ① ② ③ ④ ⑤
7 ① ② ③ ④ ⑤	17 ① ② ③ ④ ⑤	27 ① ② ③ ④ ⑤	37 ① ② ③ ④ ⑤	47 ① ② ③ ④ ⑤
8 ① ② ③ ④ ⑤	18 ① ② ③ ④ ⑤	28 ① ② ③ ④ ⑤	38 ① ② ③ ④ ⑤	48 ① ② ③ ④ ⑤
9 ① ② ③ ④ ⑤	19 ① ② ③ ④ ⑤	29 ① ② ③ ④ ⑤	39 ① ② ③ ④ ⑤	49 ① ② ③ ④ ⑤
10 ① ② ③ ④ ⑤	20 ① ② ③ ④ ⑤	30 ① ② ③ ④ ⑤	40 ① ② ③ ④ ⑤	50 ① ② ③ ④ ⑤

Answer Sheet

GED Mathematics Entry Test

Name: _____ Class: _____ Date: _____

Time started: _____

Time finished: _____

Part I

1 ① ② ③ ④ ⑤

2 ① ② ③ ④ ⑤

3 ① ② ③ ④ ⑤

4 ① ② ③ ④ ⑤

5 ① ② ③ ④ ⑤

6

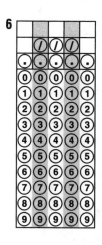

7 ① ② ③ ④ ⑤

8 ① ② ③ ④ ⑤

9 ① ② ③ ④ ⑤

10 ① ② ③ ④ ⑤

11 ① ② ③ ④ ⑤

12

Part II

13 ① ② ③ ④ ⑤

14 ① ② ③ ④ ⑤

15 ① ② ③ ④ ⑤

16 ① ② ③ ④ ⑤

17 ① ② ③ ④ ⑤

18

19 ① ② ③ ④ ⑤

20 ① ② ③ ④ ⑤

21 ① ② ③ ④ ⑤

22 ① ② ③ ④ ⑤

23 ① ② ③ ④ ⑤

24 ① ② ③ ④ ⑤

25 ① ② ③ ④ ⑤

Answer Sheet

GED Mathematics Test, Part I

Name: _____   Class: _____   Date: _____

Time started: _____

Time finished: _____

○ Simulated Test

1 ① ② ③ ④ ⑤   **9** ① ② ③ ④ ⑤   **17**

2 ① ② ③ ④ ⑤   **10** ① ② ③ ④ ⑤

3 ① ② ③ ④ ⑤   **11** ① ② ③ ④ ⑤

4   **12**

5   **13**   **18** ① ② ③ ④ ⑤   **22**

                                                   19 ① ② ③ ④ ⑤

                                                   20 ① ② ③ ④ ⑤

                          21

6 ① ② ③ ④ ⑤   **14** ① ② ③ ④ ⑤   **23** ① ② ③ ④ ⑤

7 ① ② ③ ④ ⑤   **15** ① ② ③ ④ ⑤   **24** ① ② ③ ④ ⑤

8 ① ② ③ ④ ⑤   **16** ① ② ③ ④ ⑤   **25** ① ② ③ ④ ⑤

END OF PART I

You must stop using your calculator now.

Answer Sheet

GED Mathematics Test, Part II

Name: _____ Class: _____ Date: _____

Time started: _____

Time finished: _____

○ Simulated Test

26 ① ② ③ ④ ⑤

27 ① ② ③ ④ ⑤

28 ① ② ③ ④ ⑤

29 ① ② ③ ④ ⑤

30 ① ② ③ ④ ⑤

31

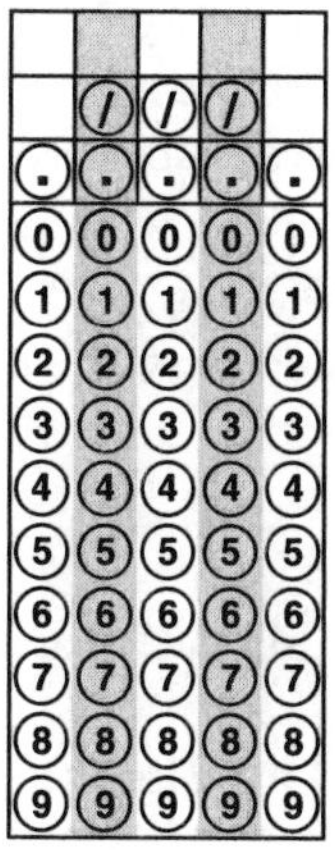

37

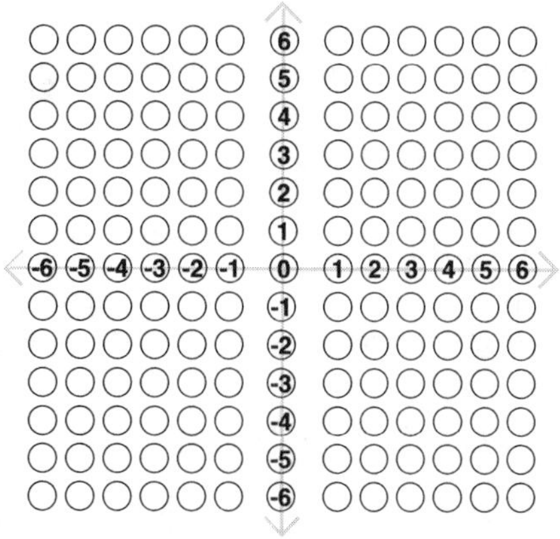

38 ① ② ③ ④ ⑤

39 ① ② ③ ④ ⑤

40 ① ② ③ ④ ⑤

41 ① ② ③ ④ ⑤

42 ① ② ③ ④ ⑤

43

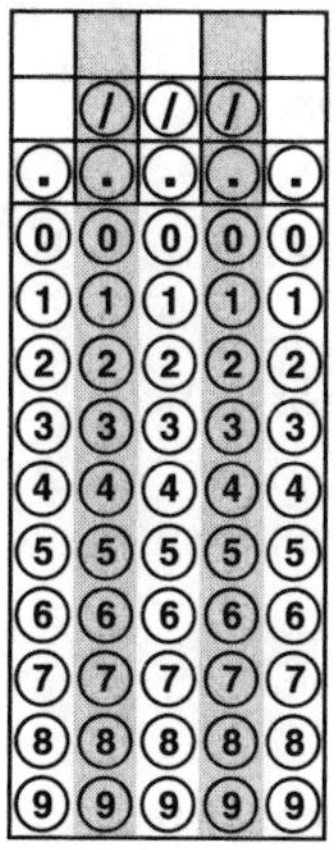

44 ① ② ③ ④ ⑤

45 ① ② ③ ④ ⑤

46 ① ② ③ ④ ⑤

47 ① ② ③ ④ ⑤

48 ① ② ③ ④ ⑤

49 ① ② ③ ④ ⑤

50 ① ② ③ ④ ⑤

32 ① ② ③ ④ ⑤

33 ① ② ③ ④ ⑤

34 ① ② ③ ④ ⑤

35 ① ② ③ ④ ⑤

36 ① ② ③ ④ ⑤

Acknowledgements

Pages 924–927 constitute an extension of the copyright page.

Grateful acknowledgement is made to the following authors, agents, and publishes for permission to use copyrighted materials. Every effort has been made to trace ownership of all copyrighted material and to secure the necessary permissions to reprint. We express regret in advance for any error or omission. Any oversight will be acknowledged in future printings.

Statistics Canada information is used with the permission of the Minister of Industry, as Minister responsible for Statistics Canada. Information on the availability of the wide range of data from Statistics Canada can be obtained from Statistics Canada's Regional Offices, its World Wide Web site at http://www.statcan.ca, and its toll-free access number 1-800-263-1136.

p. 25: Malcolm Mayes/artizans.com

p. 25 Source: Law Courts Education Society, Vancouver, BC

p. 26: Vic Davidson/Montréal Gazette/National Archives of Canada/C-053641

p. 27: "Acid rain and ... the facts," Environment Canada http://www.ec.gc.ca/acidrain/acidfact.html). Reproduced with the permission of the Minister of Public Works and Government Services, 2003

p. 28: Source: Statistics Canada (www.statcan.ca)

p. 29: Copyright © 2003 Ingrid Rice

p. 30: National Archives of Canada/C-008449

p. 43: Reprinted by permission of Farrar, Straus and Giroux, LLC. Excerpt from "Dean of Men" from THE COLLECTED STORIES by Peter Taylor. Copyright © 1968 by Peter Taylor

p. 44: Booker T. Washington, *Up from Slavery*

p. 45: "A Kite is a Victim" from *Stranger Music: Selected Poems and Songs* by Leonard Cohen. Used by permission, McClelland & Stewart Ltd., *The Canadian Publishers*

p. 47: Excerpted from GO TELL IT ON THE MOUNTAIN © 1953 by James Baldwin. Copyright renewed. Published by Dial Press. Reprinted by arrangement with the James Baldwin Estate

p. 48: Charlie Russell, *Five on the Black Hand Side*, Applause Theatre & Cinema Books, 1997

p. 49: © 1993 by Judith Ortz Cofer. All rights reserved. Published by the University of Georgia Press, Athens, Georgia 30602

p. 185: Reprinted with permission of the American Council on Education

p. 200: Courtesy of Brad Woodside.

p. 204: Heidenreich, Conrad, *Huronia. A History and Geography of the Huron Indians, 1600-1650*. Toronto: McClelland & Stewart 1971, figure 12 A. Seasonal Cycle of Activities

p. 205: Brian Young and John A. Dickinson, *A Short History of Quebec, Third Edition*, McGill-Queen's University Press, 2003. p. 21

p. 207: "Carte geographie de la Nouvelle Franse en son vray mondia," 1612 from *Les Voyages du Sieur de Champlain*, Samuel de Champlain, 1613

p. 209: *Civilization and Barbarism*, Anon., Archives of Manitoba

p. 211: National Library of Canada/National Archives of Canada/C-050336

p. 214: Department of Immigration, Canada/National Archives of Canadaa/C-085854

p. 216: Archives of Manitoba: L.B. Foote Collection 1691 (N2757)

p. 220: *Canadian Charter of Rights and Freedoms*, Department of Justice Canada

p. 222: From CANADIAN HISTORY 1900-2000 STUDENT TEXT by HUNDEY/MAGARREY. © 2000. Reprinted with permission of Nelson, a division of Thomson Learning: www.thomsonrights.com. Fax 800-730-2215

p. 223: © Dusan Petricic

p. 234: SARGENT © Austin American-Statesman. Reprinted with permission of UNIVERSAL PRESS SYNDICATE. All rights reserved

p. 235: Reprinted with Special Permission of King Features Syndicate

p. 236: Jeff Koterba/Omaha World-Herald. Reprinted by permission

p. 238: Linda Boileau, *Frankfort State Journal*, Rothco Cartoon Syndicate. Reprinted by permission

p. 245: Reprinted with permission from *The Globe and Mail*

p. 249: Reprinted with permission from *The Globe and Mail*

p. 251: *Annual Financial Report of the Government of Canada—Fiscal Year 2001-2002*, Department of Finance Canada, p. 12. Reproduced with the permission of the Minister of Public Works and Government Services, 2003

p. 252: Courtesy of the Canadian Taxpayers Federation (www.taxpayer.com)

p. 259: Source: Statistics Canada (www.statcan.ca)

p. 263: Source: *Directory of Mergers and Acquisitions in Canada* and *The Toronto Stock Exchange Review 1999*

p. 264: Source: Adapted from Statistics Canada Web site, 1996 Census Nation tables (http://www.statcan.ca/english/Pgdb/labor50a.htm), June 2003

p. 265: Source: Statistics Canada (www.statcan.ca)

p. 266: Prepared by the Canadian Council on Social Development using Statistics Canada *Income Distributions by Size Canada 1995*

p. 271: From: *The Regional Geography of Canada*, by Robert M. Bone, Copyright © Oxford University Press Canada, 2000. Reprinted by permission of Oxford University Press Canada

p. 274: From: *The Regional Geography of Canada*, by Robert M. Bone, Copyright © Oxford University Press Canada, 2000. Reprinted by permission of Oxford University Press Canada

p. 276: Cartoon by Peter Porges. Copyright © 1975 Peter Porges

p. 282: Source: Statistics Canada (www.statcan.ca)

p. 284: Data extracted from the Parliamentary Internet Parlementaire website (www.parl.gc.ca)

p. 286: Data extracted from the Parliamentary Internet Parlementaire website (www.parl.gc.ca)

p. 286: Reprinted with permission from *The Globe and Mail*

p. 287: Canadian Pacific Railway Archives (NS.1960)

p. 287 John Henry Walker. Ink. Notman Photo Archives, McCord Museum of Canadian History, Montreal/M930.50.5.262 and M930.50.5.142

p. 367: Thomas Griffith, "What's So Special About News Magazines?" *Newsweek*. © Newsweek, Inc.

p. 368: From AN AMERICAN HOMEPLACE by Donald McCaig, copyright © 1992 by Donald McCaig. Used by permission of Crown Publishers, a division of Random House, Inc.

p. 371: © Reid Goldsborough

p. 372: © Brad Templeton

p. 375: Art Daudelin, "Keys to Effective Web Searching," *Physicians Financial News*.

p. 377: Víctor Landa, "My 20-Hour Workweek Never Arrived," © 2000 Hispanic Link News Service

p. 378: © 1998 Charles W. Moore

p. 379: Michael C. Moran, "Saving downtown's gems," *Chicago Tribune*. Copyright © Chicago Tribune

p. 380: Excerpt from DAKOTA by Kathleen Norris. Copyright © 1993 by Kathleen Norris. Reprinted by permission of Houghton Mifflin Company. All rights reserved

p. 381: Robert Frost, "Education by Poetry," *The Selected Prose of Robert Frost*, Holt, Rinehart & Winston, 1966

p. 382: "Living Well," *Newsweek*. © Newsweek, Inc.

p. 383: Ira A.J. Baden as told to Robert H. Parham, "Forty-five Seconds Inside a Tornado," *Man Against nature*, Cooper Square Press, 2000

p. 384: Andy Meisler, "The Man Who Keeps E.R.'s Heart Beating," *The New York Times*. Copyright © The New York Times Company. Reprinted by permission

p. 386: Extracted from *Streeters: Rants and Raves from This Hour Has 22 Minutes* by Rick Mercer. Copyright © 1998 by Rick Mercer. Reprinted by permission of Doubleday Canada

p. 387: Excerpt from ON PHOTOGRAPHY by Susan Sontag. Copyright © 1977 by Susan Sontag. Reprinted by permission of Farrar, Straus and Giroux, LLC

p. 388: Sally R. Sommer, "Superfeet," *The Village Voice*. Copyright © Village Voice Media, Inc.

p. 389: David Patrick Stearns, "Majestic Henry V does justice to the Bard," *USA Today*. Copyright: November 10, 1989

p. 390: Robert R. Harris, "Too Embarrassed Not to Kill, " *New York Times Book Review*.

p. 392: Margaret Craven, *I Heard the Owl Call My Name*. Copyright © 1967 by Margaret Craven

p. 393: Reprinted with the permission of Simon & Schuster Adult Publishing Group from CONTACT by Carl Sagan. Copyright © 1985, 1986, 1987 by Carl Sagan

p. 396: Excerpt from "A Good Man is Hard to Find" in A GOOD MAN IS HARD TO FIND AND OTHER STORIES, copyright 1953 by Flannery O'Connor and renewed 1981 by Regina O'Connor, reprinted by permission of Harcourt, Inc.

Acknowledgements

p. 397: Excerpt from "The Red Convertible" from LOVE MEDICINE new and revised edition by Louise Erdrich, © 1984, 1993 by Louise Erdrich. Reprinted by permission of Henry Holt and Company, LLC

p. 398: Edwidge Danticat, *Krik? Krak!*, Soho Press Inc., 1995

p. 399: Reprinted with permission of Scribner, an imprint of Simon & Schuster Adult Publishing Group, from THE OLD MAN AND THE SEA by Ernest Hemingway. Copyright 1952 by Ernest Hemingway. Copyright renewed © 1980 by Mary Hemingway.

p. 400: From FOOL'S CROW by James Welch, copyright © 1986 by James Welch. Used by permission of Viking Penguin, a division of Penguin Group (USA) Inc.

p. 401: Copyright 1954 Doris Lessing. Reprinted by kind permission of Jonathan Clowes Ltd., London, on behalf of Doris Lessing.

p. 402: Charles Dickens, *Bleak House*

p. 403: Excerpt from "The Jilting of Granny Weatherall" in FLOWERING JUDAS AND OTHER STORIES, copyright 1930 and renewed 1958 by Katherine Anne Porter, reprinted by permission of Harcourt, Inc.

p. 404: "A Rose for Emily" from COLLECTED STORIES OF WILLIAM FAULKNER by William Faulkner, Random House, Inc.

p. 405: Edgar Allan Poe, "The Fall of the House of Usher," *The Fall of the House of Usher and Other Writings*.

p. 406: William Makepeace Thackeray, Vanity Fair

p. 408: Ambrose Bierce, *A Horseman in the Sky*

p. 409: Enedina Casarez Vasquez, "The House of Quilts," *Daughters of the Fifth Sun*, Riverhead Books, 1995

p. 410: Excerpt from Isaac Bashevis Singer, "The Spinoza of Market Street," *The Spinoza of Market Street*, Farrar, Straus & Giroux, 1967

p. 411: Excerpt from Toni Cade Bambera, "Raymond's Run," *Gorilla, My Love*, Vintage Books, 1992

p. 412: Mary Wilkins Freeman, "A Village Singer"

p. 414: Mark Twain, *The Adventures of Huckleberry Finn*

p. 416: William Golding, *Lord of the Flies* (Faber and Faber Ltd., 1954)

p. 417: Stephen Crane, "The Open Boat," *The Portable Stephen Crane*

p. 418: John Knowles, *A Separate Peace*. Copyright © 1959 by John Knowles.

p. 420: From CANNERY ROW by John Steinbeck, copyright 1945 by John Steinbeck. Renewed © 1973 by Elaine Steinbeck, John Steinbeck IV and Thom Steinbeck. Used by permission of Viking Penguin, a division of Penguin Group (USA) Inc.

p. 423: Robert Frost, "The Road Not Taken," *The Poetry of Robert Frost*, Holt, Rinehart & Winston, 1969

p. 425: Langston Hughes, "What happens to a dream deferred?" *The Collected Poems of Langston Hughes*, Alfred Hughes, Alfred A. Knopf, Inc., 1994

p. 426: Edgar Lee Masters, "Abel Melveny," *The Spoon River Anthology*

p. 427: By HD (Hilda Doolittle), from COLLECTED POEMS, 1912-1944, copyright © 1982 by The Estate of Hilda Doolittle. Reprinted by permission of New Directions Publishing Corp.

p. 428: Reprinted by permission of Farrar, Straus and Giroux, LLC. "The Woman at the Washington Zoo" from THE COMPLETE POEMS by Randall Jarrell. Copyright © 1969, renewed 1997 by Mary von S. Jarrell.

p. 430: Emily Dickinson, "A Narrow Fellow in the Grass," *The Poems of Emily Dickinson*

p. 431: Simon J. Ortiz, "Earth and Rain, the Plants & Sun," *Woven Stone*. Permission granted by author Simon J. Ortiz.

p. 433: "The Wind in the Trees," from FRAMELESS WINDOWS, SQUARES OF LIGHT: POEMS by Cathy Song. Copyright © 1988 by Cathy Song. Used by permission of W.W. Norton & Company, Inc.

p. 434: Karl Shapiro, "Calling the Child," *Collected Poems 1940-1978*. © Karl Shapiro by permission of Wieser & Wieser, Inc.

p. 435: "Fences" by Pat Mora is reprinted with permission from the publisher of Communion (Houston: Arte Público Press—University of Houston, 1991)

p. 436: From *Collected Poems, 1930-83*. Copyright 1983 by Josephine Miles. Used with permission of the University of Illinois Press.

p. 439: Henrik Ibsen, *A Doll's House*

p. 440: Sam Shepard, *True West*, 1981

p. 441: From FENCES by August Wilson, copyright © 1986 by August Wilson. Used by permission of Dutton Signet, a Division of Penguin Group (USA) Inc.

p. 443: Reprinted by permission of Hill & Wang, a division of Farrar, Straus and Giroux, LLC: Excerpt from NIGHT, MOTHER: A PLAY by Marsha. Copyright © 1983 by Marsha Norman

p. 444: Excerpted from THE AMEN CORNER © 1968 by James Baldwin. Copyright renewed. Published by Vintage Books. Reprinted by arrangement with the James Baldwin Estate.

p. 445: Excerpt from "The Heidi Chronicles" in THE HEIDI CHRONICLES AND OTHER PLAYS, copyright © 1990 by Wendy Wasserstein, reprinted by permission of Harcourt, Inc.

p. 446: Anton Chekhov, *The Sea Gull*

p. 448: August Strindberg, *The Stronger*

p. 450: Henry David Thoreau, "Life Without Principle," from *Major Writers of America*

p. 451: Paul Laurence Dunbar, "Sympathy," *The Complete Poems of Paul Laurence Dunbar*

p. 452: Andy Seiler, "'Love and Basketball' misses the net," *USA Today*. Copyright: April 21, 2000.

p. 453: Reprinted by permission of Don Congdon Associates, Inc. © 1953, renewed 1981 by Ray Bradbury

p. 454: From "The Devil's Disciple" by George Bernard Shaw

p. 455: "Why I Live at the P.O." from A CURTAIN OF GREEN AND OTHER STORIES, copyright 1941 and renewed 1969 by Eudora Welty, reprinted by permission of Harcourt, Inc.

p. 648: © Reuters NewMedia Inc./CORBIS/MAGMA BE023762

p. 649: Cartoon by Dean Vietor. Copyright © 1989 Dean Vietor

p. 650: "NOBLESSE OBLIGE: Queen on Moose", 1973, acrylic on canvas © Charles Pachter, used by permission of the artist.

p. 650: Source: Eulogy for Pierre Elliott Trudeau, Justin Trudeau, Tuesday, October 2, 2000

p. 651: *Gambling in Canada*, National Council of Welfare, 1996 (http://www.ncwcnbes.net/htmdocument/reportgambling/Gambling.htm). Reproduced with the permission of the Minister of Public Works and Government Services, 2003.

p. 652: *Canadian Charter of Rights and Freedoms*, Department of Justice Canada

p. 652: Source: Statistics Canada (www.statcan.ca)

p. 657: Reprinted with permission from *The Globe and Mail*

p. 659: Adapted from Statistics Canada Web site (http://www.statcan.ca/english/Pgdb/demo03.htm), June 2003

p. 660: From The Wall Street Journal—Permission, Cartoon Features Syndicate

p. 662: © The New Yorker Collection 1973 Edward Koren from cartoonbank.com. All Rights Reserved.

p. 663: South African Vote by Jack Higgins, 1994. Reprinted with special permission from the Chicago Sun-Times, Inc. @ 2003.

p. 688: From THE CHILDREN'S HOUR by Lillian Hellman, copyright 1934 by Lillian Hellman Kober and renewed 1962 by Lillian Hellman. Used by permission of Random House, Inc.

p. 690: Excerpt from COLD SASSY TREE by Olive Ann Burns. Copyright © 1984 by Olive Ann Burns. Reprinted by permission of Houghton Mifflin Company. All rights reserved.

p. 692: by Ezra Pound, from PERSONAE, copyright © 1926 by Ezra Pound. Reprinted by permission of New Directions Publishing Corp.

p. 696: Katherine Mansfield, "Bliss," *The Short Stories of Katherine Mansfield*

p. 698: Chris Buchman, "The Television Scene," *Films in Review*

p. 879: Reprinted by permission of Nanaimo Regional Transit

p. 880: Courtesy of the Trans Canada Trail Foundation (www.tctrail.ca). Copyright © 1999–2001 the Trans Canada Trail Foundation. All Rights Reserved.

p. 880: Courtesy of Thompson's Community Website (www.hubofthenorth.ca).

p. 882: Source: Adapted from *Physical and Mathematical Tables*, John B. Clark. Published by Oliver and Boyd (Edinburgh: Tweeddale Court; London: 39A Walbeck St.), 1904. Reprinted in 1968.

p. 886: Reprinted by permission of City of Nanaimo

p. 886: Source: Adapted from *Physical and Mathematical Tables*, John B. Clark. Published by Oliver and Boyd (Edinburgh: Tweeddale Court; London: 39A Walbeck St.), 1904. Reprinted in 1968.

Acknowledgements

ALL THE GED MATERIALS YOU NEED TO BE SUCCESSFUL.
WE WANT YOU TO SUCCEED!

MORE SUPPORT = MORE SUCCESS!

SV GED SATELLITE BOOKS

	ISBN
Language Arts, Writing	0-7398-2831-2
Language Arts, Reading	0-7398-2836-3
The Essay	0-7398-2832-0
Science	0-7398-2833-9
Social Studies	0-7398-2834-7
Mathematics	0-7398-2835-5
Instructor's Resource Guide	0-7398-2940-8

SV GED EXERCISE BOOKS

	ISBN
Language Arts, Reading	0-7398-3604-8
Language Arts, Writing	0-7398-3606-4
Mathematics	0-7398-3603-X
Science	0-7398-3602-1
Social Studies	0-7398-3605-6

SV GED SKILLS BOOKLETS

	ISBN	10-PACK ISBN
The Calculator Booklet	N/A	0-7398-4669-8
The Calculator Booklet w/Calculator	0-7398-5209-4	N/A
Language Arts Writing — Essay	0-7398-5419-4	0-7398-5659-6
Language Arts Writing — Sentence Structure, Organization	0-7398-5420-8	0-7398-5660-X
Language Arts Writing — Mechanics, Usage	0-7398-5421-6	0-7398-5661-8
Language Arts Reading — Literary Texts	0-7398-5422-4	0-7398-5662-6
Language Arts Reading — Nonfiction Texts	0-7398-5423-2	0-7398-5663-4
Science — Life Science	0-7398-5424-0	0-7398-5664-2
Science — Earth Space, Physical Science	0-7398-5425-9	0-7398-5665-0
Social Studies — US & World History, Geography	0-7398-5426-7	0-7398-5666-9
Social Studies — Economics, Civics, Government	0-7398-5427-5	0-7398-5667-7
Math — Number Operations, Algebra	0-7398-5428-3	0-7398-5668-5
Math — Data Analysis, Measurement, Geometry	0-7398-5429-1	0-7398-5669-3
Interpreting Visual Information	0-7398-5747-9	0-7398-5748-7
Higher Order Thinking Skills	0-7398-5749-5	0-7398-5750-9
Evaluative Test	0-7398-6390-8	0-7398-6391-6
Diagnostic Test	0-7398-6393-2	0-7398-6394-0

OFFICIAL GED CALCULATOR

	ISBN
Casio fx-260 Solar Calculator	0-7398-5054-7
Casio OH-260 Overhead Calculator	0-7398-5447-X
NEW! Complete Canadian GED Preparation Book + fx260-Casio Calculator Package	0-7747-1780-7

OFFICIAL GED PRACTICE TESTS

	ISBN
❀ **Canadian Class Pack** – including Canadian OPT Tests PA and PB (5 copies of each) Administration Manual and Universal Answer Sheets (25 sheets)	0-7398-6826-8
❀ **Canadian OPT Test PA (5 copies of same title)**	0-7398-5775-4
❀ **Canadian OPT Test PB (5 copies of same title)**	0-7398-5776-2
❀ **Canadian (PA) Test Audio Version**	0-7398-6495-5
❀ **NEW! French Class Pack** – including French OPT Test PA and PB (5 copies of each) Administration Manual and Universal Answer Sheets (25 sheets)	0-7747-1781-5
❀ **NEW! French OPT Test PA (5 copies of same title)**	0-7398-8595-2
❀ **NEW! French OPT Test PB (5 copies of same title)**	0-7398-8602-9
Administrator's Manual w/answers	0-7398-5439-9
Essay Scoring Training CD	0-7398-5436-4
Universal Answer Sheet (25 answer sheets)	0-7398-5445-3
Test PA Large Print w/Answer Sheet	0-7398-5658-8

PRE-GED PREPARATION

	ISBN
NEW! Complete Pre-GED Preparation Book	0-7398-8785-8
Language Arts — Writing	0-7398-6696-6
Language Arts — Reading	0-7398-6697-4
Mathematics	0-7398-6698-2
Science	0-7398-6700-8
Social Studies	0-7398-6699-0
Critical Thinking Skills	0-7398-6701-6
Instructor's Guide	0-7398-8062-4

ALSO AVAILABLE:

GED SOFTWARE RESOURCES:

	ISBN
GED 21st CENTURY	
Hard Drive Windows	0-7398-4921-2
Hard Drive w/Site Licence Win	0-7398-5448-8
Network Windows — LAN	0-7398-5449-6
Network Windows — WAN	0-7398-5450-X

OFFICIAL GED PRACTICE TEST SCANNING SOFTWARE

	ISBN
Hard-Drive Version (Windows)	
Scanning Program	0-7398-5647-2
Scanning and Testing Combo	
Network Version (Windows)	0-7398-5653-7
Hard-Drive Version with Site Licence	
Scanning Program	0-7398-5648-0
Scanning & Testing Combo	
Network Version (Windows)	
Scanning Program	0-7398-5649-9
Scanning and Testing Combo	0-7398-5655-3

OFFICIAL GED PRACTICE TESTS TESTING SOFTWARE

Hard Drive Version (Windows)	
Testing Program	0-7398-5650-2
Scanning & Testing Combo	0-7398-5653-7
Hard-Drive Version with Site Licence (Windows)	
Testing Program	0-7398-5651-0
Scanning & Testing Combo	0-7398-5654-5
Network Version (Windows)	
Testing Program	0-7398-5652-9
Scanning & Testing Combo	0-7398-5655-3

PRE-GED 2001 SOFTWARE

Hard Drive Windows	0-8114-9299-0
Hard Drive Macintosh	0-8114-9297-4
Hard Drive w/Site Licence Win	0-8114-9570-1
Hard Drive w/Site Licence Mac	0-8114-9569-8
Network Windows / Novell	0-7398-1824-4
Network Macintosh	0-8114-9340-7

*NOTE: For Technical Support Line please call us at 1-800-200-7109

NEED MORE PRACTICE? WE CAN HELP WITH FREE INTERNET-BASED GED PRACTICE AT www.gedpractice.com

For more information contact us at:

NELSON/STECK-VAUGHN

1120 Birchmount Road, Toronto, ON M1K 5G4
Toll Free: 1-800-668-0671   www.nelson.com